PRENTICE HALL

# UNITED STATES HISTORY
## MODERN AMERICA

Emma J. Lapsansky-Werner
Peter B. Levy
Randy Roberts
Alan Taylor
Grant Wiggins

PEARSON

Upper Saddle River, New Jersey   Boston, Massachusetts   Chandler, Arizona   Glenview, Illinois

**Cover Images:** TR, © Josef Scaylea/CORBIS; TL, © Bettmann/CORBIS; TR, © Bettmann/CORBIS; MR, Carr Clifton/Minden Pictures; BR, Pearson Curriculum; Bkgd Corbis Royalty-Free; BL, Getty Images; BFL, Fox Photos/Getty Images; BM, © Ted Streshinsky/CORBIS; BR, © Michael Macor/San Francisco Chronicle/Corbis; **Title page:** Bkgrnd, © Ilene MacDonald/Alamy; BL, © Ilene MacDonald/Alamy; BM, © Kayann Legg/istockphoto.com; BR © Jeremy Edwards/istockphoto.com; **Spine:** Corbis Royalty-Free; **Back cover:** Corbis Royalty-Free; **MI 29:** Renaissance Center, Digital Vision/Getty Images, Inc.; **MI 30:** Rock Harbor lighthouse Peter Frischmuth/Peter Arnold, Inc.;  MI 32: Detroit monorail, Richard Cummins/Corbis; **MI 34–MI 35:** Great Islands, Photolibrary; **MI 36–MI 37:** Mackinac bridge, Corbis; **MI 38:** Whitcomb Conservatory, agefotostock; **MI 40:** Grand Haven South Pier lighthouse Claver Carroll/Photolibrary.

Acknowledgments appear on page 795, which constitutes an extension of this copyright page.

ISBN-13: 978-0-13-368672-2
ISBN-10:    0-13-368672-8

3 4 5 6 7 8 9 10  V052  13 12 11 10

## Emma J. Lapsansky-Werner

Emma J. Lapsansky-Werner is Professor of History and Curator of the Quaker Collection at Haverford College. After receiving her doctorate from the University of Pennsylvania, she taught at Temple University for almost two decades. Dr. Lapsansky-Werner's recent publications include *Quaker Aesthetics,* coauthored with Ann Verplanck, and *Back to Africa: Benjamin Coates and the Colonization Movement in America, 1848–1880,* coedited with Margaret Hope Bacon.

## Peter B. Levy

Peter B. Levy is a Full Professor in the Department of History at York College of Pennsylvania, where he teaches a wide variety of courses in American history. He received his B.A. from the University of California, Berkeley, and his Ph.D. from Columbia University. Dr. Levy is the author of eight books and many articles, including: *The New Left and Labor in the 1960s; Civil War on Race Street: The Civil Rights Movement in Cambridge, Maryland;* and *100 Key Documents in American Democracy.* He lives in Towson, Maryland, with his wife, two children, and a yellow Labrador.

## Randy Roberts

Randy Roberts, Professor of History at Purdue University, specializes in twentieth-century American history and the history of popular culture. He has written, cowritten, or edited more than 20 books, including biographies of John Wayne, Jack Johnson, and Oscar Robertson. Dr. Roberts has also written histories of American sports and of the Vietnam War. His books have been nominated for and won a number of national prizes. At Purdue University, he has won the University Teacher of the Year award. Dr. Roberts has also appeared frequently on the History Channel and in documentaries for HBO, NBC, ESPN, and PBS.

## Alan Taylor

Alan Taylor, Professor of History at the University of California, Davis, earned his Ph.D. in history from Brandeis University and did a postdoctoral fellowship at the Institute of Early American History and Culture in Williamsburg, Virginia. He teaches courses in early American history and the history of the American West. Dr. Taylor is the author of five books, including *American Colonies* and *William Cooper's Town,* which won the Bancroft and Beveridge prizes, as well as the 1996 Pulitzer Prize for American history. He is a contributing editor for *The New Republic.*

## Program Consultant

**Grant Wiggins, Ed.D.,** is the President of Authentic Education in Hopewell, New Jersey. He earned his Ed.D from Harvard University and his B.A. from St. John's College in Annapolis. Wiggins consults with schools, districts, and state education departments on a variety of reform matters; organizes conferences, workshops, and develops print materials and Web resources on curricular change. He is the co-author, with Jay McTighe, of *Understanding by Design* and *The Understanding By Design Handbook,* the award-winning and highly successful materials on curriculum.

# Senior Consultants

 **John R. Chavez** is Professor of History at Southern Methodist University, Clements Department of History. He earned his Ph.D. from the University of Michigan, with a specialty in Mexican American history. Dr. Chavez's publications include *Eastside Landmark: A History of the East Los Angeles Community Union, The Lost Land: The Chicano Image of the Southwest,* and *Teaching Mexican American History,* co-authored with Neil Foley.

 **Herman Viola** specializes in the history of the American West, the American Indian, and the Civil War and has published such books on these subjects as *After Columbus* and *Little Bighorn Remembered: The Untold Indian Story of Custer's Last Stand.* He earned his Ph.D. from Indiana University. Dr. Viola currently serves as curator emeritus at the Smithsonian's National Museum of Natural History.

# Senior Reading Consultants

 **Kate Kinsella, Ed.D.,** is a faculty member in the Department of Secondary Education at San Francisco State University. A specialist in second-language and adolescent literacy, she teaches coursework addressing language and literacy development across the secondary curricula. Dr. Kinsella earned her M.A. in TESOL from San Francisco State University and her Ed.D. in Second Language Acquisition from the University of San Francisco.

 **Kevin Feldman, Ed.D.,** is the Director of Reading and Early Intervention with the Sonoma County Office of Education (SCOE) and an independent educational consultant. At the SCOE, he develops, organizes, and monitors programs related to K–12 literacy. Dr. Feldman has an M.A. from the University of California, Riverside, in Special Education, Learning Disabilities, and Instructional Design. He earned his Ed.D. in Curriculum and Instruction from the University of San Francisco.

# Differentiated Instruction Consultants

 **Don Deshler** Don Deshler, Ph.D., is the director of the Center for Research on Learning (CRL) at the University of Kansas. Dr. Deshler's expertise centers on adolescent literacy, learning strategic instruction, and instructional strategies for teaching content areas to academically diverse classes. He is the author of *Teaching Content to All: Evidence-Based Inclusive Practices in Middle and Secondary Schools,* a text which presents the instructional practices that have been tested and validated through his research at CRL.

**Anthony S. Bashir**
Director, Academic and Disability Services
Emerson College
Boston, Massachusetts

**Dr. Cathy Collins Block**
Professor of Curriculum and Instruction
Texas Christian University
Fort Worth, Texas

**Anna Uhl Chamot**
Professor of Secondary Education (ESL)
The George Washington University
Washington, D.C.

**John Guthrie**
Professor of Human Development
University of Maryland
College Park, Maryland

**Susan P. Miller**
Professor of Special Education
University of Nevada, Las Vegas
Las Vegas, Nevada

**Jennifer Platt**
Executive Associate Dean for Academic Affairs
College of Education
University of Central Florida
Orlando, Florida

# Reviewers

## Academic Reviewers

**William Childs**
Professor of History
The Ohio State University
Columbus, Ohio

**Michael Jay Friedman, Ph.D.**
Bureau of International Information
  Programs
U.S. Department of State
Washington, D.C.

**Huping Ling, Ph.D.**
Professor of History
Truman State University
Kirksville, Missouri

**Judith Ridner**
Department of History
Muhlenberg College
Allentown, Pennsylvania

**Carol Schneider**
Rock Point Community School
Rock Point, Arizona

## Contributing Editor

**Richard Snow**
former Editor in Chief
*American Heritage Magazine*
New York, New York

## Accuracy Panel

**Esther Ratner, M.L.S.**
Greyherne Information Services

**Barbara Whitney Petruzzelli, M.L.S.**

**Amy Raff, M.L.S.**

**Bernard Rosen, Ph.D.**

**Wilma Schmidt, M.L.S.**

## Teacher Reviewers

**Tom Berve**
Papillion–LaVista High School
Papillion, Nebraska

**Joyce Cooper**
Dallas Independent School District
Dallas, Texas

**Scott Crump**
Bingham High School
South Jordan, Utah

**Peter DiNardo**
Mt. Lebanon High School
Pittsburgh, Pennsylvania

**Dee Ann Holt**
Mann Magnet School
Little Rock, Arkansas

**Bruce Lesh**
Franklin High School
Reisterstown, Maryland

**Dr. Robert McAdams**
East Burke High School
Connelly Springs, North Carolina

**Cynthia Mostoller**
Alice Deal Middle School
Washington, D.C.

**Dr. Brent Muirhead**
University of Phoenix
Atlanta, Georgia

**Deborah W. Powers**
Westlake High School
Atlanta, Georgia

**Jeanne Salvado**
Montgomery County Public Schools
Rockville, Maryland

**Dr. Francis N. Sheboy**
Assistant Principal
Cornwall Central High School
New Windsor, New York

**Jim Thovson**
Rapid City Central High School

Rapid City, South Dakota

## Social Studies Master Teacher Board

**Peggy Altoff**
K-12 Social Studies Facilitator
District 11 Colorado Springs
Colorado Springs, Colorado

**David Burns**
Foothill High School
Sacramento, California

**Katherine A. Deforge**
Marcellus Central School
Marcellus, New York

**Pam Gothart**
Madison County Schools
Huntsville, Alabama

## Teacher's Edition Consultants

**Diane Hart**
Social Studies Author and Assessment
  Consultant
Menlo Park, California

**Sam Intrator**
Professor of Education
  and Child Studies
Smith College
Northampton, Massachusetts

**John Poggio**
Professor, Department of Educational
  Psychology and Research
University of Kansas
Lawrence, Kansas

## Program Adviser

**Michal Howden**
Social Studies Consultant
Zionsville, Indiana

 **Program Adviser**

**Amy B. Bloom, JD**
History/Social Studies Consultant
Oakland Schools
Waterford, Michigan

**(MI) Content Expectations**

| | |
|---|---|
| F1.1a | F2.1f |
| F1.1b | F2.1g |
| F1.1c | 6.1.1d |
| F1.1d | 6.1.1f |
| F1.1e | 6.1.2b |
| F1.2a | 6.1.3b |
| F1.2b | 6.1.3c |
| F1.2c | 6.1.3d |
| F2.1a | 6.1.3e |
| F2.1b | 6.1.4 |
| F2.1c | 6.3.1 |
| F2.1d | 6.3.2e |
| F2.1e | 6.3.3 |

# EMERGENCE OF THE MODERN UNITED STATES (1890–1920)

(MI) **Content Expectations**

| | |
|---|---|
| 6.1.1a | 6.2.2 |
| 6.1.1f | 6.2.3 |
| 6.1.2a | 6.2.4 |
| 6.1.2b | 6.3.1 |
| 6.1.3c | 6.3.2a |
| 6.1.3d | 6.3.2b |
| 6.1.4 | 6.3.2d |
| 6.1.5a | 6.3.2e |
| 6.1.5c | 6.3.3 |
| 6.2.1 | |

# PROSPERITY AND DEPRESSION (1919–1941)

**MI Content Expectations**

| | |
|---|---|
| 6.1.1e | 6.3.2e |
| 6.1.1f | 6.3.3 |
| 6.1.2b | 7.1.1 |
| 6.1.3a | 7.1.1a |
| 6.1.3b | 7.1.1b |
| 6.1.3e | 7.1.2a |
| 6.1.3d | 7.1.2b |
| 6.1.5b | 7.1.2c |
| 6.2.3 | 7.1.3a |
| 6.3.1 | 7.1.3b |
| 6.3.2a | 7.1.3c |
| 6.3.2d | 8.2.3 |

# WORLD WAR II AND POSTWAR AMERICA (1931–1960)

**MI Content Expectations**

| | |
|---|---|
| 6.1.3d | 7.2.3d |
| 6.1.5e | 7.2.4 |
| 6.2.4 | 8.1.1a |
| 6.3.1 | 8.1.1b |
| 6.3.2d | 8.1.1c |
| 7.1.2b | 8.1.2 |
| 7.1.3b | 8.1.2a |
| 7.1.3c | 8.1.2b |
| 7.2.1a | 8.1.2d |
| 7.2.1b | 8.1.2f |
| 7.2.1c | 8.2.1 |
| 7.2.1d | 8.2.2a |
| 7.2.2 | 8.2.2b |
| 7.2.3a | 8.2.3 |
| 7.2.3b | 8.3.4 |
| 7.2.3c | 8.3.5 |

# CHALLENGES AND CHANGE (1945–1980)

## Content Expectations

| | |
|---|---|
| 8.1.1a | 8.2.4 |
| 8.1.2a | 8.3.1a |
| 8.1.2c | 8.3.1b |
| 8.1.2d | 8.3.1c |
| 8.1.2e | 8.3.1d |
| 8.1.2f | 8.3.2 |
| 8.1.3 | 8.3.3 |
| 8.2.1 | 8.3.4 |
| 8.2.2a | 8.3.5 |
| 8.2.2b | 9.1.1 |
| 8.2.3 | 9.1.2b |

*MI* **Content Expectations**

| | |
|---|---|
| 8.1.3 | 9.1.2b |
| 8.2.1 | 9.1.2c |
| 8.2.3 | 9.2.1 |
| 8.3.3 | 9.2.2 |
| 9.1.1 | 9.3.1a |
| 9.1.2a | 9.3.1b |

## Witness History: The Latest Fad

As baby boomers went to school, new fads came and went with amazing speed. One such fad revolved around a popular television show about the American folk hero Davy Crockett. Steven Spielberg, who would become one of Hollywood's most successful movie directors, recalled the craze:

"I was in third grade at the time. Suddenly, the next day, everybody in my class but me was Davy Crockett. And because I didn't have my coonskin cap and my powder horn, or Old Betsy, my rifle, and my chaps, I was deemed the Mexican leader, Santa Anna. And they chased me home from school until I got my parents to buy me a coonskin cap."

—Steven Spielberg, recalling the Davy Crockett craze of 1955

**WITNESS HISTORY** ◀)) AUDIO

**Primary source audio accounts throughout the text bring the voices and sounds of history to life.**

## WITNESS HISTORY DVD

**Witness History Discovery School™ Videos bring the events you read about in the text to life.**

## History *Interactive*

**Audio, video, and animation-filled features help you explore major turning points in history.**

# Primary Source

**Full-page excerpts allow you to relive history through eyewitness accounts and documents.**

# American Humanities

**Experience great literature and arts from around the world.**

## In-Text Primary Source

**Gain insights as you read by reading the words of people who were there.**

# Make Connections

Comparing Viewpoints

## Explore issues by analyzing two opposing viewpoints.

### Comparing Viewpoints

**Can the United States Win the War in Vietnam?**

As Johnson settled into office, some urged him to get out of "Kennedy's war" in Vietnam. Despite the war's growing unpopularity, Johnson was reluctant to start his term by walking away. His own cabinet was divided on the issue.

**DEAN RUSK**

Rusk was Secretary of State from 1961 to 1968. Citing Chamberlain and Hitler as an example, Rusk refused to appease communists in Southeast Asia. He supported increased bombing and troops to force North Vietnam to negotiate a peace.

**Primary Source**

"If... North Vietnam will stop [its] campaign to destroy the Republic of Vietnam, the measures we are taking to assist South Vietnam... will no longer be necessary. ...We see no necessity for international negotiations.... [W]e cannot [think of] any points that would be negotiable."

**GEORGE BALL**

Ball was Undersecretary of State for Kennedy and Johnson. Convinced the United States could not win a guerrilla war in Asia, he urged Johnson in 1965 to start peace negotiations and stop sending U.S. soldiers to Vietnam.

**Primary Source**

"No one can assure you that we can beat the Viet Cong... no matter how many... troops we deploy. No [ground forces] of whatever size can win a guerrilla war—which is at the same time a civil war... in jungle terrain in the midst of a population that refuses cooperation...."

**Compare**
1. What stance does each official take on fighting until the communists are defeated?

2. How did these viewpoints relate to what Americans were thinking as the war progressed?

Decision Point

## Consider how you would have decided key questions in American history.

### Decision Point

**Should the United States Drop the Atomic Bomb?**

The Allies had planned an invasion of Japan for November 1945 in an attempt to end the war. But after the successful test of the first atom bomb, President Truman had to decide whether to drop the bomb on Japan instead. Read the options below. Then, you decide.

**Truman Favors Using the Bomb**

**Primary Source**

"I asked Gen. Marshall what it would cost in lives to land . . . in Japan. It was his opinion that $1/4$ million casualties would be the minimum cost. . . . I asked Sec. Stimson which cities in Japan were devoted exclusively to war production. He . . . named Hiroshima and Nagasaki. We sent an ultimatum to Japan. It was ignored. I ordered atomic bombs dropped on the two cities. . . . Dropping the bombs ended the war, saved lives and gave the free nations a chance to face the facts."

—President Harry S. Truman

**Scientists Advise Caution**

**Primary Source**

"We the undersigned scientists . . . believe that the United States ought not resort to the use of atomic bombs in the present phase of the war, at least not unless . . . Japan is given an opportunity to surrender. . . . A nation which sets the precedent of using these newly liberated forces of nature for purposes of destruction may have to bear the responsibility of opening the door to an era of devastation on an unimaginable scale."

—Scientist Leo Szilard

**You Decide**
1. Why did Truman decide to drop the bomb?
2. Why course of action did Szilard favor?
3. What decision would you have made? Why?

# Cause and Effect

## Diagrams help you see the short- and long-term causes and effects of history's most important events.

## HISTORY MAKERS

**Meet many fascinating people.**

DON'T BUY CALIFORNIA GRAPES!

## HISTORY MAKERS

**Cesar Chavez** (1927–1993)

Cesar Chavez spent his childhood and youth toiling, like his parents, as a migrant farmworker. In the 1950s, he trained to be a community organizer. His skills led him to be named chief of the group doing the training. In 1962, he formed the National Farm Workers Association. Migrant workers had tried to form unions before and failed; Chavez made the effort succeed. In an impassioned letter to the grape industry, he expressed the workers' suffering and determination. "We are men and women who have suffered and endured much," he wrote. "Generation after generation have sought to demoralize us, to break our human spirit. But God knows that we are not beasts of burden, agricultural implements or rented slaves; we are men."

# American Issues
## Connector

## Examine key issues that have endured throughout American history.

## ● INFOGRAPHIC

**Photographs, maps, charts, illustrations, and text help you understand the significance of important historical events and developments.**

**Military Casualties of World War I**

Troops (in millions) — Russia, British Empire, France, Italy, United States (Allies); Germany, Austria-Hungary (Central Powers)

☐ Troops mobilized
☒ Troops killed, wounded, or missing

SOURCE: *Encyclopædia Britannica Online*

**INFOGRAPHIC**

## American Voices From the Western Front

▲ American doughboy helmet, worn by a member of the first U.S. division in France

In 1918, Americans fought alongside other Allied troops in several key battles on the Western Front, including Belleau Wood, Château-Thierry, the Second Battle of the Marne, Saint-Mihiel, and Argonne Forest. Although all of these battles were Allied victories, they were nonetheless deadly. Machine-gun barrages and exploding artillery shells filled with shrapnel or deadly gas killed or wounded thousands of American troops. One soldier wrote home to his mother: "Don't worry. I am alright and it is worthwhile...we are blocking the road to Paris. So we don't die in vain."

"Sept 29 at 5.50 A.M. Several men were gassed before we went over. Advanced to top of ridge. Capt. Smith killed. 1st Lt. McKory and 2nd Lt. Kerr killed later. No officers left. Piece of shrapnel hit helmet and went through canister of my gas mask."
—Corporal Wilfred H. Allen, fighting in late September 1918

Private Martin P. Coogan 76th Field Artillery

Gas mask ▶

American soldiers bandaged after a gas attack ▼

"Our division, which went into action yesterday morning at practically full strength, has lost half its men. ...I am just beginning to realize what war really is."
—John Clark, fighting in the Second Battle of the Marne, July 19, 1918

American machine-gunners at Belleau Wood

Devastated battlefield near Ypres

## Document-Based Assessment

**Practice the art and science of a historian by analyzing an event through multiple historical documents, data, and images.**

## *Landmark Decisions of the Supreme Court*

**Explore key Supreme Court cases and link the decisions to today.**

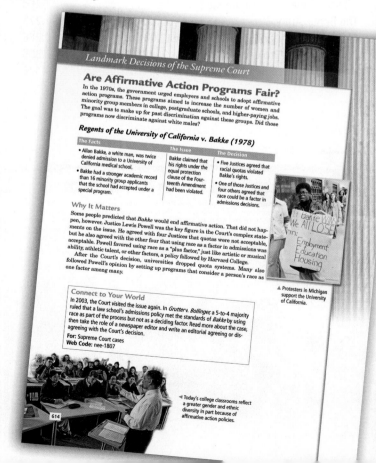

# ☑ Quick Study

**Review key information and concepts to prepare for tests.**

# Charts and Graphs

## Diagrams and data help you understand history through visuals.

## Maps Geography *Interactive*

**Interactive maps with a Web code help you understand where history happened.**

# ✓ Quick Study Timeline

**Review key events from each chapter on illustrated timelines.**

# Political Cartoons

**Examine how artists have expressed their points of view about events of their day.**

IN THE HANDS OF HIS PHILANTHROPIC FRIENDS. 1897

## Focus On Geography

### See how geography has affected events in American history.

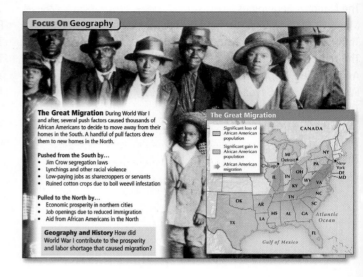

**Focus On Geography**

**The Great Migration** During World War I and after, several push factors caused thousands of African Americans to decide to move away from their homes in the South. A handful of pull factors drew them to new homes in the North.

**Pushed from the South by...**
- Jim Crow segregation laws
- Lynchings and other racial violence
- Low-paying jobs as sharecroppers or servants
- Ruined cotton crops due to boll weevil infestation

**Pulled to the North by...**
- Economic prosperity in northern cities
- Job openings due to reduced immigration
- Aid from African Americans in the North

**Geography and History** How did World War I contribute to the prosperity and labor shortage that caused migration?

## Events That Changed America

### See how certain events changed the course of our nation's history.

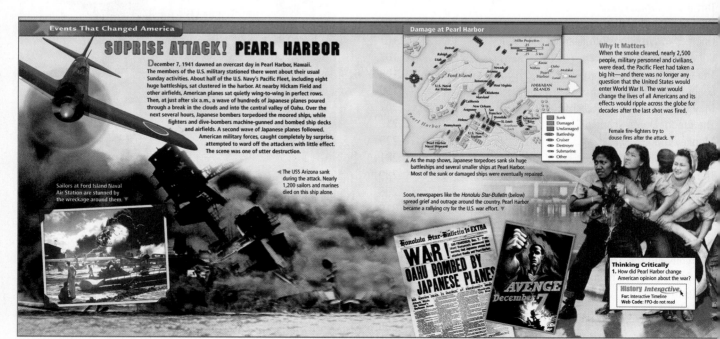

**Events That Changed America**

## SURPRISE ATTACK! PEARL HARBOR

December 7, 1941 dawned an overcast day in Pearl Harbor, Hawaii. The members of the U.S. military stationed there went about their usual Sunday activities. About half of the U.S. Navy's Pacific Fleet, including eight huge battleships, sat clustered in the harbor. At nearby Hickam Field and other airfields, American planes sat quietly wing-to-wing in perfect rows. Then, at just after six a.m., a wave of hundreds of Japanese planes poured through a break in the clouds and into the central valley of Oahu. Over the next several hours, Japanese bombers torpedoed the moored ships, while fighters and dive-bombers machine-gunned and bombed ship decks and airfields. A second wave of Japanese planes followed. American military forces, caught completely by surprise, attempted to ward off the attackers with little effect. The scene was one of utter destruction.

Sailors at Ford Island Naval Air Station are stunned by the wreckage around them. ▼

◄ The USS Arizona sank during the attack. Nearly 1,200 sailors and marines died on this ship alone.

**Damage at Pearl Harbor**

▲ As the map shows, Japanese torpedoes sank six huge battleships and several smaller ships at Pearl Harbor. Most of the sunk or damaged ships were eventually repaired.

Soon, newspapers like the *Honolulu Star-Bulletin* (below) spread grief and outrage around the country. Pearl Harbor became a rallying cry for the U.S. war effort. ▼

**Why It Matters**
When the smoke cleared, nearly 2,500 people, military personnel and civilians, were dead, the Pacific Fleet had taken a big hit—and there was no longer any question that the United States would enter World War II. The war would change the lives of all Americans and its effects would ripple across the globe for decades after the last shot was fired.

Female fire-fighters try to douse fires after the attack. ▼

**Thinking Critically**
1. How did Pearl Harbor change American opinion about the war?

**History** *Interactive*
**For:** Interactive Timeline
**Web Code:** FPO-do not read

# Develop Key Skills

**Geography** *Interactive*

Historical maps are important for understanding where events took place, so we've created easy-to-read maps for your exploration. To make sure you get the most out of each map, we've also provided you with an opportunity to interact with each map online. You can access these interactive maps through the Web Codes provided in your textbook.

Some of the maps in your textbook have interactive-online versions that will allow you to see how events shown on the map unfolded over time or will give you additional images and information to make the places shown on the map come alive.

**Go Online at PHSchool.com**

**Geography** *Interactive*

**For:** Interactive Map
**Visit:** www.PHSchool.com **Web Code:** nep-1206
Use the Web Codes that appear throughout this text-book to access additional information and activities.
1. Go to PHSchool.com
2. Enter the Web Code.
3. Click Go.

## SKILLS Handbook

The Skills Handbook at the front of this textbook allows you to brush up on important skills at the beginning of the course or at any time you need help.

- **Reading Informational Text**

  Make the most of the time you spend reading the text, and improve your reading comprehension by looking at some proven reading strategies to use before you read, while you read, and after you read.

- **Writing Handbook**

  Learning to be a good writer is key to your success in this class, on tests, and in life. Use this part of the Skills Handbook to study models of good writing and to learn hints for writing various types of essays, including expository and persuasive essays.

- **Critical Thinking About Visuals and Text**

  As a practicing historian, you need to train yourself to think criti-cally about everything you read, see, and hear. Is what you are reading accurate? Biased? Use this part of the Skills Handbook to practice your critical thinking skills.

- **Speaking and Listening**

  Speaking is another way to demonstrate what you've learned. Good listening is another key to success in every classroom. In this part of the Skills Handbook, look for key tips on how to pre-pare a presentation and how to listen actively.

# Prepare for Tests

## NoteTaking

Throughout most of this course, you'll be reading and studying information as it occurred chronologically. In each section of the textbook, you'll find suggestions for how to take notes using graphic organizers, timelines, and outlines. Complete these graphic organizers in your own notebook, in your Reading and Note Taking Study Guide, or on the Note Taking Worksheets for each section, which you can download at PHSchool.com. If you complete all of the suggested notetaking strategies, you'll be able to use your notes to prepare for chapter, midterm, and high-stakes end-of-course tests.

## Progress Monitoring *Online*

Web Codes at the end of every section take you to an online quiz with multiple-choice questions on section content and vocabulary. At the end of every chapter, you'll find an online self-test on chapter content and a crossword puzzle to test your vocabulary mastery. Both quizzes and tests provide you with instant help so you can be sure you have grasped key content.

### Go Online at PHSchool.com

**Progress Monitoring *Online***
**For:** Self-test with vocabulary practice
**Web Code:** nea-1211

## Quick Study Guide

In addition to the notetaking graphics that you create yourself, we've provided some for each chapter on the end-of-chapter Quick Study pages. Use these pages to review for tests and to make sure you have mastered the content in the chapter. The Quick Study pages also include a timeline of key events discussed in the chapter. Interactive versions of these timelines are available online at PHSchool.com.

## Document-Based Assessment

To prepare you for document-based questions on in-class and high-stakes tests, each chapter ends with a page of Document-Based Assessment. Each of these pages contains several documents followed by multiple-choice questions that help you analyze documents and practice your map, graph, visual learning, and critical reading skills. A writing task helps you analyze and draw conclusions about the various documents.

# Student Guide to Michigan High School Content Expectations

## Michigan High School Content Expectations (HSCE) ................. MI 30
Review a complete list of the Michigan High School Content Expectations for United States History and Geography.

## Your Guide to the MME ............... MI 40
Learn what to expect on the Michigan Merit Exam. This guide outlines the types of questions you will see on the test.

## MME Skills Practice .................... MI 41
Practice your skills for the **Michigan Merit Exam (MME)** while reviewing what you have learned in your United States history course.

## Skills Handbook .......................... SH1
Use these series of handbooks to strengthen your skills in reading, writing, critical thinking, speaking, and listening.

## Reading Your HSCE Codes

Michigan uses a special coding system to identify its High School Content Expectations for U.S. History and Geography. Below is an example.

7.2.1a

| **Era 7** | **Standard 2** | **Content Expectation 1** | **Topic a** |
| The Great Depression and World War II | World War II | Causes of WWII | The political and economic disputes over territory |

**The Renaissance Center along the waterfront in Detroit**

# High School Content Expectations

The following pages provide a complete list of the Michigan High School Content Expectations for United States History and Geography.

## Eras 1–5

### F1 Political and Intellectual Transformations of America to 1877

**F.1.1** Identify the core ideals of American society as reflected in the documents below and analyze the ways that American society moved toward and/or away from its core ideals

**a.** Declaration of Independence

**b.** the U.S. Constitution (including the Preamble)

**c.** Bill of Rights

**d.** the Gettysburg Address

**e.** 13th, 14th, and 15th Amendments

**F1.2** Using the American Revolution, the creation and adoption of the Constitution, and the Civil War as touchstones, develop an argument/narrative about the changing character of American political society and the roles of key individuals across cultures in prompting/supporting the change by discussing

**a.** the birth of republican government, including the rule of law, inalienable rights, equality, and limited government

**b.** the development of governmental roles in American life

**c.** and competing view of the responsibilities of governments

**d.** changes in suffrage qualifications

**e.** the development of political parties

**f.** America's political and economic role in the world

**Rock Harbor lighthouse on Lake Superior in Michigan**

**F2.1** Describe the major trends and transformations in American life prior to 1877 including

a. changing political boundaries of the United States

b. regional economic differences and similarities, including goods produced and the nature of the labor force

c. changes in the size, location, and composition of the population

d. patterns of immigration and migration

e. development of cities

f. changes in commerce, transportation, and communication

g. major changes in Foreign Affairs marked by such events as the War of 1812, the Mexican-American War, and foreign relations during the Civil War

## ERA 6: The Development of an Industrial, Urban, and Global U.S. (1870–1930)

### 6.1 Growth of an Industrial and Urban America

Explain the causes and consequences—both positive and negative—of the Industrial Revolution and America's growth from a predominantly agricultural, commercial, and rural nation to a more industrial and urban nation between 1870 and 1930.

**6.1.1 Factors in the American Industrial Revolution**—Analyze the factors that enabled the United States to become a major industrial power, including

a. gains from trade

b. organizational "revolution" (e.g., development of corporations and labor organizations)

c. advantages of physical geography

d. increase in labor through immigration and migration

e. economic policies of government and industrial leaders (including Andrew Carnegie and John D. Rockefeller)

f. technological advances

**6.1.2 Labor's Response to Industrial Growth**—Evaluate the difference responses of labor to industrial change including

a. development of organized labor, including the Knights of Labor, American Federation of Labor, and the United Mine workers

b. southern and western farmers' reactions, including the growth of populism and the populist movement (e.g. Farmers Alliance, Grange, Platform of the Populist Party, Bryan's "Cross of Gold" speech)

**6.1.3 Urbanization**—Analyze the changing urban and rural landscape by examining

a. the location and expansion of major urban centers

b. the growth of cities linked by industry and trade

c. the development of cities divided by race, ethnicity, and class

d. resulting tensions among and within groups

e. different perspectives about immigrant experiences in the urban setting

**6.1.4 Population Changes**—Use census data from 1790–1940 to describe changes in the composition, distribution, and density of the American population and analyze their causes, including immigration, the Great Migration, and urbanization.

## 6.1 Growth of an Industrial and Urban America (Continued)

**6.1.5 A Case Study of American Industrialism**—Using the automobile industry as a case study, analyze the causes and consequences of this major industrial transformation by explaining

**a.** the impact of resource availability

**b.** entrepreneurial decision making by Henry Ford and others

**c.** domestic and international migrations

**d.** the development of an industrial work force

**e.** the impact on Michigan

**f.** the impact on American society

## 6.2 Becoming a World Power

Describe and analyze the major changes – both positive and negative – in the role the United States played in world affairs after the Civil War, and explain the causes and consequences of this changing role.

**6.2.1 Growth of U.S. Global Power**—Locate on a map the territories (Cuba, Puerto Rico, Philippines, Hawaii, Panama Canal Zone) acquired by the United States during its emergence as an imperial power between 1890 and 1914, and analyze the role the Spanish American War, the Philippine Revolution, the Panama Canal, the Open Door Policy, and the Roosevelt Corollary played in expanding America's global influence and redefining its foreign policy.

**6.2.2 WWI**—Explain the causes of World War I, the reasons for American neutrality and eventual entry into the war, and America's role in shaping the course of the war.

**Elevated monorail in Detroit, Michigan**

**6.2.3 Domestic Impact of WWI**—Analyze the domestic impact of WWI on the growth of the government (e.g., War Industries Board), the expansion of the economy, the restrictions on civil liberties (e.g., Sedition Act, Red Scare, Palmer Raids), and the expansion of women's suffrage.

**6.2.4 Wilson and His Opponents**—Explain how Wilson's "Fourteen Points" differed from proposals by others, including French and British leaders and domestic opponents, in the debate over the Versailles Treaty, United States participation in the League of Nations, the redrawing of European political boundaries, and the resulting geopolitical tensions that continued to affect Europe.

## 6.3 Progressivism and Reform

Select and evaluate major public and social issues emerging from the changes in industrial, urban, and global America during this period; analyze the solutions or resolutions developed by Americans, and their consequences (positive/negative—anticipated/unanticipated) including, but not limited to, the following:

**6.3.1 Social Issues**—Describe at least three significant problems or issues created by America's industrial and urban transformation between 1895 and 1930 (e.g., urban and rural poverty and blight, child labor, immigration, political corruption, public health, poor working conditions, and monopolies).

**6.3.2 Causes and Consequences of Progressive Reform**—Analyze the causes, consequences, and limitations of Progressive reform in the following areas

a. major changes in the Constitution, including 16th, 17th, 18th, and 19th Amendments

b. new regulatory legislation (e.g., Pure Food and Drug Act, Sherman and Clayton Anti-Trust Acts)

c. the Supreme Court's role in supporting or slowing reform

d. role of reform organizations, movements and individuals in promoting change (e.g., Women's Christian Temperance Union, settlement house movement, conservation movement, and the National Association for the Advancement of Colored People, Jane Addams, Carrie Chapman Catt, Eugene Debs, W.E.B. DuBois, Upton Sinclair, Ida Tarbell)

e. efforts to expand and restrict the practices of democracy as reflected in post-Civil War struggles of African Americans and immigrants

**6.3.3 Women's Suffrage**—Analyze the successes and failures of efforts to expand women's rights, including the work of important leaders (e.g., Susan B. Anthony, Elizabeth Cady Stanton) and the eventual ratification of the 19th Amendment.

## ERA 7: The Great Depression and World War II (1920–1945)

### 7.1 Growing Crisis of Industrial Capitalism and Responses

Evaluate the key events and decision surrounding the causes and consequences of the global depression of the 1930s and World War II.

**7.1.1 The Twenties**—Identify and explain the significance of the cultural changes and tensions in the "Roaring Twenties" including

a. cultural movements, such as the Harlem Renaissance and the "lost generation"

b. the struggle between "traditional" and "modern" America (e.g., Scopes Trial, immigration restrictions, Prohibition, role of women, mass consumption)

**7.1.2** **Causes and Consequences of the Great Depression**—Explain and evaluate the multiple causes and consequences of the Great Depression by analyzing

a. the political, economic, environmental, and social causes of the Great Depression including fiscal policy, overproduction, under consumption, and speculation, the 1929 crash, the Dust Bowl

b. the economic and social toll of the Great Depression, including unemployment and environmental conditions that affected farmers, industrial workers and families

c. Hoover's policies and their impact (e.g., Reconstruction Finance Corporation)

**7.1.3** **The New Deal**—Explain and evaluate Roosevelt's New Deal Policies including

a. expanding federal government's responsibilities to protect the environment (e.g., Dust Bowl and the Tennessee Valley), meet challenges of unemployment, address the needs of workers, farmers, poor, and elderly

b. opposition to the New Deal and the impact of the Supreme Court in striking down and then accepting New Deal laws

c. consequences of New Deal policies (e.g., promoting workers' rights, development of Social Security program, and banking and financial regulation conservation practices, crop subsidies)

**7.2** World War II

Examine the causes and course of World War II, and the effects of the war on United States society and culture, including the consequences for United States involvement in world affairs.

**7.2.1** **Causes of WWII**—Analyze the factors contributing to World War II in Europe and the Pacific region, and America's entry into war including

a. the political and economic disputes over territory (e.g., failure of Versailles Treaty, League of Nations, Munich Agreement)

b. the differences in the civic and political values of the United States and those of Nazi Germany and Imperial Japan

c. United States neutrality

d. the bombing of Pearl Harbor

**7.2.2 U.S. and the Course of WWII**—Evaluate the role of the U.S. in fighting the war militarily, diplomatically and technologically across the world (e.g., Germany First strategy, Big Three Alliance and the development of atomic weapons).

**7.2.3 Impact of WWI on American Life**—Analyze the changes in American life brought about by U.S. participation in World War II including

**a.** mobilization of economic, military, and social resources

**b.** role of women and minorities in the war effort

**c.** role of the home front in supporting the war effort (e.g., rationing, work hours, taxes)

**d.** internment of Japanese-Americans

**7.2.4 Responses to Genocide**—Investigate development and enactment of Hitler's "final solution" policy, and the responses to genocide by the Allies, the U.S. government, international organizations, and individuals (e.g., liberation of concentration camps, Nurembergwar crimes tribunals, establishment of state of Israel).

## ERA 8: Post-World War II United States (1945–1989)

### 8.1 Cold War and the United States

Identify, analyze, and explain the causes, conditions, and impact of the Cold War Era on the United States.

**8.1.1 Origins and Beginnings of Cold War**—Analyze the factors that contributed to the Cold War including

**a.** differences in the civic, ideological and political values, and the economic and governmental institutions of the U.S. and U.S.S.R.

**b.** diplomatic decisions made at the Yalta and Potsdam Conferences (1945)

**c.** actions by both countries in the last years of and years following World War II (e.g., the use of the atomic bomb, the Marshall Plan, the Truman Doctrine, North American Treaty Alliance (NATO), and Warsaw Pact)

Grand Islands National
Recreation Area,
Lake Superior, Michigan

**8.1.2 Foreign Policy during the Cold War**—Evaluate the origins, setbacks, and successes of the American policy of "containing" the Soviet Union, including

a. the development of a U.S. national security establishment, composed of the Department of Defense, the Department of State, and the intelligence community

b. the armed struggle with Communism, including the Korean conflict

c. direct conflicts within specific world regions including Germany and Cuba

d. U.S. involvement in Vietnam, and the foreign and domestic consequences of the war (e.g., relationship/conflicts with U.S.S.R. and China, U.S. military policy and practices, responses of citizens and mass media)

e. indirect (or proxy) confrontations within specific world regions (e.g., Chile, Angola, Iran, Guatemala)

f. the arms race

**8.1.3 End of the Cold War**—Evaluate the factors that led to the end of the cold war including détente, policies of the U.S. and U.S.S.R. and their leaders (President Reagan and Premier Gorbachev), the political breakup of the Soviet Union, and the Warsaw Pact.

## 8.2 Domestic Policies

**Examine, analyze, and explain demographic changes, domestic policies, conflicts, and tensions in Post-WWII America.**

**8.2.1 Demographic Changes**—Use population data to produced and analyze maps that show the major changes in population distribution, spatial patterns and density, including the Baby Boom, new immigration, suburbanization, reverse migration of African Americans to the South, and the flow of population to the "Sunbelt."

**8.2.2 Policy Concerning Domestic Issues**—Analyze major domestic issues in the Post-War II era and the policies designed to meet the challenges by

a. describing issues challenging Americans such as domestic anticommunism (McCarthyism), labor, poverty, health care, infrastructure, immigration, and the environment

b. evaluating policy decisions and legislative actions to meet these challenges (e.g., G.I. Bill of Rights (1944), Taft-Hartley Act (1947), Twenty-Second Amendment to the U.S. Constitution (1951), Federal Highways Act (1956), National Defense Act (1957), E.P.A. (1970))

**8.2.3  Comparing Domestic Policies**—Focusing on causes, programs, and impacts, compare and contrast Roosevelt's New Deal initiatives, Johnson's Great Society programs, and Reagan's market-based domestic policies.

**8.2.4  Domestic Conflicts and Tensions**—Using core democratic values, analyze and evaluate the competing perspectives and controversies among Americans generated by U.S. Supreme Court decisions (e.g., Rose v Wade, Gideon, Miranda, Tinker, Hazelwood), the Vietnam War (anti-war and counter-cultural movements), environmental movement, women's rights movement, and the constitutional crisis generated by the Watergate scandal.

## 8.3  Civil Rights in the Post-WWII Era

Examine and analyze the Civil Rights Movement using key events, people, and organizations.

**8.3.1  Civil Rights Movement**—Analyze the key events, ideals, documents, and organizations in the struggle for civil rights by African American including

a. the impact of WWII and the Cold War (e.g., racial and gender integration of the military)

b. Supreme Court decisions and governmental actions (e.g., Brown v. Board (1954), Civil Rights Act (1957), Little Rock schools desegregation, Civil Rights Act (1964), Voting Rights Act (1965))

c. protest movements, organizations, and civil actions (e.g., integration of baseball, Montgomery Bus Boycott (1955-1956), March on Washington (1963), freedom rides, National Association for the Advancement of Colored People (NAACP), Southern Christian Leadership Conference (SCLC), Student Non-violent Coordinating committee (SNCC), Nation of Islam, Black Panthers)

d. resistance to Civil Rights

**Mackinac Bridge at dusk**

**8.3.2 Ideals of the Civil Rights Movement**—Compare and contrast the ideas in Martin Luther King's March on Washington speech to the ideas expressed in the Declaration of Independence, the Seneca Falls Resolution, and the Gettysburg Address.

**8.3.3 Women's Rights**—Analyze the causes and course of the women's rights movement in the 1960s and 1970s (including role of population shifts, birth control, increasing number of women in the work force, National Organization for Women (NOW), and the Equal Rights Amendment (ERA)).

**8.3.4 Civil Rights Expanded**—Evaluate the major accomplishments and setbacks in civil rights and liberties for American minorities over the 20th century including American Indians, Latinos/Latinas, new immigrants, people with disabilities, and gays and lesbians.

**8.3.5 Tensions and Reactions to Poverty and Civil Rights**—Analyze the causes and consequences of the civil unrest that occurred in American cities by comparing the civil unrest in Detroit with at least one other American city (e.g., Los Angeles, Cleveland, Chicago, Atlanta, Newark).

**Whitcomb Conservatory, Belle Isle, Michigan**

# ERA 9: America in a New Global Age

## 9.1 The Impact of Globalization on the United States

Explain the impact of globalization on the United States' economy, politics, society and role in the world.

**9.1.1 Economic Changes**—Using the changing nature of the American automobile industry as a case study, evaluate the changes in the American economy created by new markets, natural resources, technologies, corporate structures, international competition, new sources and methods of production, energy issues, and mass communication.

**9.1.2 Transformation of American Politics**—Analyze the transformation of American politics in the late 20th and early 21st centuries including

**a.** growth of the conservative movement in national politics, including the role of Ronald Reagan

**b.** role of evangelical religion in national politics

**c.** intensification of partisanship

**d.** partisan conflict over the role of government in American life

**e.** role of regional differences in national politics

## 9.2 Changes in America's Role in the World

Examine the shifting role of United States on the world stage during the period from 1980 to the present.

**9.2.1 U.S. in the Post-Cold World**—Explain the role of the United States as a super-power in the post-Cold War world, including advantages, disadvantages, and new challenges (e.g., military missions in Lebanon, Somalia, Haiti, Bosnia, Kosovo, and the Gulf War).

**9.2.2 9/11 and Responses to Terrorism**—Analyze how the attacks on 9/11 and the response to terrorism have altered American domestic and international policies (including e.g., the Office of Homeland Security, Patriot Act, wars in Afghanistan and Iraq, role of the United States in the United Nations, NATO).

## 9.3 Policy Debates

**9.3.1** Compose a persuasive essay on a public policy issue, and justify the position with a reasoned argument based upon historical antecedents and precedents, and core demographic values or constitutional principles.

**a.** role of the United States in the world

**b.** national economic policy

**c.** welfare policy

**d.** energy policy

**e.** health care

**f.** education

**g.** civil rights

# Your Guide to the MME

## A Word About the Test

The Michigan Merit Exam (MME) is an achievement test that measures your understanding of the Michigan High School Content Expectations.

The MME is composed of two types of questions, selected-response and extended-response items.

### Selected-Response Items

Selected-response items are made up of multiple choice questions. Some questions rely on a prompt. The prompt is a passage, a chart, a table, or a map. After studying the prompt, read the questions that follows. Some questions require you to use information you have learned in the course while others rely on information from the passage. Choose the best answer from four answer choices.

### Extended-Response Item

The MME has one extended-response item. This item is composed of a Data section and two tasks, or questions. Task I is similar to the selected-response items. Task II asks you to defend a position on a public policy issue.

**Task I** asks you to answer one selected-response item by interpreting the information provided in the data section.

**Task II** asks you to take a position on a public policy issue. You will evaluate the data and use what you already know to decide on a position. Then, you will develop a written response.

**Grand Haven South Pier lighthouse along Lake Michigan**

# Michigan Merit Exam Practice

**MME Skills Practice** allows you to practice answering the types of questions you will encounter on the MME. If you have difficulty answering a question, you may want to refer to the review pages provided for additional help.

| MME Skills Practice | | | |
|---|---|---|---|
| **Skills Practice** | **Skills Practice for Each Era** | **Correlation to the Michigan HSCE** | **Review Pages** |
| 1 | Connecting With Past Learnings (Beginnings–1900) | 6.1.1e, 6.1.2b, 6.1.2a, 6.2.3e | 72, 76, 87, 89, 90, 92 |
| 2 | Emergence of the Modern United States (1890–1920) | F.2.1a, F.2.1g, 6.2.1, 6.2.2, 6.3.2b | 122–123, 141, 156–163, 164, 175–177, 221–222 |
| 3 | Prosperity and Depression (1919–1941) | 7.1.1, 7.1.2a, 7.1.3a, 7.1.3c | 215–217, 240–241, 254–260, 284–289 |
| 4 | World War II and Postwar America (1931–1960) | 7.2.2, 8.1.1c, 8.1.2b, 8.1.2f, 8.2.2a | 377–379, 400, 405, 406–411, 412–415, 425–427 |
| 5 | Challenges and Change (1945–1980) | 8.1.2d, 8.3.1a, 8.3.1b, 8.3.1c, 8.3.2, 8.3.5 | 472–475, 478, 490–492, 536, 547, 553 |
| 6 | Changing and Enduring Issues (1980–Today) | 8.2.2a, 9.3.1 | 73–75, 88, 92, 119, 120, 155, 175, 187, 225–227, 459, 522–523, 580–583, 610, 679–680 |

After completing Era 1, read the following passage and use it with what you already know to answer the questions that follow.

---

### An Excerpt from the Populist Party's "The Omaha Platform," July 4, 1892

The conditions which surround us best justify our co-operation; we meet in the midst of a nation brought to the verge of moral, political, and material ruin. Corruption dominates the ballot-box, the Legislatures, the Congress, and touches even the ermine [weasels] of the bench. The people are demoralized. . . . The urban workmen are denied the right to organize . . . and they are rapidly degenerating into European conditions. . . . [O]ur annual agricultural productions amount to billions of dollars in value, which must, within a few weeks or months, be exchanged for billions of dollars' worth of commodities. . . . [T]he existing currency supply is wholly inadequate to make this exchange. . . . We believe that the power of government—in other words, of the people—should be expanded. . . . We demand that the amount of circulating medium [money supply] be speedily increased . . . [and that] transportation being a means of exchange and a public necessity, the government should own and operate the railroads in the interest of the people.

---

**1.** What group's interests did the Populist party represent?

  **A** bankers

  **B** politicians

  **C** women

  **D** farmers

**2.** Which of these positions did Populists support?

  **A** The national government should have less power.

  **B** The national government needs to regulate the economy.

  **C** The national government should halt westward expansion.

  **D** Sectional differences are a threat to the national government.

**3.** The excerpt above states "urban workmen are denied the right to organize." Which event might the statement refer to?

  **A** the formation of monopolies by the "robber barons"

  **B** the creation of the Interstate Commerce Commission to oversee railroads

  **C** the government reaction to the Homestead Strike by steel workers

  **D** the passage of Jim Crow laws in southern states

**4.** Which of the following was the result of increased immigration and productivity of factories in the late 1800s?

  **A** the rapid expansion of urban areas

  **B** the mechanization of agriculture

  **C** high wages for factory workers

  **D** overpopulation of the South

**5.** In 1896, racial segregation was upheld by the Supreme Court decision

  **A** *Brown v. Board of Education*

  **B** *Gideon v. Wainwright*

  **C** *Gibbons v. Ogden*

  **D** *Plessy v. Ferguson*

## MME Skills Practice

After completing Era 2, look at the following map and use it with what you already know to answer the questions that follow.

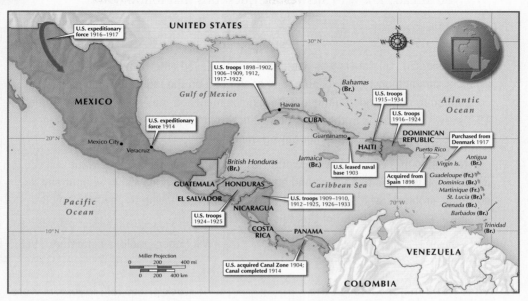

**1.** How does the map illustrate the principles of the Roosevelt Corollary to the Monroe Doctrine?

**A** The U.S. assumed the role of a "police power" in the Western Hemisphere.

**B** The U.S. was asserting its Manifest Destiny.

**C** The U.S. was responding to cries of help from Latin Americans for military protection.

**D** The U.S. no longer believed the Monroe Doctrine was applicable.

**2.** Roosevelt's Square Deal promoted which Progressive platform?

**A** reforming election rules

**B** recognizing women's right to vote

**C** ending lynching

**D** regulating of trusts and the protection of workers

**3.** What did Roosevelt's "big stick" policy advocate?

**A** using a strong military to achieve diplomatic goals

**B** expanding American investments abroad

**C** establishing national parks and forests

**D** enforcing antitrust legislation

**4.** How does the map above go against the United States' foreign policy of neutrality?

**A** It shows the US using diplomacy to solve problems.

**B** It shows the US promoting intervention.

**C** It shows how other countries threatened the US.

**D** It shows the US only wants to explore, not own, other lands.

**5.** As a result of US involvement in World War I, US foreign policy strove for

**A** political isolation and economic involvement

**B** political isolation and no economic involvement

**C** political intervention and economic involvement

**D** complete isolation

## MME Skills Practice

After completing Era 3, read the following passage and use it with what you already know to answer the questions that follow.

---

***Paying for It?***

Folksy comedian Will Rogers was one of the most beloved entertainers of his day. Whether standing onstage twirling a rope or chatting on the radio, he could always be counted on to deliver good-natured, amusing comments on the American scene. In the 1920s—with the nation in the midst of a giant economic boom—Rogers turned his keen eye on Americans' passion for buying things:

"No nation in the history of the world was ever sitting as pretty. If we want anything, all we have to do is go and buy it on credit. So that leaves us without any economic problems whatsoever, except perhaps some day having to pay for them. But we are certainly not thinking of that this early."

—Will Rogers, radio commentary, 1928

---

1. What was a major factor in the prosperity Rogers talks about?

   A the Harlem Renaissance

   B rising wages

   C increase in farm incomes

   D quota systems in immigrant law

2. How did Rogers's quote anticipate the crash of 1929?

   A It referred to the plight of rural America.

   B It exposed widespread anger for the burden of Prohibition.

   C It foreshadowed the Teapot Dome Scandal.

   D It pointed out that buying with credit would cause problems if people could not pay.

3. In the 1920s, stocks could be purchased "on margin," which is similar to credit. How did that system cause the 1929 crash?

   A It caused the price of stocks to rise above their real value.

   B Corrupt lenders were able to cheat investors out of money.

   C If stock prices fell, investors were unable to pay back loans.

   D It encouraged investors to buy only what they could afford.

4. How did the end of this prosperity affect the nations of Europe?

   A German war reparations kept the European economy relatively stable.

   B The Hawley-Smoot Tariff caused Europeans to loosen trade restrictions.

   C Britain and France began to loan money to the United States.

   D Germany ceased war reparations payments to England and France.

5. Which New Deal agency was created to help businesses?

   A Federal Reserve Board

   B National Recovery Administration

   C Civilian Conservation Corps

   D Home Owner's Loan Corporation

**MME Skills Practice**

After completing Era 4, read the following passage and use it with what you already know to answer the questions that follow.

"After I noticed the flash, white clouds spread over the blue sky. It was amazing. It was as if blue morning-glories had suddenly bloomed up in the sky. . . . Then came the heat wave. It was very, very hot. Even though there was a window glass in front of me, I felt really hot. It was as if I was looking directly into a kitchen oven."

—Isao Kita. From *Hiroshima Witness*

1. How did Truman justify his decision to use the atom bomb?
   A He claimed he wasn't aware of the destructive power.
   B He wanted to make a statement to the Soviets about American firepower.
   C Military advisers informed him an invasion of Japan would cost 1 million American lives.
   D He learned the Japanese were developing atomic weapons.

2. How did the Truman Doctrine set a new course for American foreign policy?
   A Troops were posted in South America.
   B Economic aid was set aside for nations in Asia only.
   C Aid was set aside for nations to rebuild.
   D Troops of various nations were recruited.

3. How did the Soviets' development of atomic technology affect the Cold War?
   A Truman ordered the A.E.C. to produce a more powerful hydrogen bomb.
   B The Soviets, under Khrushchev, helped provide Communist China with atomic technology.
   C Truman addressed Congress and asked for funding to help curb the spread of communism.
   D Eisenhower and Khrushchev signed a nuclear non-proliferation treaty in 1955.

4. Which was a direct result of the Cold War conflict in Korea?
   A The United States invaded China but was forced to withdraw.
   B 300,000 Chinese soldiers were either wounded or killed.
   C China extended its border beyond the Yalu River.
   D General Douglas MacArthur was fired for insubordination.

5. McCarthyism can best be described as
   A an economic backlash of the Cold War
   B Americans' fear of a Russian invasion
   C persecution of Americans suspected of Communist activities
   D Senator McCarthy's theory of how to end communism

## MME Skills Practice

After completing Era 5, read the following passage and use it with what you already know to answer the questions that follow.

> **An excerpt from Lyndon Johnson's speech to Congress on March, 15, 1965, a week after deadly racial violence erupted in Selma, Alabama.**
>
> . . . There is no Negro problem. There is no Southern problem. There is no Northern problem. There is only an American problem. And we are met here tonight as Americans—not as Democrats or Republicans—we are met here as Americans to solve that problem. . . . Many of the issues of civil rights are very complex and most difficult. But about this there can and should be no argument. Every American citizen must have an equal right to vote. . . . What happened in Selma is part of a far larger movement which reaches into every section and State of America. . . . Because it is not just Negroes, but really it is all of us, who must overcome the crippling legacy of bigotry and injustice. . . . And we shall overcome. . . .

**1. The Civil Rights Act of 1965 . . .**

  **A** gave equality in the Army

  **B** banned use of different voter registration standards for blacks and whites

  **C** eliminated literacy tests for voting

  **D** eliminated the poll tax

**2. Why did the Student Nonviolent Coordinating Committee form?**

  **A** bring change through military confrontation

  **B** protest FBI surveillance of civil rights groups

  **C** promote MLK during the bus boycott

  **D** give greater voice to young people in civil rights movement

**3. Johnson's message of unity in his speech is an echo of which Civil Rights leader?**

  **A** Cesar Chavez

  **B** John F. Kennedy

  **C** Rosa Parks

  **D** Martin Luther King, Jr.

**4. Which event led Johnson to ask Congress for complete control over US actions in Vietnam?**

  **A** Tet Offensive

  **B** Gulf of Tonkin attack

  **C** My Lai massacre

  **D** bombing of Ho Chi Minh Trail

**5. Johnson's Kerner Commission determined the major cause of violent riots in Detroit and other major cities to be**

  **A** sexism.

  **B** racism.

  **C** nativism.

  **D** classism.

**MME Skills Practice**

• Inquiry and Decision Making

After completing Era 6, read the following passage and use it with what you already know to answer the questions that follow.

---

### IMMIGRATION

The United States has always been a nation of immigrants, though the origin of the immigrants has changed. Public policy about immigration has varied greatly, and some people think that the number of immigrants should be limited. Others would like to increase the number of immigrants who are allowed to enter the country legally. Study the following information about immigration.

### Data Section

The following charts provide information about the geographic origin of immigrants to the United States from 1870 to 1910 and in 2000. Study the charts and complete the tasks on the following page.

**Part A**

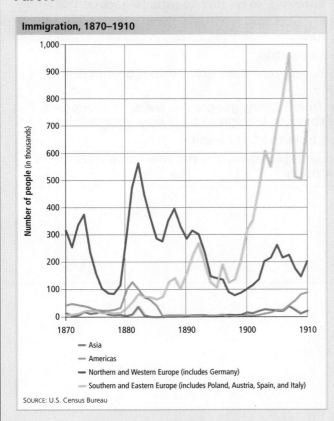

**Immigration, 1870–1910**

Number of people (in thousands)

— Asia
— Americas
— Northern and Western Europe (includes Germany)
— Southern and Eastern Europe (includes Poland, Austria, Spain, and Italy)

SOURCE: U.S. Census Bureau

**Part B**

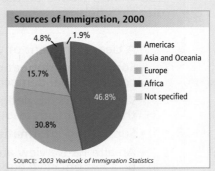

**Sources of Immigration, 2000**

4.8%   1.9%

15.7%

46.8%

30.8%

■ Americas
■ Asia and Oceania
■ Europe
■ Africa
■ Not specified

SOURCE: *2003 Yearbook of Immigration Statistics*

After studying the data section on page MI 47 complete the tasks below.

## Task I: Interpreting Information
**Which of the following statements best describes how immigration in 2000 differed from 1900?**

A In 2000, a smaller percentage of immigrants were from Asia.

B In 2000, a higher percentage of immigrants were from Europe.

C In 2000, a higher percentage of immigrants were from the Americas.

D In 2000, most immigrants came from Africa.

## Task II: Take a Stand
You will now take a stand on the following public policy issue: How should government regulate immigration? Write a letter to your senator explaining your position. Use information to provide reasons that support your position.

You will be graded on the following, so be sure to include each of the elements below:

- A clear statement of your position
- Supporting information using core democratic values of American constitutional democracy
- Supporting knowledge from history, geography, civics, or economics that you already know (It is not enough to state only your opinion.)
- Supporting information from the Data Section
- An alternative view and an explanation why the alternative view would be a less effective public policy

# Contents

*A series of handbooks provides skills instruction to help you read, learn, and demonstrate your knowledge of American history.*

## Reading Informational Texts

## Writing Handbook

## Critical Thinking About Visuals and Text Sources

## Speaking and Listening

# Reading Informational Texts

*Reading a newspaper, a magazine, an Internet page, or a textbook differs from reading a novel. You read nonfiction texts to acquire new information. Researchers have shown that the reading strategies presented below will help you maximize your understanding of such informational texts.*

## Strategies to Use Before You Read

Before you read informational text, it's important to take the time to do some prereading. These strategies will help.

### Set a Purpose for Reading

Try to focus on a goal when you're reading the text. Preview a section by reading the objectives and looking at the illustrations. Then, write a purpose for your reading, such as:

- "I'll learn about the development of the North and South and find ways to compare these regions."
- "I'll find out about the growth of railroads."

### Ask Questions

Before you read a section, consider what you'd like to know about a topic. Then, ask questions that will yield relevant information. Scan the section headings and illustrations and write a few questions in a chart like the one below. As you read, try to answer each of your questions. Use phrases and words to fill in the chart.

| Question | Answer |
|---|---|
| Why did immigrants come to the United States in the late 1800s? | To find religious freedom, to escape poverty, to flee persecution |
| What was life like for immigrants when they arrived? | It was hard at first, but opportunities opened up; sometimes they faced hostility and prejudice |

## Predict

Engage in the reading process by making predictions about what you are preparing to learn. Scan the section headings and the visuals. Then, write a prediction, such as:

• "I will find out what caused the United States to fight Spain in 1898."

Keep your predictions in mind as you read—do they turn out to be accurate or do you need to revise them?

## Use Prior Knowledge

Research shows that if you connect the new information in your reading to your prior knowledge, you'll be more likely to remember the new information. You'll also see the value of studying history if you see how it connects to the present. After previewing a section, create a chart like this one. Complete the chart as you read the section.

| What I Know | What I Want to Know | What I Learned |
|---|---|---|
| Older Americans are worried about Social Security and whether it will provide for them when they retire. | When did Social Security start? | Social Security was a program that started during the Great Depression of the 1930s to help provide for older Americans when they retire. |

# Strategies to Use As You Read

It's important to be an active reader. Use these strategies as you read informational text.

## Reread or Read Ahead

If you do not understand a certain passage, reread it to look for connections among the words and sentences. For example, look for cause-and-effect words that link ideas or sequence words that show when events took place. Or, try reading ahead to see if the ideas are clarified later on. Once you find new clarifying information, return to the confusing text and read it again with the new information in mind.

## Paraphrase/Summarize

To paraphrase is to restate information in your own words. Summarizing—a version of paraphrasing—can also help you confirm your understanding of the text. Summarizing focuses on restating the main ideas of a passage, as you can see in the example below. Include a few important details, such as the time period, to orient yourself or other readers to the text.

| Original Paragraph | Summary |
|---|---|
| During the 1920s, the National Women's Party took a more militant position, demanding complete economic, social, and political equality with men. Their primary goal was the passage of the Equal Rights Amendment. Most women, however, believed that a new constitutional amendment was premature. | In the 1920s, the National Womens Party demanded complete equality with men, working for passage of the Equal Rights Amendment. Most women thought it was too soon for such an amendment. |

## Identify Main Ideas and Details

A main idea is the most important point in a paragraph or section of text. Some main ideas are stated directly, but others are implied. You must determine these yourself by reading carefully. Pause occasionally to make sure you can identify the main idea.

Main ideas are supported by details. Record main ideas and details in an outline format like the one shown here.

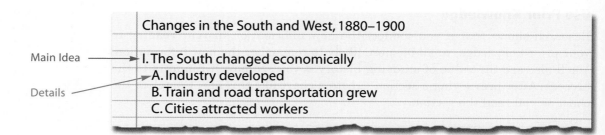

Changes in the South and West, 1880–1900

Main Idea → I. The South changed economically
A. Industry developed
Details → B. Train and road transportation grew
C. Cities attracted workers

## Analyze the Text's Structure

Just as you might organize a story about your weekend to highlight the most important parts, authors will organize their writing to stress their key ideas. Analyzing text structure can help you tap into this organization. In a social studies textbook, the author frequently uses one of the structures listed in the chart at right to organize information. Learn to identify structures in texts and you'll remember text information more effectively.

### Structures for Organizing Information

**Compare and Contrast** Here, an author highlights similarities and differences between two or more ideas, cultures, processes, people, etc. Look for clue words such as *on the other hand* or *similarly*.

**Sequence** Here, an author recounts the order in which events occurred or steps were taken. History is often told in chronological sequence but can also involve flashbacks from later times to earlier times. Look for sequence words such as *initially*, *later*, and *ultimately*.

**Cause and Effect** Here, an author highlights the impact of one event on another or the effects of key events. Cause and effect is critical to understanding history because events in one time often strongly influence those in later times. Look for clue words such as *because*, *so*, or *as a result*.

## Analyze the Author's Purpose

Different reading materials are written with different goals, or purposes. For example, this textbook is written to teach you about American history. The technical manual that accompanies a cellphone is written to explain how to use the product.

An author's purpose influences not only how the material is presented but also how you read it. Thus you must identify the purpose, whether it is stated directly or merely suggested. If it is not directly stated, use clues in the text—such as opinion words in an editorial—to identify the author's purpose.

# Vocabulary

Here are several strategies to help you understand the meaning of a word you do not recognize.

**Use Context Clues**   You can often define an unfamiliar word with clues from the surrounding text. For example, in the sentence "One campaign of the Progressives had the goal of improving sanitation in cities," the words *campaign* and *improve* are clues that Progressives were reformers. Context clues can be in the same sentence as the unfamiliar word or in nearby sentences or paragraphs.

**Analyze Word Parts**   Use your knowledge of word parts to help you define unfamiliar words. Break the word into its parts—root, prefix, suffix. What do you know about these parts? For example, the prefix *inter* means "between" and the suffix *ism* means "belief in." The word *international* means "between nations" and *internationalism* means "belief in relations between nations."

**Recognize Word Origins**   Another way to figure out the meaning of an unfamiliar word is to understand the word's origins. Use your experience with Greek or Latin roots, for example, to build meaning. The word *bilingual* contains the Latin root *lingua,* which means "tongue." *Bilingual* means "two tongues" or "two languages."

## Distinguish Between Facts and Opinions/Recognize Bias

It's important to read actively, especially when reading informational texts. Decide whether information is factual—which means it can be proven—or if it includes opinions or bias—that is, people's views or evaluations.

Anytime you read material that conveys opinions, such as an editorial, keep an eye out for author bias. This bias might be revealed in the use of emotionally charged words or faulty logic. For example, the newspaper editorial below includes factual statements (in blue) and opinion statements (in red). The emotionally charged words (underlined) will get a rise out of people. Faulty logic may include circular reasoning that returns to its beginning and either/or arguments that ignore other possibilities.

> **Editorial**
>
> Some day, Dwight Eisenhower will be remembered as the best President of the 20th century. He kept government small; he left the states alone to tend to their affairs; and the economy hummed. Any American with any sense will agree that these things contributed to the overall well-being of the nation.

## Identify Evidence

Read critically. Do not accept an author's conclusion automatically. Identify and evaluate the author's evidence. Does it justify the conclusion in quantity and content? An author may present facts to support a claim, but there may be more to the story than facts. For example, what evidence does the writer of the editorial above present to support the claim that Eisenhower was a great President? Perhaps Americans who didn't prosper in the 1950s would disagree with the assertion.

### Evaluate Credibility

After you evaluate evidence, check an author's credentials. Consider his or her level of experience and expertise about the topic. Is he or she likely to be knowledgeable *and* objective about the topic? Evaluating credibility is especially important with Web sites you may visit on the Internet. Ask the following questions to determine if a Web site and its author are reliable.

- Who sponsors the Web site? Is it a respected organization, a discussion group of individuals, or a single person?
- What is the source of the Web site's information? Does the site list sources for facts and statements?
- Does the Web site creator include his or her name and credentials?
- Is the information on the Web site balanced and objective or biased to reflect only one point of view?
- Can you verify the Web site's information using two other sources, such as an encyclopedia or news agency?
- Is the information current? Is there a date on the Web site to show when it was created or last updated?

# Strategies to Use After You Read

### Evaluate Understanding

Evaluate how well you understand what you've read.
- Go back to the questions you asked yourself before reading. Try to answer each of them.
- Check the predictions you made and revise them if appropriate.
- Draw a conclusion about the author's evidence and credibility.
- Check meanings of unfamiliar words in the dictionary to confirm your definitions.

### Recall Information

Before moving on to new material, you should be able to answer the following questions fully:
- What was the text about?
- What was the purpose of the text?
- How was the text structured?

You should also be able to place the information you have just read in the context of your prior knowledge of the topic.

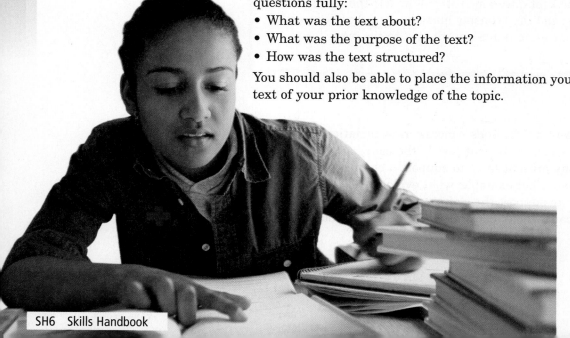

# Writing Handbook

*Writing is one of the most powerful communication tools you will use for the rest of your life. Research shows that writing about what you read actually helps you learn new information and ideas. A systematic approach to writing—including prewriting, drafting, revising, and proofreading—can always help you write better.*

## Narrative Essay

Narrative writing tells a story about a personal experience or a historical event. This story might also recount a person's life or tell about an important accomplishment.

### 1 Prewriting

**Choose a topic.** The focus of your essay will often be about a historical event from a particular point of view. Use these ideas as a guide.

- **Review the details of the event** you will be writing about.
- **Choose a person,** actual or fictional, who would have experienced the event.
- **List words** describing why the person caused the event or how he or she might have reacted to it.
- **Brainstorm** about the story you will write. Jot down ideas like the ones below.

> Teenager in the 1920s responds to hearing jazz music for the first time.
> • Circumstances: standing in the street outside an apartment building, overhearing a musician practicing
> • Reactions: startled at first because the music is different; intrigued; spellbound; wants to dance to the music; goes home and tries to play jazz

**Consider audience and purpose.**

- Keep your **audience's** knowledge and experience level in mind. Make sure you provide any necessary background information.
- Choose a **purpose** as well. If you want to entertain, include humorous details. You might also include more serious insights.

**Gather details.**

- Collect the facts and details you need to tell your story.
- Research any background about the historical event that readers might need to know about.

## 2 Drafting

**Identify the climax,** or most interesting part of your story. Then, logically organize your story into a beginning, middle, and end. Narratives are often told in chronological order.

**Open strongly** with an engaging sentence, such as the one below, that will catch your reader's attention.

**Use sensory details,** such as sights, sounds, or smells, to make the story vivid for readers. Describe people's actions and gestures. Pinpoint and use detail to describe locations.

**Write a conclusion** that sums up the significance of the event or situation you are writing about.

Strong opening engages the reader.

Sensory details help the reader envision the experience.

Insight or significance tells the reader what this event means to the person in the narrative or to history.

> I never could have imagined how a simple stroll down the street would change my life. I was walking down the street yesterday, whistling to myself, when the most strange and enticing harmonies drifted toward me from an open third-floor window. Now, I'm pretty cool, but I've never heard such music before. It set me tingling; it set me to swaying. It made me want to dance right there on the spot. I emerged from the trance as the saxophonist let the last full note drift into the air. Then, I rushed home to see if I could replicate the smooth new sound on my clarinet. I know this chance encounter has changed my life forever.

## 3 Revising

**Add dialogue or description.** Dialogue, or conveying a person's thoughts or feelings in his or her own words, can make a narrative more effective. Look for places where the emotions are especially intense. In the model, this might be when the writer began to "feel" the music.

| First Draft | Revised Original |
|---|---|
| The music made me feel very involved. It made me want to dance. | It set me tingling; it set me to swaying. It made me want to dance right there on the spot. |

**Revise word choice.** Replace general words with more specific, colorful ones. Choose vivid action verbs, precise adjectives, and specific nouns to convey your meaning. Look at the example above. Notice how much more effective the revised version is at conveying the experience.

Read your draft aloud. Listen for grammatical errors and statements that are unclear. Revise your sentences as necessary.

## 4 Publishing and Presenting

**Share by reading aloud.** Highlight text you want to emphasize and then read your essay aloud to the class. Invite and respond to questions.

# Expository Writing

Expository writing explains ideas or information in detail. The strategies on these pages examine each of several types of expository writing.

## ❶Prewriting

**Choose a topic.** In social studies, the focus of your writing might be comparing and contrasting economic trends, explaining causes and effects of current events, or exploring problems the nation has faced and the solutions it has sought. These ideas are a guide.

- **Create a compare/contrast grab bag.** With a small group, write on separate slips of paper examples from each category: ideas, events, or time periods. Mix the slips in a bag and choose two. Compare and contrast the two ideas, events, or time periods.

- **Interview** someone who made a major change in lifestyle, such as moving from one part of the country to another. Find out how and why the person did this. Understanding why is the basis of any cause-and-effect essay.

- **Take a mental walk.** Study a map and envision taking a tour of the region. Think about problems each area you visit might face, such as economic challenges or natural disasters. Choose a problem and suggest solutions for it.

**Consider audience and purpose.** Consider how much your readers know about the problem, comparison, or event you will address. Suit your writing to your audience's knowledge or plan to give explanations of unfamiliar terms and concepts.

**Gather details.** Collect the facts and details you need to write your essay.

**Research the topic.** Use books, the Internet, or interviews of local experts. List facts, details, and other evidence related to your topic. Also consider your personal experience. For example, you might know about a problem from your own experience or have witnessed the effects of a historic legal decision.

**Create a graphic organizer.** For cause-and-effect or problem-solution essays, use a two-column chart. Process writing can be listed as a bulleted list of steps. A Venn diagram can help you compare and contrast.

**World War I**
- New weapons used: machine guns, poison gas, submarines
- 8.5 million military deaths

- Fought by two powerful alliances
- Began in Europe, then spread

**World War II**
- New weapon used: atomic bomb
- 20 million military deaths

**Identify causes and effects.** List possible explanations for events. Remember that many events result from multiple causes. Identify effects both large and small. Note that some events may have effects that in turn cause other events. Look for causes and effects in all your expository essays. But be aware that sometimes there are limitations on determining cause and effect.

## ❷ Drafting

**Match structure to purpose.** Typically, cause-and-effect essays are written in sequence order. Problem-solution essays benefit from block organization, which presents the entire problem and proposes a solution. For compare/contrast essays, you can organize by subject or by point.

| |
| --- |
| **By subject:** Discuss the events and outcomes of World War I, and then compare and contrast these with those of World War II. |
| **By point:** Introduce a category, such as use of new weapons. Relate both wars to this category, comparing or contrasting them along the way. |

**Give background.** To discuss events from history, first orient the reader to time and place. Choose the important facts but don't overwhelm the reader with detail. If you need to, return to prewriting to narrow your topic further.

**Elaborate for interest and emphasis.** Give details about each point in your essay. For example, add facts that make the link between events so that a cause-and-effect relationship is clear. Also, readers will support proposed solutions more if your details clearly show how these solutions will solve the stated problem. Use facts and human experiences to make your essay vivid.

**Connect to today.** Even when you write about historical events, you may find links to today. Explore these links in your essay.

Identify the topic to orient readers.

Chronological order walks readers through the cause-and-effect sequence.

Elaboration supports the relationship you are highlighting.

Connection to today tells readers why this matters to them.

The United States population underwent tremendous change in the first half of the twentieth century. In the early part of the century, Americans moved from rural to urban areas. Later, people moved out of cities into suburbs in increasing numbers. These changes resulted from many causes.

Lured by jobs in the cities' factories, rural Americans and growing numbers of immigrants settled in cities during the late nineteenth and early twentieth centuries. By 1920, urban population had surpassed rural population.

Thirty years later, Americans were again on the move. Cities had become overcrowded, and Americans longed to own homes and live in more space. The explosion of highways also made it easier to commute from the suburbs to the cities for work.

Americans continue to be on the move today. Now they are moving to the Sunbelt or "exurbs" in a continuing effort to improve their lives.

# 3 Revising

**Add transition words.** Make cause-and-effect relationships clear with words such as *because, as a result,* and so on. To compare or contrast ideas, use linking words, such as *similarly, both,* and *equally* or *in contrast, instead,* and *yet.* Use words such as *first, second, next,* and *finally* to help readers follow steps in a sequence or chain of causes. Look at the following examples. In the revised version, a reader knows the correct order in which to perform the steps.

| First Draft | Revised |
| --- | --- |
| Historians form an educated guess called a hypothesis. They test that hypothesis with further research. | <u>Next</u>, historians form an educated guess called a hypothesis. <u>Then</u>, they test that hypothesis with further research. |

**Remember purpose.** Shape your draft so that it answers the question or thesis you began with. For a problem-solution essay—in which your purpose is to sell your solution—that means anticipating opposing arguments and responding to them. For a cause-and-effect essay, you want to stress the way one event leads to the next. Always tell readers why they should care about your topic.

**Review organization.** Confirm that your ideas flow in a logical order. Write main points on index cards. Reorganize these until you are satisfied that the order best strengthens your essay.

**Add details.** Make sure you have not left out any steps in your essay, and do not assume readers will make the connections. For example, you might forget to state explicitly that your narrative represents a particular point of view. Add more background if necessary for clarity.

**Revise sentences and words.** Look at your sentence length. Vary it to include both short and long sentences. Then, scan for vague words, such as *good.* Replace them with specific and vibrant words, such as *effective.* Use technical terms only when necessary, and then define them.

**Peer review.** Ask a peer to read your draft. Is it clear? Can he or she follow your ideas? Revise areas of confusion.

# 4 Publishing and Presenting

**Contribute to a class manual.** Include your comparison essay in a class History Journal.

**Submit to a library.** Find a specialized library, such as a presidential library. Mail your essay to the library's publications or public relations department.

**Seek publication.** If your historical events or issues are local, seek publication in a local historical magazine or contact a historical society. You might speak to their members.

**Mail to an advocacy group.** Find a local, national, or international organization that is concerned with your topic. Send them your essay and ask for comments on its ideas. Make sure to include a self-addressed stamped envelope and a note explaining your essay and offering thanks for its review.

# Research Writing

## ① Prewriting

**Choose a topic.** Often, a teacher will assign your research topic. You may have flexibility in choosing your focus or you may have the opportunity to completely define your topic. These ideas are a guide.

- **Catalog scan.** Using a card or electronic catalog in a library, or Internet search engine, search for topics that interest you. When a title looks promising, find the book on the shelves. Or follow up on your Internet search results by reviewing the linked Web sites. You can use what you find to decide on your final topic.

- **Notes review.** Review your social studies notes from the last month or so. Jot down topics that you found interesting. Then, repeat the process with your other classes. For example, you might find a starting point for research into an environmental issue from a biology experiment.

- **Social studies categories game.** With a group, brainstorm categories in social studies. For example, you might list key American leaders or important wars. Within each category, take turns adding subtopics. The chart below shows different topics related to agriculture.

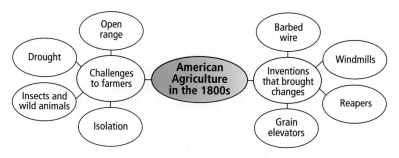

You can use sources such as newspapers to get ideas.

**Analyze the audience.** Your research and your paper should be strongly influenced by the audience. How much will readers know about this topic and how much will you have to teach them?

**Gather details.** Collect the facts and details you need to write your paper. Use resources beyond the typical history books. Look at nonfiction books such as memoirs or collections of letters. Also look at magazine and newspaper articles. Consider news magazines, as well as those focused on topics such as history or travel. Search the Internet, starting with online encyclopedias, news organizations, and history Web sites. Remember to check Web sites for reliability.

**Organize evidence and ideas.** Use note cards to record information and to help you organize your thoughts. Start with a general thesis statement in mind. Then, begin reading and taking notes. Write a heading at the top of each note card to group it under a subtopic. Note a number or title to identify the information source. In the examples below, the number 3 is used. Use the same number for an additional source card containing the bibliographic information you will need.

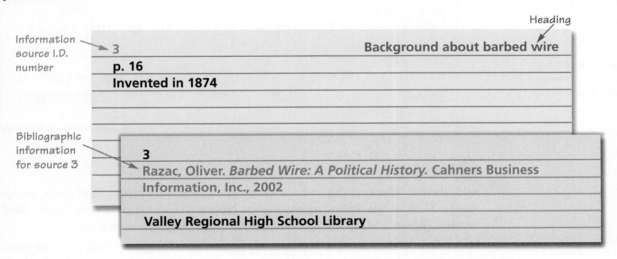

Heading

Information source I.D. number

3        **Background about barbed wire**

**p. 16**
**Invented in 1874**

Bibliographic information for source 3

**3**
Razac, Oliver. *Barbed Wire: A Political History.* Cahners Business Information, Inc., 2002

**Valley Regional High School Library**

## ② Drafting

**Fine-tune your thesis.** Review your notes to find relationships between ideas. Shape a thesis that is supported by the majority of your information, then check that it is narrow enough to address thoroughly in the allotted time and space. Remember, you can fine-tune your thesis further as you draft or even when you revise.

**Organize to fit your purpose.** Do you want to persuade readers of a particular position about your topic, compare and contrast aspects of the topic, or show a cause-and-effect relationship? Organize appropriately.

**Make an outline.** Create an outline in which you identify each topic and subtopic in a single phrase. You can then turn these phrases into sentences and later into the topic sentences of your draft paragraphs. Study the example at the top of the next page to see how to do this well.

**Write by paragraph.** Write an introduction, at least three body paragraphs, and a conclusion. Address a subtopic of your main topic in each body paragraph. Support all your statements with the facts and details you gathered.

An outline helps you structure your information.

Each body paragraph looks at a part of the whole topic.

The introduction puts the topic in a context of time and place. The entire paragraph conveys the thesis: dividing up the Plains with barbed wire had lasting effects for the region.

The conclusion recaps key points and leaves readers with a final statement to remember.

---

**The Importance of Barbed Wire**

Outline

I. Introduction
II. Why barbed wire was invented
III. How barbed wire was used
IV. Effects of the use of barbed wire
   A. End of open grazing lands for cattle
   B. End of cowboys' way of life
   C. Increased importance of farming on the Plains
V. Conclusion

Introduction

No invention was more important to the development of the American Plains than barbed wire. Until its widespread use in the late 1800s, cattle herds roamed the Plains region and farmers worried about their crops getting trampled. With the advent of barbed wire, all of this changed.

Conclusion

By the end of the nineteenth century, the Plains had been sectioned off through the use of barbed wire. The earlier life on the Plains had been changed forever.

---

## 3 Revising

**Add detail.** Mark points where more details would strengthen your statements. Look at the following examples. Notice the added details in the revised version. When adding facts, make certain that they are accurate.

**Make the connection for readers.** Help readers find their way through your ideas. First, check that your body paragraphs and the information within them flow in a logical sequence. If they do not, revise to correct this. Then, add transition words to link ideas and paragraphs.

**Give credit.** Check that you have used your own words or given proper credit for borrowed words. You can give credit easily with parenthetical notes. These include the author's last name and the relevant page number from the source. For example, you could cite the note card on the previous page as "(Razac, 16)."

| First Draft | Revised |
|---|---|
| Cowboys would ride the range with huge herds of cattle. Their goal was to bring the herd to Kansas for shipping to markets in Chicago and the East. | Cowboys worked long hours on the dusty Plains, keeping constant vigilance on their herd of hundreds of cattle. They always kept the goal in sight: reaching Kansas, a key shipping center, then taking a well-deserved rest. |

## 4 Publishing and Presenting

**Plan a conference.** Gather a group of classmates and present your research projects. You may each wish to create visual materials to accompany your presentations. After you share your papers, hold a question-and-answer session.

# Persuasive Essay

Persuasive writing supports an opinion or position. In social studies, persuasive essays often argue for or against positions on historical or current issues.

## 1 Prewriting

**Choose a topic.** Choose a topic that provokes an argument and has at least two sides. Use these ideas as a guide.

- **Round-table discussion.** Talk with classmates about issues you have studied recently. Outline pro-and-con positions about these issues.
- **Textbook flip.** Scan the table of contents or flip through the pages of your textbook. Focus on historical issues that engage your feelings.
- **Make connections.** Relate current events to history. Develop a position for or against a situation of importance today using historical evidence.

**Narrow your topic.**

- **Cover part of the topic** if you find too many pros and cons for a clear argument of the whole topic.
- **Use looping.** Write for five minutes on the general topic. Circle the most important idea. Then write for five minutes on that idea. Continue looping until the topic is manageable.

**Consider your audience.** Choose arguments that will appeal to the audience for your writing and that are likely to persuade them to agree with your views.

**Gather evidence.** Collect the evidence to support your position convincingly.

- **Identify pros and cons.** Use a graphic organizer like the one below to list points on both sides of the issue.

| The United States should increase its efforts to send astronauts to Mars. | |
| --- | --- |
| **Pro** ⟵ | ⟶ **Con** |
| • Space travel increases human knowledge about Earth and inspires young people to learn about science.<br>• Space travel leads to technologies that can be used to improve life on Earth.<br>• The United States has a history of exploration beyond its borders; this would be just one more step. | • Space travel is too expensive.<br>• Space travel is a luxury; the nation should concentrate on needs at home.<br>• There is no need to send humans to Mars when we can learn as much from robots traveling there. |

- **Interview** adults who remember the first moon landing. What do they think about sending astronauts to Mars? Ask them for reasons to support their views.
- **Research** to get your facts straight. Read articles or books about the space program.

## 2 Drafting

**State your thesis.** Clearly state your position, as in this example:

> The United States should strongly promote the space program by sending people to Mars. We have so much to learn from the challenge of space travel that can help us at home.

**Use your introduction** to provide a context for the issue. Tell your readers when and why the issue arose, and identify the important people involved.

**Sequence your arguments.** Open or close with your strongest argument. If you close with the strongest argument, open with the second-best argument.

**Acknowledge opposition.** State, and then refute, opposing arguments.

**Use facts and details.** Include quotations, statistics, or comparisons to build your case. Include personal experiences or reactions to the topic, such as those a family member might have shared when interviewed.

**Write a conclusion** that restates your thesis and closes with a strong, compelling argument.

Background orients readers.

Thesis identifies your main argument.

Supporting argument clarifies your thesis.

Opposing argument, noted and refuted, adds to your position.

For a long time, the United States led the world in space exploration. But recently, the space program has become more limited. This situation should change. The United States should strongly promote the space program by sending people to Mars. We have so much to learn from meeting the challenge of space travel that can help us here at home.

Sending people into space has already yielded great rewards in the development of technology and other advances. Improved computers, medicines, and GPS systems are all positive by-products of space exploration. Some people might argue that space exploration is too expensive and that we have problems to tackle right here at home. However, the benefits of space exploration will help us at home today and in the future. The benefits outweigh the costs....

### ❸ Revising

**Add information.** Extra details can generate interest in your topic. For example, in the essay on space travel add a quotation from a news article that assesses the importance of space exploration to solving problems on Earth.

**Review arguments.** Make sure your arguments are logically sound and clearly developed. Avoid faulty logic such as circular reasoning (arguing a point by merely restating it differently). Evidence is the best way to support your points. Look at the following examples. Notice how much more effectively the revised version supports the argument.

| First Draft | Revised |
|---|---|
| Space exploration will help our nation in many ways. | Space exploration will provide jobs, new technologies, and inspiration to young scientists. |

**Use transition words** to guide readers through your ideas.

- **To show contrast:** *however, although, despite*
- **To point out a reason:** *since, because, if*
- **To signal conclusion:** *therefore, consequently, so, then*

### ❹ Publishing and Presenting

**Persuasive Speech.** Many persuasive essays are delivered orally. Prepare your essay as a speech, highlighting words for emphasis and adding changes in tone, volume, or speed.

# Writing for Assessment

Assessment writing differs from all other writing that you do. You have many fewer choices as a writer, and you almost always face a time limit. In social studies, you'll need to write both short answers and extended responses for tests. While these contrast in some ways, they share many requirements.

## 1 Prewriting

**Choose a topic.** Short-answer questions seldom offer a topic choice. For extended-response questions, however, you may have a choice of more than one question. Use the following strategies to help you navigate that choice.

- **Examine the question.** To choose a question you can answer effectively, analyze what each question is asking. Use key words such as those listed below to help you choose topics and respond to short-answer questions in which the topic is given.

| Key Words | What You Need in an Answer |
|---|---|
| Explain | Give a clear, complete account of how something works or why something happened. |
| Compare/Contrast | Show how two or more things are alike and different. |
| Define | Give examples to explain meaning. |
| Argue, Convince, Support, Persuade | Take a position on an issue and present strong reasons to support your side of the issue. |
| Summarize | Provide the most important elements of a subject. |
| Evaluate/Judge | Assign a value or explain an opinion. |
| Interpret | Support a thesis with examples from the text. |

Notice in the examples below that the key words are underlined:

**Short answer:** Describe one way that Chief Joseph showed his military expertise.

**Extended response:** According to the author of this article, Chief Joseph was both a peace chief and a military genius. Use information from the article to support this conclusion.

- **Plot your answer.** After choosing a question, quickly plot the answer in your mind. Do you have the information to answer this question? If the answer is no, try another question.

**Measure your time.** Your goal is to show the instructor that you've mastered the material. To stay focused on this goal, divide your time: one-quarter on prewriting; half on drafting; one-quarter on revising. For short-answer questions, determine how much of the overall test time you can spend on each question. Don't spend more than that.

**Gather details.** Organize the facts and details you need to write your answer. For short-answer questions, this usually involves identifying exactly what information is required.

**Use a graphic organizer.** For extended-response questions, divide your topic into subtopics that fit the type of question. Jot down facts and details for each. For the question on Chief Joseph, the following organizer would be effective:

| Chief Joseph of the Nez Percés |
| --- |
| **Peace Chief** |
| • traded peacefully with white settlers (1) |
| • reluctantly went to war (2) |
| • famous speech, "I will fight no more forever." (3) |
| |
| **Military Genius** |
| • won battles with fewer warriors than opposing troops had (a) |
| • avoided capture for many months (b) |
| • led his people more than 1,000 miles (c) |
| • knew when to surrender for the good of his people (d) |

## ② Drafting

**Choose an organization** that fits the question. With a short-answer question, write one to three complete sentences. With extended responses, you'll need more elaborate organization. For the question on Chief Joseph, organize your points by importance within each subtopic. For a summary or explanation, use chronological order. For compare/contrast, present similarities first, then differences.

**Open and close strongly.** Start your answer by restating the question or using its language to state your position. This helps you focus and shows the instructor that you understand the question. Finish with a strong conclusion that restates your position. For short answers, include some language from the question in your response.

> One way that Chief Joseph showed his military expertise was by defeating U.S. Army troops despite having fewer warriors than they had.

**Support your ideas.** Each paragraph should directly or indirectly support your main idea. Choose facts that build a cohesive argument. The numbered sentences in the draft below show how this writer organized support.

*The opening restates the question and presents the writer's main idea.*

*The writer uses information from the graphic organizer, in order of importance.*

*The writer supports the second subtopic in a separate paragraph.*

*The conclusion recaps the main idea and again references the question's language.*

> Chief Joseph was both a peace chief and a military genius.
> He was a peace chief because he traded peacefully with white settlers for many years. (1) He went to war reluctantly after the government ordered his people to move to a reservation. (2) When he finally surrendered, he said in a famous speech, "I will fight no more forever." (3)
> Chief Joseph was also a military genius. He fought off U.S. Army forces with fewer warriors than they had, (a) and he avoided capture for many months. (b) He led his people more than 1,000 miles (c) before he made the decision to surrender. (d) Chief Joseph will long be remembered for his dual roles as peace chief and military genius.

## 3 Revising

**Examine word choice.** Replace general words with specific words. Add transitions where these improve clarity. Read the following examples. The revised version shows the relative importance of the writer's supporting evidence.

| First Draft | Revised |
|---|---|
| Chief Joseph was both a peace chief and a military genius. He was a peace chief because he traded peacefully with whites for many years. He went to war reluctantly.... | Chief Joseph was both a peace chief and a military genius. He was a peace chief for several reasons. First, he traded peacefully with whites for many years. Second, he went to war reluctantly.... |

**Check organization.** Make sure your introduction includes a main idea and defines subtopics. Review each paragraph for a single main idea. Check that your conclusion summarizes the information you've presented.

## 4 Publishing and Presenting

**Edit and proof.** Check spelling, grammar, and mechanics. Make sure that tenses match, that subjects agree with verbs, and that sentences are not too long. Finally, confirm that you have responded to all the questions you were asked to answer.

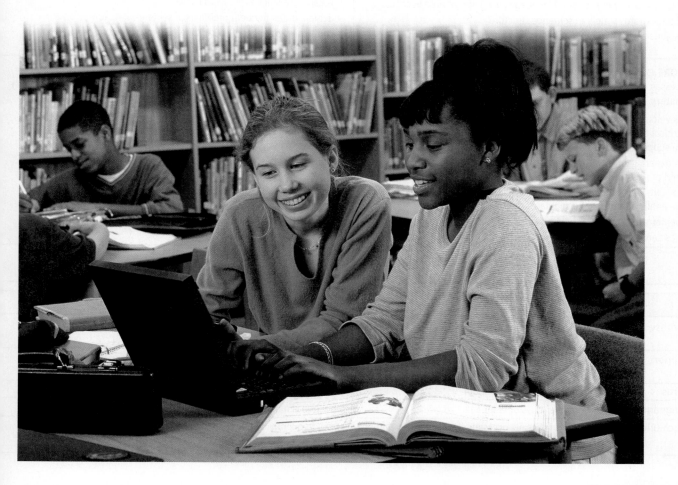

# Writing Rubrics

Use these charts, or rubrics, to evaluate your writing.

## SAT

### SCORE OF 6
An essay in this category is **outstanding**, demonstrating **clear and consistent mastery**, although it may have a few minor errors. A typical essay

- effectively and insightfully develops a point of view on the issue and demonstrates outstanding critical thinking, using clearly appropriate examples, reasons, and other evidence to support its position.
- is well organized and clearly focused, demonstrating clear coherence and smooth progression of ideas.
- exhibits skillful use of language, using a varied, accurate, and apt vocabulary.
- demonstrates meaningful variety in sentence structure.
- is free of most errors in grammar, usage, and mechanics.

### SCORE OF 5
An essay in this category is **effective**, demonstrating **reasonably consistent mastery**, although it will have occasional errors or lapses in quality. A typical essay

- effectively develops a point of view on the issue and demonstrates strong critical thinking, generally using appropriate examples, reasons, and other evidence to support its position.
- is well organized and focused, demonstrating coherence and progression of ideas.
- exhibits facility in the use of language, using appropriate vocabulary.
- demonstrates variety in sentence structure.
- is generally free of most errors in grammar, usage, and mechanics.

### SCORE OF 4
An essay in this category is **competent**, demonstrating **adequate mastery**, although it will have lapses in quality. A typical essay

- develops a point of view on the issue and demonstrates competent critical thinking, using adequate examples, reasons, and other evidence to support its position.
- is generally organized and focused, demonstrating some coherence and progression of ideas.
- exhibits adequate but inconsistent facility in the use of language, using generally appropriate vocabulary.
- demonstrates some variety in sentence structure.
- has some errors in grammar, usage, and mechanics.

### SCORE OF 3
An essay in this category is **inadequate**, but demonstrates **developing mastery**, and is marked by **one or more** of the following weaknesses:

- develops a point of view on the issue, demonstrating some critical thinking, but may do so inconsistently or use inadequate examples, reasons, or other evidence to support its position
- is limited in its organization or focus, but may demonstrate some lapses in coherence or progression of ideas
- displays developing facility in the use of language, but sometimes uses weak vocabulary or inappropriate word choice
- lacks variety or demonstrates problems in sentence structure
- contains an accumulation of errors in grammar, usage, and mechanics

### SCORE OF 2
An essay in this category is **seriously limited**, demonstrating **little mastery**, and is flawed by **one or more** of the following weaknesses:

- develops a point of view on the issue that is vague or seriously limited, demonstrating weak critical thinking, providing inappropriate or insufficient examples, reasons, or other evidence to support its position
- is poorly organized and/or focused, or demonstrates serious problems with coherence or progression of ideas
- displays very little facility in the use of language, using very limited vocabulary or incorrect word choice
- demonstrates frequent problems in sentence structure
- contains errors in grammar, usage, and mechanics so serious that meaning is somewhat obscured

### SCORE OF 1
An essay in this category is **fundamentally lacking**, demonstrating **very little** or **no mastery**, and is severely flawed by **one or more** of the following weaknesses:

- develops no viable point of view on the issue, or provides little or no evidence to support its position
- is disorganized or unfocused, resulting in a disjointed or incoherent essay
- displays fundamental errors in vocabulary
- demonstrates severe flaws in sentence structure
- contains pervasive errors in grammar, usage, or mechanics that persistently interfere with meaning

### SCORE OF 0
Essays not written on the essay assignment will receive a score of zero.

| ACT | Scores of 4–6 | Scores of 1–3 |
|---|---|---|
| **Purpose** | shows a clear understanding of the essay's purpose by articulating a perspective and developing ideas | does not clearly articulate a perspective |
| **Support** | most generalizations developed with specific examples to support the perspective | demonstrates some development of ideas but may be overly general or repetitive |
| **Focus** | clear focus maintained throughout | focus maintained on general prompt topic but is not sufficiently specific |
| **Language** | shows competent use of language | language is mostly understandable, organization is clear but simple |
| **Mechanics** | minimal errors that only occasionally distract and do not interfere with meaning | errors frequently distract and interfere with meaning |

# Critical Thinking About Visuals and Text Sources

## Analyze Graphic Data

The study of history requires that you think critically about the text you're reading as well as any visuals or media sources. This section will allow you to practice and apply some important skills for critical thinking.

Graphs show numerical facts in picture form. Bar graphs and line graphs compare things at different times or places, such as changes in school enrollment. Circle graphs show how a whole is divided into parts. To interpret a graph, look closely at its features. Use the graphs below and the steps that follow to practice analyzing graphic data.

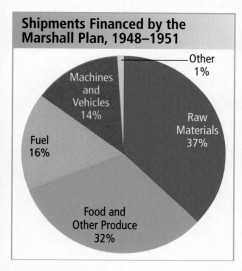

**Shipments Financed by the Marshall Plan, 1948–1951**

Other 1%
Machines and Vehicles 14%
Raw Materials 37%
Fuel 16%
Food and Other Produce 32%

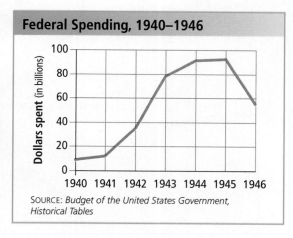

**Federal Spending, 1940–1946**

Dollars spent (in billions)

SOURCE: *Budget of the United States Government, Historical Tables*

**Read the title** to learn the main topic of the graph.

**Use labels and the key** to read the data given in the graph. The line graph is labeled in years, with single-year intervals. The different colors on the circle graph represent the different shipments.

**Interpret the graph.** Look for interesting patterns in the data. Look at changes over time or compare information for different categories.

## Practice and Apply the Skill

Use the graphs above to answer the following questions:

1. What is the title of the line graph? What is its topic?
2. In which year did federal spending increase at the fastest rate? State two generalizations that are supported by the graph.
3. The Marshall Plan was a program under which the United States helped European countries devastated by World War II. According to the circle graph, what proportion of shipments contained fuel? What proportion of shipments contained items that could help factories run?
4. Could the information in the circle graph be shown as a line graph? Explain.

# Analyze Maps

Maps can show many different types of information. A physical map represents what a region looks like by showing its major physical features, such as mountains and plains. A political map focuses on elements related to government, such as nations, borders, and cities.

A special-purpose map provides information on a specific subject—for example, land use, population distribution, natural resources, or trade routes. Road maps are special-purpose maps, as are weather maps. These maps often use a variety of colors and symbols to show different pieces of information, so the key is very important. Use the map below and the steps that follow to practice analyzing a special-purpose map.

## Louisiana Purchase

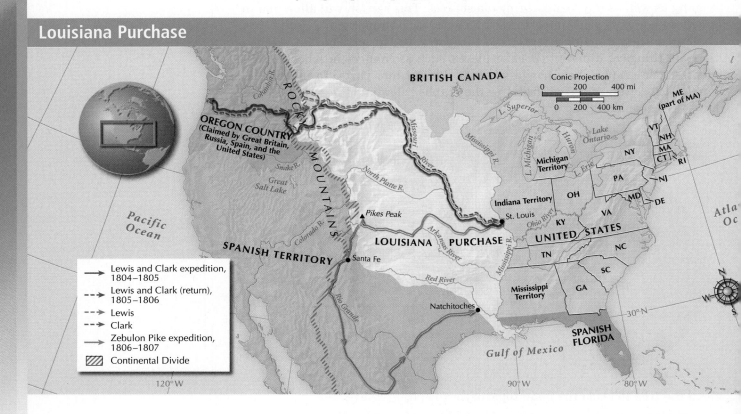

**Study the title, locator globe, scale bar, and compass rose.** Together, these features tell you the map's context—what part of the world it shows and why.

**Read the key.** Use the key to learn the specific details shown on the map.

**Apply the key and labels to the map.** Locate the symbols, lines, or colors from the key on the map. Also read any labels on the map. Then, use the information given in the key and labels to understand what the map shows.

## Practice and Apply the Skill

Use the map above to answer the following questions:

1. What is the purpose of this map? What part of the world does it show?
2. What does the red dotted line on the map represent?
3. Where did Zebulon Pike's expedition end?
4. Through which region did Lewis and Clark travel on their way to Oregon Country?
5. Does the map provide information about the effects of the Louisiana Purchase? Explain.

# Analyze Images

Television, film, the Internet, and print media all carry images that seek to convey information or influence attitudes. To respond, you must develop the ability to understand and interpret visuals. Use the photograph below and the steps that follow to practice analyzing images.

In the 1950s, people everywhere worried about nuclear attacks. This 1952 image shows schoolchildren and their teacher ducking under desks during a nuclear air raid drill.

**Identify the content.** Look at all parts of the image and determine which are most important.

**Note emotions.** Study facial expressions and body positions. Consider the emotions they may suggest.

**Read captions/credits.** Gather information about the image, such as when it was produced.

**Study purpose.** Consider who might have created this image. Decide if the purpose was to entertain, inform, or persuade.

**Consider context.** Determine the context in which the image was created—in this case, the Cold War between the United States and the Soviet Union.

**Respond.** Decide if a visual's impact achieves its purpose—to inform, to entertain, or to persuade.

## Practice and Apply the Skill

Use the photograph above to answer the following questions:

1. What is the focus of this photograph?
2. What feelings are conveyed by the children's facial expressions?
3. What do you think the photograph's purpose is?
4. When was this image produced? How did historical context influence its production?

# Analyze Primary Sources

Primary sources include official documents and firsthand accounts of events or visual evidence such as photographs, paintings, and political cartoons. Such sources provide valuable information about the past. Use the excerpt below and the steps that follow to learn to analyze primary sources.

In 1914, a great war broke out in Europe. Americans debated whether the United States should take sides in the war. In this excerpt, President Wilson expresses his views:

**Primary Source** 66The people of the United States are drawn from many nations, and chiefly from the nations now at war. It is natural and inevitable that there should be the utmost variety of sympathy and desire among them. . . . Some will wish one nation, others another, to succeed in the momentous struggle. . . . The people of the United States, whose love of their country and whose loyalty to its government should unite them as Americans all, . . . may be divided in camps of hostile opinion. . . .

Such divisions amongst us would be fatal to our peace of mind and might seriously stand in the way of the proper performance of our duty as the one great nation at peace.99

—speech by Woodrow Wilson, August 19, 1914

**Read the headnote, caption, or attribution line.** Determine the source's historical context—who wrote it, when, and why.

**Read the primary source.** Identify and define unfamiliar words. Then, look for the writer's main point.

**Identify facts and opinions.** Facts can be proven. Opinions reflect a person's views or feelings. Use clues to help identify opinion words: exaggeration, phrases such as *I think,* or descriptive words such as *gorgeous.*

**Identify bias and evaluate credibility.** Consider whether the author's opinions suggest bias. Evaluate other factors that might lead to author bias, such as his or her previous experiences. Decide if the author knows enough to be credible and was objective enough to be reliable. Determine whether the source might be propaganda, that is, material published to promote a policy, an idea, or a cause.

## Practice and Apply the Skill

Political cartoons reflect an artist's observations about events of the time. They often use symbols to represent things or exaggeration to make a point. Use the cartoon at left to answer the following questions.

**1.** What was happening in Europe when this cartoon was published?

**2.** What does the kneeling woman represent? the man?

**3.** What is exaggerated in this cartoon?

**4.** What opinion is the cartoonist expressing?

The Only Way We Can Save Her

# Compare Viewpoints

A person's viewpoint is shaped by subjective influences such as feelings, prejudices, and past experiences. For example, two politicians may recommend two different policies to address the same problem. Likewise, historians often have different interpretations of past events, based on their research and review of other historians' work. Comparing such viewpoints will help you understand issues and develop your own interpretations. The excerpts below offer two different views on why the founders wrote a new U.S. Constitution in 1787. Use the excerpts and the steps that follow to learn about comparing viewpoints.

## Comparing Viewpoints

> "[People who favored the Constitution] believed the slogans of 1776 were outmoded; . . . that certain political processes such as war, foreign affairs, and commerce, were national by nature; that the right to tax was essential to any government; and that powers wrested from king and parliament should not be divided among thirteen states, if the American government was to have any influence in the world."
>
> —Samuel E. Morison and Henry S. Commager, *The Growth of the American Republic.* New York: Oxford University Press, 1962.

> "The 55 delegates [to the Constitutional Convention] had much in common. All were white, male, and well educated, and many already knew one another. . . . Not surprisingly, all seemed to agree that the contagion of liberty had spread too far. . . . Most delegates hoped to replace the existing Confederation structure with a national government capable of controlling finances and creating [lender]-friendly [economic] policies. . . ."
>
> —Jacqueline Jones, Peter W. Wood, Elaine Tyler May, Thomas Borstelmann, and Vicki L. Ruiz, *Created Equal: A Social and Political History of the United States.* Boston: Pearson Education, 2003.

**Identify the authors.** Determine when the historians studied or wrote.

**Examine the viewpoints.** Identify each author's main idea and evaluate his or her supporting arguments. Determine whether the arguments are logical and the evidence is sufficient to support the main idea. Confirm that the evidence is valid by doing research if necessary.

**Determine the author's frame of reference.** Consider how the author's background and historical specialty might affect his or her viewpoint.

**Recognize facts and opinions.** Identify which statements are opinions and which are facts. Opinions represent the author's viewpoint.

**Evaluate each viewpoint's validity.** Decide whether the viewpoints are based on facts and/or reasonable arguments. Consider whether or not you agree with the viewpoints.

## Practice and Apply the Skill

Use the excerpts above to answer the following questions.

1. Who are the authors of these two excerpts? When was each excerpt written?
2. What is each historian's main argument about the U.S. Constitution? What evidence or supporting arguments does each provide?
3. How might each historian's frame of reference affect the viewpoint?
4. Are these two viewpoints based on reasonable arguments? Explain.

# Synthesize Information

Just as you might ask several friends about a movie before deciding to see it, you can combine information from different sources to develop a fuller understanding of any topic. This process, called synthesizing, will help you become better informed. Study the documents below about developments during the Great Depression in the 1930s. Then, use the steps that follow to learn to synthesize information.

Document A

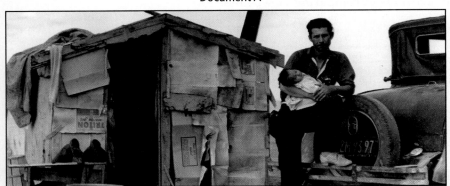

Rural poverty during the Great Depression of the 1930s.

Document B

**Unemployment, 1928–1933**

SOURCE: *Historical Statistics of the United States*

Document C

**Primary Source** 66 This great nation will endure as it has endured, will revive and will prosper. So, first of all, let me assert my firm belief that the only thing we have to fear is fear itself—nameless, unreasoning, unjustified terror which paralyzes needed efforts to convert retreat into advance. 99

—President Franklin Roosevelt, First Inaugural Address, 1933

**Identify thesis statements.** Before you can synthesize, you must understand the thesis, or main idea, of each source. Analyze how the information and ideas in the sources are the same or different. When several sources agree, the information is more reliable and thus more significant.

**Draw conclusions and generalize.** Look at all the information. Use it to draw conclusions that form a single picture of the topic. Make a generalization, or statement that applies to all the sources.

**Construct and test hypotheses.** As you learn new information about history, you can begin to form hypotheses, or educated guesses, about events and trends. You might form a hypothesis about why something happened or about the connection between two events. Then, as you learn more, you should test your hypothesis against new information. You should continue to refine your hypothesis based on the new information.

## Practice and Apply the Skill

Use the documents above to answer the following questions.

1. What is the main idea of each source?
2. Which sources support the idea that the depression affected people throughout the United States?
3. Form a hypothesis about the Great Depression, based on the information presented.

# Analyze Cause and Effect

One of a historian's main tasks is to understand the causes and effects of the event he or she is studying. Study the facts below, which are listed in random order. Then, use the steps that follow to learn how to analyze cause and effect.

---

The United States, with other nations, fought a war in North and South Korea in the 1950s. This list shows key trends and events related to that war.

- South Korea and its allies fight a 3–year war against North Korea and its allies.
- At the end of World War II, Korea was divided into North Korea, a communist nation, and South Korea, a noncommunist nation, divided at the 38th parallel.
- President Truman worried about the spread of communism in Europe and Asia.
- Communists gained control of mainland China.
- By the end of the Korean War, the border between North Korea and South Korea stood at about the 38th parallel, where it still is today.
- North Korea invaded South Korea.
- As a result of the north's invasion, the south and its allies pushed back.
- The United States continues to station troops along the border dividing North Korea from South Korea.
- Thousands of Americans were killed in the Korean War.
- The United States stations thousands of troops in West Germany.

---

**Identify the central event.** Determine to what event or issue all the facts listed relate.

**Locate clue words.** Use words such as *because, so,* and *due to* to spot causes and effects.

**Identify causes and effects.** Causes precede the central event and contribute to its occurrence. Effects come after the central event. They occur or emerge as a result of it.

**Consider timeframe.** Decide if causes have existed for a long period of time or if they emerged just prior to the central event. Short-term causes are usually single or narrowly defined events. Long-term causes usually arise from conditions that are ongoing.

**Notice relationships that are not causal.** Sometimes events are related, but the earlier event did not cause the later event. For example, although there are parallels, the Russian Revolution was not caused by the American Revolution.

## Practice and Apply the Skill

Use the list above to answer the following questions:

1. Which item on the list describes the central event whose causes and effects can be determined?
2. Name two facts that are long-term effects.
3. Name two facts that are probably causes of the central event.
4. Name one fact that is not a cause or effect of the central event, though it is related.

# Problem Solving and Decision Making

When you have a problem to solve or decision to make, you can find solutions if you think in a logical way. Study the situation outlined below. Then, use the steps that follow to learn the skills of problem solving and decision making.

## Ending the Woes of the Great Depression

In 1929, the United States entered a period of extreme economic difficulties, known as the Great Depression. Thousands of businesses closed, millions of people lost their jobs, and many people had to leave their homes because they couldn't afford the rent or other costs. When the Depression began, Herbert Hoover was President. Later, Franklin Roosevelt was elected to replace Hoover. Both Presidents tried strategies to solve the problems brought on by the Depression.

### Options for Presidents Hoover and Roosevelt

| Option | Advantages | Disadvantages |
|---|---|---|
| 1. Allow the economy to correct itself. | • The economy works better when left alone.<br>• The government does not have the right to intervene in local economic affairs. | • This could take a long time, while people continue to suffer.<br>• |
| 2. Let the federal government do whatever is necessary to relieve the effects of the Depression. | •<br><br>• | •<br><br>• |
| 3. Take certain federal actions, but rely mainly on the states and on private economic activities. | •<br><br>• | •<br><br>• |

## The Decisions
• President Hoover decided to follow Option 3.
• President Roosevelt decided to follow Option 2.

## Effects of the Decisions
• Hoover's actions did not relieve the problems of the Depression quickly enough and he lost his bid for reelection in 1932.
• Roosevelt's actions put some people back to work and relieved some hunger, but did not end the Depression.

**Identify the problem.** You cannot solve a problem until you examine it and understand it.

**Gather information and identify options.** Most problems have many solutions. Identify as many solution options as possible.

**Consider advantages and disadvantages.** Analyze each option by predicting benefits and drawbacks.

**Decide on and implement the solution.** Pick the option with the most desirable benefits and least important drawbacks.

**Evaluate the decision.** After awhile, reexamine your solution. If necessary, make a new decision.

## Practice and Apply the Skill

Use information from the box above to answer the following questions:

1. What problems did Presidents Hoover and Roosevelt face?
2. Identify at least one advantage and one disadvantage of Options 2 and 3.
3. Why do you think that neither President was able to end the Depression?

# Draw Inferences and Conclusions

Text and artwork may not contain all the facts and ideas you need to understand a topic. You may need to draw inferences, that is, to add information from your own experience or knowledge, or use information that is implied but not directly stated in the text or artwork. Study the biography below. Then, use the steps that follow to learn how to draw inferences and conclusions.

## HISTORY MAKERS

### Ida B. Wells (1862–1931)

Wells had gained fame for her campaign against the lynching of African Americans. But she was also a tireless worker for women's suffrage and joined in the famous 1913 march for universal suffrage that took place in Washington, D.C. Not able to tolerate injustice of any kind, Ida B. Wells, along with Jane Addams, successfully blocked the establishment of segregated schools in Chicago. In 1930, she ran for the Illinois State legislature, which made her one of the first black women to run for public office in the United States.

**Study the facts.** Determine what facts and information the text states.

**Summarize information.** Confirm your understanding of the text by briefly summarizing it.

**Ask questions.** Use who, what, when, where, why, and how questions to analyze the text and learn more. For example, you might compare and contrast, or look for causes or effects.

**Add your own knowledge.** Consider what you know about the topic. Use this knowledge to evaluate the information.

**Draw inferences and conclusions.** Use what you learned from the text and your own knowledge to draw inferences and conclusions about the topic.

## Practice and Apply the Skill

Use the biography above to answer these questions.

1. Who is discussed in the biography? When did she live?
2. Briefly summarize the text.
3. How might Wells's activities have been unusual for her time?
4. What inferences can you draw about Wells's character from the information in the biography?

# Speaking and Listening

*Speaking and listening are forms of communication you use every day. In certain situations, however, specific skills and strategies can increase the effectiveness of your communication. The strategies offered in this section will help you improve both your speaking and listening skills.*

## Participate in Group Discussions

A group discussion is an informal meeting of people that is used to openly discuss ideas and topics. You can express your views and hear those of others.

### Identify Issues

Before you speak, identify the issues and main points you want to address. Incorporate what you already know about these issues into your views. Then, find the best words to convey your ideas effectively.

### Interact With the Group

As with persuasive writing, in a discussion it helps to accept the validity of opposing views, then argue your position. Always acknowledge the views of others respectfully, but ask questions that challenge the accuracy, logic, or relevance of those views.

### Debating

A debate is a formal argument about a specific issue. Explicit rules govern the procedure of a debate, with each debater or team given an allotted time to make arguments and respond to opposing positions. You may also find yourself arguing a position you do not personally hold.

### Prepare Your Arguments

If you support a position, use your existing knowledge of it to direct your research. If you personally oppose an assigned position, use that knowledge to identify likely opposing arguments. Generate an outline and then number note cards to highlight key information for each of your main points.

### Avoid Common Pitfalls

Stay focused on your arguments. Be aware of words that may reveal bias, such as *unpatriotic*. Speak assertively, but avoid getting overly emotional. Vary the pitch and tone of your voice to keep listeners engaged. Try to speak actively, rather than just reading aloud, and use eye contact and gestures to emphasize your message.

# Give an Oral or Multimedia Presentation

An oral or multimedia presentation provides an audience with information through a variety of media.

## Choose Media

If you are limited to speaking only, focus your time on developing a presentation that engages listeners. If you can include other media, consider what kind of information each form of media conveys most effectively.

| Maps | Graphs/Charts | Pictures | Diagrams | Audio/Video |
|---|---|---|---|---|
| Clarify historical or geographical information | Show complicated information in an accessible format | Illustrate objects, scenes, or other details | Show links between parts and a whole or a process | Bring the subject to life and engage audiences |

## Prepare Your Presentation

Gather information using library and online sources. Develop your most important ideas in the body of your presentation. Back up assertions with solid facts and use multimedia examples to illustrate key points.

## Present With Authority

Practice your presentation to gain comfort with the ideas and the presentation sequence. Experiment with the timing of how to include multimedia elements. Make sure you have the necessary equipment and know how to use it.

# Active Listening

Active listening is a key component of the communication process. Like all communication, it requires your engaged participation.

## Focus Your Attention on Ideas

Look at and listen to the speaker. Think about what you hear and see. Which ideas are emphasized or repeated? What gestures or expressions suggest strong feelings? Can you connect the speaker's ideas to your own experiences?

## Listen to Fit the Situation

Active listening involves matching your listening to the situation. Listen critically to a speech given by a candidate for office. Listen empathetically to the feelings of a friend. Listen appreciatively to a musical performance.

## Ask Questions

Try to think of questions while you're listening. Look at these examples:

| Open-ended | Closed | Fact |
|---|---|---|
| Why do you think it is so important for young people to vote? | Do you support the current voting age of 18? | How many people between the ages of 18 and 25 voted in the most recent election? |

# MI Connect to Michigan

## Michigan: A Period of Exploration

In 1608, teenager Étienne Brûlé left France to join explorer Samuel de Champlain's expeditions in North America. Ten years later, Champlain sent Brûlé to find what he sought after most—the Northwest Passage across the continent to Asia. Brûlé didn't find the passage, but his 1618 stop at the location of Sault Ste. Marie made him the first European to explore the land that would later become Michigan. In less than four years, he returned to the area and continued exploring the coast of Lake Superior. Brûlé also acted as an interpreter between the French and Native Americans in the Michigan area..

About fifty years later, French missionaries with hopes of converting Native Americans to Christianity began moving to the area and building churches and other settlements. The priest and missionary Jacques Marquette founded two of the first settlements in Michigan: Sault Ste. Marie in 1668 and St. Ignace in 1671.

After the missionaries arrived, fur traders poured into the area. People who hunted for furs, called voyageurs, needed fur-trading posts and forts to protect their lucrative business from both hostile Native Americans and British forces. Antoine de la Mothe Cadillac founded perhaps the most important of these forts in 1701—Fort Pontchartrain du De Troit, or simply Detroit. In 1749, the Jesuit priest and scientist Joseph-Pierre de Bonnécamps joined an expedition down the Beautiful River, today called the Ohio River. His group reached Detroit in October, 1749. Impressed with the fort and the surrounding area, Bonnécamps wrote about the settlement:

> [I]ts situation appeared to me charming. A beautiful river runs at the foot of the fort; vast plains, which only ask to be cultivated, extend beyond the sight…. Moreover, we should regard Detroit as one of the most important posts of the Colony. It is conveniently situated for furnishing aid to Michilimakinak, to the St. Joseph River, to the Bay, to the Miamis, Ouiatanons, and to the Beautiful River, supposing that settlements be made thereon."
> —from *The Jesuit Relations and Allied Documents: Travels and Explorations of the Jesuit Missionaries in New France, 1610–1791*

Despite the area's long French history, first the British and then the new United States would claim the territory of Michigan over the course of the eighteenth century..

# CONNECTING WITH PAST LEARNINGS

## CONTENTS

*The Spirit of '76,* by
Archibald M. Willard,
**honors the heroes of the
American Revolution.** ▶

# 1 The Nation's Beginnings
## Prehistory–1824

### The Nation's First President

George Washington was elected President twice, serving from 1789 to 1797. Washington's second inauguration took place in Philadelphia, where he delivered the shortest inaugural speech ever given!

❝I am again called upon by the voice of my country to execute the functions of its Chief Magistrate. . . . I shall endeavor to express the high sense I entertain of this distinguished honor, and of the confidence which has been reposed in me by the people of United America.❞
—George Washington, March 4, 1793

*Listen to the* Witness History *audio to hear more about George Washington's inauguration.*

◀ This painting shows (from left to right) George Washington, John Adams, and Thomas Jefferson at Washington's second inauguration.

Navajo pottery

Three-cornered hat worn by Patriots during the American Revolution

 **Content Expectations**

**Chapter Focus Question:** What factors led to the founding of the United States and its formation as a democratic republic?

### Section 1
**Many Cultures Meet**   F2.1b, F2.1c, F2.1d

### Section 2
**The American Revolution**   F1.1a, F1.2a, F1.2c

### Section 3
**The Constitution**   F1.1b, F1.1c, F1.2a, F1.2b

### Section 4
**The New Republic**   F1.2a, F1.2b, F1.2c

Peace medal given to the Nez Percés in 1810 in honor of the expedition of Meriwether Lewis and William Clark

Use the ☑ **Quick Study Timeline** at the end of this chapter to preview chapter events.

> **Note Taking Study Guide** *Online*
> **For:** Note Taking and American Issues Connector
> **Web Code:** nee-6151

▼ An American Indian and a European exchange goods.

WITNESS HISTORY  AUDIO

**Two Cultures Meet**

In one of the great accidents of history, explorer Christopher Columbus sailed west from Spain and landed on an island he thought was in Asia. In fact, Columbus encountered lands and people that Europeans did not know existed. In an October 12, 1492, journal entry, Columbus describes his first encounter with the people who lived on the island.

❝As I saw that [the island residents] were very friendly to us, . . . I presented them with some red caps, and strings of beads to wear upon the neck, and many other trifles of small value. . . . Afterwards they came . . . bringing parrots, balls of cotton thread, javelins, and many other things which they exchanged for articles we gave them, such as glass beads, and hawk's bells; which trade was carried on with the utmost good will.❞
—Christopher Columbus, October 1492

# Many Cultures Meet

 **Content Expectations**

- **F2.1b** Describe regional American economic differences/similarities prior to 1877.
- **F2.1c** Describe changes in size, location, composition of U.S. population prior to 1877.
- **F2.1d** Describe patterns of immigration/migration.

## Terms and People

clan
Middle Passage
Christopher Columbus

conquistador
Columbian Exchange

## NoteTaking

**Reading Skill: Identify Causes and Effects**
Identify the causes and effects of European arrival in the Americas.

| Cause | Event | Effect |
|---|---|---|
| • Desire to find trade routes to Asia<br>• | Europeans arrive in the Americas | • Columbian Exchange<br>• |

**Why It Matters** Europe's Age of Exploration began in the 1400s as a quest for an all-water route to Asia. In 1492, Europeans crossed the Atlantic Ocean and began to explore North and South America. The arrival of European settlers and enslaved Africans brought traumatic changes to the Native Americans, who had developed many complex cultures in the Americas. **Section Focus Question: What were the causes and effects of European arrival in the Americas?**

## The American Indians

North and South America are remarkable for the diversity of their landscapes and their climates. Tens of thousands of years ago, humans began arriving in these vast lands.

**Ancient Peoples Migrate to the Americas** Most scientists believe that the first inhabitants of the Americas migrated from the northeastern coast of Asia between 40,000 and 15,000 years ago. Some scientists believe that Asians came over a land bridge that appeared across the Bering Strait during the last ice age. Others suggest that the first Americans arrived in boats that traveled along the Pacific coastline.

Over the generations, the American Indians expanded southward, occupying North and South America. As they filled these two continents, they adapted to dramatically different climates and landscapes, developing great cultural diversity. By 1492, the American Indians spoke at least 375 distinct languages.

**Cultures Share Many Traits** Despite their <u>diverse</u> cultures, many Indian cultures shared a number of characteristics. Most cultures were based on extended family groups called **clans.** All members of a clan had a common ancestor and identified with the spirit of a powerful animal. Several clans combined to make up a mobile band of Indians or a stationary village.

Many American Indian cultures shared similar religious beliefs. They believed that powerful spiritual forces were part of nature. Some Indians became shamans, who conducted rituals to seek benefits from spirit beings.

**Agriculture Leads to the Growth of Civilizations** About 3,500 years ago in central Mexico, the Indians learned how to grow such crops as maize (corn), squash, and beans. The methods of cultivation spread northward into the American Southwest and Midwest. The expanded food supply allowed the population to grow, which led in turn to the growth of towns and cities sometimes guided by powerful chiefs.

Many Indians did not adopt an agricultural way of life and thrived on a mix of hunting, gathering, and fishing. Crops did not thrive in the arid Great Basin between the Sierra Nevada and Rocky Mountains. In the Pacific Northwest, Indians did not need to farm because fishes and game were so plentiful.

✓ **Checkpoint** How did geography influence the American Indians' way of life?

**Vocabulary Builder**
<u>diverse</u>–(duh VERS) *adj.* different; varied

**Geography** *Interactive*
**For:** Interactive map
**Web Code:** nep-0102

## Native American Culture Regions of North America in About 1450

**Map Skills** By 1450, a great variety of Native American groups lived in North America. Within each culture area shown on the map, groups shared similar ways of life.

1. **Locate:** (a) Gulf of Mexico, (b) Arctic Ocean, (c) Hudson Bay

2. **Regions** In which region do the Cheyennes live?

3. **Make Comparisons** Based on the characteristics of their regions, describe at least one way in which Inuit culture may have differed from Navajo culture.

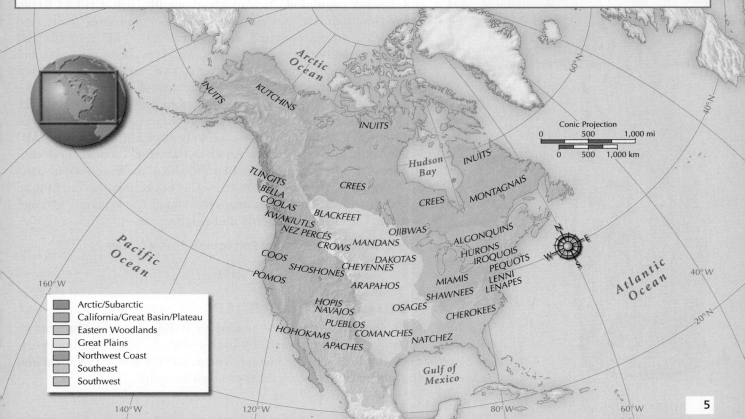

Arctic/Subarctic
California/Great Basin/Plateau
Eastern Woodlands
Great Plains
Northwest Coast
Southeast
Southwest

## The Europeans

While Native American cultures thrived in the Americas, life in Europe was changing rapidly. Changes in Europe that had begun in the fourteenth century would lead to contact between the cultures of Europe and the Americas.

**The Renaissance Changes Europe** The period from the fourteenth to the sixteenth centuries when great advances in science, economics, political thought, and art occurred in Europe is called the Renaissance. Scientific advances and an increase in economic wealth led some to sponsor early voyages of exploration. European kingdoms on the Atlantic coastline sent explorers into the sea. The monarchs and aristocrats who ruled these nations competed for access to the profitable trade in silks, gems, gold, ivory, and spices from Asia and Africa. This trade was dominated by Muslims who lived in North Africa, the Balkans, and Southwest Asia and by Italian merchants with access to the Mediterranean Sea.

**The Age of Exploration Leads to Voyages of Discovery** During the fifteenth century, the Portuguese took the lead in an era known as the Age of Exploration. By developing better ships and more advanced methods of navigation, the Portuguese regularly ventured into the Atlantic Ocean far from the sight of land. Sailing farther south and then east, Portuguese mariner Bartolomeu Dias traveled around the southern tip of Africa into the Indian Ocean from 1487 to 1488. Then in 1498, Vasco da Gama reached India, opening a profitable trade.

✔ **Checkpoint** Why did Europeans seek a sea route to Asia?

### West African Kingdoms

Songhai and Benin were powerful African kingdoms. Pictured here are the city of Timbuktu, which reached its height under the Songhai empire, and a Benin ivory saltcellar with carvings of Portuguese traders. *How did trade affect West Africa?*

## The West Africans

Sailing south into the Atlantic Ocean, Portuguese mariners reached West African kingdoms below the Sahara. Highly civilized and densely populated, African kingdoms like Songhai and Benin had a sophisticated agricultural system, made iron tools, and employed draft animals and writing systems. Their products and produce moved north by caravans of camels or along the coast and the major rivers in large canoes. To trade, the Portuguese needed the cooperation of the powerful West African kings.

The Portuguese mariners were not only interested in gold and salt, they were also interested in buying enslaved Africans. The Portuguese did not invent the slave trade, but they greatly expanded it—especially after 1500, when new colonial plantations created a demand in the Americas. During the next three centuries, slave traders from Portugal, Spain, Britain, and other European nations forced at least 11 million Africans across the Atlantic. Known as the **Middle Passage,** this brutal transatlantic commerce weakened the economy of West Africa as it enriched European merchants and empires.

✔ **Checkpoint** What effects did the Portuguese mariners have in West Africa?

## First Encounters in America

In 1492, Spain sponsored a voyage headed by Italian mariner **Christopher Columbus.** Columbus hoped to reach the Indies of East Asia by sailing westward across the Atlantic. However, he underestimated the size of the world and had no idea that the Americas were there to block his ships.

## TRACK THE ISSUE

**Is global interdependence good for the American economy?**

Like many nations, the United States depends on trade and commerce with other countries to support its economy. Employment is a part of the global economy, as a growing number of U.S. companies outsource jobs overseas. Use the timeline below to explore this enduring issue.

**1500s  Columbian Exchange**
Products and ideas are exchanged between the hemispheres.

**1812 War of 1812**
United States goes to war in part to protect its trade rights.

**1944  World Bank**
The World Bank and International Monetary Fund are established at Bretton Woods Conference.

**1990s  World Trade Increases**
NAFTA joins the United States, Mexico, and Canada in a free-trade pact, and the World Trade Organization is founded.

**2000s  Globalization Debated**
Critics and advocates debate benefits of globalization.

Europeans trade goods with Native Americans.

**MI** 9.3.1a

U.S. firms outsource work to such nations as India and Nigeria.

## DEBATE THE ISSUE

**Outsourcing Jobs**  Many American companies send work overseas where wages are lower. This is called "outsourcing." In the past, most of the jobs lost through outsourcing were factory jobs. Now office work and computer jobs are being sent abroad, too. How does outsourcing affect America?

"Sending jobs overseas is part of corporate America's quest for short-term profits at the expense of the well-being of our workers. In effect, forcing the middle class to compete with the cheapest foreign labor can only result in a decline in our nation's standard of living and a diminished quality of life."

—Lou Dobbs, News Anchor, CNN

"Will [the outsourcing of services] lead to jobs going overseas? You bet, but that is not a disaster. For a start, America runs a large and growing surplus in services with the rest of the world. The jobs lost will be low-paying ones. . . . By contrast, jobs will be created that demand skills to handle the deeper incorporation of information technology, and the pay for these jobs will be high."

—*The Economist* magazine

### *TRANSFER* Activities

1. **Compare**  How do these two views on outsourcing differ?

2. **Analyze**  Do you think either Lou Dobbs or the writer in *The Economist* would have considered the Columbian Exchange a danger to European or Native American economies? Explain.

3. **Transfer**  Use the following Web site to see a video, try a WebQuest, and write in your journal. **Web Code:** neh-6102

Columbus explored several Caribbean islands. Convinced that the islands were the Indies, he called the natives "Indians." (See the Witness History at the beginning of this section.) Columbus and those who followed worked to convert the Indians to Christianity. Europeans also took Indians' lands and enslaved Indians.

**The Conquistadores** The Spanish rapidly conquered a vast empire around the Caribbean and in Central and South America. Known as **conquistadores,** Spanish invaders were brave, resourceful, ruthless, and destructive. Between 1519 and 1521, Hernando Cortés overpowered the Aztecs in Mexico.

Other Spanish conquistadores explored and conquered other parts of North America. Juan Ponce de Leon traveled through parts of Florida in 1513. Later, from 1539 to 1542, Hernando de Soto explored other portions of Florida and parts of the Southeast, reaching the Mississippi River. Francisco Coronado searched for legendary cities of gold in the Southwest. He explored present-day Arizona and New Mexico but found no gold.

**The Columbian Exchange** The conquistadores had the advantage of horses and steel weapons. But they had an unintentional weapon, too. Native Americans had no immunity to such deadly European diseases as smallpox, measles, and cholera. Indians died by the thousands.

These plagues made it easier for the Europeans to conquer and colonize North and South America. But they also thinned the number of possible Indian slaves. To make up the loss, the colonizers forced millions of enslaved Africans across the Atlantic to the Americas.

In addition to bringing new people into the Americas, the colonizers introduced new animals, including pigs, horses, mules, sheep, and cattle. The Europeans diversified their own agriculture by adopting crops pioneered by the Indians. Maize and potatoes helped to boost the population of Europe. The traffic of goods and ideas between Europe and the Americas is called the **Columbian Exchange.**

 **Checkpoint** How did European explorations affect life in the Americas, Africa, and Europe?

---

SECTION

# 1 Assessment

**Progress Monitoring _Online_**
**For:** Self-test with vocabulary practice
**Web Code:** nea-0104

## Comprehension

**1. Terms and People** For each item below, write a sentence explaining its significance.
- clan
- Middle Passage
- Christopher Columbus
- conquistador
- Columbian Exchange

**2. NoteTaking Reading Skill: Identify Causes and Effects** Use your cause-and-effect chart to answer the Section Focus Question: What were the causes and effects of European arrival in the Americas?

## Writing About History

**3. Quick Write: Identify Effects** Write a paragraph describing the effects of the European arrival in America from a Native American point of view. Your paragraph should state a main idea and include supporting details.

## Critical Thinking

**4. Draw Inferences** How would the culture of Native American peoples who lived in a mountainous region differ from those who lived on a fertile plain? Which groups would be more likely to live in villages, and which would be more likely to hunt and gather?

**5. Summarize** What did the Europeans hope to gain by finding a sea route to Asia?

**6. Analyze Information** How did European contact with Africans affect the Africans?

**7. Recognize Bias** When Europeans and American Indians first encountered one another, they each must have been startled to see the other. What opinion do you think Columbus had of the Indians? What do you think American Indians thought of the Europeans?

DONT TREAD ON ME

**SECTION 2**

▲ American colonists protest taxes levied by the Stamp Act.

WITNESS HISTORY ◀)) AUDIO

## A Voice for Freedom

In March 1775, the 13 colonies were on the brink of war with England. Delegates from across Virginia met to debate their options. Should they give Britain another chance to resolve the problem peacefully? Or were the colonists ready to fight for their freedom? Then, Patrick Henry urged the Virginia convention to prepare for war in a speech that roused the delegates. Based on recollections of men like Thomas Jefferson, Henry's biographer, William Wirt, included the text of the speech that is attributed to Patrick Henry.

❝Gentlemen may cry peace, peace—but there is no peace. The war is actually begun! . . . Our brethren are already in the field! Why stand we here idle? . . . Is life so dear, or peace so sweet, as to be purchased at the price of chains and slavery? . . . I know not what course others may take; but as for me, give me liberty, or give me death!❞

—Patrick Henry, March 23, 1775

# The American Revolution

**Content Expectations**

- **F1.1a** Analyze American society ideals reflected in Declaration of Independence.
- **F1.2a** Discuss republican government birth, rule of law, inalienable rights, equality, limited government.
- **F1.2c** Discuss competing views of the responsibilities of governments.

## Terms and People

| | |
|---|---|
| House of Burgesses | Enlightenment |
| Mayflower Compact | Great Awakening |
| Magna Carta | Thomas Jefferson |
| English Bill of Rights | George Washington |

## NoteTaking

**Reading Skill: Recognize Sequence** Note the sequence of events that led to the American Revolution by making a series-of-events chain.

```
        French and Indian War
   ↓            ↓             ↓
```

**Why It Matters** European nations explored the Americas and began establishing colonies. England established 13 colonies along the mid-Atlantic coast of North America. Eventually, these colonies would declare their independence from England and become a new nation: the United States of America. **Section Focus Question: What important ideas and major events led to the American Revolution?**

## European Colonies in the Americas

Wealth flowed into Spain from its colonies in Mexico, Central America, and South America. Population was thin and life harder in the borderland regions in the present-day Southwest and Florida. In an effort to encourage settlement and protect these outposts, Spain established presidios, or forts. Priests and nuns established dozens of missions to convert Native Americans to Christianity.

The French established colonies in Canada along the coast of Nova Scotia and the St. Lawrence River. Besides exploiting rich fishing off the coast, they found a fortune in furs. American Indians were eager to exchange beaver pelts for European-made metal axes, knives, and kettles. During the 1690s, the French founded Louisiana, along the Mississippi River valley and the Gulf Coast.

**England Establishes Colonies in Virginia** In 1607, the English established their first enduring settlement, Jamestown, in Virginia.

Chapter 1 Section 2 9

# Roots of Democracy

**A**lthough the United States is more than 200 years old, the ideas of democracy and representative government are far older. The roots of democracy reach back to civilizations in southwest Asia and Europe.

## Judeo~Christian Roots ▲

The values found in the Bible, including the Ten Commandments and the teachings of Jesus, inspired American ideas about government and morality.

## The Enlightenment ▲

Two Enlightenment philosophers who influenced American ideas about government were John Locke and Baron de Montesquieu. Locke stated that all people have natural rights and that if a monarch violates those rights, then the people have the right to overthrow the monarch. Montesquieu declared that the powers of government should be clearly defined and limited.

## English Parliamentary Traditions ▼

Two key English documents inspired Americans. The Magna Carta (1215) and the English Bill of Rights (1689) guaranteed certain rights to citizens, including the right to trial by jury. The ideas of a two-house lawmaking body and voting rights also influenced Americans.

## Greco~Roman Roots ▶

Ancient Greek democracy and Roman republicanism have influenced American government.

### Thinking Critically

1. **Draw Conclusions** How does government in the United States reflect English Parliamentary traditions?

2. **Make Inferences** How might John Locke's ideas about natural rights lead to revolution?

**For:** More about the roots of democracy
**Web Code:** nep-0114

Despite enormous losses to disease, to starvation, and to war with the Indians, the English expanded around the Chesapeake Bay. The colonists prospered by raising tobacco for export. Claiming the political rights of Englishmen, the Virginia planters elected a legislature, known as the **House of Burgesses.** It governed the colony in partnership with a royal governor appointed by the king of England.

**New England Colonies** To the north, the English established more colonies, which they called New England. The first colonists were devout Protestants called "Puritans," who hoped to create model moral communities. They settled first in 1620 at Plymouth, where they adopted the **Mayflower Compact,** which provided a framework for self-government. By 1700, New England had four colonies: Massachusetts, Rhode Island, Connecticut, and New Hampshire.

Adapting to the cold climate and short growing season, the New Englanders supplemented farming with lumber harvested from the forests and fish taken from the seas. By building ships, they were able to trade with the other colonies and with Europe.

**Middle and Southern Colonies** The English developed a third cluster of colonies between Maryland and New England. They conquered Dutch New Netherland and renamed it New York, then added New Jersey and Pennsylvania, a haven for Quaker immigrants. The Middle Colonies offered religious toleration and a prospering economy based on exporting wheat.

South of Virginia, the English developed a fourth cluster of colonies. The Southern Colonies consisted of North Carolina, South Carolina, and Georgia. The colonists raised rice on coastal plantations and cattle on farms in the backcountry. The plantations relied on the labor of enslaved Africans.

✔ **Checkpoint** What were the major economic activities of the English colonies in America?

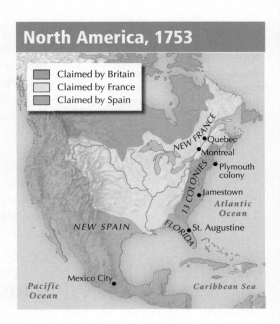

**North America, 1753**

Claimed by Britain
Claimed by France
Claimed by Spain

**Colonial America**
Three European nations controlled vast amounts of territory in North America in the mid-eighteenth century. *Which nation controlled territory that bordered the Pacific Ocean?*

# Democratic Ideals in the American Colonies

The English colonists brought ideas about democracy and republican government with them to America. Some of these ideas were from Southwest Asia while others came from Europe.

**English Traditions** As English citizens, the colonists believed that they were entitled to the same rights as English citizens in England. Many of these rights were contained in two important documents: the Magna Carta and the English Bill of Rights. The **Magna Carta,** signed by King John in 1215, limited the power of the English monarch. It protected the right of people to own private property and guaranteed the right to trial by jury. The **English Bill of Rights,** signed by King William and Queen Mary in 1688, was a written list of freedoms that the government promised to protect. The English Bill of Rights required Parliament, England's lawmaking body, to meet regularly. It also stated that the monarch could not raise taxes or build an army without Parliament's consent.

**The Enlightenment and the Great Awakening** During the 1700s, ideas based on the **Enlightenment** circulated among well-educated American colonists. The Enlightenment was a European intellectual movement. Enlightenment philosophers believed that all problems could be solved by human reason. Frenchman Baron de Montesquieu and Englishman John Locke were two thinkers who applied reason to government and politics.

**WITNESS HISTORY DVD**

Watch *The Enlightenment and the American Revolution* on the **United States Witness History DVD** to explore the effect of Enlightenment philosophy on the leaders of the American Revolution.

**Vocabulary Builder**
philosophy–(fih LAHS uh fee) *n.*
theory or logical analysis of the
fundamental principles of human
conduct, thought, knowledge, and
the nature of the universe

Enlightenment <u>philosophy</u> affected religious beliefs in the colonies. Colonists who admired these ideas wanted a religion that was less emotional and more rational. At the same time, attendance at worship services was in decline.

During the 1740s, concern about these trends led to a religious movement called the **Great Awakening.** Evangelical preachers such as Jonathan Edwards and George Whitefield toured the colonies promoting revivals where people felt a direct and transforming contact with an overwhelming Holy Spirit. The Great Awakening led to the birth of new churches. This eventually increased tolerance of religious differences. Many colonists also came to believe that if they could decide how to worship God, they could also decide how to govern themselves.

The Enlightenment and the Great Awakening would later combine to influence the American Revolution. The Enlightenment informed the writings of the political leaders, while the Great Awakening inspired the common people.

✓ **Checkpoint** **Which democratic ideas were expressed by Enlightenment thinkers?**

# Causes of the American Revolution

The tradition of a limited English monarchy, experience with self-government, and exposure to Enlightenment ideas were important ideas in the minds of leading American colonists. A war and a spirit of independence in the colonies prompted Americans to action that would change the course of world history.

Between 1689 and 1763, the British and French fought a series of wars in Europe. These conflicts spread to America and involved the French and English colonists and their Native American allies.

The last of these wars, called the French and Indian War, erupted in 1754 and ended in 1763 with a British victory. The peace treaty gave Canada, Florida, and a portion of French Louisiana to Britain. British colonists were eager to move into Louisiana, but Britain wished to keep peace with the Indians who lived on this territory. British limits on westward expansion angered the colonists.

**Taxes and Traditional Rights** The British victory was expensive, nearly doubling Britain's national debt. During the 1760s, the British Parliament <u>asserted</u> that the colonists should pay new taxes to help the empire. The proposed taxes and tighter trade regulations shocked the colonists. Valuing the prosperity and protection of the empire, they did not immediately seek independence. Instead, they wanted to remain part of the empire that had for so long produced so many benefits at so little cost to them.

**Vocabulary Builder**
assert–(uh SERT) *v.* to state
positively; declare; affirm

In resisting the taxes, colonists cited the traditional rights of Englishmen. They cited the Magna Carta and the English Bill of Rights, which blocked the king from levying taxes without the permission of Parliament. During the 1760s, their problem was with Parliament, rather than with King George III. Professing loyalty to the king, the colonists hoped to be free from Parliament's efforts to tax them. They would pay taxes levied only by their own elected assemblies in the colonies.

**Colonial Resistance** To pressure Parliament, colonists boycotted British goods. Local committees enforced this boycott, which threatened the British economy. Angry crowds harassed colonists who helped to collect the new taxes. Colonists who refused to honor the boycotts or who spoke out in favor of the taxes were considered Loyalists. Representing a large minority, the Loyalists preferred to pay the taxes and honor Parliament and the king. They also feared that the resistance would lead to a war that Britain seemed certain to win.

✓ **Checkpoint** **Why did many American colonists object to paying taxes imposed by Parliament?**

# The American Revolution

**Map legend:**
- Original 13 colonies
- Other British territories
- American victory
- British victory

**Map labels:**

Lake Superior

Lake Michigan

Lake Huron

L. Ontario

L. Erie

Quebec

Montreal    St. Lawrence R.

Maine (part of Mass.)

New York    GREEN MTS.

Saratoga (1777)    N.H.

Albany    Bunker Hill (1775)

Delaware R.    Boston

Conn.    Mass.

Princeton (1777)    R.I.

Pennsylvania    New York

Valley Forge    Trenton (1776)

Brandywine (1777)    Philadelphia

Md.    N.J.

Del.

Wabash R.

Vincennes (1779)

Potomac R.    Chesapeake Bay

Cahokia (1778)    Ohio R.

Louisiana (Spanish Territory)

Kaskaskia (1778)    Virginia    Richmond

James R.    Yorktown (1781)

APPALACHIAN

Guilford Courthouse (1781)    North Carolina

Mississippi R.    Kings Mt. (1780)

Camden (1780)    South Carolina    Wilmington

Georgia    Charles Town

Savannah R.    Savannah

New Orleans

Atlantic Ocean

Gulf of Mexico

90° W    80° W    70° W

Conic Projection

0    200    400 mi

0    200    400 km

## Conflict With Great Britain

The American colonists opposed "taxation without representation"—or taxes levied by a Parliament to which the colonists had elected no representatives. Patriot leaders staged boycotts and anti-British propaganda campaigns in order to win support for independence.

**Map Skills** The American Revolution was fought in battles along the east coast of North America and along the Mississippi River in the West. This map shows the war's major battles in the fight for American independence from Great Britain.

1. **Locate:** (a) Saratoga, (b) Brandywine, (c) Yorktown

2. **Place** Which battles were fought along the Mississippi River?

3. **Synthesize Information** Based on the dates that appear on the map, in which region were the earlier battles fought? In which region were the later battles fought?

## Roots of the American Revolution

**1763** French and Indian War ends with a British victory. King George III signs the Proclamation of 1763, ending colonial expansion west of the Appalachian Mountains.

**1764** To pay off war debt, Parliament passes the Sugar Act, imposing duties on imported sugar and other goods that colonists import from England.

**1765** Stamp Act is passed by Parliament, directly taxing all legal documents, almanacs, and other items in the colonies. Colonists form the Sons of Liberty and the Daughters of Liberty to organize protests. One year later, the Stamp Act is repealed.

**1767** Parliament passes the Townshend Acts, taxing a number of items the colonies import. Colonists boycott British goods.

**1770** Boston Massacre results in death of five colonists. Townshend Acts are repealed.

**1773** Protesting the tax on tea, colonists stage the Boston Tea Party, dumping crates of British tea into Boston Harbor.

**1774** Parliament passes the Intolerable Acts, imposing harsh measures on the colonies. The First Continental Congress meets.

**1775** First shots of the American Revolution are fired at Lexington and Concord.

# The War for Independence

In 1774, leading colonists held a convention, called the First Continental Congress. Delegates appealed to the British government to stop taxing the colonies. The British government refused.

**Americans Declare Their Independence**  In 1775, war began when British troops tried to seize arms and ammunition stored at Concord, Massachusetts. The New Englanders quickly organized an army, which the Continental Congress adopted as the army for all the colonies.

In 1776, Congress adopted a Declaration of Independence drafted by **Thomas Jefferson** of Virginia. This declared American independence and expressed Enlightenment philosopher John Locke's ideas about the natural rights of people. The Declaration stated that certain truths were "self-evident."

> **Primary Source**  "That all men are created equal; that they are endowed by their Creator with certain unalienable rights; that among these are life, liberty, and the pursuit of happiness. . . ."
>
> —Declaration of Independence, July 4, 1776

**The War Is Fought**  During the war, the British made many military mistakes because they underestimated the Patriots, who were highly motivated and benefited from the leadership of **George Washington.** Beginning in 1778, the Patriots also received military assistance from France. In 1781, a French fleet trapped the British army at Yorktown in Virginia, where Washington's army completed the victory. The treaty of Paris, signed in 1783, gave the new nation very favorable boundaries: Florida on the south; the Great Lakes to the north; and the Mississippi River to the west. The British retreated to Canada, while the Spanish claimed Florida and everything west of the Mississippi.

✔ **Checkpoint** What risks did declaring independence pose for the colonists?

**Minuteman**
This sculpture reminds Americans of the sacrifices made by minutemen, members of the Patriot militia who were ready to fight for freedom at a moment's notice.

---

## SECTION 2 Assessment

**Progress Monitoring *Online***
For: Self-test with vocabulary practice
Web Code: nea-0106

### Comprehension

1. **Terms and People** For each term and person below, write a sentence explaining how each contributed to the development of U.S. democracy or to the Revolution.
   - House of Burgesses
   - Mayflower Compact
   - Enlightenment
   - Great Awakening
   - Magna Carta
   - English Bill of Rights
   - Thomas Jefferson
   - George Washington

2. **NoteTaking Reading Skill: Recognize Sequence** Use your series-of-events chain to answer the Section Focus Question: What important ideas and major events led to the American Revolution?

### Writing About History

3. **Quick Write: Identify Effects** Make a list of one or two effects of each of the following events: the French and Indian War, the British decision to tax the colonists, the colonial boycott of British goods, and the American Revolution.

### Critical Thinking

4. **Make Inferences** What Enlightenment values are reflected in the Declaration of Independence?

5. **Draw Conclusions** What effects did the Great Awakening have on American thought?

6. **Analyze Information** How did the peace treaty that marked the end of the American Revolution change the boundaries of the United States? Which countries controlled territory on the borders of the new nation?

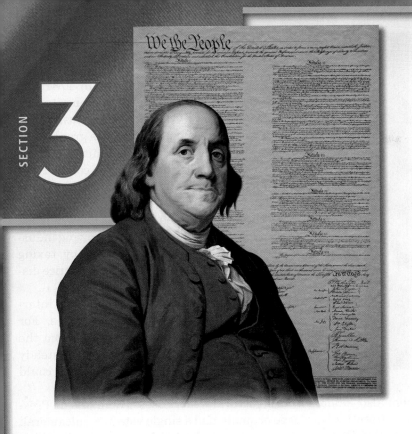

◀ Benjamin Franklin framed by the U.S. Constitution

WITNESS HISTORY 🔊 AUDIO

## A New Constitution

Delegates to the Constitutional Convention met in 1787 at Independence Hall in Philadelphia. After intense debate and compromise, they created a document that has endured for more than 200 years. Benjamin Franklin, a great patriot, diplomat, and philosopher, urged his fellow delegates to ratify the Constitution:

❝I agree to this Constitution with all its faults . . . because I think a general government necessary for us, and there is no form of government but what may be a blessing to the people if well administered. . . . On the whole, sir, I can not help expressing a wish that every member of the convention who may still have objections to it, would, with me, . . . to make manifest our unanimity, put his name to this instrument.❞

—Benjamin Franklin, Constitutional Convention, 1787

# The Constitution

 **Content Expectations**

- **F1.1b** Analyze American society ideals reflected in U.S. Constitution.
- **F1.1c** Analyze American society ideals reflected in Bill of Rights.
- **F1.2a** Discuss republican government birth, rule of law, inalienable rights, equality, limited government.

## Terms and People

bill of rights

Shays' Rebellion

James Madison

ratify

federalism

separation of powers

checks and balances

## NoteTaking

**Reading Skill: Recognize Sequence**

Complete a timeline that includes important dates that led to the formation of the U.S. government.

```
1781 Articles
of Confederation
    |_____
  1780    1785    1790    1795
```

**Why It Matters** Dissatisfied with British rule, the American colonists rebelled and created the United States of America. The leaders of the new nation faced the task of creating a system of government. Their hard work resulted in the U.S. Constitution, an enduring document that has guided the nation for more than 200 years. **Section Focus Question: What ideas and debates led to the Constitution and Bill of Rights?**

## A Confederation of States

The colonists declared their independence from Britain in 1776 and won independence with their victory in the American Revolution in 1783. Now, they faced the daunting task of organizing a new government.

**States Establish Constitutional Governments** The former colonies became states in 1776, and each wrote a constitution that created republics, or governments in which officials are representatives elected by the people. Voters elected their state legislatures and their governors. Only white male property owners could vote, except in New Jersey where women had the right to vote until 1807. African Americans—whether free or enslaved—and Native Americans were not permitted to vote. Most state constitutions included a **bill of rights,** a list of freedoms guaranteed by the state government.

## The Northwest Territory

Congress passed land ordinances to organize the Northwest Territory. Settlers then rushed in to build homes. Eventually, the states of Ohio, Indiana, Illinois, Michigan, Wisconsin, and part of Minnesota were carved out of this vast territory.

**Vocabulary Builder**
constrain–(kuhn STRAYN) *v.* to hold back; restrain

Many of them guaranteed freedom of religion, freedom of the press, and the right to trial by jury.

**The Articles of Confederation** In 1781, the 13 states adopted their first federal constitution. Under the Articles of Confederation, most power remained with the states. The Articles granted the federal government only certain limited powers. Congress had the power to declare and conduct war and could regulate trade with foreign countries and with Indian nations.

Under the Articles, each state set its own trade policy. Each state tried to protect its growing industry and agriculture from competition by taxing goods imported from other states. This practice discouraged trade among the states.

The national government had no say in interstate commerce and could not levy taxes. For money, Congress drew on contributions from the states, which were unreliable. Without a steady source of income, the federal government could not pay its immense war debt.

The government also suffered from structural weaknesses. There was no President. Each state, no matter how large or small, had a single vote in a unicameral, or one-house, Congress. On the major issues, including declaring war and making treaties, two thirds of the states (nine) had to approve. Amending the Articles was almost impossible, because all 13 states had to endorse any change.

**The Northwest Territory** Under the Articles, Congress had authority over the vast Northwest Territory, which lay north of the Ohio River and stretched west from Pennsylvania to the Mississippi River. In 1785 and 1787, Congress passed two laws to manage this land. The first, the Land Ordinance, created a system for surveying and selling the land to settlers. The second, the Northwest Ordinance, described how territories should be governed and how they could become full-fledged states. This law also banned slavery in the territory and provided for public education.

**Troubles Grow in the 1780s** Lacking an army, the weak Confederation could not defend American interests on the frontier. The Spanish in Louisiana tried to constrain western American settlements by closing the port of New Orleans. Along the Great Lakes, the British refused to abandon frontier forts on the American side of the boundary set by the terms of the peace treaty that ended the American Revolution.

During the mid-1780s, an economic depression reduced the prices paid to farmers for their produce. Unable to pay their debts, farmers faced losing their crops, livestock, and even their homes. In Massachusetts, matters worsened when the courts seized farms from farmers who did not pay taxes to the state or their loans. In rural Massachusetts in 1786, armed farmers led by Daniel Shays shut down the courts, blocking foreclosures. The state of Massachusetts sent troops to suppress this revolt, known as **Shays' Rebellion.** The rebellion highlighted the weaknesses of the federal government.

✔ **Checkpoint** What were the chief weaknesses of the Articles of Confederation?

# The Constitutional Convention

By 1787, many Americans agreed that the Articles of Confederation were flawed. To draft proposed amendments to the Articles, the states sent delegates to a special convention in Philadelphia, in May 1787. However, once delegates restructured the national government, the convention would be known as the Constitutional Convention.

Favored by the small states, the proposed New Jersey Plan would give Congress the power to regulate commerce and to tax, while keeping the basic structure of the Confederation. The plan retained a unicameral legislature representing the states as equals—no matter how large or small. The states remained sovereign except for those few powers specifically granted to the national government. Under the New Jersey Plan, the United States would stay a loose confederation of states, rather than become a unified nation.

**James Madison** of Virginia designed the Virginia Plan, which <u>advocated</u> a national union that was both strong and republican. He insisted that a large republic could be more stable than a small one, because in a large republic, the diverse interests would provide checks and balances to preserve the common good. In addition to securing the power to tax and to regulate commerce, this plan proposed major structural changes. The nation would have a bicameral legislature: a House of Representatives and a Senate. In both houses, the states with larger populations would have more members. The Virginia Plan also featured a President to command the armed forces and to manage foreign relations.

**Vocabulary Builder**
advocate—(AD vuh kayt) *v.* to speak or write in support of; be in favor of

**The Great Compromise** The delegates worked throughout the hot Philadelphia summer to resolve their differences. Roger Sherman proposed what has come to be called the Great Compromise. It settled the differences between the Virginia and the New Jersey plans by creating a bicameral, or two-house legislature. In a concession to the smaller states, the Senate would equally represent every state by allowing just two senators per state. In keeping with the Virginia Plan, the House of Representatives, which represented population, granted more power to the larger states.

Another major compromise appeased the southern states. Their delegates feared domination by the northern states, which had a larger white population. To reassure the South, the delegates adopted the three-fifths clause. It counted each enslaved person as three fifths of a person, to be added to a state's free population, which boosted the number of the South's seats in Congress. The three-fifths clause, however, gave no rights to enslaved African Americans.

✔ **Checkpoint** What key compromises did delegates to the Constitutional Convention make?

# The Struggle Over Ratification

The Constitution was now written, but it was not yet the law of the land. Before it could go into effect, 9 of the 13 states had to **ratify,** or officially approve, it.

**Federalists Argue for Ratification** Supporters of the Constitution were called Federalists. They wanted the United States to have a strong central government. Three leading Federalists—James Madison, Alexander Hamilton, and John Jay—wrote a series

## HISTORY MAKERS

**James Madison** (1751–1836)
James Madison is aptly called the "Father of the Constitution" because he was so instrumental in creating that document and securing its ratification in Virginia. He agreed to add amendments that would guarantee basic freedoms, a promise he fulfilled by introducing the Bill of Rights when the House of Representatives first met. Later, Madison served as Secretary of State and was elected President for two terms.

**Reading Skill: Compare and Contrast** As you read, identify similarities and differences between the Federalists and the Antifederalists.

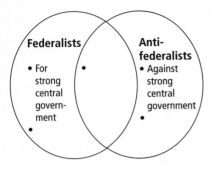

Federalists
- For strong central government

Anti-federalists
- Against strong central government

of letters to newspapers in support of the Constitution. These letters, collectively called *The Federalist Papers,* explained why they believed the Constitution was vital to the survival of the new nation. Today, the *Federalist* essays are recognized as perhaps the most sophisticated explanation of the new American political system ever written.

**Antifederalists Argue Against Ratification** Opponents of the proposed Constitution were the Antifederalists. They included some leading Americans, such as Patrick Henry and Samuel Adams. The Antifederalists objected to the Constitution because they thought it gave the national government far too much power at the expense of the states. They believed that the President had too much power, that Congress was too small and could not represent voters, and that a federal court system interfered with local courts.

**A Bill of Rights Leads to Ratification** One of the most powerful arguments of the Antifederalists was that the proposed Constitution lacked a bill of rights. To secure ratification, the Federalists promised to add a bill of rights once the new government convened.

In 1789, Congress approved the ten constitutional amendments that became the federal Bill of Rights. States ratified the amendments in 1791. The protected rights included freedom of speech, freedom of religion, freedom of the press and of assembly, the right to bear arms as part of "a well-regulated militia," and judicial protections against arbitrary arrests and trials.

✔ **Checkpoint** What were the main arguments for and against ratification of the Constitution?

---

**Decision ● Point**

# Should the states ratify the Constitution?

Delegates at the Constitutional Convention in 1787 debated the pros and cons of the new Constitution. In order for the Constitution to become law, at least 9 of the 13 states had to approve the document. Read the opinions below. Then, you decide.

**Patrick Henry Opposes Ratifying the Constitution**

**Primary Source**

❝I review . . . the subject . . . and . . . the dangers . . . in this new plan of government, and compare . . . my poor abilities to secure our rights, it will take much more time to traverse the objectionable parts of it. . . . [T]he change is dangerous . . . and the experiment ought not be made. . . .❞

—Patrick Henry, June 9, 1788

**You Decide**
1. Why did Hamilton favor ratifying the Constitution?
2. Why did Henry oppose ratifying the Constitution?
3. What decision would you have made? Why?

**Alexander Hamilton Favors Ratifying the Constitution**

**Primary Source**

❝The establishment of a Constitution, . . . by the . . . consent of a whole people, is a prodigy, to the completion of which I look forward. . . . I dread . . . the consequences of new attempts, because I know that powerful individuals, . . . are enemies to a general national government in every possible shape.❞

—Alexander Hamilton, *The Federalist Papers*

## TRACK THE ISSUE

### What should the federal government do to expand and protect civil rights?

The U.S. Constitution guarantees equal rights for all Americans. In 1789, though, African Americans, women, and Native Americans did not have the same rights given white males. Over the years, however, rights have been extended to these groups. A major question remains, though: How far should the government go to expand rights? Use the timeline below to explore this enduring issue.

**1791  Bill of Rights**
The first 10 amendments to the U.S. Constitution guarantee certain basic rights and freedoms.

**1868  Fourteenth Amendment**
Guarantees citizenship to everyone born or naturalized in the United States.

**1920  Nineteenth Amendment**
Women gain the right to vote.

**1964  Civil Rights Act**
Bans race or gender discrimination in public accommodations and jobs.

**1990  Americans With Disabilities Act**
Bans discrimination against people with disabilities.

The Bill of Rights

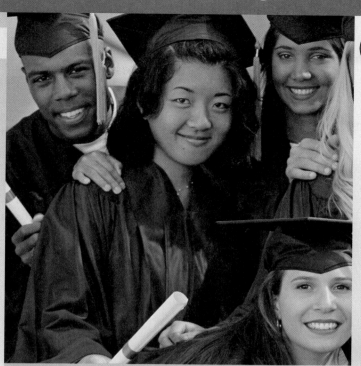

F1.1e

College graduates celebrate their achievements.

## DEBATE THE ISSUE

**Affirmative Action**  Some urge companies, colleges, and the government to use affirmative action programs to expand opportunities for women and minorities. Others argue that such steps are unfair.

"You do not take a man who for years has been hobbled by chains, liberate him, bring him to the starting line of a race, saying 'you are free to compete with all the others,' and still justly believe you have been completely fair. . . . We seek not just freedom but opportunity . . . not just equality as a right and a theory, but equality as a fact and as a result."

—President Lyndon Johnson, speech, June 4, 1965

"The civil rights laws themselves forbade employers to discriminate on the basis of race, sex, national origin, color, or religion. They didn't say anything about guaranteeing a certain number of slots to minorities or women. . . . The supporters of affirmative action everywhere seemed to believe that the only way to eliminate racial discrimination against blacks, Latinos, and women was to discriminate against white men."

—Linda Chavez, essay, October 2002

### TRANSFER Activities

1. **Compare**  Choose a statement about affirmative action you disagree with. Explain why you disagree.

2. **Analyze**  Do you think either Johnson or Chavez believed that affirmative action is a basic right? Why or why not?

3. **Transfer**  Use the following Web site to see a video, try a WebQuest, and write in your journal. **Web Code:** neh-6502

## Ideas Behind the Constitution

✓ **Quick Study**

| Principle | Definition |
| --- | --- |
| Popular sovereignty | People are the main source of the government's authority. |
| Limited government | The government has only the powers that the Constitution gives it. |
| Federalism | The federal government and the state governments share power. |
| Separation of powers | The government's power is divided among three branches: the legislative, the executive, and the judicial branch. |
| Checks and balances | Each branch of government has the power to limit the actions of the other two. |
| Representative government | Citizens elect representatives to government to make laws. |
| Individual rights | The Constitution protects citizens' individual rights, such as freedom of speech and freedom of religion. |

# Principles of the Constitution

The new Constitution divided power between the states and the nation, a division of sovereignty known as **federalism.** The states could no longer issue their own paper money. These were delegated powers belonging only to the federal government. Certain reserved powers belonged to the states, including the power to regulate elections. The federal and state governments also held some overlapping concurrent powers, among them parallel court systems.

The Constitution also promoted a **separation of powers** within the federal government by defining distinct executive, legislative, and judicial branches. Each branch had **checks and balances** on the others to prevent the emergence of a single center of power. For example, although Congress enacts laws, the President may veto them—but Congress may override the veto by a two-thirds majority. The President nominates judges, but the Senate must approve them.

The founders knew that they could not anticipate future social, economic, or political events, and so they worded parts of the Constitution to permit flexibility. For example, the Constitution gave Congress the power "to make all laws which shall be necessary and proper" to carry out its powers. This clause of the Constitution has been stretched to provide constitutional underpinning for so many laws that it is sometimes called the elastic clause. The ability to amend the Constitution also provides flexibility as well. Since its ratification, the Constitution has been amended 27 times.

✔ **Checkpoint** What major principles appear in the U.S. Constitution?

SECTION **3** Assessment

**Progress Monitoring *Online***
For: Self-test with vocabulary practice
Web Code: nea-0108

### Comprehension

1. **Terms and People** What do all of the terms and people listed below have in common? Explain.
   - bill of rights
   - Shays' Rebellion
   - James Madison
   - ratify
   - federalism
   - separation of powers
   - checks and balances

2. **NoteTaking Reading Skill: Recognize Sequence** Use your timeline to answer the Section Focus Question: What ideas and debates led to the Constitution and Bill of Rights?

### Writing About History

3. **Quick Write: Make a Cause-and-Effect Flowchart** As you prepare a cause-and-effect essay, you need to decide how to organize it. To do so, create a flowchart that shows the causes and effects of Shays' Rebellion. Do you want to write about the events in chronological order or by the importance of each event?

### Critical Thinking

4. **Draw Inferences** Under the Articles of Confederation, the federal government had limited power. Why do you think that the states were reluctant to concede power to the federal government?

5. **Identify Central Issues** Why did delegates to the Constitutional Convention create a new Constitution rather than revise the Articles of Confederation?

6. **Recognize Ideologies** Does the following quotation express the views of a Federalist or an Antifederalist? Explain. "The entire separation of the States into thirteen unconnected sovereignties is a project too extravagant and too replete with danger to have many advocates."

◄ Hard-working pioneers, like this woman, helped the new nation grow and prosper.

### Democracy in America

The French historian and politician, Alexis de Tocqueville, toured the United States for nine months in 1831 and 1832. After returning to France, he wrote *Democracy in America,* a highly regarded study of American life and customs. In one chapter, he discussed the importance of popular rule, or "sovereignty of the people," in America.

❝If there is a country in the world where the doctrine of the sovereignty of the people can be fairly appreciated, where it can be studied in its application to the affairs of society, and where its dangers and its advantages may be judged, that country is assuredly America. . . . The people reign in the American political world. . . . They are the cause and the aim of all things; everything comes from them, and everything is absorbed in them.❞

—Alexis de Tocqueville, *Democracy in America*

# The New Republic

 **Content Expectations**

- **F1.2a** Discuss republican government birth, rule of law, inalienable rights, equality, limited government.
- **F1.2b** Discuss governmental roles development in U.S. life.
- **F1.2c** Discuss competing views of the responsibilities of governments.

## Terms and People

| | |
|---|---|
| Alien Act | impressment |
| Sedition Act | embargo |
| judicial review | cotton gin |
| Louisiana Purchase | Monroe Doctrine |

## NoteTaking

**Reading Skill: Categorize** Create a chart that lists the five Presidents in this chapter. List the major accomplishments of each President in the chart.

| President | Accomplishments |
|---|---|
| George Washington | |
| John Adams | |

**Why It Matters** The new U.S. Constitution promised a stronger federal government to guide the new republic through difficult times. During the 1790s and early 1800s, both internal political issues and international affairs tested the nation's strength. Despite these challenges, the nation continued to grow in size and power. Nevertheless, economic, political, and social differences began to divide the North and the South. **Section Focus Question: How did the United States and its government change in the late 1700s and early 1800s?**

## Government and Party Politics

In 1789, a new federal government gathered in New York City. The nation was anxious as its first President took office. Washington's government set precedents of enduring importance to the nation's future. A good start would increase the strength of the nation. But early mistakes could doom it.

**The Government Under Washington** Fortunately, the United States enjoyed extraordinary leadership. Americans had the best of all possible Presidents in George Washington, whose dignity commanded respect. To conduct foreign policy, Washington appointed Thomas Jefferson as Secretary of State. To supervise domestic policy, the President depended on the Secretary of the Treasury, Alexander Hamilton.

Hamilton and Jefferson belonged to a group of executive officers known as the President's Cabinet.

### Hamilton's Financial Plan Stirs Debate

Alexander Hamilton wanted the United States to develop a commercial and industrial economy that could support a large federal government with a strong army and navy. He also wanted to pay off the nation's huge war debt. Hamilton proposed to pay off the debt by issuing government bonds, which paid interest to the bondholders. To pay the interest, Hamilton proposed new taxes on goods. To manage the debt, he asked Congress to charter a Bank of the United States with the power to regulate state banks.

To justify his ambitious program, Hamilton pointed to the Constitution's elastic clause empowering Congress to enact laws for the "general welfare." He reasoned that a national bank would promote the general welfare. In Congress, in 1791, Hamilton's supporters—the Federalists—narrowly approved his program.

### Democratic Republicans Challenge Hamilton

Hamilton's broad interpretation of the Constitution appalled critics who wanted to limit the federal government to powers explicitly granted by the Constitution. Favoring a "strict construction," Democratic Republicans led by Thomas Jefferson saw no grounds for a national bank.

The critics also pointed out that Hamilton's system favored merchants from northeastern cities who owed much of the debt. Why, southerners asked, should their tax dollars compensate creditors in the Northeast?

✔ **Checkpoint** How did Hamilton and Jefferson differ in their interpretations of the Constitution?

## The Struggle Over Foreign Policy

President Washington and other federal government officials had their hands full dealing with domestic economic and political issues. But, as a sovereign country on the world stage, they also had to define and conduct foreign policy.

### America Has Strained Relations With Europe

In 1789, the French Revolution began. Many Americans, especially Democratic Republicans, sympathized with the French revolutionaries, whom they viewed as fighting for freedom from tyranny. Many Federalists, however, saw the revolutionaries as murderous mobs. Other nations of Europe shared this view, and they declared war on the new French government. Britain was among them.

The United States declared its neutrality in this war but continued to trade with Britain and France. In 1793, the British navy tested American neutrality by seizing U.S. merchant ships trading with the French colonies in the West Indies. This added to the U.S. outrage at British forts on the American side of the Great Lakes. To avoid war, Washington sent John Jay to London to negotiate with the British. In Jay's Treaty of 1794, the British gave up the forts but kept most of their restrictions on U.S. shipping. Washington had avoided war. However, the Democratic Republicans denounced Jay's Treaty as a sellout.

### The Battle of Fallen Timbers

U.S. General Anthony Wayne led his troops against Indians in the Ohio Valley. Wayne's victory in 1794 opened the region to settlement and discouraged foreign nations from invading the region.

Meanwhile, the Americans were in conflict with Indians in the Ohio Country. In August 1794, General Anthony Wayne won the pivotal victory at Fallen Timbers. The Indians gave up two thirds of what is now Ohio as well as southern Indiana.

In 1795, the United States also benefited from a treaty negotiated by Thomas Pinckney with the Spanish. Pinckney's Treaty permitted Americans to export their produce through New Orleans. Recovering the forts, defeating the Indians, and opening New Orleans combined to encourage westward movement.

**The Alien and Sedition Acts** After two terms in office, George Washington retired. Federalist John Adams won the election of 1796. A foreign policy crisis with France dominated Adams's administration. Offended by Jay's Treaty, the French began seizing American merchant ships. In addition, the French demanded bribes from American diplomats. Soon, French and American ships were fighting a full-scale naval war on the high seas.

**Vocabulary Builder**
exploit–(ehk SPLOIT) *v.* to make use of for one's own advantage or profit

The Federalists <u>exploited</u> the crisis by trying to crush their political opponents by passing the Alien and Sedition Acts in 1798. Most immigrants voted Democratic Republican and the **Alien Act** made it more difficult for them to become citizens. The Alien Act also authorized the President to arrest and to deport immigrants who criticized the federal government.

The **Sedition Act** made it a crime for citizens publicly to discredit the federal leaders. The Federalists argued that criticism undermined trust in the government, which was dangerous at a time when the French might invade the country.

✓ **Checkpoint** Why did Jay's Treaty offend France?

# Jefferson, Madison, and the War of 1812

By 1800, support for the Federalists and for fighting France declined. In the presidential election, Jefferson defeated Adams. The Democratic Republicans also won control of Congress and most of the state governments. The victors spoke of the election as the "Revolution of 1800."

Jefferson's election established the principle that the federal government should respect public opinion and should allow public criticism. The new President encouraged Congress to abandon the Alien and Sedition Acts. He got rid of the Federalist taxes on stamps and on land. Despite reducing taxes, he cut the national debt from $80 million when he took office to $57 million in 1809. He achieved this budgetary miracle, in part, by reducing the federal government, including major cuts in the army and the navy. He benefited from the French decision to seek peace and from the increased federal revenue from customs duties.

**The Supreme Court Issues a Landmark Decision**
Thomas Jefferson's electoral revolution was limited by the growing power of the Supreme Court. In 1801, shortly before Jefferson became President, John Marshall became the Chief Justice of the Supreme Court.

Marshall served on the Supreme Court for 35 years— longer than any other Chief Justice. He had a lasting influence on the role of the Court. In 1803, Marshall first asserted **judicial review**—the power to decide the constitutionality of a federal law—in the celebrated case *Marbury* v. *Madison*. Judicial review gives the Court the power to review acts of the President or laws in Congress.

**HISTORY MAKERS**

**Thomas Jefferson** (1743–1826)
Thomas Jefferson was a writer, an inventor, an architect, and a politician. He served as the nation's first Secretary of State, second Vice President, and third President. Jefferson did not believe in a strong presidency or federal government. He thought the states should have relatively more strength. In 1798, he wrote the Virginia Resolutions, which said that states could leave the union if the federal government tried to take away their power.

**America Purchases Louisiana** In 1803, Jefferson scored a great diplomatic coup when France's new ruler, Napoleon Bonaparte, agreed to sell the Louisiana Territory. In 1801, Napoleon had forced Spain to give the territory to France. That concession alarmed the Americans, who dreaded their powerful new neighbors. Fortunately, Napoleon needed money and decided to sell the territory.

In the **Louisiana Purchase,** Jefferson bought a vast territory extending from the Mississippi River to the Rocky Mountains. The Louisiana Territory nearly doubled the size of the United States and cost the country only $15 million. Explorers Meriwether Lewis and William Clark were sent west to the Pacific, while Zebulon Pike was sent southwest to explore the territory.

**Jefferson's Embargo** After the Louisiana Purchase, Jefferson's foreign policy faltered. The British navy resumed seizing American merchant ships trading with France. The British also seized sailors from U.S. ships for the royal navy, a practice known as **impressment.**

As an alternative to war, in 1807 Jefferson persuaded Congress to declare an **embargo,** suspending trade by ordering American ships to stay in port. He expected that the embargo would pressure the British to make concessions. He reasoned that the British needed American food more than Americans needed to wear British-made clothing. In fact, however, the embargo hurt Americans more than it hurt the British.

**Geography** *Interactive*
For: Interactive map
Web Code: nep-0109

## Louisiana Purchase

**Map Skills** The Louisiana Purchase of 1803 doubled the size of the United States. In exploring Louisiana Territory, Lewis and Clark were aided by Native American groups who lived in the region.

1. **Locate:** (a) Mississippi Territory, (b) Spanish Florida, (c) Missouri River

2. **Movement** Describe the journey of Lewis and Clark. Where did they begin and end their journey? What rivers and mountain ranges did they cross?

3. **Make Comparisons** How did Zebulon Pike's expedition differ from that of Lewis and Clark?

## Industrial North and Agricultural South 🔊 AUDIO

In the North, industry relied on employing factory workers at low wages. In the South, agriculture often relied on the labor of enslaved Africans.

**The War of 1812** Congress lifted the embargo in 1809, shortly before Jefferson's term ended. Another Democratic Republican, James Madison, became President. In 1812, he and Congress decided that there was no alternative to war with the British Empire.

During the first two years of war, the Americans failed in their attempts to invade British Canada. In 1814, the British invaded the United States. They briefly captured Washington, D.C., burning the Capitol and the White House. However, the Americans defeated the British in other major attacks.

Weary of war, both sides agreed to a peace treaty that did not change any boundaries. Relieved at surviving the British counterattacks, the Americans celebrated the treaty as proving the stability of their republican form of government.

✔ **Checkpoint** What were the causes and effects of the War of 1812?

# Growing Differences Between North and South

During the 1700s, a change took place that affected the way people worked. The gradual change from using mostly hand-held tools to using machines to produce goods is called the Industrial Revolution.

**Industry Grows in the North** The Industrial Revolution began in Great Britain, where inventors had built machines that revolutionized the way textiles were produced. Slowly, British textile workers came to the United States and built factories. Industrial growth was slow until after the War of 1812. The war cut off American access to British manufactured goods. Eager for substitutes, Americans built factories to produce textiles, shoes, guns, and tools.

Most of those new factories were in the northeastern states, which had more water power than any other region. Industrialization promoted urban growth and attracted European immigrants seeking work. Consequently, the Northeast became the most populous region in the nation.

# Sectionalism and National Politics

## TRACK THE ISSUE

**How do regional differences affect national politics?**

Throughout U.S. history, people in different parts of the country have had different views on important national issues. These differences have sometimes divided American politics along regional lines. Use the timeline below to explore this enduring issue.

**1787 Three-fifths Compromise**
North and South disagree over congressional representation of enslaved people.

**1812 War of 1812**
Western and southern farmers favor war.

**1816–1832 Tariffs**
North wants protective tariffs.

**1861 Civil War**
Disagreements between the North and the South lead to the Civil War.

**1948 Dixiecrats**
Southern Democrats split from their party over civil rights.

**2004 Presidential Election**
Election confirms division between Democratic and Republican states.

Henry Clay, a senator from the western state of Kentucky, supported the War of 1812.

9.1.2d

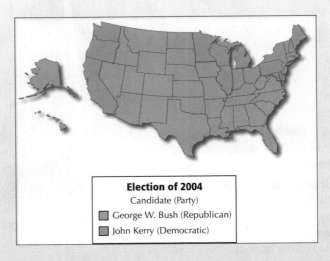

**Election of 2004**
Candidate (Party)
◼ George W. Bush (Republican)
◼ John Kerry (Democratic)

The presidential election of 2004

## DEBATE THE ISSUE

**Red and Blue States** Recent presidential elections have revealed an alleged political divide between the states. "Red" states in the South, West, and Midwest have generally voted Republican. "Blue" states in the Northeast and Pacific West have generally voted Democratic. Are regional or sectional differences affecting voting patterns?

❝Democrats and Republicans once came from the same kinds of communities. Now they don't. . . . The nation has gone through a big . . . sifting of people and politics into what is becoming two Americas. One is urban and Democratic, the other Republican, suburban and rural.❞
—Bill Bishop, *Austin American-Statesman*

❝Very little in politics, very little in life is black and white, or in this case, red and blue. There's an awful lot of gray. . . . Truth be told, if we ask about core American values and core beliefs, about opportunity, equity and how we should go about living our lives, we see very little [if] any difference.❞
—Samuel Abrams, Harvard University researcher

### *TRANSFER* Activities

1. **Compare** In what way does Bishop believe the United States is split? How does Abrams see the red-blue divide?

2. **Analyze** How do you think each of the writers quoted above would respond to the regional differences of opinion regarding the War of 1812?

3. **Transfer** Use the following Web site to see a video, try a WebQuest, and write in your journal. **Web Code:** neh-6702

**Cotton Boom in the South** While the Northeast industrialized, the southern states had an agricultural economy that relied on enslaved labor. Slavery became more profitable as cotton became the South's leading crop. In 1793, Eli Whitney of Connecticut visited Georgia, where he invented the **cotton gin.** This simple machine reduced the time and cost of separating cotton fiber from its hard shell. From 1.5 million pounds in 1790, American cotton production surged to 167 million pounds in 1820.

Cotton planters established new plantations in Tennessee, Alabama, Mississippi, Arkansas, Louisiana, and Texas. Taken from the Indians, the new lands proved more fertile for cotton than the longer-cultivated fields to the east.

Cotton was in great demand in textile factories in the northern United States and in Europe. By paying good prices for cotton, the mill owners encouraged southern planters to expand their fields and increase the number of enslaved African Americans to work them. However, as the North and South adopted different specializations, their political differences increased as well.

 **Checkpoint** How did the industrialization in the North and the spread of cotton in the South contribute to the spread of slavery?

# The Monroe Doctrine

In 1817, James Monroe of Virginia succeeded James Madison as President. The Monroe administration hoped to cure sectional differences by cultivating national strength and ambition. The President and his Secretary of State, John Quincy Adams, wanted to prevent Spain from recovering her American colonies that had declared their independence. In 1823, Monroe and Adams announced a doctrine declaring that European monarchies had no business meddling with American republics. In return, the United States promised to stay out of European affairs.

The **Monroe Doctrine** meant little in 1823, when the Americans lacked the army and navy to enforce it. The Latin American republics kept their independence with British, rather than American, help. The doctrine became much more important later in the nineteenth century, when the United States began to intervene militarily in the Caribbean and Central America.

 **Checkpoint** How did the Monroe Doctrine assert American power in the Western Hemisphere?

## SECTION 4 Assessment

**Progress Monitoring *Online***
For: Self-test with vocabulary practice
Web Code: nea-0111

### Comprehension

1. **Terms and People** For each item below, write a sentence explaining its significance.
   - Alien Act
   - Sedition Act
   - judicial review
   - Louisiana Purchase
   - impressment
   - embargo
   - cotton gin
   - Monroe Doctrine

2. **NoteTaking Reading Skill: Categorize** Use your completed chart to answer the Section Focus Question: How did the United States and its government change in the late 1700s and early 1800s?

### Writing About History

3. **Quick Write: Rank Effects** Make a list of the effects of one of the following events: the Louisiana Purchase, the War of 1812, the Industrial Revolution. Then, rank the effects in order of importance.

### Critical Thinking

4. **Identify Central Issues** Why did southerners object to Hamilton's plan to pay off America's war debt?

5. **Analyze Information** Why did the Democratic Republicans believe that Jay's Treaty did not serve American interests?

6. **Recognize Cause and Effect** What impact did the War of 1812 have on U.S. industrial growth? Explain.

# Quick Study Guide

 F1.1c

**Progress Monitoring *Online***
For: Self-test with Vocabulary Practice
Web Code: nea-0112

## ■ World in About 1500

## ■ Causes of the American Revolution

| The American Revolution | |
| --- | --- |
| **Long-Term Causes** | **Immediate Causes** |
| • Enlightenment<br>• Great Awakening<br>• French and Indian War | • British tax colonists<br>• Colonists protest and resist paying taxes<br>• British king refuses to compromise with colonists<br>• Colonists declare independence |

## ■ The Bill of Rights

| | |
| --- | --- |
| **1st:** | Guarantees freedom of religion, speech, press, assembly, and petition |
| **2nd:** | Guarantees right to bear arms |
| **3rd:** | Prohibits quartering of troops in private homes |
| **4th:** | Protects people from unreasonable searches and seizures |
| **5th:** | Guarantees due process for accused persons |
| **6th:** | Guarantees the right to a speedy and public trial in the state where the offense was committed |
| **7th:** | Guarantees the right to jury trial for civil cases tried in federal courts |
| **8th:** | Prohibits excessive bail and cruel and unusual punishments |
| **9th:** | Provides that people have rights beyond those stated in the Constitution |
| **10th:** | Provides that powers not granted to the national government belong to the states and to the people |

## ☑ Quick Study Timeline

**In America**

**1492**
**Christopher Columbus sails to the Americas**

**1607**
**Jamestown established in Virginia**

**1740s**
**Great Awakening sweeps through American colonies**

**Presidential Terms**

1400–1600

1750

**Around the World**

**1689**
**England's Glorious Revolution leads to English Bill of Rights**

**1707**
**Act of Union unites England and Scotland**

# American Issues
●—●—● **Connector**

By connecting prior knowledge with what you have learned in this chapter, you can gradually build your understanding of enduring questions that still affect America today. Answer the questions below. Then, use your American Issues Connector study guide (or go online: www.PHSchool.com **Web Code:** neh-6155).

## Issues You Learned About

● **Expanding and Protecting Civil Rights**  The United States has long embraced the idea that citizens are entitled to certain rights.

1. What new ideas about citizenship were introduced during the Enlightenment?

2. Which groups of people were not afforded all the rights stated in the Bill of Rights? Why?

● **Global Interdependence**  As Europeans explored and settled the Americas, these two regions became linked by culture and economics.

3. What caused European sailors to seek a sea route to Asia despite the dangers they faced?

4. Why were many American colonists dependent on trade with West Africa?

5. During the Industrial Revolution, Britain passed a law prohibiting textile workers from leaving the country or from sharing technological information on water-powered textile mills. Why would Britain do this?

| Connect to Your World | Michigan |
|---|---|

**Territorial Expansion of the United States**  In its early days as a territory, Michigan faced several hardships. In 1805, the year Michigan became a territory, a raging fire destroyed much of Detroit. During the War of 1812, local battles caused even more damage, including the devastation of settlements along the Detroit River. Territorial Governor Lewis Cass's post–war efforts helped Michigan recover. He created a system of roads and encouraged new settlers to move to the territory. By 1834, Michigan had a population of about 85,000 people—many more than the 60,000 required for the territory to become a state. Michiganians wrote a constitution and applied to Congress for statehood. Following the resolution of a border dispute with Ohio, Michigan became the twenty-sixth state in 1837. Research Michigan Territory's history and create a timeline of events that led to statehood.

| 1775–1781 American Revolution | 1788 U.S. Constitution is ratified | 1803 Louisiana Purchase | 1823 Monroe Doctrine issued |
|---|---|---|---|

| | George Washington 1789–1797 | John Adams 1797–1801 | T. Jefferson 1801–1809 | J. Madison 1809–1817 | J. Monroe 1817–1825 |
|---|---|---|---|---|---|

**1775** | **1800** | **1825**

| 1799 Napoleon seizes control of France | 1805 Haiti declares independence from France | **History Interactive** **For:** Interactive timeline **Web Code:** nep-0113 |
|---|---|---|

# Chapter Assessment

## Terms and People

1. Define **conquistador.** What impact did conquistadores have on American Indian societies?
2. What is the **Enlightenment**? How did the Enlightenment influence American political thought?
3. Define **separation of powers** and **checks and balances.** Give an example of how these ideas work in U.S. government.
4. Who was **James Madison**? How did he contribute to the Constitutional Convention of 1787?
5. What was the **cotton gin**? What effect did it have on American economy and culture?

## Focus Questions

The focus question for this chapter is **What factors led to the founding of the United States and its formation as a democratic republic?** Build an answer to this big question by answering the focus questions for Sections 1 through 4 and the Critical Thinking questions that follow.

**Section 1**
6. What were the causes and effects of European arrival in the Americas?

**Section 2**
7. What important ideas and major events led to the American Revolution?

**Section 3**
8. What ideas and debates led to the Constitution and Bill of Rights?

**Section 4**
9. How did the United States and its government change in the late 1700s and early 1800s?

## Critical Thinking

10. **Identify Assumptions** What were some of the values held by North American Indian cultures?
11. **Analyze Information** What advantages did the Columbian Exchange bring to the people of the Americas? What disadvantages did it bring?
12. **Categorize** Identify four English colonial regions, and name their primary resources and economic activities.
13. **Recognize Cause and Effect** In what ways did Britain demonstrate its control over the American colonies? What result did these actions have on the colonists?
14. **Make Comparisons** How was the United States government under the Constitution different from the government under the Articles of Confederation?
15. **Draw Conclusions** Why do you think the Antifederalists demanded that a bill of rights be added to the Constitution?
16. **Summarize** Describe the accomplishments of Thomas Jefferson during his presidency.
17. **Problem Solving** Identify and evaluate one effort taken by the federal government prior to the War of 1812 to ease the problems caused by Britain's seizure of American vessels.
18. **Determine Relevance** How did the Monroe Doctrine demonstrate the increased presence of the United States in the world?

## Writing About History

**Expository Essay: Cause and Effect** There were a number of reasons England established colonies on the eastern seaboard of North America. The founding of colonies had profound effects on Native Americans, Africans, and other European nations. Write an essay that explains the causes and effects of one of the 13 English colonies.

### Prewriting
• Consider what you know about the founding of each colony, and choose one that you think best shows cause and effect.
• Take time to research facts, descriptions, and examples to clearly illustrate the causes and effects in your essay.

### Drafting
• To organize the causes and effects in your essay, either show the chronological order of events or order the events from the least important to the most important.
• As you draft your essay, illustrate each cause and effect with supporting facts and details.

### Revising
• Review your entire draft to ensure you show a clear relationship between the causes and effects.
• Analyze each paragraph to check that you have provided a thorough set of facts and details.
• Use the guidelines on page SH11 of the Writing Handbook to revise your essay.

# Prepare for the MME

## Religious Freedom in Early America

America was settled by colonists who had been subjected to religious discrimination in their native countries. How did their desire to protect their religious freedom influence the formation of state and federal governments? Use your knowledge of government and Documents A, B, and C to answer questions 1 through 4.

### Document A

"Whereas Almighty God has created the mind free, so that all attempts to influence it by temporal punishments . . . are a departure from the plan of the Holy Author of our religion, . . . that to compel a man to furnish contributions of money for the propagation of opinions which he disbelieves is sinful and tyrannical; . . . that our civil rights have no dependence on our religious opinions, any more than our opinions in physics or geometry. . . .

Be it . . . enacted by the General Assembly that no man shall be compelled to frequent or support any religious worship, place, or ministry whatsoever, nor shall be enforced, restrained, molested, or burdened in his body or goods, nor shall otherwise suffer on account of his religious opinions or belief; but that all men shall be free to profess, and by argument to maintain, their opinion in matters of religion, and that the same shall in no wise diminish, enlarge, or affect their civil capacities. . . . [Y]et as we are free to declare, and do declare, that the rights hereby asserted are the natural rights of mankind, and that if any act shall hereafter be passed to repeal the present, or to narrow its operation, such act will be an infringement of natural right."

—Thomas Jefferson, Virginia Statute for Religious Freedom, 1779

### Document B

"Congress shall make no law respecting an establishment of religion, or prohibiting the free exercise thereof; or abridging the freedom of speech, or of the press; or the right of the people peacefully to assemble, and to petition the government for a redress of grievances."

—First Amendment to the U.S. Constitution, 1791

### Document C

Religion in the Colonies, 1776

| Denomination | Number of Congregations |
|---|---|
| Congregational | 668 |
| Presbyterian | 588 |
| Baptist | 497 |
| Episcopal | 495 |
| Quaker | 310 |
| German Reformed | 159 |
| Lutheran | 120 |
| Methodist | 65 |
| Catholic | 56 |
| Moravian | 31 |
| Separatist and Independent | 27 |
| Dunker | 24 |
| Mennonite | 16 |
| Huguenot | 7 |
| Sandemanian | 6 |
| Jewish | 5 |
| **Total** | **3,074** |

SOURCE: *The Churching of America, 1776–2005,* Roger Finke and Rodney Stark

---

1. What civil right is protected by Document A?
   - **A** freedom of speech
   - **B** freedom of the press
   - **C** freedom of education
   - **D** freedom of religion

2. What can you conclude about the growth of religion in the colonies based on Document C?
   - **A** By 1776, there were fewer than 2,000 congregations in America.
   - **B** There were a variety of religious denominations in Early colonial America.
   - **C** Most colonists did not practice their religion on a regular basis.
   - **D** Most colonists belonged to two establishment churches.

3. What is the relationship between Documents A and B?
   - **A** Both established the right of assembly.
   - **B** Both prohibited the government from imposing religious taxes.
   - **C** Both guaranteed the separation of church and state.
   - **D** Both guaranteed freedom of the press.

4. **Writing Task** What effect did the importance of religious liberty have on the social, moral, and political development of the new nation? Use your knowledge of the formation of the new national government and specific evidence from the primary and secondary sources above to support your answer.

By signing the Declaration of Independence, members of the Continental Congress sent a clear message to Britain that the American colonies were free and independent states. Starting with its Preamble, the document explains why the people of the United States have the right to break away from Britain.

The Declaration of Independence is made up of three parts: the Preamble and explanation of natural rights, which give the reasons for writing the Declaration; the list of grievances against British King George III; and the official statement of breaking away from Great Britain.

▲ King George III of England

◀ On July 18, 1776, the Declaration of Independence was read to the citizens of Boston from the Old State House. Later that day, the lion and unicorn, symbols of royal authority, were taken down from the roof and burned in Dock Square.

## In Congress, July 4, 1776

THE UNANIMOUS DECLARATION OF THE THIRTEEN UNITED STATES OF AMERICA,

When in the Course of human events, it becomes necessary for one people to dissolve the political bands which have connected them with another, and to assume among the powers of the earth, the separate and equal station to which the Laws of Nature and of Nature's God entitle them, a decent respect to the opinions of mankind requires that they should declare the causes which impel them to the separation.

We hold these truths to be self-evident, that all men are created equal, that they are endowed by their Creator with certain unalienable Rights, that among these are Life, Liberty and the pursuit of Happiness.—That to secure these rights, Governments are instituted among Men, deriving their just powers from the consent of the governed,—That whenever any Form of Government becomes destructive of these ends, it is the Right of the People to alter or to abolish it, and to institute new Government, laying its foundation on such principles and organizing its powers in such form, as to them shall seem most likely to effect their Safety and Happiness. Prudence, indeed, will dictate that Governments long established should not be changed for light and transient causes; and accordingly all experience hath shewn, that mankind are more disposed to suffer, while evils are sufferable, than to right themselves by abolishing the forms to which they are accustomed. But when a long train of abuses and usurpations, pursuing invariably the same Object evinces a design to reduce them under absolute Despotism, it is their right, it is their duty, to throw off such Government, and to provide new Guards for their future security.—Such has been the patient sufferance of these Colonies; and such is now the necessity which constrains them to alter their former Systems of Government. The history of the present King of Great Britain is a history of repeated injuries and usurpations, all having in direct object the establishment of an absolute Tyranny over these States. To prove this, let Facts be submitted to a candid world.

He has refused his Assent to Laws, the most wholesome and necessary for the public good.

He has forbidden his Governors to pass Laws of immediate and pressing importance, unless suspended in their operation till his Assent should be obtained; and when so suspended, he has utterly neglected to attend to them.

He has refused to pass other Laws for the accommodation of large districts of people, unless those people would relinquish the right of Representation in the Legislature, a right inestimable to them and formidable to tyrants only.

He has called together legislative bodies at places unusual, uncomfortable, and distant from the depository of their public Records, for the sole purpose of fatiguing them into compliance with his measures.

## Commentary

◀ **Preamble**
The document first lists the reasons for writing the Declaration.

◀ **Protection of Natural Rights**
People set up governments to protect their basic rights. These rights are unalienable; they cannot be taken away. The purpose of government is to protect these natural rights. When a government does not protect the rights of the people, the people must change the government or create a new one. The colonists feel that the king's repeated usurpations, or unjust uses of power, are a form of despotism, or tyranny, that has denied them their basic rights.

◀ **Grievances Against the King**
The list of grievances details the colonists' complaints against the British government and King George III. The colonists have no say in determining the laws that govern them, and they feel King George's actions show little or no concern for the well-being of the people.

The colonists refuse to relinquish, or give up, the right to representation, which they feel is inestimable, or priceless.

## Commentary

The king has refused to allow new legislators to be elected. As a result, the colonies have not been able to protect themselves against foreign enemies and convulsions, or riots, within the colonies.

The king has tried to stop foreigners from coming to the colonies by refusing to pass naturalization laws. Such laws set up the process for foreigners to become legal citizens.

The king alone has decided a judge's tenure, or term. This grievance later would result in Article 3, Section 1, of the Constitution, which states that federal judges hold office for life.

Forced by the king, the colonists have been quartering, or lodging, troops in their homes. This grievance found its way into the Constitution in the Third Amendment.

The king has taken away the rights of the people in a nearby province (Canada). The colonists feared he could do the same to the colonies if he so wished.

### ✔ Checkpoint

**Why does the Declaration list the colonists' many grievances?**

He has dissolved Representative Houses repeatedly, for opposing with manly firmness his invasions on the rights of the people.

He has refused for a long time, after such dissolutions, to cause others to be elected; whereby the Legislative powers, incapable of Annihilation, have returned to the People at large for their exercise; the State remaining in the mean time exposed to all the dangers of invasions from without, and convulsions within.

He has endeavored to prevent the population of these States; for that purpose obstructing the Laws for Naturalization of Foreigners; refusing to pass others to encourage their migration hither, and raising the conditions of new Appropriations of Lands.

He has obstructed the Administration of Justice, by refusing his Assent to Laws for establishing Judiciary powers.

He has made Judges dependent on his Will alone, for the tenure of their offices, and the amount and payment of their salaries.

He has erected a multitude of New Offices, and sent hither swarms of Officers to harass our people and eat out their substance.

He has kept among us in time of peace, Standing Armies, without the Consent of our legislatures.

He has affected to render the Military independent of and superior to the Civil power.

He has combined with others to subject us to a jurisdiction foreign to our constitutions, and unacknowledged by our laws; giving his Assent to their Acts of pretended Legislation:

For Quartering large bodies of armed troops among us:

For protecting them, by a mock Trial, from punishment for any Murders which they should commit on the Inhabitants of these States:

For cutting off our Trade with all parts of the world:

For imposing Taxes on us without our Consent:

For depriving us in many cases, of the benefits of Trial by Jury:

For transporting us beyond Seas to be tried for pretended offenses:

For abolishing the free System of English Laws in a neighbouring Province, establishing therein an Arbitrary government, and enlarging its Boundaries so as to render it at once an example and fit instrument for introducing the same absolute rule into these Colonies:

For taking away our Charters, abolishing our most valuable Laws, and altering fundamentally the Forms of our Governments:

For suspending our own Legislature, and declaring themselves invested with power to legislate for us in all cases whatsoever.

He has abdicated Government here, by declaring us out of his Protection, and waging War against us.

He has plundered our seas, ravaged our Coasts, burned our towns, and destroyed the lives of our people.

He is at this time transporting large Armies of foreign Mercenaries to compleat the works of death, desolation and tyranny, already begun with circumstances of Cruelty and perfidy scarcely paralleled in the most barbarous ages, and totally unworthy the Head of a civilized nation.

He has constrained our fellow Citizens taken Captive on the high Seas to bear Arms against their Country, to become the executioners of their friends and Brethren, or to fall themselves by their Hands.

He has excited domestic insurrections amongst us, and has endeavored to bring on the inhabitants of our frontiers the merciless Indian Savages, whose known rule of warfare, is an undistinguished destruction of all ages, sexes and conditions.

In every stage of these Oppressions We have Petitioned for Redress in the most humble terms: Our repeated Petitions have been answered only by repeated injury. A Prince, whose character is thus marked by every act which may define a Tyrant, is unfit to be the ruler of a free people.

Nor have We been wanting in attentions to our British brethren. We have warned them from time to time of attempts by their legislature to extend an unwarrantable jurisdiction over us. We have reminded them of the circumstances of our emigration and settlement here. We have appealed to their native justice and magnanimity, and we have conjured them by the ties of our common kindred to disavow these usurpations, which, would inevitably interrupt our connections and correspondence. They too have been deaf to the voice of justice and of consanguinity. We must, therefore, acquiesce in the necessity, which denounces our Separation, and hold them, as we hold the rest of mankind, Enemies in War, in Peace Friends.

We, therefore, the Representatives of the United States of America, in General Congress, Assembled, appealing to the Supreme Judge of the world for the rectitude of our intentions, do, in the Name, and by the Authority of the good People of these Colonies, solemnly publish and declare, That these United Colonies are, and of Right ought to be Free and Independent States; that they are Absolved from all Allegiance to the British Crown, and that all political connection between them and the State of Great Britain, is and ought to be totally dissolved; and that as Free and Independent States, they have full Power to levy War, conclude Peace, contract Alliances, establish Commerce, and to do all other Acts and Things which Independent States may of right do. And for the support of this Declaration, with a firm reliance on the protection of Divine Providence, we mutually pledge to each other our Lives, our Fortunes and our sacred Honor.

## Commentary

The king has hired foreign mercenaries, or soldiers, to bring death and destruction to the colonists. The head of a civilized country should never act with the cruelty and perfidy, or dishonesty, that the king has.

The colonists have repeatedly asked the king to correct these wrongs. Each time, he has failed to do so. Because of the way he treats his subjects, the king is not fit to rule.

The colonists have appealed to the British people. They have asked their fellow British subjects to support them. However, like the king, the British people have ignored the colonists' requests.

◀ **Declaring Independence**
The resolution of independence boldly asserts that the colonies are now "free and independent states." The Declaration concludes by stating that these new states have the power to wage war, establish alliances, and trade with other countries.

---

### ✓ Checkpoint

**What powers does the new nation have, now that it is independent?**

# Signatories of the Declaration of Independence

JOHN HANCOCK
PRESIDENT OF THE CONTINENTAL CONGRESS 1775-1777

NEW HAMPSHIRE
Josiah Bartlett
William Whipple
Matthew Thornton

MASSACHUSETTS BAY
Samuel Adams
John Adams
Robert Treat Paine
Elbridge Gerry

RHODE ISLAND
Stephen Hopkins
William Ellery

CONNECTICUT
Roger Sherman
Samuel Huntington
William Williams
Oliver Wolcott

NEW YORK
William Floyd
Philip Livingston
Francis Lewis
Lewis Morris

NEW JERSEY
Richard Stockton
John Witherspoon
Francis Hopkinson
John Hart
Abraham Clark

DELAWARE
Caesar Rodney
George Read
Thomas McKean

MARYLAND
Samuel Chase
William Paca
Thomas Stone
Charles Carroll
  of Carrollton

VIRGINIA
George Wythe
Richard Henry Lee
Thomas Jefferson
Benjamin Harrison
Thomas Nelson, Jr.
Francis Lightfoot Lee
Carter Braxton

PENNSYLVANIA
Robert Morris
Benjamin Rush
Benjamin Franklin
John Morton
George Clymer
James Smith
George Taylor
James Wilson
George Ross

NORTH CAROLINA
William Hooper
Joseph Hewes
John Penn

SOUTH CAROLINA
Edward Rutledge
Thomas Heyward, Jr.
Thomas Lynch, Jr.
Arthur Middleton

GEORGIA
Button Gwinnett
Lyman Hall
George Walton

▶ New Yorkers tear down a statue of King George III after a reading of the Declaration of Independence on Bowling Green. The statue was later melted down to make ammunition for the American Army.

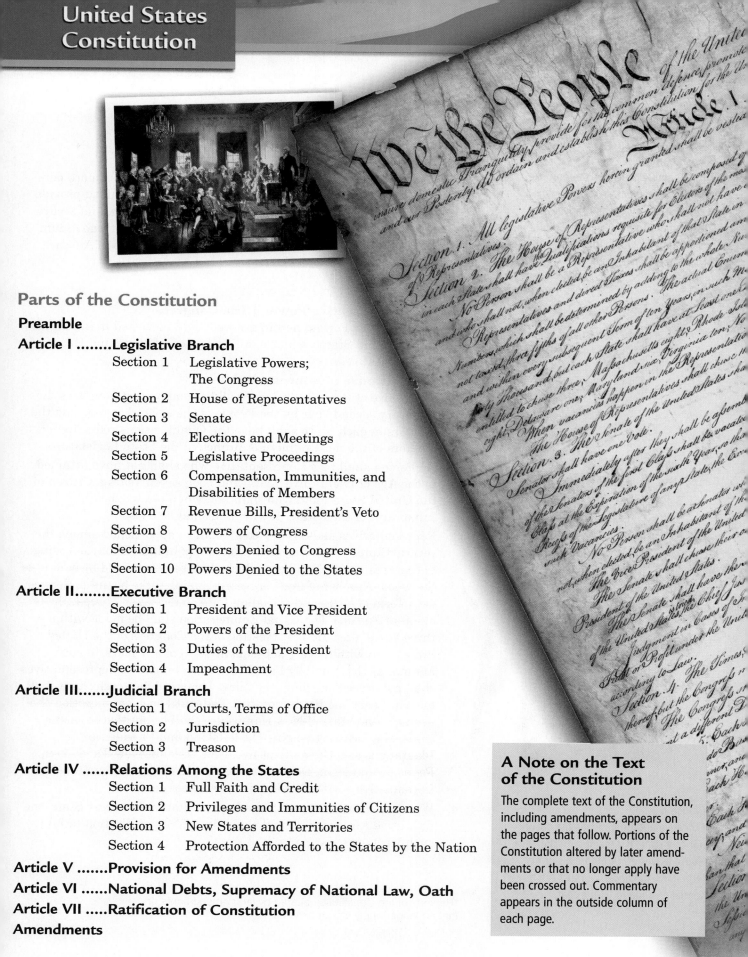

# United States Constitution

## Parts of the Constitution

## A Note on the Text of the Constitution

The complete text of the Constitution, including amendments, appears on the pages that follow. Portions of the Constitution altered by later amendments or that no longer apply have been crossed out. Commentary appears in the outside column of each page.

## Commentary

**The Preamble ▶**
The Preamble describes the purpose of the government as set up by the Constitution. Americans expect their government to defend justice and liberty and provide peace and safety from foreign enemies.

**Clause 4 ▶**
Executive authority means the governor of a state. If a member of the House leaves office before his or her term ends, the governor must call a special election to fill the seat.

## Preamble

We the People of the United States, in Order to form a more perfect Union, establish Justice, insure domestic Tranquility, provide for the common defence, promote the general Welfare, and secure the Blessings of Liberty to ourselves and our Posterity, do ordain and establish this Constitution for the United States of America.

## Article I. Legislative Branch

### Section 1. Legislative Powers; The Congress

All legislative Powers herein granted shall be vested in a Congress of the United States, which shall consist of a Senate and House of Representatives.

### Section 2. House of Representatives

1. The House of Representatives shall be composed of Members chosen every second Year by the People of the several States, and the Electors in each State shall have the Qualifications requisite for Electors of the most numerous Branch of the State Legislature.

2. No Person shall be a Representative who shall not have attained to the Age of twenty-five Years, and been seven Years a Citizen of the United States, and who shall not, when elected, be an Inhabitant of that State in which he shall be chosen.

3. Representatives ~~and direct Taxes~~* shall be apportioned among the several States which may be included within this Union, according to their respective Numbers, ~~which shall be determined by adding to the whole Number of free Persons, including those bound to Service for a Term of Years and excluding Indians not taxed, three fifths of all other Persons.~~ The actual Enumeration shall be made within three Years after the first Meeting of the Congress of the United States, and within every subsequent Term of ten Years, in such Manner as they shall by Law direct. The Number of Representatives shall not exceed one for every thirty Thousand, but each State shall have at Least one Representative; ~~and, until such enumeration shall be made, the State of New Hampshire shall be entitled to choose three, Massachusetts eight, Rhode Island and Providence Plantations one, Connecticut five, New York six, New Jersey four, Pennsylvania eight, Delaware one, Maryland six, Virginia ten, North Carolina five, South Carolina five, and Georgia three.~~

4. When vacancies happen in the Representation from any State, the Executive Authority thereof shall issue Writs of Election to fill such Vacancies.

*Portions of the Constitution altered by later amendments or that no longer apply are crossed out.

5. The House of Representatives shall choose their Speaker and other Officers; and shall have the sole Power of Impeachment.

### Section 3. Senate

1. The Senate of the United States shall be composed of two Senators from each State ~~chosen by the Legislature thereof~~ for six Years; and each Senator shall have one Vote.

2. Immediately after they shall be assembled in Consequences of the first Election, they shall be divided, as equally as may be, into three Classes. The Seats of the Senators of the first Class shall be vacated at the Expiration of the second Year; of the second Class, at the Expiration of the fourth Year; and of the third Class, at the Expiration of the sixth Year; so that one-third may be chosen every second Year; ~~and if Vacancies happen by Resignation, or otherwise, during the Recess of the Legislature of any State, the Executive thereof may make temporary Appointments until the next Meeting of the Legislature, which shall then fill such Vacancies.~~

3. No Person shall be a Senator who shall not have attained to the Age of thirty Years, and been nine Years a Citizen of the United States, and who shall not, when elected, be an Inhabitant of that State for which he shall be chosen.

## Commentary

◀ **Clause 5** The House elects a Speaker. Also, only the House has the power to <u>impeach</u>, or accuse a federal official of wrongdoing.

◀ **Clause 1** Each State has two senators.

◀ **Clause 2** Every two years, one third of the senators run for reelection. The Seventeenth Amendment changed the way of filling <u>vacancies</u>, or empty seats. Today, the governor of a state must choose a senator to fill a vacancy that occurs between elections.

---

✓ **Checkpoint**
**What is the main job of Congress?**

---

## Separation of Powers

**Legislative Branch** (Congress)
**Passes laws**

- Can override presidential veto
- Approves treaties
- Can impeach and remove President and other high officials from office
- Prints and coins money
- Raises and supports armed forces
- Can declare war
- Regulates foreign and interstate trade

**Executive Branch** (President)
**Carries out laws**

- Proposes laws
- Can veto legislation
- Serves as commander in chief of armed forces
- Negotiates foreign treaties
- Appoints federal judges, ambassadors, and other high officials
- Can grant pardons to federal offenders

**Judicial Branch**
(Supreme Court and Other Lower Federal Courts)

**Interprets Laws**
- Can declare laws unconstitutional
- Can declare executive actions unconstitutional

## Commentary

**Clause 5**
The House elects a Speaker. Also, only the House has the power to impeach, or accuse a federal official of wrongdoing.

**Clause 6** ▶
The Senate acts as a jury if the House impeaches a federal official. The Chief Justice of the Supreme Court presides if the President is on trial. Two thirds of all senators present must vote for conviction, or finding the accused guilty. No President has ever been convicted.

---

### ✔ Checkpoint

**Which branches are involved in presidential impeachment?**

---

**Clause 1** ▶
Each state legislature can decide when and how congressional elections take place, but Congress can overrule these decisions. In 1842, Congress required each state to set up congressional districts with one representative elected from each district. In 1872, Congress decided that congressional elections must be held in every state on the same date in even-numbered years.

4. The Vice President of the United States shall be President of the Senate but shall have no Vote, unless they be equally divided.

5. The Senate shall choose their other Officers, and also a President pro tempore, in the Absence of the Vice President, or when he shall exercise the Office of President of the United States.

6. The Senate shall have the sole Power to try all Impeachments. When sitting for that Purpose, they shall be on Oath or Affirmation. When the President of the United States is tried, the Chief Justice shall preside: And no Person shall be convicted without the Concurrence of two thirds of the Members present.

7. Judgment in Cases of Impeachment shall not extend further than to removal from Office, and disqualification to hold and enjoy any Office of honor, Trust, or Profit under the United States: but the Party convicted shall nevertheless be liable and subject to Indictment, Trial, Judgment and Punishment, according to Law.

### Section 4. Elections and Meetings

1. The Times, Places and Manner of holding Elections for Senators and Representatives, shall be prescribed in each State by the Legislature thereof; but the Congress may at any time by law make or alter such Regulations, except as to the Places of choosing Senators.

2. The Congress shall assemble at least once in every Year, ~~and such Meeting shall be on the first Monday in December, unless they shall by Law appoint a different Day.~~

### Section 5. Legislative Proceedings

1. Each House shall be the Judge of the Elections, Returns and Qualifications of its own Members, and a Majority of each shall constitute a Quorum to do Business; but a smaller Number may adjourn from day to day, and may be authorized to compel the Attendance of absent Members, in such Manner, and under such Penalties, as each House may provide.

2. Each House may determine the Rules of its Proceedings, punish its Members for disorderly Behavior, and, with the Concurrence of two thirds, expel a Member.

3. Each House shall keep a Journal of its Proceedings, and from time to time publish the same, excepting such Parts as may in their Judgment require Secrecy; and the Yeas and Nays of the Members of either House on any question shall, at the Desire of one fifth of those Present, be entered on the Journal.

4. Neither House, during the Session of Congress, shall, without the Consent of the other, adjourn for more than three days, nor to any other Place than that in which the two Houses shall be sitting.

### Section 6. Compensation, Immunities, and Disabilities of Members

1. The Senators and Representatives shall receive a Compensation for their Services, to be ascertained by Law, and paid out of the Treasury of the United States. They shall in all Cases, except Treason, Felony, and Breach of the Peace, be privileged from Arrest during their Attendance at the Session of their respective Houses, and in going to and returning from the same; and for any Speech or Debate in either House, they shall not be questioned in any other Place.

2. No Senator or Representative shall, during the Time for which he was elected, be appointed to any civil Office under the Authority of the United States, which shall have been created, or the Emoluments whereof shall have been increased during such time; and no Person holding any Office under the United States, shall be a Member of either House during his Continuance in Office.

### Section 7. Revenue Bills, President's Veto

1. All Bills for raising Revenue shall originate in the House of Representatives; but the Senate may propose or concur with amendments as on other Bills.

2. Every Bill which shall have passed the House of Representatives and the Senate, shall, before it become a Law, be presented to the President of the United States: If he approve he shall sign it, but if not he shall return it, with his Objections to that House in which it shall have originated, who shall enter the Objections at large on their Journal, and proceed to reconsider it. If after such Reconsideration two thirds of the House shall agree to pass the Bill, it shall be sent, together with the Objections, to the other House, by which it shall likewise be reconsidered, and if approved by two thirds of that House, it shall become a Law. But in all such Cases the Votes of both Houses shall be determined by Yeas and Nays, and the Names of the Persons voting for and against the Bill shall be entered on the Journal of each House respectively. If any Bill shall not be returned by the President within ten Days

## Commentary

◄ **Clause 4** Neither house can adjourn, or stop meeting, for more than three days unless the other house approves. Both houses must meet in the same city.

◄ **Clause 1** Tax bills must be introduced in the House, but the Senate can make changes in those bills.

◄ **Clause 2** A bill, or proposed law, that is passed by a majority of the House and Senate is sent to the President. If the President signs the bill, it becomes law. The President can veto, or reject, a bill by sending it back to the house where it was introduced. Congress can override the President's veto if each house of Congress passes the bill again by a two-thirds vote.

## Commentary

**✓ Checkpoint**

What is the role of Congress and the President in making laws?

(Sunday excepted) after it shall have been presented to him, the Same shall be a law, in like Manner as if he had signed it, unless the Congress by their Adjournment, prevent its Return, in which Case it shall not be a Law.

3. Every Order, Resolution, or Vote to which the Concurrence of the Senate and House of Representatives may be necessary (except on a question of adjournment) shall be presented to the President of the United States; and before the Same shall take Effect, shall be approved by him, or, being disapproved by him, shall be repassed by two thirds of the Senate and House of Representatives, according to the Rules and Limitations prescribed in the Case of a Bill.

## How a Bill Becomes a Law

**Start: Senate**

**❶ Introduction**
Bill introduced in Senate.

**❷ Committee Action**
Bill referred to standing committee. Moves to subcommittee for study, hearings, revisions, approval. Moves back to full committee for more hearings and revisions.

**❸ Floor Action**
Bill is debated, then passed or defeated. If passed, the bill goes to the House of Representatives. If the bill has already passed in House, the bill goes to Conference Committee.

**❹ Conference Committee**
Conference Committee resolves differences between House and Senate versions of the bill.

**Congressional Approval**
House and Senate vote on final passage. Approved bill is sent to the President.

**❺ Presidential Action**
President signs, vetoes, or allows the bill to become a law without signing. Vetoed bill returns to Congress. Veto may be overridden by two-thirds majority vote of each house.

**❸ Floor Action**
Bill is debated, then passed or defeated. If passed, the bill goes to Senate. If the bill has already passed through Senate, the bill goes to Conference Committee.

**❷ Committee Action**
Bill referred to standing committee. Moves to subcommittee for study, hearings, revisions, approval. Moves back to full committee for more hearings and revisions. Moves to Rules Committee to set conditions for debate and amendments.

**❶ Introduction**
Bill introduced in House

**Start: House**

## Section 8. Powers of Congress
The Congress shall have Power

1.  To lay and collect Taxes, Duties, Imposts and Excises to pay the Debts and provide for the common Defence and general Welfare of the United States; but all Duties, Imposts and Excises, shall be uniform throughout the United States;
2.  To borrow Money on the credit of the United States;
3.  To regulate Commerce with foreign Nations, and among the several States, and with the Indian Tribes;
4.  To establish an uniform Rule of Naturalization, and uniform Laws on the subject of Bankruptcies throughout the United States;
5.  To coin Money, regulate the Value thereof, and of foreign Coin, and fix the Standard of Weights and Measures;

6.  To provide for the Punishment of counterfeiting the Securities and current Coin of the United States;
7.  To establish Post Offices and post Roads;
8.  To promote the Progress of Science and useful Arts, by securing for limited Times to Authors and Inventors the exclusive Right to their respective Writings and Discoveries;
9.  To constitute Tribunals inferior to the supreme Court;
10. To define and punish Piracies and Felonies committed on the high Seas, and Offences against the Law of Nations;

## Commentary

◀ **Section 8** The Constitution is our social contract in which the people consent to the form and powers of government. An important part of the contract is the enumeration of legislative powers which sets the scope and limits of government authority over the people. Article I, Section 8, lists most of the expressed powers of Congress. Numbered from 1 to 18, these powers are also known as enumerated powers.

◀ **Clause 1** Duties are tariffs, or taxes on imports. Imposts are taxes in general. Excises are taxes on the production or sale of certain goods.

◀ **Clause 4** Naturalization is the process whereby a foreigner becomes a citizen. Bankruptcy is the condition in which a person or business cannot pay its debts. Congress has the power to pass laws on these two issues.

◀ **Clause 6** Counterfeiting is the making of imitation money. Securities are bonds. Congress can make laws to punish counterfeiters.

## Commentary

**Clause 11** ▶

Only Congress can declare war. Declarations of war are granted at the request of the President. <u>Letters of marque and reprisal</u> were documents issued by a government allowing merchant ships to arm themselves and attack ships of an enemy nation. They are no longer issued.

 **Checkpoint**

**Which powers of Congress relate to taking in and spending money?**

**Clause 18** ▶

Congress has the power to make laws as needed to carry out the previous 17 clauses. It is sometimes known as the "Necessary and Proper Clause."

**Clause 1** ▶

<u>Such persons</u> means slaves. In 1808, as soon as Congress was permitted to abolish the slave trade, it did so.

**Clause 2** ▶

A <u>writ of habeas corpus</u> is a court order requiring government officials to bring a prisoner to court and explain why he or she is being held. A writ of habeas corpus protects people from unlawful imprisonment. The government cannot suspend this right except in times of rebellion or invasion.

11. To declare War, grant Letters of Marque and Reprisal, and make Rules concerning Captures on Land and Water;

12. To raise and support Armies, but no Appropriation of Money to that Use shall be for a longer Term than two Years;

13. To provide and maintain a Navy;

14. To make Rules for the Government and Regulation of the land and naval Forces;

15. To provide for calling forth the Militia to execute the Laws of the Union, suppress Insurrections and repel Invasions;

16. To provide for organizing, arming, and disciplining the Militia, and for governing such Part of them as may be employed in the Service of the United States, reserving to the States respectively, the Appointment of the Officers, and the Authority of training the Militia according to the discipline prescribed by Congress;

17. To exercise exclusive Legislation in all Cases whatsoever, over such District (not exceeding ten Miles square) as may, by Cession of Particular States, and the Acceptance of Congress, become the Seat of the Government of the United States, and to exercise like Authority over all Places purchased by the Consent of the Legislature of the State in which the Same shall be, for the Erection of Forts, Magazines, Arsenals, Dockyards and other needful Buildings;—And

18. To make all Laws which shall be necessary and proper for carrying into Execution the foregoing Powers and all other Powers vested by this Constitution in the Government of the United States, or in any Department or Officer thereof.

### Section 9. Powers Denied to Congress

1. ~~The Migration or Importation of such Persons as any of the States now existing shall think proper to admit, shall not be prohibited by the Congress prior to the Year one thousand eight hundred and eight, but a Tax or duty may be imposed on such Importation, not exceeding ten dollars for each Person.~~

2. The Privilege of the Writ of Habeas Corpus shall not be suspended, unless when in Cases of Rebellion or Invasion the public Safety may require it.

3. No Bill of Attainder or ex post facto Law shall be passed.

4. No Capitation, ~~or other direct, Tax~~ shall be laid, unless in Proportion to the Census of Enumeration hereinbefore directed to be taken.

5. No Tax or Duty shall be laid on Articles exported from any State.

6. No Preference shall be given by any Regulation of Commerce or Revenue to the Ports of one State over those of another: nor shall Vessels bound to, or from, one State, be obliged to enter, clear or pay Duties in another.

7. No Money shall be drawn from the Treasury, but in Consequence of Appropriations made by Law; and a regular Statement and Account of the Receipts and Expenditures of all public Money shall be published from time to time.

8. No Title of Nobility shall be granted by the United States: And no Person holding any Office of Profit or Trust under them, shall, without the Consent of the Congress, accept of any present, Emolument, Office, or Title, of any kind whatever, from any King, Prince, or foreign State.

### Section 10.  Powers Denied to the States

1. No State shall enter into any Treaty, Alliance, or Confederation; grant Letters of Marque and Reprisal; coin Money; emit Bills of Credit; make any Thing but gold and silver Coin a Tender in Payment of Debts; pass any Bill of Attainder, ex post facto Law, or Law impairing the Obligation of Contracts, or grant any Title of Nobility.

## Commentary

◀ **Clause 3** A <u>bill of attainder</u> is a law declaring that a person is guilty of a particular crime without a trial. An <u>ex post facto</u> law punishes an act which was not illegal when it was committed.

◀ **Clause 1** The writers of the Constitution did not want the states to act like separate nations, so they prohibited states from making treaties or coining money. Some powers denied to the federal government are also denied to the states.

## The Federal System

**Powers of the National Government**
- Regulate interstate and foreign trade
- Declare war
- Create and maintain armed forces
- Establish foreign policy
- Create federal courts
- Make copyright and patent laws
- Establish postal offices
- Coin money
- Set standard weights and measures
- Admit new states

**Concurrent Powers**
- Provide for public welfare
- Administer criminal justice
- Charter banks and borrow money
- Levy and collect taxes
- Borrow money

**Powers Reserved to the States**
- Regulate trade within state
- Maintain schools
- Establish local governments
- Make laws about marriage and divorce
- Conduct elections
- Provide for public safety
- Create corporation law

## Commentary

**Clauses 2, 3** ▶
Powers listed here are forbidden to the states, but Congress can pass laws that give these powers to the states. Clause 2 forbids states from taxing imports and exports without the consent of Congress.

**Clause 3** ▶
This clause forbids states from keeping an army or navy without the consent of Congress. States cannot make treaties or declare war unless an enemy invades or is about to invade.

**Clauses 2, 3** ▶
Some writers of the Constitution were afraid to allow the people to elect the President directly. Therefore, the Constitutional Convention set up the electoral college. Clause 2 directs each state to choose underlinedelectors, or delegates to the electoral college, to vote for President. A state's electoral vote is equal to the combined number of senators and representatives. Each state may decide how to choose its electors. Members of Congress and federal officeholders may not serve as electors. This part of the original electoral college system is still in effect.

**Clause 3** ▶
This clause called upon each elector to vote for two candidates. The candidate who received a majority of the electoral votes would become President. The runner-up would become Vice President. If no candidate won a majority, the House

2. No State shall, without the Consent of the Congress, lay any Imposts or Duties on Imports or Exports, except what may be absolutely necessary for executing its inspection Laws; and the net Produce of all Duties and Imposts, laid by any State on Imports or Exports, shall be for the Use of the Treasury of the United States; and all such Laws shall be subject to the Revision and Control of the Congress.

3. No State shall, without the Consent of Congress, lay any Duty of Tonnage, keep Troops, or Ships of War in time of Peace, enter into any Agreement or Compact with another State, or with a foreign Power, or engage in War, unless actually invaded, or in such imminent Danger as will not admit of delay.

## Article II  Executive Branch

### Section 1.  President and Vice President

1. The executive Power shall be vested in a President of the United States of America. He shall hold his Office during the Term of four Years, and, together with the Vice President, chosen for the same Term, be elected as follows:

2. Each State shall appoint, in such Manner as the Legislature thereof may direct, a Number of Electors, equal to the whole Number of Senators and Representatives to which the State may be entitled in the Congress: but no Senator or Representative, or Person holding an Office of Trust or Profit, under the United States, shall be appointed an Elector.

3. The Electors shall meet in their respective States, and vote by Ballot for two Persons, of whom one at least shall not be an Inhabitant of the same State with themselves. And they shall make a List of all the Persons voted for, and of the Number of Votes for each; which List they shall sign and certify, and transmit sealed to the Seat of the Government of the United States, directed to the President of the Senate. The President of the Senate shall, in the Presence of the Senate and House of Representatives, open all the Certificates, and the Votes shall then be counted. The Person having the greatest Number of Votes shall be the President, if such Number be a majority of the whole Number of Electors appointed; and if there be more than one who have such Majority, and have an equal Number of Votes, then, the House of Representatives shall immediately choose by Ballot one of them for President; and if no Person have a Majority, then from the five highest on the List the said House shall in like Manner choose the President. But in choosing the President, the Votes shall be taken by States, the Representatives from each State having one Vote; a quorum for this Purpose shall consist of a Member or Members from two thirds of the States, and a Majority of

all the States shall be necessary to a Choice. In every Case, after the Choice of the President, the Person having the greatest Number of Votes of the Electors shall be the Vice President. But if there should remain two or more who have equal Votes, the Senate shall choose from them by Ballot the Vice President.

4. The Congress may determine the Time of choosing the Electors, and the Day on which they shall give their Votes; which Day shall be the same throughout the United States.

5. No Person except a natural born Citizen, or a Citizen of the United States, at the time of the Adoption of this Constitution, shall be eligible to the Office of President; neither shall any person be eligible to that Office who shall not have attained to the Age of thirty-five Years, and been fourteen Years a Resident within the United States.

6. In Case of the Removal of the President from Office, or of his Death, Resignation, or Inability to discharge the Powers and Duties of the said Office, the Same shall devolve on the Vice President, and the Congress may by Law provide for the Case of Removal, Death, Resignation or Inability, both of the President and Vice President, declaring what Officer shall then act as President, and such Officer shall act accordingly, until the Disability be removed, or a President shall be elected.

7. The President shall, at stated Times, receive for his Services, a Compensation, which shall neither be increased nor diminished during the Period for which he shall have been elected, and he shall not receive within that Period any other Emolument from the United States, or any of them.

8. Before he enter on the Execution of his Office, he shall take the following Oath or Affirmation:

"I do solemnly swear (or affirm) that I will faithfully execute the Office of President of the United States, and will to the best of my Ability, preserve, protect and defend the Constitution of the United States."

### Section 2. Powers of the President

1. The President shall be Commander in Chief of the Army and Navy of the United States, and of the Militia of the several States, when called into the actual Service of the United States; he may require the Opinion, in writing, of the principal Officer in each of the executive Departments, upon any Subject relating to the Duties of their respective Offices, and he shall have Power to Grant Reprieves and Pardons for Offences against the United States, except in Cases of Impeachment.

## Commentary

would choose the President. The Senate would choose the Vice President. The election of 1800, however, ended in a tie in the electoral college between Thomas Jefferson and Aaron Burr. The Twelfth Amendment changed the electoral college system so that this could not happen again.

 **Checkpoint**

**Who may become President?**

◀ **Clause 6** The powers of the President pass to the Vice President if the President leaves office or cannot discharge his or her duties. The Twenty-fifth Amendment clarifies this clause.

◀ **Clause 7** The President is paid a salary. It cannot be raised or lowered during his or her term in office. The President is not allowed to hold any other state or federal position while in office.

◀ **Clause 1** The President is the head of the armed forces and the state militias when they are called into national service. The military is under <u>civilian</u>, or nonmilitary, control. The President has the power to grant a <u>reprieve</u>, or pardon. A reprieve suspends punishment. A <u>pardon</u> prevents prosecution for a crime or overrides the judgment of a court.

## Commentary

**Clause 2 ▶**
The President has the power to make treaties with other nations. Under the system of checks and balances, all treaties must be approved by two thirds of the Senate. The President has the power to appoint ambassadors to foreign countries and to appoint other high officials. The Senate must confirm, or approve, these appointments.

**Section 4 ▶**
Civil officers include federal judges and members of the Cabinet. High crimes are major crimes. Misdemeanors are lesser crimes. The President, Vice President, and others can be forced out of office if impeached and found guilty of certain crimes.

2. He shall have Power, by and with the Advice and Consent of the Senate, to make Treaties, provided two thirds of the Senators present concur; and he shall nominate, and by and with the Advice and Consent of the Senate, shall appoint Ambassadors, other public Ministers and Consuls, Judges of the supreme Court, and all other Officers of the United States, whose Appointments are not herein otherwise provided for, and which shall be established by Law: but the Congress may by Law vest the Appointment of such inferior Officers, as they think proper, in the President alone, in the Courts of Law, or in the Heads of Departments.

3. The President shall have Power to fill up all Vacancies that may happen during the Recess of the Senate, by granting Commissions which shall expire at the End of their next Session.

### Section 3. Duties of the President
He shall from time to time give to the Congress Information of the State of the Union, and recommend to their Consideration such Measures as he shall judge necessary and expedient; he may, on extraordinary Occasions, convene both Houses, or either of them, and in Case of Disagreement between them, with Respect to the Time of Adjournment, he may adjourn them to such Time as he shall think proper; he shall receive Ambassadors and other public Ministers; he shall take Care that the Laws be faithfully executed, and shall Commission all the Officers of the United States.

### Section 4. Impeachment
The President, Vice President and all Civil Officers of the United States, shall be removed from Office on Impeachment for and Conviction of, Treason, Bribery, or other high Crimes and Misdemeanors.

## Article III  Judicial Branch

### Section 1. Courts, Terms of Office
The judicial Power of the United States, shall be vested in one supreme Court, and in such inferior Courts as the Congress may from time to time ordain and establish. The Judges, both of the supreme and inferior Courts, shall hold their Offices during good Behavior, and shall, at stated Times, receive for their Services, a Compensation, which shall not be diminished during their Continuance in Office.

## Section 2. Jurisdiction

1.  The judicial Power shall extend to all Cases, in Law and Equity, arising under this Constitution, the Laws of the United States, and Treaties made, or which shall be made, under their Authority;— to all Cases affecting Ambassadors, other public Ministers, and Consuls;— to all Cases of Admiralty and maritime Jurisdiction;— to Controversies to which the United States shall be a Party;— to Controversies between two or more States;— ~~between a State and Citizens of another State~~;— between Citizens of different States;— between Citizens of the same State claiming Lands under Grants of different States, and between a State, or the Citizens thereof, and foreign States, Citizens, or Subjects.

2.  In all Cases affecting Ambassadors, other public Ministers and Consuls, and those in which a State shall be a Party, the supreme Court shall have original Jurisdiction. In all the other Cases before mentioned, the supreme Court shall have appellate Jurisdiction, both as to Law and Fact, with such Exceptions, and under such Regulations as the Congress shall make.

3.  The trial of all Crimes, except in Cases of Impeachment, shall be by Jury; and such Trial shall be held in the State where the said Crimes shall have been committed; but when not committed within any State, the Trial shall be at such Place or Places as the Congress may by Law have directed.

## Commentary

◄ **Clause 1** <u>Jurisdiction</u> refers to the right of a court to hear a case. Federal courts have jurisdiction over cases that involve the Constitution, federal laws, treaties, foreign ambassadors and diplomats, naval and maritime laws, disagreements between states or between citizens from different states, and disputes between a state or citizen and a foreign state or citizen.

◄ **Clause 2** <u>Original jurisdiction</u> means the power of a court to hear a case when it first arises. The Supreme Court has original jurisdiction over only a few cases, such as those involving foreign diplomats. More often, the Supreme Court acts as an <u>appellate court</u>. An appellate court considers whether the trial judge made errors during the trial or incorrectly interpreted or applied the law in reaching a decision.

# Checks and Balances

Courts may declare acts of Congress to be unconstitutional.

Congress creates lower courts and may remove judges through impeachment; Senate approves or rejects appointment of judges.

**Judicial Branch**
Interprets the law

Judges are appointed for life, free from executive control; courts may declare executive actions to be unconstitutional.

President appoints Supreme Court justices and other federal judges.

President may veto legislation, call special sessions, recommend legislation and appeal to the people.

**Legislative Branch**
Makes the law

Congress makes laws, creates agencies and programs, and appropriates funds to carry out laws and programs; it may override veto with two-thirds vote and may remove President through impeachment; Senate approves treaties and presidential appointments.

**Executive Branch**
Carries out the law

# Commentary

✓ **Checkpoint**

How does the Constitution define treason?

**Clause 2** ▶
The act of returning a suspected criminal or escaped prisoner to a state where he or she is wanted is called extradition. State governors must return a suspect to another state. However, the Supreme Court has ruled that a governor cannot be forced to do so if he or she feels that justice will not be done.

**Clause 3** ▶
Persons held to service or labor refers to slaves or indentured servants. The Thirteenth Amendment replaces this clause.

**Clause 1** ▶
Congress has the power to admit new states to the Union. Existing states cannot be split up or joined together to form new states unless both Congress and the state legislatures approve. New states are equal to all other states.

## Section 3. Treason

1. Treason against the United States shall consist only in levying War against them, or in adhering to their Enemies, giving them Aid and Comfort. No Person shall be convicted of Treason unless on the Testimony of two Witnesses to the same overt Act, or on Confession in open Court.

2. The Congress shall have Power to declare the Punishment of Treason, but no Attainder of Treason shall work Corruption of Blood, or Forfeiture except during the Life of the Person attainted.

## Article IV  Relations Among the States

### Section 1.  Full Faith and Credit

Full Faith and Credit shall be given in each State to the public Acts, Records, and judicial Proceedings of every other State. And the Congress may by general Laws prescribe the Manner in which such Acts, Records and Proceedings shall be proved, and the Effect thereof.

### Section 2.  Privileges and Immunities of Citizens

1. The Citizens of each State shall be entitled to all Privileges and Immunities of Citizens in the several States.

2. A Person charged in any State with Treason, Felony, or other Crime, who shall flee from justice, and be found in another State, shall on Demand of the executive Authority of the State from which he fled, be delivered up, to be removed to the State having Jurisdiction of the Crime.

3. ~~No Person held to Service or Labor in one State, under the Laws thereof, escaping into another, shall, in Consequence of any Law or Regulation therein, be discharged from Service or Labor, but shall be delivered up on Claim of the Party to whom such Service or Labor may be due.~~

### Section 3.  New States and Territories

1. New States may be admitted by the Congress into this Union; but no new State shall be formed or erected within the Jurisdiction of any other State; nor any State be formed by the Junction of two or more States, or Parts of States, without the Consent of the Legislatures of the States concerned as well as of the Congress.

2. The Congress shall have Power to dispose of and make all needful Rules and Regulations respecting the Territory or other Property belonging to the United States; and nothing in this Constitution shall be so construed as to Prejudice any Claims of the United States, or of any particular State.

### Section 4. Protection Afforded to the States by the Nation

The United States shall guarantee to every State in this Union a Republican Form of Government, and shall protect each of them against Invasion; and on Application of the Legislature, or of the Executive (when the Legislature cannot be convened) against domestic Violence.

## Article V  Provision for Amendments

The Congress, whenever two thirds of both Houses shall deem it necessary, shall propose Amendments to this Constitution, or, on the Application of the Legislatures of two thirds of the several States, shall call a Convention for proposing Amendments, which, in either Case, shall be valid to all Intents and Purposes, as Part of this Constitution, when ratified by the Legislatures of three fourths of the several States, or by Conventions in three fourths thereof, as the one or the other Mode of Ratification may be proposed by the Congress; Provided ~~that no Amendment which may be made prior to the Year One thousand eight hundred and eight shall in any Manner affect the first and fourth Clauses in the Ninth section of the first Article; and~~ that no State, without its Consent, shall be deprived of its equal Suffrage in the Senate.

## Article VI  National Debts, Supremacy of National Law, Oath

### Section 1.

All Debts contracted and Engagements entered into, before the Adoption of this Constitution, shall be as valid against the United States under this Constitution, as under the Confederation.

### Section 2.

This Constitution, and the Laws of the United States which shall be made in Pursuance thereof; and all Treaties made, or which shall be made, under the Authority of the United States, shall be the supreme Law of the Land; and the Judges in every State shall be bound thereby, anything in the constitution or Laws of any State to the Contrary notwithstanding.

## Commentary

◀ **Article V** The Constitution can be amended, or changed, if necessary. An amendment can be proposed by (1) a two-thirds vote of both houses of Congress or (2) a national convention called by Congress at the request of two thirds of the state legislatures. (This second method has never been used.) An amendment must be ratified, or approved, by (1) three fourths of the state legislatures or (2) special conventions in three fourths of the states. Congress decides which method will be used.

◀ **Section 2** The "supremacy clause" in this section establishes the Constitution, federal laws, and treaties that the Senate has ratified as the supreme, or highest, law of the land. Thus, they outweigh state laws. A state judge must overturn a state law that conflicts with the Constitution or with a federal law.

# Commentary

**Article VII ▶**
During 1787 and 1788, states held special conventions. By October 1788, the required nine states had ratified the United States Constitution.

 **Checkpoint**

**What had to happen before the Constitution would go into effect?**

## Section 3.

The Senators and Representatives before mentioned, and the Members of the several State legislatures, and all executive and judicial Officers, both of the United States and of the several States, shall be bound by Oath or Affirmation, to support this Constitution; but no religious Test shall ever be required as a Qualification to any Office or public Trust under the the United States.

## Article VII  Ratification of Constitution

The ratification of the Conventions of nine States, shall be sufficient for the Establishment of this Constitution between the States so ratifying the same.

Done in Convention by the Unanimous Consent of the States present the Seventeenth Day of September in the Year of our Lord one thousand seven hundred and Eighty seven and of the Independence of the United States of America the twelfth. In witness whereof We have hereunto subscribed our Names.

Attest: William Jackson, SECRETARY
    George Washington, PRESIDENT and deputy from Virginia

**New Hampshire**
John Langdon
Nicholas Gilman

**Massachusetts**
Nathaniel Gorham
Rufus King

**Connecticut**
William Samuel Johnson
Roger Sherman

**New York**
Alexander Hamilton

**New Jersey**
William Livingston
David Brearley
William Paterson
Jonathan Dayton

**Pennsylvania**
Benjamin Franklin
Thomas Mifflin
Robert Morris
George Clymer
Thomas Fitzsimons
Jared Ingersoll
James Wilson
Gouverneur Morris

**Delaware**
George Read
Gunning Bedford, Jr.
John Dickinson
Richard Bassett
Jacob Broom

**Maryland**
James McHenry
Dan of St. Thomas Jenifer
Daniel Carroll

**Virginia**
John Blair
James Madison, Jr.

**North Carolina**
William Blount
Richard Dobbs Spaight
Hugh Williamson

**South Carolina**
John Rutledge
Charles Cotesworth Pinckney
Charles Pinckney
Pierce Butler

**Georgia**
William Few
Abraham Baldwin

# AMENDMENTS

**First Amendment  Freedom of Religion, Speech, Press, Assembly, and Petition**

Congress shall make no law respecting an establishment of religion, or prohibiting the free exercise thereof, or abridging the freedom of speech, or of the press; or the right of the people peaceably to assemble, and to petition the Government for a redress of grievances.

**Second Amendment  Bearing Arms**

A well-regulated Militia being necessary to the security of a free State, the right of the people to keep and bear Arms, shall not be infringed.

**Third Amendment  Quartering of Troops**

No Soldier shall, in time of peace be quartered in any house, without the consent of the Owner, nor, in time of war, but in a manner to be prescribed by law.

## Commentary

**The Amendments**  The Amendments are changes made to the Constitution, which has been amended 27 times since it was originally ratified in 1788. The first 10 amendments are referred to as the Bill of Rights.

◄ **First Amendment**  The First Amendment protects five basic rights: freedom of religion, speech, the press, assembly, and petition. Congress cannot set up an established, or official, church or religion for the nation, nor can it forbid the practice of religion.

Congress may not <u>abridge,</u> or limit, the freedom to speak or write freely. The government may not censor, or review, books and newspapers before they are printed. This amendment also protects the right to assemble, or hold public meetings. <u>Petition</u> means ask. <u>Redress</u> means to correct. <u>Grievances</u> are wrongs. The people have the right to ask the government for wrongs to be corrected.

◄ **Second Amendment**  The Supreme Court decision in the case of *District of Columbia* v. *Heller* in 2008 ruled that a ban on handguns in the District of Columbia violated the Second Amendment. This is the first case since *U.S.* v. *Miller* in which the Court moved to interpret the Second Amendment.

◄ **Third Amendment**  In colonial times, the British could quarter, or house, soldiers in private homes without permission of the owners. The Third Amendment prevents such abuses.

## Commentary

### Fourth Amendment ▶

This amendment protects Americans from unreasonable searches and seizures. Search and seizure are permitted only if a judge issues a <u>warrant</u>, or written court order. A warrant is issued only if there is probable cause. This means an officer must show that it is probable, or likely, that the search will produce evidence of a crime.

### Fifth Amendment ▶

This amendment protects the rights of the accused. <u>Capital crimes</u> are those that can be punished with death. <u>Infamous crimes</u> are those that can be punished with prison or loss of rights. The federal government must obtain an <u>indictment</u>, or formal accusation, from a <u>grand jury</u> to prosecute anyone for such crimes. A grand jury is a panel of between 12 and 23 citizens who decide if the government has enough evidence to justify a trial.

<u>Double jeopardy</u> is forbidden by this amendment. This means that a person cannot be tried twice for the same crime. However, if a court sets aside a conviction because of a legal error, the accused can be tried again. A person on trial cannot be forced to <u>testify</u>, or give evidence, against himself or herself. A person accused of a crime is entitled to <u>due process of law</u>, or a fair hearing or trial.

The government cannot seize private property for public use without paying the owner a fair price for it.

---

### Fourth Amendment  Searches and Seizures

The right of the people to be secure in their persons, houses, papers, and effects, against unreasonable searches and seizures, shall not be violated, and no Warrants shall issue, but upon probable cause, supported by Oath or affirmation, and particularly describing the place to be searched, and the persons or things to be seized.

### Fifth Amendment  Criminal Proceedings; Due Process; Eminent Domain

No person shall be held to answer for a capital, or otherwise infamous crime, unless on a presentment or indictment of a Grand Jury, except in cases arising in the land or naval forces, or in the Militia, when in actual service in time of War or public danger; nor shall any person be subject for the same offence to be twice put in jeopardy of life or limb; nor shall be compelled in any criminal case to be a witness against himself, nor be deprived of life, liberty, or property, without due process of law; nor shall private property be taken for public use, without just compensation.

## Sixth Amendment  Criminal Proceedings

In all criminal prosecutions, the accused shall enjoy the right to a speedy and public trial, by an impartial jury of the State and district wherein the crime shall have been committed, which district shall have been previously ascertained by law, and to be informed of the nature and cause of the accusation; to be confronted with the witnesses against him; to have compulsory process for obtaining witnesses in his favor, and to have the Assistance of Counsel for his defence.

## Seventh Amendment  Civil Trials

In Suits at common law, where the value in controversy shall exceed twenty dollars, the right of trial by jury shall be preserved, and no fact tried by a jury, shall be otherwise re-examined in any Court of the United States, than according to the rules of the common law.

## Eighth Amendment  Punishment for Crimes

Excessive bail shall not be required, nor excessive fines imposed, nor cruel and unusual punishment inflicted.

## Ninth Amendment  Unenumerated Rights

The enumeration in the Constitution, of certain rights, shall not be construed to deny or disparage others retained by the people.

## Tenth Amendment  Powers Reserved to the States

The powers not delegated to the United States by the Constitution, nor prohibited by it to the States, are reserved to the States respectively, or to the people.

## Commentary

◄ **Sixth Amendment** In criminal cases, the jury must be impartial, or not favor either side. The accused is guaranteed the right to a trial by jury. The trial must be speedy. The accused must be told the charges and be allowed to question all witnesses. The accused must be allowed a lawyer.

◄ **Seventh Amendment** Common law refers to rules of law established by judges in past cases. An appeals court can set aside a verdict only if legal errors make the trial unfair.

◄ **Eighth Amendment** <u>Bail</u> is money that the accused leaves with the court as a pledge to appear for trial. If the accused does not appear, the court keeps the money. This amendment prevents the court from imposing bail or fines that are <u>excessive</u>, or too high. The amendment also forbids cruel and unusual punishments, such as physical torture.

◄ **Ninth Amendment** The rights of the people are not limited to those listed in the Bill of Rights. In the Ninth Amendment, the government is prevented from claiming these are the only rights people have.

◄ **Tenth Amendment** Powers not given to the federal government belong to the states. Powers reserved to the states are not listed in the Constitution.

## Commentary

### Eleventh Amendment ▶

A private citizen from one state cannot sue the government of another state in federal court. However, a citizen can sue a state government in a state court.

### Twelfth Amendment ▶

This amendment changed the way the electoral college voted as outlined in Article II, Section 1, Clause 3. This amendment provides that each elector choose one candidate for President and one candidate for Vice President. If no candidate for President receives a majority of electoral votes, the House of Representatives chooses the President. If no candidate for Vice President receives a majority, the Senate elects the Vice President. The Vice President must be a person who is eligible to be President.

It is possible for a candidate to win the popular vote and lose the electoral college. This happened in 1888 and 2000.

## Eleventh Amendment  Suits Against States

The Judicial power of the United States shall not be construed to extend to any suit in law or equity, commenced or prosecuted against one of the United States by Citizens of another State, or by Citizens or Subjects of any Foreign State.

## Twelfth Amendment  Election of President and Vice President

The Electors shall meet in their respective States and vote by ballot for President and Vice President, one of whom, at least, shall not be an inhabitant of the same State with themselves; they shall name in their ballots the person voted for as President, and in distinct ballots the person voted for as Vice President, and they shall make distinct lists of all persons voted for as President, and of all persons voted for as Vice President, and of the number of votes for each, which lists they shall sign and certify, and transmit sealed to the seat of the government of the United States, directed to the President of the Senate;— The President of the Senate shall, in the presence of the Senate and the House of Representatives, open all the certificates and the votes shall then be counted;— the person having the greatest Number of votes for President shall be the President, if such number be a majority of the whole number of Electors appointed; and if no person have such a majority, then, from the persons having the highest numbers not exceeding three on the list of those voted for as President, the House of Representatives shall choose immediately, by ballot, the President. But in choosing the President, the votes shall be taken by States, the representation from each State having one vote; a quorum for this purpose shall consist of a member or members from two thirds of the States, and a majority of the States shall be necessary to a choice. ~~And if the House of Representatives shall not choose a President whenever the right of choice shall devolve upon them, before the fourth day of March next following, then the Vice President shall act as President, as in case of death or other constitutional disability of the President.~~ The person having the greatest number of votes as Vice President, shall be the Vice President, if such number be a majority of the whole number of Electors appointed, and if no person have a majority, then from the two highest numbers on the list, the Senate shall choose the Vice President; a quorum for the purpose shall consist of two thirds of the whole number of Senators, a majority of the whole number shall be necessary to a choice. But no person constitutionally ineligible to the office of President shall be eligible to that of Vice President of the United States.

## Thirteenth Amendment  Slavery and Involuntary Servitude

**Section 1.** Neither slavery nor involuntary servitude, except as a punishment for crime whereof the party shall have been duly convicted, shall exist within the United States, or any place subject to their jurisdiction.

**Section 2.** Congress shall have power to enforce this article by appropriate legislation.

## Fourteenth Amendment  Rights of Citizens

**Section 1.** All persons born or naturalized in the United States and subject to the jurisdiction thereof, are citizens of the United States and of the State wherein they reside. No State shall make or enforce any law which shall abridge the privileges or immunities of citizens of the United States; nor shall any State deprive any person of life, liberty, or property, without due process of law; nor deny to any person within its jurisdiction the equal protection of the laws.

**Section 2.** Representatives shall be apportioned among the several States according to their respective numbers, counting the whole number of persons in each State, excluding Indians not taxed. But when the right to vote at any election for the choice of electors for President and Vice President of the United States, Representatives in Congress, the Executive and Judicial officers of a State, or the members of the Legislature thereof, is denied to any of the male inhabitants of such State, being twenty-one years of age, and citizens of the United States, or in any way abridged, except for participation in rebellion, or other crime, the basis of representation therein shall be reduced in the proportion which the number of such male citizens shall bear to the whole number of male citizens twenty-one years of age in such State.

**Section 3.** No person shall be a Senator or Representative in Congress, or elector of President and Vice President, or hold any office, civil or military, under the United States, or under any State, who, having previously taken an oath, as a member of Congress, or as an officer of the United States, or as a member of any State legislature, or as an executive or judicial officer of any State, to support the Constitution of the United States, shall have engaged in insurrection or rebellion against the same, or given aid or comfort to the enemies thereof. But Congress may, by a vote of two thirds of each House, remove such disability.

## Commentary

◄ **Thirteenth Amendment**
The Emancipation Proclamation (1863) freed slaves only in areas controlled by the Confederacy. This amendment freed all slaves. It also forbids involuntary servitude, or labor done against one's will. However, it does not prevent prison wardens from making prisoners work. Congress can pass laws to carry out this amendment.

◄ **Fourteenth Amendment, Section 1** This amendment defines citizenship for the first time in the Constitution. It was intended to protect the rights of the freed slaves by guaranteeing all citizens "equal protection under the law."

◄ **Fourteenth Amendment, Section 2** This section replaced the three-fifths clause. It provides that representation in the House of Representatives is decided on the basis of the number of people in the states. It also provides that states that deny the vote to male citizens aged 21 or over will be punished by losing part of their representation. This provision has never been enforced.

**Checkpoint**

**What is one key provision of the Fourteenth Amendment?**

## Commentary

**Section 4.** The validity of the public debt of the United States, authorized by law, including debts incurred for payment of pensions and bounties for services in suppressing insurrection or rebellion, shall not be questioned. But neither the United States nor any State shall assume or pay any debt or obligation incurred in aid of insurrection or rebellion against the United States, or any claim for the loss or emancipation of any slave; but all such debts, obligations and claims shall be held illegal and void.

**Section 5.** The Congress shall have power to enforce, by appropriate legislation, the provisions of this article.

### Fifteenth Amendment  Right to Vote—Race, Color, Servitude

**Section 1.** The right of citizens of the United States to vote shall not be denied or abridged by the United States or by any State on account of race, color, or previous condition of servitude.

**Fifteenth Amendment, ▶
Section 1** This amendment gave African Americans the right to vote. In the late 1800s, however, southern states used grandfather clauses, literacy tests, and poll taxes to keep African Americans from voting.

**Fifteenth Amendment, ▶
Section 2** Congress can pass laws to carry out this amendment. The Twenty-fourth Amendment barred the use of poll taxes in national elections. The Voting Rights Act of 1965 gave federal officials the power to register voters where there was voting discrimination.

**Section 2.** The Congress shall have power to enforce this article by appropriate legislation.

### Sixteenth Amendment  Income Tax

The Congress shall have power to lay and collect taxes on incomes, from whatever source derived, without apportionment among the several States, and without regard to any census or enumeration.

**Sixteenth Amendment ▶**
Congress has the power to collect taxes on people's income. An income tax can be collected without regard to a state's population. This amendment changed Article I, Section 9, Clause 4.

## Seventeenth Amendment  Popular Election of Senators

**Section 1.** The Senate of the United States shall be composed of two Senators from each State, elected by the people thereof, for six years; and each Senator shall have one vote. The electors in each State shall have the qualifications requisite for electors of the most numerous branch of the State legislatures.

**Section 2.** When vacancies happen in the representation of any State in the Senate, the executive authority of such State shall issue writs of election to fill such vacancies: *Provided,* That the legislature of any State may empower the executive thereof to make temporary appointments until the people fill the vacancies by election as the legislature may direct.

**Section 3.** ~~This amendment shall not be so construed as to affect the election or term of any Senator chosen before it becomes valid as part of the Constitution.~~

## Eighteenth Amendment  Prohibition of Alcoholic Beverages

**Section 1.** ~~After one year from the ratification of this article the manufacture, sale, or transportation of intoxicating liquors within, the importation thereof into, or the exportation thereof from the United States and all territory subject to the jurisdiction thereof for beverage purposes is hereby prohibited.~~

**Section 2.** ~~The Congress and the several States shall have concurrent power to enforce this article by appropriate legislation.~~

**Section 3**. ~~This article shall be inoperative unless it shall have been ratified as an amendment to the Constitution by the legislatures of the several States, as provided in the Constitution, within seven years of the date of the submission hereof to the States by Congress.~~

## Nineteenth Amendment  Women's Suffrage

**Section 1.** The right of citizens of the United States to vote shall not be denied or abridged by the United States or by any State on account of sex.

**Section 2.** Congress shall have power to enforce this article by appropriate legislation.

## Commentary

◀ **Seventeenth Amendment**
This amendment replaced Article I, Section 3, Clause 2. Before it was adopted, state legislatures chose senators. This amendment provides that senators are elected directly by the people of each state.

◀ **Eighteenth Amendment**
This amendment, known as Prohibition, banned the making, selling, or transporting of alcoholic beverages in the United States. Later, the Twenty-first Amendment repealed, or canceled, this amendment.

◀ **Nineteenth Amendment**
Neither the federal government nor state governments can deny the right to vote on account of sex.

# Commentary

**Twentieth Amendment,** ▶
**Section 1** The date for the inauguration of the President was changed to January 20, and the date for Congress to begin its term changed to January 3. Prior to this amendment, the beginning-of-term date was set in March. The outgoing officials with little or no influence on matters were not effective in office. Being so inactive, they were called "lame ducks."

**Twentieth Amendment,** ▶
**Section 3** If the President-elect dies before taking office, the Vice President-elect becomes President. If no President has been chosen by January 20 or if the elected candidate fails to qualify for office, the Vice President-elect acts as President, but only until a qualified President is chosen. Finally, Congress has the power to choose a person to act as President if neither the President-elect nor the Vice President-elect is qualified to take office.

**Twenty-first Amendment,** ▶
**Section 1** The Eighteenth Amendment is repealed, making it legal to make and sell alcoholic beverages. Prohibition ended on December 5, 1933.

## Twentieth Amendment  Presidential Terms; Sessions of Congress

**Section 1.** The terms of the President and Vice President shall end at noon on the 20th day of January, and the terms of Senators and Representatives at noon on the 3d day of January, of the years in which such terms would have ended if this article had not been ratified; and the terms of their successors shall then begin.

**Section 2.** The Congress shall assemble at least once in every year, and such meeting shall begin at noon on the 3d day of January, unless they shall by law appoint a different day.

**Section 3.** If, at the time fixed for the beginning of the term of the President, the President elect shall have died, the Vice President elect shall become President. If a President shall not have been chosen before the time fixed for the beginning of his term, or if the President elect shall have failed to qualify, then the Vice President elect shall act as President until a President shall have qualified; and the Congress may by law provide for the case wherein neither a President elect nor a Vice President elect shall have qualified, declaring who shall then act as President, or the manner in which one who is to act shall be selected, and such person shall act accordingly until a President or Vice President shall have qualified.

**Section 4.** The Congress may by law provide for the case of the death of any of the persons from whom the House of Representatives may choose a President whenever the right of choice shall have devolved upon them, and for the case of the death of any of the persons from whom the Senate may choose a Vice President whenever the right of choice shall have devolved upon them.

**Section 5.** ~~Sections 1 and 2 shall take effect on the 15th day of October following the ratification of this article.~~

**Section 6.** This article shall be inoperative unless it shall have been ratified as an amendment to the Constitution by the legislatures of three fourths of the several States within seven years from the date of its submission.

## Twenty-first Amendment  Repeal of Prohibition

**Section 1.** The eighteenth article of amendment to the Constitution of the United States is hereby repealed.

**Section 2.** The transportation or importation into any State, Territory, or possession of the United States for delivery or use therein of intoxicating liquors, in violation of the laws thereof, is hereby prohibited.

**Section 3.** ~~This article shall be inoperative unless it shall have been ratified as an amendment to the Constitution by conventions in the several States, as provided in the Constitution, within seven years from the date of the submission hereof to the States by the Congress.~~

## Twenty-second Amendment  Presidential Tenure

**Section 1.** No person shall be elected to the office of the President more than twice, and no person who has held the office of President, or acted as President, for more than two years of a term to which some other person was elected President shall be elected to the office of the President more than once. ~~But this Article shall not apply to any person holding the office of President, when this Article was proposed by the Congress, and shall not prevent any person who may be holding the office of President, or acting as President, during the term within which this Article becomes operative from holding the office of President or acting as President during the remainder of such term.~~

**Section 2.** ~~This article shall be inoperative unless it shall have been ratified as an amendment to the Constitution by the legislatures of three fourths of the several states within seven years from the date of its submission to the States by the Congress.~~

## Twenty-third Amendment  Presidential Electors for The District of Columbia

**Section 1.** The District constituting the seat of Government of the United States shall appoint in such manner as the Congress may direct:

A number of electors of President and Vice President equal to the whole number of Senators and Representatives in Congress to which the District would be entitled if it were a State, but in no event more than the least populous State; they shall be in addition to those appointed by the States, they shall be considered, for the purposes of the election of President and Vice President, to be electors appointed by a State; and they shall meet in the District and perform such duties as provided by the twelfth article of amendment.

**Section 2.** The Congress shall have power to enforce this article by appropriate legislation.

## Commentary

◀ **Twenty-second Amendment, Section 1** This amendment provides that no President may serve more than two terms. A President who has already served more than half of someone else's term can serve only one more full term. Before Franklin Roosevelt became President, no President served more than two terms in office. Roosevelt broke with this custom and was elected to four terms.

◀ **Twenty-third Amendment, Section 1** This amendment gives the residents of Washington, D.C., the right to vote in presidential elections. Until this amendment was adopted, people living in Washington, D.C., could not vote for President because the Constitution had made no provision for choosing electors from the nation's capital. Washington, D.C., has three electoral votes.

## Commentary

**Twenty-fourth Amendment,** ▶
**Section 1** A poll tax is a tax on voters. This amendment bans poll taxes in national elections. Some states used poll taxes to keep African Americans from voting. In 1966, the Supreme Court struck down poll taxes in state elections, also.

**Twenty-fifth Amendment,** ▶
**Section 1** If the President dies or resigns, the Vice President becomes President. This section clarifies Article II, Section 1, Clause 6.

**Twenty-fifth Amendment,** ▶
**Section 3** If the President declares in writing that he or she is unable to perform the duties of office, the Vice President serves as acting President until the President recovers.

**Twenty-fifth Amendment,** ▶
**Section 4** Two Presidents, Woodrow Wilson and Dwight Eisenhower, fell gravely ill while in office. The Constitution contained no provision for this kind of emergency.

---

### Twenty-fourth Amendment  Right to Vote in Federal Elections

**Section 1.** The right of citizens of the United States to vote in any primary or other election for President or Vice President, for electors for President or Vice President, or for Senator or Representative in Congress, shall not be denied or abridged by the United States or any State by reason of failure to pay any poll tax or other tax.

**Section 2.** The Congress shall have power to enforce this article by appropriate legislation.

### Twenty-fifth Amendment  Presidential Succession; Vice Presidential Vacancy; Presidential Inability

**Section 1.** In case of the removal of the President from office or of his death or resignation, the Vice President shall become President.

**Section 2.** Whenever there is a vacancy in the office of the Vice President, the President shall nominate a Vice President who shall take office upon confirmation by a majority vote of both Houses of Congress.

**Section 3.** Whenever the President transmits to the President pro tempore of the Senate and the Speaker of the House of Representatives his written declaration that he is unable to discharge the powers and duties of his office, and until he transmits to them a written declaration to the contrary, such powers and duties shall be discharged by the Vice President as Acting President.

**Section 4.** Whenever the Vice President and a majority of either the principal officers of the executive departments or of such other body as Congress may by law provide, transmit to the President pro tempore of the Senate and the Speaker of the House of Representatives their written declaration that the President is unable to discharge the powers and duties of his office, the Vice President shall immediately assume the powers and duties of the office as Acting President.

Thereafter, when the President transmits to the President pro tempore of the Senate and the Speaker of the House of Representatives his written declaration that no inability exists, he shall resume the powers and duties of his office unless the Vice President and a majority of either the principal officers of the executive department or of such other body as Congress may by law provide, transmit within four days to the President pro tempore of the Senate and the Speaker of the House of Representatives their written declaration that the President is unable to discharge the powers and duties of his office. Thereupon Congress shall decide the issue, assembling within forty-eight hours for that purpose if not in session. If the Congress, within twenty-one days after receipt of the latter written declaration, or, if Congress is not in session, within twenty-one days after Congress is required to assemble, determines by two-thirds vote of both Houses that the President is unable to discharge the powers and duties of his office, the Vice President shall continue to discharge the same as Acting President; otherwise, the President shall resume the powers and duties of his office.

### Twenty-sixth Amendment  Right to Vote—Age
**Section 1.** The right of citizens of the United States, who are eighteen years of age or older, to vote shall not be denied or abridged by the United States or by any State on account of age.

**Section 2.** The Congress shall have the power to enforce this article by appropriate legislation.

### Twenty-seventh Amendment  Congressional Pay
No law varying the compensation for the services of the Senators and Representatives, shall take effect, until an election of Representatives shall have intervened.

## Commentary

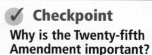

**Checkpoint**
Why is the Twenty-fifth Amendment important?

◀ **Twenty-sixth Amendment, Section 1** In 1970, Congress passed a law allowing 18-year-olds to vote. However, the Supreme Court decided that Congress could not set a minimum age for state elections.

◀ **Twenty-seventh Amendment** If members of Congress vote themselves a pay increase, it cannot go into effect until after the next congressional election. This amendment was proposed in 1789. In 1992, Michigan became the thirty-eighth state to ratify it.

# 2 Manifest Destiny, Civil War, and Reconstruction

## 1800–1877

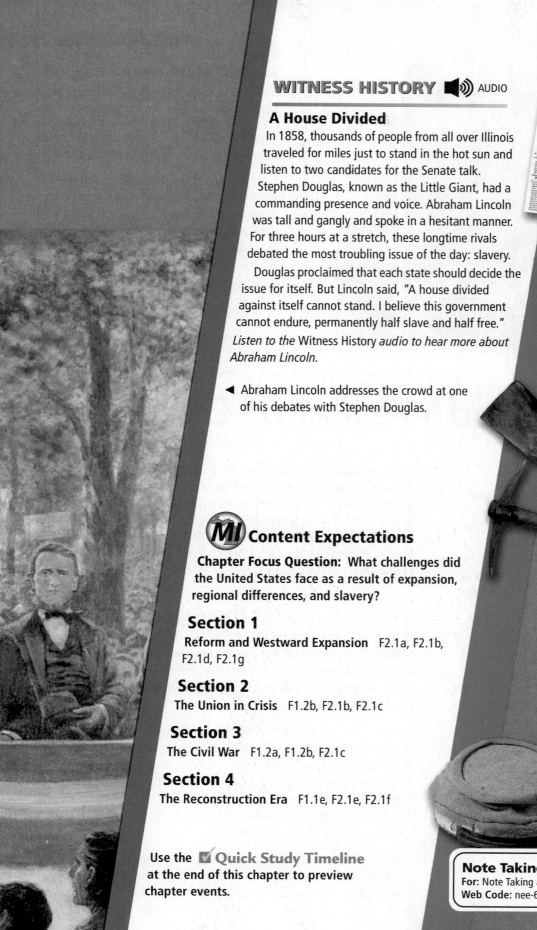

## WITNESS HISTORY ◀))) AUDIO

### A House Divided

In 1858, thousands of people from all over Illinois traveled for miles just to stand in the hot sun and listen to two candidates for the Senate talk. Stephen Douglas, known as the Little Giant, had a commanding presence and voice. Abraham Lincoln was tall and gangly and spoke in a hesitant manner. For three hours at a stretch, these longtime rivals debated the most troubling issue of the day: slavery.

Douglas proclaimed that each state should decide the issue for itself. But Lincoln said, "A house divided against itself cannot stand. I believe this government cannot endure, permanently half slave and half free."

*Listen to the* Witness History *audio to hear more about Abraham Lincoln.*

◀ Abraham Lincoln addresses the crowd at one of his debates with Stephen Douglas.

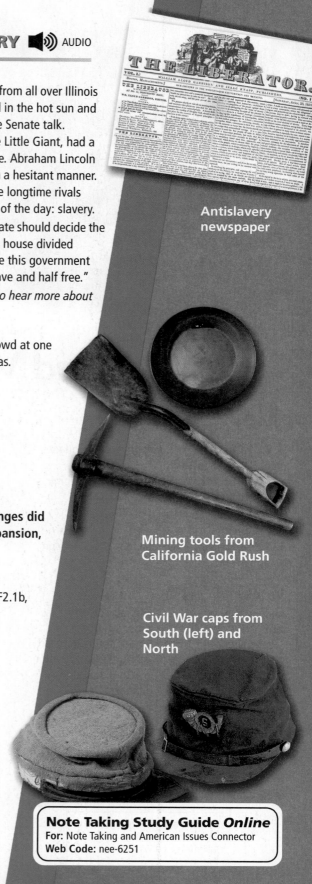

Antislavery newspaper

Mining tools from California Gold Rush

Civil War caps from South (left) and North

### (MI) Content Expectations

**Chapter Focus Question:** What challenges did the United States face as a result of expansion, regional differences, and slavery?

### Section 1

**Reform and Westward Expansion** F2.1a, F2.1b, F2.1d, F2.1g

### Section 2

**The Union in Crisis** F1.2b, F2.1b, F2.1c

### Section 3

**The Civil War** F1.2a, F1.2b, F2.1c

### Section 4

**The Reconstruction Era** F1.1e, F2.1e, F2.1f

Use the ☑ **Quick Study Timeline** at the end of this chapter to preview chapter events.

**Note Taking Study Guide** *Online*
**For:** Note Taking and American Issues Connector
**Web Code:** nee-6251

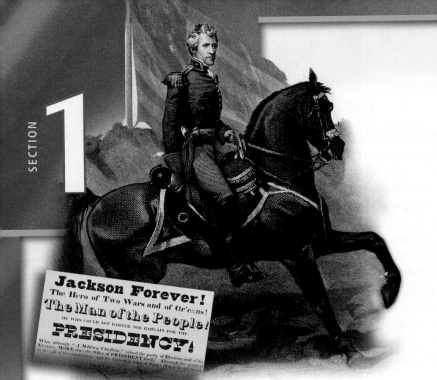

Jackson Forever!
The Hero of Two Wars and of Or'eans!
The Man of the People!
HE WHO COULD NOT BARTER NOR BARGAIN FOR THE
PRESIDENCY!

WITNESS HISTORY 🔊 AUDIO

### A "Mob" at the White House

Washington, D.C., March 4, 1829. Andrew Jackson, a popular war hero from the Tennessee frontier, had been sworn in as President. The aristocratic Margaret Bayard Smith was horrified to see the White House overrun by what she called "a rabble, a mob":

❝Cut glass and china to the amount of several thousand dollars had been broken in the struggle to get the refreshments. . . . Ladies fainted, men were seen with bloody noses and such a scene of confusion took place as is impossible to describe. . . . But it was the People's day, and the People's President and the People would rule.❞
—Margaret Bayard Smith, *The First Forty Years of Washington Society*

▲ Andrew Jackson, known as the "People's President"

# Reform and Westward Expansion

 **Content Expectations**

- **F2.1a** Describe changing political boundaries of U.S. prior to 1877.
- **F2.1b** Describe regional American economic differences/similarities prior to 1877.
- **F2.1d** Describe patterns of immigration/migration.
- **F2.1g** Describe major changes in U.S. foreign affairs prior to 1877.

## Terms and People

Andrew Jackson
tariff
Second Great
  Awakening
civil disobedience
abolitionist

Missouri Compromise
Frederick Douglass
Underground Railroad
Elizabeth Cady Stanton
Susan B. Anthony
Manifest Destiny

## NoteTaking

**Reading Skill: Identify Main Ideas** As you read, outline the main ideas.

> I. Democracy and the Age of Jackson
>   A. More Americans can vote
>     1. Suffrage grows in West
>     2.

**Why It Matters** The Constitution established the framework for a democratic government based on principles of liberty and justice. In the mid-1800s, as the nation expanded westward, some Americans also called for an expansion of democratic rights. Today, issues raised by reformers in such areas as women's rights continue to stir debate. **Section Focus Question: What trends in democratization and reform were taking shape in the United States by 1850?**

## Democracy and the Age of Jackson

In the first years of the Republic, political power was concentrated. Congressional caucuses nominated presidential candidates, and state legislatures chose the electors who cast votes for President. In general, only adult white men who owned property and paid taxes could vote.

**More Americans Can Vote** A major political shift began on the western frontier, where suffrage laws gave the vote to any white man over 21. Gradually, most eastern states also ended property requirements. Voting remained restricted—free African American men could vote in only a handful of northern states, women and Native Americans could not vote at all. Still, by 1828, more white men could vote than ever before.

**Jackson Becomes President** This new generation of voters made **Andrew Jackson** the overwhelming winner of the presidential election of 1828. Seen as a representative of the "common man," Jackson had a background quite different from earlier Presidents.

Born to poor Irish immigrant parents, he had little early education. He had made a name for himself as a military hero in the War of 1812. By the time he became President, he had acquired wealth and a plantation, but he never lost his appeal to ordinary voters.

Although the Jackson era saw increased rights for some, Jackson's policies restricted the rights of Native Americans. He supported Georgia's efforts to reverse earlier treaties that had guaranteed lands to the Cherokees. When the Supreme Court upheld the Cherokees' rights, Jackson refused to enforce the decision. Instead, he ordered the relocation of Indians across the Mississippi to the West. Beginning in 1831, tens of thousands of Indians were <u>compelled</u> to leave their homes in Florida, Mississippi, and Alabama and march to what is now Oklahoma. The forced march of the Cherokees from Georgia in 1838 caused so much suffering and death that it became known as the Trail of Tears.

**Vocabulary Builder**
<u>compel</u> – (kuhm PEHL) *v.* to force

**Tariffs Threaten National Unity** Another issue during Jackson's presidency highlighted a growing conflict between state and federal power. The federal government had imposed high **tariffs,** or taxes on imported products. These tariffs protected northern manufacturers by raising the prices of foreign-made goods. But southerners resented paying higher prices for imports. John Calhoun of South Carolina argued that the tariff gave too much authority to the federal government—and that states had the right to nullify, or cancel, any federal law that went against their interests.

When South Carolina passed a law nullifying a federal tariff, Jackson responded strongly to the Nullification Crisis. He asked Congress for the authority to use federal troops if necessary. Congress eased tensions by lowering the tariff. Though the immediate crisis passed, southern distrust of federal authority continued to fester.

✔ **Checkpoint** How did tariffs lead to a conflict between federal and state authority?

# Religion and Social Reform

Even while strife divided diverse groups, many American men and women supported religious, political, or social experiments to create a better society. Reformers came from many backgrounds and all regions of the country.

**Religious Revival Sweeps the Nation** Starting in the 1820s, a religious movement swept across America that become known as the **Second Great Awakening.** Marked by outdoor camp meetings that might last as long as a week, this movement attracted thousands of religious converts. The Second Great Awakening encouraged the belief that people could and should work to achieve a state of moral perfection. The Second Great Awakening helped bring religious fervor to social reform.

The Second Great Awakening fueled the rapid growth of several Christian denominations, especially the Baptists and Methodists. Other denominations also expanded during this period, including the African

**The Growing Electorate**
Before 1824, presidential election results did not even include a popular vote count. By 1840, the number of voters had skyrocketed. *Which Americans were not represented on the table below?*

| The Growing Electorate, 1824–1840 | |
|---|---|
| **Presidential Election** | **Total Popular Vote** |
| 1824 | 350,671 |
| 1828 | 1,155,350 |
| 1832 | 1,318,406 |
| 1836 | 1,500,802 |
| 1840 | 2,404,118 |

SOURCE: Encyclopedia Brittanica

Methodist Episcopal Church. One of the most dramatic developments was the founding of the Church of Jesus Christ of Latter-day Saints, or Mormon Church, in 1830.

**Religious Conflicts Surface** From the earliest days of the Republic, Americans debated the relationship between church and government. While some favored what Thomas Jefferson called a "wall of separation" between church and state, others felt that the government should encourage public morality by supporting religion. In the 1830s, reformers known as Sabbatarians urged the federal government to officially observe Sunday, the Christian day of rest and worship. While the post office did end Sunday mail delivery, Congress rejected petitions to ban commerce on Sundays.

Members of minority religious groups, such as Roman Catholics and Jews, often faced discrimination. Most state constitutions forbade non-Christians from holding public office. Anti-Catholic rioting broke out in Philadelphia and Boston. In Illinois, Mormon leader Joseph Smith was murdered by an angry mob. As you will read, the murder of Smith spurred the Mormons to seek a safe haven in Utah.

**Reformers Work to Improve Society** The link between religious zeal and social reform was especially clear in the temperance movement, which worked to end alcohol abuse. But social reform took many other shapes. Dorothea Dix worked to improve the treatment of prisoners and the mentally ill. Horace Mann fought for the improvement of public schools.

A group of thinkers known as Transcendentalists also became involved in social reform. They included Ralph Waldo Emerson and Margaret Fuller, who taught that it was important to follow one's conscience. Henry David Thoreau went even further, arguing that people should peacefully refuse to obey laws they considered to be immoral. He called this concept **civil disobedience.** Thoreau himself once went to jail for refusing to pay a tax to support a war that he felt encouraged the spread of slavery.

 **Checkpoint** How did the Second Great Awakening encourage reform?

## The Antislavery Movement

Thoreau was one of a small but fervent number of reformers, known as **abolitionists,** who sought a gradual or immediate end to slavery. They insisted that owning another human being was morally wrong, harming both slaves and slaveholders. Still, abolitionists faced an uphill struggle because many Americans believed their prosperity rested on the institution of slavery. Cotton produced by slave labor in the agrarian South supplied the textile mills of the industrial North.

**Slavery Causes Suffering** Some 2 million African Americans were unfairly treated by law as human property. Most labored at backbreaking tasks— picking tobacco or cotton, loading freight onto ships, or preparing meals in scorching kitchens. At any time, enslaved people could be whipped or sold away from their families.

Historians estimate that nearly 200 significant slave revolts took place in the first half of the 1800s. In 1831, Nat Turner led a rebellion in which more than 60 white Virginians were killed. Turner was later captured, tried, and executed. Fear of slave revolts led slave states to impose even harsher treatment. New laws made it a crime to teach a slave to read and write.

# Church and State

## TRACK THE ISSUE

### What is the proper relationship between government and religion?

The First Amendment says that government may not establish an official church or interfere with the free exercise of religion. But Americans differ over whether "separation of church and state" is meant to keep government out of religion or religion out of government. Use the timeline below to explore this enduring issue.

**1791 Bill of Rights**
First Amendment bars government involvement in religion.

**1840s Sabbatarian Controversy**
Congress debates whether to ban commerce and mail delivery on Sundays.

**1947 *Everson* v. *Board of Education***
Supreme Court affirms separation of government and religion.

**1984 Federal Equal Access Act**
Law allows students to form religious clubs at public high schools.

**2000 *Mitchell* v. *Helms***
Ruling allows private schools to receive federal funds for educational materials.

A church of the early 1800s

Students pray around a flagpole outside their school.

## DEBATE THE ISSUE

**Should prayer be allowed in public schools?** One controversial topic in the church-state debate is the issue of prayer in public schools. Current law prohibits public-school-sponsored prayers. Some Christians believe this ban violates their right to practice their beliefs.

"We're deeply religious. . . . And we believe that prayer in school is a necessity because, although yes, my children say blessings at home and pray at home and they learn to do that at church, most of their waking hours are spent in school. So why shouldn't they be able to pray, on the intercom, anywhere."
—Pat Mounce, high school parent, Pontotoc, Mississippi

"I'm a Catholic and I hope a devout one, but I think that the public school classroom is no place for me to try and impose my world formula for prayer on children who don't share it, and for that very reason, I don't want my children in a public school classroom to be exposed to someone else's religion or formula."
—Senator Phillip A. Hart, Michigan

### ? TRANSFER Activities

1. **Compare** What views do Mounce and Hart share? On what point do they differ?

2. **Analyze** How do you think each of these two speakers would have reacted to the issue of outlawing commerce on Sunday?

3. **Transfer** Use the following Web site to see a video, try a WebQuest, and write in your journal. **Web Code:** neh-6802

# Three Antislavery Heroes

Today, we take for granted that slavery is wrong. But in the mid-1800s, it took courage to oppose slavery. These three abolitionists took great risks to stand up for their beliefs.

## Harriet Tubman

As a conductor on the Underground Railroad, Harriet Tubman risked enslavement and death every time she returned to the South. Called the Black Moses, Tubman helped so many fugitives escape that slave-owners offered a $40,000 reward for her capture.

## William Lloyd Garrison

William Lloyd Garrison published *The Liberator*, the most influential abolitionist newspaper. In October 1835, a proslavery mob put a rope around his neck and dragged him through the streets of Boston.

## Frederick Douglass

When Frederick Douglass revealed at a public meeting that he had escaped from slavery, he knowingly ran the risk of being recaptured. Here, police break up an antislavery rally where Douglass is speaking.

---

### Thinking Critically

**Contrast** How did Tubman's method of opposing slavery differ from those of Garrison and Douglass?

**History Interactive** ✷

**For:** More about the Underground Railroad
**Web Code:** nep-0213

**Slavery Becomes a Political Issue** Slavery became one of many issues separating the slaveholding South and the northern states, which had gradually done away with slavery. American leaders sought to keep a balance of power between North and South in Congress. The **Missouri Compromise** of 1820 allowed Missouri to enter the Union as a slave state, so long as a free state—Maine—was admitted at the same time. It also set 36°30´N latitude as the dividing line between slave territory and free territory. This compromise worked until the 1840s. But by then, abolitionists had begun to increase the outcry against slavery.

**Abolitionists Call For Freedom** Some leading abolitionists had firsthand knowledge of slavery: they themselves had been born into slavery and ran away to seek freedom in the North. In 1838, **Frederick Douglass** struck out for the North from Maryland. In time, he started an antislavery newspaper and became a powerful speaker at abolitionist meetings. His booming voice filled lecture halls as he recounted the harrowing stories of his cruel master and his daring escape.

Like Douglass, Harriet Tubman had fled from slavery in Maryland. But Tubman returned to the South many times to help others escape. For this she earned the nickname Black Moses, after the biblical figure who led the Jewish people out of bondage. Tubman was one of the many "conductors" on the **Underground Railroad,** a network of abolitionists—white and black—who led enslaved people to freedom in the North or in Canada.

Douglass and Tubman added their efforts to those of a small but increasing number of white abolitionists. In January 1831, Bostonian William Lloyd Garrison began publishing *The Liberator,* which became the most influential abolitionist newspaper. Garrison proclaimed his mission: "I will be as harsh as Truth, and as uncompromising as justice. I am in earnest. I will not equivocate, I will not excuse, I will not retreat a single inch, and I WILL BE HEARD." Unlike most white abolitionists, Garrison called not only for the immediate emancipation of all people held in slavery, but also for full political and social rights for African Americans.

In several northern states, abolitionists faced violent attacks. In Alton, Illinois, an irate crowd killed abolitionist newspaper editor Elijah Lovejoy. Such violence only increased the determination of abolitionists.

 **Checkpoint** How did the goals of the abolitionist movement change over time?

## The Women's Rights Movement

While the abolitionist movement was gaining strength, another reform movement was just beginning. The focus of this movement was the political and legal rights of women.

**Women Have Limited Rights** Under the law, women could not hold office or vote. Married women could not own property in their own name. In the rare instances of divorce, husbands usually gained custody of children. When women began working in factories in the early 1800s, their wages went to their fathers or husbands. In addition, colleges and most professions were closed to women.

Slowly, some restrictions loosened. By the 1840s, a few women's labor unions asked for higher wages and more control over their own wages for women. Some women worked for educational reform. Emma Willard opened the Troy Female Academy in New York to offer women a chance at higher education.

**Women Begin to Organize** Real progress began when women began to take a leading role in the abolitionist movement. In the 1830s, the Philadelphia Female Anti-Slavery Society, an organization of middle-class white and black women, led the movement to gain economic and political rights for both women and African Americans.

### HISTORY MAKERS

**Susan B. Anthony** (1820–1906)
For five decades, Susan B. Anthony led the fight for women's right to vote. Working with close friend Elizabeth Cady Stanton, she tirelessly pushed the cause by traveling, writing, speaking, and organizing. In 1872, she was arrested for casting a ballot in the presidential election. Defiantly, she refused to pay the fine when found guilty.

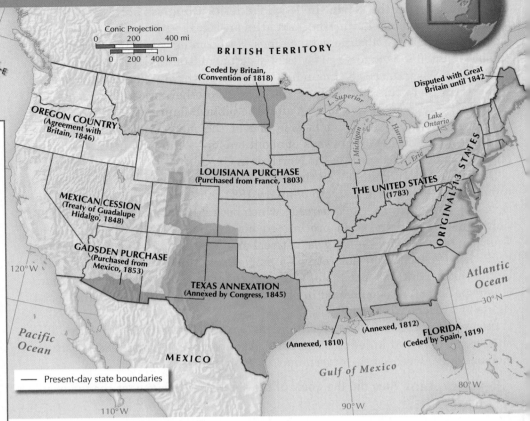

**Map Skills** By 1853, the United States had extended its borders to the Pacific Ocean, achieving the goal of Manifest Destiny.

1. **Locate:** (a) Oregon, (b) Texas, (c) the Mexican Cession, (d) the Pacific Ocean

2. **Regions** What areas did the United States gain as a result of war?

3. **Link Past to Present** Was the state in which you live part of the United States by 1803? By 1853? If so, how was it acquired?

**Geography** *Interactive*
**For:** Interactive map
**Web Code:** nep-0203

Then, in 1848, **Elizabeth Cady Stanton** and Lucretia Mott helped organize the nation's first women's rights convention. Several hundred men and women, black and white, attended this gathering at Seneca Falls, New York. There they drew up a Declaration of Sentiments, modeled after the Declaration of Independence, beginning with the lines, "We hold these truths to be self-evident: that all men and women are created equal." The document goes on to charge:

> **Primary Source** "The history of mankind is a history of repeated injuries and usurpations on the part of man toward woman, having in direct object the establishment of an absolute tyranny over her. . . . He has taken from her all right in property, even to the wages she earns. . . . He has denied her the facilities for obtaining a thorough education."
>
> —Elizabeth Cady Stanton, Declaration of Sentiments

Over the next decades, women's rights leaders such as Stanton and **Susan B. Anthony** worked to achieve greater rights for women. But their ultimate goal—suffrage, or the right to vote—would not be attained in their lifetimes.

✔ **Checkpoint** How did Elizabeth Cady Stanton try to promote women's rights?

## Manifest Destiny

As in colonial times, Americans continued to expand westward. Seeking good farmland, gold, or animal furs—or just to satisfy a sense of adventure—some men crossed the Great Plains to explore the West. They marked out trails that crossed the Rocky Mountains and the Sierra Nevadas. By 1850, St. Louis, Missouri, had become the launching point from which settlers traveled west along the Santa Fe Trail, the Oregon Trail, the Mormon Trail, or the California Trail.

In 1845, journalist John O'Sullivan predicted that it was the nation's "manifest destiny . . . to overspread the continent allotted by Providence for the free development of our yearly multiplying millions." The term **Manifest Destiny** came to stand for the idea that the United States was intended by God to stretch from the Atlantic Ocean all the way to the Pacific Ocean.

**Vocabulary Builder**
manifest—(MAN uh fehst) *adj.* obvious; clear; plain

**Conflict Erupts With Mexico** Westward expansion brought the United States into conflict with Mexico. In the 1820s, the Mexican government encouraged Americans to move into Texas. Many did so, especially southerners with slaves. By the 1830s, these American Texans sought independence from Mexico. In 1836, after a short war against Mexico, they won their independence, and Texas became the Republic of Texas. Suddenly, without having moved, many Mexicans lived in a new country—one in which they often were treated as second-class citizens.

The United States annexed Texas as a state in 1845. The following year, a dispute over the boundary between Texas and Mexico led to the outbreak of war. Some northerners opposed the Mexican-American War, viewing it as an attempt to extend slavery. Still, the United States won a quick victory. In 1848, the Treaty of Guadalupe Hidalgo set the Rio Grande as the southern boundary of Texas. Mexico also agreed to cede an immense expanse of land to the United States, including California and parts of other southwest states.

**Gold Brings Settlers to California** In 1848, gold was discovered in California. Within months, easterners were streaming into California in search of quick riches. These "forty-niners" set up campsites and hastily constructed towns as they staked a claim to a plot of land that they hoped would make them wealthy. The gold rush also attracted emigrants from as far away as China.

In 1850, enough American citizens lived in California that it was able to apply for statehood as a free state. This request would inflame the growing national conflict over slavery.

✔ **Checkpoint** What were the causes and effects of the Mexican-American War?

**Gold Rush**
News about the discovery of gold brought thousands of "forty-niners" like these rushing to California.

---

# SECTION 1 Assessment

**Progress Monitoring *Online***
**For:** Self-test with vocabulary practice
**Web Code:** nea-0204

## Comprehension

1. **Terms and People** Write a sentence explaining how each of the following was connected with reform or the growth of democracy.
   - Andrew Jackson
   - Second Great Awakening
   - civil disobedience
   - abolitionist
   - Frederick Douglass
   - Underground Railroad
   - Elizabeth Cady Stanton
   - Susan B. Anthony

2. **NoteTaking Reading Skill: Identify Main Ideas** Use your outline to answer the Section Focus Question: What trends in democratization and reform were taking shape in the United States by 1850?

## Writing About History

3. **Quick Write: Identify a Viewpoint** Write a paragraph describing one of the two viewpoints on the Nullification Crisis discussed in this section. Be sure to identify the underlying attitude about the nature of federal versus state authority.

## Critical Thinking

4. **Evaluate Information** To what extent did the presidency of Andrew Jackson represent a move toward democratization? How was this trend limited?

5. **Analyze Effects** Describe one direct and one indirect effect of the Second Great Awakening.

6. **Compare and Contrast** How were the abolitionist movement and the women's rights movement similar? How were they different?

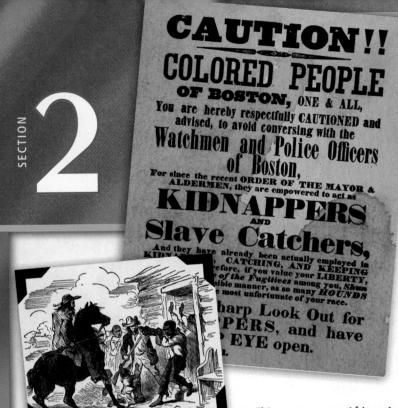

**CAUTION!!**

**COLORED PEOPLE**
OF BOSTON, ONE & ALL,
You are hereby respectfully CAUTIONED and
advised, to avoid conversing with the
**Watchmen and Police Officers**
of Boston,
For since the recent ORDER OF THE MAYOR &
ALDERMEN, they are empowered to act as
**KIDNAPPERS**
AND
**Slave Catchers,**
And they have already been actually employed in
KIDNAPPING, CATCHING, AND KEEPING
......., erefore, if you value your LIBERTY,
.... of the Fugitives among you, Shun
....ible manner, as so many HOUNDS
..... most unfortunate of your race.

....harp Look Out for
....PERS, and have
... EYE open.

▲ This poster warns African Americans in Boston about the
arrival of "slave catchers" like the ones shown at left.

**A Fugitive Escapes**

The Fugitive Slave Law of 1850 made it a crime to
help African Americans escape slavery. But that did
not stop Levi Coffin and his fellow abolitionists from
taking action when slave catchers in Indiana arrested
a fugitive named Louis. Coffin described how Louis
escaped from a public courtroom in broad daylight:

❝[Louis] slipped his chair back a little way. Neither
his master nor the marshal noticed the movement, as
they were intently listening to the judge, and he
slipped his chair again, until he was back of them. . . .
Next he rose quietly to his feet and took a step
backward. Some abolitionist friendly to his cause
gave him an encouraging touch on the foot, and he
stepped farther back. Then a good hat was placed on
his head by some one behind, and he quietly and
cautiously made his way . . . toward the door.❞
—*Reminiscences of Levi Coffin*

# The Union in Crisis

 **Content Expectations**

- **F1.2b** Discuss governmental roles development in U.S. life.
- **F2.1b** Describe regional American economic differences/similarities prior to 1877.
- **F2.1c** Describe changes in size, location, composition of U.S. population prior to 1877.

**Terms and People**

Wilmot Proviso
Free-Soil Party
Compromise of 1850
popular sovereignty
Harriet Beecher Stowe

Kansas-Nebraska Act
*Dred Scott* v. *Sandford*
Abraham Lincoln
John Brown
secede

## NoteTaking

**Reading Skill: Recognize Sequence** As you read, trace the sequence of events that led to the division of the Union.

| 1820: Missouri Compromise keeps balance between slave states and free states |
| --- |

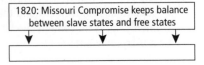

**Why It Matters** Regional differences between the North and South had existed since colonial times. These differences widened in the 1800s as the North developed an industrial economy while the South continued to depend on plantation agriculture and slavery. In time, conflict over the issue of slavery led to an armed struggle that would forever change the nation: the Civil War. **Section Focus Question: How did the issue of slavery divide the Union?**

## Slavery and Western Expansion

After the Mexican-American War, the question of slavery in the West emerged as a major issue. A Pennsylvania congressman proposed the **Wilmot Proviso,** which stated that, though slavery would continue in the South, it would be banned in the territory won from Mexico. The proposal passed the House of Representatives, where northern members held a majority, but was defeated in the Senate, where some northern Democrats opposed the measure.

**New Parties Oppose Slavery** The Wilmot Proviso helped spur the rise of antislavery political parties. In 1848, the **Free-Soil Party** nominated former President Martin Van Buren for President. Although Van Buren did not win, he and other Free-Soil candidates garnered enough votes to show that the party's motto of "free soil, free speech, free labor, and free men" would not easily be silenced.

**Congress Tries to Compromise** In 1850, California applied to enter the Union as a free state, thus threatening the balance between slave and free states in Congress. To ease southern concerns, Congress passed what became known as the **Compromise of 1850.** According to this measure, California was admitted as a free state. In the rest of the territory acquired from Mexico, voters would decide for themselves whether or not to allow slavery. This approach became known as **popular sovereignty.** By permitting slavery north of 36°30′N latitude, the Compromise of 1850 undid the Missouri Compromise.

Another provision of the Compromise of 1850, the Fugitive Slave Act, required citizens to help apprehend runaway slaves. Northern opponents of the law mounted an <u>intense</u> and disruptive resistance. In 1851, at Christiana, Pennsylvania, a small band of African Americans gathered to protect several runaways from southern slave catchers. Local white bystanders not only refused to help the slave-hunting party but, when the slave owner died in the scuffle, a white jury refused to convict the killers. In other northern cities, white and black opponents found nonviolent ways to defy the hated law.

✔ **Checkpoint** How did the Compromise of 1850 lead to conflict between the North and South?

## The Road to Disunion

Resentment against the Fugitive Slave Act spurred **Harriet Beecher Stowe** to write the antislavery novel *Uncle Tom's Cabin.* Southerners argued that Stowe presented a false picture of slavery and the South. But the novel became a best-seller in the North, increasing opposition to slavery.

**Violence Erupts in Kansas** In 1854, Congress again tried to settle the issue of slavery in the West by passing the **Kansas-Nebraska Act,** which divided the Nebraska Territory into Kansas and Nebraska. Voters in each territory would decide the issue of slavery by popular sovereignty. Many northerners complained that this plan allowed slavery in areas where it had been banned by the Missouri Compromise.

Soon, both proslavery and antislavery settlers were flocking to Kansas, each hoping to outnumber the other when the time came to vote on slavery. By 1856, Kansas had two governments, one proslavery, the other antislavery. For several months there was so much violence between the two sides that the territory became known as "Bleeding Kansas." Finally, in 1861, Kansas entered the Union as a free state.

**The Republican Party Emerges** The election of 1856 pitted Democrat James Buchanan against John C. Frémont, candidate of the new Republican Party. Like the earlier Free-Soil Party, the Republican Party opposed the extension of slavery into the western territories. Republicans included abolitionists who believed slavery was immoral, business leaders who felt that slavery stifled industry, and northerners who argued that the Fugitive Slave Act intruded into state politics.

**Bleeding Kansas**

In the dispute over slavery in Kansas, both sides turned to violence. Below, proslavery raiders attack settlers who oppose slavery.

**MI** F1.2c

## TRACK THE ISSUE

### THE ESSENTIAL ? How much power should the federal government have?

Under the Constitution, all powers not granted to the federal government belong to the states. Over time, however, the federal government has expanded its scope, especially in the area of social programs. Use the timeline below to explore this enduring issue.

### 1791 Bill of Rights
Tenth Amendment reserves most powers to the states.

### 1798 Kentucky and Virginia Resolutions
States argue that they can void federal legislation.

### 1831 Nullification Crisis
John C. Calhoun declares that states may overturn federal laws.

### 1857 *Dred Scott* v. *Sandford*
Supreme Court rules that federal government does not have power to outlaw slavery within territories.

### 1930s New Deal
Government expands power over economy and social services.

### 1965 Voting Rights Act
Law allows federal officers to register voters.

Dred Scott

Exhaust and waste gases from cars are just one of the many issues in the center of the continuing national debate about the environment.

## DEBATE THE ISSUE

**The Environment and States' Rights** Since 1967, the Environmental Protection Agency (EPA) allowed California to make its own emissions rules. California is exempt from the Clean Air Acts as long as its rules are stricter than those of the Federal Government and it obtains a waiver from the federal government. In November 2007, Governor Arnold Schwarzenegger sued the Federal Government because the EPA denied California a waiver.

> "The authority of the States to address greenhouse gas emissions from motor vehicles has been supported—by the Supreme Court [and] by a federal court here in California. On this issue, the . . . EPA . . . has failed to follow the States' lead . . . we are prepared to force it out of the way . . . to protect the environment."
> —Governor Arnold Schwarzenegger, April 2, 2008

> "I believe that Congress by passing a . . . federal standard of 35 mpg (miles per gallon) delivers significant reductions that are more effective than a state-by-state approach. This applies to all 50 states. . . . and that's great for the economy, for national security, and for the environment."
> —Stephen L. Johnson, EPA Administrator

### ? TRANSFER Activities
1. **Compare** Why does Governor Schwarzenegger feel California should oppose the federal government? Why does Stephen Johnson disagree?
2. **Analyze** Should a state have the right to determine its own environmental standards?
3. **Transfer** Use the following Web site to see a video, try a WebQuest, and write in your journal. **Web Code:** neh-7002

Buchanan won the election. But Frémont's strong showing underscored the importance of the slavery issue and the growing appeal of the new party.

**The Dred Scott Decision Inflames the Nation** In 1857, a Supreme Court decision widened the growing divisions over slavery. Dred Scott, an enslaved African American from Missouri, had sued for his freedom, based on the fact that he had traveled with his master into free territory.

In **Dred Scott v. Sandford,** the Court made a sweeping ruling that went far beyond the particulars of Scott's case. The Court declared that African Americans were not citizens, and therefore were not entitled to sue in the courts. Furthermore, the Court ruled that the federal government did not have the power to ban slavery in any territory and that the Missouri Compromise was unconstitutional, since it could deprive citizens of their property without due process of law. Southerners were delighted with the Dred Scott decision, but northerners were outraged.

**Lincoln Debates Douglas** The 1858 Senate race in Illinois crystallized the slavery issue for many Americans. At a series of debates, Republican **Abraham Lincoln** challenged Democrat Stephen Douglas, architect of the Kansas-Nebraska Act. Lincoln did not call for the immediate abolition of slavery, nor for political equality for African Americans. Still, he argued:

> **Primary Source** "There is no reason in the world why the negro is not entitled to all the natural rights enumerated in the Declaration of Independence, the right to life, liberty and the pursuit of happiness. . . . In the right to eat the bread, without leave of anybody else, which his own hand earns, he is my equal and the equal of Judge Douglas, and the equal of every living man."
> —Abraham Lincoln, debate at Ottawa, Illinois

Douglas continued to champion popular sovereignty. "This Union was established on the right of each State to do as it pleased on the question of slavery, and every other question," he insisted. Douglas won the senate race, but the debates helped Lincoln win national attention.

**John Brown Plans a Revolt** In 1859, a violent attack on slavery occurred in northern Virginia. In the fall of 1859, white abolitionist **John Brown** led a small band of white and black followers in an attempt to seize a federal arsenal in Harpers Ferry, Virginia (now in West Virginia). He hoped to inspire local enslaved African Americans to join a revolution that would destroy slavery in the South. Brown's plan failed.

Put on trial for treason, Brown proclaimed his willingness to "mingle my blood . . . with the blood of millions in this slave country whose rights are disregarded by wicked, cruel, and unjust enactments." In the eyes of many abolitionists, Brown's defense of his actions and the dignified calm with which he faced execution made him a heroic martyr to the antislavery cause. Northern support for Brown further inflamed southern anger.

✔ **Checkpoint** How did northerners and southerners react to the Dred Scott decision?

### HISTORY MAKERS

**Abraham Lincoln** (1809–1865)
Born in a log cabin to a struggling farmer, Abraham Lincoln had little formal education. "When I came of age I did not know much," he later wrote. "I could read, write, and cipher . . . but that was all. I have not been to school since." Still, he developed a thirst for learning, eventually gaining enough knowledge to practice law and enter politics. He was elected to the Illinois state legislature four times and, in 1846, was elected to the U.S. House of Representatives. While in Congress, he spoke out against the Mexican-American War—an unpopular position that cost him reelection. Ten years later, he joined the newly formed Republican Party.

# The Election of 1860

"We believe that this election is a turning-point in our history." So wrote poet James Russell Lowell a month before the presidential election of 1860. In fact, he was right. The victory of Abraham Lincoln literally split the nation in two.

▲ This 1860 cartoon shows Lincoln and Douglas (left) fighting over slavery in the West. While Breckinridge (center) tears off the South, Bell (right) vainly tries to glue the Union back together.

The issue of slavery was so divisive in 1860 that the Democratic Party nominated different candidates in the North and South. As the map and chart show, each of the four presidential candidates won support in a different region. ▼

Lincoln campaign banner ▼

FOR PRESIDENT, ABRAHAM LINCO

VICE PRESIDENT, HANNIBAL HAM

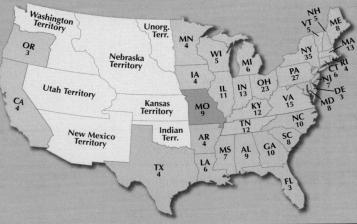

| Candidate (Party) | Electoral Vote | Popular Vote | % Electoral Vote | % Popular Vote |
|---|---|---|---|---|
| ☐ Abraham Lincoln (Republican) | 180 | 1,866,452 | 59 | 40 |
| ☐ John C. Breckinridge (Southern-Democratic) | 72 | 847,953 | 24 | 18 |
| ☐ Stephen A. Douglas (Democratic) | 12 | 1,380,202 | 4 | 29 |
| ☐ John Bell (Constitutional Union) | 39 | 590,901 | 13 | 13 |

## Thinking Critically

1. **Analyze a Map** Which party won nearly all the northern states?

2. **Synthesize Information** Does the cartoon accurately reflect the information given on the map? Explain.

# Lincoln, Secession, and War

Brown's execution and the Dred Scott decision were still fresh in voters' minds as the 1860 presidential elections approached. Meeting in Chicago, the Republican Party adopted a platform that affirmed the Wilmot Proviso and the authority of Congress to ban slavery in the territories.

**The Election Fragments the Nation** Republicans saw Abraham Lincoln, with his reputation for integrity, as the ideal candidate to carry their platform to victory. Around the country, newspapers had publicized Lincoln's positions—his objections to slavery, and his defense of the West as a land of opportunity for free white men. Meanwhile, the Democratic Party fractured over the slavery issue. Northern Democrats nominated Stephen Douglas, while Southern Democrats nominated John Breckinridge. A fourth candidate, John Bell, represented a small moderate coalition who wanted to keep the Union together.

Benefiting from the Democrat split, Lincoln easily won the election, carrying 18 northern and western free states. He ended up with only 40 percent of the popular vote but almost 60 percent of the electoral vote, even though he did not receive a single southern electoral vote.

**The South Secedes** To southerners, the election was a clear sign that the more populous free states were now in a position to control national politics. On December 20, 1860, a convention in South Carolina declared that "the union now subsisting between South Carolina and the other States . . . is hereby dissolved." South Carolina thus became the first state to **secede,** or break away, from the Union.

Six other states soon joined South Carolina to establish the Confederate States of America. They framed a constitution modeled on the U.S. Constitution but with some important differences. First, the Confederate constitution stressed the independence of each state, implying that states had the right to secede. Second, the new constitution guaranteed the protection of slavery. In time, four additional states joined the Confederacy.

**War Begins at Fort Sumter** At first, Lincoln insisted he had no authority to force Confederate states to return to the Union. Then, the Confederacy began to seize federal military bases in southern states. When Fort Sumter, in the harbor of Charleston, South Carolina, ran short of supplies, Lincoln notified the Confederacy that he was sending food but no armaments. Confederates decided to try to seize the fort before provisions could arrive.

On April 11, 1861, Confederate troops demanded that Union troops give up Fort Sumter. When the commander refused, the Confederates fired on the fort. After heavy bombardment, the federal troops surrendered. The fall of Fort Sumter marked the start of the Civil War, a four-year struggle that threatened to bring the Union to a bloody end.

✔ **Checkpoint** How did the election of 1860 split the nation in two?

### Fort Sumter Flag
The tattered Union flag shown below was flying over Fort Sumter when Confederate troops fired on the fort.

---

**Progress Monitoring *Online***
**For:** Self-test with vocabulary practice
**Web Code:** nea-0206

## Comprehension
1. **Terms and People** Write a sentence explaining how each of the following was connected with the growing rift between North and South.
   - Wilmot Proviso
   - Free-Soil Party
   - Compromise of 1850
   - popular sovereignty
   - Kansas-Nebraska Act
   - *Dred Scott* v. *Sandford*
   - Abraham Lincoln
   - John Brown
   - secede

2. **NoteTaking Reading Skill: Recognize Sequence** Use your flowchart to answer the Section Focus Question: How did the issue of slavery divide the Union?

## Writing About History
3. **Quick Write: State a Point of View** Write a paragraph defining a viewpoint on the following issue: Should states have the right to secede from the Union? Give one argument someone might use to support that viewpoint.

## Critical Thinking
4. **Draw Inferences** Why do you think southerners in Congress insisted on the passage of a Fugitive Slave Act? Why did many northerners oppose it?

5. **Analyze Information** Why was the *Dred Scott* decision a blow to those who opposed the extension of slavery?

6. **Draw Conclusions** Do you think the issue of slavery could have been settled without war? Why or why not?

SECTION
**3**

**WITNESS HISTORY** 🔊 AUDIO

### The Battle of Gettysburg: A Soldier's Story

On July 1, 1863, the Battle of Gettysburg began. The Union victory on July 3 ended General Lee's invasion of the North and was a turning point in the Civil War. A 22-year-old lieutenant from New York described the Battle of Little Round Top:

❝As we reached the crest a never to be forgotten scene burst upon us. A great basin lay before us full of smoke and fire, and literally swarming with riderless horses and fighting, fleeing and pursuing men. The air was saturated with the sulphurous fumes of battle and was ringing with the shouts and groans of the combatants. The wild cries of charging lines, the rattle of musketry, the booming of artillery and the shrieks of the wounded were the orchestral accompaniments of a scene like very hell itself. . . . But fascinating as was this terrible scene we had no time to spend upon it. Bloody work was ready for us at our very feet.❞

—Lieutenant Porter Farley, 140th New York Infantry,
Weed's Brigade

▲ Civil War soldier and gear

# The Civil War

 **Content Expectations**

- **F1.2a** Discuss republican government birth, rule of law, inalienable rights, equality, limited government.
- **F1.2b** Discuss governmental roles development in U.S. life.
- **F2.1c** Describe changes in size, location, composition of U.S. population prior to 1877.

### Terms and People

| | |
|---|---|
| Robert E. Lee | Ulysses S. Grant |
| Anaconda Plan | Battle of Gettysburg |
| Emancipation | Gettysburg Address |
|   Proclamation | William T. Sherman |
| habeas corpus | total war |
| inflation | |

### NoteTaking

**Reading Skill: Recognize Sequence** As you read, identify the events and developments that led to the final Union victory in the Civil War.

**Why It Matters** With the election of Lincoln, the slavery issue that had long divided North from South finally split the nation in two. From April 1861 to April 1865, the United States of America and the Confederate States of America faced each other in the bloody Civil War. At stake was the future not only of slavery but of the Union itself. **Section Focus Question: What factors and events led to the Union victory in the Civil War?**

## Resources, Strategies, and Early Battles

As the Civil War began, each side had a clear goal. The North was determined to preserve the Union, arguing that no state had the right to secede. The southern states who formed the Confederacy aimed to gain their independence from a Union that they felt had become hostile to their interests, especially slavery.

**Advantages and Disadvantages** Although each side faced challenges, a variety of factors favored the Union. In the Northeast, growing urban populations supported a wide range of manufacturing. Replenished by a continuing influx of immigrant workers from Europe, northern factories were able to increase production of the supplies needed to wage war: ammunition, arms, uniforms, medical supplies, food, ships, and railroad cars.

Across the North, the railroad network was well developed, as were systems for farming, mining, and processing raw materials. Banking, insurance, and financing industries were also clustered in the urbanized North. The federal government had a well-organized navy. By the end of 1861, the Union navy had outfitted and launched more than 250 warships and was constructing dozens more. Naval superiority allowed the Union to blockade the South's few vital ports.

Given such advantages, northerners <u>anticipated</u> a quick victory. But the North had distinct disadvantages as well. When the war began, the Union army consisted of only about 16,000 men. Although the South had an even smaller army, its troops at the outset of the war were generally more highly committed to the fight. In addition, some of the nation's finest military leaders were from the South. The experienced and inspiring **Robert E. Lee** had originally been offered command of Union forces but chose instead to remain loyal to his native Virginia. Throughout the war, General Lee provided the Confederacy with expert military leadership. The North struggled for much of the war to find a commander of comparable skill and daring.

**North and South Develop Their Strategies**  Each side had a clear military goal. Here, again, the South enjoyed an advantage. The Confederacy simply had to survive, keeping their armies in the field until northerners became tired of fighting. The Union, however, had to crush and conquer the Confederacy.

The North adopted a strategy designed to starve the South into submission. It was called the **Anaconda Plan** after the snake that slowly squeezes its prey to death. The plan involved seizing the Mississippi River and the Gulf of Mexico so that the South could not send or receive shipments. By the middle of 1862, with victories in Mississippi and New Orleans, the North had captured the Mississippi Valley. Union soldiers also seized the strategic railroad juncture at Chattanooga, Tennessee, and scored victories in battles as far west as New Mexico.

**Vocabulary Builder**
anticipate–(an TIHS uh payt) *v.* to expect; to look forward to

**A Confederate Victory**
Two major Civil War battles took place at Bull Run, a creek in Virginia. Both were Confederate victories. The painting below depicts the Second Battle of Bull Run (known in the South as the Second Battle of Manassas.) *What advantages might the Confederates have had at Bull Run?*

**A Stalemate Develops** On the east coast, though both sides won battles, neither side could gain a clear and decisive victory in the early part of the war. Union armies hoped to capture the Confederate capital of Richmond, Virginia. But troops outside Washington, D.C., could not seem to make progress toward that goal. Confederate troops were equally unsuccessful in pushing the war north toward Washington, D.C.

Thanks to efficient new weapons—especially more accurate rifles and deadlier bullets—a single day's battle might produce more than 10,000 casualties. This new lethal warfare stung the public consciousness. Battle sites such as Bull Run (July 1861), Shiloh (April 1862), Antietam (September 1862), and Fredericksburg (December 1862) are still remembered as the scenes of some of the deadliest encounters in American history. Limited medical care ensured that many of the wounded died of infection rather than of the wounds themselves.

**✓ Checkpoint** What advantages did the Union enjoy as the Civil War began?

## Lincoln Proclaims Emancipation

Early in the war, President Lincoln insisted that he did not have the authority to end slavery. In his public statements, he <u>emphasized</u> the fact that his chief goal was to preserve the Union. Although Lincoln personally opposed slavery, he did not want to lose the support of the four slave states—Maryland, Delaware, Kentucky, and Missouri—that had remained loyal to the Union.

However, by the autumn of 1862, Lincoln decided that he did, indeed, have the authority to proclaim the end of slavery, and that as a "practical war measure" he wished to do so. In January 1863, he issued the **Emancipation Proclamation.** This presidential decree declared that "all persons held as slaves within any State or designated part of a State, the people whereof shall then be in rebellion against the United States, shall be then, thenceforward, and forever free."

The Emancipation Proclamation did not apply to the loyal slave states or to those areas of the South already under Union control. As a result, it did not immediately free a single slave. Nevertheless, it was an important turning point because it encouraged enslaved African Americans in the South to run away to Union army encampments and to aid the Union cause. It also symbolically redefined the war as being "about slavery."

African Americans had always believed that the war should be about slavery, and they had volunteered to fight as soon as the war began. But at first they were turned away and told "this is a white man's war." After the Emancipation Proclamation, however, the Union began to actively recruit both free blacks from the North and newly freed African Americans from the South. Eventually, some 180,000 African American men served in the Union Army.

**✓ Checkpoint** What was the impact of the Emancipation Proclamation?

## War Affects Daily Life

The Civil War transformed the nation's civilian life. In the North, mines and factories stepped up production to supply military needs such as ships, railroads, weapons, uniforms, provisions, and fuel. To pay for the war, the federal government raised tariffs, imposed income taxes, and printed money. Congress also encouraged western settlement and offered free land to soldiers who would give two years of military service. Such land grants sparked agricultural growth, which helped feed Union troops.

**Vocabulary Builder**
<u>emphasize</u>–(EHM fuh sīz) *v.* to stress; to give special attention or importance

## NoteTaking

**Reading Skills: Compare and Contrast** As you read, note effects of the war on the North and South.

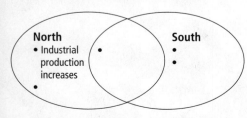

North
• Industrial production increases
•

South
•
•

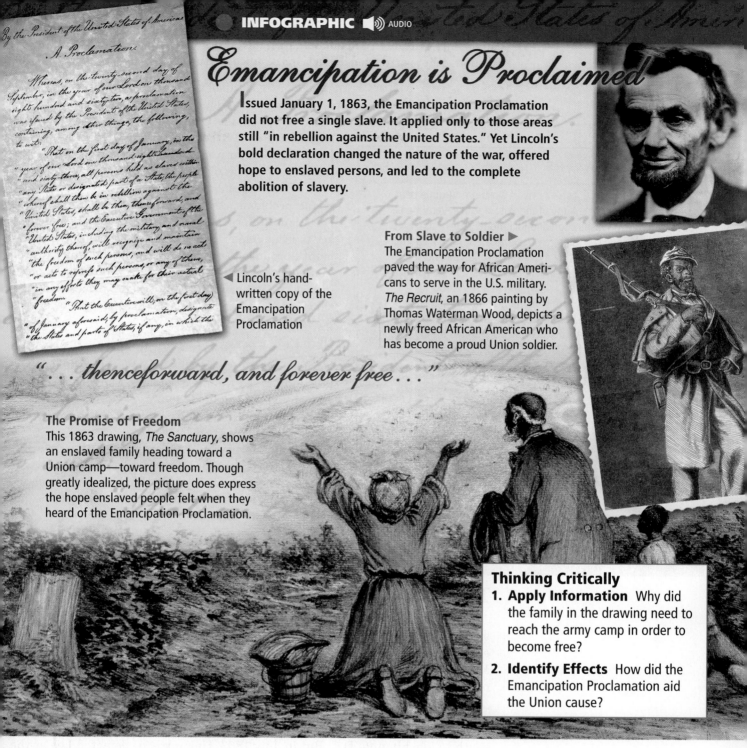

# Emancipation is Proclaimed

Issued January 1, 1863, the Emancipation Proclamation did not free a single slave. It applied only to those areas still "in rebellion against the United States." Yet Lincoln's bold declaration changed the nature of the war, offered hope to enslaved persons, and led to the complete abolition of slavery.

◄ Lincoln's hand-written copy of the Emancipation Proclamation

**From Slave to Soldier ▶**
The Emancipation Proclamation paved the way for African Americans to serve in the U.S. military. *The Recruit*, an 1866 painting by Thomas Waterman Wood, depicts a newly freed African American who has become a proud Union soldier.

*" . . . thenceforward, and forever free . . ."*

**The Promise of Freedom**
This 1863 drawing, *The Sanctuary*, shows an enslaved family heading toward a Union camp—toward freedom. Though greatly idealized, the picture does express the hope enslaved people felt when they heard of the Emancipation Proclamation.

**Thinking Critically**
1. **Apply Information** Why did the family in the drawing need to reach the army camp in order to become free?
2. **Identify Effects** How did the Emancipation Proclamation aid the Union cause?

**The North Faces Problems** As the war dragged on, the Union army experienced a shortage of volunteers. When Congress passed a draft law in 1863, requiring all able-bodied men between the ages of 20 and 45 to serve in the military if called, riots broke out in several northern cities. The most severe rioting took place in New York City in July 1863. White workers attacked free African Americans as well as wealthy New Yorkers who were able to pay a fee to avoid military service.

Some Northerners opposed Lincoln's conduct of the war and demanded immediate peace. To deal with dissent, Lincoln suspended the Constitutional right of **habeas corpus,** which guarantees that no one can be held in prison without specific charges being filed. Union troops arrested many people suspected of disloyalty. Although Lincoln felt such measures were necessary to preserve the Union, others criticized his actions as unconstitutional.

**The South Suffers Hardships** Almost all of the battles took place on southern soil. The fighting destroyed some of the South's traditional strengths, such as large-scale agriculture, and stripped the Confederacy of the resources it might have used to rebuild. By 1863, the Union plan to starve the South into submission seemed to be on the verge of succeeding.

The South seized every opportunity to ease its economic problems. As Lincoln had done, Confederate President Jefferson Davis authorized the Confederacy to issue paper money, backed only by the government's promise to pay. Doubts about the true value of Confederate money led to severe **inflation,** or price increases. The combination of rising prices and food shortages sparked food riots in some parts of the South.

**War Leads to Social Change** On both sides, the war gave women new tasks. Women set up field hospitals and nursed wounded soldiers. Many Confederate women took to the fields to harvest crops. White and black teachers from the North went south to become teachers of newly freed slaves.

Churches in both the North and South supported the war effort. Confederate soldiers often held revival meetings near the field of battle. One Virginia chaplain claimed that many southern men "have come out of this war Christian soldiers."

## HISTORY MAKERS

In May 1864, Robert E. Lee's Army of Northern Virginia beat back Ulysses S. Grant's Army of the Potomac in several fierce battles between Washington and Richmond. After each fight, Grant sidestepped Lee to march closer to the southern capital. However, as the Union army moved, Lee followed and set up strong defensive positions, which forced Grant to attack. In a month's time, the two armies suffered nearly 70,000 combined casualties. By late summer, the bloody contest between Grant and Lee had settled into a siege at Petersburg, south of Richmond. In April 1865, Lee abandoned the city and eventually surrendered to Grant.

**Ulysses S. Grant**
(1822–1885)

**Robert E. Lee**
(1807–1870)

✔ **Checkpoint** How did the Civil War affect the economies of the North and South?

# The Union Prevails

In the summer of 1863, the Union succeeded in capturing Vicksburg, Mississippi. Advancing from the Louisiana side of the Mississippi River, Union General **Ulysses S. Grant** scored five victories in three weeks, ending with the surrender of 30,000 Confederate troops. The Anaconda Plan had achieved one of its major goals: Confederate territory was split apart.

**The Union Wins a Victory at Gettysburg** Meanwhile, in the East, General Lee marched into Pennsylvania. He hoped to win a surprise victory, then swing south to Washington, D.C. But in July 1863, Union troops defeated Lee at the town of Gettysburg. The **Battle of Gettysburg** destroyed one third of Lee's forces and marked the last major Confederate attempt to invade the North.

A few months later, the President went to Gettysburg to help dedicate a battle cemetery. In a speech known as the **Gettysburg Address,** Lincoln used the occasion to reaffirm the ideas for which the Union was fighting:

> **Primary Source** "We here highly resolve that these dead shall not have died in vain—that this nation, under God, shall have a new birth of freedom—and that government of the people, by the people, for the people, shall not perish from the earth."
>
> —Abraham Lincoln, *Gettysburg Address,* November 19, 1863

**Geography** *Interactive*

**For:** Interactive map
**Web Code:** nep-0207

CANADA

Union victory
Confederate victory
Union naval blockade
Sherman's March

Lake Superior

Montana
Territory

Dakota Territory

MN

WI

MI

Lake Huron

L. Ontario

ME

VT

NH

NY

MA

CT

RI

St. Lawrence R.

Lake Michigan

Lake Erie

40° N

Nebraska
Territory

IA

PA

Gettysburg (July 1863)

NJ

Antietam (Sept. 1862)

MD

Washington, D.C.

DE

Utah
Territory

Colorado
Territory

IL

IN

OH

Bull Run (July 1861)

Fredericksburg (Dec. 1862)

Chancellorsville (May 1863)

VA

Seven Days (June 1862)

KS

MO

KY

Richmond

Colorado R.

Arizona
Territory

Santa Fe

Glorieta Pass
(March 1862)

New Mexico
Territory

Indian Territory

Fort Henry (Feb. 1862)

Fort Donelson (Feb. 1862)

NC

Pea Ridge
(March 1862)

Shiloh (April 1862)

TN

Picacho Pass
(April 1862)

Valverde
(Feb. 1862)

AR

Corinth (May 1862)

Atlanta (Sept. 1864)

SC

Tucson

MS

AL

GA

Atlantic
Ocean

Mississippi R.

Vicksburg
(Nov. 1862–July 1863)

Rio Grande

LA

30° N

TX

FL

New Orleans

New Orleans
(April 1862)

MEXICO

Gulf of Mexico

Conic Projection

0        200        400 mi

0        200        400 km

90° W

80° W

## Map Skills

The Civil War split the nation into two opposing countries. Although most of the fighting took place on Confederate land, some fighting extended north into Pennsylvania or as far west as Arizona.

1. **Locate:** (a) Gettysburg, (b) Vicksburg, (c) Richmond, (d) Washington, D.C.

2. **Regions** How would northern control of the Mississippi River affect the Confederacy?

3. **Draw Conclusions** Describe the Union naval blockade. What do you think was its goal?

### A Nation Divided, 1865

Washington
Territory

Montana
Territory

NH

VT

ME

OR

Idaho
Territory

Dakota Territory

MN

WI

MI

NY

MA

CT RI

NV

Utah
Territory

Colorado
Territory

Nebraska
Territory

IA

IL

IN

OH

PA

NJ

DE

CA

KS

MO

KY

WV

VA

MD

Arizona
Territory

New
Mexico
Territory

Indian
Territory

AR

TN

NC

SC

TX

MS

AL

GA

LA

FL

Union state
Confederate state
Territory

**The War Ends** In the fall of 1864, Union General **William T. Sherman** led more than 60,000 troops on a 400-mile march of destruction through Georgia and South Carolina. The march was part of a strategy of **total war,** which targeted not only troops but all of the resources needed to feed, clothe, and support an army. Sherman's troops burned crops in fields, tore up railroad tracks, and destroyed homes, plantations, and public buildings.

By spring 1865, the Confederacy was exhausted. Union troops captured the Confederate capital. On April 9, in the small Virginia town of Appomattox Court House, Lee surrendered to Grant.

**The Civil War Has Lasting Impact** The Civil War ushered in the harsh reality of modern warfare. More than one third of northern and southern soldiers were killed or disabled.

The southern landscape and economy were in shambles. Millions of dislocated southerners drifted north in search of new lives in Illinois, Indiana, Missouri, or other points north. Others joined the increasing migration to the West, becoming cowboys or farmers. For African Americans in the South, freedom promised them new opportunities, including a chance to work for wages and to control their own lives. Some joined the migration to the North and West.

The war ended an era in American political life. Although debates about states' rights and federal authority continue to this day, never again would states attempt to secede. More and more, Americans would see themselves not just as citizens of a state, but of a united nation.

✔ **Checkpoint** What were the goals and effects of the Union strategy of total war?

| Civil War Casualties, 1861–1865 | | | | | |
| --- | --- | --- | --- | --- | --- |
| | Total Forces | Wounded | Battle Deaths | Other Deaths in Service | Total Deaths |
| Union | 2,213,363 | 280,040 | 140,414 | 224,097 | 364,511 |
| Confederate | 1,050,000 | 226,000 | 94,000 | 166,000 | 260,000 |
| SOURCES: U.S. Department of Veterans Affairs; *Encyclopedia of the Confederacy* | | | | | |

**The Deadly Toll of War**
The Civil War was the deadliest military conflict in American history. *Why do you think a higher percentage of American troops died in the Civil War than in any other war?*

**Progress Monitoring *Online***
**For:** Self-test with vocabulary practice
**Web Code:** nea-0208

**Comprehension**

**1. Terms and People** For each item below, write a sentence explaining how it was connected with the course and outcome of the Civil War.
- Robert E. Lee
- Anaconda Plan
- Emancipation Proclamation
- habeas corpus
- Ulysses S. Grant
- Battle of Gettysburg
- Gettysburg Address
- William T. Sherman
- total war

**2. NoteTaking**  **Reading Skill: Recognize Sequence** Use your timeline to answer the Section Focus Question: What factors and events led to the Union victory in the Civil War?

**Writing About History**

**3. Quick Write: Prioritize Arguments** List three arguments in favor of or against Lincoln freeing all enslaved African Americans as soon as the war began. Then, order the three arguments from most important to least important.

**Critical Thinking**

**4. Recognize Causes and Effects** What impact did the economic differences between the North and South have on the course of the Civil War?

**5. Draw Inferences** How do you think the Anaconda Plan and Sherman's march affected southerners psychologically?

**6. Predict Consequences** List three challenges that African Americans in the South might face after emancipation from slavery.

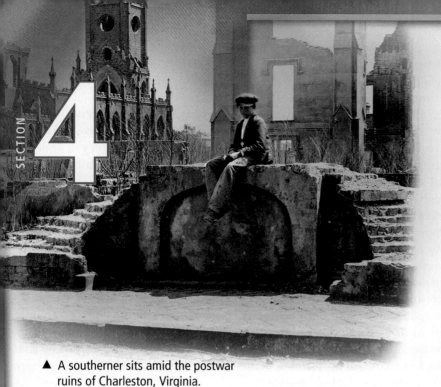

▲ A southerner sits amid the postwar ruins of Charleston, Virginia.

### The Devastated South

Mary Chesnut was the wife of a wealthy and respected South Carolina planter and politician. Now, at war's end, the family was penniless. The world they had known was gone. Chesnut described the devastation:

❝Mrs. Bartow drove me to our house at Mulberry. On one side of the house, every window was broken, every bell torn down, every piece of furniture destroyed, every door smashed in. . . . [The Yankee soldiers] carried off sacks of our books and our papers, our letters were strewed along the Charleston road. Potter's raid ruined us. He burned our mills and gins, and a hundred bales of cotton. Indeed nothing is left now but the bare land.❞

—Mary Boykin Chesnut, *A Diary From Dixie*

# The Reconstruction Era

 **Content Expectations**

- **F1.1e** Analyze American society ideals reflected in 13th, 14th, 15th Amendments.
- **F2.1e** Describe development of U.S. cities prior to 1877.
- **F2.1f** Describe changes in U.S. commerce, transportation, communication prior to 1877.

### Terms and People

| | |
|---|---|
| Reconstruction | impeachment |
| Freedmen's Bureau | Fourteenth Amendment |
| Andrew Johnson | Fifteenth Amendment |
| Thirteenth Amendment | Ku Klux Klan |
| Radical Republican | de jure segregation |

## NoteTaking

**Reading Skill: Categorize** As you read, identify the political, social, and economic aspects of Reconstruction.

| Political | Social | Economic |
|---|---|---|
| • Radical Republicans clash with President | • | • Sharecropping develops |
| • | | • |

**Why It Matters** The Civil War ended in April 1865 with the Union victorious. Now, North and South faced the challenge of reunion. Political decisions made in the next decades helped shape the modern South. And constitutional amendments passed during this period redefined American notions of citizenship and civil rights. **Section Focus Question: What were the immediate and long-term effects of Reconstruction?**

## The Nation Moves Toward Reunion

Even while the war was in progress, Union politicians had been debating ways to achieve **Reconstruction,** bringing the South back into the Union. For President Lincoln, the major goal was to reunify the nation—in the words of his Second Inaugural Address, to "bind up the nation's wounds." But some congressional leaders favored a harsh Reconstruction plan designed to punish the South.

**The Freedmen's Bureau Aids Southerners** Shortly before the war ended, Lincoln and Congress did agree on the creation of the **Freedmen's Bureau,** a federal agency designed to aid freed slaves and relieve the South's immediate needs. The black and white agents of the Bureau delivered food and healthcare and began to develop a public school system for both black and white southerners. It also helped to reunite families separated by slavery and to negotiate fair labor contracts between formerly enslaved African Americans and white landowners.

**President and Congress Clash** Meanwhile, debate over Reconstruction continued. Before he could gain support for his moderate plan, Abraham Lincoln was assassinated on April 14, 1865. As the nation mourned, Vice President **Andrew Johnson** became President.

Johnson favored a plan that restored political power to southerners if they merely swore allegiance to the United States. Under Johnson's plan, the South also had to accept the **Thirteenth Amendment,** which ended slavery in 1865. In return, the new President promised to uphold states' rights, with the laws of individual states taking precedence over federal regulations.

Many congressmen disagreed. Arguing that southerners had caused the war, these **Radical Republicans** favored punishment and harsh reorganization for the South. Radicals also advocated full citizens' rights for African Americans and wanted states' authority to be subordinate to federal power. When southern legislatures passed laws to restrict the activities of African Americans, Radicals became even more determined to impose a harsh Reconstruction policy on the South.

Johnson and the Radicals in Congress clashed repeatedly. In 1868, Congress voted to impeach Johnson. **Impeachment** is the act of bringing charges against an official in order to determine whether he or she should be removed from office. The Senate narrowly voted not to remove Johnson from office, but by that time he had lost control of Reconstruction. A few months later, Civil War hero Ulysses S. Grant was elected President.

 **Checkpoint** What were the Reconstruction goals of the Radical Republicans?

## The Reconstruction South

With Congress firmly under their control, Radical Republicans designed a sweeping Reconstruction plan. They divided the South into five military districts under the command of Union generals. As a condition of readmission to the Union, all southern states were required to grant the vote to African American men. Perhaps most important, Radicals passed the **Fourteenth Amendment,** which guaranteed full citizenship status and rights to every person born in the United States, including African Americans. The Amendment was ratified in 1868.

**African Americans Gain Political Rights** Under Radical Reconstruction, many white southerners were not eligible to vote or chose to stay away from the polls. African American men, on the other hand, eagerly signed up to exercise their new right of suffrage. Thus, by 1868, many southern states had black elected officials and were dominated by a strong Republican Party. South Carolina—the first state to secede—became the only state where, for a short time, an African American majority dominated the legislature.

At this time, no laws guaranteed the vote to African Americans in the North. To remedy this imbalance, Congress passed the **Fifteenth Amendment,** which guaranteed that no male citizen could be denied the right to vote on the basis of "race, color, or previous condition of servitude." It was ratified in 1870.

**Freedmen Rebuild Their Lives** In the South, formerly enslaved African Americans worked to carve out new lives. Some struck out for the North or West. But many more stayed in the South. They assembled their scattered families and built strong churches that also served as community centers, employment agencies, schoolhouses, and—in later years—centers of protest.

For the first time, many African American men and women could legalize and celebrate their marriages, set up housekeeping with their families and make

**Vocabulary Builder**
status–(STAT uhs) *n.* standing or position, especially with regard to the law

# Checks and Balances

## TRACK THE ISSUE

### Does any branch of the government have too much power?

Our system of checks and balances is meant to prevent any branch of government from becoming too powerful. Yet at times the balance of power between the executive, legislative, and judicial branches has shifted. Use the timeline below to explore this enduring issue.

**1803** *Marbury* v. *Madison*
John Marshall affirms Supreme Court's right of judicial review.

**1830s Jackson Presidency**
Andrew Jackson increases executive power.

**1868 Johnson Impeachment**
Congress tries to remove President Andrew Johnson from office.

**1930s New Deal**
Franklin D. Roosevelt boosts presidential power to fight the depression.

**1960s Warren Court**
Supreme Court under Earl Warren becomes a force for social reform.

**1973 War Powers Act**
Congress limits the President's power to wage war.

**2000s War on Terrorism**
Congress increases executive branch powers to combat terrorism.

Ticket to Andrew Johnson's trial

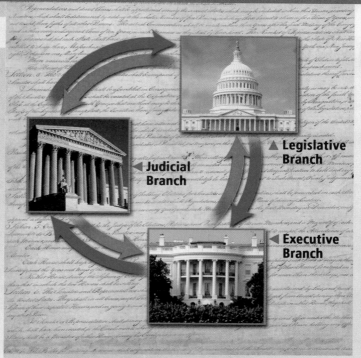

**MI** F1.1b

▲ Legislative Branch

◀ Judicial Branch

◀ Executive Branch

## DEBATE THE ISSUE

**Imbalance of Power?** During the administration of President George W. Bush, much debate focused on the relative powers of the President and Congress.

"I do have the view that over the years there had been an erosion of presidential power. . . . I served in the Congress for 10 years. I've got enormous regard for the other body, Title I of the Constitution, but . . . the President of the United States needs to have his constitutional powers unimpaired, if you will, in terms of the conduct of national security policy."

—Vice President Richard Cheney, December 20, 2005

"During the early years of the post–World War II era, power was relatively well-balanced . . . but major shifts, particularly those in the last two decades of the 20th century, have made Congress much weaker and the President dangerously stronger. . . . The Bush presidency has attained a level of power over Congress that undermines sound democratic governance."

—Walter Williams, *Seattle Times*, May 2004

 ***TRANSFER* Activities**

1. **Compare** When does Vice President Cheney feel the President should have more power? Why would Walter Williams disagree?

2. **Analyze** How did the administration of President Andrew Johnson reflect a similar power struggle?

3. **Transfer** Use the following Web site to see a video, try a WebQuest, and write in your journal. **Web Code:** neh-7202

choices about where they would reside. Freed women could care for their families and leave field labor. Freed people also realized the importance of learning to read and to count their money. So the Freedmen's Bureau schools quickly filled. By 1869, as many as 300,000 African American adults and children were acquiring basic literacy.

**The Ku Klux Klan Uses Terror Tactics** Even though the South remained under military occupation, organized secret societies, such as the **Ku Klux Klan,** used terror and violence against African Americans and their white supporters. A federal grand jury concluded that the chief goal of the Klan attacks was to keep African Americans from voting:

> **Primary Source** "The Klan . . . inflicted summary vengeance on the colored citizens of these counties by breaking into their houses at the dead of night, dragging them from their beds, torturing them in the most inhuman manner, and in many instances murdering them; and this, mainly, on account of their political affiliations."
> —42nd Congress, House Report No. 22, 1871

Congress passed federal laws making it a crime to use violence to prevent people from voting. Although Klan activities lessened somewhat, the threat of violence persisted, keeping many southern African Americans from the polls.

✔ **Checkpoint** What political gains did African Americans make in the early phases of Reconstruction?

**The Ku Klux Klan**
Ku Klux Klan members wore hoods, like those shown above, to hide their identities and terrorize their victims.

**Vocabulary Builder**
withdraw—(wihth DRAW) v. to remove; to pull back from

# Reconstruction Comes to an End

After a decade of Reconstruction, northerners began to lose interest in remaking the South and to focus on other social, political, and economic issues. In the fall of 1873, a series of bank failures sparked a severe economic downturn. At the same time, a series of political scandals in the Grant administration damaged the Radical Republicans. Under these circumstances, Reconstruction began to fade. Gradually and quietly, beginning in 1871, troops were withdrawn from the South. In 1872, Congress dissolved the Freedmen's Bureau.

**Southern Democrats Regain Power** Meanwhile, southern white Democrats patiently devised a strategy for regaining political control of the South. They argued that Republican programs for public schools and road building resulted in higher taxes. Most white southerners shunned anyone who supported Radical Republicans. Southern Democrats grasped every opportunity to discredit African American politicians as corrupt and incompetent. At the same time, the ever-present threat of violence kept African Americans from voting, thus depriving the Republicans of a large segment of their political base.

One by one, southern states reinstated wealthy white southern men as governors and sent former Confederate leaders to the U.S. Congress. In the 1874 elections, the Republicans lost control of the House of Representatives. By 1876, only South Carolina, Florida, and Louisiana—three states with large African American populations—still had Reconstruction governments and remained under military occupation.

**Election of 1876 Ends Reconstruction** The presidential election of 1876 signaled the end of Reconstruction. Democratic candidate Samuel Tilden won more popular votes than Republican candidate Rutherford B. Hayes, but the electoral vote was in dispute. The disputed votes were those of Florida, South Carolina, and Louisiana, the three southern states still controlled by Republican Reconstruction governments.

In an informal compromise, a congressional committee declared Hayes the winner. In return, he promised to pull all remaining federal troops from the South. In effect, the election of Hayes ended Reconstruction.

**Historians Evaluate Reconstruction** Was Reconstruction a success or a failure? Southerners and northerners, black and white, then and now would give different answers. All will agree, however, that some things were changed forever by those dozen years during which the victorious North tried to remake the vanquished South.

Certainly, Radical Reconstruction failed in most of its aims. By the end of the century, the political rights of African Americans in the South had eroded. Southern states slowly took away the voting rights of African Americans. **De jure segregation,** or legal separation of the races, became the law in all southern states.

Still, Reconstruction did mark the beginning of the physical and economic rebuilding of the South. Despite continuing conflicts and resentments, the nation was permanently reunited. And the constitutional amendments passed during Reconstruction, especially the Fourteenth Amendment, would eventually form the basis for a revived civil rights movement that sought political equality for all citizens.

✓ **Checkpoint** How did the influence of Radical Reconstruction in the South erode?

# Cause and Effect

## Causes

- Civil War destroys South's economy and infrastructure.
- Freed slaves and war victims need help.
- Black codes discriminate against African Americans.
- Radical Republicans want to restructure the South.
- Southern states need to rejoin Union.

## Reconstruction

### Effects

- South is divided into military districts.
- African Americans gain citizenship and voting rights.
- Union is restored.
- Sharecropping becomes the new farming system.
- White backlash leads to Ku Klux Klan and segregation.

## Connections to Today

- Constitutional amendments protect civil rights.
- Debate over states' rights and the federal government continues.

**Analyze Cause and Effect**
Although it failed in some of its major goals, Reconstruction had a lasting impact, especially on the South. *Which of the effects of Reconstruction were temporary?*

**Progress Monitoring Online**
For: Self-test with vocabulary practice
Web Code: nea-0210

## Comprehension

1. **Terms and People** For each item below, write a sentence explaining how it was connected with the reshaping of the South after the Civil War.
   - Reconstruction
   - Freedmen's Bureau
   - Andrew Johnson
   - Thirteenth Amendment
   - Radical Republican
   - impeachment
   - Fourteenth Amendment
   - Fifteenth Amendment
   - Ku Klux Klan
   - du jure segregation

2. **NoteTaking Reading Skill: Categorize** Use your table to answer the Section Focus Question: What were the immediate and long-term effects of Reconstruction?

## Writing About History

3. **Quick Write: Chart Conflicting Arguments** Make a table with two columns. In one column, list two arguments in favor of a harsh Reconstruction policy toward the South. In the other column, list two arguments in favor of a lenient Reconstruction policy.

## Critical Thinking

4. **Recognize Ideologies** How did the clash between President Johnson and Congress reflect a difference in attitudes about the role of the federal government?

5. **Evaluate Information** How did the Fifteenth Amendment guarantee the voting rights of some Americans but not others?

6. **Contrast Viewpoints** How do you think a northern Radical Republican and a southern Democrat would evaluate the long-term impact of Reconstruction?

# CHAPTER 2

# Quick Study Guide

 F2.1b

**Progress Monitoring *Online***
For: Self-test with vocabulary practice
Web Code: nea-0211

## ■ Reform Movements

## ■ Civil War Amendments to the Constitution

| Amendment | Ratified | Provisions |
|-----------|----------|------------|
| Thirteenth Amendment | 1865 | Abolishes slavery throughout United States |
| Fourteenth Amendment | 1868 | Defines citizenship; guarantees all citizens "equal protection of the laws" |
| Fifteenth Amendment | 1870 | Guarantees that right to vote cannot be denied on basis of race |

## ■ Cause and Effect: The Civil War

| Cause and Effect |
|------------------|
| **Causes** |
| • Economic differences divide agrarian South and industrial North. |
| • Abolitionist movement grows in North. |
| • Compromise of 1850, *Uncle Tom's Cabin*, violence in Kansas, and Dred Scott decision increase tensions. |
| • Election of Lincoln leads to secession of southern states. |
| • Confederate troops fire on Fort Sumter. |

| The Civil War |
|---------------|

| Effects |
|---------|
| • Confederacy is defeated; Union is restored. |
| • Much of South lies in ruins. |
| • Thirteenth Amendment abolishes slavery. |
| • Radical Reconstruction puts South under military rule. |
| • African Americans in South temporarily gain political rights. |

## ☑ Quick Study Timeline

**In America**

| 1820 Missouri Compromise | 1828 Election of Jackson marks widening of suffrage | | 1848 Seneca Falls women's rights conference |

**Presidential Terms**

| Monroe 1817–1825 | Adams 1825–1829 | Jackson 1829–1837 | Van Buren 1837–1841 | Harrison 1841 Tyler 1841–1845 | Polk 1845–1849 |

**1820**　　　　**1830**　　　　**1840**

**Around the World**

| 1822 Liberia founded as colony for freed slaves | 1832 Reform Act in Britain expands suffrage | 1840 World Anti-Slavery Convention | 1848 Democratic revolutions sweep Europe |

Jackson Forever!
The Hero of Two Wars and of Orleans!
The Man of the People!
PRESIDENCY!
BECAUSE
It should be derived from the
PEOPLE!
KNOCK DOWN
OLD HICKORY
AND THE ELECTORAL LAW.

# American Issues
## ●──●──● Connector

F1.2

By connecting prior knowledge with what you have learned in this chapter, you can gradually build your understanding of enduring questions that still affect America today. Answer the questions below. Then, use your American Issues Connector study guide (or go online: www.PHSchool.com **Web Code:** neh-6255).

## Issues You Learned About

● **Checks and Balances** Each of the three branches of the federal government has the ability to check the powers of the others.

1. How can the executive branch check the power of the legislative branch? How can the Supreme Court check both?

2. Was President Jackson's refusal to uphold the Supreme Court's decision in the debate over Cherokee rights a legitimate usage of the system of checks and balances? Explain.

3. How did Congress check the power of the President during Reconstruction? Was this effort successful?

● **Federal Power and States' Rights** Conflicting ideas about federal and state authority under the Constitution have persisted for more than 200 years.

4. According to southern leaders during the tariff crisis in the early 1800s, what could states do if the federal government passed a law that went against their interests?

5. How did the system of popular sovereignty favor state power over federal power?

● **Church and State** The United States follows a policy of keeping religion separate from matters of government.

6. What guarantees the American people the right to freedom of religion?

7. Describe the debate about the relationship between church and state that emerged during the Second Great Awakening.

8. Some communities and states have passed "blue laws" banning the sale of certain goods on Sundays. Do you think such laws violate the separation of church and state?

### Connect to Your World — Michigan

**Voting Rights** The state's first constitution, written in 1835, specified that only white men were entitled to vote. Over the next 15 years, members of churches and antislavery societies sent hundreds of petitions to the state legislature demanding voting rights for African American men in Michigan. When a new constitution was written in 1850, however, a majority of voters rejected extending the vote. It was not until the ratification of the Fifteenth Amendment to the U.S. Constitution in 1870 that African American men were able to vote in their first Michigan election. Write a short persuasive essay to the Michigan state legislature explaining why African Americans should be given the vote in the 1850 state constitution.

**History *Interactive***
**For:** Interactive timeline
**Web Code:** nep-0212

**1856**
Violence erupts in Kansas

**1861**
Civil War begins

**1865**
Civil War ends; Thirteenth Amendment

**1877**
Reconstruction ends

Taylor 1849–1850
Fillmore 1850–1853
Pierce 1853–1857
Buchanan 1857–1861
Lincoln 1861–1865
Johnson 1865–1869
Grant 1869–1877
Hayes 1877–1881

**1850**        **1860**        **1870**        **1880**

**1861**
Czar of Russia frees serfs

**1873**
Slave markets are abolished in Zanzibar

# Chapter Assessment

## Terms and People

1. Who was **Elizabeth Cady Stanton**? What was her main goal?

2. How would decisions about slavery be made under **popular sovereignty**?

3. What did the Supreme Court decide in the case of *Dred Scott v. Sandford?* Which Americans condemned this decision?

4. Who were **Robert E. Lee** and **Ulysses S. Grant**? What happened to these men in April 1865?

5. Who were the **Radical Republicans**? What were their goals?

6. What was the **Fifteenth Amendment**? To whom did it apply?

## Focus Questions

The focus question for this chapter is **What challenges did the United States face as a result of expansion, regional differences, and slavery?** Build answers to this big question by answering the focus questions for Sections 1 through 4 and the Critical Thinking questions that follow.

### Section 1
7. What trends in democratization and reform were taking shape in the United States by 1850?

### Section 2
8. How did the issue of slavery divide the Union?

### Section 3
9. What factors and events led to the Union victory in the Civil War?

### Section 4
10. What were the immediate and long-term effects of Reconstruction?

## Critical Thinking

11. **Draw Conclusions**  Andrew Jackson has been called the "People's President." How accurate do you think this nickname is? Explain your answer.

12. **Draw Conclusions**  Why do you think many preachers of the Second Great Awakening supported the temperance and abolitionist movements?

13. **Solve Problems**  What issue did the Missouri Compromise settle? How long did this compromise last, and why did it come to an end?

14. **Analyze Graphs**  Describe the information shown on this pie graph. What impact do you think this data had on the outcome of the Civil War?

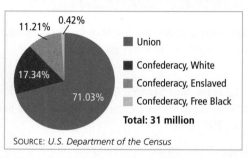

**Population of North and South, 1860**

11.21%   0.42%

17.34%

71.03%

- Union
- Confederacy, White
- Confederacy, Enslaved
- Confederacy, Free Black

**Total: 31 million**

SOURCE: *U.S. Department of the Census*

15. **Analyze Information**  How did Lincoln's and the Union's attitude toward African Americans change as the Civil War progressed?

16. **Draw Inferences**  Why did southern states develop a strong Republican Party?

---

## Writing About History

**Writing a Persuasive Essay**  In a persuasive essay, you try to identify an issue and present arguments that will persuade the readers to support a particular viewpoint. Choose one of the reform movements described in Section 1 of this chapter. Write a three-paragraph essay in which you define the issue and give reasons in support of your viewpoint.

### Prewriting
- Read the text in this chapter relating to the topic you have chosen.
- Use Internet or library sources to find additional descriptions and primary sources relating to your topic.
- Decide what viewpoint you wish to support.
- Make a list of arguments that might be used to support that viewpoint. Identify the two strongest arguments.

### Drafting
- Make an outline identifying what aspects of your topic you want to describe.
- Write an opening paragraph in which you describe the issue and explain why it is important. Include a thesis statement.
- Write two persuasive paragraphs. In each paragraph, use reasoned but forceful language that explains one of the arguments you have identified in your prewriting.
- If possible, anticipate and counter possible objections to your arguments.

### Revising
- Use the guidelines on page SH16 of the Writing Handbook to revise your writing.

# Prepare for the MME

## American Democracy in the Age of Jackson

Historians have often used the term *Jacksonian democracy* to describe the expansion of democratic government during the era of President Andrew Jackson. But how democratic was Jacksonian democracy? Use your knowledge of the chapter material and Documents A, B, C, D, and E to answer questions 1 through 4.

### Document A

"In America the people name those who make the law and those who execute it; they themselves form the jury that punishes infractions of the law. Not only are the institutions democratic in their principle, but also in all their developments; thus the people name their representatives directly and generally choose them every year in order to keep them more completely under their dependence. It is therefore really the people who direct."

—*Alexis de Tocqueville,* Democracy in America, *1835*

### Document B

The Trail of Tears, 1838

### Document C

"Jacksonians believed that there was a deep-rooted conflict in society between the 'producing' and 'non-producing' classes—the farmers and laborers, on the one hand, and the business community on the other. . . . Jacksonian democracy was [one] phase of that enduring struggle between the business community and the rest of society which is the guarantee of freedom in a liberal capitalist state."

—*Arthur M. Schlesinger, Jr.,* The Age of Jackson, *1945*

### Document D

"The Jacksonian period, our Jacksonian democracy: Arthur Schlesinger writes this glowing book about Andrew Jackson and Jacksonian democracy. What else was going on? And then I find out that Jackson is responsible for the brutal treatment of the Indians in the Southeast, driving them across the Mississippi, thousands of them dying. Jackson is a racist. Jackson is a slave owner. Under Jackson, the industrial system begins with the mill girls going to work at the age of 12 and dying at the age of 25."

—*Howard Zinn, interview, 2001*

### Document E

"These Americans . . . were champions of equality—that is, of course, for those who were white and male. . . . Women, blacks, and Indians just didn't enter the thinking of these people when they argued for equality.

To fault Americans of this period for failing to understand what the modern world means by equality is a pointless and futile exercise. But if they are examined on their own terms, with all their faults and limitations, they make an exciting bunch to watch as they changed their world and shaped so many things that became basic to the American system."

—*Robert V. Remini,* The Revolutionary Age of Andrew Jackson, *1976*

---

1. According to Document A, what was the most important feature of America democracy in the 1830s?
   A Americans had the right to trial by jury.
   B Americans considered all people equal.
   C The people were the source of political authority.
   D All Americans had the right to vote.

2. Document B best illustrates one of the main points made in
   A Document A.
   B Document C.
   C Documents C and E.
   D Documents D and E.

3. According to Document C, which of the following groups benefited most from Jacksonian Democracy?
   A Factory workers
   B Bankers
   C Westerners
   D Slaveholders

4. **Writing Task** Was Jacksonian democracy democratic by modern standards? By the standards of the time? Use your knowledge of the chapter content and specific evidence from the primary sources above to support your opinion.

# 3

# The Development of Industrial America

## 1870–1914

## WITNESS HISTORY  AUDIO

### Exciting Times

At the turn of the twentieth century, a new period of industrialization began to sweep across the United States. As waves of immigrants came into America's cities, urban areas such as New York City, Chicago, and San Francisco rapidly grew into cosmopolitan centers that offered exciting new experiences and opportunities. One such exciting experience was the opening of Coney Island in New York.

**Brooklyn Bridge newspaper ad**

66They took the lid off Coney Island May 15, 1904, and a quarter of a million men and women got a glimpse of a swaying, rocking, glittering magic city by the sea. It was Coney Island's opening day, . . . there were more dazzling, wriggling, spectacular amusements offered than had ever before been collected together at any one place at any time.99
—from "Review of Opening Night at Coney Island," *The New York Times,* May 16, 1904

*Listen to the* Witness History *audio to hear more about the development of industrial America.*

◀ Workers build one of the first skyscrapers in New York City.

**Pin from 1896 presidential campaign**

 **Content Expectations**

**Chapter Focus Question: How did industrialization affect the United States?**

### Section 1
**The Triumph of Industry** 6.1.1b, 6.1.1e, 6.1.2a, 6.1.5f

### Section 2
**Immigration and Urbanization** 6.1.3e, 6.1.4, 6.3.1

### Section 3
**The South and West Transformed** 6.1.1d, 6.1.2b, 6.1.3b

### Section 4
**Issues of the Gilded Age** 6.1.3c, 6.1.3d, 6.1.4

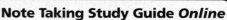

**Sears, Roebuck and Company catalog**

Use the ☑ **Quick Study Timeline** at the end of this chapter to preview chapter events.

**Note Taking Study Guide** *Online*
**For:** Note Taking and American Issues Connector
**Web Code:** nee-6351

▼ Brooklyn Bridge under construction

**WITNESS HISTORY** 🔊 AUDIO

### Building the Brooklyn Bridge

At the time of its dedication, in 1883, some hailed the Brooklyn Bridge as the "Eighth Wonder of the World." The bridge, which linked Manhattan to Brooklyn, towered over New York City. Built largely of steel, it symbolized the new industrial era and still stands as a landmark achievement in the history of engineering.

❝It is distinctly an American triumph. American genius designed it, American skill built it, and American workshops made it.❞

—New York City Mayor Seth Low,
"Dedication remarks," 1883

# The Triumph of Industry

### Content Expectations

- **6.1.1b** Analyze organizational "revolution" that enabled U.S. to become an industrial power.
- **6.1.1e** Analyze economic polices of government/industrial leaders.
- **6.1.2a** Evaluate development of organized labor.
- **6.1.5f** Analyze the automobile industry's impact on U.S. society.

### Terms and People

Thomas Alva Edison
Andrew Carnegie
John D. Rockefeller
trust
Social Darwinism

Gospel of Wealth
monopoly
Knights of Labor
AFL
anarchist

### NoteTaking

**Reading Skill: Identify Causes and Effects**
Fill in a table like the one below with the causes and effects of industrialization.

| The Industrialization of America | |
| --- | --- |
| Causes | Effects |
| • Natural resources | • Growth of cities |
| • | • |

**Why It Matters** Although manufacturing and factory towns had sprung up in the Northeast before the Civil War, an even greater period of industrial growth occurred at the end of the century. Industrial towns soon dominated the landscape throughout much of the North and had established a presence in the South. Industrialization rapidly transformed the United States into one of the most powerful nations in the world and dramatically altered how Americans lived. **Section Focus Question: What factors led to the industrialization of America, and what impact did industrialization have on society?**

## Industry and Technology Advance Rapidly

The numbers alone display the nation's emergence as an industrial power. Between the end of the Civil War and the beginning of the twentieth century, coal production skyrocketed 800 percent and steel production increased even more. The nation built tens of thousands of miles of railroads and sprouted brand-new industries, including the production of petroleum and electricity. When the Civil War began, the majority of Americans worked as farmers. By 1900, those who made a living from farming were outnumbered by nearly three to one.

**Causes of Industrial Expansion** There were many reasons for rapid industrial expansion in the United States. First, the nation's physical geography provided an abundance of natural resources— including lumber, coal, and oil—that manufacturers relied on to power their factories and lubricate their machines. Second, as industries expanded, millions of immigrants from Southern and Eastern Europe, as well as from Asia, poured into the United States to fill the demand for labor. Third, government policies encouraged the success of businesses in the late 1800s. Finally, the nation's cultural climate, with its favorable view of entrepreneurs, contributed to the growth of industry.

**New Technologies Transform the Economy** The combination of factors just described contributed to an outbreak of creative inventions, many of which had a profound impact on the economy. No one better symbolizes this inventiveness than **Thomas Alva Edison,** who designed the electric light bulb and the phonograph, in addition to numerous other inventions. Large utility companies soon formed to power his light bulbs and machines. New and better railroads, improvements in the telegraph, and the invention of the telephone all made communication and transportation less costly and more efficient.

**The Impact of Industrialization** Industrialization had a broad and long-lasting impact on American society, including a rise in most people's standard of living. The nation's cities grew upward and outward. New and more efficient production techniques, as well as improvements in transportation and communication, paved the way for the rise of mass consumerism. For example, rather than making their own clothes, Americans increasingly bought ready-made garments.

✓ **Checkpoint** What factors contributed to the industrialization of America?

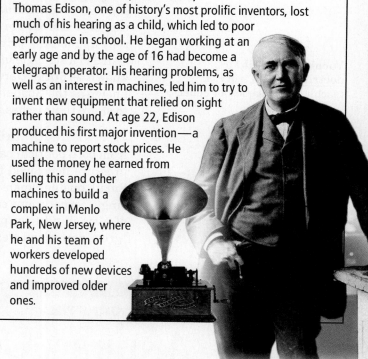

# The Rise of Big Business

Before the Civil War, most businesses were small and family-owned. By the end of the nineteenth century, large corporations dominated the American scene. The owners of these firms amassed enormous fortunes and power over the lives of hundreds of thousands of workers and related small businesses. As they did, the nation grappled with the costs and benefits of big business.

**Corporations Amass Huge Fortunes** In 1901, **Andrew Carnegie** sold his steel business to the newly formed United States Steel Corporation. At the time, investors valued U.S. Steel at $1.5 billion, making it the richest corporation in the world. It also made Carnegie one of the wealthiest men in the world—but he was not alone. During the latter decades of the nineteenth century, **John D. Rockefeller** gained control of the oil industry through his company Standard Oil, while Gustavus Swift and Philip Armour came to dominate meatpacking. Other powerful industrialists dominated the sale and production of tobacco, farm machinery, and sewing machines. These industrialists and financiers were often called robber barons, implying they "stole" their fortunes by paying their workers low wages. Others considered these men to be "captains of industry"—steering the country in the direction of economic prosperity.

Part of the success of these corporations lay in the development of new forms of business arrangements, such as cartels, or associations of producers that coordinate prices and production. Industrialists also established trusts. In a trust, companies assign their stock to a board of trustees, who combine the stocks into a new organization. The trustees then run the organization, paying the shareholders dividends on profits. To form cartels and trusts, corporations often bought out or merged with smaller firms. By joining with firms involved in different aspects of the steel industry, such as the mining of iron, Carnegie gained an edge on his competitors. In a similar manner, by taking advantage of special deals he had arranged with the railroads, Rockefeller compelled his competitors to join his firm or risk bankruptcy.

**Carnegie and the Gospel of Wealth** Carnegie and others developed sophisticated explanations to defend their business methods and the accumulation of massive sums of money. Borrowing from Darwin's theory of evolution, they applied the principle of natural selection to society, arguing that life consisted of a struggle in which only the fittest survived. This view of the world was known as **Social Darwinism.** Carnegie added to this a doctrine that came to be known as the **Gospel of Wealth,** which called on those who accumulated wealth to share their riches for the betterment of society.

**Federal Regulations Target Corporate Abuses** Even though politicians from both political parties tended to agree with the Social Darwinist view of life, pressure developed to combat the growing power of the biggest corporations. Small businessmen complained about the dangers of **monopolies,** whereby single corporations came to control entire industries. As George Rice, the owner of a small oil firm put it, John D. Rockefeller had "ruined" him by using his "great power and wealth" to run him out of business.

**Vocabulary Builder**
doctrine–(DAHK trihn) *n.*
teachings, principles, or beliefs

● **INFOGRAPHIC**

# ANDREW CARNEGIE:
## "Robber Baron" or "Captain of Industry"?

Andrew Carnegie and his poverty-stricken family immigrated to the United States from Scotland in 1848. Carnegie soon began work in a Pittsburgh cotton mill. He continued to work long hours for low pay at various jobs before he built his fortune in the steel business. Work in Carnegie's steel mills was grueling. As one steelworker said, "They wipe a man out here every little while. Sometimes a chain breaks, and a ladle tips over, and the iron explodes."

Those people who considered Carnegie to be a "robber baron" believed he "stole" his fortune by paying his workers low wages while he lived like a baron, or nobleman. Others saw Carnegie as a "captain of industry," who served the nation in a positive way by increasing productivity, creating jobs, and giving generously to public projects. By the year of his death in 1919, he had given $350 million—an amount that would equal more than $5 billion today—to fund libraries, museums, and educational institutions.

Many workers in Carnegie's steel mills worked with heavy machinery in intense heat 7 days a week, 12 hours a day. ▶

Partly in response to the complaints of small businesses, the federal government created the Interstate Commerce Commission in 1887 to oversee railroad operations. Railroad owners were often considered the worst abusers of their monopoly status. The federal government then became involved in regulating trusts and enacted the Sherman Antitrust Act in 1890, which outlawed mergers and monopolies. Initially, these reforms had little impact, in part because the nation's leaders chose not to strongly enforce them. In the spirit of Social Darwinism, leading economists such as William Graham Sumner promoted a policy of laissez faire, in which businesses operate with little or no government interference.

✓ **Checkpoint** What factors explained the emergence of large corporations, and what did Americans think of them?

# Workers Organize

The United States had been created as a land of opportunity, free from the corruption and exploitation that had existed in Europe. But as the nation industrialized, the extremes of wealth and poverty so apparent in industrial England began to appear in the United States as well.

**Workers Endure Hardships** Most industrial workers endured long days in poor conditions for low pay. Whereas Carnegie amassed a fortune, steelworkers in his plants labored 10 to 12 hours a day, six days a week, for about 15 cents an hour. They received no health benefits, no vacation time, and suffered from

▼ Carnegie devoted himself to philanthropic endeavors after his retirement. Today, people across the country enjoy the more than 2,800 libraries (top) and many museums (bottom) that he funded.

Carnegie Library and Col. Wm. Crawford Monument, Connellsville,

From his article "Wealth," this quote reflects Carnegie's belief that the wealthy had a responsibility to improve society with their riches:

*"It is . . . essential for the progress of the race that the houses of some should be homes for all that is highest and best in literature and the arts . . . . Much better this great irregularity than universal squalor."*

—Andrew Carnegie, "Gospel of Wealth," 1889

**Thinking Critically**
1. **Synthesize Information** How might Carnegie's belief in Social Darwinism have affected his views on how to run a business?

2. **Draw Conclusions** Do you think Carnegie's dedication to philanthropy offset his reputation as a "robber baron"? Explain.

**History** *Interactive* ✴
**For:** Interactive Steel Mill
**Web Code:** nep-0309

## TRACK THE ISSUE

6.1.1f

### What are the benefits and costs of technology?

Technology has had a great impact on American life. It has produced economic and social benefits for the nation, yet has also had some negative effects. What are the benefits and costs of technological change? Use the timeline below to explore this enduring issue.

**Late 1700s  Factory System**
Water-powered mills boost production but worsen conditions for workers.

**1859  Oil Refining**
Oil fuels industrial growth and raises standard of living but encourages American dependence on a single resource and worsens pollution.

**1930s  Polymers**
Manufactured materials like plastics have many uses but also increase pollution.

**1940s  Nuclear Reactor**
Nuclear energy holds promise but carries the threat of radioactive meltdown and nuclear waste.

**2000s  Genetic Engineering**
Biotechnology offers benefits but may also have harmful effects.

Factory workers circa 1900

Nuclear power plant, Illinois

## DEBATE THE ISSUE

**Nuclear Energy**  Building more nuclear plants would help meet our energy needs and limit fossil-fuel emissions that contribute to global warming. But the radioactive material used may pose grave risks to human health and safety.

"Nuclear energy supplies clean, reliable, affordable and safe electricity and is the only emission-free source that can be readily expanded to meet our nation's growing energy needs. . . . Nuclear power plants produce electricity that otherwise would be supplied by oil-, gas-, or coal-fired generating capacity, and thus *prevent* the emissions associated with that fossil-fueled capacity."

—John E. Kane, Senior Vice President, Nuclear Energy Institute

"There is strong skepticism . . . [about] the promises of the nuclear industry. . . . This is an industry that on a daily basis, as a direct result of its work, generates the most toxic and long-lived substances known to humans. It is an industry that poses a grievous threat to the health of humans and to the wider biosphere."

—Dave Sweeney, nuclear campaign, Australian Conservation Foundation

### TRANSFER Activities

1. **Compare**  Why does Mr. Kane support nuclear energy? Why does Mr. Sweeney oppose it?

2. **Analyze**  Which of the authors cited above would be more likely to question the factory system's impact on workers?

3. **Transfer**  Use the following Web site to see a video, try a WebQuest, and write in your journal. **Web Code:** neh-7302

periodic layoffs because of downturns in the business cycle. In addition, workers took little pride in what they did and often performed the same repetitive task day after day.

Women and children toiled in the nation's factories alongside the men. Mines hired young boys, known as breaker boys, to separate coal needed for fuel from slate and other rocks. Textile mills employed young girls to help operate their power looms around the clock. Women worked in textile mills, as well as in many light industries, such as manufacturing light bulbs. Nearly all women and child laborers were paid even less than men.

**Labor Unions Promote Workers' Rights** To improve their conditions, workers formed unions. The **Knights of Labor,** which sought to organize all workers—male and female, black and white, skilled and unskilled—grew rapidly in the early 1880s. Reaching a peak membership of about 700,000 in 1885, the Knights sought broad social reforms, such as transcending the wage labor system by creating cooperatives in which workers would own the factories where they labored.

In the mid-1880s, the Knights rallied tens of thousands of workers around obtaining an eight-hour workday. "Eight hours of work, eight hours of sleep, eight hours for what we will," supporters of the Knights would chant at mass rallies. For a variety of reasons, including the Haymarket Riot that you will soon read about, the Knights of Labor fell apart in the late 1880s, leaving it to others to forge a successful labor movement.

No sooner had the Knights collapsed than the **American Federation of Labor (AFL)** emerged. Unlike the Knights, the AFL did not aim for larger social gains for workers. Instead, it focused on very specific workers' issues such as wages, working hours, and working conditions. Led by Samuel Gompers, the AFL operated like a business. It was a loose organization of skilled workers from some 100 local craft unions, each devoted to a specific craft or trade.

**Workers and Socialism** In addition to unions, some workers became attracted to socialism as a means to improve their condition and place in society. They considered the Social Darwinist rationalization of cutthroat business practices inhumane and antidemocratic. Eugene V. Debs, who ran for President on the Socialist Party ticket five times, demanded government ownership of the railroads and called for workers to organize industrial unions to counter the power of big business. Although socialists enjoyed some success in local politics, they never attained nearly as large a following as did Socialist parties in Europe.

✔ **Checkpoint** How did workers respond to the rise of industrialization?

# Workers and Big Business Clash

Workers and big business often clashed violently in the latter decades of the nineteenth century. On May 4, 1886, an event known as the Haymarket Riot erupted during a labor rally in Haymarket Square, in Chicago. It began when someone threw a bomb that killed a police officer. More police officers and civilians died in the bloody fight that followed. Government authorities reacted by rounding up eight **anarchists,** political radicals opposed to any form of government, and convicted them of conspiracy to commit murder.

The following excerpt is from the Preamble of the Knights of Labor's Constitution. *What "power" do the Knights of Labor want to place limits on?*

Primary Source "**The recent alarming development and aggression of aggregated wealth, which, unless checked, will inevitably lead to the pauperization and hopeless degradation of the toiling masses, render it imperative, if we desire to enjoy the blessings of life, that a check should be placed upon its power and upon unjust accumulation.**"

—Preamble to the Constitution of the Knights of Labor, 1878

In 1892, fighting broke out between steelworkers and Andrew Carnegie's business partner, Henry Frick, in Homestead, Pennsylvania. With the help of strikebreakers, or those sent to break up the strike, and members of the National Guard, Frick and Carnegie crushed the Homestead Strike and broke apart a union that represented skilled workers in the plant. As a result, steelworkers went without a union for decades.

Two years later, in 1894, a nationwide strike erupted against the railroad companies. The Pullman Strike began with a walkout in the Illinois town where the famous Pullman passenger cars were manufactured when an economic downturn led the Pullman company to cut hours and wages. The American Railway Union, led by Eugene V. Debs (who was fired by George Pullman for protesting pay cuts and layoffs), came to the Pullman workers' aid. In turn, other railroad companies joined forces with Pullman. By the time the strike ended, President Cleveland had sent federal troops to Chicago to protect the railroads and the U.S. Attorney General had thrown Debs in jail for violating an injunction against leading the strike.

▼ Soldiers guard a mail train against rioters during the Pullman Strike, 1894.

✔ **Checkpoint** What resulted from the clashes between workers and big business during the 1880s and 1890s?

SECTION

# 1 Assessment

**Progress Monitoring *Online***
**For:** Self-test with vocabulary practice
**Web Code:** nea-0302

## Comprehension

**1. Terms and People** For each item below, write a sentence explaining how it related to the rise of big business.
- Andrew Carnegie
- John D. Rockefeller
- trust
- Social Darwinism
- Gospel of Wealth
- monopoly

**2. NoteTaking Reading Skill: Identify Causes and Effects** Use your table to answer the Section Focus Question: What factors led to the industrialization of America, and what impact did industrialization have on society?

## Writing About History

**3. Quick Write: Select a Topic** Choose a topic from this section that interests you, such as America's industrial growth or the rise of big business. To prepare for an oral presentation, write what you already know about the topic in one or two paragraphs.

## Critical Thinking

**4. Determine Relevance** How did technology impact the growth of the United States?

**5. Draw Inferences** How did the rise of big business lead to the formation of labor unions?

**6. Summarize** What occurred during the Pullman Strike?

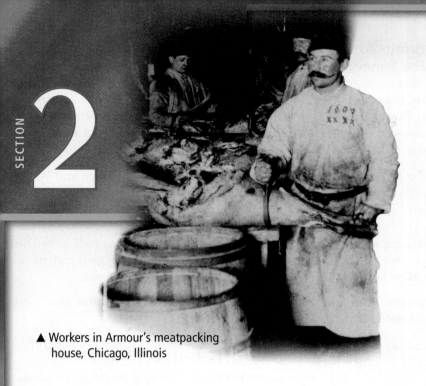

▲ Workers in Armour's meatpacking house, Chicago, Illinois

WITNESS HISTORY  AUDIO

**The New Urban America**

Chicago—with its enormous stockyards and packinghouses, railroad depots, and machine-making plants—symbolized the new urban America perhaps more than any other city. Chicago attracted waves of immigrants who filtered into the city's ever-expanding ethnic neighborhoods. The poet Carl Sandburg describes the city:

❝Hog Butcher for the World,
Tool Maker, Stacker of Wheat,
Player with Railroads and the Nation's
   Freight Handler;
Stormy, husky, brawling,
City of the Big Shoulders. . . .
Come and show me another city with lifted head
   singing so proud to be alive and coarse and strong
   and cunning.❞

—Carl Sandburg, "Chicago,"
from *Chicago Poems*, 1916

# Immigration and Urbanization

 **Content Expectations**

- **6.1.3e** Analyze perspectives about immigrant experiences in the urban setting.
- **6.1.4** Describe changes in composition, distribution, and density of U.S. population.
- **6.3.1** Describe problems/issues created by U.S.'s industrial/urban transformation between 1895–1930.

## Terms and People

Ellis Island          suburb
Angel Island          tenement

## NoteTaking

**Reading Skill: Understand Effects** As you read the section, use a concept web to record the various effects of immigrants on American society.

**Why It Matters** "Give me your tired, your poor, your huddled masses yearning to breathe free," Emma Lazarus wrote in the poem *The New Colossus* in 1883. But many Americans did not share her sentiments that the United States should welcome all newcomers. Instead, they feared that the waves of immigrants from Southern and Eastern Europe, as well as from Asia, posed a threat to their American way of life. They feared immigrants would take their jobs and undermine their culture. Today, however, nearly all acknowledge that these immigrants helped build America into one of the most powerful nations in the world. Lazarus's poem now appears at the main entrance to the Statue of Liberty, reflecting the nation's vision of itself as a refuge for the immigrants of the world. **Section Focus Question: Why did immigrants come to the United States, and how did they impact society?**

## New Immigrants Come to America

Immigration is central to American history. In the 1840s and 1850s, millions of Europeans came to America, especially from Ireland and Germany. Between 1880 and 1920, the United States experienced a second, even larger, wave of immigration. From afar, these immigrants saw America in biblical terms, as a "land of milk and honey." Yet upon arrival, some, because of the hardships they had to endure, cursed their new homeland as a place of tears.

**New Immigrants Arrive From Many Lands** Between 1880 and 1920, more than 18 million European immigrants poured into the United States. Another quarter million immigrants came from Asia, especially from China. Unlike most who had preceded them, the European newcomers came from Southern and Eastern Europe. Most were Catholic or Jewish (instead of Protestant), which changed the religious makeup of the nation. They also did not speak English, had few skills, and had little experience living in cities.

**Push-and-Pull Factors** Much like those who came from Northern and Western Europe, the new wave of immigrants left their homelands for a variety of "push-and-pull" reasons. Religious persecution and mandatory military service were among the "push" factors. They were "pulled" to the United States by the prospect of finding work in the expanding industrial economy, as well as by the promise of greater political and religious freedom. Like earlier generations of immigrants, they hoped to provide a better future for their children.

✅ **Checkpoint** How did pre–Civil War immigrants differ from those who entered America between 1880 and 1920?

▲ Chinese immigrants on Angel Island, San Francisco Bay

# The Immigrant Experience

Although no two immigrants had exactly the same experience, all of them had to endure the long journey to America and then find a job and a place to live. In addition to very difficult living and working conditions, they had to overcome prejudice, both from those who had been in the United States for generations and, in many cases, from their own assimilated countrymen who derided them as "greenhorns," meaning they looked green, or new, to the American way of life.

**Arriving in a New Land** After a journey that could range from a week to several months, the immigrants would arrive in New York City, Boston, Philadelphia, Galveston, or another American port. Starting in 1892, the vast majority first stepped on American soil at **Ellis Island** in New York Harbor. Government clerks asked the immigrants a series of questions at these entry points. If authorities believed the newcomers posed a risk to public health, perhaps because they had polio or another disease, they would send them back to Europe.

From the early 1850s to 1882, hundreds of thousands of Chinese immigrants came to the West Coast, mostly to work on the new railroads that were being built. Between 1910 and 1940, most Asian immigrants disembarked at **Angel Island** in San Francisco Bay, where they experienced much harsher conditions than those at Ellis Island. Some waited months or even years before processing and questioning came to an end.

**Opportunities and Challenges** Some immigrants received help from fraternal organizations, such as the Irish Hibernian Association, the Hebrew Immigrant Aid Society, and the Italian Knights of Columbus. Most had some kin or contacts from the old country who helped them find work and a place to live. Still, adjusting to urban industrial life could prove extremely difficult. Neighborhoods and living quarters were overcrowded; work was long, dangerous, and poorly paid; and the threat of disease, such as tuberculosis, was ever present.

**Vocabulary Builder**
urban–(ER buhn) *adj.* of, relating to, or characteristic of a city

# ELLIS ISLAND

**O**n a typical day in the early 1900s, thousands of immigrants steamed past the Statue of Liberty in New York Harbor and landed at Ellis Island. As soon as immigrants arrived, they checked their baggage and then walked up to the Great Hall on the second floor. Doctors watched closely, looking for signs of illness. About one tenth of the immigrants were marked with chalk and sent for a closer medical examination. In the Great Hall, immigrants waited in long lines for an interview with a customs officer who checked their paperwork and determined whether they would be able to support themselves. If approved and admitted to the United States, immigrants would meet up with family members, whom they may not have seen in years. By 1924, an estimated 17 million immigrants had passed through this process at Ellis Island.

A city health ▲ official examines this woman's eyes for infection.

People sit at long ▶ tables in Ellis Island's dining hall.

◀ Immigrants land at Ellis Island, New York. Some carry a piece of paper in their mouth that they hope to exchange for a visa.

A ship's log contains passengers' names and information, such as who paid for their tickets and where they are going. ▼

## Thinking Critically
1. **Identify Point of View**  What did immigrants experience upon their arrival at Ellis Island?
2. **Draw Conclusions**  How might the culture of the United States be different if immigrants were not an integral part of its history? Explain.

▲ Aerial view of Ellis Island

The new immigrants contributed to the American economy and culture in countless ways. They built churches and synagogues, established foreign-language newspapers, and established cultural institutions, such as Yiddish theaters. Irving Berlin, who immigrated to the United States in 1893, composed "God Bless America" and "White Christmas," two of the most popular songs in American history. Still, some Americans did not recognize the new immigrants' contributions for many years.

✔ **Checkpoint** What experiences were common to most immigrants who came to America?

# Cities Experience Growth and Change

Throughout most of U.S. history, the vast majority of Americans lived in rural areas. In the latter half of the nineteenth century, however, cities grew so rapidly that it became clear that urban Americans would soon make up the majority. At the same time, cities themselves changed. They grew larger, more complex, and much more diverse in terms of the ethnic heritage of their residents.

**Immigrants and Farmers Move to Cities** Both foreign-born immigrants and American-born farmers moved to cities for a variety of reasons. Foremost, as the centers of industry and commerce, cities offered newcomers jobs. They also promised a more cosmopolitan lifestyle than rural areas. Residents could attend the theater and sporting events; socialize at neighborhood bars, coffee-houses, and dance halls; and shop at department stores. Theodore Dreiser described the allure of a department store in *Sister Carrie,* a novel about a farm girl who moves to the big city.

**Primary Source** "Carrie passed along the busy aisles, much affected by the remarkable display of trinkets, dress goods, station[e]ry, and jewelry. Each separate counter was a show place of dazzling interest and attraction. . . . There was nothing there, which she could not have used—nothing which she did not long to own. The dainty slippers and stockings, the delicately frilled skirts and petticoats, the laces, ribbons, hair combs, purses, all touched her with individual desire."
—Theodore Dreiser, *Sister Carrie,* 1900

Of course, as Sister Carrie soon discovered, she could not afford the items in the store. Like most immigrant workers, she had to adjust to the difficulties of urban life—overcrowding, vice, and crime. Most newcomers barely made enough money for necessities in their new neighborhoods.

**Technology Improves Urban Life** As cities grew, city planners and workers scrambled to take advantage of new technologies to make life better for everyone. For example, new electric streetlights allowed factory workers to travel to and from work safely. New forms of transportation—from the horse-drawn trolley to the elevated railroad and electric trolleys—allowed cities to expand. These new forms of transportation eased travel and made possible the first **suburbs,** residential areas surrounding the cities. Those who could not afford the new suburbs lived in densely populated urban ghettos, or areas where one ethnic or racial group dominates.

Although urban boosters celebrated the construction of the first skyscrapers and subways as symbols of technological advancement, perhaps the most important progress took place in the innards of the nation's cities. Public-works departments constructed miles of sewers and massive reservoirs, along with intricate systems of underground pipes to carry fresh water to residents and wastewater away from their homes. The ability of America's cities to quickly create the infrastructure necessary to support such a huge influx of residents remains one of the nation's greatest industrial accomplishments.

**Urban Life Creates Problems** Despite some of the technological advances, urban dwellers faced

## Urban Life

New electric streetlights (top) line the streets in St. Louis, Missouri. Mulberry Street (bottom) in New York City is filled with life as the streets teem with people. *What was the impact of the rapid growth that occurred in cities during this time?*

# Migration and Urbanization

 6.1.1d

## TRACK THE ISSUE

**How does migration affect patterns of settlement in America?**

Several migration trends have shaped settlement patterns in the United States. One is the movement of people to the West and to the southern "Sunbelt." Another is the movement from rural to urban areas, which then developed suburbs. These migrations have had a great influence on American life. Use the timeline below to explore this enduring issue.

**1862 Homestead Act**
Offer of free land brings settlers to the Great Plains.

**1880-1920 Urban Migration**
Millions of Americans leave farms for the city. By 1920, urban population exceeds rural population.

**1910–1930 Great Migration**
Southern blacks move north, giving rise to the first large African American neighborhoods in northern cities.

**1950s Suburban Flight**
Mass movement begins from central cities to suburbs.

**1970s Present Sunbelt Growth**
Sunbelt states grow rapidly as Americans move to the warmer, southern half of the country.

A modern suburb of Las Vegas, Nevada

A poster advertising a new suburb

## DEBATE THE ISSUE

**Expanding Suburbs** American suburbs began in the 1800s but mushroomed after World War II. By 1990, nearly half of all Americans lived in suburbs. These communities offered many benefits. But critics say they have contributed to urban sprawl, traffic congestion, and other problems.

"Suburbanization represents a significant improvement in the quality of life for people who settle there. Most people who move out of their older homes do so because their needs have changed. Suburban and rural areas often meet these new needs better than older, more densely populated central cities."

—Samuel Stanley, Reason Public Policy Institute

"Sprawling patterns of growth are an inefficient use of land that scatters jobs, houses, schools and shopping across the landscape. . . . It leaves people little choice but to use their auto for any trip. . . . It fragments the ecosystems that protect our drinking water and wildlife habitat and that provide recreational opportunities that we all enjoy."

—Robert J. Pirani, Regional Plan Association, New York

### ? TRANSFER Activities

1. **Compare** How do the two quotations differ in their perspective on suburbs?

2. **Analyze** How did the growth of the suburbs affect urban life and growth?

3. **Transfer** Use the following Web site to see a video, try a WebQuest, and write in your journal. **Web Code:** neh-7402

▲ A traffic jam of people, horse-drawn trolleys, and electric trolleys in Chicago, Illinois

the problem of overcrowding. Rapid growth led to a shortage of housing, and unscrupulous landlords often took advantage of the newcomers' desperate need for a place to live. Immigrants crowded into subdivided homes called **tenements**. These tenements often housed twenty families, each in a virtually airless, tiny, cramped space where parents and children slept, ate, and often worked together. With few windows and little sanitation, tenements were unhealthy and dangerous. To make matters worse, few parks or public squares existed, leaving children only the streets as play areas. There, they encountered heaps of garbage, thieves, and rival street gangs.

✔ **Checkpoint** What was urban life like for most city residents?

## Social and Cultural Trends

Even with its problems, industrialization and urbanization created the foundation for the emergence of a more modern society. Instead of providing just basic needs for survival, the economy began to generate a wide variety of consumer goods and leisure activities. Besides the wealthy elite, a growing middle class had the ability to take advantage of many of these new goods and services. The working classes also occasionally had the opportunity to attend a ballgame or visit an amusement park.

**A New Middle Class Emerges** As industries grew larger and more sophisticated, they generated a demand for skilled white-collar workers—engineers, accountants, and attorneys. Big businesses hired salesclerks to sell their goods and managers to supervise their workers. In turn, these workers (mostly men) and their families had enough money to purchase items that historically only the elite could afford. Advances in technology and greater business efficiency and productivity further expanded the variety of goods and services within their reach.

One place where the middle class could find the things they desired was at the modern department store. New York shoppers flocked to Macy's, and Philadelphians flooded Wanamaker's. To boost sales, these department stores advertised in local newspapers and magazines, creating an atmosphere that made shopping fun.

**Culture and Entertainment Abound** The growing middle class also supported an expansion of higher education. At the same time, colleges and universities began to transform their curriculums. Some even began to focus on training graduate students. An increasing number of women went to college. Overall, illiteracy declined and a high school diploma came within reach for more and more people.

Alongside the expansion of education, the arts thrived. Some of the nation's greatest authors wrote during this time period. Among them were Edith Wharton and Mark Twain. Ironically, Twain considered the era crass and often satirized it. Other well-known authors included the poet Emily Dickinson and the novelist Henry James.

Perhaps one of the most important cultural developments of the era was the rise of mass entertainment, from collegiate and professional sports to amusement parks. Major league baseball, with teams in many of the nation's largest cities and in stadiums that charged admission, led the way. Mark Twain touted baseball as "the very symbol, the outward and visible expression of the drive and push and rush and struggle of the raging, tearing, booming nineteenth century." Daily newspapers advanced the fortunes of professional sports by establishing sports pages dedicated to covering the games.

**Religion Attracts Urban Masses** As America's cities grew, religious leaders appealed to the urban masses. Liberal theologians stressed the importance and value of each individual person. Building on this idea, Walter Rauschenbusch and others developed the Social Gospel movement, which promoted better working conditions and decent wages.

Dwight L. Moody and other evangelical Protestants traveled from city to city with their religious revival meetings. Moody used preaching, inspirational prayer, and gospel songs to spread a message of Christian love and compassion. After Moody left town, local congregations would swell with new members.

✓ **Checkpoint** How did religious leaders appeal to city residents?

**The Department Store**
Pedestrians peer into a Marshall Field's department store (below). Even people in rural areas had access to department-store items from a Sears, Roebuck and Company catalog (below left).

---

**Progress Monitoring *Online***
For: Self-test with vocabulary practice
Web Code: nea-0303

**Comprehension**

1. **Terms and People** For each term below, write a sentence explaining how it relates to either immigration or urbanization.
   • Ellis Island
   • Angel Island
   • suburb
   • tenement

2. **NoteTaking Reading Skill: Understand Effects** Use your completed concept web to answer the Section Focus Question: Why did immigrants come to the United States, and how did they impact society?

**Writing About History**

3. **Quick Write: Gather Evidence** In order to prepare for an oral presentation, you should gather information on your selected topic. Research to gather evidence on the growth and development of cities as discussed in this section. List several sources and image ideas after your preliminary research.

**Critical Thinking**

4. **Identify Point of View** What challenges did immigrants face upon their arrival in America?

5. **Recognize Cause and Effect** **(a)** How did technology affect the growth of cities? **(b)** How did the growth of cities affect housing within them?

6. **Identify Central Issues** How did industrialization and urbanization lead to the rise of the middle class?

Workers lay railroad track in Nebraska, 1866.

▲ Golden spike that joined Central Pacific and Union railroads, Promontory, Utah, 1869

WITNESS HISTORY  AUDIO

## Working on the Railroad

Railroad construction boomed in the latter half of the nineteenth century. The railroads opened the West to a rush of settlers and played a key role in the rise of a number of southern cities. Hundreds of thousands of workers constructed about a quarter of a million miles of railroad tracks. Thousands more worked for the railroads after the tracks had been completed. As they toiled, many sang one of America's most popular folk tunes:

❝I've been working on the railroad,
All the livelong day.
I've been working on the railroad,
Just to pass the time away.
Don't you hear the whistle blowing?
Rise up so early in the morn.
Don't you hear the captain shouting,
'Dinah, blow your horn'?❞

—from "I've Been Working on the Railroad,"
Unknown

# The South and West Transformed

## Content Expectations

- **6.1.1d** Analyze increase in labor through immigration that enabled U.S. to become an industrial power.
- **6.1.2b** Evaluate southern/western farmers' reactions to industrial growth.
- **6.1.3b** Analyze growth of cities linked by industry/trade.

## Terms and People

sharecropping
Dawes Act

assimilate
open range

## NoteTaking

**Reading Skill: Summarize** Prepare an outline to summarize the main events of the section.

> I. The South and West Transformed
>   A. The New South
>     1. Industries and Cities Grow
>       a. Railroad construction
>       b.

**Why It Matters** In the wake of the Civil War, southerners sought to rebuild their economy, knowing they could not simply revive the old system of plantation agriculture based on slave labor. The end of the war also unleashed a massive wave of migration to the West, which led to a boom in ranching, mining, and farming. This migration would cause the end to a way of life for most American Plains Indians. These developments transformed the way people in the South and the West lived. **Section Focus Question: What were the most important developments in the South and the West?**

## The New South

After Reconstruction came to an end, some of the South's leading citizens hoped to create a new economy. Henry Grady, the editor of the *Atlanta Constitution,* touted what he called a "New South." Unlike the Old South, the New South would have a mixed economy. Rather than shipping its raw products, namely cotton, to northern textile mills, it would develop its own manufacturing firms.

**Industries and Cities Grow** To an extent, Grady's vision took hold. Textile mills cropped up in the Carolina hill country, and the timber industry expanded in the Gulf States. Making use of nearby iron deposits, Birmingham, Alabama, developed into a steel-producing center. In the years following Reconstruction, railway construction boomed. Taking note of these developments, Wilbur Fisk Tillett of Vanderbilt University concluded that few if any parts of the country had made "such a marvelous advance" in such a short period of time.

Yet, such optimistic assessments glossed over persistent problems that beset the region. While the southern economy grew, it did not grow as rapidly as the economies of the North and the Midwest. Shortages of capital compelled southern industrialists to borrow from northern financiers, to the benefit of New York bankers. High illiteracy rates, persistent discrimination against African Americans, and a distrust of foreign immigrants weighed down the South.

**Southern Farmers Face Difficult Times** Hard times especially hit southern farmers. Overly dependent on a single product—cotton—southern farmers, white and black, suffered from declining prices for their crops. Also, beginning in 1890, farmers faced a new pest called the boll weevil. This beetle could completely destroy an entire planting, leaving farmers with little choice but to move north for jobs.

The **sharecropping** system also contributed to the hardships that southern farmers faced. Under this system, landowners dictated the crop and provided the sharecropper with a place to live, as well as seeds and tools, in exchange for a share of the harvested crop. Landowners and merchants often cheated sharecroppers at harvest time and discouraged them from diversifying their crops. Often, sharecroppers had to forfeit their entire crop just to pay off their previous debt and then had to take on further debt to survive.

**African Americans Suffer Setbacks** Although some African Americans managed to buy land and gain a higher education, overall the post-Reconstruction

# The Sharecropping System

In theory, sharecropping provided an opportunity for poor, landless freedmen and white southerners to save money to purchase their own land. However, as the chart at right illustrates, sharecropping proved to be an endless cycle of debt and poverty that southern farmers could rarely escape. As agriculture was key to the southern economy, the sharecropping system remained a major source of labor until mechanized farming reduced the need for human laborers by the 1940s.

**Why was the sharecropping system considered an endless cycle for southern farmers?**

◀ Cotton was the primary crop of sharecroppers.

**Sharecropping Cycle of Poverty**

❶ Landowner provides land, seed, and tools to sharecropper in exchange for a large share of the harvested crop.

❷ Sharecropper purchases supplies from landowner's store on credit, often at high interest rates.

❸ Sharecropper plants and harvests the crop.

❹ Landowner sells the crop and takes the predetermined share. The sharecropper's portion of the crop is worth less than the amount owed to the landowner.

❺ Sharecropper must promise the landowner a larger share of the next year's crop and becomes trapped in a cycle of debt.

era was a bleak one. Undeterred by northern military forces, which the federal government withdrew from the South after the election of 1876, the white southern majority slowly stripped African Americans of the political and civil rights they had gained following the Civil War. Groups like the Ku Klux Klan terrorized African Americans who sought to exercise their new political rights.

✓ **Checkpoint** What were the advances and setbacks in the development of the New South?

## Cultures Clash in the West

For centuries, European settlers and their descendants had pressed westward, pushing Native Americans off their lands. Although Native Americans were lumped together in the minds of most Americans as "Indians," they embraced many different belief systems, languages, and ways of life. In the 1830s, Congress enacted the Indian Removal Act and forced tribes in the Southeast to move beyond the Mississippi River to Indian Territory in present-day Oklahoma.

**Plains Indians Under Pressure** After the Civil War and a brief period of Indian wars, the federal government compelled Plains Indians to move to reservations, or public land specifically reserved for them. "All who cling to their old hunting-grounds," declared one federal army commander, "will be killed off." The Indians fell into a cycle of poverty and despair. Even when they sought to revive their traditional customs and religious practices, they encountered resistance and persecution.

Approximately 250,000 Plains Indians lived west of the Mississippi River at the end of the Civil War. Their livelihoods were based on hunting buffalo and other wild game. Even before large numbers of farmers and ranchers migrated west, hunters had already started to undermine their culture by decimating the great buffalo herds that roamed the Plains. Killing the animals for their hides and for sport, hunters nearly drove them into extinction and with them, the Native Americans' traditional way of life.

**Native Americans Resist** Although some Native Americans moved to the reservations without a fight, others decided to defend land they believed was rightfully theirs. In the middle of the Civil War, following a conflict between the Dakota tribe and settlers in Minnesota, the U.S. military captured 300 Dakota warriors and sentenced them to death. Ultimately, the army executed 39 of them, the largest public hanging in American history.

In a reversal of fortune, the Sioux crushed American troops commanded by General George Custer at the Battle of Little Bighorn in 1876. Not a single American soldier survived the famous fight. Custer's Last Stand, as the battle became known, however, proved to be the exception, not the rule.

**HISTORY MAKERS**

**Chief Joseph**
(1840?–1904)
For almost three months, starting in June 1877, Chief Joseph led about 700 of his people on a 1,000-mile retreat toward Canada. Despite being outnumbered by at least ten to one, the Nez Percés won several battles and outmaneuvered the army through the month of September. When troops surrounded the Nez Percés, however, Chief Joseph surrendered with this famous speech:

❝I am tired of fighting. Our chiefs are killed. . . . The little children are freezing to death. . . . Hear me, my chiefs! I am tired. My heart is sick and sad. From where the sun now stands I will fight no more forever.❞

—Chief Joseph, "I Will Fight No More Forever," 1877

Chief Joseph's retreat is considered one of the great military actions in American history, despite the fact that he and his people were eventually taken to a reservation.

# American Indian Policy

## TRACK THE ISSUE

### How should the federal government deal with Indian nations?

From its earliest days, the federal government has grappled with the issue of relations with Native Americans. Since Indians in the West were forced to move onto reservations, government policy has shifted several times. Use the timeline below to explore this enduring issue.

**1787 U.S. Constitution**
Federal government given power to regulate trade with Native Americans.

**1824 Bureau of Indian Affairs**
Agency created to handle relations with Native Americans.

**1887 Dawes Act**
Government divides reservations into individual land holdings.

**1934 Indian Reorganization Act**
Tribal governments gain more control over their own affairs.

**1975 Indian Self-Determination and Educational Assistance Act**
Indians win control over reservation schools and government services.

Comanche girls, 1892

*MI* 6.1.4

Native Americans in traditional garb press for Indian rights in Washington, D.C.

## DEBATE THE ISSUE

**Native American Land Claims** Today, several Native American nations have made claims to their original lands, arguing that old treaties were illegal. Opponents say that to recognize these claims after so many years would lead to injustice of a different kind to the people now living on those lands.

> ❝For over 200 years, we have endured hardship and indignities from the unjust taking of our ancestral land. We have been confined to a small reservation. We have suffered the painful loss of our traditional way of life. . . . There will be no actions to evict our neighbors from their homes as we know all too well the pain and suffering displacement causes.❞
>
> —Tadodaho (Sidney Hill) of the Onondaga Nation, March 10, 2005

> ❝Employing a unique body of laws, today's courts have decided to hear cases based on alleged violations of federal law that occurred over 200 years ago. Even more incredible than the ability and willingness of our judicial system to resurrect these ancient claims, is its [tendency] to apply modern legal interpretations to ancient events and blatantly disregard the historical record.❞
>
> —Scott Peterman, May 25, 2002

### *TRANSFER* Activities

1. **Compare** How do Tadodaho and Peterman differ on the subject of land claims?

2. **Analyze** How do you think Tadodaho would view the Dawes Act?

3. **Transfer** Use the following Web site to see a video, try a WebQuest, and write in your journal. **Web Code:** neh-7502

**WITNESS HISTORY DVD**

Watch *A Clash of Cultures* on the *United States Witness History* DVD to learn more about the conflicts between white settlers and Native Americans in the west.

The story of the Nez Percé tribe better depicted the fate of Native Americans. The leaders of the peaceful Nez Percé tribe did not want to desert their ancestral homelands in the Northwest. When General Oliver Otis Howard threatened to force them onto the reservation, however, they realized they could not match the firepower of the United States Army. Therefore, the chief of the Nez Percés, Chief Joseph, reluctantly agreed to lead his people toward a reservation in Idaho. Soon after, however, about 20 young warriors, unhappy about losing their homeland, attacked nearby white settlements. The army immediately began a pursuit of the Nez Percés. With little choice left, Chief Joseph led a fighting retreat toward Canada that is remembered to this day for its skill and audacity. Within 40 miles of the Canadian border, American troops surrounded the Nez Percés. Finally, Chief Joseph surrendered.

**The Government Promotes Assimilation** Only after the federal government crushed most of the resistance and placed the remaining Indians on reservations did expressions of regret about the nation's Native American policy appear. In 1881, Helen Hunt Jackson wrote *A Century of Dishonor*. As the title of her book suggests, Jackson contended that the United States had pursued a dishonorable policy toward Native Americans since its founding.

Partly in response to her work, which became a bestseller, the United States enacted the **Dawes Act** in 1887. This act sought to destroy the Native American way of life by urging Native Americans to **assimilate,** or to be absorbed into the main culture of American society. The act gave the federal government the authority to divide the reservations into 160-acre privately owned plots of land and to give Native Americans the opportunity to become citizens. However, the act utterly failed to achieve its goal. Indians lost more than 50 percent of their land over the next 50 years, largely to unscrupulous investors, and fell further into poverty.

Yet another tragic chapter in the history of Native Americans took place in 1890. In the northern plains, many Indians looked to their traditions as a way to regain their spirit. Following the advice of some of their shamans, or religious leaders, they took part in the Ghost Dance, an ancient religious ritual. Fearing that the Ghost Dances would lead to an armed insurrection, federal officials banned them. Ultimately, this led to the massacre at Wounded Knee, in which the federal cavalry killed 250 Native Americans, mostly women and children. Black Elk, a Sioux Chief, later wrote about the massacre in *Black Elk Speaks,* one of the most widely read books written by a Native American.

✔ **Checkpoint** What impact did U.S. policies have on Native Americans?

# The Transformation of the West

Millions of American citizens poured into the West in the latter half of the nineteenth century. They came searching for gold and silver, to establish farms and ranches, and to work in the cities that sprang up along the railroad lines that stretched as far west as San Francisco. This mass migration would eventually transform the West into a mainstay of the American economy.

**Miners and Railroaders** The discovery of gold and silver—first in California and later in Nevada, Colorado, Montana, Idaho, and the Black Hills of South Dakota—attracted hordes of prospectors in the middle decades of the 1800s. These prospectors gathered in mining towns, many of which quickly became ghost towns when the gold and silver ran out.

**Vocabulary Builder**
decade–(DEHK ayd) *n.* ten-year period

# Economic Development of the West

**Geography** *Interactive*
For: Interactive map
Web Code: ncp-1502

**Map Skills** Miners, ranchers, and railroads all played a role in the development of the West in the late 1800s.

1. **Location** How did the location of these cities enable them to become centers of economic activity: Denver, Abilene, Omaha?

2. **Draw Conclusions** How did the railroads contribute to the growth and prosperity of the West?

Map legend:
- Mining center
- Railroad
- Cattle trail

While gold and silver provided the first impetus for the migration westward, the transcontinental railroad opened the West to long-term economic development. The construction of the railroads was a massive undertaking. To encourage private corporations to lay the tracks, the federal government granted them nearly 200 million acres of land. In May 1869, the first transcontinental railroad was completed when Leland Stanford drove the final golden spike into the ground at Promontory, Utah.

By the turn of the century, railroads had transformed a country of isolated communities into an interconnected nation of towns and cities. Without the railroads, farmers and ranchers would have found it difficult to get their products to market. In turn, they could not have acquired the farm machinery and home amenities that they wanted. Over time, however, tensions increased between the owners of the railroads, who charged high rates for carrying freight, and the farmers who had no other way to ship their crops to the East.

**Ranchers and Farmers** Americans from the East who migrated west encountered a strange land. The Great Plains had few trees, very little rainfall, and the land from Missouri to the Rocky Mountains stretched on that way for miles. To heat their homes—initially constructed of sod—they had to burn dried buffalo chips, or dung. They relied on barbed wire for fencing. Moreover, spread out over vast expanses of land, they often lived in social isolation. Ida Lindgren's letter to her mother reflected these difficulties:

"Beloved Mamma,
It has been a long time since I have written, hasn't it? . . . [W]hen one never has anything fun to write about, it is not fun to write. . . . We have not had rain since the beginning of June, and then with this heat and often strong winds as well, you can imagine how everything has dried out. . . . Then one fine day there came millions, trillions of grasshoppers in great clouds, hiding the sun, and coming down onto the fields, eating up everything that was still there."
—Ida Lindgren, *Letters,* August 25, 1874, Manhattan, Kansas

In spite of these obstacles, millions of Americans moved west. They came to realize the American dream of owning their own land and working for themselves or, in the case of miners and the first cowboys, to make a fortune. At the end of the Civil War, approximately 5 million head of cattle roamed freely in Texas under a herding system created by Mexican ranchers. The demand for meat back east led to the great cattle drives and the era of the cowboy.

On these cattle drives, entrepreneurs herded cattle from Texas to towns in Missouri and Kansas for shipment to the Midwest and the East. Immortalized in fiction and the movies, the long drives ended in Abilene, Dodge City, Tombstone, and other cities that had railroad depots. Beginning in the late 1870s, cowboys and cattlemen realized it made more sense to raise steers on the northern plains. There, the herds could feed on the **open range**—a vast area of grassland owned by the federal government—and then cowboys could ship their steer from nearby railroads without the difficulty of the long drive.

The era of open-range ranching came to an abrupt end with a series of terrible winters. Many of the animals could not get to sheltered areas because of fencing, which resulted in the death of millions of cattle. To avoid such terrible occurrences in the future, ranchers built fences around their land and raised enough feed for their herds.

**Era of the Cowboy**
*Cold Morning on the Range* by Frederic Remington (top); American cowboy, *c.* 1885 (bottom)

 **Checkpoint** Who moved west in the latter half of the nineteenth century and why?

---

SECTION

# 3 Assessment

**Progress Monitoring *Online***
**For:** Self-test with vocabulary practice
**Web Code:** nea-0304

## Comprehension

1. **Terms and People** For each term below, write a sentence explaining its significance to the South or the West.
   - sharecropping
   - Dawes Act
   - open range

2. **NoteTaking Reading Skill: Summarize** Use your completed outline to answer the Section Focus Question: What were the most important developments in the South and the West?

## Writing About History

3. **Quick Write: Prepare an Outline** Make an outline for an oral presentation on the development of the New South. This will help you structure the information in a logical way. Identify main ideas with Roman numerals and supporting details with capital letters.

## Critical Thinking

4. **Synthesize Information** What factors led to the rise of the New South, and what resulted?

5. **Make Generalizations** How did the United States change as settlers moved westward?

6. **Make Comparisons** What were the similarities and differences between the economic development of the South and that of the West?

▲ Members of the
Populist Party, 1890

"Gold Bug" from the 1896 McKinley-
Bryan presidential campaign ▶

**WITNESS HISTORY** 🔊 AUDIO

## The Populist Platform

By the 1890s, numerous Americans felt that the United States lay on the verge of ruin. In reaction, they joined various political movements, such as the Populist, or People's, Party. Made up largely of farmers, the Populists met in Omaha, Nebraska, in 1892, to draft a party platform. The preamble of this platform reflected the angry mood that had set in across much of the nation:

❝The conditions which surround us best justify our cooperation; we meet in the midst of a nation brought to the verge of moral, political, and material ruin. Corruption dominates the ballot-box, the legislatures, the Congress, and touches even the ermine [weasels] of the bench. The people are demoralized. . . .❞

—The Preamble of the Platform of the
Populist Party, 1892

# Issues of the Gilded Age

 **Content Expectations**

- **6.1.3c** Analyze development of cities divided by race, ethnicity, class.
- **6.1.3d** Analyze resulting tensions among/within groups.
- **6.1.4** Describe changes in composition, distribution, and density of U.S. population.

## Terms and People

Gilded Age
Jim Crow laws
graft
Pendleton Act
gold standard
Populist Party
William Jennings Bryan

## NoteTaking

**Reading Skill: Recognize Multiple Causes**
Create a chart in which you record key events and developments that led to the Populist movement.

| Causes | | Event |
|---|---|---|
| • Declining crop prices<br>•<br>• | → | Populist movement |

**Why It Matters** The pace of industrialization and westward expansion in the latter part of the nineteenth century suggested that the United States had reached a new golden age. Yet the nation still faced many troubles, including the distance between people's dreams of wealth and the reality of their sometimes difficult lives. This period during the late nineteenth century is often referred to as the **Gilded Age,** implying that under the glittery, or gilded, surface of prosperity lurked troubling issues, including poverty, unemployment, and corruption. **Section Focus Question: What challenges arose for the nation during the Gilded Age?**

## Segregation and Social Tensions

One issue that troubled the nation was the persistence of racial inequality. During the last decades of the nineteenth century, African Americans, other minorities, and women found themselves fighting a losing battle to gain equality.

**Separate but Equal** During the decades after Reconstruction, southern states passed laws that separated blacks and whites. These laws were known as **Jim Crow laws.** In the 1896 case *Plessy* v. *Ferguson*, the Supreme Court upheld segregation as long as states maintained "separate but equal" facilities for both races. Yet facilities for blacks almost always were inferior. During the same time period, southern states enacted laws such as poll taxes and literacy tests that stripped blacks of the vote. As W.E.B. Du Bois, a leading civil rights activist, observed: "The freedman has not yet found in freedom his promised land."

In spite of these setbacks, some hope for a brighter future emerged. Booker T. Washington, who had been born a slave, built the Tuskegee Institute in Alabama into an important symbol of black self-help. In the same time period, Ida B. Wells's brave crusade against lynching gained some traction, especially among northern blacks who began to organize into clubs and civil rights organizations to demand full equality.

### Mexican Americans and Chinese Immigrants Face Discrimination

During the same period, Mexican Americans struggled against long odds to maintain their lands in the Southwest. Prominent whites prodded the federal government to grant them title over property pledged to Mexicans who lived in the Southwest before it became part of the United States. Federal courts tended to side with the whites when Mexican Americans pressed their legal case for the land. Some Mexican Americans resorted to warlike tactics to protect their lands. For instance, masked men known as *Las Gorras Blancas,* or the White Caps, sabotaged railroad lines and cut holes in fences to protest the displacement of Mexican Americans.

Asian immigrants, especially the Chinese, faced persistent discrimination, too. Western states enacted laws that prohibited the Chinese from working at certain jobs. Mobs of white workers terrorized Chinese migrants, claiming the migrants were taking the white workers' jobs. In 1882, the federal government temporarily banned further immigration from China for 10 years under the Chinese Exclusion Act. In 1902, the government made the ban permanent.

### Women's Suffrage Makes Gains

Women experienced both gains and setbacks during the Gilded Age. In spite of tireless efforts by Susan B. Anthony and Elizabeth Cady Stanton, the fight to gain a women's suffrage amendment stalled, although a few western states granted women the vote. At the same time, educational opportunities for women grew. By 1900, women made up one third of all college students.

✔ **Checkpoint** How did racial minorities and women fare during the Gilded Age?

## Political Challenges

As future President Woodrow Wilson lamented in 1885, "the conditions of public life in this country are not what they were in the early years of the Republic. We . . . are perplexed at finding ourselves denied a new order of statesmanship to suit the altered conditions." As a result, many of the nation's problems went unresolved.

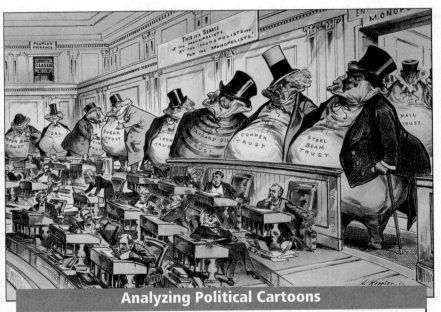

**Analyzing Political Cartoons**

This nineteenth-century political cartoon titled "The Bosses of the Senate" shows the influence that large corporations exerted on government.
1. How does the cartoonist illustrate the corruption of the time?
2. What do the men towering over the senators represent?

**Corruption Plagues Government** As cities grew, politicians gained power by providing jobs or patronage and services in exchange for political support. **Graft,** or bribery and corruption, touched nearly all aspects of public life. Some politicians, such as George Washington Plunkitt of New York City's Tammany Hall political club, even defended their actions.

**Tariffs, Civil Service, and Monetary Policy** On the national level, few issues divided the major political parties as much as the tariff, with the Republicans supporting high protective tariffs and the Democrats favoring lower duties, or taxes, on imported goods. Following the assassination of President James Garfield by a disgruntled former federal employee, the Democrats supported the **Pendleton Act,** which created a civil service system for the federal government. This meant that individuals who wanted to work for the government were required to take an exam. They were then given a job based on their performance on the exam, instead of on who they knew. Both Republican and Democratic Presidents also favored a hard monetary policy, the **gold standard,** much to the chagrin of many farmers who felt that this hurt them by keeping prices low.

✔ **Checkpoint** What issues plagued the government during the Gilded Age?

**Farmers' Alliance Seeks Lower Storage Rates**
Farmers waiting to unload wheat at a grain elevator, 1879

# Farmers and Populism

In the late 1880s and early 1890s, a massive political insurgency developed called populism. It grew out of the frustration that many Americans felt toward the federal government. Farmers in particular displayed their anger.

**Farmers Face Complex Problems** Farmers migrated to the West knowing that they would have to toil long hours in difficult conditions. But they expected that their circumstances would improve and that their children would be better off. Instead, as the nineteenth century drew to a close, many farmers felt that they were losing ground.

Several interrelated problems beset American farmers during this era. The prices paid for the main crops—corn, wheat, and cotton—declined significantly between the end of the Civil War and the early 1890s. At the same time, farmers accumulated growing debts that they found harder and harder to repay. Government monetary policies contributed to both of these <u>trends</u>.

**Vocabulary Builder**
<u>trend</u>—(trehnd) *n.* general course of events

**Farmers Organize and Demand Reforms** Immediately following the Civil War, farmers came together to address their problems. First, farmers in the Midwest banded together in the Grange movement. Their counterparts in the South and the Plains states established the Farmers' Alliance. These organizations sought to lower shipping and storage rates, either through government regulation of the railroads or use of grain elevators, or both.

Members of the Farmers' Alliance, in both the South and the West, soon formed the People's Party, or the **Populist Party,** and met in Omaha, Nebraska, to spell out its views. They endorsed General James Weaver for the presidency in 1892, as well as slates of candidates for state and local offices. They did well in several

Plains states, leading some to believe that they could challenge the two major political parties on the national level.

The Populists favored reforms that addressed their main problems. To lower the cost of transportation, they sought regulation or ownership of the railroads. In order to make it easier for farmers to borrow money and pay off their debts, they called for the creation of subtreasury banks and the coinage of silver or "free silver." **William Jennings Bryan,** the Democratic and Populist candidate for the presidency in 1896, made the call for free silver the centerpiece of his campaign. The Populists also sought political and economic reforms, such as the secret ballot, the direct election of senators, and a graduated income tax.

**Economic Crisis and Populism's Decline** During the election of 1896, the Populists hoped to gain the support of many industrial workers whose situations had taken a turn for the worse because of an economic depression. In one of the hardest fought campaigns in American history, Bryan crisscrossed the country, championing the cause of the American farmer and denouncing the monetary policies of the Republicans, namely the gold standard.

> **Primary Source** "If they [the Republicans] dare to come out in the open field and defend the gold standard as a good thing, we will fight them to the uttermost. Having behind us the producing masses of this nation . . . we will answer their demand for a gold standard by saying to them: You shall not press down upon the brow of labor this crown of thorns, you shall not crucify mankind upon a cross of gold."
> —William J. Bryan, "Cross of Gold" Speech, 1896

In part because he failed to convince industrial workers that the policy of free silver would benefit them, Bryan failed to win a state outside of the South and the West. As a result, William McKinley, the Republican candidate, won the presidency. The Populist Party never recovered from its defeat in 1896. Yet, even in defeat, the Populist movement had an impact upon the political system. Bryan's style of appealing directly to the people became the norm rather than the exception. In addition, a number of the Populist's specific proposals, such as the graduated income tax, became law during the Progressive Era.

▲ William J. Bryan, during a speech made in the 1896 presidential campaign

✓ **Checkpoint** What factors led to the rise of the Populists?

---

SECTION
# 4 Assessment

**Progress Monitoring *Online***
**For:** Self-test with vocabulary practice
**Web Code:** nea-0305

### Comprehension

1. **Terms and People** For each term below, write a sentence explaining its significance.
   - Gilded Age
   - Pendleton Act
   - gold standard
   - Populist Party

2.  **NoteTaking Reading Skill: Recognize Multiple Causes** Use your completed chart to answer the Section Focus Question: What challenges arose for the nation during the Gilded Age?

### Writing About History

3. **Quick Write: Use Numbered Note Cards** It is helpful to use numbered note cards to organize the main points for an oral presentation. On note cards, write the main ideas about the rise of populism. Determine the order in which you will likely deliver your speech on this topic, and number each card accordingly.

### Critical Thinking

4. **Identify Main Ideas** Describe several factors that caused the public to feel demoralized during the late 1800s.

5. **Predict Consequences** What additional actions might the government have taken to address the political corruption of the Gilded Age?

6. **Determine Relevance** What impact did the Populists have on society?

# Women in American Society

**MI** 6.3.3

## TRACK THE ISSUE

### THE ESSENTIAL ? Why do Americans disagree over women's rights?

In early America, women had few legal rights. They could not vote, hold office, or work at most jobs. Married women could not own property and were under the legal authority of their husbands. The women's movement helped change this, but Americans are still divided over women's rights. Use the timeline below to explore this enduring issue.

**1848 Seneca Falls Convention**
Women meet in upstate New York to declare support for women's rights.

**1869 The National Woman Suffrage Association**
Anthony and Stanton form organization to fight for women's suffrage.

**1920 Nineteeth Amendment**
Women gain right to vote.

**1964 Title VII of the Civil Rights Act**
Law protects women against job discrimination.

**1972 Title IX of the Education Codes**
Law bans sex discrimination in schools.

Supporters of women's suffrage gather in protest.

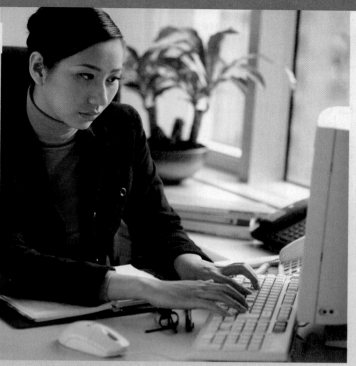

While many women today have successful careers, some still feel limited in their efforts to land higher positions in their chosen fields.

## DEBATE THE ISSUE

**Women in the Workplace** On average, women earn less than men in the workplace. This wage gap has led to charges of sex discrimination. Feminists also argue that a "glass ceiling" keeps many women from rising to the top of their profession. But other factors may be involved, too.

"The wage gap is the result of a number of factors in addition to discrimination, such as the differences in women's education, their shorter time in the workforce, and their concentration in a narrow range of jobs that are underpaid because women are in them. Nonetheless, a significant portion is attributable to discrimination."

—Sonia Pressman Fuentes, founding member, National Organization for Women

"[Feminists] often portray working women as victims of rampant discrimination . . . [which] renders women powerless in the face of an impenetrable glass ceiling. While discrimination does exist in the workplace, levels of education . . . and time spent in the workforce play a far greater role in determining women's pay and promotion."

—Naomi Lopez, Director, Center for Enterprise and Opportunity

###  ? TRANSFER Activities

1. **Compare** How do the two writers agree? How do they disagree?

2. **Analyze** Affirmative action makes it possible for women and minorities to compete in the workplace. Which of the two women quoted above might support this?

3. **Transfer** Use the following Web site to see a video, try a WebQuest, and write in your journal. **Web Code:** neh-7602

# CHAPTER 3

# Quick Study Guide

 6.1.4

**Progress Monitoring *Online***
For: Self-test with vocabulary practice
**Web Code:** nea-0306

## ■ Causes of Industrialization

| Civil War | Natural Resources | Growing Workforce | Technology/ Innovation | Government Policies |
|---|---|---|---|---|
| The war encouraged production, innovation, and expansion of railroads. | Ample natural resources, including oil, fueled growth. | Immigrants willing to work for low wages flowed into the country. | New technology and innovative business practices spurred growth. | Government policies encouraged investment in businesses and new technology. |

↓ ↓ ↓ ↓ ↓

**Industrialization**

## ■ Reasons For Immigrating

| Push and Pull Factors | |
|---|---|
| **Push Factors** | **Pull Factors** |
| • Religious persecution<br>• War and mandatory military service<br>• Economic hardship<br>• Lack of jobs | • Religious freedom<br>• Political freedom<br>• Affordable land<br>• Factory jobs |

## ■ The "New South"

| Economic Growth | Limits to Growth |
|---|---|
| • Development of new industries such as textiles, lumber, iron, steel<br>• Expansion of rail lines<br>• Some agricultural diversification to reduce dependence on cotton | • Shortage of skilled workers<br>• Wealth concentrated in hands of a few<br>• Few banks to finance business expansion |

## ■ The Populist Party Platform

• Increase in money supply
• Graduated income tax
• Federal loan program for farmers
• Election of U.S. senators by popular vote
• Eight-hour workday
• Restriction on immigration
• Government ownership of railroads

## ☑ Quick Study Timeline

| | 1869 | 1876 | 1882 | 1887 |
|---|---|---|---|---|
| **In America** | **Workers finish construction of transcontinental railroad** | **Custer and his men are killed at Battle of Little Bighorn** | **Standard Oil Trust is formed** | **Dawes Act allots land to individual Indians** |

| Presidential Terms | Ulysses S. Grant 1869–1877 | Rutherford B. Hayes 1877–1881 | James Garfield 1881 Chester Arthur 1881–1885 | Grover Cleveland 1885–1889 |
|---|---|---|---|---|

1870                                                    1880

| **Around the World** | 1869 **Suez Canal is completed** | 1876 **Korea becomes an independent nation** | 1882 **Britain takes control of Egypt** |
|---|---|---|---|

# American Issues
●─●─●─● **Connector**

By connecting prior knowledge with what you have learned in this chapter, you can gradually build your understanding of enduring questions that still affect America today. Answer the questions below. Then, use your American Issues Connector study guide (or go online: www.PHSchool.com **Web Code:** neh-6356).

## Issues You Learned About

● **Migration and Urbanization** Immigrants have overcome many obstacles in their quest to improve their lives in the United States.

1. **The Immigrant Experience** Millions of immigrants moved to American cities in the late 1800s and early 1900s. Write a short narrative describing the life of one of these immigrants. Consider the following:
   • reasons for immigration
   • working conditions
   • life in the cities
   • the process of adapting to American culture

● **Technology and Society** New technology can bring both positive and negative changes to society.

2. List the three main causes of industrial expansion in the United States.

3. What positive effects did industrialization have on American society? What negative effects did it have?

4. Identify and describe one invention that impacted the lives of industrial workers.

● **American Indian Policy** During the 1800s, Native Americans lost their native lands to white settlers.

5. In the post–Civil War years, what policy did the federal government impose on Native Americans? How did they respond?

6. Why did Chief Joseph surrender to federal troops?

7. What were the causes and effects of the Dawes Act?

---

**Connect to Your World**  |  **Michigan**

**Poverty and Prosperity: Wealthy Companies and Individuals** Automobile pioneer Henry Ford contributed significantly to American industrialization. Ford was born on a Michigan farm in 1863, but he was more interested in machines than farm work. In 1891, Ford took a job in the emerging electricity industry as an engineer for Detroit's Edison Illuminating Company. In his spare time, he worked on internal combustion engines. In 1903, he founded the tiny Ford Motor Company in Detroit. By 1914, Ford employed 14,000 workers. He had developed a phenomenally popular automobile and revolutionized the industry with his use of the moving assembly line and other production methods that lowered company costs. Do research on Ford and another industrialist from this time period. Then create a Venn diagram to compare and contrast the two.

---

**1890**
**Congress passes Sherman Antitrust Act**

**1894**
**Pullman Strike occurs**

**1907**
**Immigration to United States reaches all-time high**

Benjamin Harrison
1889–1893

Grover Cleveland
1893–1897

William McKinley
1897–1901

Theodore Roosevelt
1901–1909

**1890**          **1900**          **1910**

**1889**
**Eiffel Tower is completed in Paris**

**1893**
**New Zealand grants women the right to vote**

**1899**
**Boer War breaks out in southern Africa**

**History** *Interactive*
**For:** Interactive timeline
**Web Code:** nep-0307

# Chapter Assessment

## Terms and People

1. Define **monopoly.** How did the federal government attempt to prevent the formation of monopolies?

2. What was **Social Darwinism**?

3. What were **Ellis Island** and **Angel Island**? What happened at these locations?

4. Explain how **sharecropping** worked. Did sharecroppers have a fair chance to get ahead economically?

5. What were the **Jim Crow laws**?

## Focus Questions

The focus question for this chapter is **How did industrialization affect the United States?** Build an answer to this big question by answering the focus questions for Sections 1 through 4 and the Critical Thinking questions that follow.

### Section 1

6. What factors led to the industrialization of America, and what impact did industrialization have on society?

### Section 2

7. Why did immigrants come to the United States, and how did they impact society?

### Section 3

8. What were the most important developments in the South and the West?

### Section 4

9. What challenges arose for the nation during the Gilded Age?

## Critical Thinking

10. **Explain Effects** How did the rise of industrialization change the nature of American businesses?

11. **Predict Consequences** What would a modern-day entrepreneur who believed in the Gospel of Wealth do with his or her fortune?

12. **Determine Relevance** Explain the relationship between the growth of the middle class, the changes in the economy, and new forms of mass entertainment.

13. **Analyze Information** According to Henry Grady, what would characterize the "New South"? Did the society he envisioned develop? What was the "New South" like for African Americans?

14. **Draw Conclusions** Would farmers and ranchers have settled in the West without the construction of the transcontinental railroad?

15. **Explain Causes** Why was the Pendleton Act passed?

16. **Evaluate Credibility of Sources** The editor of a farmers' paper wrote in 1890, "There are three great crops raised in Nebraska. One is the crop of corn, one a crop of freight rates, and one a crop of interest." Do you think this statement should be taken at face value? Explain your reasoning.

## Writing About History

**Preparing for an Oral Presentation** The late 1800s were a time of growth and great change in the United States. As industrialization took hold, immigrants arrived, businesses boomed, and cities expanded as people moved there to live and to work. Soon, industrialization also spread to the South and led to the development of the West. Write an oral presentation that you might deliver to a private corporation during this time to encourage it to play a role in the development of the West.

### Prewriting

- Gather information on why corporations might have been interested in the development of the West in the late 1800s.

- Make a graphic organizer to arrange the information you find. In a two-column chart, for example, one column could be entitled "Why People Are Moving West" and the other "Why Businesses Should Move West."

### Drafting

- Develop a working thesis in which you clearly state the purpose of your speech.

- Write an introduction that will hook your listeners with the top three reasons they should agree with your position and take action.

- Make an outline for your presentation, and fill in facts and examples that support your position.

### Revising

- Use the guidelines on page SH31 of the Writing Handbook to revise your presentation.

# Prepare for the MME

## Attitudes of business and government toward organized labor

Were labor unions successful in working out their disputes with big-business owners? What roles did the federal government and the courts play in settling these disputes? Use your knowledge of the organized labor movement and Documents A, B, C, and D to answer questions 1 through 4.

### Document A

"The workers at the blast furnaces in our steel-rail works once sent in a 'round-robin' stating that unless the firm gave them an advance of wages by Monday afternoon at four o'clock they would leave the furnaces. . . . Gentlemen of the Blast Furnace Committee, you have threatened our firm that you will break your agreement and that you will leave these blast furnaces . . . unless you get a favorable answer to your threat by four o'clock today. It is not three but your answer is ready. You may leave the blast furnaces. . . . The worst day that labor has ever seen in this world is that day in which it dishonors itself by breaking its agreement. You have your answer."

—The Autobiography of Andrew Carnegie, *August 1920*

### Document B

THE CHIVALRY OF MODERN KNIGHTS.

### Document C

"There was a time when workmen were denied the right of leaving their employers, when they were part of the soil, owned by their employers. . . . Not many years ago, when workmen counseled with each other for the purpose of resisting a reduction in their wages or making an effort to secure an increase, it was held to be a conspiracy punishable by imprisonment. Through the effort of organized labor, an enlightened public sentiment changed all this until to-day the right to unite for material, moral, and social improvement on the part of workers is accepted by all."

—*Samuel Gompers to Editor,* Washington Evening Star, *May 15, 1900*

### Document D

"In the winter of 1893–1894 the employees of the Pullman Palace Car Company . . . were greatly disturbed because of a wage reduction. . . . They joined the new American Railway Union . . . attempting to organize all workers connected with the railways. . . . The [Pullman] company refused to consider arbitration and the boycott went into effect. . . . Indictments charging Debs [president of the American Railway Union] and others of violations of the Sherman Act were secured. . . . As a result of the various injunctions, indictments, and the activities of federal troops which reached Chicago, following directions from President Cleveland, the strike and the consequent violence were practically at an end by the middle of July."

—Labor and the Sherman Act *by Edward Berman, 1930*

---

1. In Document A, what view does Andrew Carnegie take toward organized labor?
   A He believes that businesses should bargain with employees.
   B He believes that workers should be paid fair wages.
   C He believes that employees should honor their original work agreement.
   D He believes that business owners should take workers' threats seriously.

2. Which document is a secondary source that describes how the Sherman Act was used as a legal tool to end a strike?
   A Document A
   B Document B
   C Document C
   D Document D

3. Who does the cartoonist make fun of in Document B?
   A The government
   B The Knights of Labor
   C The Sherman Antitrust Act
   D George Pullman

4. **Writing Task** What were the goals of the labor movement? How did big business, the government, and the courts respond to labor unions? Use your knowledge of the chapter content and specific evidence from the primary sources above to support your opinion.

## MI Connect to Michigan

### May Stocking Knaggs

As you will read, women living in the United States in the late 1800s and early 1900s lacked many basic rights, including the right to vote. During this time, the women's suffrage movement began to gain momentum. That was when May Stocking Knaggs of Bay City, Michigan, entered the scene.

A clear and persuasive speaker, Knaggs used her talents to promote women's suffrage. In 1894, she joined the famous suffragist Susan B. Anthony on a speaking tour through New York State. Together, the two women gave more than 60 speeches in support of women's rights. On January 28, 1896, Knaggs addressed a committee of the U.S. Senate about the issue of women's suffrage:

> "I stand before you representing nearly 600,000 women of the age of 21 years and upward in the great State of Michigan. Of these, about 100,000 are wage-earning women, in the trades, industries, and professions. These women are asking for the ballot [so] that they may protect their industrial interests, as the ballot has been given to all classes of men to protect their various interests. There are also about 76,000 property-holding women, owning $34,000,000, and paying into the Treasury yearly something over $2,000,000 in taxes.
>
> Our forefathers rebelled against British domination upon the principle that "taxation without representation is tyranny," and if it is tyranny for men it is tyranny for women also."
>
> —May Stocking Knaggs, 1896

Knaggs was also active in the women's suffrage movement at the state level. Throughout her career, she wrote articles about women's issues and rights for her hometown's newspaper, the *Bay City Tribune*. When the state held a constitutional convention that began in 1907, she led a committee representing the Michigan Equal Suffrage Association. Knaggs's committee tried unsuccessfully to persuade the delegates not to use the word "male" in the state constitution's list of voter qualifications.

May Stocking Knaggs died in 1917, but her influence had a lasting effect. The very next year, Michigan legislators and voters approved an amendment to the state constitution that paved the way for women's suffrage. The following year, Michigan became the second state to ratify the Nineteenth Amendment to the United States Constitution, which extended voting rights to women throughout the country in 1920.

# EMERGENCE OF THE MODERN UNITED STATES

## CONTENTS

In France, a Red Cross nurse
tends American soldiers
wounded in World War I. ▶

### Slum Sisters

In 1865, Methodist minister William Booth opened a street-corner mission in the slums of London. This was the beginning of the Salvation Army. By 1889, the Salvation Army had taken root in New York City. The Army sent pairs of women, known as 'slum sisters,' to visit tenement dwellers. Carrying mops and buckets along with religious pamphlets, these volunteers scrubbed floors, cooked meals, and cared for the sick. As cities grew and industry boomed, the slum sisters of the Salvation Army were just a few of the reformers who dedicated themselves to the needs of the poorest of the poor. *Listen to the* Witness History *audio to hear more about efforts to help the poor.*

◄ The Salvation Army delivers baskets of food to the poor in New York City on Christmas day.

**THE JUNGLE**

UPTON SINCLAIR

*The Jungle* exposed the abuses of the meatpacking industry

 **Content Expectations**

**Chapter Focus Question:** What were the causes and effects of the Progressive Movement?

### Section 1
**The Drive for Reform**   6.1.3c, 6.3.2d, 6.3.3

### Section 2
**Women Make Progress**   6.3.1, 6.3.2a, 6.3.3

### Section 3
**The Struggle Against Discrimination**   6.1.5c, 6.3.1, 6.3.2d

### Section 4
**Roosevelt's Square Deal**   6.1.1f, 6.3.2d, 6.3.2e

### Section 5
**Wilson's New Freedom**   6.3.1, 6.3.2a, 6.3.2b

1912 Progressive Party presidential campaign button

Women's suffrage statuette

Use the ☑ **Quick Study Timeline** at the end of this chapter to preview chapter events.

**Note Taking Study Guide** *Online*
**For:** Note Taking and American Issues Connector
**Web Code:** nee-7701

WITNESS HISTORY  AUDIO

## Children in the Coal Mines

Progressive reformers were appalled by the child labor that was common in coal mines, textile mills, and other industries. John Spargo, a union organizer and socialist, sadly described the terrible conditions endured by boys working in the coal mines.

"The coal is hard, and accidents to the hands, such as cut, broken, or crushed fingers, are common among the boys. Sometimes there is a worse accident: a terrified shriek is heard, and a boy is mangled and torn in the machinery, or disappears in the chute to be picked out later smothered and dead. Clouds of dust fill the breakers and are inhaled by the boys, laying the foundations for asthma and miners' consumption."

—John Spargo, *The Bitter Cry of the Children*, 1906

▲ These boys toiled in a West Virginia coal mine.

# The Drive for Reform

 **Content Expectations**

- **6.1.3c** Analyze development of cities divided by race, ethnicity, class.
- **6.3.2d** Analyze causes/consequences of reform organizations, movements, individuals promoting change.
- **6.3.3** Analyze successes/failures to expand women's rights.

### Terms and People

Progressivism
muckraker
Lincoln Steffens
Jacob Riis
Social Gospel
settlement house
Jane Addams
direct primary
initiative
referendum
recall

## NoteTaking

**Reading Skill: Identify Details** Fill in a chart like this one with details about Progressivism.

| Progressivism | | |
| --- | --- | --- |
| **Problems** | **Muckrakers** | **Reforms** |
| • Industrial hazards | • Exposed conditions | • Factory laws |
| • | • | • |

**Why It Matters** Industrialization, urbanization, and immigration brought many benefits to America, but they also produced challenging social problems. In response, a movement called **Progressivism** emerged in the 1890s. Progressives believed that new ideas and honest, efficient government could bring about social justice. Progressive ideas brought lasting reforms that still affect society today. **Section Focus Question: What areas did Progressives think were in need of the greatest reform?**

## Origins of Progressivism

The people who made up the Progressive Movement came from many walks of life. They came from all political parties, social classes, ethnic groups, and religions. Many Progressive leaders emerged from the growing middle class, whose power and influence was rapidly spreading. Dissatisfied industrial workers also joined the Progressive Movement. So did a few wealthy Americans driven by a desire to act for the good of society.

**Progressives Share Common Beliefs** What the Progressives shared in common was a belief that industrialization and urbanization had created troubling social and political problems. Progressives wanted to bring about reforms that would correct these problems and injustices. They encouraged their state legislatures and the federal government to enact laws to address the issues faced by the poor. Progressives wanted to use logic and reason to make society work in a more efficient and orderly way. Many, motivated by religious faith, sought social justice.

Progressivism was similar to the Populist Movement of the late 1800s. Both were reform movements that wanted to get rid of corrupt government officials and make government more responsive to people's needs. Both sought to eliminate the abuses of big business. Still, the two movements differed. At the forefront of Progressivism were middle-class people. They believed that highly educated leaders should use modern ideas and scientific techniques to improve society. Leaders of the Populist Movement, on the other hand, consisted mostly of farmers and workers.

**Progressives Target a Variety of Problems** Some Progressives thought that political reform was the most urgent need. For many women, the number one goal was winning the right to vote. Other Progressives considered honest government to be the most important goal. Reformers targeted city officials who built corrupt organizations, called political machines. The bosses of these political machines used bribery and violence to influence voters and win elections. They counted on the loyalty of city workers who looked the other way when they took public money for themselves. Bosses also helped people solve personal problems, which often kept voters loyal.

Corrupt and ineffective government combined with the booming growth of cities produced other problems. The people living in America's crowded cities needed paved streets, safe drinking water, decent housing, and adequate municipal services. The lack of adequate services led to wretched living conditions for the urban poor. Too often, dishonest business owners and politicians controlled municipal services. Bribes and shady deals made them rich while conditions for urban residents remained unsafe and little changed.

While some Progressives focused on government, others were worried about big business. As you have learned, wealthy industrialists took over businesses and built huge trusts that limited competition and raised prices. Middle-class Progressives wanted the government to "bust the trusts" and so create more economic opportunities for smaller businesses. Progressives complained that the Sherman Antitrust Act of 1890 was inadequate and ineffective in limiting the abuses of big business.

Other Progressive reformers, often motivated by their religious faith, sought to reduce the growing gap between the wealthy and the poor. Progressives attacked the harsh conditions endured by miners, factory workers, and other laborers. They wanted better conditions for poor people living in city slums. They wanted social welfare laws to help children, as well as government regulations to aid workers and consumers.

✓ **Checkpoint** What problems did Progressive reformers hope to solve?

THE SHARP METHOD.—IT WORKS WITH ANY BOARD OF ALDERMEN.

## Analyzing Political Cartoons

**Business and Government Corruption** In the 1880s, Jacob Sharp expanded his streetcar business by bribing New York City aldermen and other government officials.
1. What symbols represent the corruption of city government?
2. According to the cartoonist, what is the effect of the street railroad monopoly on the taxpayer?

## Muckrakers Reveal the Need for Reform

Socially conscious journalists and other writers dramatized the need for reform. Their sensational investigative reports uncovered a wide range of ills afflicting America in the early 1900s. Even though Theodore Roosevelt agreed with much of what they said, he called these writers **muckrakers** because he thought them too fascinated with the ugliest side of things. (A muckrake is a tool used to clean manure and hay out of animals' stables.) The writers were angry at first but in time took up Roosevelt's taunting name as a badge of honor. The muckrakers' articles appeared in magazines and newspapers that entered millions of American homes. People across the nation were horrified by the conditions that were revealed to them.

**Journalists Uncover Injustices** One leading muckraker was **Lincoln Steffens,** managing editor at *McClure's,* a magazine known for uncovering social problems. In 1903, Steffens published *The Shame of the Cities,* a collection of articles on political corruption. His reports exposed how the government of Philadelphia let utility companies charge their customers excessively high fees. He showed how corrupt politicians won elections by bribing and threatening voters, and revealed how political corruption affected all aspects of life in a city.

Jacob Riis ▼

> **Primary Source** "The visitor [to St. Louis] is told of the wealth of the residents, of the financial strength of the banks, and of the growing importance of the industries; yet he sees poorly paved, refuse-burdened streets, and dusty or mud-covered alleys; he passes a ramshackle firetrap crowded with the sick and learns that it is the City Hospital. . . . Finally, he turns a tap in the hotel to see liquid mud flow into [the] wash basin or bathtub."
>
> —Lincoln Steffens and Claude Wetmore, "Corruption and Reform in St. Louis," *McClure's Magazine*, October 1902

● **INFOGRAPHIC**

## EXPOSING HOW THE OTHER HALF LIVES

"Long ago it was said that 'one half of the world does not know how the other half lives.' . . . It did not know because it did not care." Jacob Riis, believing that the "poor were the victims rather than the makers of their fate," used images and words to make the public confront the conditions of New York City's tenement slums.

Riis's 1890 book ▼

HOW THE OTHER HALF LIVES STVDIES AMONG THE TENEMENTS OF NEW YORK

▲ A horse lies dead in a New York City street as children play nearby. A lack of city services forced slum-dwellers to live in unsanitary conditions.

Another influential muckraker was **Jacob Riis,** a photographer for the *New York Evening Sun.* Riis turned his camera on the crowded, unsafe, rat-infested tenement buildings where the urban poor lived. Between 1890 and 1903, he published several works, including *How the Other Half Lives* (see Infographic below), that shocked the nation's conscience and led to reforms.

Other outraged writers joined Riis and Steffens. In *The History of Standard Oil,* Ida Tarbell reported that John D. Rockefeller used ruthless methods to ruin his competitors, charge higher prices, and thereby reap huge profits. Others proclaimed the need to improve schools or warned of the breakdown of family life because mothers had to work long hours in factories. John Spargo focused attention on the dangerous and difficult lives of child workers. (See the Witness History at the beginning of this section.)

**Novelists Defend the Downtrodden**  Fiction writers put a human face on social problems. They developed a new genre—the naturalist novel—that honestly portrayed human misery and the struggles of common people. Theodore Dreiser, a midwesterner raised in poverty, published *Sister Carrie* in 1900. His provocative novel traces the fate of a small-town girl drawn into the brutal urban worlds of Chicago and New York.

Naturalist novels became very popular. Frank Norris's *The Octopus* fascinated readers by dramatizing the Southern Pacific Railroad's stranglehold on struggling California farmers. In *The Jungle,* Upton Sinclair related the despair of immigrants working in Chicago's stockyards and revealed the unsanitary conditions in the industry. (See an excerpt from the novel at the end of this section.) African American author Frances Ellen Watkins portrayed some of the struggles of black Americans in her 1892 novel *Iola Leroy.*

✓ **Checkpoint** What role did journalists and other writers play in the Progressive Movement?

**WITNESS HISTORY DVD**

Watch *The Jungle: A View of Industrial America* on the **United States Witness History DVD** to learn more about city life in the industrial age.

▼ Adults and children sew knee-pants in a New York tenement, many of which served as both homes and workshops. "[F]rom earliest dawn until mind and muscle give out together," people toiled unprotected by the laws governing factory work.

▲ A New York City cobbler prepares for the Jewish Sabbath Eve dinner in a Ludlow Street coal cellar.

**Thinking Critically**
**Analyze Visuals**  What do Riis's images reveal about the conditions of city slums?

**History** *Interactive* ✷
**For:** A look at tenement life
**Web Code:** nep-0403

## Progressives Reform Society

The work of the muckrakers increased popular support for Progressivism. Progressive activists promoted laws to improve living conditions, public health, and schools. They urged government to regulate businesses. They believed that careful social planning would make American life better.

**The Social Gospel Guides Reform Efforts** Many reformers, like Walter Rauschenbusch, thought that Christianity should be the basis of social reform. A child of German immigrants, Rauschenbusch had become a Baptist minister. He blended ideas from German socialism and American Progressivism into a plan for building a better society. His book *Christianity and the Social Crisis* outlined what he called the **Social Gospel.** By following the Bible's teachings about charity and justice, he explained, people could make society "the kingdom of God."

Many Protestant leaders followed Rauschenbusch's program. They began to urge the end of child labor and a shorter workweek. They also pushed for the federal government to limit the power of corporations and trusts.

**Settlement House Workers Aid the Urban Poor** An important goal of many Progressives was to improve the lives of poor people in the cities. One approach was the **settlement house,** a community center that provided social services to the urban poor. Before settlement houses, there were private charities that helped poor people. Settlement house workers gave mothers classes in child care and taught English to immigrants. They ran nursery schools and kindergartens. They also provided theater, art, and dance programs for adults.

A young woman named **Jane Addams** became a leading figure in the settlement house movement. After graduating from college, she pursued several different careers. On a trip to Europe in 1888, however, she was inspired by the work at Toynbee Hall, a "settlement house" in London. In 1889, Addams opened Hull House, a settlement house in Chicago. Over the years, Hull House grew to include 13 buildings. Its success inspired other college-educated, middle-class women to become social workers. By 1911, the country had more than four hundred settlement houses.

### The 1911 Triangle Shirtwaist Factory Fire

Victims of the Triangle Shirtwaist Factory fire lie at the feet of a police officer as he looks up at the deadly blaze. *How did the fire help or hurt Progressives' efforts to reform workplace conditions?*

**Protecting Children and Improving Education** Progressives also tried to help children. Leading the effort was a lawyer named Florence Kelley. Kelley helped convince the state of Illinois to ban child labor, and other states soon passed similar laws. In 1902, Kelley helped form the National Child Labor Committee, which successfully lobbied the federal government to create the U.S. Children's Bureau in 1912. This new agency examined any issue that affected the health and welfare of children. The agency still works to protect children today.

But progress in children's rights had a long way to go. In 1916, Congress passed the Keating-Owens Act, which banned child labor. However, two years later, the Supreme Court ruled the law unconstitutional. It was not until 1938 that Congress would end child labor for good.

Progressives also tried to better children's lives by improving education. A number of states passed laws that required children to attend school until a certain age. However, there were heated debates about what children should learn and how they should learn. Some argued that they should be taught only work skills. Others said they should learn to appreciate literature and music. Most educators agreed that girls should learn different things from boys.

Educator John Dewey criticized American schools for teaching children to memorize facts but not to think creatively. Dewey wanted schools to teach new subjects such as history and geography, as well as practical skills like cooking and carpentry. His ideas were not adopted at once, but in later years, many states put them into effect.

**Progressives Help Industrial Workers** In the early 1900s, the United States had the highest rate of industrial accidents in the world. Long hours, poor ventilation, hazardous fumes, and unsafe machinery threatened not only workers' health but also their lives. Each year some thirty thousand workers died on the job, while another half a million were injured.

In March 1911, a fire at the Triangle Shirtwaist Factory in New York City shocked Americans and focused attention on the need to protect workers. Workers in the factory had little chance to escape the raging fire because managers had locked most of the exits. The fire killed 146 workers, most of them young Jewish women. Many jumped from the windows in desperation. Inside the smoldering ruins, firefighters found many more victims, "skeletons bending over sewing machines."

After the blaze, outraged Progressives intensified their calls for reform. New York passed laws to make workplaces safer, and other cities and states followed suit. Many states also adopted workers' compensation laws, which set up funds to pay workers who were hurt on the job.

Progressives also persuaded some states to pass laws limiting the workday to 10 hours. However, their efforts suffered a blow in 1905 when the Supreme Court ruled in *Lochner* v. *New York* that such laws were unconstitutional.

✔ **Checkpoint** How did Progressives work to help the urban poor?

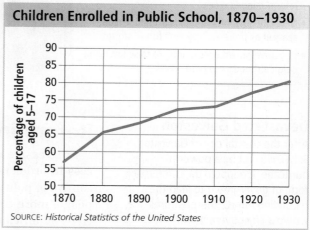

**Children Enrolled in Public School, 1870–1930**

SOURCE: *Historical Statistics of the United States*

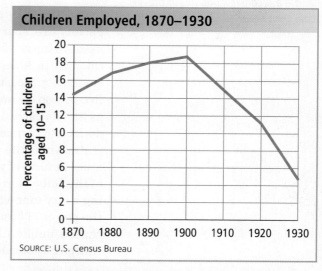

**Children Employed, 1870–1930**

SOURCE: U.S. Census Bureau

**Graph Skills** During the Progressive Era, child labor declined sharply while school enrollment increased. *According to the graphs, how did the percentage of children employed change from 1890 to 1920? How did school enrollment change during the same period?*

### Devastated Galveston

After the coastal city of Galveston, Texas, was hit by a powerful hurricane, it adopted the commission form of government to lead the rebuilding effort. *What features would a city government need to handle a reconstruction job of the scale seen here?*

# Reforming Government

Progressive reformers realized that they needed to reform the political process in order to reform society. They would have to free government from the control of political bosses and powerful business interests. They wanted to give people more control over their government and make government more effective and efficient in serving the public.

**Reformers Improve City Government** Just as the Triangle Shirtwaist Factory fire spurred reformers to action, so did another disaster. In 1900, a massive hurricane left the city of Galveston, Texas, in ruins. The greatest national calamity in American history, the hurricane killed more than 8,000 people. As an emergency measure, Galveston replaced its mayor and board of aldermen with a five-person commission. The commission form of government proved very efficient as the city carried out a tremendous rebuilding effort. The following year, Galveston decided to permanently adopt the commission form of government.

Known as the Galveston plan, many other cities decided to take up the commission form of government. By 1918, nearly 500 cities had adopted some form of the Galveston plan. Dayton, Ohio, and other cities modified the plan by adding a city manager to head the commission. The new city governments curbed the power of bosses and their political machines. The reform governments purchased public utilities so that electric, gas, and water companies could not charge city residents unfairly high rates.

**Progressives Reform Election Rules** Progressives also pushed for election reforms, taking up some Populist ideas. Traditionally, it was the party leaders who picked candidates for state and local offices. But in Wisconsin, reform governor Robert M. La Follette established a **direct primary,** an election in which citizens themselves vote to select nominees for upcoming elections. By 1916, all but four states had direct primaries.

Progressives also wanted to make sure that elected officials would follow citizens' wishes. To achieve this goal, they worked for three other political reforms: the initiative, the referendum, and the recall. The **initiative** gave people the power to put a proposed new law directly on the ballot in the next election by collecting citizens' signatures on a petition. This meant that voters themselves could pass laws instead of waiting for elected officials to act. The **referendum** allowed citizens to approve or reject laws passed by a legislature. The **recall** gave voters the power to remove public servants from office before their terms ended.

Progressives won yet another political reform: They adopted the Populist call for the direct election of senators by voters, not state legislators. That reform became law in 1913 when the Seventeenth Amendment to the Constitution was approved.

**Progressive Governors Take Charge** <u>Dynamic</u> Progressives became the leaders of several states, and chief among them was Robert La Follette of Wisconsin. Elected governor in 1900, "Fighting Bob" won the passage of many reform laws. Under his leadership, the Wisconsin state government forced railroads to charge lower fees and pay higher taxes. La Follette helped his state to improve education, make factories safer, and adopt the direct primary. Progressives called Wisconsin the "laboratory of democracy."

Hiram Johnson, governor of California, shattered the Southern Pacific Railroad's stranglehold on state government. He put in place the direct primary, initiative, referendum, and recall. He also pushed for another goal of some Progressives—planning for the careful use of natural resources such as water, forests, and wildlife.

Other Progressive governors included Theodore Roosevelt of New York and Woodrow Wilson of New Jersey. Roosevelt worked to develop a fair system for hiring state workers and made some corporations pay taxes. Wilson reduced the railroads' power and pushed for a direct primary law. Both Roosevelt and Wilson later became President and brought reforms to the White House.

**✓ Checkpoint** How did Progressive reformers change local and state governments?

**Vocabulary Builder**
<u>dynamic</u>—(dī NAM ihk) *adj.* energetic; relating to change or productive activity

---

SECTION

# 1 Assessment

**Progress Monitoring *Online***
For: Self-test with vocabulary practice
Web Code: nea-0402

## Comprehension

1. **Terms** Explain how each of the following terms is an example of a social or political reform.
   - settlement house
   - direct primary
   - initiative
   - referendum
   - recall

2. **NoteTaking Reading Skill: Identify Details** Use your flowchart to answer the Section Focus Question: What areas did Progressives think were in need of the greatest reform?

## Writing About History

3. **Quick Write: Compare and Contrast Points of View** In a narrative essay, you may compare and contrast points of view on an issue through the opinions of various individuals. Compare and contrast Social Darwinism with Social Gospel through the personalities of William Graham Sumner, Billy Sunday, and Dwight L. Moody. Use library or Internet resources to complete this assignment.

## Critical Thinking

4. **Recognize Cause and Effect** What problems did muckrakers expose and what effects did their work have on Progressive reform?

5. **Summarize** Describe Walter Rauschenbusch's ideas about Social Gospel and the Progressive Movement.

6. **Identify Points of View** Which groups in American society might have opposed Progressive reform? Explain.

# *The Jungle* by Upton Sinclair

When Upton Sinclair published *The Jungle* in 1906, he meant to open America's eyes to the plight of workers in the filthy, dangerous Chicago stockyards. Instead, popular outrage focused on the wider-reaching threat of spoiled meat. Congress quickly passed the nation's first legislation regulating the meat, food, and drug industries. Sinclair, disappointed by his failure to provoke more sympathy for the overworked, underpaid workers, noted "I aimed at the public's heart, and by accident I hit it in the stomach."

There was never the least attention paid to what was cut up for sausage. . . . There would be meat that had tumbled out on the floor, in the dirt and sawdust, where the workers had tramped and spit uncounted billions of consumption [tuberculosis] germs. There would be meat stored in great piles in rooms; and the water from leaky roofs would drip over it, and thousands of rats would race about on it. It was too dark in these storage places to see well, but a man could run his hand over these piles of meat and sweep off handfuls of the dried dung of rats. These rats were nuisances, and the packers would put poisoned bread out for them; they would die, and then rats, bread, and meat would go into the hoppers together. This is no fairy story and no joke; the meat would be shoveled into carts, and the man who did the shoveling would not trouble to lift out a rat even when he saw one—there were things that went into the sausage in comparison with which a poisoned rat was a tidbit. There was no place for the men to wash their hands before they ate their dinner, and so they made a practice of washing them in the water that was to be ladled into the sausage. There were the butt-ends of smoked meat, and the scraps of corned beef, and all the odds and ends of the waste of the plants, that would be dumped into old barrels in the cellar and left there. Under the system of rigid economy which the packers enforced, there were some jobs that it only paid to do once in a long time, and among these was the cleaning out of the waste barrels. Every spring they did it; and in the barrels would be dirt and rust and old nails and stale water—and cartload after cartload of it would be taken up and dumped into the hoppers with fresh meat, and sent out to the public's breakfast.

## Thinking Critically
1. **Analyze Literature** Describe the author's style in this excerpt.
2. **Evaluate Literature** How does Sinclair's way of writing boost his credibility?

◀ A woman working at a Pittsburgh cigar factory in 1909

▲ A week's wages—only $1.50!

**WITNESS HISTORY** 🔊 AUDIO

### Women at Work

As the Progressive Movement wore on, many reformers took up causes that affected women. Although women spearheaded a number of Progressive reforms, they did not have the right to vote in national elections. In workplaces like the Triangle Shirtwaist Factory, women endured the awful conditions described by one worker:

❝It was a world of greed; the human being didn't mean anything. The hours were from 7:30 in the morning to 6:30 at night when it wasn't busy. When the season was on we worked until 9:00. No overtime pay, not even supper money. . . . When you were told Saturday afternoon, through a sign on the elevator, 'If you don't come in on Sunday, you needn't come in on Monday,' what choice did you have? You had no choice.❞

—Pauline Newman, organizer of the International Ladies Garment Workers Union

# Women Make Progress

 **Content Expectations**

- **6.3.1** Describe problems/issues created by U.S.'s industrial/urban transformation between 1895–1930.
- **6.3.2a** Analyze causes/consequences of 16th, 17th, 18th, 19th Amendments.
- **6.3.3** Analyze successes/failures to expand women's rights.

### Terms and People

Florence Kelley
NCL
temperance movement
Margaret Sanger
Ida B. Wells

suffrage
Carrie Chapman Catt
NAWSA
Alice Paul
Nineteenth Amendment

### NoteTaking

**Reading Skill: Identify Main Ideas** As you read this section, complete an outline like the one below to capture the main ideas.

> I. Women Expand Reforms
>   A. Hardships for women
>     1.
>     2.
>   B.

**Why It Matters** In the early 1900s, a growing number of women were no longer content to have a limited role in society. Women activists helped bring about Progressive reforms and won the right to vote. In the years ahead, women would continue the struggle to expand their roles and rights. **Section Focus Question: How did women of the Progressive Era make progress and win the right to vote?**

## Progressive Women Expand Reforms

In the early 1900s, a growing number of women wanted to do more than fulfill their roles as wives and mothers. They were ready to move beyond raising children, cooking meals, keeping the home tidy, and caring for family members. They wanted to expand their role in the community.

Education helped women achieve their goals. By the 1890s, a growing number of women's colleges prepared them for careers as teachers or nurses. Some, such as Bryn Mawr College in Pennsylvania and the School of Social Work in New York, trained them to lead the new organizations working for social reform. Armed with education and modern ideas, many middle-class white women began to tackle problems they saw in society.

**Working Women Face Hardships** For most women, however, working outside the home meant difficult jobs, with long hours and dangerous conditions. And these women were usually expected to

011135

hand over their wages to their husbands, fathers, or brothers. Many women labored in factories that made cigars or clothing. Others toiled as laundresses or servants. Immigrants, African Americans, and women from rural areas filled these jobs, and most of them had little or no education. As a result, they could easily be cheated or bullied by their employers. Without being able to vote, women had little influence on the politicians who could expand their rights and look after their interests.

### Reformers Champion Working Women's Rights

A key goal of women reformers was to limit the number of work hours. They succeeded in several states. For example, a 1903 Oregon law capped women's workdays at ten hours. Five years later, in *Muller* v. *Oregon*, the Supreme Court reviewed that law. Lawyer Louis D. Brandeis argued that long working hours harmed working women and their families.

The Supreme Court agreed with Brandeis. Based on their role as mothers, it said, women could be "properly placed in a class" by themselves. As a result, laws could limit their work hours, even if similar laws would not be allowed for men. At the time, Progressives viewed this decision as a victory for women workers. In later years, however, this ruling was used to justify paying women less than men for the same job.

**Florence Kelley** believed that women were hurt by the unfair prices of goods they had to buy to run their homes. In 1899, she helped found the **National Consumers League (NCL),** which is still active today. The NCL gave special labels to "goods produced under fair, safe, and healthy working conditions" and urged women to buy them and avoid products that did not have these labels. The NCL pushed for other reforms as well. It backed laws calling for the government to inspect meatpacking plants, to make workplaces safer, and to make payments to the unemployed.

Florence Kelley also helped form the Women's Trade Union League (WTUL), another group that tried to improve conditions for female factory workers. It was one of the few groups in which upper-class and working-class women served together as leaders. The WTUL pushed for federal laws that set a minimum wage and an eight-hour workday. It also created the first workers' strike fund, which could be used to help support families who refused to work in unsafe or unfair conditions.

### Women Work for Changes in Family Life

A main goal of Progressive women was to improve family life. They pushed for laws that could help mothers keep families healthy and safe. One focus of this effort was the **temperance movement** led by the Women's Christian Temperance Union (WCTU). This group promoted temperance, the practice of never drinking alcohol. Members felt that alcohol often led men to spend their earnings on liquor, neglect their families, and abuse their wives. Formed in the 1870s, the WCTU gained strength during the Progressive Era. Their work led to the passage of the Eighteenth Amendment, which outlawed the production and sale of alcohol.

Nurse **Margaret Sanger** thought that family life and women's health would improve if mothers had fewer children. In 1916, Sanger, herself one of 11 children, opened the country's first birth-control clinic. Sanger was jailed several times as a "public nuisance." But federal courts eventually said doctors could give out information about family planning. In 1921, Sanger founded the American Birth Control League to make this information available to more women.

### Women Campaign for Temperance

Minnesota women march to ban alcohol. The temperance movement gained a victory when Congress passed the 18th Amendment in 1917.

African American women also worked for social change. In 1896, **Ida B. Wells,** a black teacher, helped form the National Association of Colored Women (NACW). The group aimed to help families strive for success and to assist those who were less fortunate. With money raised from educated black women, the NACW set up day-care centers to protect and educate black children while their parents went to work.

 **Checkpoint** What steps did women take to win workers' rights?

# Women Fight for the Right to Vote

One of the boldest goals of Progressive women was **suffrage**—the right to vote. They argued that this was the only way to make sure that the government would protect children, foster education, and support family life. As Jane Addams explained, women needed the vote because political issues reached inside people's homes.

> **Primary Source** "If the street is not cleaned by the city authorities no amount of private sweeping will keep the tenement free from grime; if the garbage is not properly collected and destroyed a tenement-house mother may see her children sicken and die of diseases from which she alone is powerless to shield them, although her tenderness and devotion are unbounded. She cannot even secure untainted meat for her household, . . . unless the meat has been inspected by city officials."
>
> —Jane Addams, *Ladies Home Journal,* 1910

Since the 1860s, reformers such as Susan B. Anthony and Elizabeth Cady Stanton had tirelessly struggled for the right for women to have a voice in political issues. They failed at the federal level, but by the end of the 1890s women in western states, such as Wyoming and Colorado, had won the right to vote.

**Catt Takes Charge of the Movement** In the 1890s, the national suffrage effort was reenergized by **Carrie Chapman Catt.** Catt had studied law and worked as one of the country's first female school superintendents. A captivating speaker, Catt traveled around the country urging women to join the **National American Woman Suffrage Association (NAWSA).** In 1900, she became the president of the NAWSA. Catt promoted what became known as her "winning plan," which called for action on two fronts. Some teams of women lobbied Congress to pass a constitutional amendment giving women the right to vote. Meanwhile, other teams used the new referendum process to try to pass state suffrage laws. By 1918, this <u>strategy</u> had helped women win the right to vote in New York, Michigan, and Oklahoma.

Catt introduced a "society plan" to recruit wealthy, well-educated women. She and her army of workers signed on women from all levels of society, including African Americans, Mexican Americans, and Jewish immigrants. All these women, called "suffragettes," helped promote suffrage in their own areas.

While the suffrage movement gained ground, some women worked against it. The National Association Opposed to Woman Suffrage (NAOWS) believed that the effort to win the vote would take women's attention away from family and volunteer work that benefited society in many ways. But as the pressure for women's suffrage grew stronger, the NAOWS faded away.

## HISTORY MAKERS

### Ida B. Wells (1862–1931)
Wells had gained fame for her campaign against the lynching of African Americans. But she was also a tireless worker for women's suffrage and joined in the famous 1913 march for universal suffrage that took place in Washington, D.C. Not able to tolerate injustice of any kind, Ida B. Wells, along with Jane Addams, successfully blocked the establishment of segregated schools in Chicago. In 1930, she ran for the Illinois State legislature, which made her one of the first black women to run for public office in the United States.

Ida B. Wells

Black Heritage USA 25

**Vocabulary Builder**
<u>strategy</u>–(STRAT uh jee) *n.* plan or an action based on a plan

Activists Carry on the Struggle Some women, known as social activists, grew more daring in their strategies to win the vote. **Alice Paul,** their best-known leader, was raised in a Quaker home where she was encouraged to be independent. Paul attended a Quaker college and the New York School of Social Work before earning a Ph.D. from the University of Pennsylvania in 1912. She believed that drastic steps were needed to win the vote. By 1913, she was organizing women to recruit others across the nation. They drew in women of many backgrounds, from Maud Younger, known as the "millionaire waitress" because she organized California's first waitresses' union, to Nina Otero-Warren, a Hispanic who headed New Mexico's State Board of Health.

By 1917, Paul formed the National Woman's Party (NWP), which used public protest marches. The NWP became the first group to march with picket signs

# SUFFRAGISTS WIN THE VOTE

**The National Woman's Party began picketing the White House,** urging President Wilson to back the woman's suffrage amendment. Susan B. Anthony had introduced the amendment nearly 40 years earlier, but the Senate had rejected it twice. So when America entered World War I, and Wilson proclaimed, "The world must be made safe for democracy," the weary suffragists were astounded. They wondered how could America be a democracy if women could not vote?

Then, when envoys from Russia visited Wilson in June, Alice Paul and her activists saw a golden opportunity. The Russians had just overthrown the czar, established a republic, and granted women the right to vote. As the envoys neared the White House, the suffragists stunned and embarrassed Wilson by unveiling a new banner that claimed America was not a democracy. The women set in motion a series of events that would change America.

TO THE RUSSIAN ENVOYS
President Wilson and Envoy Root are deceiving Russia. They say we are a democracy. Help us win a world war so that democracies may survive".
We, the Women of America, tell you that America is not a democracy. Twenty million American Women are denied the right to vote. President Wilson is the chief opponent of their national enfranchisement.
Help us make this nation really free. Tell our government that it must liberate its people before it can claim free Russia as an ally.

▲ "America is Not a Democracy"
An angry mob shredded protestors' banners. The police warned the women not to return.

VOTE FOR THE WOMAN SUFFRAGE AMENDMENT
NOV. 2ND 1915.

**Suffrage Poster** ▶
In marches on Washington, D.C., women urged Congress to vote for suffrage.

outside the White House. Hundreds of women were arrested in these protests. Some went on hunger strikes, refusing to eat until they could vote. The NWP methods angered many people, including women in other suffrage groups. Nevertheless, they did help win women the right to vote, because the NWP's actions made less-radical groups like the NAWSA look tame by comparison.

**The Nineteenth Amendment Becomes Law** When the United States entered World War I in 1917, Carrie Catt and Florence Kelley led the NAWSA to support the war effort. Their actions and those of the NWP convinced a growing number of legislators to support a women's suffrage amendment. In June 1919, Congress approved the **Nineteenth Amendment,** which stated that the right to vote "shall not be denied or abridged on account of sex." On August 18, 1920, the

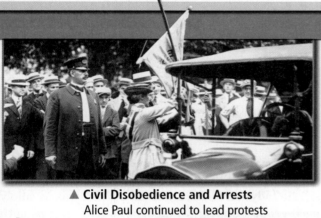

▲ **Civil Disobedience and Arrests**
Alice Paul continued to lead protests in front of the White House. She and 168 others were arrested and jailed.

**Suffering for the Cause** ▶
The jailed women went on hunger strikes. They endured forced-feedings, beatings, disease, and poor medical treatment.

◀ **Spreading the Word**
The suffragists traveled the country, telling their story. They kept attention focused on women's suffrage when the issue might otherwise have been eclipsed by World War I.

**Why It Matters**
The efforts of these women swayed public opinion and helped the Susan B. Anthony Amendment become law. The House passed the amendment in 1918. Then the Senate passed it by one vote in 1919. Finally, in 1920, Tennessee became the 36th state to ratify the 19th Amendment. At long last, women in every state of the nation could vote. America had changed.

**Thinking Critically**
Why was the banner that was unveiled when the Russians visited Wilson so effective in stirring public opinion?

# Passage of Women's Suffrage

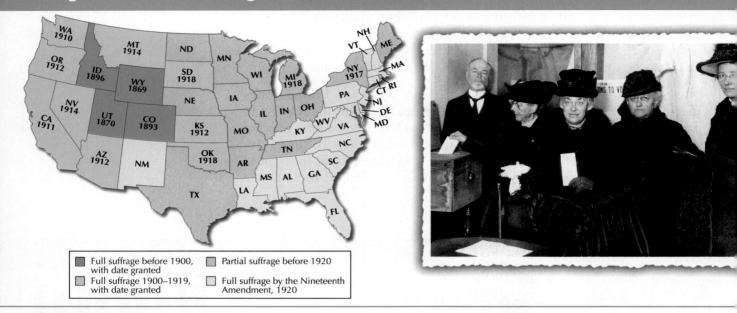

Full suffrage before 1900, with date granted
Full suffrage 1900–1919, with date granted
Partial suffrage before 1920
Full suffrage by the Nineteenth Amendment, 1920

## Women's Suffrage

What pattern do you see in the passage of suffrage at the state level?

Tennessee State House of Representatives passed the amendment by one vote. With Tennessee's ratification, enough states had passed the amendment that it became official.

Alice Paul and Carrie Catt both claimed responsibility for the victory. In fact, according to historian Nancy Cott, "neither the shocking militancy of the National Women's Party nor the ladylike moderation of NAWSA was so solely responsible for victory as each group publicly claimed." The rival groups both contributed to the triumph of the women's suffrage movement. As a result, on November 2, 1920, Catt, Paul, and millions of other American women voted for the first time in a U.S. presidential election.

✓ **Checkpoint** What tactics did Progressive women use to win the right to vote?

---

## SECTION 2 Assessment

**Progress Monitoring Online**
For: Self-test with vocabulary practice
Web Code: nea-0404

### Comprehension

1. **People** Explain how each of the following people changed the lives of women.
   - Florence Kelley
   - Margaret Sanger
   - Ida B. Wells
   - Carrie Chapman Catt
   - Alice Paul

2.  **NoteTaking Reading Skill: Identify Main Idea** Use your outline to answer the Section Focus Question: How did women of the Progressive Era make progress and win the right to vote?

### Writing About History

3. **Quick Write: Communicate Perspective** Look at the map on the passage of women's suffrage in this section. In one paragraph, describe the map from the perspective of a supporter of suffrage for women. In a second paragraph, describe the map as viewed by a suffrage opponent.

### Critical Thinking

4. **Draw Conclusions** Why would education have led middle-class women to address societal problems?

5. **Solve Problems** Choose one specific social problem and explain how Progressive women reformers proposed to solve that problem.

6. **Analyze Effects** How did suffragists' efforts at the state level affect their effort to win the right to vote at the national level?

# Social Problems and Reforms

## TRACK THE ISSUE

**THE ESSENTIAL ?**

## What are the most pressing problems, and how can we solve them?

There have been many movements for social reform in the United States. But Americans do not always agree on the need for reform or on the best way to achieve it. In fact, some reform ideas face strong opposition. Why do some reform movements win support, while others do not? Use the timeline below to explore this enduring issue.

● **1790s–1820s**
**Second Great Awakening**
Revival of Christian faith sparks moral and spiritual reform.

● **1830s–1850s  Abolitionism**
Antislavery forces demand an end to the slave system.

● **1890–1920  Progressivism**
Reformers urge a broad range of social and political changes.

● **1950s–1960s  Civil Rights**
African Americans lead movement for racial equality.

● **1990s–2000s**
**Healthcare Reform**
Reformers combat the spiraling costs of healthcare and insurance.

Young children line up to receive vaccinations in a school clinic.

**MI** 6.3.1

***HEALTH CARE ACCOUNT SUMMARY***

| 01/11/05 | MRI LUMBAR W/O CONTRAST | $1,874.00 |
| 01/12/05 | INSURANCE/PAYMENTS | $250.00 |
| | AMOUNT DUE FROM PATIENT | $1,624.00 |

Healthcare costs are a major issue.

## DEBATE THE ISSUE

**Health Insurance**  Medical costs are soaring. Many Americans lack health insurance and cannot pay their bills. Some reformers want the government to provide universal health insurance, also known as a single-payer system. Others say this approach will cause more harm than good.

"... Everybody has ... to be covered. There's only three ways of doing it. You can have a single-payer system, you can require employers, or you can have individual responsibility. My plan combines employers and individual responsibility, while maintaining Medicare and Medicaid. The whole idea of universal health care is ... a core Democratic principle ..."
—Senator Hillary Clinton, 2008

"A single-payer system promotes higher taxes, limits technology, produces waiting lists, rations care, and prolongs suffering. ... A universal healthcare system run by government will reduce the quality and access to health care for all Americans. It's a prescription for disaster."
—Sally Pipes, President, Pacific Research Institute

**? TRANSFER Activities**

1. **Compare**  Why does Hillary Clinton support universal health care? Why does Sally Pipes oppose it?

2. **Analyze**  Do you think Sally Pipes would support the efforts of some Progressive Era city governments to purchase public utilities? Explain.

3. **Transfer**  Use the following Web site to see a video, try a WebQuest, and write in your journal. **Web Code:** neh-7702

**WITNESS HISTORY**  AUDIO

## Voices of Protest

The sympathy that reformers felt for the plight of the poor did not often extend to minorities. In 1912, Progressive journalist Samuel Bryan wrote an investigative article about Mexican immigrants. Displaying a common bias, Bryan concluded that the immigrants did not work hard enough. Yet, he was forced to admit that Mexican Americans faced discrimination. He wrote:

❝[Mexican Americans] are now employed to a considerable extent in the coal mines of Colorado and New Mexico, in the ore mines of Colorado and Arizona, in the smelters of Arizona, in the cement factories of Colorado and California, . . . and in fruit growing and canning in California. . . . Where they are employed in other industries, the same wage discrimination against them as was noted in the case of railroad employees is generally apparent.❞

—Samuel Bryan, *The Survey,* September 1912

▲ Cuero family, Warner Springs, California, 1904

# The Struggle Against Discrimination

 **Content Expectations**

- **6.1.5c** Analyze the automobile industry's impact on domestic and international migrations.
- **6.3.1** Describe problems/issues created by U.S.'s industrial/urban transformation between 1895–1930.
- **6.3.2d** Analyze causes/consequences of reform organizations, movements, individuals promoting change.

## Terms and People

Americanization
Booker T. Washington
W.E.B. Du Bois
Niagara Movement

NAACP
Urban League
Anti-Defamation League
mutualistas

## NoteTaking

**Reading Skill: Main Idea and Details**
Outline the section's main ideas and details.

> I. The Struggle Against Discrimination
>   A.

**Why It Matters** Prejudice and discrimination against minorities continued even as the Progressive Movement got underway. But in the spirit of Progressivism, African Americans, Latinos, Catholics, Jews, and new immigrant groups worked to help themselves. Their efforts paved the way for the era of civil rights that would follow decades later. **Section Focus Question: What steps did minorities take to combat social problems and discrimination?**

## Progressivism Presents Contradictions

The Progressive Era was not so progressive for nonwhite and immigrant Americans. Most Progressives were white Anglo-Saxon Protestant reformers who were indifferent or actively hostile to minorities. They tried to make the United States a model society by encouraging everyone to follow white, middle-class ways of life.

**Social Reform or Social Control?** Settlement houses and other civic groups played a prominent role in the **Americanization** efforts of many Progressives. While they taught immigrants English, their programs also tried to change how immigrants lived. They advised immigrants how to dress like white middle-class Americans and pushed them to replace the foods and customs of their homelands with

Protestant practices and values. These reformers believed that assimilating immigrants into American society would make them more loyal and moral citizens.

Many Progressives found the immigrants' use of alcohol especially alarming. In many European countries, it was customary for families to serve wine or beer with meals. Many reformers, however, believed that these practices showed moral faults. As a result, prejudice against immigrants was one of the forces behind the temperance movement.

**Racism Limits the Goals of Progressivism** Many Progressives shared the same prejudice against nonwhites held by other white Americans of the time. They believed that some people were more fit than others to play a leading role in society. They agreed with so-called scientific theories that said that dark-skinned peoples had less intelligence than whites. In the late 1800s, southern Progressives used these misguided theories to justify the passage of laws that kept African Americans from voting. Some southern Progressives urged an end to the violence and terrorism waged against African Americans. Edgar Gardner Murphy, an Episcopal minister and a leading Alabama Progressive, advised that African Americans "will accept in the white man's country the place assigned him by the white man, . . . not by stress of rivalry, but by genial cooperation with the white man's interests."

After the Supreme Court issued its *Plessy* v. *Ferguson* decision, states across the North and the South had passed segregation laws. By 1910, segregation was the norm across the nation. After 1914, even the offices of the federal

**Vocabulary Builder**
so-called–(SOH kawld) *adj.* commonly named; falsely or improperly named

**Comparing** Viewpoints

# How should we respond to discrimination?

African Americans were freed from slavery, but discriminatory laws and racist attitudes kept them oppressed and threatened. African Americans debated how they should respond to this discrimination.

## BOOKER T. WASHINGTON

Washington (1856–1915) believed that African Americans had to achieve economic independence before civil rights. Black people must tolerate discrimination while they proved themselves equal to white people. Slowly, civil rights would come.

**Primary Source**

"[The Negro must] live peaceably with his white neighbors . . . the Negro [must] deport himself modestly . . . depending upon the slow but sure influences that proceed from the possessions of property, intelligence, and high character for the full recognition of his political rights."

## W.E.B. DU BOIS

Du Bois (1868–1963) believed that black Americans had to demand their social and civil rights or else become permanent victims of racism. African Americans must fight every day for the rights given to them in the Constitution.

**Primary Source**

"We claim for ourselves every single right that belongs to a freeborn American . . . and until we get these rights we will never cease to protest. . . . How shall we get them? By voting where we may vote, by persistent, unceasing agitation, by hammering at the truth, by sacrifice and work."

**Compare**

1. How did the views of Washington and Du Bois about the nature of civil rights differ?

2. How do these leaders' opinions reflect the era in which they lived? Would leaders today make similar arguments? Explain.

government in Washington, D.C., were segregated as a result of policies approved by President Woodrow Wilson, a Progressive.

✓ **Checkpoint** What attitudes did most Progressives hold about minorities and immigrant groups?

## African Americans Demand Reform

In the face of these injustices, the nation's most visible African American leader urged patience. **Booker T. Washington** told blacks to move slowly toward racial progress. By working hard and waiting patiently, he believed, African Americans would gradually win white Americans' respect and eventually would be able to exercise their full voting and citizenship rights.

Other African Americans rejected this view. The most outspoken among them were **W.E.B. Du Bois** and William Monroe Trotter. Both men had been raised in New England and educated at Harvard University. Both urged African Americans to demand immediately all the rights guaranteed by the Constitution.

**African Americans Form the Niagara Movement** Du Bois and Trotter were especially concerned that all across the South, black men were being denied the right to vote. In the summer of 1905, they and other leading African American thinkers met at Niagara Falls. They had to meet in Canada because no hotel on the New York side of the border would give them rooms.

The **Niagara Movement,** as the group called itself, denounced the idea of gradual progress. Washington, they said, was too willing to compromise African Americans' basic rights. They also condemned his notion of teaching only trade skills. This kind of education, Du Bois said, "can create workers, but it cannot make *men*." Talented blacks should be taught history, literature, and philosophy, so they could think for themselves.

Despite its bold ideas, the Niagara Movement never grew to more than a few hundred strong. To make a difference, African Americans needed a more powerful voice.

**Riots Lead to Formation of NAACP** In the summer of 1908, a white mob in Springfield, Illinois, attempted to lynch two African American prisoners in the city jail. Upon learning that the prisoners had been removed to safety, the rioters turned their anger against the city's black residents, killing two people and burning 40 homes. The Niagara Movement members were outraged that such an attack could happen in Abraham Lincoln's hometown.

**Niagara Movement**
The original leaders of the Niagara Movement met in response to W.E.B. Du Bois's call to "organize thoroughly the intelligent honest Negroes throughout the United States."

This lynching occurred during the 1908 Springfield, Illinois, riot.

The Springfield riot also got the attention of a number of white reformers. They now <u>acknowledged</u> the need to help African Americans protect their lives, win the right to vote, and secure their civil rights. In 1909, they joined with leaders of the Niagara Movement to form the **National Association for the Advancement of Colored People (NAACP)**. The NAACP aimed to help African Americans be "physically free from peonage [forced, low-paid labor], mentally free from ignorance, politically free from disfranchisement, and socially free from insult."

NAACP leaders included white and black Progressives who had worked in other areas of social reform. Among them were Jane Addams, Ray Stannard Baker, and Florence Kelley. Ida B. Wells, owner of a Tennessee newspaper, used her publication to make clear the horror of lynching. She and the others planned the group's strategy—to use the courts to challenge unfair laws. In the early 1900s, the NAACP focused on the battle for equal access to decent housing and professional careers like teaching.

**African Americans Form the Urban League** Across the country, African Americans were migrating from rural to urban areas during this period. Local black clubs and churches set up employment agencies and relief efforts to help African Americans get settled and find work. In 1911, more than 100 of these groups in many cities joined into a network called the **Urban League.** While the NAACP helped middle-class blacks struggle for political and social justice, the Urban League focused on poorer workers. It helped families buy clothes and books and send children to school. It helped factory workers and maids find jobs. Both the NAACP and the Urban League still aid African Americans today.

✔ **Checkpoint** Why did African Americans and others decide it was time to organize against discrimination?

# Reducing Prejudice and Protecting Rights

African Americans were not alone in seeking their rights. Individuals and organizations of diverse ethnic groups spoke out against unfair treatment and took action by creating self-help agencies. For example, in northern cities, Catholic parishes offered a variety of social services to immigrants. In Chicago, a network of Polish Catholic groups grew so strong that it earned the nickname American Warsaw.

**The Anti-Defamation League Aids Jews** Jews in New York had formed the B'nai B'rith in 1843 to provide religious education and to help Jewish families. In response to growing anti-Semitism, the group founded the **Anti-Defamation League** in 1913. Its goal was—and still is—to defend Jews and others against physical and verbal attacks, false statements, and "to secure justice and fair treatment to all citizens alike. . . ."

**Mexican Americans Organize** Mexican Americans also organized to help themselves. Those living in Arizona formed the Partido Liberal Mexicano (PLM), which offered Mexican Americans many of the same services that the Urban League gave to African Americans. In several states, Mexican Americans formed **mutualistas,** groups that made loans and provided legal assistance. The mutualistas also had insurance programs to help members if they were too sick to work.

**Vocabulary Builder**
<u>acknowledge</u>–(ak NAHL ihj) *v.* to admit to be true

## HISTORY MAKERS

**Octaviano Larrazolo** (1859–1930)
Larrazolo was a Progressive governor in New Mexico who worked for many reforms. He helped make sure that New Mexico's first state constitution protected Latinos from discrimination. Elected governor in 1918, he pushed for laws aimed at helping children and improving public health. He also favored bilingual education and voting rights for women. That last stand cost him the support of his Republican Party, and he served only one term as governor.

**Japanese Field Workers**

Japanese immigrants, like those above, often found work tending the fruit orchards of California. Through hard work, many were later able to buy land and orchards of their own.

Many Mexican Americans were forced to sign unfair labor contracts that kept them in debt to people whose land they worked. In 1911, the Supreme Court struck down a law that enforced that system.

**Native Americans Take Action** Progressives did little to help Native Americans. The Dawes Act, passed in 1887, had divided reservations into plots for individuals to farm. But the law also said that lands not given to individual Indians could be sold to the general public. By 1932, nearly two thirds of the lands held by tribes in 1887 were in the hands of whites.

Carlos Montezuma, a Native American from Arizona, helped establish the Society of American Indians in 1911, the first organization for Indian rights to protest federal Indian policy. A doctor, Montezuma treated Native Americans living on reservations. He urged Native Americans to preserve their cultures and avoid being dependent on the government.

**Asian Americans Fight Unfair Laws** Asian Americans also had to protect themselves. A 1913 California law said that only American citizens could own land. Because Japanese immigrants could not become citizens, the law forced them to sell their land. Japanese Americans found a way around this, however, by putting the land in their children's names. Because their children had been born in the United States, they were American citizens.

Takao Ozawa fought the law in court that blocked Asian Americans from becoming citizens. In 1922, however, the Supreme Court ruled against him. A newspaper read by Japanese Americans commented, "The slim hope that we had entertained . . . has been shattered completely."

✔ **Checkpoint** What strategies did other minority groups use to defend their rights?

---

**Progress Monitoring Online**
For: Self-test with vocabulary practice
Web Code: nea-0406

## Comprehension

1. **Terms and People** For each item below, write a sentence explaining its significance.
   - Booker T. Washington
   - W.E.B. Du Bois
   - Niagara Movement
   - NAACP
   - Urban League
   - Anti-Defamation League
   - mutualistas

2. **NoteTaking Reading Skill: Main Ideas and Details** Use your outline to answer the Section Focus Question: What steps did minorities take to combat social problems and discrimination?

## Writing About History

3. **Quick Write: Gather Details** Suppose you want to write a narrative about the effect of the Urban League's work in the Progressive Era. Conduct research to find descriptions and images of African American life before and during this period.

## Critical Thinking

4. **Analyze Information** How did Progressives' views about race and values foster prejudice?

5. **Draw Inferences** What do the differing approaches of Booker T. Washington and W.E.B. Du Bois suggest about their views of American society?

6. **Compare** Were the goals and actions of the mutualistas more similar to those of the Urban League or to those of the Anti-Defamation League? Explain.

▲ Theodore Roosevelt speaking in New York City

"Teddy" bear ▶

## A Bold Leader Takes Control

When Theodore Roosevelt entered the White House, never before had the country had so young a leader. He brought to the presidency tremendous energy, vision, and a willingness to expand presidential power in order to improve American lives. In a rousing speech, he urged some young supporters:

❝The principles for which we stand are the principles of fair play and a square deal for every man and every woman in the United States. . . . I wish to see you boys join the Progressive Party, and act in that part and as good citizens in the same way I'd expect any one of you to act in a football game. In other words, don't flinch, don't fold, and hit the line hard.❞

—Theodore Roosevelt, Address to Boy's Progressive League, 1913

# Roosevelt's Square Deal

### MI Content Expectations

- **6.1.1f** Analyze technological advances that enabled the U.S. to become an industrial power.
- **6.3.2d** Analyze causes/consequences of reform organizations, movements, individuals promoting change.
- **6.3.2e** Analyze causes/consequences of expanding/restricting democracy practices of African Americans/immigrants.

### Terms and People

Theodore Roosevelt
Square Deal
Hepburn Act
Meat Inspection Act
Pure Food and Drug Act
John Muir

Gifford Pinchot
National Reclamation Act
New Nationalism
Progressive Party

## NoteTaking

**Reading Skill: Identify Main Ideas** As you read this section, use a concept web like the one below to record the main ideas.

Roosevelt's Square Deal — Environmental policies — Economic policies

**Why It Matters** In the late 1800s, the United States had several weak and ineffective Presidents. The arrival of Theodore Roosevelt, a charismatic figure who embraced Progressive ideals, ushered in a new era. Roosevelt passed Progressive reforms and expanded the powers of the presidency. He changed the way Americans viewed the roles of the President and the government. **Section Focus Question: What did Roosevelt think government should do for citizens?**

## Roosevelt Shapes the Modern Presidency

In 1901, when **Theodore Roosevelt** became President of the United States, he was only 43 years old. However, Roosevelt had packed quite a lot into those years, gaining a reputation for being smart, energetic, and opinionated. The sickly child of wealthy parents, he had used his family's resources to develop both his strength and his mind. Observers said he generated so much energy that if you met him, you left the event with bits of his personality "stuck to your clothes."

**Roosevelt Rises to the Presidency** Roosevelt had graduated with honors from Harvard University in 1880. He spent only a few months studying law at Columbia University before being elected to the New York State Assembly. After three years' service there, and after the deaths of both his mother and his wife, Alice, Roosevelt retired to a ranch in the West. There he developed a love of the wilderness.

# A Rough Rider in the White House

Theodore Roosevelt's energetic leadership style enabled him to redefine the presidency. He took on industry and tackled tough issues. Roosevelt used his presidential power to bust illegal monopolies, reduce abusive business practices, and make a symbolic statement against segregation.

This 1909 cartoon shows ► Roosevelt's differing approaches to "good" and "bad" trusts.

Roosevelt could not remain long out of the spotlight, however. By 1889, he had returned to politics. As president of New York City's Board of Police Commissioners, he gained fame by fighting corruption. President William McKinley noticed him and named him Assistant Secretary of the Navy. When the Spanish-American War broke out in 1898, Roosevelt resigned the post to form the Rough Riders, a volunteer cavalry unit that became famous during the war.

After the end of the conflict, the young war hero was elected governor of New York, where he pushed for Progressive reforms. His reform efforts annoyed Republican leaders in the state, though. They convinced McKinley to choose Roosevelt as his running mate so Roosevelt would leave New York—and them—alone. McKinley was reelected President in 1900, but within a few months he was assassinated, and Roosevelt became President. Roosevelt soon <u>dominated</u> public attention. Journalists vied for interviews with him and children begged their parents for a teddy bear, the new stuffed animal named for him.

Roosevelt greatly expanded the power of the President. He used his office and its powers to convince Americans of the need for change and to push through his reform proposals. He called his program the **Square Deal,** and its goals were to keep the wealthy and powerful from taking advantage of small business owners and the poor. His idea of fair government did not mean that everyone would get rich or that the government should take care of the lazy. He compared his Square Deal to a hand of cards.

**Vocabulary Builder**
<u>dominate</u> – (DAHM ih nayt) *v.* to have a commanding place or position in

**Primary Source** ❝When I say I believe in a square deal, I do not mean to give every man the best hand. If good cards do not come to any man, or if they do come, and he has not got the power to play them, that is his affair. All I mean is that there shall be no crookedness in the dealing.❞

—Theodore Roosevelt, 1905

✔ **Checkpoint** What did Roosevelt want his Square Deal program to achieve?

The illustration shows that ▶ in 1901, Booker T. Washington accepted Roosevelt's invitation to dinner. Roosevelt's actions angered those who favored segregation.

EQUALITY

◀ "Patent medications" sometimes made fraudulent claims or contained harmful chemicals. Roosevelt helped restore consumer confidence by supporting laws that regulated the food and drug industries.

**Thinking Critically**
1. **Analyze Visuals** Look at the image of Roosevelt's dinner with Washington. Why would the artist have placed a painting of Abraham Lincoln in the background?

2. **Make Generalizations** Using the information in these visuals, make one generalization about Theodore Roosevelt as President.

# Trustbusting and Regulating Industry

Roosevelt often stepped in with the authority and power of the federal government. One example was in 1902, when Pennsylvania coal miners went on strike. The miners wanted a pay raise and a shorter workday. Roosevelt sympathized with the overworked miners, but he knew that a steady supply of coal was needed to keep factories running and homes warm. He wanted the strike ended quickly.

First, Roosevelt tried to get mine owners to listen to workers' concerns. When this failed, he threatened to send federal troops to take control of the mines and to run them with federal employees. His threat forced the mine owners to give the miners a small pay raise and a nine-hour workday. For the first time, the federal government had stepped in to help workers in a labor dispute.

The coal strike was one of many steps Roosevelt took to control the power of corporations. Within a year, Roosevelt convinced Congress to establish the Department of Commerce and Labor to monitor businesses engaged in interstate commerce and to keep capitalists from abusing their power.

**Roosevelt Takes on the Railroads** The cost of shipping freight on railroads had been an issue since the 1870s. Railroad companies could charge whatever they wanted. The railroads' power was especially troublesome for western farmers. They had no other way to move their products to eastern markets.

In 1887, Congress had created the Interstate Commerce Commission (ICC) to oversee rail charges for shipments that passed through more than one state. The ICC was supposed to make sure that all shippers were charged the same amounts. By 1900, though, the Supreme Court had stripped away most of the ICC's power. So Roosevelt pushed Congress to pass the Elkins Act in 1903, which imposed fines on railroads that gave special rates to favored shippers. In 1906, he got Congress to pass the **Hepburn Act,** which gave the ICC strong enforcement powers. This law gave the government the authority to set and limit shipping costs. The act also set maximum prices for ferries, bridge tolls, and oil pipelines.

**Roosevelt Enforces the Sherman Antitrust Act** It did not take long for the President and his administration to earn a reputation as "trustbusters." In response to an antitrust suit filed by Roosevelt's attorney general, the Supreme Court ruled in 1904 that the Northern Securities Company—a big railroad company—was an illegal trust. The decision forced the company to split into smaller companies. The next year, the Court found that a beef trust and several powerful agricultural companies broke antitrust laws.

Roosevelt was not interested in bringing down all large companies. He saw a difference between "good trusts" and "bad trusts." Big businesses could often be more efficient than small ones, he believed. Big business was bad, he said, only if it bullied smaller outfits or cheated consumers. So he supported powerful corporations as long as they did business fairly. His supporters called him a "trust-tamer," but some wealthy Progressives criticized his trustbusting.

**Regulating Food and Drug Industries** In 1906, Upton Sinclair published his novel *The Jungle*. His descriptions of the filthy, unhealthy conditions in meatpacking plants revolted the public and infuriated the President. Roosevelt urged Congress to pass the **Meat Inspection Act** that same year. It provided federal agents to inspect any meat sold across state lines and required federal inspection of meat-processing plants. Today, when we eat lunchmeat or grilled chicken, we trust that federal inspectors have monitored the plant where it is produced. If there is a serious problem, the government can force the meat-packer to pull the product off the shelves before many people become sick. This regulation is one lasting result of Progressives' insistence that the government take responsibility for food safety.

The **Pure Food and Drug Act** placed the same controls on other foods and on medicines. It also banned the interstate shipment of impure food and the mislabeling of food and drugs. Today, the Food and Drug Administration (FDA) still enforces this law and others. The FDA monitors companies to make sure people are not hurt by dangerous substances or dishonest labels. For example, before a drug can be sold, it must be tested and approved by the FDA.

 **Checkpoint** What impact did Roosevelt's actions have on the government's role in the economy?

# The Government Manages the Environment

Roosevelt's deep reverence for nature also shaped his policies. The books he published on hunting and the rugged West reflected his fascination with the competition between humans and the wilderness. He was pleased that the federal government had established Yellowstone National Park in 1872 to protect wildlife, and he admired California naturalist **John Muir,** whose efforts had led Congress to create Yosemite National Park in 1890.

**Should National Forests Be Conserved or Preserved?** In 1891, Congress had given the President the power to protect timberlands by setting aside land as federal forests. Following Muir's advice, Roosevelt closed off more than 100 million acres of forestland. However, the President did not agree with Muir that all wild areas should be preserved, or left untouched. Some wild lands held valuable resources, and Roosevelt thought those resources were meant to be used. This view became clear in his forest policy. In typical Progressive style, he called on experts to draw up plans for both conserving and using the forests.

Roosevelt drew on the "<u>rational</u> use" ideas of **Gifford Pinchot,** who led the Division of Forestry in the U.S. Department of Agriculture. Pinchot recommended a different approach—that forests be preserved for public use. By this, he meant

**Vocabulary Builder**
<u>rational</u> – (RASH uhn uhl) *adj.* relating to or based on reason; reasonable

# National Land Conservation

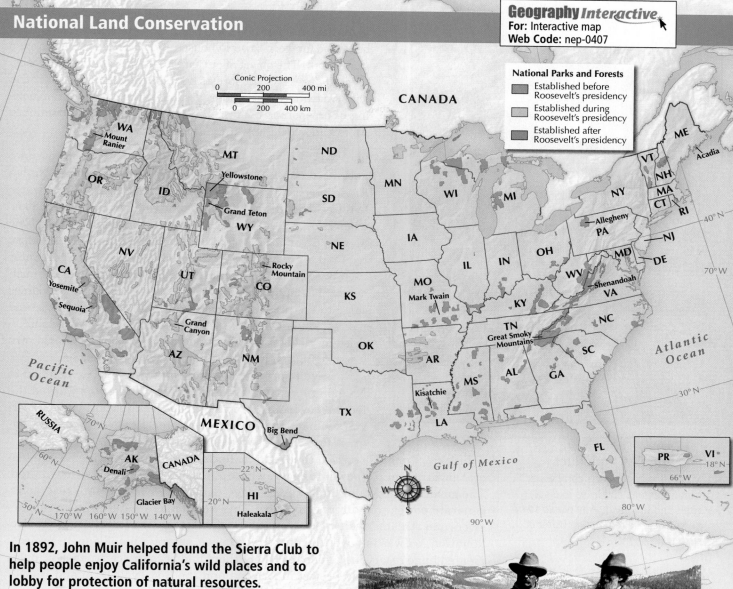

**National Parks and Forests**
- Established before Roosevelt's presidency
- Established during Roosevelt's presidency
- Established after Roosevelt's presidency

In 1892, John Muir helped found the Sierra Club to help people enjoy California's wild places and to lobby for protection of natural resources.

**Primary Source** "Climb the mountains and get their good tidings, Nature's peace will flow into you as sunshine flows into trees. The winds will blow their own freshness into you and the storms their energy, while cares will drop off like autumn leaves. As age comes on, one source of enjoyment after another is closed, but nature's sources never fail."

—John Muir, *Our National Parks,* 1901

**Map Skills** The land conservation movement of the Progressive Era led to the conservation of millions of acres of United States land.

1. **Human-Environment Interaction** How does preserving land for national parks and forests benefit people?

2. **Regions** What region of the country has the greatest area of conservation lands? Why do you think this is so?

President Theodore Roosevelt and conservationist John Muir at California's Yosemite National Park in 1903

125

**Los Angeles Aqueduct**

Massive water projects carry water from reservoirs and lakes to distant cities and farmland. *Why would some people oppose redirecting water in such ways?*

that forests should be protected so that trees would have time to mature into good lumber. Then, the protected areas should be logged for wood to build houses and new areas placed under protection. "The object of our forest policy," explained Pinchot, "is not to preserve the forests because they are refuges for the wild creatures of the wilderness, but rather they are the making of prosperous homes." Pinchot's views came to dominate American policies toward natural resources.

**Roosevelt Changes Water Policy** A highly controversial natural resource issue was water. Over centuries, Native Americans had used various irrigation methods to bring water to the arid Southwest. The situation changed in the late 1800s, when prospectors began mining and farming in Utah, New Mexico, Colorado, Nevada, and California. Mining machinery required a great deal of water, and systems of sharing water used by Mexican Americans were fought by people and businesses moving into these states. Private irrigation companies came to the area, staked claims to sections of riverbeds and redirected the water so farmers could revive—or "reclaim"—dried-up fields. Bitter fights developed over who should own water rights and how the water should be shared.

Roosevelt sprang into action on this issue. He listened to Nevada representative Francis Newlands, who wanted the federal government to help western states build huge reservoirs to hold and to conserve water. Roosevelt pushed Congress for a law that would allow it.

In 1902, Congress passed the **National Reclamation Act,** which gave the federal government the power to decide where and how water would be distributed. The government would build and manage dams that would create reservoirs, generate power, and direct water flow. This would make water from one state's rivers and streams available to farmers in other states. The full effect of the Reclamation Act was felt over the next few decades, as water management projects created huge reservoirs and lakes where there had been dry canyons. Examples include the Salt Valley Project in Arizona and the Roosevelt Dam and Hoover Dam on the Colorado River.

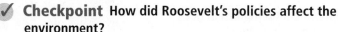 **Checkpoint** How did Roosevelt's policies affect the environment?

## NoteTaking

**Reading Skill: Compare and Contrast** As you read, fill in the Venn diagram with similarities and differences between Roosevelt and Taft.

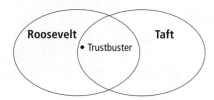

# Roosevelt and Taft Differ

Roosevelt left the presidency after two terms in office, saying he wished to enjoy private life. He was still a powerful force in the Republican Party, however, and he used that power to help Secretary of War William Howard Taft win the presidency in 1908. Roosevelt expected Taft to continue his programs of managing business and natural resources. Political cartoonists made caricatures of Roosevelt handing over what he called "my policies" to Taft, who seemed to have no ideas of his own.

**Taft Takes His Own Course** But Taft soon set his own agenda. He approved the Payne-Aldrich Act (1909), which did not lower tariffs as much as Roosevelt had wanted. He also pushed Congress to pass the Mann-Elkins Act (1910), which gave the government control over telephone and telegraph rates. He encouraged Congress to propose an income tax. Perhaps, most importantly, he dropped Roosevelt's distinction between good trusts and bad trusts.

Taft's Justice Department brought lawsuits against twice as many corporations as Roosevelt's had done. As a result, in 1911, the Supreme Court "busted" the trust built by the Standard Oil Company. But Taft also supported what the Court called its "rule of reason," which relaxed the hard line set by the Sherman Antitrust Act. The rule of reason allowed big monopolies so long as they did not "unreasonably" squeeze out smaller companies. Roosevelt publicly criticized these decisions. Then, Taft's attorney general sued to force U.S. Steel to sell a coal company it had bought. Roosevelt, who had approved the purchase of the company, fumed.

Taft further infuriated Roosevelt and other Progressives in the Republican Party when he fired Gifford Pinchot for publicly criticizing Secretary of the Interior Richard Ballinger. Pinchot charged that Ballinger, who opposed Roosevelt's conservation policies, had worked with business interests to sell federal land rich in coal deposits in Alaska.

**Analyzing Political Cartoons**

**Taft in the White House** Theodore Roosevelt looks on as President Taft is entangled in troubles.
1. What details illustrate Taft's troubles?
2. What does the cartoon suggest about Roosevelt's reaction to Taft's situation?

**Roosevelt Strikes Back** Roosevelt began traveling the country speaking about what he called the **New Nationalism**—a program to restore the government's trustbusting power. (See an excerpt from Roosevelt's New Nationalism speech at the end of this book.) Declaring himself as "strong as a bull moose," Roosevelt vowed to tackle the trusts in a third presidential term. The Taft-Roosevelt battle split the Republican Party as an election neared. Progressives bolted from the Republican party and set up the **Progressive Party**. Reformer Jane Addams nominated Roosevelt as the Progressive Party's candidate for the 1912 presidential election. The Republicans nominated Taft. A bitter election loomed.

✓ **Checkpoint** How did William Howard Taft's policies compare with Theodore Roosevelt's?

**SECTION 4 Assessment**

**Progress Monitoring *Online***
**For:** Self-test with vocabulary practice
**Web Code:** nea-0408

**Comprehension**

1. **Terms** Explain how each of the following acts and policies reflects Progressivism's influence.
   • Square Deal
   • Hepburn Act
   • Meat Inspection Act
   • Pure Food and Drug Act
   • National Reclamation Act
   • New Nationalism

2. NoteTaking **Reading Skill: Identify Main Ideas** Use your concept web to answer the Section Focus Question: What did Roosevelt think government should do for citizens?

**Writing About History**

3. **Quick Write: Present a Point of View** Choose one of the industries that President Roosevelt regulated. Imagine that you are a worker or business owner in the industry. In one or two paragraphs, describe your reaction to the President's actions. Use details to relate the effect of the government's actions on your work.

**Critical Thinking**

4. **Recognize Causes** Why might Theodore Roosevelt's push for reforms have angered some political leaders?

5. **Apply Information** How did Roosevelt's use of presidential and federal power differ from that of earlier Presidents? Give two examples.

6. **Analyze** How did Theodore Roosevelt's national forest policy reflect his ideas about conservation and preservation?

7. **Draw Conclusions** Do you think Roosevelt's public criticisms of Taft were justified? Why or why not?

◄ Woodrow Wilson, 1919

### A History of Reform

Before becoming President of the United States, Woodrow Wilson was president of Princeton University in New Jersey. At the time, most Princeton students were sons of wealthy families. These students joined "eating clubs" that excluded poor students and other outsiders.

Wilson objected. The eating clubs, he said, made social life more important than learning. Furthermore, he said, the clubs were unfair and damaging to those students who were excluded. Wilson lost his fight to do away with the eating clubs. But he won a reputation as a high-minded reformer who would speak out against social injustice. Wilson's reform efforts would continue in his role as President of the United States.

▲ Wilson campaign button

# Wilson's New Freedom

### Content Expectations

- **6.3.1** Describe problems/issues created by U.S.'s industrial/urban transformation.
- **6.3.2a** Analyze causes/consequences of 16th, 17th, 18th, 19th Amendments.
- **6.3.2b** Analyze causes/consequences of new regulatory legislation.

### Terms and People

Woodrow Wilson
New Freedom
Sixteenth Amendment
Federal Reserve Act
Federal Trade
  Commission
Clayton Antitrust Act

### NoteTaking

**Reading Skill: Identify Details** As you read this section, fill in a concept web like the one below to record details from the section.

**Why It Matters** Republicans Theodore Roosevelt and William Howard Taft introduced the country to forceful Progressive Presidents. Democrat Woodrow Wilson used the expanded power of the presidency to promote a far-reaching reform agenda. Some of Wilson's economic and antitrust measures are still important in American life today. **Section Focus Question: What steps did Wilson take to increase the government's role in the economy?**

## Wilson and the Democrats Prevail

In 1912, the Republican Party split over the issue of reform. Those who wanted a more active government formed the Progressive Party and chose Theodore Roosevelt as their candidate for President. Loyal Republicans gave the nod to President William Howard Taft.

The split created an opportunity for the Democrats and their candidate, **Woodrow Wilson,** to win the White House. Wilson's ideas had caught the attention of William Jennings Bryan, who helped Wilson win the Democratic nomination. As a student and later as a professor, Wilson had thought a great deal about good government. His doctoral thesis, *Congressional Government,* had launched him on a career teaching in college before he became the reforming governor of New Jersey.

Wilson shaped his ideas into a program he called the **New Freedom.** His plan looked much like Roosevelt's New Nationalism. It, too, would place strict government controls on corporations.

In a speech on the New Freedom, Wilson outlined his aim to provide more opportunities—more freedom—for small businesses.

**Primary Source** "The man with only a little capital is finding it harder and harder to get into the field, more and more impossible to compete with the big fellow. Why? Because the laws of this country do not prevent the strong from crushing the weak."

—Woodrow Wilson, "The New Freedom," 1913

Though he did not win the majority of the popular vote, Wilson received more than four times the number of Electoral College votes that went to Roosevelt or to Taft. The pious and <u>intellectual</u> son of a Virginia minister, Wilson was the first man born in the South to win the presidency in almost 60 years.

✔ **Checkpoint** How did Republican divisions help Wilson win the presidency?

**Vocabulary Builder**
<u>intellectual</u>–(ihn tuh LEHK choo uhl) *adj.* guided by thought; possessing great power of thought and reason

# Wilson Regulates the Economy

President Wilson attacked what he called the "triple wall of privilege"—the tariffs, the banks, and the trusts—that blocked businesses from being free. Early in his first term, he pushed for new laws that would bring down those three walls and give the government more control over the economy.

**Congress Lowers Tariffs and Raises Taxes** First, Wilson aimed to prevent big manufacturers from unfairly charging high prices to their customers. One way to do this was to lower the tariffs on goods imported from foreign countries so, if American companies' prices were too high, consumers could buy foreign goods. Wilson called a special session of Congress and convinced its members to pass the Underwood Tariff Bill, which cut tariffs.

The Underwood Tariff Act of 1913 included a provision to create a graduated income tax, which the recently passed **Sixteenth Amendment** gave Congress the power to do. A graduated income tax means that wealthy people pay a higher percentage of their income than do poor people. The revenue from the income tax more than made up for the money the government lost by lowering tariffs on imports.

**Federal Reserve Act** Next, Wilson tried to reform the banking system. At the time, the country had no central authority to supervise banks. As a result, interest rates for loans could fluctuate wildly, and a few wealthy bankers had a great deal of control over the national, state, and local banks' reserve funds. This meant that a bank might not have full access to its reserves when customers needed to withdraw or borrow money.

Wilson pushed Congress to pass the **Federal Reserve Act** (1913). This law placed national banks under the control of a Federal Reserve Board, which set up regional banks to hold the reserve funds from commercial banks. This system, still in place today, helps protect the American economy from having too much

Progressive Party button

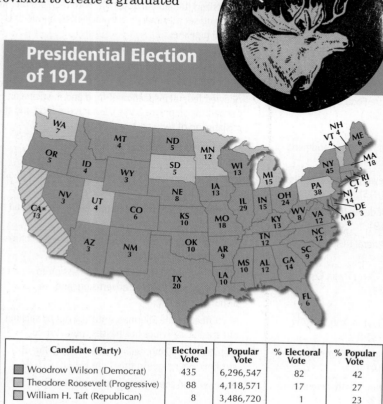

**Presidential Election of 1912**

| Candidate (Party) | Electoral Vote | Popular Vote | % Electoral Vote | % Popular Vote |
|---|---|---|---|---|
| Woodrow Wilson (Democrat) | 435 | 6,296,547 | 82 | 42 |
| Theodore Roosevelt (Progressive) | 88 | 4,118,571 | 17 | 27 |
| William H. Taft (Republican) | 8 | 3,486,720 | 1 | 23 |

*Two of California's electors voted for Wilson

money end up in the hands of one person, bank, or region. The Federal Reserve Board also sets the interest rate that banks pay to borrow money from other banks, and it supervises banks to make sure they are well run. Historians have called the Federal Reserve Act the most important piece of economic legislation before the 1930s.

**Wilson Strengthens Antitrust Regulation** Like Presidents before him, Wilson focused on trusts. Wilson agreed with Roosevelt that trusts were not dangerous as long as they did not engage in unfair practices. In 1914, he persuaded Congress to create the **Federal Trade Commission (FTC)**. Members of this group were named by the President to monitor business practices that might lead to monopoly. The FTC was also charged with watching out for false advertising or dishonest labeling. Congress also passed the **Clayton Antitrust Act** (1914), which strengthened earlier antitrust laws by spelling out those activities in which businesses could not engage.

These laws are still in effect today, protecting both businesses and consumers from abusive business activities. In recent years, the FTC has prosecuted companies that traded stocks dishonestly and fined companies that published false ads. The FTC also regulates buying on the Internet.

## Progressive Era Legislation and Constitutional Amendments

| Legislation/Amendment | Effect |
|---|---|
| Sherman Antitrust Act (1890) | Outlawed monopolies and practices that restrained trade, such as price fixing |
| National Reclamation Act (1902) | Provided for federal irrigation projects by using money from the sale of public lands |
| Elkins Act (1903) | Imposed fines on railroads that gave special rates to favored shippers |
| Hepburn Act (1906) | Authorized the federal government to regulate railroad rates and set maximum prices for ferries, bridge tolls, and oil pipelines |
| Meat Inspection Act (1906) | Allowed the federal government to inspect meat sold across state lines and required inspection of meat-processing plants |
| Pure Food and Drug Act (1906) | Allowed federal inspection of food and medicine and banned the shipment and sale of impure food and the mislabeling of food and medicine |
| Sixteenth Amendment (1913) | Gave Congress the power to collect taxes on people's income |
| Seventeenth Amendment (1913) | Instituted the direct election of senators by the people of each state |
| Underwood Tariff Act (1913) | Lowered tariffs on imported goods and established a graduated income tax |
| Federal Reserve Act (1913) | Created the Federal Reserve Board to oversee banks and manage reserve funds |
| Federal Trade Commission Act (1914) | Established the Federal Trade Commission to monitor business practices, false advertising, and dishonest labeling |
| Clayton Antitrust Act (1914) | Strengthened the Sherman Antitrust Act by spelling out specific activities businesses could not do |
| Eighteenth Amendment (1919) | Banned the making, selling, and transporting of alcoholic beverages in the United States |
| Nineteenth Amendment (1920) | Gave women the right to vote in all elections |

**Workers' Rights Protected** The Clayton Antitrust Act also ushered in a new era for workers by protecting labor unions from being attacked as trusts. Now, workers could organize more freely. Samuel Gompers of the American Federation of Labor (AFL) praised the new law as the "Magna Carta" of labor.

On the heels of these protections came the Workingman's Compensation Act (1916), which gave wages to temporarily disabled civil service employees. That same year, Wilson pushed for the Adamson Act to prevent a nationwide railroad strike, which would have stopped the movement of coal and food, leaving millions of Americans cold and hungry. Railroad union leaders insisted on the eight-hour day, but railroad managers would not accept it. Wilson called many company leaders to the White House, pleading with them to change their minds and avert a strike. When those efforts failed, he worked with Congress to pass the Adamson Act, which limited railroad employees' workdays to eight hours.

However, Wilson did not always support organized labor, as a tragic incident known as the Ludlow Massacre showed. In the fall of 1913, coal miners in Ludlow, Colorado, demanded safer conditions, higher pay, and the right to form a union. When the coal company refused, they walked off the job. Evicted from company housing, the miners and their families set up in a tent city near the mines. The strike continued through the winter. Then, on April 20, 1914, the Colorado National Guard opened fire on the tent city and set fire to the tents, killing some 26 men, women, and children. In the end, Wilson sent federal troops to restore order and break up the strike. The miners' attempt to form a union had failed.

✓ **Checkpoint** What policies did Wilson pursue in support of his New Freedom program?

# Progressivism Leaves a Lasting Legacy

The political reforms of the Progressives had a lasting effect on the American political system. The initiative, referendum, and recall and the Nineteenth Amendment expanded voters' influence. Progressive reforms also paved the way for future trends. Starting in this period, the federal government grew to offer more protection to Americans' private lives while at the same time, gaining more control over peoples' lives.

The American economy today showcases the strength of the Progressives' legacy. Antitrust laws, the Federal Reserve Board, and the other federal agencies watch closely over the economy. The controls that Roosevelt and Wilson put in place continue to provide consumer protections. In later years, the government built on those actions to extend regulation over other aspects of business.

The Progressive years also greatly expanded the government's role in managing natural resources. Especially in the West, federal action on dams, national parks, and resource use remain major areas of debate. Those debates and decisions affect people in other regions as well. For example, while farmers in California, Arizona, or New Mexico worry about getting enough water to grow crops, the rest of the nation awaits the delivery of the food they grow.

It is true that many of the problems identified by the Progressives still plague us today. There are still dishonest sellers, unfair employment practices, and problems in schools, cities, the environment, and public health. However, the Progressive reformers passed on the idea that government can take action to help people fix those problems.

✓ **Checkpoint** What was the long-term impact of the Progressive Era on American life?

---

**Progress Monitoring _Online_**
For: Self-test with vocabulary practice
Web Code: nea-0409

**Comprehension**

1. **Terms and People** For each item below, write a sentence explaining its significance.
   • Woodrow Wilson
   • New Freedom
   • Sixteenth Amendment
   • Federal Reserve Act
   • Clayton Antitrust Act

2. <u>NoteTaking</u> **Reading Skill: Identify Details** Use your flowchart to answer the Section Focus Question: What steps did Wilson take to increase the government's role in the economy?

**Writing About History**

3. **Quick Write: Use Vivid Language** Choose an event discussed in this section. In one or two paragraphs, retell a portion of the event. Be sure to use vivid language and include details. Do additional research if needed.

**Critical Thinking**

4. **Compare and Contrast** How were the goals and actions of Wilson's New Freedom similar to Roosevelt's New Nationalism? How were they different?

5. **Draw Conclusions** Describe how each of the following met Progressive goals: the Sixteenth Amendment; the Clayton Antitrust Act; the FTC.

6. **Demonstrate Reasoned Judgment** In which area do you think government reforms had the greatest impact? Why?

# Quick Study Guide

 6.3.1

**Progress Monitoring *Online***
For: Self-test with vocabulary practice
Web Code: nea-0410

## ■ Effects of Social Progressivism

| Living Conditions | • Immigrants gain access to child care and English classes.<br>• Municipal governments are pressured to improve sanitation and tenement safety.<br>• Minority groups organize, create self-help agencies, and fight discrimination.<br>• Immigrants are encouraged to become "Americanized."<br>• Laws regulate safety of foods and medicine. |
|---|---|
| Working Conditions | • City and state laws improve workplace safety.<br>• Workers' compensation laws provide for payments to injured workers.<br>• Laws limit workday hours; Supreme Court upholds limits for women but not for men.<br>• State and federal governments were urged to adopt minimum wage and make other reforms.<br>• Strike fund aids workers who reject unsafe working conditions.<br>• Minority job seekers gain access to more jobs. |
| Children | • State and federal laws ban child labor; Supreme Court overturns federal ban.<br>• Compulsory-education laws require children to attend school.<br>• Poor children gain access to nursery schools and kindergartens. |

## ■ Progressive Organizations That Worked for Rights

NAACP
National Consumers League
Partido Liberal Mexicano
**Worked to Protect or Expand Rights**
National American Woman Suffrage Association
Anti-Defamation League
Urban League

## ■ Municipal Reforms

| Government Reforms | Election Reforms |
|---|---|
| • Commission form of government<br>• City managers<br>• Trained administrators<br>• City-owned public utilities | • Direct primary<br>• Initiative<br>• Referendum<br>• Recall |

## ☑ Quick Study Timeline

| | **In America** | | | |
|---|---|---|---|---|
| **1892**<br>John Muir helps found Sierra Club | | **1899**<br>Florence Kelley helps found National Consumers League | **1900**<br>Hurricane devastates Galveston, Texas | **1902**<br>President Roosevelt signs the National Reclamation Act |

| **Presidential Terms** | Grover Cleveland 1893–1897 | William McKinley 1897–1901 | Theodore Roosevelt 1901–1909 |
|---|---|---|---|

**1895**      **1900**

| **Around the World** | **1893**<br>New Zealand becomes first nation to grant women the right to vote | **1900**<br>Boxer Rebellion erupts in China | **1901**<br>Britain outlaws employing children under the age of 12 in factories or workshops |
|---|---|---|---|

# American Issues
## ●—●—● Connector

By connecting prior knowledge with what you have learned in this chapter, you can gradually build your understanding of enduring questions that still affect America today. Answer the questions below. Then, use your American Issues Connector study guide (or go online: www.PHSchool.com **Web Code:** neh-7703).

## Issues You Learned About

● **Social Problems and Reforms** Again and again, Americans have worked to reform problems that afflict society.

1. Think about the social problems that you have read about in this chapter. Identify the five problems that you think posed the biggest threat to society or to groups of Americans. Create a chart showing the following:
   - social problems
   - reform efforts
   - reformers involved
   - results of reform efforts

● **Voting Rights** Over the years, Americans have gradually expanded the democratic right to vote.

2. Who were some of the nineteenth-century leaders of the women's suffrage movement?

3. What methods did Carrie Chapman Catt use to help women win voting rights?

4. How did Alice Paul's methods differ from Catt's?

● **Government's Role in the Economy** Americans often debate the proper balance between free enterprise and government regulation of the economy.

5. What is a trust?

6. How did Roosevelt's and Taft's attitudes toward trusts differ?

7. What effect did Wilson have on trusts?

| Connect to Your World | Michigan |
|---|---|

**Expanding and Protecting Civil Rights** As you have read, African American and white reformers founded the National Association for the Advancement of Colored People (NAACP) in 1909 to protect African Americans' rights and freedom. Three years later, the NAACP chartered its eleventh local branch in Detroit, Michigan. The Detroit NAACP quickly became one of the largest and most active branches in the country. The organization has challenged housing discrimination, supported efforts to desegregate schools, promoted African-American-owned businesses, arranged college tours for local youth, provided aid to African countries, and registered African American voters. Today, the Detroit NAACP has more than 42,000 members and continues to actively sponsor community services. Learn more about one achievement of the Detroit NAACP. Write a newspaper article about the significance of that achievement.

**1906**
Congress passes the Meat Inspection and Pure Food and Drug acts

**1909**
NAACP is formed

**1913**
Congress passes the Federal Reserve Act

**1920**
Nineteenth Amendment is ratified

William H. Taft 1909–1913    Woodrow Wilson 1913–1921

| 1905 | 1910 | 1915 | 1920 |

**1910**
Mexican Revolution begins

**1914**
World War I begins in Europe

**History Interactive**
**For:** Interactive timeline
**Web Code:** nep-0412

# Chapter Assessment

## Terms and People

1. Who were the **muckrakers**? Explain the effect the muckrakers had on American life.

2. Define **suffrage.** Why did Progressive women demand suffrage?

3. Who were **Booker T. Washington** and **W.E.B. Du Bois**? What different ideas did they hold?

4. What was the **Pure Food and Drug Act?** Which government agency enforces this act, and how does it do so?

5. Define the **Sixteenth Amendment.** How did it help the government?

## Focus Questions

The focus question for this chapter is **What were the causes and effects of the Progressive Movement?** Build an answer to this big question by answering the focus questions for Sections 1 through 5 and the Critical Thinking questions that follow.

### Section 1
6. What areas did Progressives think were in need of the greatest reform?

### Section 2
7. How did women of the Progressive Era make progress and win the right to vote?

### Section 3
8. What steps did minorities take to combat social problems and discrimination?

### Section 4
9. What did Roosevelt think government should do for citizens?

### Section 5
10. What steps did Wilson take to increase the government's role in the economy?

## Critical Thinking

11. **Analyze Visuals** Study the photograph of the child coal miners on the opening page of Section 1. What does this image tell you about the life of young laborers?

12. **Identify Point of View** Explain the different points of view Progressives held on the education of children. What point of view did John Dewey hold?

13. **Draw Inferences** In what way did the Court ruling in *Muller* v. *Oregon* contradict the ideas behind the women's rights movement?

14. **Draw Inferences** What factors may have pushed African Americans to migrate from rural areas to urban areas?

15. **Make Generalizations** How did nonwhites and minority groups seek to better themselves during the Progressive Era?

16. **Determine Relevance** How important was Upton Sinclair's *The Jungle* to passage of the Meat Inspection Act? Explain.

17. **Explain Effects** How did the Progressive Party affect the presidential election of 1912?

18. **Analyze Information** Why do historians believe that the Federal Reserve Act was the most important piece of economic legislation before the 1930s?

19. **Analyze Ideas and Effects** Compare the Social Gospel Movement and its results with Social Darwinism, which you read about earlier.

20. **Predict Consequences** Do you think that either the NAWSA or the NWP could have succeeded in gaining suffrage for women on its own? Explain.

## Writing About History

**Writing a Narrative Essay** Write a narrative essay that tells a story about one of the reform efforts of the Progressive Era in the United States. Tell the story from the point of view of a historical individual or a fictional character of the period.

### Prewriting
- Choose a reform effort that interests you most. Take notes about the people and locations involved.
- Choose a purpose for your essay. For example, you may want to highlight a certain event or result that you think deserves attention.
- Gather the facts and details you will need to tell your story, including any historic background.

### Drafting
- Identify the climax, or most important part, of your story. Then, decide what will happen in the beginning, middle, and end of the essay.

- Write an opening for the essay that will grab a reader's interest and make sure to include sensory details.
- Use many details to make the story vivid. Include dialogue when possible to convey the thoughts of your character.
- Write a conclusion that summarizes the significance of the experience to the character.

### Revising
- Use the guidelines on page SH11 of the Writing Handbook to revise your narrative essay.

## Regulation of the Economy

During the Progressive Era, Presidents such as Theodore Roosevelt and Woodrow Wilson called for the federal government to take on a greater role in regulating the economy. But not all Americans approved of the expansion of federal power. Use your knowledge of the Progressive Era and Documents A, B, C, and D to answer questions 1 through 4.

### Document A

"This country belongs to the people who inhabit it. Its resources, its businesses, its institutions, and its laws should be utilized, maintained, or altered in whatever manner will best promote the general interest. It is time to set the public welfare in the first place. . . .

We demand . . . that those who profit by control of business affairs shall justify that profit and that control by sharing with the public the fruits thereof. We therefore demand a strong national regulation of interstate corporations. . . .

We pledge our party to establish a Department of Labor, with a seat in the Cabinet, and with wide jurisdiction over matters affecting the conditions of labor and living."

—*Progressive "Bull Moose" Party Platform, 1912*

### Document B

#### Federal Reserve System

| Board of Governors | • Appointed by the President; confirmed by the Senate<br>• Sets cash-reserve requirements for member banks<br>• Reviews the short-term rates set by reserve banks |
|---|---|
| 12 Federal Reserve Banks | • Each serves one of 12 regional districts<br>• Set short-term interest rates for member banks |

| All nationally chartered banks required to be members |
|---|

### Document C

"What effect is what you may do here going to have upon the future welfare, productiveness, and value of the greatest single industrial interest of the country?. . . . Gentlemen, you may pass an act that will so compromise the value of the property and the prosperity of the communities of this country that it will bring widespread disaster. . . .

What I say, gentlemen, is that [it] is a very, very serious moment when an Anglo-Saxon government undertakes the charge of the people's money and says how much they shall earn by the exercise of their constitutional rights of liberty and property. And it should be recognized that possibly we are at the parting of the ways, and that if this be done it will go on until those constitutional guarantees have but little value, and the only profession worth exercising in the country will be that of holding office in some administrative board."

—*David Wilcox, President of Delaware and Hudson Railroad, testimony to Congress, 1905*

### Document D

"We have studied, as perhaps no other nation has, the most effective means of production, but we have not studied cost or economy as we should either as organizers of industry, as statesmen, or as individuals. Nor have we studied and perfected the means by which government may be put to the service of humanity, in safeguarding the health of the nation, the health of its men and its women and its children, as well as their rights in the struggle for existence. . . .

The first duty of law is to keep sound the society it serves. Sanitary laws, pure-food laws, and laws determining conditions of labor, which individuals are powerless to determine for themselves, are intimate parts of the very business of justice and legal efficiency."

—*Woodrow Wilson, First Inaugural Address, 1913*

---

1. Which of the documents above most closely reflects a belief in laissez-faire economics?
   - **A** Document A
   - **B** Document B
   - **C** Document C
   - **D** Document D

2. Why does the Progressive Party platform favor the creation of a federal Department of Labor?
   - **A** It would increase the profits of corporations.
   - **B** It would promote the good of the people.
   - **C** It would lead to the regulation of interstate commerce.
   - **D** It would limit the growing power of the federal government.

3. Based on Document B, how did the Federal Reserve Act increase the role of the federal government?
   - **A** It gave a federal board greater power to regulate interest rates.
   - **B** It increased the number of commercial banks.
   - **C** It made the Board of Governors independent of the President and Senate.
   - **D** It gave the people the right to elect the Board of Governors of the Federal Reserve.

4. **Writing Task** Should the federal government have broad power over the economy and people's lives? Use your knowledge of the Progressive Era and specific evidence from the primary sources above to support your opinion.

# 5 An Emerging World Power

## 1890–1917

## Americans Charge to Victory

When Theodore Roosevelt assumed command of the First U.S. Regiment of Volunteer Cavalry, the press nicknamed his new unit "Roosevelt's Rough Riders." On July 1, 1898, the Rough Riders, together with other units—including African American troops from the U.S. Ninth and Tenth Cavalries—stormed into battle outside Santiago, Cuba. A junior officer who would later become a decorated general remembered the unity of his fellow soldiers as the Americans charged up Spanish-held San Juan Hill:

66 White regiments, black regiments, regulars and Rough Riders, representing the young manhood of the North and South, fought shoulder to shoulder, unmindful of race or color . . . mindful only of their common duty as Americans. 99

—Lieutenant John J. Pershing

*Listen to the* Witness History *audio to hear more about America's rise to global power.*

◀ Future President Theodore Roosevelt poses with his victorious Rough Riders atop San Juan Hill.

Carving of Commodore Matthew Perry on an animal tusk

Poster from the Spanish-American War

### Content Expectations

**Chapter Focus Question: How did the United States become a global power?**

## Section 1
**The Roots of Imperialism** 6.1.1a, 6.1.5a, 6.3.1

## Section 2
**The Spanish-American War** 6.1.2a, 6.1.2b, 6.2.1

## Section 3
**The United States and East Asia** 6.1.2a, 6.1.2b, 6.2.1

## Section 4
**The United States and Latin America** 6.1.2a, 6.1.2b, 6.2.1

Medal won by African American soldier in Spanish-American War

Use the ☑ **Quick Study Timeline** at the end of this chapter to preview chapter events.

**Note Taking Study Guide** *Online*
For: Note Taking and American Issues Connector
**Web Code:** nee-7801

John Stevens

◀ A Hawaiian plantation worker harvests pineapples.

## WITNESS HISTORY 🔊 AUDIO

### America Eyes Hawaii

"The Hawaiian pear is now fully ripe and this is the golden hour for the United States to pluck it." John Stevens, U.S. minister to Hawaii, was not talking about fruit when he sent this note to the Secretary of State in 1893. He was talking about the United States taking over the Hawaiian Islands—along with their rich fields of sugar cane and pineapples. And Stevens did more than just talk. He ordered the United States Marines to aid in a revolt against the queen of Hawaii.

Five years later, the Senate finally agreed to annex Hawaii. The "Hawaiian pear" became part of the United States.

# The Roots of Imperialism

## Content Expectations

- **6.1.1a** Analyze gains from trade that enabled U.S. to become an industrial power.
- **6.1.5a** Analyze the automobile industry's impact of resource availability.
- **6.3.1** Describe problems/issues created by U.S.'s industrial/urban transformation between 1895–1930.

## Terms and People

imperialism
extractive economy
Alfred T. Mahan
Social Darwinism

Frederick J. Turner
Matthew Perry
Queen Liliuokalani

## NoteTaking

**Reading Skill: Identify Main Ideas** As you read, fill in a concept web like the one below with the key events that marked America's first steps toward world power.

Seward purchases Alaska

First Steps to World Power

**Why It Matters** For most of its early history, America played a small role in world affairs. But in the late 1800s, this began to change. With leading spokesmen calling for the United States to join the ranks of the world's major powers, the United States began to acquire influence and territories outside its continental borders. The United States was abandoning isolationism and emerging as a new power on the global stage. **Section Focus Question: How and why did the United States take a more active role in world affairs?**

## The Causes of Imperialism

During the Age of Imperialism, from the mid-1800s through the early 1900s, powerful nations engaged in a mad dash to extend their influence across much of the world. European nations added to colonies they had established during the Age of Exploration by acquiring new colonies in Africa and Asia. Following European success, Japan and the United States also began to consider the benefits of **imperialism,** the policy by which strong nations extend their political, military, and economic control over weaker territories.

**Imperialists Seek Economic Benefits** One reason for the rush to grab colonies was the desire for raw materials and natural resources. This was especially true for European nations and Japan. They sought colonies to provide tea, rubber, iron, petroleum, and other materials for their industries at home. These colonial economies were examples of **extractive economies.** The imperial country extracted, or removed, raw materials from the colony and shipped them to the home country. Possession of colonies gave nations an edge in the competition for global resources. In contrast to other world powers, the resource-rich United States had fewer concerns about shortages of raw materials in the nineteenth century.

For Americans, the problem was not a shortage of materials, but a surplus of goods. The booming U.S. economy of the late 1800s was producing more goods than Americans could consume. Farmers complained that excess production resulted in declining crop prices and profits. Industrialists urged expanding trade into new overseas markets where American <u>commodities</u> could be sold. Otherwise, they warned, American factories would close and unemployment would rise. Senator Albert J. Beveridge, a Progressive and friend of Theodore Roosevelt, explained why the United States needed to become a world power:

**Vocabulary Builder**
<u>commodity</u>—(kuh MAHD uh tee) *n.* anything bought or sold; any article of commerce

> **Primary Source**  "Today we are raising more [crops] than we can consume. Today we are making more than we can use. . . . Therefore we must find new markets for our produce, new occupation for our capital, new work for our labor."
> —Senator Albert J. Beveridge, "The March of the Flag," 1898

**Imperialists Stress Military Strength** To expand and protect their interests around the world, imperialist nations built up their military strength. **Alfred T. Mahan,** a military historian and an officer in the United States Navy, played a key role in transforming America into a naval power. In *The Influence of Sea Power Upon History*, Mahan asserted that since ancient times, many great nations had owed their greatness to powerful navies. He called upon America to build a modern fleet. Mahan also argued that the United States would need to acquire foreign bases where American ships could refuel and gather fresh supplies. Influenced by the ideas of Mahan and others, the United States expanded and modernized its navy by building new steel-plated, steam-powered battleships such as the USS *Maine*. By 1900, the United States had the third largest navy in the world.

**A Strong Navy**
Prominent imperialists like Alfred T. Mahan called for a strong American navy to protect U.S. interests overseas. *How could a strong navy benefit American exporters?*

## HISTORY MAKERS

**Alfred T. Mahan** (1840–1914)
Mahan, a naval officer and historian, urged American leaders to build a stronger navy and to obtain naval bases in Cuba, Hawaii, and the Philippines. He also argued that the United States should build a canal across Central America so its ships could move quickly between the Atlantic and Pacific oceans. American leaders eventually adopted all of Mahan's ideas to bolster the power of the United States Navy.

**Imperialists Believe in National Superiority** Imperialists around the world used ideas of racial, national, and cultural superiority to justify imperialism. One of these ideas was **Social Darwinism,** the belief that life consists of competitive struggles in which only the fittest survive. Social Darwinists felt that certain nations and races were superior to others and therefore were destined to rule over inferior peoples and cultures. Prominent Americans worried that if the United States remained isolated while European nations gobbled up the rest of the world, America would not survive.

One reason that these Americans embraced Social Darwinism was that they had long believed that God had granted them the right and responsibility to settle the frontier. They spoke of America's "Manifest Destiny" to expand all the way to the Pacific Ocean. In a best-selling work titled *Our Country,* Josiah Strong picked up on this theme. A religious missionary, Strong argued that Americans had a responsibility to spread their Western values. "God is training the Anglo-Saxon race," he asserted, "for its mission [to civilize] weaker races." American missionaries who shared Strong's belief journeyed to foreign lands to gain converts to Christianity.

In *The Significance of the Frontier in American History,* historian **Frederick Jackson Turner** noted that the frontier had been closed by gradual settlement in the nineteenth century. Throughout American history, he continued, the frontier had traditionally supplied an arena where ambitious Americans could pursue their fortunes and secure a fresh start. It had thus served as a "safety valve," siphoning off potential discontent. Now that America had spanned the continent, advocates of Turner's thesis urged overseas expansion as a way to keep the "safety valve" open and avoid internal conflict.

✔ **Checkpoint** What factors influenced Americans to play a more active role in the world?

## America's First Steps Toward World Power

Beginning in the mid-1800s, with little fanfare, America focused more and more on expanding its trade and acquiring new territories. One of America's first moves toward world power came before the Civil War.

**U.S. Power Grows in the Pacific** In 1853, Commodore **Matthew Perry** sailed a fleet of American warships into present-day Tokyo Bay, Japan. Prior to Perry's arrival, Japan had denied the rest of the world access to its ports. In fact, because most Japanese people had never seen steamships before, they thought the ships in Perry's fleet were "giant dragons puffing smoke." Perry cleverly won the Japanese emperor's favor by showering him with lavish gifts. Japanese leaders also realized that by closing off their nation to the outside world, they had fallen behind in military technology. Within a year, Perry negotiated a treaty that opened Japan to trade with America.

Perry's journey set a precedent for further expansion across the Pacific Ocean. In 1867, the United States took possession of the Midway Islands. Treaties in 1875 and 1887 increased trade with the Hawaiian Islands and gave the United States the right to build a naval base at Pearl Harbor.

**Seward Purchases Alaska** In 1867, Secretary of State William Seward bought Alaska from Russia for $7.2 million. Journalists scoffed at the purchase and referred to Alaska as "Seward's Folly" and "Seward's Icebox." They wondered why the United States would want a vast tundra of snow and ice 1,000 miles north

## Nationalism Fuels Pursuit of Empire

In the late nineteenth century, patriotic songs by composers such as John Philip Sousa reinforced Americans' widespread belief in the national superiority of the United States. *How did nationalism contribute to the rise of American imperialism?*

| Causes of Imperialism | ☑ Quick Study |
|---|---|
| **Economic gain** | • Industrialists want raw materials for industries in their home countries.<br>• Entrepreneurs want to sell their goods and invest in new overseas markets. |
| **Militarism** | Colonial powers seek bases for naval forces that protect their global trade networks. |
| **Nationalism and Social Darwinism** | Imperialists feel a moral duty to spread their culture to peoples they consider inferior. |

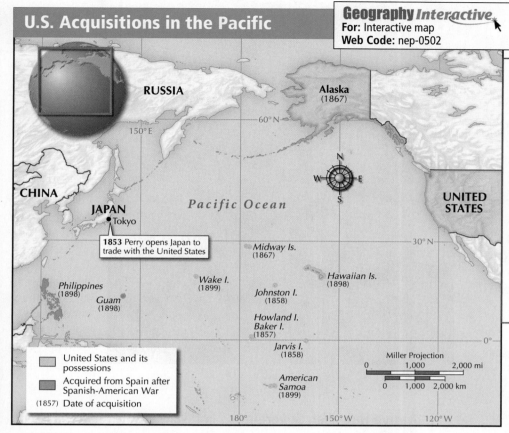

## U.S. Acquisitions in the Pacific

**Geography** Interactive.
For: Interactive map
Web Code: nep-0502

RUSSIA

Alaska
(1867)

60° N

150° E

N
W E
S

CHINA

JAPAN
• Tokyo

*Pacific Ocean*

UNITED
STATES

**1853** Perry opens Japan to
trade with the United States

Midway Is.
(1867)

30° N

Hawaiian Is.
(1898)

Philippines
(1898)

Wake I.
(1899)

Guam
(1898)

Johnston I.
(1858)

Howland I.
Baker I.
(1857)

Jarvis I.
(1858)

Miller Projection

0        1,000        2,000 mi
0     1,000    2,000 km

0°

American
Samoa
(1899)

☐ United States and its
  possessions
☐ Acquired from Spain after
  Spanish-American War
(1857) Date of acquisition

180°        150° W        120° W

**Map Skills** Between 1853
and 1898, the United States
opened Japan to American trade
and gained valuable possessions
across the Pacific Ocean.

**1. Locate:** (a) Japan, (b) Alaska,
  (c) Hawaiian Islands

**2. Place** Which islands lie about
  halfway between the United
  States and Japan?

**3. Analyze** Why were the
  Hawaiian Islands important to
  U.S. naval and merchant
  ships?

Engraving of Matthew Perry on an
animal tusk

of its border. But Seward's purchase almost doubled the country's size, and the "ice-box" turned out to be rich in timber, oil, and other natural resources. Alaska also greatly expanded America's reach across the Pacific. Scholars today see Seward's purchase as a key milestone on America's road to power.

### U.S. Influence in Latin America Grows
U.S. businessmen saw Latin America as a natural place to expand their trade and investments. Secretary of State James Blaine helped them by sponsoring the First International Pan-American Conference in 1889. Blaine preached the benefits of economic cooperation to delegates of 17 Latin American countries. The conference also paved the way for the construction of the Pan-American Highway system, which linked the United States to Central and South America.

In 1895, tensions rose between America and Great Britain because of a border dispute between British Guiana and Venezuela. Claiming that Britain was violating the Monroe Doctrine, President Cleveland threatened U.S. intervention. After some international saber-rattling, the British accepted a growing U.S. sphere of influence in Latin America. Relations between Britain and the United States soon improved.

✔ **Checkpoint** Why did journalists criticize Seward for his purchase of Alaska?

## The United States Acquires Hawaii

The Hawaiian Islands had been economically linked to the United States for almost a century. Since the 1790s, American merchant ships had stopped at Hawaii on their way to East Asia. Missionaries had established Christian churches and schools on the islands. Americans had also established sugar cane

## TRACK THE ISSUE

### Should the United States expand its territory?

The United States has expanded its territory many times. It has done so through various means, including negotiation, treaty, annexation, and war. But territorial expansion has often aroused strong debate among Americans. Use the timeline below to explore this enduring issue.

**1803 Louisiana Purchase**
Jefferson buys Louisiana Territory despite doubts about constitutionality.

**1845 Texas Annexation**
Texas joins the Union despite opposition from Mexico and nonslave states.

**1848 Mexican Cession**
United States gains vast lands in the Southwest as a result of war with Mexico.

**1867 Alaska Purchase**
Critics say Alaska is an icebox and call the deal "Seward's Folly."

**1893 Hawaiian Revolt**
American planters overthrow Queen Liliuokalani and pave way to annexation in 1898.

**1898 Spanish-American War**
Victory over Spain puts Cuba, Puerto Rico, the Philippines, and Guam under U.S. control.

Queen Liliuokalani

 6.2.1

Protesters want to restore the native sovereignty of the Hawaiian Islands.

## DEBATE THE ISSUE

**Native Hawaiian Sovereignty** In 1898, the United States annexed Hawaii without the consent of native Hawaiians. In recent years, some Hawaiians have called for the return of native sovereignty. One possible solution is the establishment of some form of self-rule for natives, much like the "nation within a nation" status of Native Americans.

❝For the overwhelming majority of Hawaiians, justice means political status and federal recognition, the restoration of our inherent sovereignty and redress from the United States for the illegal overthrow of the Kingdom of Hawaii. . . . Although there are more Hawaiians than . . . any other native peoples in the United States, Hawaiians have remained without recognition of our right to self-govern.❞

—Clayton Hee, Office of Hawaiian Affairs

❝Would the citizens of [a] Native Hawaiian government—like reservation Indians—be immune from state laws, regulations and taxes? . . . If Congress were to create a separate tribal government for Native Hawaiians, it would be imposing just such a system on the people of Hawaii. Persons of different races, who live together in the same society, would be subject to different legal codes. This . . . is a recipe for permanent racial conflict.❞

—John Kyl, senator from Arizona

### ? TRANSFER Activities

1. **Compare** How do the two speakers differ on the issue of self-rule for Hawaiians?

2. **Analyze** If Native Hawaiians gain sovereignty, how would their lives change?

3. **Transfer** Use the following Web site to see a video, try a WebQuest, and write in your journal. **Web Code:** neh-7802

plantations there. In 1887, American planters convinced King Kalakaua (kah LAH kah oo ah) to amend Hawaii's constitution so that voting rights were limited to only wealthy landowners, who were, of course, the white planters.

**American Planters Increase Their Power** In the early 1890s, American planters in Hawaii faced two crises. First, a new U.S. tariff law imposed duties on previously duty-free Hawaiian sugar. This made Hawaiian sugar more expensive than sugar produced in the United States. The sugar-growers in Hawaii therefore feared that they would suffer decreasing sales and profits.

The other problem was that in 1891, Kalakaua died and his sister Liliuokalani (lih lee oo oh kah LAH nee) was his <u>successor</u>. A determined Hawaiian nationalist, **Queen Liliuokalani** resented the increasing power of the white planters, who owned much of the Hawaiian land. She abolished the constitution that had given political power to the white minority.

With the backing of U.S. officials, the American planters responded quickly and forcefully. In 1893, they overthrew the queen. John Stevens, U.S. minister to Hawaii, ordered United States Marines to help the rebels seize power. The new government, led by wealthy planter Sanford B. Dole, asked President Benjamin Harrison to annex Hawaii into the United States.

**The United States Annexes Hawaii** President Harrison signed the treaty of annexation but could not get the required Senate approval before Grover Cleveland became President. Cleveland ordered a full investigation, which revealed that the majority of the Hawaiian people did not approve of the treaty. Cleveland refused to sign the agreement and apologized for the "flagrant wrong" done by the "reprehensible conduct of the American minister."

However, American sentiment for annexation remained strong, especially on the West Coast, where California business interests had close ties with the planters in Hawaii. In 1897, a new President entered the White House. William McKinley's administration favored annexation, and in 1898, after the outbreak of the Spanish-American War, Congress proclaimed Hawaii an official U.S. territory.

**Vocabulary Builder**
<u>successor</u>–(suhk SEHS uhr) *n.* person or thing that succeeds, or follows, another

✔ **Checkpoint** How did American planters react to Queen Liliuokalani's actions when she gained power?

---

## Assessment

**Progress Monitoring *Online***
For: Self-test with vocabulary practice
Web Code: nea-0504

**Comprehension**

1. **Terms and People** For each person listed below, write a sentence explaining his or her significance to American imperialism.
   - Alfred T. Mahan
   - Frederick J. Turner
   - Matthew Perry
   - Queen Liliuokalani

2. NoteTaking **Reading Skill: Identify Main Ideas** Use your concept web to answer the Section Focus Question: How and why did the United States take a more active role in world affairs?

**Writing About History**

3. **Quick Write: Choose a Topic** To write a narrative essay, start by choosing a topic. Suppose that you want to write a narrative from the perspective of the American imperialist Alfred T. Mahan. Make a list of topics that interest you, such as the construction of new battleships for the United States Navy or an account of a U.S. exploration for unclaimed territory in the Pacific Ocean. You may want to do research in books and on the Internet before you decide on a topic.

**Critical Thinking**

4. **Evaluate Information** Which of the motives for American imperialism do you think was the most important? Why?

5. **Compare Points of View** How did public opinion about the purchase of Alaska in 1867 differ from the view of historians today?

6. **Make Decisions** If you had been President in 1894, would you have supported or opposed the annexation of Hawaii? Give reasons for your answer.

YOUR
COUNTRY
CALLS YOU

R·M·WRIGH
'98.

▲ Nameplate from the *Maine's* wreckage

**WITNESS HISTORY** 🔊 AUDIO

### Remember the *Maine*!

On February 15, 1898, an explosion ripped through the hull of the USS *Maine* in Havana harbor, in the Spanish colony of Cuba. More than 250 American sailors died. The incident ignited a furor as Americans clamored for war with Spain. In newspapers, speeches, and songs, patriots implored their fellow citizens to remember the *Maine*:

❝And shall our country let it pass, this deed of foul intent? And shall our country dare believe it was an accident? . . . Come arm, we all, and let us teach a lesson to bold Spain. We will avenge, by more than speech the destruction of the *Maine*!❞

—H. W. Petrie, lyrics from "The Wreck of the *Maine*," 1898

# The Spanish-American War

 **Content Expectations**

- **6.1.2a** Evaluate development of organized labor.
- **6.1.2b** Evaluate southern/western farmers' reactions to industrial growth.
- **6.2.1** Locate territories acquired by U.S. during emergence as imperial power.

### Terms and People

José Martí
William Randolph
  Hearst
Yellow Press
jingoism

George Dewey
Emilio Aguinaldo
Rough Riders
Treaty of Paris

### NoteTaking

**Reading Skill: Identify Causes and Effects**
Note the causes, key events, and effects of the Spanish-American War.

| Cause | Spanish-American War | Effect |
|---|---|---|
| • | • Dewey destroys Spanish fleet | • U.S. acquires Philippines |
| • | | |

**Why It Matters** American power and economic interests around the world were growing. Still, the United States remained reluctant to risk war with other powers to acquire colonies. That changed, however, in 1898, when America went to war against Spain. The United States acquired colonies and became a world power. **Section Focus Question: What were the causes and effects of the Spanish-American War?**

## Causes of the War

At the end of the nineteenth century, Spain was an imperial nation in decline. Its formerly vast empire had dwindled to a small number of possessions, including the Philippine Islands in the Pacific and the Caribbean islands of Puerto Rico and Cuba.

**Cubans Rebel Against Spanish Rule** By 1897, American entrepreneurs had invested $50 million in sugar cane plantations and other ventures in Cuba, which lay just 90 miles off the Florida coast. These businessmen saw Cuba as a growing market for American products. However, the island was very unstable. Yearning for freedom, the Cubans repeatedly rebelled against Spanish rule.

In 1895, Cuban patriot **José Martí** launched a war for independence from Spain. With cries of *"Cuba Libre!"* ("Free Cuba!"), rebel fighters used guerrilla tactics of hit-and-run raids against Spanish forces. In response, Spanish General Valeriano Weyler devised a

**Rebellion in Cuba**
Spain sent 150,000 troops and one of its best generals, Valeriano Weyler, to smash the uprising. Here, rebel cavalry forces charge into battle. *What attitude do you think the artist had toward the rebels? How can you tell?*

plan to deprive the rebels of food and recruits. He herded the rural population into reconcentration camps, where tens of thousands died from disease and starvation. Meanwhile, the Cubans and Spanish destroyed American property.

Many Americans favored the Cubans, whose struggle for freedom and democracy reminded Americans of their own revolutionary heritage. The brutality of Spanish tactics intensified American affection and sympathy for the rebels. But other Americans, especially business people, were worried about U.S. economic interests in Cuba and hoped that Spain would quickly put down the rebellion.

**The Yellow Press Inflames Opinion** Rival newspaper publishers Joseph Pulitzer and **William Randolph Hearst** heightened the public's dislike of the Spanish government. Their publications were called the **Yellow Press** because they featured a popular comic-strip character called The Yellow Kid. To boost readership, Pulitzer's *New York World,* Hearst's *New York Journal,* and similar newspapers pasted sensational headlines and pictures on their front pages. Their stories exaggerated Spanish atrocities and compared Cuban rebels to the patriots of the American Revolution.

President William McKinley warned the Spanish to quickly establish peace, or the United States would take whatever steps it "should deem necessary to procure this result." Spain recalled General Weyler and offered the Cuban rebels some reforms. But the rebels insisted on independence, which Spain refused to grant. McKinley ordered the battleship *Maine* to Havana harbor to protect American citizens in Cuba.

Then, in February 1898, the *Journal* published a private letter written by Enrique Dupuy de Lôme, Spain's ambassador to Washington, D.C. The letter, stolen by Cuban rebels and leaked to Hearst, called McKinley a weak and stupid politician. Hearst published the letter under the sensational headline, "Worst Insult to the United States in Its History." The letter fueled American **jingoism,** or aggressive nationalism, and inflamed relations with Spain.

**The *Maine* Blows Up** Soon after the *Journal* published de Lôme's letter, the *Maine* exploded in Havana harbor. Of the 350 officers and crew on board at the time, 266 died. The Yellow Press promptly accused Spain of blowing up the battleship. One *Journal* headline even declared: "War? Sure!"

But President McKinley did not ask Congress to declare war just yet. Instead, he ordered a special naval board of inquiry to investigate the cause of the explosion. On March 28, 1898, the board concluded that a mine had destroyed the battleship. Years later, follow-up investigations raised doubts about the naval board's findings, but, at the time, most people blamed Spain.

**The Nation Goes to War** War fever gripped the nation. In newspapers, speeches, and songs, patriotic Americans implored their fellow citizens to "Remember the *Maine*!" In response to American demands, Spain agreed to abolish the reconcentration camps and make other concessions, but it was too little too late. On April 11, 1898, McKinley asked Congress for the authority to use force against Spain to end the fighting in Cuba "in the name of humanity, in the name of civilization, in behalf of endangered American interests."

Eight days later, Congress enacted four resolutions that amounted to a declaration of war on Spain. The fourth resolution—the Teller Amendment—stipulated that the United States had no intention of annexing Cuba. The navy quickly blockaded Cuban ports, and McKinley called for more than 100,000 volunteers to join the army. In response, Spain declared war on the United States.

✓ **Checkpoint** Why did Americans object to Spanish actions in Cuba?

**Vocabulary Builder**
stipulate – (STIHP yuh layt) *v.* to include specifically in the terms of an agreement

Spanish misrule of Cuba and the sinking of the USS *Maine* moved the nation toward war with Spain. ▼

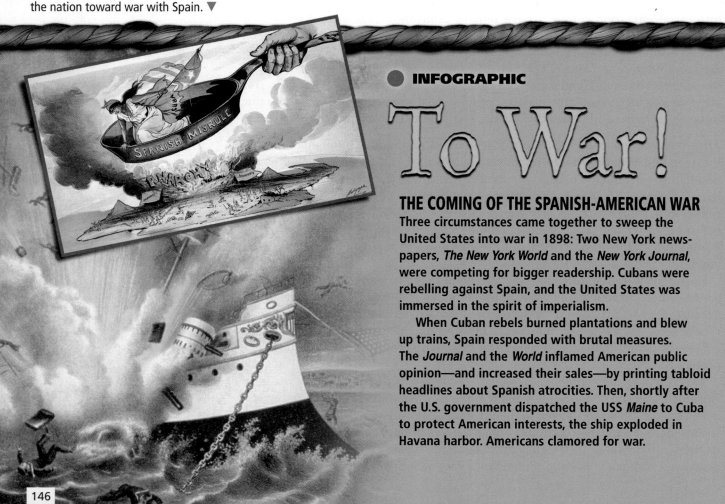

● **INFOGRAPHIC**

# To War!

### THE COMING OF THE SPANISH-AMERICAN WAR

Three circumstances came together to sweep the United States into war in 1898: Two New York newspapers, *The New York World* and the *New York Journal*, were competing for bigger readership. Cubans were rebelling against Spain, and the United States was immersed in the spirit of imperialism.

When Cuban rebels burned plantations and blew up trains, Spain responded with brutal measures. The *Journal* and the *World* inflamed American public opinion—and increased their sales—by printing tabloid headlines about Spanish atrocities. Then, shortly after the U.S. government dispatched the USS *Maine* to Cuba to protect American interests, the ship exploded in Havana harbor. Americans clamored for war.

# American Troops Battle the Spanish

Americans responded enthusiastically to the war. About 200,000 men enlisted in the army, up from the 25,000 that enlisted at the beginning of 1898. In early May, as the United States Army prepared to attack, Americans heard news of a great naval victory over Spain. But, surprisingly, the victory was not in Cuba. Rather, it was in the Pacific Ocean, on the opposite side of the world.

**Dewey Takes the Philippines** On May 1, 1898, Commodore **George Dewey** steamed his squadron of vessels into Manila Bay, in the Spanish-held Philippines. The Americans completely surprised the Spanish fleet that was stationed in the bay. Upon issuing the order to "fire when ready," Dewey watched his ships quickly destroy the Spanish force. While no American died during the naval battle, nearly 400 Spanish sailors lost their lives. Americans gleefully received news of the victory and proclaimed Dewey a hero.

While Dewey was winning an astounding victory over the Spanish navy, Filipino nationalists led by **Emilio Aguinaldo** (ahg ee NAHL doh) were defeating the Spanish army. Like the Cubans, the Filipinos were fighting for freedom from Spain. In August, after some 15,000 U.S. soldiers had landed on the islands, Spanish troops surrendered to the United States.

**U.S. Forces Win in Cuba** Meanwhile, American troops landed in Cuba in June 1898. U.S. Marines captured Guantánamo Bay, and a force of 17,000 soldiers under U.S. Army General William Shafter stormed ashore east of Santiago.

In spite of their excitement for the war, the troops faced deplorable conditions. They were poorly trained and supplied. As they assembled for duty around

With each new headline, the Yellow Press sold more papers to Americans angry with Spain. ▼

**New York Journal Sales**

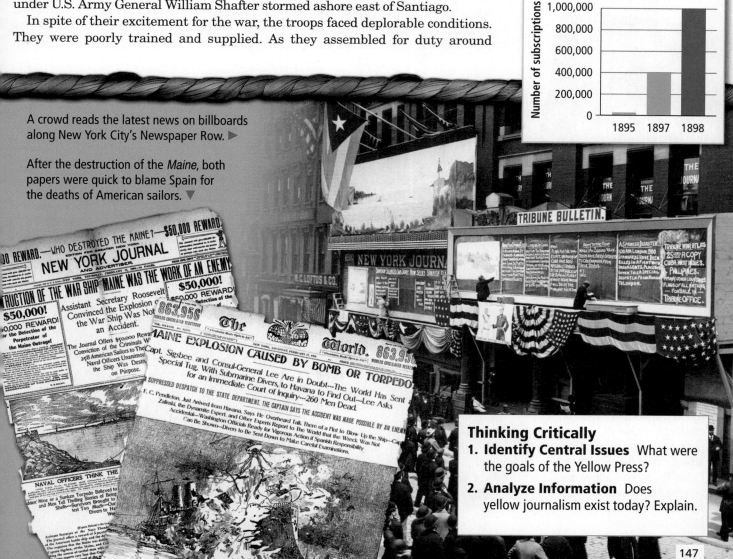

A crowd reads the latest news on billboards along New York City's Newspaper Row. ▶

After the destruction of the *Maine*, both papers were quick to blame Spain for the deaths of American sailors. ▼

**Thinking Critically**
1. **Identify Central Issues** What were the goals of the Yellow Press?
2. **Analyze Information** Does yellow journalism exist today? Explain.

Tampa, Florida, the soldiers were issued obsolete weapons and heavy wool uniforms that were unsuitable for Cuba's tropical climate. Corrupt and inefficient officials provided the men with rotting and contaminated food.

General Shafter's army consisted of state National Guard units and regular army units, including the African American Ninth and Tenth Cavalry regiments from the western frontier. Another cavalry unit was organized and commanded by the future President Theodore Roosevelt. His **Rough Riders** consisted of rugged westerners and upper-class easterners who relished what Roosevelt called the "strenuous life."

The Rough Riders and Roosevelt gained fame for the role they played in the battles for Kettle and San Juan hills outside Santiago, Cuba. Joined by African American soldiers from the Ninth and Tenth Cavalries, the Riders stormed up those hills to secure high ground surrounding Santiago. One war correspondent described a charge of the African American soldiers:

**Primary Source** "[T]hey followed their leader up the terrible hill from whose crest the desperate Spaniards poured down a deadly fire of shell and musketry. They never faltered. . . . [T]heir aim was splendid, their coolness was superb. . . . The war had not shown greater heroism."

—War correspondent, 1898

Two days after the battle of San Juan Hill, the Spanish navy made a desperate attempt to escape from Santiago's harbor. U.S. forces, which had blockaded the harbor, destroyed the Spanish fleet as it tried to break out. Surrounded, outnumbered, and dispirited, Spanish forces in Santiago surrendered. Although a few battles followed when U.S. forces occupied the island of Puerto Rico, another Spanish

▼ Regimental flag carried by African American soldiers

## African Americans Serve Their Country

African American soldiers of the Ninth and Tenth Cavalry regiments stand at attention after fighting the Spanish in Cuba. The medals above were won by Augustus L. Reed, an African American officer in the United States Navy.

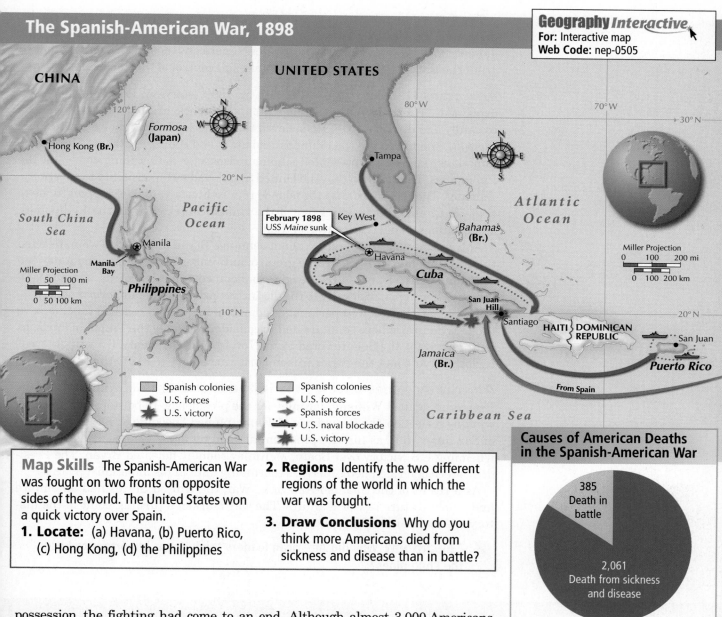

# The Spanish-American War, 1898

**Geography** *Interactive*

For: Interactive map
Web Code: nep-0505

CHINA

UNITED STATES

Formosa (Japan)

Hong Kong (Br.)

Pacific Ocean

South China Sea

Manila

Manila Bay

Miller Projection
0   50   100 mi
0   50 100 km

Philippines

Tampa

80° W

70° W

30° N

20° N

Atlantic Ocean

February 1898
USS *Maine* sunk

Key West

Bahamas (Br.)

Havana

Cuba

San Juan Hill

Santiago

HAITI   DOMINICAN REPUBLIC

San Juan

Puerto Rico

From Spain

Jamaica (Br.)

Caribbean Sea

Miller Projection
0   100   200 mi
0   100   200 km

20° N

10° N

**Legend (left):**
- ☐ Spanish colonies
- ➤ U.S. forces
- ✴ U.S. victory

**Legend (right):**
- ☐ Spanish colonies
- ➤ U.S. forces
- ➤ Spanish forces
- ····· U.S. naval blockade
- ✴ U.S. victory

**Map Skills** The Spanish-American War was fought on two fronts on opposite sides of the world. The United States won a quick victory over Spain.

**1. Locate:** (a) Havana, (b) Puerto Rico, (c) Hong Kong, (d) the Philippines

**2. Regions** Identify the two different regions of the world in which the war was fought.

**3. Draw Conclusions** Why do you think more Americans died from sickness and disease than in battle?

**Causes of American Deaths in the Spanish-American War**

385 Death in battle

2,061 Death from sickness and disease

SOURCE: *Historical Statistics of the United States*

possession, the fighting had come to an end. Although almost 3,000 Americans died during the war, only around 380 died in combat. Disease, especially malaria and yellow fever, caused most of the deaths.

✓ **Checkpoint** How did the Rough Riders and African American cavalry units contribute to the war effort?

# Effects of the War

Secretary of State John Hay referred to the conflict with Spain as a "splendid little war" because of the ease and thoroughness of America's victory. Although the war may have been "splendid," it created a new dilemma for Americans: What should the United States do with Spain's former possessions?

**The Treaty of Paris** Signed by Spain and the United States in December 1898, the **Treaty of Paris** officially ended the war. Spain gave up control of Cuba, Puerto Rico, and the Pacific island of Guam. It also sold the Philippines to the United States for $20 million.

The Teller Amendment, passed by Congress when it declared war on Spain, prevented the United States from taking possession of Cuba. The amendment did not, however, apply to the Philippines. Americans disagreed over whether to grant the Philippines independence or take full control of the Pacific nation.

**Americans Debate Imperialism** In an 1899 interview, President McKinley explained, "We could not give [the Philippines] back to Spain—that would be cowardly and dishonorable." He believed that America had no choice but to "take them all, and to educate the Filipinos, and uplift and civilize . . . them." McKinley's imperialist supporters presented similar reasons for maintaining control of the Philippines. They argued that the United States had a responsibility to govern the Filipinos. They reasoned that the islands represented a valuable stepping stone to trade in China. They warned that if the United States gave up the Philippines, other nations would take control of them.

Anti-imperialists, including William Jennings Bryan and Mark Twain, rejected these arguments. In 1899, a large group of anti-imperialists formed the American Anti-Imperialist League. The league condemned imperialism as a crime and attacked it as "open disloyalty to the distinctive principles of our government."

The debate between imperialists and anti-imperialists reached its climax in the U.S. Senate, where senators had to consider ratifying the Treaty of Paris. In February 1899, the Senate voted 57 to 27 in favor of the treaty. By a single "yes" ballot, the vote met the two-thirds majority necessary to ratify the treaty.

**America Assumes a New Role in the World** In 1900, William Jennings Bryan ran against William McKinley for the presidency. To bolster his chances of winning reelection, the Republican McKinley named Theodore Roosevelt, the "hero of San Juan Hill," as his vice-presidential running mate. Emphasizing the overwhelming U.S. victory over Spain, McKinley soundly defeated Bryan. The President's reelection signaled America's continuing faith in his imperialist policies.

As a result of the Spanish-American War, the United States had an empire and a new stature in world affairs. The war marked a turning point in the history of American foreign policy.

 **Checkpoint** Why did American leaders think it was important to keep the Philippines?

**Progress Monitoring *Online***
**For:** Self-test with vocabulary practice
**Web Code:** nea-0506

### Comprehension

**1. Terms and People** What do the following terms and people have in common?
- José Martí
- William Randolph Hearst
- Yellow Press
- jingoism

**2. NoteTaking Reading Skill: Identify Causes and Effects** Use your cause-and-effect chart to answer the Section Focus Question: What were the causes and effects of the Spanish-American War?

### Writing About History

**3. Quick Write: Gather Details** When you write a narrative essay, you often need to gather details about your topic. Suppose that you want to write a narrative diary entry as a witness to the destruction of the USS *Maine*. Conduct research to find descriptions of the explosion and illustrations of the event from newspapers of the time. You may want to research particular newspapers such as the *New York World* and the *New York Journal*.

### Critical Thinking

**4. Draw Conclusions** Do you think the United States would have gone to war with Spain without the explosion of the *Maine*? Why or why not?

**5. Identify Points of View** Who might agree with John Hay's opinion that the Spanish-American War was a "splendid little war"? Who might disagree? Why?

**6. Summarize** What were the principal issues dividing imperialists and anti-imperialists?

▲ An American soldier and two Filipino women

**WITNESS HISTORY** 🔊 AUDIO

**A Plea for Peace**

Sixto Lopez, a leading Filipino spokesman, wrote to President McKinley to express his disapproval of America's decision to keep control of the Philippines. When he wrote the letter, many Filipinos had already taken up arms against the U.S. military.

❝I only know that the Filipino people are asking for [what] the American people have enjoyed for more than a hundred years. . . . At this season of peace I plead for peace. I plead on behalf of the wife and mother whose cheeks are coursing the silent tears . . . on behalf of the sad little faces, too young to realize what has happened. . . .❞

—Sixto Lopez, 1900

# The United States and East Asia

## Content Expectations

- **6.1.2a** Evaluate development of organized labor.
- **6.1.2b** Evaluate southern/western farmers' reactions to industrial growth.
- **6.2.1** Locate territories acquired by U.S. during emergence as imperial power.

## Terms and People

insurrection
guerrilla warfare
William Howard Taft
sphere of influence
John Hay
Boxer Rebellion

Open Door Policy
Russo-Japanese War
"Gentlemen's Agreement"
Great White Fleet

**NoteTaking**

**Reading Skill: Recognize Sequence** As you read, use a timeline to trace events and developments in East Asia that tested America's new global power.

Filipino insurrection begins

1898    1901    1904    1907

**Why It Matters** America's decision to keep the Philippines reflected a desire to expand its influence, compete with European colonial powers, and gain new trade in Asia. American leaders devised policies to open China and other Asian markets to U.S. producers. They also wanted to extend the benefits of American culture to the people of the region. Imperialism in East Asia brought greater power and wealth to Americans, but it also increased international tensions in Asia. **Section Focus Question: How did the United States extend its influence in Asia?**

## Filipinos Rebel Against U.S. Rule

The Filipino nationalist leader Emilio Aguinaldo had thought that the United States was an ally in the Filipino struggle for independence. His forces had fought side by side with the Americans against the Spanish. However, after the United States decided to maintain possession of the Philippines, Aguinaldo grew disillusioned with America. He helped organize an **insurrection,** or rebellion, against U.S. rule. The rebels believed they were fighting for the same principle of self-rule that had inspired America's colonial patriots during the American Revolution.

**Guerrilla War Erupts in the Philippines** Outgunned by American troops, Filipino insurgents relied on **guerrilla warfare,** a form of non-traditional warfare generally involving small bands of fighters

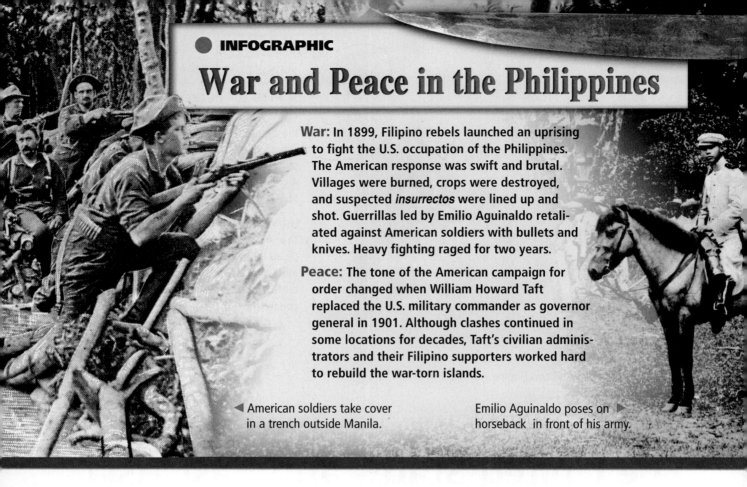

# War and Peace in the Philippines

**War:** In 1899, Filipino rebels launched an uprising to fight the U.S. occupation of the Philippines. The American response was swift and brutal. Villages were burned, crops were destroyed, and suspected *insurrectos* were lined up and shot. Guerrillas led by Emilio Aguinaldo retaliated against American soldiers with bullets and knives. Heavy fighting raged for two years.

**Peace:** The tone of the American campaign for order changed when William Howard Taft replaced the U.S. military commander as governor general in 1901. Although clashes continued in some locations for decades, Taft's civilian administrators and their Filipino supporters worked hard to rebuild the war-torn islands.

◀ American soldiers take cover in a trench outside Manila.

Emilio Aguinaldo poses on ▶ horseback in front of his army.

to attack behind American lines. In turn, the American military used extraordinary measures to crush the rebellion. Like the Spanish in Cuba, U.S. soldiers gathered civilians into overcrowded concentration camps. General Jacob Smith ordered his soldiers not to take prisoners. "I wish you to kill and burn, the more you kill and burn the better you will please me," he commented. A California newspaper defended such actions:

> **Primary Source** "Let us all be frank. WE DO NOT WANT THE FILIPINOS. WE DO WANT THE PHILIPPINES. All of our troubles in this annexation matter have been caused by the presence in the Philippine Islands of the Filipinos. . . . The more of them killed the better. It seems harsh. But they must yield before the superior race."
>
> —San Francisco *Argonaut,* 1902

In the spring of 1901, the Americans captured Aguinaldo. Although the fighting did not end immediately, his capture marked the beginning of the end of the insurrection. The war in the Philippines took more lives than the Spanish-American War. Nearly 5,000 Americans and 200,000 Filipinos died in the fighting. The U.S. government sent more than 100,000 troops to fight in the war and spent upwards of $400 million to defeat the insurgency. The conflict highlighted the rigors of fighting against guerrilla insurgents.

**Reforms Lead to Promise of Self-Rule** In 1901, **William Howard Taft**—a future President of the United States—became governor of the Philippines. Taft had large ambitions for helping the islands recover from the rebellion. He censored the press and placed dissidents in jail to maintain order and to win the support of the Filipino people. At the same time, he extended limited self-rule and ordered the construction of schools, roads, and bridges.

**Vocabulary Builder**
rigor – (RIHG uhr) *n.* extreme hardship or difficulty

▲ Filipino rebels often used bolo knives in addition to rifles to fight American soldiers.

The American presence in the Philippines provided several benefits for Filipinos:

- **Political reform:** After 1901, Taft's civilian government extended limited self-rule to Filipinos. The Philippine Assembly (shown above) convened in Manila in 1907.
- **Healthcare:** U.S. administrators established a public health system to care for Filipinos. At right, American doctors aid a Filipino woman wounded during the insurrection.
- **Education:** The American commission also built new schools for Filipino children and staffed them with teachers from the United States. (See photo at far right.)

In 1916, Congress passed the Jones Act, which pledged that the Philippines would ultimately gain their independence. Thirty years later, after U.S. forces liberated the islands from Japanese occupation at the end of World War II, the Philippines finally became an independent nation.

✔ **Checkpoint** Why did hostilities erupt in the Philippines after the Spanish-American War?

## The United States Pursues Interests in China

By 1899, once-mighty China had fallen into political, economic, and military disarray. Its huge population, however, was a tempting target for other nations' imported goods. Rather than compete for Chinese trade, Britain, France, Germany, and Russia carved China into distinct **spheres of influence.** Within its zone, each power had privileged access to Chinese ports and markets. Japan also expanded its regional influence, grabbing territory in China and Korea. Since the United States did not have a zone, this system of "special privileges" threatened to limit American trade in China.

**America Declares Equal Trade in China** In order to overcome these barriers, U.S. Secretary of State **John Hay** issued the first of a series of notes to foreign diplomats in 1899. He notified the leaders of imperialist nations that the United States expected "perfect equality of treatment for commerce" in China. Hay's note had little immediate impact on the actions of European nations or Japan. However, it served as a guiding principle of American foreign policy in Asia for years to come.

**Thinking Critically**
1. **Make Generalizations** How did the Filipino uprising present a new challenge to American soldiers?
2. **Explain Effects** What two things happened in 1901 that signaled a shift in the rebellion?

**History** *Interactive*

**For:** To discover more about the Filipino insurrection
**Web Code:** nep-0509

**The U.S. Intervenes in the Boxer Rebellion** In response to the growing influence of outsiders in their country, some Chinese joined secret societies. One such society, the Righteous and Harmonious Fists, won the nickname "Boxers" from Europeans because its members trained in martial arts. The secret societies celebrated traditional Chinese customs and criticized Western ways. They also condemned Chinese converts to Christianity. Over time, simmering anger exploded into an outright rebellion against the "foreign devils."

In May 1900, the Boxers killed foreign missionaries and besieged the foreign diplomats' district in Beijing. A multinational force of European, American, and Japanese troops was sent to the Chinese capital to quash the **Boxer Rebellion.** An initial force of 2,100 soldiers grew to more than 20,000, including 2,000 Americans. After putting down the rebellion, European powers compelled China's imperial government to pay an indemnity, or money to repair damage caused by the rebellion. This poured more fuel onto the nationalist fire. Chinese nationalists would eventually revolt and overthrow the emperor in 1911.

**Hay Reaffirms the Open Door Policy** As the Boxer Rebellion engulfed China, Secretary of State Hay reasserted America's **Open Door Policy.** In a second note to European powers, Hay stated that the United States wanted to "preserve Chinese territorial and administrative entity." In other words, America did not want colonies in China; it just wanted free trade there. As an act of goodwill, the United States used some of the indemnity money it received from China to fund scholarships for Chinese students to study in America.

✓ **Checkpoint** How did the United States protect its commercial interests in China?

## Tensions Rise Between America and Japan

Like the United States, Japan wanted to expand its influence in China. Japan also disapproved of the European "carve-up" of the region. Furthermore, the Japanese took offense to the presence of Russian troops in Manchuria, a region of China that bordered Russia. In February 1904, without a declaration of war, Japan attacked and bottled up Russia's Pacific fleet stationed at Port Arthur, China. The Japanese followed up on this victory with a series of major land engagements in Manchuria that caused more than 100,000 Russian casualties. However, Japan also suffered heavy losses in the fighting.

**American Soldiers Rescue Diplomats in China**
U.S. troops went into the Chinese capital of Beijing in 1900 to help put an end to the Boxer Rebellion. Below, the troops march through the Forbidden City in close ranks.

**Roosevelt Settles the Russo-Japanese War** In 1905, representatives from Russia and Japan met in Portsmouth, New Hampshire, to negotiate an end to the **Russo-Japanese War.** When the talks stalled, President Theodore Roosevelt intervened and convinced the two sides to sign a peace treaty. (Roosevelt had become President when McKinley was assassinated in 1901.) For his efforts, Roosevelt won the Nobel Peace Prize. The President's intervention—and his receipt of the famous award—prominently displayed America's growing role in world affairs.

**Anti-Asian Prejudice Troubles Relations** Despite Roosevelt's achievement, America entered troubled waters in its relations with Japan. A root cause of this trouble was anti-Asian sentiment on the West Coast of the United States. In the fall of 1906, the San Francisco School Board banned Japanese, Chinese, and Korean children from attending public schools with white children. The incident drew Japan's immediate wrath. One Tokyo journal demanded that Japan retaliate. "Stand up Japanese nation! Our countrymen have been HUMILIATED on the other side of the Pacific," the newspaper cried out.

Roosevelt disapproved of the decision to segregate Asian children in the San Francisco schools. He understood Japan's anger with America. To calm tensions, he negotiated a **"Gentlemen's Agreement"** with Japan. According to the pact, the school board pledged to end its segregation policy. In return, Japan agreed to limit the emigration of its citizens to the United States.

**The Great White Fleet Sets Sail** While Roosevelt used diplomacy to ease tensions with Japan, he also promoted military preparedness to protect U.S. interests in Asia. Expressing rising concerns about Japan's territorial expansion at the expense of China, Korea, and Russia—the President won congressional support for a new force of navy ships, known as the **Great White Fleet.** In 1907, Roosevelt sent this armada of 16 white battleships on a "good will cruise" around the world. The voyage of the Great White Fleet demonstrated America's increased military power to the world.

**A Mighty American Fleet**
After stopping at several Latin American ports, the Great White Fleet moved on to Asia and made a friendly visit to the Japanese port city of Yokohama. *How do you think the Japanese felt about the U.S. warships' visit?*

✓ **Checkpoint** What were some of the difficulties America faced in maintaining good relations with Japan?

---

**Progress Monitoring *Online***
For: Self-test with vocabulary practice
Web Code: nea-0507

**Comprehension**

1. **Terms and People** For each item below, write a sentence explaining its significance.
   • insurrection
   • guerrilla warfare
   • William Howard Taft
   • Boxer Rebellion
   • Open Door Policy

2.  **NoteTaking Reading Skill: Recognize Sequence** Use your timeline to answer the Section Focus Question: How did the United States extend its influence in Asia?

**Writing About History**

3. **Quick Write: Write an Introduction** A narrative essay needs an introduction that "hooks" a reader and draws him or her into your story. Suppose that you want to write a narrative from the perspective of an American sailor aboard a battleship in the Great White Fleet. Draft an introduction that captures the excitement and purpose of the fleet's departure from America.

**Critical Thinking**

4. **Recognize Bias** Based on what you have read, what role do you think racial attitudes played in U.S. policy in the Philippines?

5. **Analyze Information** Identify two threats to U.S. interests in China, and describe how the U.S. government responded to those threats.

6. **Apply Information** How do President Roosevelt's actions toward Japan illustrate the use of diplomacy and compromise?

TAFT BIDS NATION BE WORLD POWER

DOLLARS VERSUS BULLETS

American Capital Must Be Employed if We Are to Get Our Share of Markets.

CY ABOVE PARTIES

Efficient Representatives and of Broad Policies place Expediency.

Dec. 3.—Declaring that on the threshold having the

▲ William Howard Taft

◀ Newspaper announcing Taft's goal

**WITNESS HISTORY**  AUDIO

### Dollars for Bullets

Like President Roosevelt, President William Howard Taft stressed the need to assert American power around the world. Taft's "dollar diplomacy" aimed to expand American investments abroad:

❝The diplomacy of the present administration . . . has been characterized as substituting dollars for bullets. . . . It is [a policy] frankly directed to the increase of American trade upon the axiomatic principle that the government of the United States shall extend all proper support to every legitimate and beneficial American enterprise abroad.❞

—President William Howard Taft, 1912

# The United States and Latin America

 **Content Expectations**

- **6.1.2a** Evaluate development of organized labor.
- **6.1.2b** Evaluate southern/western farmers' reactions to industrial growth.
- **6.2.1** Locate territories acquired by U.S. during emergence as imperial power.

## Terms and People

Foraker Act
Platt Amendment
"big stick" diplomacy
Panama Canal

Roosevelt Corollary
"dollar diplomacy"
"moral diplomacy"
Francisco "Pancho" Villa

## NoteTaking

**Reading Skill: Identify Supporting Details** Complete a table like the one below to note how the U.S. dealt with Puerto Rico and Cuba.

| American Policy After Spanish-American War | |
|---|---|
| **Puerto Rico** | **Cuba** |
| • Foraker Act establishes civil government in 1900 | • |
| • | • |

**Why It Matters** As the United States tentatively asserted its interests in East Asia, Americans called for a more aggressive role in Latin America. American entrepreneurs and government leaders viewed the region as the nation's backyard and as a sphere of influence from which other great powers should be excluded. American influence in Latin America brought obvious benefits to the United States, but it also contributed to anti-American hostility and instability in the region. **Section Focus Question: What actions did the United States take to achieve its goals in Latin America?**

## U.S. Policy in Puerto Rico and Cuba

America's victory over Spain liberated the Puerto Rican and Cuban people from Spanish rule. But victory left the fates of these islands unresolved. Would Puerto Rico and Cuba become independent nations? Or would they become colonies of the United States? As questions lingered in the aftermath of war, the United States assumed control in Puerto Rico and Cuba.

**Civil Government in Puerto Rico** As the smoke from the Spanish-American War cleared, Puerto Rico remained under direct U.S. military rule. In 1900, Congress passed the **Foraker Act,** which established a civil government in Puerto Rico. The act authorized the President of the United States to appoint a governor and part of the Puerto Rican legislature. Puerto Ricans could fill the rest of the legislature in a general election.

Whether Puerto Ricans could enjoy citizenship rights in the United States, however, remained unclear. This unusual situation led to a series of court cases, known as Insular Cases, in which the Supreme Court determined the rights of Puerto Ricans. One case examined whether the U.S. government could <u>assess</u> taxes on Puerto Rican goods sold in the United States. The Supreme Court ruled the taxes legal and determined that Puerto Ricans did not enjoy the same rights as U.S. citizens.

In 1917, President Woodrow Wilson signed the Jones-Shafroth Act. It granted Puerto Ricans more citizenship rights and gave the islanders greater control over their own legislature. Still, many Puerto Ricans expressed their discontent because they did not enjoy all of the same rights as Americans.

**United States Establishes Cuban Protectorate** Although the Treaty of Paris granted Cuban independence, the United States Army did not withdraw from the island until 1902. But before the U.S. military left, Congress obliged Cuba to add to its constitution the **Platt Amendment.** The amendment restricted the rights of newly independent Cubans and effectively brought the island within the U.S. sphere. It prevented Cuba from signing a treaty with another nation without American approval. It also required Cuba to lease naval stations to the United States. Additionally, the Platt Amendment granted the United States the "right to intervene" to preserve order in Cuba.

Many Cubans strongly disliked the Platt Amendment but soon realized that America would not otherwise end its military government of the island. The United States, for its part, was unwilling to risk Cuba's becoming a base for a potentially hostile great power. Cuba thus added the Platt Amendment to its constitution as part of a treaty with the United States. The treaty made Cuba a protectorate of the United States and governed their relationship for decades.

✔ **Checkpoint** Why did Cubans dislike the Platt Amendment?

# Roosevelt Pursues "Big Stick" Diplomacy

Upon assuming the presidency after McKinley's assassination, Theodore Roosevelt promoted a new kind of diplomacy based on America's success in the Spanish-American War. Beyond determining what would happen to Puerto Rico and Cuba, Roosevelt developed a broader policy for U.S. action in Latin America. Historians have called this Roosevelt's **"big stick" diplomacy** since it depended on a strong military to achieve America's goals. "Big stick" stemmed from the President's admiration for an old African saying, "Speak softly and carry a big stick; you will go far."

Roosevelt's view that America needed to carry a big stick during the Age of Imperialism flowed from his adherence to balance-of-power principles and from his view of the United States as a special nation with a moral responsibility to "civilize," or uplift, weaker nations. In this sense, the new President held beliefs similar to those of other imperial powers in Europe and Asia. Roosevelt also felt that America's elite—its statesmen and captains of industry—had to accept the challenge of international leadership.

**Vocabulary Builder**

<u>assess</u>—(uh SEHS) *v.* to impose a fine, tax, or special payment on a person or property

## HISTORY MAKERS

### Theodore Roosevelt (1858–1919)

As a boy, Theodore Roosevelt suffered from asthma and poor eyesight. Determined not to be held back by physical limitations, he took on an active program of exercise that included boxing and horseback riding.

In 1898, when Roosevelt was Assistant Secretary of the Navy, he again showcased his determination. Two months before the United States declared war on Spain, he secretly ordered Commodore George Dewey to sail for Hong Kong, within striking distance of the Philippines. Thus, when the war began, U.S. ships were instantly ready to attack the Spanish fleet in Manila Bay. Soon after Dewey's victory, Roosevelt resigned from his post and organized the Rough Riders.

# The Panama Canal

The construction of the Panama Canal was a monumental engineering feat. It fulfilled a vision of shortening the travel distance between the Atlantic and Pacific oceans that traced back to when the Spanish first began shipping gold and silver from the Americas in the 1500s. To complete the canal, workers built a series of locks to raise ships to the level of Gatún Lake, 85 feet above sea level, to cross the isthmus. (See the diagram below.) From 1904 to 1913, tens of thousands of laborers worked on the canal. In the end, the challenge of the landscape was overshadowed by the threat of the deadly mosquito, which spread yellow fever and malaria. "If we do not control malaria, our mortality is going to be heavy," warned Dr. William Gorgas, a United States Army surgeon. He convinced the chief engineer that fighting the mosquito was vital to keeping American steam shovels in action.

▲ In 1898, the U.S. battleship *Oregon* raced around South America to fight the Spanish in Cuba. Without a Central American canal to shorten its voyage to Florida, the *Oregon* spent more than two months at sea.

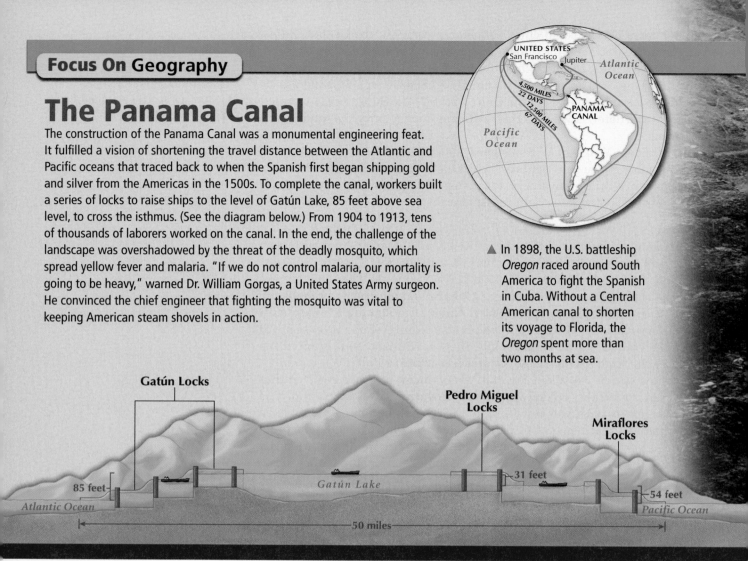

**Gatún Locks**

**Pedro Miguel Locks**

**Miraflores Locks**

**31 feet**

**85 feet**

**54 feet**

*Atlantic Ocean*

*Gatún Lake*

*Pacific Ocean*

50 miles

**Vocabulary Builder**
nevertheless–(nehv er thuh LEHS) *adv.* in spite of that; however

**America Builds the Panama Canal** Although the plan to dig a canal across Central America did not originate with Roosevelt, he <u>nevertheless</u> played a crucial role in its history. In the late 1800s, a French company had tried to link the Atlantic to the Pacific across the Isthmus of Panama but failed. Afterward, some suggested building a canal through Nicaragua. However, those plans came to nothing. Eventually, an agent from the French company that had abandoned its canal attempt convinced the United States to buy the company's claim. In 1903, the U.S. government bought the Panama route for $40 million.

Before it could build a canal through Panama, however, the United States needed the consent of the Colombian government. At that time, Panama was part of independent Colombia. American efforts to negotiate a purchase of land across the isthmus stalled when Colombia demanded more than the United States was willing to provide.

So Roosevelt stepped in. The President dispatched U.S. warships to the waters off Panama to support a Panamanian rebellion against Colombia. The appearance of the United States Navy convinced the Colombians not to suppress the uprising. Panama soon declared its independence from Colombia. The new nation immediately granted America control over the "Canal Zone." To secure this land for its vital trade link, America agreed to pay Panama $10 million and an annual rent of $250,000.

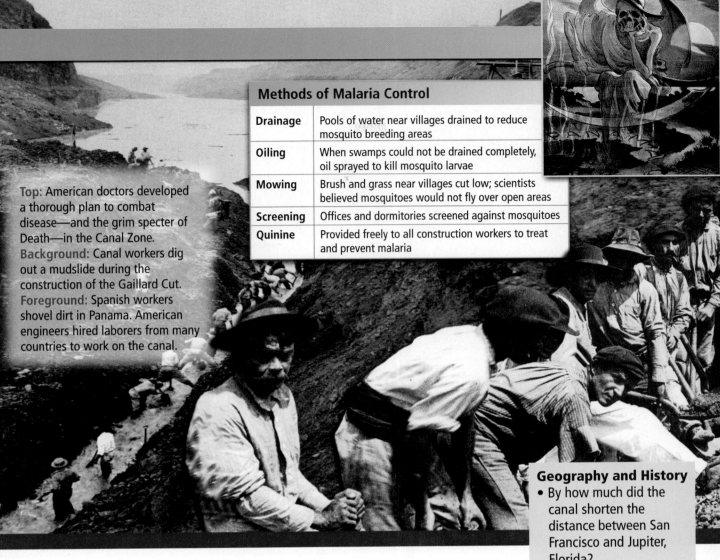

| Methods of Malaria Control | |
|---|---|
| **Drainage** | Pools of water near villages drained to reduce mosquito breeding areas |
| **Oiling** | When swamps could not be drained completely, oil sprayed to kill mosquito larvae |
| **Mowing** | Brush and grass near villages cut low; scientists believed mosquitoes would not fly over open areas |
| **Screening** | Offices and dormitories screened against mosquitoes |
| **Quinine** | Provided freely to all construction workers to treat and prevent malaria |

**Top:** American doctors developed a thorough plan to combat disease—and the grim specter of Death—in the Canal Zone.
**Background:** Canal workers dig out a mudslide during the construction of the Gaillard Cut.
**Foreground:** Spanish workers shovel dirt in Panama. American engineers hired laborers from many countries to work on the canal.

**Geography and History**
- By how much did the canal shorten the distance between San Francisco and Jupiter, Florida?
- Which methods of malaria control involved direct changes to the physical environment of the Canal Zone?

More than 35,000 workers helped dig the **Panama Canal,** often in very difficult conditions. Completion of the canal depended on scientific breakthroughs by doctors as they learned how to combat tropical diseases. Still, more than 5,000 canal workers died from disease or accidents while building the canal. When the finished waterway opened in 1914, it cut some 8,000 nautical miles off the trip from the west coast to the east coast of the United States.

**Roosevelt Updates the Monroe Doctrine** In the early 1900s, the inability of Latin American nations to pay their debts to foreign investors raised the possibility of European intervention. In 1903, for example, Germany and Britain blockaded Venezuelan ports to ensure that debts to European bankers were repaid. Roosevelt concluded: "If we intend to say hands off to the powers of Europe, then sooner or later we must keep order ourselves." So in a 1904 message to Congress, he announced a new Latin American policy.

The President's **Roosevelt Corollary** updated the Monroe Doctrine for an age of economic imperialism. In the case of "chronic wrongdoing" by a Latin American nation—the kind that Europeans might use to justify military intervention—the United States would assume the role of police power, restoring order and depriving other creditors of the excuse to intervene. This change, Roosevelt argued, merely reasserted America's long-standing policy of keeping the Western Hemisphere free from European intervention.

# U.S. Interventions in Latin America

**Geography** *Interactive*
For: Interactive map
Web Code: nep-0508

**UNITED STATES**

U.S. expeditionary force 1916–1917

U.S. troops 1898–1902, 1906–1909, 1912, 1917–1922

*Gulf of Mexico*

**MEXICO**

*Bahamas* **(Br.)**

U.S. troops 1915–1934

*Atlantic Ocean*

U.S. expeditionary force 1914

Havana

**CUBA**

U.S. troops 1916–1924

30°N

20°N

Mexico City

Veracruz

Guantanamo

**DOMINICAN REPUBLIC**

Purchased from Denmark 1917

**HAITI**

*Puerto Rico*

*Virgin Is.*

*Antigua* **(Br.)**

*Jamaica* **(Br.)**

U.S. leased naval base 1903

Acquired from Spain 1898

*Guadeloupe* **(Fr.)**

*Dominica* **(Br.)**

*Martinique* **(Fr.)**

*St. Lucia* **(Br.)**

*Grenada* **(Br.)**

*Barbados* **(Br.)**

*British Honduras* **(Br.)**

*Caribbean Sea*

70°W

**GUATEMALA**

**HONDURAS**

**EL SALVADOR**

**NICARAGUA**

U.S. troops 1909–1910, 1912–1925, 1926–1933

*Trinidad* **(Br.)**

*Pacific Ocean*

U.S. troops 1924–1925

**COSTA RICA**

**PANAMA**

10°N

**VENEZUELA**

Miller Projection

0   200   400 mi

0   200   400 km

U.S. acquired Canal Zone 1904; Canal completed 1914

**COLOMBIA**

100°W          90°W          80°W

---

**Map Skills**  The United States repeatedly intervened in the affairs of its Latin American neighbors from the time of the Spanish-American War through the early 1900s.

**1. Locate:**  (a) Cuba, (b) Mexico, (c) Veracruz, (d) Nicaragua, (e) Panama Canal Zone

**2. Place**  Why was Panama an ideal place for the construction of a canal?

**3. Analyze**  Why was Cuba vital to U.S. operations in Central America and the Caribbean?

**◄ Wielding the Big Stick**

With his update to the Monroe Doctrine, Roosevelt wanted only "to see neighboring countries stable, orderly, and prosperous." But if those governments were to collapse, the United States stood ready to restore order and prevent European intervention.

**Latin Americans React to the Roosevelt Corollary** Many Latin Americans resented America's role as the hemisphere's police force. They disagreed with Roosevelt's belief that Latin Americans could not police themselves. Francisco García Calderón, a Peruvian diplomat, contended that the Monroe Doctrine had taken on an "aggressive form with Mr. Roosevelt." Like Calderón, Nicaraguan spokesman Augusto Sandino felt that the United States threatened the "sovereignty and liberty" of his people. Sandino eventually led an army of guerrillas against U.S. Marines in Nicaragua in the 1920s.

**Taft Switches to Dollar Diplomacy** Roosevelt handpicked William Howard Taft to succeed him as the Republican candidate for President in 1908. Taft shared Roosevelt's basic foreign policy objectives. After defeating William Jennings Bryan in the general election, Taft wanted to maintain the Open Door Policy in Asia and ensure ongoing stability in Latin America. The new President pursued both goals with the aim of expanding American trade.

Taft hoped to achieve these ends by relying less on the "big stick" and more on **"dollar diplomacy."** As Taft commented in 1912, he looked to substitute "dollars for bullets." The policy aimed to increase American investments in businesses and banks throughout Central America and the Caribbean. Americans busily invested in plantations, mines, oil wells, railways, and other ventures in those regions. Of course, "dollar diplomacy" sometimes required a return to the "big stick" and military intervention. Such was the case when President Taft dispatched troops to Nicaragua in 1909—and again in 1912—to protect the formation of a pro-American government there.

 **Checkpoint** What were Roosevelt's most important foreign-policy initiatives in Latin America?

# Wilson Pursues Moral Diplomacy

During the 1912 presidential election campaign, Democratic candidate Woodrow Wilson criticized the foreign policies of his Republican predecessors Theodore Roosevelt and William Howard Taft. After his election victory, Wilson appointed the anti-imperialist William Jennings Bryan as Secretary of State, which sent a strong message to the American people.

**The U.S. Supports Honest Government in Latin America** The new President intended to take U.S. foreign policy in a different direction. He promised that the United States would "never again seek one additional foot of territory by conquest" but would instead work to promote "human rights, national integrity, and opportunity." Wilson spelled out his new **"moral diplomacy"** in a message to the American people:

> **Primary Source** "We must prove ourselves [Latin America's] friends and champions upon terms of equality and honor. . . . We must show ourselves friends by comprehending their interest, whether it squares with our own interest or not. . . . Comprehension must be the soil in which shall grow all the fruits of friendship. . . . I mean the development of constitutional liberty in the world."
> —Woodrow Wilson, October 27, 1913

In spite of his stated preference for "moral diplomacy" over "big stick" or "dollar diplomacy," Wilson used the military on a number of occasions to guide Latin Americans in the directions that he thought proper. In 1915, Wilson sent marines to Haiti to protect American investments and to guard against the potential of German or French aggression in the nation. Wilson prodded the government of Haiti to sign an agreement that essentially gave the United

## NoteTaking

**Reading Skill: Compare** As you read, compare Wilson's moral diplomacy with the foreign policies of Roosevelt and Taft by completing a flowchart like the one below.

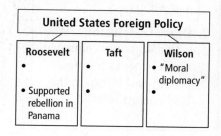

| United States Foreign Policy | | |
|---|---|---|
| **Roosevelt** | **Taft** | **Wilson** |
| • | • | • "Moral diplomacy" |
| • Supported rebellion in Panama | • | • |

# INTERVENTION IN MEXICO: THE HUNT FOR PANCHO VILLA

On March 9, 1916, the Mexican rebel Francisco "Pancho" Villa and his gang of outlaws attacked Columbus, New Mexico, killing 18 Americans. An enraged President Wilson dispatched General John J. Pershing to hunt Villa down. Equipped for the first time with airplanes such as the Curtiss JN-3 to support its movements in the field, the U.S. Army pushed 400 miles into Mexico. The Americans chased Villa for 11 months in spite of protests from the Mexican government and occasional clashes with the Mexican army. Preoccupied more by the ongoing war in Europe than by the apprehension of Villa, Wilson ultimately withdrew Pershing's army in early 1917.

▲ Painting of a Curtiss JN-3

New Mexico

Columbus

① Villa raids Columbus and kills 18 Americans

Ascension

② Pershing gives chase as Villa flees south

Dublan

Carrizal

⑤ U.S. troops fight Mexican government soldiers

Rio Grande

MEXICO

N
W E
S

UNITED STATES
Map area
MEXICO

▲ General Pershing leads American cavalry in Mexico in 1916.

Guerrero        Agua Caliente

Temochic

Ojos Azules

④ U.S. troops kill most of Villa's men but Villa escapes

Valle de Zaragoza

◄ Pancho Villa was eventually killed by unknown assassins in 1923.

Parral

③ U.S. troops repel attack by Mexican government forces

→ Villa's route
→ Pershing's route
✳ Villa's raid
⚔ Skirmish

0        50 miles
0        50 kilometers

## Thinking Critically

1. **Analyze Information** Do you think Pershing's expedition violated the ideals of "moral diplomacy"? Explain.

2. **Draw Conclusions** Why would American commanders be eager to test new military technology in the field against Villa?

States the right to control its financial and foreign affairs. The marines did not leave until 1934. Under Wilson, U.S. soldiers and sailors also intervened in the Dominican Republic and in Mexico.

**Revolution Grips Mexico** For decades, Mexican dictator Porfirio Díaz had benefited his country's small upper class of wealthy landowners, clerics, and military men. With Díaz's encouragement, foreign investments in Mexico grew. As a result, American business people owned large portions of Mexico's industries. While foreign investors and Mexico's aristocracy grew rich, Mexico's large population of farmers struggled in poverty.

In 1911, Francisco Madero led the Mexican Revolution that toppled Díaz. Madero was committed to reforms but was a weak administrator. In 1913, General Victoriano Huerta seized power and executed Madero. Under "dollar diplomacy," Taft probably would have recognized Huerta as the leader of Mexico because Huerta pledged to protect American investments. But under "moral diplomacy," Wilson refused to do so, declaring that he would not accept a "government of butchers." Instead, Wilson favored Venustiano Carranza, another reformer, who had organized anti-Huerta forces.

**Wilson Sends U.S. Troops Into Mexico** In 1914, the President used the Mexican arrest of American sailors as an opportunity to help Carranza attain power. Wilson sent marines to occupy the Mexican port of Veracruz. The action caused Huerta's government to collapse, and Carranza assumed the presidency.

Huerta's fall from power cheered many Mexicans and appeared to validate Wilson's "moral diplomacy." However, Wilson soon discovered that he faced more trouble in Mexico. The new Carranza government was slow in bringing about reforms, and rebels again rose up, this time under the leadership of **Francisco "Pancho" Villa.** For a while, Wilson courted Villa. After American support disappeared in 1916, Villa's forces crossed into New Mexico and raided the town of Columbus, leaving 18 Americans dead. President Wilson responded by sending General John J. Pershing and more than 10,000 troops on a "punitive expedition" to Mexico.

Pershing's forces chased Villa for several months but failed to capture the rebel leader. Wilson eventually withdrew American troops from Mexico in 1917, mostly because of his concerns about World War I raging in Europe. Not long afterward, the United States declared war on Germany. Free from hunting Villa, Pershing took command of the American Expeditionary Force in France.

A generation earlier, few would have believed it possible that more than one million American troops would engage in a large-scale war in Europe. But the triumph over Spain and U.S. actions in Asia and Latin America demonstrated that America had emerged as a world power. Now, World War I would test that new global strength.

✔ **Checkpoint** What was "moral diplomacy"?

---

**Progress Monitoring *Online***
For: Self-test with vocabulary practice
Web Code: nea-0510

## Comprehension

1. **Terms and People** Define each term below. How are they similar? How are they different?
   - "big stick" diplomacy
   - "dollar diplomacy"
   - "moral diplomacy"

2. **NoteTaking Reading Skill: Identify Supporting Details** Use your table to answer the Section Focus Question: What actions did the United States take to achieve its goals in Latin America?

## Writing About History

3. **Quick Write: Write a Conclusion** A narrative essay should include a conclusion that wraps up the events described in your story. Suppose that you want to write a narrative from the perspective of United States Army General John J. Pershing as he pursued "Pancho" Villa through northern Mexico. Write a conclusion to the story Pershing would tell of the pursuit.

## Critical Thinking

4. **Analyze Geography** What impact did the building of the Panama Canal have on American trade?

5. **Identify Assumptions** How do the Platt Amendment and the Roosevelt Corollary reflect similar assumptions about the governments of Latin American nations?

6. **Draw Conclusions** Do you think Woodrow Wilson succeeded in carrying out the principle of "moral diplomacy" in Latin America? Explain.

# Quick Study Guide

 6.2.1

## ■ Cause and Effect: American Imperialism

**Causes**
- Industrialized nations compete for raw materials and markets.
- Nations seek overseas bases to support naval and commercial interests.
- Imperialists believe in a superior American culture.

↓

**American Imperialism**

↓

**Effects**
- The United States purchases Alaska from Russia in 1867.
- American planters, supported by U.S. Marines, overthrow Hawaii's Queen Liliuokalani in 1893; the United States annexes Hawaii in 1898.
- The United States wins the Spanish-American War and acquires colonies in the Caribbean Sea and in the Pacific.
- In 1899, U.S. Secretary of State John Hay establishes the Open Door Policy to protect American trading rights in China.
- Panama rebels against Colombian rule; President Roosevelt acquires land for the construction of the Panama Canal.
- President Wilson sends U.S. troops on a "punitive expedition" into Mexico to hunt and capture the rebel Pancho Villa.

## ■ The Panama Canal

## ■ U.S. Interventions in Latin America

| Country | Type of Intervention | Year |
|---------|---------------------|------|
| Cuba | Occupation | 1898–1902, 1906–1909, 1912, 1917–1922 |
| Dominican Republic | Military intervention Occupation | 1905–1907 1916–1924 |
| Haiti | Occupation | 1915–1934 |
| Mexico | Military intervention | 1914, 1916–1917 |
| Nicaragua | Occupation | 1912–1925, 1927–1933 |
| Panama | Acquisition of Canal Zone | 1904 |
| Puerto Rico | Military invasion and territorial acquisition | 1898 |

## ✔ Quick Study Timeline

**1890**
**Mahan publishes**
***The Influence of Sea Power Upon History***

**1898**
**United States annexes Hawaii; Spanish-American War**

**In America**

**Presidential Terms**   Benjamin Harrison 1889–1893   Grover Cleveland 1893–1897   William McKinley 1897–1901

**1890**   **1895**   **1900**

**Around the World**

**1893**
**Americans overthrow Queen Liliuokalani in Hawaii**

**1899**
**Filipino insurrection**

**1900**
**Boxer Rebellion**

# American Issues
## ●—●—● Connector

By connecting prior knowledge with what you have learned in this chapter, you can gradually build your understanding of enduring questions that still affect America today. Answer the questions below. Then, use your American Issues Connector study guide (or go online: www.PHSchool.com **Web Code:** neh-7803).

## Issues You Learned About

● **Territorial Expansion of the United States** The United States has acquired land inside and outside of the continental United States.

1. Think about the events that led to the annexation of Hawaii. Write a paragraph explaining whether you think the United States had the right to take control of Hawaii. Consider the following:
   • the initial status of the Hawaiian Islands
   • changes made to the Hawaiian constitution by the monarchy
   • the role of American planters in Hawaii's government and society
   • the reasons that some Americans sought annexation
   • the Senate's initial response to the treaty of annexation

● **America and the World** At times, the United States chooses to get involved in the affairs of other countries.

2. Who proclaimed the Monroe Doctrine, and why?

3. How did the Roosevelt Corollary demonstrate Roosevelt's belief in "big stick" diplomacy?

4. What policies did Taft and Wilson develop for their involvement in Latin American affairs?

● **America Goes to War** The United States sometimes becomes involved in regional conflicts in other parts of the world.

5. Why did many Americans favor the Cuban revolutionaries in their struggle for freedom from Spain?

6. What event caused President McKinley and Congress to prepare for war with Spain?

### Connect to Your World | Michigan

**Michigan Goes to War** When the United States began mobilizing for the Spanish-American War in April 1898, President McKinley called for individuals to volunteer for military service. Almost every member of the Michigan National Guard answered the call. Michigan women contributed to the war effort as well. Ellen May Tower, from Byron, Michigan, went to Puerto Rico as a U.S. Army nurse. After contracting typhoid fever, Tower became the first Army nurse to die overseas. Tower's funeral on January 17, 1899, marked the first time in Michigan history—and only the third time in United States history up to that point—that a woman received the honor of a military funeral. Write a journal entry from the point of view of a Spanish-American War volunteer. Explain your decision to serve in the war despite the many risks.

**1907**
**Great White Fleet**

**1908**
**President Taft embraces "dollar diplomacy"**

**1916**
**Pershing hunts Pancho Villa in Mexico**

| Theodore Roosevelt 1901–1909 | William H. Taft 1909–1913 | Woodrow Wilson 1913–1921 | |
|---|---|---|---|
| **1905** | **1910** | **1915** | **1920** |

**1904**
**U.S. gains control of Canal Zone in Panama**

**1910**
**Mexican Revolution begins**

**1914**
**World War I breaks out in Europe**

**History Interactive**
**For:** Interactive timeline
**Web Code:** nep-0513

# Chapter Assessment

## Terms and People

1. Define **Social Darwinism.** How did some imperialists make use of this concept?
2. Who was **Queen Liliuokalani**? What changes did she bring to her country?
3. What was the **Treaty of Paris**? What were its terms?
4. Define **guerrilla warfare.** Who relied on guerrilla warfare?
5. Define the **Foraker Act** and **Platt Amendment.** Did they settle the debate over U.S. policy in Puerto Rico and Cuba?

## Focus Questions

The focus question for this chapter is **How did the United States become a global power?** Build an answer to this big question by answering the focus questions for Sections 1 through 4 and the Critical Thinking questions that follow.

### Section 1

6. How and why did the United States take a more active role in world affairs?

### Section 2

7. What were the causes and effects of the Spanish-American War?

### Section 3

8. How did the United States extend its influence in Asia?

### Section 4

9. What actions did the United States take to achieve its goals in Latin America?

## Critical Thinking

10. **Recognize Ideologies** How did U.S. expansion in the late nineteenth century extend and change the principle of Manifest Destiny?
11. **Make Comparisons** Choose two of the following: Commodore Perry's mission to Japan; the revolt in Hawaii; the Open Door Policy; the building of the Panama Canal. Explain how the two were similar yet different in terms of U.S. goals and actions.
12. **Recognize Propaganda** How did the Yellow Press contribute to U.S. actions against Spain?
13. **Compare Points of View** Explain the different opinions held by imperialists and anti-imperialists in the debate over the Philippines.
14. **Analyze Line Graphs** How were growing tensions with Japan linked to the trend shown on the graph below?

**U.S. Navy Yearly Federal Budget, 1898–1908**

SOURCE: *Historical Statistics of the United States*

15. **Draw Conclusions** What was the goal of U.S. policy toward China? Why do you think Hay did not favor establishing colonies in China?
16. **Predict Consequences** If Wilson had been President when the United States was seeking to build the Panama Canal, do you think he would have supported Panama's rebellion against Colombia? Justify your answer.

## Writing About History

**Write a Narrative Essay** Write a narrative essay telling a story about America's emergence as a global power in the late 1800s and early 1900s. Write your essay from the point of view of an imperialist or an anti-imperialist. Consult page SH11 of the Writing Handbook for additional help.

**Prewriting**
• Choose a chapter event that interests you most to write about.
• Choose a purpose for your essay. You might highlight a certain aspect of the event that you think deserves attention.
• Gather details related to your essay topic.

**Drafting**
• Identify the climax, or the most important part, of your story. Then, decide what will happen in the beginning, middle, and end of the essay.

• Write an introduction for the essay that will grab a reader's interest.
• Use many details to make the story vivid. When possible, include dialogue to convey the thoughts of the character.
• Write a conclusion that summarizes the significance of the experience to the character.

**Revising**
• Use the guidelines on page SH11 of the Writing Handbook to revise your essay.

YOUR COUNTRY CALLS YOU

# Prepare for the MME

## American Imperialism

Should the United States annex territories in order to establish a global empire? Or should it honor American roots by granting self-rule to the native peoples of those lands? Use your knowledge of the debate over American imperialism and the following documents to answer questions 1 through 4.

### Document A

Uncle Sam Wrestles With Filipino Insurgency

### Document B

The taking of the Philippines does not violate the principles of the Declaration of Independence, but will spread them among a people who have never known liberty and who in a few years will be unwilling to leave the shelter of the American flag. . . . The form of government natural to the Asiatic has always been despotism. . . . [T]o abandon those islands is to leave them to anarchy, [and] to short-lived military dictatorships. . . .

*Senator Henry Cabot Lodge, March 1900*

### Document C

I wanted the American eagle to go screaming into the Pacific. It seemed tiresome and tame for it to content itself with the Rockies. Why not spread its wings over the Philippines, I asked myself? And I thought it would be a real good thing to do. . . . But I have thought some more, since then, and I have read carefully the treaty of Paris, and I have seen that we do not intend to free, but to subjugate the people of the Philippines. We have gone there to conquer, not to redeem. . . . And so I am an anti-imperialist. I am opposed to having the eagle put its talons on any other land.

*Mark Twain, October 1900*

### Document D

WELL, I HARDLY KNOW WHICH TO TAKE FIRST!

---

1. Which of the documents is a primary source that supports the maintenance of American control over the Philippines to ensure a stable government there?
   A Document A
   B Document B
   C Document C
   D Document D

2. According to Document A, how did the cartoonist choose to portray the Filipino population?
   A Filipinos are resisting the American presence in the Philippines.
   B Filipinos are cooperating with American officials to maintain U.S. control.
   C Filipinos are fleeing their homes in fear of American soldiers.
   D Filipinos are celebrating their independence from Spain.

3. Mark Twain most closely agrees with which of the other documents?
   A Documents A and D
   B Documents A and B
   C Document B
   D Document D

4. **Writing Task** How did the principles of the American Revolution influence the debate over American imperialism in the Philippines? Use your knowledge of the aftermath of the Spanish-American War and specific evidence from the primary sources above to support your opinion.

## American Soldiers Arrive "Over There"

During World War I, nearly 4 million American soldiers went "over there"—to France—to help the Allies win the war. A British volunteer nurse working near the front in France described the arrival of the new American troops:

> **"**I pressed forward with the others to watch the United States physically entering the War, so god-like, so magnificent, so splendidly unimpaired in comparison with the tired, nerve-racked men of the British Army. So these were our deliverers at last, marching up the road to Camiers in the spring sunshine!**"**
> —Vera Brittain, *Testament of Youth*

*Listen to the* Witness History *audio to learn more about America in World War I.*

◄ A French couple greets American soldiers in France in 1918.

American soldier's helmet

American recruitment poster

###  Content Expectations

**Chapter Focus Question:** What caused the United States to become involved in World War I, and how did the United States change as a result of its involvement?

## Section 1
**From Neutrality to War**   6.1.1f, 6.1.3d, 6.3.1, 6.3.3

## Section 2
**The Home Front**   6.1.3d, 6.1.4, 6.3.3

## Section 3
**Wilson, War, and Peace**   6.2.2, 6.2.3, 6.2.4

## Section 4
**Effects of the War**   6.1.4, 6.3.1, 6.3.3

World War I–era airplane

Use the ☑ **Quick Study Timeline** at the end of this chapter to preview chapter events.

**Note Taking Study Guide *Online***
**For:** Note Taking and American Issues Connector
**Web Code:** nee-7901

A 1917 cartoon shows the German leader William II considering the U.S. flag looming on the horizon. ▶

WITNESS HISTORY 🔊 AUDIO

## To Fight or Not to Fight?

When war broke out in Europe in 1914, the United States decided to stay neutral. However, incidents like the senseless destruction of Louvain, a medieval university town in Belgium, by German troops turned American opinion against Germany.

❝For two hours on Thursday night I was in what for six hundred years had been the city of Louvain. The Germans were burning it . . . the story . . . was told to us by German soldiers incoherent with excesses; and we could read it in the faces of the women and children being led to concentration camps and of the citizens on their way to be shot.❞

—American journalist Richard Harding Davis, August 1914

# From Neutrality to War

 **Content Expectations**

- **6.1.1f** Analyze technological advances that enabled the U.S. to become an industrial power.
- **6.3.1** Describe problems/issues created by U.S.'s industrial/urban transformation between 1895–1930.
- **6.3.3** Analyze successes/failures to expand women's rights.

## Terms and People

| | |
|---|---|
| Alsace-Lorraine | casualty |
| militarism | contraband |
| Francis Ferdinand | U-boat |
| William II | *Lusitania* |
| Western Front | Zimmermann note |

## NoteTaking

**Reading Skill: Identify Causes** As you read, identify the causes of World War I, the conditions facing soldiers, and the reasons for U.S. involvement.

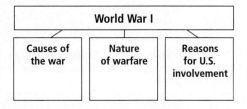

**Why It Matters** In 1914, nationalism, militarism, imperialism, and entangling alliances combined with other factors to lead the nations of Europe into a brutal war. The war quickly stretched around the globe. The United States remained neutral at first but ended up abandoning its long tradition of staying out of European conflicts. **Section Focus Question: What caused World War I, and why did the United States enter the war?**

## What Caused World War I?

Until 1914, there had not been a large-scale European conflict for nearly one hundred years. However, bitter, deep-rooted problems simmered beneath the surface of polite diplomacy. Europe was sitting on a powder keg of nationalism, regional tensions, economic rivalries, imperial ambitions, and militarism.

**Nationalism and Competition Heighten Tension** Nationalism, or devotion to one's nation, kick-started international and domestic tension. In the late 1800s, many Europeans began to reject the earlier idea of a nation as a collection of different ethnic groups. Instead, they believed that a nation should express the nationalism of a single ethnic group. This belief evolved into an intense form of nationalism that heightened international rivalries. For example, France longed to avenge its humiliating defeat by a collection of German states in 1871 and regain **Alsace-Lorraine,** the territory it lost during that conflict. Nationalism also threatened minority groups within nation-states. If a country existed as the expression of "its people," the majority ethnic group, where did ethnic minorities fit in?

The spread of the theory of Social Darwinism did not help soothe the competitive instinct. Social Darwinism applied biologist Charles Darwin's ideas of natural selection and "survival of the fittest" to human society. Social Darwinists believed that the best nation would come out ahead in the constant competition among countries.

Nationalism also destabilized old multinational empires such as Austria-Hungary and the Ottoman Empire. This was particularly true in the Balkan region of southeastern Europe. For example, when Serbia emerged as an independent nation in 1878, it challenged the nearby empire of Austria-Hungary in two ways: by trying to gain territory controlled by the empire, where Serbs lived, and by the example it offered to Austria-Hungary's diverse peoples.

The nationalist sentiments of the period sometimes spilled over into the economic goals of each nation. Industrial output, trade, and the possession of an overseas empire were the yardsticks of wealth and greatness. The leading industrial nations competed for lands rich in raw materials as well as for places to build military bases to protect their empires. Britain already had a large empire, and France commanded a smaller one. But Germany, Italy, Belgium, Japan, and the United States also rushed to join the imperial race. Together, industrialized nations jostled among themselves as they carved colonies out of Africa, claimed islands in the Pacific, and began to nibble away at China.

**Militarism Produces an Arms Race** For some European leaders, the question was not so much *if* a great war would start but *when*. To prepare, leaders increased the size of their armies and stockpiles of weapons. No nation readied its war machinery more than Germany. By 1914, it had a huge standing army and the largest, deadliest collection of guns in the world. It also built up its navy enough to rival Britain's, the world's strongest at that time. To keep up, Britain, too, increased the size of its navy. A spirit of **militarism,** or glorification of the military, grew in the competing countries and fueled this arms race even more.

The contest between Germany and Britain at sea and between Germany, France, and Russia on land guaranteed one important thing: The next major war would involve more troops and more technologically advanced weapons than ever before. Machine guns, mobile artillery, tanks, submarines, and airplanes would change the nature of warfare.

### Building the War Machine
In the early 1900s, European countries raced to keep up with one another's military might. Below, workers build artillery in Essen, a German city, in 1904. *According to the chart, which country had the largest army in 1914? Which had the largest navy?*

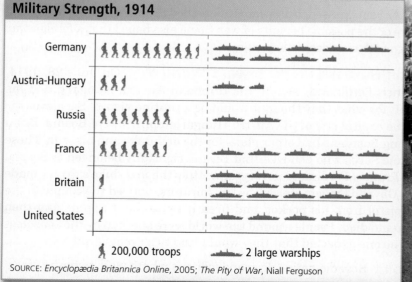

**Military Strength, 1914**

Germany
Austria-Hungary
Russia
France
Britain
United States

🚶 200,000 troops    🚢 2 large warships

SOURCE: *Encyclopædia Britannica Online,* 2005; *The Pity of War,* Niall Ferguson

**Geography** *Interactive*
For: Interactive map
Web Code: nep-0602

Legend:
- Allies, 1917
- Central Powers, 1917
- Neutral countries, 1917
- Front line, 1914
- Front line, 1915–1916
- Front line, 1917
- Russian offensive, June–September 1916
- Battle site

Occupied by Central Powers at end of 1915

Conic Projection
0   100   200 mi
0   100 200 km

**Map Skills** The war on most fronts was a stalemate by 1916.

1. **Locate:** (a) Belgium, (b) Western Front, (c) Battle of Verdun

2. **Location** What challenge did Germany's location present to its pursuit of victory in the war?

3. **Synthesize Information** Describe the movement of the opposing lines of the Western Front between 1914 and 1917.

**Vocabulary Builder**
<u>ally</u>–(AL ī) *n.* person, nation, or group joined with another for a common purpose

**Alliances Make Nations Overconfident and Reckless** European leaders also prepared for war by forming alliances. Before 1914, two major ones emerged. Germany, Austria-Hungary, and Italy joined together in the Triple Alliance (although Italy never fought with it). Opposed to the Triple Alliance was the Triple Entente, made up of France, Russia, and Great Britain. Alliances emboldened leaders to act recklessly. They knew that if they did declare war, powerful <u>allies</u> were obligated to fight along with them. No country wanted to be seen as an unreliable partner. As years passed, European leaders thought less of the advantages of peace and more of the possible benefits of war. Some also hoped that a foreign war would help to smooth over domestic problems.

**Assassination Hurtles Europe Toward World War** On June 28, 1914, Archduke **Francis Ferdinand,** heir to the throne of Austria-Hungary, and his wife Sophie left for what they thought would be a routine visit to Sarajevo (sar uh YAY voh), the capital city of the Austro-Hungarian province of Bosnia. But a handful of young Bosnians had other plans for the archduke and his wife. These men were ethnic Serbs who believed that Bosnia rightfully belonged to Serbia, and they saw Francis Ferdinand as a tyrant. After the archduke's driver made a wrong turn, Gavrilo Princip, one of the conspirators, noticed the couple in the car, pulled a pistol from his pocket, and fired it twice. First Sophie and then Francis Ferdinand died. People around the world were shocked by the senseless murders. But no one expected that they would lead to a great world war.

✓ **Checkpoint** How did nationalism and militarism both work to push Europe toward war?

# The Fighting Begins

Everything was in place for a great conflict—nationalist ambitions, large armies, stockpiles of weapons, alliances, and military plans. The nations of Europe were hurtling like giant trains toward a great collision. Archduke Francis Ferdinand's assassination was the incident that triggered this conflict.

**Alliances Cause a Chain Reaction** Soon after the assassination, Kaiser **William II,** the German emperor, assured Austria-Hungary that Germany would stand by its ally if war came. Confident in Germany's support, Austria-Hungary then sent a harsh ultimatum to Serbia demanding Serbia's total cooperation in an investigation into the assassination. When Serbia did not agree to all of the demands, Austria-Hungary declared war on July 28, 1914.

Because of the alliance system, what otherwise might have been a localized quarrel quickly spread. In early August, Russia mobilized for war to help its ally Serbia against Austria. This caused Germany to declare war against Russia. France, Russia's ally, promptly declared war against Germany. The very next day, Germany declared war against neutral Belgium, so that it could launch an invasion of France through that small country. Great Britain, which had treaties with France and Belgium, immediately declared war against Germany. In less than one week, the Central Powers of Germany and Austria-Hungary were at war against the Allied Powers of Britain, France, Russia, and Serbia. The Ottoman Empire later joined the Central Powers.

German soldiers fought through Belgium and moved southwest into France, toward Paris. Then in September, with the German advance only 30 miles from Paris, the French and the British counterattacked and stopped the German forces near the Marne River.

**Deadly Technology Leads to Stalemate** After the Battle of the Marne, the Germans settled onto high ground, dug trenches, and fortified their position. When the French and British attacked, the German troops used machine guns and artillery to kill thousands of them. The French and British then dug their own trenches and used the same weapons to kill thousands of counterattacking Germans. Soon, 450 miles of trenches stretched like a huge scar from the coast of Belgium to the border of Switzerland. Although fighting went on in Eastern Europe, the Middle East, and in other parts of the world, this **Western Front** in France became the critical battle front. The side that won there would win the war.

The war dragged on for years, and it was hideously deadly—much more so than anyone had expected. The primary reason for the length of the war and its deadly nature was the simple fact that the defensive weapons of the time were better and more devastating than the offensive ones. Generals on each side threw their soldiers into assaults against the enemy without fully considering the new technology. Charging toward trenches that were defended by artillery, machine guns, and rifles was futile. In virtually every battle on the Western Front, the attacking force suffered terribly. Even the use of poison gas did nothing to benefit the offense, despite its horrifying effects. Ineffective offensives and effective defensives produced only a deadly stalemate.

## War in the Trenches

German soldiers hunker down in a shallow trench that stretches into the distance to protect themselves from enemy fire. *How did new technology make defenses such as trenches necessary?*

173

**WITNESS HISTORY DVD**

Watch *World War I: A New Kind of War* on the **United States Witness History DVD** to learn more about the nature of warfare during World War I.

**The Reality of Trench Warfare** The stalemate led to gruesome conditions for the men in the trenches of the Western Front. The soldiers battled the harsh conditions of life often as fiercely as they attacked the enemy. They developed "trench foot" from standing for hours in wet, muddy trenches. They contracted lice from the millions of rats that infested the trenches. Dug into the ground, the soldiers lived in constant fear, afraid to pop their heads out of their holes and always aware that the next offensive might be their last.

Even on a quiet day, soldiers could be killed by snipers or a surprise gas attack, like the one described by French officer Paul Truffaut at Verdun:

**Primary Source** "The special shells the men call "shells on wheels" [shells filled with poison gas] are whizzing by continuously. They explode silently and have no smell but can be deadly. They killed several men yesterday. One of my men refused to put his mask on because he couldn't smell anything. All of a sudden, he was dizzy, foaming at the mouth and his skin went black, then he went rigid and died."
—Paul Truffaut, March 5, 1917

In between enemy lines was an area known as "no man's land." Artillery barrages had blasted no man's land until any fields, trees, or homes, that had once existed there, were charred beyond recognition. Soldiers went "over the top" of their trenches into this muddy, nearly impassable wasteland when they attempted to attack the entrenched enemy.

**Casualties**—or soldiers killed, wounded, and missing—mounted first in thousands, then hundreds of thousands, and finally in millions. Almost one million French soldiers were killed or wounded in just the first three months of the war. The Germans lost only slightly fewer. In two battles in 1916—Verdun (ver DUHN) and the Somme (suhm)—the British, French, and Germans sustained more than 2 million casualties. The British suffered 60,000 casualties on the first day alone at the Somme and achieved virtually nothing. And still the stalemate dragged on.

✔ **Checkpoint** Why did both sides embrace trench warfare as a strategy to win the war?

**Horror of Modern Warfare**
Although gas masks were soon developed to counter poison gas, gas attacks were still particularly horrifying to soldiers. *According to the chart, which type of weapon caused the most casualties?*

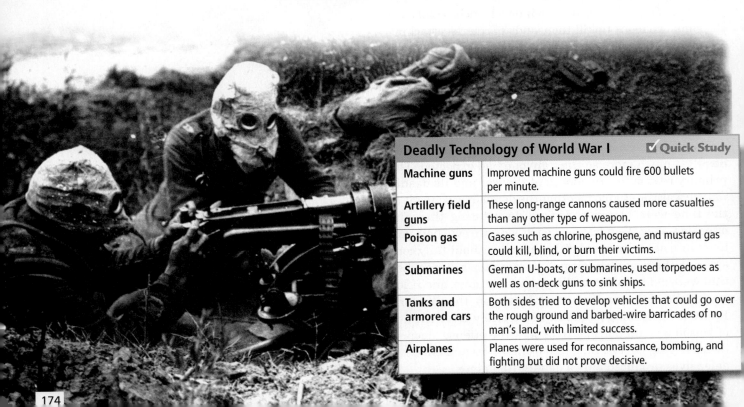

| Deadly Technology of World War I | ✓ Quick Study |
|---|---|
| Machine guns | Improved machine guns could fire 600 bullets per minute. |
| Artillery field guns | These long-range cannons caused more casualties than any other type of weapon. |
| Poison gas | Gases such as chlorine, phosgene, and mustard gas could kill, blind, or burn their victims. |
| Submarines | German U-boats, or submarines, used torpedoes as well as on-deck guns to sink ships. |
| Tanks and armored cars | Both sides tried to develop vehicles that could go over the rough ground and barbed-wire barricades of no man's land, with limited success. |
| Airplanes | Planes were used for reconnaissance, bombing, and fighting but did not prove decisive. |

# Wilson Urges Neutrality

As the war spread in Europe, President Woodrow Wilson called for Americans to be "impartial in thought as well as action." In a "melting pot" nation that tried to make Americans of peoples from diverse origins, Wilson did not want to see the war set Americans against one another. At first, most Americans viewed the conflict as a distant European quarrel for land and influence. Unless the nation's interests were directly threatened, Americans wanted no part of it. They preferred to maintain what they viewed as traditional American isolation from European disputes. Still, many Americans felt the war's effects and few were truly impartial in thought. Most held a preference for one or another combatant, and many businesses benefited from the increased demand by warring nations for American goods.

**Americans Have Divided Loyalties** In 1914, one third of Americans were foreign-born. Many still thought of themselves in terms of their former homelands—as German Americans, Irish Americans, Polish Americans, and so on. With relatives in Europe, many people supported the nation in which they were born.

Some German Americans in the Midwest and some Irish Americans along the East Coast felt strongly that the Central Powers were justified in their actions. Many Americans had emigrated from Germany or Austria-Hungary. Millions of Irish Americans harbored intense grudges over the centuries of Great Britain's domination of their homeland. They hoped that Ireland would gain its independence as Britain became entangled in the war. Many Jewish Americans who had fled Russia to escape the Czarist regimes' murderous pogroms against Jews hoped for Russia's defeat.

Most Americans, however, sided with Britain and France, both of which had strong historic ties with the United States. America's national language was English, its cultural heritage was largely British, and its leading trading partner was Britain. France had aided the American cause during the Revolutionary War.

**American Opinion Crystallizes** No event at the beginning of the war swayed American opinion more than the vicious German invasion of neutral Belgium. German soldiers marching through Belgium committed numerous atrocities, killing unarmed civilians and destroying entire towns. British journalists and propagandists stressed, and sometimes exaggerated, the brutality of the Germans' actions. Americans might have only dimly understood the causes of the war, but they clearly perceived the human cost of the war for Belgium.

Eventually, three distinct positions on the war crystallized among Americans. One group, the isolationists, believed that the war was none of America's business and that the nation should isolate itself from the hostilities. A second group, the interventionists, felt that the war did affect American interests and that the United States should intervene in the conflict on the side of the Allies. A third group, the internationalists, occupied the middle ground. Internationalists believed that the United States should play an active role in world affairs and work toward achieving a just peace but not enter the war.

✔ **Checkpoint** Why did President Wilson fear that the war would set Americans against one another?

Stop!

## Analyzing Political Cartoons

**The Question of Neutrality** In this 1916 cartoon, President Wilson tries to neutralize German Kaiser William II's bloody sword (representing Germany's policy of unrestricted submarine warfare) by pointing it toward the ground.

1. How does the cartoonist portray Kaiser William II?
2. What position do you think the cartoonist holds on American involvement in the war?

## Neutrality Gives Way to War

An internationalist, President Wilson sincerely desired peace in his country and around the world. Between the start of the war in 1914 and America's entry into it in 1917, Wilson attempted to use his influence to end the conflict among the warring countries. He failed in this great effort. Ultimately, he also failed to keep the United States out of the war.

**Britain Blockades Germany**  Early in the war, British leaders decided to use their navy to blockade Germany to keep essential goods from reaching the other country. International law generally allowed **contraband** goods, usually defined as weapons and other articles used to fight a war, to be confiscated legally by any belligerent nation. Noncontraband goods, such as food, medical supplies, and other nonmilitary items, could not be confiscated. Britain, however, contested the definition of noncontraband articles. As the war continued, Britain expanded its definition of contraband until it encompassed virtually every product, including gasoline, cotton, and even food—in spite of international law.

**German Submarines Violate Neutral Rights**  Germany responded by attempting to blockade Britain—even though it lacked the conventional naval forces to do so. Instead, in February 1915, Germany began sinking Allied ships using its **U-boats,** or submarines. The reality of the German blockade struck America on May 7, 1915, when a German U-boat sank the British passenger liner *Lusitania* off the coast of Ireland. German officials correctly claimed that

# U-Boats
## Sink American Neutrality

**O**n May 7, 1915, the British passenger ship *Lusitania* cruised off the coast of Ireland. The German submarine *U-20*, lurking underwater, sighted the ship and fired a torpedo into its starboard side. It sank within 20 minutes, killing nearly 1,200 passengers. Among the dead were 128 Americans.

The sinking of the *Lusitania* was part of Germany's submarine blockade of Britain. The sinking of passenger ships carrying American neutrals angered the United States when it occurred in 1915 and again in 1916. Nonetheless, in early 1917, desperate German leaders declared unrestricted submarine warfare—causing the United States to enter the war.

### Ships Sunk by U-boats, May 1917–Jan. 1918

• Ship sunk

Conic Projection
0    50    100 mi
0  50 100 km

North Sea

Edinburgh

Belfast

Dublin

UNITED KINGDOM

Queenstown

London

Portsmouth
Falmouth    Dover

Le Havre
Cherbourg

Atlantic Ocean

Brest

FRANCE

During World War I, German U-boats, like the *U-166* shown below, destroyed more than 11 million tons of Allied shipping and killed nearly 14,000 people.

the ship was carrying ammunition and other contraband. Americans protested that an unarmed and unresisting ship should not be sunk without first being warned and provided with safety for its passengers. President Wilson was stunned but still wanted peace. "There is such a thing as a man being too proud to fight," he told his fellow citizens. "There is such a thing as a nation being so right that it does not need to convince others by force that it is right."

Germany helped to keep the United States out of the war by eventually promising not to sink any more passenger ships. But in 1916, Germany violated that promise by sinking the unarmed French passenger ship *Sussex*. Another storm of protest erupted in America. Again, Germany pledged not to sink unarmed ships. This promise, called the Sussex Pledge, would not last long.

**Wilson Prepares for War** President Wilson wanted to remain at peace, but even he must have realized the futility of that hope. At the end of 1915, Wilson began to prepare the nation for war. Many believed that "preparedness" was a dangerous course that could actually provoke war. Even so, Congress passed two pieces of legislation in 1916 to prepare for the possibility of U.S. involvement. The National Defense Act expanded the size of the army, and the Naval Construction Act ordered the building of more warships.

Still, Wilson hoped to avoid the conflict. In 1916, he ran for reelection with the slogan, "He kept us out of war." It was a close election, but Wilson won a narrow victory over Republican Charles Evans Hughes.

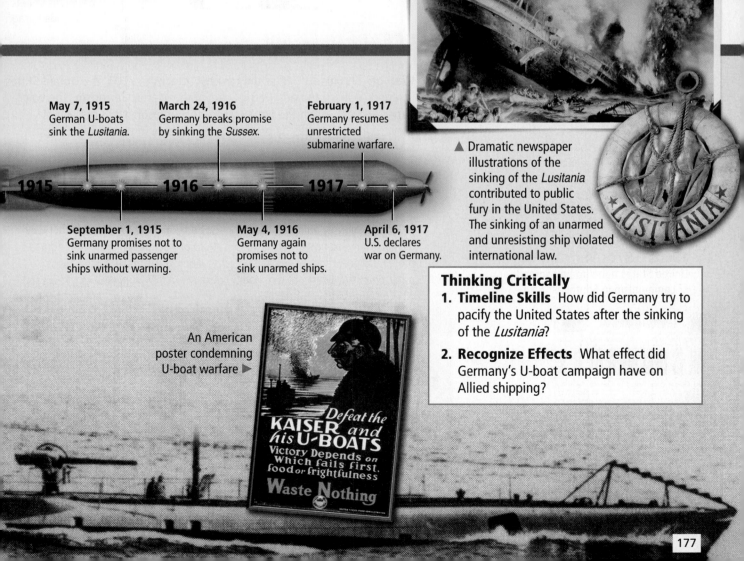

**May 7, 1915**
German U-boats sink the *Lusitania*.

**March 24, 1916**
Germany breaks promise by sinking the *Sussex*.

**February 1, 1917**
Germany resumes unrestricted submarine warfare.

**1915** — **1916** — **1917**

**September 1, 1915**
Germany promises not to sink unarmed passenger ships without warning.

**May 4, 1916**
Germany again promises not to sink unarmed ships.

**April 6, 1917**
U.S. declares war on Germany.

▲ Dramatic newspaper illustrations of the sinking of the *Lusitania* contributed to public fury in the United States. The sinking of an unarmed and unresisting ship violated international law.

An American poster condemning U-boat warfare ▶

Defeat the KAISER and his U-BOATS
Victory Depends on Which fails first, food or frightfulness
Waste Nothing

**Thinking Critically**
1. **Timeline Skills** How did Germany try to pacify the United States after the sinking of the *Lusitania*?
2. **Recognize Effects** What effect did Germany's U-boat campaign have on Allied shipping?

# America Goes to War

6.2.2

## TRACK THE ISSUE

### When should America go to war?

Over the years, the United States has had many motives for going to war. The nation has gone to war to protect itself, gain economic benefits, aid its allies, expand its borders, or increase its power and influence. Under what circumstances is war justified? Americans debate this issue each time the country fights. Use the timeline below to explore this enduring issue.

**1812 War of 1812**
Americans fight to stop Britain from seizing American ships and sailors.

**1860s Civil War**
North and South fight over slavery, states' rights, and preservation of the Union.

**1917–1918 World War I**
United States goes to war after Germany violates American neutrality.

**1940s World War II**
The Japanese attack on Pearl Harbor draws America into the conflict.

**1960s–1970s Vietnam War**
United States fights to halt spread of communism in Southeast Asia.

U.S. soldiers patrol the streets in Baghdad, Iraq.

## DEBATE THE ISSUE

**War on Terrorism** After the terrorist attacks of 2001, the United States invaded Afghanistan and Iraq as part of the War on Terrorism. The war aimed to track down the perpetrators of the terrorist attacks and to prevent future attacks by promoting democracy in the Middle East.

❝The use of military force against terrorist networks and regimes abetting their crimes is certainly justifiable. . . . Our leaders are, in my judgment, morally obligated to use as much force as necessary . . . to protect innocent Americans and other potential victims of terrorism.❞
—Robert P. George, professor, Princeton University

❝When you make the argument that there is a 'just war,' what you are saying is that there is an aggression, a major offense is being committed and you do not have any other way to protect people from that aggression except to use force.❞
—Reverend J. Brian Hehir, Catholic theologian

A newspaper announces America's entry into World War I on April 6, 1917.

### ❓ *TRANSFER* Activities

1. **Compare** Why does Professor George support the War on Terrorism? Why does Reverend Hehir oppose it?

2. **Analyze** Do you think Hehir would have supported the decision to enter World War I? Explain.

3. **Transfer** Use the following Web site to see a video, try a WebQuest, and write in your journal. **Web Code:** neh-7902

**America Enters the War** Wilson did not have much time to enjoy his victory. In early 1917, two events occurred that helped to push the United States into the war. American trade with the Allies had sustained Britain and France in the war, while the British blockade of Germany had stopped the flow of American goods to the Central Powers. As far as Germany was concerned, desperate times demanded desperate measures.

In January 1917, suffering severe supply shortages due to the blockade, Germany took action. First, German Foreign Minister Arthur Zimmermann sent a telegram to Mexico. The **Zimmermann note** proposed an alliance with Mexico, stating that if the United States declared war on Germany, Mexico should declare war on the United States. In return, after a German victory, Mexico would get back the states of Texas, New Mexico, and Arizona, which it had lost in 1848 after its defeat in the Mexican-American War. The telegram was intercepted by the British, who gave it to American authorities. Next, Germany once again announced unrestricted submarine warfare against Britain.

Although most leaders knew Mexico had no intention of attacking the United States, Americans were shocked by the publication of the Zimmermann note. Even Wilson no longer called for peace. On April 2, 1917, he asked Congress for a declaration of war against Germany:

## HISTORY MAKERS

### Jeannette Rankin (1880–1973)

In 1916, Jeannette Rankin became the first woman elected to Congress. Committed to women's rights, she was also a dedicated pacifist. She and 49 other members of Congress voted against declaring war on Germany in 1917. Twenty-four years later, in 1941, she was the only member of Congress to vote against the declaration of war against Japan. "As a woman," Rankin said, "I can't go to war, and I refuse to send anyone else." She lost her bid for reelection in the election years that followed both votes.

**Primary Source** "The world must be made safe for democracy. Its peace must be planted upon the tested foundations of political liberty. . . . We are but one of the champions of the rights of mankind. We shall be satisfied when those rights have been made as secure as the faith and the freedom of nations can make them."
—Woodrow Wilson, April 2, 1917

Congress responded on April 6, 1917, with a declaration of war. Wilson's long struggle to keep America at peace was over.

✔ **Checkpoint** What German actions led the United States to enter World War I?

---

## SECTION 1 Assessment

**Progress Monitoring Online**
For: Self-test with vocabulary practice
Web Code: nea-0603

### Comprehension

1. **Terms and People** For each item below, write a sentence explaining its significance to the outbreak and course of World War I.
   - militarism
   - Francis Ferdinand
   - William II
   - casualty
   - U-boat
   - *Lusitania*

2. **NoteTaking Reading Skill: Identify Causes** Use your chart to answer the Section Focus Question: What caused World War I, and why did the United States enter the war?

### Writing About History

3. **Quick Write: Identify Causes** List each cause of U.S. entry into World War I, and then organize them in order of importance. Finally, turn your list into a paragraph describing the causes of U.S. involvement in the war.

### Critical Thinking

4. **Draw Conclusions** Why did a stalemate develop on the Western Front?

5. **Compare Points of View** Compare the three positions Americans took on the issue of whether or not the United States should enter the war.

6. **Synthesize Information** Why did the United States decide to enter the war and fight on the side of the Allies?

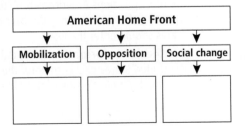

Little
AMERICANS
*Do your bit*

Eat Oatmeal-Corn meal mush-
Hominy - other corn cereals-
and Rice with milk.
*Save the wheat for our soldiers.*
Leave nothing on your plate

UNITED STATES FOOD ADMINISTRATION

▲ Girl Scouts collect peach pits to be used in gas-mask filters.

## WITNESS HISTORY ◀)) AUDIO

### Supporting the War

While soldiers trained to fight in the war, Americans on the home front supported the war by working in war industries, lending money to the government, and conserving food to feed the troops abroad.

❝Perhaps it will not be long before we will read each day long lists of American boys killed or wounded in the trenches of France. There will be boys in those lists that you know, boys that I know. And as our eyes film over with tears it will be at least some comfort to us to be able to say, 'I am helping too. I am saving food for the boys who are fighting.'❞

—Committee on Public Information bulletin, July 1917

# The Home Front

 **Content Expectations**

- **6.1.3d** Analyze resulting tensions among/ within groups.
- **6.1.4** Describe changes in composition, distribution, and density of U.S. population.
- **6.3.3** Analyze successes/failures to expand women's rights.

## Terms and People

Selective Service Act
Bernard Baruch
CPI
George Creel

conscientious objector
Espionage Act
Great Migration

## NoteTaking

**Reading Skill: Summarize** As you read, summarize the key points made in the section in a chart like the one below.

```
            American Home Front
        ┌─────────────┼─────────────┐
        ▼             ▼             ▼
   Mobilization   Opposition   Social change
        ▼             ▼             ▼
   ┌─────────┐   ┌─────────┐   ┌─────────┐
   │         │   │         │   │         │
   └─────────┘   └─────────┘   └─────────┘
```

**Why It Matters** Before the war, the federal government played a minor role in the daily lives of most Americans. But during World War I, the government assumed new powers. It regulated industrial and agricultural production, worked to shape public opinion, and established a new military draft. While war required sacrifice, it also brought new economic opportunities and many Americans migrated to other parts of the country in search of these opportunities. The war permanently changed Americans' relationship with their government. **Section Focus Question: How did the war affect Americans at home?**

## America Mobilizes for War

War affects many things, but its greatest impact is on the lives of ordinary people. People fight, sacrifice, and sometimes die in war. People work to produce the food that soldiers eat and the guns that soldiers fire. People shape the information that others receive about the war. War may be the result of conflicts between nations, but it touches the lives of millions of individuals.

**Building an Army** When the United States entered World War I, the United States Army was only a fraction of the size of European armies. To build the army, President Wilson encouraged Americans to volunteer for service and pushed Congress to pass the **Selective Service Act.** The act, which Congress passed in May 1917, authorized a draft of young men for military service in Europe. On the first day of its enactment, June 5, 1917, more than 9.6 million Americans registered for the draft and were assigned a number. The government held a "great national lottery" in July to decide the order in which the first draftees would be called into service. Blindfolded, Secretary of War Newton D. Baker pulled number 258 out of a jar. The group of men assigned that number became the very first draftees.

Over the course of the war, more than 24 million Americans registered for the draft. Of these, about 2.8 million were actually drafted into the armed forces. Including volunteers, the total number of American men in uniform during World War I reached nearly 4.8 million. More than 4 million of these were sent to help the Allies in France.

**Constructing a War Economy** While the Selective Service Commission raised an army, President Wilson worked to shift the national economy from peacetime to wartime production. This process proved slow and frustrating. First, the Council of National Defense, which was formed in August 1916, created an array of new federal administrative agencies to oversee different phases of the war effort. Individual agencies regulated food production, coal and petroleum distribution, and railway use. In practical terms, this meant that the government determined what crops farmers grew, what products industries produced, and how supplies moved around on the nation's trains.

Problems and administrative overlap soon led to the creation of the War Industries Board (WIB). The WIB eventually became independent of the Council of National Defense. Headed by **Bernard Baruch** (buh ROOK), an influential Wall Street investment broker who reported directly to the President, the WIB regulated all industries engaged in the war effort. Baruch's agency determined what products industries would make, where those products went, and how much they would cost. The system of free enterprise was curtailed to fulfill the nation's acute need for war materials. Americans realized that they had to cooperate rather than compete in order to defeat the Central Powers.

What Baruch did for industry, future U.S. President Herbert Hoover achieved for agriculture. As head of the Food Administration, he set prices high for wheat and other foodstuffs to encourage farmers to increase production. He also asked

**Wartime Production**

These women worked during the war inspecting bullets for rifles. *According to the graph, by what percentage did manufacturing increase between 1915 and 1918?*

**Rising U.S. Production, 1915–1918**

Percentage of increase over 1914 production levels

| | Textiles | Manufacturing | Agriculture |
|---|---|---|---|

* In 1916, agricultural output did not increase above the 1914 levels.
SOURCE: *The American Home Front*, James L. Abrahamson

Americans to <u>conserve</u> food as a patriotic gesture. If the American people ate less, then more food could be shipped to American and other Allied soldiers fighting the war overseas. To this end, Hoover instituted wheatless Mondays and Wednesdays, meatless Tuesdays, and porkless Thursdays and Saturdays.

**Shaping Public Opinion** Hoover's efforts would have been fruitless if the American people did not believe in supporting the war. Most Americans did not understand the reasons for the war in 1914, and many questioned why the United States became involved in 1917. It was the job of the **Committee on Public Information (CPI)** to educate the public about the causes and nature of the war. The CPI had to convince Americans that the war effort was a just cause.

Wilson appointed **George Creel** as the director of the CPI. A former journalist and a passionate admirer of American institutions, Creel combined education and a widespread advertising campaign to "sell America." The CPI distributed 75 million pamphlets and 6,000 press releases, and it assembled an army of 75,000 speakers who gave lectures and brief speeches on America's war aims and the nature of the enemy. In addition, the CPI designed, printed, and distributed millions of posters that dramatized the needs of America and its allies. The CPI also stressed the cruelty and wickedness of the enemy, particularly Germany, which in some cases aggravated resentment toward German Americans. Still, using these methods, Creel and the CPI earned widespread support for the American war effort.

✔ **Checkpoint** How did the United States ready its military, economy, and people for war?

## Opposition and Its Consequences

The CPI's work was important because Americans did not always peacefully agree with one another about the war. Members of two large ethnic groups, German Americans and Irish Americans, tended to oppose the Allies for different reasons. Swept up in patriotic fervor, some people treated German Americans with prejudice, or intolerance. Other Americans were pacifists who opposed war for any reason. To quiet dissent, or differing opinions, the government acted in ways that sometimes trespassed on individual liberties.

**Resistance to the Draft** Without a doubt, the draft created controversy. Some Americans believed it was an illegal intrusion of the federal government into their private lives. Some men refused to cooperate with the Selective Service process. They were often court-martialed and imprisoned. Others simply tried to avoid the draft. Perhaps as many as 12 percent of men who received draft notices never responded to them.

Another group resisted the draft by becoming **conscientious objectors,** people whose moral or religious beliefs forbid them to fight in wars. In theory, the Selective Service Act exempted from combat service members of "any well recognized religious sect or organization . . . whose existing creed or principles forbid its members to participate in war." In practice, this policy was widely ignored. Some conscientious objectors were treated badly by their local draft boards, and others were humiliated in training camps. As America's participation in the war increased, however, the government improved its treatment of conscientious objectors.

**Noble Goals**
Postcards like this one emphasized Wilson's goal of making the world "safe for democracy."

# HE'S IN THE ARMY NOW!

**W**hile the presence of millions of American soldiers in France helped the Allies, their absence at home had dramatic consequences. Families lived in constant fear for their fathers, husbands, brothers, or sons overseas, some of whom would never return. Many people had to take on the jobs of the absent soldiers. Meanwhile, the government encouraged Americans to go to work in war industries, conserve food and other goods, and buy Liberty bonds to support the war effort.

## Effects of the War on the Workforce

| Workers Lost | Workers Gained |
| --- | --- |
| In addition to the millions of workers who went into the military, immigrants from Europe, who had swelled the workforce in the early 1900s, dropped from one million in 1914 to only 31,000 in 1918. | Nearly 500,000 women joined the workforce for the first time, 400,000 African Americans left the rural South for industrial jobs in the North, and nearly 240,000 Mexicans immigrated to the United States, filling mainly agricultural jobs in the Southwest. |

**Result:** Despite gains, the United States still faced a shortage of workers when it joined the war in 1917.

SOURCE: *The American Home Front,* James L. Abrahamson

Private T. P. Loughlin says goodbye to his family (above right). A poster with a stirring message urges Americans to buy Liberty bonds (far right). Two women deliver ice, a job formerly done by men (left).

OVER THE TOP
FOR YOU

Buy U.S. Gov't Bonds
**THIRD LIBERTY LOAN**

## Thinking Critically

1. **Draw Conclusions** How did conserving food on the home front help the war effort?

2. **Predict Consequences** What do you think will happen to the women and African Americans who took new jobs during the war when the war ends?

**Women Work for Peace** Some American women also opposed the war. Before the war, a number of leading American feminists, including reformer Jane Addams, formed the Women's Peace Party and, with pacifist women from other countries, the Women's International League for Peace and Freedom. Jeannette Rankin, the first woman to serve in the U.S. House of Representatives, voted against the declaration of war. After America joined the Allies, some women continued to oppose the war, but most supported American war efforts. For example, the influential National American Woman Suffrage Association (NAWSA) dropped its initial peace initiatives and supported America's war objectives. After adopting this new policy, NAWSA doubled in size.

**Vocabulary Builder**
objective–(uhb JEHK tihv) *n.* something worked toward; goal

**The Government Cracks Down on Dissent** The work of the CPI created a mood in America that did not welcome open debate. Some felt the CPI stifled the free expression of controversial opinions and worried about the impact of a rigorous military campaign on democracy. They did not want the freedoms that Americans held most dear to become victims of the conflict. As in previous and future wars, the government navigated a difficult path between respecting and restricting individual rights. Authorities tended to treat harshly individuals who worked against the goal of winning the war.

In June 1917, Congress passed the **Espionage Act,** allowing postal authorities to ban treasonable or seditious newspapers, magazines, or printed materials from the mail. It also enacted severe penalties for anyone engaged in disloyal or treasonable activities. Anyone found obstructing army recruiters, aiding the enemy, or generally interfering with the war effort could be punished with up to a $10,000 fine and 20 years of imprisonment.

In 1918, Congress limited freedom of speech even further with the passage of the Sedition Act. The act made it unlawful to use "disloyal, profane, scurrilous, or abusive language" about the American form of government, the Constitution, or the military forces. The government employed the Sedition Act to prosecute socialists, political radicals, and pacifists. Eugene V. Debs, the leader of the Socialist Party in America, was imprisoned under the act. For his crime—giving a mildly antiwar speech to a convention of socialists in Canton, Ohio—he was sentenced to a 10-year term in a federal prison.

The Supreme Court upheld the constitutionality of the Sedition Act in the case of *Schenck* v. *United States* (1919). The Court ruled that there are times when the need for public order is so pressing that First Amendment protections of speech do not apply. The Debs case and others like it show that the war did lead to some suppression of personal freedoms and individual rights.

**Prejudice Against German Americans** Sometimes, the war enthusiasm created by the CPI and other groups took an ugly turn. Some German Americans were treated harshly during the war. Americans regarded Germany—with its arrogant kaiser, ruthless generals, and spike-helmeted soldiers—as the primary foe among the Central Powers. Popular movies, such as *The Kaiser, the Beast of Berlin,* as well as some CPI posters and speeches intensified this feeling by portraying Germany as a cruel enemy. Some Americans wrongly generalized that if Germany was cruel, then all German people were cruel.

As a result, Americans stopped teaching German in public schools and discontinued playing the music of Beethoven and Brahms. They renamed German measles "liberty measles," cooked "liberty steaks" instead of hamburgers, and walked their "liberty pups" instead of dachshunds. German Americans were pressured to prove their loyalty to America by condemning the German government, giving up speaking German and reading German-language newspapers, and participating enthusiastically in any patriotic drive. Occasionally, hatred of the German enemy boiled over into violence against German Americans. Some German Americans were harassed, others were beaten, and a few were killed for no other reason than they were born in Germany or spoke with a German accent.

✔ **Checkpoint** Compare and contrast the reasons some Americans did not support the war.

## Eugene V. Debs Protests

In June 1918, Socialist leader Eugene V. Debs was arrested for making an antiwar speech in Canton, Ohio (below). While in prison, Debs accepted the Socialist Party's nomination for President and won more than 900,000 votes in the 1920 election.

## The War Changes American Society

The war not only changed the economic and political lives of Americans, but it also brought substantial social changes. New opportunities opened up for women, African Americans, and Mexican Americans. Some left their homes to seek new ones where they could take advantage of these opportunities.

**Women Embrace New Opportunities** Before the war, some American women campaigned for women's suffrage. They won the vote in several western states and still hoped to gain the franchise nationally. Many feared that the war would draw attention away from their efforts. In fact, the war gave women new chances and won them the right to vote.

As men entered the armed forces, many women moved into the workforce for the first time. Women filled jobs that were vacated by men who had gone to fight. They worked in munitions factories, on the railroads, as telegraph operators and trolley conductors, and in other jobs that were previously open only to men. Others labored on farms. Some joined the Red Cross or the American Women's Hospital Service and went overseas. They worked as doctors, nurses, ambulance drivers, and clerks. Thousands enlisted when the Army Corps of Nurses was created in 1918. Women proved that they could succeed in any type of job, regardless of difficulty or risk.

By their efforts and sacrifices during the war, women convinced President Wilson to support their suffrage demands. He contended that granting the vote to women was "vital to winning the war." If women could do the work of men, they certainly deserved the same voting privileges as men. Finally, in 1919, Congress passed the Nineteenth Amendment giving the vote to women. The required two thirds of states ratified the amendment in the summer of 1920, a victory more than 70 years in the making.

### Nursing the Wounded

Red Cross workers were a symbol of caring in the midst of fear during World War I. About 18,000 American Red Cross nurses cared for wounded soldiers and civilians during the war. Their job was difficult and often dangerous—nearly 300 nurses lost their lives.

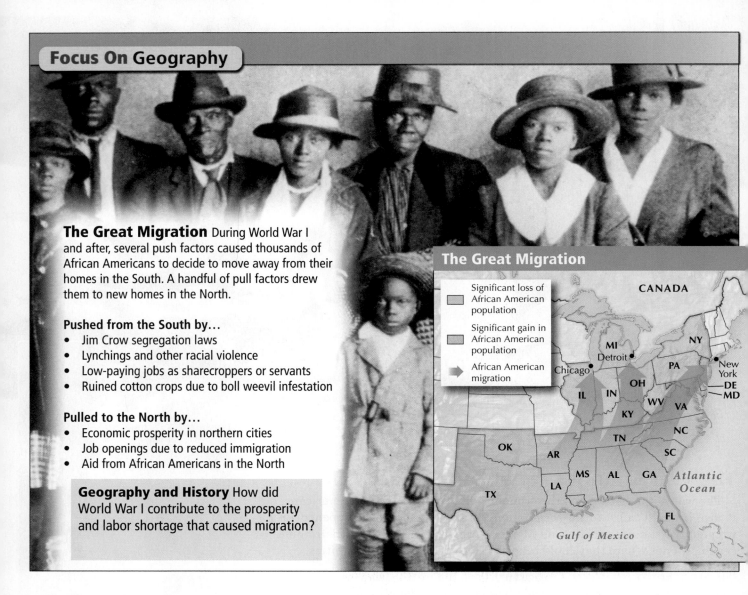

**The Great Migration** During World War I and after, several push factors caused thousands of African Americans to decide to move away from their homes in the South. A handful of pull factors drew them to new homes in the North.

**Pushed from the South by...**
- Jim Crow segregation laws
- Lynchings and other racial violence
- Low-paying jobs as sharecroppers or servants
- Ruined cotton crops due to boll weevil infestation

**Pulled to the North by...**
- Economic prosperity in northern cities
- Job openings due to reduced immigration
- Aid from African Americans in the North

**Geography and History** How did World War I contribute to the prosperity and labor shortage that caused migration?

### The Great Migration

Significant loss of African American population

Significant gain in African American population

African American migration

CANADA

MI
Detroit
Chicago
IL  IN  OH
WV  VA
KY
TN
AR
OK
MS  AL  GA
LA
TX
FL
NY
New York
PA
DE
MD
NC
SC

*Atlantic Ocean*

*Gulf of Mexico*

**African Americans Follow Opportunity North** The war similarly presented new opportunities to African Americans. From the outset, most African American leaders supported the war. "If this is our country, then this is our war," wrote African American leader W.E.B. Du Bois. He viewed the struggle as an excellent opportunity to show all Americans the loyalty and patriotism of African Americans. Thousands of them enlisted or were drafted into the army and sailed for the battlefields of France. On the battlefield, they fought in segregated units under the command of white officers. Altogether, 367,000 African Americans served in the military. Hundreds died for their country.

Meanwhile, a great movement of African Americans from the rural South to the industrial North was taking place. This movement to the "Land of Hope," as many African Americans referred to the North at that time, is called the **Great Migration.** African Americans left their homes in the South for many reasons. Some hoped to escape the violent racism of the South. Others desired better jobs and a chance for economic advancement, which wartime industry in the North offered. Still others dreamed of a better future for their children. Between 1910 and 1920, more than 1.2 million African Americans moved to the North.

Some whites in the South tried to get blacks to stay in the region of their birth, using methods that ranged from persuasion to violence. Meanwhile, African

Americans who already lived in the North encouraged migration. Newspapers in the North, such as the Chicago *Defender*, an African American newspaper that was widely read in the South, pushed home this point:

**Primary Source** "I beg you, my brother, to leave the benighted land. . . . Get out of the South. . . . Come north then, all you folks, both good and bad. . . . The *Defender* says come."

—*Chicago Defender*

African Americans moved to Chicago, as the *Defender* encouraged, where they found work in meatpacking plants. They migrated to Detroit, where they obtained jobs in auto factories. They traveled to smaller industrial towns in the Midwest and to the giant cities of the Northeast. Millions eventually made the exodus, and although they did not entirely escape discrimination, many did forge better futures. The Great Migration was one of the most important episodes in African American history.

**Mexican Americans Move North** Some of the same reasons that led African Americans to move north caused Mexicans to cross the border into the United States. Many Mexicans also faced violence and desperate poverty, and they also wanted better lives for themselves and their children. Most immigrated to the American West, where they sought work on large ranches and farms in Texas and along the Pacific Coast. Increased demands for food and a decrease in American farmworkers created jobs that Mexican migrants filled.

Some of the Mexican migration was seasonal. Many workers crossed the border to harvest fruits or grains or to pick cotton while each crop was in season, then crossed back into Mexico. But others stayed and made the United States their home. Some Mexican workers migrated first to the Southwest and then to the northern states in search of factory jobs, but a large population stayed in California. They formed *barrios* (BAHR ee ohz), or Hispanic neighborhoods, in Los Angeles and in smaller cities in California's Imperial Valley. California had always had a rich Hispanic heritage, but these new immigrants added an important economic dimension to that heritage.

 **Checkpoint** How did the war provide new opportunities for women, African Americans, and Mexican Americans?

**Progress Monitoring Online**
For: Self-test with vocabulary practice
Web Code: nea-0604

## Comprehension

**1. Terms and People** For each item below, write a sentence explaining how it affected the American home front during World War I.
- Selective Service Act
- Bernard Baruch
- CPI
- George Creel
- conscientious objector
- Espionage Act
- Great Migration

**2. NoteTaking Reading Skill Summarize** Use your chart to answer the Section Focus Question: How did the war affect Americans at home?

## Writing About History

**3. Quick Write: Identify Multiple Effects** Write a paragraph describing three effects that World War I had on the American home front. Think about economic and social changes caused by the war. Be sure to include at least one example of each effect to support your statements.

## Critical Thinking

**4. Categorize** In what ways did Americans support the war effort?

**5. Identify Point of View** How did the Supreme Court justify the restrictions of the Sedition Act?

**6. Predict Consequences** How do you think returning soldiers reacted to changes at home when the war ended?

# What Are the Limits of Free Speech?

 6.3.2a

The First Amendment guarantees that each person has the right to free speech, both spoken and written. It protects the right of people to have their say and to hear what others have to say. But can the government limit freedom of speech in order to protect the rights or safety of individuals and the nation?

## *Schenck* v. *United States* (1919)

| The Facts | The Issue | The Decision |
|---|---|---|
| • During World War I, Charles Schenck was convicted of violating the Espionage Act of 1917, which made it a crime to cause refusal of duty in the military.<br><br>• Schenck had distributed pamphlets urging men to resist the military draft. | Schenck's appeal to the Supreme Court argued that his actions were protected by the First Amendment. | The Court unanimously upheld Schenck's conviction and said that in times of war the government may place reasonable limitations on freedom of speech. |

## Why It Matters

The Supreme Court reasoned that there are limits to freedom of speech. Justice Oliver Wendell Holmes pointed out that one does not have the right to falsely shout "Fire!" in a crowded theater and cause a panic. He then set his famous "clear and present danger" test for determining the limits of the First Amendment protection of speech.

> "The question in every case is whether the words used are used in such circumstances and are of such a nature as to create a clear and present danger that they will bring about the substantive evils that Congress has a right to prevent."

NOTHING STOPS THESE MEN LET NOTHING STOP *YOU*

UNITED STATES SHIPPING BOARD — EMERGENCY FLEET CORPORATION

▲ A World War I–era poster

Over the years, the Supreme Court has protected the individual's right to express unpopular ideas. But the Court has also said that free speech is limited. Restricted speech includes obscenities, libel, slander, words that incite violence, and words that pose an immediate threat to the rights of individuals or national security.

### Connect to Your World

What are the limits of free speech in schools? Select one of the cases below. Research and summarize the facts of the case, the Court's decision, and the reasoning behind the decision. Explain why you agree or disagree with the decision.

- *Tinker* v. *Des Moines School District* (1969)
- *Hazelwood School District* v. *Kuhlmeier* (1988)

**For:** Supreme Court cases
**Web Code:** nee-0613

◀ **Free Speech in School**
In 1969, Mary Beth Tinker went to the Supreme Court to test her right to protest the Vietnam War in school.

▲ "Over There" sheet music

WITNESS HISTORY  AUDIO

### War Enthusiasm

Although the first American troops arrived in France in 1917, American soldiers did not reach France in great numbers until 1918. George M. Cohan's song "Over There" was used effectively to recruit troops and raise morale.

❝Over there, over there.
Send the word, send the word over there,
That the Yanks are coming,
The Yanks are coming . . .
So prepare, say a pray'r,
Send the word, send the word to beware.
We'll be over, we're coming over,
and we won't come back till it's over
Over there.❞

—From the song "Over There," written by George M. Cohan in 1917

▲ American troops disembark in France.

# Wilson, War, and Peace

### Content Expectations

- **6.2.2** Explain causes of WWI/U.S.'s role in it.
- **6.2.3** Analyze domestic impact of WWI on growth of government, economy, civil liberties restrictions.
- **6.2.4** Explain Wilson's "Fourteen Points".

### Terms and People

convoy
Vladimir Lenin
John J. Pershing
Fourteen Points
self-determination

League of Nations
Henry Cabot Lodge
reparations
"irreconcilables"
"reservationists"

### NoteTaking

**Reading Skill: Sequence** As you read, sequence the events leading to the end of World War I in a timeline.

| U-boat war intensifies. | | Armistice ends war. |
|---|---|---|
| **March 1917** | | **Nov. 1918** |

**Why It Matters** When the United States entered World War I in the spring of 1917, the conflict had become a deadly, bloody stalemate. The war would be won or lost on the Western Front in France. Since 1914, both sides had tried desperately to break the stalemate there—and failed. The American entry into the war would play a key role in the Allied victory. **Section Focus Question: How did Americans affect the end of World War I and its peace settlements?**

## America Gives the Allies the Edge

To European leaders, the United States was a great unknown. Ethnic divisions in America raised questions about how committed American troops would be in combat. Some doubted that the United States could raise, train, equip, and transport an army fast enough to influence the outcome of the war. Desperate German military leaders renewed unrestricted submarine warfare, hoping to end the conflict before the Americans could make a difference.

**Allied Convoys Protect Shipping** The Allies immediately felt the impact of the renewed unrestricted submarine warfare. German U-boats sank merchant ships in alarming numbers, faster than replacements could be built. As one merchant ship after another sank to the bottom of the sea, the Allies lost crucial supplies.

Together, the Allies addressed the problem of submarine warfare by adopting an old naval tactic: convoying. In a **convoy,** groups of merchant ships sailed together, protected by warships. The arrangement was designed to provide <u>mutual</u> safety at sea. Convoys made up of British and American ships proved to be an instant success. Shipping losses from U-boat attacks fell as sharply as they had risen. Germany's gamble had failed.

**The Allies Struggle** Meanwhile, the situation on land began to swing in favor of the Central Powers. The Allies were exhausted by years of combat. Russia was torn by revolutions. In March 1917, a moderate, democratic revolution overthrew Czar Nicholas II but kept Russia in the war. In November 1917, radical communists led by **Vladimir Lenin** (LEHN ihn) staged a revolution and gained control of Russia. Russia stopped fighting in mid-December, and on March 3, 1918, the Treaty of Brest-Litovsk ended the war between Russia (soon to become the Soviet Union) and Germany. The end of the war on the Eastern Front allowed Germany to send more soldiers to the Western Front.

In the spring of 1918, Germany launched an all-out offensive on the Western Front. The fierce attacks threatened to break through Allied defenses and open a path to Paris. The hard-pressed Allies organized a joint command under French General Ferdinand Foch (fawsh).

**American Troops Join the Fight** General **John J. Pershing,** the commander of American forces in Europe, arrived in France in June 1917, with a small American force. However, it was not until early 1918 that American troops began arriving in larger numbers. At about the same time, the German offensive began to stall. By the end of March 1918, Allied counterattacks and German exhaustion ended the great German offensive.

More fighting followed, and with each passing week, American troops assumed more of the burden on the battlefield. Germany launched several more offensives. Allied defenses buckled and stretched but did not break. Each failed offensive weakened Germany a bit more and raised Allied hopes.

**American Troops Distinguish Themselves** American troops called "doughboys," saw significant action in the late spring and summer of 1918. Americans fought on the defensive along with the French at the Second Battle of the Marne and on the offensive at the Battle of Cantigny (kahn tee NYEE), where they dislodged a large German force from fortified positions. They battled valiantly at Château-Thierry (sha TOH tir EE) and Belleau (beh LOH) Wood, Meuse-Argonne (myooz ahr GAHN) and Saint-Mihiel (mee YEHL). Although it took some time, American troops learned quickly and fought bravely.

One of America's greatest war heroes was Alvin York of Tennessee. On October 8, 1918, York was one of thousands of Americans fighting in the Meuse-Argonne region of northeastern France. Trapped behind enemy lines, York and 16 other Americans took cover from blistering machine-gun fire. As half of the American force fell to German bullets, York took aim with his rifle and silenced a nearby German machine-gun nest. He then dodged a flurry of bullets to attack several other machine gunners and even charged one German position with only a pistol! When the firefight died down, York and the surviving Americans had taken the German position against amazing odds. York's battlefield heroics earned him a Congressional Medal of Honor.

## HISTORY MAKERS

**John J. Pershing** (1860–1948)
John J. Pershing was an experienced soldier and leader who had fought in several wars before the beginning of American involvement in World War I. After the U.S. declaration of war, Pershing guided the creation of the American Expeditionary Force. He faced the difficult task of turning millions of untrained men into an effective fighting force. He then led this force in France. His skill in doing so helped the Allies win the war.

# American Involvement in World War I, 1918

**Geography** *Interactive*
For: Interactive map
Web Code: nep-0605

**Legend:**
- Allies, 1918
- Central Powers, 1918
- Neutral countries, 1918
- Allied front line, July 1918
- Armistice line, November 1918
- American offensives
- British offensives
- French offensives
- Battle, 1918

*North Sea*

NETHERLANDS

52°N

London

UNITED KINGDOM

0°

*English Channel*

50°N

★ Brussels
BELGIUM

Rhine River

GERMANY

Meuse River

LUX.

Moselle River

**❶ Late May–July 1918**
Americans help stop the German advance at Cantigny, Château-Thierry, Belleau Wood, and the Second Battle of the Marne.

Amiens

Cantigny

Aisne River

**❹ Late September–November 11, 1918**
Americans attack through the Argonne Forest, reaching the Germans' vital railway line as the armistice brings the war to an end.

Oise R.

Miller Projection
0    50    100 mi
0    50    100 km

Seine River

Belleau Wood

Marne

Argonne

Saint-Mihiel

Château-Thierry

Paris

Marne River

**❷ Late July–Early September 1918**
American forces help the Allies launch counteroffensives at the Marne and Amiens.

**❸ Mid-September 1918**
American forces and French forces attack the Germans at Saint-Mihiel.

FRANCE

SWITZERLAND

When the American General Pershing reached France, he is said to have remarked "Lafayette, we are here!" He was referring to the French General Marquis de Lafayette, who aided the American cause during the Revolutionary War. Now was the time for America to repay that debt.

**Map Skills** American troops helped their allies stop the German offensive and launch successful counteroffensives.

1. **Locate:** (a) Allied front line, (b) Second Battle of the Marne, (c) armistice line

2. **Region** In what region of France did American troops have their greatest impact?

3. **Summarize** Describe the American contribution to the Allied victory on the Western Front.

## The Convoy System in World War I

A cruiser directed the convoy.

Destroyers, or fast, armed ships, protected the merchant ships.

Armed trawlers and torpedo boats provided close protection and detected torpedoes.

Merchant ships, sometimes camouflaged, carried vital war supplies.

Alvin York was only one of thousands of heroes, many of whom died and most of whom were never recognized for their deeds. They followed orders, fought bravely, and made great sacrifices. Although African American soldiers often faced discrimination in the United States Army, they demonstrated their patriotism in dozens of engagements. For example, an entire African American unit, the 369th Infantry Regiment, received the *Croix de Guerre*, a French award for bravery, for its members' actions in the Meuse-Argonne campaign. By the end of the war, 1.3 million American soldiers had served on the front, more than 50,000 had lost their lives, and about 230,000 had been wounded.

**The War Ends** The American troops, added to those of France, Britain, and Italy, gave the Allies a military advantage. By the fall of 1918, the German front was collapsing. Both the German and Austro-Hungarian armies had had enough. Some men deserted, others mutinied, and many refused to fight. Their leaders faced little choice but to surrender. On November 11, 1918, Germany surrendered to the Allies in a railway car in Compiegne (kohn PYEHN), France.

The war was over. Of the millions of soldiers who mobilized to fight, almost 5 million Allied and 8 million Central Power troops were dead. Nearly 6.5 million civilians were also dead, victims of the terrible conflict. It was left to the peacemakers to determine whether the results would justify the costs.

✓ **Checkpoint** How did American involvement help the Allies win World War I?

## INFOGRAPHIC

# American Voices From the Western Front

▲ American doughboy helmet, worn by a member of the first U.S. division in France

In 1918, Americans fought alongside other Allied troops in several key battles on the Western Front, including Belleau Wood, Château-Thierry, the Second Battle of the Marne, Saint-Mihiel, and Argonne Forest. Although all of these battles were Allied victories, they were nonetheless deadly. Machine-gun barrages and exploding artillery shells filled with shrapnel or deadly gas killed or wounded thousands of American troops. One soldier wrote home to his mother: "Don't worry. I am alright and it is worthwhile…we are blocking the road to Paris. So we don't die in vain."

"Our division, which went into action yesterday morning at practically full strength, has lost half its men. …I am just beginning to realize what war really is."

—John Clark, fighting in the Second Battle of the Marne, July 19, 1918

American machine-gunners at Belleau Wood

# Wilson Promotes Peace Without Victory

Vladimir Lenin, leader of the communist revolution in Russia, maintained that the entire war was nothing more than an imperialistic land-grab. Once in power, he exposed secret treaties that Russia had made with the other Allies in which they agreed to divide among themselves the empires of their enemies. These revelations undercut the morality of the Allied cause in the war.

For President Woodrow Wilson, however, the war was not about acquisitions and imperialism—it was about peace and freedom. In January 1917, Wilson had introduced the idea of a "peace without victory" in an address to Congress:

**Primary Source** "Only a tranquil Europe can be a stable Europe. . . . [There] must be a peace without victory. . . . Victory would mean peace forced upon the loser, a victor's terms imposed upon the vanquished. It would be accepted in humiliation . . . and would leave a sting, a resentment, a bitter memory upon which terms of peace would rest, not permanently, but only as upon quicksand."
—Woodrow Wilson, "Peace Without Victory" speech, January 22, 1917

In another address to Congress in January 1918, Wilson answered Lenin's charges about the nature of the conflict by outlining America's war aims in what became known as the **Fourteen Points**. At the heart of the Fourteen Points was his idea of "peace without victory." Wilson proposed a peace inspired by noble ideals, not greed and vengeance.

## Military Casualties of World War I

Troops (in millions): categories at 12, 10, 8, 6, 4, 2, 0

Allies: Russia, British Empire, France, Italy, United States
Central Powers: Germany, Austria-Hungary

☐ Troops mobilized
▨ Troops killed, wounded, or missing

SOURCE: *Encyclopædia Britannica Online*

Private Martin P. Coogan
75th Field Artillery

"Sept 29 at 5.50 A.M. Several men were gassed before we went over. Advanced to top of ridge. Capt. Smith killed. 1st Lt. McKory and 2nd Lt. Kerr killed later. No officers left. Piece of shrapnel hit helmet and went through canister of my gas mask."

—Corporal Wilfred H. Allen, fighting in late September 1918

Gas mask ▶

American soldiers bandaged after a gas attack ▼

Devastated battlefield near Ypres

## Thinking Critically
Why do you think American casualties were relatively few compared with the casualties of the other combatants?

**History** *Interactive*✶
**For:** Interactive content
**Web Code:** nep-0611

**Reading Skill: Summarize** As you read, summarize Wilson's goals for peace and whether or not each goal was fulfilled.

| Wilson's Ideas for Peace | Decision Made at Paris Peace Conference |
| --- | --- |
| Peace without victory | Great Britain and France make Germany pay reparations. |
| Open diplomacy | |
| Freedom of seas and free trade | |
| Move toward ending colonialism | |
| Self-determination | |
| League of Nations | |

The Fourteen Points sought to fundamentally change the world by promoting openness, encouraging independence, and supporting freedom. Critical of all secret treaties, Wilson called for open diplomacy. He insisted on freedom of the seas, free trade, a move toward ending colonialism, and a general reduction of armaments. He also championed national **self-determination,** or the right of people to choose their own form of government. This would lead to the creation of several new, independent states, but also raised many questions of which populations would achieve statehood and under what circumstances. Finally, he asked for a **League of Nations** to secure "mutual guarantees of political independence and territorial integrity to great and small states alike."

In early 1919, the victorious Allies held a peace conference in Versailles (ver Sī), a suburb of Paris, in the former palace of Louis XIV. President Wilson believed that the peace conference was too important to be left to career diplomats and lesser politicians, so he crossed the Atlantic Ocean himself to represent the United States at the conference, something no President had ever done.

Wilson did not invite any leading Republicans to join him in his peace delegation. Senator **Henry Cabot Lodge,** a Republican foreign policy expert, was left behind because Wilson disliked him intensely. Wilson's decision angered Republicans, who had won control of Congress in the 1918 elections. However, when the American President arrived in France, adoring crowds greeted him. "Never has a king, never has an emperor received such a welcome," wrote one journalist.

 **Checkpoint** Why did Wilson believe that a "peace without victory" would help avoid future wars?

## Wilson at the Paris Peace Conference

Wilson's idealism did not inspire the other Allied leaders at the peace conference. They blamed Germany for starting the war, reminded Wilson that they had suffered more in the war than the United States, and insisted that Germany make **reparations,** or payment for war damages. They wanted to weaken Germany so that it would never threaten Europe again.

**Allied Leaders Reject Wilson's Ideas** British prime minister David Lloyd-George and French premier Georges Clemenceau (klay mahn SOH) knew that the citizens of their countries expected both peace and victory. Lloyd-George insisted on protecting the existing colonial status quo and punishing Germany. Clemenceau wanted to make Germany pay dearly for what it had done to France. In addition to reparations, he demanded the return of Alsace-Lorraine and several key German colonies. Besides Britain and France, other Allies also had goals of their own and were skeptical of Wilson's grand vision.

**Allies Create a League of Nations** Once the Versailles conference began, Clemenceau, Lloyd-George, Italian Premier Vittorio Orlando, and other Allied leaders started to chip away at Wilson's Fourteen Points. Onto the scrap heap of failed proposals they piled freedom of the seas, free trade, the liberation of colonial empires, a general disarmament, and several other ideas.

### HISTORY MAKERS

**Woodrow Wilson** (1856–1924)
Before entering politics, Woodrow Wilson was first a professor and then the president of Princeton University. He brought his intellect and his idealism to the presidency. Wilson believed that relations between nations should be based on the principles of collective security and the common good. During the Paris Peace Conference, he urged other nations to form an international organization that could be used to promote peace. Although the League of Nations was ultimately unable to ensure peace in Europe, it laid the groundwork for the United Nations, which the United States took an active role in creating after World War II.

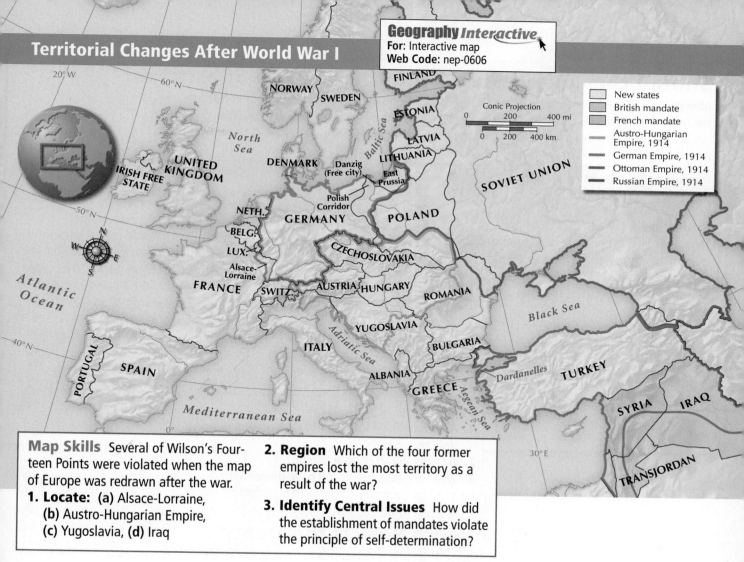

## Territorial Changes After World War I

**Geography** *Interactive*
For: Interactive map
Web Code: nep-0606

Legend:
- New states
- British mandate
- French mandate
- Austro-Hungarian Empire, 1914
- German Empire, 1914
- Ottoman Empire, 1914
- Russian Empire, 1914

Conic Projection
0   200   400 mi
0   200   400 km

**Map Skills** Several of Wilson's Fourteen Points were violated when the map of Europe was redrawn after the war.

1. **Locate:** (a) Alsace-Lorraine,
   (b) Austro-Hungarian Empire,
   (c) Yugoslavia, (d) Iraq

2. **Region** Which of the four former empires lost the most territory as a result of the war?

3. **Identify Central Issues** How did the establishment of mandates violate the principle of self-determination?

Wilson lost a number of battles but kept fighting to salvage a League of Nations, a world organization where countries could gather and peacefully resolve their quarrels. On this point, Wilson refused to compromise. The other delegates finally voted to make the League of Nations part of the treaty.

**Problems With the Peace** In the end, the various peace treaties created almost as many problems as they solved. In the new map that emerged from the conference, national self-determination was violated almost as often as it was confirmed. In Europe, several populations of Germans found themselves attached to non-German nations. The same was true of several Austrian populations.

Furthermore, in the Middle East, the breakup of the Ottoman Empire led to new states in which ethnic groups were clustered together randomly. To form Iraq, for example, the Versailles peacemakers threw together three provinces of the defeated Ottoman Empire—Basra, Baghdad, and Mosul. But Basra had natural links to the Persian Gulf and India, Baghdad to Persia, and Mosul to Turkey and Syria. The various regions had no sense of Iraqi nationalism. In addition, Iraq, like other holdings in the Middle East, Asia, and Africa, was not allowed to practice self-determination. It was attached to Britain as a mandate, or territory overseen by another nation.

✔ **Checkpoint** How did the decisions at the Paris Peace Conference violate the Fourteen Points?

## Should the United States Join the League of Nations?

After the Paris Peace Conference, the United States had to decide whether to join the League of Nations. The League's purpose was to help maintain peace in the world. In the political cartoon below, Wilson overloads a dove, a symbol of peace, with a large, heavy branch representing the League of Nations. Read the options below. Then you make the call.

### President Wilson Favors Joining

**Primary Source**

"A general association of nations must be formed . . . for the purpose of affording mutual guarantees of political independence and territorial integrity to great and small states alike. . . . It is the principle of justice to all peoples . . . and their right to live on equal terms . . . with one another, whether they be strong or weak."

—President Woodrow Wilson,
January 8, 1918

### Senator Borah Opposes Joining

**Primary Source**

"Mr. President, there is another reason . . . why I shall record my vote against this treaty. It imperils what I conceive to be the underlying, the very first principles of this Republic. It is in conflict with the right of our people to govern themselves free from all restraint, legal or moral, of foreign powers. It challenges every tenet of my political faith."

—Senator William Borah,
November 19, 1919

**You Decide**
1. Why did Wilson favor joining the League of Nations?
2. Why did Borah oppose joining?
3. What decision would you have made? Why?

## America Rejects the Treaty

When Wilson left Versailles to return to the United States, he knew the treaty was not perfect. But he believed that over time the League could correct its problems. He still thought that a lasting peace could emerge.

**Wilson Faces Troubles at Home** Wilson did not leave his problems in France when he boarded a ship bound for the United States. German Americans thought the treaty was too harsh toward Germany, especially the "war guilt clause" that suggested that Germany had caused the war. Irish Americans criticized the failure to create an independent Ireland. Most importantly, however, the treaty would need to be submitted to the Republican-controlled Senate Foreign Relations Committee and then ratified, or approved, by the Republican-controlled Senate. In both bodies, as well as in his own Democratic Party, Wilson faced stiff opposition.

A handful of senators believed that the United States should not get entangled in world politics or involved in world organizations. Known as **"irreconcilables,"** these isolationist senators opposed any treaty that had a League of Nations folded into it. They particularly disliked Article 10 of the League covenant. Article 10 called for mutual defense by the signers of the treaty, a pledge that each nation would "respect and preserve . . . the territorial integrity and existing political inde-pendence of all the Members of the League."

A larger group of senators, led by Henry Cabot Lodge and known as **"reservationists,"** were opposed to the treaty as it was written. Some wanted only small changes, while others demanded larger ones. For example, many felt

Article 10 could lead the United States into a war without the consent of Congress, which was unconstitutional. Reservationists believed that the language of the article was too vague and demanded that it not <u>contradict</u> the power of Congress to declare war. But with some changes, the reservationists were prepared to vote for the Treaty of Versailles. They knew that polls indicated that the American people favored the League of Nations.

Wilson had compromised in Versailles, but he was not ready to compromise in Washington, D.C. When the Senate delayed its ratification vote, Wilson took his case directly to the people. The League of Nations had become his personal crusade. Even though he was ill and weak, he set himself the grueling task of crossing the country and giving 32 addresses in 33 days. But his health failed on September 25, 1919, in Pueblo, Colorado. He was rushed back to Washington, D.C., but suffered a debilitating stroke a few days later. As the Senate prepared to vote on the treaty, Wilson lay close to death, barely able to speak.

**The Senate Rejects the Versailles Treaty** In November 1919, one year after the war ended, a treaty revised to eliminate the complaints of the reservationists reached the Senate for a vote. Wilson would not compromise and told his Democratic supporters to vote with the irreconcilables against it. They did, and it was defeated. Next, the Senate voted on the treaty without any changes. The Democrats voted for it, but the combined strength of the irreconcilables and reservationists defeated it. Once more it was voted on, this time with only modest changes. Again, Wilson told his followers to vote against it. Although some Democrats voted for it, the combination of Wilson Democrats and irreconcilables defeated the treaty.

The problem was not that most of the Senate was isolationist. Except for the irreconcilables, most senators wanted the United States to participate in world affairs. They differed slightly on what form that participation would take. However, at a moment that demanded compromise, Wilson and his opponents refused to put aside personal and political differences for the good of the country. The tragedy of the failed votes was that without full American support, the League of Nations proved unable to maintain peace among nations.

✔ **Checkpoint** What reservations did Henry Cabot Lodge and his followers have about the peace treaty?

**Vocabulary Builder**
<u>contradict</u>—(kahn truh DIHKT) v. to go against

---

SECTION

# 3 Assessment

**Progress Monitoring *Online***
For: Self-test with vocabulary practice
Web Code: nea-0607

## Comprehension

1. **Terms and People** For each item below, write a sentence explaining why it is significant to the end of World War I.
   - convoy
   - Fourteen Points
   - self-determination
   - League of Nations
   - Henry Cabot Lodge
   - reparations
   - "irreconcilables"
   - "reservationists"

2. **NoteTaking Reading Skill: Sequence** Use your timeline and chart to answer the Section Focus Question: How did Americans affect the end of World War I and its peace settlements?

## Writing About History

3. **Quick Write: Create an Effects Diagram** Predict at least three problems that could stem from the Treaty of Versailles. Create a diagram showing these effects.

## Critical Thinking

4. **Summarize** Describe America's contributions to the Allied war effort.

5. **Express Problems Clearly** What problems did the peace treaties solve? What problems did they create?

6. **Draw Conclusions** Why did the United States Senate ultimately reject the peace treaty and the League of Nations?

6.2.4

# Woodrow Wilson:
## *The Fourteen Points*

In a speech to Congress on January 8, 1918, President Wilson laid out America's war aims and his vision for peace after the war. His speech included fourteen key points upon which he believed that the peace following the war must be based. However, not all of Wilson's ideas were adopted at the Paris Peace Conference.

| | Summary of the Fourteen Points |
|---|---|
| 1. | Make no secret diplomatic agreements. |
| 2. | Allow freedom of the seas in peace and war. |
| 3. | Remove as many economic trade barriers as possible between countries. |
| 4. | Reduce stockpiles of military armaments to lowest point needed for domestic safety. |
| 5. | Adjust colonial claims, giving more weight to the views of the colonized peoples. |
| 6. | Evacuate and restore Russian territories seized during the war. |
| 7. | Restore and protect Belgium's sovereignty. |
| 8. | Restore French territory and settle the debate over Alsace-Lorraine. |
| 9. | Adjust Italy's boundaries according to the nationalities of populations living there. |
| 10. | Allow the peoples of the former Austro-Hungarian Empire to choose their own governments. |
| 11. | Redraw boundaries of Balkan states based on nationalities and historical allegiances. |
| 12. | Separate the Ottoman Empire into independent countries according to nationality; guarantee all nations access to the Dardanelles. |
| 13. | Restore and protect Poland as a sovereign state with access to the sea. |
| 14. | Establish an association of nations to provide collective security and to ensure peace. |

W hat we demand in this war, therefore, is nothing peculiar to ourselves. It is that the world be made fit and safe to live in; and particularly that it be made safe for every peace-loving nation which, like our own, wishes to live its own life, [and] determine its own institutions. . . . The program of the world's peace, therefore, is our only program; and that program, the only possible program as we see it, is this:

1. Open covenants[1] of peace, openly arrived at, after which there shall be no private international understandings of any kind but diplomacy shall proceed always frankly and in the public view.

2. Absolute freedom of navigation upon the seas, outside territorial waters, alike in peace and in war, except as the seas may be closed in whole or in part by international action for the enforcement of international covenants.

3. The removal, so far as possible, of all economic barriers and the establishment of an equality of trade conditions among all the nations consenting to the peace and associating themselves for its maintenance.

4. Adequate guarantees given and taken that national armaments will be reduced to the lowest point consistent with domestic safety.

5. A free, open-minded, and absolutely impartial adjustment of all colonial claims, based upon a strict observance of the principle that in determining all such questions of sovereignty the interests of the populations concerned must have equal weight with the equitable claims of the government whose title is to be determined. . . .

14. A general association of nations must be formed under specific covenants for the purpose of affording mutual guarantees of political independence and territorial integrity to great and small states alike.

▼ President Wilson giving a speech in 1916

## Thinking Critically

1. **Make Inferences** Why does President Wilson think that the Fourteen Points are "the only possible program" for the world's peace?

2. **Synthesize Information** Which of the Fourteen Points introduced the idea of the League of Nations?

**1. covenant** (KUHV uh nuhnt) *n.* formal agreement.

WELCOME HOME

▲ Members of the famous 369th Infantry Regiment are welcomed home in New York City, 1919.

**WITNESS HISTORY** ◀)) AUDIO

## A Difficult Transition

The service of African Americans during the war renewed hopes for equal rights for African Americans. However, the reality changed little.

❝It is necessary now as never before that the black man press his claims as an American citizen. . . . The Government laid claim to him, both body and soul, and used him as freely as if he were the equal of any other man behind the guns. . . . The path he had to walk was just as rough, the load he had to carry was just as heavy, and the life he gave just as sweet, as that of any other man who laid his all upon the altar. He should contend, therefore, for every privilege, every comfort, every right which other men enjoy.❞

—Dr. A. A. Graham, African American leader

# Effects of the War

 **Content Expectations**

- **6.1.4** Describe changes in composition, distribution, and density of U.S. population.
- **6.3.1** Describe problems/issues created by U.S.'s industrial/urban transformation between 1895–1930.
- **6.3.3** Analyze successes/failures to expand women's rights.

## Terms and People

influenza
inflation
Red Scare
Palmer Raids

Nicola Sacco
Bartolomeo Vanzetti
Warren G. Harding
creditor nation

### NoteTaking

**Reading Skill: Identify Main Ideas** As you read, identify and record the main ideas of this section in a concept web like the one below.

**Why It Matters** The end of World War I produced an unstable international order. The loss of territory and the harsh reparations imposed by the Allies encouraged a strong desire for revenge in Germany. Meanwhile, Lenin's Soviet Russia threatened revolution throughout the industrial world. In the United States, the horrors of the war along with widespread fear of communists and radicals led Americans to question their political, if not their economic, role in the world. **Section Focus Question: What political, economic, and social effects did World War I have on the United States?**

## America Adjusts to Peace

World War I produced significant economic, social, political, and cultural changes in America and throughout the world. This led to important, occasionally painful, adjustments.

**Flu Epidemic Grips the Nation** The movement from war to peace would have been difficult even in the best of times. But the end of 1918 and 1919 were not the best of times. In September 1918, an unusually deadly form of the **influenza,** or flu, virus appeared. Research in recent years shows that the 1918 influenza virus was originally a bird flu that mutated to spread to humans. Many historians now believe that the virus originated in the United States, then traveled around the world. Once the virus began, it spread like a wildfire and killed millions worldwide like a predator feasting on its prey. The great influenza pandemic, coming on the heels of the Great War, gave a sense of doom and dread to people around the globe.

# The Influenza Pandemic Hits the United States

The influenza attack of 1918 was a pandemic, an epidemic that affects many people all over the world. Oddly, the virus hit men and women in their twenties and thirties the hardest, rather than children and the elderly. The flu pandemic killed 550,000 Americans, including 50,000 soldiers. Worldwide, it probably claimed between 50 and 100 million lives. **Describe how the influenza virus spread in the United States.**

## The Spread of Influenza in the United States

Most of the virus' victims in the United States died between mid-September and early December 1918.

Before September 14
September 14–September 21
After September 21

People who contracted the influenza virus (above) often complained of "body aches so intense they felt like bones breaking." Many people avoided public places, and others, like these ballplayers (right), wore masks when they went outside.

**Women and African Americans Confront New Realities** Women and African Americans made significant advances during the war. However, the end of the war also spelled the end of wartime economic opportunities for both groups. A postwar recession, or economic slowdown, created a competitive job market. By 1920, there were fewer women in the workforce than there had been in 1910.

In northern industrial cities, African American workers vied with returning soldiers for jobs and housing. During the hot summer of 1919, race riots erupted in cities throughout the country. The worst, in Chicago, was triggered by the drowning of a young black man by whites, and went on for 13 days. In 1921, violence erupted in Tulsa, Oklahoma, when armed African American men—many of them returning veterans—tried to protect a young black man from lynching. By the time the Tulsa race riots were over, at least 10 whites and 26 African Americans were dead. In one African American neighborhood, white rioters burned 35 city blocks to the ground.

**Inflation Leads to Labor Unrest** During the war, **inflation,** or rising prices, had been held in check. After the conflict, Americans rushed to buy consumer goods rather than war bonds. The scarcity of these goods, coupled with widespread demand, caused inflation. During the war, the price of corn, wheat, cotton, cattle, and other agricultural goods had risen, encouraged by Hoover's policies. After the war, prices fell sharply, making it difficult for farmers to pay their mortgages or buy what they needed for the next growing season. This began a long period of tough times for farmers.

Industrial workers also felt the pain of inflation when their wages did not buy as much as they had during the war. In 1919, more than 4 million workers, or 20 percent of the workforce, went on strike at one time or another. Demanding rewards for their wartime patriotism, workers struck for higher wages and shorter workdays. In Boston, even the police force struck. The workers won some of the strikes, but they lost far more. When some strikes turned violent, the pro-management press blamed the presence of radicals among the strike leaders.

 **Checkpoint** How did the economic situation after the war lead to labor unrest?

# The Red Scare

The reaction against labor was partly spurred by a wave of fear of radicals and communists. The <u>emergence</u> of the Soviet Union as a communist nation, which began in 1917, fed these fears. Communist ideology called for an international workers' revolution as a prelude to the death of capitalism. To this end, Soviet leader Vladimir Lenin encouraged and supported revolutions outside of his country. In Central and Eastern Europe, a series of communist revolts did break out, making it seem like the worldwide revolution was starting.

**Fear of Communism Starts the Red Scare** This revolutionary activity abroad, coupled with strikes across the United States, prompted the first American **Red Scare,** a wave of widespread fear of suspected communists and radicals thought to be plotting revolution within the United States. Real revolutionary activity inside America gave substance to the scare. Authorities discovered bombs mailed to important industrialists and government officials, including Attorney General A. Mitchell Palmer. Suspected anarchists, members of a radical political movement, exploded bombs in cities across America.

As the leading law-enforcement official, Palmer mounted a broad offensive against radicals in the United States in 1919 and 1920. In a series of raids in early 1920, known as the **Palmer Raids,** police arrested thousands of people, some who were radicals and some who were simply immigrants from southern or Eastern Europe. Most were never charged or tried for a crime. The government then deported hundreds of radicals.

To many, these actions seemed to attack the liberties that Americans held most dear. A group of people in New York City formed the American Civil Liberties Union (ACLU) in 1920 to protect these liberties. The ACLU tried to do this by becoming involved in important court cases. To this end, the ACLU became involved in one of America's most controversial court cases: the trial of Nicola Sacco and Bartolomeo Vanzetti.

**Sacco and Vanzetti Are Executed** **Nicola Sacco** (SAH koh) and **Bartolomeo Vanzetti** (van ZEHT ee) were Italian immigrants and known anarchists. They were charged with shooting and killing two men during a holdup at a shoe factory in a town

**Vocabulary Builder**
emergence–(ee MER juhns) *n.* rise or development

### Guilty or Innocent?

Rosina Sacco visits her husband, Nicola Sacco, and Bartolomeo Vanzetti as the two men wait in the prisoners' dock during their famous trial. Debate whether both were truly guilty still continues.

## The Wall Street Bombing

On September 16, 1920, just days after Sacco and Vanzetti's murder indictment, a horsecart filled with dynamite exploded in the financial heart of New York City. The explosion and flying debris killed about 40 people and caused the New York Stock Exchange to close early that day. Investigators suspected that anarchists had staged the bombing, but the culprits were never found.

near Boston. Eyewitnesses of the event said the robbers "looked Italian." Sacco and Vanzetti were arrested and charged with the crime. Even though the ACLU provided defense counsel, the two men were found guilty in a swift and decisive trial, despite the fact that there was little hard evidence against them. Some prominent legal scholars, intellectuals, and liberal politicians charged that the convictions were based more on Sacco and Vanzetti's ethnicity and political beliefs than on the facts of the crime. Nevertheless, on August 23, 1927, the two men were put to death in the electric chair.

At its worst, hysteria accompanied by violence characterized the Red Scare. Mobs attacked suspected radicals, abused immigrants, and committed crimes in the name of justice. But eventually, the great fear ended. Americans saw that democracy and capitalism were more powerful in the United States than Lenin's call for worldwide revolution. By the summer of 1920, the Red Scare hysteria, like the great influenza, had run its course.

 **Checkpoint** How did the rise of communism in the Soviet Union contribute to the Red Scare?

## Americans Embrace Normalcy

Woodrow Wilson hoped that the presidential election of 1920 would prove that Americans supported both the League of Nations and his vision of the role the United States should play in the world. He suggested that electing Democratic presidential candidate James M. Cox of Ohio would show support for the League. The election of Republican candidate **Warren G. Harding** of Ohio would serve as a final rejection of the League.

Harding had a different view of the presidential race. He knew that national elections seldom turned on a single issue. Harding campaigned for a rejection of Wilsonian idealism. He was tired of progressive reforms and foreign crusades. Harding called for a return to "normalcy," by which he meant the "normality" of what he believed had been a simpler time before Wilson took office in 1913. Harding won in a landslide, and Republicans won control of Congress, as well. Americans had decisively rejected Wilson's ideas.

**A Quiet American Giant** Despite Harding's election and all it implied, the United States did not plan to totally withdraw from world affairs. By 1920, the United States was an economic giant. It was the richest, most industrialized country in the world. Even before the war, America led all other nations in industrial output. Now, British and French demands for American goods created an immense trade imbalance. Europeans had to borrow money from American bankers and obtain lines of credit with American business firms to pay for the goods.

This situation fundamentally changed America's economic standing in the world. The United States was now the largest **creditor nation** in the world, meaning that other countries owed the United States more money than the United States owed them. World War I shifted the economic center of the world from London to New York City. The United States embraced its new role as a quiet giant. A world without America playing a major economic role had become simply impossible to conceive.

**The World Adjusts to a New Order** World War I had caused sweeping changes around the globe. German and Russian monarchies toppled, and new forms of government were created. The Austro-Hungarian and Ottoman empires ceased to exist. Britain and France emerged from the war victorious but economically and politically weakened. In contrast, the victorious United States came out of the war strong, confident, and prosperous.

An old order five hundred years in the making had collapsed in just a few years. It was as if the world's compass was out of whack and no one knew where to turn for directions. The United States was unsure of the requirements of its new status. Could America retreat into isolationism in political but not economic affairs? After rejecting the League of Nations, how could it exert its moral authority in the world? Americans would wrestle with these questions—and many others—in the decades ahead.

✔ **Checkpoint** Why did the United States become the leading economic power after World War I?

### A Return to "Normalcy"
The election of 1920 was the first presidential election in which women were allowed to vote under the Nineteenth Amendment. American voters overwhelmingly elected Warren G. Harding, who promised a return to simpler days.

---

SECTION

# 4 Assessment

**Progress Monitoring *Online***
For: Self-test with vocabulary practice
Web Code: nea-0608

### Comprehension

1. **Terms and People** For each item below, write a sentence explaining its significance to events in the United States after World War I.
   - influenza
   - inflation
   - Red Scare
   - Palmer Raids
   - Nicola Sacco
   - Bartolomeo Vanzetti
   - Warren G. Harding

2. **NoteTaking Reading Skill: Summarize** Use your concept web to answer the Section Focus Question: What political, economic, and social effects did World War I have on the United States?

### Writing About History

3. **Quick Write: Write a Thesis Statement** Write a thesis statement for a cause-and-effect essay on the effects of World War I on the United States. Your thesis statement should state a point you will argue.

### Critical Thinking

4. **Analyze Information** How did the influenza pandemic make the transition from war to peace more difficult?

5. **Determine Relevance** How does the Sacco and Vanzetti case demonstrate the mindset of the Red Scare?

6. **Draw Inferences** How did Americans both reject and embrace the new global influence of the United States?

# Quick Study Guide

 6.2.2

**Progress Monitoring *Online***
For: Self-test with vocabulary practice
**Web Code:** nea-0609

## ■ Causes and Effects of America's Entry into World War I

### Causes
- Many Americans have cultural ties with Britain and France.
- Reports of German atrocities in Belgium outrage Americans.
- Germany continues its policy of unrestricted submarine warfare, despite promises to stop.
- In the Zimmermann note, Germany offers Mexico the chance to regain lost U.S. territory.

↓

### America's Entry Into World War I

↓

### Effects
- The Allies defeat the Central Powers.
- The Government's role in daily life increases.
- African Americans and Mexican Americans migrate north.
- More women enter the workforce.
- The United States refuses to join the League of Nations.
- The United States becomes a leading economic power.

## ■ Views on America's Decision to Fight or Not to Fight

| | |
|---|---|
| Isolationists | Believed the United States should isolate itself from all foreign conflicts |
| Internationalists | Believed the United States should actively work for peace but not enter the war |
| Interventionists | Believed the United States should intervene in the war on the side of the Allies, protect U.S. interests, and fulfill U.S. obligations |

## ■ Key Military Engagements Involving American Troops

- Cantigny
- Château-Thierry
- Belleau Wood
- Second Battle of the Marne
- Amiens
- Saint-Mihiel
- Meuse-Argonne Offensive

## ☑ Quick Study Timeline

**In America**

**1914**
**President Wilson announces American neutrality in World War I**

**1915**
**Sinking of the *Lusitania* angers Americans**

**Presidential Terms**     **Woodrow Wilson 1913–1921**

**Around the World**

**1914**
**Assassination of Austrian archduke triggers World War I**

**1915**
**Poison gas first used on Western Front**

**1916**
**More than 2 million casualties suffered i[n] battle of Verdun and battle of the Somme on Western Front**

# American Issues
### •─•─•─• Connector

By connecting prior knowledge with what you have learned in this chapter, you can gradually build your understanding of enduring questions that still affect America today. Answer the questions below. Then, use your American Issues Connector study guide (or go online: www.PHSchool.com **Web Code:** neh-7903).

## Issues You Learned About

● **America Goes to War**  The United States has been involved in two global conflicts.

1. How has the United States made the decision to declare war in past conflicts?

2. In 1916, Wilson won reelection using the campaign slogan "He kept us out of war," but less than a year later, the United States joined World War I. What happened to change Wilson's mind?

3. Why did some Americans oppose American involvement in World War I?

● **Civil Liberties and National Security**  At times, Americans' civil liberties are curtailed, resulting in major debates over constitutional rights and powers.

4. How does the Constitution guarantee that accused criminals will receive fair trials?

5. Why did some people protest the execution of Sacco and Vanzetti?

6. Describe another event during the Red Scare that seemed to curtail civil liberties.

● **Checks and Balances**  Responsibilities are shared among the three branches of the federal government.

7. Which branch of the government has the power to make treaties?

8. How did the battle over the Treaty of Versailles demonstrate the ways in which the different branches of the federal government may void one another's decisions?

### Connect to Your World | Michigan

**Michigan Goes to War**  Michigan institutions played a key role in U.S. mobilization for World War I. In 1918, the University of Michigan opened its doors to the U.S. military, offering to help teach military trainees special skills such as gunsmithing and machine work. Meanwhile the Fisher Body Company, a Detroit automobile manufacturer, started producing military aircraft, including J-1 training planes and DH-4 fighters. As war industries boomed, the need for workers increased. However, thousands of Michiganians were joining the military, creating a lack of available laborers. Southerners looking for work began pouring into Michigan to fill job vacancies. This influx of workers helped Detroit's population leap from about 466,000 in 1910 to nearly 1 million ten years later. Make a poster about Michigan's contributions during World War I.

**1917**
**United States declares war on Germany**

**1919**
**United States Senate rejects membership in League of Nations**

**History *Interactive***
**For:** Interactive timeline
**Web Code:** nep-0610

| 1917 | 1918 | 1919 | 1920 |

**1918**
**Armistice with Germany ends war**

**1918–1919**
**Deadly influenza pandemic sweeps across the world**

# Chapter Assessment

## Terms and People

1. Define **Western Front.** What characterized this region during World War I?

2. Who was **George Creel**? What methods did he introduce to "sell America"?

3. What was the **League of Nations**? How successful was the League of Nations?

4. Define **reparations.** What stance did Britain and France take on reparations?

5. Define **influenza.** What effect did it have on the world's population immediately after World War I?

## Focus Questions

The focus question for this chapter is **What caused the United States to become involved in World War I, and how did the United States change as a result of its involvement?** Build an answer to this big question by answering the focus questions for Sections 1 through 4 and the Critical Thinking questions that follow.

**Section 1**

6. What caused World War I, and why did the United States enter the war?

**Section 2**

7. How did the war affect Americans at home?

**Section 3**

8. How did Americans affect the end of World War I and its peace settlements?

**Section 4**

9. What political, economic, and social effects did World War I have on the United States?

## Critical Thinking

10. **Recognize Causes** Identify and explain the causes of World War I.

11. **Analyze Credibility** How do you know the Zimmermann note was a reliable source? Explain.

12. **Distinguish False From Accurate Images** Is the image to the right an accurate or inaccurate image of Germans during World War I? Why do you think the artist chose this representation?

13. **Draw Conclusions** How did Wilson arrive at the decision that women deserved the right to vote?

14. **Summarize** What was the main goal that Wilson wanted to accomplish with the Fourteen Points?

15. **Categorize** Who were the main groups of senators opposed to the Versailles Treaty, and what positions did they hold? Who supported the treaty?

16. **Express Problems Clearly** What problems led to a weak postwar economy?

17. **Determine Relevance** How did the presidential election of 1920 show Americans' rejection of Wilson's ideas?

## Writing About History

**Write a Cause-and-Effect Essay** World War I both caused and affected many different events around the world. Write an essay in which you explain how several different causes led to an event or trend that occurred during World War I. Consider one of the following topics: the stalemate on the Western Front, the increased role of women in the war effort, or the defeat of the Treaty of Versailles in the United States.

**Prewriting**

- Choose the topic above that interests you the most. Consider what caused the event in question.

- List the multiple causes. Conduct research if necessary to gather more information.

**Drafting**

- Develop a thesis that clearly states the causal relationship between your event and its main causes.

- Choose an organizational structure for your essay.

- Write an introduction, several body paragraphs, and a conclusion.

**Revising**

- Use the guidelines on page SH11 of the Writing Handbook to revise your essay.

# Prepare for the MME

## Americans for and Against the War

Both before and after the U.S. entry into World War I, Americans differed in their opinions about the war. While most Americans demonstrated their patriotism with enthusiasm by buying war bonds, conserving food, and enlisting in the army, others, including Quakers and pacifists, continued to oppose the war. Use your knowledge of Americans' opinions on World War I and the following documents to answer questions 1 through 4.

### Document A

"I find myself a soldier among millions of others in the great Allied Armies, fighting for all I believe to be right and civilized and humane against a power which is evil and which threatens the existence of all the rights we prize and the freedom we enjoy, although some of you in California as yet fail to realize it. It may seem to you that for me this is all quite uncalled for, that it can only mean the supreme sacrifice for nothing or some of the best years of my life wasted, but I tell you that not only am I willing to give my life to this enterprise . . . but that I firmly believe if I live through it to spend a useful lifetime with you, that never will I have an opportunity to gain so much honorable advancement for my own soul, or to do so much for the cause of the world's progress. . . ."

—*Harry Butters, an American volunteering with the Allies in 1915*

### Document B

"I could not look at those long lines of fine looking men, marching so gaily along, and with so little realization of what it all means, without a fresh outburst of tears. How little they realized that they were endorsing a system which means that great armies of splendid manhood shall go forth and slay other great armies. And why? Because stupid diplomats were too avaricious [greedy], too selfish, too ambitious to sanely handle the affairs entrusted to their care. . . . And yet we, blind and stupid as we are, are rushing into the same horrible cataclysm [disaster]."

—*Lella Secor*

### Document C

"It was quite black out there on the Atlantic and in the blackness the [*Lusitania*'s] life-boats alternately rose on the crests of the waves and sank into the black valley between. The boats carried women and children whose hair hung in icicles over their shoulders. . . . Now and then a half-dead passenger uttered a shriek of pain or of anguish as she realized that a friend or relative had died in her arms. . . . Meanwhile, in the dark hull of the German submarine, the captain watching through the periscope finally turned his head away. Even this man, agent of Prussian cruelty, had witnessed a scene upon which he did not care to gaze."

—*Wesley Frost, giving a speech sponsored by the Committee on Public Information*

### Document D

MAY THE SPARKS NEVER REACH IT!

---

1. Which of the documents above reflects the views of a pacifist opposed to the war?
   - **A** Document A
   - **B** Document B
   - **C** Document C
   - **D** Document D

2. The speech in Document C is designed to promote
   - **A** sympathy for the sailors on the German U-boats.
   - **B** sympathy for the innocent victims of a U-boat attack.
   - **C** support for pacifists.
   - **D** support for the British.

3. What point of view does Document D express?
   - **A** Interventionist
   - **B** Internationalist
   - **C** Isolationist
   - **D** Pacifist

4. **Writing Task** Why did some Americans support the war effort while others opposed it? Use your knowledge of World War I and specific evidence from the documents to support your answer.

# Ml Connect to Michigan

## Michigan Autoworkers' Discontent

During the early 1900s, Michigan automobile workers earned low pay and faced stressful, often dangerous, working conditions. As the country's economic situation weakened in the 1920s, then plunged during the Great Depression of the 1930s, many workers turned to labor unions for protection. The United Automobile Workers (UAW), founded in 1935, grew rapidly during its first year, and included many workers from the General Motors (GM) plants in Flint, Michigan.

However, GM refused to recognize or negotiate with the UAW. Concerned about the UAW's increasing strength, GM decided to move one of its Flint plants to an area with less union activity. On December 30, 1936, workers discovered plant equipment packed and ready for moving. Union leaders called an emergency meeting. At the crowded meeting, workers decided to hold a sit-down strike. By staying in the plant indefinitely, they believed they could prevent GM from removing the equipment and force the company to negotiate with the union. One worker at the meeting described going to the plant to start the strike:

> "The men stood still facing the door. It was like trying to chain a natural force. They couldn't hold back and started crowding forward. Then suddenly, they broke through the door and made a race for the plant gates, running in every direction."
>
> —Henry Kraus

The workers inside the plant stayed in place and blocked all entrances, but GM still refused to negotiate.

As the strike continued into January, strikers braved freezing temperatures inside plants where GM had turned off the heat. The union organized chores and activities to keep the workers' minds off their hardships. City bus drivers and family members of striking workers also helped by delivering food. Then, on January 11, 1937, police and company guards blocked the plant entrance—and the food deliveries. Thousands of angry strikers attacked the police with fire hoses and glass bottles. The police responded with teargas and fired pistols into the crowd of strikers with little success. The strikers won this "battle" after a total of 27 people were injured in the fighting.

Fearing more violence, President Franklin Roosevelt urged GM to negotiate with the union. The two sides reached an agreement on February 11. GM agreed to recognize and bargain with the union, keep the plant in Flint, increase workers' pay, and improve working conditions, and the union ended its strike. The sit-down strike's success made it a model for other unions around the country.

# PROSPERITY AND DEPRESSION

## CONTENTS

*Construction of the Dam,*
*by William Gropper,*
*celebrates American*
*workers who struggled*
*through hard times.* ▶

### Kings of Jazz

When he was 14 years old, Louis Armstrong began to haunt the jazz clubs of New Orleans, Louisiana. King Oliver, an experienced musician, took the boy under his wing and bought him his first cornet. Before long, young Armstrong—nicknamed Satchmo—was making a name for himself playing in clubs and on riverboats.

Then, he got a telegram from King Oliver asking him to come to Chicago to join his Creole Jazz Band. Armstrong was scared, but he made the move north. Satchmo would become America's ambassador of jazz, and jazz would become the music that made the "Roaring Twenties" roar. *Listen to the Witness History audio to hear more about jazz.*

◄ King Oliver's Creole Jazz Band, left, helped create the jazz sound.

Dancing the Charleston

Campaign button for Warren G. Harding

###  Content Expectations

**Chapter Focus Question:** How did the United States experience both economic growth and social change in the decade after World War I?

### Section 1
**A Booming Economy**   6.1.1f, 6.1.3a, 6.1.3b, 6.1.5b

### Section 2
**The Business of Government**   6.1.1e, 6.2.3, 7.1.1

### Section 3
**Social and Cultural Tensions**   6.1.3d, 6.3.2a, 7.1.1a, 7.1.1b

### Section 4
**A New Mass Culture**   6.1.1f, 7.1.1a, 7.1.1b

### Section 5
**The Harlem Renaissance**   6.3.2d, 6.3.2e, 7.1.1a

Ford Model T

Use the ☑ **Quick Study Timeline** at the end of this chapter to preview chapter events.

**Note Taking Study Guide *Online***
**For:** Note Taking and American Issues Connector
**Web Code:** nee-8001

▲ Will Rogers

◄ 1920s magazine ad

**WITNESS HISTORY** 🔊 AUDIO

### Paying for It?

Folksy comedian Will Rogers was one of the most beloved entertainers of his day. Whether standing onstage twirling a rope or chatting on the radio, he could always be counted on to deliver good-natured, amusing comments on the American scene. In the 1920s—with the nation in the midst of a giant economic boom—Rogers turned his keen eye on Americans' passion for buying things:

"No nation in the history of the world was ever sitting as pretty. If we want anything, all we have to do is go and buy it on credit. So that leaves us without any economic problems whatsoever, except perhaps some day having to pay for them. But we are certainly not thinking of that this early."
—Will Rogers, radio commentary, 1928

# A Booming Economy

 **Content Expectations**

- **6.1.1f** Analyze technological advances that enabled the U.S. to become an industrial power.
- **6.1.3a** Analyze location/expansion of major urban centers.
- **6.1.3b** Analyze growth of cities linked by industry/trade.
- **6.1.5b** Analyze entrepreneurial decision-making by Henry Ford and others.

## Terms and People

Henry Ford
mass production
Model T
scientific management
assembly line

consumer revolution
installment buying
bull market
buying on margin

## NoteTaking

**Reading Skill: Identify Supporting Details**
Note specific economic changes of the 1920s.

**Why It Matters** In the decade after World War I, the American economy experienced tremendous growth. Using revolutionary mass-production techniques, American workers produced more goods in less time than ever before. The boom fundamentally changed the lives of millions of people and helped create the modern consumer economy. **Section Focus Question: How did the booming economy of the 1920s lead to changes in American life?**

## The Automobile Drives Prosperity

Rarely, if ever, has the nation enjoyed such an economic boom as it did in the 1920s. The recession that had followed World War I quickly ended. All signs pointed to economic growth. Stock prices rose rapidly. Factories produced more and more goods and, with wages on the rise, more and more people could afford to buy them.

Much of this explosive growth was sparked by a single business: the automobile industry. Carmaker **Henry Ford** introduced a series of methods and ideas that revolutionized production, wages, working conditions, and daily life.

**Ford Pioneers Mass Production** Ford did not originate the idea of **mass production,** the rapid manufacture of large numbers of identical products. It had been used, for example, to make sewing machines and typewriters. But such products involved only hundreds of parts—not the thousands that go into the production of cars. Ford brought mass production to new heights.

Early in the century, only wealthy city dwellers could afford cars. The automobile was often seen as a symbol of the class divisions in the country. City drivers who ventured out onto country roads frightened horses and cows, coated crops with dust, and rutted dirt roads. "To the countryman," said Woodrow Wilson in 1906, cars "are a picture of the arrogance of wealth."

Ransom Olds had introduced a less expensive car, the Oldsmobile in 1901. But it was Henry Ford who truly brought the automobile to the people. In 1908, he introduced the **Model T,** a reliable car the average American could afford. The first Model T sold for $850. Soon after, Ford opened a new plant on the Detroit River. The Detroit location gave Ford easy access to steel, glass, oil, and rubber manufactured in Pennsylvania, Ohio, Indiana, and Illinois.

Ford hired **scientific management** experts to improve his mass-production techniques. Scientific management was a relatively new method of improving efficiency, in which experts looked at every step of a manufacturing process to find ways to reduce time, effort, and expense. Ford also studied the techniques of Chicago meatpacking houses, where beef carcasses were moved on chains past a series of meat cutters, each of whom cut off a specific part of the carcass. Ford reversed the process. He put his cars on moving **assembly lines.** At each step, a worker added something to construct the automobile. In two years, assembly line techniques reduced the time it took to manufacture a Model T— from more than 12 hours to just 90 minutes.

The assembly line allowed Ford to keep dropping the sale price. The cost of a Model T fell to $350 by 1916 and to $290 by 1927. It was slow, dull, and available only in black. But the Model T was the first car that ordinary people could afford. In 1919, only 10 percent of American families owned an automobile. By 1927, 56 percent did.

**Graph Skills** The economic boom of the 1920s was reflected in many aspects of the economy, from wages to industrial production to stock prices. *By how much did wages increase between 1910 and 1925? During what years did stock prices soar the most?*

**Average Price of Selected Stocks, 1921–1929**

SOURCE: *Standard and Poor's*

**Earnings of Nonagricultural Employees, 1910–1930**

SOURCE: *Historical Statistics of the United States*

**Gross Domestic Product**

| Year | Value of goods produced (in millions of dollars) |
|------|--------------------------------------------------|
| 1921 | 68,355 |
| 1923 | 82,994 |
| 1925 | 87,359 |
| 1927 | 94,161 |
| 1929 | 101,444 |

SOURCE: *National Bureau of Economic Research*

◀ The automobile gave Americans new freedom to enjoy picnics, camping, and Sunday drives.

YELLOWSTONE PARK

# Impact of the *Automobile*

**H**enry Ford made the automobile affordable for the average American. By the 1920s, the growing "car culture" was changing the nation in deeper ways than even Ford might have imagined.

**The Gas Station ▶**
Automobiles encouraged the growth of related industries—especially the oil industry. The gas station—and gas fumes—became a permanent feature of the U.S. landscape.

STANDARD

U1223

US 66

**U.S. HIGHWAY SYSTEM**
**1926**

N

Pacific Ocean

Atlantic Ocean

— Major U.S. highway

**◀ The Highway System**
By 1925, states had built hundreds of highways, and the federal government organized them into a numbered system. One of the first federal highways was Route 66, which ran from Illinois to California.

**Advertising ▶**
Ads stressed what cars gave their owners—speed, status, and a new sense of freedom.

CADILLAC
A NOTABLE PRODUCT OF GENERAL MOTORS

**◀ Vacation Industry**
Americans used their new cars and expanded leisure time to travel. Motels and motor camps sprung up all over the nation.

Enjoy our Southern Hospitality

HARBIN'S TOURIST COURT
MEMPHIS, TENN.
U.S. HIGHWAY 51 SOUTH.
4 MILES SOUTH OF CITY LIMITS

## Connect to Your World
Which of the features of "car culture" shown here are still part of American life today?

**History *Interactive* ★**
**For:** More on the automobile
**Web Code:** nep-0712

When it came to managing the men who worked along his assembly lines, Ford also proved that he was not afraid of <u>innovation</u>. In 1914, he more than doubled the wages of a large number of his workers, from $2.35 to $5 a day. He also reduced their workday from 9 hours to 8 hours. In 1926, he became the first major industrialist to give his workers Saturday and Sunday off. Before Ford, the idea of a "weekend" hardly existed. Ford shrewdly realized that if workers made more money and had more leisure time, they would become potential customers for his automobiles. The combination of the Model T and the "five-dollar day, forty-hour week" made Ford not only a very rich man but also one of the shapers of the modern world.

**Vocabulary Builder**

<u>innovation</u>–(ihn uh VAY shuhn) *n.* change in the way of doing something; act of introducing such a change

**The Automobile Changes America** The boom in the automotive industry <u>stimulated</u> growth in other industries related to car manufacture or use. The steel, glass, rubber, asphalt, wood, gasoline, insurance, and road-construction industries all benefited. For example, one seventh of all steel output was used to make automobiles. The need for gasoline prompted a nationwide search for oil deposits. Oil discoveries in California, Texas, New Mexico, and Oklahoma brought workers and money to the Southwest.

**Vocabulary Builder**

<u>stimulate</u>–(STIHM yuh layt) *v.* to excite to action; to cause to grow or act

Road construction boomed, especially when the federal government introduced the system of numbered highways in 1926. The millions of cars on American roads led to the rapid appearance of thousands of service stations, diners, and motor hotels (a term later shortened to *motels*). The growth in all these industries created new and often better-paying jobs, spurring national prosperity.

The automobile caused additional economic effects. Other forms of ground transportation, such as railroads and trolleys, suffered a decline in use. With cars, people could go where they wanted, when they wanted. They did not have to travel along set tracks on set schedules.

The automobile prompted a new sense of freedom and prosperity. Never had Americans been so mobile. Entire families crowded into their cars for cross-country vacations or Sunday drives to the country. Ownership of an automobile came to symbolize participation in the American dream of success.

Finally, automobiles altered residential patterns. The ability to drive to work permitted people to live farther from their places of employment. This led to the development of suburban communities linked to cities by arteries of highways and roads. Los Angeles, one of the first cities whose growth was influenced by the automobile, developed in a sprawling, haphazard fashion. It became, according to one observer, "a series of suburbs in search of a city."

 **Checkpoint** How did Henry Ford increase the production and sale of automobiles?

# A Bustling Economy

The 1920s saw what has been called a **consumer revolution,** in which a flood of new, affordable goods became available to the public. The widespread availability of electrical power supported the consumer revolution. Electric washing machines, vacuum cleaners, and irons made housekeeping easier and less time-consuming. Accessible electricity also contributed to radio and refrigerator sales.

**Advertising and Credit Build a Consumer Culture** The growing advertising industry also played its part. Using new "scientific" techniques and psychological research, advertisers were able to sell more products to more Americans than ever before. Magazine and newspaper ads often focused on the desires and fears of Americans more than on what people really needed.

Advertisers celebrated consumption as an end in itself, convincing people that they could be the person they wanted to be just by buying the right products. From Kleenex to Listerine, Americans bought products that years earlier they could never have imagined they needed.

Finally, new ways of buying fueled the consumer revolution. People who did not have enough ready cash could buy what they wanted on credit. **Installment buying,** in which a consumer would make a small down payment and then pay off the rest of the debt in regular monthly payments, allowed Americans to own products they might otherwise have had to save up for years in order to buy.

**The Big Bull Market Makes Fortunes** Consumers were not the only Americans buying and selling in a big way. During the 1920s, the stock market enjoyed a dizzying **bull market,** a period of rising stock prices. More and more Americans put their money into stocks in an effort to get rich quick. By 1929, around 4 million Americans owned stocks.

The pounding desire to strike it rich often led investors to ignore financial risks. As the market soared, people began **buying on margin**—another form of buying on credit. By purchasing stock on margin, a buyer paid as little as 10 percent of the stock price upfront to a broker. The buyer then paid the broker for the rest of the stock over a period of months. The stock served as collateral, or security, for the broker's loan. As long as the price of the stock rose, the buyer had no trouble paying off the loan and making a profit. But if the price fell, the buyer still had to pay off the loan. Buyers gambled that they would be able to sell the stock at a profit long before the loan came due.

In truth, the big bull market stood on very shaky ground. But most people ignored the dangers. By the middle of 1929, economic authorities proclaimed that America and the stock market had entered a "new era." Stock prices would continue their march upward, they said, while boom-and-bust economics would become a thing of the past.

✔ **Checkpoint** How did buying on margin allow more people to invest in the stock market?

## Cities, Suburbs, and Country

The economic boom did not affect all parts of the nation equally. While urban and suburban areas prospered, rural Americans faced hardships.

**People Flock to Cities** In the 1920s, the movement of people was toward cities. Immigrants settled in cities. Farmers left their fields for cities. The direction of the African American Great Migration was toward northern cities. Mexican Americans crossing the border relocated to southwestern cities.

As in the late nineteenth century, cities grew and changed shape. In addition, the adoption of skyscraper technology caused cities to stretch skyward. Steel-framed skyscrapers with light coverings of masonry and glass began to dominate the skylines of the nation's cities. New York's Empire State Building, finished in 1931, symbolized the power and majesty of the United States.

**The Suburbs Grow** Improved mass transportation and the widespread use of automobiles caused cities to expand outward. More urban workers moved to the suburbs. Western and southern cities, developed after the automobile revolution, encompassed suburban areas as well as inner cities. Suburbs mushroomed, growing much faster than inner cities.

**Urban Growth**

Built by automaker Walter P. Chrysler in 1928, New York's Chrysler Building (below) was the world's tallest skyscraper—but only for a short time. *Look at the table below. Why do you think Detroit grew so fast after 1910?*

| Population of Selected U.S. Cities, 1910–1930 | | | |
|---|---|---|---|
| City | 1910 | 1920 | 1930 |
| New York | 4,766,883 | 5,620,048 | 6,930,446 |
| Chicago | 2,185,283 | 2,701,705 | 3,376,478 |
| St. Louis | 687,029 | 772,897 | 821,960 |
| Los Angeles | 319,198 | 576,673 | 1,238,048 |
| Detroit | 465,766 | 993,078 | 1,568,662 |

SOURCE: U.S. Census Bureau

Slowly at first, but more rapidly as the century progressed, suburbs drained people and resources from the cities. Catering to middle- and upper-class residents, suburbs tended to be more conservative and Republican. Meanwhile, the inner cities at the heart of older urban areas began a slow but steady decline.

**Many Americans Face Hardship** In the cities and suburbs, Americans enjoyed prosperity and the fruits of growth. They participated in the consumer economy and in the joys of automobile ownership. The wealthiest urban residents—owners and managers of businesses—reaped fabulous rewards, which they often pumped back into the bull market. But there were problems looming ahead. America's wealth was poorly distributed. Industrial wages rose at a much slower rate than corporate salaries.

Worst yet, farm incomes declined during the decade. Many people living in the country did not participate in the consumer benefits and economic gains of the decade. They formed part of another America—poorer and outside the economic boom. In particular, farmers suffered from growing debt and falling farm prices. A protest song of 1928 expressed their frustration:

**Earnings of Agricultural Employees, 1918–1928**

SOURCE: *Historical Statistics of the United States*

### Rural Struggles

American farmers did not share in the prosperity of the 1920s. *Compare this graph to the economic graphs at the beginning of this section and make a generalization about farm wages versus nonfarm wages in the 1920s.*

**Primary Source**

❝'Leven-cent cotton, forty-cent meat,
How in the world can a poor man eat?
Mule's in the barn, no crop's laid by,
Corncrib empty and the cow's gone dry.❞
—Bob Miller and Emma Dermer,
"Eleven Cent Cotton"

If the wealthy believed that the country had entered an age of permanent prosperity, the "other Americans" saw things differently.

✔ **Checkpoint** What impact did the development of suburbs have on American society?

---

**SECTION 1 Assessment**

**Progress Monitoring *Online***
For: Self-test with vocabulary practice
Web Code: nea-0702

**Comprehension**

1. **Terms and People** For each of the following, write a sentence explaining how that person or item was connected with the changing economy of the 1920s.
   - Henry Ford
   - mass production
   - assembly line
   - consumer revolution
   - installment buying
   - bull market
   - buying on margin

2. **NoteTaking Reading Skill: Identify Supporting Details** Use your concept web to answer the Section Focus Question: How did the booming economy of the 1920s lead to changes in American life?

**Writing About History**

3. **Summarize a Historical Interpretation** Using information from the text, write a paragraph summarizing the reasons for the historical viewpoint that Henry Ford was one of the chief makers of the modern world.

**Critical Thinking**

4. **Analyze Effects** How is the rise of the automobile an example of technology affecting attitudes or values?

5. **Draw Conclusions** Why do you think many advertisers began to focus on the benefits of their products rather than on the products themselves?

6. **Predict Consequences** Identify two potential signs of weakness in the economy of the 1920s, and predict what might happen if those problems are not solved.

Harding campaign button ▶

**SECTION 2**

▲ President Harding joins a parade.

**WITNESS HISTORY** 🔊 AUDIO

### A Fun-Loving President

In 1920, voters turned from the intellectualism and rigid idealism of Woodrow Wilson to someone who presented himself as an average American, Warren G. Harding. "I am a man of limited talents from a small town," Harding admitted. "I don't seem to grasp that I am President." The genial politician from Marion, Ohio, got more pleasure from golf, poker, and music. He once claimed that he could play every band instrument "but the slide trombone and the e-flat cornet." But what Harding loved most was shaking hands with tourists who visited the White House:

❝I love to meet people. It is the most pleasant thing I do; it is really the only fun I have. It does not tax me, and it seems to be a very great pleasure to them.❞

—Warren G. Harding, U.S. President

# The Business of Government

 **Content Expectations**

- **6.1.1e** Analyze economic polices of government/industrial leaders.
- **6.2.3** Analyze domestic impact of WWI on growth of government, economy, civil liberties restrictions.
- **7.1.1** Explain significance of cultural changes/tensions "Roaring Twenties."

## Terms and People

Andrew Mellon
Herbert Hoover
Teapot Dome scandal
Calvin Coolidge

Washington Naval
   Disarmament
   Conference
Kellogg-Briand Pact
Dawes Plan

## NoteTaking

**Reading Skill: Compare and Contrast**
Note similarities and differences between Presidents Harding and Coolidge.

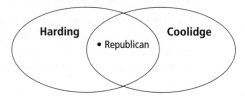

Harding    • Republican    Coolidge

**Why It Matters** In 1920, Warren G. Harding was elected President on a pledge of a "return to normalcy." Rather than pursue reform, as the Progressives had done, Harding and his successor, Calvin Coolidge, favored more conservative policies that aided the growth of business. This pattern—a period of activism followed by a more laissez-faire approach—would repeat itself in the 1950s and 1980s. **Section Focus Question: How did domestic and foreign policy change direction under Harding and Coolidge?**

## The Harding Administration

What exactly did a "return to normalcy" mean? Different voters saw different things in the vague phrase. Some saw it as a retreat from involvement in world affairs, others as a rejection of Progressive reform efforts or a swing back to laissez-faire economics. Once in office, however, Harding had to give substance to his promise.

**New Policies Favor Big Business** Harding signaled the economic direction of his administration by naming wealthy banker **Andrew Mellon** Secretary of the Treasury. Mellon's idea of prudent economic policy was to support legislation that advanced business interests. He disliked the relatively new income tax, favoring instead low taxes on individuals and corporations. Mellon also cut the fat from the budget. By 1925, Congress had reduced spending from a wartime high of $18 billion to $3 billion. Instead of sinking deeper into debt, the Treasury actually showed a surplus.

Harding signed a bill raising protective tariff rates by about 25 percent. The tax on imports made it easier for American producers to sell goods at home. However, in retaliation, European nations also hiked tariffs, making American goods harder to sell overseas. This tariff war weakened the world economy.

Under the Progressive leadership of Roosevelt and Wilson, the federal government had passed laws to break up monopolies, protect workers, and restrict the absolute freedom of business leaders. By contrast, Harding favored a return to a more traditional laissez-faire approach. He and Mellon worked to reduce government regulation of business.

Still, the Harding administration did not abandon social goals. Harding's thoughtful and energetic Secretary of Commerce, **Herbert Hoover,** worked with business and labor leaders to achieve voluntary advancements. What the Progressives hoped to achieve through legislation, Hoover attempted to attain with the cooperation of interest groups. He enjoyed great successes at getting people to work together instead of battling one another.

**The Ohio Gang Cashes In** Harding was a kind, likable man, but he was not especially intelligent. Perhaps no President was friendlier, and few had less sense of what was expected of a President. Faced with a tax issue, Harding lamented, "I listen to one side and they seem right . . . I talk to the other side, and they seem just as right, and here I am where I started. . . . What a job!"

Rather than struggle to master the complexities of the job, Harding trusted others to make decisions. Many were his close friends, men he enjoyed relaxing and gambling with at late-night poker games. Known as the Ohio Gang, they were not honest public servants like Mellon and Hoover. They were mostly greedy, small-minded men who saw government service as a chance to get rich at the expense of the very citizens they were supposed to serve.

Charles Forbes, head of the Veterans' Bureau, practiced graft on an immense scale and wasted hundreds of millions of taxpayers' dollars. For example, his department bought $70,000 worth of floor cleaner—enough to last 100 years—at more than 24 times the fair price. Another Harding pal, Attorney General Harry Daugherty, used his position to accept money from criminals.

**The Teapot Dome Scandal Explodes** The worst scandal involved Secretary of the Interior Albert Fall. In 1921, Fall arranged to transfer oil reserves in Elk Hills, California, and Teapot Dome, Wyoming, from the Navy Department to the Interior Department. The oil reserves were intended for the navy's use in time of emergency. Harding signed the transfer.

Once Fall had control of the oil, he forgot about the needs of the navy. He leased the properties to private oilmen in return for "loans"—which were actually bribes. Rumors of the deal led to a Senate investigation, and, by 1924, the entire

**Analyzing Political Cartoons**

**The Teapot Dome Scandal** This cartoon comments on the most notorious scandal of the Harding administration.
1. What object is used to represent the scandal? Why?
2. According to the cartoon, what is the impact of the scandal?

**Silent Cal**

In the picture (above right), President Coolidge reenacts the scene when his father swore him in as President. At above left, Coolidge wears a proper business suit to go fishing.

sordid affair was revealed to the public. Later, the oil reserves were returned to the government. Fall was sentenced to a year in prison.

Harding himself never saw the full extent of the **Teapot Dome scandal.** In fact, he only had a growing suspicion that his friends were up to no good. But that was enough, as he said, to keep him "walking the floor nights." In July 1923, he visited Alaska during a speaking tour. On his return voyage, he suffered a heart attack and died on August 2. Americans mourned Harding as they had mourned no other President since Lincoln. When the full extent of the scandals emerged, however, the public formed a different opinion of him.

 **Checkpoint** What were the causes and effects of the Teapot Dome scandal?

## Coolidge Prosperity

News of Harding's death reached Vice President **Calvin Coolidge** during a visit to his father's Vermont farm. Almost immediately, the elder Coolidge, a justice of the peace, used the family Bible to swear in his son as President.

In personality, Coolidge was far different from the outgoing, back-slapping Harding. Known as Silent Cal, he was quiet, honest, and frugal—a man who measured his words carefully. He placed his trust in business, and put his administration in the hands of men who held to the simple virtues of an older America. Political sharpies out to make a quick buck had no place in the Coolidge administration. Neither did Progressives who believed in an activist government bent on sweeping reforms.

**Silent Cal Supports Big Business** Coolidge admired productive business leaders. "The man who builds a factory," Coolidge once said, "builds a temple." He believed that the creation of wealth benefited the nation as a whole. In 1925, he expressed this view in his best-known speech:

**Primary Source** "The chief business of the American people is business. They are profoundly concerned with producing, buying, selling, investing, and prospering in the world. . . . We make no concealment of the fact that we want wealth, but there are many other things that we want very much more. We want peace and honor, and that charity which is so strong an element of all civilization. The chief ideal of the American people is idealism."

—Calvin Coolidge, speech to the American Society of Newspaper Editors

Coolidge's statement of values and principles has often been oversimplified as "the business of America is business."

In his approach to the economy, Coolidge continued to follow the goals of Secretary of the Treasury Mellon by reducing the national debt, trimming the federal budget, and lowering taxes to give <u>incentives</u> for businesses. Coolidge thus oversaw a spectacular boom in the national economy. For almost six years, the economy soared, generating industrial profits, spectacular growth in the stock market, and general prosperity, especially for urban Americans.

**Troubles Brew Beneath the Surface** Yet, there were grave problems breeding in the nation. Farmers struggled to keep their land as the prices of their goods fell. Labor unions demanded higher wages and better working conditions. African Americans faced severe discrimination, especially in the South, where Jim Crow laws made enforced segregation a way of life. African American leaders urged Congress to pass an antilynching law. In the Southwest, Mexican Americans confronted shamefully low wages and efforts to force them to return to Mexico.

To all of these concerns, Silent Cal remained silent. Like Harding, he mistrusted the use of legislation to achieve social change. Unlike Progressive Presidents, he believed that it was not the business of the federal government to help create an ideal nation.

 **Checkpoint** **What policies did Calvin Coolidge favor to support economic growth?**

**Vocabulary Builder**
<u>incentive</u>–(ihn SEHNT ihv) *n.* something intended to encourage someone to take action or work harder

# America's Role in the World

Under both Harding and Coolidge, America continued to play an increasingly important role in world business and trade. Beyond that, U.S. foreign policy was largely shaped by reaction to World War I. No previous war had been as deadly. Citizens of all nations agreed: It must never happen again. But how could this goal be achieved?

**Seeking an End to War** One solution was to avoid another arms race, such as the naval rivalry between Germany and Britain that had contributed to the outbreak of the war. In 1921 and 1922, diplomats gathered in Washington, D.C., to halt another naval arms race before it got out of control. World leaders agreed to limit construction of large warships and hammered out a settlement on several problems between Japan and the West. This **Washington Naval Disarmament Conference** did not end the world's naval problems, but it raised hopes that nations could solve disagreements without resorting to war.

A later attempt to prevent war was the **Kellogg-Briand Pact** of 1928. Secretary of State Frank B. Kellogg and French Foreign Minister Aristide Briand

| The United States in International Affairs, 1920–1929 | | ✓ Quick Study |
|---|---|---|
| | **Goal** | **U.S. Action** |
| **League of Nations** | To prevent war and settle disputes between nations | U.S. membership favored by Wilson; rejected by Senate |
| **World Court** | To make judgments in international disputes voluntarily submitted by nations | U.S. participation favored by Harding; rejected by Senate |
| **Washington Naval Conference** | To reduce arms race and size of navies of major powers | U.S. agreed with leading naval powers to limit construction of warships. |
| **Kellogg-Briand Pact** | To "outlaw war … as an instrument of national policy" | U.S. agreed with many other nations to renounce war as a means of settling international disputes. |

(bree AHN) drew up a treaty to "outlaw" war "as an instrument of national policy." Eventually, 62 nations ratified the pact. But, in reality, the pact was unenforceable. Kellogg knew it, Briand knew it, and so did the rest of the diplomats. No sooner was the ink dry than everyone involved forgot about it.

Although Congress applauded the useless Kellogg-Briand Pact, it refused to join the World Court, an international body which at least promised to help <u>mediate</u> international disputes. As much as possible, most American leaders in the 1920s hoped to avoid another war by keeping the rest of the world at arm's length.

**Vocabulary Builder**
<u>mediate</u>–(MEE dee ayt) v. to bring about the settlement of a dispute between two parties

### Collecting War Debts
Money issues were another matter. The United States insisted that Britain and France repay their huge war debts to the United States. For this to happen, though, Germany had to make the reparation payments to Britain and France imposed by the Treaty of Versailles. The complex financial issue threatened to undermine the international economy. Some statesmen suggested reducing or even canceling both war debts and reparations. But the frugal Coolidge insisted that a debt was a debt and had to be paid.

In 1924, an agreement known as the **Dawes Plan** arranged U.S. loans to Germany. By enabling Germany to make reparation payments to Britain and France, the Dawes Plan helped Britain and France to repay their debts to the United States. Of course, the entire scheme was financed by U.S. money. After the stock market crash of 1929, however, the well of U.S. money went dry. Germany stopped reparation payments, and Britain and France ended war-debt payments to the United States.

In the end, the war-debt situation damaged America's reputation in the eyes of the world. People from England and France thought that it was heartless for American bankers and politicians to insist on repayment of debts and not to take into account the human costs of the war. In the next war, the United States would take a more flexible approach to war loans.

 **Checkpoint** How did the United States support world peace efforts during the 1920s?

---

**Progress Monitoring *Online***
**For:** Self-test with vocabulary practice
**Web Code:** nea-0703

## Comprehension

**1. Terms and People** For each of the following, write a sentence explaining its importance to national politics of the 1920s.
- Teapot Dome scandal
- Washington Naval Disarmament Conference
- Kellogg-Briand Pact
- Dawes Plan

**2. NoteTaking Reading Skill: Compare and Contrast** Use your Venn diagram to answer the Section Focus Question: How did domestic and foreign policy change direction under Harding and Coolidge?

## Writing About History

**3. Comparing Historical Interpretations** Some people view Coolidge as a moral, idealistic President who restored integrity to government and promoted prosperity. Others see him as a stiff, unimaginative President who retreated from the idealism of the Progressive Era and cared only for the interests of business. Make a Venn diagram comparing these differing historical interpretations.

## Critical Thinking

**4. Make Comparisons** How did the approach to government of Harding and Coolidge differ from that of the Progressives?

**5. Draw Conclusions** Do you think that Harding should be held responsible for the scandals in his administration? Why or why not?

**6. Evaluate Information** Many Americans in the 1920s seemed to support both isolationism and an active role in international affairs. Do you agree?

◀ Billy Sunday

▲ Crowd at a Billy Sunday revival meeting

## WITNESS HISTORY 🔊 AUDIO

### Kicking, Fighting, Butting, and Biting

In a time of rapid social change, with a deadly war behind them, many Americans sought a return to more traditional values. They found comfort and strength in the words of preachers such as Billy Sunday. A former pro baseball player, Sunday never lost the dynamic energy of an athlete. Arms flailing, fists punching the air, he railed against the evils of greed, card playing, dancing, and, especially, drinking. He liked to tell audiences:

❝I'm against sin. I'll kick it as long as I've got a foot, and I'll fight it as long as I've got a fist. I'll butt it as long as I've got a head. I'll bite it as long as I've got a tooth. And when I'm old and fistless and footless and toothless, I'll gum it 'till I go home to Glory.❞

—Billy Sunday, sermon

# Social and Cultural Tensions

 **Content Expectations**

- **6.1.3d** Analyze resulting tensions among/within groups.
- **6.3.2a** Analyze causes/consequences of 16th, 17th, 18th, 19th Amendments.
- **7.1.1a** Explain significance of Harlem Renaissance/"lost generation."
- **7.1.1b** Explain struggle between "traditional" and "modern" U.S.

## Terms and People

| | |
|---|---|
| modernism | Ku Klux Klan |
| fundamentalism | Prohibition |
| Scopes Trial | Eighteenth Amendment |
| Clarence Darrow | Volstead Act |
| quota system | bootlegger |

## NoteTaking

**Reading Skill: Contrast** As you read, look for issues that divided Americans in the 1920s.

| Differing Viewpoints | |
|---|---|
| Education | • Viewpoint 1<br>• Viewpoint 2 |
| Evolution | |

**Why It Matters** In the 1920s, while many city dwellers enjoyed a rising standard of living, most farmers suffered through hard times. Conflicting visions of what the nation should be heightened the urban-rural division. Some of these issues, such as immigration policy and teaching the theory of evolution, still divide Americans today. **Section Focus Question: How did Americans differ on major social and cultural issues?**

## Traditionalism and Modernism Clash

The 1920 census reported that, for the first time in American history, more people lived in urban areas than in rural regions. This simple fact had profound consequences. The nation had been divided before, but usually along north-south or east-west lines. In the 1920s, however, the split was between urban America and rural America. On virtually every important social and cultural issue, the two groups were divided.

Urban Americans enjoyed new consumer products and a wide array of leisure activities. They generally showed an openness toward social change and the new discoveries of science. The growing trend to emphasize science and secular values over traditional ideas about religion became known as **modernism.**

By contrast, rural Americans did not participate fully in the consumer bonanzas, and they missed out on many of the new forms of leisure. People in the country generally embraced a more traditional view of religion, science, and culture.

| High School Education, 1900–1930 | |
| --- | --- |
| Year | High School Graduates (percentage of 17-year-olds) |
| 1900 | 6.3 |
| 1910 | 8.6 |
| 1920 | 16.3 |
| 1930 | 28.8 |

SOURCE: U.S. Census Bureau

**Americans Go to School**
Although school attendance grew steadily, fewer than half of American children graduated from high school by 1930. *How much did the high school graduation rate increase during the 1920s?*

**Education Becomes More Important** Rural and urban Americans differed in their attitudes toward formal education. In rural America, prolonged formal education had not seemed vital. Farmers expected their children to master the "Three R's"—reading, writing, and arithmetic. But beyond that, education collided with the many farm tasks that needed to be done. Muscle, endurance, and knowledge of crops and animals seemed more important to farmers than "book learning."

Formal education took on more importance in urban America. Mental ability, not muscular fitness, was seen as the essential ingredient for success. Mastery of mathematics and language could spell the difference between a low-paying, unskilled job and a higher-paying position as an office worker. By 1930, more American teens were graduating from high school, and more Americans than ever before went to college.

**Religious Fundamentalism Grows** In the 1920s, many devout Americans believed that Christianity was under siege throughout the world. They pointed to Soviet communist attacks on the Orthodox Church in Russia and to the Mexican revolutionary assaults on the Roman Catholic Church in Mexico.

At home, a growing number of Christians were upset by what they saw as secular trends in religion and culture. They reaffirmed their belief in the fundamental, or basic, truths of their religion. This approach, often called **fundamentalism,** emphasized Protestant teachings and the belief that every word in the Bible was literal truth. Fundamentalists believed that the answer to every important moral and scientific question was in their holy book. Their ideas took root all over the country but were especially strong in rural America.

**Americans Clash Over Evolution** Fundamentalism and modernism clashed head-on in the **Scopes Trial** of 1925. At issue was the theory of evolution, developed by English scientist Charles Darwin. Darwin believed that complex forms of life, such as human beings, had developed gradually from simpler forms of life. This theory clashed with the description of creation in the Bible.

In 1925, Tennessee passed a law making it illegal to teach Darwin's theory in the state's public schools. The American Civil Liberties Union convinced John Scopes, a high school biology teacher in Dayton, Tennessee, to challenge the law. When Scopes taught evolution in his classroom, he was promptly arrested.

The Scopes Trial drew nationwide attention. Journalists flocked to Dayton to cover the emotionally charged event, which many dubbed the "Monkey Trial" because of the mistaken belief that Darwin claimed that human beings descended from monkeys. **Clarence Darrow,** the most celebrated defense attorney in America, traveled from his home in Chicago to defend Scopes. Three-time presidential candidate William Jennings Bryan, a long-time defender of rural values, served as an expert for the prosecution.

The highlight of the trial came when Darrow called Bryan to the stand as an expert on the Bible. Bryan affirmed that the Bible stated the literal truth. He testified that he believed that God created Adam and Eve and that Joshua made the sun stand still. Darrow tried to use science to cast doubt on such beliefs, but Bryan firmly stated, "I accept the Bible absolutely."

Scopes was found guilty of breaking the law—a fact that was never in question—and fined $100. While the Scopes Trial showcased a major cultural and religious division, it did not heal the conflict or answer its central questions. When the trial was over, each side still believed in the truth of its position. The conflict over evolution continues today.

 **Checkpoint** How did the Scopes Trial illustrate the urban-rural split in the 1920s?

# Restricting Immigration

Another cultural clash involved the ongoing boom in immigration. As in the past, Americans known as nativists argued that the new arrivals took jobs away from native-born workers and threatened American religious, political, and cultural traditions.

**Nativists Oppose Immigration**  Although nativist politicians had been able to restrict immigration from China in 1882, they had failed to push through laws to restrict immigration from southern and eastern Europe. On the eve of World War I, however, Congress did pass a law requiring immigrants to take a literacy test. Immigrants who could not read or write their own language were prohibited from entering the United States. President Wilson vetoed the law, but Congress overrode Wilson's veto.

During the postwar Red Scare, fear that communists and socialists from eastern Europe were traveling to the United States with their revolutionary doctrines added an emotional edge to the debate. The problem that confronted nativists was traditional immigration policy. All Americans who could trace their ancestry back far enough discovered foreign origins. Many viewed the immigration experience as part of what made an American an American.

**Quota Laws Limit Newcomers**  World War I, the Russian Revolution, and the Red Scare strengthened the nativist position. Two important laws—the Emergency Quota Act of 1921 and the National Origins Act of 1924—established a **quota system** to govern immigration from specific countries.

## Comparing Viewpoints

## Should a State Ban Teaching of Darwin's Theory of Evolution?

The Scopes Trial of 1925 revolved around a Tennessee law that banned the teaching of Darwin's theory of evolution. The deeper issue involved a clash between traditional religious beliefs and modern science.

### THE PROSECUTION

William Jennings Bryan believed that Tennessee had a right to protect its children from ideas that violated biblical teachings.

**Primary Source**

"Science is a magnificent force, but it is not a teacher of morals. . . . In war, science has proven itself an evil genius; it has made war more terrible than it ever was before."

"It is for the jury to determine whether this attack upon the Christian religion shall be permitted in the public schools of Tennessee by teachers employed by the state."

*"When Shall We Three Meet Again?"*

### THE DEFENSE

Dudley Field Malone, who joined Clarence Darrow in the defense of Scopes, argued against a state determining what should be taught.

**Primary Source**

"We feel we stand with progress. We feel we stand with science. We feel we stand with intelligence. We feel we stand with fundamental freedom in America."

"Let the children have their minds kept open. Close no doors to their knowledge. Shut no door from them. Make the distinction between theology and science. Let them have both. Let them be taught both. Let them both live."

### Compare
1. How does Bryan's view of science differ from that of Malone?
2. What does each man feel should happen when science clashes with religion?

# U.S. Immigration Policy

MI 6.1.4

## TRACK THE ISSUE

 THE **ESSENTIAL** ?

### How should government regulate immigration?

The first major effort to limit immigration to the United States came in the late 1800s. By then, immigrants were streaming into the country. Many Americans worried about losing their jobs or their sense of national identity. Since then, immigration and immigration policy have remained controversial issues. Use the timeline below to explore this enduring issue.

**1882 Chinese Exclusion Act**
Federal government makes first law to exclude a specific national group.

**1924 National Origins Act**
Law sets quotas on numbers of immigrants from each country.

**1952 McCarran-Walter Act**
Law establishes political beliefs as criteria for exclusion.

**1965 Immigration Act Amended**
Congress abolishes national quotas but sets ceiling for each hemisphere.

**1986 Immigration Reform and Control Act**
Law offers amnesty to some illegal aliens.

**2004 Guest Worker Program**
President Bush proposes law allowing temporary foreign workers.

Immigrants enter New York's Ellis Island in the 1920s.

Immigrants and foreign visitors go through a careful check before they are allowed to enter the country.

## DEBATE THE ISSUE

**Amnesty for Illegal Immigrants** In recent years, Americans have hotly debated the question of amnesty for illegal immigrants. Some Americans favor laws providing a legal route to citizenship. Critics say that laws curbing further illegal immigration would be more effective.

❝Amnesty combined with serious penalties for employers that hire undocumented workers . . . is the only real way out of [this] situation. . . . It . . . is . . . the option most likely to secure the border and end the system of undocumented worker exploitation—which is precisely why our well-funded leaders in Washington have no intention of pursuing it.❞
—Tom Head, author

❝Amnesty for illegal aliens is simply a reward for law-breaking. No system depending on a strict regard for the rule of law can treat law-breaking so casually. Amnesty will be a magnet for further illegal immigrants, who hope to be future recipients of the nation's compassion.❞
—Edward J. Erler, Senior Fellow, Claremont Institute

 ?

### *TRANSFER* Activities

1. **Compare** Why does Tom Head support amnesty? Why does Erler oppose it?

2. **Analyze** How does the issue debated today differ from the issues that led to the passage of the National Origins Act?

3. **Transfer** Use the following Web site to see a video, try a WebQuest, and write in your journal. **Web Code:** neh-8002

The National Origins Act set up a simple formula: The number of immigrants of a given nationality each year could not exceed 2 percent of the number of people of that nationality living in the United States in 1890. The year 1890 was chosen because it came before the great wave of immigration from southern and eastern Europe. For example, the act permitted about 65,721 immigrants from England and Northern Ireland to come to America every year, but it allowed only about 5,802 immigrants from Italy. The act also continued to exclude most Asian immigrants. America had closed its "golden door" to many of the people trying to enter.

**More Mexicans Come North** The quota system did not apply to Mexico, which was still reeling from the chaos of the 1910 revolution. Mexicans settled in sparsely populated regions of the Southwest and made major contributions to the local economies. Most Mexican newcomers found work harvesting crops in Texas and California. A smaller number sought jobs in the factories and farms of the North or Midwest.

Many Mexican immigrants faced discrimination and hostility in their new homes. They often competed with native-born Americans for jobs and were frequently subjected to brutality and violence.

✓ **Checkpoint** How did new laws change U.S. immigration policy in the 1920s?

# The New Ku Klux Klan

Immigration restriction was an attempt to turn back the clock to what many saw as a simpler, better time—a time before the nation became ethnically diverse. As rural Americans saw the country become increasingly urban and their own position in the nation slip in relative importance, many lashed out against symbols of change. Some even turned to organizations that supported doctrines of hate and employed violence and terror to achieve their ends.

**The Klan Rises Again** In 1915, on Stone Mountain in Georgia, a group of angry men revived the **Ku Klux Klan.** The original Klan had been formed in the South during Reconstruction largely to terrorize African Americans who sought to vote. Although the revived Klan continued to promote hatred of African Americans, it was also aimed at the new America taking shape in the cities. It targeted Jews, Catholics, and immigrants. The Klan also claimed to stand against lawbreaking and immorality. One of their leaders claimed that "every criminal, every gambler . . . every crooked politician . . . is fighting the Klan."

At its height, the Klan's "Invisible Empire" had perhaps 4 to 5 million members. Most were in the South, but there were also branches in the Midwest, Northeast, and West—in both rural areas and in small industrial cities. One center of Klan strength was Indiana, where Klan leader David Stephenson ruled with an iron fist and controlled numerous politicians. They burned crosses, boycotted businesses owned by anyone who was Jewish, Catholic, or African American, and terrorized citizens in the darkness of night. Klansmen

**The New Ku Klux Klan**
In 1925, thousands of Klansmen (below) staged a huge march in Washington, D.C.

**Vocabulary Builder**

imperial–(ihm PIR ee uhl) *adj.*
relating to an empire or emperor;
having supreme authority

usually wore masks to conceal their identities, met to wave flags and preach hate, and followed leaders with such titles as Grand Dragon and <u>Imperial</u> Wizard. But behind the Klan's confident facade were Americans fearful of change.

**Americans Oppose the Klan** Individuals, as well as organizations such as the NAACP and the Jewish Anti-Defamation League, battled against the Klan and its values. They embraced the idea of racial, ethnic, religious, and cultural diversity. For them, the notion of the "melting pot" was as old as America itself, and they drew strength from American traditions and saw hope in the American future. Journalist William Allen White noted:

> **Primary Source** "To make a case against a birthplace, a religion, or a race is wickedly un-American and cowardly. The whole trouble with the Ku Klux Klan is that it is based upon such deep foolishness that it is bound to be a menace to good government in any community."
> —William Allen White, letter to the editor of the *New York World,* 1921

The Klan itself became thoroughly corrupt. Its leaders bribed politicians, stole from its members' dues, and lied to its members. Stephenson ended up going to prison for assault and second-degree murder. By the late 1920s, the Klan stood exposed. Although it never disappeared, it withered in importance.

✔ **Checkpoint** How did the goals of the new Ku Klux Klan differ from those of the old Klan?

● **INFOGRAPHIC**

# PROHIBITION AND CRIME

Supporters of Prohibition rightly pointed out that alcohol was at the root of many social ills, from child abuse to lost productivity on the job. Sadly, the attempt to ban alcohol opened the door to a new set of social problems.

During Prohibition, many ordinary Americans—rich and poor—became lawbreakers. Ignoring the Volstead Act, they found creative ways to hide alcohol. This woman has a flask hidden in her boot. ▼

Federal agents destroy a still used to manufacture illegal alcohol. Although these "feds" worked tirelessly, there were not enough of them to enforce Prohibition effectively. ▼

# Prohibition and Crime

Another divisive issue was **Prohibition,** the banning of alcohol use. Since the early 1800s, temperance reformers had crusaded against alcohol. By 1917, some 75 percent of Americans lived in "dry" counties that had banned liquor. World War I increased support for temperance. It seemed unpatriotic to use corn, wheat, and barley to make alcohol when soldiers overseas needed bread.

**Government Bans Alcoholic Beverages** In 1919, the states ratified the **Eighteenth Amendment** to the Constitution. It forbade the manufacture, distribution, and sale of alcohol anywhere in the United States. The amendment had been passed largely on the strength of rural votes. Congress then passed the **Volstead Act,** a law that officially enforced the amendment.

Advocates of Prohibition, known as "drys," called it a "noble experiment." They argued that Prohibition improved individuals, strengthened families, and created better societies. In fact, drinking—as well as alcoholism and liver disease caused by drinking—did decline during Prohibition.

Opponents of Prohibition, dubbed "wets," countered that the ban on alcohol did not stop people from drinking. Instead, they argued, Prohibition helped create an atmosphere of hypocrisy and increased organized crime.

**Americans Break the Law** As the wets noted, the Volstead Act did not stop Americans from drinking, but it did prevent them from purchasing drinks

**Vocabulary Builder**
advocate–(AD vuh kiht) *n.* supporter; one who argues in favor of something

Critics of Prohibition argued that it encouraged political corruption. In this cartoon, a row of officials from federal agents to judges hold their hands out for bribe money.

Prohibition encouraged a new breed of organized crime. Racketeers like Al Capone (left) and his rival, Bugs Moran, thumbed their nose at the law and ruthlessly murdered their competitors (below).

7 CHICAGO GANGSTERS SLAIN BY FIRING SQUAD OF RIVALS SOME IN POLICE UNIFORM

Special to The New York Times.
...AGO, Feb. 14.--Chicago gang-
...aders observed Valentine's
... machine guns and a stream

VICTIMS LINED UP IN

## Thinking Critically
1. **Summarize** What three types of lawbreaking are illustrated here?
2. **Analyze** How were these three types of lawbreaking related to one another?

229

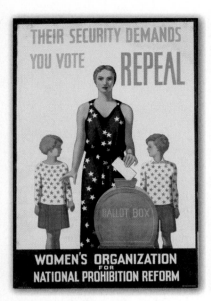

**Wets Seek Repeal**
Supporters of the Eighteenth Amendment had often used images of mothers and children to press for a ban on alcohol. This propaganda poster uses similar images to press for the repeal.

legally. The gap between the law and individual desires was filled by a large illegal network. People made alcohol in homemade stills or smuggled it in from other countries. **Bootleggers** sold illegal alcohol to consumers. In cities, secret drinking establishments, known as speakeasies, attracted eager customers.

Government agents worked tirelessly to stop the flow of illegal liquor. However, they were short-handed, and the demand for alcohol was too great. There were millions of dollars to be made by both organized and unorganized criminals. Particularly in cities, policemen and politicians tended to look the other way when liquor was concerned. They rationalized their actions by saying that if people wanted to drink they would drink.

Al Capone, a Chicago gang leader, was the most famous criminal of the Prohibition era. He defended his illegal actions:

 **Primary Source** "I make my money from supplying a public demand. If I break the law, my customers, who number hundreds of the best people in Chicago, are as guilty as I am. The only difference between us is that I sell and they buy. Everybody calls me a racketeer. I call myself a businessman."
—Al Capone, quoted in *Era of Excess* (Sinclair)

The problem was that under the guise of providing a glass of beer or scotch, organized crime spread into other areas of society. Capone's other "businesses" included prostitution, drugs, robbery, and murder. Thus, Prohibition contributed to the growth of organized crime in America.

**Prohibition Divides the Nation** By the mid-1920s, most city politicians clamored for the repeal of the Eighteenth Amendment. But to many rural Americans, liquor and crime were tied to other divisive cultural issues of the day. Thus, like immigration and evolution, the debate over Prohibition became part of a battle over the future of America.

In the culturally divided 1920s, Americans could not reach a satisfactory settlement on the issue. Not until 1933 did the Twenty-first Amendment finally repeal Prohibition.

✔ **Checkpoint** What were the effects of the Eighteenth Amendment and the Volstead Act?

**Progress Monitoring *Online***
**For:** Self-test with vocabulary practice
**Web Code:** nea-0705

**Comprehension**

1. **Terms and People** For each of the following, write a sentence explaining its importance to the social and cultural clashes of the 1920s.
   - modernism
   - fundamentalism
   - Scopes Trial
   - quota system
   - Ku Klux Klan
   - Prohibition
   - Eighteenth Amendment
   - Volstead Act
   - bootlegger

2. NoteTaking **Reading Skill:** **Contrast** Use your table to answer the Section Focus Question: How did Americans differ on major social and cultural issues?

**Writing About History**

3. **Compare and Contrast** Write the opening paragraph for an essay comparing supporters and opponents of Prohibition. Use the information in this section as well as your own thoughts. Consider the goals and values that wets and drys might have had in common as well as the ways in which they differed.

**Critical Thinking**

4. **Recognize Ideologies** How did the two sides in the Scopes Trial represent conflicting value systems? What did each side value most?

5. **Identify Points of View** Why did both supporters and opponents of immigration quotas believe they were defending American traditions and values?

6. **Draw Conclusions** Why do you think the revived Ku Klux Klan was able to spread beyond the South and even into some urban areas?

◄ Couple dancing to phonograph music

## WITNESS HISTORY  AUDIO

### "Ain't We Got Fun?"

The phonograph had come a long way from that day in 1877 when inventor Thomas Edison had recorded himself reciting "Mary Had a Little Lamb." By the 1920s, Americans were buying thousands of phonographs and millions of shiny phonograph records. In the comfort of their living rooms, they listened and danced to popular songs that reflected the carefree spirit of the age. One hit tune of 1921 told of a young couple who were determined to enjoy themselves even though they didn't have much money:

❝Night or daytime, it's all playtime,
Ain't we got fun?
Hot or cold days, any old days,
Ain't we got fun?
If wifie wishes to go to a play,
Don't wash the dishes, just throw them away!❞

—Gus Kahn and Raymond B. Egan,
"Ain't We Got Fun?"

# A New Mass Culture

## Content Expectations

- **6.1.1f** Analyze technological advances that enabled the U.S. to become an industrial power.
- **6.3.2d** Analyze causes/consequences of reform organizations, movements, individuals promoting change.
- **7.1.1a** Explain significance of Harlem Renaissance/"lost generation."
- **7.1.1b** Explain struggle between "traditional" and "modern" U.S.

## Terms and People

Charlie Chaplin
*The Jazz Singer*
Babe Ruth
Charles Lindbergh
flapper

Sigmund Freud
"Lost Generation"
F. Scott Fitzgerald
Ernest Hemingway

## NoteTaking

**Reading Skill: Summarize** Look for ways in which culture changed during the 1920s.

**Why It Matters** The automobile reshaped American culture, creating new forms of recreation and making it easier for people to travel. Other factors also contributed to changing ways of daily life. Americans listened to the radio, went to the movies, and followed the exploits of sports heroes. In the process, a new mass culture emerged—one whose shape and character closely resemble our own. **Section Focus Question: How did the new mass culture reflect technological and social changes?**

## New Trends in Popular Culture

The 1920s was in many respects the first decade of our modern era. Even as cultural issues divided Americans from different regions or economic levels, technology was beginning to break down other barriers. Nowhere is this more evident than in the leisure interests of the American people.

**Americans Enjoy More Leisure Time** The growth of cities changed leisure patterns. On farms, people worked from dawn to dusk, with little time to spare. In the evenings, a farm family might play games, read, or sing together around the piano. Occasionally, they joined other farm families and townsfolk for picnics or a game of baseball. They did not have the time or the money for more extensive leisure pursuits.

City life was different. The average workweek in all industries fell from 70 hours in 1850 to 55 in 1910 to 45 by 1930. The workweek itself also changed from seven days a week to six and at last to five. At the same time, salaries and wages were on the rise.

▼ **Charlie Chaplin,** the comic "common man"

▲ **Douglas Fairbanks,** athletic star of adventure movies

▶ **Lon Chaney,** star of horror films like *The Phantom of the Opera*

▲ **Mary Pickford,** known as America's Sweetheart

## Silent Movie Stars

Each silent movie star had his or her own special appeal. The four shown above were among the most popular not only in the United States but around the world.

**Americans Flock to the Movies**  With more free time and disposable income, urban and suburban Americans looked to new sources of entertainment. Motion pictures helped supply that demand.

The technology to make motion pictures had been around for a generation, but the movie industry rose to new heights in the 1920s. A handful of huge studios in Hollywood, California, established monopolies that controlled the production, distribution, and exhibition of movies. During the 1920s, from 60 to 100 million Americans went to the movies each week. Ornate movie palaces or small local theaters became America's cultural classrooms.

For most of the decade, the studios made silent pictures. They were an ideal entertainment at a time when millions of immigrants spoke little English. Motion pictures transcended languages and even literacy, treating universal themes in familiar ways that allowed any viewer to follow the stories. Motion pictures became America's democratic art. Unlike theatrical productions or classical concerts, movies were available to anyone with a few cents to spare. In addition, the fact that movies were silent made it easier for them to cut across geographic boundaries. Hollywood's biggest movies and stars became nearly as popular in far corners of the world as they were at home.

Many stars of the silent era portrayed ordinary folks. Comedian **Charlie Chaplin,** the most popular silent film star, played the Little Tramp. The character was equal parts hobo, dreamer, and poet but an eternal optimist in his ability to charm his audience and continually reinvent himself. Other stars played more romantic types. Handsome Rudolph Valentino was the sheik, as exotic to ordinary Americans as the deserts of Arabia. William S. Hart was a steely-eyed cowboy who came into town to restore law and order.

In 1927, film history changed, suddenly and forever, with the release of ***The Jazz Singer,*** the first movie with sound synchronized to the action. Audiences were amazed when Al Jolson said—not pantomimed—"You ain't heard nothin' yet" and then launched into a song. Silent pictures quickly faded out, replaced by "talkies." But whether silent or sound, movies spoke directly to the desires, needs, fears, and fantasies of millions of people in the United States and around the world.

**The Radio and Phonograph Break Barriers** Like the movies, the phonograph and the radio also became powerful instruments of mass popular culture. Each was the result of both technological advances and business enterprise. Millions of radios and phonographs (as well as phonograph records) were marketed in the 1920s. On a deeper level, the phonograph and radio helped produce a standardized culture. Americans in the East and West and North and South listened to the same songs, learned the same dances, and shared the same popular culture as they never had before.

The radio, or wireless, had been developed in the 1890s by Italian inventor Guglielmo Marconi. Before the 1920s, the radio had been an innovation for a small group of military technicians, telephone operators, and amateur "wireless" operators. Then, in 1920, an executive of the Westinghouse company started radio station KDKA in Pittsburgh, Pennsylvania. It was an immediate success. Within three years, there were almost 600 licensed stations broadcasting to more than 600,000 radio sets. Americans listened to music, educational lectures and religious sermons, and news and weather reports. They also heard commercials for a wide variety of consumer products.

Radios brought distant events into millions of homes in a way unmatched by newspapers or magazines. In 1927, much of America listened to a championship boxing match between Gene Tunney and Jack Dempsey. That night, theaters and movie houses played to empty seats as Americans huddled next to their sets. Even the men on death row at Sing Sing prison listened to the broadcast. Before the 1920s, such coverage of an event had been impossible.

The phonograph allowed people to listen to the same music they heard on the radio, but whenever they wanted. Early phonographs employed difficult-to-use wax cylinders and suffered from poor sound quality. In the 1920s, grooved disc recordings and superior sound reproduction improved the sound of the earlier machines. Recordings helped spread country and western music from the South and West to the North and East, while pop tunes from New York City's Tin Pan Alley traveled in the other direction. As they listened to the same songs, Americans also learned the same fashionable dances, from the fox trot to the Charleston.

 **Checkpoint** How did movies and the radio cut across geographic barriers?

## An Age of Heroes

Hollywood's chief rivals for the creation of heroes were the nation's baseball parks, football fields, and boxing rings. Before the 1920s, there were relatively few nationally famous athletes, such as boxer John L. Sullivan and all-around athlete Jim Thorpe. Most sports stars were local heroes. This changed by the 1920s, often called the Golden Age of Sports.

**Sports Heroes Win Fans** Thanks to increased newspaper readership and the rise of radio coverage, every major sport boasted nationally famous performers. Perhaps the leading sports hero was baseball home-run king **Babe Ruth.** Others included Red Grange in football, Jack Dempsey in boxing, Bobby Jones in golf, and Bill Tilden in tennis. Women athletes, too, gained fame, from tennis player Helen Wills to Gertrude Ederle, the first woman to swim the English Channel.

### HISTORY MAKERS

**Babe Ruth** (1895–1948)
Babe Ruth—also known as the Bambino and the Sultan of Swat—towered over major league baseball, not only while he was playing but for decades after. Originally a standout pitcher for the Boston Red Sox, Ruth gained fame as a slugging outfielder for the New York Yankees. In 1920, baseball was suffering from a gambling scandal. Ruth's amazing home runs and great appeal helped the sport win back fans. His record for most home runs in a season stood for more than 30 years, and his record for most home runs in a career lasted even longer.

Why did athletes reach such heights of popularity? Part of the answer is that the Golden Age of Sports was also the Golden Age of the Sportswriter. Such journalists as Damon Runyon and Grantland Rice captured the excitement of sports events in their colorful prose. Turning the finest athletes into seemingly immortal gods, the sportswriters nicknamed Babe Ruth the Sultan of Swat and dubbed Notre Dame's football backfield the Four Horsemen.

The other part of the answer is that the decade needed heroes. World War I had shattered many Americans' faith in progress, making the world seem cheap and flawed. Athletic heroes reassured Americans that people were capable of great feats and lofty dreams. If in our heroes we see our idealized selves, the sports heroes of the 1920s gave Americans a sense of hope.

**Lucky Lindy Crosses the Atlantic** Even the biggest sports stars could not match the adoration given aviator **Charles Lindbergh.** In the 1920s, the airline industry was in its infancy. Flying aces had played a role in World War I, and a few small domestic airlines carried mail and passengers. But airplanes were still a novel sight to most Americans. The pilot became a new breed of hero, a romantic daredevil who risked death with every flight.

Lindbergh outdid them all. In May 1927, he took off from Long Island, New York, in his tiny single-engine plane, the *Spirit of St. Louis*, and headed east— to Paris, France. Other pilots had flown across the Atlantic Ocean before, but Lindbergh was the first to do it solo and non-stop. The flight took more than 33 hours, and the lone pilot had to stay awake the entire time. He also recalled, "In the daytime I knew where I was going, but in the evening and at night it was largely a matter of guesswork."

When Lindbergh landed in Paris, he became an instant media celebrity, dubbed Lucky Lindy and the Lone Eagle. The radio reported on his landing, and movie newsreels showed his triumphant return home. The modest young man from the Midwest became the greatest hero of his time.

## Lucky Lindy Crosses the Atlantic

"Well, I made it," Charles Lindbergh said simply as he landed his airplane, the *Spirit of St. Louis,* in Paris. Moments later, soldiers had to rescue him from the thousands of well-wishers who crowded the airfield.

 **Checkpoint** How did the new mass media contribute to the popularity of heroes?

## NoteTaking

**Reading Skill: Summarize** As you read, classify the various types of changes that took place in women's lives in the 1920s.

| Women in the 1920s | | |
|---|---|---|
| Social Changes | Political Changes | Economic Changes |
| | | |
| | | |
| | | |

## Women Assume New Roles

In a 1931 book, *Only Yesterday*, journalist Frederick Lewis Allen attempted to make sense of the fads, heroes, and problems of the 1920s. Featured prominently was the New Woman. During the decade, many women challenged political, economic, social, and educational boundaries, to prove that their role was as vital outside the home as inside it.

**Flappers Challenge Older Limits** During the Victorian Age of the late 1800s and early 1900s, women had been expected to center their lives on the home and family. The New Woman of the 1920s, noted Allen, was more liberated. She wore dresses with shorter hemlines, put on more makeup, danced to the latest crazes, and generally assumed that she had the same political and social rights as any man.

# THE NEW Woman?

What was new about the "New Woman" of the 1920s? The flapper—exciting to some and shocking to others—became the most familiar symbol of women's new freedom. But for most women, change came more slowly and subtly.

◄ **New Products for the Housewife**
Even for the majority of women who stayed at home to care for the house and children, life changed. New consumer products such as dishwashers and vacuum cleaners made housework easier.

**The Flapper** ▲
"Flappers are we/ Flappers wild and free," crowed a song of the 1920s. "Never too slow/ All on the go." But although flappers influenced styles and attitudes, relatively few women were full-fledged flappers.

◄ **Women Pioneers**
In the 1920s, individual women seized opportunities to blaze new trails in fields from politics to auto mechanics.

| "Firsts" for American Women, 1920s | |
| --- | --- |
| Florence Allen | First woman state judge (1920) |
| Marie Luhring | First woman automotive engineer (1920) |
| Rebecca Felton | First woman in U.S. Senate (1922) |
| Nellie Tayloe Ross | First woman governor (1924) |
| Gertrude Ederle | First woman to swim English Channel (1926) |
| Dorothy Arzner | First woman to direct a talking movie (1927) |
| Phoebe Omlie | First woman to earn a federal pilot's license (1927) |

**Office Workers** The trend toward more women entering the workforce continued throughout the decade. Some white-collar jobs, such as stenographers and telephone ◄ operators, became predominantly female.

## Thinking Critically

1. **Evaluate Information** Why were the "Firsts" shown on the table at left important?

2. **Draw Conclusions** Why do you think the flapper became a major symbol even though relatively few women were flappers?

235

Popular magazines, <u>sociological</u> studies, novels, and movies all echoed Allen's observations. The rejection of Victorian morality seemed so total and the New Woman so novel that the change amounted to a "revolution in manners and morals." The symbol of all these changes was the **flapper,** a young woman with short skirts and rouged cheeks who had her hair cropped close in a style known as a bob.

There was only a germ of truth in the various observations. The Victorian code of separate spheres for men and women was disappearing but not as rapidly or as completely as Allen indicated. The flapper was undoubtedly more publicized than imitated. Still, the image of the flapper underscores an important aspect of the decade. Not all women aspired to be flappers, but many wanted more control over their lives—and got it.

**Women Make Strides** The great fight for suffrage had been won with the passage of the Nineteenth Amendment. What was the next step? Some groups, such as the National American Woman Suffrage Association, called on women to work in reform movements, run for office, or fight for laws to protect women and children in the workplace. Some women had success in public life. In 1925, Nellie Tayloe Ross of Wyoming and Miriam Ferguson of Texas became the first women elected as their state's governor.

The National Women's Party took a more militant position, demanding complete economic, social, and political equality with men. Their primary goal was the passage of an Equal Rights Amendment. Most women, though, believed that a new constitutional amendment was premature. They set more achievable goals and made significant strides in employment. Although most working women continued to toil in domestic service and manufacturing, others moved into clerical, sales, and management positions. Women also won jobs in journalism, aviation, banking, and the legal and medical professions.

**Family Life Changes** Perhaps the most widespread revolution taking place in women's lives was a quiet one. During the decade, women tended to live longer, marry later, and have fewer children, freeing their time to pursue other interests. Some entered the workforce, others devoted more time to charitable work, and still others joined clubs that discussed books and ideas. All these pursuits enlarged the intellectual world of women.

The consumer economy of the 1920s benefited women. Electric vacuum cleaners and irons took some of the labor and drudgery out of household chores. Of course, not all women shared in the blessings of technology. Many homes in rural America had no access to electricity. For women in these regions, household labor continued to involve intense, even painful, work. They drew and carried water from wells, heated irons on stoves, and washed clothes by hand. Here again, the split between urban and rural Americans was distinct.

 **Checkpoint** What political gains did American women make during the 1920s?

# Modernism in Art and Literature

No area of American life, however, reflected the impact of World War I more than literature and the arts. The war altered the way writers and artists viewed the world, changed the way they approached their craft, and inspired them to experiment with new forms and fresh ideas.

**The Arts Reflect a Mood of Uncertainty** During the Victorian era, most poets and novelists had expressed a belief in progress, placing boundless faith in human potential. But World War I called the notion of progress into question.

How could a society ruled by the idea of progress embark on a war that killed millions of people, destroyed monuments of civilization, and left survivors hungry, homeless, and hopeless? This was not an action of a rational people, a new generation of writers argued, but the irrational exploits of civilization without a sense of direction. This pessimistic, skeptical worldview sparked an artistic movement known as modernism.

The theories of Austrian <u>psychologist</u> **Sigmund Freud** (SIHG muhnd froid) also contributed to literary and artistic modernism. Freud argued that much of human behavior is driven not by rational thought but by unconscious desires. To live in society, people learn to suppress these desires. But the tension between outward behavior and the subconscious, said Freud, could lead to mental and even physical illness. Freud's theories led writers and artists to explore the subconscious mind.

**Modern Painting Challenges Tradition** Modernism clashed head-on with traditionalism most dramatically in the field of modern art. Since the late 1800s, European painters had led the way in seeking a fresh visual idiom, or language. They moved away from representational paintings that simply reproduced real life and experimented with more abstract styles.

**Vocabulary Builder**

<u>psychologist</u>—(sī KAHL uh jihst) *n.* scientist who studies the human mind and the process of thought and emotion

## Modern Art

By the 1920s, many artists had broken away from purely representational styles. The two American artists shown here used vastly different methods in their work. *How do these paintings reflect the changing world of the 1920s? How do they express differing moods?*

**Edward Hopper: *Automat***
Basically realistic, Edward Hopper's works often reflect the loneliness and anonymity of urban life. In this 1927 painting, a woman dressed in flapper style eats in a restaurant where even the food is dispensed by machine.

**Joseph Stella: *Brooklyn Bridge***
Joseph Stella was one of the few American painters to follow a European style called futurism, which celebrated change and technology. This 1920 painting is more abstract than Hopper's, but the subject matter is still recognizable.

▼ Willa Cather

▲ Original cover of *Main Street*

| American Postwar Novelists | | ☑ Quick Study |
|---|---|---|
| **Novelist** | **Major Themes** | **Representative Work** |
| **Willa Cather** (1873–1947) | Frontier life on the Great Plains | ***My Ántonia*** (1918) depicts the passing of the American frontier through the life of an immigrant girl in Nebraska. |
| **William Faulkner** (1897–1962) | Life in the South; inner workings of mind | ***The Sound and the Fury*** (1929) uses different narrators to tell the story of the complex inner workings of a Southern family. |
| **F. Scott Fitzgerald** (1896–1940) | The Jazz Age | ***The Great Gatsby*** (1925) shows the emptiness of the Jazz-Age world of flappers and bootleggers. |
| **Ernest Hemingway** (1899–1961) | Disillusionment of postwar generation | ***A Farewell to Arms*** (1929) tells the story of doomed love between a cynical American ambulance driver and a nurse during World War I. |
| **Sinclair Lewis** (1885–1951) | Small-town life in the Midwest | ***Main Street*** (1920) paints a satirical portrait of small-minded people in an American town. |
| **Edith Wharton** (1862–1937) | Life among the rich in New York | ***The Age of Innocence*** (1920) depicts a wealthy young man prevented by social conventions from marrying the woman he loves. |

Most Americans got their first real glimpse of the new European approach at a major art show at New York's 69th Infantry Regimental Armory in 1913. Traditionalists were outraged by the Armory Show, and Theodore Roosevelt said that most of it represented the "lunatic fringe" of the art world. But many American painters were inspired by the bold new styles. They began their own search for artistic honesty in abstract patterns. In the 1920s, paintings by Edward Hopper, Man Ray, Joseph Stella, and Georgia O'Keeffe demonstrated the richness and varied styles of American artists. At the same time, the works of artists such as Archibald Motley and William H. Johnson portrayed African American perspectives on modern life.

**Postwar American Literature Flowers** American writers of the 1920s are often referred to as the **"Lost Generation"** because they no longer had faith in the cultural guideposts of the Victorian era. But many were inspired by their "lost" condition to search for new truths and fresh ways of expressing those truths. Never in American history had one decade seen the emergence of so many great literary talents. A list of writers who rose to distinction in the 1920s includes F. Scott Fitzgerald, Ernest Hemingway, Edith Wharton, Sinclair Lewis, William Faulkner, Gertrude Stein, Eugene O'Neill, and T. S. Eliot. Each of these writers remains today on any list of distinguished American authors.

Novelist **F. Scott Fitzgerald** explored the reality of the American dream of wealth, success, and emotional fulfillment. In *This Side of Paradise*, he wrote that his generation had "grown up to find all Gods dead, all wars fought, and all faiths in man shaken." In *The Great Gatsby* (1925), his most accomplished work, Fitzgerald showed the American dream ending in nightmare. In the novel, through hard work and careful planning, James Gatz re-creates himself as Jay Gatsby, a successful tycoon. Gatsby fills his home with wild parties, dancing, bootleg liquor, and endless activity:

> **Primary Source** "In the main hall a bar with a real brass rail was set up, and stocked with gins and liquors and with cordials so long forgotten that most of his female guests were too young to know one from another. By seven o'clock the orchestra had arrived, no thin five-piece affair, but a whole pitful of oboes and trombones and saxophones. . . . People were not invited—they went there. They got into automobiles which bore them out to Long Island, and somehow they ended up at Gatsby's door."
> —F. Scott Fitzgerald, *The Great Gatsby*

But in the end, Gatsby is destroyed by the very things he hoped to achieve. His lofty dreams end in a violent, meaningless death.

Fitzgerald's fellow novelist and good friend **Ernest Hemingway** explored similar themes but in a new idiom. Hemingway felt betrayed, not only by the American dream, but also by literary language itself. In *A Farewell to Arms*, his 1929 novel about World War I, Hemingway's narrator says:

**Primary Source** "I was always embarrassed by the words sacred, glorious, and sacrifice. . . . I had seen nothing sacred, and the things that were glorious had no glory and the sacrifices were like the stockyards at Chicago if nothing was done with the meat except to bury it. . . . Abstract words such as glory, honor, courage, or hallow were obscene beside the concrete names of villages, the numbers of roads, the names of rivers, the numbers of regiments and the dates."
—Ernest Hemingway, *A Farewell to Arms*

In his short stories and novels, Hemingway worked to develop a writing style that reflected his insights. He wrote in unadorned sentences, stripped of vague adjectives and adverbs. He created a style that was as concrete and as powerful as a rifle shot.

Influenced by Freud, other writers explored the subconscious mind. Playwright Eugene O'Neill experimented with techniques that put the subconscious right on stage. In *The Emperor Jones,* the title character gets lost in a jungle and is attacked by imaginary beings called Little Formless Fears. In *Strange Interlude,* characters turn away from their conversations with other people on stage and speak their thoughts directly to the audience.

Certainly, many poets and novelists of the decade were disillusioned. Like Hemingway and Fitzgerald, they wrestled with the meaning of the war and life itself. But in the end, their efforts resulted in the creation of literary masterpieces, not worthless products of aimless despair.

✔ **Checkpoint** What impact did World War I have on postwar American literature?

## HISTORY MAKERS

**Gertrude Stein** (1874–1946)
Gertrude Stein lived for a while in Europe as a child and returned there after college. A poet and writer, her poetry was highly experimental and often difficult to understand. But her Paris home became a gathering place for writers and artists. She supported new styles and encouraged several American writers, including Ernest Hemingway and F. Scott Fitzgerald. It was Stein who called this group the "Lost Generation."

**Progress Monitoring *Online***
**For:** Self-test with vocabulary practice
**Web Code:** nea-0706

## Comprehension

1. **Terms and People** For each of the following, write a sentence explaining the importance of that person or item to American culture of the 1920s.
   - Charlie Chaplin
   - *The Jazz Singer*
   - flapper
   - Sigmund Freud
   - "Lost Generation"
   - F. Scott Fitzgerald
   - Ernest Hemingway

2. **NoteTaking Reading Skill: Summarize** Use your concept web to answer the Section Focus Question: How did the new mass culture reflect technological and social changes?

## Writing About History

3. **Compare** Write a paragraph comparing the mass culture of today with the mass culture of the 1920s. Consider: What technologies form part of the mass culture? What role do they play in our lives?

## Critical Thinking

4. **Analyze Information** How did the increased popularity of sports heroes and the disillusionment of the "Lost Generation" writers represent different responses to the same events?

5. **Identify Main Ideas** How did the political role of American women change in the years after World War I?

6. **Analyze Literature** Reread the selection from *The Great Gatsby,* on the previous page. How does it reflect other information you have learned about the society of the 1920s?

# EXPERIENCE THE ROARING TWENTIES

**T**urn on the radio! Let's go to the movies! In the 1920s, Americans were having fun in ways that hadn't even been invented half a century earlier. And, with new forms of mass communication, fads and entertainment were spreading faster and wider than ever before. For a few pennies, a farmer in Indiana could go to the movies and enjoy the same laughs and thrills as a factory worker in New York or a businessman in San Francisco. Practically every American knew ballplayer Ty Cobb, actress Mary Pickford, and singer Rudy Vallee.

Today, the technology and the fads have changed. But the age of mass culture has never left us. ◀)) AUDIO

◀ **The Charleston**
No fad symbolizes the Roaring Twenties more than the Charleston. Here, two young people demonstrate the wild, loose-limbed dance that swept the nation.

**Saturday Night at the Movies** ▼
By the 1920s, Americans were going to the movies so often that attendance at other forms of public entertainment, such as theater, suffered. Decades later, the rise of television would have the same effect on movie attendance.

**Average Weekly Movie Attendance, 1922–1930**

People per week (in millions)

100
75
50
25
0

1922   1924   1926   1928   1930

SOURCE: *Historical Statistics of the United States*

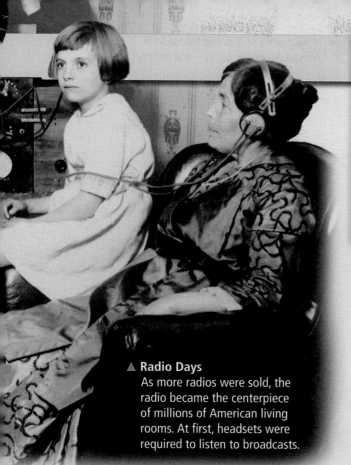

## Households With Radios, 1922–1930

Chart: Households (in millions) by year

- 1922: ~0.5
- 1924: ~1.3
- 1926: ~4.5
- 1928: ~8
- 1930: ~13.5

SOURCE: *Historical Statistics of the United States*

**▲ Radio Days**
As more radios were sold, the radio became the centerpiece of millions of American living rooms. At first, headsets were required to listen to broadcasts.

**The Great American Pastime**
Baseball remained America's favorite sport, but mass media brought it to an entirely new audience. Here, veteran superstar Ty Cobb (below) of the Detroit Tigers greets some young fans. ▼

**▲ Casual Reading**
Mass-market magazines with eye-catching covers were more popular than ever. This *Life* magazine cover (left) highlights the growing popularity of golf among both men and women. *Amazing Stories* (right) was the first "pulp" magazine devoted exclusively to science fiction.

## Thinking Critically

1. **Analyze Visuals** Identify two ways that technology affected leisure activities.

2. **Draw Conclusions** Do you think mass entertainment, such as movies and radio, would promote greater understanding and unity among Americans? Explain.

**Connect to Today** Many people worry that some of today's leisure activities, such as video games and the Internet, have a negative impact on family togetherness. Do you agree or disagree? Give reasons for your answer.

## History *Interactive* ✶

**For:** Experience the Mass Culture of the 20s video, audio, and analysis
**Web Code:** nep-0707

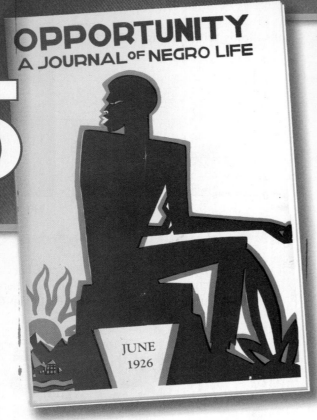

**OPPORTUNITY**
**A JOURNAL OF NEGRO LIFE**

JUNE 1926

◀ Magazines like this one focused on African American culture and history.

**WITNESS HISTORY** ◀)) AUDIO

### The Excitement of Harlem

In the early 1920s, the New York City neighborhood known as Harlem was the most vibrant African American community in the nation. Teeming with people and teeming with activity, it was also, as one observer noted, "a great magnet for the Negro intellectual." Among those who were drawn to Harlem was a young Missouri-born poet named Langston Hughes. He later recalled what he felt like as he stepped off the subway:

❝I can never put on paper the thrill of the underground ride to Harlem. I went up the steps and out into the bright September sunlight. Harlem! I stood there, dropped my bags, took a deep breath and felt happy again.❞

—Langston Hughes, *The Big Sea*

# The Harlem Renaissance

**Ml** **Content Expectations**

- **6.3.2d** Analyze causes/consequences of reform organizations, movements, individuals promoting change.
- **6.3.2e** Analyze causes/consequences of expanding/restricting democracy practices of African Americans/immigrants.
- **7.1.1a** Explain significance of Harlem Renaissance/"lost generation."

**Terms and People**

Marcus Garvey      Harlem Renaissance
jazz      Claude McKay
Louis Armstrong      Langston Hughes
Bessie Smith      Zora Neale Hurston

**NoteTaking**

**Reading Skill: Identify Main Ideas** As you read, identify the main ideas.

> I. New "Black Consciousness"
>   A. New Chances, New Challenges
>     1. Migration to North continues
>     2.
>   B.
> II.

**Why It Matters** As a result of World War I and the Great Migration, millions of African Americans relocated from the rural South to the urban North. This mass migration continued through the 1920s and contributed to a flowering of music and literature. Jazz and the Harlem Renaissance made a lasting impact, not only on African Americans but on the culture all Americans share. **Section Focus Question: How did African Americans express a new sense of hope and pride?**

## A New "Black Consciousness"

Like the immigrants who traveled from Europe and Asia, African Americans who left the South dreamed of a better future. They had heard stories of economic opportunity, social advancement, and greater political rights. The South, they reasoned, was a dead end. Locked into low-paying rural jobs, barred from decent schools, faced with the reality of Jim Crow oppression and the threat of lynching, they pointed their compasses north.

**Migrants Face Chances and Challenges** Most African American migrants to the north probably found a better life. Wages in a Detroit auto plant or a Pittsburgh steel mill were far better than what a sharecropper earned in the South. In such cities as New York, Chicago, Pittsburgh, and Cleveland, African Americans had a growing political voice. In those towns, there also existed black middle and upper classes. African American ministers, physicians, lawyers, teachers, and journalists practiced their professions and served as role models to the younger generation.

But in coming North, African Americans had certainly not escaped racism and oppression. On average, they were forced to live in the worst housing and labor in the lowest paying jobs. In addition, as the race riots of the summer of 1919 demonstrated, violence was a threat to African Americans north as well as south of the Mason-Dixon line. After World War I, African Americans increased their demand for a real solution to the country's racial problems.

New York City's Harlem became the focal point for the aspirations of hundreds of thousands of African Americans. Some 200,000 blacks settled in Harlem. Migrants from the South mixed with recently arrived immigrants from Caribbean islands, such as Jamaica. This dynamic blend of different cultures and traditions bred new ideas.

**Garvey Calls for Racial Pride** The most prominent new African American leader to emerge in the 1920s was **Marcus Garvey.** Born in Jamaica, Garvey traveled widely before immigrating to Harlem in 1916. From his travels, Garvey drew one important conclusion: Everywhere blacks were exploited. To combat the problem, he promoted the idea of universal black nationalism and organized a "Back to Africa" movement. Unlike Booker T. Washington or W.E.B. Du Bois, Garvey did not call for blacks and whites to work together to improve America. Instead, Garvey advocated the separation of the races.

Garvey's message found willing converts in American cities. By the mid-1920s, his Universal Negro Improvement Association boasted almost 2.5 million members and sympathizers. His advocacy of black pride and black support of black-run businesses won considerable support.

Garvey's movement fell apart in the second half of the decade. The federal government sent him to prison for mail fraud and then deported him to Jamaica. Without his powerful leadership, the Universal Negro Improvement Association lost its focus and appeal.

Although Garvey's movement died, his ideas did not fade. The nationalist and separatist aspects of the Nation of Islam and the Black Power movement in the 1960s owed much to Garvey. So, too, did later appeals to black pride, self-reliance, and cultural ties to Africa. Harlem's major newspaper, the *Amsterdam News*, later wrote, "In a world where black is despised, he taught [African Americans] to admire and praise black things and black people."

 **Checkpoint** How did Marcus Garvey encourage African American pride?

**Marcus Garvey**
Dressed in a ceremonial uniform, Marcus Garvey rides in a New York City parade on the opening day of a 1922 convention of a group called Negro Peoples of the World.

# The Jazz Age

It was F. Scott Fitzgerald who called the 1920s the "Jazz Age." However, it was African Americans who gave the age its jazz. A truly <u>indigenous</u> American musical form, **jazz** is a musical form based on improvisation. Jazz musicians creatively recombine different forms of music, including African American blues and ragtime, and European-based popular music.

**A Unique American Music Emerges** Jazz emerged in the South and Midwest, particularly New Orleans, where different cultures and traditions came together and influenced each other. Early jazz artists won fame playing in

**Vocabulary Builder**
<u>indigenous</u>—(ihn DIHJ uh nuhs) *adj.* native to; growing out of a particular region or country

Storyville, a section of New Orleans known for its night life. From the South, it spread north with the Great Migration of African Americans.

Trumpet player **Louis Armstrong** became the unofficial ambassador of jazz. After playing with King Oliver's band in New Orleans and Chicago and with Fletcher Henderson's orchestra in New York, Armstrong began to organize his own groups. His ability to play the trumpet and his subtle sense of improvisation made him a legend and influenced the development of jazz. After Armstrong, all jazz bands featured soloists. Many also began to feature vocal soloists, such as **Bessie Smith,** the "Empress of the Blues."

**Jazz Wins Worldwide Popularity** Jazz was more than a musical style. It was also a symbol of the Roaring Twenties. It was part of the Prohibition era, played in speakeasies and nightspots in New York, Chicago, St. Louis, and Los Angeles. It was the sound of the Cotton Club, one of Harlem's most famous attractions, where African Americans played African American music to all-white audiences. Phonograph records and radio spread the influence of jazz across the country and beyond. By the end of the decade, the popularity of jazz had spread to Europe as well.

But jazz was still more. It was a demonstration of the depth and richness of African American culture. Gerald Early, a modern scholar of English and African American studies, predicted that, in the future, America will be best remembered for three great contributions—the Constitution, baseball, and jazz. All three enriched lives, opened windows to new possibilities, and lifted the human spirit. Jazz announced that the United States was a land of shared cultures and traditions, a place where people came together and created something greater than their parts.

Jazz quickly bridged the races. Trumpeter Bix Beiderbecke (BĪ der behk) became the first white musician to contribute to the styles and popularity of jazz. Jazz sounds influenced such white songwriters and composers as Cole

**Stars of the Jazz Age** 🔊 AUDIO
Not only was Louis Armstrong (below left) an influential trumpeter, he also pioneered "scat," a style in which the singer improvises meaningless syllables that mimic the sounds of musical instruments. The recordings and concerts of blues singer Bessie Smith (below right) made her the highest-paid African American entertainer of the 1920s.

Porter, Irving Berlin, and George Gershwin, whose jazz-inspired orchestral work *Rhapsody in Blue* premiered in 1924. The title of a song by African American band leader Duke Ellington best captures how jazz changed popular music: "It Don't Mean a Thing If It Ain't Got That Swing."

✔ **Checkpoint** How did jazz spread from its roots in the South to the North in the 1920s?

### Duke Ellington (1899–1974)
Duke Ellington became one of the most important early figures in jazz and probably its greatest composer. He gained fame in the 1920s, when his band played in Harlem nightclubs. Hiring many skilled musicians, he arranged his music to showcase their talents. Ellington wrote or arranged about two thousand pieces of music that range from popular songs to ballets and movie music. Before his death, he had been awarded the highest honors from the governments of both the United States and France.

# The Harlem Renaissance

Jazz and blues were expressions of the African American experience. The pain of the African American experience can be heard in the blues, and the joy of that experience in the soaring notes of jazz. The range of such African American musicians as Duke Ellington and Cab Calloway speaks to the varieties of African American life. But in the 1920s, there were other expressions of African American culture. Novelists, poets, and artists celebrated their culture and explored questions of race in America. This flowering of African American culture became known as the **Harlem Renaissance**. The Harlem Renaissance helped give a new vocabulary and dynamic to race relations in the United States.

**African American Literature Flowers** In the 1920s, the term the "New Negro" entered the American vocabulary. It suggested a radical break with the past. No longer would African Americans silently endure the old ways of exploitation and discrimination. The new mood was most vividly expressed in Harlem, which attracted African American novelists, essayists, poets, and journalists from all over the country and beyond. In their work, these writers explored the pains and joys of being black in America, leaving a literary legacy that spoke to all Americans of all times.

Jean Toomer's *Cane* (1923) set the tone for the Harlem Renaissance. A collection of short stories, poems, and sketches, *Cane* presented African American life and folk culture in all its richness. It was not a blueprint for where African Americans needed to move politically in the future, but a plea to remember and preserve the past.

Soon, other African American writers joined Toomer at the forefront of the Harlem Renaissance. Jamaican immigrant **Claude McKay** was the most militant of these writers. In his novels and poems, McKay showed ordinary African Americans struggling for dignity and advancement in the face of discrimination and economic hardships. A poem that McKay wrote after Chicago was stricken by violent race riots captured his sense of anger and militancy:

### Primary Source
"If we must die—let it not be like hogs,
Hunted and penned in an inglorious spot.
While round us bark the mad and hungry dogs,
Marking their mark at our accursed lot. . . .
What though before us lies the open grave?
Like men we will face the murderous, cowardly pack,
Pressed to the wall, dying but fighting back!"
—Claude McKay, "If We Must Die"

McKay represented the political and ideological left wing of the Harlem Renaissance. More in the center was **Langston Hughes,** probably the most powerful African American literary voice of his time. For Hughes, the force of the movement was not politics but a celebration of African American culture and life. (See the American Literature feature on the next page.) In more than 50 works of fiction, poetry, journalism, and criticism, he captured the remarkable diversity of everyday African American life. In the last line of his autobiography *The Big Sea*, Hughes wrote, "Literature is a big sea full of many fish. I let down my nets and pulled. I'm still pulling."

Another powerful voice was **Zora Neale Hurston.** Hurston traveled the rural back roads of her native Florida, collecting folk tales in books such as *Mules and Men*. But Hurston also looked to the future. Her 1937 novel *Their Eyes Were Watching God* expressed the new longing for independence felt by many women, black and white.

**The Harlem Renaissance Has Lasting Impact** The Harlem Renaissance gave a voice to African American culture, just as jazz and blues gave it a tune. It altered the way many white Americans viewed African American culture, and even the way African Americans viewed themselves. James Weldon Johnson, poet and secretary of the NAACP, noted:

> **Primary Source** "A great deal has been accomplished in this decade of 'renaissance.' . . . Today, one may see undesirable stories, but one may also read stories about Negro singers, Negro actors, Negro authors, Negro poets. The connotations of the very word *Negro* have changed. A generation ago many Negroes were half or wholly ashamed of the term. Today, they have every reason to be proud of it."
> —James Weldon Johnson, article in *Harper's* magazine, 1928

The Harlem Renaissance ended with the national financial collapse that also ended the nation's decade of prosperity. But the sense of group identity and African American solidarity that it created would become part of the bedrock on which the later civil rights movement would be constructed.

✓ **Checkpoint** What themes did Langston Hughes and Zora Neale Hurston explore?

▲ Zora Neale Hurston

---

SECTION **5** Assessment

**Progress Monitoring *Online***
For: Self-test with vocabulary practice
Web Code: nea-0708

## Comprehension

**1. Terms and People** For each of the following, write a sentence explaining the importance of that person or item to the development of African American culture.
- Marcus Garvey
- jazz
- Louis Armstrong
- Bessie Smith
- Harlem Renaissance
- Claude McKay
- Langston Hughes
- Zora Neale Hurston

**2. NoteTaking Identify Main Ideas** Use your section outline to answer the Section Focus Question: How did African Americans express a new sense of hope and pride?

## Writing About History

**3. Compare and Contrast** Write a thesis statement and introductory paragraph for an essay in which you compare the influence of jazz to the influence of the Harlem Renaissance. Consider both the similarities and differences in the two cultural developments.

## Critical Thinking

**4. Identify Points of View** Why do you think Marcus Garvey rejected the goals of earlier African American leaders such as Washington and Du Bois?

**5. Analyze Information** How did jazz blend cultural influences and cross-cultural divides?

**6. Identify Main Ideas** Restate the main idea of Claude McKay's poem "If We Must Die" in your own words.

▲ Langston Hughes

**MI** 6.3.2e

## *Two Poems* by Langston Hughes

Langston Hughes wrote about how it felt to be African American, from the pain of racial prejudice to his deep pride in his culture and heritage. The two poems below are among his most famous.

### The Negro Speaks of Rivers
I've known rivers:
I've known rivers ancient as the world and older than the flow of human
    blood in human veins.

My soul has grown deep like the rivers.

I bathed in the Euphrates when dawns were young.[1]
I built my hut near the Congo and it lulled me to sleep.
I looked upon the Nile and raised the pyramids above it.
I heard the singing of the Mississippi when Abe Lincoln went down to
    New Orleans, and I've seen its muddy bosom turn all golden in the
    sunset.

I've known rivers:
Ancient, dusky rivers.

My soul has grown deep like the rivers.

### My People
The night is beautiful,
So the faces of my people.

The stars are beautiful,
So the eyes of my people.

Beautiful, also, is the sun.
Beautiful, also, are the souls of my people.

Harlem street scene,
1920s ▶

### Thinking Critically
1. **Analyze Literature** In "The Negro Speaks of Rivers," what point do you think Hughes is making when he names four rivers at four different periods of history?

2. **Make Inferences** How would you describe the speaker's attitude toward being African American in these poems?

1. The Euphrates is a river in the Middle East. The Nile and the Congo are rivers in Africa.

# Quick Study Guide

 6.1.5e

**Progress Monitoring *Online***
**For:** Self-test with vocabulary practice
**Web Code:** nea-0709

## ■ Rise of the Automobile

- Decline of railroads, trolleys
- Higher wages for auto workers
- Mass production; lower prices
- **Rise of the Automobile**
- Greater freedom
- Growth of suburbs
- Highway system
- Growth in related industries

## ■ Economic Policies of Harding and Coolidge

| Goal: Support Economic Growth | | |
|---|---|---|
| **Policy: Raise Tariffs** | **Policy: Cut Government Spending** | **Policy: Support Business** |
| • Increased sales of domestic goods<br>• Led to tariff war with foreign nations | • Cut national debt<br>• Created federal budget surplus | • Encouraged business growth through tax incentives and reduced regulations<br>• Caused organized labor to lose ground |

## ■ Urban and Rural Population, 1900–1930

SOURCE: U.S. Census Bureau

## ■ New Cultural Trends

| Mass culture | Radio and movies unite people of different regions. |
|---|---|
| Prohibition | Crime rises as people find ways to avoid the ban on alcohol. |
| Fundamentalism | Many Christians promote a literal interpretation of the Bible and return to traditional values. |
| Modernism | Literature and art depict postwar disillusionment and the influence of the subconscious on human behavior. |
| Jazz | Musical style blends elements of African American and European forms. |
| Harlem Renaissance | Literature and art express pride and aspirations of African Americans. |

## ☑ Quick Study Timeline

**In America**

**1919** Eighteenth Amendment is ratified

**1920** Warren Harding elected President

**1922** Investigations into Teapot Dome scandal begin

| Presidential Terms | Woodrow Wilson 1913–1921 | Warren Harding 1921–1923 |
|---|---|---|

**1919** — **1921** — **1923**

**Around the World**

**1919** Paris peace conference meets

**1921** World Court is founded in the Netherlands

**1923** Reparations contribute to inflation in Germany

# American Issues
## Connector

6.1.3c

By connecting prior knowledge with what you have learned in this chapter, you can gradually build your understanding of enduring questions that still affect America today. Answer the questions below. Then, use your American Issues Connector study guide (or go online: www.PHSchool.com **Web Code:** neh-8003).

## Issues You Learned About

● **U.S. Immigration Policy** The U.S. government makes decisions about how many immigrants to allow into the country.

1. In the mid-1800s, the United States experienced a wave of immigration. From which countries did the majority of these immigrants come?

2. What measures had been taken to restrict immigration before the 1920s?

3. Was the National Origins Act biased? Explain.

● **Women in American Society** Women's roles in society continue to change and evolve, allowing women greater opportunities.

4. What amendment gave women the right to vote, and when was it ratified?

5. What immediate changes were the result of women's winning the right to vote?

6. How did the role of women in society change in the 1920s?

● **Technology and Society** New technological developments continually change the way Americans work and play.

7. Prior to the automobile, what inventions in transportation transformed the way people and goods traveled in the United States?

8. What social changes did the automobile bring to America?

9. What other technological changes affected American culture in the 1920s?

### Connect to Your World | Michigan

**Migration and Urbanization** The new laws that sharply reduced immigration to the United States in the 1920s had a major impact on Detroit. Thousands of booming Detroit factories—including almost 300 related to the automobile industry—needed a new source of affordable labor to replace immigrant workers. Ford had already started recruiting African American workers for low-level jobs during World War I. African Americans, suffering from poverty and discrimination in the South, needed little urging. In 1920, just over 40,000 African Americans lived in Detroit. In 1922, 3,500 African Americans came to Detroit each month. By the end of the decade, the city's African American population had nearly tripled to more than 120,000. Do research to learn more about the opportunities and challenges that faced African Americans in 1920s Detroit and discuss your findings with a small group.

---

**History** *Interactive*

**For:** Interactive timeline
**Web Code:** nep-0711

**1924**
**National Origins Act sets up quota system for immigration**

**1925**
**Scopes trial begins in Tennessee**

**1927**
*The Jazz Singer*, **first talking movie, opens**

**1929**
**Stock market crash marks end of 1920s prosperity**

Calvin Coolidge 1923–1929

Herbert Hoover 1929–1933

**1925**　　　　　**1927**　　　　　**1929**

**1924**
**Stalin comes to power in the Soviet Union**

**1927**
**Civil war begins in China**

**1928**
**Major nations sign Kellogg-Briand Pact to ban war**

# Chapter Assessment

## Terms and People

1. Define **bull market.** How did it affect the investment activities of Americans?

2. Who was **Andrew Mellon**? What economic goals did he achieve?

3. What was the **Eighteenth Amendment**? Which lawmakers supported it?

4. Define **modernism.** Explain how modernist ideas could be viewed in literature.

5. What was the **Harlem Renaissance**? Name and describe the accomplishments of two people who took part in it.

## Focus Questions

The focus question for this chapter is **How did the United States experience both economic growth and social change in the decade after World War I?** Build an answer to this big question by answering the focus questions for Sections 1 through 5 and the Critical Thinking questions that follow.

### Section 1

6. How did the booming economy of the 1920s lead to changes in American life?

### Section 2

7. How did domestic and foreign policy change direction under Harding and Coolidge?

### Section 3

8. How did Americans differ on major social and cultural issues?

### Section 4

9. How did the new mass culture reflect technological and social changes?

### Section 5

10. How did African Americans express a new sense of hope and pride?

## Critical Thinking

11. **Analyze Evidence** What evidence supports the conclusion that Henry Ford cared about the quality of life of his workers?

12. **Predict Consequences** What likely happened in the 1930s to people who, in the 1920s, bought goods they could not afford on the installment plan?

13. **Analyze Information** Did Harding show good leadership of the country? Explain.

14. **Draw Inferences** Why did Congress support the Kellogg-Briand Pact even when lawmakers knew that its provision could not be enforced?

15. **Summarize** How could you describe the cultural differences between rural and urban Americans in the 1920s? What issues led to cultural clashes between the two groups?

16. **Analyze Information** What did athletes represent for Americans in the 1920s?

17. **Evaluate Information** List four changes that affected women in the 1920s. Which of these do you think had the most immediate effect? Which do you think was most important in the long term?

18. **Identify Central Issues** What did southern African Americans hope to find by moving north? Did they achieve their goals?

## Writing About History

**Writing a Comparison-and-Contrast Essay** Evaluations and interpretations of historical eras often change over time or differ from historian to historian. Write the introductory paragraph and outline for an essay comparing two historical views on one of the following topics: the prosperity of the 1920s; the presidency of Calvin Coolidge; the role of the United States in world affairs after World War I; the "New Woman."

### Prewriting

• Use Internet or library sources to find two different interpretations or descriptions of one of the topics above. You may use this textbook as one of your sources.

• Make a Venn diagram to identify similarities and differences in the two articles.

### Drafting

• Develop a working thesis in which you define the differences between the two historical interpretations.

• Write an opening paragraph in which you introduce the topic and summarize the major differences between your two sources.

• Make an outline organizing your supporting details.

### Revising

• Use the guidelines on page SH11 of the Writing Handbook to revise your writing.

# Prepare for the MME

6.1.5b,
6.1.5d

## Scientific Management and Mass Production

The legacy of Henry Ford included not only the popularly priced automobile but techniques of mass production. What were his goals in introducing these techniques, and what impact did they have? Use your knowledge of the chapter material and Documents A, B, C, and D to answer questions 1 through 4.

### Document A

"If you and your workman have become so skillful that you and he together are making two pairs of shoes in a day, while your competitor and his workman are making only one pair, it is clear that after selling your two pairs of shoes you can pay your workman much higher wages than your competitor who produces only one pair of shoes is able to pay his man, and that there will still be enough money left over for you to have a larger profit than your competitor. . . . The greatest permanent prosperity for the workman, coupled with the greatest prosperity for the employer, can be brought about only when the work of the establishment is done with the smallest combined expenditure of human effort, plus nature's resources, plus the cost for the use of capital in the shape of machines, buildings."

—*Frederick Taylor*, Principles of Scientific Management, *1911*

### Document B

"[In 1914], Ford announced that he would nearly double the minimum salary paid to his 13,600 workers to $5 a day, and reduce the workday from nine hours to eight. In a stroke, he transformed the people who manufacture automobiles into the people who buy them. . . . The reaction from business thinkers was generally negative. 'He's crazy, isn't he?' asked Adolph Ochs, publisher of the *New York Times*. . . . The *Wall Street Journal* went even further, accusing Ford of having 'committed economic blunders, if not crimes' and applying 'spiritual' principles where they don't belong.'"

—*Kevin Baker*, "Ford's Paradox," *2000*

### Document C

Assembly line at Ford auto plant, 1928

### Document D

"We have decided upon and at once put into effect through all the branches of our industries the five day week. Hereafter there will be no more work with us on Saturdays and Sundays. These will be free days, but the men, according to merit, will receive the same pay equivalent as for a full six day week. . . . It does not pay to put men at work, excepting in continuous operations, from midnight until morning. As a part of low cost production—and only low cost production can pay high wages—one must have a big investment in machinery and power plants. Expensive tools cannot remain idle. They ought to work twenty-four hours a day, but here the human element comes in, for although many men like to work all night and have part of their day free, they do not work so well and hence it is not economical, or at least that is our experience, to go through the full twenty-four hours."

—*Henry Ford*, "Why I Favor Five Days' Work With Six Days' Pay," *1926*

---

1. Documents C and D provide evidence that Henry Ford
   A applied the principles described in Document A.
   B disagreed with the principles described in Document A.
   C had influenced the writer of Document A.
   D had listened to the criticisms of the business leaders quoted in Document B.

2. According to Document B, why did many business leaders disapprove of Ford's wage plan?
   A It did not take the well-being of his workers into account.
   B It was not based on accepted business principles.
   C It violated antitrust laws.
   D It would give Ford an unfair advantage over his competitors.

3. According to Document D, why did Ford institute the five-day workweek?
   A If his machinery was not used over the weekend, it would last longer.
   B His company would save money if he could pay his workers for only five days' work instead of six.
   C He was giving in to the demands of labor unions for a shorter workweek.
   D The five-day workweek would allow maximum productivity and efficiency.

4. **Writing Task** Who was right: Henry Ford or his critics? Use your knowledge of the chapter content and specific evidence from the primary sources above to support your opinion.

# 8

# The Great Depression
## 1928–1932

## The Depression Descends on America

No one who lived through the Great Depression ever forgot it. Panicked investors watched their fortunes dwindle to nothing overnight. Jobless men trudged anywhere and everywhere looking for work. The hungry lined up for handouts from churches and charitable organizations. Misery stalked Americans at virtually every turn. One survivor of the Depression remembered:

❝There were many beggars, who would come to your back door, and they would say they were hungry. I wouldn't give them money because I didn't have it. But I did take them in and put them in my kitchen and give them something to eat.❞
—Kitty McCulloch

*Listen to the* Witness History *audio to hear more about the Great Depression.*

◄ A poor family from rural Maryland poses for a photograph.

Stock ticker machine

Magazine cover from the early 1930s

 **Content Expectations**

**Chapter Focus Question: How did the Great Depression happen, and how did Americans respond to it?**

### Section 1
Causes of the Depression    7.1.2a, 7.1.2b, 7.1.2c

### Section 2
Americans Face Hard Times    6.1.3e, 7.1.2a, 7.1.2b

### Section 3
Hoover's Response Fails    6.3.1, 7.1.2b, 7.1.2c

World War I victory medal worn by Bonus Army veteran

Use the ☑ **Quick Study Timeline** at the end of this chapter to preview chapter events.

> **Note Taking Study Guide *Online***
> **For:** Note Taking and American Issues Connector
> **Web Code:** nee-8101

▲ Stock ticker tape

◀ An affluent middle-class family, 1925

WITNESS HISTORY 🔊 AUDIO

**Stock Market Prosperity**

As the 1920s roared along, millions of Americans poured their savings into the soaring "bull" market. Excited investors bought and sold stocks based on "tips" from friends or brokers. Many investors amassed huge fortunes on the strength of rising stock prices. Families who had to scrimp and save at the beginning of the decade found themselves fabulously wealthy by its end. In 1929, a prominent magazine printed a poem that captured the essence of America's market fever:

❝Oh, hush thee, my babe, granny's bought some more shares,
Daddy's gone out to play with the bulls and the bears,
Mother's buying on tips and she simply can't lose,
And baby shall have some expensive new shoes!❞
—*The Saturday Evening Post,* 1929

# Causes of the Depression

### Content Expectations

- **7.1.2a** Analyze political, economic, environmental, social causes of Great Depression.
- **7.1.2b** Analyze economic/social toll of Great Depression.
- **7.1.2c** Analyze Hoover's policies and their impact.

### Terms and People

| | |
|---|---|
| Herbert Hoover | business cycle |
| speculation | Great Depression |
| Black Tuesday | Hawley-Smoot Tariff |

### NoteTaking

**Reading Skill: Recognize Multiple Causes**
Identify the causes of the Great Depression.

Uneven distribution of wealth

Depression Causes

**Why It Matters** During the Roaring Twenties, many Americans enjoyed what seemed like an endless era of prosperity. Then, in October 1929, the mighty bull market crashed. As production fell and unemployment rose, the U.S. economy lurched into a period of dramatic decline. Years after the Great Depression began, many Americans came to see this contraction as a regular feature of the nation's business cycle. **Section Focus Question: How did the prosperity of the 1920s give way to the Great Depression?**

## Prosperity Hides Troubles

In 1928, Republican leaders exuded confidence about both their party and their country. The Roaring Twenties had been a Republican decade. In 1920, Americans sent Warren G. Harding to the White House, and four years after that they sent Calvin Coolidge. Neither election had been close.

Once in office, both Presidents watched the country grow increasingly prosperous. As the decade passed, consumption went up, the gross national product went up, and the stock market went up. No matter what index an economist chose to consult, the conclusion was always the same: Times were good in America—and they were getting better. Republicans took credit for the bullish economy, and Americans heartily agreed.

**Optimism Sweeps Hoover to Victory** When the Republicans met at their 1928 nominating convention, they chose **Herbert Hoover**—an accomplished public servant—to run for the White House. Born in Iowa, Hoover was orphaned as a child. But he overcame this personal tragedy and eventually graduated from Stanford University with a degree in geology. He became a mining engineer and worked all over the world. By 1914, after amassing a vast fortune, he retired from engineering and devoted himself to public service.

Herbert Hoover came to the attention of Americans during World War I, first as the brilliant coordinator of the Belgium relief program and then as head of the Food Administration. During the Harding and Coolidge administrations, Hoover served as Secretary of Commerce. His philosophy was simple but effective. He stressed the importance of competition, but he also believed in voluntary cooperation between labor and management. American greatness showed itself, Hoover maintained, when owners, workers, and government officials <u>converged</u> on common goals.

With a solid record of accomplishments behind him and seemingly endless prosperity in front of him, Hoover was a formidable presidential candidate in 1928. While his campaign ads noted how Republicans had "put the proverbial 'chicken in every pot,'" Hoover spoke glowingly of ending poverty in America:

> **Primary Source** "By adherence to the principles of decentralized self-government, ordered liberty, equal opportunity, and freedom to the individual, our American experiment in human welfare has yielded a degree of well-being unparalleled in all the world. It has come nearer to the abolition of poverty, to the abolition of fear of want, than humanity has ever reached before."
>
> —Herbert Hoover, campaign speech, 1928

Hoover's contest with Democratic nominee Alfred E. Smith of New York was, in the end, no contest at all. Americans voted overwhelmingly for Hoover, prosperity, and the continuation of Republican government. When the new President took office in March 1929, America was awash in a sea of confidence. Few imagined that an economic disaster lay just seven months in the future.

But even as Hoover delivered his victory speeches, economic troubles were beginning to worry some Americans. The prosperity of the 1920s was not as deep or as sturdy as Hoover claimed. Throughout the U.S. economy, there were troubling signs.

**Problems Plague the Agricultural Sector** American farmers faced difficult times during the 1920s. Farmers made up one fourth of the American workforce during the decade. To meet the unprecedented crop demands created by World War I, they had increased harvest yields and bought more land to put under the plow. They also bought costly tractors and other mechanized farm equipment. Farmers contracted huge debts doing this, and the additional mortgage payments followed them into the 1920s.

After the war, the demand for American crops fell sharply. Despite this drop, postwar production remained high because of increasingly mechanized farm equipment and more intensive farming methods. Farms were getting bigger and yielding bumper crops at harvest. However, farmers were failing to sell off their huge crop surpluses and to pay the debts they owed banks and other institutions.

The result was a rural depression that affected millions of Americans. Hard-pressed to pay their debts, forced to sell in a glutted and competitive world market, and confronted by several natural disasters, farmers did not share in the boom times of the 1920s. They did not have the cash to buy the new consumer goods produced by

**Vocabulary Builder**
<u>converge</u>–(kuhn VERJ) *v.* to move or be directed toward the same purpose or result

**Farmers Struggle to Get By**
Farmers who could not meet their debts faced bank foreclosures on their land, equipment, and livestock. Here, a horse is paraded in front of prospective buyers at a Missouri farm sale.

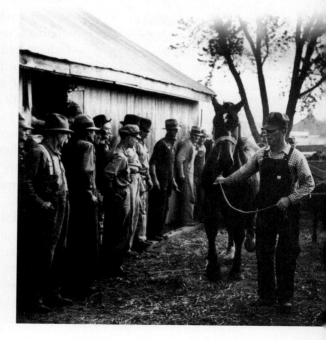

# Causes of the Great Depression

Lured by luxury and easy credit, many Americans bought expensive new cars during the 1920s. ▼

**H**istory remembers the 1920s as a decade of bull markets and new fortunes. However, by 1929, the surging American economy was on the brink of financial collapse. Soaring stock prices made rich people richer and concentrated more wealth into fewer hands. Excited by a stream of new products and buyer-friendly payment plans, consumers piled up huge debts as they purchased goods on credit. Everywhere, the economy expanded, soaring toward its peak in the summer of 1929 and then pausing on the verge of contraction—and economic chaos. (See the diagram below.)

### The Business Cycle

Peak — Expansion — Contraction — Trough — Expansion — Peak — Contraction — Expansion — Trough

Declining production, employment, and income

Rising production, employment, and income

## Consumer Debt, 1921–1929

Dollars (in billions)

8
6
4
2
0

1921 1923 1925 1927 1929

SOURCE: *Historical Statistics of the United States*

▲ American consumers racked up more than $6 billion of debt by 1929—more than double what they owed at the beginning of the decade.

American industries. They lived largely on credit from month to month, often teetering on the brink of financial ruin. Any downward slide in the economy was likely to hit America's struggling farmers first and hardest.

**Wealth Is Distributed Unevenly** Unlike farmers, industrial workers participated in the great national success story. During the 1920s, their wages rose steadily, as did their disposable income. Many purchased Model T Fords along with a variety of other consumer products. Though they were certainly not wealthy, industrial laborers were in a better financial position than their fathers had been a generation before.

But the problem was that while wages rose gradually, worker productivity increased astronomically. Between 1923 and 1929, output per person-hour jumped 32 percent, but workers' wages inched up only 8 percent. During that same period, corporate profits from worker output skyrocketed 65 percent. All these figures pointed to the fact that during the 1920s, the rich became much, much richer, while industrial workers simply became less poor. In few periods of the country's history have so small a number of rich Americans dominated such a large percentage of the country's total wealth. In 1929, for example, the wealthiest 1 percent of the population earned about the same amount of money as the bottom 42 percent.

This uneven distribution of the nation's wealth created economic problems. More than 60 percent of all American families had yearly incomes of less than $2,000 per year. Twenty-four thousand of the country's wealthiest families enjoyed annual incomes of more than $100,000, which was 50 times more than what most families were earning. But these wealthy families did not eat 50 times more food than lower-income families. The wealthiest households did not

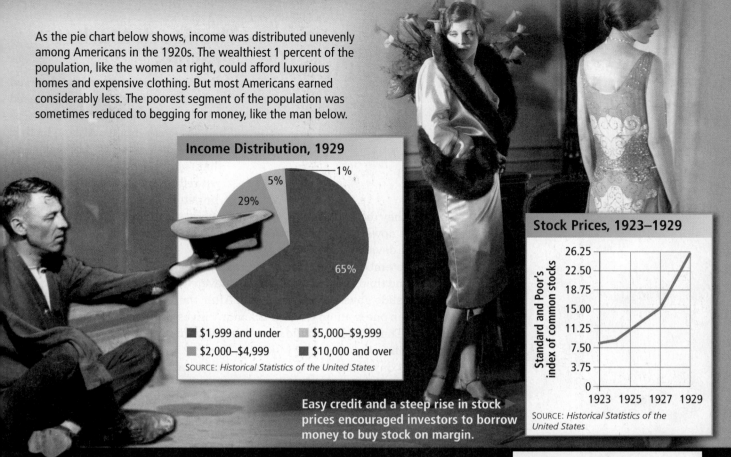

As the pie chart below shows, income was distributed unevenly among Americans in the 1920s. The wealthiest 1 percent of the population, like the women at right, could afford luxurious homes and expensive clothing. But most Americans earned considerably less. The poorest segment of the population was sometimes reduced to begging for money, like the man below.

**Income Distribution, 1929**

- 1%
- 5%
- 29%
- 65%

Legend:
- $1,999 and under
- $2,000–$4,999
- $5,000–$9,999
- $10,000 and over

SOURCE: *Historical Statistics of the United States*

**Stock Prices, 1923–1929**

Standard and Poor's index of common stocks

26.25, 22.50, 18.75, 15.00, 11.25, 7.50, 3.75, 0

1923 1925 1927 1929

SOURCE: *Historical Statistics of the United States*

Easy credit and a steep rise in stock prices encouraged investors to borrow money to buy stock on margin.

purchase 50 times more automobiles or radios or ovens. The rich undoubtedly spent a lot on consumer products. The problem was that the wealthiest few did not buy enough to keep the economy booming.

A healthy economy needs more people to buy more products, which in turn creates even more wealth. In this way, a healthy economy avoids underconsumption that can limit economic growth. The uneven distribution of wealth in the 1920s pointed to an uncertain future for the American economy.

From the overproduction of the struggling farmer to the underconsumption of the lower-income industrial worker, deep-seated problems created economic instability. Too many Americans did not have enough money to buy what they needed or wanted.

**Easy Credit Hides Problems** For a time, the expansion of credit partially hid this problem. Americans bought automobiles, appliances, radios, and other goods on credit. Using the installment plan, they paid a small percentage down and the rest over a period of months or years. By the end of the decade, 80 percent of radios and 60 percent of cars were purchased on installment credit. Americans even bought stock on credit, making such stock purchases on margin. Every year, Americans accumulated more debt. In the past, they had feared debt and put off buying goods until they had the cash to pay for those items. However, easy credit changed this behavior during the 1920s. The growing credit burden could mask the problem of Americans living beyond their means for only so long before the economy imploded.

✔ **Checkpoint** What economic problems lurked beneath the general prosperity of the 1920s?

**Thinking Critically**

1. **Make Generalizations** Is it fair to suggest that the American economy stood "on thin ice" in 1929? Why or why not?

2. **Analyze Costs and Benefits** How did easy credit and buying stock on margin provide both costs and benefits to the U.S. economy?

## The Stock Market Crashes

By 1929, some economists observed that soaring stock prices were based on little more than confidence. Prices had no basis in reality. Although other experts disagreed, it became clear that too much money was being poured into stock **speculation.** Investors were gambling, often with money they did not even have, on stock increases to turn quick profits. If the market's upward climb suddenly reversed course, many investors would face economic devastation.

On September 3, 1929, the stock market began to sputter and fall. Prices peaked and then slid downward in an uneven way. At the end of October, however, the slide gave way to a free fall. After the Dow Jones average dropped 21 points in one hour on October 23, many investors concluded that the boom was over. They had lost confidence—the very thing that had kept the market up for so long.

The next day, October 24, came to be known as Black Thursday. With confidence in the stock market failing, nervous investors started to sell. Stock in General Electric that once sold at $400 a share plunged to $283. Across the United States, investors raced to pull their money out of the stock market. On October 29, **Black Tuesday,** the bottom fell out. More than 16 million shares were sold as the stock market collapsed in the Great Crash. Billions of dollars were lost. Whole fortunes were wiped out in hours. Many speculators who had bought stock on margin lost everything they had. President Hoover tried to soothe Americans by insisting that the "business of the country is on a sound and prosperous basis." But by November 13, the Dow Jones average had dropped like a brick from its September high of 381 to 198.7. The Great Crash represented another hallmark of the nation's **business cycle,** which explained the periodic growth and contraction of the economy.

 **Checkpoint** What happened on October 29, 1929?

## The Great Depression Begins

The stock market crash marked the beginning of the **Great Depression,** a period lasting from 1929 to 1941 in which the economy faltered and unemployment soared. Though it did not start the depression by itself, the crash sparked a chain of events that quickened the collapse of the U.S. economy.

**The Banks Collapse** One of the first institutions to feel the effects of the stock market crash was the country's banking system. The crisis in confidence continued as frightened depositors feared for their money and tried to withdraw it from their banks. Few banks could survive a sustained "run" of requests by depositors for their money. In 1929, 641 commercial banks failed. A year later, 1,350 failed. And a year after that, 1,700 went under. By 1932, many Americans believed that no banks would be left standing.

Another cause of many bank failures was misguided monetary policy. During the 1920s, the Federal Reserve, which regulates the amount of money in circulation, cut interest rates to stimulate economic growth. But in 1929, worried about investor overspeculation, the "Fed" limited the money supply to discourage lending. As a

### The Panic Spreads

The sudden collapse of stock prices sent brokers and investors into a panic throughout New York's financial district and across the country. A cartoonist for the *New York World* captured the feelings of many Americans in the aftermath of the Great Crash.

result, there was too little money in circulation to help the economy after the stock market crash. When plummeting stock prices sent investors to the banks to secure whatever hard money they had left, the banks were cleaned out of currency and forced to close.

**Businesses Close and Unemployment Rises** Banks were not the only institutions to face the harsh financial realities of the depression. The collapse of stock prices, combined with reduced consumer spending, spelled trouble for American businesses. Business leaders believed that the survival of their companies depended on production cutbacks, to maintain price levels, and layoffs, to reduce payroll. While their stocks were still falling, companies began closing plants and forcing workers onto the growing lists of the unemployed. In August 1931, Henry Ford closed several of his Detroit automobile factories, putting nearly 75,000 people out of work.

Like a snowball rolling down a hill, the problem of production cuts kept getting bigger and bigger. As businesses closed plants and fired workers to save money, more Americans lost their jobs. As unemployment grew and incomes shrank, consumers spent less money. So businesses cut production even more, closing more plants and firing more workers. By 1933, nearly 25 percent of all American workers had lost their jobs.

**Tariffs Add to the Woes** Hoping to reverse the downward slide, the government moved to protect American products from foreign competition. In June 1930, Congress passed the **Hawley-Smoot Tariff,** which raised prices on foreign imports to such a level that they could not compete in the American market. The tariff inspired European countries to retaliate and enact protective tariffs of their own.

Far from solving the problems of the depression, the Hawley-Smoot Tariff added to them. At a time when American manufacturers and farms had a glut of unsold products, the international move toward high protective tariffs closed markets. This closure was not just harmful to American producers. It was equally disastrous to the global economy. The ripple effect caused by the Hawley-Smoot Tariff helped to destroy international trade.

**The Depression Goes Global** The Hawley-Smoot Tariff was only one of the causes of a depression spreading across the globe. As we saw earlier, the European problems of reparation payments, war debt payments, and international imbalance of trade had already created a shaky economic structure. In the early 1930s, the structure collapsed. Germany ceased their reparation payments, and the United States agreed to suspend France and Britain's war debt payments. The international economy had largely been funded by American loans to Europe, but the crisis in the United States drastically curtailed those loans. As a result, European nations

## NoteTaking

**Reading Skill: Recognize Sequence** Use a flowchart to note what happened in the wake of the stock market crash.

| Stock market crashes |
|---|
| Commercial banks fail |
|  |
|  |

## Banks Fail

In 1931, more than 1,500 banks ran out of money and closed their doors. Depositors lost untold savings. Here, a crowd gathers outside the closed doors of a bank in New York City. *How might Americans react today if hundreds of banks failed?*

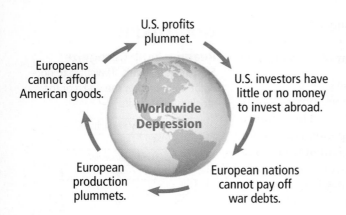

U.S. profits plummet.

Europeans cannot afford American goods.

Worldwide Depression

U.S. investors have little or no money to invest abroad.

European production plummets.

European nations cannot pay off war debts.

**Diagram Skills** The diagram above shows how the stock market collapse contributed to a global economic crisis. *How did European war debts affect the U.S. economy?*

experienced the same cycle of business failures, bank collapses, and high unemployment as the United States. The depression had become a global nightmare.

 **Checkpoint** How did the stock market crash contribute to the onset of the depression?

# What Caused the Great Depression?

Historians and economists disagree on the exact causes of the Great Depression. Some have stressed a single root cause in their explanations of the financial crisis. Milton Friedman, one economist, believed that the depression resulted from a contraction in the money supply. The twin events of the stock market crash in 1929 and the run of bank failures in 1930 left too little money in circulation for the nation's economic needs.

John Maynard Keynes was one of the most influential economists of the depression. He argued that the lack of government interference in the economy led to the depression. Critical problems in money supply, distribution of wealth, stock speculation, consumer spending, productivity, and employment could have been controlled, he said, by proactive government policies. Keynes's work points to a fundamental difference between many economists regarding the depression. While Keynes recommended that governments spend more money to keep people employed when the economy slows, other noted economists like Ludwig von Mises and Friedrich von Hayek criticized centralized economic planning and management.

There will never be a fully accepted answer to the question of what caused the Great Depression. But clearly, problems in consumption contributed heavily to it. Economic hardships before 1929 in Europe and rural America, coupled with an uneven distribution of wealth and overspeculation in the stock market, created dangerous economic conditions. When this was combined with poor or misinformed economic decisions by Congress and President Hoover, the Great Depression resulted.

 **Checkpoint** What were the primary causes of the Great Depression?

**Progress Monitoring *Online***
**For:** Self-test with vocabulary practice
**Web Code:** nea-0802

## Comprehension

1. **Terms** For each term below, write a sentence explaining its significance.
   • speculation
   • business cycle
   • Great Depression
   • Hawley-Smoot Tariff

2. **NoteTaking Reading Skill: Recognize Causes** Use your concept web to answer the Section Focus Question: How did the prosperity of the 1920s give way to the Great Depression?

## Writing About History

3. **Quick Write: Define a Problem** Choose one topic from this section that you could use to write a problem-solution essay. For example, you could write about the weaknesses in the agricultural sector of the economy. Make a list of details, facts, and examples that define the problems that this weakness poses to a stable economy.

## Critical Thinking

4. **Explain Causes** How did the uneven distribution of the nation's wealth weaken the American economy?

5. **Analyze Information** Why was recovery so difficult after the stock market crash?

6. **Draw Conclusions** Do you think the nation would have experienced an economic depression even if the stock market had not crashed? Why or why not?

◀ Hobos walk along a railroad line.

### Riding the Rails

As the country plunged deeper into the Great Depression, many young people left home, either out of necessity or to follow their dreams of a better life. Nearly a quarter million teenagers hit the road during the early 1930s, jumping freight trains to ride from town to town. Some looked for work, others thirsted for adventure, but all faced the dangers of the hobo life. Charley Bull, who left his California home at 18, recalled:

❝You could ride on top of a freight car and then you just had to be careful. If a train is going sixty or seventy miles an hour and hits a curve and you're walking and your back's to the turn and you don't see it coming—a little tiny turn can throw you right off the train. A lot of people have been killed like that.❞

—Charley Bull, from a PBS presentation "The American Experience—Riding the Rails"

# Americans Face Hard Times

## Content Expectations

- **6.1.3e** Analyze perspectives about immigrant experiences in the urban setting.
- **7.1.2a** Analyze political, economic, environmental, social causes of Great Depression.
- **7.1.2b** Analyze economic/social toll of Great Depression.

## Terms and People

bread line
Hooverville
tenant farmer

Dust Bowl
Okies
repatriation

## NoteTaking

**Reading Skill: Categorize** As you read, use a Venn diagram to note how the Great Depression affected both urban and rural America.

**In Cities**
- Production cutbacks in factories

• Unemployment
•

**On Farms**
- Falling commodity prices

**Why It Matters** The stock market crash signaled the end of boom times and the beginning of hard times. As investors mourned their losses, Americans watched the economy stagger into the Great Depression. In the cities and on the farms, desperate poverty gripped the nation. Even after prosperity returned, those who lived through the crisis would remember the pain and worries of the depression. Tested by extreme hardship, this generation of Americans forged a character and will strong enough to overcome economic ruin and restore prosperity. **Section Focus Question: How did the Great Depression affect the lives of urban and rural Americans?**

## Misery and Despair Grip America's Cities

The Great Depression had a deep and lasting impact on the lives of the people who lived through it. Few Americans grasped the underlying problems of the 1920s economy or the subtle reasons for the stock market crash. Fewer still comprehended how the crash led to the Great Depression. But they did understand the *impact* of the economic crisis. Workers understood having a job one day and being unemployed the next. Whole families knew the shame and fear of losing their homes.

The Great Depression touched every American because every American either experienced or knew someone who experienced the hardships and loss caused by the economic catastrophe. For many, their lives were never the same again.

## Bank Failures

## Business Failures

## Per Capita Income and Spending

- Average yearly income
- Average yearly spending

SOURCE: *Historical Statistics of the United States*

**Graph Skills** The year 1929 marked the start of a pronounced downturn in the American economy. *In what year did the largest number of banks fail? By roughly how much did Americans' average yearly income decrease between 1929 and 1933?*

**Searching for a Job and a Meal** The threat of unemployment and destitution haunted workers in cities and towns across the United States. Between 1921 and 1929, annual average unemployment rates had never risen above 3.7 percent. But then, the depression hit, and the rate shot up. By 1933, it had climbed to a shocking 24.9 percent.

Despite this high rate, millions of workers were able to keep their jobs. However, most had their wages or hours cut. Many workers brought home paychecks that were 10, 20, sometimes 30 percent less than their pre-depression checks.

Yet statistics tell only part of the story. The human drama of unemployment unfolded over and over again, in city after city across the nation. For a man employed as a factory worker, the 1920s had promised a chance at upward economic mobility. He had been able to provide for his family, enjoy a decent standard of living, and save something for retirement. Then, the depression hit. The man saw his hours cut and his workweek shortened. Eventually, he was laid off. Looking for another job, he trudged from one factory to the next. "No help wanted here" or "We don't need nobody" greeted him at every turn. The man's clothes began to look worn. His collars and cuffs became frayed, and his pants became shiny at the knees. He said less, stared more, moved slower.

Maybe his wife was able to find work washing and ironing clothes or laboring as a maid. But those jobs were hard to find, too. At home, children ate smaller meals. Water replaced milk. Meat disappeared from the table. Hunger lurked about the home like an unwanted guest. Sometimes, the parents and children received free meals in public soup kitchens. Often, the only place for the family to get a free scrap of food was in a **bread line,** where people lined up for handouts from charities or public agencies.

**Descending Into Poverty** Men like the factory worker just described moved from unemployed to unemployable. Whole families descended into hunger and homelessness. Their dreams of success and prosperity turned into nightmares of failure and poverty.

This feeling of loss—this sense of the "American Dream" betrayed—wove through the cultural fabric of the Great Depression. The widespread despair found expression in an early-1930s song by E. Y. Harburg. It tells the story of an American "Everyman," a worker who labored to build the country and a citizen soldier who fought to defend it. However, the depression has left him out of work, out of money, and out of dreams:

### Primary Source

"They used to tell me I was building a dream
And so I followed the mob.
When there was earth to plow or guns to bear,
I was always there, right on the job.
They used to tell me I was building a dream
With peace and glory ahead—
Why should I be standing in line,
Just waiting for bread?
Once I built a railroad, I made it run,
Made it run against time.
Once I built a railroad, now it's done—
Brother can you spare a dime?"

—song lyrics, "Brother Can You Spare a Dime?"

# Effects of the Great Depression

After the stock market crash, the American economy slowed to a crawl in the face of a devastating global Depression. Bank failures more than quadrupled from 1929 to 1933. Companies fired thousands of workers to keep from going out of business. As a result, unemployment soared, condemning a quarter of the American workforce to poverty. (See the line graph below.) Jobless people crowded outside employment offices, clamoring for work to put food on their tables. Life became a daily struggle for many Americans during these lean times.

**Top:** Women and children wait in a bread line set up by a religious mission.
**Center:** This 1932 cartoon summarized the feelings of many depositors when their banks failed.
**Bottom right:** Unable to support their families, some men gave in to despair.

Unemployed men wait for a chance to register for municipal jobs in New York City in 1933. ▼

**Unemployment, 1928–1933**

3% of workforce

25% of workforce

People (in millions) — 0, 3, 6, 9, 12, 15

1928 1929 1930 1931 1932 1933

SOURCE: *Historical Statistics of the United States*

**Thinking Critically**

1. **Analyze Information** How did the shrinking economy lead to increased layoffs of workers?

2. **Draw Conclusions** What effect might a high unemployment rate have on the wages of Americans who still had jobs?

Harburg said the song asked a simple question about the nature of the depression. "This is a man who says: I built the railroads. . . . I fought your wars. . . . [Why] should I be standing in line now? What happened to all this wealth I created?"

**Looking for a Place to Live** As Americans lost their jobs and ran through their savings, they had to scrounge wherever they could to keep from going hungry. They sold furniture, pawned jewelry, and moved to cheaper lodgings—anything to keep their pantries stocked and rents paid. In many cities, they ran out of money, were evicted from their homes, and ended up on the streets.

A field-worker's home in California

A family in Alabama

### Americans Face Hard Times

Photographs of the 1930s conveyed the gritty realism of daily life under the boot heels of hunger, homelessness, and destitution. Cartoonists of the time criticized political leaders, President Hoover foremost among them, for the parts they played in bringing about, or failing to prevent, the depression. *Judging from these images, what would it have been like to live in a Hooverville?*

Homeless people slept on park benches, in empty railway cars, or in cardboard boxes. Many grouped together in **Hoovervilles,** makeshift shantytowns of tents and shacks built on public land or vacant lots. Homeless people, some of whom had worked as skilled carpenters before the crisis, cobbled houses together out of lumber scraps, tar paper, tin, and glass. One of the largest Hoovervilles in the country sprang up in the middle of Central Park in New York City. There, the homeless covered themselves with newspapers, called Hoover blankets, to stay warm at night. They walked around looking for jobs with their empty pants pockets turned inside out, a sign of poverty known as Hoover flags.

Despite the difficulties of life during the depression, many Americans did what they could to boost morale and help their neighbors. During a New York City newspaper strike, Mayor Fiorello LaGuardia read comic strips to children over the radio. In Reading, Pennsylvania, members of the Taxpayers Protection League staged nonviolent protests to thwart evictions. Nevertheless, thousands of other Americans found no such escapes from their misery.

✓ **Checkpoint** How did the Great Depression affect American cities in the early 1930s?

## Poverty Devastates Rural America

In cities and towns across the nation, Americans faced a terrible plight. The numbers of the unemployed, homeless, and hopeless increased like a casualty list in some great war. In rural America, people fared no better. In fact, sometimes their condition was even worse. Farmers had been suffering even before the Great Depression. Falling commodity prices and accumulating debt had made it a struggle for farmers to keep their heads above water. Many failed to stay afloat and sank so deep that they lost their farms.

**Commodity Prices Plunge** But then the bottom fell out of the economy and the depression added more woes. Crop prices fell even further, and new debts were added to old debts. To make matters even worse, the Great Plains was suffering through a choking drought, an ecological disaster that lasted for years. As a result, many more farmers lost their farms and moved. They traveled about the country, looking for work and fighting for survival.

A sprawling Hooverville in Seattle, Washington

▲ A 1935 political cartoon criticizing Hoover

The basic reality of farm life was the low prices paid to farmers for crops they grew for market. In 1919, a bushel of wheat sold for $2.16; in 1932, it sold for 38 cents. A pound of cotton fetched 35.34 cents in 1919; the same pound fetched 6.52 cents in 1932. The sharp fall in prices was evident with other farm products—corn and beans, cattle and hogs. The income farmers generated was not enough to allow them to continue farming. They could not pay their debts, purchase more seed, repair equipment, and buy what their families needed to survive. Overburdened by the diminishing returns for their labor, some farmers buckled under the stress.

In Sioux City, Iowa, in 1932, the Sioux City Milk Producers Association threatened to strike if its members did not see higher profits for their milk. When the association's threats were ignored by local storeowners, farmers dumped 1,000 gallons of milk on a road outside the city. Despite such a <u>drastic</u>—and for many Americans unthinkable—action like this, farmers everywhere feared losing everything.

**Vocabulary Builder**
<u>drastic</u>–(DRAS tihk) *adj.* harsh or severe

**Farmers Lose Their Farms** Between 1930 and 1934, nearly one million farmers failed to pay their mortgages and lost their farms. Banks foreclosed on their lands and houses and repossessed their farming equipment. The bankers sold what they could at public auctions. Some farmers remained on the land as **tenant farmers,** working for bigger landowners rather than for themselves. Others drifted away from their communities, looking for some other kind of work.

Cesar Chavez, who later became a well-known labor organizer, recalled the troubles his proud father had during the depression. A California bank repossessed his father's small ranch, and the family was evicted from their house. Chavez remembered how it felt to lose his home:

> **Primary Source** 66We had been poor, but we knew every night there was a bed *there*, and *this* was our room. . . . But that all of a sudden changed. When you're small, you can't figure these things out. You know something's not right and you don't like it, but you don't . . . let that get you down. You sort of just continue to move.99
> —Cesar Chavez

Like the Chavez family, other farmers moved on after their losses. But for those who remained, Mother Nature dealt a cruel blow to already cruel times.

**History** *Interactive*

**For:** To learn more about the Dust Bowl
**Web Code:** nep-0809

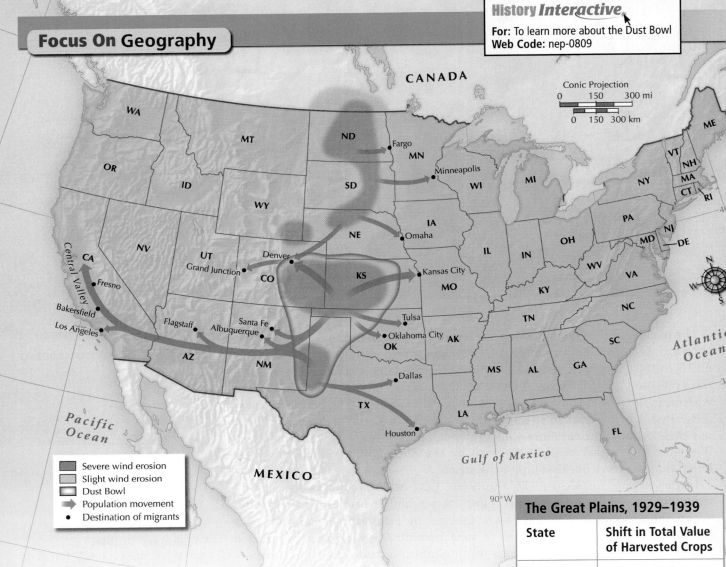

Legend:
- Severe wind erosion
- Slight wind erosion
- Dust Bowl
- → Population movement
- • Destination of migrants

Conic Projection
0   150   300 mi
0   150   300 km

| The Great Plains, 1929–1939 | |
| --- | --- |
| **State** | **Shift in Total Value of Harvested Crops** |
| Colorado | −51% |
| Kansas | −53% |
| Nebraska | −61% |
| New Mexico | −32% |
| North Dakota | −47% |
| Oklahoma | −49% |
| South Dakota | −57% |
| Texas | −45% |
| Wyoming | −40% |

# The Dust Bowl

By the middle of the 1930s, drought and wind had cut a huge swath of destruction down the middle of the continental United States. The "black blizzards" of the Dust Bowl soared to heights of 8,000 feet and swept like waves across towns and farms. Outside, rabbits, birds, and field mice suffocated and died in the swirling dust. Inside, dirt seeped through every crack and covered everything and everyone in layers of grit. "We live with the dust, eat it, sleep with it," observed one witness. A single storm could carry more than 300 million tons of dust, and constant storms in the "dirty thirties" destroyed as many as 5 million acres of wheat. Much of the Great Plains "breadbasket" simply blew away.

Whole harvests could be destroyed wherever dust storms struck. Many farmers went out of business as a result of their crop failures. ▶

A massive dust storm threatens the town of Stratford, Texas, in this photograph from 1935.

**Geography and History**
How did environmental change affect farmers living on the Great Plains during the 1930s?

**The Great Plains Becomes a Dust Bowl** Farmers who survived the tumble in prices were still not safe. Through the mid-1930s, a drought in the Great Plains added to their problems. Water was a constant problem in the region. Normal rainfall seldom exceeded the 20 inches a year that traditional American agricultural practices demanded. As a result, droughts on the Great Plains were often more devastating than those in the East and Midwest. In the years before America's western rivers were dammed and irrigation practices became widespread, there were few answers to the drought threat.

New farming methods made drought conditions worse. Intensive farming came to prominence throughout the region in the late nineteenth and early twentieth centuries. Farmers then had moved onto the plains and plowed under much of the natural grasses in order to plant oceans of winter wheat. The landscape shift tipped the ecological balance of the region. In the past, plains grasses prevented the topsoil from blowing away during periods of drought. By the early 1930s, that dwindling grassy safety net could no longer do the job.

By 1932, the combination of drought, loose topsoil, and high winds resulted in disaster on the Great Plains. The winds kicked up towering dust storms that began to blow east. These gigantic clouds of dust and dirt could rise from ground level to a height of 8,000 feet. The dust storms moved as fast as 100 miles per hour and blotted out the sun, plunging daylight into darkness.

Most of the dust storms started in the southern Great Plains, especially the high plains regions of Texas, Oklahoma, Kansas, New Mexico, and Colorado. This swath of parched earth became known as the **Dust Bowl.** For people living in these hardest hit regions, depression and dust storms defined the misery of the "dirty thirties."

Those unfortunate enough to be caught in a dust storm were temporarily choked and blinded by the swirling dirt. The storms killed cattle and birds, blanketed rivers, and suffocated fish. Dirt seeped into houses, covering everything with a thick coat of grime. Some dust clouds blew east as far as the Atlantic coast, dumping acres of dirt on Boston, New York, and Washington. Altogether, dust storms displaced twice as much dirt as Americans had scooped out to build the Panama Canal.

## Desperation Causes Migration
Many farm families trapped in the Dust Bowl had no choice but to migrate out of the region. They had lost their farms to the banks. Dust storms had destroyed most remaining opportunities. They were low on everything except despair. Although only some came from Oklahoma, Dust Bowl refugees were generally referred to as **Okies,** regardless of their states of origin.

Okie families packed onto rickety trucks and headed toward California or Oregon or Washington, any place where a job might be found. Before the pace slowed, 800,000 people migrated out of Missouri, Arkansas, Oklahoma, and Texas alone.

Agricultural collapse and the Great Plains Dust Bowl forced millions of Americans to leave the midwestern and southern regions where they had been born. Many moved to California, lured by the promise of jobs, but were crushed when that promise too often proved empty. Others headed to the cities of the Northeast and Midwest, again looking for jobs, shelter, and relief. As a result of the migration, rural states lost population while states with large cities gained population.

## WITNESS HISTORY DVD
Watch *The Dust Bowl* on the **United States Witness History DVD** to learn more about the causes and effects of the Dust Bowl.

## Okies Flee the Dust Bowl
The Okie exodus from the Great Plains carried thousands of Americans west to the rich farmlands of California. Okies also packed up and headed east to great industrial centers like Chicago, Pittsburgh, and New York. Here, a migrant family arrives in California.

There were other effects of the Dust Bowl. The farmers best able to survive the Great Depression were the ones with the biggest operations. They often bought repossessed land at rock-bottom prices and expanded their holdings into large commercial farms. The Dust Bowl also motivated the government to help Great Plains farmers. After the initial crisis, immense federal projects dammed western rivers. Dams eventually provided irrigation that made farm profits possible on the Great Plains.

✓ **Checkpoint** How did the Dust Bowl make life even more difficult for farmers on the Great Plains?

## Fierce Job Competition in California

As Okies flowed into California, Mexican and Mexican American migrants already there faced stiff new competition for scarce jobs. Here, a family of migrant farmworkers gathers outside their home in California's Imperial Valley. *What does the photograph suggest about the economic status of migrant workers in California?*

# Few Americans Escape Hard Times

One of the ironies of the depression was the word itself. In the nineteenth and early twentieth centuries, an economic slump was called a "panic" or a "crisis." President Hoover used the word *depression* to describe the state of affairs because he thought it sounded less severe than the other terms. But before long, Hoover's "depression" gave way to the "Depression" and then the "Great Depression." The term described not only a state of mind, but also an economic reality. It showed a despondent America, filled with people overwhelmed by seemingly inescapable poverty. Not only did the depression make victims of the men and women who lost jobs, it also was an economic and emotional crisis that profoundly affected Americans in all walks of life.

**The Depression Attacks Family Life** For millions of Americans, the depression was an intensely personal affair. Men who lost their jobs and could not find other work often felt that they had betrayed their families. They had been the "breadwinners," the providers, the ones whose paychecks fed and clothed the family and kept a roof over everyone's head. The loss of a job meant a reduction in status. Different men reacted differently to unemployment. Many labored tirelessly to find a new job, while others sank into shame and despair. Some even deserted their families.

The unemployed were not the only ones who suffered. Men lucky enough to have jobs lived in constant fear that the next paycheck would be their last. They often felt guilty for being employed while so many of their relatives and friends were suffering. Few Americans were spared from the crisis.

Wives and children experienced the pain of their husbands and fathers. Birthrates plummeted to the lowest marks in American history—a sure sign of family distress. Mothers worked constantly to stretch meager family incomes. They sewed clothes, searched for odd jobs, and valiantly tried to meet their families' needs. With both parents preoccupied with making something out of nothing, family discipline often declined. Some children quit school. Others ran away from home. Families coped with the depression as best they could. Some huddled together, working to survive the hard times. Others broke apart, making those times even harder and lonelier.

**Minorities Suffer Hardships** The depression affected everyone, but it did not affect them equally. Americans on the bottom rung of the economic ladder—the poorest of the poor, often minorities with no financial resources—felt the sting of the depression the keenest. A Howard University sociologist noted early in the crisis that African Americans were "the last to be hired and the first to be fired." In the South, landowners threw African American sharecroppers off the plots they had been farming. Many of these workers migrated to northern cities, but there were no jobs waiting there. Only more poverty greeted them. In 1932, unemployment among African Americans hovered around 50 percent, nearly double the national rate.

However, African Americans had long stood firm against the challenges of poverty. They relied on the emotional resources of family and religion to cope with grim times. During his interview with a depression historian, an African American man explained what the depression meant to African Americans:

> **Primary Source** "The Negro was born in depression. It didn't mean too much to him, The Great American Depression, as you call it. There was no such thing. The best he could be was a janitor or a porter or shoeshine boy. It only became official when it hit the white man."
>
> —Clifford Burke, quoted in *Hard Times,* 1970

Hard times came upon Mexican Americans as well. As more Okies headed west out of the Dust Bowl, the competition for jobs between those migrants and Mexican American farmworkers in states like California heated up. A flood tide of workers struggled to find and keep farm jobs. Often, Mexican Americans faced the additional burden of discrimination when competing with white farmhands for those jobs. In the Southwest, many white Americans clamored for Mexican American **repatriation.** Repatriation involved efforts by local, state, and federal governments to encourage or coerce Mexican immigrants and their naturalized children to return to Mexico. Hundreds of thousands of people of Mexican ancestry—many of them U.S. citizens—were pushed out of the United States. Even so, many more remained. By the end of the 1930s, Mexican Americans were working in most industries of the Southwest, including farming, ranching, and industry.

**Poverty in the South**
African Americans who had long faced discrimination and segregation were especially hard-hit by the depression. Many moved from the South to seek jobs in the North. Here, a man sits forlornly outside his home in Atlanta, Georgia.

✔ **Checkpoint** How did the depression take a toll on women, children, and minorities in America?

**SECTION 2 Assessment**

**Progress Monitoring *Online***
**For:** Self-test with vocabulary practice
**Web Code:** nea-0803

**Comprehension**

1. **Terms and People** What do each of the following terms have in common? Explain.
   - bread line
   - Hooverville
   - tenant farmer
   - Okies

2. **NoteTaking Reading Skill: Categorize** Use your Venn diagram to answer the Section Focus Question: How did the Great Depression affect the lives of urban and rural Americans?

**Writing About History**

3. **Quick Write: Brainstorm for Possible Solutions** Choose one topic from this section, such as skyrocketing unemployment in American cities, about which you could write a problem-solution essay. Use the text and your own knowledge to list possible solutions to the problem. Next, organize your list by ranking the solutions from most effective to least effective.

**Critical Thinking**

4. **Compare and Contrast** How were the experiences of the urban unemployed and the rural poor similar? How were they different?

5. **Recognize Effects** How do you think the arrival of so many Okies affected native Californians?

6. **Draw Inferences** Where might Americans have laid the blame for their difficulties during the early 1930s?

# EXPERIENCE THE GREAT DEPRESSION

**M**oviegoers cheered as Shirley Temple sang "Prosperity Is Just Around the Corner." Salvation Army volunteers handed out clothing and food to the needy. While some of the unemployed sold apples on sidewalks, others rioted in the streets.

There were many reactions to the Great Depression, some hopeful and some desperate, but everywhere Americans struggled to ease the daily burden of their poverty. The mayor of Youngstown, Ohio, captured the universality of the Depression when he described its victims laid low in his city: "These were old men gnarled by heavy labor, young mechanics tasting the first bitterness of defeat, clerks and white-collar workers learning the equality of misery, derelicts who fared no worse in bad times than in good, Negroes who only a short time before had come from Southern cotton fields, immigrants who had been lured to [the] 'land of youth and freedom'—each one a personal tragedy, and all together an overwhelming catastrophe for the nation. . . ."

As unemployment soared, the jobless often demonstrated against their former employers. A protest at a Ford Motor Company plant in March 1931 erupted in violence that left four workers dead. Here, a man is carried off during a demonstration in New York City. ▼

UNEMPLOYED BUY A...

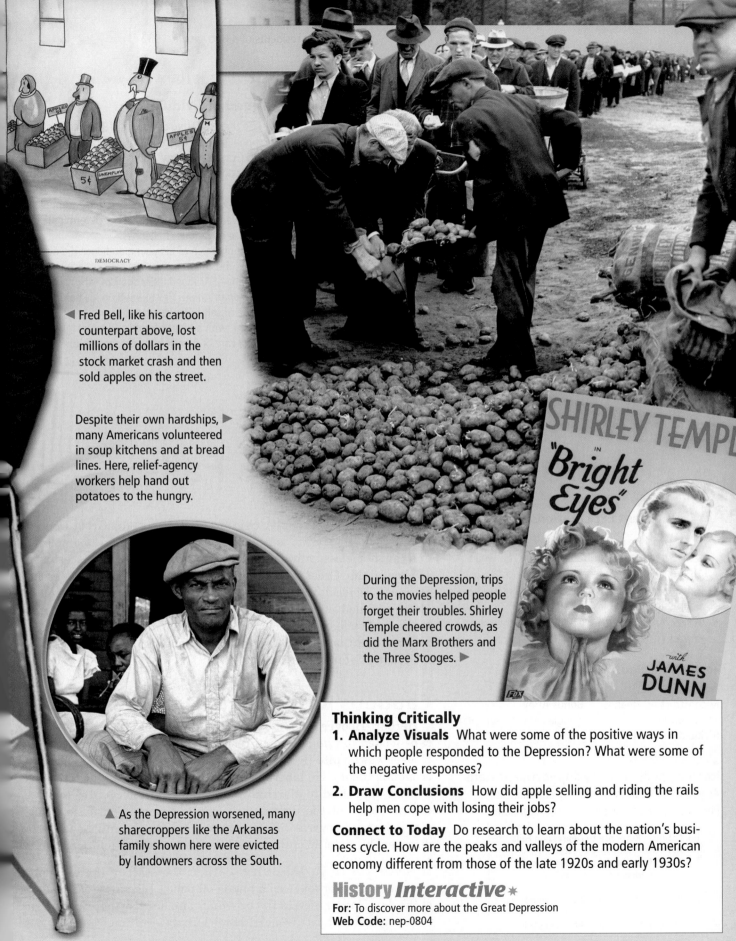

DEMOCRACY

◄ Fred Bell, like his cartoon counterpart above, lost millions of dollars in the stock market crash and then sold apples on the street.

Despite their own hardships, ► many Americans volunteered in soup kitchens and at bread lines. Here, relief-agency workers help hand out potatoes to the hungry.

During the Depression, trips to the movies helped people forget their troubles. Shirley Temple cheered crowds, as did the Marx Brothers and the Three Stooges. ►

SHIRLEY TEMPLE IN "Bright Eyes" with JAMES DUNN

▲ As the Depression worsened, many sharecroppers like the Arkansas family shown here were evicted by landowners across the South.

## Thinking Critically

1. **Analyze Visuals** What were some of the positive ways in which people responded to the Depression? What were some of the negative responses?

2. **Draw Conclusions** How did apple selling and riding the rails help men cope with losing their jobs?

**Connect to Today** Do research to learn about the nation's business cycle. How are the peaks and valleys of the modern American economy different from those of the late 1920s and early 1930s?

**History** *Interactive* ✴
**For:** To discover more about the Great Depression
**Web Code:** nep-0804

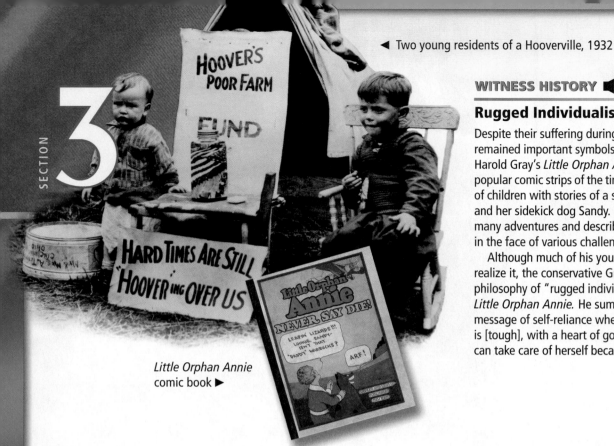

Two young residents of a Hooverville, 1932

*Little Orphan Annie*
comic book ▶

### Rugged Individualism

Despite their suffering during the 1930s, children remained important symbols of hope and resilience. Harold Gray's *Little Orphan Annie,* one of the most popular comic strips of the time, entertained millions of children with stories of a strong-willed orphan and her sidekick dog Sandy. Gray depicted Annie's many adventures and described her determination in the face of various challenges.

Although much of his young audience did not realize it, the conservative Gray was preaching a philosophy of "rugged individualism" through *Little Orphan Annie.* He summed up his heroine's message of self-reliance when he noted that "Annie is [tough], with a heart of gold and a fast left, [and] can take care of herself because she has to."

# Hoover's Response Fails

## Content Expectations

- **6.3.1** Describe problems/issues created by U.S.'s industrial/urban transformation between 1895–1930.
- **7.1.2b** Analyze economic/social toll of Great Depression.
- **7.1.2c** Analyze Hoover's policies and their impact.

## Terms and People

localism
Reconstruction Finance
 Corporation
trickle-down economics

Hoover Dam
Bonus Army
Douglas MacArthur

## NoteTaking

**Reading Skill: Identify Supporting Details**
As you read, fill in the outline with details about President Hoover's response to the depression.

> I. Cautious Response to Depression Fails
>   A. Hoover Turns to Volunteerism
>     1. Calls on business leaders to maintain employment, wages, prices
>     2.
>   B. Volunteerism Fails to Bring Relief
>     1.
> II. Hoover Adopts More Activist Policies

**Why It Matters** From big cities to small towns, the Great Depression spread misery far and wide across America. The unemployed and the homeless crowded into shantytowns. Giant dust storms swallowed the Great Plains. Yet as the crisis deepened, Herbert Hoover struggled to respond to the nation's problems. As a result of Hoover's failed response, in 1932 Americans would turn to a new leader and increased government intervention to stop the depression. **Section Focus Question: Why did Herbert Hoover's policies fail to solve the country's economic crisis?**

## Cautious Response to Depression Fails

Herbert Hoover did not cause the Great Depression. But Americans looked to him as their President to solve the crisis. He tried. Hoover was an intelligent man, familiar with business methods and economic theory. He labored long hours, consulted a wide range of experts, and tried to marshal the resources of the country to solve the problems of the depression. As the economic situation worsened, he tried several different approaches. In the end, he failed to discover the right formula, but it was not because of a lack of effort.

**Hoover Turns to Volunteerism** At the start of the economic downturn, Hoover followed a hands-off policy. Like most economists of the day, Hoover viewed the upswings and downswings of business cycles as natural occurrences. He felt that government should not interfere with such events. Periodic depressions were like storms. They could not be avoided, but strong businesses could weather them without the support of the government.

A policy of doing nothing, however, was no policy at all. Hoover soon recognized this fact and turned to a policy he had used in the past. As Secretary of Commerce during the 1920s, Hoover had motivated businessmen and laborers to voluntarily work toward common goals. To address the current crisis, he asked business and industrial leaders to keep employment, wages, and prices at current levels. He simultaneously called for the government to reduce taxes, lower interest rates, and create public-works programs. The plan was to put more money into the hands of businesses and individuals to encourage more production and consumption. This, Hoover said, would reverse the cycle that led to the depression.

**Vocabulary Builder**
simultaneously—(sī muhl TAY nee uhs lee) *adv.* done at the same time

Lastly, Hoover requested that wealthier individuals give more money to charity. Millions of Americans gave money, clothing, and food to private and religious charities, which in turn distributed the goods to those in need. The idea was for all Americans to voluntarily join forces to combat the depression.

**Volunteerism Fails to Bring Relief** Although the ideas behind the plan were sound, Hoover's program relied too much on voluntary cooperation. The President believed he could persuade Americans to act not in their own best interests but in those of the country as a whole. He was cautious to encourage, not legislate, America's recovery. But volunteerism did not work. Businesses cut wages and laid off workers because it was in their own best interests. Farmers boosted production because it was in the best interests of their families. Most Americans followed individual, not cooperative, courses.

Hoover had also asked state and local governments to provide more jobs and relief measures. He had faith in **localism,** the policy whereby problems could best be solved at local and state levels. However, towns and states simply did not have the financial or human resources to successfully combat the crisis. Making matters worse, the President strongly resisted using federal resources to provide direct relief to individuals. Believing it to be unconstitutional, Hoover opposed public assistance and instead favored "rugged individualism" so that people could better themselves through their own efforts. Yet as the months wore on, unemployment increased, charities ran low on money, and local and state governments could no longer plug the leaks in the economy. The crisis demanded decisive federal action.

✔ **Checkpoint** Why was Hoover reluctant to have the federal government interfere with the economy?

# Hoover Adopts More Activist Policies

With Hoovervilles and homelessness on the rise, the President's failed policies were laid bare. Poor Americans called trucks pulled by horse or mule "Hoover wagons," campfires "Hoover heaters," and cardboard boxes "Hoover houses." The association of the President's name with suffering and want indicated Americans' negative feelings about their leader.

## HISTORY MAKERS

**Herbert Hoover** (1874–1964)
After the depression hit, President Hoover eventually embraced an active economic plan. He urged Congress to fund construction projects that would provide jobs and pushed for legislation that would loan money to businesses to kick-start the economy. Yet at the same time, Hoover insisted that local governments and charities should provide direct aid to people out of work. "Economic depression cannot be cured by legislative action or executive pronouncement," he said. As a result, many Americans blamed him for their troubles.

## Hoover Dam Energy Use

- Arizona 19%
- Nevada 24%
- California 57%

SOURCE: U.S. Bureau of Reclamation

### Hoover Dam Powers the West

Hoover Dam contains 325 million cubic yards of concrete—enough to pave a highway 16 feet wide from New York City to San Francisco—and provides power to more than a million people each year. It also irrigates millions of acres of farmland in western states.

Hoover decided to reverse course and use federal resources to battle the depression. Believing the economy suffered from a lack of credit, Hoover urged Congress to create the **Reconstruction Finance Corporation (RFC).** Passed in 1932, the RFC gave more than a billion dollars of government loans to railroads and large businesses. The act also lent money to banks so that they could extend more loans to struggling businesses. Hoover believed that if the government lent money to bankers, they would lend it in turn to businessmen. Businessmen would then hire workers, production and consumption would increase, and the depression would end. This theory, known as **trickle-down economics,** held that money poured into the top of the economic pyramid will trickle down to the base.

Although the RFC put the federal government at the center of economic life, it did not work well under Hoover's guidance. The RFC lent out billions, but all too often bankers did not increase their loans to businesses. Additionally, businesses often did not use the loans they received to hire more workers. In the end, the money did not trickle down to the people who needed it the most.

Despite the failings of the RFC, Hoover succeeded with one project that made a difference. During the 1920s, Secretary of Commerce Hoover had called for the construction of a dam on the Colorado River. By the time Hoover became President in 1929, Congress had approved the project as part of a massive public-works program. Workers broke ground on Boulder Dam (later renamed **Hoover Dam**) in 1930. Construction brought much-needed employment to the Southwest during the early 1930s.

 **Checkpoint** What actions did Herbert Hoover take to fight the effects of the depression?

## Americans Protest Hoover's Failures

From the Oval Office, Hoover worked hard to end the depression. But to many out-of-work Americans, the President became a symbol of failure. Some people blamed capitalism, while others questioned the responsiveness of democracy. Many believed the American system was due for an overhaul.

**Some Urge Radical Change** Some Americans thought the answer to the country's problems was the rejection of capitalism and the acceptance of socialism or communism. They argued that capitalism created great inequities of wealth and an unhealthy atmosphere of competition in society. In fact, they saw the depression as a sign that capitalism was about to collapse. Looking at the Soviet Union, they maintained that a state-run economy was the only avenue out of the depression. Even during the worst of the crisis, though, communist calls for revolution proved no match for American dreams of progress, opportunity, and individual freedom.

Fascist appeals from the political right also failed to hold any attraction. Economic troubles in Europe contributed to the rise to power of fascist leaders like Benito Mussolini in Italy and Adolf Hitler in Germany. Despite this political shift abroad, no fascist gained power in the United States. Although some questioned the ability of America's capitalistic and democratic institutions to overcome the crisis, most Americans never lost faith in their country.

**The Bonus Army Marches on Washington** Most Americans did not want a revolution, but many did desire substantial changes. In 1932, one such group arrived in Washington, D.C., demanding a solution to their particular problem. From across the country came World War I veterans seeking the bonus Congress had promised them. They became known as the **Bonus Army**. In 1924, Congress had passed the Adjusted Compensation Act, which provided for a lump-sum payment to the veterans in 1945. But in 1931, many veteran groups began to call for an early payment of the bonus, arguing that out-of-work vets needed the money to support themselves. Congress agreed and passed a bill to provide for early payment of the bonuses. However, President Hoover vetoed the bill, saying that many of the vets did not need the early payment.

▼ The Bonus Army gathers on Capitol Hill.

● INFOGRAPHIC 🔊 AUDIO

# THE BONUS ARMY

**D**uring the economic boom of the 1920s, Congress promised a bonus to World War I veterans to be paid out in 1945. In the summer of 1932, as the nation struggled in the grasp of the Depression, the "Bonus Expeditionary Force" of veterans converged on Washington, D.C., seeking immediate payment. When the Senate rejected their demands, President Hoover called upon the army to keep order. General Douglas MacArthur brought in troops to drive the protesters out of the city. Evalyn McLean, a Washington, D.C., resident, remembered the federal action: "I saw in a news reel the tanks, the cavalry, and the gas-bomb throwers running those wretched Americans out of our capital. I was so raging mad . . . ." Memories of the event influenced the next presidential election.

Honorary medal given to veterans of World War I ▼

◀ U.S. troops set fire to the Bonus Army camps after driving out the protesters.

General MacArthur (left) and his aide, ▶ Colonel Dwight Eisenhower (right), supervise the removal of the Bonus Army.

## Thinking Critically
1. **Identify Points of View** How might the veterans and regular soldiers have felt about one another during the standoff?

2. **Make Generalizations** Was the Bonus Army justified in its protest? Why or why not?

In protest, veteran groups marched on Washington. In the summer of 1932, almost twenty thousand veterans arrived in the capital, setting up camps and occupying empty government buildings. A riot broke out in July when police tried to evict the marchers from their makeshift settlements.

**Hoover Orders the Bonus Army Out** Although President Hoover sympathized with the marchers, he called for General **Douglas MacArthur** and federal troops to "[s]urround the affected area and clear it without delay." MacArthur exceeded his order, deciding to move the marchers out of the city altogether. He ordered his troops to ready tear gas and fix bayonets.

The Army force that pushed the marchers out included not only MacArthur but also the future World War II generals Dwight Eisenhower and George Patton. While Eisenhower regretted the use of the Army to solve a political problem, Patton ordered his troops to brandish their sabers in a show of force. Force, perhaps excessive, was exactly what MacArthur used. More than one thousand marchers were tear-gassed, and many were injured, some very badly.

After the removal, MacArthur said that the marchers were a gang of revolutionaries bent on taking over the government:

> **Primary Source**  "They had come to the conclusion, beyond a shadow of a doubt, that they were about to take over . . . direct control of the government. . . . It is my opinion that had the president let it go on another week the institutions of our government would have been very severely threatened."
>
> —Douglas MacArthur, 1932

**The Aftermath Dooms Hoover** Hoover had not ordered the use of such force against the veterans. Nevertheless, photographs of American troops marching with fixed bayonets against ragged veterans shocked the nation. Any chance that Hoover had for winning reelection in November ended after the summer of 1932. With unemployment nearing 25 percent, stomachs grumbling from hunger, and the number of homeless people increasing every day, Hoover's policies had failed completely. Americans were ready for a change.

✔ **Checkpoint** Why did Hoover order the removal of the Bonus Army from its camps?

---

SECTION **3** Assessment

**Progress Monitoring *Online***
**For:** Self-test with vocabulary practice
**Web Code:** nea-0805

### Comprehension

1. **Terms and People** For each of the following terms, write a sentence explaining its significance.
   - localism
   - RFC
   - Hoover Dam
   - Bonus Army

2. NoteTaking **Reading Skill: Identify Supporting Details** Use your outline to answer the Section Focus Question: Why did Herbert Hoover's policies fail to solve the country's economic crisis?

### Writing About History

3. **Quick Write: Analyze Solutions** Based on what you have read, list supporting information—such as details, data, and facts—for the following thesis statement of a problem-solution essay: Although President Hoover responded to the developing economic crisis, he ultimately failed to stop it.

### Critical Thinking

4. **Recognize Ideologies** How did Hoover's views on government influence his response to the depression? Give two examples.

5. **Analyze Evidence** What facts show that Hoover's policies to reverse the depression failed?

6. **Recognize Effects** How did MacArthur's tactics in removing the Bonus Army affect Hoover's political future?

## *The Grapes of Wrath* by John Steinbeck

Published during the depths of the depression, *The Grapes of Wrath* won its author the Pulitzer Prize in 1940. Steinbeck's sympathetic portrayal of dispossessed Okies, along with his searing criticism of the rich and powerful who profited from their plight, caused an immediate sensation. The novel tells the story of the Joad family, hardy Dust Bowl farmers who are forced off their land by the bank. The Joads join the mass migration west, to the "promised land" of California. There, instead of opportunity, they find low wages, harsh conditions, discrimination—and finally, after years of drought, the cruel irony of a killing flood.

▲ First edition cover of the novel

In the barns, the people sat huddled together; and the terror came over them, and their faces were gray with terror. The children cried with hunger, and there was no food.

Then the sickness came, pneumonia, and measles that went to the eyes and to the mastoids.[1]

And the rain fell steadily, and the water flowed over the highways, for the culverts[2] could not carry the water.

Then from the tents, from the crowded barns, groups of sodden men went out, their clothes slopping rags, their shoes muddy pulp. They splashed out through the water, to the towns, to the country stores, to the relief offices, to beg for food, to cringe and beg for food, to beg for relief, to try to steal, to lie. And under the begging, and under the cringing, a hopeless anger began to smolder. And in the little towns pity for the sodden men changed to anger, and anger at the hungry people changed to fear of them. Then sheriffs swore in deputies in droves, and orders were rushed for rifles, for tear gas, for ammunition. Then the hungry men crowded the alleys behind the stores to beg for bread, to beg for rotting vegetables, to steal when they could.

Frantic men pounded on the doors of the doctors; and the doctors were busy. And sad men left word at country stores for the coroner to send a car. The coroners were not too busy. The coroners' wagons backed up through the mud and took out the dead.

And the rain pattered relentlessly down, and the streams broke their banks and spread out over the country.

▲ The Joads, from the 1940 film *The Grapes of Wrath,* starring Henry Fonda

### Thinking Critically

1. **Draw Inferences** Why did the townspeople's pity for the hungry migrant workers change to anger and then to fear?

2. **Analyze Literature** Notice the words Steinbeck uses to describe the rain and flooding. What might the flood symbolize in the story?

1. **mastoids** (MAS toidz) *n.* infection-prone areas of the skull behind the ears.
2. **culverts** (KUHL vertz) *n.* drainage ditches crossing under roads.

# Quick Study Guide

 7.1.2a

**Progress Monitoring *Online***
**For:** Self-test with vocabulary practice
**Web Code:** nea-0806

## ■ The Cycle of Production Cutbacks

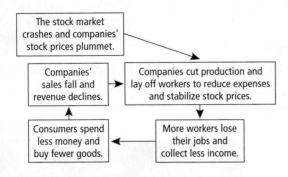

The stock market crashes and companies' stock prices plummet.

Companies' sales fall and revenue declines.

Companies cut production and lay off workers to reduce expenses and stabilize stock prices.

Consumers spend less money and buy fewer goods.

More workers lose their jobs and collect less income.

## ■ Cause and Effect: The Great Depression

**Causes**
- Overproduction and underconsumption of agricultural crops
- Uneven distribution of income
- Gradual accumulation of consumer debt
- Widespread stock market speculation

**The Great Depression**

**Effects**
- Banks and businesses fail.
- Unemployment soars.
- Personal incomes shrink.
- Countries enact high tariffs to protect their products from foreign competition; world trade declines.
- American loans to Europe dry up.

## ■ Causes of the Dust Bowl

Severe drought scorches the land.
+
Farmers plow deep-rooted grasses to plant crops.
+
Livestock overgraze the land.
=
Windstorms blow topsoil away.

## ☑ Quick Study Timeline

**In America**

1928
**Hoover elected President**

October 1929
**Stock market crashes**

June 1930
**Hawley-Smoot Tariff**

**Presidential Terms**     Calvin Coolidge 1923–1929     Herbert Hoover 1929–1933

1928          1929          1930

**Around the World**

1928
**Stalin launches first Five-Year Plan in the Soviet Union**

1930
**Haile Selassie becomes emperor of Ethiopia**

# American Issues Connector

7.1.2b

By connecting prior knowledge with what you have learned in this chapter, you can gradually build your understanding of enduring questions that still affect America today. Answer the questions below. Then, use your American Issues Connector study guide (or go online: www.PHSchool.com **Web Code:** neh-8102).

## Issues You Learned About

● **Government's Role in the Economy** Like other Presidents, Hoover sought the right balance between free enterprise and government intervention in the economy.

1. Think about the problems that emerged in society during the Great Depression and Hoover's response to them. Write a paragraph suggesting what Hoover might have done to improve the nation's economic situation and morale. Consider the following:
   - the depression's impact on families, businesses, industries, agriculture, and the banking system
   - the rising unemployment rate
   - the falling prices for farm products
   - Hoover's belief in volunteerism
   - responses to Hoover's policies

● **Migration and Urbanization** Economic changes often lead to migration around the country.

2. Why did thousands of people who lived in the Great Plains leave the region in the 1930s?

3. How did the drought on the Great Plains change population distribution in the country?

4. What other migrations took place as a result of the Great Depression?

● **Global Interdependence** The economies of nations around the world are impacted by distant events.

5. What economic practice of the 1920s contributed to the weakening of European economies?

6. What happened to European economies as a result of the Great Depression in the United States?

### Connect to Your World | Michigan

**Social Problems and Reforms** During the Great Depression, many Michigan automobile workers began organizing unions to protect their interests. The United Automobile Workers of America (UAW) labor union held its first convention in Detroit in 1935. As part of the larger American Federation of Labor (AFL), the new union had a difficult beginning. AFL leaders appointed a president for the UAW, Francis Dillon, who was unpopular among auto workers because of his conservative ideas. The AFL also limited the UAW to representing only assembly line operators, not all automobile workers. In response, UAW members elected a new president and joined the Congress of Industrial Organizations (CIO), a union that accepted unskilled industrial workers. The UAW went on to organize several successful sit-down strikes in the 1930s. With a partner, make a list of possible benefits that auto workers gained by joining a union.

**1931**
**Bank failures cause panic**

**January 1932**
**Congress sets up the RFC**

**July 1932**
**Bonus Army driven from Washington, D.C.**

**History Interactive**
For: Interactive timeline
Web Code: nep-0808

**Franklin D. Roosevelt 1933–1945**

**1931**

**1932**

**1933**

**1931**
**Japanese troops occupy Manchuria**

**1932**
**Britain and France agree to suspend German reparations**

**1933**
**Hitler becomes chancellor of Germany**

# Chapter Assessment

## Terms and People

**1.** Who was **Herbert Hoover**? What did he represent to the American people in 1928?

**2.** What is the **business cycle**? If you were to chart the business cycle of 1929, how would you represent the period from mid-October through mid-November?

**3.** Define **bread line.** Who ran bread lines during the depression?

**4.** What was Mexican American **repatriation**? How did Mexican Americans respond to this effort?

**5.** Define **trickle-down economics.** Explain how the depression proved whether or not this theory worked.

## Focus Questions

The focus question for this chapter is **How did the Great Depression happen, and how did Americans respond to it?** Build an answer to this big question by answering the focus questions for Sections 1 through 3 and the Critical Thinking questions that follow.

### Section 1

**6.** How did the prosperity of the 1920s give way to the Great Depression?

### Section 2

**7.** How did the Great Depression affect the lives of urban and rural Americans?

### Section 3

**8.** Why did Herbert Hoover's policies fail to solve the country's economic crisis?

## Critical Thinking

**9. Identify Central Issues** What weaknesses existed in the U.S. economy before the stock market crash?

**10. Recognize Causes** How did the Dust Bowl cause Okies to prefer life in California over life on the Great Plains?

**11. Analyze Line Graphs** Based on the graph below, between which two years did unemployment rise the most? Based on your reading, explain why the increase was especially great during this period.

**U.S. Unemployment Rate, 1925–1933**

SOURCE: *Historical Statistics of the United States*

**12. Synthesize Information** Why did some men find their role in the family diminished during the depression? What were some of the different ways these men reacted?

**13. Identify Central Issues** Do you think the depression changed people's goals and expectations? Why or why not?

**14. Draw Conclusions** Why did Hoover turn from volunteerism and localism to more activist policies to fight the depression?

**15. Identify Fact Versus Opinion** What demands did the Bonus Army make? What did General MacArthur think about the Bonus Army?

## Writing About History

**Writing a Problem-Solution Essay** Throughout its history, the United States has experienced periods of economic decline. However, not all these downturns ended in a general depression. In 1929, underlying problems surfaced to sink the American economy in the wake of the stock market crash. Write a problem-solution essay about one of these causes of the depression or choose your own topic relating to the content in this chapter.

### Prewriting

• Choose the topic that interests you the most. If you have a personal interest in a problem and its solution, your essay will be easier to develop.

• Narrow your topic.

• Make a list of details, facts, and examples that prove there is a problem. Then, identify the specific parts of your solution.

### Drafting

• Develop a working thesis and choose information to support it.

• Organize the paragraphs in a logical order so that readers can understand the solution you propose.

### Revising

• Use the guidelines on page SH16 of the Writing Handbook to revise your essay.

# Prepare for the MME

## Worldwide Depression

In 1929, the stock market crash echoed across the Atlantic Ocean to a European continent still suffering the aftereffects of war. Use your knowledge of the Great Depression and the following documents to answer questions 1 through 4.

### Document A

"Values decreased, prices fell, production lessened. The American faith began its decline as extremely as had its illusions been created. Simultaneously, with the misfortunes of business in America came the catastrophes of Europe. . . . The [American] government made unheard-of efforts in the last three years to contain the avalanche. . . . But they made the big mistake of believing they could save the nation in isolation."

—El Sol, *Madrid newspaper, March 7, 1933*

### Document B

Nations indebted to the United States, 1914–1925
Loans given by the United States, 1914–1918
Loans given by the United States for reconstruction, 1919–1925
$160 Total debt (in millions of dollars)
*Debt repudiated in 1918

### Document C

"The Hawley-Smoot Tariff went into effect in June 1930, in the full blast of the depression. Under the circumstances there was great indignation and resentment on the part of the majority of the countries of the world, but that of the debtor countries of Europe was extreme. This intense indignation, coupled with the absolute necessity of securing a favorable trade balance, could result in but one course of action: retaliatory tariff increases against the United States."

—*Joseph M. Jones, Jr.*, Tariff Retaliation: Repercussions of the Hawley-Smoot Bill

### Document D

PASSING THE BUCK.

---

1. Which of the documents is a primary source that explains how the stock market crash snowballed into an international economic crisis?
   A Document A
   B Document B
   C Document C
   D Document D

2. In Document D, how did the cartoonist choose to portray the problem of reparations after World War I?
   A The United States does not need its loans repaid.
   B Germany has plenty of money available to repay Britain and France.
   C Britain and France cannot repay U.S. loans because Germany is bankrupt.
   D The United States is loaning more money to Germany.

3. According to Joseph Jones, which of the following statements is an accurate assessment of the Hawley-Smoot Tariff?
   A It caused European countries to pass their own protective tariffs.
   B It opened international markets and stimulated world trade.
   C It put limits on Allied war debts.
   D It established the funds for the Reconstruction Finance Corporation.

4. **Writing Task** How did the structure of loans to rebuild Europe after World War I collapse under the weight of economic depression? Use your knowledge of the war, the Great Depression, and specific evidence from the primary sources above to support your opinion.

### A New Beginning

Still suffering through the worst economic crisis in the nation's history, depression-weary Americans anxiously awaited Franklin D. Roosevelt's Inaugural Address.

"Saturday, March 4, 1933.

Turn on the radio. It's time for the inauguration.

There is a tension in the air today—a sense of momentousness and of expectation. When you went downtown this morning you found the banks shut. . . . But what next? . . . The one thing you want to hear, that everybody wants to hear, is the Inaugural Address. All over the country people are huddled round their radios, wondering what Roosevelt's answer to disaster will be."

—Frederick Lewis Allen, *Since Yesterday: The 1930s In America*

*Listen to the* Witness History *audio to learn more about FDR's inauguration.*

Movie poster for *King Kong*

1932 presidential campaign button

◄ On the campaign trail in West Virginia, Governor Roosevelt greets a coal miner.

### (MI) Content Expectations

**Chapter Focus Question:** How did the New Deal respond to the ravages of the Depression and change the role of the federal government?

## Section 1
**FDR Offers Relief and Recovery**  6.1.2b, 7.1.3a, 8.2.3

## Section 2
**The Second New Deal**  6.1.5e, 7.1.2b, 7.1.3b, 7.1.3c

## Section 3
**Effects of the New Deal**  6.3.2e, 6.3.3, 7.1.3a

## Section 4
**Culture of the 1930s**  7.1.1a, 7.1.2a, 7.1.3c

The CCC provided government jobs for unemployed young men.

Use the ☑ **Quick Study Timeline** at the end of this chapter to preview chapter events.

**Note Taking Study Guide *Online***
**For:** Note Taking and American Issues Connector
**Web Code:** nee-8201

▼ Franklin Delano Roosevelt

▼ Roosevelt campaign banner

**VELT FOR PRESIDENT**

WITNESS HISTORY 🔊 AUDIO

### Overcoming Fear

Franklin D. Roosevelt's March 1933 inauguration came at a somber moment in American history. The U.S. economy had hit rock bottom. Many Americans wondered if they would ever find work again. With the first words of his Inaugural Address, FDR reassured the American people:

❝This is preeminently the time to speak the truth, the whole truth, frankly and boldly. Nor need we shrink from honestly facing conditions in our country today. This great Nation will endure as it has endured, will revive and will prosper. So, first of all, let me assert my firm belief that the only thing we have to fear is fear itself—nameless, unreasoning, unjustified terror which paralyzes needed efforts to convert retreat into advance.❞

—*Franklin D. Roosevelt, First Inaugural Address, March 4, 1933*

# FDR Offers Relief and Recovery

### Content Expectations

- **6.1.2b** Evaluate southern/western farmers' reactions to industrial growth.
- **7.1.3a** Explain expanding federal government responsibility.
- **8.2.3** Compare/contrast Roosevelt's New Deal initiatives, Johnson's Great Society programs, Reagan's market-based domestic policies.

### Terms and People

| | |
|---|---|
| Franklin D. Roosevelt | CCC |
| Eleanor Roosevelt | NRA |
| New Deal | PWA |
| fireside chat | Charles Coughlin |
| FDIC | Huey Long |
| TVA | |

### NoteTaking

**Reading Skill: Connect Ideas** Fill in a chart like the one below with the problems that FDR faced and the steps he took to overcome them.

| FDR Tackles Tough Problems | |
|---|---|
| **Problem** | **FDR's Policy** |
| Failing banks | |

**Why It Matters** The Great Depression challenged the faith of Americans that democracy could handle the crisis. Faced with similar circumstances, people in Germany, Italy, and Japan had turned to dictators to deliver them from despair. The New Deal had great significance because America's response to the Great Depression proved that a democratic society could overcome the challenges presented by the severe economic crisis. **Section Focus Question: How did the New Deal attempt to address the problems of the depression?**

## Roosevelt Takes Charge

In 1928, Herbert Hoover had almost no chance of losing his bid for the presidency. In 1932 however, Hoover had almost no chance of winning reelection. The depression had taken its toll. About 25 percent of the population was unemployed. Bank failures had wiped out peoples' savings. The hungry waited on long lines at soup kitchens.

Americans were ready for a change. In July of 1932, the relatively unknown governor of New York, **Franklin D. Roosevelt,** accepted the Democratic Party's nomination for President.

**Roosevelt Overcame Obstacles** Strangely enough, Americans had chosen a presidential candidate who had never known economic hardship. As a child, Franklin Delano Roosevelt had enjoyed all the privileges of an upper-class upbringing, including education at elite schools and colleges. From his parents and teachers, FDR gained a great deal of self-confidence and a belief that public service was a noble calling.

In 1905, Franklin married his distant cousin **Eleanor Roosevelt.** President Theodore Roosevelt, Eleanor's uncle and Franklin's fifth cousin gave the bride away. In time, Eleanor would become deeply involved in public affairs.

Like Teddy Roosevelt, Franklin rose quickly through the political ranks. After election to the New York State Senate, he served as Woodrow Wilson's Assistant Secretary of the Navy. In 1920, Roosevelt was the Democratic Party's vice presidential nominee. Although the Democrats lost the election, many considered him the rising star of the party.

Then, in the summer of 1921, tragedy struck. While vacationing, FDR slipped off his boat into the chilly waters of the North Atlantic. That evening, he awoke with a high fever and severe pains in his back and legs. Two weeks later, Roosevelt was diagnosed with polio, a dreaded disease that at the time had no treatment. He never fully recovered the use of his legs.

FDR did not allow his physical disability to break his spirit. With Eleanor's encouragement, Roosevelt made a political comeback. In 1928, he was elected governor of New York and earned a reputation as a reformer. In 1932, he became the Democrat's presidential candidate, pledging "a new deal for the American people."

**Voters Elect a New President** When FDR pledged a **"New Deal,"** he had only a vague idea of how he intended to combat the depression. Convinced that the federal government needed to play an active role in promoting recovery and providing relief to Americans, he experimented with different approaches to see which one worked best.

> **Primary Source** "The country needs and, unless I mistake its temper, the country demands bold, persistent experimentation. It is common sense to take a method and to try it. If it fails, admit it frankly and try another. But above all, try something!"
> —Franklin D. Roosevelt, speech at Oglethorpe University, May 22, 1932

The 1932 election campaign pitted Roosevelt against President Herbert Hoover. The two men advocated very different approaches to the problems of the Great Depression. Hoover believed that depression relief should come from state and local governments and private agencies. Roosevelt believed that the depression required strong action and leadership by the federal government. As Hoover noted, "This campaign is more than a contest between two men. . . . It is a contest between two philosophies of government."

Hoover's popularity declined as the Great Depression worsened. Even longtime Republicans deserted him. FDR—with the support of those who embraced his ideas as well as those who opposed Hoover's approach—won a landslide presidential victory, defeating Hoover by more than 7 million votes.

Americans had to wait four long months between Roosevelt's election, in November 1932, and his inauguration, in March 1933. Meanwhile, they watched helplessly as thousands of banks collapsed and unemployment soared. What would Roosevelt do to combat the depression? Even the experts did not know what to expect.

**Putting Together a Winning Team** To help him plan the New Deal, FDR sought the advice of a diverse group of men and women. Among the most influential was a group of professionals and academics whom the press nicknamed the

## FDR Not Slowed by Polio

Despite the debilitating effects of polio, FDR continued to serve in public office. *How do you think FDR's earlier jobs and experiences prepared him to serve as President?*

- **1903** Earned BA in history from Harvard University
- **1910** Elected to the New York State Senate
- **1913** Appointed Assistant Secretary of the Navy
- **1920** Campaigned as Democratic nominee for Vice President
- **1921** Contracted polio, which paralyzed his legs
- **1928** Elected governor of New York State
- **1933** Inaugurated as President of the United States

"Brain Trust." Roosevelt, a Democrat, displayed his openness by nominating two Republicans, Henry Wallace and Harold Ickes (IHK uhs), to serve as his Secretary of Agriculture and Secretary of Interior. Roosevelt also nominated Frances Perkins, a social worker, to serve as his Secretary of Labor. She became the first woman Cabinet member in U.S. history.

Throughout his presidency, FDR depended heavily on his wife, Eleanor. She traveled widely, interacting with the American people and serving as FDR's "eyes and ears." For example, in 1933, the Bonus Army, which had marched on Washington, D.C., in 1932, returned to the capital, seeking an early payment of its bonus for World War I service. Like Hoover, FDR informed the marchers that the government could not afford to pay them their bonus. But unlike Hoover, who had sent the army to evict the Bonus Army, FDR sent Eleanor. She sang songs with the veterans and made them feel that the government cared.

✔ **Checkpoint** How did FDR's background and actions help build confidence among the American people?

# The First Hundred Days Provide Instant Action

During his first hundred days in office, Roosevelt proposed and Congress passed 15 bills. These measures, known as the First New Deal, had three goals: relief, recovery, and reform. Roosevelt wanted to provide relief from the immediate hardships of the depression and achieve a long-term economic recovery. He also instituted reforms to prevent future depressions.

**FDR Swiftly Restores the Nation's Confidence** Roosevelt wasted no time dealing with the nation's number one crisis. Late in 1932, banks had begun to fail in great numbers. A banking panic gripped the nation as frightened depositors lined up outside banks, trying to withdraw their savings.

The day after his inauguration, Roosevelt called Congress into a special session and convinced them to pass laws to shore up the nation's banking system. The Emergency Banking Bill gave the President broad powers—including the power to declare a four-day bank "holiday." Banks all over the country were ordered to close. The closings gave banks time to get their accounts in order before they reopened for business.

Eight days after becoming President, Roosevelt delivered an informal radio speech to the American people. This was the first of many presidential **fireside chats.** They became an important way for Roosevelt to communicate with the American people. In the first fireside chat, FDR explained the measures he had taken to stem the run on banks. His calming words reassured the American people. When the bank holiday ended, Americans did not rush to their banks to withdraw their funds. Roosevelt had convinced them that the banks were a safe place to keep their money.

**Reforming the Financial System** A number of Roosevelt's proposals sought to reform the nation's financial institutions. One act created the **Federal Deposit Insurance Corporation (FDIC),** which insured bank deposits up to $5,000. In the following year, Congress established the Securities and Exchange Commission (SEC) to regulate the stock market and make it a safer place for investments.

These financial reforms helped restore confidence in the economy. Runs on banks ended, largely because Americans now had confidence that they would not lose their lifetime savings if a bank failed. The stock markets also stabilized as regulated trading practices reassured investors.

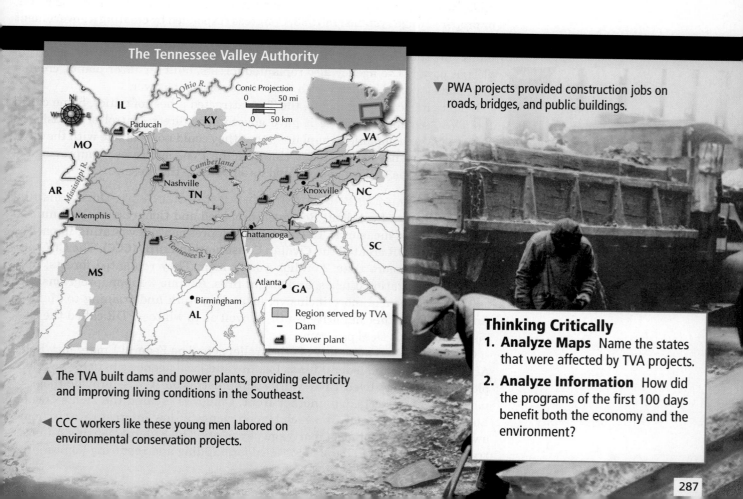

### The Tennessee Valley Authority

Conic Projection
0    50 mi
0    50 km

IL
KY
Paducah
MO
VA
AR
Cumberland
Nashville
TN
Knoxville
NC
Memphis
Chattanooga
Tennessee R.
SC
MS
Atlanta
GA
Birmingham
AL

Region served by TVA
Dam
Power plant

▲ The TVA built dams and power plants, providing electricity and improving living conditions in the Southeast.

◄ CCC workers like these young men labored on environmental conservation projects.

▼ PWA projects provided construction jobs on roads, bridges, and public buildings.

**Thinking Critically**

1. **Analyze Maps** Name the states that were affected by TVA projects.

2. **Analyze Information** How did the programs of the first 100 days benefit both the economy and the environment?

## Government Puts People to Work

The Works Progress Administration poster (above) promoted the benefits of putting people to work. These TVA workers (right) assembled generators at the Cherokee Dam in Tennessee. *If you had been out of work during the depression, what effect might these images have had on you? Why?*

**Helping Farmers** A number of New Deal programs aimed at easing the desperate plight of American farmers. For years, the supply of crops grown by American farmers had far exceeded demand. Prices dropped to the point where it was no longer profitable to grow some crops. To counter this, Congress passed the Agricultural Adjustment Act (AAA), which sought to end overproduction and raise crop prices. To accomplish these goals, the AAA provided financial aid, paying farmers subsidies not to plant part of their land and to kill off excess livestock. Many Americans believed it was immoral to kill livestock or destroy crops while people went hungry. However, by 1934, farm prices began to rise.

**The TVA Aids Rural Southerners** Americans living in the Tennessee River valley were among the poorest in the nation. Few had electricity, running water, or proper sewage systems. In 1933, Congress responded by creating a government agency called the **Tennessee Valley Authority (TVA).** The TVA built a series of dams in the Tennessee River valley to control floods and to generate electric power. The agency also replanted forests, built fertilizer plants, created jobs, and attracted industry with the promise of cheap power.

Despite its accomplishments, the TVA attracted a host of critics. Some called the TVA "socialist," because it gave government direct control of a business. Private power companies complained that they could not compete with the TVA, because the agency paid no taxes. However, the TVA's successes in improving life in the Tennessee Valley have ensured its survival to the present.

**Providing Relief and Promoting Industrial Recovery** During his first hundred days as President, Roosevelt proposed and Congress enacted numerous other relief measures. To counter the depression's devastating impact on young men, FDR created the **Civilian Conservation Corps (CCC).** The CCC provided jobs for more than 2 million young men. They replanted forests, built trails, dug irrigation ditches, and fought fires. As time went on, programs such as the CCC became more inclusive, extending work and training to Mexican American and other minority youth, as well as to whites. FDR called the CCC his favorite New Deal program.

Congress passed a number of other relief acts. The Federal Emergency Relief Act (FERA) granted federal funds to state and local agencies to help the unemployed. The short-lived Civil Works Administration (CWA) provided jobs on public-works projects. On another front, Congress created the Home Owners Loan Corporation (HOLC), which loaned money at low interest rates to homeowners who could not meet mortgage payments. The Federal Housing Administration (FHA) insured bank loans used for building and repairing homes.

These New Deal measures marked a clear break from the policies of the Hoover administration, which had disapproved of direct relief to individuals. The $500 million appropriated for FERA represented the largest peacetime expenditure by the federal government to that time.

The centerpiece of the early New Deal's recovery program was the National Industrial Recovery Act, which established the **National Recovery Administration (NRA).** Roosevelt called the NIRA "the most important and far-reaching legislation ever enacted by the American Congress." Working with business and labor leaders, the NRA developed codes of fair competition to govern whole industries. These codes established minimum wages for workers and minimum prices for the goods that businesses sold. The idea behind these codes was to increase the wages of workers so they could buy more goods and raise prices so companies could make a profit.

Another New Deal legislative achievement was the **Public Works Administration (PWA),** which built bridges, dams, power plants, and government buildings. The PWA was responsible for building many important projects still in use today, such as New York City's Triborough Bridge, the Overseas Highway linking Miami and Key West, and the Bonneville Dam on the Columbia River in the Pacific Northwest. These public-works projects improved the nation's infrastructure and created millions of new jobs for workers.

✔ **Checkpoint** **What actions did Roosevelt take during his first hundred days in office?**

## Opposition to the New Deal Emerges

While Roosevelt had little difficulty gaining support from Congress for his proposals, a minority of Americans expressed their opposition to the New Deal. Some thought the changes it brought were too radical. Others thought that the New Deal was not radical enough. Several of FDR's critics attracted mass followings and made plans to challenge him for the presidency in 1936.

**The Right Says "Too Much"** The chief complaint against the New Deal was that it made the government too powerful. Critics contended that the government was telling business how to operate, spending large sums of money, and piling up a huge national debt.

To many conservatives, the New Deal was destroying free enterprise and undermining individualism. In a 1934 book entitled *The Challenge to Liberty,* former President Herbert Hoover described the New Deal as "the most stupendous invasion of the whole spirit of liberty" in the nation's history. Robert Taft, the son of former President William Howard Taft and a leading Republican in Congress, claimed Roosevelt's programs threatened individual freedom.

In 1934, these critics formed the American Liberty League. Supporters included prominent business leaders, such as Alfred Sloan and William Knudsen of General Motors. Leading Democrats, such as John W. Davis, the Democrat's presidential nominee in 1924, and Al Smith, the nominee in 1928, joined the Liberty League because they felt Roosevelt had deserted the Democratic Party's principles of a limited federal government.

## Analyzing Political Cartoons

**The Galloping Snail** This cartoon represents the relationship between President Roosevelt and Congress during FDR's first hundred days in office.

Ⓐ President Roosevelt

Ⓑ Congress

Ⓒ Roosevelt's New Deal agenda

1. Why did the cartoonist use a snail to represent Congress?
2. What is the cartoonist saying about the relationship between the President and Congress?

# The New Deal: Too Much—or Not Enough?

Franklin Roosevelt's New Deal raised the issue of how involved the government should be in the economy and in the lives of its citizens. This question divided many Americans.

## ALFRED E. SMITH

Smith (1873–1944) served as governor of New York and ran for President in 1928. He believed the New Deal made the government too powerful and described it as a "trend toward Fascist control" and "the end of democracy."

### Primary Source

"... Something has taken place in this country—there is a certain kind of foreign 'ism' crawling over [it]. ... There can be only one Capitol, Washington or Moscow! There can be only one atmosphere of government, [the] clear, pure, fresh air of free America, or the foul breath of Communistic Russia."

## FRANCIS TOWNSEND

Townsend (1867–1960) was a medical doctor who felt the New Deal did not do enough to help older Americans devastated by the depression. He proposed a pension plan funded by a national sales tax.

### Primary Source

THE TOWNSEND PLAN
$200, PER MONTH FOR THOSE OVER 60 YRS OF AGE - THE SPENDING OF THIS MONEY WILL PUT THE CONTROL OF CREDIT IN THE HANDS OF THE PEOPLE - PREVENTING ECONOMIC CHAOS

### Compare

1. Which man thought that the New Deal went too far? Which man thought that the New Deal did not go far enough?

2. Why does each oppose the New Deal?

**Vocabulary Builder**
ensure–(ehn SHUR) v. to make safe; guarantee

**The Left Says "Not Enough"** While conservatives accused FDR of supporting socialism, some leading socialists charged that the New Deal did not do enough to end the depression. Norman Thomas, the Socialist Party's presidential candidate, claimed that FDR's only concern was saving the banking system and <u>ensuring</u> profits for big business. The American Communist Party described the New Deal as a "capitalist ruse."

**Populist Critics Challenge FDR** The most significant criticism of FDR came from a cluster of figures whose roots were in the Populist movement. They saw themselves as spokesmen for poor Americans, challenging the power of the elite. Roosevelt's strongest critics were Francis Townsend, Father Charles Coughlin, and Huey Long.

Townsend, a doctor from California, had a simple program. It called for the federal government to provide $200 a month to all citizens over the age of 60. These funds, he argued, would filter out to the rest of society and produce an economic recovery. To promote this plan, he established "Townsend Clubs" and held meetings that resembled old-time church revivals.

Father **Charles Coughlin** presented an even bigger challenge to FDR. Coughlin, a Roman Catholic priest, had attracted millions of listeners to his weekly radio show. At first, Coughlin supported the New Deal, but in time he broke with FDR, accusing him of not doing enough to fight the depression. Coughlin said that Roosevelt had "out-Hoovered Hoover" and called the New Deal "the raw deal."

Coughlin mixed calls for the nationalization of industry with anti-Semitic remarks and attacks on "communists" who, he charged, were running the country. By the early 1940s, Coughlin's views became so extreme that Roman Catholic officials forced him to end his broadcasts.

Canadian by birth, Coughlin could not run against FDR in the 1936 election. However, he threatened to throw his support behind an even more popular New Deal critic, Senator **Huey Long** of Louisiana. Long was an expert performer whose folksy speeches delighted audiences. Long's solution to the depression was his "Share Our Wealth" program that proposed high taxes on the wealthy and large corporations, and the redistribution of their income to poor Americans.

**Huey Long Challenges the Roosevelt Administration**

Huey Long used his Share Our Wealth Society to promote the redistribution of wealth in the country. *How might Long's efforts have influenced FDR's policies?*

> **Primary Source** "God invited us all to come and eat and drink all we wanted. He smiled on our land and we grew crops of plenty to eat and wear. . . . [But then] Rockefeller, Morgan, and their crowd stepped up and took enough for 120,000,000 people and left only enough for 5,000,000 for all the other 125,000,000 to eat. And so the millions must go hungry and without those good things God gave us unless we call on them to put some of it back."
>
> —Huey Long radio broadcast, 1934

Roosevelt viewed Long as a serious political threat. But unlike Roosevelt, Long did not have a deep faith in democracy. Ruling Louisiana as if he owned the state, he made many enemies. In 1935, a political enemy assassinated Long, ending the most serious threat to Roosevelt's presidency.

✓ **Checkpoint** What were the two major criticisms of FDR's New Deal economic policies?

---

**Progress Monitoring *Online***
For: Self-test with vocabulary practice
Web Code: nea-0902

## Comprehension

1. **Terms and People** For each item below, write a sentence explaining how it affected the lives of people during the New Deal.
   • Eleanor Roosevelt
   • fireside chat
   • TVA
   • PWA
   • Charles Coughlin
   • Huey Long

2. **NoteTaking Reading Skill: Connect Ideas** Use your problem-solution table to answer the Section Focus Question: How did the New Deal attempt to address the problems of the depression?

## Writing About History

3. **Quick Write: Identify Main Ideas** Before you can synthesize, you must understand the main idea, or thesis, of each source. Study the political cartoon in this section and write a sentence summarizing its main idea about FDR. Then, review the Alfred E. Smith primary source quote. Write a sentence summarizing Smith's view of FDR.

## Critical Thinking

4. **Draw Inferences** Why did President Roosevelt need his wife, Eleanor, to serve as his "eyes and ears"?

5. **Make Comparisons** How did FDR's economic policies differ from those of Herbert Hoover?

6. **Identify Central Issues** Why do you think the depression led to the development of some extreme proposals?

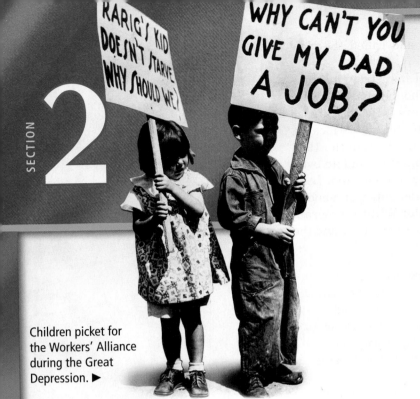

Children picket for the Workers' Alliance during the Great Depression. ▶

### Trying to Survive

During the Great Depression, people found themselves desperate for work. Daily visits to the unemployment office and workplaces often turned up nothing. Some of the jobless lost their homes. Others could not feed their children. One 12-year-old boy wrote to President Roosevelt to ask for help for his family.

❝My father hasn't worked for 5 months. . . . Please you do something. . . . We haven't paid the gas bill, and the electric bill, haven't paid grocery bill. . . . I have a sister she's twenty years, she can't find work. My father he staying home. All the time he's crying because he can't find work.❞

—Anonymous 12-year-old boy, Chicago, 1936

# The Second New Deal

### Content Expectations

- **6.1.5e** Analyze the automobile industry's impact on Michigan.
- **7.1.2b** Analyze economic/social toll of Great Depression.
- **7.1.3b** Explain opposition to New Deal/impact of Supreme Court striking down/accepting New Deal laws.
- **7.1.3c** Explain consequences of New Deal policies.

### Terms and People

Second New Deal
WPA
John Maynard Keynes
pump priming
Social Security Act
Wagner Act

collective bargaining
Fair Labor Standards Act
CIO
sit-down strikes
court packing

## NoteTaking

**Reading Skill: Connect Ideas** Complete a table like the one below to record problems and the second New Deal's solutions.

| The Second New Deal ||
|--------------|----------|
| Problem | Solution |
| Unemployment | |
| | |

**Why It Matters** FDR's goals for the first New Deal were relief, recovery, and reform. Progress had been made, but there was still much work that needed to be done. Beginning in early 1935, Roosevelt launched an aggressive campaign to find solutions to the ongoing problems caused by the Great Depression. This campaign, known as the Second New Deal, created Social Security and other programs that continue to have a profound impact on the everyday lives of Americans. **Section Focus Question: What major issues did the Second New Deal address?**

## Extending Social and Economic Reform

In his fireside chats, press conferences, and major addresses, Roosevelt explained the challenges facing the nation. He said that the complexities of the modern world compelled the federal government to "promote the general welfare" and to intervene to protect citizens' rights. Roosevelt used legislation passed during the **Second New Deal** to accomplish these goals. The Second New Deal addressed the problems of the elderly, the poor, and the unemployed; created new public-works projects; helped farmers; and enacted measures to protect workers' rights. It was during this period that the first serious challenges to the New Deal emerged.

**New Programs Provide Jobs** In the spring of 1935, Congress appropriated $5 billion for new jobs and created the **Works Progress Administration (WPA)** to administer the program. Roosevelt placed his longtime associate Harry Hopkins in charge. The WPA built or improved a good part of the nation's highways, dredged rivers and harbors, and promoted soil and water conservation. The WPA even provided programs in the arts for displaced artists. As Hopkins explained, artists "have to eat just like other people."

By 1943, the WPA had employed more than 8 million people and spent about $11 billion. Its workers built more than 650,000 miles of highways and 125,000 public buildings. Among the most famous projects funded by the WPA were the San Antonio River Walk and parts of the Appalachian Trail.

All of these programs were expensive, and the government paid for them by spending money it did not have. The federal deficit—$461 million in 1932— grew to $4.4 billion in 1936. The enormous expenditures and growing debt led many to criticize the government's public-works projects as wasteful. Some economists disagreed. British economist **John Maynard Keynes** argued that deficit spending was needed to end the depression. According to Keynes, putting people to work on public projects put money into the hands of consumers who would buy more goods, stimulating the economy. Keynes called this theory **pump priming.**

## Social Security Eases the Burden on Older Americans

The United States was one of the few industrialized nations in the world that did not have some form of pension system for the elderly. During the depression, many elderly people had lost their homes and their life savings and were living in poverty. On January 17, 1935, President Roosevelt unveiled his plans for Social Security.

In addition to creating a pension system for retirees, the **Social Security Act** that Congress enacted established unemployment insurance for workers who lost their jobs. The law also created insurance for victims of work-related accidents and provided aid for poverty-stricken mothers and children, the blind, and the disabled.

The Social Security Act had many flaws. At first, it did not apply to domestics or farmworkers. Since African Americans were disproportionately employed in these fields, they were not eligible for many of the benefits of Social Security. Widows received smaller benefits than widowers, because people presumed that elderly women could manage on less money than elderly men. Despite these shortcomings, Social Security proved the most popular and significant of the New Deal programs.

## More Aid Goes to Farmers

The Second New Deal included further help for farmers. When the depression began, only 10 percent of all farms had electricity, largely because utility companies did not find it profitable to run electric lines to communities with small populations. To bring farmers into the light, Congress established the Rural Electrification Administration (REA). The REA loaned money to electric utilities to build power lines, bringing electricity to isolated rural areas. The program was so successful that by 1950, more than 80 percent of American farms had electricity.

New Deal programs changed the relationship of the federal government to the American farmer. The government was now committed to providing price supports, or subsidies, for agriculture. Critics attacked price supports for undermining the free market. Others observed that large

**Electricity Comes to Rural Farms**

The success of the REA allowed farm families to light their homes, pump water, and run radios, refrigerators, and washing machines.

**Farms With Electricity, 1930–1950**

Percentage of farms

100
80
60
40
20
0

1930  1935  1940  1945  1950

SOURCE: *Statistical Abstract of the United States*

farms, not small farmers, benefited most from federal farm programs. Even during the 1930s, many noticed that tenant farmers and sharecroppers, often African Americans, did not fully share in the federal programs. Yet farm prices stabilized, and agriculture remained a productive sector of the economy.

**Water Projects Change the Face of the West** Many of the New Deal public-works water projects had an enormous impact on the development of the American West. The government funded the complex Central Valley irrigation system in California. The massive Bonneville Dam in the Pacific Northwest controlled flooding and provided electricity to a vast number of citizens. In 1941, the Department of the Interior's Bonneville Power Administration (BPA) hired folk singer Woody Guthrie for one month to write songs for a movie they had made

# Milestones in SOCIAL SECURITY

During the Great Depression, many elderly Americans had lost their life savings and were struggling to survive. The 1935 Social Security Act created a pension system as well as unemployment insurance for workers who had lost their jobs. Financed through a payroll tax on employers and workers, Social Security is one of the country's most important legislative achievements.

SOCIAL SECURITY ACT
ACCOUNT NUMBER
002-03-3122
HAS BEEN                                    ESTABLISHED FOR
RICHARD LANCASTER KRAYBILL
WORKER'S
SIGNATURE
FOR SOCIAL SECURITY PURPOSES • NOT FOR IDENTIFICATION

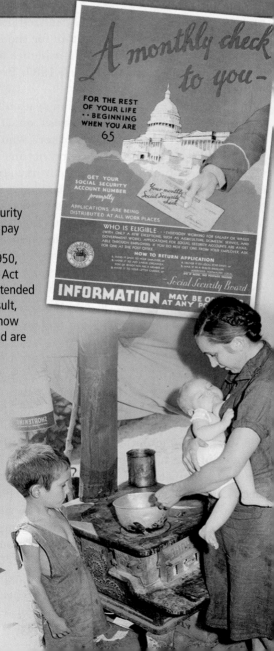

A monthly check to you—

FOR THE REST
OF YOUR LIFE
•• BEGINNING
WHEN YOU ARE
65

GET YOUR
SOCIAL SECURITY
ACCOUNT NUMBER
promptly

APPLICATIONS ARE BEING
DISTRIBUTED AT ALL WORK PLACES

WHO IS ELIGIBLE

HOW TO RETURN APPLICATION

Social Security Board

INFORMATION MAY BE O... AT ANY P...

**1935–1950** The Social Security program was expanded in 1939 to pay benefits to the widows and young children of deceased workers. In 1950, amendments to the Social Security Act increased benefit payments and extended coverage to more workers. As a result, almost all working Americans now contribute to Social Security and are eligible for benefits.

◀ Since 1940, senior citizens have depended on their monthly Social Security retirement checks.

Social Security benefits ▶ helped widows feed their children.

promoting the benefits of electricity. Guthrie's song, "Roll on, Columbia," pays tribute to the projects that harnessed the power of the Columbia River.

"Your power is turning our darkness to dawn,
And on up the river is the Grand Coulee Dam,
The Mightiest thing ever built by a man,
To run the great factories and water the land."
—Woody Guthrie, "Roll On, Columbia," 1941

✓ **Checkpoint** Why did the onset of the depression make it essential to have some form of Social Security?

▲ Medicaid makes healthcare more available to low-income families.

**1950–1970** During the 1950s and 1960s, Social Security expanded to provide benefits to people with disabilities. In 1965, two new Social Security programs, Medicare and Medicaid, were introduced. Medicare is a health-insurance program for Americans age 65 and older, and Medicaid provides health insurance to needy persons of any age.

**The Elderly and Poverty, 1940–2000**

Percentage living in poverty

| | | | |
|---|---|---|---|
| 100 | | | |
| 80 | | | |
| 60 | | | |
| 40 | | | |
| 20 | | | |
| 0 | | | |
| 1940 | 1960 | 1980 | 2000 |

SOURCE: U.S. Census Bureau

**1970–Today** The Supplemental Social Security Income (SSI) program, begun in 1974, provides monthly payments to the needy elderly and to people who are blind or who have a disability. The Medicare Prescription Drug program, passed in 2003, provides Medicare recipients with voluntary prescription-drug coverage and discounts. President George W. Bush's proposal to allow younger workers to invest Social Security tax money in personal retirement accounts was rejected by the public in 2005.

▼ Supplemental Security Income benefits help people who are blind.

The Medicare Prescription ▶ Drug program helps seniors manage rising drug costs.

**Why It Matters**
For more than 70 years, Social Security has provided basic economic security to millions of Americans. Social Security programs act as a safety net for senior citizens, the poor, and others in financial need. Popular support for Social Security continues, although concern mounts over the program's long-term funding.

**Thinking Critically**
Describe four different kinds of benefits that the Social Security system provides today.

**History Interactive**

**For:** More about Social Security
**Web Code:** nep-0903

# Labor Unions Find a New Energy

Even before the Great Depression, most industrial workers labored long hours for little pay. Few belonged to labor unions. However, during the Great Depression, there was an upsurge in union activity. New unions enlisted millions of workers from the mining and automobile industries.

**Vocabulary Builder**

upsurge–(UHP serj) *n.* a sudden, rapid increase

**Granting New Rights to Workers**  Roosevelt believed that the success of the New Deal depended on raising the standard of living for American industrial workers. This, he believed, would improve the entire economy. The National Labor Relations Act was the most important piece of New Deal labor legislation. Called the **Wagner Act,** it recognized the right of employees to join labor unions and gave workers the right to **collective bargaining.** Collective bargaining meant that employers had to negotiate with unions about hours, wages, and other working conditions. The law created the National Labor Relations Board (NLRB) to look into workers' complaints.

The **Fair Labor Standards Act** of 1938 provided workers with additional rights. It established a minimum wage, initially at 25 cents per hour, and a maximum workweek of 44 hours. It also outlawed child labor. The minimum wage remains one of the New Deal's most controversial legacies. In the years ahead, the minimum wage would be gradually raised. Today, whenever a raise in the minimum wage is proposed, economists and political leaders debate the wisdom of such an increase.

**Workers Use Their Newfound Rights**  The upsurge in union activity came at the same time as a bitter feud within the major labor federation, the American Federation of Labor (AFL). The AFL represented skilled workers—such as plumbers, carpenters, and electricians—who joined trade or craft unions. Few workers in the major industries belonged to the AFL, and the union made little effort to organize them.

Fed up with the AFL's reluctance to organize, John L. Lewis, the president of the United Mine Workers, and a number of other labor leaders, established the **Congress of Industrial Organizations (CIO).** The workers targeted by the CIO-organizing campaigns tended to be lower paid and ethnically more diverse than those workers represented by the AFL.

## Sit-Down Strikes Lead to Union Gains

The success of the UAW's sit-down strike against General Motors led the U.S. Steel Company to recognize the steelworkers' union. *How do you think strikes affected union membership?*

### Labor Union Membership, 1920–1960

Union members (in millions)

```
20
15
10
 5
 0
   1920  1930  1940  1950  1960
```

SOURCE: *Historical Statistics of the United States*

## The Second New Deal

| Program | Year | Effects |
|---------|------|---------|
| Social Security Act (SSA) | 1935 | Established a pension system and unemployment insurance; provided payments to workers injured on the job, the poor, and people with disabilities |
| Works Progress Administration (WPA) | 1935 | Employed millions of people on government projects ranging from highway construction to arts programs |
| Rural Electrification Administration (REA) | 1935 | Provided loans to electric companies to build power lines, bringing electricity to isolated rural areas |
| National Labor Relations Act (Wagner Act) | 1935 | Outlawed unfair labor practices; granted workers the right to organize unions and to bargain collectively; created the National Labor Relations Board |
| National Youth Administration (NYA) | 1935 | Trained and provided jobs and counseling for unemployed youth between the ages of 16 and 25 |
| Banking Act of 1935 | 1935 | Finalized the creation of the FDIC and made insurance for bank deposits permanent; created a board to regulate the nation's money supply and interest rates on loans |
| United States Housing Authority (USHA) | 1937 | Subsidized construction of low-cost public housing by providing federal loans |
| Fair Labor Standards Act | 1938 | Banned child labor, established a minimum hourly wage, and set the workweek at 44 hours |
| Food, Drug, and Cosmetic Act | 1938 | Prohibited the mislabeling of food, drugs, and cosmetics, and ensured the safety and purity of these products |

This commemorative postage stamp honors the many programs of FDR's New Deal. Critics mocked the abbreviated titles, or acronyms, of the New Deal programs as "alphabet soup." *Use the chart to identify five programs from the second New Deal that helped workers.*

In December 1936, members of the CIO's newly formed United Automobile Workers Union (UAW) staged a **sit-down strike,** occupying one of General Motors' most important plants in Flint, Michigan. In a sit-down strike, workers refuse to leave the workplace until a settlement is reached. When the police and state militia threatened to remove them by force, the workers informed Michigan governor Frank Murphy that they would not leave.

> **Primary Source** "We fully expect that if a violent effort is made to oust us many of us will be killed and we take this means of making it known to our wives, to our children, to the people of the State of Michigan and the country, that if this result follows from the attempt to eject us, you are the one who must be held responsible for our deaths!"
>
> —Auto workers sit-down committee, Flint, Michigan, January 1936

The strike lasted for 44 days until General Motors, then the largest company in the world, agreed to recognize the UAW. This union success led to others. By 1940, 9 million workers belonged to unions, twice the number of members in 1930. Just as important, union members gained better wages and working conditions.

 **Checkpoint** How did the New Deal affect trade unions?

## Challenges to the New Deal

Franklin Roosevelt won an overwhelming victory in the presidential election of 1936. He received 61 percent of the vote, compared to just 37 percent for his Republican challenger, Alfred M. Landon. Roosevelt carried every state but Maine and Vermont. FDR entered his second term determined to challenge the group that he considered the main enemy of the New Deal—a Supreme Court that had struck down many of his programs.

**The Supreme Court Opposes the New Deal** A year before the 1936 election, the Supreme Court had overturned one of the key laws of Roosevelt's first hundred days. In the case of *Schechter Poultry* v. *United States,* the Supreme Court unanimously ruled that since the President has no power to regulate interstate commerce, the National Industrial Recovery Act was unconstitutional. One pro–New Deal newspaper captured the mood of many Democrats: "AMERICA STUNNED; ROOSEVELT'S TWO YEARS' WORK KILLED IN TWENTY MINUTES."

Not long afterward, the Court ruled a key part of the Agricultural Adjustment Act unconstitutional. Roosevelt charged that the Court had taken the nation back to "horse-and-buggy" days. He expected the Court to strike down other New Deal measures, limiting his ability to enact new reforms.

**FDR Proposes "Packing" the Court** So on February 5, 1937, in a special address to Congress, FDR unveiled a plan that would dilute the power of the sitting Justices of the Supreme Court. He called for adding up to six new Justices to the nine-member Court. He justified his proposal by noting that the Constitution did not specify the number of judges on the Court. He added that many of the Justices were elderly and overworked. Critics, recognizing that Roosevelt's new appointees would most likely be New Deal supporters, called his plan **court packing.** They accused him of trying to increase presidential power and upsetting the delicate balance between the three branches of the federal government. Some critics urged Americans to speak out.

> **Primary Source** "If the American people accept this last audacity of the President without letting out a yell to high heaven, they have ceased to be jealous of their liberties and are ripe for ruin."
>
> —Dorothy Thompson, newspaper columnist, 1937

Given Roosevelt's enormous popularity, he might have convinced Congress to enact his plan but he did not have to because the Court began to turn his way. On March 29, 1937, the Court ruled 5 to 4 in favor of a minimum wage law. Two weeks later, again by a vote of 5 to 4, the Supreme Court upheld the constitutionality of the Wagner Act. In both cases, Justice Owen J. Roberts provided the deciding vote. Pundits called it the "switch in time to save nine," because Roberts had previously voted against several New Deal programs. Roberts's two votes in support of the New Deal removed FDR's main reason for packing the Court.

Shortly after this switch, Judge Willis Van Devanter, who had helped strike down several New Deal programs, resigned from the Court. This enabled FDR to nominate a Justice friendlier to the New Deal. With more retirements, Roosevelt nominated a number of other new Justices, including Felix Frankfurter, one of his top advisers.

Indeed, 1937 marked a turning point in the history of the Court. For years to come, the Court more willingly accepted a larger role for the federal government. Yet the court-packing incident weakened FDR politically. Before the court-packing plan, FDR's popularity prevented critics from challenging him. Now that Roosevelt had lost momentum, critics felt free to take him on. And even though the Court did not strike down any more laws, after 1937 Roosevelt found the public much less willing to support further New Deal legislation.

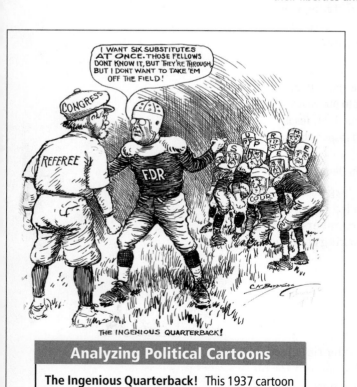

THE INGENIOUS QUARTERBACK!

**Analyzing Political Cartoons**

**The Ingenious Quarterback!** This 1937 cartoon makes fun of FDR's court-packing plan.
1. Why did the cartoonist make FDR the quarterback and Congress the referee?
2. What is the cartoonist's message?

**A New Downturn Spurs Conservative Gains** The turmoil over the Supreme Court had barely faded when the Roosevelt administration faced another crisis. During 1935 and 1936, economic conditions had begun to improve. Unemployment had fallen 10 percent in four years. With the economy doing better, FDR cut back on federal spending in order to reduce the rising deficit. But he miscalculated.

While Roosevelt reduced federal spending, the Federal Reserve Board raised interest rates, making it more difficult for businesses to expand and for consumers to borrow to buy new goods. Suddenly, the economy was in another tailspin. Unemployment soared to more than 20 percent. Nearly all of the gains in employment and production were wiped out.

Largely because of the downturn, the Democrats suffered a setback in the 1938 congressional elections. Republicans picked up 7 Senate and 75 House seats. Although Democrats still maintained a majority in both houses of Congress, Roosevelt's power base was shaken because many southern Democrats were lukewarm supporters of the New Deal. Needing their support for his foreign policies, FDR chose not to try to force more reforms through Congress.

**Unemployment, 1933–1941**

SOURCE: *Historical Statistics of the United States*

**Millions Look for Jobs**
While New Deal programs employed many Americans, millions of others continued to search for work. *What happened to the unemployment rate in 1937?*

✓ **Checkpoint** What setbacks did Roosevelt face during his second term as President?

---

SECTION

**2 Assessment**

**Progress Monitoring *Online***
**For:** Self-test with vocabulary practice
**Web Code:** nea-0904

**Comprehension**

1. **Terms** For each act or New Deal agency below, explain how it eased conditions during the depression.
   • WPA
   • Social Security Act
   • Wagner Act
   • Fair Labor Standards Act

2. <u>NoteTaking</u> **Reading Skill: Connect Ideas** Use your table to answer the Section Focus Question: What major issues did the second New Deal address?

**Writing About History**

3. **Quick Write: Compare and Contrast** In order to synthesize, you need to compare and contrast different sources. List some emotions expressed by the photos on the first and last pages of this section. Do these images convey the same idea as the graph above? Explain in one or two sentences.

**Critical Thinking**

4. **Identify Central Issues** What were the most important reforms of the Second New Deal?

5. **Make Comparisons** Why did American labor make greater progress during the 1930s than during the prosperous 1920s?

6. **Demonstrate Reasoned Judgment** Do you think that FDR's court-packing plan was justified? Explain your answer.

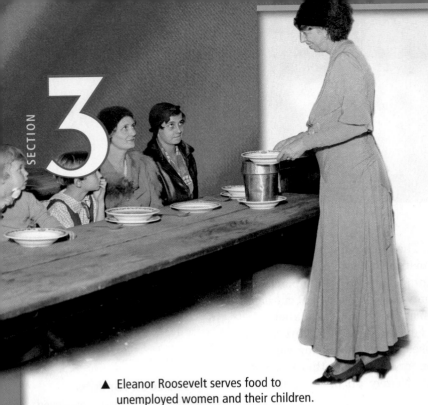

▲ Eleanor Roosevelt serves food to unemployed women and their children.

WITNESS HISTORY  AUDIO

### The Caring First Lady

Eleanor Roosevelt played a crucial role in the New Deal. She traveled to places FDR could not, advised her husband, and served as an inspiration to millions of Americans. Mrs. Roosevelt also corresponded with thousands of citizens. The following letter reflects the affection that many citizens felt for the first lady.

❝Ridley Park, Pennsylvania
Dear Mrs. Roosevelt:
. . . Just to look at your picture and that of our President seems to me like looking at the picture of a saint. So when you answered my letter and promised to have some one help me it only proved that you are our own Mrs. Roosevelt. I have told everyone what you have done for me. I want them to know you are not too busy to answer our letters and give us what help and advice you can. You hold the highest place any woman can hold still you are not to[o] proud to befriend the poor. . . . Thank you and God bless you both.❞
—Letter to Eleanor Roosevelt, September 1, 1935

# Effects of the New Deal

 **Content Expectations**

- **6.3.2e** Analyze causes/consequences of expanding/restricting democracy practices of African Americans/immigrants.
- **6.3.3** Analyze successes/failures to expand women's rights.
- **7.1.3a** Explain expanding federal government responsibility.

### Terms and People

Black Cabinet
Mary McLeod Bethune
Indian New Deal

New Deal coalition
welfare state

### NoteTaking

**Reading Skill: Identify Main Ideas** As you read, identify the lasting effects of the New Deal upon American society.

Expanded role
of government

Effects of
New Deal

**Why It Matters** The New Deal provided desperately needed relief from the depression and enacted reforms that guarded against economic catastrophe. It did not end the depression. World War II, with its massive military spending, would do that. Yet, the New Deal mattered enormously because it brought fundamental changes to the nation. It changed the role of the federal government in the economy, the power of the presidency, and the relationship of the American people to their government. **Section Focus Question: How did the New Deal change the social, economic, and political landscape of the United States for future generations?**

## Women Help Lead the New Deal

The New Deal provided some women with the opportunity to increase their political influence and to promote women's rights. Foremost among them was Eleanor Roosevelt, who transformed the office of First Lady from a largely ceremonial role to a position of action and deep involvement in the political process. Representing the President, she toured the nation. She visited farms and Indian reservations and traveled deep into a coal mine. She helped FDR on his campaigns and offered advice on policy issues. In her newspaper column, "My Day," she called on Americans to live up to the goal of equal justice for all.

"Eleanor Roosevelt is the First Lady of Main Street," explained magazine writer Margaret Marshall. "She occupies the highest social position in the land. Yet she makes friends on a plane or a train even as you and I." Mrs. Roosevelt's causes included advancing public health and education, promoting the arts in rural areas, and even addressing flood control. She exhibited boundless energy, traveling more than 60,000 miles in two years.

Molly Dewson, head of the Women's Division of the Democratic Party, observed that Eleanor Roosevelt provided women with an unprecedented access to the President. "When I wanted help on some definite point, Mrs. Roosevelt gave [me] the opportunity to sit by the President at dinner and the matter was settled before we finished our soup."

The Roosevelt Administration included the first female Cabinet member, Secretary of Labor Frances Perkins. She played a leading role in establishing Social Security. Perkins also helped win approval of the Fair Labor Standards Act, which ended child labor and established a minimum wage.

However, the New Deal did not fight to end gender discrimination in the workplace. Indeed, some historians have argued that a number of New Deal programs reinforced traditional <u>gender</u> differences. The WPA and other relief programs employed women but made a much greater effort to provide work to men first. For example, women were not eligible to work for the CCC. However, the increased homeownership and insured savings accounts brought by the New Deal were of special benefit to the widows of men who were covered.

**Vocabulary Builder**
<u>gender</u>—(JEHN der) *n.* a person's sex

✔ **Checkpoint** What impact did the New Deal have on women?

# African Americans Make Advances and Face Challenges

When the depression hit, African American workers were often the first to lose their jobs. By 1934, the unemployment rate for African Americans was almost 50 percent, more than twice the national average. Eleanor Roosevelt and others urged the President to improve the situation of African Americans.

As the New Deal progressed, Eleanor Roosevelt increasingly used her position to protest against racial discrimination. At a meeting held by the Southern Conference on Human Welfare, a biracial group that sought to promote racial reforms, the first lady sat with the black delegates—a daring move in segregated Birmingham, Alabama. When a white police officer told her that she was violating local segregation laws, Mrs. Roosevelt moved her chair to the space between the black and white sides. She then delivered a rousing and provocative keynote address in favor of racial reform.

**Primary Source** "We are the leading democracy of the world and as such must prove to the world that democracy is possible and capable of living up to the principles upon which it was founded. The eyes of the world are upon us, and often we find they are not too friendly eyes."
—Eleanor Roosevelt, November 22, 1938

## HISTORY MAKERS

**Frances Perkins** (1882–1965)
After graduating from college, Frances Perkins earned her master's degree in economics. From 1912, until being named Secretary of Labor, she held various jobs in New York State government. She was a strong voice for consumers and workers, especially working women and children.

**Mary McLeod Bethune** (1875–1955)
Mary McLeod Bethune was a teacher who worked to improve educational opportunities for African Americans. Bethune served as FDR's special adviser on minority affairs. As the director of Negro Affairs of the National Youth Administration, Bethune was the first black woman to head a federal agency.

The President invited many African American leaders to advise him. These unofficial advisers became known as the **Black Cabinet.** They included Robert Weaver and William Hastie, Harvard University graduates who rose to high positions within the Department of the Interior. Hastie later became a federal judge, and Weaver was the first African American Cabinet member.

**Mary McLeod Bethune** was another member of the Black Cabinet. The founder of what came to be known as Bethune Cookman College, she was a powerful champion of racial equality. In her view, the New Deal had created a "new day" for African Americans. She noted that African Americans gained unprecedented access to the White House and positions within the government during Roosevelt's presidency.

Nevertheless, Roosevelt did not always follow the advice of his Black Cabinet. Racial discrimination and injustice continued to plague African Americans. When the NAACP launched an energetic campaign in favor of a federal anti-lynching law, the President refused to support it. FDR told black leaders that he could not support an antilynching law, because if he did, southern Democrats "would block every bill I ask Congress to pass." Hence, no civil rights reforms became law during the 1930s.

Several New Deal measures also unintentionally hurt African Americans. Federal payments to farmers to produce fewer crops led white landowners to evict unneeded black sharecroppers from their farms. Even though they benefited from the WPA and other relief measures, African Americans often did not receive equal wages. Social Security and the Fair Labor Standards Act exempted domestic workers and farm laborers, two occupations in which African Americans were employed in great numbers.

 **Checkpoint** How did the New Deal affect African Americans?

### Native Americans Benefit From Building Projects
Navajo medicine men attend the opening of a new hospital in Fort Defiance, Arizona, in 1938. *How was this project part of the Indian New Deal?*

# The New Deal Affects Native Americans

Attempting to improve the lives of Native Americans, the Roosevelt administration made major changes in long-standing policies. The 1887 Dawes Act had divided tribal lands into smaller plots. By the early 1930s, it was clear that the act had worsened the condition of the people it was designed to help. Of the original 138 million acres American Indians had owned in 1887, only 48 million remained in American Indian hands, and much of it was too arid to farm. John Collier, the New Deal's Commissioner of Indian Affairs, warned that the Dawes Act was resulting in "total landlessness for the Indians."

To prevent further loss of land and improve living conditions for Native Americans, Collier developed the **Indian New Deal,** a program that gave Indians economic assistance and greater control over their own affairs. Collier got funding from New Deal agencies for the construction of new schools and hospitals and to create an Indian Civilian Conservation Corps. In addition, the Bureau of Indian Affairs, in a reversal of previous policies, encouraged the practice of Indian religions, native languages, and traditional customs. Collier also convinced Congress to pass the Indian Reorganization Act of 1934, considered the centerpiece of the Indian New Deal. This law restored tribal control over Native American land.

Although it did not immediately improve their standard of living, the Indian Reorganization Act gave Native Americans greater control over their destiny. But some New Deal measures actually hurt Native Americans. For example, federal authorities determined that large herds of sheep tended by the Navajos were causing soil erosion on the Colorado Plateau. As a result, the federal government enacted a Navajo Livestock Reduction program, which mandated that the Navajo sell or kill thousands of sheep. The Navajo deeply resented this act. They did not believe that their sheep threatened the soil and they did not trust the motives of government agents.

✔ **Checkpoint** In what ways did the New Deal alter the U.S. policies toward Native Americans?

# The New Deal Creates a New Political Coalition

By the time he died in 1945, Roosevelt had been elected to four terms as President. His legendary political skills had united an unlikely group of Americans into a strong political force called the **New Deal coalition.** This coalition brought together southern whites, northern blue-collar workers—especially those with immigrant roots—poor midwestern farmers, and African Americans.

African American voting patterns show the importance of the New Deal coalition. Before the New Deal, most African Americans voted Republican, the party of Abraham Lincoln. Responding to the efforts of Franklin and Eleanor Roosevelt, African Americans began to vote Democratic during the 1930s. This trend was strongest in the West and the North. For example, in 1934, Arthur W. Mitchell, an African American Democrat, defeated Oscar De Priest, an African American Republican, to represent the largely black south side of Chicago. Mitchell became the first African American Democrat elected to Congress.

The New Deal coalition gave the Democratic Party a sizable majority in both houses of Congress. Before FDR's election, the Democrats had been the minority party in the House of Representatives for all but eight years since 1895. But from 1932 to 1995, the Democrats controlled the majority of seats in the House of Representatives for all but four years. The coalition that elected Roosevelt in 1932 went on to secure the White House for the Democrats in six of the next eight presidential elections.

### African Americans Join New Deal Coalition

In Atlanta, African Americans register to vote in a Democratic primary election. *What percentage of African American voters voted Democratic in 1932? What was the percentage in 2004?*

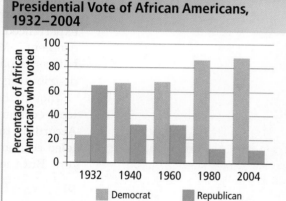

**Presidential Vote of African Americans, 1932–2004**

Percentage of African Americans who voted

■ Democrat  ■ Republican

SOURCES: Joint Center for Political and Economic Studies; Donald L. Grant, *The Way It Was in the South: The Black Experience in Georgia*; Sean J. Savage, *Roosevelt: The Party Leader, 1932–1945*; CNN.com

Besides forging a powerful political coalition, Roosevelt and the New Deal helped to unify the nation. Social and <u>ethnic</u> divisions, so much a part of the 1920s, diminished significantly during the 1930s. Immigrant communities, in particular, gained a greater sense of belonging to the mainstream. Programs such as the CCC and WPA allowed individuals of varied backgrounds to get to know one another, breaking down regional and ethnic prejudices. As one CCC worker observed:

> **Primary Source** "The Civilian Conservation Corps is a smaller melting pot within the big one. We are thrown together in such a way that we have to get acquainted whether or not we want to. . . . Different races and nationalities look each other in the face, work and eat together for the first time. And it is a safe bet, we think, that this process many times results in the elimination of traditional prejudices based on ignorance and misinformation."
>
> —C. W. Kirkpatrick, CCC worker

 **Checkpoint** How did New Deal policies affect ethnic and social divisions?

## The Role of Government Expands

New Deal programs greatly increased the size and scope of the federal government. "For the first time for many Americans," writes historian William Leuchtenburg, "the federal government became an institution that was directly experienced. More than the state and local governments, it came to be *the* government." Moreover, the government began to do things it had never done before, from withdrawing taxes directly from workers' paychecks to distributing benefits to the elderly.

Though the New Deal did not end the depression, it did help restore the American economy. It created the foundation for sustained and stable growth. According to Pulitzer Prize–winning historian David Kennedy, "the unparalleled economic vitality of the post-1940 decades was attributable to many factors. But the [economic expansion] . . . owed much to the New Deal."

**Playing a Larger Role in the Economy** With the New Deal, the federal government broke from the tradition of laissez faire, or leaving the economy alone, which had characterized most of American history. Now the federal government accepted responsibility for spurring economic growth, or pump priming. For the first time, the government had acted as an employer of the unemployed and a sponsor of work projects. FDR accepted the idea that the federal government had to do something to get the economy going again, and Democrats and many Republicans agreed.

FDR's rejection of laissez-faire policies led a number of New Deal critics to accuse him of promoting socialism. However, many New Deal measures actually strengthened capitalism and helped make possible the economic boom of the post–World War II era. The FDIC and SEC restored Americans' trust in banks and the stock market. The Federal Housing Authority (FHA) provided low-interest loans, increasing homeownership.

The New Deal affected millions of workers and their families. The Wagner Act boosted union membership, which continued to grow after World War II. Minimum wage increases improved the purchasing power of minorities and those at the bottom rung of the economic ladder. New Deal legislation created child labor laws, workers' compensation laws, and unemployment insurance, programs that had important and enduring impacts on the U.S. economy.

## TRACK THE ISSUE

### What is the proper balance between free enterprise and government regulation of the economy?

In theory, a free-enterprise system should function with little government interference. In practice, though, our government often plays a strong economic role. How much government regulation of the economy is appropriate? Use the timeline below to explore this enduring issue.

**1890  Sherman Antitrust Act**
Congress tries to curb the power of monopolies.

**1906  Pure Food and Drug Act**
Progressive law regulates the safety of food and medicine.

**1913  Federal Reserve Act**
Federal Reserve system is established to control the money supply.

**1933  Agricultural Adjustment Act**
New Deal law pays farmers to reduce production, causing higher crop prices and farm profits.

**2001 Tax Cuts**
Government lowers taxes in an effort to promote economic growth.

### Federal Social Welfare Spending

Percentage of gross national product (GNP)

| Year | Percentage |
| --- | --- |
| 1930 | ~4 |
| 1950 | ~9 |
| 1970 | ~15 |
| 1990 | ~17.5 |

SOURCES: *Historical Statistics of the United States; Social Security Bulletin; Statistical Abstract of the United States*

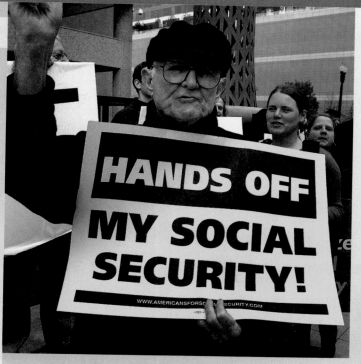

MI 7.1.3c

Activists protest plans to privatize Social Security.

## DEBATE THE ISSUE

**Social Security's Effectiveness**  The government manages retirement accounts for millions of Americans through the Social Security system. But with the coming retirement of millions of baby boomers, some people believe that Social Security can no longer achieve its original goals.

"Well, the system is facing serious financial problems, but more than that it has become an increasingly bad deal for today's workers. Workers are paying 12 1/2 percent of their income into a system that is providing a poorer and poorer return. It's a system in which workers don't own their assets, have no legal rights to their benefits, don't control their money, and a system that penalizes groups like African Americans and working women."

—Michael Tanner, Cato Institute

"Social Security is one of the most successful government programs. It has consistently provided a safety net for seniors so that retirees are able to support themselves through their retirement and pay for food, housing, and medical costs. By helping to support the elderly and vulnerable among us, Social Security provides Americans with the guarantee of security for life."

—Center for American Progress

### TRANSFER Activities

1. **Compare**  Do you think that today's Center for American Progress would support or oppose New Deal laws like the AAA?

2. **Analyze Costs and Benefits**  Compare the data on this page to the data in the Section 2 Social Security feature. Do you think that the costs of Social Security outweigh the benefits?

3. **Transfer**  Use the following Web site to see a video, try a WebQuest, and write in your journal. **Web Code:** neh-8202

The New Deal had a great impact on rural Americans. Regional public-works projects, such as the TVA and Bonneville Dam, reduced flooding and provided water for irrigation. Along with the Rural Electrification Administration, these dams brought electricity to farmers in the Southeast and the Northwest. Rose Dudley Scearce of Shelby, Kentucky, recalled what the REA meant to her farm family:

**Primary Source** "The first benefit we received from the REA was light, and aren't lights grand? My little boy expressed my sentiments when he said, 'Mother, I didn't realize how dark our house was until we got electric lights.' . . . Like the rest of the people, we changed our storage-battery radio into an electric radio. . . . Next we bought an electric refrigerator. . . . The next benefit we received from the current was our electric stove. . . . Now with a vacuum cleaner, I can even dust the furniture before I clean the carpet, the carpet gets clean, and I stay in good humor."
—Rose Dudley Scearce, "What the REA Service Means to Our Farm House"

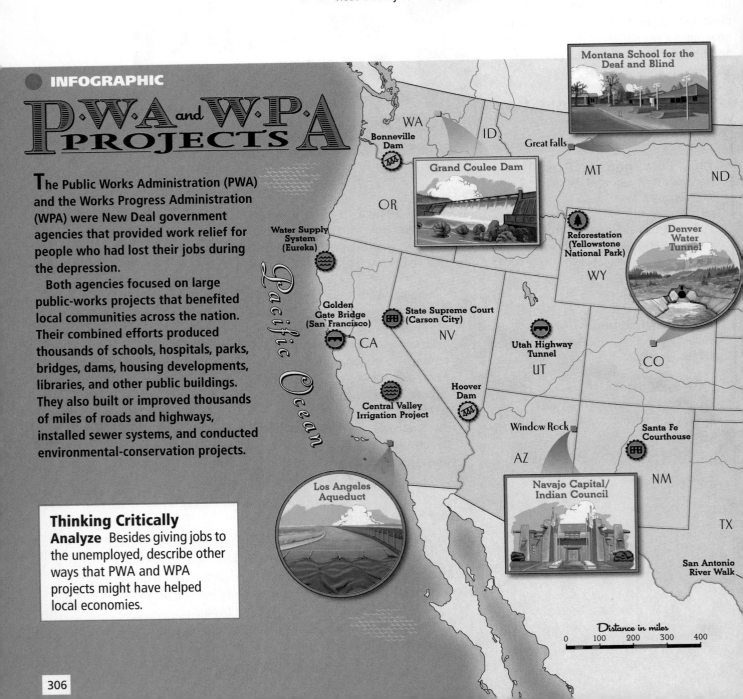

**INFOGRAPHIC**

# P·W·A and W·P·A PROJECTS

The Public Works Administration (PWA) and the Works Progress Administration (WPA) were New Deal government agencies that provided work relief for people who had lost their jobs during the depression.

Both agencies focused on large public-works projects that benefited local communities across the nation. Their combined efforts produced thousands of schools, hospitals, parks, bridges, dams, housing developments, libraries, and other public buildings. They also built or improved thousands of miles of roads and highways, installed sewer systems, and conducted environmental-conservation projects.

**Thinking Critically**
**Analyze** Besides giving jobs to the unemployed, describe other ways that PWA and WPA projects might have helped local economies.

Montana School for the Deaf and Blind

WA
Bonneville Dam
Great Falls
ID
MT
ND

Grand Coulee Dam

OR

Reforestation (Yellowstone National Park)

Denver Water Tunnel

WY

Water Supply System (Eureka)

Golden Gate Bridge (San Francisco)

State Supreme Court (Carson City)

CA
NV

Utah Highway Tunnel

UT
CO

Central Valley Irrigation Project

Hoover Dam

Window Rock

Santa Fe Courthouse

AZ
NM

Los Angeles Aqueduct

Navajo Capital/ Indian Council

TX

San Antonio River Walk

*Pacific Ocean*

Distance in miles
0    100   200   300   400

**Creating a Welfare State** "We are going to make a country in which no one is left out," Franklin Roosevelt once told Frances Perkins. The many programs he enacted to realize this goal led to the rise of a **welfare state** in the United States, a government that assumes responsibility for providing for the welfare of children and the poor, elderly, sick, disabled, and unemployed.

The creation of the American welfare state was a major change in government policy. With the exception of military veterans, most Americans had never received any direct benefits from the federal government. State and local governments, private charities, and families had long served as the safety net for needy Americans. True, the New Deal did not achieve FDR's goal of "a country in which no one is left out," because it exempted many Americans from Social Security and other programs. Still, the New Deal established the principle that the federal government was responsible for the welfare of all Americans. In the latter half of the twentieth century, the reach of government programs would grow greatly.

## Causes

- Stock market crash
- Failure of farms and businesses
- Sharp decline in prices and production
- Failure of banks
- Massive unemployment and low wages
- Homelessness and Hoovervilles
- Drought, crop failures, and Dust Bowl

## The New Deal

## Effects

- Millions employed in new government programs
- Banking system is stabilized
- Regulated stock market restores confidence
- Social-insurance programs aid elderly and poor
- Agricultural subsidies help farmers
- Government takes more active role in economy

## Connections to Today

- Social Security and other New Deal programs still exist
- Size and role of federal government still debated
- Costs and benefits of social welfare programs still debated

**Analyze Cause and Effect** The New Deal brought dramatic changes to the United States. *Identify one economic and one political effect of the New Deal.*

New Deal reforms provided the framework for the debate over the proper role of the federal government in the private lives of Americans. It energized liberals who would push for an even greater role for the federal government in future years. But it troubled conservatives who would argue that the expansion of the federal government limited American rights. Indeed, this very debate divides liberals and conservatives to this day.

**Restoring the Environment** Reared in New York State's beautiful Hudson River valley, Franklin Roosevelt had a great love of nature. As a child, FDR also loved outdoor sports and became an expert swimmer and sailor. A number of his New Deal programs, such as the CCC, aimed at restoring forests and preserving the environment. Other federal agencies started soil conservation efforts. Perhaps most visibly, New Dealers worked hard to end the Dust Bowl, a symbol of the degraded state of the land at the beginning of the depression.

Franklin Roosevelt also continued the conservation work of his cousin, President Theodore Roosevelt. Although funds were short, the government set aside about 12 million acres of land for new national parks, including Shenandoah National Park in Virginia, Kings Canyon National Park in California, and Olympic National Park in Washington State.

However, not all New Deal programs helped the environment. Several of the large public-works projects, such as the TVA and the string of dams along the Columbia River, had a mixed impact. The dams controlled floods, generated electric power, and provided irrigation, but they also upset the natural habitats of some aquatic life. Massive reservoirs created by these projects also displaced some people and destroyed some traditional Native American burial, hunting, and fishing grounds.

**Changing the Nature of the Presidency** In no area did FDR have a greater impact than on the office of the President itself. The expanding role of the government, including the creation of many new federal agencies, gave the executive branch much more power. New Deal administrators, such as Harry Hopkins, head of the WPA, commanded large bureaucracies with massive budgets and little supervision by Congress. Their authority increased Roosevelt's influence. Indeed, some commentators even began to speak of the rise of an imperial presidency, an unflattering comparison to the power exercised in the past by rulers of great empires.

FDR also affected the style of the presidency. His mastery of the radio captivated Americans. His close relations with the press assured a generally popular response to his projects from the major media. Because he served for such a long time and was such an outstanding communicator, FDR set a standard that future Presidents had a hard time fulfilling.

Later, during World War II, FDR's presidential power grew even greater. As commander in chief of the nation's armed forces, he exercised enormous authority over many aspects of life. Most Americans accepted the President's increased

- Increased power of the President and the executive branch
- Made mass media, such as radio, an essential tool in advertising and promoting policies
- Expanded role of the President in managing the economy
- Expanded role of the President in developing social policy
- Won third and fourth terms, leading to passage of Twenty-second Amendment, which limited Presidents to two consecutive terms

authority as a necessary condition of wartime. But after the war, they sought to protect the delicate balance between the different branches of government and between the federal and state governments.

One way that Americans sought to guard against the growing power of the President was by amending the Constitution. When Roosevelt ran for an unprecedented third term in 1940, he knew that he had broken an unwritten rule, established by George Washington, that Presidents should serve only two terms. He won that election and then ran and won again in 1944. But after Roosevelt's death in 1945, there was a growing call for limiting a President's term in office. In 1951, the Twenty-second Amendment was ratified, limiting the President to two consecutive terms.

### The Presidency After Roosevelt

Franklin Roosevelt had a dramatic impact on the role of the presidency. *Was FDR's impact positive or negative?*

✔ **Checkpoint** In what ways did the role of the federal government grow during Franklin Roosevelt's presidency?

---

SECTION **3** Assessment

**Progress Monitoring Online**
For: Self-test with vocabulary practice
Web Code: nea-0906

### Comprehension

**1. Terms and People** What is the relationship between each of the following terms or people and the enduring significance of the New Deal?
- Black Cabinet
- Mary McLeod Bethune
- Indian New Deal
- New Deal coalition
- welfare state

**2. NoteTaking Reading Skill: Identify Main Ideas** Use your concept web to answer the Section Focus Question: How did the New Deal change the social, economic, and political landscape of the United States for future generations?

### Writing About History

**3. Quick Write: Draw Conclusions** After comparing information from different sources, the next step in synthesizing is to draw conclusions. Compare the photograph of Eleanor Roosevelt with the primary source on the section's opening page. Write a paragraph that describes Mrs. Roosevelt's personality.

### Critical Thinking

**4. Recognize Cause and Effect** Why do you think African Americans suffered more extensive discrimination during the depression than during more prosperous times?

**5. Determine Relevance** Has the New Deal coalition affected politics in your community today? Explain your answer.

**6. Synthesize Information** Did the growth in the powers of the federal government during the New Deal benefit the nation? Explain your answer.

▲ *The Wizard of Oz's* Dorothy, Tin Man, and Scarecrow

**SECTION 4**

## WITNESS HISTORY 🔊 AUDIO

### "Somewhere Over the Rainbow"

Americans eager to escape the gloom of the depression regularly sought refuge in the fantasy world presented by the movies. One of their favorites was *The Wizard of Oz,* which opened in 1939. In an early scene, the farm girl Dorothy sings of better times:

❝Somewhere over the rainbow
  Way up high,
  There's a land that I've heard of
  Once in a lullaby.

Somewhere over the rainbow
  Skies are blue,
  And the dreams that you dare to dream
  Really do come true.

Some day I'll wish upon a star
  And wake up where the clouds are far behind me.
  Where troubles melt like lemon drops
  Away above the chimney tops
  That's where you'll find me.❞
— "Over the Rainbow," E. Y. Harburg, 1939

# Culture of the 1930s

### Content Expectations

- **7.1.1a** Explain significance of Harlem Renaissance/"lost generation."
- **7.1.2a** Analyze political, economic, environmental, social causes of Great Depression.
- **7.1.3c** Explain consequences of New Deal policies.

### Terms and People

Frank Capra
Federal Art Project
mural

Dorothea Lange
John Steinbeck
Lillian Hellman

### NoteTaking

**Reading Skill: Identify Main Ideas and Details** Complete a table like the one below to record examples of cultural or popular media.

| Cultural or Popular Media | Example |
|---|---|
| Movies | |
| | |

**Why It Matters** Mass entertainment, such as *The Wizard of Oz,* flourished during the New Deal years as Americans sought escape from the worries of the depression. And, for the first time, the government played an active role in the arts, creating programs that put artists to work. It was a golden age for entertainment, and the movies, music, and works of literature produced during this era hold a unique place in American culture. **Section Focus Question: How did the men and women of the depression find relief from their hardships in the popular culture?**

## Movies and Radio Captivate Americans

Entertainment became big business during the 1930s. Large radio networks, such as NBC and CBS, were broadcasting giants while a cluster of film companies—including MGM, Warner Brothers, Twentieth Century Fox, and Paramount—dominated the silver screen. By 1935, two in three homes owned a radio; by the end of the decade, about nine in ten did. In 1939, nearly two thirds of all Americans attended at least one movie a week. Stars in both industries made fortunes and attracted loyal followings. Glossy fan magazines tracked the stars' personal and professional lives.

**Enjoying Escapism** Above all, when Americans went to the movies during the Great Depression, they did so as a means of escapism. They sought relief from their concerns through a good laugh, a good cry, a lyrical song, or by seeing good triumph over evil. *The Wizrd of Oz,* one of the most memorable depression-era films, delivered all four. It promised weary audiences that their dreams really would come true.

The big movie studios churned out musicals, romantic comedies, and gangster films. Children marveled at the colorful animation of Walt Disney's *Snow White and the Seven Dwarfs.* For a good scare, teens and young adults flocked to *Frankenstein.* Adults watched dancers Fred Astaire and Ginger Rogers glide effortlessly across the ballroom floor in *Top Hat.* And millions wept as they watched the stormy love affair between Clark Gable and Vivien Leigh in the Civil War epic *Gone With the Wind.*

**Providing Social Commentary** In the early 1930s, many films reflected the public's distrust of big business and government. Gangster movies, such as *Public Enemy* starring James Cagney, were very popular. These films showed a declining faith in government and law enforcement, with characters turning to crime to survive the depression. But as the New Deal restored confidence, the government regained its glow, and movies began portraying government officials as heroes. In 1935, Cagney portrayed an FBI agent who captured the bad guys in *G-Men.*

Other films focused on the strength of average Americans. Director **Frank Capra** was a leader of this genre. The characters in his films were everyday people struggling with the hardships of the time. In Capra's *Mr. Smith Goes to Washington,* actor James Stewart plays a junior senator who fights against the greed and corruption he finds in the nation's capital. Depression-era audiences cheered Capra's films, which celebrate American idealism and the triumph of the common man over the forces of adversity.

**Radio's Golden Age** The success of the movie industry was matched by that of radio. The national radio networks broadcast popular shows starring comedians such as Bob Hope and Jack Benny. Americans avidly followed soap operas,

### Radio Captures the Nation
Americans united in their love for the radio and its stars, including mainstays George Burns and Gracie Allen (below).

variety shows, and humorists, such as Will Rogers. Dramatic shows were also popular. *The Lone Ranger* started its run in 1933 and ran for more than 20 years. The detective serial *The Shadow* began each thrilling episode with the haunting line, "Who knows what evil lurks in the hearts of men?"

In addition to providing entertainment, the family radio provided information. FDR used his fireside chats to explain and promote his New Deal programs. Newscasters delivered the daily news and political commentary.

On at least one occasion, radio listeners had a hard time recognizing the difference between news and entertainment. It happened on the night of October 30, 1938, when millions of Americans tuned in to a drama called *War of the World,* directed by Orson Welles. The Mercury Theatre broadcast was so realistic that many people believed that Martians were actually invading. Panic gripped areas of the country until announcers insisted that it was all make-believe.

**Swinging to the Sounds of the Era** Like films and radio shows, music provided a diversion from hard times. Whether listening to the radio at home or dancing in nightclubs, Americans enjoyed the popular music of the day. "Swing" music played by "big bands" topped the charts. Duke Ellington, Benny Goodman, Artie Shaw, Glenn Miller, and Jimmy and Tommy Dorsey were some of the top swing musicians, a term probably derived from Ellington's tune "It Don't Mean a Thing If It Ain't Got That Swing." *Your Hit Parade* and *Make Believe Ballroom*—the program that introduced disc jockeys—were just two of the radio shows that brought the latest tunes to listeners. The most popular vocalist of the era was Bing Crosby.

Latin music was very popular. The rhythms of the rumba and the samba had a special appeal for dancers, and Latin bands were prominently featured in films and on the radio. Folk and ethnic music also gained a following during the 1930s. Black singers focused on the harsh conditions faced by African Americans. Huddie Ledbetter, a folk singer known as Leadbelly, described experiences of African Americans with the songs "Cotton Fields" and "The Midnight Special." Woody Guthrie wrote ballads about the Okies, farmers who fled Dust Bowl states and headed to California. Guthrie's song "Dust Bowl Refugee" helped listeners understand the Okies' plight.

✔ **Checkpoint** What were some of the most important popular cultural trends of the 1930s?

**Funding the Arts**
The Federal Art Project poster (below) promotes an exhibition of works by WPA artists. William Gropper's mural, *Construction of a Dam,* was a tribute to the strength and dignity of labor inspired by the construction of two western dams.

# The New Deal and the Arts

During the New Deal, the federal government provided funding for the arts for the first time in American history. Recognizing that many artists and writers faced dire circumstances, WPA administrator Harry Hopkins established a special branch of the WPA to provide artists with work. Programs such as the **Federal Art Project,** the Federal Writers' Project, and the Federal Theater Project offered a variety of job opportunities to artists.

In federally funded theaters, musicians and actors staged performances that were often free to the public. In a series of new state guidebooks, WPA writers recorded the history and folklore of the nation. Artists painted huge, dramatic **murals** on public buildings across the nation. These paintings celebrated the accomplishments of the workers who helped build the nation. Many of the murals can still be seen in public buildings today.

Photographers also benefited from federal arts programs. The Resettlement and Farm Security Administration (FSA) sought to document the plight of America's farmers. Roosevelt's top aide, Rexford Tugwell, told the head of the FSA, "Show the city people what it's like to live on the farm." Walker Evans and **Dorothea Lange** were among the FSA photographers who created powerful images of impoverished farmers and migrant workers, including Lange's famous photo "Migrant Mother."

> **Primary Source** ❝When Dorothea took that picture that was the ultimate. She never surpassed it. . . . She has all the suffering of mankind in her but all the perseverance too. A restraint and a strange courage.❞
> —Roy Stryker, FSA, on Dorothea Lange's "Migrant Mother"

Some members of Congress attacked the Federal Art programs for promoting radical values. Congressman J. Parnell Thomas described the Federal Writers' and Theater projects as "a hotbed for Communists." Eleanor Roosevelt and others defended the Federal Art programs on the grounds that they did not "believe in censoring anything." Nonetheless, congressional support for the programs declined. Although the Federal Art programs ceased to exist in the early 1940s, they set a precedent for further federal funding of the arts and humanities in the 1960s.

✓ **Checkpoint** In what ways did the New Deal support American arts?

### California

One of several WPA murals in San Francisco's Coit Tower, *California* was painted by Maxine Albro, an artist who painted many scenes of Mexican life after studying with noted Mexican muralist Diego Rivera.

## Native Son

Richard Wright's novel about the psychological pressures that lead a young black man to commit murder sold more than 200,000 copies in one month. During the 1930s, the author worked as a writer and editor for the Federal Writers' Project in Chicago.

# The Literature of the Depression

The literature of the 1920s, from authors such as F. Scott Fitzgerald and Ernest Hemingway, sometimes overshadowed the literature of the 1930s. Still, the depression era produced some memorable works.

During the depression, many writers drifted to the left and crafted novels featuring working-class heroes. They believed that the American economic system no longer worked and they blamed this failure on political and business leaders. Many artists of the 1930s saw "ordinary Americans" as the best hope for a better day.

The most famous novel of the 1930s was **John Steinbeck**'s *The Grapes of Wrath.* Steinbeck follows the fictional Joad family from their home in Oklahoma, which has been ravaged by Dust Bowl conditions, to California, where they hope to build a better life. But instead of the Promised Land, the Joads encounter exploitation, disease, hunger, and political corruption.

African American writers captured the special plight of blacks, facing both the depression and continuing prejudice. Richard Wright's *Native Son* explored racial prejudice in a northern urban setting. Wright was an outspoken critic of racial discrimination.

In New York, some important playwrights had their first successes during the New Deal period. **Lillian Hellman,** a New Orleans native, wrote several plays featuring strong roles for women. Hellman's plays *The Children's Hour, The Little Foxes,* and *Watch on the Rhine* are also notable for their socially conscious subject matter. Clifford Odets was another dramatist who achieved prominence in the 1930s. His plays *Waiting for Lefty* and *Awake and Sing!* chronicle the struggles of the working class during the Great Depression.

On a lighter note, many Americans devoured comic strips and comic books during the 1930s. Among the most popular comic strips were *Flash Gordon,* a science-fiction saga; *Dick Tracy,* a detective story; and *Superman,* the first great "superhero" comic. The success of *Superman,* which began in 1938, quickly led to a radio show and later to a popular television series and several feature films. *Superman* reassured Americans that ordinary citizens, like mild-mannered Clark Kent, could overcome evil.

 **Checkpoint** Describe the most notable works of literature of the 1930s.

---

SECTION

# 4 Assessment

**Progress Monitoring *Online***
**For:** Self-test with vocabulary practice
**Web Code:** nea-0907

## Comprehension

**1. Terms and People** For each item below, write a sentence explaining how it affected the people of the era.
- *The Wizard of Oz*
- Frank Capra
- *War of the Worlds*
- Federal Art Project

**2. NoteTaking Reading Skill: Identify Main Ideas and Details** Use your table to answer the Section Focus Question: How did the men and women of the depression find relief from their hardships in the popular culture?

## Writing About History

**3. Quick Write: Make Generalizations** Compare *The Wizard of Oz* and *War of the Worlds.* Write a few sentences describing how both were escapist fare that helped people forget their troubles.

## Critical Thinking

**4. Make Generalizations** What values did the movies and other popular entertainment of the depression reinforce for Americans?

**5. Identify Effects** How did federal support of the arts benefit both artists and the public?

**6. Identify Point of View** How did the work of New Deal era artists and writers contribute to our appreciation today of the New Deal?

# The Golden Age of Hollywood

The 1930s were a Golden Age for Hollywood—and for moviegoers. Depression-era audiences watched the latest Hollywood spectacles in beautiful theaters that were a far cry from today's multiplexes. Advancements in color and sound added even more realism to movies that depicted lives of glamour and adventure unknown to most Americans. But it was the outstanding quality of the movies that made the 1930s Hollywood's Golden Age.

▲ *King Kong* (1933)
*King Kong* was the thrilling adventure tale of a giant ape and the woman he loved. The film's innovative special effects helped make it a huge box-office hit.

◄ *Gone With the Wind* (1939)
Clark Gable was Rhett Butler, and Vivien Leigh was Scarlett O'Hara in the Civil War saga adapted from Margaret Mitchell's Pulitzer Prize–winning novel.

▲ *Swing Time* (1936)
Fred Astaire and Ginger Rogers became one of the silver screen's legendary teams as they danced their way through a series of popular musicals.

▼ *Dead End* (1937)
A gritty social drama about life in a Manhattan slum, *Dead End* starred Humphrey Bogart and introduced the Dead End Kids.

## Thinking Critically

1. **Make Inferences** Why would people who were struggling just to get by enjoy films portraying extravagant upper-class lifestyles?

2. **Connect to Today** Do you think Hollywood movies give an accurate picture of contemporary American life? Explain.

# Quick Study Guide

 7.1.3c

## ■ New Deal Legislation

| New Deal Program | Effects |
|---|---|
| Federal Deposit Insurance Corporation (FDIC), 1933 | Guaranteed bank deposits up to $5,000 to ease banking crisis |
| National Recovery Administration (NRA), 1933 | Established codes to regulate wages and prices, stimulate consumer activity, and promote fair competition |
| Securities and Exchange Commission (SEC), 1934 | Regulated the stock market and restored investor confidence |
| Civilian Conservation Corps (CCC), 1933 | Provided jobs for millions of young, single men on conservation projects |
| Public Works Administration (PWA), 1933 | Sponsored large-scale government construction projects to create new jobs and improve the nation's infrastructure |
| Agricultural Adjustment Act (AAA), 1933 | Paid subsidies to lower production on farms and raise crop prices |
| Tennessee Valley Authority (TVA), 1933 | Built dams and hydroelectric plants in the Tennessee River valley to control flooding, generate power, and attract industry to the South |
| Home Owners' Loan Corporation (HOLC), 1933 | Provided low-interest loans to homeowners who were unable to make mortgage payments |

## ■ Effects of the New Deal

**Immediate Effects**
- Banking system is stabilized.
- Federal payments help farmers.
- Work-relief programs provide jobs.
- Social Security provides safety net.
- New Deal helps to unify the nation.

**Long-term Effects**
- Power of the presidency increases.
- Government takes active role in economy.
- New Deal coalition is powerful political force.
- Wagner Act protects workers and raises standard of living.
- Minorities and women gain positions in government.

## ■ Opposition to the New Deal

| On the Left | On the Right |
|---|---|
| • New Deal does not do enough to end the depression.<br>• FDR's only concern is saving banks and big business.<br>• New Deal does not address redistribution of wealth.<br>• New Deal does not help the elderly. | • New Deal makes government too powerful.<br>• Increased government role in economy equals socialism.<br>• New Deal destroys free enterprise and individual freedom.<br>• New Deal creates huge national debt. |

## ☑ Quick Study Timeline

**In America**

**1932** More than 5,000 banks close

**1933** FDR begins New Deal

**1934** Dust Bowl worsens

**1935** Social Security Act passed

**Presidential Terms** Herbert Hoover 1929–1933     Franklin D. Roosevelt 1933–1945

**1932**                                                                          **1935**

**Around the World**

**1932** Aldous Huxley's *Brave New World* is published

**1933** Nazis begin burning of books

**1935** Italy invades Ethiopia

# American Issues
●━━●━━● **Connector**

By connecting prior knowledge with what you have learned in this chapter, you can gradually build your understanding of enduring questions that still affect America today. Answer the questions below. Then, use your American Issues Connector study guide (or go online: www.PHSchool.com **Web Code:** neh-8203).

## Issues You Learned About

● **Government's Role in the Economy** Political leaders disagree on how much control the government should have over the national economy.

1. Do you agree with the statement that many Americans probably thought that Herbert Hoover should have let his administration take a greater role in the economy? Explain.

2. Following the tradition of laissez faire, how did the federal government respond to the downturn of the economy under Hoover? How did it respond under Roosevelt?

● **American Indian Policy** The U.S. government has followed different policies toward Native Americans.

3. What did the Indian Removal Act demand? What action did some Indian tribes, that did not want to follow the Indian Removal Act, take?

4. What was the Dawes Act? Did it achieve its goals?

5. How did John Collier bring changes to American Indian life and culture?

● **Federal Power and States' Rights** At times, the national government may seem to go beyond its constitutional rights.

6. According to the Constitution, what powers does the national government have over trade? What powers does each state government have?

7. In response to the Supreme Court ruling in *Schechter Poultry* v. *United States*, one newspaper proclaimed this headline: "ROOSEVELT'S TWO YEARS' WORK KILLED IN TWENTY MINUTES." What did the headline mean?

| Connect to Your World | Michigan |
|---|---|

**Interaction with the Environment** As you have read, President Franklin Roosevelt created the Civilian Conservation Corps (CCC) to help provide jobs to young American men during the Great Depression. The Michigan CCC, however, had a special mission. In the late 19th century, Michigan became the national leader in the logging industry. Even as lumber sales reached into the billions of dollars, logging and related fires ruined nearly 20 million acres of Michigan land. When lumber companies abandoned the barren land, the state government took ownership of much of the area. Michigan CCC members planted more than 485 million new trees there between 1933 and 1942. Do research and prepare a presentation about current efforts to preserve Michigan's forests.

**1936** UAW stages sit-down strike

**1939** *Gone With the Wind* breaks box-office records

**1940** FDR reelected to third term

**History** *Interactive*
**For:** Interactive timeline
**Web Code:** nep-0910

| 1938 | | 1941 |
|---|---|---|

**1936** Spanish Civil War begins

**1937** Pablo Picasso paints *Guernica*

**1939** Radio broadcasts WWII events

**1941** Japanese attack Pearl Harbor

# Chapter Assessment

## Terms and People

1. What was the **CCC**? How did it help individual Americans as well as the country?
2. Define **pump priming.** Give an example of pump priming in the second New Deal.
3. Define **collective bargaining** and **sit-down strikes.** How effective did workers find these methods?
4. Who was **Mary McLeod Bethune**? How did she feel about the New Deal?
5. What were the Federal Theater Project, the Federal Writers' Project, and the **Federal Art Project**? When and why did they come to an end?

## Focus Questions

The focus question for this chapter is **How did the New Deal respond to the ravages of the depression and change the role of the federal government?** Build an answer to this big question by answering the focus questions for Sections 1 through 4 and the Critical Thinking questions that follow.

### Section 1
6. How did the New Deal attempt to address the problems of the depression?

### Section 2
7. What major issues did the second New Deal address?

### Section 3
8. How did the New Deal change the social, economic, and political landscape of the United States for future generations?

### Section 4
9. How did the men and women of the depression find relief from their hardships in the popular culture?

## Critical Thinking

10. **Analyze Information** The first New Deal had three goals: relief, recovery, and reform. Choose one of the laws or programs created by the first New Deal and explain how the program met one, two, or all of these goals.
11. **Compare Points of View** Why did both the right and the left protest the New Deal?
12. **Summarize** What impact did New Deal programs and legislation have on the lives of industrial workers?
13. **Analyze Graphs** Study the graph below.

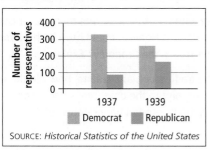

SOURCE: *Historical Statistics of the United States*

What political shift does this graph show? What caused this change?

14. **Draw Inferences** Why did New Deal work programs place a greater emphasis on employing men than women?
15. **Determine Relevance** What does the creation of a welfare state say about the changing priorities of the United States? Does this principle still hold today? Give examples to support your answer.
16. **Identify Point of View** Why might filmmakers have chosen to produce movies that drew on America's historical past?
17. **Evaluate Credibility of Sources** Do you think the work of depression-era writers can be read for historical value? Explain.

## Writing About History

**Synthesize Information** In this chapter there are different images of President Roosevelt. One photograph might present FDR as weak, while another shows him as strong and confident. A cartoon might praise or criticize him. Write a few paragraphs in which you compare several different viewpoints on FDR, and then draw your own conclusion about him.

### Prewriting
• Find four different images of Roosevelt that you will compare and contrast.
• Identify the main idea or viewpoint that is conveyed by each photograph or cartoon.

### Drafting
• For each image, write a brief paragraph describing the main idea of the image.

• Then, write a paragraph in which you point out how the portrayals of FDR are similar and different.
• Finally, write a concluding paragraph in which you draw your own conclusions and make some generalizations about the nature of FDR.

### Revising
• Use the guidelines on page SH11 of the Writing Handbook to revise your essay.

# Prepare for the MME

## The Tennessee Valley Authority

Was the Tennessee Valley Authority (TVA) a federal program that would bring jobs and electricity to rural towns in the region? Or was it an expensive, poorly planned federal program that taxpayers would have to shoulder and that would also cause many environmental problems? Use your knowledge of the TVA and Documents A, B, C, and D to answer questions 1 through 4.

### Document A

"... The continued idleness of a great national investment in the Tennessee Valley leads me to ask Congress for legislation necessary to enlist this project in the service of the people. It is clear that the Muscle Shoals development is but a small part of the potential public usefulness of the entire Tennessee River. Such use, if envisioned in its entirety, transcends mere power development; it enters the wide fields of flood control, soil erosion, afforestation, elimination from agricultural use of marginal lands, and distribution and diversification of industry."
—President Franklin D. Roosevelt, April 10, 1933

### Document B

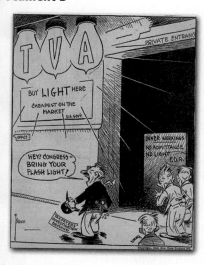

### Document C

"... The TVA has therefore appeared to be on the side of the angels in the controversy between it and the utilities. But the conservation program of the TVA is only a masquerade. It has no functional connection with the power program of the Authority, and the amount spent on it is only an insignificant portion of the Authority's total expenditures. Other departments of government, both state and national, are charged with the duty of caring for soil erosion and are doing such work effectively without the building of dams and power facilities. ... The American people are paying more than half a billion dollars for eleven dams, chiefly designed to supply power to one area. But this power is to be supplied to this area at less than cost. ... [The] TVA will operate annually at a deficit, and these deficits must ... be paid for out of the pockets of the taxpayers."
—From "Political Power" by Wendell L. Willkie from *Atlantic Monthly* 160 (August 1937) pp. 211–214

### Document D

"One of TVA's original missions was to manage the region's natural resources, but the agency has long invoked the ire of environmentalists. TVA ... was the leading promoter of destructive coal strip-mining. ... TVA still remains the nation's worst violator of the Clean Air Act. The agency, in fact, is the largest emitter among eastern utilities of nitrogen oxide (NOx), which causes smog. It is the third largest emitter of sulfur dioxide ($SO_2$) and carbon dioxide ($CO_2$), which has been identified as the leading cause of global warming. TVA's nuclear program has been so plagued with safety and economic problems that consumer activist Ralph Nader in 1998 declared: 'The TVA ... has the most expensive set of nuclear reactors, has a debt of $29 billion, has the poorest safety record with TVA reactors spending more time on the Nuclear Regulatory Commission's watch list than any other utility.'"
—"Restructure TVA: Why the Tennessee Valley Authority Must Be Reformed" by Richard Munson (September 17, 2001)

---

1. Which document is a secondary source that criticizes the environmental impact of the Tennessee Valley Authority?
   A Document A
   B Document B
   C Document C
   D Document D

2. According to Documents B and C, why were taxpayers concerned about the Tennessee Valley Authority?
   A It provided cheap electricity only to people in Tennessee.
   B Taxpayers demanded an investigation because it operated at a deficit.
   C Taxpayers in Tennessee wanted the government to promise better flood control.
   D It did not build enough dams to provide adequate electricity.

3. In Document A, what message is President Roosevelt trying to convey to Congress?
   A He wanted Congress to view the TVA as a way to control the region's environmental problems.
   B He wanted Congress to build the TVA only to provide electricity.
   C He wanted Congress to provide money to the region's farmers.
   D He wanted Congress to plan many additional watershed projects throughout the country.

4. **Writing Task** Who was right about the impact of the Tennessee Valley Authority: President Roosevelt or his critics? Use your knowledge of the chapter and evidence from the primary sources above to support your opinion.

## MI Connect to Michigan

### World War II's "Arsenal of Democracy"

On December 29, 1940, President Franklin Roosevelt addressed the nation over the radio. The United States had not yet entered World War II, but it was already providing military aid to Great Britain. The President stressed the importance of American industry in meeting the challenges of wartime production.

> "American industrial genius, unmatched throughout the world in the solution of production problems, has been called upon to bring its resources and talents into action. Manufacturers of watches, of farm implements, linotypes, cash registers, automobiles, sewing machines, lawn mowers, and locomotives are now making fuses, bomb-packing crates, telescope mounts, shells, pistols, and tanks…. I have the profound conviction that the American people are now determined to put forth a mightier effort than they have ever yet made to increase our production of all the implements of defense, to meet the threat to our democratic faith."
>
> —President Franklin Roosevelt, December 29, 1940

Michigan companies quickly stepped up to meet the President's challenge. And after the United States entered World War II in December 1941, wartime production in Michigan exploded, led by the state's major automakers. Within three months, automakers stopped producing cars and switched over entirely to war materials such as tanks, aircraft engines, and ammunition. Chrysler produced tanks. Ford designed a new four-wheel drive military vehicle called the "Jeep." Between 1940 and 1945, the U.S. government bought $12.3 billion of GM military materials. Hundreds of smaller companies contributed to the war effort as well.

Throughout the war, the U.S. military depended on Michigan's war production to help American forces win World War II. To increase production and replace white male workers who went to war, Michigan companies hired large numbers of women and African Americans. One woman worker from Ann Arbor became the model for the famous "Rosie the Riveter" poster promoting women's wartime work. By the end of the war, the automobile industry had produced 12.5 billion rounds of ammunition, 245 million shells, and other military equipment worth a total of $29 billion. Detroit had earned its nickname as the nation's "arsenal of democracy."

# WORLD WAR II AND POSTWAR AMERICA

## CONTENTS

This famous photo, taken
in New York City's Times
Square, captured the
nation's joy at the end of
World War II. ▶

# 10

# The Coming of War
## 1931–1942

## A Rendezvous With Destiny

In the 1930s, Adolf Hitler, a ruthless dictator, rose to power in Germany. Early in 1939, American President Franklin Roosevelt contrasted American life with life under a dictatorship like Hitler's:

“Dictatorship, however, involves costs which the American people will never pay: The cost of our spiritual values. . . . The cost of having our children brought up, not as free and dignified human beings, but as pawns molded and enslaved by a machine. . . . Once I prophesied that this generation of Americans had a rendezvous with destiny. That prophecy comes true. To us much is given; more is expected.”
—Franklin Roosevelt, State of the Union Address, January 4, 1939

*Listen to the* Witness History *audio to hear more about World War II.*

◄ German dictator Adolf Hitler at a Nazi Party rally in the 1930s

**Button for the America First Committee, an isolationist group**

 **Content Expectations**

**Chapter Focus Question:** What events caused World War II, and how did the United States become involved?

### Section 1
**Dictators and Wars** 6.1.3d, 6.2.4, 6.3.1, 7.2.1a

### Section 2
**From Isolation to Involvement** 7.1.3b, 7.2.1b, 7.2.1c

### Section 3
**America Enters the War** 7.2.1d, 7.2.3a, 7.2.3b

Use the ☑ **Quick Study Timeline** at the end of this chapter to preview chapter events.

**Japanese "Zero" plane**

**Board game that spread Nazi ideals to German children**

---

**Note Taking Study Guide *Online***
**For:** Note Taking and American Issues Connector
**Web Code:** nee-8301

▲ Hitler's manifesto, *Mein Kampf*

WITNESS HISTORY  AUDIO

## Hitler's Brutal Determination

For the German dictator Adolf Hitler, war was an ennobling experience. War united a nation, demanded righteous sacrifices, and culminated in territorial acquisitions. Hitler believed that there was no morality in war, just victory and defeat. He instructed his generals:

❝The victor will not be asked afterwards whether he told the truth or not. When starting and waging a war it is not right that matters, but victory. Close your hearts to pity. Act brutally. Eighty million people [Germans] must obtain what is their right. Their existence must be made secure. The stronger man is right.❞
—Adolf Hitler, August 1939

◀ Hitler speaks to the German people.

# Dictators and War

### Content Expectations

- **6.1.3d** Analyze resulting tensions among/within groups.
- **6.2.4** Explain Wilson's "Fourteen Points."
- **6.3.1** Describe problems/issues created by U.S.'s industrial/urban transformation between 1895–1930.
- **7.2.1a** Analyze political/economic disputes over territory.

### Terms and People

| | |
|---|---|
| totalitarianism | Spanish Civil War |
| Joseph Stalin | appeasement |
| Benito Mussolini | Anschluss |
| Adolf Hitler | Munich Pact |
| anti-Semitic | |

### NoteTaking

**Reading Skill: Summarize** As you read, summarize the actions in the 1930s of each of the countries listed in the table below.

| Soviet Union | Italy | Germany | Japan |
|---|---|---|---|
| | | | |

**Why It Matters** The effects of World War I and the Great Depression touched almost every corner of the world. In some countries, these upheavals led to the rise of a new kind of brutal dictatorship—the totalitarian state. Led by aggressive dictators, these states would destroy the peace established after World War I and spark a new, even deadlier, global conflict. **Section Focus Question: Why did totalitarian states rise after World War I, and what did they do?**

## A Bitter Peace Unravels

In November 1918, World War I ended when Germany surrendered to the Allies. In 1919, delegates from 27 nations met in Versailles to hammer out a peace agreement, but only Britain, France, and the United States had a real say in most of the important decisions. Germany and Russia were not even present. From the first, many Germans resented the resulting Treaty of Versailles. Other nations also grumbled over the peace settlements. Italy and Japan, both Allies, had expected far more land for their sacrifices. The war that American President Woodrow Wilson had called "a war to end all wars" had left behind a mountain of bitterness, anger, frustration, and despair, often capped by a burning desire for revenge.

During the 1920s many nations, new and old, moved steadily toward democracy and freedom. Others, however, took the opposite direction, embracing repressive dictatorships and **totalitarianism,** a theory of government in which a single party or leader controls the economic, social, and cultural lives of its people. Throughout history there have been dictatorships, countries ruled by one person or small groups of people. But totalitarianism was a twentieth-century phenomenon. It was more extreme than a simple dictatorship, as the chart below shows. Why were totalitarian regimes able to take hold in the years leading up to World War II? As you will read, historians lay much of the blame on the destruction and bitterness left behind by World War I and the desperation caused by the Great Depression.

✓ **Checkpoint** What legacy did World War I leave behind?

# Repression in the Soviet Union and Italy

The 1917 communist revolution in Russia inaugurated the first totalitarian state. The communist leader Vladimir Lenin created the beginnings of a totalitarian system of control to maintain power. His programs resulted in civil war, starvation, famine, and the death of millions of Russians.

**Stalin's Grip on the Soviet Union** After Lenin's death in 1924, **Joseph Stalin** took Lenin's place as the head of the Communist Party. In Russian, *Stalin* means "man of steel," and it is an apt description of the dictator's personality. Stalin was suspicious, cruel, ruthless, and tyrannical. He did not think twice about killing rivals or sentencing innocent people to death. His efforts to transform the Soviet Union into an industrial power and form state-run collective farms resulted in the deaths of at least 10 million people. In what became known as the Great Terror, Stalin purged the Communist Party of real or suspected traitors in the 1930s, ordering the deaths or imprisonment of up to a million people. The purge also included most of the higher officers of the Red Army, among many others. A combination of fear and massive propaganda kept Stalin in power.

**Mussolini's Fascist Party Controls Italy** Italian totalitarianism was in many ways a direct result of the war and the peace treaties. Although Italy was on the winning side, it did not get the land along the Adriatic coast it had hoped to obtain from the division of Austria-Hungary. Added to this frustration, the postwar economic depression made it difficult for returning veterans to find jobs, a communist movement was growing, and the government seemed weak and inept.

It was during this period that **Benito Mussolini** entered the world stage. In 1919, Mussolini founded the *Fasci di Combattimento* (FAH shee dee kohm ba tee MEHN toh), or Fascist Party, a right-wing organization that trumpeted nationalism and promised to make Italy great again. Followers of Mussolini, known as Black Shirts, fought in the streets against socialists and communists. Fearing revolution, in 1922, Italian King Victor Emmanuel III asked Mussolini to form a government. Calling himself *Il Duce* (ihl DOO chay), or "the leader," Mussolini consolidated his control over the government and the army within a few years. He outlawed political parties, took over the press, created a secret police, organized youth groups to indoctrinate the young, and suppressed strikes. He opposed liberalism and socialism. Still, his hold over Italy was never as powerful as Stalin's grip on the Soviet Union.

✓ **Checkpoint** How did Stalin and Mussolini maintain their power?

## Stalin: A Gentle Father?

In this staged photo, a fatherly Stalin poses with a young girl, Galia Markifova. Years later, Stalin's government sent Galia to the dreaded Gulag, a chain of labor camps where millions of Soviets were imprisoned during Stalin's rule. *How is this photo an example of propaganda?*

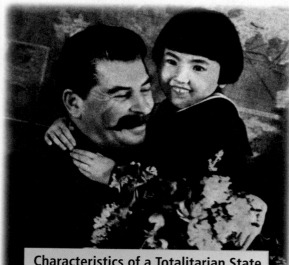

### Characteristics of a Totalitarian State

- Single-party dictatorship exerting control over all aspects of life
- Strong, charismatic leader often at head of government
- State control of the economy
- Use of police, spies, and terror to enforce the will of the state
- Government control of the media and use of propaganda to indoctrinate citizens
- Use of schools and youth organizations to spread ideology to children
- Strict censorship of artists, intellectuals, and political rivals with dissenting opinions

## Aggressive Leaders in Germany and Japan

After World War I, Germany became a democracy. The Weimar (VĪ mahr) Republic (named after the town of Weimar where the government was created) struggled throughout the 1920s to establish a functional democracy. However, Germany was beset by severe economic troubles in the 1920s, including runaway inflation. Anger over the Treaty of Versailles and internal disunity also plagued the young government. The Weimar Republic's ship of state was slowly sinking.

**The Nazis Rise** In the early 1930s, the worldwide Great Depression hit the Weimar Republic hard, worsening the problems that already existed. Increasingly, antidemocratic parties on the right, especially the National Socialist German Workers' Party, or Nazi (NAHT see) Party, threatened the republic. Regardless of the party's name, Nazis were not socialists. They bitterly opposed socialism, communism, or any other *ism* that promoted class interests or workers' rights above German ethnic solidarity. **Adolf Hitler** led the Nazi Party. The son of a minor Austrian civil servant, Hitler was a failed artist, a wounded and decorated World War I soldier, and a person who teetered on the brink of madness.

Hitler joined the small Nazi Party after the war and soon gained control of it. While in prison after the party attempted a rebellion, Hitler dictated the book *Mein Kampf* ("My Struggle"), in which he stated his explanations for the problems facing Germany. He criticized many people, political programs, and

● **INFOGRAPHIC**

# HITLER'S STRANGLEHOLD ON GERMANY

**W**hen Adolf Hitler came to power, he promised that Germany would rise again from the quagmire of reparations and the economic Depression that it had floundered in since World War I. For many, those promises seemed to come true in the 1930s. "[O]nce Hitler came to power, it was wonderful. Everybody had a job and there weren't any more unemployed people," remembers one German citizen. But from the beginning, Hitler's promises had dark undertones of oppression, based on extreme antisemitism and the rejection of democracy. Hitler maintained his power by alternately brainwashing the public with lies and propaganda drives or terrifying them into silence through ruthless violence. His rule led ultimately to genocide and the devastation of World War II.

Propaganda images like this presented Hitler as Germany's savior. Medals (above right) rewarded German mothers who bore several children.

German soldiers humiliate a Jewish boy and his father by forcing the boy to cut off his father's beard in 1933.

ideologies, but his sharpest assaults were against communists and Jews. Hitler was violently **anti-Semitic,** or prejudiced against Jewish people. Anti-Semitism had troubled Europe for centuries, mainly motivated by religious intolerance and economic resentment. In the late nineteenth century, new pseudo-scientific theories about Jews as a race, along with the rise of nationalism, caused Jews to be marginalized as ethnic outsiders. Hitler believed and spread this type of thinking. He preached that the greatest threat confronting Germany was the Jewish people who lived there. In *Mein Kampf,* which quickly became a national bestseller, Hitler presented a blueprint of his hatreds and plans for world domination.

**Hitler Seizes Power** The shattered German economy—the widespread unemployment, homelessness, and hunger—played into the Nazis' hands. Recognizing the power of Hitler's party, in January 1933, the president of the Weimar Republic appointed Hitler chancellor of Germany. Over the next two years, Hitler became president as well as chancellor, consolidated his power, and ruled unchecked by the Reichstag (RĪKS tahg), or the German parliament. By 1935, the democratic institutions of the Weimar Republic were silenced, and Hitler spoke alone as the voice of Germany.

Like Stalin and Mussolini, Hitler was the symbol of his totalitarian regime. Aided by a secret police that crushed all opposition, a state-controlled press that praised his accomplishments, and a state-controlled educational system that

**Vocabulary Builder**
ideology–(ī dee AHL uh jee) *n.* a system of ideas that guides an individual, movement, or political program

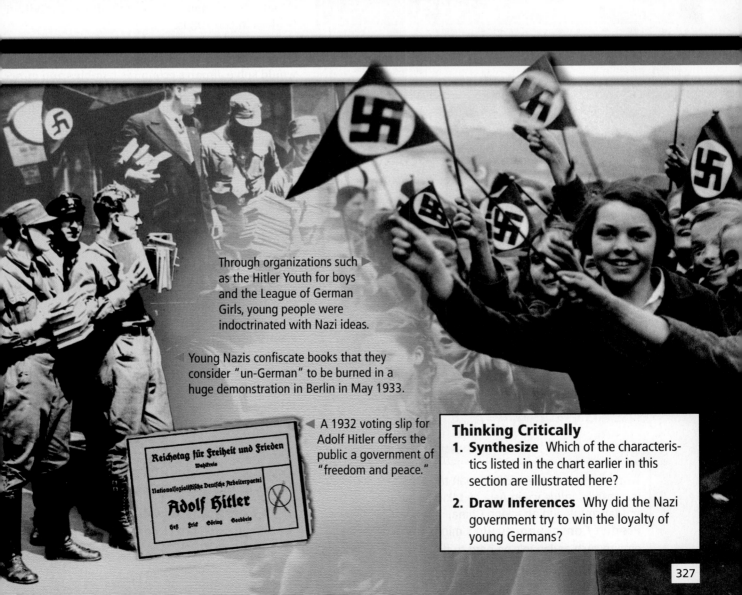

Through organizations such as the Hitler Youth for boys and the League of German Girls, young people were indoctrinated with Nazi ideas.

Young Nazis confiscate books that they consider "un-German" to be burned in a huge demonstration in Berlin in May 1933.

A 1932 voting slip for Adolf Hitler offers the public a government of "freedom and peace."

Reichstag für Freiheit und Frieden
Wahlkreis

Nationalsozialistische Deutsche Arbeiterpartei
**Adolf Hitler**
Heß  Frick  Göring  Goebbels

**Thinking Critically**
1. **Synthesize** Which of the characteristics listed in the chart earlier in this section are illustrated here?

2. **Draw Inferences** Why did the Nazi government try to win the loyalty of young Germans?

indoctrinated the young, Hitler assumed a godlike aura. One German described the emotions of seeing Hitler address a crowd:

> **Primary Source** "There stood Hitler in a simple black coat and looked over the crowd. . . . How many look up to him with a touching faith! As their helper, their savior, their deliverer from unbearable distress—to him who rescues . . . the scholar, the clergyman, the farmer, the worker, the unemployed, who leads them from the [jumbled political] parties back into the nation."
> —Louise Solmitz, a schoolteacher who observed an early Nazi rally

By the late 1930s, Hitler's economic policies, including rearmament and massive public-works projects, had ended the depression in Germany. Many Germans followed his lead and cheered for him at Nazi rallies. Meanwhile, his political initiatives restricted freedom. He openly attacked Jewish people, communists, and socialists.

**Militarists Gain Power in Japan** In Japan, as in Germany, the 1920s was a period of increased democracy and peaceful change. The Japanese government reduced the power of the military, passed laws to give all men the right to vote, legalized trade unions, and allowed several diverse political parties to be established. This period ended when the Great Depression discredited Japan's civilian leaders in the 1930s.

Reasserting their traditional powers, military leaders argued that expansion throughout Asia would solve Japan's economic troubles and guarantee future security. Throughout the 1930s, the military played a significant role in shaping Japanese civilian and military policy.

Japan, however, did not become a totalitarian dictatorship. No charismatic leader like Stalin or Hitler emerged. Instead, Japan continued as a constitutional monarchy headed by a mainly aloof emperor.

**The Japanese Expand Their Empire** As the power shifted toward military control, Japan started on a course of aggressive military expansion. In 1931, Japan attacked Manchuria (man CHUR ee uh), a region in northeastern China, and established a puppet state. The new nation was named Manchukuo (man choo kwoh). Japan controlled its domestic and foreign policies, as well as its abundant natural resources. In 1937, Japan moved against China, gaining control over major Chinese railroad links and coastal areas. In the then-capital city of Nanjing, Japanese soldiers acted with such brutality—murdering more than 200,000 residents and burning a large section of the city—that the incident became known as the "Rape of Nanjing."

✔ **Checkpoint** How did the Great Depression affect political life in Germany and Japan?

**Geography Interactive**
For: Interactive map
Web Code: nep-1002

**Japanese Expansion, 1931–1939**

SOVIET UNION

MONGOLIA

Manchuria (Manchukuo)

Miller Projection
0   200   400 mi
0   200 400 km

Beijing

Korea

Sea of Japan

JAPAN

Tokyo

Osaka

CHINA

Nanjing

Huang River

Yellow Sea

Shanghai

Chang River

50° N
40° N
30° N

Pacific Ocean

Taiwan

130° E   140° E

Hong Kong (Britain)

20° N

110° E   120° E

South China Sea

■ Japanese Empire, 1930
▨ Japanese sphere of influence, 1930
■ Japanese conquests, 1931–1933
□ Japanese conquests, 1937–1939

**Map Skills** In the 1930s, Japan tried to increase its influence in Asia by taking control of Manchuria and attacking China.
**Predict Consequences** How might an empire such as Japan's be hard to defend?

# Dictators Turn to Aggression

In the 1930s, Italy and Germany resorted to acts of aggression similar to those of Japan in Asia. Throughout the decade, neither the League of Nations nor democratic nations succeeded in stopping the aggression. It was a time that recalled a line from Irish poet William Butler Yeats: "The best lack all conviction and the worst are full of passionate intensity."

**Weakness of the League of Nations** In many ways, the League of Nations never recovered from America's refusal to join it. The League was also handicapped by its own charter. It had no standing army and no real power to enforce its decrees. It was only as strong as its members' resolve, and during the worldwide depression of the 1930s, those members lacked resolve. When aggressive nations began to test the League, they discovered that the organization was long on words and short on action.

**Hitler and Mussolini Threaten the Peace** From the first, Hitler focused on restoring Germany's strength and nullifying the provisions of the Treaty of Versailles. From 1933 to 1936, he rebuilt the German economy and dramatically enlarged the army, navy, and air force in direct defiance of the Treaty of Versailles. In the mid-1930s, Hitler began to move toward his goal of reunifying all Germanic people into one Reich, or state. He spoke often of the need for Germany to expand to gain *Lebensraum* (LAY buhns rowm), or living space, for its people. In 1935, he reclaimed the Saar (sahr) region from French control. In 1936, in a direct challenge to the League, he sent German troops into the Rhineland. The League failed to respond.

Meanwhile, Mussolini commenced his own imperial plans. In 1935, Italy invaded Ethiopia, an independent country in east Africa. Its emperor, Haile Selassie (HĪ luh suh lah SEE), appealed to the League of Nations for support. The organization did almost nothing, and Ethiopia fell.

**Fighting Breaks Out in Spain** Fascists were also victorious in the **Spanish Civil War,** a bloody conflict that raged from 1936 until 1939. The Nationalists, who had fascist tendencies, rebelled against Spain's democratic Republican government. Both Hitler and Mussolini sent military and economic aid to the Nationalist leader, General Francisco Franco, using the conflict to test some of their new military technology. Though the Soviet Union provided some support for the Republican side, France, Britain, and the United States remained largely on the sidelines, deploring the bloodshed but refusing to provide weapons to the Republican forces.

✔ **Checkpoint** Why did the League of Nations fail to halt German and Italian aggression?

## HISTORY MAKERS

**Benito Mussolini** (1883–1945)
**Adolf Hitler** (1889–1945)
Benito Mussolini's involvement in radical politics began when he was a young man. In 1919, he formed the Fascist Party and quickly gained followers with his powerful speaking style and by terrorizing opponents. Other world leaders criticized him when he sent Italian armies to invade Ethiopia in 1935. Only Germany's Adolf Hitler supported the move, and the two leaders became allies.

Before World War I, Adolf Hitler lived in Vienna and tried to make his living as an artist. During the war, he fought for Germany and was wounded several times. In 1933, Hitler became head of the German government. He quickly took absolute power using propaganda and violence. Though never close, he and Benito Mussolini supported each other in their efforts to control Europe.

## NoteTaking

**Reading Skill: Identify Main Ideas** Use a concept web like the one below to record the main ideas about the policies of Great Britain, France, and the United States toward aggressive nations.

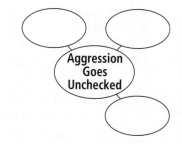

Aggression Goes Unchecked

# Aggression Goes Unchecked

The policy that France and Britain pursued against aggressive nations during the 1930s is known as **appeasement.** It is a policy of granting concessions to a potential enemy in the hope that it will maintain peace. Unfortunately, appeasement only spurred the fascist leaders to become more bold, adventurous, and aggressive.

Why did France and Britain appease the fascist powers? There were a number of reasons. World War I was so horrible that some leaders vowed never to allow another such war to break out. Other leaders believed that the Soviet Union posed a greater threat than Nazi Germany. They maintained that a strong Germany would provide a buffer against the Soviet menace. Still other leaders questioned the resolve of their own people and their allies—particularly the United States.

The United States played an important role in this appeasement policy. Although, in the 1930s, President Franklin Roosevelt pursued a Good Neighbor policy with Latin America and improved relations with the Soviet Union, he did not take a forceful line against German aggression. Instead, the country concerned itself with its own economic troubles and embraced a policy of isolationism.

Hitler took advantage of the lack of commitment and unity among France, Britain, and the United States. In the spring of 1938, he brought Austria into his Reich. Austria was given little choice but to accept this union, called the **Anschluss** (AHN shloos). In the fall, Hitler turned toward the Sudetenland, a portion of western Czechoslovakia that was largely populated by ethnic Germans.

Many people expected the conflict over the Sudetenland to lead to a general war. But once again, Britain and France appeased Germany. At the Munich Conference with Hitler, British prime minister Neville Chamberlain and French premier Edouard Daladier sacrificed the Sudetenland to preserve the peace. On his return to London, Chamberlain told a cheering crowd that the **Munich** (MYOO nihk) **Pact,** the agreement reached at the conference, had preserved "peace for our time." He was wrong. It merely postponed the war for 11 months.

## Appeasement at Munich

British prime minister Neville Chamberlain greets Hitler at the Munich Conference in 1938. Historians still debate why Britain and France pursued the policy of appeasement leading up to World War II.

 **Checkpoint** Why did Britain, France, and the United States not stop fascist aggression in the 1930s?

---

# Assessment

**Progress Monitoring *Online***
**For:** Self-test with vocabulary practice
**Web Code:** nea-1003

## Comprehension

1. **Terms and People** Write several sentences describing what the items listed below have in common.
   - totalitarianism
   - Joseph Stalin
   - Benito Mussolini
   - Adolf Hitler
   - anti-Semitic
   - Anschluss

2. **NoteTaking Reading Skill: Summarize** Use your table and concept web to answer the Section Focus Question: Why did totalitarian states rise after World War I, and what did they do?

## Writing About History

3. **Quick Write: Analyze Primary Sources** Reread the Primary Source in this section describing the crowd at one of Hitler's speeches. Write one paragraph analyzing the source. Consider the following questions: What key words are used to describe Hitler? What do these words suggest about how the crowd viewed Hitler?

## Critical Thinking

4. **Recognize Effects** How did World War I contribute to the rise of dictators in Europe?

5. **Make Comparisons** How were Germany and Japan similar in the 1930s? How were they different?

6. **Express Problems Clearly** How did the policy of appeasement encourage aggression?

▲ Women protesting the Lend-Lease Act

SECTION

2

WITNESS HISTORY  AUDIO

**An Isolationist Voice**

As war erupted in Europe, Americans debated what stance the United States should take on the global conflict. Charles A. Lindbergh, the popular aviation hero, felt strongly that it would be a mistake for the United States to enter the new war in Europe:

❝We must band together to prevent the loss of more American lives in these internal struggles of Europe. . . . Modern war with all its consequences is too tragic and too devastating to be approached from anything but a purely American standpoint. We should never enter a war unless it is absolutely essential to the future welfare of our nation. . . . Our safety does not lie in fighting European wars. It lies in our own internal strength, in the character of the American people and of American institutions.❞
—Charles Lindbergh, radio address, September 15, 1939

# From Isolation to Involvement

 **Content Expectations**

- **7.1.3b** Explain opposition to New Deal/impact of Supreme Court striking down/accepting New Deal laws.
- **7.2.1b** Analyze differences in civic/political values of U.S., Nazi Germany, Imperial Japan.
- **7.2.1c** Analyze U.S. neutrality.

## Terms and People

blitzkrieg

Axis Powers

Allies

Winston Churchill

Neutrality Act of 1939

Tripartite Pact

Lend-Lease Act

Atlantic Charter

## NoteTaking

**Reading Skill: Sequence** Sequence the major events described in the section in a timeline.

Germany invades Poland.

Atlantic Charter issued.

Sept. 1939

Aug. 1941

**Why It Matters** While Britain and France appeased the dictator in Germany at Munich, American President Franklin Roosevelt condemned aggression in Asia but did little to stop it. As war exploded in Europe, it became increasingly difficult for the United States to maintain its neutrality. Once again, Americans would have to decide what role they were willing to play in shaping world events. **Section Focus Question: How did Americans react to events in Europe and Asia in the early years of World War II?**

## Roosevelt Opposes Aggression

The unrestrained violence of the 1937 Japanese attack on China shocked Americans, even before the notorious Rape of Nanjing in December 1937. Japan attacked without a declaration of war. Its planes rained terror on Chinese cities, especially Shanghai and Nanjing. The Japanese had even killed three American sailors when Japanese warplanes sank the United States gunboat *Panay* on the Chang River.

In the midst of these bloody events, President Franklin Roosevelt criticized Japan's aggression in a speech in Chicago on October 5, 1937. He lamented the "reign of terror and international lawlessness," the bombing of civilian populations, and the horrible acts of cruelty. Speaking in a city where American isolationist sentiments were strong, Roosevelt suggested that no part of the world was truly isolated from the rest of the world. He warned:

> **Primary Source** "When an epidemic of physical disease starts to spread, the community approves and joins in a quarantine of the patients in order to protect the health of the community against the spread of the disease. . . . War is a contagion, whether it be declared or undeclared. It can engulf states and peoples remote from the original scene of hostilities. We are determined to keep out of war, yet we cannot insure ourselves against the disastrous effects of war and the dangers of involvement."
> —President Franklin Roosevelt, Quarantine speech, October 5, 1937

Roosevelt's solution for stopping aggression involved an informal alliance of the peace-loving nations, but he did not suggest what steps the peaceful nations should take in quarantining the aggressive ones. Roosevelt's speech was widely criticized, and for a time, the President backed away from his more interventionist stance. The speech did, however, alert some Americans to the threat Japan posed to the United States.

✔ **Checkpoint** How did President Roosevelt react to Japan's aggression in China in the late 1930s?

## War Erupts in Europe

Roosevelt's words failed to prevent Japan from extending its control over much of China. Similarly, France and Britain's efforts to appease Hitler in Europe failed to limit the dictator's expansionist plans. By the end of 1938, even the leaders of France and Britain realized that Hitler's armed aggression could only be halted by a firm, armed defense. The urgency of the situation grew in the spring of 1939 when Hitler violated the Munich Pact by absorbing the remainder of Czechoslovakia into his German Reich.

**Hitler Launches a Blitzkrieg Against Poland** Finally, British and French leaders saw the need to take action. They vowed not to let Hitler take over another country without consequences. Realizing that Hitler's next move would be against Poland, Britain and France signed an alliance with Poland, guaranteeing aid if Hitler attacked. Hitler, however, was more concerned about war with the Soviet Union than with Britain and France. Not wanting to fight a war on two fronts, Germany signed the Nazi-Soviet Nonaggression Pact with the Soviets on August 23, 1939. The two former rivals publicly promised not to

**The German Juggernaut Rolls Through Europe**

As the map on the next page shows, the Nazi war machine rampaged through Europe from 1939 through 1941. Below, victorious German troops parade through the Arc de Triomphe in Paris, France (left), after Nazi tanks had rolled through Belgium (right).

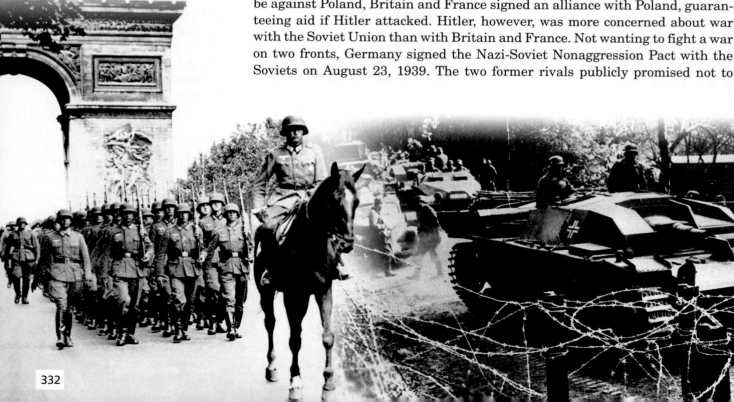

attack one another. Secretly, they agreed to invade and divide Poland and recognize each other's territorial ambitions. The public agreement alone shocked the West and guaranteed a German offensive against Poland.

War came to Europe in the early hours of September 1, 1939, when a massive German **blitzkrieg** (BLIHTS kreeg), or sudden attack, hit Poland from three directions. *Blitzkrieg* means "lightning war." It was a relatively new style of warfare that emphasized the use of speed and firepower to penetrate deep into the enemy's territory. The newest military technologies made it devastatingly effective. Using a coordinated assault by tanks and planes, followed by motorized vehicles and infantry, Germany broke through Poland's defenses and destroyed its air force. The situation became even more hopeless on September 17 when the Soviet Union invaded Poland from the east. Although France and Britain declared war against Germany, they did nothing to help save Poland. By the end of the month, a devastated Poland fell in defeat.

A woman weeps as she salutes her new rulers.

**France Falls to the Axis Powers** Europe was at war, just as it had been 21 years earlier. The **Axis Powers** eventually included Germany, Italy, Japan, and several other nations. The **Allies** included Britain, France, and eventually many other nations, including the Soviet Union, the United States, and China. But after the Polish campaign, the war entered an eight-month period of relative quiet, known in Britain as the "phony war." Things would not remain quiet for long, however.

The next storm erupted with raging fury in the spring of 1940. Germany's nonaggression pact with the Soviet Union freed Hitler to send his army west. On April 9, 1940, Germany attacked Denmark and Norway. The two countries fell almost immediately. On May 10, he sent his blitzkrieg forces into the

## German Aggression, 1936–1941

**Geography** *Interactive*
For: Interactive map
Web Code: nep-1004

**Map Skills** In 1939, Hitler used force, rather than diplomatic gymnastics to add territory to the German Reich.

1. **Locate:** (a) Sudetenland, (b) Poland, (c) Vichy France

2. **Location** What made Poland a difficult ally for France and Britain to protect?

3. **Synthesize Information** How does this map illustrate the dire situation of the Allies in 1941?

Netherlands, Belgium, and Luxembourg. The small nations fell like tumbling dominoes. Hitler seemed invincible; his army unstoppable.

Hitler next set his sights on France. France had prepared for Germany's invasion by constructing an interconnected series of fortresses known as the Maginot Line along its border with Germany. Additionally, France had stationed its finest armies along its border with Belgium—the route that Germany had used to attack France in 1914. In between the Maginot Line and Belgium lay the Ardennes, a hilly, forested area that military experts considered invasion proof.

But once again the military experts were wrong. In early May 1940, German tanks rolled through the Ardennes, ripped a hole in the thin French line there, and raced north toward the English Channel. The German plan involved attacking the French and British forces from the front and the rear and trapping them against the channel. It almost worked. Only a few tactical German mistakes gave Britain enough time to evacuate its forces from the French port of Dunkirk. Some 338,000 British and French troops escaped, to Britain. Had they not escaped, it is doubtful if Britain could have remained in the war.

The Miracle of Dunkirk was a proud moment for Britain, but as the new prime minister **Winston Churchill** cautioned Parliament, "wars are not won by evacuations." Although the British army escaped, the Germans took Paris and forced the French to surrender in the same railway car that the French had used for the German surrender in 1918. France was then divided into two sections: a larger northern section controlled by the Germans and known as Occupied France, and a smaller southern section administered by the French and known as Unoccupied France, or Vichy France, after its capital city. Although Vichy France was officially neutral, it collaborated with the Nazis.

**The Battle of Britain Is Fought in the Air** France had fallen to Hitler in just 35 days. Hitler next turned his fury on Britain. After the evacuation at Dunkirk, Churchill made it clear that he had no intention of continuing the policy of appeasement. He told his nation:

> **Primary Source** "We shall go on to the end. We shall fight in France, we shall fight on the seas and oceans, we shall fight with growing confidence and growing strength in the air, we shall defend our island, whatever the cost may be, we shall fight on the beaches, we shall fight on the landing grounds, we shall fight in the fields and in the streets, we shall fight in the hills; we shall never surrender."
>
> —Winston Churchill, June 4, 1940

Churchill's words stirred his nation as the British readied themselves for battle. Hitler's plan to invade Britain, codenamed Operation Sea Lion, depended upon Germany's Luftwaffe, or air force, destroying the British Royal Air Force and gaining control over the skies above the English Channel. The Battle of Britain, then, was an air battle, fought over the English Channel and Great Britain. It began in July 1940. The British lost nearly 1,000 planes, the Germans more than 1,700. Germany bombed civilian as well as military targets, destroying houses, factories, and churches and conducted a months-long bombing campaign against London itself, known as "the blitz." But the British held on and, sensing failure, Hitler made a tactical decision to postpone the invasion of Britain indefinitely.

✓ **Checkpoint** Which side seemed to be winning the war at the end of 1940?

## The Miracle of Dunkirk

Almost cut off from escape by the German army, British and French troops evacuated from Dunkirk using almost any sailing vessel available, including private yachts and fishing boats as small as 14 feet long! Some of the small boats were used to get close to shore to pick up men and then ferry them to larger naval vessels waiting in deeper waters. *Why do you think the evacuation from Dunkirk raised morale in Britain?*

# Edward R. Murrow Reports on the Blitz

American news correspondent Edward R. Murrow (above) broadcast live from London as the Luftwaffe bombed the city. He described the purpose of his reports: "I have an old-fashioned belief that Americans like to make up their own minds on the basis of all available information." 🔊 AUDIO

**How do you think Murrow's reports influenced Americans?**

A milkman (above) delivers milk as usual in October 1940 amid the devastation of an air raid. Londoners (left) take refuge in an underground train station converted into an air-raid shelter.

## Americans Debate Involvement

Winston Churchill referred to the United States in many of his speeches during the crisis in France and the Battle of Britain. The fight against Hitler, Churchill implied, was more than simply a European struggle. Nazi aggression threatened the freedoms and rights cherished by democratic nations everywhere. The contest was between ideologies as well as nations.

**America Favors Isolation** President Roosevelt shared Churchill's concerns, but at the beginning of the war in Europe he understood that the majority of Americans opposed U.S. intervention. The severe economic crisis of the Great Depression had served to pin the nation's attention firmly on domestic affairs throughout the 1930s. In addition, many believed that U.S. involvement in World War I had been a deadly, expensive mistake. The rise of fascism in Europe made the sacrifices of World War I seem even more pointless.

In the 1930s, numerous books and articles presented a new theory about why the United States had become involved in World War I that disturbed many Americans. The theory held that big business had conspired to enter the war in order to make huge fortunes selling weapons. In 1934, a senate committee chaired by Gerald Nye of South Dakota looked into the question. Although the Nye Committee discovered little hard evidence, its findings suggested that "merchants of death"—American bankers and arms manufacturers—had indeed pulled the United States into World War I. The committee's findings further reinforced isolationist sentiments.

In order to avoid making the "mistakes" that had led to U.S. involvement in World War I, Congress passed the Neutrality Acts of 1935, 1936, and 1937.

The acts imposed certain restrictions on Americans during times of war. For example, Americans were prohibited from sailing on ships owned by belligerents or nations at war. The acts also prevented Americans from making loans to belligerents or selling them arms and munitions. The acts did not distinguish between aggressors like Germany and Italy and victims like Poland, or their allies, France and Britain.

**Interventionists Urge Support for the Allies** Once war began in Europe, Roosevelt felt confined by the limitations of the Neutrality Acts. Though he issued a proclamation of American neutrality, he was firmly anti-Nazi and wanted to aid the democracies of Europe. In the end, Congress agreed and passed the **Neutrality Act of 1939,** which included a cash-and-carry provision. This provision allowed belligerent nations to buy goods and arms in the United States if they paid cash and carried the merchandise on their own ships. Since the British navy controlled the seas, cash-and-carry in effect aided the Allies.

Many Americans disagreed with Roosevelt's openly pro-Allies position. They argued that FDR's policies violated American neutrality and threatened to push the United States into the war. Between early 1940 and late 1941, a great debate raged in America between isolationists and interventionists. The debate became particularly heated after the fall of France left Britain standing by itself in Europe against Germany. Interventionist organizations such as the Committee to Defend America by Aiding the Allies claimed that Britain was fighting for free countries everywhere. Sending aid to Britain was a way for America to stay out of the conflict.

**Isolationists Argue for Neutrality** Isolationists countered by claiming that giving aid to the Allies was automatically harming the Axis and would culminate with the United States entering the conflict. They argued that the only way to keep America safe was to follow a policy of complete neutrality. The America First Committee, an isolationist group, held rallies and sponsored speeches that criticized Roosevelt's openly pro-British policies. Charles Lindbergh became the leading isolationist voice. Lindbergh believed that the real threats to America were the Soviet Union and Japan, and he did not want to see his country weaken itself fighting in Western Europe to save Britain. Lindbergh's addresses were measured and clear. He appealed to Americans' minds but not their hearts.

**Roosevelt Inches Toward Involvement** Events in Europe shocked Americans out of strict neutrality. Reports by Edward R. Murrow, a CBS reporter stationed in London, during the blitz brought the war into American living rooms. His frequent live radio reports, which began with the words "This is London," emphasized that the Germans were bombing not armies or military sites but civilians—grandparents, parents, and children.

These reports and the turn of events in Europe against the Allies convinced many Americans that the United States needed to at least prepare to defend itself. Shortly after the fall of France in September 1940, Germany, Italy, and Japan signed the **Tripartite Pact** and became

The Only Way We Can Save Her

"STAY OUT! STAY OUT FOR MY SAKE, AS WELL AS YOUR OWN!"

WAR MAD EUROPE

DEMOCRACY

AMERICA THE LAST REFUGE OF DEMOCRACY

**Analyzing Political Cartoons**

**The Only Way to Save Democracy?** In this cartoon, a figure symbolizing democracy begs Uncle Sam to stay out of the war in Europe.
1. What does this cartoonist think has happened to democracy in Europe?
2. According to this cartoonist's vision, how will the United States be able to save democracy?

| Should the United States Enter World War II? | ☑ Quick Study |
|---|---|
| **Isolationist Viewpoint** | **Interventionist Viewpoint** |
| • The United States should avoid alliances with other nations.<br><br>• Americans should focus on issues at home, such as the depression.<br><br>• Complete neutrality was the way to keep the United States safe.<br><br>• Intervention in a foreign war would be a mistake, just as World War I was. | • The United States should work with other nations to promote collective security.<br><br>• Axis aggressions were wrong and threatened American interests.<br><br>• The United States should aid the Allies, who were fighting for democracy and freedom.<br><br>• The United States should put pressure on the Axis Powers and prepare for war. |

allies. In that same month, after a heated debate between isolationists and interventionists, Congress passed a Selective Service Act—a peacetime draft—providing for the military training of 1.2 million troops and 800,000 reserve troops each year.

At the same time, President Roosevelt took an additional step to strengthen Britain. He gave Britain 50 World War I–era battleships in exchange for eight British defense bases. Britain needed the destroyers to convoy goods across the Atlantic. Believing the act to be an emergency measure, Roosevelt made the transfer without the consent of Congress.

The American people <u>evaluated</u> FDR's leadership the next month in the presidential election. Roosevelt ran for an unprecedented third term against Republican nominee Wendell L. Willkie of Indiana. Willkie was critical of FDR's handling of both the economy and foreign affairs but not of the President's basic positions on either. Given such little differences between candidates, Americans voted overwhelmingly not to change leaders in the middle of a crisis.

 **Checkpoint** According to interventionists, how would aiding the Allies actually keep the United States out of the war?

## America Takes Steps Toward War

Once safely reelected, President Roosevelt increased his support of Britain. When Britain began to run short on funds to purchase cash-and-carry goods in the United States, FDR took the opportunity to address Congress. On January 6, 1941, he spoke about "four freedoms"—freedom of speech, freedom of worship, freedom from want, and freedom from fear—that were threatened by Nazi and Japanese militarism. Roosevelt believed that the best way to stay out of the conflict with Germany was to aid Britain.

**Lend-Lease Gives Aid to the Allies** Roosevelt compared America's situation to the scenario of a fire in a neighbor's home. If a neighbor asked to borrow your fire hose to put out the fire, you would not debate the issue or try to sell the hose. Extending help was both being a good neighbor and acting to keep the fire from spreading to your own home.

Britain, Roosevelt said, needed American aid, and it had run out of money to pay for it. The President called for America to become "the great arsenal for democracy." Once again, America answered Britain's plea for help. In March 1941, Congress approved the **Lend-Lease Act,** symbolically numbered 1776, after another heated debate between isolationists and interventionists. The act authorized Roosevelt to

**Aid to Britain**
The president of Bundles for Britain (above) collects money for her organization, which sent food and clothing to help British people suffering from the effects of the war. *Is Bundles for Britain an example of the interventionist or isolationist viewpoint?*

**Vocabulary Builder**
<u>evaluate</u>–(ee VAL yoo ayt) *v.* to judge or find the value of

**Roosevelt and Churchill**
President Roosevelt (left) met with British prime minister Winston Churchill (right) in August 1941. Although the United States was still not at war with Germany, the two leaders set out some common goals in the Atlantic Charter. *How did President Roosevelt's actions reveal his interventionist stance?*

"sell, transfer title to, exchange, lease, lend, or otherwise dispose of, to any such government any defense article" whenever he thought it was "necessary in the interests of the defense of the United States." By 1945, the United States had sent more than $40 billion of Lend-Lease aid to the Allies, including the Soviet Union. The Lend-Lease Act was nothing less than an economic declaration of war against Germany and the Axis Powers.

**The Atlantic Charter Reinforces America's Support of Britain** In August 1941, President Roosevelt and prime minister Churchill met secretly on a warship off the misty coast of Newfoundland. They talked not only about Britain's problems in the war but also about their hopes for the world after Hitler's defeat. On board the ship they signed the **Atlantic Charter,** a document that endorsed national self-determination and an international system of "general security." The signing of the Atlantic Charter signaled the deepening alliance between the two nations.

**U.S. Navy Battles German U-Boats** Hitler was not blind to America's actions in support of the Allies. Nor did he fail to notice the fact that the United States had begun to escort arms shipments to Iceland, where the British picked them up and transported them to England.

In the fall of 1941, he ordered his German U-boats, or submarines, to attack American ships. The U-boats shot at the USS *Greer,* hit the USS *Kearny,* and sunk the USS *Reuben James,* killing more than a hundred sailors. The attacks shocked and angered Americans, moving them closer to declaring war on Germany. Though the United States was still officially a neutral nation, Roosevelt gave orders to the navy to attack German U-boats on sight. In June 1941, Germany had gone to war against the Soviet Union, and by November, war against the United States seemed inevitable.

✓ **Checkpoint** How did the United States support the Allies after Roosevelt's reelection?

**Progress Monitoring *Online***
For: Self-test with vocabulary practice
Web Code: nea-1005

**Comprehension**

1. **Terms and People** For each item below, write a sentence explaining its significance.
   - blitzkrieg
   - Axis Powers
   - Allies
   - Winston Churchill
   - Neutrality Act of 1939
   - Tripartite Pact
   - Lend-Lease Act
   - Atlantic Charter

2. NoteTaking **Reading Skill: Sequence** Use your timeline to answer the Section Focus Question: How did Americans react to events in Europe and Asia in the early years of World War II?

**Writing About History**

3. **Quick Write: Compare Points of View** Compare the image of the women protesting the Lend-Lease Act to the excerpt from Roosevelt's Quarantine speech in this section. Write a paragraph summarizing the two different points of view presented by these two documents.

**Critical Thinking**

4. **Summarize** Describe the course of World War II in Europe until the end of 1940.

5. **Identify Point of View** Why did members of the America First Committee believe that the United States should avoid war with Germany?

6. **Recognize Causes** Why did the United States give more and more help to the Allies?

# Franklin Delano Roosevelt: The "Four Freedoms" Speech

In his State of the Union address to Congress on January 6, 1941, President Roosevelt stressed the danger that aggressive fascist powers presented to the United States. He urged the American people to support those "who are resisting aggression and are thereby keeping war away from our Hemisphere"—namely the Allies. Congress passed the Lend-Lease Act three months later to do just that. Finally, Roosevelt set out the ideals that he believed Americans should fight for: the Four Freedoms.

Inspired by Roosevelt's speech, the illustrator Norman Rockwell created four paintings, each illustrating one of the Four Freedoms. In *Freedom of Speech,* Rockwell shows a man speaking at his town meeting.

I address you, the Members of the Seventy-Seventh Congress, at a moment unprecedented[1] in the history of the Union. I use the word "unprecedented" because at no previous time has American security been as seriously threatened from without as it is today. . . .

In the future days, which we seek to make secure, we look forward to a world founded upon four essential human freedoms.

The first is freedom of speech and expression—everywhere in the world.

The second is freedom of every person to worship God in his own way—everywhere in the world.

The third is freedom from want—which, translated into world terms, means economic understandings which will secure to every nation a healthy peace time life for its inhabitants—everywhere in the world.

The fourth is freedom from fear—which, translated into world terms, means a worldwide reduction of armaments to such a point and in such a thorough fashion that no nation will be in a position to commit an act of physical aggression against any neighbor—anywhere in the world.

That is no vision of a distant millennium. It is a definite basis for a kind of world attainable in our own time and generation. That kind of world is the very antithesis[2] of the so-called new order of tyranny which the dictators seek to create with the crash of a bomb. . . . The world order which we seek is the cooperation of free countries, working together in a friendly, civilized society.

This nation has placed its destiny in the hands and heads and hearts of its millions of free men and women; and its faith in freedom under the guidance of God. Freedom means the supremacy of human rights everywhere. Our support goes to those who struggle to gain those rights and keep them. Our strength is our unity of purpose.

To that high concept there can be no end save victory.

---

1. **unprecedented** (uhn PREHS uh dehn tihd) *adj.* new, having no previous example.
2. **antithesis** (an TIHTH uh sihs) *n.* exact opposite.

## Thinking Critically

1. **Summarize** What are the Four Freedoms?

2. **Predict Consequences** How do you think an isolationist would respond to Roosevelt's speech?

WITNESS HISTORY  AUDIO

**A Date Which Will Live in Infamy**

In December 1941, the Japanese mounted a surprise attack on the U.S. naval base at Pearl Harbor, Hawaii. The next day Franklin Delano Roosevelt spoke to the shocked American public:

66 Yesterday, December 7, 1941—a date which will live in infamy—the United States of America was suddenly and deliberately attacked by naval and air forces of the Empire of Japan. . . . The facts of yesterday speak for themselves. The people of the United States have already formed their opinions and well understand the implications to the very life and safety of our nation. . . . No matter how long it may take us to overcome this premeditated invasion, the American people in their righteous might will win through to absolute victory.99

—Franklin Roosevelt, Message Asking for War Against Japan, December 8, 1941

▲ President Roosevelt addresses Americans after the attack on Pearl Harbor

# America Enters the War

 **Content Expectations**

- **7.2.1d** Analyze bombing of Pearl Harbor.
- **7.2.3a** Analyze mobilization of U.S. economic, military, social resources during WWII.
- **7.2.3b** Analyze role of women/minorities in war effort.

**Terms and People**

Hideki Tojo
Pearl Harbor
WAC

Douglas MacArthur
Bataan Death March
Battle of Coral Sea

**NoteTaking**

**Reading Skill: Identify Causes and Effects**
As you read, record the causes and effects of the attack on Pearl Harbor, as well as details about the attack itself, in a chart like the one below.

**Why It Matters** In the beginning of December 1941, the United States had engaged in warlike activity but had yet to commit itself. A surprise attack on Pearl Harbor, an American naval base in Hawaii, ended all debate and brought the United States into the war. The participation of the United States in this war, as in World War I, would decide the struggle's conclusion. **Section Focus Question: How did the United States react to the Japanese attack on Pearl Harbor?**

## Japan Attacks the United States

Although Japan and the United States had been allies in World War I, conflict over power in Asia and the Pacific had been brewing between the two nations for decades prior to 1941. Japan, as the area's industrial and economic leader, resented any threats to its authority in the region. America's presence in Guam and the Philippines and its support of China posed such a threat. Yet Japan relied on trade with the United States to supply much-needed natural resources.

**Trouble in the Pacific** As war broke out in Europe, the Japanese Empire continued to grow in China and began to move into Indochina. President Roosevelt tried to stop this expansion, in July of 1940, by placing an embargo on important naval and aviation supplies to Japan, such as oil, iron ore, fuel, steel, and rubber. After Japan signed the Tripartite Pact in 1940 with Germany and Italy, FDR instituted a more extensive embargo. The embargo slowed, but did not stop, Japanese expansion as the Japanese were able to secure the resources they needed within their new possessions.

In 1941, General **Hideki Tojo** (hī DEHK ee TOH joh) became the Japanese prime minister. Known as "the Razor" for his sharp mind, he focused intently on military expansion but sought to keep the United States neutral. Throughout the summer of 1941, Japan and the United States attempted to negotiate an end to their disagreement, but with little success. Japan was bent on further expansion, and the United States was firmly against it. Finally, in late November 1941, Cordell Hull, the U.S. Secretary of State, rejected Japan's latest demands. Formal diplomatic relations continued for the next week, but Tojo had given up on peace. By the beginning of December he had made the decision to deliver a decisive first blow against the United States.

**The Japanese Attack Pearl Harbor** As Japanese diplomats wrangled in the U.S. capital, Japan's navy sailed for **Pearl Harbor,** Hawaii, the site of the United States Navy's main Pacific base. The forces that Tojo sent from Japan under the command of Vice Admiral Chuichi Nagumo (joo EE chee nah GOO moh) included 6 aircraft carriers, 360 airplanes, an assortment of battleships and cruisers, and a number of submarines. Their mission was to eradicate the American naval and air presence in the Pacific with a surprise attack. Such a blow would prevent Americans from mounting a strong resistance to Japanese expansion.

The attackers struck with devastating power, taking the American forces completely by surprise. A sailor aboard the hospital ship USS *Solace* recalled the destruction of the USS *Arizona:*

> **Primary Source** "I saw more planes coming in, passing over Battleship Row dropping bombs. I remember very clearly what looked like a dive-bomber coming in over the *Arizona* and dropping a bomb. I saw that bomb go down through what looked like a stack, and almost instantly it cracked the bottom of the *Arizona*, blowing the whole bow loose. It rose out of the water and settled. I could see flames, fire, and smoke coming out of that ship, and I saw two men fling through the air and the fire, screaming as they went."
> —Corpsman James F. Anderson, aboard the USS *Solace* in Pearl Harbor

**Results of the Attack** The Americans suffered heavy losses: nearly 2,500 people killed, 8 battleships severely damaged, 3 destroyers left unusable, 3 light cruisers damaged, and 160 aircraft destroyed and 128 more damaged. The U.S. battlefleet was knocked out of commission for nearly six months, allowing the Japanese to freely access the needed raw materials of their newly conquered territories, just as they had planned.

Despite these losses, the situation was not as bad as it could have been. The most important ships—aircraft carriers—were out at sea at the time of the attack and survived untouched. In addition, seven heavy cruisers were out at sea and also avoided detection by the Japanese. Of the battleships in Pearl Harbor, only three—the USS *Arizona,* the USS *Oklahoma,* and the USS *Utah*—suffered irreparable damage. American submarine bases also survived the morning, as did important fuel supplies and maintenance facilities. In the final analysis, Nagumo proved too conservative. He canceled a third wave of bombers, refused to seek out the aircraft carriers, and turned back toward home because he feared an American counterstrike. The American Pacific Fleet survived.

**America Declares War** As the news about Pearl Harbor spread across the nation and FDR prepared to address Congress, Americans rallied together. Many did not know what to expect, but they anticipated monumental changes. Journalist Marquis Child recalled thinking, "Nothing will ever be the same," and added, "it never was the same."

**Japanese Ambitions**
In late 1941, General Hideki Tojo (below) decided to stage a surprise attack on American forces. Items like this matchbook (below left) glorified Japan's military might. On the matchbook, planes emerge from a Japanese flag and fly in the direction of the flags of Britain and the United States.

The attack on Pearl Harbor left little doubt about declaring war on Japan. The Soviet Union's conversion to the Allied side, following Germany's invasion in June 1941, made some Americans doubt the wisdom of supporting the Allies. The attack on Pearl Harbor changed that. It made the necessity of declaring war on Japan clear and ended any continuing political divisions between isolationists and interventionists. After President Roosevelt's speech, the House voted 388 to 1 to declare war, and the Senate joined them unanimously. True to their military commitments with Japan, Germany and Italy declared war on America. Both Democrats and Republicans put aside their political differences to unify the nation in facing the task of winning a global war.

✔ **Checkpoint** What did the Japanese military leaders hope to achieve by attacking Pearl Harbor? Were they successful in this goal?

## Events That Changed America

# SURPRISE ATTACK! PEARL HARBOR

December 7, 1941, dawned an overcast day in Pearl Harbor, Hawaii. The members of the U.S. military stationed there went about their usual Sunday activities. About half of the United States Navy's Pacific Fleet, including eight huge battleships, sat clustered in the harbor. At nearby Hickam Field and other airfields, American planes sat quietly wing-to-wing in perfect rows.

Just before 8 A.M., the Japanese attack on the unsuspecting Americans below had begun. Over the next several hours, Japanese bombers torpedoed the moored ships, while fighters and dive-bombers machine-gunned and bombed ship decks and airfields. American military forces, caught completely by surprise, attempted to ward off the attackers with little effect. The scene was one of utter destruction.

◄ The USS *Arizona* sank during the attack. Nearly 1,200 sailors and marines died on this ship alone.

Sailors at Ford Island Naval Air Station are stunned by the wreckage around them. ▼

# Mobilizing for War

Following the Japanese attack, a spirit of patriotism and service swept across the country. Americans looked for ways to contribute to the war effort. They joined the military, volunteered with the Red Cross and other organizations, and moved into new jobs to help.

**Responding to the Call** During the course of the war, more than 16 million Americans served in the military. From 1941 to 1942 alone, the army grew from about 1.4 million to more than 3 million, the navy increased from under 300,000 to more than 600,000, and the marines expanded from only about 54,000 to almost 150,000. Americans from all ethnic and racial backgrounds joined the fight. Approximately 300,000 Mexican Americans and 25,000 Native Americans

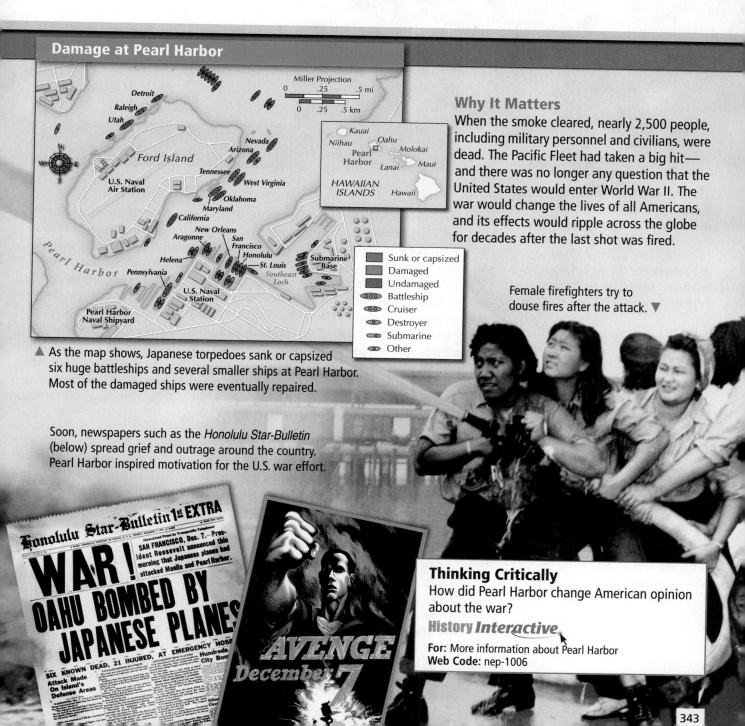

### Damage at Pearl Harbor

Miller Projection

0  .25  .5 mi
0  .25  .5 km

Detroit
Raleigh
Utah
Ford Island
Nevada
Arizona
Tennessee
West Virginia
U.S. Naval Air Station
Oklahoma
Maryland
California
New Orleans
Aragonne
San Francisco
Honolulu
Helena
St. Louis
Pennsylvania
Southeast Loch
U.S. Naval Station
Pearl Harbor Naval Shipyard
Pearl Harbor
Submarine Base

Kauai
Niihau    Oahu
          Molokai
Pearl
Harbor    Lanai    Maui
HAWAIIAN
ISLANDS   Hawaii

Sunk or capsized
Damaged
Undamaged
Battleship
Cruiser
Destroyer
Submarine
Other

▲ As the map shows, Japanese torpedoes sank or capsized six huge battleships and several smaller ships at Pearl Harbor. Most of the damaged ships were eventually repaired.

Soon, newspapers such as the *Honolulu Star-Bulletin* (below) spread grief and outrage around the country. Pearl Harbor inspired motivation for the U.S. war effort.

#### Why It Matters

When the smoke cleared, nearly 2,500 people, including military personnel and civilians, were dead. The Pacific Fleet had taken a big hit—and there was no longer any question that the United States would enter World War II. The war would change the lives of all Americans, and its effects would ripple across the globe for decades after the last shot was fired.

Female firefighters try to douse fires after the attack. ▼

**Honolulu Star-Bulletin 1st EXTRA**

(Associated Press by Transpacific Telephone)
SAN FRANCISCO, Dec. 7.—President Roosevelt announced this morning that Japanese planes had attacked Manila and Pearl Harbor.

# WAR!
## OAHU BOMBED BY JAPANESE PLANES

SIX KNOWN DEAD, 21 INJURED, AT EMERGENCY HOSP
Hundreds
City Bom
Attack Made
On Island's
Defense Areas

AVENGE
December 7

### Thinking Critically
How did Pearl Harbor change American opinion about the war?

**History** *Interactive*

**For:** More information about Pearl Harbor
**Web Code:** nep-1006

**World War II Aircraft Production**

SOURCE: U.S. Department of Defense

## The Production Miracle

America's productive capability proved to be one of the Allies' main advantages in World War II. Above, female workers inspect the noses of A-20 attack bomber aircraft. *By how much did U.S. aircraft production increase between 1941 and 1944?*

served in integrated units. Nearly one million African Americans also joined the military. They served mostly in segregated units, however, and were at first limited to supporting roles. However, as casualties mounted, African Americans saw more active combat, and some eventually served in white combat units.

Over 350,000 women also responded to the call. In 1941, Congresswoman Edith Nourse Rogers introduced a bill to establish a Women's Army Auxiliary Corps—which became the **Women's Army Corps (WAC)** in 1943—to provide clerical workers, truck drivers, instructors, and lab technicians for the United States Army. More than 150,000 women volunteered for the service; 15,000 served abroad over the course of the war and over 600 received medals for their service. More than 57,000 nurses served in the Army Nurse Corps, putting themselves in danger to care for the wounded in Europe and the Pacific. Tens of thousands more American women joined similar navy and Coast Guard auxiliaries.

**Mobilizing Industry** From the start, Roosevelt and the other Allied leaders knew that American production would play a key role in helping the Allies win the war. Although America's industry had started to mobilize in response to the Lend-Lease Act, American production still needed to increase the rate at which it churned out war materials. In January 1942, the government set up the War Production Board (WPB) to oversee the conversion of peacetime industry to war industry. Later, the government created a host of other agencies that worked together to <u>allocate</u> scarce materials into the proper industries, regulate the production of civilian goods, establish production contracts, negotiate with organized labor, and control inflation, with the Office of War Mobilization (OWM) to supervise all of these efforts.

Under the direction of the government, Americans worked to create a "production miracle." The massive defense spending finally ended the Great Depression; for the first time in more than a decade there was a job for every worker. Each year of the war, the United States raised its production goals for military

**Vocabulary Builder**
<u>allocate</u>–(AL oh kayt) *v.* to distribute according to a plan

materials, and each year it met these goals. The Ford Motor Company poured all of its resources into war production, building over 8,000 B-24 Liberator bombers. Henry J. Kaiser's shipyards produced large merchant "Liberty Ships" in as little as four and a half days. In 1944, American production levels were double those of all the Axis nations put together, giving the Allies a crucial advantage. In a toast at a wartime conference, even Joseph Stalin, an Allied leader, praised American production: "To American production, without which the war would have been lost."

✔ **Checkpoint** What were the first actions taken by the United States once war was declared?

# Fierce Fighting in the Pacific

With Pearl Harbor smoldering, the Japanese knew they had to move fast to gain important footholds in Asia and the Pacific. Although Japan's population was smaller than America's, the Japanese did have military advantages, including technologically advanced weapons and a well-trained and highly motivated military. At the start of the Pacific war the outlook was grim for America.

**Japanese Forces Take the Philippines** In December 1941, General **Douglas MacArthur,** commander of United States Army forces in Asia, struggled to hold the U.S. positions in the Philippines with little support. This task grew even more daunting when the Japanese destroyed half of the army's fighter planes in the region and rapidly took Guam (gwahm), Wake Island, and Hong Kong. The main land attack came on December 22. MacArthur positioned his forces to repel the Japanese invasion, but he badly miscalculated the strength of the enemy and was forced to retreat. U.S. forces fell back from Manila to the Bataan (buh TAN) Peninsula and a fortification on Corregidor (kuh REHG uh dor) Island, where they dug in for a long siege. Trapped in Corregidor, Americans suffered, lacking necessary military and medical supplies and living on half and quarter rations.

Although MacArthur was ordered to evacuate to Australia, the other Americans remained behind. They held out until early May 1942, when 75,000 Allied soldiers surrendered. Japanese troops forced the sick and malnourished prisoners of war, or POWs, to march 55 miles up the Bataan Peninsula to reach a railway that took them inland where they were forced to march 8 more miles. More than 7,000 American and Filipino troops died during the grueling journey, which is known as the **Bataan Death March.**

**Japanese Forces Advance** Throughout the Pacific, Japanese forces attacked and conquered. These advances secured important oil and rubber supplies for Japan, and brought Southeast Asia and the western Pacific securely under Japanese control. By the summer of 1942, Japan appeared ready to dominate the Indian Ocean, Australia, New Zealand, and the central Pacific. If the Allies did not regroup quickly, they would have little hope of victory in the Pacific.

## NoteTaking

**Reading Skill: Sequence**
Sequence the fighting that followed Pearl Harbor in a table like the one below.

| Early War in the Pacific | |
| --- | --- |
| May 1942 | The Philippines fall to the Japanese. |
| | |
| | |
| | |

## America Mobilizes

These young men train to fight abroad. Training went on for months before soldiers were considered ready for combat.

## Japanese Aggression, December 1941–June 1942

**Geography** *Interactive*
For: Interactive map
Web Code: nep-1007

SOVIET UNION

MONGOLIA

Manchuria
(Manchukuo)

• Vladivostok

• Beijing

CHINA

Korea

Sea of
Japan

JAPAN

Tokyo

Yellow
Sea

• Shanghai

Kuril Islands

Aleutian Islands (U.S.)

**Doolittle Raid** Successful
American raid on Tokyo shocks
the Japanese in April 1942.

**Manila** Japanese forces land near Manila
in late December 1941. American forces
hold out in the Bataan Peninsula until April
9 and on Corregidor Island until May 5.

Burma
(U.K.)

French
Indochina

• Bangkok

Hong Kong
(U.K.)

South
China
Sea

Manila

Philippines
(U.S.)

THAILAND

Malaya (U.K.)
Singapore

Sumatra

Borneo

Celebes

Java Sea

D u t c h     E a s t     I n d i e s

Batavia • Java

Indian
Ocean

Darwin •

Mariana
Islands

• Saipan
• Guam
(U.S.)

Caroline
Islands

New  Guinea

Rabaul •

Coral Sea

Solomon Islands
(U.K. & Aust.)

Gilbert Islands
(U.K.)

Wake Island
(U.S.)

Marshall
Islands

Midway
Island
(U.S.)

Hawaiian
Islands
(U.S.)

Pacific
Ocean

**Pearl Harbor** Japan attacks Pearl Harbor
in Hawaii, Wake Island, Midway Island,
Guam, the Philippines, and Hong Kong
on December 7 and 8, 1941.

**Battle of Coral Sea** Outcome of
battle between Allied aircraft carriers
and Japanese aircraft carriers is
inconclusive, but Japan calls off
attack on New Guinea in 1942.

• Coral Sea

Miller Projection
0   500   1,000 mi
0   500   1,000 km

120° E

180°

AUSTRALIA

Extent of Japanese control, December 1941
Extent of Japanese control, June 1942
Areas under Japanese control, 1942
Japanese advance, December 1941
Japanese advance, January–May 1942
Major battle
Route of Doolittle Raid

**Map Skills** By mid-1942, the Japanese controlled
much of Southeast Asia and the Pacific region.

1. **Locate:** (a) Philippines, (b) New Guinea, (c) Wake
   Island, (d) Pearl Harbor

2. **Movement** What targets other than Pearl
   Harbor did the Japanese attack in December 1941?

3. **Recognize Cause and Effect** Why did the
   Doolittle Raid shock the citizens of Tokyo?

**Prisoners of War on the Bataan Peninsula** American and Filipino
troops surrender to the Japanese after holding out for months with
little food. They did not yet know that this would be only the beginning of their ordeal.

**America Strikes Back With the Doolittle Raid** After Pearl Harbor, FDR wanted America to retaliate against Japan. American military leaders devised a plan for a nighttime bombing raid from the deck of the aircraft carrier USS *Hornet,* led by Colonel James Doolittle. While still 800 miles away from mainland Japan, the *Hornet* was detected, so rather than wait for night, Doolittle led a force of 16 B-25 bombers against Tokyo. They delivered their payload on the Japanese capital just after noon.

The raid killed 50 Japanese people and damaged 100 buildings. The pilots then flew to China, where they crash-landed. Doolittle's Raid proved a <u>minimal</u> military gain, but it bolstered American morale for the long fight ahead.

**Vocabulary Builder**
<u>minimal</u>–(MIHN uh muhl) *adj.* smallest or least amount possible

**The Battle of Coral Sea Gives Hope** A second event, the **Battle of Coral Sea,** also helped to kindle hope for the American military in the Pacific. In early May 1942, the Japanese moved to take Port Moresby in New Guinea. From that position they could threaten Australia and protect their important military bases at Rabaul (also in New Guinea). To counter Japan's move, the United States sent two aircraft carriers, the USS *Lexington* and USS *Yorktown*, along with support vessels.

On May 7 and 8, in the middle of a Pacific storm, Japanese and U.S. aircraft carriers engaged in battle. It was the first sea fight in which enemy warships never sighted one another. Instead, U.S. airplanes attacked Japanese ships and vice versa. Although technically the Battle of Coral Sea proved a draw, strategically it was a victory for the United States because it forced the Japanese to call off their attack on New Guinea. It marked a shift in momentum toward the Americans. From that day on, the Pacific theater of battle would be won or lost on the strength of aircraft carriers and planes—and here, America's productive capacity gave Americans a marked advantage over their adversaries.

The Battle of Coral Sea and the Doolittle Raid gave the United States a renewed sense of confidence. The war would last three more years, but the dark days of early 1942 were over.

✔ **Checkpoint** What military advantages did the United States have over Japan?

---

SECTION

# 3 Assessment

**Progress Monitoring *Online***
For: Self-test with vocabulary practice
Web Code: nea-1008

## Comprehension

1. **Terms and People** For each item below, write a sentence explaining how it related to the entry of the United States into World War II.
   - Hideki Tojo
   - Pearl Harbor
   - WAC
   - Douglas MacArthur
   - Bataan Death March
   - Battle of Coral Sea

2. **NoteTaking Reading Skill: Identify Causes and Effects** Use your chart and table to answer the Section Focus Question: How did the United States react to the Japanese attack on Pearl Harbor?

### Writing About History

3. **Quick Write: Compare Primary Sources** Compare the primary source describing the attack on Pearl Harbor to the images of the attack in this section. Write one paragraph describing what information both sources convey about the event.

## Critical Thinking

4. **Identify Points of View** Was the Japanese attack on Pearl Harbor a success or failure from the Japanese point of view? Explain.

5. **Predict Consequences** What role do you think the productive capacity of the United States played in World War II?

6. **Draw Conclusions** Why was the Battle of Coral Sea a turning point for the Allies?

# Quick Study Guide

 7.2.1a

**Progress Monitoring** *Online*
For: Self-test with vocabulary practice
**Web Code:** nea-1009

## ■ Key Causes of World War II

| Destruction caused by World War I | Failure of World War I peace settlements | Global economic Depression |
| --- | --- | --- |

**Causes of World War II**

| Weakness of the League of Nations | Militaristic, nationalist leaders in Germany, Italy, and Japan | Acts of aggression by Axis Powers | British and French appeasement |
| --- | --- | --- | --- |

## ■ Key Allied Powers and Axis Powers and Their Leaders

| Allies | Leaders |
| --- | --- |
| Great Britain | Winston Churchill, prime minister |
| France | Charles de Gaulle, leader of French not under German control |
| Soviet Union | Joseph Stalin, communist dictator |
| United States | Franklin D. Roosevelt, President |

| Axis Powers | Leaders |
| --- | --- |
| Germany | Adolf Hitler, Nazi dictator |
| Italy | Benito Mussolini, fascist dictator |
| Japan | Hideki Tojo, army general and prime minister; Hirohito, emperor |

## ■ Steps Toward American Entry Into World War II

| 1935–1937 | Congress passes Neutrality Acts to help prevent the United States from being drawn into any foreign wars. |
| --- | --- |
| 1939 | The Neutrality Act of 1939 allows belligerent nations to buy supplies from the United States on a cash-and-carry basis; The act favors the Allies. |
| September 1940 | Roosevelt tightens trade embargo against Japan; Congress passes Selective Service Act, instituting a peacetime draft. |
| March 1941 | Congress passes the Lend-Lease Act, allowing the United States to give aid to the Allies. |
| August 1941 | Roosevelt and Churchill issue the Atlantic Charter. |
| Summer 1941 | Japanese and American diplomats try to resolve differences. |
| October–November 1941 | German U-boats sink United States Navy ships; U.S. merchant ships are armed and given permission to sink U-boats. |
| December 1941 | Japan attacks Pearl Harbor; the United States declares war on Japan and later on Germany and Italy. |

## ☑ Quick Study Timeline

**In America**

| | 1933 Nearly one in four American workers is unemployed | 1934–1936 Nye Committee scrutinizes reasons for U.S. involvement in World War I | 1935 Congress bans the sale of arms to countries at war |
| --- | --- | --- | --- |

Presidential Terms — Franklin D. Roosevelt 1933–1945

**1931** — **1933** — **1935**

**Around the World**

| 1931 Japanese army overruns Manchuria | 1933 Hitler becomes chancellor of Germany | 1935 Italy invades Ethiopia |
| --- | --- | --- |

# American Issues
## ●─●─●─● Connector

 7.1.3a

By connecting prior knowledge with what you have learned in this chapter, you can gradually build your understanding of enduring questions that still affect America today. Answer the questions below. Then, use your American Issues Connector study guide (or go online: www.PHSchool.com **Web Code:** neh-8302).

## Issues You Learned About

● **America and the World** Americans debated involvement in World War II.

1. What viewpoint on the war did isolationists hold? What viewpoint did interventionists hold?

2. Write a speech as if you were a Congress member who is either an isolationist or an interventionist. In your speech, you should express your view and attempt to persuade others to believe as you do. Consider the following:
   • the spread of fascist governments
   • the aggression of Japan, Italy, and Germany
   • the lessons of World War I
   • the Neutrality Acts
   • the Tripartite Pact

● **Global Interdependence** Countries develop specific policies about ways to deal with other countries' aggressive acts.

3. What was decided at the Munich Conference?

4. What happened after Hitler absorbed Czechoslovakia into the German Reich in the spring of 1939?

5. Did the appeasement policies of Britain and France prove to be effective? Explain.

● **America Goes to War** The United States became involved in World War II after an attack on its own soil.

6. What earlier global conflict had the United States been involved in? Why did the country get involved in that conflict?

7. How did the attack on Pearl Harbor draw the United States into war with Germany and Italy?

### Connect to Your World | Michigan

**Poverty and Prosperity** As you have read, the Civilian Conservation Corps (CCC) employed millions of Americans beginning in 1933. That May, 200 unemployed men between the ages of 17 and 23 left their homes in Detroit and Hamtramck to join the CCC's first camp in Michigan. At Camp Raco in the Hiawatha National Forest, the men planted trees, created a trail for trucks, and worked on fire prevention. The work at Camp Raco lasted until the CCC ended in 1942, longer than any other CCC camp in the area. The camp also served as an invaluable recruitment tool, as many men there went on to become soldiers, sailors, and marines. For the remainder of World War II, Camp Raco served as a camp for German prisoners of war. Create a pamphlet recruiting young Michiganians for the CCC.

---

**1937**
Roosevelt condemns aggression in Quarantine speech

**1940**
Roosevelt wins third term

**1941**
Pearl Harbor is attacked

WAR!
OAHU BOMBED BY JAPANESE PLANES

**1937**

**1938**
Germany annexes Austria

**1939**

**1939**
Germany invades Poland, beginning World War II

**1941**

**1941**
Germany invades the Soviet Union

**History Interactive**
**For:** Interactive timeline
**Web Code:** nep-1010

# Chapter Assessment

## Terms and People

1. Who was **Adolf Hitler**? How did he rise to power?

2. What was the **Spanish Civil War**? Describe other European countries' involvement in that war.

3. What was the **Lend-Lease Act**? How did it involve the United States in World War II?

4. What happened as a result of Japan's attack on **Pearl Harbor**?

5. Who was General **Douglas MacArthur**? What happened to him and his soldiers in the Philippines?

## Focus Questions

The focus question for this chapter is **What events caused World War II, and how did the United States become involved?** Build an answer to this big question by answering the focus questions for Sections 1 through 3 and the Critical Thinking questions that follow.

### Section 1

6. Why did totalitarian states rise after World War I, and what did they do?

### Section 2

7. How did Americans react to events in Europe and Asia in the early years of World War II?

### Section 3

8. How did the United States react to the Japanese attack on Pearl Harbor?

## Critical Thinking

9. **Make Comparisons** What did the governments in Italy and Germany in the 1930s have in common?

10. **Draw Conclusions** Do you think the League of Nations followed a policy of appeasement toward aggressors? Explain.

11. **Recognize Causes** Why do you think Germany wanted to sign a nonaggression pact with the Soviet Union?

12. **Draw Inferences** Why did Hitler decide to call off Operation Sea Lion?

13. **Determine Relevance** When did the United States declare war on Japan? How much Lend-Lease aid had the United States provided to Allies by this time?

### Lend-Lease Aid Given by the United States

| Year | To British Empire | To Soviet Union |
|---|---|---|
| 1941 (March–December) | $1.1 billion | $20.0 million |
| 1942 | $4.8 billion | $1.4 billion |
| 1943 | $9.0 billion | $2.4 billion |
| 1944 | $10.8 billion | $4.1 billion |
| 1945 (January–August) | $4.4 billion | $2.8 billion |
| **Total** | **$30.1 billion** | **$10.7 billion** |

SOURCE: *British War Economy*, W. K. Hancock and M. M. Gowing

14. **Predict Consequences** Do you think the United States would have eventually joined World War II if the Japanese had not attacked Pearl Harbor?

15. **Identify Central Issues** What was Japan's primary goal in taking part in World War II?

16. **Summarize** Describe the war in the Pacific from December 1941 through May 1942.

## Writing About History

**Analyzing Point of View** Between early 1940 and late 1941, a great debate raged in America between isolationists and interventionists. Go online to **www.PHSchool.com** and enter **Web Code: nep-1012** to read a series of primary sources on the Lend-Lease Act, each reflecting a different point of view. Then, write an essay comparing and contrasting the different viewpoints on the act.

### Prewriting

• On note cards, summarize each of the primary sources in your own words focusing on the writer's particular argument(s) in support of or opposed to the Lend-Lease Act.

• Organize your summaries into two piles: those supporting and those opposing the Lend-Lease Act.

### Drafting

• Develop a working thesis and choose information to support the thesis.

• Make an outline organizing your essay.

• Write an introduction in which you point out what you think were the strongest arguments of both sides of the debate.

• Write a body and a conclusion. Be sure to include and cite quotes from the primary sources to support your main points.

### Revising

• Use the guidelines on page SH11 of the Writing Handbook to revise your essay.

# Prepare for the MME

## American Contributions to the War Effort

Both prior to and during World War II, Americans mobilized to produce the material needed to win the war. Factories quickly converted from producing consumer goods to military goods, and each year the country increased and met its production goals. The following documents illustrate the role of American industrial output during the war. Use your knowledge of American production during World War II and Documents A, B, C, and D to answer questions 1 through 4.

### Document A

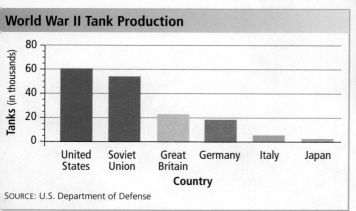

**World War II Tank Production**

SOURCE: U.S. Department of Defense

### Document B

"The superiority of the United Nations [Allies] in munitions and ships must be overwhelming—so overwhelming that the Axis nations can never hope to catch up with it. In order to attain this overwhelming superiority the United Nations must build planes and tanks and guns and ships to the utmost limit of our national capacity. . . . This production of ours in the United States must be raised far above its present levels. . . . Let no man say it cannot be done. It must be done—and we have undertaken to do it."

*President Franklin D. Roosevelt, Annual Message to Congress, January 6, 1942*

### Document C

*The Liberty Ship* Robert E. Peary *was built in a matter of days.*

### Document D

"The reliance on American aid indicates just how much the Allied war effort owed to the exceptional material and logistical strength of the United States.

The ability of the world's largest industrial economy to convert to the mass production of weapons and war equipment is usually taken for granted. Yet the transition from peace to war was so rapid and effective that the USA was able to make up for the lag in building up effectively trained armed forces by exerting a massive material superiority.

This success owed . . . a great deal to the character of American industrial capitalism, with its 'can-do' ethos, high levels of engineering skill and tough-minded entrepreneurs. After a decade of recession the manufacturing community had a good deal of spare, unemployed capacity to absorb. . . ."

*From* World War Two: How the Allies Won, *Professor Richard Overy*

---

1. According to Document A, which of the following countries produced the most tanks during World War II?
   A Germany and Italy
   B Italy and Japan
   C the United States and the Soviet Union
   D the Soviet Union and the United Kingdom

2. In Document B, President Roosevelt is calling for
   A the immediate recruitment of troops.
   B a dramatic increase in the production of armaments.
   C a dramatic increase in the workforce.
   D production levels to match those of the Axis Powers.

3. According to the author of Document D,
   A the Allied victory is often taken for granted.
   B America's transition to war production was slow but effective.
   C Allied success was partly a result of American know-how and effort.
   D the training of American troops was superior to that of the enemies' troops.

4. **Writing Task** Do you agree that America's role in the war was crucial to the Allies eventual success? Why? Use your knowledge from the chapter and specific evidence from the documents to support your view.

# 11

# World War II
## 1941–1945

## The Slow March to Victory

In June 1944, Allied troops landed in German-held France and began their push toward the defeat of Hitler. An American soldier later described his memories:

"Trying to stay clean, trying to rest when possible, eating when possible. . . . Feeling very thankful that one of the guys just looking upwards into a tree observed a German and without hesitation fired his rifle from the hip—Hollywood fashion—killing the German, who no doubt was waiting for the last GI in the platoon to pass by and would then open fire from the rear. . . . On the move constantly, pushing inland, small villages with buildings burning."

—Dick Biehl, quoted in *June 6, 1944: The Voices of D-Day*

*Listen to the* Witness History *audio to hear more about American soldiers in France.*

◄ Near a French village, an American soldier fires a cannon at retreating German soldiers in 1944.

 **Content Expectations**

**Chapter Focus Question:** What impact did World War II have on America and the world?

### Section 1
**The Allies Turn the Tide**  7.2.1a, 7.2.1b, 7.2.2

### Section 2
**The Home Front**  6.3.2d, 7.2.3b, 7.2.3c, 7.2.3d

### Section 3
**Victory in Europe and the Pacific**  7.2.3a, 7.2.3b, 7.2.4

### Section 4
**The Holocaust**  7.2.1b, 7.2.2, 7.2.4

### Section 5
**Effects of the War**  7.2.2, 7.2.3b, 7.2.3c

Use the ☑ **Quick Study Timeline** at the end of this chapter to preview chapter events.

Navajos in the United States Marines sent coded messages in their native language.

Patch commemorating the Battle of Guadalcanal

American tank

**Note Taking Study Guide** *Online*
**For:** Note Taking and American Issues Connector
**Web Code:** nee-8401

▲ American marines on Guadalcanal

### Spiders as Big as Your Fist

World War II placed U.S. soldiers in a dazzling variety of settings, from mountains to deserts to forests to tropical isles. One marine described the ordeal of fighting on a Pacific island:

“It was beautiful, but beneath the loveliness . . . Guadalcanal was a mass of slops and stinks and pestilence; of scum-crusted lagoons and vile swamps inhabited by giant crocodiles; a place of spiders as big as your fist and wasps as long as your finger . . . of ants that bite like fire, of tree leeches that fall, fasten and suck; of scorpions, of centipedes whose foul scurrying across human skin leaves a track of inflamed flesh, of snakes and land crabs, rats and bats and carrion birds and of a myriad of stinging insects.”

—Robert Leckie, *Delivered From Evil: The Saga of World War II*

# The Allies Turn the Tide

### Content Expectations

- **7.2.1a** Analyze political/economic disputes over territory.
- **7.2.1b** Analyze differences in civic/political values of U.S., Nazi Germany, Imperial Japan.
- **7.2.2** Evaluate U.S. role in fighting war militarily, diplomatically, technologically across the world.

### Terms and People

| | |
|---|---|
| Dwight Eisenhower | strategic bombing |
| George S. Patton, Jr. | Tuskegee Airmen |
| unconditional surrender | Chester Nimitz |
| saturation bombing | Battle of Midway |

### NoteTaking

**Reading Skill: Summarize** List the ways in which the Allies turned back the Axis advance.

| Turning Back the Axis | |
|---|---|
| **In Europe** | **In the Pacific** |
| • Battle against U-boats in Atlantic | • |
| • | • |

**Why It Matters** The attack on Pearl Harbor brought America into World War II on the Allied side. In 1942, the Allies began to stop the seemingly unstoppable Axis onslaught. Though years of fighting lay ahead, the most aggressive threat to world peace and democracy in modern times had been halted. **Section Focus Question: How did the Allies turn the tide against the Axis?**

## Axis and Allies Plan Strategy

By June 1942, the Allies were battered but still fighting. As you have read, British pilots had fought off a Nazi invasion of their island, while at the Battle of Coral Sea, the U.S. Navy had frustrated Japanese plans to extend their domination in the Pacific. Although the war was not close to being over, the Allies spied signs of hope.

The Axis Powers never had a coordinated strategy to defeat the Allies. Germany, Italy, and Japan shared common enemies but nurtured individual dreams. Hitler wanted to dominate Europe and eliminate "inferior" peoples. Mussolini harbored dreams of an Italian empire stretching from the eastern Adriatic to East Africa. Tojo sought Japanese control of the Western Pacific and Asia.

The Allies shared more unified goals. Roosevelt, Churchill, and Stalin considered Germany the most dangerous enemy. None felt Japan or Italy posed a serious long-term threat. Only Germany had the resources to bomb Britain, fight U.S. and British navies on the

Atlantic, and invade the Soviet Union across a 1,200-mile front. Thus, although their <u>ultimate</u> goal was to fight and win a two-front war, the Allies agreed to pursue a "Europe First" strategy. Until Hitler was defeated, the Pacific would be a secondary theater of war.

✓ **Checkpoint** Why did the Allies decide to concentrate first on the war in Europe?

# Turning the Tide in Europe

The first blow America struck against the Axis was by fulfilling FDR's promise to be the "arsenal of democracy." American industries turned out millions of tons of guns, tanks, and other supplies—enough to keep the Soviets and British battling Germany for years. The problem was delivering the supplies.

**Allies Battle U-Boats in the Atlantic** Hitler was determined to cut the sea lines between the United States and Europe before American aid could make a difference. "Wolf packs" of German U-boats patrolled the Atlantic and Caribbean, sinking more than 3,500 merchant ships and killing tens of thousands of Allied seamen. "The only thing that ever really frightened me during the war was the U-boat peril," Churchill later wrote.

Finally, in mid-1943, the Allies began to win the war in the North Atlantic. As in World War I, convoys of escort carriers protected Allied shipping. A new invention, radar, helped Allied vessels locate U-boats on the surface at night. Long-range aerial bombers and underwater depth charges allowed Allied forces to sink U-boats faster than Germany could manufacture them.

**Soviets Turn Back Nazis at Stalingrad** Germany had attacked Russia in June 1941, sending one army north toward Leningrad, a second east toward Moscow, and a third south toward Stalingrad. Although Hitler's forces penetrated deep into Soviet territory, killing or capturing millions of soldiers and civilians, they did not achieve their main objective of conquering the Soviet Union. Soviet resistance and a brutal Russia winter stopped the German advance.

In 1942, Hitler narrowed his sights and concentrated his armies in southern Russia. His goal this time was to control the rich Caucasus oil fields. To achieve this objective, he would have to capture the city of Stalingrad.

The struggle for Stalingrad was especially ferocious. German troops advanced slowly, fighting bitter block-by-block, house-by-house battles in the bombed-out buildings and rubble. Soviet troops then counterattacked, trapping the German forces. Yet Hitler refused to allow his army to retreat. Starving, sick, and suffering from frostbite, the surviving German troops finally surrendered on January 31, 1943.

The battle of Stalingrad was the true turning point of the war in Europe. It ended any realistic plans Hitler had of dominating Europe. Nazi armies were forced to retreat westward back toward Germany. Instead, it was the Soviet Union that now went on the offensive.

**Surrender at Stalingrad**
The long Battle of Stalingrad ended in January 1943 with the surrender of German troops like these. Of the 91,000 prisoners taken by the Soviets, only about 5,000 eventually survived and returned to Germany.

**Desert Warfare** American soldiers had to fight in many unfamiliar types of terrain. But the Sahara of North Africa—the world's largest desert—presented special challenges:

- In hot, dry weather, sandstorms choked and blinded troops.
- In wet weather, mud halted machinery.
- The high visibility of the desert terrain made it difficult for troops to move without being seen.
- Poisonous reptiles, ants, and scorpions added to the problems.

Brilliant tank strategists like Patton and Rommel were able to overcome such challenges. But the tanks themselves caused other problems, such as kicking up enormous dust clouds that could be seen miles away.

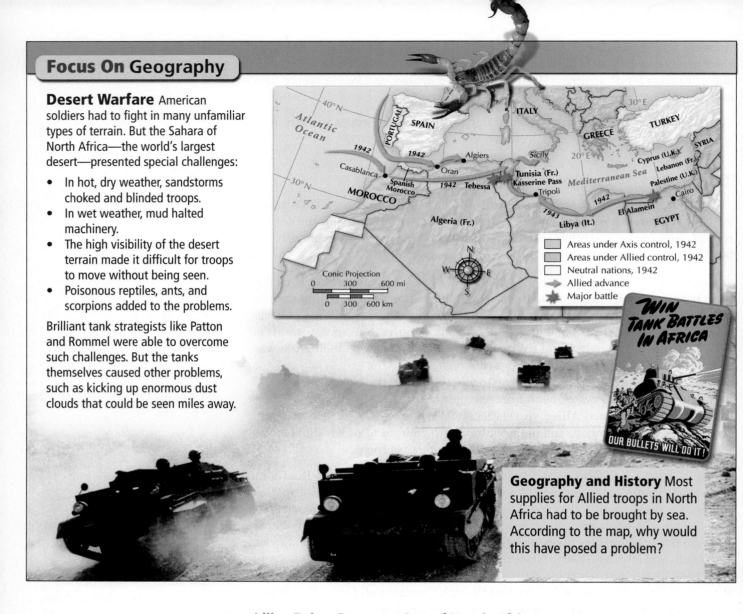

**Geography and History** Most supplies for Allied troops in North Africa had to be brought by sea. According to the map, why would this have posed a problem?

**Allies Drive Germans Out of North Africa** Meanwhile, another important campaign was taking place in the deserts and mountains of North Africa, where the British had been fighting the Germans and Italians since 1940. Several goals motivated the Allied campaign in North Africa. Stalin had wanted America and Britain to relieve the Soviet Union by establishing a second front in France. However, FDR and Churchill felt they needed more time to prepare for an invasion across the English Channel. An invasion of North Africa, however, required less planning and fewer supplies. In addition, forcing Germany out of North Africa would pave the way for an invasion of Italy.

In October 1942, the British won a major victory at El Alamein (ehl al uh MAYN) in Egypt and began to push westward. The next month, Allied troops landed in Morocco and Algeria and began to move east toward key German positions. An energetic American officer, General **Dwight Eisenhower**—known as Ike—commanded the Allied invasion of North Africa.

In February 1943, German general Erwin Rommel (known as the Desert Fox) led his Afrika Korps against the Americans at the Kasserine Pass in Tunisia. Rommel broke through the American lines in an attempt to reach the Allied supply base at Tebessa in Algeria. Finally, American soldiers stopped the assault. Lack of supplies then forced Rommel to retreat.

The fighting at the Kasserine Pass taught American leaders valuable lessons. They needed aggressive officers and troops better trained for desert fighting. To that end, Eisenhower put American forces in North Africa under the command of **George S. Patton, Jr.,** an innovative tank commander. A single-minded general known as Blood and Guts, Patton told his junior officers:

**Primary Source** "You usually will know where the front is by the sound of gunfire, and that's the direction you should proceed. Now, suppose you lose a hand or an ear is shot off, or perhaps a piece of your nose, and you think you should walk back to get first aid. If I see you, it will be the last . . . walk you'll ever take."

—George S. Patton, Jr., 1943

Patton's forces advanced east with heightened confidence. Simultaneously, the British pressed westward from Egypt, trapping Axis forces in a continually shrinking pocket in Tunisia. Rommel escaped, but his army did not. In May 1943, German and Italian forces—some 240,000 troops—surrendered.

✓ **Checkpoint** Why was the Battle of Stalingrad a turning point in World War II?

# Increasing the Pressure on Germany

Germany was now on the defensive, and the Allies planned to keep it that way. In January 1943, Roosevelt and Churchill met in Casablanca, Morocco, to plan their next move. The conference resulted in two important decisions. First, the Allies decided to increase bombing of Germany and invade Italy. Second, FDR announced that the Allies would accept only **unconditional surrender,** or giving up completely without any concessions. Hitler, Mussolini, and Tojo could not hope to stay in power through a negotiated peace.

**Allies Invade Italy** The Allies next eyed Italy. Situated across the Mediterranean from Tunisia and 2 miles from the Italian mainland, Sicily was the obvious target for an invasion. The Allies could invade Sicily without great risk from U-boats and under the protection of air superiority. In July 1943, British and American armies made separate landings in Sicily and began to advance across the island before joining forces in the north. Once again, Eisenhower commanded the joint American-British forces.

Ike hoped to trap Axis forces on Sicily, but they escaped to the Italian mainland. Still, the 38-day campaign achieved important results: It gave the Allies complete control of the western Mediterranean, paved the way for an invasion of Italy, and ended the rule of Benito Mussolini. On September 3, 1943, Italy surrendered to the Allies and five weeks later declared war on Germany.

But Hitler was not through with Italy. After a small German airborne force rescued Mussolini from a mountaintop fortress, Hitler installed him as head of a puppet state in northern Italy. In the south, German military forces continued the fight against the Allies.

**On the Beach at Sicily**
Using only a small foldable shovel, an American soldier digs himself a foxhole on the beach at Sicily.

The invasion of Italy was a slow, grinding slog. Italy was crisscrossed with mountains and rivers. Heavy rains and mountain snows made combat difficult and painful. Men fought in ankle-deep mud. In the mountains, where tanks and heavy artillery were useless, Allied forces depended on mules to haul supplies up slippery and steep roads. To make matters worse, the Germans occupied the best defensive positions. Fighting continued into 1945. The Allies won battles, but none were important enough to alter the basic German defensive policy.

**Bombers Batter Germany** Stalin continued his demand that Roosevelt and Churchill open a second front in France. While the Allies did not launch a massive invasion of France until 1944, they did open a second front of another kind in early 1942. From bases in England, Allied bombers launched nonstop attacks against Germany. Flying by night in order to avoid being shot down in large numbers, British planes dropped massive amounts of bombs on German cities. The goal of this **saturation bombing** was to inflict maximum damage.

By day, American bombers targeted Germany's key political and industrial centers. The goal of this campaign of **strategic bombing** was to destroy Germany's capacity to make war. A Nazi official later commented that "the fleets of bombers might appear at any time over any large German city or important factory."

An African American fighter squadron known as the **Tuskegee Airmen** played a key role in the campaign, escorting bombers and protecting them from enemy fighter pilots. In more than 1,500 missions over enemy territory in Europe, the Tuskegee Airmen did not lose a single bomber.

Overall, though, the bombing missions cost the Allies dearly. Bomber crews suffered an incredibly high 20 percent casualty rate. But they successfully

# Air War Over Europe

INFOGRAPHIC ◀)) AUDIO

129445

**D**uring World War II, the B-24 *Liberator* was the king of American bombers, faster than previous planes and with a greater long-range flight capacity. The B-24s and the men who flew them played a critical and demanding role in the air war over Europe.

◀ Hollywood hero Jimmy Stewart (seated) became a real hero: He emerged from the Air Force as a Brigadier General.

▼ Silver Air Force Gunner Wings pin

### U.S. Air War in Europe

| | |
|---|---|
| Flight crew members killed | 30,099 |
| Flight crew members wounded | 13,360 |
| Combat missions | 1,693,565 |
| Tons of bombs dropped | 1,554,463 |
| Planes lost in combat | 18,418 |
| Enemy aircraft destroyed | 29,916 |

SOURCE: Army Air Force Statistical Digests

carried the war into Germany, day after day and night after night. This second front in the sky did indeed relieve some of the pressure on the Soviet armies on the Eastern Front and helped pave the way for an all-out Allied offensive.

✓ **Checkpoint** What were the goals of British and American bombing runs over Germany?

# Turning the Tide in the Pacific

While the Allies pursued their "Europe First" strategy, they did not ignore the Pacific. Through May 1942, Japanese forces continued to advance with seemingly unstoppable <u>momentum</u>. They had attacked American, British, and Dutch colonies, winning control of the Philippines, Malaya, Dutch East Indies, Hong Kong, Wake Island, Guam, and Burma. Then, the United States struck back. As you have read in the last chapter, the Battle of Coral Sea served as a warning that America might be down in the Pacific, but it was not out.

**Turning Point: Americans Triumph at Midway** Admiral Yamamoto, commander of Japanese forces in the Pacific, knew that the United States Navy was still a powerful threat. Before the Americans could retaliate for Pearl Harbor, Yamamoto sought to destroy American aircraft carriers in the Pacific. He turned his attention to Midway, an American naval base in the Central Pacific that was vital to the defense of Hawaii. Losing Midway would force American defenses back to the California coast. Yamamoto's ambitious plan entailed taking Midway and establishing a military presence in the Aleutians, a string of islands off the coast of Alaska.

**Vocabulary Builder**

<u>momentum</u>–(moh MEHN tuhm) *n.* forward motion; push

The B-24 took more crew members to operate than any flying machine ever built. Each member of the 10-man crew had a vital job. **1, 2, 3, 4, 5, 10** **Gunners:** defend the B-24 from attacking enemy planes coming from any direction **5 Flight Engineer:** handles any mechanical problems; doubles as gunner **6 Radio Operator:** communicates with ground, other planes **7 Pilot:** responsible for entire mission **8 Co-pilot:** assists pilot in flying plane **9 Navigator:** plots course of plane; also doubles as Bombardier in charge of aiming and dropping bomb

**Tuskegee Airmen** Rather than carrying bombs, some planes escorted and protected the planes that did. The most celebrated of these escort crews were the Tuskegee Airmen, a special unit of African American pilots. In more than 1,500 missions over Europe, the Tuskegee Airmen did not lose a single bomber.

## Thinking Critically

1. **Draw Inferences** Which members of the flight crew carried out the main objective of the mission? What was the chief job of the other members?

2. **Synthesize Information** How did the Tuskegee Airmen affect the casualty figures listed in the chart at left?

What Yamamoto did not realize was that Admiral **Chester Nimitz,** commander of the United States Navy in the Pacific, knew the Japanese plans. Navy code breakers had intercepted Japanese messages. To meet the expected assault, Nimitz sent his only available aircraft carriers to Midway. The Japanese navy was stretched out across more than a thousand miles, from the Aleutians to well west of Midway. American forces were all concentrated near Midway.

The Japanese commenced their attack on June 4, 1942. In the most important naval battle of World War II, the United States dealt Japan a decisive defeat. Torpedo planes and dive bombers sank 4 Japanese aircraft carriers, along with all 250 aircraft on board and many of Japan's most experienced pilots. America lost only one aircraft carrier.

The **Battle of Midway** was the turning point of the war in the Pacific, ending the seemingly unstoppable Japanese advance. Japan still had a powerful navy, committed troops, and fortified positions. But it would never again threaten Hawaii or Pacific domination. Japan was now on the defensive end of the war.

**Americans Take the Offensive** The first American offensive in the Pacific took place in August 1942, with an assault on Guadalcanal in the Solomon Islands. (See the Witness History at the beginning of this section.) After three months of intense fighting, the United States Marines drove the Japanese off the island.

Guadalcanal was the first leg in a strategy to approach Japan from both the southwest Pacific and the central Pacific, using combined U.S. Marine, Navy, and Army forces. The logic behind the dual offensives was to force Japan to fight a two-front war and to capture bases from which to bomb the Japanese home islands. In jungles and coral reefs, under torrential monsoons and the blistering sun, fighting for every new piece of territory, American servicemen began their slow, painful trek toward Japan.

### The Battle of Midway

Midway was a new kind of naval battle. Instead of armed ships facing each other directly, the fighting was carried on by swift airplanes that took off from the decks of aircraft carriers to bomb vessels many miles away.

✔ **Checkpoint** What impact did the Battle of Midway have on Japanese expansion in the Pacific?

---

# 1 Assessment

**Progress Monitoring _Onlin_**
For: Self-test with vocabulary practice
Web Code: nea-1102

## Comprehension

1. **Terms and People** Write a sentence explaining how each of the following was connected with the Allied effort to turn back the Axis offensive.
   - Dwight Eisenhower
   - George S. Patton, Jr.
   - unconditional surrender
   - saturation bombing
   - strategic bombing
   - Tuskegee Airmen
   - Chester Nimitz
   - Battle of Midway

2. NoteTaking **Reading Skill: Summarize** Use your table to answer the Section Focus Question: How did the Allies turn the tide against the Axis?

## Writing About History

3. **Quick Write: Describe a Photograph** Look at the photograph from Stalingrad in this section. Write a two-sentence factual description of what is happening in the picture. Use at least one descriptive adjective and one action verb.

## Critical Thinking

4. **Analyze Causes** Why did Roosevelt support a "Europe First" strategy even though it was Japan that had first attacked the United States?

5. **Evaluate Information** Was the Allied invasion of Italy a success? Give reasons for your answer.

6. **Apply Information** How does the Battle of Midway illustrate the importance of intelligence gathering and espionage in modern warfare?

◄ Workers in an aircraft plant

WITNESS HISTORY 🔊 AUDIO

### Rosie the Riveter

Who was Rosie the Riveter? The image of a muscular, determined worker, hair tucked under a kerchief, graced countless magazines and posters. And several real-life Rosies won nationwide publicity, including Rose Hicker, a worker in a Tarrytown, New York, aircraft plant, who set a record for driving rivets into the wing of a bomber. But, in fact, Rosie was not based on one woman. The name was first used in a 1942 song:

❝All the day long, whether rain or shine,
She's a part of the assembly line.
She's making history,
Working for victory,
Rosie the Riveter.❞

—Redd Evans and John Jacob Loeb,
"Rosie the Riveter"

◄ "Rosie the Riveter" poster

# The Home Front

### Content Expectations

- **6.3.2d** Analyze causes/consequences of reform organizations, movements, individuals promoting change.
- **7.2.3b** Analyze role of women/minorities in war effort.
- **7.2.3c** Analyze role of home front in supporting war effort.
- **7.2.3d** Analyze internment of Japanese-Americans.

### Terms and People

A. Philip Randolph
Executive Order 8802
bracero program
internment

442nd Regimental
 Combat Team
rationing
OWI

### NoteTaking

**Reading Skill: Identify Main Ideas** As you read, identify the major effects of World War II on the home front.

| The Home Front, World War II | | |
| --- | --- | --- |
| **Economy** | **Effects on Women** | **Effects on Minorities** |
| • War bonds<br>• Wage controls | •<br>• | •<br>• |

**Why It Matters** World War II engaged the peoples and resources of the countries involved. The war effort stirred patriotism and promoted economic recovery. And, while wartime fears and tensions tested civil liberties, new opportunities for women and minorities would spur stronger efforts to ensure equal rights after the war was over. **Section Focus Question: How did the war change America at home?**

## New Economic Opportunities

American industry quickly converted to war production to meet the nation's military needs. Once industry exhausted the available men, women found more jobs for the taking. Government and industry launched an all-out publicity campaign urging women to do their part to meet wartime production quotas. In time, women made up one third of the wartime workforce.

**Women Work for Victory** A woman working outside the home was nothing new, but wartime pressures created two sharp breaks from the past. Many women found jobs, especially in heavy industry, that fell outside the traditional realm of women's work. The need for labor also weakened the common practice that a woman quit her job once she married. Three fourths of women working in war industries were married, and 60 percent were older than 35 years.

The image of Rosie the Riveter's rolled up sleeves, red kerchief, and rivet gun gave Americans an enduring image of women in wartime production. Still, women labored in both blue-collar and white-collar jobs. Most factory owners expected women to step aside once men returned home at war's end. In white-collar settings, however, the war accelerated long-term trends toward increased employment. During the 1940s, the number of women employed in secretarial and clerical work increased five-fold.

The benefits that women gained from wartime work cannot be underestimated. They earned paychecks, formed new and different relationships, and gained organizational experience. "I decided that if I could learn to weld like a man," noted one laborer, "I could do anything it took to make a living." The confidence and knowledge women developed enriched their postwar experiences and helped create opportunities for their daughters in the years ahead.

With fathers in the military and mothers in the workplace, children's lives began to change. The federal government spent $50 million building day-care centers for children of working mothers. Still, only about 130,000 kids ended up in day-care centers. Many women preferred to leave their children in the care of neighbors or relatives.

**African Americans Demand Fair Employment** Many African American leaders hoped the war might provide jobs and alleviate their dismal economic situations. However, few found meaningful employment with national defense employers. Out of 100,000 Americans working in the aircraft industry in 1940, for example, only 240 were African Americans. Even jobs provided by the government and military remained segregated.

African American leaders stressed the need for a "Double V" campaign— victory against fascism abroad and victory against discrimination at home. The charismatic and savvy labor leader **A. Philip Randolph** asserted that African Americans would no longer accept second-class citizenship. "We loyal Negro American citizens demand the right to work and fight for our country," he proclaimed. Randolph presented President Roosevelt a list of demands, including the end of discriminatory practices in government-funded training, employment, and the armed services. He also took steps to organize a massive protest march on Washington, D.C.

FDR had hoped to put civil rights reform on the back burner while fighting the Axis Powers. But Randolph persisted in his plans. Roosevelt feared that the sight of a huge protest march on the nation's capital would undermine wartime unity and provide ammunition for enemy propaganda. So, under pressure, he issued **Executive Order 8802.** This measure assured fair hiring practices in any job funded with government money and established the Fair Employment Practices Committee to enforce these requirements.

Such victories encouraged African Americans to join organizations dedicated to promoting equal rights. The NAACP grew to 500,000 members. In 1942, civil rights leaders founded the Congress of Racial Equality (CORE), an organization that sought to apply nonviolent protest as a means of fighting segregation. Although segregation still prevailed in the military, the South, and other parts of the nation, wartime developments helped set the agenda for the civil rights struggles of the coming decades.

## HISTORY MAKERS

### A. Philip Randolph (1889–1979)

In 1925, A. Philip Randolph became head of the Brotherhood of Sleeping Car Porters. At the time, virtually all the nation's porters were African American. The Pullman Corporation, which employed them, refused to deal with labor unions. In fact, the Brotherhood had to be organized in secret. For 12 years, the company fired or threatened union members and attacked Randolph as a dangerous radical. But Randolph refused to give up. Finally, in 1937, the Pullman company gave in and signed the first contract in history between a major company and an African American labor union.

 **Checkpoint** How did the war create new opportunities for African Americans?

# Workers on the Move

Wartime needs encouraged migration as people moved in search of work. California alone gained 2 million new residents seeking work in the state's many shipyards and other wartime industries. Although the South lost residents in its rural areas, it grew by a million new people as a whole. Older industrial cities in the North, such as Detroit, Gary, Chicago, and Cleveland, also boomed.

**The Population Starts to Shift** The ebb and flow of people fostered long-term changes. After receiving billions of dollars to fund industry, the South and Southwest became a growing cultural, social, economic, and political force. This trend continues to this day.

To alleviate the rural population drain, especially in the West, the United States partnered with Mexico to operate the **bracero program,** bringing laborers from Mexico to work on American farms. During the war years, several hundred thousand braceros migrated to the United States. Although they often faced discrimination, they contributed greatly to the war effort. In the long term, the bracero program <u>initiated</u> decades of migratory labor in the West.

**Migration Triggers Conflict** In the summer of 1943, wartime migration led to racial violence in a number of cities. The worst occurred in Detroit, Michigan, where conflict erupted over the construction of housing for black workers drawn north to defense plants. Finally, some 100,000 whites and blacks broke into scattered fights at a city park. By the next morning, full-scale riots erupted in which 34 people were killed. Federal troops ended the violence, but nobody found a real resolution to the city's problems.

Mexican Americans had long dealt with similar tensions. Few had mastered the English language, and many languished in slums while struggling to find work. A violent incident highlighted the problems. In the Los Angeles area, many Mexican and Mexican American youths dressed in stylish "zoot suits" with baggy pants and long jackets. In June 1943, mobs of off-duty sailors roamed through the Mexican sections of Los Angeles, attacking "zooters." Once the fighting ended, police arrested the zoot-suited victims, not their attackers.

**Vocabulary Builder**
initiate–(ih NIHSH ee ayt) *v.* to begin or originate

## After the Zoot Suit Riots

Los Angeles police arrest a group of young Mexican Americans after a spate of violence in June 1943. Some, like the second prisoner from the right, wear the flashy, baggy zoot suits that gave the incident its name.

Japanese internment camp

**Manzanar Internment Camp**

At the Manzanar internment camp in California's Owens Valley (above, right), Japanese Americans lived in bleak barracks, subject to heat and dust storms. Above, a mother and her children await relocation. *Which western states housed internment camps?*

After the riots, an indignant Governor Earl Warren formed a committee to investigate the causes of the outbreak and demanded that the guilty parties be punished. Although the committee blamed the lack of sufficient recreation for the violence, long-brewing racial tensions acted as the true spark.

✔ **Checkpoint** How did the war affect the location of industries and workers in the United States?

## A Challenge to Civil Liberties

The attack on Pearl Harbor spread fear across America. The federal government began drafting policies toward immigrants and aliens from the Axis nations. All resident "enemy aliens" were required to register with the government, submit to fingerprinting, and list their organizational affiliations.

**Aliens Face Restrictions** Originally, laws made no distinction among nationalities. German, Italian, and Japanese aliens were subject to arrest or deportation if deemed dangerous to national security. Some 11,000 German immigrants and hundreds of Italian immigrants were held in camps; others faced curfews or travel restrictions. Federal orders also forced all three groups to vacate the West Coast temporarily in the winter of 1942. Once public fears subsided, FDR removed Germans and Italians from the enemy aliens list.

Japanese aliens and Japanese American citizens received no such respite. Believing Japanese Americans to be inherently disloyal, West Coast leaders pressed FDR to address the "threat." In February 1942, the President issued Executive Order 9066, designating certain areas as war zones from which anyone might be removed for any reason. By September, the government evacuated more than 100,000 Japanese Americans on the West Coast. Evacuees—including both Issei, Japanese immigrants, and Nisei, native-born American citizens of Japanese descent—were forced to sell their property at a loss and allowed to take only necessary items.

Why did Japanese Americans generally face harsher treatment than Italian or German Americans? Several factors help explain the difference: racism, the smaller numbers of Japanese Americans, their lack of political clout, and their relative isolation from other Americans. In Hawaii, where Japanese Americans <u>comprised</u> one third of a multiracial society, they escaped a similar fate.

**Japanese Americans Are Interned** The first orders stipulated only that Japanese Americans must leave designated military zones, but leaders in interior states objected. The governor of Arizona insisted his state did not want to become a "dumping ground for enemy aliens." The War Department then initiated a policy of **internment,** or temporary imprisonment of members of a specific group. Japanese American men, women, and children were transported to camps in isolated locations such as Poston, Arizona, and the Gila River Indian Reservation. With few exceptions, Nisei and Issei remained in the camps for the duration of the war.

Families huddled into stark one-room shacks, while single people were herded into drafty bunkhouses. Camp schools were hopelessly underfunded. Internees often suffered from food shortages and substandard medical care. The psychological effects could be just as severe. One internee reported:

> **Primary Source**  ❝The resettlement center is actually a jail—armed guards in towers with spotlights and deadly tommy guns, fifteen feet of barbed-wire fences, everyone confined to quarters at nine. . . . What really hurts [is being called] 'Japs.' 'Japs' are the guys we are fighting.❞
> —Ted Nakashima, *The New Republic,* June 5, 1942

Some Japanese Americans went to court to seek their rights. In the 1944 case of Korematsu v. United States, the Supreme Court upheld the government's wartime internment policy. (See Landmark Decisions of the Supreme Court at the end of this section.) Not until 1988 did the government offer an apology and $20,000 payments to surviving internees.

Japanese Americans also faced another form of discrimination. At first, they were not accepted into the armed forces. But after the government lifted the ban in early 1943, many eagerly enlisted. The all-Nisei **442nd Regimental Combat Team** fought in the Italian campaign and became the most decorated military unit in American history. The 442nd helped counter the notion that Japanese Americans were not loyal citizens.

✓ **Checkpoint** Why were Japanese Americans interned during World War II?

# Supporting the War Effort

The war eventually cost Americans $330 billion, which was double the total amount of federal expenditures since the founding of the nation. In six years, the national debt skyrocketed from $42 billion to $269 billion. To help raise funds, Congress levied a 5 percent tax on all working Americans. In addition, millions of Americans bought war bonds to save income and invest in the war effort. The government reminded Americans that every dollar spent on war bonds meant another bullet or bomb and another step closer to victory. (See the American Experience feature at the end of this section.)

**The Government Manages the Economy** Increased production of war goods created a scarcity of consumer products. As shortages led to price increases, many feared that inflation

**Vocabulary Builder**
comprise–(kuhm PRĪZ) *v.* to include; to make up

## The Cost of Waging War

The cost of building arms and paying and equipping military personnel caused the federal budget to skyrocket. *Based on the combined information on the two graphs, approximately how much was spent on national defense in 1945?*

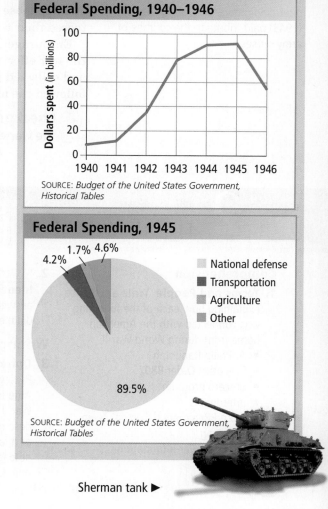

**Federal Spending, 1940–1946**

Dollars spent (in billions): 0, 20, 40, 60, 80, 100
Years: 1940 1941 1942 1943 1944 1945 1946

SOURCE: *Budget of the United States Government, Historical Tables*

**Federal Spending, 1945**

- 4.2%
- 1.7%
- 4.6%
- 89.5%

- National defense
- Transportation
- Agriculture
- Other

SOURCE: *Budget of the United States Government, Historical Tables*

Sherman tank ▶

## Hollywood Goes to War

The two films above dealt with the fall of the Philippines. *Back to Bataan* (1945) told the story of anti-Japanese guerrilla fighters. *So Proudly We Hail* (1943) paid tribute to the courage of army nurses.

would run wild. To manage this problem, FDR created the Office of Price Administration, which had the authority to control wages and set maximum prices. Another form of economic control was **rationing.** Americans were issued coupon books that limited the amount of certain goods, such as butter and tires, that they could buy. Rationing ensured that raw materials such as rubber and oil found their way into war production.

Although most Americans accepted the need for wartime controls, others resented the restrictions. Unscrupulous profiteers manipulated the ration coupon system to create a "black market," an illegal underground network for the sale of restricted goods. Because the government restricted job mobility to ensure constant production and because wages lagged behind rising prices and profits, some workers accused their employers of unfair practices. Still, Americans created a powerful industrial network that contributed to victory and carried long-term consequences.

**Media Boosts Morale** Sacrifices on the home front took a toll on morale. The federal **Office of War Information (OWI)** worked closely with the media to encourage support of the war effort. The OWI tried to spotlight common needs, minimize racial and economic divisions, and downplay problems of poverty and crime. The radio, print, and film industries reminded Americans that they were in a struggle between dictatorship and democracy.

Hollywood proved a capable and willing ally in this cause. Documentaries like Frank Capra's *Why We Fight* series highlighted the need to defeat fascism. Fiction films showed patriotic Americans pitching in overseas or on the home front and stirred hatred of the enemy with stereotypical portrayals of treacherous Japanese and brutal Germans. Movie stars and popular singers volunteered their time to sell war bonds and entertain the troops.

Encouraged by government and media, Americans voluntarily contributed to the war effort in dozens of large and small ways. They planted victory gardens and collected paper, scrap metal, and fat. Instead of buying new, many people followed the motto "Use it up, wear it out, make it do, and do without."

✓ **Checkpoint** How did the federal government control resources needed for the war effort?

**Progress Monitoring *Online***
**For:** Self-test with vocabulary practice
**Web Code:** nea-1103

### Comprehension

1. **Terms and People** Write a sentence explaining how each of the following was connected with the American home front during World War II.
   - A. Philip Randolph
   - Executive Order 8802
   - bracero program
   - internment
   - 442nd Regimental Combat Team
   - rationing
   - Office of War Information

2. **NoteTaking Reading Skill: Identify Main Ideas** Use your table to answer the Section Focus Question: How did the war change America at home?

### Writing About History

3. **Quick Write: Describe a Scene** Review the text relating to Japanese American internment during World War II. Write a two-sentence factual description of what you might witness as a family is being sent to a camp. Use at least one descriptive adjective and one action verb.

### Critical Thinking

4. **Predict Consequences** Predict two possible consequences for wartime women factory workers when men began to return from overseas after the war.

5. **Compare** How were the causes of the Detroit race riots and the Los Angeles Zoot Suit Riots similar?

6. **Draw Conclusions** Do you think the federal government was justified in limiting individual freedom by imposing wage and price controls and by rationing during wartime? Why or why not?

# Can Government Limit a Group's Liberties During Wartime?

**MI** 7.2.3b

Because some leaders feared that some Japanese Americans might be disloyal, the government took action against the whole group. How should national security be balanced against civil rights?

## *Korematsu* v. *United States* (1944)

| The Facts | The Issue | The Decision |
|---|---|---|
| • In 1942, President Roosevelt ordered that select people could be banned from war zones.<br><br>• The army relocated Japanese Americans on the West Coast to internment camps.<br><br>• Fred Korematsu was arrested for resisting the army's order. | Korematsu argued that he was denied equal protection under the law simply because he was a Japanese American. | The Court held that the military order was justified for security reasons. Three judges dissented. Justice Frank Murphy wrote that internment "falls into the ugly abyss of racism." |

▲ A Japanese American is arrested in 1943.

## Why It Matters

Most experts today agree with Murphy that the *Korematsu* case was a triumph of prejudice over justice. In recent years, the war on terrorism has revived talk of *Korematsu* in discussions of "racial profiling." Racial profiling is a law enforcement technique in which police or federal investigators single out members of a particular racial or ethnic group for questioning. Defenders of profiling argue that, because several deadly terrorist attacks were carried out by radical Muslims, it is only logical for law enforcement officials to pay special attention to Muslims. Critics insist that racial profiling is a form of prejudice that violates the civil rights of individuals.

## Connect to Your World

Discussing racial profiling in 2004, Fred Korematsu warned, "No one should ever be locked away simply because they share the same race, ethnicity, or religion as a spy or terrorist. If that principle was not learned from the internment of Japanese Americans, then these are very dangerous times for our democracy." Write an editorial agreeing or disagreeing with Fred Korematsu's position.

**For:** Supreme Court cases
**Web Code:** neh-1115

◄ Americans today protest against racial profiling by law enforcement officials.

# EXPERIENCE THE WORLD WAR II HOME FRONT

While fathers, sons, husbands, and brothers were serving overseas, their families served on the home front. Every American was expected to help boost morale and make sacrifices to shoulder the cost of the war.

Since World War II, the United States has not experienced a war that required so much of Americans on the home front. However, soldiers today continue to face combat, homesickness, and occasional boredom. That is why the USO and ordinary citizens still work to provide support for America's troops. ◀)) AUDIO

▲ **Collecting Scrap**
Here, children collect junk metal that might be turned into bullets or old clothes that could be recycled into blankets and uniforms.

▼ **Victory Gardens**
With so much farm produce going to feed the troops, people planted "victory gardens" in vacant lots (below) or in their backyards.

## HOW TO SHOP WITH WAR RATION BOOK TWO
### ... to Buy Canned, Bottled and Frozen Fruits and Vegetables; Dried Fruits, Juices and all Canned Soups

YOUR POINT ALLOWANCE MUST LAST FOR THE FULL RATION PERIOD
*Plan How Many Points You Will Use Each Time Before You Shop*

BUY EARLY IN THE WEEK    Foods are going to our fighting men. They come first! Your ration gives you your fair share of the foods that are left.    BUY EARLY IN THE DAY

▲ **Rationing**
Households were issued ration books and stamps, which told them how much of certain items, such as sugar or butter, they were allowed to buy. The above poster explains how the rationing system worked.

**▼ USO**

Through the United Service Organizations (USO), volunteers boosted the morale of those who were fighting the war. At the USO's Hollywood Canteen in Los Angeles, a soldier could get a hot meal served by a celebrity or dance with their favorite movie star. Here, servicemen pose with glamorous actress Hedy Lamarr.

**War Bonds Poster ▶**

They're fighting harder than ever

are you buying
MORE WAR BONDS THAN EVER?

**Thinking Critically**

1. **Analyze Visuals** Choose one of the posters shown on this spread and describe what message it gave to people.

2. **Draw Conclusions** Do you think the effort on the home front helped to win the war? Explain.

**Connect to Today** How do Americans today give support and encouragement to people serving in the military?

**History Interactive** ★

**For:** More about the home front in World War II
**Web Code:** nep-1115

Lieutenant
Audie
Murphy ▶

## WITNESS HISTORY 🔊 AUDIO

### Audie Murphy, American Hero

Audie Murphy received more medals than any other American in World War II. In January 1945, his squad was set upon by German troops near Holtzwihr, France. Ordering his men to withdraw, Murphy climbed atop a burning tank that was in danger of exploding. For an hour, the young lieutenant used the tank's machine gun to hold off the enemy on three sides:

❝Germans reached as close as 10 yards, only to be mowed down by his fire. He received a leg wound, but ignored it and continued the single-handed fight until his ammunition was exhausted. He then made his way to his company, refused medical attention, and organized the company in a counterattack.❞

—Medal of Honor Citation for Audie Murphy

# Victory in Europe and the Pacific

 **Content Expectations**

- **7.2.2** Evaluate U.S. role in fighting war militarily, diplomatically, technologically across the world.
- **7.2.3a** Analyze mobilization of U.S. economic, military, social resources during WWII.
- **7.2.3b** Analyze role of women/minorities in war effort.
- **7.2.4** Investigate development/enactment of Hitler's "final solution" policy and response from U.S.

## Terms and People

D-Day
Battle of the Bulge
Harry S. Truman
island hopping

kamikaze
Albert Einstein
Manhattan Project
J. Robert Oppenheimer

## NoteTaking

### Reading Skill: Recognize Sequence

Identify the steps that led to the Allied victory.

| Europe | The Pacific |
|---|---|
| • Allies land at Normandy on D-Day | • |
| | • |

**Allies Win World War II**

**Why It Matters** In 1942 and 1943, the Allies turned back the Axis advances. In the last two years of the war, 1944 and 1945, they delivered the final, crushing blow. They attacked Germany from the west and east, and the United States advanced across the Pacific to the doorstep of Japan. In the process, Americans created a new form of weapon that would change both warfare and global politics. **Section Focus Question: How did the Allies defeat the Axis Powers?**

## Planning Germany's Defeat

Throughout 1943, Roosevelt, Churchill, and Stalin squabbled over when they would start a second front in France. Up to that point, Soviet troops had done most of the fighting in Europe. Stalin insisted that Britain and the United States carry more of the military burden by attacking Germany in the west, thereby forcing Germany to divide its troops.

Roosevelt sympathized with Stalin's position, but Churchill hesitated and delayed. Recalling the slaughter of British troops on the Western Front in World War I, he was not anxious to see history repeat itself. He argued that the German U-boat presence was too great in the English Channel and that the Allies needed more landing craft, more equipment, and better-trained soldiers.

In November 1943, Roosevelt and Churchill traveled to Teheran, Iran, for their first face-to-face meeting with Stalin. Churchill continued to voice reservations about a cross-channel invasion, but

FDR sided with Stalin. Reluctantly, Churchill agreed. After years of war, British and American soldiers would invade France and begin their march toward Germany. At the end of the Teheran Conference, the Big Three issued a joint statement that gave no hint of their earlier disagreements:

**Primary Source** "We have reached complete agreement as to the scope and timing of the operations to be undertaken from the east, west and south. The common understanding which we have here reached guarantees that victory will be ours. . . . No power on earth can prevent our destroying the German armies by land, their U Boats by sea, and their war planes from the air."
—Declaration of the Three Powers, December 1, 1943

Six months after the Teheran Conference, the plan to open a second front in France became reality. The massive Allied invasion of France was given the code name Operation Overlord.

✓ **Checkpoint** On what issues did Stalin, Roosevelt, and Churchill disagree?

# D-Day Invasion of Normandy

Overlord involved the most experienced Allied officers in Europe. American General Dwight D. Eisenhower again served as Supreme Commander. British General Bernard Montgomery served as commander of the ground forces, while General Omar Bradley led the United States First Army.

**Eisenhower Plans the Invasion** Overlord involved landing 21 American divisions and 26 British, Canadian, and Polish divisions on a 50-mile stretch of beaches in Normandy. The fleet was the largest ever assembled, comprising more than 4,400 ships and landing crafts.

The plan dictated striking five beaches in Normandy (code-named Utah, Omaha, Gold, Juno, and Sword), but it also involved an elaborate deception. The Allies created a fictional army under General Patton. Although the army existed only on paper, the Allies set up fake headquarters in southeast England across the English Channel from Calais, equipped with wood and cardboard tanks, useless ships, and detectable radio traffic. The Allies hoped to convince the Germans that the Allied attack would come at Calais, not farther west in Normandy. In the end, the deception worked. Hitler ordered his top tank division to Calais.

**Heroes Storm the Beaches** On June 6, 1944—known as **D-Day**—the Allies hit Germany in force. More than 11,000 planes prepared the way, attempting to destroy German communication and transportation networks and soften Nazi beach defenses. At 6:30 A.M., after a rough crossing of the English Channel, the first troops landed.

On four of the beaches, the landings were only lightly opposed and casualties relatively low. But at Omaha, one of the two beaches assigned to American forces, the Germans offered stiff opposition. On the cliffs overlooking the beach, the Germans had dug trenches and built small concrete pillbox structures from which heavy artillery could be fired. They had the beach covered with

## HISTORY MAKERS

### Dwight D. Eisenhower (1890–1969)
As a young man, Dwight Eisenhower had not been considered a brilliant student at the U.S. Military Academy at West Point. During the 1930s, though, his career rose due to his organizational skill and ability to work with others. In 1942, Ike was given command of all American forces in Europe—even though more than 350 other generals had more seniority. After strong performances in North Africa and Italy, he was made Supreme Commander of Allied Forces. His skillful handling of the D-Day invasion and the drive to Germany won wide respect. Eisenhower went on to serve two terms as President before retiring.

a wide variety of deadly guns. They had also heavily mined the beaches. When the first American soldiers landed, they stepped out of their landing crafts into a rainstorm of bullets, shells, and death. Some crafts dumped their occupants too far from the beach; soldiers, weighted down by heavy packs, drowned.

One writer called D-Day "the longest day." For many Americans, it was a very short day—and their last on Earth. Some fought bravely and died. Others fought bravely and survived. By the end of the day, the Allies had gained a toehold in France. Within a month, more than one million Allied troops had landed at Normandy. Berlin, the capital of Germany, was still a long road ahead, but the Allies had taken the first, and most important, step on that road.

✓ **Checkpoint** What was the primary objective of the D-Day invasion at Normandy?

---

**Events That Changed America**

# THE ALLIES LAND ON D-DAY

**"You are about to embark upon the Great Crusade,** toward which we have striven these many months." General Eisenhower gave this message to Allied troops on the morning of June 6, 1944. "You will bring about the destruction of the German war machine, the elimination of Nazi tyranny over oppressed peoples of Europe, and security for ourselves in a free world." That day, Allied troops stormed the beaches of Normandy, paving the way for the liberation of France and the final defeat of the Nazis. But victory came at a tremendous cost. Wave after wave of soldiers were mowed down by German fire. One American later recalled, "As our boat touched sand and the ramp went down, I became a visitor to hell."

▲ The invasion of Normandy was truly a massive international effort. U.S., Canadian, and British forces were assigned to different beaches. Members of the French Underground were waiting to offer aid and support.

"*The carnage on the beach was indescribable.... Although many wounded men were crying for help, aid-men were scarce and others could not help because they had an assigned task to accomplish.*"
—Thomas E. Herring, C Company

# Liberation of Europe

After D-Day, Germany faced a hopeless two-front war. Soviet soldiers were advancing steadily from the east, forcing German armies out of Latvia, Romania, Slovakia, and Hungary. Mile by mile, Germany lost the lands it had once dominated and the natural resources it had once plundered.

**Allies Advance** Allied armies were also on the move in the west. In August 1944, the Allies liberated Paris. Hitler had ordered his generals to destroy the French capital, but they disobeyed him, leaving the "City of Lights" as beautiful as ever. As Parisians celebrated, Allied troops kept advancing.

As a mood of hopelessness fell over Germany, Rommel and other leading generals plotted to overthrow Hitler. On July 20, 1944, an officer planted a bomb at Hitler's headquarters. The explosion killed or wounded 20 people, but Hitler

*I remember the bullets flying over our craft and seeing the ricochets of the bullets hitting the water. The landing craft's door fell open and we ran into the surf. We were in very deep water and I thought I was either going to drown or be shot before getting to land. By the grace of God, I made it ashore and started running through the deep water toward the seawall.*
—Jack Fox, combat medic

Sixty years after D-Day, an American veteran revisits the cemetery in Normandy where so many of his comrades are buried.

## Why It Matters
Six decades later, Americans still take pride in the young heroes who secured Omaha Beach. Whether they died on the blood-soaked sands or survived against impossible odds, the D-Day invaders helped create an enduring standard of courage, sacrifice, and patriotism. Books like Tom Brokaw's *The Greatest Generation* and movies like Steven Spielberg's *Saving Private Ryan* honor their memory.

## Thinking Critically
Why do you think a veteran of D-Day would choose to return to a place where so many people died?

**History Interactive** ✷
**For:** Eyewitness accounts of D-Day
**Web Code:** nep-1105

**Geography** *Interactive*
**For:** Interactive map
**Web Code:** nep-1106

Axis Powers, 1942
Greatest extent of Axis control, 1942
Allied territory, 1942
Neutral nations, 1942
Allied advance
Major battle

NORWAY
SWEDEN
FINLAND
*Leningrad*
*Moscow*
*North Sea*
DENMARK
*Baltic Sea*
*1945*
*1944*
SOVIET UNION
*1943*
*Stalingrad*
IRELAND
UNITED KINGDOM
*Warsaw* 1944
*Kursk* 1943
1945
Berlin
1945
1945
*London*
NETH.
1945
GERMANY
1944
BELG.
1945
D-Day
NORMANDY
1944
Battle of the Bulge (see below)
SLOVAKIA
1945
*Paris*
FRANCE
HUNGARY
1944
*Atlantic Ocean*
1944
SWITZ.
ROMANIA
*Yalta*
*Vichy*
Vichy France
ITALY
1944
*Black Sea*
*Conic Projection*
0   200   400 mi
0   200   400 km
CROATIA  SERBIA
MONT.
BULGARIA
PORTUGAL
SPAIN
ALB.
*Rome*
Anzio
1944
*Salerno*
TURKEY
SYRIA
GREECE
*Mediterranean Sea*
1944
1943
*Palermo*
*Sicily*
Lebanon (Fr.)
*Tunis*
1943

Winston Churchill gave U.S. forces full credit for the Allied victory at the Battle of the Bulge:

**Primary Source** "The United States troops have done almost all the fighting and have suffered almost all the losses. They have suffered losses almost equal to those of both sides at the Battle of Gettysburg. . . . [The Battle of the Bulge] will, I believe, be regarded as an ever-famous American victory."

—Winston Churchill, Address to the House of Commons, January 18, 1945

### Battle of the Bulge

*Conic Projection*
0   10   20 mi
0   10   20 km
*Meuse R.*
BELGIUM
St. Vith
Prüm
Ciergnon
La Roche
Rochefort
*Ourthe R.*
Houffalize
GERMANY
St. Hubert
Bastogne
Clervaux
Wiltz
*Our R.*
Libramont
Vianden
Neufchâteau
Echternach
LUXEMBOURG
Tri
Luxembourg
*Moselle R.*
FRANCE

Axis control, Dec. 15, 1944
Allied control, Dec. 15, 1944
German offensive
Allied counterattack
Front line, Dec. 16, 1944
Front line, Dec. 25, 1944
Front line, Jan. 16, 1945

**Map Skills** In the final phases of the war in Europe, the Allies hemmed in Germany from the east, west, and south.
1. **Locate:** (a) Stalingrad, (b) Sicily, (c) Normandy, (d) Berlin
2. **Movement** Describe American and German troop movements at the Battle of the Bulge.
3. **Draw Conclusions** Why do you think there was no Allied attempt to approach Germany from the north?

### Battle of the Bulge ▲
The Battle of the Bulge was the last Nazi offensive of the war. After its failure, the German armies were in constant retreat.

survived. Rommel took poison to escape being put on trial. Claiming that fate was on his side, Hitler refused to surrender to the advancing troops.

**Germany Counterattacks** In December 1944, Hitler ordered a counterattack. With Allied troops strung out between the English Channel and the Alps, German forces massed near the Ardennes. Hitler's <u>scenario</u> called for English-speaking German soldiers in U.S. uniforms to cut telephone lines, change road signs, and spread confusion. German tanks would then secure communication and transportation hubs.

**Vocabulary Builder**
<u>scenario</u>—(suh NAIR ee oh) *n.* outline for a proposed series of events; script

The counterattack, known as the **Battle of the Bulge,** almost succeeded. The Germans caught the Allies by surprise, created a bulge in the American line, and captured several key towns. Snowy, cloudy skies prevented the Allies from exploiting their air superiority. But at the Belgian town of Bastogne (bas TOHN), American forces held despite frostbite and brutal German assaults. Then, on December 23, the skies cleared and Allied bombers attacked German positions. After reinforcements arrived, the Allies went back on the offensive, steadily pushing the Germans out of France.

The Battle of the Bulge was a desperate attempt to drive a wedge between American and British forces. Instead, it crippled Germany by using its reserves and demoralizing its troops. Ultimately, it shortened the time Hitler had left.

**Allies Push to Victory** By January, the Soviet Army had reached the Oder River outside Berlin. The Allies also advanced northward in Italy. In April 1945, Mussolini tried to flee to Switzerland but was captured and executed. By this time, American and British troops had crossed the Rhine River into Germany. In April, a U.S. army reached the Elbe River, 50 miles west of Berlin. Allied forces were now in position for an all-out assault against Hitler's capital.

Hitler was by now a physical wreck: shaken by tremors, paranoid from drugs, and kept alive by mad dreams of a final victory. He gave orders that no one followed and planned campaigns that no one would ever fight. Finally, on April 30, he and a few of his closest associates committed suicide. His "Thousand Year Reich" had lasted only a dozen years.

On May 7, in a little French schoolhouse that had served as Eisenhower's headquarters, Germany surrendered. Americans celebrated V-E (Victory in Europe) Day. Sadly, FDR did not see the momentous day. He had died a few weeks earlier. It would be up to the new President, **Harry S. Truman,** to see the nation through to final victory.

✓ **Checkpoint** What were the results of the Battle of the Bulge?

# Advancing in the Pacific

While war still raged in Europe, American forces in the Pacific had been advancing in giant leaps. They followed an **island-hopping** strategy, capturing some Japanese-held islands and ignoring others in a steady path toward Japan. From Tarawa and Makin in the Gilbert Islands, American forces jumped ahead to Eniwetok and Kwajalein in the Marshall Islands. Then, they took another leap to Saipan, Tinian, and Guam in the Mariana Islands.

**Japanese Troops Fight to the Death** American forces took each island only after a nearly unbelievable life-and-death struggle. Time and again, Japanese defenders fought

**Navajo Code Talkers**
Navajo troops played a vital role in the Pacific island-hopping campaign. Using a code based on their own language—which was a mystery to the Japanese—Navajo radio operators sent critical messages from island to island. *What other special ethnic units played a role in the American war effort?*

**Legend:**
- Areas under Japanese control, 1942
- Extent of Japanese control, June 1942
- Extent of Japanese control, June 1944
- Allied advance
- Atomic bomb target
- Major battle

SOVIET UNION

MONGOLIA

Manchuria (Manchukuo)

Vladivostok

Sea of Japan (East Sea)

Beijing

Korea

CHINA

Yellow Sea

Hiroshima (Aug. 1945)

Tokyo

JAPAN

Shanghai

Nagasaki (Aug. 1945)

East China Sea

Okinawa (April–June 1945)

Iwo Jima (Feb.–March 1945)

Kuril Islands

Aleutian Islands (U.S.)

Pacific Ocean

Midway (June 1942)

Hawaiian Islands (U.S.)

INDIA

Burma (U.K.)

French Indochina

Bangkok

THAILAND

South China Sea

Hong Kong (U.K.)

Philippines (U.S.)

Manila

Philippine Sea (June 1944)

Mariana Islands

Saipan (June–July 1944)

Guam (July–Aug. 1944)

Wake Island (U.S.)

Leyte Gulf (Oct. 1944)

Caroline Islands

Marshall Islands (U.S.)

Malaya (U.K.)

Singapore

Sumatra

Borneo

Celebes

Batavia

Java

Dutch East Indies

New Guinea

Rabaul

New Britain (Dec. 1944)

Solomon Islands (U.K./Aust.)

Guadalcanal (Aug. 1942–Feb. 1943)

Eastern Solomons (Aug. 1942)

Santa Cruz (Oct. 1942)

Tarawa (Nov. 1943)

Gilbert Islands (U.K.)

Darwin

Coral Sea

Coral Sea (May 1942)

AUSTRALIA

Indian Ocean

Miller Projection

0    500    1,000 mi

0    500    1,000 km

**Map Skills** The island-hopping strategy brought U.S. forces closer and closer to the Japanese home islands, but it took even more drastic measures to bring the war in the Pacific to an end.

1. **Locate:** (a) Guadalcanal, (b) Okinawa, (c) Iwo Jima, (d) Hiroshima, (e) Nagasaki

2. **Movement** Describe the two separate island-hopping paths that brought American marines to Okinawa.

3. **Predict Consequences** What might have happened in the Pacific if Japan had been able to take Midway and Hawaii early in the war?

virtually to the last man. Rather than surrender, many Japanese troops readily killed themselves. At the same time, Japanese **kamikaze** (kah muh KAH zee) pilots deliberately crashed their planes into American ships. By the end of the war, more than 3,000 Japanese pilots had died in kamikaze missions. Their deaths, however, did not prevent General Douglas MacArthur from retaking the Philippines or the United States Navy from sinking Japanese ships.

**American Forces Near Japan** One of the fiercest battles in the island-hopping campaign took place in February and March 1945. On Iwo Jima (EE woh JEE muh), a 5-mile-long island 650 miles southeast of Tokyo, United States Marines faced a dug-in, determined enemy. In 36 days of fighting, more than 23,000 marines became casualties. But they took the island. The famous photograph of six marines (including Native American Ira Hayes) planting the American flag on Iwo Jima symbolized the heroic sacrifice of American soldiers.

The fight for Okinawa (oh kuh NAH wuh) in April 1945 was even deadlier. Only 340 miles from Japan, Okinawa contained a vital air base, necessary for the planned invasion of Japan. Taking Okinawa was the most complex and costly operation in the Pacific campaign, involving half a million troops and 1,213 warships. U.S. forces finally took Okinawa but at a cost of roughly 50,000 casualties.

From Okinawa and other Pacific bases, American pilots could bomb the Japanese home islands. Short on pilots and aircraft, low on fuel and ammunition, Japan was virtually defenseless. American bombers hit factories, military bases, and cities. In a single night in March 1945, B-29 bombers destroyed 16 square miles of Tokyo. The raid killed over 83,000 Japanese—more than either of the later atomic bombs—and injured 100,000 more.

✔ **Checkpoint** Why was the island-hopping campaign in the Pacific so deadly to both sides?

# The Atomic Bomb Ends the War

Advances in technology, as well as the troops, helped determine the outcome of World War II. (See the Quick Study chart.) Allied and Axis scientists labored to make planes faster, bombs deadlier, and weapons more accurate. The most crucial scientific development of all was the atomic bomb.

▼ A soldier reading a radar screen

**The Manhattan Project Develops the A-Bomb** The atomic bomb began with an idea. In the early 1930s, scientists learned how to split the nuclei of certain elements. They also discovered that this process of nuclear fission released tremendous energy. Over the next decade, they learned more about the nature of the atom, the effect of a chain reaction, and the military uses of uranium.

| Science and Technology of World War II | | ☑ **Quick Study** |
|---|---|---|
| **Advance** | **Military Use in WWII** | **Civilian Applications** |
| Radar | Detected objects such as bombs, incoming gunfire, or enemy ships | Used to track weather systems and monitor automobile speed |
| Calculating machines | Allowed cryptographers to break enemy codes by detecting letter patterns and frequencies | Developed into small personal computers |
| Jet engines | Enabled planes to fly much faster than non-jet-powered planes | Used in commercial airplanes |
| Penicillin | Cured soldiers' infected wounds, saving many lives | Used to treat bacterial infections |

Early in the war, **Albert Einstein,** the world's most famous scientist, signed a letter that alerted President Roosevelt about the need to proceed with atomic development. In 1942, FDR gave the highest national <u>priority</u> to the development of an atomic bomb. The program, code-named the **Manhattan Project,** cost several billion dollars and employed tens of thousands of people.

The two primary leaders of the project were General Leslie Groves and physicist **J. Robert Oppenheimer.** Groves was responsible for building facilities, acquiring the necessary materials, recruiting scientists, and providing security. Oppenheimer ran the scientific aspect of the project from the construction site in Los Alamos, New Mexico. Scientists working on the project included many refugees from Europe, including Enrico Fermi, developer of the first atomic reactor. Security on the Manhattan Project was tight. People worked on small parts of the puzzle, little realizing the whole picture.

On the morning of July 16, 1945, in a barren area outside of Alamogordo, New Mexico, the first atomic bomb was tested. The flash of light was clearly visible 180 miles away, and the sound was heard at a distance of 100 miles. Watching the blast, Oppenheimer recalled the following line from a Hindu poem: "Now I am become Death, the destroyer of Worlds."

The general's thoughts were less poetic. Turning to an aide, Groves said, "The war's over. One or two of those things and Japan will be finished."

**Truman Makes His Decision** The decision to use the bomb fell directly on the narrow shoulders of Harry Truman. The new President fully understood the ethical issues presented by using the bomb, especially against civilians. At the same time, he also knew that the Axis Powers had nuclear scientists, and there was no way to tell how close they were to developing their own bomb. Ultimately, Truman's chief priority was to save American lives. His military advisers predicted that, in light of the ferocious defense waged by Japanese soldiers during

**Vocabulary Builder**
<u>priority</u>–(prī AHR uh tee) *n.* degree of importance or urgency

## Decision ◯ Point

# Should the United States Drop the Atomic Bomb?
President Truman had to decide whether to drop the bomb on Japan. Read the options below. Then, you decide.

**Truman Favors Using the Bomb**

Primary Source

"I asked Gen. Marshall what it would cost in lives to land . . . in Japan. It was his opinion that 1/4 million casualties would be the minimum cost. . . . I asked Sec. Stimson which cities in Japan were devoted exclusively to war production. He . . . named Hiroshima and Nagasaki. We sent an ultimatum to Japan. It was ignored. I ordered atomic bombs dropped on the two cities. . . . Dropping the bombs ended the war, saved lives and gave the free nations a chance to face the facts."

—President Harry S. Truman

**Scientists Advise Caution**

Primary Source

"We the undersigned scientists . . . believe that the United States ought not resort to the use of atomic bombs in the present phase of the war, at least not unless . . . Japan is given an opportunity to surrender. . . . A nation which sets the precedent of using these newly liberated forces of nature for purposes of destruction may have to bear the responsibility of opening the door to an era of devastation on an unimaginable scale."

—Scientist Leo Szilard

**You Decide**
1. Why did Truman decide to drop the bomb?
2. What course of action did Szilard favor?
3. What decision would you have made? Why?

the island-hopping campaign, an invasion of Japan might cost as many as 1,000,000 American casualties.

In truth, Truman did not agonize over the decision to use the atomic bomb against Japan. For the President, abstract ethical issues did not outweigh very real American lives and an opportunity to end the war. Later, some critics would condemn Truman's decision. But in the late summer of 1945, no one close to him did so.

**Hiroshima and Nagasaki Are Destroyed** On August 6, 1945, U.S. pilots dropped an atomic bomb on Hiroshima. It exploded at 8:15 A.M. One survivor of the blast later recalled the first moments:

> **Primary Source** ❝After I noticed the flash, white clouds spread over the blue sky. It was amazing. It was as if blue morning-glories had suddenly bloomed up in the sky. . . . Then came the heat wave. It was very, very hot. Even though there was a window glass in front of me, I felt really hot. It was as if I was looking directly into a kitchen oven.❞
>
> —Isao Kita, *Hiroshima Witness*

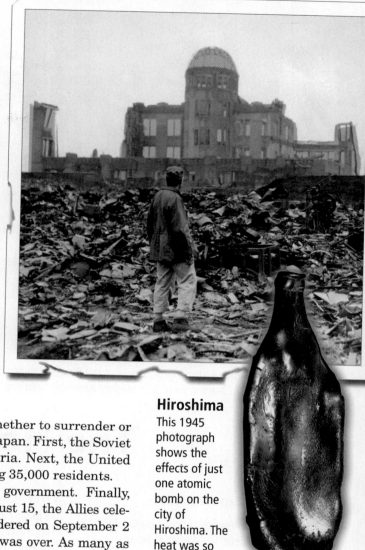

**Hiroshima**
This 1945 photograph shows the effects of just one atomic bomb on the city of Hiroshima. The heat was so intense that it melted this bottle (right).

Within two minutes, more than 60,000 of Hiroshima's 344,000 residents were dead or missing.

Over the next three days, Japanese leaders debated whether to surrender or continue to fight. Then, on August 9, two events rocked Japan. First, the Soviet Union declared war against Japan and invaded Manchuria. Next, the United States dropped a second atomic bomb on Nagasaki, killing 35,000 residents.

Debate continued at the highest levels of Japanese government. Finally, Emperor Hirohito made the decision to surrender. On August 15, the Allies celebrated V-J (Victory in Japan) Day. Japan officially surrendered on September 2 aboard the USS *Missouri*. The most costly war in history was over. As many as 60,000,000 people, mostly civilians, had died in the conflict.

✔ **Checkpoint** What were the consequences of the decision to bomb Hiroshima and Nagasaki?

---

SECTION **3** **Assessment**

**Progress Monitoring *Online***
**For:** Self-test with vocabulary practice
**Web Code:** nea-1108

**Comprehension**

1. **Terms and People** Write a sentence explaining how each of the following was connected with the Allies' final push toward victory in World War II.
   • D-Day
   • Battle of the Bulge
   • Harry S. Truman
   • island hopping
   • kamikaze
   • Manhattan Project
   • J. Robert Oppenheimer

2. NoteTaking **Reading Skill: Recognize Sequence** Use your table to answer the Section Focus Question: How did the Allies defeat the Axis Powers?

**Writing About History**

3. **Quick Write: Identify Impressions** Review the text description of the D-Day landings, including the Events That Changed America feature. Then, make a list of sights, sounds, and smells associated with the event.

**Critical Thinking**

4. **Summarize** Summarize the arguments for and against an Allied invasion of France before 1944.

5. **Compare and Contrast** How were the final phases of the war in Europe similar to the final phases of the war in the Pacific? How were they different?

6. **Predict Consequences** What effect do you think possession of the atomic bomb will have on the role of the United States in the postwar world?

▲ These starving prisoners at the Ebensee death camp in Austria were liberated by American soldiers.

WITNESS HISTORY  AUDIO

## "I Have No Words"

On April 15, 1945, American radio listeners sat stunned as newsman Edward R. Murrow told of a horror beyond belief. Murrow was reporting about his visit to the Nazi concentration camp at Buchenwald. He described the emaciated, hollow-eyed prisoners, the stink which was "beyond all description," the children with identification numbers tattooed on their arms, and the hundreds of "bodies stacked up like cordwood." Toward the end of his report, Murrow said:

❝I pray you to believe what I have said about Buchenwald. I have reported what I saw and heard, but only part of it. For most of it I have no words. Dead men are plentiful in war, but the living dead, more than twenty thousand of them in one camp. . . . If I've offended you by this rather mild account of Buchenwald, I'm not in the least sorry.❞

—Edward R. Murrow, CBS Radio Broadcast, April 15, 1945

# The Holocaust

## Content Expectations

- **7.2.1b** Analyze differences in civic/political values of U.S., Nazi Germany, Imperial Japan.
- **7.2.2** Evaluate U.S. role in fighting war militarily, diplomatically, technologically across the world.
- **7.2.4** Investigate development/enactment of Hitler's "final solution" policy and response from U.S.

## Terms and People

| | |
|---|---|
| Holocaust | genocide |
| anti-Semitism | concentration camp |
| Nuremberg Laws | death camp |
| Kristallnacht | War Refugee Board |

## NoteTaking

**Reading Skill: Recognize Sequence** As you read, identify the steps that led to Hitler's attempt to exterminate European Jews.

| 1933: Hitler becomes dictator of Germany; begins persecution of Jews |
|---|

**Why It Matters** From the time he came to power, Adolf Hitler had targeted Jews for persecution. By the end of the war, the Nazis had murdered 6 million Jews and 5 million other people they considered inferior. Today, we continue to remember this tragedy and seek ways to prevent anything like it from ever happening again. **Section Focus Question: How did the Holocaust develop and what were its results?**

## Roots of the Holocaust

What Edward R. Murrow saw at Buchenwald was just a fragment of the most horrific chapter of the Nazi era. In 1945, there was no word for it. Today, it is called the **Holocaust,** the Nazi attempt to kill all Jews under their control. The mass murders of Jews, as well as other "undesirables," were a direct result of a racist Nazi ideology that considered Aryans (white gentiles, especially those of Germanic, Nordic, and Anglo-Saxon blood) superior to other people.

**Hitler Preaches Hate** From the start, the Nazi movement trafficked in hatred and **anti-Semitism.** Hitler blamed Jews for all the ills of Germany, from communism to inflation to abstract painting—and, especially, for the defeat of Germany in World War I.

Other extremists influenced Hitler's ideas and shared his prejudices. In the 1920s, his was just another angry voice in the Weimar Republic, advancing simplistic answers for the nation's grave economic, political, and social troubles. In 1933, however, Hitler became chancellor of Germany.

## Nazis Begin the Persecution

Hitler's persecution of the Jews began as soon as he came to power. At first, his focus was economic. He urged Germans to boycott Jewish-owned businesses, and he barred Jews from jobs in civil service, banking, the stock exchange, law, journalism, and medicine. In 1935, Hitler moved to a broader legal persecution. The **Nuremberg Laws,** named for the city that served as the spiritual center of Nazism, denied German citizenship to Jews, banned marriage between Jews and non-Jews, and segregated Jews at every level of society. Yet even these measures were not enough for Hitler. He hinted that, in the future, there might be what he called the "Final Solution to the Jewish question."

Hitler employed the full power of the state in his anti-Semitic campaigns. Newspapers printed scandalous attacks against Jews. Children in schools and the Hitler Youth movement were taught that Jews were "polluting" German society and culture. Comic books contained vile caricatures of Jews.

## Violence Erupts on Kristallnacht

Acts of violence against Jews were common. The most serious attack occurred on November 9, 1938, and is known as **Kristallnacht** (KRIHS tahl nahkt), or the "Night of the Broken Glass." After a Jewish refugee killed a German diplomat in Paris, Nazi officials ordered attacks on Jews in Germany, Austria and the Sudetenland. Secret police and military units destroyed more than 1,500 synagogues and 7,500 Jewish-owned businesses, killed more than 200 Jews, and injured more than 600 others. The Nazis arrested thousands of Jews.

## Jewish Refugees Face Obstacles

Between 1933 and 1937, about 129,000 Jews fled Germany and Nazi-controlled Austria. They included some of the most notable figures in the scientific and artistic world, including physicist Albert Einstein.

More Jews would have left, but they were not generally welcomed into other countries. During the Great Depression, with jobs scarce, the United States and other countries barred their doors to many Jews. In 1939, the ocean liner *St. Louis* departed Germany for Cuba with more than 900 Jewish refugees on board. Only 22 of the passengers received permission to stay in Cuba. U.S. officials refused to accept any of the refugees. The ship returned to Germany. Almost 600 of the Jews aboard the *St. Louis* later died in Nazi concentration camps.

✔ **Checkpoint** How did Hitler enforce anti-Semitism as chancellor of Germany?

### German Jews Face Persecution

In Nazi Germany, Jews were forced to wear yellow stars (below right) with the word *Jude* ("Jew"). By the time of Kristallnacht (below left), Hitler's policy of anti-Semitism had progressed from discrimination to organized violence—but there was even worse to come.

# CONCENTRATION CAMP

Auschwitz . . . Buchenwald . . . Dachau . . . The names of these and other concentration camps are a roll call of horror. Above, the motto over the gate at Auschwitz reads "Work makes you free." It gave no hint of what prisoners faced inside. Whether they died of disease or starvation, survived, or were murdered, all were dehumanized by a regime that treated them as less than human.

Prisoners are shipped to a camp in railroad cattle cars.

The youngest "enemies of the state"

Inside the barracks, jammed onto bunks

Wedding rings stolen from Holocaust victims

The crematorium, where human bodies were burned

Prisoners wore triangular, color-coded patches like these (left) from Dachau.
**Yellow:** Jew
**Purple:** Jehovah's Witness
**Pink:** homosexual
**Red:** political prisoner
**Blue:** immigrant
**Green:** criminal
**Black:** "antisocial"

## Thinking Critically

1. **Identify Central Issues** How did Nazi Germany use concentration camps to carry out genocide?

2. **Predict Consequences** After the war, what do you think will happen to the Nazi officials who ran the camps?

# Nazis Adopt the "Final Solution"

Since 1933, the Nazis had denied Jews the rights of citizenship and committed acts of brutality against them. These acts of persecution were steps toward Hitler's "Final Solution to the Jewish question": nothing short of the systematic extermination of all Jews living in the regions controlled by the Third Reich. Today, we call such willful annihilation of a racial, political, or cultural group **genocide.**

### Nazis Build Concentration Camps

In 1933, the year he became chancellor, Hitler opened the first Nazi **concentration camps,** where members of specially designated groups were confined. The earliest camps included Dachau, Sachsenhausen, and Buchenwald. Later, Ravensbruck, not far from Berlin, was opened for female prisoners.

In theory, the camps were designed not to kill prisoners, but to turn them into "useful members" of the Third Reich. The Nazis imprisoned political opponents such as labor leaders, socialists, and communists, as well as anyone—journalists or novelists, ministers or priests—who spoke out against Hitler. Many Jews as well as Aryans who had intimate relations with Jews were sent to camps. Other groups targeted as "undesirable" included Gypsies, Jehovah's Witnesses, homosexuals, beggars, drunkards, conscientious objectors, the physically disabled, and people with mental illness.

Camp administrators tattooed numbers on the arms of prisoners and dressed them in vertically striped uniforms with triangular insignias. For example, political prisoners wore red insignias, homosexuals pink, Jews yellow, and Jehovah's Witnesses purple. Inside the walls of the concentration camps, there were no real <u>restraints</u> on sadistic guards. They tortured and even killed prisoners with no fear of reprisals from their superiors.

Death by starvation and disease was an everyday occurrence. In addition, doctors at camps such as Dachau conducted horrible medical experiments that either killed inmates or left them deformed. Prisoners were made subjects of bogus experiments on oxygen deprivation, hypothermia, and the effects of altitude. Bodies were mutilated without anesthesia. Thousands of prisoners died in agonizing pain, including some 5,000 mentally or physically disabled children.

### Millions Are Murdered in Death Camps

When Germany invaded Poland and the Soviet Union, the Nazis gained control of large territories that were home to millions of Jews. Under Nazi rule, Jews in Warsaw, Lodz, and other Polish cities were forced to live in crowded, walled ghettos. Nazis also constructed additional concentration camps in Poland and Eastern Europe.

At first, the murder of Jews and other prisoners tended to be more <u>arbitrary</u> than systematic. But at the Wannsee Conference in January 1942, Nazi leaders made the decision to move toward Hitler's "Final Solution." Reinhard Heydrich, an SS leader known as "the man with an iron heart," outlined a plan to exterminate about 11,000,000 Jews. Although the minutes of the meeting do not use the word "kill," everyone there understood that killing was their goal.

Many concentration camps, especially in Poland, were designated as **death camps,** where prisoners were systematically exterminated. The largest death camp was Auschwitz in southern Poland. Others included Treblinka, Maidenek, Sobibor, Belsec, and Chelmno. Prisoners from various parts of the Reich were transported by trains to the death camps and murdered. Nazis forced

## Nazi Concentration Camps

The Nazi system of concentration and slave labor camps extended over several countries. The six death camps in Poland were designed specifically for the extermination of Jewish prisoners.

**Concentration Camps in Europe**

**Vocabulary Builder**

<u>restraint</u>–(rih STRAYNT) *n.* control; something that holds someone back from action

**Vocabulary Builder**

<u>arbitrary</u>–(AR buh trer ee) *adj.* not following any fixed rule or plan; random

prisoners into death chambers and pumped in carbon monoxide or crammed the prisoners into showerlike facilities and released the insecticide Zyklon B.

Some concentration camps that the Nazis converted into death camps did not have gassing equipment. In these camps, Nazi guards shot hundreds of thousands of prisoners. Nazi "Action Groups" that followed the army into Eastern Europe also shot several million Jews and buried them in ditches.

In fully functioning death camps, the bodies of murdered prisoners were further desecrated. Human fat was turned into soap; human hair was woven into wigs, slippers, and mattresses; cash, gold fillings, wedding rings, and other valuables were stripped off the victims. After the Nazis had taken what they wanted, they burned the bodies in crematoriums.

By 1945, about 6 million European Jews had been murdered. But Jews were not the only victims. As many as 5 million others lay dead, including nearly 2 million non-Jewish Poles. While many survivors lived with constant nightmares of the experience, or with the sorrow and guilt of being the last members of their families, many others determined to rebuild their lives and families in the United States, Israel, or elsewhere and continue to be productive citizens.

 **Checkpoint** What actions did the Nazis take to carry out Hitler's "Final Solution"?

## The Allies and the Holocaust

The inevitable question about the Holocaust is: Could it have been prevented? Could the nations in the democratic West—especially Britain, France, and the United States—have intervened at some point and stopped the slaughter of millions of innocent people? There are no simple answers to these questions. However, many people today believe that the West could have done more than it did.

**Early Response Was Weak** Before the war, the United States (as well as other countries) could have done more if it had relaxed its immigration policy. It could have accepted more Jewish refugees and saved the lives of many German and Austrian Jews. However, the State Department at first made a conscious effort to block Jewish immigration. Later commentators have blamed this failure to help European Jews on a variety of factors: anti-Semitism, apathy, preoccupation with the problems of the Great Depression, and a tendency to underestimate Hitler's genocidal plans.

**American Government Takes Action** Once the war started, news of the mass killings had filtered to the West. By the end of 1942, the allies issued a statement acknowledging that Jews were being taken to Poland and killed there. In April 1943, British and American officials hosted the Bermuda Conference to discuss the possibility of rescuing the surviving Jewish refugees from Europe. However, no concrete action was taken.

By early 1944, however, FDR began to respond to the reports. He established the **War Refugee Board,** which worked with the Red Cross to save thousands of Eastern European Jews, especially in Romania and Hungary.

Tragically, too few were saved. Of the Allies, the Soviet Union was closest to the death camps, but Stalin showed no concern. Britain and the United States expressed sympathy, but their resources and strategy were focused on defeating Hitler not on stopping his genocidal campaign. They might have bombed railway lines to the death camps, but the camps were not military targets. A War Department official told the Refugee Board that bombing the railway lines "could be executed only by the diversion of considerable air support essential to

**NoteTaking**

**Reading Skill: Summarize** As you read, identify different ways in which the United States and other nations responded to the treatment of Jews in Nazi Germany before, during, and after the war.

Response to the Holocaust

United States recognizes Israel.

the success of our forces now engaged in decisive operations elsewhere." The Allies also refused to pressure countries within the Nazi sphere of influence to stop the transportation of Jews to Germany.

**Allied Soldiers Liberate the Camps** For most Americans, the enormity of the Nazi crime became real only when soldiers began to liberate the concentration camps that dotted the map of Germany. When they saw it all—the piles of dead bodies, the warehouses full of human hair and jewelry, the ashes in crematoriums, the half-dead emaciated survivors—they realized as never before that evil was more than an abstraction.

Hardened by war, accustomed to the sight and smell of death, the soldiers who liberated the camps were nevertheless unprepared for what they saw. Major Richard Winters—who had parachuted behind enemy lines on D-Day, defended Bastogne at the Battle of the Bulge, and risked his life in a number of other engagements—was stunned almost beyond belief:

> **Primary Source** "The memory of starved, dazed men, who dropped their eyes and heads when we looked at them through the chain-link fence, in the same manner that a beaten, mistreated dog would cringe, leaves feelings that cannot be described and will never be forgotten. The impact of seeing those people behind that fence left me saying, only to myself, 'Now I know why I'm here.'"
> —Richard Winters, quoted in *Band of Brothers* (Ambrose)

The liberation of the camps led to an outpouring of American sympathy and sincere longing to aid the victims. Many survivors found temporary or permanent homes in the United States.

The revelation of the Holocaust also increased demand and support for an independent Jewish homeland. In 1948, when the Jewish community in Palestine proclaimed the State of Israel, President Truman immediately recognized the new nation. The United States became perhaps the staunchest ally of the new Jewish State.

**A Survivor Bears Witness**
This 90-year-old Holocaust survivor continues to speak to young Germans about his time in the Auschwitz death camp. He still bears a physical reminder of his suffering: the identification number tattooed on his arm.

✔ **Checkpoint** How did the U.S. government respond to the German campaign against European Jews?

---

**Progress Monitoring *Online***
For: Self-test with vocabulary practice
Web Code: nea-1109

### Comprehension

**1. Terms and People** For each term below, write a sentence explaining how it was connected with the Nazi campaign against the Jews and the U.S. reaction.
- Holocaust
- anti-Semitism
- Nuremberg Laws
- Kristallnacht
- genocide
- concentration camp
- death camp
- War Refugee Board

**2. NoteTaking Reading Skill: Recognize Sequence** Use your flowchart to answer the Section Focus Question: How did the Holocaust develop and what were its results?

### Writing About History

**3. Quick Write: Describe Emotions** Write three sentences describing the emotions of an American soldier liberating a concentration camp in Germany. Be sure to use adjectives and nouns that express specific inner feelings.

### Critical Thinking

**4. Identify Ideologies** How were Hitler's racial ideas and policies connected to his concept of extreme nationalism?

**5. Analyze Information** One historian has said that the Holocaust began on "the day that the Jews started to be treated differently." Explain what this statement means and what evidence supports it.

**6. Make Decisions** Do you think that the U.S. military should have decided to bomb railway lines leading to the death camps? Why or why not?

▲ Defendant Hermann Goring (right) at the Nuremberg Trials

WITNESS HISTORY  AUDIO

### Nazism on Trial

In October 1945, a historic trial unlike any other began. The 21 defendants were the cream of the Third Reich, leaders of Hitler's war machine and architects of the Holocaust. Robert Jackson, the American prosecutor, scoffed as men like Hermann Goring, Hitler's handpicked successor, claimed to be tools of Hitler, unaware of his true plans. In his closing speech, Jackson turned the spotlight not on the defendants alone, but on the future of humanity:

❝No half-century ever witnessed slaughter on such a scale, such cruelties and inhumanities. . . . If we cannot eliminate the causes and prevent the repetition of these barbaric events, it is not an irresponsible prophecy to say that this twentieth century may yet succeed in bringing the doom of civilization.❞

—Robert Jackson, closing speech, Nuremberg War Crimes Trials, 1946

# Effects of the War

## Content Expectations

- **7.2.2** Evaluate U.S. role in fighting war militarily, diplomatically, technologically across the world.
- **7.2.3b** Analyze role of women/minorities in war effort.
- **7.2.3c** Analyze role of home front in supporting war effort.

## Terms and People

Yalta Conference
superpower
GATT
United Nations

Universal Declaration of Human Rights
Geneva Convention
Nuremberg Trials

## NoteTaking

**Reading Skill: Understand Effects** As you read, look for various developments in the postwar world that resulted from World War II.

**Why It Matters** World War II changed the nation in profound ways. Many Americans came home determined to extend the ideals of democracy and freedom at home as well as abroad. In addition, the United States emerged from the war prepared to take on the complex and vital role in world affairs that it still holds today. **Section Focus Question: What were the major immediate and long-term effects of World War II?**

## Allies Set Postwar Goals

World War II differed from World War I in several ways. One major difference was that it was fought to the bitter end. In 1918, the Kaiser had surrendered before the Allies could invade Germany. By contrast, in World War II, Japan and Germany kept fighting long after their defeat was certain. In the last year of the war, they lost battle after battle, retreated from the lands they had conquered, and saw the slow destruction of their military forces. Allied bombing devastated their cities and industries. Yet Germany fought on until Hitler committed suicide, and Japan refused to surrender until after the bombing of Hiroshima and Nagasaki.

**Allies Make Plans at Yalta** The protracted fighting gave the Allies time to make plans for a postwar world. Roosevelt, Churchill, and Stalin met at Yalta on the Black Sea in February 1945 to discuss final strategy and crucial questions concerning postwar Germany, Eastern Europe, and Asia. At the **Yalta Conference,** the Big Three agreed that Poland, Bulgaria, and Romania would hold free elections. However, Stalin later reneged on this promise.

Roosevelt and Churchill were not in a good position to press Stalin too hard. The Red Army already occupied much of Eastern Europe, and Roosevelt wanted Soviet help in the war against Japan. Vague promises were about as much as Stalin would give.

**Truman Faces Stalin at Potsdam** A dramatically altered Big Three met in July 1945 in the Berlin suburb of Potsdam. Although Stalin remained in power in the Soviet Union, Harry S. Truman had become U.S. President upon the death of FDR. After the start of the conference, Clement Atlee replaced Churchill as prime minister of Britain.

While in Potsdam, Truman learned of the successful test of the atomic bomb. But he was more focused on Europe and the Soviet Union than on Asia. At the meeting, the Big Three formalized the decision to divide Germany into four zones of occupation: Soviet, American, British, and French. They agreed to new borders and free elections for Poland, and they recognized the Soviets' right to claim reparations for war damages from the German sector they controlled. Stalin also reaffirmed his Yalta pledge to enter the war against Japan.

✔ **Checkpoint** What goals did the Allies set for Eastern Europe at the Yalta Conference?

# A New World Takes Shape

After the war ended in August 1945, plans for the postwar world had to be turned into realities. However, the changes that took place were not often what the Allies had envisioned at Yalta and Potsdam.

**The World Map Changes** World War II altered the political realities of the world. The borders of Poland, for example, shifted slightly to the west. In time, as you will read in the next chapter, differences between the Soviet Union and its former Allies led to the division of Germany into two countries: communist East Germany and noncommunist West Germany. Nearly all the nations of Eastern Europe became communist states under Soviet control.

Other countries experienced profound political changes. Communist and non-communist interests clashed in Eastern Europe. In China, a long-standing civil war between Nationalists and communists resumed.

In Japan, General Douglas MacArthur headed an American military occupation and supervised the writing of a new constitution. It abolished the armed forces except for purposes of defense, gave women the right to vote, enacted democratic reforms, and established the groundwork for full economic recovery.

**Imperialism Goes Into Decline** The war also marked the end of Western European domination of the world.

**The Big Three at Yalta**
This famous photo shows (left to right) Churchill, Roosevelt, and Stalin at the Yalta Conference. Their glum looks seem to say: Here are not victors, but potential enemies. In addition, FDR looks ill and tired—he died only months after this picture was taken.

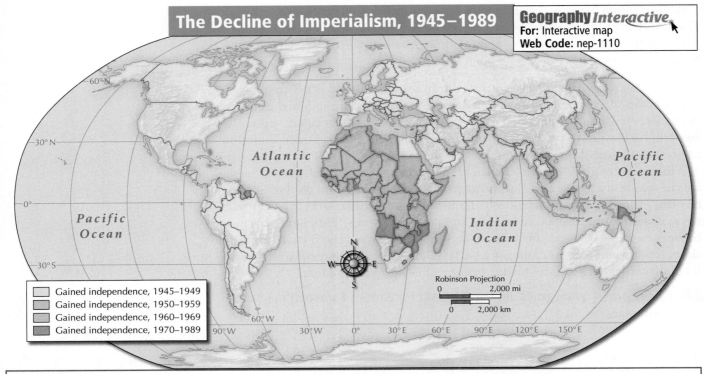

## The Decline of Imperialism, 1945–1989

**Geography** *Interactive*
**For:** Interactive map
**Web Code:** nep-1110

Legend:
- Gained independence, 1945–1949
- Gained independence, 1950–1959
- Gained independence, 1960–1969
- Gained independence, 1970–1989

Robinson Projection
0    2,000 mi
0    2,000 km

**Map Skills** In the decades following World War II, the Age of Imperialism ended as colony after colony won independence.

1. **Locate:** (a) Europe, (b) Africa, (c) Asia, (d) the Soviet Union

2. **Regions** On what continent did the largest number of nations win independence?

3. **Predict Consequences** How might the appearance of so many new nations affect the balance of power in the postwar world?

Since the 1500s, nations such as Britain, France, and Spain had exerted paramount influence on global developments. They colonized much of Africa, the Middle East, Asia, and the Americas. They had controlled world trade and finance, led the industrial revolution, and stood at the forefront of world military power.

The aggressive acquisition of territories by Japan and Germany underscored the abuses of imperialism. After World War II, colonial peoples renewed their drive for independence from European powers. Freed from Japanese domination, the East Indies had no interest in returning to Dutch colonial status. Nor did Indochina want to see the return of French rule. India, Burma, colonies in the Middle East and Africa—all had their sights set on independence.

By the end of the war, it was clear that the Age of Imperialism was in the twilight of its existence. The British Empire, the <u>predominant</u> power of the nineteenth century, came out of the war suffering severe economic shortages and, within decades, would see the loss of most of its colonies.

**The Balance of Power Shifts** Into the power vacuum stepped the United States and the Soviet Union. They had played the most decisive roles in defeating the Axis Powers, and they emerged from the war confident and strong. Indeed, they so dominated the postwar world that they became known as **superpowers.**

Of the two superpowers, the United States was clearly the stronger. Except for the attack on Pearl Harbor, no major battle had been fought on U.S. soil. In addition, American industry had boomed during the war. By 1945, America was wealthy, militarily powerful, and confident. By contrast, much of the war had

**Vocabulary Builder**
<u>predominant</u>–(pree DAHM uh nuhnt) *adj.* having the greatest amount of authority or dominance

been fought on Soviet soil. Its industries, cities, and peoples had suffered terribly. Still, the Red Army controlled most of Eastern Europe and threatened to move farther west. Militarily, although the Americans had the atomic bomb, the Soviets had the Red Army, the world's largest military force.

✓ **Checkpoint** What impact did World War II have on the relative roles of the United States and Britain in the world?

# International Cooperation

Americans were quick to recognize that their nation had taken on a new position in the world. After World War I, the Senate had rejected the Treaty of Versailles and refused to join the League of Nations. Many Americans now viewed these decisions as mistakes that contributed to the rise of fascism and the outbreak of another war. As World War II drew to a close, Americans were ready to embrace the idea of world organizations.

**A New World Economy Takes Shape** The United States took on major responsibilities in shaping the postwar world economy. After meeting in 1944 with the Allies in Bretton Woods, New Hampshire, the U.S. government pushed for establishment of the International Monetary Fund and the World Bank. The United States provided most of the working capital for these new organizations, which worked to foster global economic and financial stability. The United States also signed the **General Agreement on Tariffs and Trade (GATT),** a 1948 treaty designed to expand world trade by reducing tariffs.

**The United Nations Is Formed** Even more importantly, the United States led the charge for the establishment of the **United Nations (UN),** an organization that, many hoped, would succeed where the League of Nations had failed. In April 1945, delegates from 50 nations met in San Francisco to write the charter for the UN. The Senate overwhelmingly ratified the charter, and the UN later set up its permanent home in New York City.

The United Nations was organized on the basis of cooperation between the Great Powers, not on the absolute equality of all nations. All member nations sat on the General Assembly. However, the five major World War II Allies—the United States, the Soviet Union, Britain, France, and China—were assigned permanent seats on the most powerful arm of the UN, the Security Council.

Over the next decades, the UN aided the move away from colonialism, helped to create the Jewish state of Israel, mediated regional conflicts, and provided food and other aid to much of the world. The UN also issued the **Universal Declaration of Human Rights** in 1948. This idealistic document states:

**Primary Source** "Recognition of the inherent dignity and of the equal and inalienable rights of all members of the human family is the foundation of freedom, justice and peace in the world. . . . All human beings are born free and equal in dignity and rights. They are endowed with reason and conscience and should act toward one another in a spirit of brotherhood."

—Universal Declaration of Human Rights

## HISTORY MAKERS

**Eleanor Roosevelt** (1884–1962)
As First Lady, Eleanor Roosevelt had been a valuable, if unofficial, part of her husband's presidential administration. After FDR's death, President Truman named her to represent the United States at the United Nations. As elected chair of the Commission on Human Rights, she guided the drafting of the Universal Declaration of Human Rights, which she hoped would "become the international Magna Carta for all men everywhere." Her work on behalf of human rights won Roosevelt the nickname First Lady of the World. Shortly before her death, President John F. Kennedy named Roosevelt to head his Commission on the Status of Women.

## Cause and Effect

### Causes

- Europe suffers massive destruction in World War I
- Germans and Italians resent Versailles Treaty
- Great Depression leads to rise of fascist dictators
- European appeasement fails to end Axis aggression
- Japanese attack on Pearl Harbor

### World War II

### Effects

- Europe and Japan lay in ruins
- European colonies gradually gain independence
- Soviets dominate Eastern Europe
- Cold War between United States and Soviet Union begins
- America becomes a world power
- African Americans gain momentum to pursue civil rights

### Connections to Today

- United States remains a global superpower
- U.S. government plays a large role in guiding the nation's economy

**Analyze Cause and Effect** In its overall impact, World War II is often considered the single most important event of the twentieth century. *How did World War II contribute to the two effects listed above under Connections to Today?*

The Declaration condemns slavery and torture, upholds freedom of speech and religion, and affirms that "everyone has the right to a standard of living adequate for the health and well-being of himself and his family." Though the document sets lofty goals it has proved difficult to enforce.

**War Criminals Go on Trial** In the effort to create a better world, the Allies did not forget to punish the people who had caused so much destruction and death. During the war, the Axis Powers had repeatedly violated the **Geneva Convention,** an international agreement governing the humane treatment of wounded soldiers and prisoners of war.

The Allies tried more than a thousand Japanese citizens for committing atrocities in China, Korea, and Southeast Asia and brutally mistreating prisoners of war. Hundreds were condemned to death, including Prime Minister Hideki Tojo and the general responsible for the Bataan Death March.

Americans more closely followed the **Nuremberg Trials,** in which the Allies prosecuted Nazis for war crimes. The trials turned a glaring spotlight on the evils of the Third Reich. The first of the Nuremberg Trials involved key leaders of Nazi Germany, such as Hermann Goring. Day by day, prosecutors described their crimes, detailing especially the horrors of the Holocaust. Most of the defendants pleaded that they were just following orders, that Hitler was the source of all the crimes. The judges at Nuremberg did not accept their excuses. Some of the Nazis were hanged; others received long prison terms.

In the following decades, Allied or Israeli authorities captured and tried such other Nazis as Adolf Eichmann, a leading architect of the "Final Solution." The periodic trials kept alive the memory of the Nazi crimes against humanity.

 **Checkpoint** **What steps did the United States take to increase its role in the postwar world?**

# A New American Identity

A new American identity rose from the ashes of World War II, one formed as the antithesis of the Nazi ideal. Americans regarded the Nazis as totalitarian, racist, and warlike. They defined themselves as democratic, tolerant, and peaceful. During the war, U.S. leaders and American popular culture had emphasized these positive themes, repeating constantly that the Allies were fighting a "people's war" for tolerance, freedom, democracy, and peace. Although many Americans felt that their country had not always lived up to that ideal, they hoped that the postwar period would usher in significant changes.

**The United States Assumes Global Leadership** Millions of Americans had spent several years closely following the war. They had attached world maps to their walls and traced the paths of U.S. troops in the deserts of North Africa, the forests of Europe, and the coral islands of the Pacific. For this generation of Americans, the world had somehow become a smaller, more interconnected place. They had learned to think in global terms.

Few Americans called for a return to a policy of isolationism or retreat from their global responsibilities. They recognized that what happened in the far reaches of the globe affected them, that the economic and political health of

America was tied to world peace and economic development. They knew that America's national security involved world security.

**Commitment to Civil Rights Grows** African American soldiers in World War II had clearly believed they were fighting two foes: dictatorship overseas and racism in the United States. As the great African American poet Langston Hughes put it:

### Primary Source

66You tell me that Hitler
Is a mighty bad man.
I guess he took lessons
From the Ku Klux Klan.99

—Langston Hughes, quoted in *The Fight of the Century* (Hietala)

World War II gave renewed vigor to the fight for civil rights. In this battle, African Americans were not alone. A growing number of white Americans also called for the nation to fully live up to its promise as a beacon of freedom, democracy, and justice.

**The Nation Prospers** World War II ended the Great Depression and ushered in decades of economic growth. It also redistributed wealth across the country. Defense industries and military bases in the South and West spurred people to move to these regions, which in turn created more wealth and encouraged further migration.

The driving force for all the jobs and prosperity was the federal government. Like other wars, World War II led to a greater governmental influence in economic affairs. From the collection of raw materials to attempts to control inflation, the government had made the important decisions to guide the economy. In the process, it established the expanded economic role that government would play in postwar America.

**A Hero Comes Home**
For millions of Americans, World War II was not truly over until their loved ones came home from overseas. Here, a wounded G.I. embraces his parents.

✓ **Checkpoint** How did World War II foster support for civil rights?

---

SECTION

# 5 Assessment

**Progress Monitoring** *Online*
**For:** Self-test with vocabulary practice
**Web Code:** nea-1111

## Comprehension

1. **Terms and People** For each term below, write a sentence explaining how it was connected with the building of the postwar world.
   • Yalta Conference
   • superpower
   • GATT
   • United Nations
   • Universal Declaration of Human Rights
   • Geneva Convention
   • Nuremberg Trials

2. **NoteTaking Reading Skill: Understand Effects** Use your concept web to answer the Section Focus Question: What were the major immediate and long-term effects of World War II?

## Writing About History

3. **Quick Write: Write a Descriptive Paragraph** Write a paragraph describing the look and feel of the Nuremberg Trials. Describe both what you might see and the emotional mood in the room.

## Critical Thinking

4. **Predict Consequences** Identify one possible postwar consequence of the Allied disagreements at Yalta and Potsdam.

5. **Recognize Causes and Effects** Why do you think Americans supported participation in the UN after World War II when they had opposed participation in the League of Nations after World War I?

6. **Compare** In what way were both the Universal Declaration of Human Rights and the postwar push for civil rights reactions to the war?

# Quick Study Guide

 7.2.2

## ■ Allied Leaders, World War II

| World Political | U.S. Military |
|---|---|
| • Winston Churchill, Britain<br>• Joseph Stalin, Soviet Union<br>• Franklin D. Roosevelt, United States<br>• Harry S. Truman, United States | **In Europe**<br> • Dwight Eisenhower<br> • George S. Patton<br> • Omar Bradley<br>**In the Pacific**<br> • Douglas MacArthur<br> • Chester Nimitz |

## ■ World War II Home Front

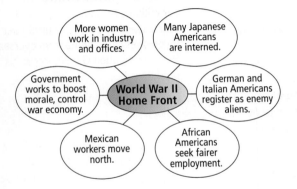

More women work in industry and offices.

Many Japanese Americans are interned.

Government works to boost morale, control war economy.

**World War II Home Front**

German and Italian Americans register as enemy aliens.

Mexican workers move north.

African Americans seek fairer employment.

## ■ Five Turning Points of World War II

| | |
|---|---|
| 1942 | **Battle of Midway** halts Japanese expansion in Pacific. |
| 1942–1943 | **Battle of Stalingrad** ends Nazi advances in Europe. |
| 1942 | **Battle of El Alamein** begins Allied offensive against Axis Powers in North Africa. |
| 1944 | **D-Day** invasion opens second front in Europe, paving way f⬤ final defeat of Germany. |
| 1945 | **Manhattan Project** develops atomic bomb, used to end wa⬤ in Pacific. |

## ■ World War II Deaths, Selected Nations

| Country | Military Deaths | Civilian Deaths |
|---|---|---|
| **Axis** | | |
| Germany | 3,500,000 | 780,000 |
| Italy | 242,000 | 153,000 |
| Japan | 1,300,000 | 672,000 |
| **Allies** | | |
| France | 213,000 | 350,000 |
| Britain | 264,000 | 93,000 |
| China | 1,310,000 | 1,000,000 |
| Soviet Union | 7,500,000 | 15,000,000 |
| United States | 292,000 | 6,000 |

SOURCES: Henri Michel, *Encyclopaedia Britannica; Harper Encyclopedia of Military History*
All figures are estimates.

## ✓ Quick Study Timeline

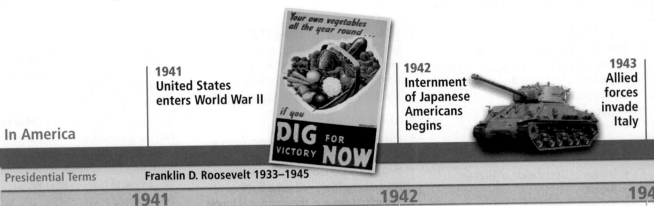

**In America**

**1941**
**United States enters World War II**

**1942**
**Internment of Japanese Americans begins**

**1943**
**Allied forces invade Italy**

*Your own vegetables all the year round . . .*
*if you*
**DIG** FOR
VICTORY **NOW**

**Presidential Terms**     Franklin D. Roosevelt 1933–1945

1941                1942                1943

**Around the World**

1941
**Germany invades Soviet Union**

1942
**Battle of Midway**

1943
**Germans surrender at Stalingrad**

# American Issues
●—●—●—● **Connector**

7.2.3a

By connecting prior knowledge with what you have learned in this chapter, you can gradually build your understanding of enduring questions that still affect America today. Answer the questions below. Then, use your American Issues Connector study guide (or go online: www.PHSchool.com **Web Code:** neh-8402).

## Issues You Learned About

● **Protecting and Expanding Civil Rights** Americans may organize to demand fair treatment and civil rights.

1. Why did Roosevelt decide to issue an executive order assuring fair hiring practices in any job funded by the government?

2. What was the NAACP, when was it founded, and why did its membership grow during the war years?

3. How did World War II motivate African Americans' fight for civil rights? What do you think African Americans did after the war ended to win more civil rights?

● **Civil Liberties and National Security** During wartime, the government has often taken steps to suspend civil liberties.

4. During World War I, which groups of people suffered from persecution? Did the U.S. government violate these groups' civil liberties? Explain.

5. How did the United States defend its internment of Japanese Americans? How did some Japanese Americans respond?

6. Was there any evidence that Japanese Americans threatened national security? Present evidence that supports or weakens this claim.

● **Technology and Society** New technological developments can hurt society as well as help it.

7. What new technology contributed to the high casualties of World War I?

8. What was the atomic bomb? How powerful was the first one that was tested?

9. What effect did the dropping of atomic bombs on Hiroshima and Nagasaki have on the progress of World War II?

### Connect to Your World | Michigan

**Michigan Goes to War** During World War II, the Ford Motor Company was one of the many contributors to the U.S. war effort. In 1941, the Ford Motor Company opened the United States Naval Service Training School at the Ford plant in Dearborn, Michigan, in order to share the company's mechanical expertise with enlisted men. Over the next five years, more than 20,000 sailors learned skills ranging from engine repair to sheet metal work. Those who completed the three-month course emerged as trained machinists and electricians, ready to put their new skills to work for the U.S. Navy. The skills that the sailors learned often helped them get promoted more quickly than other sailors. Write a speech about the importance of the Naval Service Training School to the American war effort.

---

**1944**
**D-Day landing in France**

**1945**
**World War II ends**

**History *Interactive***
**For:** Interactive timeline
**Web Code:** nep-1114

Harry S. Truman 1945–1953

**1944**

**1945**

**1946**

**1945**
**Nazi death camps liberated**

**1946**
**Nuremberg war crimes trials**

# Chapter Assessment

## Terms and People

1. Who were **Dwight D. Eisenhower** and **George S. Patton, Jr.**? How were the two men linked?

2. What Americans were sent to **internment camps**? What were conditions like in these camps?

3. Define **D-Day**. What was the result of this strategy?

4. What was the goal of the **Manhattan Project**?

5. Define **genocide**. How did Hitler attempt to accomplish genocide?

6. What was the purpose of the **Nuremberg Trials**?

## Focus Questions

The focus question for this chapter is **What impact did World War II have on America and the world?** Build an answer to this big question by answering the focus questions for Sections 1 through 5 and the Critical Thinking questions that follow.

### Section 1
7. How did the Allies turn the tide against the Axis?

### Section 2
8. How did the war change America at home?

### Section 3
9. How did the Allies defeat the Axis Powers?

### Section 4
10. How did the Holocaust develop and what were its results?

### Section 5
11. What were the major immediate and long-term effects of World War II?

## Critical Thinking

12. **Recognize Effects** Explain the significance of Allied victories at Stalingrad and in North Africa.

13. **Evaluate Information** The Americans who fought in World War II have been called the "Greatest Generation." What do you think this means? What evidence supports this claim?

14. **Summarize** Summarize the contributions of two of these groups to the war effort: women, Mexican Americans, African Americans, Navajos.

15. **Interpreting a Political Cartoon** What is the main point of the cartoon below? How do you think American soldiers reacted to this cartoon?

16. **Make Decisions** Do you think Truman's decision to drop the atomic bomb was justified at the time? Was it justified in light of future events?

17. **Recognize Propaganda** How did Hitler use propaganda in his campaign against German Jews?

18. **Synthesize Information** **(a)** How do the meetings at Yalta and Potsdam reflect a new balance of global power? **(b)** What type of relationship do you think the United States and the Soviet Union will have in the post–World War II years?

---

## Writing About History

**Writing a Descriptive Essay** In a descriptive essay, you try to convey in words the look, sound, and mood of an event. Write a three-paragraph descriptive essay on one of the following topics: an American flight crew making a bombing run over Germany; women going to work in defense industries during World War II; soldiers walking on Omaha Beach after D-Day; American soldiers liberating a concentration camp.

### Prewriting
- Look at the pictures and read the text in this chapter relating to the topic you have chosen.
- Use Internet or library sources to find additional pictures and descriptions relating to your topic.
- Make a list of sights, sounds, impressions, and connections to your topic.

### Drafting
- Make an outline identifying what aspects of your topic you want to describe.
- Write an opening paragraph in which you introduce the topic and identify the setting.
- Write descriptions using precise adjectives and specific action verbs. Avoid generalizations that are too broad or too vague.

### Revising
- Use the guidelines on page SH8 of the Writing Handbook to revise your writing.

# Prepare for the MME

## The Battle of Midway

The Battle of Midway is considered a major turning point of World War II. But why was it so important? How was it viewed by the participants? Use your knowledge of the chapter material and Documents A, B, C, and D to answer questions 1 through 4.

### Document A

| War in Asia and the Pacific, December 1941–August 1942 | |
| --- | --- |
| December 7, 1941 | Japan bombs Pearl Harbor. |
| December 23, 1941 | Japan captures Wake Island. |
| December 25, 1941 | Japan captures Hong Kong. |
| February 15, 1942 | Japan captures Singapore. |
| April 8, 1942 | Japan captures Bataan, Philippines. |
| May 4, 1942 | Japanese offensive stalls at Battle of the Coral Sea. |
| May 20, 1942 | Japan drives British out of Burma. |
| June 4–7, 1942 | United States Navy wins Battle of Midway. |
| August 7, 1942 | Americans begin assault on Guadalcanal. |

### Document B

"In numerous and widespread engagements lasting from the 3rd to 6th of June, with carrier based planes as the spearhead of the attack, combined forces of the Navy, Marine Corps and Army in the Hawaiian Area defeated a large part of the Japanese fleet and frustrated the enemy's powerful move against Midway that was undoubtedly the keystone of larger plans. All participating personnel, without exception, displayed unhesitating devotion to duty, loyalty and courage. This superb spirit in all three services made possible the application of the destructive power that routed the enemy. . . . These results were achieved at the cost of the *Yorktown* and *Hamman* sunk and about 150 planes lost in action or damaged beyond repair. Our total personnel losses were about ninety-two (92) officers and two hundred and fifteen (215) men."

—*Admiral Chester A. Nimitz, official report of the Battle of Midway, filed June 28, 1942*

### Document C

"Had Yamamoto fulfilled his projects of taking Midway and destroying Nimitz's carriers, the next program on his agenda was to turn to the Australian campaign. And with the aerial striking power of the U.S. Pacific Fleet out of the running, there would have been precious little to stop him. . . . And in the meantime, possession of Midway would have given Japan the means to harass at least the Hawaiian Islands and even the West Coast. . . . At Midway, the United States laid aside the shield and picked up the sword, and through all the engagements to follow, never again yielded the strategic offensive."

—*Gordon W. Prange,* Miracle at Midway, *1982*

### Document D

"It was Japan that had attacked the United States, and it was Japan on which the anger of the American people had focused. . . . Had it not been for Midway, Roosevelt could not have persevered with a Europe-first policy. Public opinion would not have allowed it. . . . Through an extraordinary combination of the skill and courage of our pilots, splendid intelligence, prudent risk-taking by our commanders that paid off, and sheer good luck, the apparently inferior American forces were victorious. This victory occurred despite the inferiority of our aircraft, the ineffectiveness of our torpedoes, the substantial absence of backup surface ships, and our overall numerical inferiority. You know the rest! Four Japanese carriers had been sunk. . . . The Japanese offensive had now been blunted. The Japanese fleet turned back toward the Home Islands and the opportunity for victory had been lost forever. . . . After Midway, the United States could, to the chagrin of Douglas MacArthur, turn its primary attention back to the European theatre."

—*Former Secretary of Defense James R. Schlesinger, June 5, 2003*

---

1. Which conclusion is best supported by Document A?
   A Japan lost the war as a direct result of the Battle of Midway.
   B Before the Battle of Midway, Japan had been on the offensive.
   C The Japanese invasion of Burma led to the Battle of Bataan.
   D The Battle of Midway was the last Japanese victory in the Pacific.

2. On what point do Document B and Document C agree?
   A The Battle of Midway was a setback for Japan.
   B The Battle of Midway was a setback for the United States.
   C The Battle of Midway was equally damaging to both sides.
   D U.S. forces were undamaged at the Battle of Midway.

3. According to Document D, how did the Battle of Midway make it easier for Roosevelt to pursue a "Europe First" strategy?
   A It convinced Americans that Japan was no longer a threat.
   B It roused public anger against Germany.
   C It satisfied immediate public demand for action against Japan.
   D It showed that the United States could not win in the Pacific unless it conquered Germany first.

4. **Writing Task** What might have happened if Japanese forces had won the Battle of Midway? Use your knowledge of the chapter content and specific evidence from the primary sources above to support your opinion.

# 12

## The Cold War
### 1945–1960

## Preparing for Attack

June 15, 1955—Wailing sirens announce that Soviet nuclear weapons are on the way. Their targets are New York, Los Angeles, and dozens of other U.S. cities. Schoolchildren duck for cover under their desks. People flee their homes and offices and rush to underground shelters. President Eisenhower is whisked away to a secret mountain location. Millions of casualties are expected. . . .

But this was only a drill. Called Operation Alert, it was one of numerous drills that took place during the Cold War, when the United States was locked in a desperate worldwide struggle against communism and the Soviet Union. *Listen to the* Witness History *audio to hear more about Operation Alert.*

◄ Schoolchildren try to stay calm during a "duck and cover" nuclear air-raid drill.

Korean War medal

Sign marking a nuclear bomb fallout shelter

 **Content Expectations**

**Chapter Focus Question:** What were the causes, main events, and effects of the early Cold War?

### Section 1
**The Cold War Begins**   8.1.1a, 8.1.1b, 8.1.2a

### Section 2
**The Korean War**   8.1.1c, 8.1.2b, 8.1.2d, 8.2.2a

### Section 3
**The Cold War Expands**   8.1.2, 8.1.2f, 8.2.3

### Section 4
**The Cold War at Home**   8.1.1c, 8.2.2a, 8.2.2b

Comic book warning about the threat of communism

Use the ☑ **Quick Study Timeline** at the end of this chapter to preview chapter events.

**Note Taking Study Guide** *Online*
**For:** Note Taking and American Issues Connector
**Web Code:** nee-8501

◀ General George Patton

▲ U.S. and Soviet soldiers celebrate the Allied victory.

**WITNESS HISTORY**  AUDIO

**A New Enemy**

After World War II, U.S. General George Patton administered western Germany, while Soviet officials governed eastern Germany. Patton looked to the east and proclaimed:

❝Russia knows what she wants. World domination! . . . Let's keep our boots polished, bayonets sharpened, and present a picture of force and strength to the Russians. This is the only language that they understand and respect. If we fail to do this, then I would like to say that we have had a victory over the Germans and have disarmed them, but we have lost the war.❞
—General George S. Patton, October 1945

# The Cold War Begins

## Content Expectations

- **8.1.1a** Analyze differences in civic/political values, economic/governmental institutions of U.S./U.S.S.R.
- **8.1.1b** Analyze diplomatic decisions made at Yalta/Potsdam Conferences.
- **8.1.2a** Evaluate development of U.S. national security establishment.

## Terms and People

| | |
|---|---|
| satellite state | containment |
| Cold War | Marshall Plan |
| iron curtain | Berlin airlift |
| Truman Doctrine | NATO |
| George F. Kennan | Warsaw Pact |

## NoteTaking

**Reading Skill: Contrast** As you read, contrast the conflicting goals of the United States and the Soviet Union.

| American Goals | Soviet Goals |
|---|---|
| | |
| | |
| | |

**Why It Matters** In the 1930s, the policies of isolationism and appeasement had contributed to the rise of dictatorships and the outbreak of global war. After World War II, U.S. leaders viewed these past policies as mistakes. They sought new ways to keep the United States safe and to protect its interests around the world. **Section Focus Question: How did U.S. leaders respond to the threat of Soviet expansion in Europe?**

## Roots of the Cold War

When Franklin Roosevelt died in April 1945, the nation was at a critical point. The United States was still at war. In addition, relations with the Soviet Union—one of the most important wartime allies—were beginning to break down.

**American and Soviet Systems Differ** The United States and the Soviet Union had been united only in their opposition to Nazi Germany. Beyond that, they had little in common. The United States was a capitalist democracy. Its citizens believed in free elections, economic and religious freedom, private property, and respect for individual differences. The Soviet Union was a dictatorship. Under Joseph Stalin, the Communist Party made all key economic, political, and military decisions. The Soviet people could not worship as they pleased, own private property, or express their views freely. Those who opposed or questioned Stalin risked imprisonment and death.

**Allies Disagree on Future of Eastern Europe** By the time Roosevelt, Stalin, and Churchill met at Yalta in February 1945, it was clear that the Allies would defeat Germany. But it was unclear how Germany and the nations of Eastern Europe would be governed after the war. Soviet troops already occupied much of Eastern Europe and some of Germany.

Stalin wanted to keep Germany weak and divided. He also wanted Eastern Europe to remain under the control of the Soviet Union. The United States and Great Britain sought a stronger, united Germany and independent nations in Eastern Europe. At the conference, Stalin agreed to establish "broadly representative" governments and free elections in Eastern Europe and to divide Germany only temporarily into zones of occupation.

Despite Stalin's promises, nearly all of the lands occupied by the Soviet Red Army in the spring of 1945 remained under Soviet control after the war. The Eastern European countries of Poland, Czechoslovakia, Hungary, Romania, and Bulgaria, as well as the eastern portion of Germany, became **satellite states** controlled by the Soviet Union.

**Truman and Stalin Clash at Potsdam** By the time Soviet, British, and U.S. leaders met at Potsdam in the summer of 1945, Harry Truman had succeeded Roosevelt as President. Truman and Clement Attlee, the new British prime minister, hoped that Stalin would confirm the decisions made at Yalta. However, Stalin refused to make a commitment to allow free elections in Eastern Europe.

## Comparing Viewpoints

# What Will Happen to Postwar Europe?

The Soviet Union and United States disagreed on what should happen to Europe after World War II. The disagreement had much to do with the conflicting values of the two countries and their leaders.

### JOSEPH STALIN

Stalin was a dictator who ruled the Soviet Union from the 1920s to the 1950s. His policy of collectivizing land led to famine and to the death of millions. He also ordered the execution of thousands of communist officials.

**Primary Source**

"To choose one's victims, to prepare one's plan minutely, to slake an implacable vengeance, and then to go to bed . . . there is nothing sweeter in the world."

"This war is different from all earlier ones; the conqueror of a region imposes his own social system on it."

### HARRY S. TRUMAN

As President from 1945 until 1953, Truman tried to stop the spread of communism. He promoted a "Fair Deal" program that included more social security benefits, public health insurance, and an end to racial discrimination.

**Primary Source**

"I would rather have peace in the world than be President."

"The American people desire, and are determined to work for, a world in which all nations and all peoples are free to govern themselves as they see fit, and to achieve a decent and satisfying life."

**Compare**
1. How did Truman's views on power differ from those of Stalin?
2. How did the two leaders disagree on the issue of self-government in Eastern Europe?

Truman left Potsdam believing that the Soviet Union was "planning world conquest" and that the alliance with the Soviet Union was falling apart. With the Soviet Red Army at his command, Stalin seemed to present a real threat. Thus, the stage was set for a worldwide rivalry between the United States and the Soviet Union. The 46-year struggle became known as the **Cold War** because the two superpowers never faced each other directly in a "hot" military conflict.

✔ **Checkpoint** How did the goals of U.S. and Soviet foreign policy differ after World War II?

## Meeting the Soviet Challenge

President Truman was not the only world leader who believed that Stalin had <u>aspirations</u> toward world domination. Winston Churchill also spoke out forcefully against the Soviet Union. On March 5, 1946, he gave an important speech at Fulton College in Missouri, Truman's home state. Referring to a map of Europe, Churchill noted that "an **iron curtain** has descended across the Continent." (See the Primary Source on the opposite page.) East of that iron curtain, the Soviet Union was gaining more control by installing communist governments and police states and by crushing political and religious dissent. In addition, Churchill feared, the Soviets were attempting to spread communism to Western Europe and East Asia. The only solution, Churchill said, was for the United States and other democratic countries to stand firm.

**Truman Faces a Crisis** Truman shared Churchill's beliefs. Born in a small town in Missouri, Truman had been too poor to attend college. He was the only president in the twentieth century with no college education. Instead, he worked the family farm, fought in France during World War I, and eventually began a political career. His life was a testament to honesty, integrity, hard work, and a willingness to make difficult decisions. "The buck stops here," was his motto as President. It meant that the person sitting in the Oval Office had the obligation to face problems head-on and make hard decisions.

In 1947, no issue was more weighty than the growing crisis between the United States and the Soviet Union. After the war, a number of European and Asian countries were struggling against communist movements supported by the Soviets. In particular, the governments of Greece and Turkey were battling communist forces seeking to gain control. Greece and Turkey needed aid, and in 1947 the United States was the only country with the resources to help them.

**The Truman Doctrine Opposes Communist Expansion** On March 12, 1947, President Truman addressed both houses of Congress. With emotion in his voice, Truman described the plight of the Greek and Turkish people. The fight they were waging, he said, was the fight that all free people had to confront. Truman requested money from Congress "to support free peoples who are resisting attempted subjugation [conquest] by armed minorities or by outside pressures." If the United States retreated into isolationism, he warned, the peace of the world and the welfare of the nation would be in danger.

Congress responded by voting to give $400 million in aid for Greece and Turkey. President Truman's promise to aid nations struggling against communist movements became known as the **Truman Doctrine,** and it set a new course for American foreign policy.

✔ **Checkpoint** What events caused President Truman to propose what became known as the Truman Doctrine?

## NoteTaking

**Reading Skill: Recognize Sequence** As you read, trace events and developments in Europe that contributed to the growth of Cold War tensions.

| Yalta and Potsdam: Allies have conflicting goals for Eastern Europe |
| --- |

# Cold War Europe, 1949

**Geography Interactive**
For: Interactive map
Web Code: nep-1202

Legend:
- Communist nations
- Annexed by Soviet Union, 1939–1945
- Noncommunist nations
- Iron curtain

Conic projection
0     200     400 mi
0     200     400 km

NORWAY
FINLAND
SWEDEN
ESTONIA
LATVIA
LITHUANIA
Moscow
DENMARK
IRELAND
UNITED KINGDOM
NETH.
London
BELGIUM
EAST GER.
POLAND
SOVIET UNION
LUX.
Paris
WEST GERMANY
CZECHOSLOVAKIA
FRANCE
SWITZ.
AUST.
HUNG.
ROMANIA
PORTUGAL
SPAIN
ITALY
YUGOSLAVIA
BULGARIA
Rome
ALB.
GREECE
TURKEY
Atlantic Ocean
North Sea
Baltic Sea
Black Sea
Mediterranean Sea

In his speech at Fulton, Missouri, Winston Churchill described the extent of the Soviet "iron curtain," shown on the map above.

**Primary Source** "From Stettin in the Baltic to Trieste in the Adriatic, an iron curtain has descended across the Continent. Behind that line lie all the capitals of . . . Central and Eastern Europe. . . . The Communist parties, which were very small in all these Eastern States of Europe, have been raised to pre-eminence and power far beyond their numbers and are seeking everywhere to obtain totalitarian control."

— "Iron Curtain" speech,
Winston Churchill, March 5, 1946

**Map Skills** Europe became a divided continent as the Cold War developed after World War II.

1. **Region** Why did the Soviet Union support the creation of communist states in Eastern Europe?

2. **Draw Conclusions** Based on the map, in what ways might the Soviet Union have benefited from gaining control of Greece and Turkey?

## Churchill and the Iron Curtain

The day after Churchill gave his "Iron Curtain" speech, this cartoon appeared in a British newspaper. It shows Churchill peeping under the barrier built by "Joe" Stalin.

## Containing Soviet Expansion

In the July 1947 issue of the magazine *Foreign Affairs*, a writer who called himself "X" published an article titled "The Sources of Soviet Conduct." The author was really **George F. Kennan,** an American diplomat and a leading authority on the Soviet Union. His article presented a blueprint for the American policy that became known as **containment** because its goal was to keep communism contained within its existing borders.

**Kennan Argues for Containment** Kennan contended that while Stalin was determined to expand the Soviet empire, he would not risk the security of the Soviet Union for expansion. In Kennan's view, the Soviet Union would only expand when it could do so without serious risks. Stalin would certainly not chance war with the United States—a war that might destroy his power in the Soviet Union—just to spread communism.

Kennan cautioned his readers that there would be no quick, easy solution to the Soviet threat. Containment would require a full commitment of American economic, political, and military power:

> **Primary Source** ❝We are going to continue for a long time to find the Russians difficult to deal with. It does not mean that they should be considered as embarked upon a do-or-die program to overthrow our society by a given date. . . . In these circumstances, it is clear that the main element of any United States policy toward the Soviet Union must be that of long-term, patient but firm and vigilant containment of Russian expansive tendencies.❞
> —George Kennan, "The Sources of Soviet Conduct"

**The Marshall Plan Aids Europe's Economies** The containment policy's first great success was in Western Europe. After World War II, people there confronted severe shortages of food, fuel, and medical supplies, as well as brutally cold winters. In this environment of desperate need, Secretary of State George C. Marshall unveiled a recovery plan for Europe. In a speech at Harvard University, he warned that without economic health, "there can be no political stability and no assured peace."

In early 1948, Congress approved the **Marshall Plan.** Over the next four years, the United States gave about $13 billion in grants and loans to nations in Western Europe. The program provided food to reduce famine, fuel to heat houses and factories, and money to jump-start economic growth. Aid was also offered to the Soviet satellite states in Eastern Europe, but Stalin refused to let them accept it.

The Marshall Plan provided a vivid example of how U.S. aid could serve the ends of both economic and foreign policy. The aid helped countries that desperately needed assistance. The prosperity it stimulated then helped the American economy by increasing trade. Finally, the good relationships that the aid created worked against the expansion of communism.

✔ **Checkpoint** Why did George Kennan think that containment would work against Soviet expansion?

## The Cold War Heats Up

The front lines of the Cold War were located in Germany. The zones that were controlled by France, Britain, and the United States were combined to form West Germany. West Germany was bordered on the east by the Soviet-controlled East Germany. The Allies also controlled the western part of Berlin, a city tucked deep inside communist East Germany. (See the map on the opposite page.)

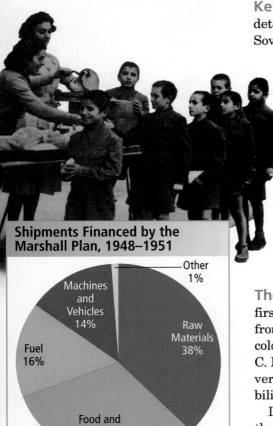

### Marshall Plan Aids European Recovery

These Greek children benefited from U.S. aid designed to promote stable democracies in Europe. *According to the pie chart, what portion of U.S. aid was devoted to reducing famine?*

**Shipments Financed by the Marshall Plan, 1948–1951**

- Other 1%
- Machines and Vehicles 14%
- Raw Materials 38%
- Fuel 16%
- Food and Other Produce 32%

**Berlin Airlift Saves West Berlin** West Berlin was, as one Soviet leader later described it, "a bone in the throat" of the Soviet Union. Its relative prosperity and freedom stood in contrast to the bleak life of East Berliners. Stalin was determined to capture West Berlin or win other concessions from the Western allies. In June 1948, he stopped all highway, railway, and waterway traffic from western Germany into West Berlin. Without any means of receiving aid, West Berlin would fall to the communists.

Stalin was able to close roads, stop barges, and block railways, but he could not blockade the sky. For almost a year, the United States and Britain supplied West Berlin through a massive airlift. Food, fuel, medical supplies, clothing, toys—everything the residents of West Berlin needed was flown into the city.

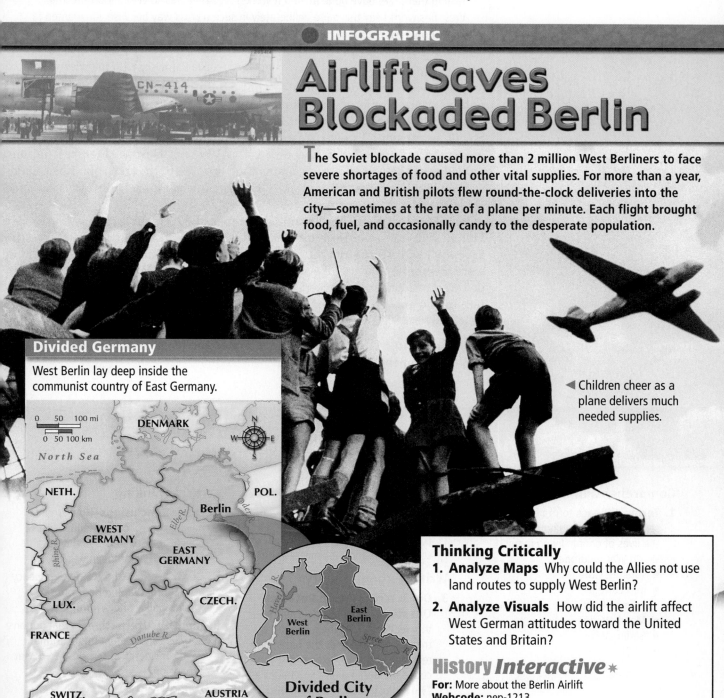

### INFOGRAPHIC

# Airlift Saves Blockaded Berlin

The Soviet blockade caused more than 2 million West Berliners to face severe shortages of food and other vital supplies. For more than a year, American and British pilots flew round-the-clock deliveries into the city—sometimes at the rate of a plane per minute. Each flight brought food, fuel, and occasionally candy to the desperate population.

◀ Children cheer as a plane delivers much needed supplies.

### Divided Germany

West Berlin lay deep inside the communist country of East Germany.

0    50    100 mi
0   50 100 km

DENMARK

North Sea

NETH.

POL.

Berlin

WEST GERMANY

EAST GERMANY

CZECH.

LUX.

FRANCE

Danube R.

SWITZ.

AUSTRIA

**Divided City of Berlin**

West Berlin

East Berlin

Havel R.

Spree R.

### Thinking Critically
1. **Analyze Maps** Why could the Allies not use land routes to supply West Berlin?
2. **Analyze Visuals** How did the airlift affect West German attitudes toward the United States and Britain?

**History *Interactive* ***

**For:** More about the Berlin Airlift
**Webcode:** nep-1213

Even through rain and snow, goods arrived regularly. The **Berlin airlift** demonstrated to West Berlin, the Soviet Union, and the world how far the United States would go to protect noncommunist parts of Europe and contain communism.

**Vocabulary Builder**
acknowledge–(ak NAHL ihj) *v.* to admit or recognize

**Cold War Rivals Form Alliances** In May 1949, Stalin was forced to acknowledge that his attempt to blockade Berlin had failed. The Berlin airlift was a proud moment for Americans and Berliners and a major success for the policy of containment. One Berlin resident later recalled her feelings when the blockade was finally lifted:

> **Primary Source** "Sheer joy—nothing else. Nothing else. Joy, and [the feeling that], 'We have done it! And it works!' . . . That was so very important. The West has won! I say this quite deliberately in such a crass way because you wanted to know how I felt emotionally. The West—well, we have succeeded. And the West has won and the others have not!"
> —Ella Barowsky, CNN interview, 1996

The Berlin airlift demonstrated that Stalin could be contained if Western nations were prepared to take forceful action. The **North Atlantic Treaty Organization (NATO),** formed in 1949, provided the military alliance to counter Soviet expansion. Twelve Western European and North American nations agreed to act together in the defense of Western Europe. Member nations agreed that "an armed attack against one or more of them . . . shall be considered an attack against all of them." This principle of mutual military assistance is called collective security.

In 1955, West Germany became a member of NATO. In response, the Soviet Union and its satellite states formed a rival military alliance, called the **Warsaw Pact.** All the communist states of Eastern Europe except Yugoslavia were members. Like members of NATO, nations of the Warsaw Pact pledged to defend one another if attacked. Although members agreed on paper not to interfere in one another's internal affairs, the Soviet Union continued to exert firm control over its Warsaw Pact allies.

✔ **Checkpoint** How did the United States and its allies apply the containment policy in Europe?

---

SECTION **1** Assessment

**Progress Monitoring *Online***
For: Self-test with vocabulary practice
Web Code: nea-1203

**Comprehension**

1. **Terms** For each term below, write a sentence explaining how it changed the lives of people living in post-World War II Europe.
   - satellite state
   - iron curtain
   - Truman Doctrine
   - Marshall Plan
   - Berlin airlift
   - NATO

2. **NoteTaking Reading Skill: Contrast** Use your chart to answer the Section Focus Question: How did U.S. leaders respond to the threat of communism and the Soviet Union?

**Writing About History**

3. **Quick Write: Frame Research Questions** Choose one event from this section. Write three questions that you could use as the basis for a research paper. For example, if you chose the Berlin airlift, you might ask, "How much food was flown into Berlin?"

**Critical Thinking**

4. **Draw Conclusions** How would having control over satellite states benefit the Soviet Union if it became involved in a European war?

5. **Contrast** How did U.S. foreign policy after World War II differ from U.S. foreign policy after World War I?

6. **Identify Alternatives** What options besides containment might Truman have considered in response to Soviet expansion?

8.1.1c

## Harry S. Truman:
### *The Truman Doctrine*

In this address to Congress, President Truman stressed the duty of the United States to combat totalitarian regimes worldwide. His March 12, 1947, speech called for $400 million in aid to Greece and Turkey, both of which he said were threatened by communism. Congress approved the financial aid as well as the commitment of U.S. troops to administer postwar reconstruction.

The peoples of a number of countries of the world have recently had totalitarian regimes forced upon them against their will. The government of the United States has made frequent protests against coercion[1] and intimidation, in violation of the Yalta agreement, in Poland, Romania, and Bulgaria. I must also state that in a number of other countries there have been similar developments.

At the present moment in world history nearly every nation must choose between alternative ways of life. The choice is too often not a free one. One way of life is based upon the will of the majority, and is distinguished by free institutions, representative government, free elections, guarantees of individual liberty, freedom of speech and religion, and freedom from political oppression. The second way of life is based upon the will of a minority forcibly imposed upon the majority. It relies upon terror and oppression, a controlled press and radio, fixed elections and the suppression of personal freedoms.

I believe that it must be the policy of the United States to support free peoples who are resisting attempted subjugation[2] by armed minorities or by outside pressures.

I believe that we must assist free peoples to work out their own destinies in their own way.

I believe that our help should be primarily through economic and financial aid which is essential to economic stability and orderly political processes. . . .

The seeds of totalitarian regimes are nurtured by misery and want. They spread and grow in the evil soil of poverty and strife. They reach their full growth when the hope of a people for a better life has died. We must keep that hope alive.

The free peoples of the world look to us for support in maintaining their freedoms. If we falter in our leadership, we may endanger the peace of the world—and we shall surely endanger the welfare of our own nation.

▲ President Truman delivering a speech

1. **coercion** (koh ER zhuhn) *n.* government by force.
2. **subjugation** (suhb juh GAY shuhn) *n.* condition of being under the control of a conqueror.

### Thinking Critically

1. **Make Inferences** What is President Truman referring to when he mentions the two "alternative ways of life"?

2. **Recognize Causes and Effects** According to Truman, how would economic aid support freedom in Greece and Turkey?

**SECTION 2**

▲ American machine-gunners in Korea

**WITNESS HISTORY** 🔊 AUDIO

### They Won't Escape This Time

General Lewis B. Puller was the only U.S. marine in history to win five Navy Crosses. Since the time he enlisted in 1918, Puller had fought in Haiti and Nicaragua, commanded marines in China, and waded ashore island after island in the Pacific during World War II. Pinned down by a surprise communist Chinese attack into North Korea, badly outnumbered, and cut off from reinforcement, Puller retained his courage and humor. He informed his regiment:

❝The enemy is in front of us, behind us, to the left of us, and to the right of us. They won't escape this time.❞

—Lewis "Chesty" Puller, November 1950

# The Korean War

**MI Content Expectations**

- **8.1.1c** Analyze actions in last years of/years following WWII.
- **8.1.2b** Evaluate armed struggle with Communism/Korean conflict.
- **8.1.2d** Evaluate U.S. involvement in Vietnam, foreign/domestic consequences of the war.
- **8.2.2a** Describe issues challenging Americans.

**Terms and People**

Jiang Jieshi
Mao Zedong
38th parallel

Douglas MacArthur
limited war
SEATO

## NoteTaking

**Reading Skill: Categorize** As you read, note problems and the steps that President Truman took to solve them. Use a problem-solution table like the one below.

| Problem | Solution |
|---|---|
| Communists threaten takeover of China | |

**Why It Matters** Europe had been the first focus of the Cold War. But in the early 1950s, U.S. involvement in the Korean War made East Asia the prime battleground in the long, hard Cold War struggle. The division between North and South Korea remains a source of international tension today. **Section Focus Question: How did President Truman use the power of the presidency to limit the spread of communism in East Asia?**

## Communists Gain Control of China

Since the time of the Russian Revolution in 1917, the Soviets had hoped to spread communism to every corner of the world, training foreigners in Marxist theory and revolutionary strategy. The Soviets were confident that communism would reach worldwide influence. In 1949, events in China seemed to justify their confidence.

**Civil War Divides China** Before Japan invaded China in 1937, Nationalist leader **Jiang Jieshi** (zhee AHNG zhǐ SHEE), known in the United States as Chiang Kai-shek, had been fighting a civil war against communists led by **Mao Zedong** (mow zeh DUHNG). Although Jiang and Mao temporarily joined forces in an uneasy alliance to fight Japan, the civil war resumed with a new fury after the war ended.

The Soviet Union supported Mao, while the United States sent several billion dollars in aid to Jiang. American leaders feared that Jiang's defeat would create a communist superpower spanning most of Asia.

Jiang's regime proved unequal to the task. Nationalist generals were reluctant to fight. And, while masses of Chinese people faced starvation, corrupt officials diverted U.S. aid dollars into their own pockets. By promising to feed the people, Mao won increased support.

**Communists Win in China** In 1948, Mao's forces dominated the war. Jiang appealed for American military intervention. However, the U.S. government had no intention of sending American troops to support the corrupt Jiang. In 1949, Jiang fled the Chinese mainland, taking control of the large offshore island of Taiwan. Mao's communists then took control of the world's most populous country, renaming it the People's Republic of China.

Mao's victory was an immense shock to Americans. Not only was China under the control of sworn enemies of the United States, but communist regimes controlled about one fourth of the world's landmass and one third of its population. "Who lost China?" Americans asked. Many critics blamed the Truman administration, saying that the United States had failed to give enough support to Jiang. But Secretary of State Dean Acheson argued:

**Communist Victory in China**
Carrying hundreds of pictures of their leader, Mao Zedong, these Chinese communists celebrate the defeat of Jiang Jieshi in 1949.

**Primary Source** "The unfortunate but inescapable fact is that the ominous result of the civil war in China was beyond the control of the government of the United States. Nothing that this country did or could have done within the reasonable limits of its capabilities could have changed the result."
—Secretary of State Dean Acheson, "White Paper on China," August 1949

✔ **Checkpoint** Why were the communists able to win the Chinese Civil War?

# Americans Fight in Korea

The focus of attention turned to the peninsula of Korea, separated from northeast China by the Yalu River. Once controlled by Japan, Korea had been divided into two independent countries by the United States and the Soviet Union after World War II. The dividing line was set at the **38th parallel** of latitude. In North Korea, the Soviets installed a communist government and equipped its armed forces. The United States provided smaller amounts of aid to noncommunist South Korea.

**North Korea Invades South Korea** American occupation troops remained in South Korea until June 1949. Their departure coincided with the communist victory in China. Soon after, North Korea began a major military buildup.

On June 25, 1950, North Korean forces attacked across the 38th parallel. The 90,000 North Korean troops were armed with powerful tanks and other Soviet weapons. Within days, the northerners overtook the South Korean capital city of Seoul and set out after the retreating South Korean army.

**U.S. Forces Defend South Korea** President Truman remembered how the policy of appeasement had failed to check the German aggression that sparked World War II. Determined that history would not repeat itself, he announced that the United States would aid South Korea.

Within days, the UN Security Council unanimously voted to follow Truman's lead, recommending that "the Members of the United Nations furnish such assistance to the Republic of Korea as may be necessary to repel the armed attack and to restore international peace and security in the area." Undoubtedly, the Soviet Union would have used its veto power to block the UN resolution if it had been present for the vote. However, it had been boycotting Security Council sessions because the UN had refused to seat Mao's People's Republic of China.

## WITNESS HISTORY DVD

Watch *A Land Divided: The Korean War* on the **United States Witness History DVD** to explore how Cold War rivalries brought the United States into a deadly armed conflict.

Truman did not ask Congress for a formal declaration of war, as required by the Constitution. However, supported by the UN resolution, Truman ordered American troops who were stationed in Japan to move to South Korea. The soldiers were mainly occupation troops who had not been trained for forced marches in monsoon rains or heavy combat in rice paddies, nor did they have the military equipment needed to stop the invasion. Soon, they joined their South Korean allies in retreating to the southeast corner of the peninsula near the city of Pusan. There, the allies held fast. As fresh supplies and troops arrived from Japan, soldiers from other UN countries joined the American and South Korean forces.

**MacArthur Drives Back the North Koreans** By September 1950, the UN forces were ready to counterattack. General **Douglas MacArthur,** the World War II hero, had a bold plan to drive the invaders from South Korea. He suspected that the rapid advance of North Korean troops had left North Korea with limited supply lines. He decided to strike at this weakness by launching a surprise attack on the port city of Inchon, well behind enemy lines. Because Inchon was such a poor landing site, with swift currents and treacherous tides, MacArthur knew that the enemy would not expect an attack there.

# The Korean War

**Geography** *Interactive*
**For:** Interactive map
**Web Code:** nep-1204

**North Korea Invades**

▲ American GIs advance as South Korean civilians retreat from the North Korean onslaught.

**1**
**June 1950**
North Korea invades South Korea.

**2**
**July 1950**
U.S. and South Korean forces halt their retreat near Pusan.

MacArthur's bold gamble paid off handsomely. On the morning of September 15, 1950, U.S. Marines landed at Inchon and launched an attack into the rear guard of the North Koreans. Communist forces began fleeing for the North Korean border. By October 1950, the North Koreans had been driven north of the 38th parallel.

With the retreat of North Korean forces, U.S. officials had to decide what to do next. Should they declare their UN mandate accomplished and end the war? Or should they send their forces north of the 38th parallel and punish the communists for the invasion? Truman was concerned about the action China would take if the United States carried the war into North Korea. Chinese leaders publicly warned the Americans not to advance near its borders. But MacArthur did not take this warning seriously. He assured Truman that China would not <u>intervene</u> in the war. Based on this advice, the United States pushed a resolution through the UN, calling for a "unified, independent, and democratic" Korea.

**China Forces a Stalemate** Highly confident, MacArthur attacked north of the 38th parallel. Despite mountainous terrain and freezing temperatures, by Thanksgiving the Allied advance had reached the Chinese border at the Yalu River. Then, on November 25, 1950, some 300,000 Chinese soldiers attacked

**Vocabulary Builder**
<u>intervene</u>—(ihn ter VEEN) *v.* to become involved in; to take action to settle a dispute or influence a course of action

**Map Skills** During the Korean War, UN troops supported South Korea, while China backed North Korea. Advantage seesawed between the two sides.
1. **Locate:** (a) 38th parallel, (b) Pusan, (c) Inchon, (d) Yalu River

2. **Movement** Describe the movement of communist troops after November 1950.

3. **Compare** How does the first map differ from the last one?

North Korean control
Communist attack
South Korean control
UN attack
— Line of control
Conic Projection
0          100 mi
0          100 km

**UN Fights Back**   **China Enters the War**   **Stalemate**

**3** Sept. 15, 1950
UN forces land at Inchon and break out of Pusan.

**4** Nov. 24, 1950
MacArthur starts offensive toward Yalu River.

**5** Nov. 25, 1950
Chinese attack. UN and South Korean forces retreat.

**6** Jan. 10, 1951
Communists push UN forces to 37th parallel.

**7** Jan. 16, 1951
UN forces push communists back to 38th parallel.

**8** June 27, 1951
Cease-fire is signed, with border at 38th parallel.

South Korean and U.S. positions. Badly outnumbered, the UN troops were forced back.

With China now in the war, the United States confronted a major land war in Asia. It was possible that this war could not be won without huge commitments of troops and even atomic weapons. Truman steadfastly ruled out both of these options. MacArthur, who favored an invasion of China, was enraged. He distrusted Truman's policy of a **limited war** fought to achieve only specific goals. As a soldier, MacArthur favored total victory.

Unable to sway Truman, the general sent a letter to the House Republican leader attacking the President's policies. After the letter became public, Truman fired MacArthur for insubordination. There was a huge outcry in the United States, and MacArthur returned home a national hero.

✔ **Checkpoint** How did President Truman react to the North Korean invasion of South Korea?

## The Korean War Has Lasting Effects

By the spring of 1951, Allied forces had regrouped and stabilized their position near the 38th parallel. The stalemate lasted until 1953. During that time, the two sides fought small, bloody battles with limited results. At the same time, diplomats tried to devise an acceptable peace agreement.

**The War Becomes a Political Issue** The stalemate was a key issue in the presidential election of 1952. Republican candidate Dwight D. Eisenhower promised that if elected he would end the war. Upon his election, he visited Korea, spoke with the troops, and studied the enemy's fortifications.

**Decision Point**

## Should the United States Invade China?

China's troops advanced, driving U.S. soldiers and marines back into South Korea. General Douglas MacArthur favored a strong response that included an invasion of China. President Truman disagreed. Read the options below. Then, you decide.

**MacArthur Favors Invasion**

**Primary Source**

"I made it clear that if not permitted to destroy the enemy built-up bases north of the Yalu, if not permitted to utilize the friendly Chinese force of some 600,000 men on Formosa [Taiwan], if not permitted to blockade the China coast . . . the position of the command from the military standpoint forbade victory."

—General Douglas MacArthur, April 19, 1951

**Truman Opposes Invasion**

**Primary Source**

"We do not want to see the conflict in Korea extended. We are trying to prevent a world war—not to start one. . . . Why can't we take other steps to punish the aggressor? Why don't we bomb Manchuria and China itself? Why don't we assist Chinese Nationalist troops to land on mainland China? If we were to do these things we would . . . become entangled in a vast conflict on the continent of Asia. . . ."

—President Truman, April 11, 1951

**You Decide**
1. Why did MacArthur want to invade China?
2. Why did Truman oppose invasion?
3. What decision would you have made? Why?

| Korean War's Impact on America | ☑ Quick Study |
|---|---|
| **Immediate Effects** | **Long-Term Effects** |
| • 37,000 Americans killed <br> • 103,000 Americans wounded <br> • Relations with China worsen <br> • Armed forces racially integrated | • Military spending increases <br> • Military commitments increase worldwide <br> • Relations with Japan improve <br> • Future presidents send military into combat without Congressional approval |

**U.S. Troops Remain in Korea**
American soldiers have stayed in Korea since the war. They patrol the border between the Koreas to prevent another North Korean invasion of South Korea.

Eisenhower became convinced that only strong action would break the stalemate. When peace talks threatened to fail, he hinted that he might introduce nuclear weapons into the conflict. That warning, along with the death of Joseph Stalin, convinced the communists to settle the conflict. On July 27, 1953, after slightly more than three years of fighting, the two sides signed a cease-fire. That cease-fire is still in effect today.

**Examining the Lessons of the Korean War** There was no victory in the Korean War. North Korea remained a communist country allied to China and the Soviet Union, and South Korea stayed a noncommunist country allied to the United States and the major democracies. The two Koreas remained divided at about the 38th parallel.

Yet, the war had an important long-term result. Truman had committed U.S. troops to battle without a congressional declaration of war. This set a precedent that future Presidents would follow. The Korean War also led to increased military spending. By 1960, military spending accounted for nearly half of the federal budget. More than a million U.S. soldiers were stationed around the world.

A new alliance underscored U.S. interest in Asia. Like NATO, the **Southeast Asia Treaty Organization (SEATO)** was a defensive alliance aimed at preventing the spread of communism. Its members included Pakistan, Thailand, the Philippines, Australia, New Zealand, France, Britain, and the United States.

✓ **Checkpoint** What were the most important results of U.S. participation in the Korean War?

---

**SECTION**

# 2 Assessment

**Progress Monitoring** *Online*
**For:** Self-test with vocabulary practice
**Web Code:** nea-1205

### Comprehension

1. **Terms and People** What is the relationship between each of the following items and American policy in East Asia?
   • Jiang Jieshi
   • Mao Zedong
   • 38th parallel
   • limited war
   • SEATO

2.  **Reading Skill: Categorize** Use your problem-solution table to answer the Section Focus Question: How did President Truman use the power of the presidency to limit the spread of communism in East Asia?

### Writing About History

3. **Quick Write: Plan an Interview** Suppose that you were going to interview some American veterans of the Korean War. Write five questions that you might ask about their experiences and their views of the war.

### Critical Thinking

4. **Identify Central Issues** Why did American aid to Jiang's Nationalists fail to prevent Mao's communists from taking control of China?

5. **Demonstrate Reasoned Judgment** How did General MacArthur's decision to advance toward the Yalu River change the course of the Korean War?

6. **Identify Central Issues** How did the way in which Truman handled the Korean crisis affect the powers of the presidency?

Nuclear fallout shelter sign ▶

◀ Civil defense poster

### The Threat of War

After the Soviet Union tested an atomic bomb in 1949, President Truman reported to the nation that the nature of war had forever changed:

❝[W]ar has undergone a technological change which makes it a very different thing from what it used to be. War today between the Soviet empire and the free nations might dig the grave not only of our Stalinist opponents, but of our own society. . . . Such a war is not a possible policy for rational men.❞

—President Harry S. Truman

# The Cold War Expands

 **Content Expectations**

- **8.1.2** Evaluate origins, setbacks, successes of U.S. policy of "containing" Soviet Union.
- **8.1.2f** Evaluate the arms race.
- **8.2.3** Compare/contrast Roosevelt's New Deal initiatives, Johnson's Great Society programs, Reagan's market-based domestic policies.

## Terms and People

arms race
mutually assured destruction
John Foster Dulles
massive retaliation
brinkmanship

Nikita Khrushchev
nationalize
Suez crisis
Eisenhower Doctrine
CIA
NASA

## NoteTaking

**Reading Skill: Identify Main Ideas** Identify the tactics used to wage the Cold War.

**Why It Matters** By 1950, the United States and the Soviet Union were the two most powerful nations in the world. The conflicting ideologies and goals of these rival nations led to a worldwide struggle for influence. The policies followed by the two superpowers helped shape the modern history of much of the world, from Latin America to the Middle East. **Section Focus Question: What methods did the United States use in its global struggle against the Soviet Union?**

## The Arms Race Heightens Tensions

A change in the balance of world power is usually gradual, taking place over decades or even centuries. But sometimes, the shift happens in a blink of an eye. Such a major shift in the balance of power in the Cold War took place on September 2, 1949. Instruments in an American B-29 aircraft flying over Alaska detected unusual atmospheric radiation. The radiation cloud was drifting eastward from the direction of Siberia.

American nuclear scientists analyzed the data that the aircraft had gathered. They then reached an inescapable conclusion: The Soviet Union had set off an atomic bomb.

**Communist Advances Shock the Nation** The news shook U.S. leaders. They had believed that the Soviet Union was years away from developing an atomic bomb. Now, the Americans no longer had a monopoly on atomic weaponry.

The news that the Soviets had the bomb was followed the next month by news of the communist takeover of China. In a very short time, Americans sensed that the world was a much more dangerous and threatening place.

**Nuclear Arsenals Expand** Three months later, Truman ordered the Atomic Energy Commission to produce a hydrogen bomb. Developers predicted that the H-Bomb would be 1,000 times as powerful as an atomic bomb. They hoped it would restore the United States advantage over the Soviets.

Some scientists, such as J. Robert Oppenheimer and Albert Einstein, opposed developing the H-Bomb, claiming it would only lead to a <u>perpetual</u> **arms race.** Others argued that Stalin would continue to develop more powerful weapons no matter what the United States did.

**Vocabulary Builder**
<u>perpetual</u>—(per PEHCH oo uhl) *adj.* constant; continuing without interruption

In 1952, the United States tested the first hydrogen bomb. The next year, the Soviets tested one of their own. More bombs and tests followed. Most of these tests were conducted aboveground, spewing radioactive waste into the atmosphere. Atomic testing in the American west, at sites such as the Nevada desert, led to increased atmospheric radiation and long range health problems for people living downwind of the test sites.

During the next four decades, the United States and the Soviet Union developed and stockpiled increasingly powerful nuclear weapons. They armed planes, submarines, and missiles with nuclear warheads powerful enough to destroy each other many times over. Both sides hoped that this program of **mutually assured destruction** would prevent either country from actually using a nuclear device against the other. Still, the threat of nuclear destruction seemed to hang over the world like a dark cloud.

✔ **Checkpoint** Why did the United States government decide to build a hydrogen bomb?

# Eisenhower Introduces New Policies

President Dwight Eisenhower knew firsthand the horrors of war and the need to defend democracy. He had led the World War II Allied invasions of North Africa, Italy, and Normandy. Having worked with top military and political leaders during the war, he was capable of speaking the language of both.

Eisenhower accepted much of Truman's foreign policy. He believed strongly in a policy to actively contain communism. Eisenhower's secretary of state, **John Foster Dulles,** was an experienced diplomat who had helped organize the United Nations after World War II. Dulles endorsed the President's vision of the role the United States should play in the world.

In their approach toward foreign policy, Eisenhower and Dulles differed significantly from Truman and his Secretary of State, Dean Acheson. Both teams of men considered the spread of communism the greatest threat to the free world. But Eisenhower believed that Truman's approach to foreign policy had dragged the United States into an endless series of conflicts begun by the Soviet Union. These limited, regional conflicts threatened to drain the country's resources.

**Eisenhower Favors Massive Retaliation** Eisenhower opposed spending billions of dollars on conventional forces, such as troops, ships, tanks, and artillery. Instead, he focused on stockpiling nuclear weapons and building the planes, missiles, and submarines needed to deliver them. He assumed that if there were a major war, it would be nuclear.

Ike's new policy drew some criticism: Conservatives felt that downgrading conventional forces would weaken American defense, while liberals feared that preparing for nuclear

### The Arms Race

**Nuclear Warhead Proliferation**

| Year | U.S. | USSR | Britain | France | China |
|------|------|------|---------|--------|-------|
| 1945 | 6 | 0 | 0 | 0 | 0 |
| 1950 | 369 | 5 | 0 | 0 | 0 |
| 1955 | 3,057 | 200 | 10 | 0 | 0 |
| 1960 | 20,434 | 1,605 | 30 | 0 | 0 |
| 1965 | 31,642 | 6,129 | 310 | 4 | 1 |

**Chart Skills** The chart above shows effects of the arms race. *How did the Soviet Union's development of nuclear weapons affect U.S. defense spending? How did Eisenhower's policies affect defense spending? Explain.*

SOURCE: *Bulletin of the Atomic Scientists*

war made such a war more likely. Still, Eisenhower's approach did save money by providing a "bigger bang for the buck." In 1953, the defense budget was $50.5 billion; in 1955, it dropped down to $35.8 billion.

In 1954, Dulles announced the policy of **massive retaliation.** The United States would respond to communist threats to its allies by threatening to use crushing, overwhelming force, perhaps even nuclear weapons.

> **Primary Source** "A potential aggressor must know that he cannot always prescribe battle conditions to suit him. . . . The way to deter aggression is for the free community to be willing and able to respond vigorously at places and with means of his choosing."
>
> —John Foster Dulles, 1954

Dulles believed that only by going to the brink of war could the United States protect its allies, discourage communist aggression, and prevent war. "You have to take some chances for peace, just as you must take chances in war," he said in 1956. Dulles's approach became known as **brinkmanship.**

## INFOGRAPHIC

# Domestic Uses Of
# COLD WAR Technology

To give their nations a military advantage, Cold War scientists rushed to invent advanced weaponry, transportation, and communication. Inventions whose origins go back to the Cold War include space travel, satellites, the Internet, and more.

### Military Technology Led to These Inventions

| 1946 | • Microwave oven |
|------|------------------|
| 1946 | • Computer |
| 1948 | • Hang glider |
| 1958 | • Nuclear energy plant |
| 1960 | • Communications satellite |
| 1970s | • Smoke detector |
| 1980s | • Global Positioning System |

▲ **MONSTER COMPUTERS!**
This 1946 computer calculated artillery trajectories and other military computations. Unlike today's laptop, it filled an entire room, required extensive wiring, and weighed about 30 tons.

▲ **5-FOOT-TALL MICROWAVE!**
In 1946, a scientist working on radar-related military research noticed that the candy bar in his pocket had melted. Knowing a good thing when he saw it, he eventually invented the "Radarange." The early model above was about 5 feet tall.

### Connect to Your World
How did military technology indirectly affect the way of life in American homes?

**Stalin's Death Eases Tensions** On March 5, 1953, Joseph Stalin died, setting off a short power struggle. **Nikita Khrushchev** soon emerged as the new head of the Soviet Union. Although a communist and a determined opponent of the United States, Khrushchev was not as suspicious or as cruel as Stalin. He condemned the excesses of the Stalin regime and inched toward more peaceful relations with the democratic West.

In July 1955, Khrushchev met with Eisenhower at a conference in Geneva, Switzerland. Although the meeting yielded few significant results, it did seem to be a small move toward "peaceful co-existence" of the two powers.

✓ **Checkpoint** How was Eisenhower's approach to foreign affairs different from that of Truman?

## The Cold War Goes Global

Peaceful co-existence was easier to imagine than it was to practice. The United States and the Soviet Union remained deeply divided. The Soviet Union would not allow free elections in the areas it controlled, and it continued to attempt to spread communism around the world. Dulles talked about "rolling back" communism and liberating the countries under Soviet rule.

**Unrest Explodes Behind the Iron Curtain** American talk of "rolling back" communist borders and Khrushchev's talk of "peaceful co-existence" were taken seriously by people in Soviet-dominated countries behind the iron curtain. People in Poland, Hungary, and Czechoslovakia resented the control exerted by the Soviet Union. Many hungered for more political and economic freedom.

In 1956, two uprisings shook Eastern Europe. First, workers in Poland rioted against Soviet rule and won greater control of their government. Since the Polish government did not attempt to leave the Warsaw Pact, Soviet leaders permitted the actions.

Then, encouraged by Khrushchev's words and Poland's example, Hungarian students and workers organized huge demonstrations. They demanded that pro-Soviet Hungarian officials be replaced, that Soviet troops be withdrawn, and that noncommunist political parties be organized. Khrushchev responded brutally, sending Soviet soldiers and tanks to crush the Hungarian revolution. The Soviets executed many of the revolution's leaders, killed hundreds of other Hungarians, and restored hard-line communists to power.

Americans could only watch these events in horror. Eisenhower's massive retaliation approach was powerless. The United States would not use nuclear weapons—or any other weapons—to guarantee Hungarian independence from the Soviet Union.

The Hungarian revolt added a new level of hostility to international relations. At the 1956 Olympic Games, held that November in Melbourne, Australia, the bitter feelings surfaced. A water-polo match between the Soviet Union and Hungary turned violent. Sportswriters called it the "blood in the water" match.

**The U.S. Defuses the Suez Crisis** The United States found itself involved in another world conflict, this time in the Middle East. As Cold War tensions increased, Egypt's president Gamal Abdel Nasser tried to use the U.S.–Soviet rivalry to his advantage.

Nasser wanted to construct a dam on the Nile River at Aswan. The United States and Britain initially offered to fund the project, but when Nasser recognized the People's Republic of China and

**Revolt in Hungary**
Americans admired the brave men and women who sacrificed their lives fighting against Soviet domination in Hungary. *Time* magazine even chose the Hungarian Freedom Fighter as its "Man of the Year" for 1956.

opened talks with the Soviet Union, the Eisenhower administration withdrew its offer. In response, Nasser **nationalized** the Suez Canal, placing it under government control. The canal, which connects the Mediterranean Sea with the Red Sea, had originally been managed by a British-French company and was protected by British armed forces.

Nasser's action threatened the flow of Middle Eastern oil to Europe. Without consulting with Eisenhower, Britain and France plotted to get the canal back into Western hands. They joined forces with Israel, a young nation that had long suffered from raids along its border with Egypt. Britain and France used the **Suez crisis** as an excuse to seize control of the Suez Canal.

President Eisenhower was outraged by these actions. Rather than support his Western allies, Ike criticized them and refused to supply them with U.S. oil. The three nations had counted on Eisenhower's support, and when it did not come, they were forced to withdraw their troops from Egypt.

**Eisenhower Promises Strong Action** In response to Soviet influence in the Middle East and elsewhere, the President made a statement in January 1957 that became known as the **Eisenhower Doctrine**. Eisenhower announced that the United States would use force to help any Middle Eastern nation threatened by communism. Eisenhower used his doctrine in 1958 to justify

**Geography** *Interactive*
For: Interactive map
Web Code: nep-1206

## Global Cold War, 1946–1956

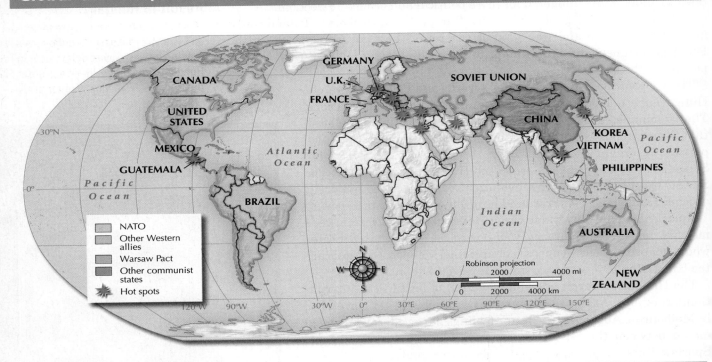

**Map Skills** The Cold War spread globally as the United States and the Soviet Union formed alliances and competed for power around the world. NATO and the Warsaw Pact were the two strongest alliances.

1. **Region** Identify a region where there were many Cold War hot spots. Why do you think there were so many conflicts in that region?

2. **Compare** How was Latin America important to the United States in the same way that Eastern Europe was important to the Soviet Union?

sending troops to Lebanon to put down a revolt against its pro-American government.

The Eisenhower administration also used the **Central Intelligence Agency (CIA)** in its struggle against communism. Congress had created the CIA in 1947 as an intelligence-gathering organization. Eisenhower gave it a new task. He approved covert, or secret, CIA operations to protect American interests. In 1953, the CIA aided a coup that installed a new government in Iran. In 1954, it accomplished a similar mission in Guatemala. While both operations helped to place anticommunist leaders in power, they also created long-term resentment against the United States.

**The Cold War Blasts Off Into Space** Although the United States successfully contained the spread of communism on the ground, it did suffer a setback in outer space. On October 4, 1957, the Soviet Union launched a 184-pound steel ball containing a small transmitter into an orbit of Earth. The Soviets named the tiny satellite *Sputnik 1*. The following month they launched a much larger satellite. It carried a dog, named Laika, to see how a living creature would react to life in outer space. Since there was no way to return the satellite to Earth, Laika died in orbit.

**Russians Succeed in Space**
The dog Laika, aboard *Sputnik 2*, was the first living creature to orbit Earth. He was hailed as a Soviet hero.

The launches shocked many Americans, who had long believed that superior technology would keep the United States ahead of the Soviet Union. Would Soviet space technology give them the rocket power to launch missiles onto American cities?

In a state of crisis, Congress quickly approved the National Defense Education Act, a $1 billion program intended to produce more scientists and teachers of science. The act authorized money for loans to enable high school and college graduates to continue their education in science. In addition, Congress created the **National Aeronautics and Space Administration (NASA)** to coordinate the space-related efforts of American scientists and the military.

 **Checkpoint** How did the Hungarian and Suez crises of 1956 raise Cold War tensions?

---

**Progress Monitoring** *Online*
**For:** Self-test with vocabulary practice
**Web Code:** nea-1207

## Comprehension

1. **Terms** For each term below, write a sentence explaining its importance to the United States during the Cold War.
   - arms race
   - mutually assured destruction
   - massive retaliation
   - brinkmanship
   - Eisenhower Doctrine

2. **NoteTaking Reading Skill: Identify Main Ideas** Use your completed charts to answer the Section Focus Question: What methods did the United States use in its global struggle against the Soviet Union?

## Writing About History

3. **Quick Write: Identify Sources** Identify two sources you might use to find answers to research questions about the arms race. One source should be a book from your school or public library. The other should be a reliable site on the Internet.

## Critical Thinking

4. **Identify Point of View** Do you think that the massive retaliation policy favored by John Foster Dulles successfully deterred the Soviet Union? Explain your answer.

5. **Contrast** How were the covert operations of the CIA in Guatemala and Iran different from the military operations of the United States Army in Korea?

6. **Demonstrate Reasoned Judgment** Were Americans justified in being alarmed when the Soviets launched *Sputnik 1*? Explain.

# EXPERIENCE THE COLD WAR

Fathers built bomb shelters in backyards, mothers stocked survival kits in basements, and children practiced ducking under their school desks. Across the nation, Americans prepared for the possibility that the Soviet Union might launch nuclear weapons against American cities. This was all part of the civil defense system of the early Cold War.

Throughout the 1950s and early 1960s, the civil defense system shaped American attitudes about their country and the Cold War. As the Cold War ended, civil defense became less important. But since 2001 and the rise of terrorism, it reemerged in a new form known as homeland security.

▼ **Stay Tuned!**
Emergency information would be broadcast on AM radio stations.

▲ **Evacuate!**
In 1955, wailing sirens signaled a simulated nuclear attack and sent New Yorkers scurrying into underground fallout shelters. Similar drills took place across the nation.

**Duck and Cover!** ▶
Schoolchildren were taught to "duck and cover" under their desks during nuclear air-raid drills.

ATTEND A HOME PREPAREDNESS WORKSHOP

Earn this award

this HOME is prepared

FOR SURVIVAL YOU WILL NEED

food and water ..enough for at least 14 days

first aid and home care of the sick ..when there is no trained medical help

sanitation ..safeguard your family's health

firefighting and rescue ..self-reliance for safety

Conelrad, utilities ..a guide to family action

receive this CITATION

by acquiring FAMILY FALLOUT SHELTER and completing the READINESS REQUIREMENTS

Kidde Kokoon

CANNED FOOD

CANNED WATER

**▲ Be Prepared!**
The Civil Defense Administration taught Americans how to survive a nuclear attack.

**◄ Take Shelter!**
Homeowners built backyard bomb shelters stocked with radiation suits and medical kits.

DO YOU QUALIFY AS A RADEF VOLUNTEER?

IF YOU DO, YOU MAY BECOME A NUCLEAR AGE MINUTEMAN

**◄ Volunteer!**
Citizens monitored the skies for enemy planes, stocked air-raid shelters, and maintained emergency equipment.

## Thinking Critically

1. **Analyze Visuals** How did civil defense literature appeal to Americans' sense of duty and citizenship?

2. **Draw Conclusions** Do you think the civil defense program made Americans feel safer or more fearful? Explain.

**Connect to Today** Do research to learn about today's homeland security system. How are the methods and goals of this system similar to and different from the civil defense system of the 1950s?

**History *Interactive* ✶**

**For:** To discover more about the Cold War
**Web Code:** nep-1208

IS THIS TOMORROW

AMERICA UNDER COMMUNISM!

▲ Anticommunist comic

WITNESS HISTORY  AUDIO

## Battling the Communist Menace

In the 1950s, Americans were alarmed by charges that communists had infiltrated their government and other institutions. Cold War themes made their way into movies, television shows, and novels. Even comic-book heroes like Superman battled the communist menace. In a 1952 comic book, a character states the concerns of many Americans:

❝Today's headlines shout of battles with Communist hordes in Korea—of Red riots in Rome and Paris and Berlin! But there's another secret battle taking place—right here, right now! A [secret] underground fight between Communism and democracy for the youth of America.❞

— "Backyard Battleground," in
*Daring Confessions*, 1953

# The Cold War at Home

 **Content Expectations**

- **8.1.1c** Analyze actions in last years of/years following WWII.
- **8.2.2a** Describe issues challenging Americans.
- **8.2.2b** Evaluate policy decisions/legislative actions to meet challenges.

## Terms and People

Red Scare
Smith Act
HUAC
Hollywood Ten
blacklist

Alger Hiss
Julius and Ethel
  Rosenberg
Joseph R. McCarthy
McCarthyism

## NoteTaking

**Reading Skill: Identify Causes and Effects**
List efforts taken to protect Americans from communism and how these policies affected rights.

| Anticommunist Policy | Effect on Rights |
| --- | --- |
|  |  |
|  |  |

**Why It Matters** Americans have often faced the difficult task of balancing the need to provide national security with the need to protect people's rights and freedoms. In times of crisis, rights have sometimes been limited. Beginning in the late 1940s, the Cold War dominated American life. For some of those years, the nation was in the grip of a new Red Scare. The hunt for communists netted some spies, but it also disrupted the lives of thousands of innocent Americans. **Section Focus Question: How did fear of domestic communism affect American society during the Cold War?**

## Worrying About Communists at Home

The Cold War influenced many aspects of American life. American soldiers fought and died in Korea. Industries hummed with activity, turning out weapons and supplies. Americans read newspaper articles about who "lost" China or who was winning the "space race." Popular culture reflected an us-versus-them attitude—democrats versus totalitarians, capitalists versus communists, the West versus the East. In the end, the Cold War was turning out to be every bit as global and as encompassing as World War II had been.

**Truman Roots Out Communists** The fear that communists both outside and inside America were working to destroy American life created a reaction known as a **Red Scare.** This fear was not unique to the late 1940s and 1950s. The 1917 Russian Revolution and the communists' call for worldwide revolution had led to a similar Red Scare in 1919 and 1920. However, the Red Scare that followed World War II went deeper and wider—and lasted far longer—than the earlier Red Scare. Truman's Attorney General, J. Howard McGrath, expressed the widespread fear of communist influence when he warned that communists "are everywhere—in factories, offices, butcher stores, on street corners, and private businesses. And each carries in himself the death of our society."

The spread of communism into Eastern Europe and Asia raised concerns that American communists, some in influential government positions, were working for the enemy. In truth, some American communists were agents of the Soviet Union, and a handful of them held high-ranking positions in government. However, overwhelmingly, government officials were loyal to the United States.

Recognizing public concern about domestic communism, President Truman created a Federal Employee Loyalty Program in March 1947. The order permitted the FBI and other government security agencies to screen federal employees for signs of political disloyalty. About 3,000 federal employees either were dismissed or resigned after the investigation. The order also empowered the Attorney General to compile a list of "totalitarian, fascist, or subversive organizations" in the United States. Americans who belonged to or supported organizations on the Attorney General's list were singled out for more intense scrutiny. Many were labeled "security risks" and dismissed from their jobs.

The Truman administration also used the 1940 **Smith Act** to cripple the Communist Party in the United States. This act made it unlawful to teach or advocate the violent overthrow of the U.S. government. In 1949, a New York jury found 11 communists guilty of violating the Smith Act and sent them to prison.

**Congress Hunts Communists** Congress joined in the search for communists. In 1938, the House of Representatives had created the **House Un-American Activities Committee (HUAC)** to investigate possible subversive activities by fascists, Nazis, or communists. After the war, the committee conducted several highly publicized hearings on communist activities in the United States. HUAC investigators probed the government, armed forces, unions, education, science, newspapers, and other aspects of American life.

The best-known HUAC hearings targeted the movie industry in 1947. The HUAC investigations uncovered people who were, or had been, communists during the 1930s and 1940s. A group of left-wing writers, directors, and producers known as the **Hollywood Ten** refused to answer questions, asserting their Fifth Amendment rights against self-incrimination. The hearings turned into a war of attacks and counterattacks as committee members and witnesses yelled at each other and pointed accusatory fingers.

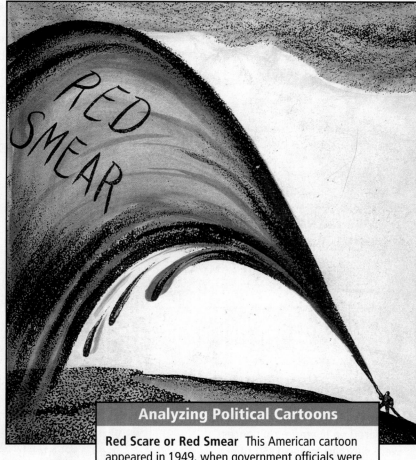

RED SMEAR

### Analyzing Political Cartoons

**Red Scare or Red Smear** This American cartoon appeared in 1949, when government officials were prosecuting communists and others for subversive activities.

1. What is the cartoonist's attitude toward the attempt to uncover communists?
2. How do you think President Truman might have responded to this cartoon?

After the hearings, the Hollywood Ten were cited for contempt of Congress and were tried, convicted, and sent to prison. Movie executives circulated a **blacklist** of entertainment figures who should not be hired because of their suspected communist ties. The careers of those on the list were shattered. Not until the case of *Watkins* v. *United States* (1957) did the Supreme Court decide that witnesses before HUAC could not be forced to name radicals they knew.

The HUAC investigation had a powerful impact on filmmaking. In the past, Hollywood had been willing to make movies about controversial subjects such as racism and anti-Semitism. Now, most producers concentrated only on entertainment and avoided addressing sensitive social issues.

**Freedom of Speech Takes a Hit** The case of the Hollywood Ten demonstrated that in the mood of fear created by Soviet aggression, freedom of speech was not guaranteed. Americans lost their jobs because they had belonged to or contributed to an organization on the Attorney General's list. Others were fired for associating with people who were known communists or for making remarks that were considered disloyal. Teachers and librarians, mail carriers and longshoremen, electricians and construction workers—people from all walks of life—might be accused and dismissed from their jobs.

The effort to root out communist influence from American life cut across many levels of society. Communists were exposed and blacklisted in the country's <u>academic</u> institutions, labor unions, scientific laboratories, and city halls.

**Government Investigates Oppenheimer** The case of J. Robert Oppenheimer illustrates the difficulty of distinguishing loyalty from disloyalty. During World War II, Oppenheimer had led the Manhattan Project, which developed the atomic bomb. After the war, he became chairman of the General Advisory Committee of the U.S. Atomic Energy Commission (AEC). However, Oppenheimer

**Vocabulary Builder**
<u>academic</u>–(ak uh DEHM ihk) *adj.* related to education

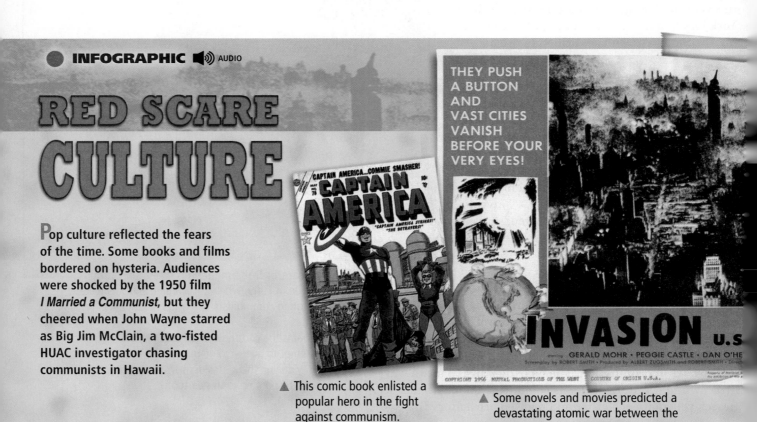

# INFOGRAPHIC ◀)) AUDIO

# RED SCARE CULTURE

Pop culture reflected the fears of the time. Some books and films bordered on hysteria. Audiences were shocked by the 1950 film *I Married a Communist,* but they cheered when John Wayne starred as Big Jim McClain, a two-fisted HUAC investigator chasing communists in Hawaii.

THEY PUSH A BUTTON AND VAST CITIES VANISH BEFORE YOUR VERY EYES!

INVASION U.S.

▲ This comic book enlisted a popular hero in the fight against communism.

▲ Some novels and movies predicted a devastating atomic war between the United States and the Soviet Union.

had ties to people who belonged to the Communist Party, including his wife and brother.

In 1954, the AEC denied Oppenheimer access to classified information. Although the AEC had no evidence that Oppenheimer himself had ever been disloyal to the United States, it questioned whether his communist ties disqualified him from holding this position.

✓ **Checkpoint** What steps did Truman and Congress take to investigate communist influence in the United States?

## Spy Cases Worry Americans

Two sensational spy trials drew the nation's attention to the threat posed by communist agents working to subvert the United States. The accused in the two cases could not have been more different. **Alger Hiss** had been educated at Johns Hopkins University and Harvard Law School. **Julius and Ethel Rosenberg** were from the poor, lower east side of Manhattan. Although Hiss and the Rosenbergs never met, their crimes and their trials have linked them in the public's imagination.

**Whittaker Chambers Accuses Alger Hiss** Until 1948, Alger Hiss's career seemed flawless. A seemingly dedicated government servant, Hiss had worked on several important New Deal agencies and helped to organize the United Nations. But a man named Whittaker Chambers disrupted Hiss's image.

As a young man, Chambers had become a communist espionage agent. But Chambers later turned against communism because of the brutality of Stalin's rule. Chambers began writing compellingly about the evils of communism. In 1948, he testified before HUAC about his

## NoteTaking

**Reading Skill: Compare and Contrast** As you read, identify similarities and differences between the Hiss case and the Rosenberg case. Consider both the facts and the impact of the two spy cases.

**Alger Hiss**
• Accused of stealing government documents

**Rosenbergs**
• Accused of passing on atomic secrets

THE SATURDAY EVENING POST SERIAL THAT JOLTED MILLIONS!

I WAS A COMMUNIST FOR THE F.B.I. FRANK LOVEJOY

◀ *I Was a Communist for the F.B.I.* thrilled movie-goers in 1951.

In this science-fiction classic, aliens invade Earth and take over people's minds. Many viewed this as a warning about communist influence. ▶

WALTER WANGER CREATES THE ULTIMATE IN SCIENCE-FICTION

INVASION OF THE BODY SNATCHERS

KEVIN McCARTHY · DANA WYNTER

SUPERSCOPE

## Thinking Critically
1. **Draw Conclusions** Do you think the investigations of the HUAC influenced the nature of pop culture? Explain.

2. **Recognize Cause and Effect** Do you think the culture of the 1950s made Americans feel safe? Explain.

# Civil Liberties and National Security

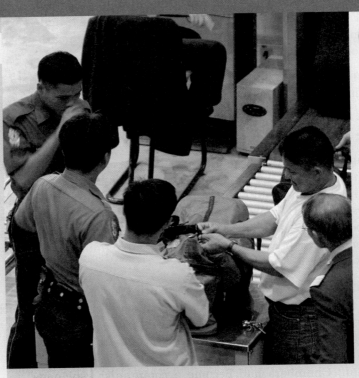

MI 8.1.2a

## TRACK THE ISSUE

### What is the proper balance between national security and civil liberties?

The Constitution guarantees rights and freedoms to all American citizens. But during war and other crises, government leaders have limited such civil liberties in order to protect citizens' lives. Should they? Use the timeline below to explore this enduring issue.

**1790s Undeclared War With France**
Alien Act allows President to imprison or deport resident aliens. Sedition Act limits freedoms of speech and press.

**1860s Civil War**
Lincoln suspends the right of habeas corpus.

**1940s World War II**
Government sends more than 100,000 Japanese Americans into internment camps.

**1950s Cold War**
Anticommunist investigations violate some people's rights.

**2001 War on Terrorism**
Patriot Act helps catch terrorists but may reduce privacy rights.

The World Trade Center towers in New York City burn after the September 11, 2001, terrorist attacks.

A traveler has his baggage searched at an airport security checkpoint.

## DEBATE THE ISSUE

**Terrorism and the Patriot Act**  After the devastating terrorist attacks of September 11, 2001, the United States declared a "War on Terrorism." Congress passed the Patriot Act to help law enforcement agencies prevent future terrorist attacks. The Act was to expire in 2005. In spite of controversy regarding it, Congress voted to extend the provisions of the Patriot Act to 2009.

"I have a lot of problems with the Patriot Act. . . . It gives the government the ability to spy on its citizens and on foreign nationals without probable cause of a crime, to get wiretaps and warrants. It gives them the ability to get records from libraries and bookstores on people who are not targets of any criminal investigation."

—David Cole, professor, Center for Constitutional Rights

"Right after 9-11, the President turned to the Attorney General and said very simply, "John, you make sure this does not happen again." Preventing another catastrophic attack on the American homeland would have been extremely difficult if not impossibly so without the tools that Congress provided in the USA Patriot Act."

—Viet Dinh, Assistant U.S. Attorney General

### ? TRANSFER Activities

1. **Compare**  Why does Professor Cole oppose the Patriot Act? Why does the Assistant Attorney General support it?

2. **Analyze**  Which of the two people above would have been more likely to oppose the work of HUAC during the Cold War? Why?

3. **Transfer**  Use the following Web site to see a video, try a WebQuest, and write in your journal. **Web Code:** neh-8502

communist past and named Alger Hiss as one of his contacts in the federal government.

Hiss soon appeared before HUAC. He denied that he was a communist and an espionage agent, and he denied that he even knew Whittaker Chambers. But Richard Nixon, a young member of Congress from California, convinced the other committee members to press the case. Slowly, Hiss's story began to unravel. Chambers proved that he did know Hiss and that Hiss had given him confidential government documents. Chambers had even kept a microfilm copy of some of those documents, storing them in a hollowed-out pumpkin on his Maryland farm.

Hiss was tried for perjury. The first trial ended in a hung jury. At his second trial, he was found guilty and sentenced to five years in prison. Even after his conviction, many Americans continued to believe that Hiss was innocent. However, as years passed, the evidence grew overwhelmingly against him. The fact that someone as influential as Hiss was a communist agent raised serious concerns. The Hiss case had another unexpected effect. The congressional hearings thrust Richard Nixon into the national spotlight. In 1952, he was named Eisenhower's running mate and would later become President.

0068310   ROSENBERG EXECUTION, 1953.
Credit: The Granger Collection, New York

**Rosenbergs Executed**
Julius and Ethel Rosenberg were executed after being found guilty of spying for the Soviet Union.

**The Rosenbergs Are Executed** Nothing created more concern about internal security than the charge that some Americans had helped the Soviets build an atomic bomb. The case began when a scientist named Klaus Fuchs was charged with sending atomic secrets to the Soviet Union. The investigation against Fuchs ultimately led to the arrest of Ethel and Julius Rosenberg in 1950. The Rosenbergs were charged with conspiring to pass secret information about nuclear science to Soviet agents.

The trial of the Rosenbergs generated intense controversy in America and around the world. The case against them was based largely on the word of one confessed spy. Pleading innocent, the Rosenbergs claimed that they were being persecuted for being Jewish and for holding unpopular beliefs. In the end, both were found guilty and sentenced to death. Many believed that the harsh sentence was intended as a lever to force them to identify other members of the alleged spy ring. But the Rosenbergs claimed they had no such information.

After 26 months on death row, the Rosenbergs were electrocuted in 1953. Years of debate followed the executions. Some believe that anti-Semitic sentiment did influence the outcome. In the 1990s, tangible evidence emerged indicating that Julius Rosenberg was guilty. Ethel Rosenberg appears to have played only a minor role in the espionage. Many people continue to believe that the death penalty was too severe for the little involvement she may have had.

**Vocabulary Builder**
tangible—(TAN juh buhl) adj.
solid; definite; capable of being felt or understood

✔ **Checkpoint** Why did the Rosenberg case attract nationwide attention and controversy?

# McCarthy Uses Ruthless Tactics

The early Cold War years saw one ominous event after another. The fall of China, Soviet nuclear bombs, and the exposure of Soviet agents in the United States all undermined American confidence. At that time, as Americans worried about the nation's security, a clever and unscrupulous man began to take advantage of this sense of fear and helplessness. He suggested that these setbacks were really caused by the work of traitors inside the United States.

**McCarthy Makes Accusations** In February 1950, a little-known senator from Wisconsin made a speech in Wheeling, West Virginia. The senator, **Joseph R. McCarthy,** charged that the State Department was infested with communist agents. He waved a piece of paper, which, he said, contained the names of State Department employees who were secretly communists.

> **Primary Source** "The reason why we find ourselves in a position of [weakness] is not because the enemy has sent men to invade our shores, but rather because of the traitorous actions of those who have had all the benefits that the wealthiest nation on earth has had to offer—the finest homes, the finest college educations, and the finest jobs in Government we can give. . . . I have here in my hand a list of 205 [individuals] that were known to the Secretary of State as being members of the Communist Party and who nevertheless are still working and shaping the policy of the State Department."
>
> —Joseph McCarthy, February 9, 1950

The charge provoked a furor. When challenged to give specific names, McCarthy said he had meant that there were "205 bad security risks" in the department. Then, he claimed that 57 employees were communists. Over the next months, the numbers on his list changed. McCarthy never did produce the list of communists. Still, with the outbreak of the Korean War in June 1950, McCarthy's accusations grabbed the attention of the American public.

At the time of the above speech, McCarthy was finishing his first term in the Senate. He had accomplished very little in that term and was looking for a popular issue on which to focus his 1952 reelection campaign. Anticommunism seemed to be just the issue. McCarthy was easily reelected to a second term.

**McCarthy's Power Increases** In the following four years, McCarthy put forward his own brand of anticommunism—so much so that the term **McCarthyism** became a catchword for extreme, reckless charges. By making irresponsible allegations, McCarthy did more to discredit legitimate concerns about domestic communism than any other single American.

Between 1950 and 1954, McCarthy was perhaps the most powerful politician in the United States. Piling baseless accusations on top of charges that could not be proved, McCarthy became chairman of an investigations subcommittee. Merely being accused by McCarthy caused people to lose their jobs and destroyed their reputations. He attacked ruthlessly. When caught in a lie, he told another. When one case faded, he introduced a new one.

Confident because of his increasing power, McCarthy took on larger targets. He attacked former Secretary of State George Marshall, a national hero and author of the Marshall Plan. Even other senators came to fear McCarthy. They worried that he would brand them as communist sympathizers.

**McCarthy Falls From Power** In 1954, McCarthy went after the United States Army, claiming that it, too, was full of communists. Army leaders responded that McCarthy's attacks were personally motivated.

## HISTORY MAKERS

### Margaret Chase Smith (1897–1995)
In 1950, Margaret Chase Smith of Maine was the only woman in the U.S. Senate. Like McCarthy, Smith was a Republican, but she strongly opposed her colleague's tactics. In June 1950, she spoke out, delivering what she called her "Declaration of Conscience" on the Senate floor. "Those of us who shout the loudest about Americanism in making character assassinations," she said, "are all too frequently those who . . . ignore some of the basic principles of Americanism: the right to criticize, the right to hold unpopular beliefs, the right to protest."

Her stand against McCarthyism won Smith nationwide attention. In 1964, she ran for president— the first woman nominated for that office at the convention of a major party. She finally retired in 1972 after 32 years in the Senate.

**McCarthy Accuses**
Day after day, from April to June 1954, Americans watched the Army-McCarthy hearings on TV. Here, the senator displays a piece of evidence. *How can TV coverage influence government and court proceedings?*

Finally, the Senate decided to hold televised hearings to sort out the allegations. For weeks, Americans were riveted to their television sets. Most were horrified by McCarthy's bullying tactics. For the first time, the public saw McCarthy badger witnesses, twist the truth, and snicker at the suffering of others. It was an upsetting sight for many Americans.

By the time the hearings ended in mid-June, the senator had lost many of his strongest supporters. The Senate formally censured, or condemned, him for his reckless accusations. Although McCarthy continued to serve in the Senate, he had lost virtually all of his power and influence.

The end of the Korean War in 1953 and McCarthy's downfall in 1954 signaled the decline of the Red Scare. The nation had been damaged by the suppression of free speech and by the lack of open, honest debate. However, Americans had come to realize how important their democratic institutions were and how critical it was to preserve them.

✓ **Checkpoint** What events led to Senator McCarthy being censured by the U.S. Senate?

---

**SECTION 4 Assessment**

**Progress Monitoring *Online***
For: Self-test with vocabulary practice
Web Code: nea-1209

### Comprehension

1. **Terms and People** For each of the following items, write a sentence explaining its significance.
   - HUAC
   - blacklist
   - Alger Hiss
   - Julius and Ethel Rosenberg
   - McCarthyism

2.  **NoteTaking Reading Skill: Identify Causes and Effects** How did fear of domestic communism affect American society during the Cold War?

### Writing About History

3. **Quick Write: Plan Research** Choose one specific topic from this section as the basis for a possible research paper. Write a paragraph describing how you would begin doing research on this topic. Identify one question you would like to answer. Then, describe how you would try to find the information. Be specific about the steps you would take in your research.

### Critical Thinking

4. **Identify Central Issues** Were Americans correct in worrying that domestic communists endangered their security?

5. **Draw Conclusions** How effective was McCarthy's campaign against communists in government?

6. **Identify Points of View** How do movies reflect the values of a society?

# Quick Study Guide

 8.1.1c

**Progress Monitoring *Online***
**For:** Self-test with vocabulary practice
**Web Code:** nea-1210

## ■ Early Cold War Flashpoints

| Flashpoint | Action and Reaction |
|---|---|
| Poland | • U.S. urges democratic elections.<br>• USSR installs communist government. |
| Turkey | • USSR demands territory from Turkey and communist rebels threaten Greece.<br>• U.S. approves Truman doctrine to aid Turkey, Greece, and other states resisting communism. |
| Berlin | • USSR blockades West Berlin.<br>• U.S., Britain, and France airlift supplies to the city. |
| Korea | • North Korea invades South Korea.<br>• U.S. and UN enter war on South Korean side.<br>• China enters war on North Korean side. |
| Europe | • U.S. forms NATO for mutual defense.<br>• USSR forms Warsaw Pact for mutual defense. |

## ■ Cold War at Home

Loyalty Review Board
Smith Act
Hollywood blacklists
**Cold War at Home**
Oppenheimer case
Senator McCarthy
Spy cases

## ■ Divided Europe

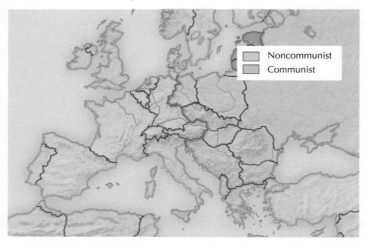

Noncommunist
Communist

## ■ Cold War Alliances, 1955

| NATO | | Warsaw Pact |
|---|---|---|
| Belgium | Netherlands | Albania |
| Canada | Norway | Bulgaria |
| Denmark | Portugal | Czechoslovakia |
| France | Turkey | East Germany |
| Greece | United Kingdom | Hungary |
| Iceland | United States | Poland |
| Italy | West Germany | Romania |
| Luxembourg | | Soviet Union |

## ✓ Quick Study Timeline

**1947**
**Truman proposes the Truman Doctrine to fight communism**

**1948**
**Marshall Plan brings relief to Europe**

**1949**
**United States joins NATO**

### In America

| Presidential Terms | Harry S. Truman 1945–1953 |
|---|---|

**1945** **1947** **1949**

### Around the World

**1945**
**United Nations is established**

**1948**
**State of Israel is established**

**1949**
**China becomes a communist nation**

**Soviet Union tests an atomic bomb**

# American Issues
●—●—●—● **Connector**

By connecting prior knowledge with what you have learned in this chapter, you can gradually build your understanding of enduring questions that still affect America today. Answer the questions below. Then, use your American Issues Connector study guide (or go online: www.PHSchool.com **Web Code:** neh-8503).

## Issues You Learned About

● **Civil Liberties and National Security** From the beginning of the American republic, Americans have debated to what extent individual freedom should be limited when the safety of the nation is at stake.

1. How does the Bill of Rights guarantee the rights of people accused of crimes?

2. During the Civil War, what action did President Lincoln take that limited these guaranteed rights? Why?

3. During the Cold War, what effect did the actions of HUAC and Senator McCarthy have on individual rights?

● **Balance of Power in Government** The balance of power in American government changes over time.

4. According to the Constitution, which branch of government has the power to declare war?

5. How did U.S. soldiers fight in Korea without a declaration of war?

6. How did Truman's actions affect the balance of power between the executive and legislative branches of the government?

● **America Goes to War** During times of conflict, Americans debate whether U.S. entry into war is justified.

7. What were arguments in favor of the United States going to war against North Korea?

8. What were arguments against U.S. entry into the Korean War?

| **Connect to Your World** | **Michigan** |
| --- | --- |

**Technology and Society** During the early days of the Cold War, Michiganians began a massive construction project to build a bridge over the Mackinac Straits, which separate Michigan's Upper and Lower Peninsulas. Until 1957, people used boats to cross the Straits to get to their jobs and homes. However, waiting lines to get on the ferries could last for hours. Although people advocated for a bridge as early as 1884, construction of the Mackinac Bridge did not begin until seventy years later. It took 2,500 workers three years and 71,000 tons of steel to build the five-mile-long bridge. By 1998, 100 million vehicles had traveled across the Mackinac Bridge. Today it is vital to the movement of workers and products, including timber and other forest products. Discuss with a partner the impact you think the Mackinac Bridge has had on Michigan's economy.

| 1950 | 1954 | 1957 |
| --- | --- | --- |
| **Senator McCarthy starts an anticommunist campaign** | **Senate censures McCarthy** | **Eisenhower Doctrine combats Soviet influence in the Middle East** |

Dwight D. Eisenhower 1953–1961

| **1951** | **1953** | **1955** |
| --- | --- | --- |

| 1950 | 1954 | 1956 |
| --- | --- | --- |
| **United States and China clash in Korea** | **CIA helps overthrow Guatemala's government** | **Soviets crush the Hungarian uprising** |

**History** *Interactive*
**For:** Interactive timeline
**Web Code:** nep-1212

429

# Chapter Assessment

## Terms and People

1. Define **satellite state**. Why did the Soviets want satellite states?

2. Define the **Truman Doctrine**. How was it implemented in Berlin?

3. Who were **Jiang** and **Mao**? What role did the United States play in their conflict?

4. Define **arms race**. How did the nuclear arms race promote the Red Scare in the United States?

5. What was the **HUAC**? How did its tactics help lead to McCarthyism?

## Focus Questions

The focus question for this chapter is **What were the causes, main events, and effects of the early Cold War?** Build an answer to this big question by answering the focus questions for Sections 1 through 4 and the Critical Thinking questions that follow.

**Section 1**
6. How did U.S. leaders respond to the threat of Soviet expansion in Europe?

**Section 2**
7. How did President Truman use the power of the presidency to limit the spread of communism in East Asia?

**Section 3**
8. What methods did the United States use in its global struggle against the Soviet Union?

**Section 4**
9. How did fear of domestic communism affect American society during the Cold War?

## Critical Thinking

10. **Explain Causes** What were the causes of the Cold War?

11. **Problem Solving** What problem did the Marshall Plan help solve?

12. **Compare and Contrast** How were Soviet activities in Berlin and Hungary similar? How were they different?

13. **Decision Making** Identify two key decisions made by President Truman regarding the Korean War. Explain the reasons that Truman had for his decisions. Explain the significant effects of each decision.

14. **Analyzing Tables** The table below shows Korean war casualties. Did communists or non-communists suffer more casualties? What are some possible reasons for the difference between communist and noncommunist losses?

| Country or Organization | Total Killed and Wounded |
|---|---|
| China | 900,000 |
| South Korea | 843,572 |
| North Korea | 520,000 |
| United States | 157,530 |
| United Nations | 15,465 |

SOURCE: U.S. Department of Defense

15. **Explain Effects** How did the arms race affect the United States economy?

16. **Compare** How was the Eisenhower Doctrine similar to the Truman Doctrine?

17. **Explain Effects** How did the Cold War affect freedom of speech and freedom of the press in the United States?

## Writing About History

**Writing a Research Report** The early Cold War includes many stories of great courage and personal sacrifice. Write a research report that describes the actions of the person or group and explains why their actions were heroic. Write your report on one of the following topics: Pilots in the Berlin airlift, U.S. troops at Inchon, Senator Margaret Chase Smith opposing Senator McCarthy.

**Prewriting**
• Choose the topic that most interests you, and create a set of questions about the topic.
• Take notes about the people involved and the personal risks they took.
• Gather additional resources.

**Drafting**
• Develop a working thesis, and choose supporting information to support the thesis.
• Make an outline to organize the report.
• Write an introduction that explains why the topic is interesting, and then write a body and a conclusion.

**Revising**
• Use the guidelines on page SH14 of the Writing Handbook to revise your report.

# Prepare for the MME

## Analysis of Senator McCarthy

Was Senator McCarthy a power-hungry politician who deliberately misled and manipulated people? Or was he a product of the time, working like other officials to defend the American people against the threat of communism? Use your knowledge of the Cold War and Documents A, B, C, and D to answer questions 1 through 4.

### Document A

In my opinion the State Department, which is one of the most important government departments, is thoroughly infested with communists. I have in my hand 57 cases of individuals who would appear to be either card-carrying members or certainly loyal to the Communist Party, but who nevertheless are still helping to shape our foreign policy.

*Senator Joseph McCarthy, February 1950*

### Document B

### Document C

[He] was in many ways the most gifted demagogue ever bred on these shores. No bolder seditionist ever moved among us—nor any politician with a surer, swifter access to the dark places of the American mind. The major phase of McCarthy's career was mercifully short. It began in 1950, three years after he had taken his seat in the Senate, where he had seemed a dim and inconsiderable figure. . . . If he was anything at all in the realm of ideas, principles, doctrines, he was a species of nihilist; he was an essentially destructive force, a revolutionist without any revolutionary vision, a rebel without a cause.

*Richard H. Rovere,* Senator Joe McCarthy

### Document D

Emotions ran very, very high about how to conduct the Cold War, about how to deal with the threat of Stalinism, both abroad but also at home. You had American soldiers dying in Korea. The Korean War formed the vivid backdrop for all of McCarthy's career. There was a bitter, bitter partisan battle in which people were prepared to say almost anything to blacken the reputations and to smear their political opponents. McCarthy did it, and his Republican allies did it. You also have to remember that the Democrats were quite prepared to do the same thing, and often did against McCarthy, calling him a Nazi sympathizer, talking about his investigations as posing a threat to American democracy and so on, charges which really don't, in the light of historical evidence and historical perspective, hold any kind of water.

*Arthur Herman,* The Rise and Fall of Joseph McCarthy

1. Which of the documents is a secondary source that claims that McCarthy was like other politicians of his time and not a significant threat to the American political system?
   A Document A
   B Document B
   C Document C
   D Document D

2. According to Richard Rovere, which of the following statements is the most accurate assessment of McCarthy?
   A He was a power-hungry politician who destroyed people without good reason.
   B He was a gifted politician who protected Americans from destructive forces.
   C He was a man with high ideals whose career in politics was too short.
   D He was evil, but he helped defeat communism.

3. The political cartoon most closely agrees with which of the other documents?
   A Documents A and D
   B Documents C and D
   C Document C
   D Document D

4. **Writing Task** With which of the historians quoted in the documents above do you most strongly agree? Use your knowledge of the Cold War, the Red Scare, and specific evidence from the primary sources above to support your opinion.

# 13 Postwar Confidence and Anxiety

## 1945–1960

### Postwar Prosperity

World War II was over, and Americans wanted nothing more than to put it and all its horrors behind them. Government spending helped new families make ends meet and helped change the economy from making bombs and warplanes to making cars and refrigerators. Americans were eager to buy these newly available items. They bought houses in the suburbs, cars, washing machines, automatic mixers, radios, and cameras. The future seemed rosy. *Listen to the* Witness History *audio to hear more about the prosperity and anxiety of the nation after World War II.*

1950s car ad

◄ A favorite family pastime was taking a long afternoon drive in the family car.

A cosmetic container served as an Eisenhower campaign item.

###  Content Expectations

**Chapter Focus Question:** How did social and economic changes after World War II affect Americans?

### Section 1
**An Economic Boom**   8.2.1, 8.2.2a, 8.2.2b

### Section 2
**A Society on the Move**   8.2.1, 8.2.2b, 8.2.3

### Section 3
**Mass Culture and Family Life**   8.2.1, 9.1.1, 9.1.2b

### Section 4
**Dissent and Discontent**   8.1.1a, 8.3.4, 8.3.5

Elvis Presley

Use the ☑ **Quick Study Timeline** at the end of this chapter to preview chapter events.

**Note Taking Study Guide** *Online*
**For:** Note Taking and American Issues Connector
**Web Code:** nee-8601

▼ Returning veterans, aided by the GI Bill of Rights, filled university classrooms.

**WITNESS HISTORY** 🔊 AUDIO

### The GI Bill of Rights

Passed in 1944, the Serviceman's Readjustment Act, known as the GI Bill of Rights, was intended to ease the soldier's transition from wartime to peacetime. One veteran remembers how the GI Bill affected his life:

❝You were able to go to any school that accepted you . . . So I . . . found the best school that I [could] go to, regardless of tuition, which was Columbia in New York, and they accepted me. I graduated [with] a Bachelor of Science in Business Administration and they accepted me into the Master's program in business at Columbia and I was amazed that [the government] paid the entire tuition. . . . [It] was a revolution that all these people, who never would go to college, went to college because of the GI Bill.❞

—Interview with Harvey S. Lowy, Rutgers Ora History Archives of World War I

# An Economic Boom

 **Content Expectations**

- **8.2.1** Use population data to analyze maps that show changes in population distribution, spatial patterns, density.
- **8.2.2a** Describe issues challenging Americans.
- **8.2.2b** Evaluate policy decisions/legislative actions to meet challenges.

## Terms and People

| | |
|---|---|
| demobilization | productivity |
| GI Bill of Rights | Taft-Hartley Act |
| baby boom | Fair Deal |

## NoteTaking

**Reading Skill: Understand Effects** List the problems raised by the shift to a peacetime economy and the steps taken to solve them.

| United States After WWII | |
|---|---|
| **Problem** | **Solution** |
| • Returning soldiers need jobs | • GI Bill |

**Why It Matters** After World War II, many Americans worried that the war's end would bring renewed economic depression Numerous economists shared this pessimistic view of the future predicting that the American economy could not produce enough jobs to employ all those who were returning from the military. Yet instead of a depression, Americans experienced the longest period of economic growth in American history, a boom that enabled millions of Americans to enter the middle class. This era of sustained growth fostered a widespread sense of optimism about the nation's future. **Section Focus Question: How did the nation experience recovery and economic prosperity after World War II?**

## The Nation Recovers From War

At the end of the war in August 1945, more than 12 million Americans were in the military. Thousands of American factories were churning out ships, planes, tanks, and all the materials required to help fight the war in the Pacific. Virtually overnight both the need for such a huge military machine and the focus on war production came to an end. Orders went out from Washington, D.C. canceling defense contracts, causing millions of defense workers to lose their jobs. Wartime industries had to be converted to meet peacetime needs.

As Americans set about enjoying the fruits of peace, President Harry Truman responded to calls to "bring the boys home for Christmas" by starting the **demobilization,** or sending home members, of the army. By July 1946, only 3 million remained in the military.

Americans were happy that the war was over, but they retained some sense of unease about the future. One poll taken in the fall of 1945 showed that 60 percent of Americans expected their earnings to fall with the return of a peacetime economy. "The American soldier is . . . worried sick about postwar joblessness," *Fortune* magazine observed.

**The GI Bill Aids Returning Soldiers** To help deal with this anxiety, the federal government enacted a law popularly known as the **GI Bill of Rights.** It granted veterans a variety of benefits. It provided a year of unemployment payments to veterans who were unable to find work. Those who attended college after the war received financial aid. The act also entitled veterans to government loans for building homes and starting businesses.

The GI bill had an enormous impact on American society. Home loans to veterans fueled an <u>upsurge</u> in home construction, which led to explosive growth in suburban areas. Perhaps the greatest contribution of the GI bill came in education. The average soldier was inducted into the armed forces at the time when he or she would have been finishing high school. The bill encouraged veterans to enter or return to college. Each veteran was eligible to receive $500 a year for college tuition. The bill also provided $50 a month for living expenses and $75 a month for married veterans. Eight million veterans eventually took advantage of the education benefits.

**A Baby Boom Fills Classrooms** Upon their return, soldiers quickly made up for lost time by marrying and having children. Americans had put off having children because of the depression and war. Now, confident that the bad times were behind them, many married couples started families. This led to what population experts termed a **baby boom.** In 1957, at the peak of the baby boom, one American baby was born every 7 seconds, a grand total of 4.3 million for the year. One newspaper columnist commented, "Just imagine how much these extra people . . . will absorb—in food, in clothing, in gadgets, in housing, in services. . . ." Between 1940 and 1955, the U.S. population experienced its greatest increase, growing 27 percent from about 130 to about 165 million.

**Converting From a Wartime Economy** Fortunately, unemployment did not materialize, nor did a depression return. However, Americans experienced some serious economic problems. The most painful was skyrocketing prices. With war's end, the federal government ended rationing and price controls, both of which had helped keep inflation in check during the war. A postwar rush to buy goods created severe inflationary pressures. There was just too much money to spend on too few goods. Overall, prices rose about 18 percent in 1946. The price of some products, such as beef, nearly doubled within a year.

**Vocabulary Builder**
upsurge—(UHP suhrj) *n.* sudden increase

## New Families

Marriage rates soared as soldiers returned home. Confident that the bad times were behind them, newlywed couples bought new homes and started families. The increase in the birthrate began in 1946 and slowed by 1964.

**Birthrate, 1940–1960**

Number of births (in millions)

4.5
4.0
3.5
3.0
2.5
2.0

1940  1945  1950  1955  1960

SOURCE: *Historical Statistics of the United States*

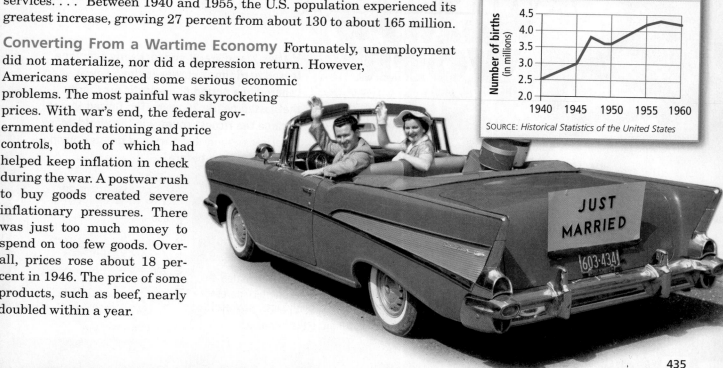

**The U.S. Dominates the World Economy** During the depression, Americans could not buy the goods they desired. The economy improved during the war, but wartime restrictions kept spending down and limited economic growth. The end of wartime restrictions finally opened the floodgates to consumer purchases. As demand soared, businesses employed more people to produce goods. This created a cycle in which people bought new goods, leading businesses to hire more workers, who in turn bought more goods.

At the end of World War II, the United States was the only developed nation untouched by the devastation. Although it had only 6 percent of the world's population, the United States produced about 50 percent of the world's total output. This allowed Americans to enjoy a higher standard of living than any other nation in the world.

**Technological Progress Boosts Productivity** The American economy benefited from numerous technological advances during the postwar period. Some developments, such as the use of atomic energy, were the result of war research. The use of computers increased, and businesses gradually began to depend on them. Worker **productivity**—the rate at which goods are produced or services performed—continued to improve, largely because of new technology.

**Government Spending Supports Growth** Increased government spending boosted the economy, too. With the outbreak of the Korean War, the United States once again committed a significant part of its budget to defense spending. Military spending led to the development of new technologies and new materials, such as plastics and new light metal alloys, that found widespread use outside the military. Other large federal spending programs, such as the Marshall Plan, <u>initiated</u> foreign demand for goods made in the United States.

✓ **Checkpoint** What did many Americans expect to happen to the American economy after World War II?

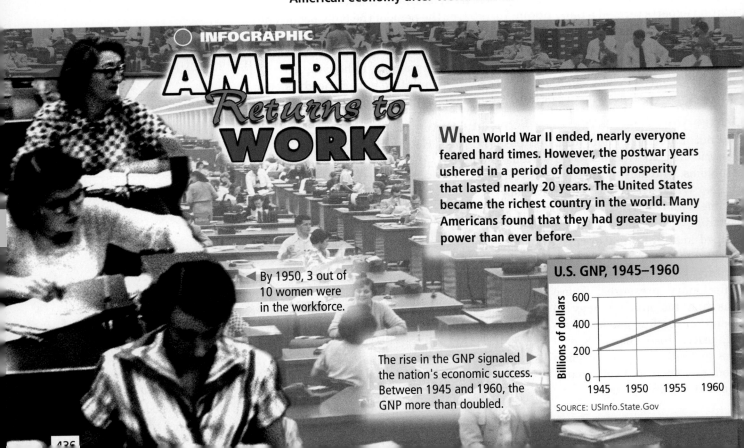

## INFOGRAPHIC
# AMERICA
## *Returns to*
# WORK

**W**hen World War II ended, nearly everyone feared hard times. However, the postwar years ushered in a period of domestic prosperity that lasted nearly 20 years. The United States became the richest country in the world. Many Americans found that they had greater buying power than ever before.

◀ By 1950, 3 out of 10 women were in the workforce.

The rise in the GNP signaled ▶ the nation's economic success. Between 1945 and 1960, the GNP more than doubled.

**U.S. GNP, 1945–1960**

Billions of dollars

600
400
200
0

1945   1950   1955   1960

SOURCE: USInfo.State.Gov

# Truman Overcomes Huge Obstacles

On April 12, 1945, when Franklin Roosevelt died, Harry S. Truman had been Vice President for only 4 months. When Eleanor Roosevelt told him that her husband had died, Truman responded "Is there anything I can do for you?" She replied, "Is there anything we can do for you? For you are the one in trouble now."

Eleanor Roosevelt's remark captured Harry Truman's predicament. He had to preside over one of the more difficult times in American history. The postwar years saw the beginning of the Cold War and communist takeovers in Europe and Asia. At home, there was inflation and labor unrest. Communist advances and a troubled domestic economy created a sense of deep unrest in the American public during the Truman years.

**Grappling With Congress and Labor** From the first days of his presidency, Truman faced a double-barreled challenge: a restless labor movement and a combative Republican Party. Trade unionists demanded pay increases to keep up with inflation. When employers refused to meet labor's demands, millions of steel, coal, railroad, and automotive workers went on strike.

The wave of strikes was one of the largest in American history. It prompted Congress to enact the **Taft-Hartley Act,** a law that outlawed the closed shop—a workplace in which only union members can be hired. Taft-Hartley rolled back some of the rights that labor unions had gained during the New Deal. Although Truman vetoed the Taft-Hartley Act, Congress overrode his veto.

**Angering Segregationists** Unlike FDR, who feared challenging the power of white southern senators and representatives, Truman refused to remain passive. He established a special committee on civil rights to investigate race relations. The committee made several recommendations for civil rights reforms. However, Congress rejected the recommendations

American families wanted their own homes. Home construction contributed to the booming economy. ▼

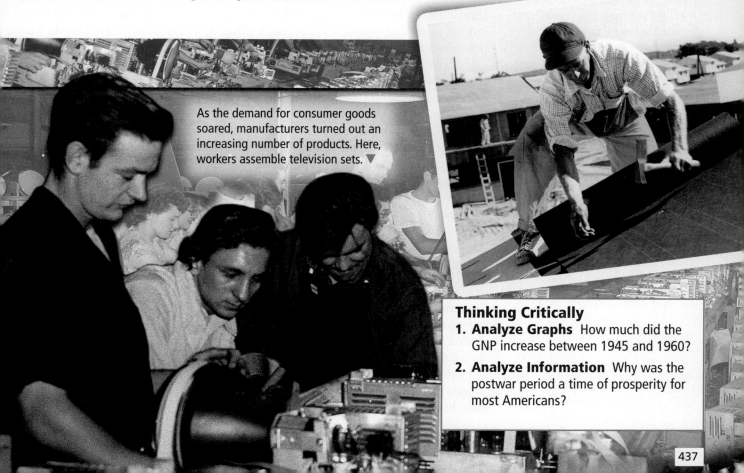

As the demand for consumer goods soared, manufacturers turned out an increasing number of products. Here, workers assemble television sets. ▼

## Thinking Critically
1. **Analyze Graphs** How much did the GNP increase between 1945 and 1960?
2. **Analyze Information** Why was the postwar period a time of prosperity for most Americans?

## Presidential Election of 1948

| Candidate (Party) | Electoral Vote | Popular Vote | % Electoral Vote | % Popular Vote |
|---|---|---|---|---|
| Truman (Democratic) | 303 | 24,105,182 | 57 | 50 |
| Dewey (Republican) | 189 | 21,970,065 | 36 | 46 |
| Thurmond (States' Rights) | 39 | 1,169,063 | 7 | 2 |
| Wallace (Progressive) | — | 1,157,172 | — | 2 |

*One of Tennessee's electors voted for Thurmond

## A Truman Victory

Despite the mistaken headline, Truman defeated Dewey in a close election. The Democrats won with a popular vote of 24 million to the Republicans' popular vote of nearly 22 million. The campaign button promoted Truman's opponents, Thurmond and Wright from the States' Rights Party. *What role should the media have in elections?*

and did not pass any meaningful civil rights reforms until the late 1950s. Truman also issued an executive order desegregating the military. This was more successful. By 1951, most units had been integrated.

**Truman Upsets Dewey** By the spring of 1948, Truman's standing had sunk so low that he faced challenges from both the right and the left in his own Democratic Party. Southern Democrats, angry at Truman's support for civil rights, left the party and established the States' Rights Party. They named South Carolina governor Strom Thurmond as their candidate for President. At the other end of the political spectrum, Henry Wallace, who had been Vice President during FDR's third term, broke with Truman over foreign policy issues. Wallace became the candidate of a new Progressive Party.

The breakaway of two large blocs of Democrats was accompanied by the Republican Party's nomination of Thomas Dewey, the well-known governor of New York, for President. Few people thought that Truman had any chance of winning the 1948 election. Truman, however, did not see it that way. He staged an energetic "whistle stop" train tour of the nation, delivering over 300 speeches and traveling 31,000 miles in a matter of weeks. At train stops in small towns, Truman attacked the current Congress as "do nothing" and the worst in history. "Give 'em hell, Harry!" some in the crowd would cry out during his speeches. Although every political poll predicted that Dewey would win easily, Truman won by a narrow victory. He had managed the political upset of the century.

**Truman Proposes a Fair Deal** Shortly after the election, Truman announced a far-ranging legislative program, which he called the **Fair Deal.** The Fair Deal, he explained, would strengthen existing New Deal reforms and establish new programs, such as national health insurance. But Congress was not in a reforming mood, and Truman failed to win approval for most of his Fair Deal proposals.

Legislative failure and a stalled war in Korea contributed to Truman's loss of popularity. He chose not to seek the 1952 Democratic nomination. His reputation, however, has improved through the years. Today, many historians applaud him for his common-sense approach, as the first President to challenge public discrimination and as a determined opponent of communist expansion.

✓ **Checkpoint** Why were workers dissatisfied during the postwar period?

# Eisenhower Charts a Middle Path

The 1952 election was hardly a contest. The Republican candidate, Dwight Eisenhower, was so popular that both the Democratic and Republican parties had wanted him as their presidential candidate. Eisenhower, whose nickname was Ike, charmed the public with his friendly smile, reassuring personality, and record of service and honesty. The Democratic candidate, Adlai Stevenson, a senator from Illinois, failed to catch the popular imagination the way Eisenhower did.

Dwight Eisenhower had spent nearly his entire adult life in the military and had never held a political office before 1952. Thus, Americans could not know for certain which way he would guide the nation upon taking office. However, most Americans believed that Eisenhower's calm personality mirrored his political views and that he would keep to the "middle road," achieving a balance between liberal and conservative positions.

Eisenhower charted a middle course as President. While he shared the conservative view that the federal government had grown too strong, he did not repeal existing New Deal programs, such as Social Security and the minimum wage. Federal spending actually increased during his presidency. Eisenhower even introduced several large new programs. For example, he created an interstate highway system and began to spend federal dollars for education, specifically to train more scientists.

One reason for Eisenhower's popularity was the strength of the American economy during the 1950s. His presidency was one of the most prosperous, peaceful, and politically tranquil in the twentieth century.

Dwight Eisenhower

✓ **Checkpoint** Why did federal spending increase during Eisenhower's presidency?

---

SECTION 1

## Assessment

**Progress Monitoring *Online***
**For:** Self-test with vocabulary practice
**Web Code:** nea-1302

## Comprehension

1. **Terms and People** Explain how each of the following changed the lives of Americans during the postwar years.
   • GI Bill of Rights
   • baby boom
   • productivity
   • Fair Deal

2.  **Reading Skill: Understand Effects** Use your problem-and-solution chart to answer the Section Focus Question: How did the nation experience recovery and economic prosperity after World War II?

## Writing About History

3. **Quick Write: Gather Information** Use the library and reliable Internet sources to find information about the Taft-Hartley Act. Use the words *Taft-Hartley Act* as key words to begin a search. Once you have found several sites, create note cards to gather the information you have found.

## Critical Thinking

4. **Identify Assumptions** Why was the government willing to give billions of dollars in assistance to returning World War II veterans?

5. **Draw Conclusions** After the war, Truman faced challenges with labor unions. Would you consider Truman as working for or against organized labor? Explain.

6. **Synthesize Information** How did the baby boom impact the postwar economy?

WITNESS HISTORY 🔊 AUDIO

### Homes for Veterans

In 1949, developer William Levitt purchased thousands of acres of farmland in Hempstead, on Long Island, New York. Drawing on modern production techniques, he constructed thousands of homes that he sold for just under $8,000 each. Advertisements for Levittown captured the mood of the country as it stood poised to begin an era of unprecedented prosperity.

❝This is Levittown! All yours for $58 [a month]. You're a lucky fellow, Mr. Veteran. Uncle Sam and the world's largest builder have made [it] possible for you to live in a charming house in a delightful community without having to pay for them with your eyeteeth.❞

—Advertisement for Levittown homes,
*The New York Times,* March 1949

▲ Moving vans line the street of a new suburban neighborhood.

# A Society on the Move

## MI Content Expectations

- **8.2.1** Use population data to analyze maps that show changes in population distribution, spatial patterns, density.
- **8.2.2b** Evaluate policy decisions/legislative actions to meet challenges.
- **8.2.3** Compare/contrast Roosevelt's New Deal initiatives, Johnson's Great Society programs, Reagan's market-based domestic policies.

## Terms and People

| | |
|---|---|
| Interstate Highway Act | multinational |
| Sunbelt | corporation |
| service sector | AFL-CIO |
| information industry | California Master Plan |
| franchise business | |

## NoteTaking

**Reading Skill: Identify Main Ideas**
Complete a chart like the one below to capture the main ideas.

| Postwar Changes | | |
|---|---|---|
| Society | Economy | Education |
| • Growth of suburbs | • Service economy | • |

**Why It Matters** Since the first colonists arrived in Jamestown, Virginia, Americans have been on the move. In the years following World War II, mobility became especially important. People moved to the suburbs and to the Sunbelt. They also moved into white-collar jobs. At the same time, the American economy was changing. The impact of these changes still affects us today. **Section Focus Question: What social and economic factors changed American life during the 1950s?**

## Americans Move to the Suburbs

Between 1940 and 1960, more than 40 million Americans moved to the suburbs, one of the largest mass migrations in history. Rural regions suffered the most dramatic decline in population, but people also came by the thousands from older industrial cities, seeking, as one father put it, a place where "a kid could grow up with grass stains on his pants." During the same time period, many older industrial cities lost population.

**Suburbs Attract Young Americans** People flocked to the suburbs in part because the nation suffered from a severe shortage of urban housing. During the depression and World War II, new housing construction had come to a near standstill. At war's end, as Americans married and formed families, they went in search of a place they could call their own.

Fortunately, at this time of peak demand, developers figured out how to build affordable housing in a hurry. William Levitt became a leader in mass producing suburban homes. Entire rows of houses in Levittown were built using the same plan. This method enabled workers to build houses in weeks rather than in months. On the installment plan, buyers could pay $58 a month toward the cost of a home. Demand for the homes was so great that Levitt built two other Levittowns—one outside Philadelphia, Pennsylvania, and the other in New Jersey. These houses were ideal for young couples starting out because they were affordable and comfortable. Other developers adopted Levitt's techniques, and suburbs were soon springing up across the country.

Suburban development depended on help from the government. State and federal governments constructed thousands of miles of highways that linked the suburbs to cities. New home buyers benefited from the GI bill and the Federal Housing Administration (FHA), which provided low-interest loans. FHA-backed loans allowed home buyers to pay as little as 5 to 10 percent of the purchase price and to pay off their mortgages over 30 years.

Residents of new suburbs faced the challenge of establishing new towns with churches and schools and police and fire departments. Through these institutions, the suburbanites forged a sense of community. During the 1950s, the suburbs became increasingly self-contained. While suburban residents of earlier generations had depended on the city for entertainment and shopping, the postwar suburban dweller could find a vast array of goods and services in nearby shopping centers.

**The "Car Culture" Takes Over** During the 1920s, automobile ownership had soared in the United States. With the explosion of suburban growth in the 1950s, Americans grew even more dependent upon their cars. The number of registered automobiles jumped from 26 million in 1945 to 60 million in 1960.

## The Car Culture

The automobile industry thrived and, as a result, led to new businesses. As shown here, Americans were happy to spend leisure time in their cars and watch a movie at the local drive-in theater. The number of families that owned cars increased drastically between 1950 and 1960. *Do you think increased car ownership may have had negative effects?*

**Car Ownership, 1950–1965**

Percentage of families owning one car

| Year | |
|---|---|
| 1950 | ~59 |
| 1955 | ~70 |
| 1960 | ~77 |
| 1965 | ~78 |

SOURCE: *Historical Statistics of the United States*

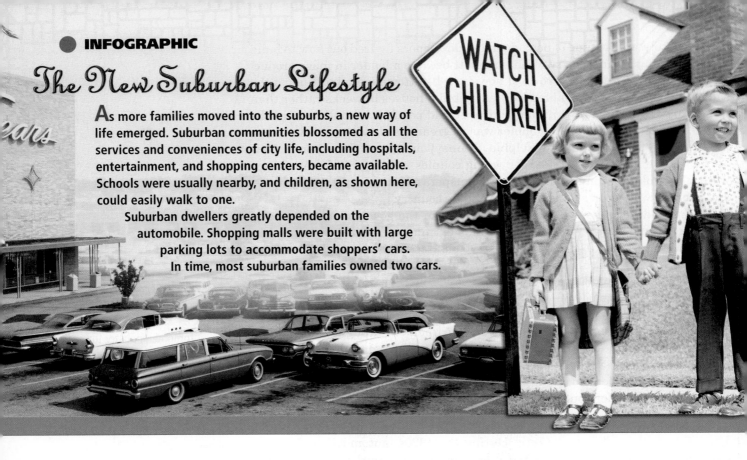

## The New Suburban Lifestyle

**A**s more families moved into the suburbs, a new way of life emerged. Suburban communities blossomed as all the services and conveniences of city life, including hospitals, entertainment, and shopping centers, became available. Schools were usually nearby, and children, as shown here, could easily walk to one.

Suburban dwellers greatly depended on the automobile. Shopping malls were built with large parking lots to accommodate shoppers' cars. In time, most suburban families owned two cars.

These new automobiles tended to have big engines and enormous horsepower. They came with the newest technology, such as power steering and brakes and automatic transmission. Harley Earl of the Ford Motor Company captured the mood of the 1950s by designing cars with lots of chrome that reminded people of jet planes.

While some suburbanites rode the train or other forms of mass transportation, Americans increasingly depended upon their cars to commute to work. Suburbanites also needed their cars to shop at suburban shopping malls. Entrepreneurs opened fast-food restaurants and drive-in movie theaters, both of which catered to the car culture. While these businesses flourished, many older businesses, often located in older city neighborhoods, struggled to survive.

✔ **Checkpoint** How did Americans living in the suburbs benefit from the "car culture"?

## Eisenhower Interstate Highway System

The scale of suburban growth would not have been remotely possible without a massive federal program of highway building. Committed to the idea of easing automobile travel, President Eisenhower authorized the first funding of the interstate system in 1953. Further legislation passed by Congress in 1956 resulted in the **Interstate Highway Act,** which authorized funds to build 41,000 miles of highway consisting of multilane expressways that would connect the nation's major cities. This represented the biggest expenditure on public works in history, bigger by far than any project <u>undertaken</u> during the New Deal. In 1990, further recognition of President Eisenhower's role in establishing the massive highway system led to a renaming of the highways. It became the Dwight D. Eisenhower System of Interstate and Defense Highways.

**Vocabulary Builder**
<u>undertake</u>–(uhn der TAYK) *v.* to take upon oneself; agree to do

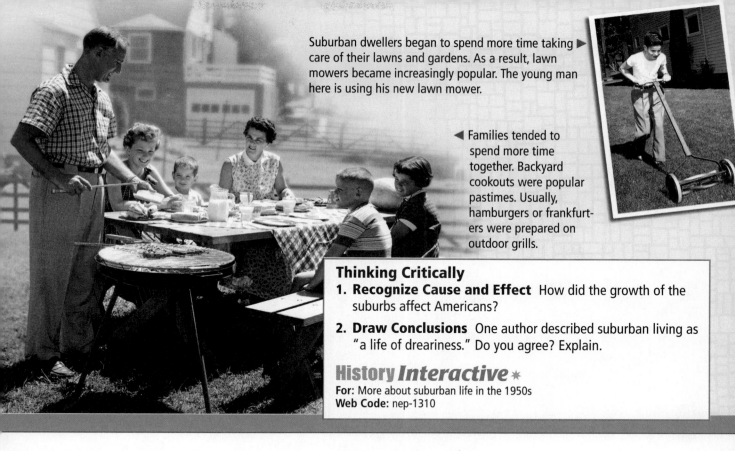

Suburban dwellers began to spend more time taking ▶ care of their lawns and gardens. As a result, lawn mowers became increasingly popular. The young man here is using his new lawn mower.

◀ Families tended to spend more time together. Backyard cookouts were popular pastimes. Usually, hamburgers or frankfurters were prepared on outdoor grills.

**Thinking Critically**
1. **Recognize Cause and Effect** How did the growth of the suburbs affect Americans?
2. **Draw Conclusions** One author described suburban living as "a life of dreariness." Do you agree? Explain.

**History *Interactive* ⋆**
**For:** More about suburban life in the 1950s
**Web Code:** nep-1310

Besides easing commutes from suburbs to cities, the new highways boosted the travel and vacation industries. Families traveled to national and state parks, to the beach, and to new destinations, such as Las Vegas. With more money and more children, American families avidly sought entertainment and leisure activity. Walt Disney met this demand by building an extraordinary amusement park in Southern California. Disneyland exhibits excited the imagination with spectacular visions of the future, including make-believe rides in space and a special exhibit based on the movie *20,000 Leagues Under the Sea.*

 **Checkpoint** How did the Interstate Highway System spur the growth of the suburbs?

## Migrating to the Sunbelt

In 1958, the Brooklyn Dodgers and the New York Giants, two well-known baseball teams, moved from New York City to Los Angeles and San Francisco, respectively. Their move reflected another crucial trend of the postwar era, the growth of the **Sunbelt,** the name given to the southern and western states. By the mid-1960s, California passed New York as the state with the largest population. The migration to Sunbelt cities, such as Houston, Texas, and Los Angeles, California, continued for the rest of the twentieth century.

**Seeking the Benefits of the Sunbelt** Many factors played a role in attracting so many people to the Sunbelt. California, which added more than 5 million new residents in the 1940s and 1950s, had both an appealing climate and a large number of jobs in defense industries. The explosive growth of the aerospace and electronics industries also attracted newcomers to the Sunbelt. The booming petrochemical industry boosted Houston's population. The development of air conditioning made it easier to live in hotter climates, too.

**NoteTaking**

**Reading Skill: Identify Causes and Effects** As you read, identify the effects of the population shift to the Sunbelt.

| Moving to the Sunbelt | |
|---|---|
| **Causes** | **Effects** |
| • Jobs | • |
| • | • |

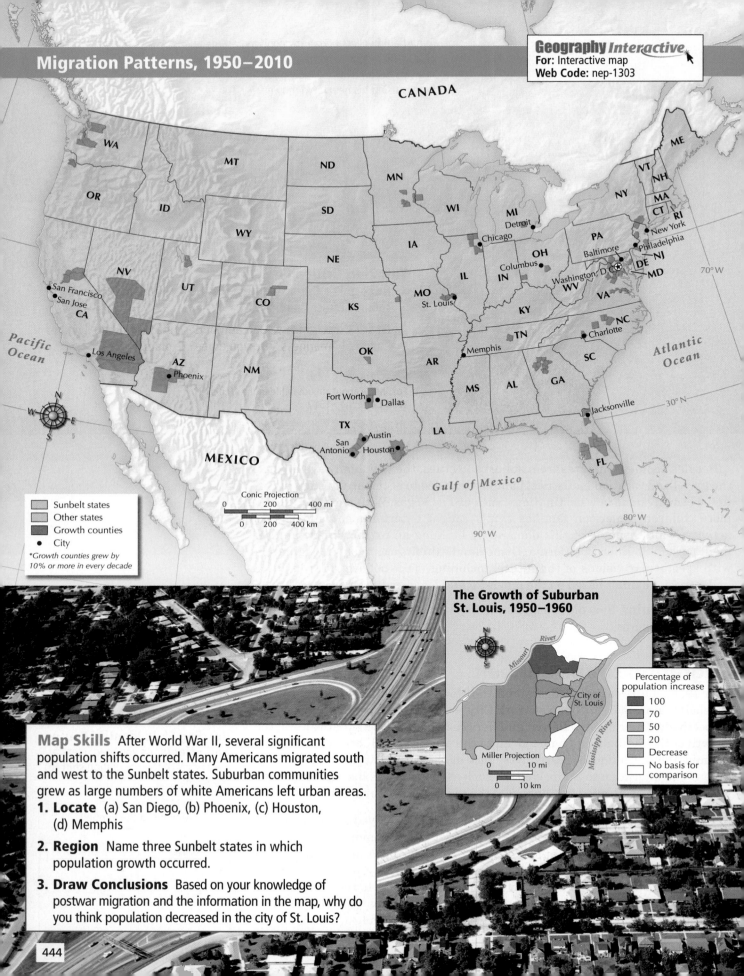

# Migration Patterns, 1950–2010

**Geography** *Interactive*
**For:** Interactive map
**Web Code:** nep-1303

CANADA

CA
NV
UT
CO
OR
WA
ID
MT
WY
ND
SD
NE
KS
OK
TX
NM
AZ
MN
IA
MO
AR
LA
MS
AL
GA
FL
WI
IL
IN
KY
TN
MI
OH
WV
VA
NC
SC
PA
NY
ME
VT
NH
MA
CT
RI
NJ
DE
MD

San Francisco
San Jose
Los Angeles
Phoenix
Fort Worth
Dallas
San Antonio
Austin
Houston
Memphis
St. Louis
Detroit
Chicago
Columbus
Baltimore
Washington, D.C.
New York
Philadelphia
Charlotte
Jacksonville

Pacific Ocean

Atlantic Ocean

MEXICO

Gulf of Mexico

70° W
80° W
90° W
30° N

Conic Projection

0    200    400 mi
0    200    400 km

**Legend:**
- Sunbelt states
- Other states
- Growth counties
- ● City

*Growth counties grew by 10% or more in every decade

## The Growth of Suburban St. Louis, 1950–1960

Missouri River
Mississippi River
City of St. Louis

**Percentage of population increase**
- 100
- 70
- 50
- 20
- Decrease
- No basis for comparison

Miller Projection

0    10 mi
0    10 km

**Map Skills** After World War II, several significant population shifts occurred. Many Americans migrated south and west to the Sunbelt states. Suburban communities grew as large numbers of white Americans left urban areas.

1. **Locate** (a) San Diego, (b) Phoenix, (c) Houston, (d) Memphis

2. **Region** Name three Sunbelt states in which population growth occurred.

3. **Draw Conclusions** Based on your knowledge of postwar migration and the information in the map, why do you think population decreased in the city of St. Louis?

Latinos contributed to the growth of the Sunbelt. In the late 1950s and early 1960s, many Cubans, who were escaping the new regime of Fidel Castro, made Miami, Florida, their new home. Prior to World War II, most Mexican Americans lived in rural areas. However, by the 1960s, the majority of them migrated to urban areas, such as Los Angeles, El Paso, and Phoenix.

**Impact of Migration** The shift to the suburbs and the Sunbelt had a momentous impact on American society. As people moved, their political power went with them. Thus, suburbs and the Sunbelt gained representation. Urbanites in the Northeast and Midwest lost political power. California's representation in the House of Representatives, for example, more than doubled between 1948 and 1998.

Urban and suburban growth created environmental concerns, ranging from traffic jams and smog to water shortages. In the 1960s and 1970s, environmental groups would begin to grapple with some of the byproducts of this growth.

✔ **Checkpoint** **What motivated so many Americans to migrate to the Sunbelt?**

# The American Economy Changes Focus

These important postwar population shifts were matched by equally groundbreaking structural changes in the American economy. For the first time in American history, more people found employment in the **service sector,** businesses that provide services, such as healthcare, law, retail, banking, or insurance, than in the manufacturing sector. These shifts led some to describe the United States as a postindustrial society.

**The Service Sector Grows** Between 1947 and 1957, the percentage of the American workforce employed in industrial or blue-collar jobs declined 4 percent. During the same time period, employment in the service sector, or white-collar jobs, rapidly grew. The new workforce included many who worked in **information industries,** including those who built or operated the first computers. These computers were enormous. One of the first, named ENIAC, short for Electronic Numerical Integrator and Computer, took up roughly 18,000 square feet, or the size of three basketball courts! Despite its size, it was less powerful than today's desktop computer.

Still, ENIAC was a remarkable advance. By the 1960s, the government and private industry had found many uses for the computer. Hotels used computers to help make reservations, and banks used them to keep track of accounts. Industries started using computers to automate work or perform jobs once done by people.

Meanwhile, the number of women in the labor force continued to grow, doubling between 1940 and 1960. Many of these women worked part time. Few pursued long-term careers and most remained underpaid. Yet, without their paychecks, their families would have found it difficult to remain in the middle class.

While the service sector grew rapidly, both the number and percentage of Americans who made a living by farming continued to decline. In 1935, one fourth of the nation's families lived on farms. By 1960, less than one in ten families did. At the same

**White-Collar Jobs**
The number of white-collar workers, such as the office workers shown here, greatly increased in the 1950s.

time, improvements in technology, ranging from mechanical cotton pickers to chemical pesticides, made agriculture much more productive. This allowed fewer workers to grow even more food. New irrigation systems helped transform much of the land in the Southwest from arid to fertile fields.

**Entrepreneurs Start Businesses** At home, the postwar era saw the rise of **franchise businesses.** A franchise business allows a company to distribute its products or services through retail outlets owned by independent operators. Franchises were attractive to consumers because they stressed quality and sameness, no matter where one was in the United States. The Holiday Inn franchise came into existence following a trip that home builder Kemmons Wilson took to Washington, D.C., with his family of five children. Frustrated, Wilson found hotels difficult to locate, overpriced, and lacking adequate parking facilities. As he traveled, according to author David Halberstam, "Wilson became more irritated until he turned to his wife and announced that he was going into the hotel business. Everyone in this country, he thought, had a car and a family, and sooner or later everyone had to go somewhere." Today, there are tens of thousands of Holiday Inn hotels all over the world.

Many postwar critics lamented the growth of franchise businesses. For them, the franchises represented a growing lack of originality, evidence that the United States was becoming a "bland" nation in which people ate bland food, lived in bland look-a-like houses, and watched bland television shows that followed the same plot line.

**American Corporations Go Multinational** As the postwar economy expanded, so did **multinational corporations,** companies that produced and sold their goods and services all over the world and established branches abroad. General Motors, General Electric, and IBM, produced a larger and larger share of all of the goods sold. Many of these corporations earned large portions of their profits abroad. Coca Cola, for instance, sold its soft drinks all over the globe. Hollywood movies found eager audiences in Tokyo, Mexico City, and Germany.

**Unions Consolidate Their Gains** The prosperity of the 1950s was reflected in generally good times for the labor movement. In 1955, the AFL and the CIO, which had split in the mid-1930s, united to form the **AFL-CIO.** The new organization enjoyed a good deal of political clout, especially within the Democratic Party. Yet, trade unions also lost some momentum during the late 1940s and early 1950s. Most of the new white-collar workers did not join unions, and labor's image was tarnished by a corruption scandal involving the Teamsters Union. Government investigators accused the Teamsters, who represented truck drivers, of illegally using their members' funds.

✓ **Checkpoint** In what ways did American businesses change during the postwar period?

# Educational Opportunities Expand

As the economy grew, so too did opportunities for Americans to attain higher education. A more educated workforce boosted economic productivity. In 1940, only about 15 percent of college-age Americans attended college. By the early 1960s, however, close to 40 percent did. The percentage of Americans who completed high school also rose sharply. "The astonishing growth of education in the late

**Vocabulary Builder**
frustrate–(FRUHS trayt) v. to annoy; disappoint

**Labor Leader**
George Meany served as the first president of the AFL-CIO.

1940s (and thereafter)," wrote historian James Patterson, "seemed yet another sign that the American Dream was well and alive."

**Government Provides Funding for Education** Large sums of money were needed to meet the education needs of the baby-boom generation. In the 1950s and early 1960s, California opened a new school about once a week. Most of the funding for education came from local and state governments, but after the Soviet Union launched *Sputnik 1* in 1957, many Americans called for more federal funds for education.

In a mood of crisis, Congress quickly approved the National Defense Education Act. Its $1 billion program was aimed at producing more scientists and science teachers. The act authorized money for loans to high school and college graduates to continue their scientific education.

**Growing Classrooms**
Class sizes increased as baby-boom children reached school age. The number of high school and college graduates soared.

**Education Is "Democratized"** The postwar era saw the stirrings of a movement to make education more accessible. Many states poured funds into their public universities, making it easier for ordinary Americans to attend college. California, for example, established a **California Master Plan,** which called for three tiers of higher education: research universities, state colleges, and community colleges. All of them were to be accessible to all of the state's citizens. Other states also built or expanded their college systems. On another front, in 1954, the Supreme Court ruled in *Brown* v. *Board of Education of Topeka* that segregated schools were unconstitutional. However, it would be years before many schools were actually integrated.

✔ **Checkpoint** How did American education change in the years following World War II?

---

SECTION

# 2 Assessment

**Progress Monitoring *Online***
**For:** Self-test with vocabulary practice
**Web Code:** nea-1303

## Comprehension

1. **Terms and People** What is the relationship between each of the following terms and the social and economic changes that took place in the postwar period?
   - Interstate Highway Act
   - Sunbelt
   - service sector
   - information industries
   - franchise business

2.  **Reading Skill: Identify Main Ideas** Use your chart to answer the Section Focus Question: What social and economic factors changed American life during the 1950s?

## Writing About History

3. **Quick Write: Evaluate Sources** Choose a topic from this section for further research. Use the Internet or the library to find one source that provides information about your selected topic. Determine the reliability of the source. Consider the following:
   - Is it a primary or secondary source?
   - Is the information supported by the evidence?
   - Is the information mostly facts or mostly opinions?
   - If you are using the Internet, is the information from a Web site that is known for being reliable?

## Critical Thinking

4. **Draw Conclusions** What were the benefits of the Interstate Highway Act? What were the disadvantages?

5. **Demonstrate Reasoned Judgment** Do you think it was easy for people in declining manufacturing industries to switch into the service sector? Explain your answer.

6. **Synthesize Information** How did the Sunbelt states benefit from the growth of the automobile and air conditioning industries?

◀ Baby-boomer fads were often based on popular television shows.

### The Latest Fad

As baby boomers went to school, new fads came and went with amazing speed. One such fad revolved around a popular television show about the American folk hero Davy Crockett. Steven Spielberg, who later would become one of Hollywood's most successful movie directors, recalled the craze.

❝I was in third grade at the time. Suddenly, the next day, everybody in my class but me was Davy Crockett. And because I didn't have my coonskin cap and my powder horn, or Old Betsy, my rifle, and my chaps, I was deemed the Mexican leader, Santa Anna. And they chased me home from school until I got my parents to buy me a coonskin cap.❞

—Steven Spielberg, recalling the Davy Crockett craze of 1955

# Mass Culture and Family Life

 **Content Expectations**

- **8.2.1** Use population data to analyze maps that show changes in population distribution, spatial patterns, density.
- **9.1.1** Evaluate changes in U.S. economy.
- **9.1.2b** Analyze role of evangelical religion in national politics.

### Terms and People

consumerism
median family income
nuclear family

Benjamin Spock
rock-and-roll
Elvis Presley

## NoteTaking

**Reading Skill: Identify Main Ideas** Identify postwar changes in daily life and popular culture.

> I. The Culture of Consumerism
>   A. Americans spend more
>     1. Increased family income
>     2.

**Why It Matters** During the 1950s, the ideal family was one in which men worked and supported their families and women stayed home and reared their children. Television and other forms of mass culture suggested that this ideal was the norm. Whether most American families actually lived like the ones they saw on prime-time television, however, remains unclear. The family values of the 1950s still affect who we are and who we want to be. **Section Focus Question: How did popular culture and family life change during the 1950s?**

## The Culture of Consumerism

For much of our history, Americans had been taught to save their money. "A penny saved is a penny earned," advised Benjamin Franklin. However, as the U.S. economy began to boom in the postwar era, Americans were caught up in a wave of **consumerism,** buying as much as they could, much of it on credit. What accounted for this spending spree?

**Spending Is Easy** One reason Americans spent more was that they had more money to spend. During the 1950s, **median family income,** or average family income, rose from $3,319 to $5,417. The average American family now had twice as much real income as the average family had during the prosperous years of the 1920s. Consumer-oriented companies found new and innovative ways to encourage buying on credit. For example, General Motors advertised its cars with the slogan "Buy Now, Pay Later." The Diner's Club introduced the first credit card.

**Buying New Conveniences** Home appliances topped the list of the goods that Americans bought. Families purchased electric washing machines and dryers, refrigerators and ranges. These labor-saving appliances helped transform housework, lessening the physical demands of everything from washing clothes to preserving foods.

With money to spend, easy credit, and new goods to buy, shopping became a new pastime for Americans. Supermarkets, where customers could buy everything from milk to mops, appeared. Shopping centers sprouted all over suburbia.

One product that Americans bought in record numbers was a television. In 1946, manufacturers produced fewer than 6,000 TV sets. Seven years later, Americans purchased 7 million sets and by the end of the decade, 90 percent of all households owned a television.

✔ **Checkpoint** What were some reasons why consumer spending skyrocketed in the postwar era?

## Family Life in the Fifties

During World War II, many women—including married women with children—had gone off to work in factories. In 1943, women made up 25 percent of the workers in the wartime auto industry. With the war's end, however, most of the women who had entered the workforce returned to being homemakers. Now, a more traditional image of the family took hold, one in which women stayed home and men served as "breadwinners." Women who wanted a career outside the home faced social pressures to rethink their decisions.

**Portraying the "Ideal" Family** In the popular magazines of the postwar era, social scientists and other opinion makers described the **nuclear family,** or a household consisting of a mother and father and their children, as the backbone of American society. For the nuclear family to function smoothly, experts claimed, women had to accept their role as homemakers. Television shows and movies made similar assertions. For example, in the 1955 Hollywood movie *The Tender Trap*, actress Debbie Reynolds declared, "A woman isn't a woman unless she's been married and had children."

As the 1950s progressed, however, more women were willing to challenge the view that a woman could not have a career outside the home. By 1960, women held one third of the nation's jobs. Approximately half of these women workers were married.

**Children Are the Focus** More so than in the past, family life revolved around children. Not surprisingly, the best-selling book of the era was Dr. **Benjamin Spock**'s *Common Sense Book of Baby and Child Care*. Parents bought and read his book because they wanted expert advice on how to raise their children. Spock emphasized the importance of nurturing children, from their earliest days as infants through their teen years. Mothers, Spock suggested, should not

**The Homemaker**
The ideal housewife stayed at home and raised the children. She used the latest appliances, dressed well, and took advantage of faster ways to prepare meals. The ad is for a convenience food—rice that can be prepared in a few minutes.

worry about spoiling their children because children could not get too much comfort and love. Some criticized Spock for promoting what they called "a permissive culture." Nevertheless, Spock's book remained extremely popular for several decades.

**Vocabulary Builder**
<u>nevertheless</u>—(nehv er thuh LEHS) *adv.* in spite of that; however

Another sign of the degree to which family life revolved around children was the amount of money parents spent on their children. Some parents even defended their spending by arguing that such spending guaranteed against the <u>recurrence</u> of another depression.

**Vocabulary Builder**
<u>recur</u>—(rih KUHR) *v.* to happen or occur again, especially after some lapse of time

As baby boomers became teens, their impact on the economy and American culture became even more noticeable. While as children they received toys, such as Davy Crockett caps and Barbie dolls, as teens they purchased very expensive items. As *LIFE* magazine observed:

> **Primary Source** "The time is past when a boy's chief possession was his bike and a girl's party wardrobe consisted of a fancy dress worn with a string of dime-store pearls. . . . Today's teenagers surround themselves with a fantastic array of garish and often expensive baubles and amusements. They own 10 million phonographs, over a million TV sets, 13 million cameras."
>
> —*LIFE*, August 31, 1959

**Celebrating a Religious Revival** The 1950s also witnessed a revival of religion in the United States. Organized religious groups became more powerful and more church buildings were built. Regular church attendance rose from about 50 million in 1940 to about 80 million in 1958. The increased number of churches in suburban communities across the country helped to strengthen community ties. The evangelist Billy Graham attracted millions to religious revivals that he held around the nation. Roman Catholic bishop Fulton Sheen effectively used television to reach audiences estimated at 10 million a week. During the 1950s, Congress added the words "In God We Trust" to the dollar bill and "under God," to the Pledge of Allegiance. These additions were aimed at making clear the contrast between the centrality of religion in American society and the atheist basis of communist societies.

**Improved Healthcare Benefits Baby Boomers** During the 1950s, American families benefited from numerous advances in medicine. In 1954, Dr. Jonas Salk developed a vaccine against polio, the disease that had struck down Franklin Roosevelt and that, in 1952 alone, had crippled tens of thousands and killed 1,400, mostly children. By 1960, the widespread distribution of Salk's new vaccine and an oral vaccine developed by Albert Sabin had nearly eliminated the disease.

At the same time, antibiotics, such as penicillin, came into widespread use. The antibiotics helped control numerous infectious diseases caused by bacteria, such as whooping cough and tuberculosis. As a result of these medical advances and a better understanding of the importance of diet, children born after 1946 had a longer life expectancy than those born before 1946.

✔ **Checkpoint** In what ways did family life revolve around children during the 1950s?

## HISTORY MAKERS

### Jonas Salk (1914–1995)
As a doctor, Salk showed early interest in developing vaccines. In the late 1940s, he turned his attention to polio, which was becoming an alarmingly serious problem. Some researchers thought a polio vaccine would have to use live virus cells, which carried risks. Salk believed dead cells could be used and succeeded in 1952 in developing such a vaccine. When tests proved it successful, the vaccine was ordered for all American children. Eventually, it was used around the world and contributed to eliminating polio.

## Television Takes Center Stage

In 1938, when television was still just a curiosity, E. B. White, author of *Charlotte's Web,* wrote that it "is going to be the test of the modern world. . . . We shall stand or fall by the television." While White's view may have been exaggerated, clearly television has had an enormous impact on American society.

Between 1945 and 1960, Americans purchased television sets at a faster pace than they had bought either radios or cars during the 1920s. The popularity of this new technology threatened the movie industry because families stayed home to watch TV rather than go out to watch movies at the theater.

● **INFOGRAPHIC**

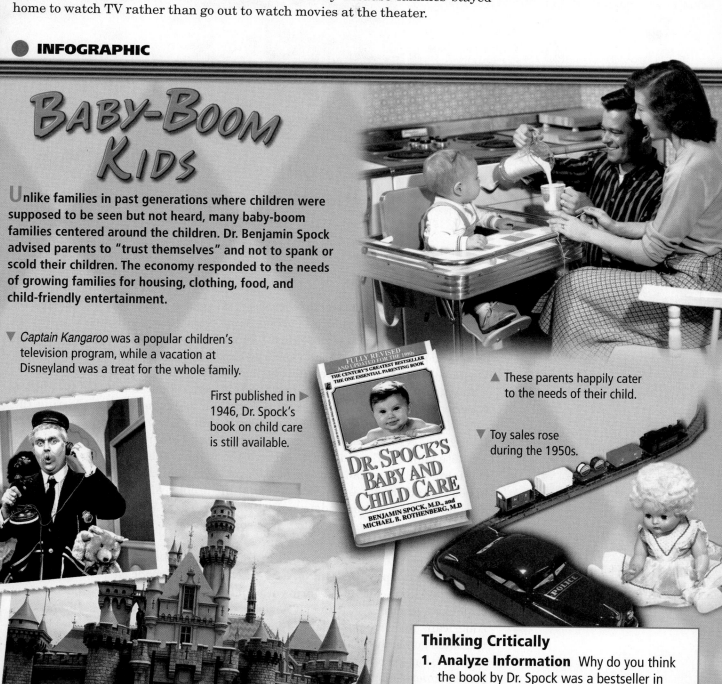

# BABY-BOOM KIDS

Unlike families in past generations where children were supposed to be seen but not heard, many baby-boom families centered around the children. Dr. Benjamin Spock advised parents to "trust themselves" and not to spank or scold their children. The economy responded to the needs of growing families for housing, clothing, food, and child-friendly entertainment.

▼ *Captain Kangaroo* was a popular children's television program, while a vacation at Disneyland was a treat for the whole family.

First published in ▶ 1946, Dr. Spock's book on child care is still available.

FULLY REVISED AND UPDATED FOR THE 1990s
THE CENTURY'S GREATEST BESTSELLER
THE ONE ESSENTIAL PARENTING BOOK
DR. SPOCK'S BABY AND CHILD CARE
BENJAMIN SPOCK, M.D., and
MICHAEL B. ROTHENBERG, M.D

▲ These parents happily cater to the needs of their child.

▼ Toy sales rose during the 1950s.

### Thinking Critically

1. **Analyze Information** Why do you think the book by Dr. Spock was a bestseller in the 1950s?

2. **Draw Conclusions** How did the baby boom affect American society and economy?

# A New Entertainment

Each week, families gathered to watch their favorite television shows. Viewers followed the adventures of a masked Lone Ranger and his Indian companion Tonto. The beloved sitcom "I Love Lucy," starring Lucille Ball, ran for nearly six years. "Beat the Clock," a popular game show, challenged participants to engage in unusual stunts. Ads such as the one below urged Americans to keep buying televisions.

◀ Lucille Ball

◀ The Lone Ranger and Tonto

VITAMEATAVEGAMIN FOR HEALTH

▲ Beat The Clock

Give your family a new thrill this Christmas morning

**Motorola TV**

GIVE A MOTOROLA AND YOU KNOW YOU GIVE THE BEST

Although television attracted viewers of all ages, it had a special influence on children. Baby boom children rushed home from school to watch the *Howdy Doody Show* or the *Mickey Mouse Club*. Children also watched hours of cartoons and shows featuring their favorite superheroes, such as the Lone Ranger. Westerns were especially popular during the 1950s and early 1960s.

Among the most memorable shows were sitcoms about families. Fifty million Americans tuned in each week to watch the *I Love Lucy* show, starring the comedic actress Lucille Ball. Other popular family sitcoms included *Leave It to Beaver, The Adventures of Ozzie and Harriet,* and *Father Knows Best.*

These shows reflected and reinforced the ideal of the 1950s family. None of the family sitcoms had important African American characters. None of the major characters got divorced. Major real-life problems, such as mental illness, alcoholism, and personal depression, rarely, if ever, appeared. Writes David Halberstam, "No family problem was so great that it could not be cleared up within the allotted twenty-two minutes."

Even before television emerged in the 1950s, a mass national culture had begun to develop in the United States. Nationally broadcast radio programs, Hollywood films, and other forms of popular culture had helped erode distinct regional and ethnic cultures. Television sped up and reinforced this process. Americans in every region of the country watched the same shows and bought the same goods they saw advertised.

Television changed political campaigns. During the 1952 presidential campaign, Americans could see the candidates in action. Usually, candidates with more money could buy more advertising time. The impact of television on elections continues today.

✔ **Checkpoint** How did television reflect and reinforce the ideal of the nuclear family in the postwar period?

# Rock-and-Roll Shakes the Nation

In the summer of 1951, a relatively unknown white disc jockey named Alan Freed began broadcasting what commonly had been called "race" music to listeners across the Midwest. Renaming the music **rock-and-roll,** Freed planted the seed for a cultural revolution that would blossom in the mid-1950s.

**Drawing on African American Roots** Rock music originated in the rhythm and blues traditions of African Americans. As African Americans began to move north, they brought their musical traditions with them. Independent recording companies began recording rhythm and blues (R&B) music. Rock-and-roll borrowed heavily from rhythm and blues. As Chuck Berry, known as the pioneer of rock-and-roll, put it, "It used to be called boogie-woogie, it used to be called blues, used to be called rhythm and blues. . . . It's called rock now."

**Attracting a Wider Audience** Live performances of rhythm and blues music was long kept separate from whites by Jim Crow laws in the South or by more subtle forms of segregation in the North. Through the radio, it began to attract a wider white audience in the postwar era. For example, a young **Elvis Presley** listened to a Memphis radio station that played African American gospel tunes. He began to integrate those tunes into the music he played. Meanwhile, in the early 1950s, Sam Phillips set up a recording studio in Memphis to record and play the music of some of Memphis's best African American blues performers, such as B. B. King. One day Phillips heard Presley and almost immediately recognized that he had found the person he had been looking for.

Presley's arrival set off the new rock craze. His first hit, "Heartbreak Hotel," sold in the millions and his success sparked popularity for rock music.

Yet, not everyone liked Elvis or the new rock craze. When Ed Sullivan, the host of a famous TV variety show, invited Elvis to sing on his show, he directed cameramen to show Elvis only from the waist up, because many parents objected to Elvis's gyrating hips and tight pants. Ministers complained about the passions that rock music seemed to unleash among so many youngsters. Congress held hearings on the subversive nature of rock music. Nonetheless, it became a symbol of the emerging youth culture and of the growing power of youth on mass culture.

✔ **Checkpoint** How did rock-and-roll gain popularity?

**Popular Music**
The record business boomed during the 1950s. Phonograph records, such as the one shown here, were made from vinyl, a plastic material. Listeners could enjoy nearly 30 minutes of music on each side.

---

## SECTION 3 Assessment

**Progress Monitoring *Online***
**For:** Self-test with vocabulary practice
**Web Code:** nea-1304

### Comprehension

1. **Terms and People** For each item below, write two or three sentences explaining its significance.
   - consumerism
   - median family income
   - Benjamin Spock
   - Elvis Presley

2. **NoteTaking Reading Skill: Identify Main Ideas** Use your outline about changes in daily life and popular culture to answer the Section Focus Question: How did popular culture and family life change during the 1950s?

### Writing About History

3. **Quick Write: Create an Annotated Bibliography** Choose one topic from this section, such as family life in the 1950s or the impact of suburban growth on the nation. Using the library or the Internet, find three or more sources on your chosen topic. Use these sources to prepare an annotated bibliography in which you record the information each source provides.

### Critical Thinking

4. **Make Comparisons** In what ways was the mood of the 1950s different from the mood of the 1930s?

5. **Identify Point of View** Why do you think the nuclear family became more important during the 1950s?

6. **Identify Central Issues** Why was television a better medium than radio for consumerism?

History *Interactive*.

🔊 AUDIO

**For:** To discover more about American music during the 1950s
**Web Code:** nep-1305

*MI* 8.1.2d

# Rock-and-Roll

Rock-and-roll music burst on the scene in the 1950s, thrilling teenagers and horrifying their parents. A faster version of the rhythm and blues played by B. B. King and other Memphis musicians, rock-and-roll made stars of singers such as Little Richard and Chuck Berry. The biggest rock-and-roll idol was Elvis Presley. Girls screamed and fainted at the sight of Elvis, and his concerts were mobbed. He sold 40 million records in two years. Critics said the new music was just a fad, but disc jockeys and TV hosts such as Dick Clark, whose *American Bandstand* got 45,000 fan letters a week, knew rock-and-roll was here to stay.

Elvis Presley and fans

On his hit television show, Dick Clark (above) played the records of Little Richard, Chuck Berry (top), and other rock-and-roll stars.

**Thinking Critically**
1. **Make Inferences** Why would Elvis Presley have achieved greater success than African American musicians in the 1950s?

2. **Connect to Today** How do reactions to current music resemble the early responses to rock-and-roll?

# 4

▼ Claude Brown, author of *Manchild in the Promised Land*

## WITNESS HISTORY ◀))) AUDIO

### Troubles in the Promised Land

In the twentieth century, millions of African Americans left the rural South and migrated to cities in the North and West. Yet, many of these migrants were disappointed. Claude Brown, who grew up in Harlem, wrote about their disillusionment in his novel *Manchild in the Promised Land*.

❝The children of these disillusioned colored pioneers inherited the total lot of their parents— their disappointments, the anger. To add to their misery, they had little hope of deliverance. For where does one run to when he's already in the Promised Land?❞

—Claude Brown, *Manchild in the Promised Land*

# Dissent and Discontent

 **Content Expectations**

- **8.1.1a** Analyze differences in civic/political values, economic/governmental institutions of U.S./U.S.S.R.
- **8.3.4** Evaluate major accomplishments/setbacks in civil rights/liberties for U.S. minorities.
- **8.3.5** Analyze causes/consequences of civil unrest that occurred in U.S. cities.

## Terms and People

beatnik
inner city
urban renewal
termination policy

## NoteTaking

**Reading Skill: Identify Main Ideas** Record the main ideas and supporting details.

**Why It Matters** Despite the prosperity of the 1950s, not all people benefited. Some, such as Claude Brown, were left out and had little hope of deliverance. Others, who had benefited, wondered whether all of the material things they acquired had actually led to a better life. The discontents of the 1950s would manifest the first signs of the dissent that would dominate the 1960s. **Section Focus Question: Why were some groups of Americans dissatisfied with conditions in postwar America?**

## Critics Reject the Fifties Culture

The failure of society to provide equal opportunities to minorities was one source of discontent during the postwar era. Another was the belief that while material conditions were better in the 1950s, the *quality* of life had not improved. Many intellectuals and artists did not consider homes in the suburbs, shopping centers, and an unending supply of new gadgets as representing a better life.

**Objecting to Conformity** Many social critics complained about an emphasis on conformity. In a book called *The Lonely Crowd*, sociologists David Riesman and Nathan Glazer lamented that Americans had sacrificed their individualism in order to fit into the larger community. They also criticized the power of advertising to mold public tastes. The theme of alienation, or the feeling of being cut off from mainstream society, dominated a number of the most popular novels of the era. The bestseller *The Man in the Gray Flannel Suit*, by Sloan

**The Rebel**
James Dean starred in the movie *Rebel Without a Cause*, which seemed to symbolize the way many young people felt at the time.

**Vocabulary Builder**
affluence–(AF loo uhns) *n.* abundance or riches; wealth

Wilson, followed a World War II veteran who could not find real meaning in life after the war. Holden Caulfield, the main character in J. D. Salinger's *Catcher in the Rye*, a favorite among many teens, mocked what Salinger saw as the phoniness of adult society.

Although published in 1963, Betty Friedan's *The Feminine Mystique* would describe the plight of the suburban housewife during the 1950s. By the 1960s, Friedan would be at the forefront of a movement to change the social and political status of women in American society.

**The Beats Reject Middle-Class Life** An additional critique of American society came from a small group of writers and artists called **beatniks,** or the beats. The beats refused to conform to accepted ways of dressing, thinking, and acting. Conformity, they insisted, stifled individualism. They displayed their dislike of American society by careless dress and colorful jargon.

In their poems, such as Allen Ginsberg's "Howl," and novels, such as Jack Kerouac's *On the Road,* the beats lambasted what they saw as crass materialism and conformity of the American middle class. Many Americans, in turn, were outraged by their behavior.

 **Checkpoint** Why did many intellectuals and artists criticize American culture during the 1950s?

# Rural and Urban Poverty

Hidden behind the new household appliances, the spreading suburbs, the burgeoning shopping malls, and the ribbons of highways was a very different United States. It was a nation of urban slums, desperate rural poverty, and discrimination. People who were poor and dispossessed were well hidden.

In an influential 1962 book entitled *The Other America,* Michael Harrington shocked many Americans by arguing that poverty was widespread in the United States. Harrington claimed that 50 million Americans, one fourth of the nation, lived in poverty. Despite American affluence, Harrington said, poverty plagued African Americans in the inner cities, rural whites in areas such as Appalachia, and Hispanics in migrant farm labor camps and urban barrios. Harrington argued that Americans could not afford to ignore the existence of the poor:

> **Primary Source** "The poor live in a culture of poverty. [They] get sick more than anyone else in the society. . . . Because they are sick more often and longer than anyone else, they lose wages and work and find it difficult to hold a steady job. And because of this, . . . their prospect is to move to an even lower level . . . toward even more suffering."
>
> —Michael Harrington, *The Other America*, 1962

**Cities Suffer a Decline** During the decades that followed World War II, African Americans and other nonwhite minorities moved in great numbers from rural areas to cities. Most migrated in search of better economic opportunities. In the same period, however, American cities were suffering a severe decline as middle-class white families moved to the suburbs.

The loss of the middle class hurt cities economically because the middle class paid a large share of the taxes. It hurt them politically, as well, because as the suburbs gained population, they also gained representation in state legislatures and the national government. This combination of declining economic and political power put a serious strain on cities, leading to a deterioration of services, such as garbage removal and street repair. In turn, as the conditions worsened and crime increased in what was now called the **inner city,** more of the middle class decided to move to the suburbs. Inner city refers to the older, central part of a city with crowded neighborhoods in which low-income, usually minority, groups live. Inner cities are often plagued with problems such as inadequate housing and schools, as well as crime.

Federal, state, and local governments tried to reverse the downward <u>trend</u> in American cities by developing **urban renewal** projects. With these projects, the government cleared large tracts of older housing and built freeways and developments which, it was hoped, would "revitalize" downtown areas. Unfortunately, the projects often backfired. Urban renewal drove people from their homes to make room for the new projects and highways. The poor were forced to seek housing in neighborhoods that were already overcrowded and overburdened. One resident of East Harlem, New York, who lost his home to an urban renewal project observed:

**Vocabulary Builder**
<u>trend</u>–(trehnd) *n.* general or prevailing course, as of events, a discussion, etc.

> **Primary Source** ❝Nobody cared what we wanted when they built this place. They threw our houses down and pushed us there and pushed our friends somewhere else. We don't have a place around here to get a cup of coffee or a newspaper even, or borrow fifty cents.❞
>
> —*America's History Since 1865*

The federal government tried to ease the shortage of affordable housing by constructing public housing. At the time, these housing projects seemed a godsend to those who lived there. Rent was cheap and the residents often enjoyed certain services, like hot running water, for the first time in their lives. Yet, since the public housing was often built in poor neighborhoods, the projects led to an even greater concentration of poverty. This, in turn led to other problems, such as crime.

**The Rural Poor Also Suffer** The plight of the rural poor was just as bad if not worse than that of the urban poor. Mississippi Delta sharecroppers, coal

## The Faces of Poverty
As revealed in Michael Harrington's *The Other America,* poverty existed in urban and rural America. Crowded city tenements, such as the one shown at left below, were usually homes to large numbers of poor African Americans. In rural areas, poor whites and blacks endured lives of hardship. Below, a mother and her children stand in the doorway of a ragged shack.

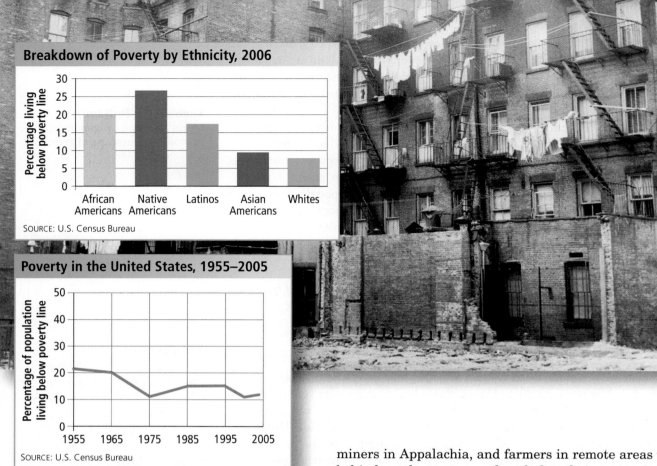

### Breakdown of Poverty by Ethnicity, 2006

Percentage living below poverty line

African Americans | Native Americans | Latinos | Asian Americans | Whites

SOURCE: U.S. Census Bureau

### Poverty in the United States, 1955–2005

Percentage of population living below poverty line

1955 1965 1975 1985 1995 2005

SOURCE: U.S. Census Bureau

**Graph Skills** The number of people living below the poverty line decreased between 1955 and 2006. However, many Americans continue to struggle to find the steady jobs and decent housing that will help them break through the poverty cycle. *What percentage of Americans lived below the poverty line in 1965? Why do you think the poverty rate remains higher among minorities?*

miners in Appalachia, and farmers in remote areas were left behind as others prospered, and often their economic situation got worse as time passed. A major transformation in farming was taking place. Corporations and large-farm owners came to dominate farm production. Many independent small-farm owners found it difficult to compete with the large farms and slipped into poverty.

Many farmers responded by leaving their rural communities behind, joining the waves of the poor who relocated to the city. Others remained behind, wondering if they would ever get to enjoy the benefits of the new economy.

✓ **Checkpoint** How did the federal government respond to the decline of American cities?

## "Other Americans" Face Injustice

During the postwar years, the battle for civil rights in the South began to gain headlines. Yet, in the same time period, African Americans and other minorities also fought for equality in the urban north and west. Central to their struggles were efforts to overcome housing and employment discrimination.

**Puerto Ricans** Latinos from Puerto Rico and Mexico and Native Americans faced many of the same problems that African Americans encountered in the years following World War II. Puerto Rican migrants to New York City, for example, often found themselves clustered together in many of the poorest inner city neighborhoods with employment opportunities limited by both formal and informal forms of discrimination. As newcomers whose native language was not English, they enjoyed little political power. Thus, they received little help from city governments in getting better services, education, or an end to discriminatory practices.

**Mexicans** Both Mexicans and Mexican Americans faced a similar situation in the United States. During World War II, the U.S. government had established the bracero program as a means to address the shortage of agricultural workers. *Braceros* was a term for Mexican migrant farmworkers in the United States. The program gave temporary visas to Mexican immigrants. By 1964, 3 million Mexicans had worked in the United States under the program, most of them as farm laborers. Many were exploited and cheated by their employers. Mexican workers followed crops from state to state. Often, children worked alongside their parents. The migrants had little power to oppose the exploitation, for if they complained about conditions, employers threatened to deport them back to Mexico. One U.S. Department of Labor official called the program "legalized slavery."

One champion of the rights of Mexican migrant workers, Ernesto Galarza, joined the effort to organize unions for Mexican farm laborers.

## HISTORY MAKERS

### Ernesto Galarza
(1905–1984)
Born in Mexico, Galarza came with his family to Sacramento, California, at age six. For a time, he worked as a farm laborer. More fortunate than most Mexican American children, he succeeded in school and eventually received a Ph.D. He began to help migrant farmworkers—many of them Mexican Americans—organize unions. His book, *Merchants of Labor,* exposed the poor working conditions of the braceros.

**Native Americans** In 1953, the federal government enacted the **termination policy,** a major change in the rules governing Native Americans. The law sought to end tribal government and to relocate Native Americans to the nation's cities. It also terminated federal responsibility for the health and welfare of Native Americans. Proponents of the policy argued that it would free American Indians to assimilate, or merge, into American society. While some Native Americans praised the intent of the program, most came to agree with Senator Mark Hatfield of Oregon who argued that it made things worse for them. "[T]he social and economic devastation which these policies have wrought upon many groups has been tremendous. . . . While these problems were already severe among Indian societies generally, they have become epidemic among terminated Indians."

✔ **Checkpoint** What were some of the problems that minorities had to overcome in the postwar era?

---

**Progress Monitoring *Online***
**For:** Self-test with vocabulary practice
**Web Code:** nea-1306

### Comprehension

1. **Terms and People** Explain how each term below relates to problems or issues in the 1950s.
   • beatnik
   • urban renewal
   • termination policy

2.  **NoteTaking Reading Skill: Identify Main Ideas** Use your concept web to answer the Section Focus Question: Why were some groups of Americans dissatisfied with conditions in postwar America?

### Writing About History

3. **Quick Write: Credit Sources** When you use quotes or ideas from sources in your research paper, you must provide proper credit. One way to do this is to list the author and page number of the material you have used in parentheses following the statement. If you have used the Internet, list the Web site. Research a topic from this section and write a paragraph using two sources. Credit the sources where appropriate and list them at the end.

### Critical Thinking

4. **Summarize** Summarize the arguments made by critics who rejected the culture of the fifties.

5. **Synthesize Information** During the 1950s, many middle-class Americans were unaware of poverty. Are poor people invisible today? Explain.

6. **Draw Conclusions** Why would the bracero program attract Mexican workers? What disadvantages did these workers face compared with other workers in the United States?

# Quick Study Guide

 8.2.2b

**Progress Monitoring *Online***
**For:** Self-test with vocabulary practice
**Web Code:** nea-1307

## ■ The Postwar Years

| |
|---|
| Worker productivity improves. |
| Wages increase. |
| Consumerism rises. |
| Baby boom boosts population. |
| GI Bill helps veterans. |
| Government spending increases. |

## ■ Population Shifts, 1950–1970

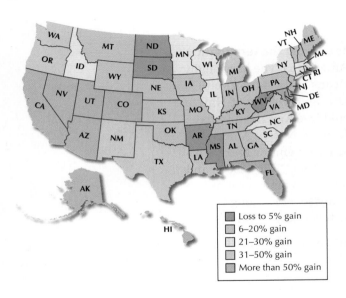

Loss to 5% gain
6–20% gain
21–30% gain
31–50% gain
More than 50% gain

## ■ Life in America, 1950s

Suburban migration

Baby boom

Seeds of discontent

**Life in America During the 1950s**

Consumerism

Car culture

Importance of family

Mass media

## ■ Causes of Discontent

| |
|---|
| Farmers suffer hardships and begin to migrate to cities. |
| Cities experience political and economic decline. |
| African Americans, Latinos, and Native Americans continue to suffer discrimination. |
| Poverty is widespread among Americans in urban and rural areas. |
| Writers and artists protest values of life in the 1950s. |

## ☑ Quick Study Timeline

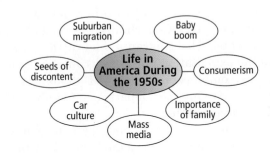

**In America**

**1944**
**GI Bill helps returning veterans**

**1947**
**Taft-Hartley Act limits power of unions**

**1951**
**Levittown, the first postwar suburb, is built on Long Island**

**Presidential Terms**

Harry S. Truman 1945–1953

**1945**

**1950**

**Around the World**

1945
**World War II ends**

1950
**Korean War begins**

# American Issues
## ●━●━●━● Connector

 9.1.1

By connecting prior knowledge with what you have learned in this chapter, you can gradually build your understanding of enduring questions that still affect America today. Answer the questions below. Then, use your American Issues Connector study guide (or go online: www.PHSchool.com **Web Code:** neh-8602).

## Issues You Learned About

● **Poverty and Prosperity** Not all Americans have shared in the nation's more prosperous times.

1. In the postwar decades, some Americans enjoyed new prosperity while others sank deeper into poverty. Write a paragraph contrasting the haves and have nots in American postwar society.

● **Technology and Society** New technological advances impact American cultural life.

2. How did technology change American society in the 1950s? What were the effects of these inventions?

3. What view of American society did television programs of the 1950s present? How accurate was this view?

4. How did Elvis Presley's appearance on Ed Sullivan's TV variety show reflect the clash of values among Americans in the 1950s?

● **Migration and Urbanization** Americans are constantly moving, leading to the rise and fall of populations in cities, states, and regions.

5. In the 1950s and 1960s, more and more Americans moved to the Sunbelt. Describe another specific migration movement in the United States.

6. Why might the Brooklyn Dodgers have made the decision to relocate to Los Angeles in 1958?

### Connect to Your World | Michigan

**Global Interdependence** The 1959 opening of the Great Lakes-Saint Lawrence Seaway had an immediate impact on North American imports and exports, contributing to the post-World War II economic boom. The 2,340-mile-long Seaway connected the Atlantic Ocean with the Great Lakes through a series of manmade canals, locks, and dams, allowing ocean-going ships to transport cargo farther inland than ever before. Today, ships from all over the world transport an average of 200 million tons of grain, iron ore, coal, limestone, cement, steel products, machinery, and other cargo through the Seaway every year. The Seaway's major ports include two in Michigan: Detroit/Wayne County and Monroe. Create a map of the Great Lakes-St. Lawrence Seaway showing the locations of ten of its major ports.

Touchstone, © 1981

**History Interactive**
**For:** Interactive timeline
**Web Code:** nep-1309

**1954**
Salk develops polio vaccine

**1956**
Interstate Highway Act expands highway construction

**1962**
Michael Harrington's *The Other America* defines poverty in America

Dwight D. Eisenhower 1953–1961

John F. Kennedy 1961–1963

**1955**

**1960**

**1965**

**1955**
Soviet Union establishes Warsaw Pact

**1959**
Fidel Castro gains power in Cuba

**1963**
Military coup ends Diem government in South Vietnam

# Chapter Assessment

## Terms and People

1. Define **baby boom.** Explain the effect of the baby boom on American life.

2. What was the **Interstate Highway Act**? How did it help boost the postwar economy?

3. Who was **Benjamin Spock**? What different ideas did he have that changed people's views?

4. Define **beatnik.** Why was such a person dissatisfied?

## Focus Questions

The focus question for this chapter is **How did social and economic changes after World War II affect Americans?** Build an answer to this big question by answering the focus questions for Sections 1 through 4 and the Critical Thinking questions that follow.

**Section 1**
5. How did the nation experience recovery and economic prosperity after World War II?

**Section 2**
6. What social and economic factors changed American life during the 1950s?

**Section 3**
7. How did popular culture and family life change during the 1950s?

**Section 4**
8. Why were some groups of Americans dissatisfied with conditions in postwar America?

## Critical Thinking

9. **Analyze Information** How did the development of the interstate highway contribute to postwar prosperity?

10. **Synthesize Information** What measures did the government take to spark the economy after the war?

11. **Explain Effects** How did automobile production affect the economy?

12. **Draw Conclusions** How did technology both help and harm the farming industry?

13. **Analyzing Visuals** Study the visual below. In which election was this campaign button used? What voters would have supported these candidates and political party? Why?

14. **Identify Point of View** When describing company workers during the 1950s, one sociologist said, "When white-collar people get jobs, they sell not only their time and energy but their personalities as well." Why do you think some people agreed with this point of view?

15. **Analyze Information** Do you think life in the suburbs became the model for the American dream? Explain.

## Writing About History

**Writing a Research Report** Musicians were not the only artists who responded to the changing culture of the postwar years. Painters experimented and began to record their vision of the postwar culture. Write a research report in which you choose two artists and explain the significance of their works. Here are some possible choices: Jackson Pollock, Romare Bearden, Willem de Kooning, Mark Rothko, Robert Rauschenberg, John T. Biggers.

**Prewriting**
• Do online research to read about the artists.
• Choose two artists. Gather information about the artists and their works.
• Create a set of questions about the artists you have chosen. Gather any additional information you need.

**Drafting**
• Develop a working thesis, and choose supporting information to support the thesis.
• Make an outline to organize the report.
• Write an introduction that explains why the topic is interesting, and then write a body and a conclusion.

**Revising**
• Use the guidelines on page SH14 of the Writing Handbook to revise your report.

# Prepare for the MME

## Impact of the Suburbs

During the postwar era, the population began to shift from the cities to the suburbs. What impact did this population shift have on American life? What impact did it have on the economy? Use your knowledge of the postwar era and Documents A, B, C, and D to answer questions 1 through 4.

**Document A**

**Document B**

\* The first year in which Hawaii and Alaska are included
SOURCE: *Historical Statistics of the United States*

**Document C**

This is the way you live at LEVITTOWN

**Document D**

"William Levitt . . . looked upon a green expanse of woods . . . in . . . Bucks County, Pa., and dreamed of instant suburbia. . . . When he marketed his mass-produced homes in beautiful color brochures, thousands of young families wanted to buy. . . . They came to escape crowded cities like Trenton . . . or Philadelphia. . . . They came to own their own home, cook with their own appliances, mow their own lawn. They had GI loans in hand, babies on the way, and a '50s brand of pioneering spirit. . . . 'We were young, all of us who moved to Levittown, and we thought Bill Levitt was the greatest man in the world. Imagine it—$10 deposit, $90 at settlement, and you had a house of your own!' . . . Levittown was a fresh marvel of modern planning to a Northeast corridor bursting at its seams in the early 1950s. . . . It took only $100 . . . to make a down payment on a Levittown home. Levitt, . . . said . . . 'that every family in the United States is entitled to decent shelter.'"

"1951: American dream houses, all in a row"
—by Jon Blackwell, *The Trentonian*, June 20, 1999

1. According to Document D, what caused the shift of population from the cities to the suburbs?
   **A** The availability of affordable housing.
   **B** Fewer apartment buildings were built.
   **C** People saved more money to buy a home.
   **D** Cities provided good public transportation.

2. Which document most clearly explains the impact of housing on the natural environment?
   **A** Document D
   **B** Document A
   **C** Document C
   **D** Document B

3. What can you conclude about life in the postwar era from Documents A and C?
   **A** Most people wanted homes close to the city.
   **B** People looked at cheap houses as a way to escape crowded cities.
   **C** Most Americans could not afford new houses.
   **D** Cities were attractive and affordable places to live.

4. **Writing Task** What role did home ownership play in the population shift from cities to suburbs? What impact did it have on the economy? Use your knowledge of the chapter content and specific evidence from the primary sources above to support your opinion.

# MI Connect to Michigan

### The 1967 Riots in Detroit, Michigan, and Newark, New Jersey

During the summer of 1967, violent protests over racial inequality took place in two major American cities—Detroit, Michigan and Newark, New Jersey. These two cities shared many of the same problems. Because of segregated neighborhoods and housing discrimination, African American residents in both cities paid high rents for crowded, poor-quality homes. In Newark, the loss of manufacturing jobs led to high unemployment. In Detroit too, African Americans had fewer job opportunities than white workers.

In the end, police action sparked both riots. In Newark on July 14, 1967, police arrested and beat an African American cab driver named John Smith for allegedly driving around a double-parked police car. Protesters who gathered at the police station became violent and began looting area stores. Then in Detroit on July 23, police raided an after hours drinking club in an African American neighborhood and arrested 82 people. The remaining club members broke into stores and set fires. Soon the violence spread.

Detroit photographer Jim Hubbard later recalled his experience that morning:

> "I grabbed my cameras and drove toward the neighborhood where most of the smoke and fire seemed to be coming from. As I turned my car onto 12th Street the chaos instantly looked like a scene from a war film. Buildings were burning, people were running from one store to another to loot the goods and there were no police present. . . . I photographed the violence and destruction in Detroit for three straight days."
>
> —Jim Hubbard, photographer

The state and federal governments sent reinforcements to both cities. The fighting between Newark rioters and the New Jersey State Police and National Guard lasted for six days. It took five days for the police, National Guard troops, and U.S. Army paratroopers to restore calm in Detroit.

Both the Detroit riots and the Newark riots resulted in thousands of arrests, millions of dollars in property damage, hundreds of injuries, and several deaths. African Americans faced tremendous struggles to overcome the challenges they faced in the post-World War II era. It was out of these struggles that the Civil Rights Movement emerged.

# CHALLENGES AND CHANGE

## CONTENTS

Cesar Chavez leads a United
Farm Workers rally in 1966. ▶

# 14

# The Civil Rights Movement

## 1945–1975

## Human Chain of Freedom

In the 1950s and 1960s, African Americans intensified their efforts to gain equal rights. During civil rights marches, peaceful protesters had to find the strength to face taunts and violence. Often, they found that strength in music. Hand in hand, they would face their opponents and sing. In the stirring civil rights anthem "Eyes on the Prize," they proclaimed:

> "Freedom's name is mighty sweet,
> Soon one day we're gonna meet. . . .
> The only thing we did wrong,
> Stayed in the wilderness a day too long.
> But the one thing we did right,
> Was the day we started to fight."
> —Alice Wine, "Eyes on the Prize"

*Listen to the* Witness History *audio to hear more about the civil rights movement.*

◀ Protesters hold hands and sing during a 1965 civil rights march in Selma, Alabama.

 **Sign protesting segregated restaurants**

 **James Meredith, first black student at the University of Mississippi**

### (MI) Content Expectations

**Chapter Focus Question:** What were the causes, main events, and effects of the civil rights movement?

### Section 1
**Early Demands for Equality** 8.3.1c, 8.3.1d, 8.3.4, 8.3.5

### Section 2
**The Movement Gains Ground** 8.3.1c, 8.3.2, 8.3.4

### Section 3
**New Successes and Challenges** 8.3.1b, 8.3.1d, 8.3.2

Use the ☑ **Quick Study Timeline** at the end of this chapter to preview chapter events.

 **Button of a militant African American organization**

> **Note Taking Study Guide *Online***
> **For:** Note Taking and American Issues Connector
> **Web Code:** nee-8701

◄ Medgar Evers

**WITNESS HISTORY** 🔊 AUDIO

## A Different Kind of Enemy

After serving in the army in Europe in World War II, Medgar Evers returned home to the South, where he faced a different kind of enemy: discrimination. When he and some other African American veterans tried to register to vote, a mob of armed whites blocked their way. "All we wanted to be was ordinary citizens," Evers later said, frustrated to find his life at risk in his own country. "We fought during the war for America, Mississippi included." Evers retreated that day, but he did not give up on his goal. He became an active member of the NAACP and a leader in the fight for civil rights.

◄ Sign at a segregated bus station

# Early Demands for Equality

 **Content Expectations**

- **8.3.1c** Analyze protest movements, organizations, civil actions.
- **8.3.1d** Analyze resistance to Civil Rights Movement.
- **8.3.4** Evaluate major accomplishments/setbacks in civil rights/liberties for U.S. minorities.
- **8.3.5** Analyze causes/consequences of civil unrest that occurred in U.S. cities.

## Terms and People

| | |
|---|---|
| de jure segregation | Civil Rights Act of 1957 |
| de facto segregation | Rosa Parks |
| Thurgood Marshall | Montgomery bus boycott |
| Earl Warren | Martin Luther King, Jr. |

## NoteTaking

**Reading Skill: Summarize** Copy the timeline below and fill it in with events of the early civil rights movement. When you finish, write two sentences that summarize the information in your timeline.

**Why It Matters** The postwar period brought prosperity to many, but most African Americans were still treated as second-class citizens. The civil rights movement, a broad and diverse effort to attain racial equality, compelled the nation to live up to its ideal that all are created equal. The movement also demonstrated that ordinary men and women could perform extraordinary acts of courage and sacrifice to achieve social justice, a lesson that continues to inspire people around the world today. **Section Focus Question: How did African Americans challenge segregation after World War II?**

## Segregation Divides America

African Americans had a long history of fighting for their rights. After World War II, the struggle intensified, as African Americans grew increasingly dissatisfied with their second-class status.

**Jim Crow Laws Limit African Americans** In the South, Jim Crow laws enforced strict separation of the races. Segregation that is imposed by law is known as **de jure segregation.** In 1896, in *Plessy* v. *Ferguson,* the Supreme Court had ruled that such segregation was constitutional as long as the facilities for blacks and whites were "separate but equal." But this was seldom the case. The facilities for African Americans were rarely, if ever, equal.

In the South and elsewhere, segregation extended to most areas of public life. Officials enforced segregation of schools, hospitals, transportation, restaurants, cemeteries, and beaches. One city even forbade blacks and whites from playing checkers together.

**Segregation Prevails Around the Nation** In the North, too, African Americans faced segregation and discrimination. Even where there were no explicit laws, **de facto segregation,** or segregation by unwritten custom or tradition, was a fact of life. African Americans in the North were denied housing in many neighborhoods. They faced discrimination in employment and often could get only low-paying jobs.

Jim Crow laws and more subtle forms of discrimination had a widespread and severe impact on African Americans. Black Americans occupied the bottom rungs of the economic ladder. Compared to white Americans, they had significantly higher rates of poverty and illiteracy, as well as lower rates of homeownership and life expectancy. Although African Americans living in the North could vote, most who lived in the South could not. Very few African Americans held public office.

In the West and Southwest, Asian Americans and Mexican Americans, too, faced de facto segregation and, in some cases, legal restrictions. (Their struggle for equality will be discussed in a later chapter.)

**The Civil Rights Movement Grows** In many ways, World War II set the stage for the rise of the modern civil rights movement. President Roosevelt banned discrimination in defense industries in 1941. Gunnar Myrdal's publication in 1944 of *An American Dilemma* brought the issue of American prejudice to the forefront of public consciousness. Lastly, after risking their lives defending freedom abroad, African Americans were unwilling to accept discrimination at home.

In the 1940s, new efforts arose to try to bring an end to racial injustice. James Farmer and several others founded the Congress of Racial Equality (CORE). Its members were deeply influenced by Henry David Thoreau and Mohandas Gandhi. They became convinced that African Americans could apply direct nonviolent methods to gain civil rights. CORE organized protests against segregation in Chicago, Detroit, Denver, and other northern cities.

Success was limited, but one highly visible break in the wall of segregation did take place in 1947. Jackie Robinson joined the Brooklyn Dodgers, becoming the first African American to play major league baseball. Robinson braved death threats and rough treatment, but throughout his career he won the hearts of millions and paved the way for integration of other sports.

Nevertheless, African Americans continued to face discrimination and felt that racial equality was long overdue.

### African Americans Are Segregated

In some parts of the country, even drinking fountains were segregated (below, left). On public buses, African Americans had to sit in the back. *Were the separate facilities for African Americans shown here "equal"?*

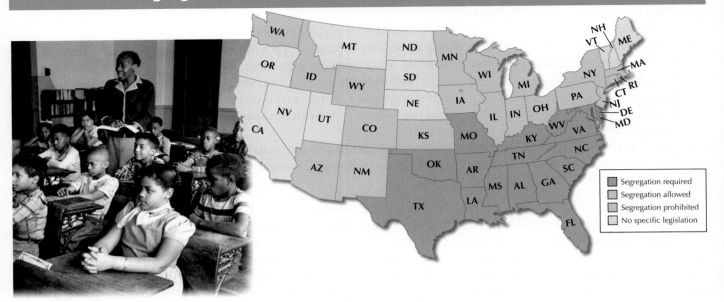

Segregation required
Segregation allowed
Segregation prohibited
No specific legislation

**Map Skills** Before the *Brown* decision, many states had laws mandating segregation in public schools. Even in states that had no laws regarding segregation, there was de facto segregation in schools. The photograph shows

Linda Brown, the student at the center of the *Brown* case, in her classroom in Topeka, Kansas.

**1. Region** Which states had laws requiring school segregation? What was the status of segregation in the state where Linda Brown lived?

**2. Draw Conclusions** Why did school segregation exist even where it was not mandated by law?

However, the vast majority of white Americans took the opposite view. Racial violence erupted in the South, sometimes against veterans who were just trying to register to vote.

In the wake of this violence, President Truman appointed a Committee on Civil Rights to investigate race relations. In its report, the committee recommended a number of measures to ensure equal opportunity for all Americans, including an antilynching law and federal protection of voting rights. Unfortunately, Truman was unable to win congressional support for these initiatives. However, in 1948, he did use his executive power to order the desegregation of the military. Over time, the U.S. armed forces would become one of the most integrated institutions in the United States.

✓ **Checkpoint** How did segregation affect the lives of African Americans?

## *Brown* v. *Board of Education*

Although the civil rights movement had made some gains in the 1940s, it stalled in the early 1950s. Feeling that the executive and legislative branches of government were unwilling to promote additional reforms, the NAACP decided to turn to the federal courts to attain its goals.

**The NAACP Challenges Segregation** By the end of World War II, the NAACP had become the largest and most powerful civil rights organization in the nation. It attracted a wide array of individuals, both black and white, including a number of lawyers. In the 1940s, a team of NAACP attorneys pursued a strategy to challenge in the courts the legality of segregation. **Thurgood Marshall,** an African American lawyer from Baltimore, Maryland, headed the legal team that mounted this challenge.

In 1950, the NAACP won a number of key cases. In *Sweatt* v. *Painter,* the Supreme Court ruled that the state of Texas had violated the Fourteenth Amendment by establishing a separate, but unequal, all-black law school. Similarly, in the *McLaurin* v. *Oklahoma State Regents,* the Court ruled that the state of Oklahoma had violated George McLaurin's constitutional rights. Even though McLaurin had been admitted to the graduate school of the University of Oklahoma, he was denied equal access to the library, dining hall, and classrooms. According to the Supreme Court, a truly equal education involved more than simply admitting African Americans to previously all-white universities.

**The Court Strikes Down Segregated Schools** Not long after it won these cases, the NAACP mounted a much broader challenge to segregated public education at all grade levels. This challenge became known as Brown v. Board of Education, *Topeka, Kansas.* In the *Sweatt* and *McLaurin* cases, the NAACP had asserted that Texas and Oklahoma had failed to provide equal educational experiences. In the *Brown* case, however, the NAACP challenged the "separate but equal" principle itself, which had been established in the 1896 *Plessy* v. *Ferguson* case.

The Supreme Court agreed with the NAACP's argument that segregated public education violated the U.S. Constitution. All nine of the Court's Justices supported the *Brown* decision, which was written by newly appointed Chief Justice **Earl Warren.** "Does segregation of children in public schools solely on the basis of race . . . deprive the children of the minority group equal education opportunities?" Warren asked in his decision. "We believe that it does." The Chief Justice and the Court declared, "in the field of public education the doctrine of 'separate but equal' has no place."

In the same month as the *Brown* decision, the Supreme Court decided another civil rights case, this time involving Mexican Americans. In *Hernandez* v. *Texas,* the Court ended the exclusion of Mexican Americans from trial juries. The *Hernandez* decision was the first Supreme Court ruling against discrimination targeting a group other than African Americans.

**Reaction to *Brown*** The *Brown* decision was one of the most significant and controversial in American history. Because public education touched so many Americans, it had a much greater impact than cases involving only professional and graduate schools. Moreover, by overturning the principle of "separate but equal," the Court lent its support to the views of many civil rights advocates that all forms of segregation were wrong.

In a separate ruling, known as *Brown II,* the Court called for the implementation of its decision "with all deliberate speed" across the nation. However, most southerners had no intention of desegregating their schools without a fight. In 1956, about 100 southern members of Congress endorsed "The Southern Manifesto." They pledged to oppose the *Brown* ruling through all "lawful means," on the grounds that the Court had misinterpreted the Constitution.

More ominously, the Ku Klux Klan staged a revival. Many prominent white southerners and businessmen

## HISTORY MAKERS

### Thurgood Marshall (1908–1993)
An excellent student, Thurgood Marshall applied to the University of Maryland Law School but was turned down because he was an African American. He went to the law school at Howard University, an historically all-black school. The law school dean, Charles Hamilton Houston, trained the students to use the law to fight segregation, and in 1936, Marshall joined the NAACP legal team. *Brown* v. *Board of Education* was just one victory among many that he won. From 1965 until 1991, Marshall himself was a Justice on the Supreme Court.

organized "White Citizens Councils" that declared that the South would not be integrated. The Citizens Councils imposed economic and political pressure against those who favored compliance with the Supreme Court's decision.

 **Checkpoint** Why was the *Brown* v. *Board of Education* decision important?

## Federal and State Governments Clash

Historically, education had been a state matter. States and local school boards ran the schools, and the federal government had little involvement. Local and state officials resisted the *Brown* decision's order to desegregate, and clashes with the federal government resulted. The most famous battle took place in 1957 in Little Rock, Arkansas.

**A Conflict Erupts in Little Rock** The Little Rock school board had established a plan to gradually desegregate its schools, beginning with Central High School. Nine young African American students volunteered to enroll. But Arkansas governor Orval Faubus announced his opposition to integration and called out the Arkansas state National Guard. When the nine students arrived at Central High, the soldiers blocked their way.

One of the nine, Elizabeth Eckford, has described the scene. An angry white mob began to approach her, with some screaming, "Lynch her! Lynch her!" Eckford sought out a friendly face, someone who might help. "I looked into the face of an old woman and it seemed a kind face," she recalled, "but when I looked at her again she spat on me." Fortunately, another white woman whisked Eckford away on a public bus before the mob could have its way. None of the nine African American students gained entrance to the school that day.

Up until the Little Rock crisis, President Eisenhower had provided little leadership on the civil rights front. Following the *Brown* decision, he did not urge the nation to rapidly desegregate its schools. Privately, he expressed his misgivings

### Integrating Little Rock Schools

Angry white students surrounded Elizabeth Eckford (below, right) as she tried to enter Central High in Little Rock. *How is Eckford responding to the white students?*

about the ruling. But when Governor Faubus resisted the will of the federal courts, Eisenhower realized he had to act. He sent federal troops to Little Rock to protect the students and to enforce the Court's decision. Eisenhower explained this action in a nationally televised address:

**Primary Source** ❝It is important that the reasons for my action be understood by all our citizens. . . . A foundation of our American way of life is our national respect for law. . . . If resistance to the federal court orders ceases at once, the further presence of federal troops will be unnecessary and the City of Little Rock will return to its normal habits of peace and order and a blot upon the fair name and high honor of our nation in the world will be removed.❞
—President Dwight D. Eisenhower, "Address on Little Rock," 1957

For the entire school year, federal troops stayed in Little Rock, escorting the nine students to and from Central High and guarding them on the schoolgrounds. On the last day of class, Ernest Green, the one senior of the nine, became the first African American to graduate from Central High School. The showdown demonstrated that the President would not tolerate open defiance of the law. Still, most southern states found ways to resist full <u>compliance</u> with the Court's decision. Many years would pass before black and white children went to school together.

**Vocabulary Builder**
<u>compliance</u>—(kuhm PLī uhns) *n.* the act of obeying a rule or law

**Congress Passes a Civil Rights Law** Civil rights forces enjoyed a small victory when Congress passed the **Civil Rights Act of 1957** and President Eisenhower signed it into law. This law established the United States Civil Rights Commission, which had the power to investigate violations of civil rights. The law also gave the U.S. Attorney General greater power to protect the voting rights of African Americans. But overall, the law lacked teeth. Its main significance was that it was the first civil rights bill passed by Congress since Reconstruction.

✓ **Checkpoint** Why did President Eisenhower send federal troops to Little Rock?

# The Montgomery Bus Boycott

In addition to legal efforts during this era, some civil rights activists took direct action to end segregation. On December 1, 1955, **Rosa Parks,** an African American seamstress, boarded a bus in Montgomery, Alabama, and sat down in an empty seat. Several stops later, the bus driver requested that she give up her seat to a white passenger. Montgomery law required African American passengers to give up their seats to whites. After Rosa Parks refused to obey the law, she was arrested. "The [policemen] asked if the driver had asked me to stand up, and I said yes, and they wanted to know why I didn't," Parks later recalled. "I told them I didn't think I should have to stand up. After I had paid my fare and occupied a seat, I didn't think I should have to give it up."

**Rosa Parks Launches a Movement** Parks's action set in motion a chain of events that transformed the civil rights movement. Over the next few days, a core of civil rights activists in Montgomery organized a one-day bus boycott. They called upon the black community

**HISTORY MAKERS**

**Rosa Parks** (1913–2005)
On December 1, 1955, in Montgomery, Alabama, Rosa Parks was arrested for refusing to give up her bus seat to a white passenger. African Americans responded with a boycott of city buses that lasted more than a year. Parks later moved to Detroit and worked for many years for Representative John Conyers, an African American member of Congress. She founded a nonprofit institute whose goal was to help young people improve their school, work, and interpersonal skills. When she died in 2005, her body was laid in honor at the Capitol in Washington, D.C., making her the first woman ever to be recognized in this way.

to refuse to ride the buses as a way to express their opposition to Parks's arrest, in particular, and segregation, in general. Meanwhile, during the **Montgomery bus boycott,** the NAACP began preparing a legal challenge.

For a long while, many people thought that Parks had refused to give up her seat simply because she was tired after a long day of work. But, in reality, Parks had a record of fighting for civil rights. She had been active in the Montgomery chapter of the NAACP for years. This does not mean that she set out to get arrested and spark a movement. But Parks and other activists welcomed the chance to use the incident to protest bus segregation.

# King's Philosophy of
# NONVIOLENT PROTEST

**F**or Martin Luther King, Jr., the strategy of nonviolent protest had diverse roots. As the son and grandson of Baptist preachers, King absorbed the teachings of Jesus at an early age. Later, a deep interest in philosophy led him to explore the writings of the American author Henry David Thoreau, who advocated civil disobedience, or refusing to obey unjust government or laws. Mohandas Gandhi was another critical influence on King. During India's struggle for independence from British rule, Gandhi expanded on Thoreau's approach, preaching nonviolence as the only way to achieve victory against much stronger foes.

King read Thoreau's *Essay on Civil Disobedience.* ▶

CIVIL DISOBEDIENCE

HENRY DAVID THOREAU

LITERARY CLASSICS

*"Fascinated by the idea of refusing to cooperate with an evil system, I was so deeply moved that I reread the work several times. This was my first intellectual contact with the theory of nonviolent resistance."*

King was a Baptist preacher with a deep faith in God and in the teachings of Jesus. ▼

*"In the midst of ... dangers I have felt an inner calm and known resources of strength that only God could give.... I have felt the power of God transforming the fatigue of despair into the buoyancy of hope."*

Gandhi's tactics inspired King. ▶

*"It was in this Gandhian emphasis on love and nonviolence that I discovered the method for social reform that I had been seeking."*

## Thinking Critically

1. **Apply Information** How did King put his belief in nonviolence into practice in the Montgomery bus boycott?

2. **Draw Conclusions** What are the advantages and disadvantages of nonviolent protest?

**Martin Luther King Urges Nonviolence** On the evening following the boycott, the Montgomery Improvement Association (MIA), the organization that sponsored the bus boycott, held a meeting. Dr. **Martin Luther King, Jr.,** a Baptist minister, addressed the group. Though he had had little time to prepare, King delivered an inspirational speech that brought the audience to its feet. Noting that African Americans were tired of segregation and oppression, King declared that there was no alternative but to protest. However, he called for the protest to be nonviolent. He urged them not to become resentful, which would lead to hatred toward whites, but rather to follow Christian doctrine and love them.

After King spoke, the MIA vowed to continue the boycott and chose King as its leader. For more than a year, African Americans in Montgomery maintained their boycott of the buses. They did so despite economic pressures from their employers and threats of violence by the Ku Klux Klan. King himself survived a bombing of his house. Fortunately, his wife and baby daughter were not home at the time. Finally, in 1956, the Supreme Court ruled that the Montgomery city law that segregated buses was unconstitutional. After more than a year, the MIA ended its boycott, and African Americans began to ride the buses again.

**Ministers Form the SCLC** The bus boycott represented a tremendous victory for African Americans in Montgomery and across the nation. The boycott revealed the power that African Americans could have if they joined together. The protest also elevated King and his philosophy of nonviolence into a prominent position within the civil rights movement.

After the boycott, King and another Montgomery minister, Ralph Abernathy, established the Southern Christian Leadership Conference (SCLC) to continue the struggle for civil rights. Made up largely of southern African American ministers, the SCLC advocated nonviolent resistance to fight injustice. The SCLC went on to organize a series of protests, including a Prayer Pilgrimage in Washington, D.C., in 1957, which helped convince Congress to pass civil rights legislation. Still, discrimination and segregation remained widespread.

 **Checkpoint** What role did Rosa Parks and Martin Luther King, Jr., play in the Montgomery bus boycott?

---

**SECTION** **1** **Assessment**

**Progress Monitoring *Online***
**For:** Self-test with vocabulary practice
**Web Code:** nea-1403

## Comprehension

**1. Terms and People** For each item below, write a sentence explaining its significance:
- de jure segregation
- de facto segregation
- Thurgood Marshall
- *Brown v. Board of Education*
- Earl Warren
- Civil Rights Act of 1957
- Rosa Parks
- Montgomery bus boycott
- Martin Luther King, Jr.

**2. NoteTaking Reading Skill: Summarize** Use your timeline to answer the Section Focus Question: How did African Americans challenge segregation after World War II?

## Writing About History

**3. Quick Write: Identify Questions** Historical research begins with identifying unanswered questions. Such questions often relate to the causes of an event or development. Reread this section and identify two events or developments that raise unanswered questions in your mind. Try to write questions that begin with *Why* or *How.*

## Critical Thinking

**4. Recognize Cause and Effect** Why did the struggle for equal rights intensify after World War II?

**5. Analyze Information** How did the *Brown* decision lead to conflict between federal and state governments?

**6. Synthesize Information** Why is the Montgomery bus boycott considered a turning point in the civil rights movement?

# How Does Segregation Affect Education?

MI 8.3.1b

Until the 1950s, public schools throughout the United States were segregated by race. This separation of students was legal because of the 1896 *Plessy* v. *Ferguson* decision, in which the Supreme Court ruled that "separate but equal" facilities did not violate the Constitution. However, many believed that segregated schools could never provide an equal education.

▼ Linda Brown

## Brown v. Board of Education (1954)

| The Facts | The Issue | The Decision |
|---|---|---|
| • Linda Brown was an African American student in the segregated school district of Topeka, Kansas.<br><br>• Linda's parents tried to enroll her in an all-white school closer to home, but school officials denied the application on the basis of race.<br><br>• The NAACP filed a lawsuit against the Board of Education on behalf of the Browns and several other black families. | The NAACP argued that segregated schools deprived African American students the equal protection of the law required by the Fourteenth Amendment. | The Supreme Court ruled unanimously that segregated schools were inherently unequal and violated the Fourteenth Amendment. |

## Why It Matters

*Brown* v. *Board of Education* was a major legal victory in the civil rights movement. This landmark decision brought America one step closer to securing equal rights for all. Chief Justice Earl Warren declared that segregation in education was unconstitutional because it prevented an equal education for all races:

"In these days, it is doubtful that any child may reasonably be expected to succeed in life if he is denied the opportunity of an education. Such an opportunity . . . is a right which must be made available to all on equal terms. . . . To separate them [children in grade and high schools] from others of similar age and qualifications solely because of their race generates a feeling of inferiority . . . that may affect their hearts and minds in a way unlikely to ever be undone. . . ."

▼ Students at a high school in Texas

### Connect to Your World

Use the data in the table to create a graph, and describe the trend that you see. Then, research school segregation today. Have schools become more or less segregated since 2001? What might explain this change?

### School Desegregation After *Brown*

(Percentage of African American students in 90 percent minority schools)

| | 1968 | 1988 | 1991 | 2001 |
|---|---|---|---|---|
| South | 78 | 24 | 26 | 31 |
| Northeast | 43 | 48 | 50 | 51 |
| Midwest | 58 | 42 | 40 | 47 |
| West | 51 | 29 | 27 | 30 |

SOURCE: *National Center for Education Statistics Common Core of Data*

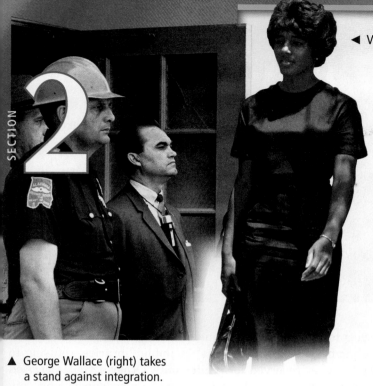

◀ Vivian Malone

▲ George Wallace (right) takes a stand against integration.

WITNESS HISTORY 🔊 AUDIO

### Blocking the Schoolhouse Door

Alabama governor George Wallace made it clear where he stood on civil rights: "I say segregation now! Segregation tomorrow! Segregation forever!" Wallace vowed to stand "in the schoolhouse door" and personally block any attempt to integrate Alabama schools. On June 11, 1963, he got his chance. As federal marshals escorted two African American students to register at the University of Alabama, Wallace stood on the steps of the school. He proclaimed the right of states to regulate their own schools. One of the students later recalled:

❝I didn't feel I should sneak in. I didn't feel I should go around the back door. If [Wallace] were standing in the door, I had every right in the world to face him and to go to school.❞

—Vivian Malone Jones, 2003

# The Movement Gains Ground

 **Content Expectations**

- **8.3.1c** Analyze protest movements, organizations, civil actions.
- **8.3.2** Compare/contrast March on Washington speech to Declaration of Independence, Seneca Falls Resolution, Gettysburg Address.
- **8.3.4** Evaluate major accomplishments/setbacks in civil rights/liberties for U.S. minorities.

## Terms and People

sit-in
SNCC
freedom ride
James Meredith

Medgar Evers
March on Washington
filibuster
Civil Rights Act of 1964

## NoteTaking

**Reading Skill: Summarize** Use a concept web like the one below to record information about the civil rights protests of the 1960s.

**Why It Matters** Despite the *Brown* decision and other civil rights victories, little changed in the everyday lives of most African Americans. Nonetheless, activists continued to struggle for civil rights. In the early 1960s, the movement experienced a groundswell of support. This surge produced a dramatic shift in race relations, led to the passage of landmark civil rights legislation in 1964, and set the stage for future reforms. **Section Focus Question: How did the civil rights movement gain ground in the 1960s?**

## Student Activists Make a Difference

After the *Brown* decision, many black youths expected that their schools would integrate quickly and that other racial reforms would follow. Change was not quick to come, however. Disappointed by the lack of progress, young African Americans began to challenge segregation with new vigor and determination.

**Sit-ins Challenge Segregation** On February 1, 1960, four African American college students ordered doughnuts and coffee at a Woolworth's lunch counter in Greensboro, North Carolina. As they expected, the white waitress refused to serve them. In the South, nearly all restaurants that served whites refused to serve blacks. To protest this discrimination, the four students sat down on the stools at the lunch counter, where they stayed until closing time.

Word of the Greensboro **sit-in** spread rapidly, sparking a wave of similar protests across the nation. In Nashville, Tennessee, for instance, students led by the Reverend James Lawson staged sit-ins

## Protesting Segregation

Protesters challenged segregation at lunch counters by picketing (above, left). Later activists held sit-ins, like the one (above, right) in Jackson, Mississippi. Sit-in participants were trained not to react, even when hostile onlookers dumped food on them. *How would you describe the atmosphere at this lunch counter?*

and, later, marches to protest racial inequality. Elsewhere, protesters held "wade-ins" at public beaches and "read-ins" at public libraries, refusing to leave beaches or libraries reserved for whites only. Other activists carried picket signs in demonstrations and wrote letters to newspapers and government officials to express their support of the protests in the South.

**SNCC Promotes Nonviolent Protest** The sit-ins marked the birth of a new militancy, especially among young African Americans. To build on the momentum they had gained, about 175 students from 30 states met at Shaw University, in Raleigh, North Carolina. There, on Easter weekend in 1960, they listened to James Lawson deliver an inspiring address:

> **Primary Source** ❝We who are demonstrators are trying to raise what we call the 'moral issue.' That is, we are pointing to the viciousness of racial segregation and prejudice and calling it evil or sin. . . . [We are also] asserting, 'get moving.' The pace of change is too slow. At this rate it will be another generation before the major forms of segregation disappear. . . . Most of us will be grandparents before we can live normal human lives.❞
>
> —James Lawson, "From a Lunch Counter Stool," 1960

Ella Baker, a veteran of the struggle for civil rights, had organized the meeting. The granddaughter of enslaved African Americans, Baker had been active in the NAACP and SCLC. She helped the young activists to establish a new civil rights organization, the **Student Nonviolent Coordinating Committee,** or **SNCC.** Its goal was to create a grass-roots movement that involved all classes of African Americans in the struggle to defeat white racism and to obtain equality.

✔ **Checkpoint** How did young people energize the civil rights movement in the 1960s?

## Riding for Freedom

The next battleground was interstate transportation. Activists targeted this industry because they knew that travel between states was subject to federal rather than state regulation. In fact, the Supreme Court had recently ruled in *Boynton* v. *Virginia* (1960) that segregation on interstate buses and in waiting rooms was illegal. Civil rights activists were now going to test the federal government's willingness to enforce the law.

**Freedom Riders Face Angry Mobs** In the spring of 1961, CORE staged a **"freedom ride"** through the Deep South. Riders set off in two separate buses from Washington, D.C., bound for New Orleans. En route, they defied segregationist codes. African Americans sat in the front of the bus and used "white" restrooms in bus stations.

In Alabama, the trip took a dangerous turn. After departing from Anniston, prosegregationists firebombed one of the buses. When the second bus arrived in Birmingham, a white mob attacked the riders.

## INFOGRAPHIC

Troops stand guard on the bus to Jackson. ▶

# RIDING FOR FREEDOM

**I**n 1961, a group of freedom riders set out to challenge segregation in buses and bus terminals in the South.

**A** **May 4: Freedom riders depart.** Six white and seven African American freedom riders leave Washington, D.C.

**B** **May 14: Attacks in Alabama** Riders travel in two groups through Alabama. Outside of Anniston, one bus is firebombed. A mob attacks the second bus in Birmingham.

**C** **May 20: Federal marshals arrive.** Riders meet more violence when they reach Montgomery. U.S. marshals are sent in.

**D** **May 24: Mass arrests** Troops escort riders to Jackson, where they are arrested and sent to jail.

**New volunteers kept the freedom rides going. By the end of the summer, more than 300 had been arrested.**

Freedom rider James Zwerg reels ▶ after being beaten in Montgomery.

Washington, D.C. ✪
Virginia
Nashville •
Tennessee
North Carolina
Anniston
Birmingham •
Mississippi
South Carolina
Georgia
Jackson •
Montgomery
Louisiana
New Orleans •
Alabama
Florida

→ Route of Freedom Riders

Passengers watch as their bus burns near Anniston. ▼

E DRIVING TO US

### Thinking Critically
1. **Analyze Information** Why do you think the freedom riders chose the route that they did?
2. **Draw Inferences** Do you think they anticipated the opposition they encountered?

**President Kennedy Takes Action** Photographs of the bombed-out bus and the injured riders appeared in newspapers and on television screens around the world, prodding President John F. Kennedy to intervene. Kennedy had intervened before. The previous year, when he was running for the presidency, Kennedy had helped to win Martin Luther King's release from a Georgia prison after state officials had sentenced King to 6 months in jail for a traffic violation. King was freed and Kennedy, with the help of African American voters, went on to win the presidential election of 1960.

Kennedy now took action to stem the violence against the freedom riders. His administration worked out a deal with Mississippi's leaders. Police and state troopers agreed to protect the riders. The Federal Transportation Commission also issued an order mandating the desegregation of interstate transportation. In exchange, the Kennedy administration agreed not to intervene when Mississippi authorities arrested the activists and sentenced them to jail for disturbing the peace.

The freedom riders achieved their immediate goal. They compelled a reluctant federal government to act. By refusing to allow violent mobs to deter them, the riders also displayed that intimidation would not defeat the movement.

✓ **Checkpoint** What did the freedom rides accomplish?

## Protests and Confrontations Intensify

In the fall of 1962 and spring of 1963, protests against racial discrimination intensified. The protesters put pressure on the federal government to help break down legal, or de jure, segregation.

### Integrating Ole Miss

Accompanied by federal marshals, James Meredith arrived at the University of Mississippi in 1962. He went on to graduate from the university in 1963.

### Meredith Integrates the University of Mississippi

One struggle that gained international attention involved **James Meredith.** Meredith was an Air Force veteran who sought to enroll at the all-white University of Mississippi, known as "Ole Miss." In September 1962, with the support of the NAACP, Meredith won a federal court case that ordered the university to desegregate. Civil rights activist **Medgar Evers** was instrumental in this effort.

Mississippi governor Ross Barnett was determined to prevent the integration of the university. The issue became a standoff between the governor and the federal government.

On September 30, rumors of Meredith's arrival on the university's campus began to spread. Federal marshals had been assigned to protect him. Over the course of the night, a full-scale riot erupted, with federal marshals battling white protestors intent on scaring Meredith away.

As the rioting took place, President Kennedy addressed the nation on television. "Americans are free . . . to disagree with the law but not to disobey it," he declared. "For any government of laws . . . , no man, however prominent and powerful . . . is entitled to defy a court of law." The rioting went on throughout the night. By the time it ended, 160 people had been injured and 2 men had been killed.

The following morning, Meredith registered as a student and took his first class. He graduated from Ole Miss in 1963 and went on to obtain his law degree from Columbia University in New York City. Tragically, Medgar Evers was assassinated, on his front doorstep, in June 1963. Three years later, Meredith himself was shot and nearly killed. Both shootings stand as historical reminders of the high costs of fighting racial discrimination.

**King Campaigns in Birmingham** In the spring of 1963, Martin Luther King, Jr., and the SCLC targeted Birmingham, Alabama, for a major civil rights campaign. They chose Birmingham because of its reputation as the most segregated city in the South.

The campaign began nonviolently at first with protest marches and sit-ins. City officials got a court order prohibiting the demonstrations. On Good Friday, April 12, 1963, King decided to violate the order and join the demonstration personally, even though he knew it would lead to his arrest. From his jail cell, King wrote a letter explaining why he and other civil rights activists were tired of waiting for reform: "For years now I have heard the word 'wait!' It rings in the ear of every Negro with piercing familiarity. This 'Wait!' has almost always meant 'Never.'"

One of the most poignant passages of the letter describes King's concern about the impact of discrimination on his children:

**Clash in Birmingham**
Police in Birmingham, Alabama, used police dogs to break up civil rights marches in 1963. *How do you think Americans reacted when they saw images like these on television and in newspapers?*

**Primary Source** "Perhaps it is easy for those who have never felt the stinging darts of segregation to say, 'Wait.' But . . . when you suddenly find your tongue twisted and your speech stammering as you seek to explain to your six-year-old daughter why she can't go to the public amusement park that has just been advertised on television, and see tears welling up in her eyes when she is told that Funtown is closed to colored children. . . . Then you will understand why we find it difficult to wait."
—Martin Luther King, Jr., "Letter From Birmingham Jail," 1963

After King was released from jail, the SCLC increased the frequency of the demonstrations. For the first time, schoolchildren joined the "freedom marches." Finally, Birmingham's Public Safety Commissioner, T. Eugene "Bull" Connor, would not <u>tolerate</u> the demonstrations any longer. He used police dogs and fire hoses on the protesters. Many Americans were shocked by photographs and news coverage of nonviolent protesters set upon by dogs and overwhelmed by the powerful jets of water from fire hoses. They sent telegrams and letters by the thousands to the White House, calling on the President to act.

**Vocabulary Builder**
<u>tolerate</u>—(TAHL er ayt) *v.* to allow or put up with

**Kennedy Backs Civil Rights** In addition to the conflict in Birmingham, civil rights protests were taking place in cities from Jackson, Mississippi, to Cambridge, Maryland. President Kennedy became convinced that he had to take a more active role in promoting civil rights.

On June 11, 1963, Kennedy delivered a moving televised address. Calling civil rights a "moral issue," he declared that the nation had an obligation to "fulfill its promise" of giving all Americans "equal rights and equal opportunities." President Kennedy sent to Congress a proposal for sweeping civil rights legislation. His brother, Attorney General Robert F. Kennedy, led the charge for passage of the bill.

✓ **Checkpoint** How did James Meredith and Martin Luther King, Jr., prompt President Kennedy to promote civil rights?

## The Movement Marches on Washington

To put pressure on Congress to pass the new civil rights bill, supporters made plans for a massive demonstration in Washington, D.C. The event brought together the major civil rights groups—including the NAACP, SCLC, and SNCC—as well as labor unions and religious groups.

The **March on Washington** took place on August 28, 1963. Organizers had hoped for 100,000 demonstrators. More than double that number showed up, having made the journey to the capital from around the country. Before the march, there had been some concern about maintaining order at such a huge demonstration. Yet despite the massive numbers, the day was peaceful and even festive. Popular celebrities and entertainers were on hand to perform for the crowd.

The main rally took place in front of the Lincoln Memorial, where a distinguished roster of speakers addressed the crowd. The highlight of the day came

**Events That Changed America**

# THE MARCH ON WASHINGTON

The March on Washington drew more than 200,000 people to Washington, D.C. The demonstrators were a diverse group from all parts of the country. They were young and old and came from various classes and religious backgrounds. More than a quarter of them were white.

The Washington Monument was the starting point for the day's events. Prominent singers performed songs, including the civil rights movement's unofficial anthem, "We Shall Overcome." Then, the throng marched to the Lincoln Memorial for the main rally. A. Philip Randolph, the elder statesman of the civil rights movement, gave the opening remarks, followed by representatives of various religious and labor groups. The final speaker was Martin Luther King, Jr., whose moving speech enthralled the crowd—and the millions more watching on television.

▼ King addresses the crowd around the reflecting pool between the Lincoln Memorial and Washington Monument.

when Martin Luther King, Jr., took the podium. King held the audience spell-bound as he described his dream of a colorblind society "when all God's children" would be free and equal. Millions more watched King's address live on television. This powerful and eloquent speech has come to be known as the "I Have a Dream" speech. (You will read an excerpt from the "I Have a Dream" speech later in this chapter.)

Behind the scenes, there was some tension between the organizations that had planned the March. SNCC, in particular, had wanted to stage a more militant protest, to show its dissatisfaction with the pace of change. Yet for the public at large and for most who took part, the March on Washington represented a magical moment in American history.

✓ **Checkpoint** What is considered the highlight of the March on Washington?

## Why It Matters

The March on Washington was one of the largest political demonstrations in U.S. history. Widely covered in the media, the march increased awareness of the movement and built momentum for the passage of civil rights legislation. Despite the huge numbers and the emotional intensity of the day, the march remained orderly and is considered a model for peaceful protest. The March on Washington has come to symbolize the civil rights movement itself.

▲ Button from the march urging interracial cooperation

▼ The crowd erupts in cheers after hearing King's speech.

### Thinking Critically
Why was the March on Washington a symbolic and appropriate choice for a civil rights demonstration?

**History** *Interactive*

**For:** More on the March on Washington
**Web Code:** nep-1405

MARCH ON WASHINGTON
FOR JOBS AND FREEDOM
AUGUST 28, 1963
LINCOLN MEMORIAL PROGRAM

483

# Congress Passes the Civil Rights Act of 1964

On September 15, 1963, less than three weeks after the march, a bomb exploded in the Sixteenth Street Baptist Church in Birmingham. The church had been the SCLC's headquarters earlier that spring. Four young African American girls, all dressed in their Sunday best, were killed in the bombing.

Two months later, on November 22, 1963, President John F. Kennedy was assassinated in Dallas, Texas. Vice President Lyndon B. Johnson assumed the presidency.

Johnson was a southerner with an undistinguished record on racial matters. However, he surprised many Americans by immediately throwing his support behind the cause of civil rights. "No eulogy could more eloquently honor President Kennedy's memory," Johnson told Congress and the nation, "[than the] earliest passage of the civil rights bill for which he fought so long."

The civil rights bill faced strong opposition in Congress, but Johnson put his considerable political skills to work for its passage. The bill passed in the House of Representatives, but it faced a more difficult fight in the Senate, where a group of southern senators attempted to block it by means of a **filibuster.** This is a tactic by which senators give long speeches to hold up legislative business. The filibuster went on for more than 80 days until supporters finally put together enough votes to overcome it. In the end, the measure passed in the Senate, and President Johnson signed the **Civil Rights Act of 1964** into law in July.

The act banned segregation in public accommodations and gave the federal government the ability to compel state and local school boards to desegregate their schools. The act also allowed the Justice Department to prosecute individuals who violated people's civil rights and outlawed discrimination in employment on account of race, color, sex, or national origin. It also established the Equal Employment Opportunity Commission (EEOC), which is responsible for enforcing these provisions and investigating charges of job discrimination.

 **Checkpoint** How did the Civil Rights Act of 1964 try to end discrimination?

---

## SECTION 2 Assessment

**Progress Monitoring *Online***
For: Self-test with vocabulary practice
Web Code: nea-1406

### Comprehension

**1. Terms and People** For each item below, write a sentence explaining its significance:
- sit-in
- SNCC
- freedom ride
- James Meredith
- Medgar Evers
- March on Washington
- filibuster
- Civil Rights Act of 1964

**2. NoteTaking Reading Skill: Summarize** Use your concept web to answer the Section Focus Question: How did the civil rights movement gain ground in the 1960s?

### Writing About History

**3. Quick Write: Construct a Hypothesis** After identifying an unanswered question, a historian might form a hypothesis, an unproven answer to that question. Write a one-sentence hypothesis to answer the following question: Why was Johnson more successful than Truman in getting civil rights legislation passed? Remem-ber, your statement is not a fact but a theory that might or might not be supported by further research. The sentence you write could later become the thesis statement for a research paper.

### Critical Thinking

**4. Draw Conclusions** Why were sit-ins often a successful tactic?

**5. Analyze Information** Why did the freedom rides lead to violence?

**6. Recognize Cause and Effect** What events led to passage of the Civil Rights Act of 1964?

8.3.2

# Martin Luther King, Jr.:
# *I Have a Dream*

Martin Luther King, Jr., delivered the closing address at the March on Washington. For approximately 20 minutes, he mesmerized the crowd with one of the most powerful speeches ever delivered. In this excerpt, King speaks of his dream for America:

▲ Martin Luther King, Jr., at the March on Washington

I say to you today, my friends, that in spite of the difficulties and frustrations of the moment I still have a dream. It is a dream deeply rooted in the American dream.

I have a dream that one day this nation will rise up and live out the true meaning of its creed[1]: "We hold these truths to be self-evident; that all men are created equal."

I have a dream that one day on the red hills of Georgia the sons of former slaves and the sons of former slaveowners will be able to sit down together at the table of brotherhood.

I have a dream that one day even the state of Mississippi . . . will be transformed into an oasis of freedom and justice.

I have a dream that my four little children will one day live in a nation where they will not be judged by the color of their skin but by the content of their character.

I have a dream today.

I have a dream that one day the state of Alabama . . . will be transformed into a situation where little black boys and black girls will be able to join hands with little white boys and girls and walk together as sisters and brothers. . . .

This is our hope. This is the faith with which I return to the South. With this faith we will be able to hew[2] out of the mountain of despair a stone of hope. With this faith we will be able to transform the jangling discords of our nation into a beautiful symphony of brotherhood. . . .

This will be the day when all of God's children will be able to sing with new meaning, "My country 'tis of thee, sweet land of liberty, of thee I sing. Land where my father died, land of the Pilgrims' pride, from every mountainside, let freedom ring." . . .

When we let freedom ring, when we let it ring from every village and every hamlet, from every state and every city, we will be able to speed up that day when all of God's children, black men and white men, Jews and Gentiles[3], Protestants and Catholics, will be able to join hands and sing in the words of the old Negro spiritual, "Free at last! Free at last! Thank God Almighty, we are free at last!"

**1. creed** (kreed) *n.* beliefs or principles
**2. hew** (hyoo) *v.* carve
**3. Gentiles** (JEHN tīlz) *n.* non-Jews

---

**Thinking Critically**
1. **Identify Central Issues** What is the "American dream" to which King refers?
2. **Draw Inferences** How well does King think the nation has lived up to its promises?

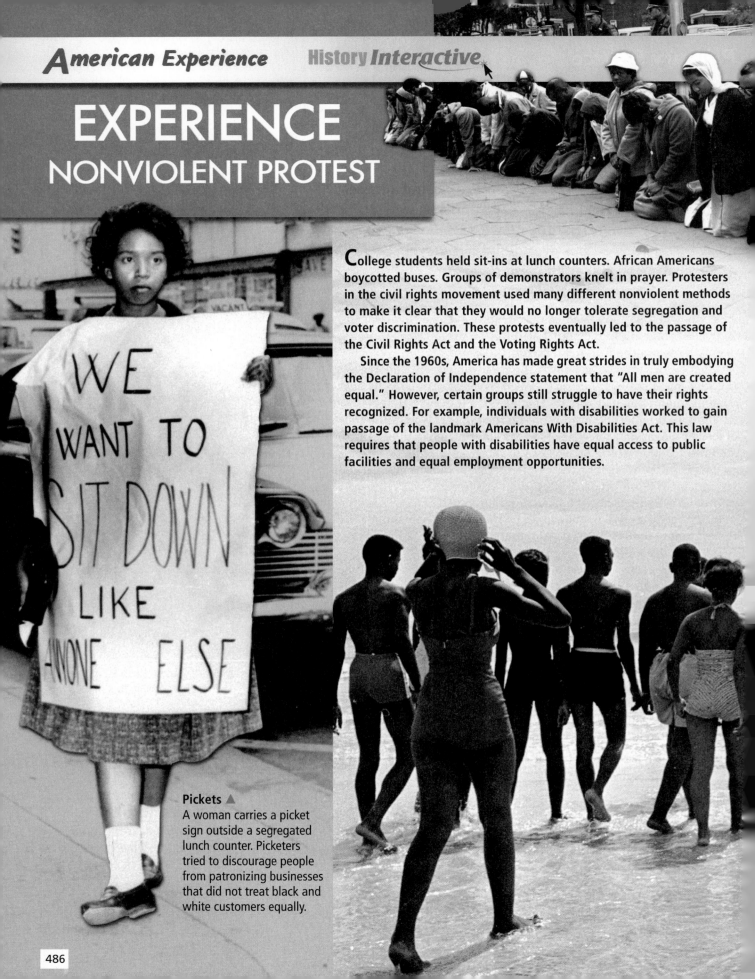

# EXPERIENCE
## NONVIOLENT PROTEST

College students held sit-ins at lunch counters. African Americans boycotted buses. Groups of demonstrators knelt in prayer. Protesters in the civil rights movement used many different nonviolent methods to make it clear that they would no longer tolerate segregation and voter discrimination. These protests eventually led to the passage of the Civil Rights Act and the Voting Rights Act.

Since the 1960s, America has made great strides in truly embodying the Declaration of Independence statement that "All men are created equal." However, certain groups still struggle to have their rights recognized. For example, individuals with disabilities worked to gain passage of the landmark Americans With Disabilities Act. This law requires that people with disabilities have equal access to public facilities and equal employment opportunities.

**Pickets** ▲
A woman carries a picket sign outside a segregated lunch counter. Picketers tried to discourage people from patronizing businesses that did not treat black and white customers equally.

**Prayerful Protests** ▲
A group of demonstrators kneel in prayer during a hearing for arrested freedom riders in Albany, Georgia, in 1961. Nonviolent protests often took the form of prayer vigils like this.

**Boycotts** ▲
African American students at Florida A&M College jeer at a nearly empty city bus as it passes through the campus. Protesters in Tallahassee were boycotting the buses to protest segregation on the bus lines.

**Wade-ins** ▼
Black protesters march onto a "whites only" public beach, ready to swim. Whites who did not want the beach desegregated face off against them as police stand guard.

## Thinking Critically

1. **Analyze Visuals** How did whites support or oppose black protesters?

2. **Draw Conclusions** Do you think the civil rights movement would have been as effective if protesters had not used peaceful protest methods?

**Connect to Today** Do research to learn about the passage of the Americans With Disabilities Act. How were the methods and goals of that movement similar to and different from the movement for racial equality in the 1960s? Did the bill succeed in gaining equal rights and opportunities for people with disabilities?

**History Interactive** ✳
**For:** Learn more about civil rights tactics
**Web Code:** nep-1407

◄ Malcolm X

▲ Button honoring Malcolm X

### Entering a New Era

Although the Civil Rights movement was making headway, many black activists were impatient with King's nonviolent methods and his emphasis on integration. Some believed that integration was not the solution. Others felt that more needed to be done to remove what they saw as oppression by white society.

Malcolm X (also known by his religious name, el-Hajj Malik el-Shabazz) became one of the most prominent voices for this faction. As a minister of the Nation of Islam, he preached a message of self-reliance and self-protection. He called for black pride and spread the idea of black nationalism, a belief in the separate identity and racial unity of the African American community. Malcolm was a "charismatic speaker who could play an audience as great musicians play instruments." His dynamic speeches won many adherents to his cause. The Civil Rights Movement had entered a new era.

# New Successes and Challenges

## Content Expectations

- **8.3.1b** Analyze Supreme Court decisions/governmental actions during Civil Rights Movement.
- **8.3.1d** Analyze resistance to Civil Rights Movement.
- **8.3.2** Compare/contrast March on Washington speech to Declaration of Independence, Seneca Falls Resolution, Gettysburg Address.

### Terms and People

| | |
|---|---|
| Freedom Summer | Kerner Commission |
| Fannie Lou Hamer | Malcolm X |
| Voting Rights Act | Nation of Islam |
| Twenty-fourth | black power |
| Amendment | Black Panthers |

### NoteTaking

**Reading Skill: Summarize** Complete an outline to summarize the contents of this section.

> I. Push for Voting Rights
>   A. Freedom Summer
>     1.
>     2.

**Why It Matters** During the 1950s and 1960s, the civil rights movement made great strides forward. Yet racial injustice was not fully eradicated. Frustration with this situation led some African Americans to turn to more radical and sometimes violent methods. African Americans achieved further successes, but for some the radicalism of the times left a bitter legacy. **Section Focus Question: What successes and challenges faced the civil rights movement after 1964?**

## The Push for Voting Rights

None of the federal court decisions or civil rights measures passed through 1964 fundamentally affected the right to vote. The problem was a southern political system that used literacy tests, poll taxes, and intimidation to keep blacks from voting. In Mississippi, in 1964, for instance, not a single African American person was registered to vote in five counties that had African American majorities. All of the major civil rights organizations sought to overcome these political injustices.

**SNCC Stages Freedom Summer** SNCC had spent several years organizing voter education projects in Mississippi. It met with little success and a great deal of violent opposition. But in 1964, it called for a major campaign, known as **Freedom Summer.** About 1,000 volunteers, mostly black and white students, were to flood Mississippi. They would focus on registering African Americans to vote. They would also form the Mississippi Freedom Democratic Party (MFDP), an alternative to the state's all-white regular Democratic Party.

Even before most of the volunteers had arrived, three civil rights workers—Michael Schwerner, James Chaney, and Andrew Goodman—disappeared. SNCC claimed that they had been murdered; state authorities denied these charges. President Johnson ordered a massive search for the three, which ended when their bodies were found buried in an earthen dam. All had been shot at point-blank range. Yet, despite the obvious dangers, almost all of the other volunteers remained in the state.

After Freedom Summer ended in August 1964, an MFDP delegation traveled to the Democratic Convention in New Jersey, seeking to be recognized as Mississippi's only Democratic Party. At the convention, **Fannie Lou Hamer,** one of the MFDP's leaders, gave powerful testimony. She described how she and other activists had been beaten, fired from their jobs, and displaced from their homes all because, as she put it, they wanted "to register" and "live as decent human beings."

Despite Hamer's testimony, the Democrats refused to seat the MFDP. Instead, party officials offered a compromise: They would seat two MFDP members as "at-large delegates" and reform the nomination rules to guarantee greater minority representation in the future. The MFDP rejected this offer. Ironically, Mississippi's regular Democratic delegation left the convention in protest because the national party had made the offer to the MFDP.

**Marching on Selma** Early in 1965, Martin Luther King, Jr., and the SCLC organized a major campaign in Selma, Alabama, to pressure the federal government to enact voting rights legislation. The protests climaxed in a series of <u>confrontations</u> on the Edmund Pettus Bridge, on the main route from Selma to Montgomery. The first of these confrontations took place on March 7, 1965, a day that became known as "Bloody Sunday." Heavily armed state troopers and other authorities attacked the marchers as they tried to cross the bridge. Sheyann Webb, a six-year-old girl at the time, recalled the scene:

> **Primary Source** ❝I heard all of this screaming and . . . somebody yelled, 'Oh God, they're killing us!' . . . And I looked and I saw the troopers charging us . . . swinging their arms and throwing canisters of tear gas. . . . Some of them had clubs and others had ropes and whips. . . . It was like a nightmare. . . . I just knew then that I was going to die.❞
>
> —Sheyann Webb, *Selma, Lord, Selma*

**Vocabulary Builder**
<u>confrontation</u>–(kahn fruhn TAY shuhn) *n.* situation in which there is angry disagreement between opposing people or groups

**Standoff in Selma**
Police officers block the path of protesters attempting to march to Selma, Alabama.

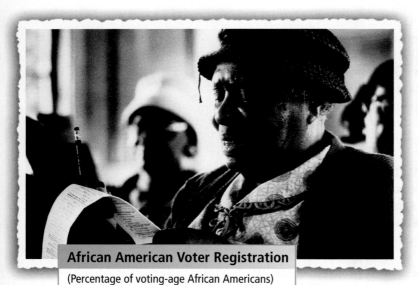

| African American Voter Registration | | |
| --- | --- | --- |
| (Percentage of voting-age African Americans) | | |
| State | 1964 | 1968 |
| Alabama | 23.0 | 56.7 |
| Louisiana | 32.0 | 59.3 |
| Mississippi | 6.7 | 59.4 |
| Texas | 57.7 | 83.1 |
| Virginia | 45.7 | 58.4 |

SOURCE: Stanley, Harold W. *Voter Mobilization and the Politics of Race: The South and Universal Suffrage, 1952–1984*

## Voting Rights Legislation Takes Effect

The table shows voter registration rates in some southern states before and after the Voting Rights Act of 1965. The women shown above are learning how to mark the ballot at a voter education class in Alabama in 1966. *Which state listed in the table had the greatest increase in voter registration between 1964 and 1968?*

Webb survived, but the rampage continued. Television coverage of the violence outraged the nation. On March 15, President Johnson went on national television and called for a strong federal voting rights law. Historically, regulation of voting rights had been left to the states, but Johnson argued that "it is wrong to deny any of your fellow citizens the right to vote." He added, "Their cause is our cause too, because it is not just Negroes, but really it is all of us, who must overcome the crippling legacy of bigotry and injustice. And, *we shall overcome.*"

**New Legislation Guarantees Voting Rights** Spurred by the actions of protesters and the words of the President, Congress passed the **Voting Rights Act** of 1965. The act banned literacy tests and empowered the federal government to oversee voting registration and elections in states that had discriminated against minorities. In 1975, Congress extended coverage to Hispanic voters in the Southwest.

Another legal landmark was the **Twenty-fourth Amendment** to the Constitution, ratified in 1964. It banned the poll tax, which had been used to keep poor African Americans from voting. In addition, the federal courts handed down several important decisions. *Baker* v. *Carr* and *Reynolds* v. *Simms* limited racial gerrymandering, the practice of drawing election districts in such a way as to dilute the African American vote, and established the legal principle of "one man, one vote."

These laws and decisions had a profound impact. Particularly in the Deep South, African American participation in politics skyrocketed. In Mississippi, the percentage of African Americans registered to vote jumped from just under 7 percent in 1964 to about 70 percent in 1986. Nationwide, the number of African American elected officials rose from fewer than 100 to more than 6,000 by the mid-1980s.

✔ **Checkpoint** What impact did the protests in Selma, Alabama, have on the nation?

## Frustration Explodes Into Violence

Many celebrated the passage of the Voting Rights Act of 1965. Yet for some African Americans, things had not changed much. In many urban areas, there was anger and frustration over continuing discrimination and poverty. That anger exploded into violence in several cities.

**Racial Violence Plagues Cities** Less than a week after Johnson signed the Voting Rights Act, one of the worst race riots in American history erupted in the predominantly African American neighborhood of Watts in Los Angeles. Violence, looting, and arson spread for several days before National Guard troops restored order.

Watts was one of many race riots that erupted in the 1960s. The worst violence occurred in Newark, New Jersey, and Detroit, Michigan, in the summer of 1967. In Detroit, 43 people died, and property damage reached $50 million. The outbursts frightened many white Americans. In most previous race riots, whites had used violence to keep African Americans "in their place." But now, blacks were using violence against police and white business owners in black neighborhoods.

# Voting Rights

**MI** 8.3.1a

## TRACK THE ISSUE

### What should the government do to promote voting rights?

Although the right to vote is a corner-stone of American democracy, many restrictions have been placed on voting rights over the years. As the history of the civil rights movement shows, gaining full electoral rights has been a struggle. How can the government ensure fair and free suffrage in America? Use the timeline below to explore this enduring question.

**1820s–1830s Age of Jackson**
States move toward universal white male suffrage.

**1870 Fifteenth Amendment**
Vote is extended to African American men, but this right is often violated.

**1920 Nineteenth Amendment**
Women's suffrage becomes law.

**1965 Voting Rights Act**
Law strengthens African American voting rights.

**1971 Twenty-sixth Amendment**
Voting age is lowered from 21 to 18.

**2000 Presidential Election**
Polling-place irregularities lead some states to reform voting process.

African Americans in Alabama voting for the first time after passage of the Voting Rights Act

A voter registration drive for ex-felons

## DEBATE THE ISSUE

**Voting Rights for Convicted Felons** Most states do not allow felons to vote while they are in prison. In some states, this ban continues even after they are released. Should ex-convicts have their voting rights restored?

"About 4.7 million Americans, more than 2 percent of the adult population, are barred from voting because of a felony conviction. Denying the vote to ex-offenders is antidemocratic and undermines the nation's commitment to rehabilitating people who have paid their debt to society."
—*The New York Times*, editorial

"Individuals who have shown they are unwilling to follow the law cannot claim the right to make laws for the rest of us. We don't let everyone vote—not children, for instance, or noncitizens. . . . We have . . . standards of trustworthiness before we let people participate in the serious business of self-government, and people who commit serious crimes don't meet those standards."
—Roger Clegg, General Counsel, Center for Economic Opportunity

### ? TRANSFER Activities

1. **Compare** How do these two views of felon voting rights differ?

2. **Contrast** How does the issue of voting rights for felons differ from the issue of voting rights in the 1960s?

3. **Transfer** Use the following Web site to see a video, try a WebQuest, and write in your journal. **Web Code:** neh-8702

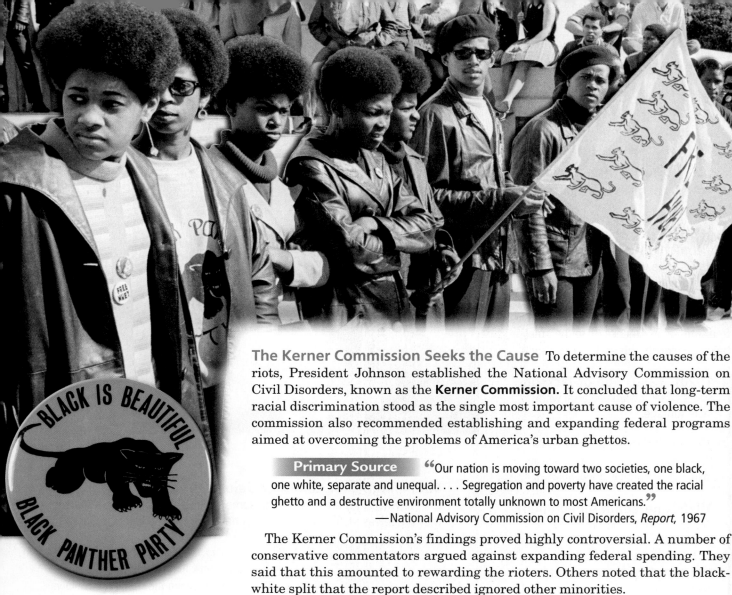

**Increasing Militancy**
Black Panthers (above) demonstrated outside the courthouse where Huey Newton was on trial, charged with killing a police officer.

**The Kerner Commission Seeks the Cause** To determine the causes of the riots, President Johnson established the National Advisory Commission on Civil Disorders, known as the **Kerner Commission.** It concluded that long-term racial discrimination stood as the single most important cause of violence. The commission also recommended establishing and expanding federal programs aimed at overcoming the problems of America's urban ghettos.

> **Primary Source** "Our nation is moving toward two societies, one black, one white, separate and unequal. . . . Segregation and poverty have created the racial ghetto and a destructive environment totally unknown to most Americans."
> —National Advisory Commission on Civil Disorders, *Report,* 1967

The Kerner Commission's findings proved highly controversial. A number of conservative commentators argued against expanding federal spending. They said that this amounted to rewarding the rioters. Others noted that the black-white split that the report described ignored other minorities.

President Johnson did not follow up on the commission's recommendations, largely because the Vietnam War was consuming enormous sums of federal money. The riots also fueled a white backlash. Many whites opposed further reforms.

✓ **Checkpoint** Why was the Kerner Commission formed?

## New Voices for African Americans

The racial rioting of the mid-1960s coincided with the radicalization of many African Americans, particularly young urban African Americans. Rather than advocating nonviolence and integration, they called for another approach.

**Malcolm X Offers a Different Vision** The most well-known African American radical was **Malcolm X,** who was born Malcolm Little in Omaha, Nebraska, in 1925. He adopted the *X* to represent his lost African name. Little, he argued, was his slave name. Malcolm had a difficult childhood. In his teens, Malcolm moved to Boston and then to New York City, where he became involved in drugs and crime and landed in prison on burglary charges at age 21.

While in prison, Malcolm became a convert to the **Nation of Islam,** a religious sect headed by Elijah Muhammad. The group prescribed strict rules of behavior, including no drugs or alcohol, and demanded a separation of the races.

After his release from prison, Malcolm became the Nation of Islam's most prominent minister. In 1964, however, he broke away from the Nation of Islam and formed his own organization. He then made a pilgrimage to Mecca, the holy city of Islam. Returning to the United States, he seemed willing to consider limited acceptance of whites. In February 1965, however, Malcolm X was shot and killed. Three members of the Nation of Islam were convicted of the murder.

**Young Leaders Call for Black Power** Many young African Americans saw themselves as heirs of the radical Malcolm X. They began to move away from the principle of nonviolence. They also began to question the goal of integration. As SNCC leader Stokely Carmichael put it:

> **Primary Source** "Integration . . . has been based on complete acceptance of the fact that in order to have a decent house or education, blacks must move into a white neighborhood or send their children to a white school. This reinforces the notion . . . that 'white' is automatically better and 'black' is by definition inferior."
>
> — "What We Want," 1966

Carmichael first used the term **"black power"** in 1966. In that year, James Meredith had set off on a "March Against Fear" across the state of Mississippi to encourage African Americans to register and vote. Meredith traveled only 20 miles before he was shot and left for dead by a white supremacist. SNCC, CORE, and SCLC members vowed to continue the march.

When they reached Greenwood, Mississippi, Carmichael and some other marchers were arrested. After his release, Carmichael told a crowd that African Americans needed "black power!" He later said that black power meant African Americans should collectively use their economic and political muscle to gain equality. Yet, many white Americans felt threatened. They believed that black power meant black violence.

**Militants Form the Black Panthers** Not long after Carmichael's "black power" speech, Huey Newton and Bobby Seale formed the Black Panther Party in Oakland, California. Almost overnight, the **Black Panthers** became the symbol of young militant African Americans. The Black Panthers organized armed patrols of urban neighborhoods to protect people from police abuse. They also created antipoverty programs, such as free breakfasts for poor African American children. The Black Panthers gained national attention when they entered the state

**Olympic Protest**
At the 1968 Summer Olympics, U.S. athletes Tommie Smith and John Carlos raised gloved fists in protest against discrimination.

# Turbulent Times

The civil rights movement reached its peak in the 1960s but at a terrible cost. During the "long, hot summers" of 1965 to 1968, pent-up anger and frustration exploded into riots in African American communities across the nation. By the time the violence had subsided, hundreds of people had been killed, thousands were wounded, and neighborhoods lay in rubble. In addition to this heavy toll, assassins' bullets claimed the lives of key figures in the civil rights movement. Malcolm X was slain in 1965. Three years later, the assassination of Martin Luther King, Jr., shocked and grieved the nation.

King's funeral procession in Atlanta (above). A woman weeps as she pays her final respects. ▶

| Long, Hot Summers | |
|---|---|
| Six days of arson, looting, and rioting rock the Watts section of Los Angeles. | 1965 |
| Riots break out in Chicago, San Fransisco, and other cities. | 1966 |
| Unrest continues. Riots occur in Detroit and Newark within a week of each other in July. | 1967 |
| King's assassination triggers riots in more than 100 cities, the worst in Washington, D.C. | 1968 |

A pall of smoke ▲ envelops a city street during riots in Detroit in 1967.

## Thinking Critically

1. **Recognize Cause and Effect** What factors contributed to the outbreak of riots in the 1960s?

2. **Predict Consequences** How do you think the events depicted here affected the civil rights movement?

capitol in Sacramento carrying shotguns and wearing black leather jackets and berets to protest attempts to restrict their right to bear arms.

The Panthers' style appealed to many young African Americans, who began to wear their hair in "Afros" and to refer to themselves as "black" rather than "Negro" or "colored." Some, following the lead of Malcolm X, changed their name and celebrated their African heritage. At the same time, the Panthers' militancy often led to violent confrontations with police. Each side accused the other of instigating the violence.

 **Checkpoint** What impact did Malcolm X have on the civil rights movement?

## Martin Luther King's Final Days

Martin Luther King understood the anger and frustration of many urban African Americans whose lives had changed little despite the civil rights reforms of the 1960s. However, he disagreed with the call for "black power" and sought a nonviolent alternative to combat economic injustice. After spending about a year in Chicago's slums to protest conditions there, King made plans for a massive "Poor People's Campaign." The campaign's goal was to pressure the nation to do more to address the needs of the poor.

As part of this effort, King journeyed to Memphis, Tennessee, in early April 1968. There, he offered his assistance to sanitation workers who were striking for better wages and working conditions.

On April 3, King addressed his followers. He referred to threats that had been made against his life. "Like anybody, I would like to live a long life," King declared. "But I'm not concerned about that now. I just want to do God's will."

The following day, as King stood on the balcony outside his motel room, he was struck by a shot from a high-powered rifle. He died at a hospital shortly afterward, at the age of 39. James Earl Ray, a white ex-convict, was later charged with King's murder.

Robert F. Kennedy was campaigning for the presidency in Indianapolis when he heard of King's death. RFK stopped his campaign speech to give the audience the sad news. He reminded them that he had lost his own brother to an assassin's bullet. Kennedy asked those assembled to honor King's memory by replacing their anger and desire for revenge "with an effort to understand with compassion and love." Despite Kennedy's plea, riots broke out in hundreds of cities after King's assassination. Two months later, Robert Kennedy's life, too, was cut short by an assassin.

 **Checkpoint** Why did King go to Memphis in 1968?

## Significant Gains and Controversial Issues

King's assassination marked an important turning point. The protests for black freedom and racial equality that began in the mid-1950s crested in the late 1960s around the time of King's death. By then, the civil rights movement had made significant gains. Yet, white racism and the social and economic gap between many blacks and whites remained. New measures aimed at closing this gap tended to provoke more controversy than consensus in America.

**Civil Rights Are Advanced** The civil rights movement of the 1950s and 1960s succeeded in eliminating legal, or de jure, segregation and knocking down barriers to African American voting and political participation. During the same period, African American poverty rates fell and the median income of African American men and women rose rapidly, as did the number of African

**WITNESS HISTORY DVD**

Watch *Civil Rights Martyrs* on the **United States Witness History DVD** to learn more about some of those who lost their lives in the struggle for equal rights.

## Effects of the Civil Rights Movement ☑ Quick Study

- End of legal segregation
- Passage of federal laws to protect civil rights
- End of legal barriers to African American voting and political participation
- Creation of affirmative action programs

Americans who graduated from high school. One symbol of the progress that had been made was the appointment of Thurgood Marshall as the first African American Supreme Court Justice in 1967. The following year, in the wake of King's murder, Congress passed one final civil rights measure, the Fair Housing Act, which banned discrimination in housing.

**Controversial Issues Remain** Attempts to increase the economic opportunities for African Americans and to integrate neighborhoods and schools encountered more difficulties. To achieve desegregated schools, the federal courts had ordered the use of forced busing. Richard Nixon, who succeeded Lyndon Johnson, criticized busing as a means of attaining racial balance.

At the same time, the Nixon administration formally established affirmative action as a means of closing the economic gap between blacks and whites. In a short period of time, colleges and universities, businesses, and local and state governments followed the federal government's lead and implemented their own affirmative action plans to increase African American representation in schools and the workforce.

Affirmative action proved controversial almost from the start. Some whites argued that it constituted reverse discrimination and violated the goal of creating a colorblind society. Justice Thurgood Marshall disagreed. "Three hundred and fifty years ago, the Negro was dragged to this country in chains to be sold into slavery," Marshall wrote. "The position of the Negro today in America is the tragic but inevitable consequence of centuries of unequal treatment."

Until the nation addressed the legacy of this unequal treatment, Marshall asserted, it would not fulfill its promise of providing equal rights and opportunities to all. This debate or controversy, as you will see in future chapters, remained unresolved.

✔ **Checkpoint** What gains did the civil rights movement make by the early 1970s?

---

SECTION **3** Assessment

**Progress Monitoring *Online***
For: Self-test with vocabulary practice
Web Code: nea-1409

## Comprehension

**1. Terms and People** For each of the items below, write a sentence explaining its significance:
- Freedom Summer
- Fannie Lou Hamer
- Voting Rights Act
- Twenty-fourth Amendment
- Kerner Commission
- Malcolm X
- Nation of Islam
- black power
- Black Panthers

**2. NoteTaking Reading Skill: Summarize** Use your outline to answer the Section Focus Question: What successes and challenges faced the civil rights movement after 1964?

### Writing About History

**3. Quick Write: Identify Sources** After constructing a hypothesis, historians look for evidence that might either prove or disprove the hypothesis. List three sources of information that you might use to test the following hypothesis: The drive for voting rights in the South could have succeeded without the involvement of the federal government.

## Critical Thinking

**4. Recognize Cause and Effect** How did the Selma march help lead to the passage of civil rights legislation?

**5. Make Comparisons** How did Malcolm X's views differ from Martin Luther King, Jr.'s views?

**6. Identify Points of View** Why did Justice Thurgood Marshall support affirmative action?

# A Raisin in the Sun
# by Lorraine Hansberry

8.3.4

The 1940s and 1950s brought an explosion of literature that exposed the harsh discrimination African Americans faced. One of the most powerful writers of the period was the playwright Lorraine Hansberry. Her most famous work, *A Raisin in the Sun,* focuses on the struggles of a black family living in the South Side of Chicago.

**In this excerpt, Lindner—a white man—tries to dissuade the family from moving into his neighborhood.**

**LINDNER:** I am sure you people must be aware of some of the incidents which have happened in various parts of the city when colored people have moved into certain areas—Well—because we have what I think is going to be a unique type of organization in American community life—not only do we deplore that kind of thing—but we are trying to do something about it. We feel—we feel that most of the trouble in this world, . . . exists because people just don't sit down and talk to each other.

**RUTH:** You can say that again, mister.

**LINDNER:** That we don't try hard enough in this world to understand the other fellow's problems. The other guy's point of view.

**RUTH:** Now that's right.

**LINDNER:** Yes—that's the way we feel out in Clybourne Park. And that's why I was elected to come here this afternoon and talk to you people. Friendly like, you know, the way people should talk to each other. . . . As I say, the whole business is a matter of *caring* about the other fellow. Anybody can see that you are a nice family of folks, hard working and honest I'm sure. Today everybody knows what it means to be on the outside of *something*. And of course, there is always somebody who is out to take the advantage of people who don't always understand."

**WALTER:** What do you mean?

**LINDNER:** Well—you see our community is made up of people who've worked hard as the dickens for years to build up that little community. They're not rich and fancy people; just hard-working, honest people who don't really have much but those little homes and a dream of the kind of community they want to raise their children in. Now I don't say we are perfect and there is a lot wrong in some of the things they want. But you've got to admit that a man, right or wrong, has the right to want to have the neighborhood he lives in a certain kind of way. And at the moment the overwhelming majority of our people out there feel that people get along better, take more of a common interest in the life of the community, when they share a common background. I want you to believe me when I tell you that race prejudice simply doesn't enter into it. It is a matter of the people of Clybourne Park believing, rightly or wrongly, as I say, that for the happiness of all concerned that our Negro families are happier when they live in their *own* communities.

**BENETHEA:** This, friends, is the Welcoming Committee!

▲ Scene from a production of *A Raisin in the Sun*

## Thinking Critically
1. **Synthesize Information** What reasons did Lindner give for not wanting the family to move into his neighborhood?

2. **Make Inferences** What obstacles did African Americans face in gaining social equality in the 1950s?

Progress Monitoring *Online*
For: Self-test with vocabulary practice
Web Code: nea-1410

## Struggle for Equality

## Civil Rights Legislation

| Civil Rights Act of 1964 | • Banned segregation in public accommodations<br>• Increased federal authority to enforce school desegregation<br>• Outlawed discrimination in employment on basis of race, color, and sex |
|---|---|
| Twenty-fourth Amendment (1964) | • Eliminated poll tax as voting requirement |
| Voting Rights Act of 1965 | • Banned literacy tests as voting requirement<br>• Empowered the federal government to supervise voter registration and elections |
| Fair Housing Act of 1968 | • Banned discrimination in housing |

## Civil Rights Organizations

| Organization and Date Founded | Key People | Key Features |
|---|---|---|
| National Association for the Advancement of Colored People (NAACP) 1909 | Thurgood Marshall | Focused on legal cases to end segregation and gain legal equality |
| Nation of Islam 1930 | Elijah Muhammad; Malcolm X | Advocated separation of the races |
| Congress of Racial Equality (CORE) 1942 | James Farmer | Organized peaceful protests to gain civil rights |
| Southern Christian Leadership Conference (SCLC) 1957 | Martin Luther King, Jr.; Ralph Abernathy | Church-based group dedicated to nonviolent resistance; organized demonstrations and protest campaigns |
| Student Nonviolent Coordinating Committee (SNCC) 1960 | James Lawson; Ella Baker; Stokely Carmichael | Grass-roots movement of young activists; organized voter education projects in the South |
| Black Panther Party 1966 | Huey Newton; Bobby Seale | Militant group advocating armed confrontation; organized antipoverty programs |

## ☑ Quick Study Timeline

**In America**

**1954**
Supreme Court rules school segregation unconstitutional

**1955**
Bus boycott begins in Montgomery, Alabama

**1957**
Desegregation of Central High in Little Rock, Arkansas

Presidential Terms **Harry S. Truman 1945–1953**  **Dwight D. Eisenhower 1953–1961**

**1953**     **1956**     **1959**

**Around the World**

**1956**
Crisis over Suez Canal

**1959**
Castro comes to power in Cuba

# American Issues
## Connector

 8.3.4

By connecting prior knowledge with what you have learned in this chapter, you can gradually build your understanding of enduring questions that still affect America today. Answer the questions below. Then, use your American Issues Connector study guide (or go online: www.PHSchool.com **Web Code:** neh-8703).

## Issues You Learned About

● **Voting Rights** Minority groups in America sometimes have had to fight for their political rights.

1. Do you think the Voting Rights Act of 1965 did enough to ensure that African Americans would be allowed to exercise their voting rights? Consider the following:
   • the results of Freedom Summer
   • the number of African American elected officials before and after 1965
   • the percentage of southern African Americans registered to vote before and after 1965
   • the black power movement

● **Federal Power and States' Rights** The national government and the state governments sometimes disagree over the delegation of power.

2. *Brown* v. *Board of Education* sparked a clash between the federal government and several southern state governments. Describe an earlier incident in which the federal government and state government disagreed over the authority of the federal government.

3. How did Arkansas governor Orval Faubus attempt to assert his authority over that of the Supreme Court? How did President Eisenhower respond on behalf of the federal government?

● **Sectionalism and National Politics** Different regions of the country often respond to events in contradictory ways.

4. Why was the civil rights movement centered in the South?

5. How do you think the South and the North responded to the Voting Rights Act of 1965? Explain.

### Connect to Your World | Michigan

**Expanding and Protecting Civil Rights** For much of the 20th century, racial discrimination and mortgage programs that favored white homebuyers had made it difficult for African Americans to purchase homes in Michigan. As the Civil Rights movement swept the nation, however, state legislators voted on a bill that aimed to change that forever. On June 11, 1968, Governor George Romney signed the Michigan Fair Housing Act into law. The act prohibited real estate agents, mortgage lenders, and homeowners from discriminating against renters or buyers because of their race, skin color, or religion. Romney continued to promote fair housing at the national level after President Nixon appointed him the nation's first secretary of Housing and Urban Development in 1969. Research George Romney's work for civil rights and equal housing opportunities and discuss your findings with a partner.

**History Interactive**
**For:** Interactive timeline
**Web Code:** nep-1412

**1960** Greensboro sit-ins

**1963** King speaks at March on Washington

**1965** Riots break out in Watts section of Los Angeles

**1968** Martin Luther King, Jr., is assassinated

John F. Kennedy 1961–1963 | Lyndon B. Johnson 1963–1969

**1962** | **1965** | **1968**

**1961** East Germany builds the Berlin Wall

**1962** Mandela is jailed in South Africa

**1966** Cultural Revolution in China

# Chapter Assessment

## Terms and People

1. Who was **Martin Luther King, Jr.**? What did he achieve in his lifetime?

2. Define **sit-ins.** What response did the first sit-in of the civil rights movement—at a Woolworth's lunch counter in 1960—provoke throughout the South?

3. What did the **Civil Rights Act of 1964** accomplish? Who worked to push this bill through Congress?

4. What did the **Twenty-fourth Amendment** do? How did it help African Americans?

5. What was the **Kerner Commission**? What recommendations did it make?

## Focus Questions

The focus question for this chapter is **What were the causes, main events, and effects of the civil rights movement?** Build an answer to this big question by answering the focus questions for Sections 1 through 3 and the Critical Thinking questions that follow.

### Section 1

6. How did African Americans challenge segregation after World War II?

### Section 2

7. How did the civil rights movement gain ground in the 1960s?

### Section 3

8. What successes and challenges faced the civil rights movement after 1964?

## Critical Thinking

9. **Decision Making** What reasoning did the Supreme Court apply in the *Brown* v. *Board of Education* ruling?

10. **Analyze Maps** Study the map below. What civil rights campaign does this map show? Was this campaign successful?

**May 14, 1961** Buses attacked; one firebombed

Washington, D.C. VA

TN NC

SC

**May 24, 1961** Mass arrests in bus terminal

MS GA

LA AL

New Orleans

FL

**May 20, 1961** More violence; Federal marshals arrive

11. **Categorize** In what general areas did civil rights activists focus their efforts? List at least three general categories along with their key victories.

12. **Analyze Information** What role did television play in the civil rights movement of the 1950s and early 1960s? Do you think television contributed to the success of the movement? Explain.

13. **Comparing Points of View** How did Stokely Carmichael's and Martin Luther King, Jr.'s attitudes toward the civil rights movement differ?

14. **Express Problems Clearly** Why was affirmative action begun? Explain the controversy surrounding it.

## Writing About History

**Writing a Research Paper** Write a hypothesis about one of the following aspects of the civil rights movement: the growth of de facto segregation in the North; the Montgomery bus boycott; the role of northern volunteers in the southern civil rights movement; the urban riots of the 1960s; the conflict between Malcolm X and Martin Luther King, Jr. Use your hypothesis as the basis of an essay that tests the hypothesis.

### Prewriting

- Identify an unanswered question about the topic you have chosen.
- Write a one-sentence hypothesis that provides a possible answer to the question.
- Use the library or Internet to find three different sources of information that can be used to support or disprove your hypothesis.

### Drafting

- Write an introductory paragraph in which you identify the question you are trying to answer and propose one hypothesis. Use your hypothesis as a thesis statement for the paragraph.
- In separate paragraphs, explain how each piece of evidence you have found either supports or disproves your hypothesis.
- Write a concluding paragraph in which you restate, modify, or reject your original hypothesis.

### Revising

- Use the guidelines on page SH14 of the Writing Handbook to revise your writing.

# Prepare for the MME

## Civil Disobedience

During the 1960s, Martin Luther King, Jr., advocated the use of civil disobedience to end segregation in the South. What forms of civil disobedience were effective tools in ending segregation? Was nonviolence more effective than violence in achieving civil rights for African Americans? Use your knowledge of the civil rights movement and Documents A, B, C, and D to answer questions 1 through 4.

### Document A

"... Unjust laws exist; shall we be content to obey them, or shall we endeavor to amend them, and obey them until we have succeeded, or shall we transgress them at once? Men generally, under such a government as this, think that they ought to wait until they have persuaded the majority to alter them. They think that, if they should resist, the remedy would be worse than the evil. But it is the fault of the government itself that the remedy *is* worse than the evil. It makes it worse. Why is it not more apt to anticipate and provide for reform? Why does it not cherish its wise minority? Why does it cry and resist before it is hurt? Why does it not encourage its citizens to be on the alert to point out its faults, and do better than it would have them?"

—*Henry David Thoreau,* Civil Disobedience, *1849*

### Document B

"The only time I hear people talk about nonviolence is when black people move to defend themselves against white people. . . . White people beat up black people every day— Don't nobody talk about nonviolence. But as soon as black people start to move, the double standard comes into being. . . . We are on the move for our liberation. . . . We are concerned with getting the things we want, the things that we have to have to be able to function. . . . The question is, Will white people overcome their racism and allow for that to happen in this country? If that does not happen, brothers, and sisters, we have no choice but to say very clearly, 'Move over, or we're going to move on over you.'"

—*Stokely Carmichael speech, 1966*

### Document C
Birmingham, 1963

### Document D

"Oppressed people cannot remain oppressed forever. The yearning for freedom eventually manifests itself, and that is what has happened to the American Negro. . . . If one recognizes this vital urge that has engulfed the Negro community, one should readily understand why public demonstrations are taking place. The Negro has many pent-up resentments and latent frustrations, and he must release them. So let him march; let him make prayer pilgrimages to the city hall; let him go on freedom rides—and try to understand why he must do so. If his repressed emotions are not released in nonviolent ways, they will seek expression through violence; this is not a threat but a fact of history. So I have not said to my people: 'Get rid of your discontent.' Rather, I have tried to say that this normal and healthy discontent can be channeled into the creative outlet of nonviolent direct action."

—*Martin Luther King, Jr.,* "Letter From Birmingham Jail," *1963*

---

1. Which document advocates the use of violence if racism against African Americans is not ended?
   A Document A
   B Document B
   C Document C
   D Document D

2. According to Document D, how does Martin Luther King, Jr., describe demonstrations such as freedom rides?
   A unjust laws
   B expression through violence
   C nonviolent direct action
   D discrimination

3. According to Document A, what does Thoreau think about the role of government in addressing unjust laws?
   A The government should listen only to the majority viewpoint.
   B The government should listen to the minority viewpoint.
   C Violence should be used as an option to end oppression.
   D The public should be content with the laws.

4. **Writing Task** What do you think about the role of government depicted in Document C? How does that image contrast with the ideas of King, Thoreau, and Carmichael? Use your knowledge of the chapter content and evidence from the primary sources above to support your opinion.

# 15 The Kennedy and Johnson Years

## 1960–1968

### The Trumpet Summons Us

On January 20, 1961, John F. Kennedy was sworn in as President of the United States. His stirring Inaugural Address announced the dawn of a new era and rallied the nation to battle against the common enemies of man.

> "Now the trumpet summons us again—not as a call to bear arms, though arms we need—not as a call to battle, though embattled we are—but a call to bear the burden of a long twilight struggle, year in and year out, 'rejoicing in hope; patient in tribulation,' a struggle against the common enemies of man: tyranny, poverty, disease, and war itself. . . .
>
> And so, my fellow Americans, ask not what your country can do for you; ask what you can do for your country."
>
> —John F. Kennedy, Inaugural Address

The challenge of fulfilling these goals would inspire the agenda of President Kennedy and that of his successor, Lyndon B. Johnson. *Listen to the* Witness History *audio to learn more about the Kennedy and Johnson years.*

◄ Senator John F. Kennedy, the 1960 Democratic presidential candidate, is greeted by his supporters.

Kennedy campaign button

Peace Corps logo

The space rocket *Saturn V*

###  Content Expectations

**Chapter Focus Question: How did the policies of Presidents Kennedy and Johnson affect the nation?**

## Section 1

**Kennedy and the Cold War** 8.1.1a, 8.1.2c, 8.1.2e, 8.3.1a

## Section 2

**Kennedy's New Frontier** 8.1.2a, 8.1.2f, 8.2.2b, 8.3.4

## Section 3

**Johnson's Great Society** 8.2.3, 8.3.1b, 8.3.5

Use the ☑ **Quick Study Timeline** at the end of this chapter to preview chapter events.

**Note Taking Study Guide *Online***
For: Note Taking and American Issues Connector
Web Code: nee-8801

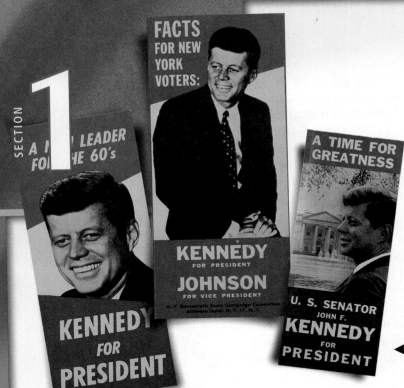

KENNEDY
FOR
PRESIDENT

FACTS
FOR NEW
YORK
VOTERS:

KENNEDY
FOR PRESIDENT
JOHNSON
FOR VICE PRESIDENT

A TIME FOR
GREATNESS

U. S. SENATOR
JOHN F.
KENNEDY
FOR
PRESIDENT

◄ Kennedy campaign posters

**WITNESS HISTORY**  AUDIO

### The Democratic Candidate

During the election of 1960, John F. Kennedy's Catholicism became an important issue. Some Americans openly questioned whether a Catholic was independent enough from his church to serve as President. Kennedy dismissed such questions, insisting that a candidate's religion should not be a factor in running for office:

❝I am not the Catholic candidate for President. I am the Democratic Party's candidate for President, who happens also to be a Catholic.❞

—John F. Kennedy, address to Southern Baptist Leaders, 1960

# Kennedy and the Cold War

## Content Expectations

- **8.1.1a** Analyze differences in civic/political values, economic/governmental institutions of U.S./U.S.S.R.
- **8.1.2c** Evaluate direct conflicts within world regions: Germany/Cuba.
- **8.1.2e** Evaluate indirect confrontations within specific world regions.
- **8.3.1a** Analyze impact of WWII and Cold War.

## Terms and People

| | |
|---|---|
| John F. Kennedy | Bay of Pigs invasion |
| Richard M. Nixon | Cuban missile crisis |
| Fidel Castro | Nikita Khrushchev |
| flexible response | hot line |
| Peace Corps | Nuclear Test Ban Treaty |
| Alliance for Progress | Berlin Wall |

### NoteTaking

**Reading Skill: Understand Effects** As you read, list the Cold War crises Kennedy faced and the effects of each event.

| Cold War Crisis | Result |
|---|---|
| Bay of Pigs Invasion | |
| | |
| | |

**Why It Matters** As the Cold War continued into the 1960s, Kennedy took office facing the spread of communism abroad and the threat of nuclear war. Determined to succeed where he felt Eisenhower had failed, Kennedy's enthusiasm and commitment to change offered the hope that with hard work and persistence the United States could win the Cold War. **Section Focus Question: How did Kennedy respond to the continuing challenges of the Cold War?**

## Kennedy Defeats Nixon in 1960

For eight years, President Dwight Eisenhower had presided over a nation that had generally enjoyed peace and prosperity. But even so, there were a number of issues that caused Americans grave concern. The launch of *Sputnik 1* showed that the rivalry between the United States and the Soviet Union was still intense. The U-2 spy plane incident demonstrated that the Cold War might heat up at a moment's notice. The Montgomery bus boycott provided clear evidence that the *Brown* decision had not ended racial discrimination in the land. Deep, unsettled problems remained—problems for a new decade and a new generation of political leadership.

**The Candidates** In the presidential election of 1960, Democrat **John F. Kennedy** and Republican **Richard M. Nixon** were quite similar in a variety of ways. For the first time in U.S. history, both candidates had been born in the twentieth century, Nixon in 1913 and Kennedy in 1917. Both had served in the navy during World War II.

Both had been elected to Congress in 1946 and to the Senate in the early 1950s. Both were passionate about foreign affairs and supported the Cold War fight against communism. Young and energetic, intelligent and hard-working, both wanted to be the first of their generation to lead the country.

Their differences, however, were as significant as their similarities. Kennedy was the son of a wealthy Boston businessman. His grandfather had been a state senator, and his father had served as the ambassador to Great Britain. Kennedy attended Harvard University. Although he was a Catholic and his religion was an issue in the election, he insisted that what church he attended should not be a factor.

Nixon, born in California, did not enjoy the advantages of a wealthy upbringing. His father struggled to make a living. As a young man, Nixon had to balance his time between his school studies and work to help support the family. Many voters, however, respected him for his experiences as Vice President under Eisenhower.

### Televised Debates Make the Difference

The 1960 election highlighted the growing power and influence of television. The candidates agreed to four televised debates. During the campaign, Nixon was hospitalized with a knee infection. After getting out of the hospital, he committed himself to a grueling schedule of public appearances. By the time of the first debate, held in late September in Chicago and watched by about 70 million people, Nixon looked pale and exhausted. Nixon arrived at the television studio an hour early, but he refused the offer to have makeup applied to hide his newly-growing beard. By contrast, Kennedy, tanned from open-air campaigning in California, looked healthy and confident. His relaxed manner, easy charm, and quick sense of humor added to his appeal.

In many ways, the debate boiled down to how the candidates looked and spoke, rather than what they said. Most Americans who listened to the debate on radio believed that Nixon had won. But the larger audience who watched the debate on television concluded that Kennedy was the clear victor. Although Nixon tried to change his image in the later debates, he was unable to significantly alter the country's initial impression of him. Kennedy's "victory" in the Chicago debate proved crucial in the election.

### Kennedy Wins a Close Election

Kennedy not only looked better on television, he also demonstrated an ability to react more quickly to unexpected events. For example, several weeks before the election, civil rights leader Martin Luther King, Jr., and a group of African American students were imprisoned during a protest in Atlanta, Georgia. Nixon said nothing publicly about the episode. Kennedy, however, telephoned King's wife, Coretta Scott King, to express his concern. He also worked behind the scenes to obtain King's release on bail. Kennedy's actions attracted the strong support of African Americans in the election.

The election of 1960 was the tightest presidential election since 1888.

**Televised Debate**

Richard Nixon (left) and John Kennedy (right) face each other in a televised debate. Kennedy won the election by a slim margin. *How did TV change political campaigns?*

| The Presidential Election of 1960 | | | | |
|---|---|---|---|---|
| Candidate | Electoral Vote | Popular Vote | % Electoral Vote | % Popular Vote |
| John Kennedy (Democrat) | 303 | 34,227,096 | 56.4 | 49.7 |
| Richard Nixon (Republican) | 219 | 34,107,646 | 40.8 | 49.6 |

In an election that witnessed the largest voter turnout in the country's history, Kennedy won by less than 120,000 of the 68 million popular votes cast. Had a few thousand people voted differently in Illinois and Texas, the election would have gone to Nixon. Kennedy's electoral victory was more convincing. He carried enough states to give him 303 electoral votes to Nixon's 219.

✓ **Checkpoint** How did the television debates affect the 1960 presidential election?

## Kennedy Launches New Cold War Strategies

John Kennedy's 1960 campaign stressed the need for the United States to move forward with vigor and determination. Kennedy argued that during the Eisenhower years America had lost ground in the Cold War struggle against communism. He pointed to the new communist regime under **Fidel Castro** in Cuba and charged that there was now a "missile gap" that left the U.S. nuclear missile force inferior to that of the Soviet Union. The first goal of the Kennedy administration would be to build up the nation's armed forces.

Nowhere was the difference between Eisenhower and Kennedy more evident than in two important 1961 addresses. In his Farewell Address, Eisenhower counseled caution in foreign affairs. "The potential for the disastrous rise of misplaced power exists and will persist," he said.

---

**Comparing Viewpoints**

## How Should the United States Fight the Cold War?

Both Presidents Eisenhower and Kennedy were strongly committed to containing communism. Their differences lay in their beliefs about the amount of military spending needed to carry out their goals.

### DWIGHT D. EISENHOWER

In spite of numerous Cold War challenges, Eisenhower prided himself on having maintained peace. In his Farewell Address, he warned Americans about the effects of heavy defense spending.

**Primary Source**

"We annually spend on military security more than the net income of all United States corporations. . . . This . . . immense military establishment . . . is new in the American experience. We recognize the . . . need for this development. Yet we must not fail to comprehend its grave implications. Our toil, resources and livelihood are all involved."

### JOHN F. KENNEDY

Determined to prepare the United States against nuclear attack, Kennedy supported programs that resulted in a $6 billion rise in defense spending. He defends his action in a State of the Union address:

**Primary Source**

"Our moral and physical strength begins at home. . . . But it includes our military strength as well. . . . [W]e must arm to deter others from aggression. We have increased the previous defense budget . . . not in the expectation of war but for the preservation of peace."

**Compare**
1. How does Eisenhower's plan for containing communism differ from Kennedy's?
2. Which plan may have prevented an attack on the United States? Explain.

As the first President born in this century, Kennedy proclaimed that a "new generation of Americans" was ready to meet any challenge. In his Inaugural Address, Kennedy warned his country's enemies:

**Primary Source**  "Let every nation know, whether it wishes us well or ill, that we shall pay any price, bear any burden, meet any hardship, support any friend, oppose any foe to assure the survival and the success of liberty."
—John F. Kennedy, Inaugural Address, January 20, 1961

Kennedy issued a challenge to Americans: "Ask not what your country can do for you; ask what you can do for your country."

**Building the Nation's Military** Eisenhower's defense policy of "massive retaliation" had emphasized the construction of nuclear weapons. Although Kennedy did not ignore the possibility of a nuclear war, he wanted to make sure that the United States was prepared to fight both conventional wars and conflicts against guerrilla forces. Kennedy therefore gave increased funding to conventional United States Army and Navy forces as well as to Army Special Forces, such as the Green Berets. He wanted a **"flexible response"** defense policy, one that prepared the United States to fight any type of conflict.

**Pursuing New Initiatives in the "Third World"** The "Third World," as it was known at the time, was the developing nations in Africa, Asia, and Latin America that did not <u>align</u> with the United States or the Soviet Union. According to Soviet propaganda, Western capitalism created poverty and inequalities in the Third World, whereas communism promoted equality.

Like previous American leaders, Kennedy believed that democracy combined with prosperity would contain or limit the spread of communism. Therefore, he initiated programs to economically and politically strengthen the Third World. The **Peace Corps,** created in 1961, sent American volunteers around the world on "missions of freedom" to assist developing countries. They worked to provide technical, educational, and health services. Other programs stressed purely economic development. The **Alliance for Progress** promised to resurrect America's Good Neighbor policy toward Latin America. During the 1950s, many Latin Americans had grown increasingly resentful of the United States, claiming that it had too much influence in their region. Kennedy hoped to change that view with this program. It promoted economic assistance to Latin America. Unlike the Peace Corps, the Alliance for Progress was not successful.

✓ **Checkpoint** What strategies did Kennedy use to improve relations between the United States and developing countries?

**Kennedy's Plan**
Special fighting forces (left), such as the Green Berets, were ready at all times for any attack. But Kennedy's Cold War strategy also involved creating goodwill among nations. The establishment of the Peace Corps (right) fulfilled that goal. *How could the Peace Corps help America win the Cold War?*

**Vocabulary Builder**
align–(uh LĪN) v. to decide to publicly support or not support a political group or country

# Confronting Communism in Cuba

**Vocabulary Builder**
regime–(ruh ZHEEM) *n.*
particular administration or government

In 1959, Cuban revolutionary Fidel Castro had succeeded in overthrowing the regime of Fulgencio Batista. Initially, the United States attempted to cultivate good relations with Castro. However, it soon became clear that the Cuban leader was determined to nationalize land held by private U.S. citizens, enforce radical reform measures, and accept Soviet economic and military aid. Thousands of wealthy and middle-class Cubans fled their country, many settling in Miami and southern Florida. Proud of their heritage and deeply anticommunist, they made new lives for themselves and their families in the United States.

**Bay of Pigs Invasion** After breaking diplomatic relations with Cuba in 1961, the Eisenhower administration authorized the Central Intelligence Agency (CIA) to plan an invasion of Cuba to overthrow Castro. The CIA recruited Cuban exiles and trained them in Guatemala. But when Eisenhower left office, the invasion plan was still that—an unexecuted, untried plan.

Pressured by members of the CIA and his own aides, Kennedy decided to implement the plan. On April 17, 1961, a CIA-led force of Cuban exiles attacked Cuba in the **Bay of Pigs invasion.** The invasion was badly mismanaged. The poorly equipped forces landed at the site with no protective cover. All but 300 of the 1,400 invaders were killed or captured. Not only did the Bay of Pigs invasion fail, it probably strengthened Castro's position in Cuba. It also turned many Cuban Americans against Kennedy.

Kennedy took personal responsibility for the failed invasion. However, he emphasized that the United States would continue to resist "communist penetration" in the Western Hemisphere.

### Effects of the Cuban Missile Crisis ✓ Quick Study

- The Soviet Union removes missiles from Cuba.
- The United States removes missiles from Turkey.
- The United States and the Soviet Union avoid nuclear war.
- Kennedy and Khrushchev establish a "hot line" telephone system to keep communications open.
- In 1963, the United States, Great Britain, and the Soviet Union sign the Nuclear Test Ban Treaty.

**WITNESS HISTORY DVD**

Watch *Showdown: The Cuban Missile Crisis* on the **United States Witness History DVD** to explore the tense confrontation between the United States and the Soviet Union that nearly resulted in a nuclear war.

**The Cuban Missile Crisis** Kennedy's efforts to contain communism were severely threatened during the **Cuban missile crisis.** In August and September of 1962 U.S. intelligence discovered that the Soviets were building nuclear missile sites in Cuba, apparently to protect Castro from another American invasion. When the sites were completed, major East Coast cities and the Panama Canal would be in range of the missiles.

Kennedy demanded the removal of the missiles. In a dramatic television address on October 22, 1962, he blamed **Nikita Khrushchev,** the Soviet premier, for causing a "reckless and provocative threat to world peace." He also announced that he had approved a naval quarantine (blockade) of Cuba to prevent the Soviets from completing the bases. Behind the scenes, however, Kennedy worked toward a diplomatic settlement. He indicated that he would remove U.S. missiles in Turkey and Italy if the Soviets removed their missiles in Cuba.

After six tense days when nuclear war seemed a real possibility, Khrushchev agreed to honor the blockade and remove the missiles. As Secretary of State Dean Rusk later told a reporter, "Remember, when you report this, that, eyeball to eyeball, they blinked first."

**The Results of the Crisis** During the Cuban missile crisis, Kennedy and Khrushchev stood on the edge of a nuclear war and then slowly backed away. In the Soviet Union, Khrushchev lost prestige and more hard-line leaders chipped away at his power. In the United States, Kennedy emerged as a more mature and thoughtful leader, one who had faced a frightening test and had remained calm and resolute. The crisis prompted both leaders to move toward détente. They installed a **"hot line"** telephone system between Moscow and Washington, D.C.,

# The Cuban Missile Crisis

**Geography** *Interactive*
**For:** Interactive map
**Web Code:** nep-1502

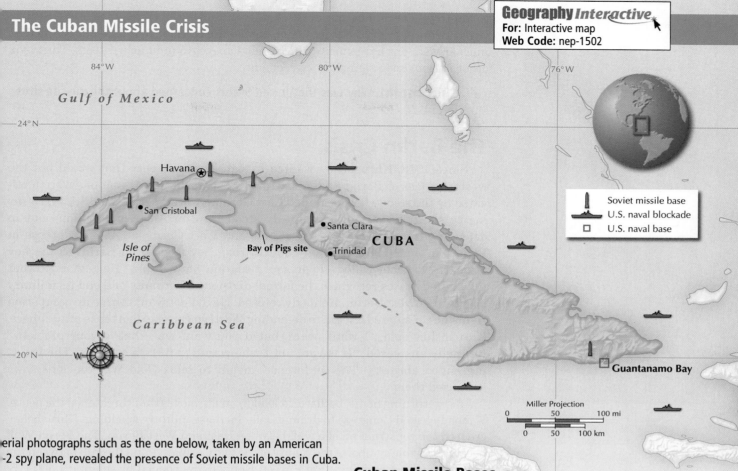

*Gulf of Mexico*

84°W    80°W    76°W

24°N

Havana ⊛
San Cristobal

Isle of Pines

Bay of Pigs site

Santa Clara

Trinidad

**CUBA**

*Caribbean Sea*

N W E S

20°N

Guantanamo Bay

Soviet missile base
U.S. naval blockade
U.S. naval base

Miller Projection

0    50    100 mi
0    50    100 km

erial photographs such as the one below, taken by an American
-2 spy plane, revealed the presence of Soviet missile bases in Cuba.

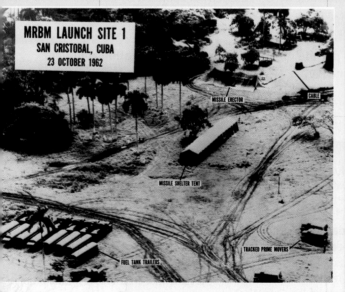

MRBM LAUNCH SITE 1
SAN CRISTOBAL, CUBA
23 OCTOBER 1962

MISSILE ERECTOR    CABLE

MISSILE SHELTER TENT

TRACKED PRIME MOVERS

FUEL TANK TRAILERS

## Cuban Missile Bases

Conic Projection

0    250    500 mi
0    250    500 km

2,000 miles, 17 minutes

Chicago    New York

Washington, D.C. ⊛

**UNITED STATES**

2,299 miles

Los Angeles

1,500 miles, 15 minutes

1,000 miles, 12 minutes

Atlanta

761 miles

1,333 miles

1,139 miles

1,317 miles

**CUBA**

The location of missile bases in Cuba posed an immediate threat to several major American cities.

**Map Skills** Kennedy, aware of the Soviet arms buildup in Cuba, faced a difficult crisis.

1. **Place** Which U.S. city shown on the map was in the greatest danger from a nuclear attack? How long would it take a missile to reach that city?

2. **Draw Conclusions** How did the crisis affect U.S. relations with Cuba and the Soviet Union?

to improve communication. In 1963, the year after the crisis, the United States, Great Britain, and the Soviet Union signed the **Nuclear Test Ban Treaty,** the first nuclear-weapons agreement, which ended aboveground nuclear tests. Thirty-six other nations soon signed the agreement.

 **Checkpoint** Why was the United States concerned about the missile sites in Cuba?

## The Berlin Crisis

Since 1958, Khrushchev wanted to sign a peace treaty that would put the western zones of Berlin under control of East Germany. His actions were motivated by the steady flow of skilled East German workers into West Berlin. Desiring to show his strength, Kennedy stood firm on America's commitment to defending the rights of West Berliners and West Germans. At a conference in Vienna in June 1961, Kennedy and Khrushchev focused on Berlin as the key issue. Khrushchev called the present situation "intolerable." He demanded that the United States recognize the formal division of Germany and end its military presence in West Berlin. Kennedy refused. He did not want to give up occupation rights he considered critical to defending Western Europe. In a tense atmosphere, Khrushchev said, "I want peace, but if you want war, that is your problem." Kennedy answered, "It is you, not I who wants to force a change." The meeting ended abruptly. The conference, meant to relax Cold War tensions, only increased them.

After returning home, both world leaders made moves that threatened the peace. Kennedy asked Congress to dramatically increase military spending. Khrushchev ordered the construction of a wall between East and West Berlin. The **Berlin Wall** became a visible symbol of the reality of the two Germanys and the gulf between the communist East and democratic West. Kennedy responded by sending 1,500 U.S. troops to West Berlin. For a time, Russian and American tanks moved within sight of each other. Yet, neither side could fully claim a victory.

 **Checkpoint** How did the meeting in Vienna affect relations between Kennedy and Khrushchev?

---

**Progress Monitoring *Online***
**For:** Self-test with vocabulary practice
**Web Code:** nea-1503

### Comprehension

1. **Terms and People** For each item below, explain its significance to the relations between the United States and the Soviet Union.
   • John F. Kennedy
   • Fidel Castro
   • Bay of Pigs invasion
   • Cuban missile crisis
   • Nikita Khrushchev
   • Berlin Wall

2. **NoteTaking Reading Skill: Understand Effects** Use your chart to answer the Section Focus Question: How did Kennedy respond to the continuing challenges of the Cold War?

### Writing About History

3. **Quick Write: Support a Point of View** Identify one point of view regarding President Kennedy's actions in starting the Peace Corps. List three arguments in favor of this point of view. Then, prioritize them by identifying the most persuasive argument.

### Critical Thinking

4. **Draw Conclusions** Television played an important role in the 1960 presidential election. How influential is television in presidential elections today? Explain.

5. **Synthesize Information** The flexible response policy increased the military budget. How do you think this affected the nuclear arms race?

6. **Identify Point of View** How did the Cuban missile crisis affect public opinion about President Kennedy?

### Civil Rights

Although Kennedy did not have a strong civil rights record while in the Senate, he did portray himself as a crusader for African American rights during his campaign. Toward the end of his presidency, he abandoned his cautious approach. In a special report to the American people on civil rights, he talked about the racial inequality that had long endured in the nation:

❝It ought to be possible for American students of any color to attend any public institution. . . . It ought to be possible for American consumers of any color to receive equal service in places of public accommodation . . . and it ought to be possible for American citizens of any color to register and to vote in a free election. . . . We preach freedom around the world, and we mean it, and we cherish it here at home, but are we to say to the world and, much more importantly, to each other that this is the land of the free except for the Negroes . . .?❞

—John F. Kennedy, June 11, 1963

▲ President Kennedy with prominent civil rights and labor leaders in 1963. Dr. Martin Luther King, Jr., is at the far left.

# Kennedy's New Frontier

### Content Expectations

- **8.1.2a** Evaluate development of U.S. national security establishment.
- **8.1.2f** Evaluate the arms race.
- **8.2.2b** Evaluate policy decisions/legislative actions to meet challenges.
- **8.3.4** Evaluate major accomplishments/setbacks in civil rights/liberties for U.S. minorities.

### Terms and People

New Frontier
Equal Pay Act
deficit spending

space race
Warren Commission

### NoteTaking

**Reading Skill: Identify Main Ideas** List the characteristics of John F. Kennedy's style that appealed to the American people.

| The Kennedy Image |
| --- |
| • Youthful |
| • |
| • |

**Why It Matters** Kennedy's determination to change life at home resulted in his domestic agenda called the New Frontier. Faced with a conservative Congress, Kennedy met with opposition as he fought to turn his vision into a reality. Still, he had some success in making changes in Social Security benefits, dealing with poverty and racial discrimination, and spurring new interest and expectations for the space program. **Section Focus Question: What were the goals of Kennedy's New Frontier?**

## The Kennedy Style

As John Kennedy showed in his 1960 campaign and in his Inaugural Address, he had a special quality—or charisma—that separated him from other politicians. With his exquisitely tailored clothes, quick smile, and sense of humor, he seemed closer to a movie star than to a run-of-the-mill politician. Although he suffered many health problems, he projected youthful health and energy.

He surrounded himself with other distinguished men. Reporters dubbed them "the best and the brightest." They came from some of the country's most prestigious businesses and universities. Robert McNamara, president of Ford Motor Company, agreed to serve as Secretary of Defense. Dean Rusk, president of the Rockefeller

Foundation, signed on as Secretary of State. Arthur Schlesinger, Jr., a Pulitzer Prize-winning historian, worked at the White House as a spokesperson for liberal causes and was a source of ideas for the President.

President Kennedy promised Americans that his administration would blaze a **"New Frontier."** The term described Kennedy's proposals to improve the economy, education, healthcare, and civil rights. He also hoped to jump-start the space program. In his presidential acceptance speech on July 15, 1960, in Los Angeles, California, Kennedy said,

> **Primary Source**   "I stand tonight facing west on what was once the last frontier. . . . From the lands that stretch three thousand miles behind me, the pioneers of old gave up their safety, their comforts and sometimes their lives to build a new world here in the West. . . . But the problems are not all solved and the battles are not all won, and we stand today on the edge of a new frontier—the frontier of the 1960s—the frontier of unknown opportunities and perils—a frontier of unfulfilled hopes and threats."
>
> —John F. Kennedy, July 15, 1960

✓ **Checkpoint** Why did people feel that Kennedy was a different kind of politician?

## Kennedy's Domestic Program

Early in his presidency, occupied by events in Cuba and Berlin, Kennedy devoted most of his attention to foreign affairs. But by 1963 he had become more concerned about pressing problems at home.

Kennedy—like millions of other Americans—was troubled by the high levels of poverty in the United States. *The Other America*, Michael Harrington's best-selling and influential 1962 exposé of poverty in America, shocked Kennedy and many other Americans.

While Kennedy failed to get Congress to accept his more ambitious social programs, he did push through an increase in the minimum wage, an extension in Social Security benefits, and improvements in the welfare system.

In addition, in 1962 Kennedy established the President's Commission on the Status of Women, a blue-ribbon panel that studied how poverty and

## NoteTaking

**Reading Skill: Identify Main Ideas** As you read, identify details of Kennedy's domestic program.

Space Program

**Domestic Program**

discrimination affected women. The differences in wages received by men and women for the same work was an especially glaring problem. The **Equal Pay Act** (1963) required equal wages for "equal work" in industries engaged in commerce or producing goods for commerce. Although it contained various loopholes, the law was a <u>crucial</u> step on the road to fair and equal employment practices. The next year Congress would prohibit discrimination by employers on the basis of race, color, religion, national origin, or sex.

**Vocabulary Builder**
crucial–(CROO shuhl) *adj.* of vital importance

**Stimulating a Sluggish Economy** Kennedy believed that increased prosperity would help to eliminate some of the nation's social problems. When he became President, the country was suffering from a high unemployment rate and a sluggish economy. To help the sagging economy, Kennedy proposed tax credits to encourage business investment in new factory equipment. At the same time, increased military spending created new jobs and boosted the economy. Finally, Kennedy accepted the "new economics" of theorist John Maynard Keynes that <u>advocated</u> **deficit spending** to stimulate the economy. Deficit spending is the government practice of borrowing money in order to spend more than is received from taxes. In 1963, Kennedy called for dramatic tax cuts for middle-class Americans as a way to put more money in the pockets of more people. At the same time, he increased the tax burden on wealthier citizens. Kennedy's economic initiatives jump-started the tremendous economic growth of the late 1960s.

**Vocabulary Builder**
advocate–(AD vuh kayt) *v.* to speak or write in support of; be in favor of

**Moving Cautiously on Civil Rights** Kennedy pursued a timid approach toward civil rights. He had narrowly won the 1960 election, and he had little real influence in Congress or even complete partisan support. He did not want to anger conservative, white southern members of Congress in his own party. They stood ready to block any civil rights legislation.

While Kennedy remained largely passive on civil rights issues, African Americans and their white allies challenged segregation in the South. In 1961, they took "freedom rides" to desegregate interstate bus travel. In 1963, Martin Luther King, Jr., took the civil rights struggle to Birmingham, Alabama. Such actions took courage and were met by angry, oftentimes violent, responses by white southerners.

In early 1963, Kennedy introduced a civil rights bill that demanded prosecution for voting-rights violations and federal money to aid school desegregation. Further violence in the South prompted Kennedy to introduce stronger civil rights legislation.

**Racing Into Space** The launching of the satellite *Sputnik 1* by the Soviet Union in 1957 called into question American technological superiority. Although Congress created the National Aeronautics and Space Administration (NASA) in 1958, the Soviets' space program remained several steps ahead of the American program. In April 1961, for example, the Soviet cosmonaut Yuri Gagarin became the first human to orbit Earth.

Kennedy recognized that the United States and the Soviet Union were locked in a **"space race."** *Space race* was the term used to describe the competition between the Soviet Union and the United States to develop technology to successfully land on the moon. In May 1961, NASA put astronaut Alan Shepard into a suborbital space flight aboard the Project Mercury space capsule *Freedom 7*. Encouraged by the success of Project Mercury, Kennedy committed the United States to landing a man on the moon by 1970.

—from Straight Herblock
(Simon & Schuster, 1964)

**Analyzing Political Cartoons**

**Civil Rights** This cartoon, titled "Eclipse," appeared in 1963, at a time when the civil rights struggle reached national prominence.
1. Define *eclipse*. Why do you think the cartoonist chose this title?
2. Do you think all Americans responded the same way to this cartoon? Explain.

# SPACE EXPLORATION

After the successful space flight of Soviet cosmonaut Yuri Gagarin in April 1961, President Kennedy announced the goal of the United States to place a man on the moon before the end of the decade. In July 1969, the launching of the *Apollo 11* (shown left) was the first successful manned mission to land on the moon. Nearly forty years later, President Bush would announce his vision for the program—continued missions to the moon and further exploration of Mars.

Ed White ▶ floats outside *Gemini 4* during a mission in 1965.

▲ President Kennedy congratulates Alan Shepard.

▲ By 1995, Soviet and American crew members worked together on MIR, the Russian space station.

Edwin Aldrin stands ▶ on the surface of the moon next to the American flag in 1969.

**October 1958** NASA is created

**May 1961** Alan Shepard becomes the first American to make a space flight.

**February 1962** John Glenn is the first American to orbit Earth.

**January 1967** Fire kills *Apollo* astronauts Roger Chaffee, Virgil Grissom, and Edward White.

**July 1969** *Apollo 11* astronauts successfully land on the moon.

**June 1976** *Viking 1* transmits the first close-up images of Mars.

**January 1986** Spacecraft *Challenger* explodes 73 seconds after takeoff. Seven astronauts are killed.

**April 1990** Hubble Space Telescope is launched.

**April 1997** *Pathfinder* lands on Mars.

**November 1998** Construction of the International Space Station begins.

**November 2000** The first crew takes residence in the International Space Station.

**Thinking Critically**

1. **Identify Causes** How did international competition lead to space exploration?

2. **Identify Central Issues** How did the loss of *Challenger* lead Americans to reexamine the costs and benefits of the space program?

America's quest to reach the moon was punctuated by enormous successes and heartbreaking failures. Astronaut John Glenn became the first American to orbit Earth in February 1962. But astronauts Virgil Grissom, Edward White, and Roger Chaffee burned to death when their docked capsule exploded in fire during a routine test. Finally, in July of 1969, astronaut Neil Armstrong left his spacecraft *Columbia*'s landing vehicle and became the first man to step on the moon. The mission was a successful completion of Kennedy's bold dream.

**A Son's Farewell**
John F. Kennedy, Jr., salutes his father's casket as it passes by in the funeral procession.

✔ **Checkpoint** Why did Kennedy change the way in which he addressed civil rights issues?

# The President Is Assassinated

During his first two and a half years in office, Kennedy made the transition from politician to national leader. In foreign affairs he confronted Soviet challenges, made hard decisions, and won the respect of Soviet leaders and American citizens. He also spoke eloquently about the need to move toward a peaceful future. In domestic affairs he finally came to the conclusion that the federal government had to lead the struggle for civil rights. Added to his new maturity was his ability to inspire Americans to dream noble dreams and work toward lofty ends.

In November 1963, Kennedy traveled to Dallas, Texas, to mend political fences for his 1964 reelection bid. He never lived to see 1964. While his motorcade moved through the city, assassin Lee Harvey Oswald, perched by a window on the sixth floor of the Texas School Book Depository, fired three shots at the President. The third shot hit Kennedy in the back of his head. A half hour later, doctors at Parkland Memorial Hospital pronounced him dead. Texan Lyndon B. Johnson, Kennedy's Vice President, was sworn in as the new President. Although many people would later question whether Oswald acted alone, the **Warren Commission,** which conducted the official investigation of the assassination, described Oswald as the "lone killer."

The senseless murder deeply saddened Americans across the nation. Millions of people watched Kennedy's funeral procession on television, and many reacted as if they had lost a family member. It seemed as if part of America's innocence had died with him.

✔ **Checkpoint** What was the purpose of the Warren Commission?

---

**Progress Monitoring *Online***
For: Self-test with vocabulary practice
Web Code: nea-1504

## Comprehension

1. **Terms and People** Discuss how each of the following terms met a goal of Kennedy's domestic program.
   - New Frontier
   - Equal Pay Act
   - deficit spending

2. **NoteTaking Reading Skill: Identify Main Ideas** Use your concept web to answer the Section Focus Question: What were the goals of Kennedy's domestic program?

## Writing About History

3. **Quick Write: Identify Counterarguments** Identify one point of view regarding President Kennedy's decision to move cautiously on civil rights. Then, identify one argument that someone might use *against* this point of view. Remember, an effective counterargument does not simply state that the original argument was wrong but gives specific reasons for the opposing point of view.

## Critical Thinking

4. **Analyze Information** Why did Kennedy consider foreign policy to be the most important issue of his administration?

5. **Draw Inferences** Why do you think Kennedy called his domestic program the New Frontier?

6. **Draw Conclusions** Was Kennedy's commitment to the space program an extension of the Cold War? Explain.

# Can a Poor Person Get a Fair Trial?

 8.3.1b

The Sixth Amendment gives a person accused of a crime the right to "the assistance of counsel." But what about poor defendants? They don't have the money to pay for a lawyer. If a poor person goes to trial without a lawyer and is convicted, was justice done?

## *Gideon* v. *Wainwright* (1963)

| The Facts | The Issue | The Decision |
|---|---|---|
| • Clarence Gideon was tried in a Florida court for breaking into a building.<br><br>• Gideon said he was too poor to afford a lawyer and asked the court to appoint one.<br><br>• After the judge refused, Gideon defended himself and was found guilty. | Gideon claimed he had been denied his rights to an attorney and to due process. | The Supreme Court ruled unanimously that Florida should have provided an attorney for Gideon. |

### Why It Matters

The Court's ruling in *Gideon* was forceful. All nine justices agreed that Florida should have given Gideon an attorney. They clearly stated why having an attorney is so important:

> "Any person hauled into court, who is too poor to hire a lawyer, cannot be assured a fair trial unless counsel is provided for him. This seems to us to be an obvious truth."

▲ Clarence Gideon

The decision had a tremendous impact on the country's legal system. Public defenders are state-paid officials who defend people who are too poor to hire their own lawyers.

But has the promise of *Gideon* been fulfilled? Critics say problems still remain. Many states do not fully fund the public defenders' offices that furnish lawyers for poor defendants. These defenders are overworked and underpaid, making it harder for them to do their job well. They lack the resources to hire experts to evaluate evidence. Many public defenders are not brought into a case as soon as a charge is made. This prevents them from properly advising their clients. Finally, public defenders do not have the time or resources to effectively carry out appeals to higher courts.

---

### Connect to Your World

Research the use of public defenders in your state or community. Then, write an essay titled "*Gideon* Today," in which you explain whether you think the justice system is fair for poor people or not.

**For:** Supreme Court cases
**Web Code:** nee-1509

---

◀ A public defender and his client face the judge during a court hearing.

**President Johnson's Hopes for America**

In 1965, President Lyndon B. Johnson addressed a joint session of Congress. In the speech he talked about some of his hopes for America and how he wished to be remembered by history. He explained,

❝I do not want to be the President who built empires, or sought grandeur, or extended dominion. I want to be the President who educated young children . . . who helped to feed the hungry . . . who helped the poor to find their own way. . . .❞

—President Johnson, speech before Congress, March 15, 1965

◀ Lyndon Johnson is sworn in as President, in 1963, after Kennedy's assassination.

# Johnson's Great Society

## Content Expectations

- **8.2.3** Compare/contrast Roosevelt's New Deal initiatives, Johnson's Great Society programs, Reagan's market-based domestic policies.
- **8.3.1b** Analyze Supreme Court decisions/ governmental actions during Civil Rights Movement.
- **8.3.5** Analyze causes/consequences of civil unrest that occurred in U.S. cities.

## Terms and People

Lyndon B. Johnson
Civil Rights Act
War on Poverty
Economic Opportunity Act
Great Society

Medicare
Medicaid
Immigration and Nationality Act of 1965
Warren Court

## NoteTaking

**Reading Skill: Identify Main Ideas** Identify details about the Great Society programs.

| The Great Society | | | |
|---|---|---|---|
| Education | Healthcare | Immigration | Poverty |
| • | • Medicare | • | • |

**Why It Matters Lyndon B. Johnson,** who became President after Kennedy's assassination, shared the same goals as his predecessor. These goals shaped the purpose of Johnson's Great Society program. A seasoned politician, Johnson successfully pushed through significant domestic legislation that he hoped would become the first step to achieving the quality of life he thought all Americans should enjoy. **Section Focus Question: How did Johnson's Great Society programs change life for most Americans?**

## Johnson's Rise to Leadership

Born in Stonewall, Texas, Lyndon B. Johnson was raised in the Hill Country town of Johnson City. He attended Southwest Texas State College and then taught for several years in Cotulla, Texas. There, at a tiny segregated school for Mexican Americans, he confronted firsthand the challenges faced by poverty-stricken minority students, and the lessons he learned remained with him for the rest of his life.

**A Determined Texan** After teaching for several years, Johnson entered politics—first as a Texas congressman's secretary and then as the head of the Texas National Youth Administration.

In 1937, Johnson was elected to Congress, and during the next several decades he became the most powerful person on Capitol Hill. Elected to the Senate in 1948, Johnson proved himself a master of party politics and rose to the position of Senate majority leader in 1955. In the Senate, he was adept at avoiding conflict, building political coalitions, and working out compromises. His skill was instrumental in pushing the 1957 Civil Rights Act through Congress.

In 1960, he hoped to be chosen by the Democratic Party to run for President, but when Kennedy got the nomination Johnson agreed to join him on the ticket as the vice presidential nominee. A New Englander and a Catholic, Kennedy needed Johnson to help carry the heavily Protestant South. Johnson was also popular both with Mexican American voters and in the Southwest. He was an important part of Kennedy's victory in 1960.

**The Kennedy Legacy** On becoming President after Kennedy's assassination, Johnson radiated reassurance and strength. His every action indicated that he was ready for the job and that the government was in good hands. Less than a week after the assassination, Johnson addressed a joint session of Congress.

## Job Training

President Johnson visits a job training center in Texas. The success of Johnson's antipoverty programs is reflected in the declining numbers of Americans living below the poverty line.

**Primary Source** "... [N]o memorial oration or eulogy could more eloquently honor President Kennedy's memory than the earliest possible passage of the Civil Rights Bill for which he fought so long."
—President Johnson, speech before a Joint Session of Congress, 1963

With Johnson's ability to build consensus, or agreement on an issue by a group, the **Civil Rights Act** became law in the summer of 1964. It outlawed discrimination in voting, education, and public accommodations. The act demanded an end to discrimination in hospitals, restaurants, theaters, and other places open to the public. It also created the Equal Employment Opportunity Commission to fight discrimination in hiring. African Americans and Mexican Americans who faced almost daily discrimination benefited immeasurably from the legislation. Finally, Title VII of the 1964 Civil Rights Act prohibited discrimination on the basis of sex.

**Johnson Declares a War on Poverty** Johnson had made his intentions clear in his first State of the Union address when he said it was time to "declare an unconditional war on poverty." The new President planned to fuse his own dreams for America onto Kennedy's legislative agenda. Although Kennedy had failed to get Congress to approve his tax bill calling for dramatic tax cuts for middle-class Americans, Johnson was able to maneuver it through. In addition, he had added a billion-dollar **War on Poverty** to the bill.

Johnson's War on Poverty introduced measures to train the jobless, educate the uneducated, and provide healthcare for those in need. The 1964 **Economic Opportunity Act** created the Job Corps to train young men and women between the ages of 16 and 21 in the work skills they needed to acquire better jobs and move out of poverty. The act also established Volunteers in Service to America, or VISTA, patterned after Kennedy's Peace Corps, which sent American volunteers into poverty-stricken American communities in an effort to solve the country's pressing economic, educational, and medical problems. The volunteers served in inner-city schools and on Indian reservations. They worked in rural health clinics and urban hospitals.

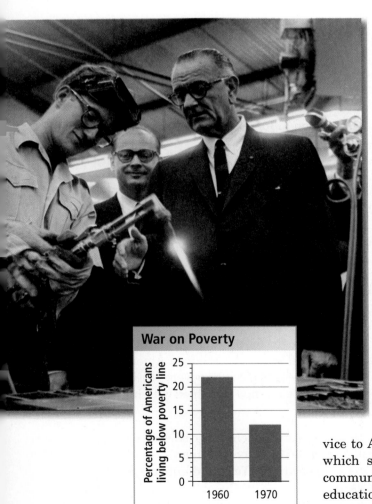

**War on Poverty**

Percentage of Americans living below poverty line

| Year | |
|---|---|
| 1960 | 22 |
| 1970 | 12 |

SOURCE: U.S. Census Bureau

# Poverty and Prosperity

## TRACK THE ISSUE

### How should Americans deal with the gap between rich and poor?

Over the years, Americans have tried to balance the extremes of wealth and poverty in society. Some have favored private charity to help the poor, while others have backed government policies to distribute wealth. Still, the gap remains. Use the timeline below to explore this enduring issue.

**1800s  Community Aid**
Private charities provide aid for the poor.

**1900  Poverty Level**
An estimated 40 percent of Americans live in poverty.

**1933  New Deal**
Federal government provides aid for the poor.

**1964  War on Poverty**
President Johnson expands programs to reduce poverty.

**1980s  Reaganomics**
President Reagan promotes business growth to reduce poverty.

**1996  Welfare Reform**
Government limits welfare programs.

Migrant farm family in Virginia

 7.1.3c

Many workers, such as the grocery clerk shown here, hold minimum-wage jobs.

## DEBATE THE ISSUE

**The Minimum Wage**  The government has tried to reduce poverty for working people by setting a minimum wage. Supporters say this wage is too low to provide a decent living. Critics say an increase would hurt employers and make it harder for them to provide low-level jobs.

"We all lose when American workers are underpaid. It's a myth that small businesses can't pay a higher minimum wage. . . . When businesses don't pay a living wage, all society pays. We pay through poverty . . . [and] needless disease. . . . We pay as businesses and communities suffer economic decline."

—Margot Dorfman, CEO, U.S. Women's Chamber of Commerce

"Decades of economic research confirm that increasing the minimum wage destroys jobs for low-skilled workers while doing little to address poverty. When faced with higher labor costs, employers tend to hire fewer, more highly-skilled and experienced employees. That leaves unskilled or low-skilled workers . . . out in the cold."

—from The Economics Policy Institute

### TRANSFER Activities

1. **Compare**  Why does Margot Dorfman support the minimum wage? Why does the Economic Policy Institute oppose it?

2. **Analyze**  Would a minimum wage help reduce poverty? Explain.

3. **Transfer**  Use the following Web site to see a video, try a WebQuest, and write in your journal. **Web Code:** neh-8802

Perhaps the most successful element of the Economic Opportunity Act was the Head Start program. Funds were provided for play groups, day care, and activities designed to help underprivileged children get ready for elementary school. Head Start enjoyed bipartisan support for decades.

**Johnson Defeats Goldwater** If Johnson was to continue his War on Poverty and other social goals, he needed to win the 1964 presidential election. In that year, the Republicans nominated Arizona senator Barry Goldwater, whose economic and social views were directly opposed to Johnson's. Whereas Johnson believed the federal government could best regulate the economy and promote social justice, Goldwater maintained that the federal government was the problem not the solution. According to Goldwater, social and economic issues, such as racism and poverty, should not be addressed by the federal government.

If elected, Goldwater would rein in the federal government by reducing its size and restricting its activities. He favored significant tax cuts and right-to-work laws, and he opposed social welfare legislation and government spending on educational, public housing, and urban renewal programs.

In 1964, most Americans were not ready either for Goldwater's belligerent tone or his conservative message. Johnson's campaign played up Goldwater's extremism, suggesting that his election would ensure the repeal of civil rights legislation and economic ruin.

Johnson had prosperity on his side, as well as his own impressive legislative record and the legacy of Kennedy. In the November election, he won a landslide

**History *Interactive***

**For:** To discover more about the Great Society programs
**Web Code:** nep-1509

● **INFOGRAPHIC**

# The Great Society
## Arts and Education

At a 1965 news conference, President Johnson declared, "When I was young, poverty was so common that we didn't know it had a name. And education was something you had to fight for . . . ." Seemingly inspired by his own upbringing, Johnson set out to create the Great Society. The program included support for education and the arts.

▲ President Johnson signs the Higher Education Act on November 8, 1965, at the one-room school-house near Stonewall, Texas, where his own education began.

▼ Project Head Start and the Elementary and Secondary Education Act committed the federal government to providing resources for individuals and schools. At left, a teacher works with students at a preschool program. Below, students work together in a school library.

victory, capturing more than 60 percent of the popular vote and carrying all but six states. Goldwater carried only Arizona and five southern states—Louisiana, Mississippi, Alabama, Georgia, and South Carolina. Furthermore, the <u>outcome</u> of the election was significant. The South was no longer solidly Democrat. Not only had Johnson won a ringing victory, but Democrats had captured both houses of Congress.

**Vocabulary Builder**
<u>outcome</u>—(OWT kuhm) *n.* final result of a meeting, process, or series of events

✔ **Checkpoint** **How did Johnson continue Kennedy's plan to eliminate poverty in the United States?**

## The Great Society

In the spring of 1964, in a speech at the University of Michigan, Johnson outlined his vision for America, calling it the **Great Society.** He said that during the previous several centuries, Americans had spread across the continent, developed industrially, and created great wealth. But the work of America was not complete. He added,

**Primary Source** ❝The challenge of the next half century is whether we have the wisdom to use that wealth to enrich and elevate our national life, and to advance the quality of our American civilization. . . . [W]e have the opportunity to move not only toward the rich society and the powerful society, but upward to the Great Society.❞
—President Johnson, University of Michigan, May 22, 1964

For Johnson, the Great Society demanded "an end to poverty and racial injustice" and opportunity for every child.

◀ Public radio and television gained support through the sponsorship of the Corporation for Public Broadcasting. *Sesame Street*, featuring Big Bird and the Muppets, combines education and entertainment for children.

▲ The National Endowment for the Arts financially assists artists, arts education, and arts organizations. Wynton Marsalis (above) and Helen Frankenthaler (left) each won the National Medal of Honor.

**Thinking Critically**
1. **Draw Inferences** How might education programs be used to create a great society?
2. **Identify Point of View** Should the government provide funds to support the arts? Explain.

521

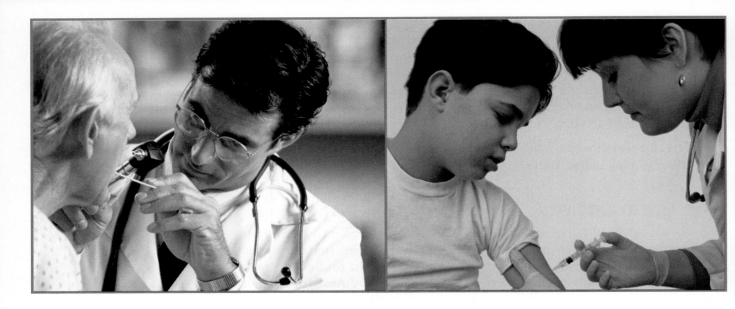

## Healthier Citizens

President Johnson gave healthcare special attention. With Medicare and Medicaid, more Americans could receive basic healthcare.

**Healthcare Insurance** In the first half of 1965, Congress passed parts of Johnson's Great Society legislation. Kennedy had supported similar legislation that failed to win congressional support. Johnson's agenda amended the Social Security Act by adding the Medical Care for the Aged Program, or **Medicare** as it was more popularly called. Medicare provided basic hospital insurance for Americans in the Social Security system who were age 65 and older. It also included a **Medicaid** feature that provided basic medical services to poor and disabled Americans who were not part of the Social Security system.

Johnson signed the bill into law in Independence, Missouri, home of former President Harry Truman, who had called for a national health insurance program almost 20 years earlier.

**Education** Along with health, education was one of the centerpieces of the Great Society program. Improved healthcare and education were necessary steps toward the goal of ending poverty. The 1965 Elementary and Secondary Education Act was designed to aid schools in poorer communities. It provided federal funds to improve school libraries, learning centers, language laboratories, and services in impoverished school districts. The act dramatically increased funding for Indian, inner city, and Mexican American schools.

**Protecting the Environment and the Consumer** The Great Society program extended to improving the overall quality of American life. In the early 1960s, several best-selling books raised Americans' awareness about environmental and consumer problems. Rachel Carson's *Silent Spring* (1962) detailed how chemical fertilizers and pesticides were damaging the fragile ecosystem. Ralph Nader's *Unsafe at Any Speed* (1965) attacked the automotive industry for its lack of concern for passenger safety.

Both these books helped to foster environmental and consumer activity and led to several important pieces of legislation. The Water Quality Act (1965) and the Clean Water Restoration Act (1966) aimed at improving water and air standards in the country. The National Traffic and Motor Vehicle Safety Act (1966) established safety standards for automotive vehicles.

**New Immigration Policies** Meanwhile, the civil rights movement was raising questions about America's long-standing immigration policy. The National Origins Acts of 1921 and 1924 had established a quota system that favored Western European immigrants and limited immigrants from other parts of the world. Such a discriminatory policy was clearly out of touch with the mood of the country in the early 1960s.

The **Immigration and Nationality Act of 1965** altered America's quota system. Nearly 170,000 immigrants from the Eastern Hemisphere were allowed into the country. Nearly 120,000 immigrants from the Western Hemisphere were welcomed. Immigrants from Latin America, Central America, the Caribbean, and Asia soon began to pour into the United States, providing the country with a pool of ideas, talent, and skills. During the 1960s and 1970s, millions of immigrants would arrive on American shores. Once again, the doors of America were open to immigrants from around the world. As in the late nineteenth and early twentieth centuries, New York and the urban East and West coasts attracted many of the country's newest immigrants.

**The Legacy** While the Great Society programs did not completely alter America, they did improve the lives of millions of individual Americans. Poverty and infant mortality rates declined. Medicare and Medicaid delivered needed healthcare to millions of elderly and poor Americans. Head Start and other anti-poverty programs provided the educational tools many underprivileged Americans needed to escape poverty. Furthermore, Congress also provided artists and scholars with assistance through the National Endowment for the Arts and Humanities, created in 1965. The Great Society victories may not have been as grandiose as Johnson predicted, but they were victories. The simple fact that 22.2 percent of all Americans lived below the poverty line in 1960 and 12.6 percent lived below the poverty line in 1970 says something about the triumphs of the Great Society.

✔ **Checkpoint** Which immigrant groups were affected by the Immigration and Nationality Act of 1965?

# The Supreme Court and Reform

During the 1960s, the Supreme Court demonstrated a willingness to take the lead on controversial social, religious, and political issues. Led by Chief Justice Earl Warren, the Supreme Court at this time—often called the **Warren Court**—became the most liberal in American history. Its decisions supported civil rights, civil liberties, voting rights, and personal privacy.

**Congressional Districts and Voters' Rights** In several decisions the Supreme Court ruled in favor of the "one man, one vote" principle. The problem was one of apportionment of seats in state legislatures. During the twentieth century, large numbers of voters moved from rural to urban areas, but many state governments had not changed, or reapportioned, electoral districts to reflect the new conditions. This led to an electoral imbalance. In many states, rural areas had more power and urban areas had less power than their populations actually mandated.

In *Baker* v. *Carr* (1962), the Supreme Court ruled in favor of reapportionment on the basis of "one man, one vote." Electoral districts, it said, had to reflect the numbers of people in those districts. In *Reynolds* v. *Sims* (1964), the Court reaffirmed its decision, adding that any arrangement other than "one man, one vote" violated the equal protection clause of the Fourteenth Amendment.

HISTORY MAKERS

**Earl Warren** (1891–1974)
One of the country's most influential Chief Justices, Earl Warren was governor of California before being named to head the Supreme Court. As Chief Justice, he guided the Court to a unanimous ruling outlawing school segregation in *Brown* v. *Board of Education*. The Warren Court issued many landmark rulings in the areas of civil rights, criminal justice, First Amendment issues, and legislative districting. These decisions led many Americans to call for Warren's removal, though he remained on the Court until retiring in 1969.

**Rights of the Accused** The Warren Court also showed a heightened concern for the constitutional rights of accused lawbreakers. In four landmark cases, the Court broadened the individual rights of accused criminals and narrowed those of federal, state, and local government officials. In *Mapp* v. *Ohio* (1961), the Court ruled that evidence obtained illegally violated the Fourth Amendment and had to be excluded from federal and state trials. In *Gideon* v. *Wainwright* (1963), the Court decided that all accused criminals had the right to a lawyer whether or not they could pay for one. In *Escobedo* v. *Illinois* (1964), the Warren Court expanded on *Gideon* v. *Wainwright* by adding that every accused lawbreaker had to be offered access to a lawyer before questioning, and all evidence obtained from a suspect who had not been informed of his or her right to a lawyer could not be used in court. Finally, in *Miranda* v. *Arizona* (1966), the Court ruled that an accused criminal had to be informed of his or her Fifth and Sixth Amendment rights before being questioned.

Critics of these decisions argued that the Warren Court had tipped the balance of justice in favor of the rights of accused criminals. Today, many conservative justices still side with this opinion. The majority of the members of the Warren Court, however, have countered that the rights of individuals had to be protected, especially when freedom hung in the balance.

**Separation of Church and State** The Warren Court addressed the separation of church and state in the case of *Engel* v. *Vitale* (1962). The case involved whether or not a public school could require students to recite a state-sanctioned prayer. The Court ruled that school prayer was a violation of the First Amendment and an attempt by a governmental body to promote religion. The next year, the Court ruled in *Abington* v. *Schempp* that Bible reading in public schools also violated the First Amendment. The two decisions divided religious groups and the American people. Some welcomed the rulings, saying the government should have no say in personal religious matters. Others insisted the decisions were hostile to religion. The two decisions ignited, and continue to ignite, controversy. For more than 40 years, various religious groups have railed against these decisions.

 **Checkpoint** What major court ruling gave a person accused of a crime the right to have a lawyer?

---

**Progress Monitoring *Online***
For: Self-test with vocabulary practice
Web Code: nea-1505

**Comprehension**

1. **Terms and People** Explain the relationship of the following terms to social reform.
   - War on Poverty
   - Great Society
   - Medicare
   - Medicaid

2. **NoteTaking Reading Skill: Identify Main Ideas** Use your chart to answer the Section Focus Question: How did Johnson's Great Society programs change life for most Americans?

**Writing About History**

3. **Quick Write: Chart Arguments and Counterarguments** Identify one point of view regarding the use of government funds to support massive social programs. Then, make a chart with two columns. In the first column, list two arguments in favor of that point of view. In the second column, list two arguments against that point of view.

**Critical Thinking**

4. **Make Comparisons** Were there differences in the goals of the New Frontier and the Great Society? Explain.

5. **Recognize Cause and Effect** How do you think the Immigration and Nationality Act of 1965 changed political activity in the nation?

6. **Identify Point of View** Why did some Americans feel that Supreme Court decisions during the 1960s considered only the rights of the poor?

# What Rights Should an Accused Person Have?

Police officers try to obtain confessions from suspects. Yet, the Fifth Amendment protects people from self-incrimination—stating facts that will result in their being accused of a crime. The Sixth Amendment gives them the right to an attorney. How do those guaranteed rights come into play when a person is being questioned by police?

**MI** 8.3.4

## *Miranda* v. *Arizona* (1966)

| The Facts | The Issue | The Decision |
|---|---|---|
| • Ernesto Miranda, under questioning by police, confessed that he had kidnapped and assaulted a woman.<br><br>• Miranda was convicted in state court of the crimes in part because of the confession. | Miranda claimed the confession should not be used because police had not warned him of his right to avoid self-incrimination or to have a lawyer present. | A 5:4 majority ruled that the conviction should be thrown out because police had violated Miranda's rights when it obtained the confession. |

▲ A suspect is advised of his Miranda rights.

## Why It Matters

The majority based its reasoning on "the necessity for procedures which assure" the protection of Fifth Amendment rights. It spelled out those procedures:

> "Prior to any questioning, the person must be warned that he has a right to remain silent, that any statement he does make may be used as evidence against him, and that he has a right to the presence of an attorney."

That statement is familiar to many Americans from hearing it on television crime dramas. The majority also ruled that people who request a lawyer must be provided with one, even if they are too poor to pay for one themselves.

The decision has had a profound effect on the criminal justice system. Police officers must inform suspects of their rights. Only then can statements made by the suspect be used in a trial.

### Connect to Your World

The Court addressed the issue of confessions by minors in *Yarborough* v. *Alvarado* (2004). Research the case. Write a summary that explains the facts, the Court's decision, Justice Sandra Day O'Connor's concerns about the rights of minors, and the views of the dissent.

**For:** Supreme Court Cases
**Web Code:** nee-1508

◄ A police officer holds the Miranda Warning card.

# Quick Study Guide

 8.3.1b

**Progress Monitoring *Online***
**For:** Self-test with vocabulary practice
**Web Code:** nea-1506

## ■ The New Frontier Paves the Way

| New Frontier | Great Society |
|---|---|
| • Anti-poverty legislation<br>• Peace Corps, Alliance for Progress<br>• Education legislation<br>• Healthcare legislation<br>• Civil rights goals | • Economic Opportunity Act<br>• Volunteers in Service to America<br>• Head Start<br>• Medicare, Medicaid<br>• Civil Rights Act, 1964 |

## ■ NASA Spending 1950–1965

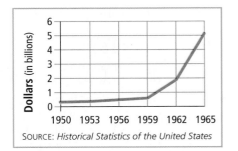

SOURCE: *Historical Statistics of the United States*

## ■ The Warren Court

- Baker v. Carr
- Mapp v. Ohio
- Engel v. Vitale
- Miranda v. Arizona
- **The Warren Court**
- Gideon v. Wainwright
- Escobedo v. Illinois
- Reynolds v. Sims
- Abington v. Schempp

## ■ Cold War Challenges

| Bay of Pigs | Berlin | Cuban Missile Crisis |
|---|---|---|
| • American CIA arms and trains anti-Castro forces.<br>• Bay of Pigs invasion fails.<br>• Soviets suspect weakness in Kennedy. | • Kennedy meets with Khrushchev in Vienna.<br>• East Germans and Soviets build Berlin Wall.<br>• In West Berlin, Kennedy delivers speech assuring West Germans of continued U.S. support. | • United States discovers Soviet missile sites in Cuba.<br>• Kennedy imposes blockade of Cuba.<br>• Khrushchev removes missiles from Cuba. |

## ☑ Quick Study Timeline

**In America**

**1961**
**Peace Corps established**

**1962**
**Cuban missile crisis**

**1963**
**President Kennedy assassinated**

**Presidential Terms**        John F. Kennedy 1961–1963                    Lyndon B. Johnson 1963–196

**1960**                                                                    **1963**

**Around the World**

1961
**Berlin Wall is built**

1963
**Civil War breaks out in Cyprus between Greeks and Turks**

# American Issues
## ●—●—● Connector

8.2.3

By connecting prior knowledge with what you have learned in this chapter, you can gradually build your understanding of enduring questions that still affect America today. Answer the questions below. Then, use your American Issues Connector study guide (or go online: www.PHSchool.com **Web Code:** neh-8803).

## Issues You Learned About

● **Poverty and Prosperity** While some people find America to be a true "land of opportunity," others face a daily struggle to make ends meet.

1. What was revealed in Michael Harrington's book *The Other America*? How did Kennedy respond to this book?

2. Did Kennedy's new tax policies benefit upper-class Americans? Explain.

3. What did Johnson hope to accomplish with his War on Poverty? Describe one new program that was part of this effort.

● **America and the World** As part of the Cold War, the United States combated communism in Latin America.

4. What was the Cold War, and when and why did it begin?

5. Did the Peace Corps serve as a tool for promoting democracy or for helping developing nations? Explain.

6. Why do you think that the U.S. government was willing to invade communist Cuba in hopes of overthrowing its leader, but was not willing to invade other communist countries?

● **Social Problems and Reforms** In the 1960s, the government grew concerned with social problems and made efforts to fix them.

7. In 1963, Kennedy told the nation in a televised address that civil rights was a "moral issue . . . as clear as the American Constitution." Did Kennedy always hold this belief about civil rights? Explain.

8. List at least five different areas in which reform legislation was passed in the 1960s. Which was the most significant? Explain your choice.

### Connect to Your World | Michigan

**Poverty and Prosperity** Thanks to federal funding and other support under the Economic Opportunity Act of 1964, local Michigan community organizations took the lead in fighting poverty in the 1960s. For example, in June 1968, the Allegan County Board of Supervisors formed the Allegan County Resource Development Committee (ACRDC) to "combat the causes and effects of human suffering and poverty in Allegan County, Michigan." Founded in 1965, the Monroe County Opportunity Program (MCOP) today provides a food bank, housing for the homeless, and other vital services to elderly, disabled, and poor residents of Monroe County, Michigan. Create a brochure about one of these groups or an antipoverty organization in your community.

**1965**
**Immigration and Nationality Act**

**1966**
*Miranda* v. *Arizona* protects rights of the accused

**History Interactive**
**For:** Interactive timeline
**Web Code:** nep-1507

**1966**

**1969**

**1965**
**India and Pakistan fight over control of Kashmir**

**1968**
**Fighting breaks out between Catholics and Protestants in Northern Ireland**

# Chapter Assessment

## Terms and People

1. Define a **"flexible response"** defense policy. How did this defense policy differ from Eisenhower's defense policy?

2. What was the **Nuclear Test Ban Treaty**? Why was it so important?

3. What was the **Warren Commission**? What were its findings?

4. What was the purpose of **Medicare** and **Medicaid**? Who led the campaign for this legislation, and which legislation were they part of?

5. What was the **Immigration and Nationality Act of 1965**? Where did most of the new immigrants come from?

## Focus Questions

The focus question for this chapter is **How did the policies of Presidents Kennedy and Johnson affect the nation?** Build an answer to this big question by answering the focus questions for Sections 1 through 3 and the Critical Thinking questions that follow.

### Section 1
6. How did Kennedy respond to the continuing challenges of the Cold War?

### Section 2
7. What were the goals of Kennedy's New Frontier?

### Section 3
8. How did Johnson's Great Society programs change life for most Americans?

## Critical Thinking

9. **Identify Central Issues** How did the education legislation passed during the Great Society build upon the War on Poverty's education program?

10. **Investigate Problems** How did the issues surrounding East and West Germany contribute to Cold War tensions between the United States and the Soviet Union?

11. **Analyze Information** The Equal Pay Act of 1963 required that women be paid the same wages as men for "equal work." Do you think this legislation had an effect on the passage of the Civil Rights Act of 1964? Explain.

12. **Analyze Charts** The chart below shows successful space launches. Use the chart, as well as your reading of the chapter, to describe the progress of the space race for the years shown. According to one source, the space program is a way to "unite" all nations. Do you agree or disagree? Explain.

| Country | 1957–1964 | 1965–1969 | 1970–1974 |
|---|---|---|---|
| Soviet Union | 82 | 302 | 405 |
| United States | 207 | 279 | 139 |
| Japan | | | 5 |
| China | | | 2 |
| France | | | 3 |
| United Kingdom | | | 1 |
| Total | 289 | 581 | 555 |

13. **Analyze Information** In what ways might Johnson's career as a teacher have made him aware that the nation faced serious social problems that needed to be addressed and reformed?

## Writing About History

**Writing a Persuasive Essay** An effective persuasive essay does not simply argue its own point of view. It also anticipates and counters arguments that might be used by the other side. Write a three-paragraph persuasive essay on the subject of the Warren Court and its decisions regarding the rights of the accused.

### Prewriting
- Identify the point of view that you will take in your essay.
- List any arguments you can think of in favor of your point of view. Prioritize them from the most persuasive to the least persuasive.
- Make a chart listing the two most persuasive arguments in one column and a possible counterargument to each argument in the other.

### Drafting
- Write an introductory paragraph in which you define the issue and state your viewpoint.
- In the first paragraph, state your most persuasive argument.
- In the second paragraph, identify a counterargument to your argument. Give specific reasons why you disagree with the counterargument.
- Throughout your essay, use clear, direct language that makes your argument sound both reasonable and forceful. Remember, overly emotional language and name-calling can sometimes make your argument seem less persuasive not more persuasive.

### Revising
- Use the guidelines on page SH22 of the Writing Handbook to revise your writing.

## The Effectiveness of President Johnson's Great Society Programs

In 1964, President Johnson proposed his vision for the United States called the Great Society. Johnson's goal was to end poverty and racial injustice and to give every child an opportunity to receive a good education. Would President Johnson's Great Society programs meet his goals or would they become a burden to taxpayers? Use your knowledge of Johnson's Great Society legislation and Documents A, B, and C to answer questions 1 through 4.

### Document A

"Project Head Start was created during the heady, idealistic days of the mid-1960s. President Lyndon Johnson believed that it was the nation's duty to provide not just legal equality but also equality of opportunity. In his 1965 commencement address at Howard University, he called for the 'next and the more profound stage' in the civil rights struggle. 'We seek not just freedom but opportunity.' . . . Johnson's War on Poverty would include a host of initiatives designed to bring blacks and other disadvantaged Americans to what he called 'the starting line' of American life with the skills and abilities necessary to compete on a level playing field. The War on Poverty focused on education as a tool for upward mobility, and Head Start was to become one of the cornerstones of the federal effort."

—"Competing Visions," Ron Haskins, 2004

### Document B

**Head Start Budget, 1965–2005**

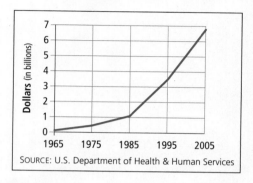

SOURCE: U.S. Department of Health & Human Services

### Document C

"On many domestic issues, [Senator] Dirksen continued the balancing act so central to his effectiveness, as he saw it: maintain a constructive relationship with the opposition and the loyalty of the Republican troops. He took issue with Medicare, for example: 'I would be eligible,' he said indignantly. 'Why should I be allowed to use dollars the government is taking from some young factory worker in Cleveland in the promise of providing for his old age?' The accumulation of Great Society spending programs appalled Dirksen. The taxpayers would have to come up with nearly $160 billion to fund them. Moreover, the programs brought with them an expanding federal bureaucracy and increasing centralization. To Dirksen, the Great Society was a misguided attempt at creating an immediate, utopian 'blueprint for paradise.'"

—*The Education of a Senator,* Frank H. Mackaman, 1998

---

1. According to Document A, why did President Johnson use Head Start as part of his War on Poverty?
   A He wanted to use Head Start to provide legal equality for disadvantaged Americans.
   B He wanted to create Head Start for Americans with exceptional abilities.
   C He wanted to use Head Start as a tool to help people achieve upward mobility.
   D He wanted to use Head Start to maintain a constructive relationship with the Republicans.

2. Which documents imply that the Great Society had a positive effect on the lives of Americans?
   A Documents A and C
   B Documents B and C
   C Documents A and B
   D Documents A, B, and C

3. In Document C, what viewpoint does Senator Dirksen take toward the Great Society programs?
   A He believed that Medicare would not help him.
   B He opposed the Republican view of the Great Society programs.
   C He proposed his own Great Society programs.
   D He believed that the Great Society programs would lead to an expanding federal government.

4. **Writing Task** Would President Johnson's Great Society programs meet his goals, or would they become a burden to taxpayers? Use your knowledge of the chapter content and specific evidence from the primary sources above to support your opinion.

### War in Vietnam

During the Vietnam War, the United States Army used helicopters to transport troops. One helicopter pilot remembered a mission to evacuate injured soldiers:

Ping-pong paddles commemorating Nixon's trip to China

❝We landed in front of the Jeep, or what was left of it. It was twisted like a child's discarded toy. . . . A sergeant ran up to my door. He told me through my extended microphone that two of the guys in the back were still alive. . . . They started loading up. The two wounded were unconscious, torn and bloody and gray.❞
—Captain Robert Mason, First Air Cavalry Division, 1965

*Listen to the* Witness History *audio to hear more about the Vietnam War Era.*

◄ U.S. troops evacuate a wounded American soldier from a firefight during the Vietnam War.

 **Content Expectations**

**Chapter Focus Question: How did the United States confront communism in East Asia after the Korean War?**

Antiwar poster

### Section 1

**Origins of the Vietnam War**  8.1.2a, 8.1.2d, 8.1.2e

### Section 2

**U.S. Involvement Grows**  8.1.2d, 8.2.3, 8.2.4

### Section 3

**The War Divides America**  8.1.2d, 8.3.1a, 8.3.5

### Section 4

**The War's End and Impact**  8.2.4, 8.3.1a, 8.3.5

Land mine used against American soldiers

### Section 5

**Nixon and the Cold War**  8.1.2a, 8.1.2d, 8.1.2f

Use the ☑ **Quick Study Timeline** at the end of this chapter to preview chapter events.

**Note Taking Study Guide *Online***
**For:** Note Taking and American Issues Connector
**Web Code:** nee-8901

▲ Ho Chi Minh depicted in a Vietnamese propaganda poster

**WITNESS HISTORY**  AUDIO

## Hope for Independence

After World War II, a spirit of nationalism and revolution spread among European colonies around the world. As colonial peoples strived for independence, their struggles sometimes became mixed up with the Cold War conflict between communist states and western democracies. Such was the case in French Indochina, which consisted of the lands of Laos, Cambodia, and Vietnam. Unaware of the long and bloody war that lie ahead, a Vietnamese communist named Ho Chi Minh dreamed of a Vietnam free from French rule:

❝The oppressed the world over are wresting back their independence. We should not lag behind. . . . Under the Vietminh banner, let us valiantly march forward!❞
—Ho Chi Minh, 1945

# Origins of the Vietnam War

### Content Expectations

- **8.1.2a** Evaluate development of U.S. national security establishment.
- **8.1.2d** Evaluate U.S. involvement in Vietnam, foreign/domestic consequences of the war.
- **8.1.2e** Evaluate indirect confrontations within specific world regions.

### Terms and People

Ho Chi Minh
domino theory
SEATO

Vietcong
Gulf of Tonkin Resolution

### NoteTaking

**Reading Skill: Summarize** As you read, describe the Vietnam policies of Presidents Truman, Eisenhower, Kennedy, and Johnson.

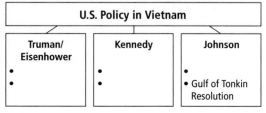

| U.S. Policy in Vietnam | | |
|---|---|---|
| Truman/ Eisenhower | Kennedy | Johnson |
| • | • | • |
| • | • | • Gulf of Tonkin Resolution |

**Why It Matters** Presidents Kennedy and Johnson shared a vision for a better America in the 1960s. They also shared a vision for a better world in which America would emerge victorious from its Cold War struggle against global communism. As part of this strategic and ideological battle, the United States established a new line of defense against communism in Vietnam. The conflict in Southeast Asia would grow to be one of the costliest wars in American history. **Section Focus Question: Why did the United States become involved in Vietnam?**

## America and the War in Indochina

Situated far away in Southeast Asia, Vietnam did not attract significant American attention until the 1960s. Television news shows rarely mentioned it, and most Americans could not locate it on a map. But over a span of more than ten years, the United States sent several million soldiers to fight in Vietnam. America's involvement in Vietnam had roots in European colonialism, Cold War politics, and Vietnamese calls for national independence.

**France Rules Indochina in Southeast Asia** In the 1800s, French military forces established control over Indochina, a peninsula in Southeast Asia that includes the modern countries of Vietnam, Cambodia, and Laos. Slightly larger than the state of Texas, Indochina included almost 27 million people by the end of World War II. French colonial officials ruled Vietnam with an iron fist. They transplanted French laws into Vietnam and imposed high taxes. French business people acquired large rice and rubber

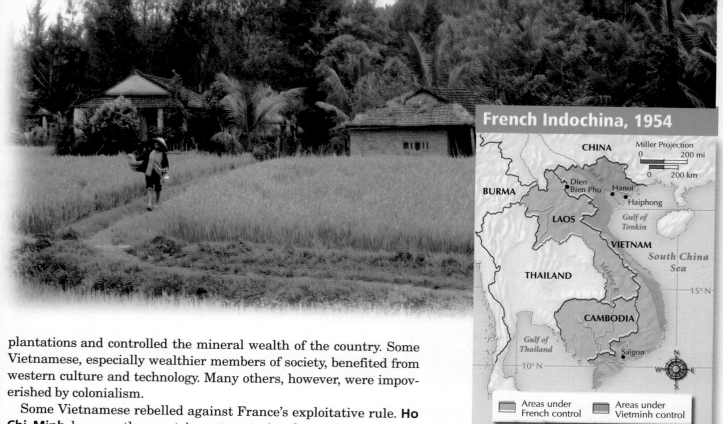

### French Indochina, 1954

CHINA

Miller Projection

BURMA

Dien Bien Phu

Hanoi

Haiphong

LAOS

*Gulf of Tonkin*

VIETNAM

*South China Sea*

THAILAND

*Mekong R.*

15° N

CAMBODIA

*Gulf of Thailand*

Saigon

10° N

Areas under French control

Areas under Vietminh control

105° E

110° E

plantations and controlled the mineral wealth of the country. Some Vietnamese, especially wealthier members of society, benefited from western culture and technology. Many others, however, were impoverished by colonialism.

Some Vietnamese rebelled against France's exploitative rule. **Ho Chi Minh** became the most important voice demanding independence for Vietnam. Born in 1890, Ho became involved in anti-French organizations as a young man and fled Vietnam in 1912. He traveled the world, visiting American ports and living periodically in London, Paris, and Moscow. During his 30-year absence, Ho constantly thought and wrote about Vietnam, and he searched for westerners who would support his plans for Vietnamese independence. Ho embraced communism, and eventually Soviet communists rallied to his cause.

### The French Battle Nationalism and Communism

During World War II, Japan had undermined French control over Vietnam. But when the conflict ended, France reasserted its colonial aims there. France's problem, however, was that colonialism was a dying institution. World War II had strengthened nationalist movements while weakening the economic and military positions of traditional European powers. In Vietnam, Ho Chi Minh clamored for independence as France struggled to maintain its dwindling global power.

Meanwhile, the United States faced a difficult decision. On the one hand, it supported decolonization. On the other hand, America wanted France as an ally in its Cold War effort to contain the Soviet Union. President Harry S. Truman believed that if he supported Vietnamese independence, he would weaken anticommunist forces in France. So, to ensure a strong, anticommunist Western Europe, Truman sacrificed his own anticolonial sentiments.

Vietnam thus became a pawn in Cold War politics. To <u>ensure</u> French support in the Cold War, Truman agreed to aid France's efforts to regain control over Vietnam. After communist forces won the civil war in China in 1949, America increased its aid to the French in Vietnam. Truman did not want to see another communist victory in Asia. Between 1950 and 1954, the United States contributed $2.6 billion to France's war efforts. Containing Ho Chi Minh's communist Vietminh—an abbreviation of the League for the Independence of Vietnam—became a national priority.

### Vietnam Under French Rule

During the French colonial era, rural villagers failed to see the same profits as French plantation owners. Ho Chi Minh found many supporters for his anticolonial efforts in villages like the one above. *In 1954, what regions of Indochina were under communist control?*

**Vocabulary Builder**
ensure–(en SHOR) *v.* to guarantee; secure

## Dien Bien Phu Under Siege

For almost two months, Vietminh soldiers hammered at French military positions around Dien Bien Phu. At left, Vietnamese communists take cover in a trench during the siege. At right, French troops guard Vietminh soldiers taken captive during the fighting.

**The Domino Theory and Dien Bien Phu** When President Dwight D. Eisenhower took office in early 1953, he continued Truman's policies toward Vietnam. He sent monetary aid to the French, arguing that by battling Ho Chi Minh, they were containing the spread of communism. Eisenhower told a journalist that the fight in Vietnam involved more than the future of just one country:

> **Primary Source** "You have a row of dominos set up, you knock over the first one, and what will happen to the last one is the certainty that it will go over very quickly. So you could have a beginning of a disintegration that would have the most profound influences."
>
> —Dwight D. Eisenhower, 1954

The **domino theory** was the idea that if Vietnam fell to communism, its closest neighbors would follow. This in turn would threaten Japan, the Philippines, and Australia. In short, stopping the communists in Vietnam was important to the protection of the entire region.

In 1954, however, the French lost their eight-year struggle to regain Vietnam. The Vietminh trapped a large French garrison at Dien Bien Phu, a military base in northwest Vietnam, and laid siege to it for 55 days. During the siege, which one Frenchman described as "hell in a very small place," Vietminh troops destroyed the French airstrip, cut French supply lines, and dug trenches to attack key French positions. Finally, on May 7, 1954, after suffering some 15,000 casualties, the French surrendered.

The very next day at an international peace conference in Geneva, Switzerland, France sued for peace. According to the Geneva Accords, France granted independence to Vietnam, Laos, and Cambodia. The accords also divided Vietnam at the seventeenth parallel into two countries, North Vietnam and South Vietnam. Ho Chi Minh's communist forces ruled in North Vietnam, and an anticommunist government, supported by the United States, assumed power in South Vietnam. The accords also called for free elections in 1956 to unify Vietnam.

✓ **Checkpoint** Why did Presidents Truman and Eisenhower support French efforts against Ho Chi Minh?

# America Opposes Communism in Vietnam

During the Battle of Dien Bien Phu, France appealed to the United States for military support. President Eisenhower was willing to supply money but not soldiers. Ike would not commit American troops to defend colonialism in Asia. Nevertheless, the President firmly supported the new anticommunist government of South Vietnam.

**The United States Aids South Vietnam** America channeled aid to South Vietnam in different ways. In 1954, the United States and seven other countries formed the **Southeast Asia Treaty Organization (SEATO).** Similar to NATO, SEATO's goal was to contain the spread of communism in Southeast Asia.

The United States provided economic and military aid to the South Vietnamese government led by Ngo Dinh Diem. Diem was an ardent nationalist and anticommunist. Although he lacked popular appeal, his anticommunism guaranteed American support. When it came time for the 1956 unification elections, American intelligence analysts predicted that Diem would lose to the more popular Ho Chi Minh. Rather than risk losing, Diem refused to participate in the elections, a move made under the <u>auspices</u> of the United States government.

**Communist Opposition Grows** By 1957, a communist rebel group in the South, known as the National Liberation Front (NLF), had committed themselves to undermining the Diem government and uniting Vietnam under a communist flag. NLF guerrilla fighters, called **Vietcong,** launched an insurgency in which they assassinated government officials and destroyed roads and bridges. Supplied by communists in North Vietnam, the Vietcong employed surprise hit-and-run tactics to weaken Diem's hold on South Vietnam.

Diem's own policies also weakened his position in South Vietnam. A devout Roman Catholic in an overwhelmingly Buddhist nation, Diem did little to build a broad political base. Instead, he signed anti-Buddhist legislation and refused to enact significant land reforms. His lack of popular support hurt him in the civil war against North Vietnam. Only the support of the United States kept the unpopular leader in power.

**Kennedy Sends U.S. Troops to Vietnam** After his election in 1960, President John F. Kennedy took a more aggressive stand against the communists in Vietnam. Beginning in 1961, he sent Special Forces troops to South Vietnam to advise the Army of the Republic of Vietnam (ARVN) on more effective ways to fight the communist forces. By 1963, more than 15,000 American "advisers" were fighting in Vietnam.

Although U.S. advisers fought bravely and achieved some success, Diem continued to alienate South Vietnamese citizens. By late 1963, his regime was in shambles. Buddhists protested his restrictive policies, occasionally by setting themselves on fire. The Kennedy administration eventually concluded that South Vietnam needed new leadership. Working behind the scenes, Americans plotted with anti-Diem generals to overthrow Diem's government. On November 1, 1963, Diem was removed from power and later assassinated.

✓ **Checkpoint** How did the United States help the South Vietnamese government resist communism?

**WITNESS HISTORY DVD**

Watch *Causes of the Vietnam War* on the **United States Witness History DVD** to learn more about how the United States became involved in Vietnam.

**Vocabulary Builder**
auspices—(AWS puh sihz) *n.* approval and support

▼ A Buddhist monk sets himself on fire in Saigon to protest the Diem regime.

# Johnson Leads the Nation Into War

Three weeks after Diem's fall, an assassin's bullet struck down President Kennedy. Vice President Lyndon B. Johnson was sworn in as the new President. Johnson was a Cold War traditionalist who held a monolithic view of communism. For this "Cold Warrior," communism in the Soviet Union, China, and Vietnam were all the same. He did not recognize subtle differences. He also knew that the American people expected victory in Vietnam.

**North Vietnamese and U.S. Forces Clash** In 1964, President Johnson faced his first crisis in Vietnam. On August 2, North Vietnamese torpedo boats fired on the American destroyer USS *Maddox* as it patrolled the Gulf of Tonkin off the coast of North Vietnam. The *Maddox* was not hit, and it returned fire on the North Vietnamese boat. Johnson promptly responded to the attack and to other North Vietnamese provocations. He announced that "aggression by terror against peaceful villages of South Vietnam has now been joined by open aggression on the high seas against the United States of America." Troubled by increasing strikes against an American ally, Johnson ordered an airstrike against North Vietnam.

**Congress Gives Johnson Broad Military Powers** The President next asked Congress to authorize the use of force to defend American troops. With little debate and only two senators voting against it, Congress agreed to Johnson's request and passed the **Gulf of Tonkin Resolution.** The resolution authorized the President "to take all necessary measures to repel any armed attack against the forces of the United States and to prevent further aggression." The resolution gave Johnson tremendous war powers. It allowed him to commit U.S. troops to South Vietnam and fight a war against North Vietnam without ever going back to Congress to ask for a declaration of war.

 **Checkpoint** What was the significance of the Gulf of Tonkin Resolution?

## Analyzing Political Cartoons

**The Opposing Forces** Early in the war, this American cartoon focused on the technological differences between the two opposing forces.
1. Is the cartoon an accurate or exaggerated representation of the technological differences? Explain.
2. Who do you think the cartoonist expected to win the war? Why?

---

## SECTION 1 Assessment

**Progress Monitoring *Online***
**For:** Self-test with vocabulary practice
**Web Code:** nea-1602

### Comprehension

1. **Terms and People** For each item below, write a sentence explaining its significance.
   - Ho Chi Minh
   - domino theory
   - Vietcong
   - Gulf of Tonkin Resolution

2. **NoteTaking Reading Skill: Summarize** Use your flowchart to answer the Section Focus Question: Why did the United States become involved in Vietnam?

### Writing About History

3. **Quick Write: Generate an Argument** Choose a topic from this section that could be the subject of a persuasive essay. For example, you might choose the domino theory. Then, write a thesis statement arguing in favor of or against U.S. intervention in Southeast Asia. Make sure that the argument clearly explains your opinion on the topic.

### Critical Thinking

4. **Identify Central Issues** Identify one argument for and one argument against Truman's decision to support the French rather than the Vietnamese nationalists.

5. **Make Decisions** What goals motivated President Kennedy's policy decisions regarding Vietnam?

6. **Recognize Cause and Effect** How did the *Maddox* incident contribute to the outbreak of war? How did it lead to a change in the balance of power in the American government?

Vietcong land mine used against American soldiers

◀ A young American soldier in Vietnam

**WITNESS HISTORY** 🔊 AUDIO

### American Soldiers on Patrol

The war in Vietnam was different from previous wars. There were no front lines—the enemy was everywhere. The terrain was difficult and littered with mines and booby traps. Drenched in sweat, the men waded through flooded rice paddies and along tangled paths, stopping occasionally to pick leeches out of their boots. One soldier recalled the difficulties of maneuvering in the overgrown and disorienting jungle during the war:

❝You carried 50 to 70 pounds of equipment, and it was tough going, particularly in forested areas. Often you'd have to pull yourself along from one tree branch to the next, or we'd have to help each other by gripping hands. And you couldn't see anything, so you didn't know what was there around you.❞

—Sergeant William Ehrhart,
United States Marines

# U.S. Involvement Grows

### Content Expectations

- **8.1.2d** Evaluate U.S. involvement in Vietnam.
- **8.2.3** Compare/contrast Roosevelt's New Deal initiatives, Johnson's Great Society programs, Reagan's market-based domestic policies.
- **8.2.4** Analyze competing perspectives/controversies among Americans generated by U.S. Supreme Court decisions.

### Terms and People

William Westmoreland    hawk
napalm                dove

### NoteTaking

**Reading Skill: Identify Supporting Details**
As you read, fill in the outline with details about the escalation of the American war effort.

> I. "Americanizing" the War
>    **A.**
>       1.
>       2.

**Why It Matters** After the Gulf of Tonkin Resolution, President Johnson began to shift U.S. military efforts in Vietnam into high gear. But America's leaders and soldiers soon found themselves stuck in a deadly quagmire with no quick victory in sight. The war began to weaken the economy, divide the American people, and erode the nation's morale. **Section Focus Question: What were the causes and effects of America's growing involvement in the Vietnam War?**

## "Americanizing" the War

In February 1965, President Johnson dramatically altered the U.S. role in the Vietnam War. In response to a Vietcong attack that killed American troops at Pleiku, Johnson ordered the start of Operation Rolling Thunder, the first sustained bombing campaign against North Vietnam. Johnson hoped that this new strategy of intensive bombing would convince North Vietnam to stop reinforcing the Vietcong in South Vietnam.

The bombs rained down destruction, but they failed to convince North Vietnam to make peace. As the communist forces continued to fight, the United States committed more troops to battle them on the ground. American soldiers moved beyond their adviser roles and assumed greater military responsibilities, while South Vietnamese troops accepted a secondary, more limited role in the war. U.S. military and civilian leaders hoped that American airstrikes, along with the troops on the ground, would eventually force the communists to the peace table.

**American Assumptions and Strategies** Johnson's change in strategy in 1965 stemmed primarily from the counsel of Secretary of Defense Robert McNamara and General **William Westmoreland,** the American commander in South Vietnam. These two advisers believed that the United States needed to increase its military presence in Vietnam and do more of the fighting in order to win the war. Operation Rolling Thunder and increased troop commitments fulfilled this need to "Americanize" the war effort.

Beginning in March 1965, U.S. airstrikes hammered North Vietnam and Vietcong strong points in South Vietnam. Between 1965 and 1973, American pilots dropped more than 6 million tons of bombs on enemy positions—almost three times the tonnage dropped by all the combatants during World War II. In addition to conventional bombs, American pilots dropped napalm and sprayed Agent Orange. **Napalm** is a jellied gasoline which was dropped in large canisters that exploded on impact, covering large areas in flames. It clung to anything it touched and was difficult to extinguish. Agent Orange is an herbicide meant to kill plant life. Almost half of South Vietnam's forested areas were sprayed at least once, and the ecological impact was devastating. U.S. forces used it to defoliate the countryside and disrupt the enemy's food supply. Many scientists believe that Agent Orange causes cancers and other physical problems.

As airstrikes intensified, American ground troops landed in South Vietnam. On March 8, 1965, U.S. Marines arrived to defend the airbase at Da Nang. They were soon followed by other troops. The soldiers accepted a wide range of missions. Some guarded bases. Others conducted search-and-destroy missions to kill as many Vietcong guerrillas as they could. Helicopters ferried commandos to and from remote locations for quick strikes against enemy positions.

**An Elusive and Determined Enemy** Large-scale battles against Vietcong or North Vietnamese Army units were not typical of America's strategy in Vietnam. American soldiers generally fought lightly armed Vietcong guerrillas in small engagements. Ho Chi Minh's military <u>doctrine</u> hinged on fighting only when victory was assured, which meant never fighting on his opponents' terms. He compared his troops to a tiger, while the Americans were like an elephant. If the tiger stands still, the elephant will crush it. But if the tiger keeps moving and occasionally jumps on the elephant to take a bite out of it, the elephant will slowly bleed to death.

During the war, the Vietcong behaved like Ho's tiger. They traveled light, often carrying just a rifle and a few handfuls of rice. They dug tunnels to hide in during the day and emerged at night to ambush American patrols. They infiltrated American bases and set off explosives. They set booby traps that maimed and crippled American troops. Their strategy was to wear the American elephant down. The leaders of North Vietnam and the Vietcong remained convinced that if they could avoid losing the war, the Americans would eventually leave.

**A Costly and Frustrating War** American strategy during this stage of the war yielded limited results. U.S. bombers did disrupt North Vietnamese industry and slow the movement of supplies to the Vietcong. But when the communists did not sue for peace, American troop commitments and battlefield deaths escalated rapidly. By the end of 1965, there were 184,300 U.S. troops in Vietnam and only 636 American soldiers had died in the war. Three years later, there were more than half a million U.S. troops in Vietnam and the number of American dead had risen to more than 30,000.

**Vocabulary Builder**
<u>doctrine</u>–(DAHK trihn) *n.* teachings

# Vietnam War, 1963–1967

**Geography** *Interactive*
**For:** Interactive map
**Web Code:** nep-1603

CHINA

BURMA

NORTH VIETNAM

Red R.

Dien Bien Phu

Hanoi

Haiphong

*Gulf of Tonkin*

LAOS

Mekong R.

Vientiane

*South China Sea*

**2. August 1964**
Gulf of Tonkin incident escalates war

**4. March 1965**
Operation Rolling Thunder

**3. February 1965**
Vietcong attack at Pleiku

Hué

Da Nang

**5. March 1965**
First U.S. combat troops arrive

Ho Chi Minh Trail

THAILAND

**6. December 1967**
More than 480,000 U.S. soldiers in South Vietnam

CAMBODIA

SOUTH VIETNAM

*Gulf of Thailand*

Phnom Penh

**1. November 1963**
Diem government overthrown

Saigon

*Mekong Delta*

100° E · 110° E · 115° E · 10° N

20° N · 15° N

Miller Projection
0 · 100 · 200 mi
0 · 100 · 200 km

## The Vietnam War Escalates

| Year | Event |
|------|-------|
| 1961 | President Kennedy sends military advisers to train South Vietnamese troops. |
| 1963 | More than 10,000 American military advisers train and fight in South Vietnam. |
| 1964 | Gulf of Tonkin Resolution passes; Number of U.S. troops doubles to more than 20,000. |
| 1965 | President Johnson authorizes bombing of North Vietnam; more than 180,000 U.S. troops are in South Vietnam. |
| 1966–1967 | Number of American soldiers in South Vietnam rises to nearly half a million. |

**Map Skills** The Vietcong were resupplied with weapons, food, and fighters along the Ho Chi Minh Trail.

1. **Locate:** (a) Saigon, (b) Hanoi, (c) Ho Chi Minh Trail

2. **Movement** Through what countries did the Vietcong travel as they moved supplies from North Vietnam to South Vietnam?

3. **Draw Conclusions** Why might a U.S. attack against the Ho Chi Minh Trail cause an international backlash against the United States?

# The Hardships of War in Vietnam

By 1968, the morale of American troops in Vietnam was on the wane. Units would fight to drive the Vietcong out of a village only to return weeks later to do the same job all over again. In a land where anyone could be the enemy, U.S. soldiers lived in a state of constant tension. Survival demanded remaining on the lookout for snipers, ambushes, and booby traps. The amount of rice cooking in a pot could be a clue to an impending attack. Was there just enough food for the people in view, or had others disappeared as the Americans approached? A moment of inattention could spell disaster.

Concealed entrance under cooking pot

Upper trench

Vent

Lower tunnel and hiding place

▲ Vietcong guerrillas relied on large tunnel networks to hide from—and launch surprise attacks against— American forces.

Each year, the war cost more American dollars and claimed more American lives. But at the end of each year, the United States seemed no closer to success. America's mission was to help South Vietnam build a stable noncommunist nation and thereby win the "hearts and minds" of its citizens. But corruption plagued the South Vietnamese administrative structure. Outside of the major cities, the government enjoyed little real support. Although American forces won most of the larger battles, they did not achieve a successful end to the war. By 1967, the war had devolved into a stalemate. Some U.S. critics of the war compared it to a quagmire—muddy terrain that sinks underfoot and is difficult to exit.

✓ **Checkpoint** What was the strategic aim of Operation Rolling Thunder?

## Patriotism, Heroism, and Sinking Morale

For American soldiers in the field, the Vietnam War presented difficult challenges that demanded courage and patience. Unlike World War II, the Vietnam War did not emphasize territorial acquisition. The United States and its allies did not invade North Vietnam, march on Ho Chi Minh's capital of Hanoi, or attempt to destroy the communist regime. As in the Korean War, the United States was fearful of triggering both Chinese and Soviet entry into the conflict. Instead, American forces supported the survival and development of South Vietnam, which was besieged by the Vietcong and their North Vietnamese allies. In this fight, U.S. troops could never fully tell their friends from their enemies. Yet from the outset, they faced the dangers of Vietnam's battlefields with dedication and bravery.

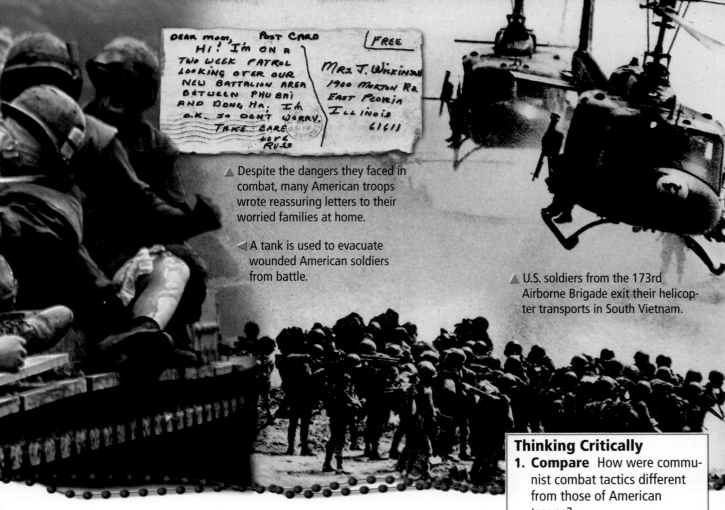

DEAR MOM, POST CARD
HI! I'm ON A
TWO WEEK PATROL
LOOKING OVER OUR
NEW BATTALION AREA
BETWEEN PHU BAI
AND DONG HA; I'M
O.K. SO DON'T WORRY,
TAKE CARE
LOVE
RUSS

FREE

MRS. J. WILKINSON
1900 MORTON RD.
EAST PEORIA
ILLINOIS
61611

▲ Despite the dangers they faced in combat, many American troops wrote reassuring letters to their worried families at home.

◄ A tank is used to evacuate wounded American soldiers from battle.

▲ U.S. soldiers from the 173rd Airborne Brigade exit their helicopter transports in South Vietnam.

**Thinking Critically**

1. **Compare** How were communist combat tactics different from those of American troops?

2. **Draw Conclusions** How did images such as these, shown on television news shows, affect the home front?

**History** *Interactive* ✳
**For:** To learn more about the hardships of the Vietnam War
**Web Code:** nep-1606

**Danger on a New Battlefield** Although American troops won numerous battles, they could not win the war outright. The problem was that the Vietcong and North Vietnamese avoided significant engagements. Rather than expose themselves to superior American firepower, the communists fought smaller skirmishes where their small-unit abilities and their knowledge of the landscape bettered their chances for victory.

U.S. forces often had no alternative but to fight indecisive battles in the jungles, rice paddies, and mountains of Vietnam. Most of these battlefields abounded with natural cover. Clad in black pajamas, Vietcong gunmen would spring out of the dense foliage, attack with automatic rifles and grenades, and disappear back into the landscape. Much of this fighting took place at night, which reduced the effectiveness of American planes, artillery, and troop tactics.

**American Soldiers Fulfill Their Duty** Despite the trials of war, American soldiers adapted to adverse conditions in Vietnam and fought with the same intensity that U.S. forces had shown in World Wars I and II. Many fought to prevent the spread of communism. Some fought to protect villagers in South Vietnam and win their trust and respect. Others fought because their country was at war and they felt it was their duty. A medic in the First Infantry Division explained his reason for going to Vietnam:

**Primary Source** ❝I volunteered. . . . Ever since the American Revolution my family had people in all the different wars, and that was always the thing—when your country needs you, you go. You don't ask a lot of questions. . . .❞
—David Ross, United States Army medic

Later, many did ask questions about America's involvement in the war, but overwhelmingly while they were in Vietnam, the soldiers met their duties with courage. More than 58,000 of them gave their lives for their country.

Women also displayed courage and valor. About 10,000 American military women served in Vietnam during the war. Most female military personnel were nurses. Not only did they face danger working close to the front, but they also had to cope with the emotional toll of constantly working with injured and dying soldiers and civilians.

Lynda Van Devanter volunteered to go to Vietnam and spent a year there as a nurse. Like other nurses, she confronted war and death on a daily basis. However, on one occasion she had to deliver a baby. She later recalled:

> **Primary Source** "It was creation of life in the midst of all that destruction. And creation of life restored your sanity. . . . Those were the things that kept you going. That there was life coming. There was still hope."
> —Lynda Van Devanter, United States Army nurse

### Nurses in Vietnam

U.S. Army nurses Capt. Gladys E. Sepulveda, left, of Puerto Rico, and 2nd Lt. Lois Ferrari of Pittsburgh, rest on sandbags at Cam Ranh Bay in South Vietnam on July 14, 1965. They were awaiting transportation to Nha Trang where they were set to work in the 8th field hospital.

**Morale Declines as War Wears On** As the war lengthened, many Americans began to question U.S. involvement. The earliest soldiers in Vietnam had been volunteers, men committed to the fight against communism. But by the end of 1965, most American soldiers in Vietnam had been drafted into military service, and they were not as certain that preserving the government in South Vietnam was crucial to American interests. They sensed that many South Vietnamese people were indifferent—if not openly hostile—to their own nation. Increasingly, it seemed that Americans were dying to defend a nation whose people were unwilling to die to defend themselves.

 **Checkpoint** Why did the morale of American troops decline as the war continued?

## Doubt Grows on the Home Front

The lack of progress toward victory in Vietnam also led to doubt in the United States. When President Johnson had begun to send troops to war, Americans had expected a relatively quick victory. After all, the United States was a militarily powerful, technologically advanced country, and North Vietnam was a poor country with comparatively little technology. Over the next few years, the Johnson administration kept <u>asserting</u> that an American victory was close at hand. But when that did not come, many began to question the President's foreign policy.

**The War Weakens the Economy** The war strained government finances. President Johnson's Great Society plan called for enormous domestic spending to eliminate poverty, improve education and medical care, and fight racial discrimination. The costs of fighting a war on the other side of the world were just as mammoth. Although massive government spending lowered the unemployment rate, it also led to rising prices and inflation. The combination of heavy government spending, rising prices, and inflation forced Johnson to raise taxes.

**Vocabulary Builder**
<u>assert</u>—(uh SERT) *v.* to state positively; declare

Ultimately, Johnson had to cut back on his Great Society reform initiatives to help pay for the war.

**Antiwar Movement Begins to Emerge** As long as America's involvement in Vietnam had been small and relatively inexpensive, few politicians voiced serious opposition. Despite its bipartisan support for the Vietnam policies of Johnson's predecessors, after the Gulf of Tonkin Resolution, Congress soon split over the President's escalation of the war.

Beginning in 1967, Congress—and eventually most of America—divided into two camps: hawks and doves. The mostly conservative **hawks** supported Johnson's war policy. Believing strongly in the containment of communism and the domino theory, they accepted rising troop levels, escalating costs, and increasing numbers of battlefield deaths. For the hawks, Vietnam was a crucial front in the Cold War. **Doves,** however, broke with Johnson's war policy. A diverse group of liberal politicians, pacifists, student radicals, and civil rights leaders, doves questioned the war on both moral and strategic grounds. For them, the conflict was a localized civil war, not a vital Cold War battleground.

Senator J. William Fulbright, chairman of the Senate Foreign Relations Committee, emerged as the early leader of the doves in Congress. A Democrat who had supported the Gulf of Tonkin Resolution, Fulbright soon came to believe that the war in Vietnam was a national civil war, not a Cold War conflict whose shots were called in Moscow or Beijing. In 1967 and 1968, Fulbright held public hearings on the war, providing a platform for critics of the conflict.

✓ **Checkpoint** What were the opposing viewpoints of hawks and doves?

Onward And Upward And Onward And—

### Analyzing Political Cartoons

**The Bombing Campaign** U.S. officials promised that increased bombing would bring America closer to victory.
1. Does the emotion on the person's face suggest that the plan is working? Explain.
2. Do you think the cartoonist was a hawk or a dove? Explain.

---

SECTION **2 Assessment**

**Progress Monitoring Online**
**For:** Self-test with vocabulary practice
**Web Code:** nea-1604

### Comprehension

**1. Terms and People** For each item below, write a sentence explaining its significance.
   - William Westmoreland
   - napalm
   - dove

**2. NoteTaking Reading Skill: Identify Supporting Details** Use your outline to answer the Section Focus Question: What were the causes and effects of America's growing involvement in the Vietnam War?

### Writing About History

**3. Quick Write: Support an Opinion With Evidence** Consider the following topic from the section: America's escalation of the war in Vietnam. Gather and present evidence from the text that supports the Americanization of the war effort.

### Critical Thinking

**4. Evaluate Information** What military strategies did the United States employ in Vietnam? How successful were these strategies?

**5. Summarize** What difficulties did American soldiers face in Vietnam? What effect did these difficulties have?

**6. Contrast** How did the disagreements between hawks and doves reflect different views about war and world politics?

◀ A Vietnam veteran protests the war in 1970.

**WITNESS HISTORY** 🔊 AUDIO

### The "Living-Room War"

Walter Cronkite, the anchor of the CBS Evening News, was the most respected television journalist of the 1960s. His many reports on the Vietnam War were models of balanced journalism and inspired the confidence of viewers across the United States. But during the Tet Offensive, Cronkite was shocked by the disconnect between Johnson's optimistic statements and the gritty reality of the fighting. After visiting Vietnam in February of 1968, he told his viewers:

❝We have been too often disappointed by the optimism of the American leaders, both in Vietnam and Washington, to have faith any longer in the silver linings they find in the darkest clouds. . . . [I]t seems now more certain than ever that the bloody experience of Vietnam is to end in stalemate.❞

—Walter Cronkite, 1968

▲ Walter Cronkite

# The War Divides America

 **Content Expectations**

- **8.1.2d** Evaluate U.S. involvement in Vietnam.
- **8.3.1a** Analyze impact of WWII and Cold War.
- **8.3.5** Analyze causes/consequences of civil unrest that occurred in U.S. cities.

### Terms and People

draftee
SDS
"credibility gap"

Tet Offensive
Eugene McCarthy
Robert Kennedy

### NoteTaking

**Reading Skill: Recognize Sequence** Note the events leading up to the 1968 election.

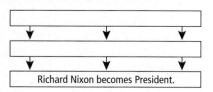

Richard Nixon becomes President.

**Why It Matters** President Johnson sent more American troops to Vietnam in order to win the war. But with each passing year, casualty lists got longer and victory seemed further away. As soldiers died abroad and hawks and doves argued at home, the Vietnam War opened up a deep emotional rift in American society. After the war ended, it would take years for the country to heal itself. **Section Focus Question: How did the American war effort in Vietnam lead to rising protests and social divisions back home?**

## Antiwar Protests Increase

The war in Vietnam divided Americans more deeply than any conflict since the Civil War. Although most Americans initially supported President Johnson's bombings and troop deployments, by 1966 critics began speaking out. Senator Fulbright's opposition to the war hurt Johnson in Congress, and the senator was soon joined by like-minded activists who believed that American soldiers were dying in a war that had little to do with American interests.

**The Draft Becomes Increasingly Unpopular** By 1965, most of the troops sent to Vietnam were no longer volunteers who had enlisted in the army. Instead, they were **draftees**—young men drafted into military service—who had been assigned a tour in Vietnam. In accordance with the Selective Service Act of 1948, the government drafted more than 1.5 million men into military service during the Vietnam War. All males had to register for the draft when they turned 18, and the Selective Service System called up draftees based on projected military needs.

Critics of the Selective Service System argued that the draft was not fair. The system gave local draft boards considerable influence in selecting men for service, and it also granted <u>deferments</u> to college students and men who worked in certain designated occupations. Most of the 2.5 million men who served in Vietnam came from working-class and poor backgrounds.

During the Johnson presidency, the number of African American troops fighting and dying in Vietnam was also disproportionately high. At the beginning of the war, African Americans suffered more than 20 percent of the total combat deaths, roughly twice their percentage of the U.S. population. Additionally, African American soldiers were more likely to serve in combat positions and less likely to become commissioned officers.

Civil rights leader Martin Luther King, Jr., spoke out against the added war burden shouldered by African American soldiers. Speaking at a New York church in 1967, King said that the war was hurting both poor blacks and whites. Vietnam was drawing human and economic resources away from America's other wars on poverty and discrimination. He added that it hindered poor Americans in other more direct ways:

**Primary Source**   ❝It was sending their sons and their brothers and their husbands to fight and to die in extraordinary high proportions relative to the rest of the population. . . . [W]e have been repeatedly faced with the cruel irony of watching Negro and white boys on TV screens as they kill and die together for a nation that has been unable to seat them together in the same schools.❞

—Martin Luther King, Jr., 1967

Perceived inequities in the draft led to widespread resistance. Antiwar advocates sponsored a Stop-the-Draft week in October 1967, and some draft-eligible males burned their draft cards in protest. Finally, in 1969, the Selective Service System adopted a lottery that was designed to eliminate deferment abuses and create a more diverse army of draftees.

**Vocabulary Builder**
deferment—(dee FER muhnt) n. postponement

**African American Soldiers in Battle**
The Vietnam War witnessed the highest proportion of African Americans ever to serve in an American war. Here, an African American Marine ducks behind a wall for cover while firing on an enemy position. *Based on the line graph, why might African American recruits be unhappy with the draft?*

**African Americans and the Vietnam War**

Percentage of African Americans

— African American combat deaths (U.S. Army)
— African Americans in U.S. population

SOURCES: Department of Defense; *Historical Statistics of the United States*

**Activism Spreads on College Campuses** Across America, college campuses became centers of antiwar sentiment. Professors and students criticized the war for a variety of reasons, ranging from pacifism and the war's effects on the economy to a personal desire to avoid military service. Antiwar activity on college campuses did not, however, reflect the attitudes of Americans as a whole. In fact, many professors remained vocal in their defense of the war effort during lectures and at protest rallies. For the most part, though, colleges and universities represented the extreme antiwar opinion.

Antiwar activities were part of more significant changes taking place on college campuses. Never before the 1960s had so many Americans entered colleges and universities. Between 1946 and 1970, the number of students enrolled in institutions of higher education increased from 2 million to 8 million. Many college students became a class unto themselves—segregated from the workforce, free from many adult responsibilities, and encouraged by their professors to think critically. Most of the students who embraced the antiwar cause came from upper-middle-class families. Students from working-class families were less likely to protest against the war.

The University of Michigan and the University of California at Berkeley became important hubs of the antiwar movement. The **Students for a Democratic Society (SDS)** was founded in 1960 at the University of Michigan. Originally formed to campaign against racism and poverty, the SDS soon began campaigning to end the war in Vietnam. By 1964, SDS had organized campus "teach-ins" and demonstrations against the war and encouraged draft-age males to sign "We Won't Go" petitions.

**Students Clash With Authorities** Student activism led to a clash with administrators and police in 1964. Students at the University of California at Berkeley protested against the school's decision not to allow them to use university grounds to organize off-campus political activities. The students formed the Free Speech Movement to contest the decision. When protesters occupied a university building, the police arrested them. In response, students cut classes to march in support of the FSM. University officials eventually relented and allowed students to engage in free speech activities on school grounds. The victory by students at Berkeley led to challenges at other colleges and universities.

**More and More Americans Oppose the War** Outside college campuses, other Americans soon enlisted in the antiwar cause. The war in Vietnam was the first "living-room war." Americans watched the progress—or lack of it—in their living rooms on nightly newscasts. The intimacy of television made news of the war unavoidable. But unlike World War II, there was no march to victory. Americans could not put maps of Vietnam on their walls and trace the routes the troops were taking to Hanoi.

Hawks and doves drifted farther apart. More groups organized against the war, their names corresponding with whom they represented—Vietnam Veterans Against the War, Catholic Peace Fellowship, Another Mother for Peace. Antiwar Americans— rich and poor, black and white—read reports from war correspondents who questioned U.S. progress in Vietnam. They watched government officials issue optimistic statement after optimistic statement. Soon, a **"credibility gap"** emerged between what the Johnson administration said and what many journalists reported. This gap referred to the American public's growing distrust of statements made by the government.

✔ **Checkpoint** Why did the antiwar movement grow across the nation?

## Hawks Respond to Protests

Despite doves' vocal opposition to the war, hawks organized their own demonstrations to support U.S. policy in Vietnam. Below, New York City union members rally behind the American war effort in 1967.

# Tet Offensive Is the Turning Point

In November 1967, President Johnson brought General Westmoreland home from Vietnam to address the nation's concerns about the war. Westmoreland said that the Vietcong were declining in strength and could no longer mount a major offensive. As Westmoreland made his claims, however, the North Vietnamese and Vietcong were planning just such an attack.

## Communist Assault Shocks Americans

In early 1968, U.S. officials anticipated a communist offensive. As expected, on January 21, the North Vietnamese Army hit Khe Sanh in northwest South Vietnam. However, nine days later, the communists expanded their attack by hitting U.S. and ARVN positions throughout South Vietnam. The **Tet Offensive**—named after the Vietnamese lunar new year—was a coordinated assault on 36 provincial capitals and 5 major cities, as well as the U.S. embassy in Saigon.

The communists planned to take and hold the cities until the urban population took up arms in their support. They thought the Tet Offensive had a good chance of ending the war. The fighting was fierce, but in the end, American and South Vietnamese forces repelled the offensive and there was no popular uprising against the government of South Vietnam. Although U.S. forces won a tactical victory by preventing the Vietcong and North Vietnamese Army from achieving their primary objectives, the Tet Offensive was a strategic blow to the Americans. It demonstrated that the communists had not lost the will or the ability to fight on.

## Tet Offensive, 1968

**Map Skills** In launching the Tet Offensive, the Vietcong and North Vietnamese Army wanted to demoralize South Vietnam and deal American forces a devastating blow.

1. **Regions** Identify two regions of South Vietnam that were hard-hit by the Tet Offensive.
2. **Draw Conclusions** How do you think the Tet Offensive affected the morale of North Vietnam? Explain.

## War's End Is Nowhere in Sight

After the Tet Offensive, American military leaders seemed less confident of a quick end to the war. When Westmoreland requested more troops, President Johnson asked his new Secretary of Defense Clark Clifford to take an objective look at the military and political situation in Vietnam. The deeper Clifford delved into the matter, the more pessimistic he became. Sending more troops would <u>inevitably</u> require raising taxes, increasing draft rolls, and calling up reserves. It would lead to increased casualties in the field and dissent at home. And it still might not lead to victory. Clifford concluded that the President should radically shift U.S. policy from one that pursued victory to one that pursued a negotiated peace.

## Johnson Steps Down

While Clifford deliberated, many Americans began to turn dramatically against the war. Some marched in protest and engaged in antiwar activities. Others registered their disapproval at the polls. In early

**Vocabulary Builder**
inevitable–(ihn EHV ih tuh buhl) *adj.* certain to happen

# Can the United States Win the War in Vietnam?

Despite the war's growing unpopularity, Johnson was reluctant to withdraw from Vietnam. Some urged him to get out of "Kennedy's war." His own Cabinet was divided on the issue.

## DEAN RUSK

Citing Chamberlain and Hitler as an example, Secretary of State Rusk opposed appeasement. He supported increased bombing and troops to force North Vietnam to negotiate a peace.

### Primary Source

"If . . . North Vietnam will stop [its] campaign to destroy the Republic of Vietnam, the measures we are taking to assist South Vietnam . . . will no longer be necessary. . . . We see no necessity for international negotiations. . . . [W]e cannot [think of] any points that would be negotiable."

—Dean Rusk, 1963

## GEORGE BALL

Undersecretary of State Ball urged President Johnson in 1965 to stop sending U.S. soldiers to Vietnam.

### Primary Source

"No one can assure you that we can beat the Viet Cong . . . no matter how many . . . troops we deploy. No [ground forces] of whatever size can win a guerrilla war—which is at the same time a civil war . . . in jungle terrain in the midst of a population that refuses cooperation. . . ."

—George Ball, 1965

### Compare

1. According to Rusk, when should the United States end its participation in the war?

2. Why does Ball think that Rusk's strategy will not work?

1968, Minnesota senator **Eugene McCarthy,** the antiwar candidate for the Democratic Party nomination, made a surprisingly strong showing in the New Hampshire primary. Sensing that Johnson was in a politically weakened position, New York's Democratic senator **Robert Kennedy** announced his candidacy for the presidency. Both McCarthy and Kennedy believed that the war had divided America and drained resources away from the fights against poverty and discrimination. What Johnson feared most was happening: The war was undermining his presidency.

On March 31, 1968, two months after the Tet Offensive, the President addressed the nation on television. He announced that America would limit its bombing of North Vietnam and seek a negotiated settlement to the war. Johnson then shocked the nation by announcing that he would not run for another term as President. The speech marked another turning point in the war. The fight for victory was over. Peace was now the official government policy.

✓ **Checkpoint** How was the Tet Offensive both a victory and a defeat for the United States?

## Violence Rocks 1968 Presidential Race

Johnson's decision not to seek reelection in 1968 threw the presidential race wide open. Many Americans believed it provided an opportunity to enact fundamental political and social changes. They argued that the future of the country was at stake. It was a time of new ideas and new plans. But the optimism and high hopes of the early campaign would soon die amidst political infighting, violence, and assassination.

# Chicago 1968: Politics and Protest

As Democrats prepared to select a new presidential candidate at their convention in Chicago (see campaign artifacts at left), antiwar activists converged on the city in August 1968. Inside the main hall, dissension between hawks and doves in the party sparked angry outbursts. On the streets outside, violent clashes broke out between antiwar protesters and the Chicago police. The crowds chanted, "The whole world is watching! The whole world is watching!" And indeed it was. Television viewers saw a vivid display of the political strife and social unrest besieging America.

### Opposition to the Vietnam War

*In view of the developments since we entered the fighting in Vietnam, do you think the United States made a mistake sending troops to fight in Vietnam?*

|  | March 1966 | April 1967 | April 1968 |
|---|---|---|---|
| **Yes** | 26% | 37% | 48% |
| **No** | 59% | 50% | 40% |
| **Don't Know** | 16% | 13% | 12% |

SOURCE: American Institute of Public Opinion (Gallup Poll)

◄ As U.S. combat deaths in Vietnam increased from roughly 5,000 in 1966 to more than 14,000 in 1968, American public opinion turned against the war.

▲ Chicago mayor Richard J. Daley shouts insults at Senator Abraham Ribicoff during the senator's speech criticizing the tactics of the Chicago police.

Many protesters sought only ► to exercise their right to free speech. Others, eyeing the ever-present television cameras, sought—and succeeded in attracting— a police response. Here, a melee erupts outside a hotel where delegates are gathered.

### Thinking Critically
1. **Analyze Information** How did American casualties in Vietnam affect public opinion back home?

2. **Draw Conclusions** How do you think events in Chicago affected the U.S. soldiers in Vietnam?

**Geography** *Interactive*

For: Interactive map
Web Code: nep-1607

| Candidate (Party) | Electoral Vote | Popular Vote | % Electoral Vote | % Popular Vote** |
|---|---|---|---|---|
| Richard M. Nixon (Republican) | 301 | 31,710,470 | 56 | 43.6 |
| Hubert H. Humphrey (Democratic) | 191 | 30,898,055 | 36 | 42.5 |
| George C. Wallace (American Independent) | 46 | 9,906,473 | 8 | 13.6 |

* One Nixon elector voted outside the party's endorsement
** Minor parties received 0.3% of the popular vote

**Map Skills** In 1968, Richard Nixon defeated Vice President Hubert Humphrey and third-party candidate George Wallace, who had split from the Democratic Party.

1. **Regions** From where did Wallace draw most of his support?

2. **Draw Conclusions** What might have happened if Wallace had renounced his candidacy and rejoined the Democratic ranks?

**Two Leaders Fall** In the spring and summer of the campaign season, bullets struck down two Americans who spoke out eloquently for peace in Vietnam and peaceful change in American society. Martin Luther King, Jr., the most prominent leader of the civil rights movement, had publicly turned against the war in 1967. He contributed compelling social and moral reasons to the argument for peace. But his voice was tragically silenced on April 4, 1968, when a racist assassin shot and killed him in Memphis, Tennessee.

Robert Kennedy was the next leader to fall. He had based his campaign for the presidency on compassion and idealism, and millions of Americans rallied to his camp. On June 5, 1968, at a rally celebrating his victory in the California primary, Kennedy asserted that "we are a great country, an unselfish country, a compassionate country," and that he intended "to make that the basis of my running." Minutes later, a Palestinian immigrant named Sirhan Sirhan shot Kennedy in the head, killing him instantly. Sirhan may have wanted revenge for America's support for Israel in that country's war with Egypt the year before.

**Protesters Disrupt Chicago Democratic Convention** The murders of King and Kennedy cast a dark shadow over the election campaigns. In August 1968, the Democrats convened in Chicago to choose a presidential candidate to represent their party in the November election. As the delegates arrived, so too did antiwar protesters. Chicago's mayor deployed police and members of the National Guard to prevent any outbreaks of violence.

Inside the convention, the Democrats angrily debated placing an antiwar plank in the party platform. They chose Hubert Humphrey, Johnson's Vice President, over Eugene McCarthy, who had garnered support from many antiwar groups. As the delegates cast their votes, violence erupted outside the convention between police and protesters. After police beat activists with nightsticks, some protesters retaliated by throwing rocks and bottles at the onrushing tide of police.

The television coverage of the fierce fighting in the streets and bitter arguments on the convention floor shocked Americans. Chaos and civil disorder appeared to have replaced civil debate in the political arena. The divisions and violence in Chicago mirrored the deep divisions in American politics and the heartbreaking violence on the front lines in Vietnam.

**Richard Nixon Wins the Presidency** At a much more peaceful convention in Miami, Republicans nominated Richard M. Nixon, who promised if elected he would deliver "peace with honor." He wanted the United States out of Vietnam, but he also demanded honorable peace terms. He promised to listen to "the great, quiet forgotten majority—the nonshouters and the nondemonstrators." This large group of Americans, described by one commentator as "the young, the unblack, and the unpoor," was dubbed the "silent majority." Throughout his campaign, Nixon used a "southern strategy" of courting more conservative southern voters with appeals to law and order, striving to pull them away from their traditional support of the Democratic Party.

Alabama governor George Wallace also ran for the presidency on a third-party ticket. A lifelong Democrat prior to his entry into the race, Wallace said that neither of the traditional political parties represented southern voters who were unsettled by the cultural and social changes in the country. He had no sympathy for the demands of antiwar radicals, counterculture hippies, or African American militants. He represented the "white backlash" against the civil rights movement and the desire to press forward to victory in Vietnam.

The combination of Nixon's "southern strategy" and Wallace's third-party candidacy siphoned traditionally Democratic votes away from Humphrey. In a close election, Nixon captured victory by winning 43.6 percent of the popular vote and 301 electoral votes. Humphrey received 42.5 percent of the popular vote and Wallace 13.6 percent. The election marked the end of the Democratic "Solid South" and signaled significant changes in the nation's political landscape. Richard Nixon's ascendancy marked a new Republican domination of the American presidency.

**"Silent" Supporters**
In 1969, President Nixon called his supporters the "silent majority." Especially strong in the South and West, the silent majority consisted of patriotic veterans of World War II and the Korean War, middle class blue-collar workers, conservative young Americans, and many others.

✔ **Checkpoint** What happened at the 1968 Democratic Convention in Chicago?

---

**Progress Monitoring *Online***
**For:** Self-test with vocabulary practice
**Web Code:** nea-1608

**Comprehension**

1. **Terms and People** For each item below, write a sentence explaining its significance.
   - draftee
   - "credibility gap"
   - Tet Offensive
   - Eugene McCarthy

2.  **Reading Skill: Recognize Sequence** Use your flowchart to answer the Section Focus Question: How did the American war effort in Vietnam lead to rising protests and social divisions back home?

**Writing About History**

3. **Quick Write: Answer Opposing Arguments** To write a strong persuasive essay, you need to address arguments that could be raised to refute your own position. Choose a topic from this section, such as whether Johnson made the right decision by withdrawing from the 1968 presidential race. Then, create a chart listing arguments on both sides of the debate.

**Critical Thinking**

4. **Evaluate Information** Identify three factors that led to the growth of the antiwar movement. Which do you think was the most important?

5. **Identify Effects** How did the military outcome of the Tet Offensive differ from its impact on the American people?

6. **Draw Conclusions** What were the chief weaknesses of the Democrats in the 1968 election? How did these weaknesses aid the election of Richard Nixon?

▲ Antiwar demonstrators march in Washington, D.C.

### Antiwar Protests Spread

As Richard Nixon entered the White House in January 1969, students across the country continued to protest the war. And their words were starting to reach ordinary Americans, not just "long-haired radicals." In late 1969, antiwar protesters organized a series of peaceful demonstrations called "moratoriums." On October 15, the mayor of New York City addressed a crowd of these protesters:

66We cannot [accept] the charge from Washington that this peaceful protest is unpatriotic. We heard that charge five years ago and three years ago. . . . The fact is that this dissent is the highest form of patriotism. It is the peaceful American way to turn the nation away from a self-defeating course.99

—New York mayor John Lindsay, 1969

# The War's End and Impact

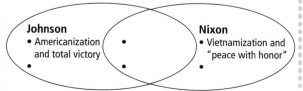

### Content Expectations

- **8.2.4** Analyze competing perspectives/ controversies among Americans generated by U.S. Supreme Court decisions.
- **8.3.1a** Analyze impact of WWII and Cold War.
- **8.3.5** Analyze causes/consequences of civil unrest that occurred in U.S. cities.

### Terms and People

Vietnamization     Paris Peace Accords
My Lai     War Powers Act
Pentagon Papers

### NoteTaking

**Reading Skill: Compare and Contrast**
Note the similarities and differences between Nixon's Vietnam policy and that of Lyndon Johnson.

**Johnson**
- Americanization and total victory
- •

•
•

**Nixon**
- Vietnamization and "peace with honor"
- •

**Why It Matters** As a presidential candidate, Richard Nixon promised "peace with honor" and an end to a war that had fractured American society. Nixon did indeed withdraw American troops, and the Vietnam War finally ended. But the impact of the war endured. As the nation recovered from war, Americans reexamined the struggle against communism, the power of the presidency, and America's role in the world. **Section Focus Question: How did the Vietnam War end, and what were its lasting effects?**

## Nixon Starts the Pullout

Nixon's defenders argued that he was a hard-working patriot with a new vision for America. His critics charged that he was a deceitful politician bent on acquiring power and punishing his enemies. There were elements of truth to both views. But defenders and critics alike agreed that Richard Nixon was a determined man with abundant political talent. From his first day in office, the new President realized that ending the Vietnam War was the key to everything else he hoped to achieve.

**Peace Talks Stall** Though formal peace talks between the warring parties had begun in May 1968, they were bogged down from the outset by disagreements and a lack of compromise. When Richard Nixon took office in January 1969, his peace delegation firmly believed they could break the impasse. The Americans and South Vietnamese wanted all communist troops out of South Vietnam.

They also wanted prisoners of war (POWs) returned. Meanwhile, the North Vietnamese demanded an immediate American withdrawal from Vietnam and the formation of a coalition government in South Vietnam that would include representatives from the Vietcong. Still hoping to win the war in the field, North Vietnam refused to budge from its initial position. And South Vietnam refused to sign any agreement that compromised its security.

**Nixon's Plan: Vietnamization and Peace With Honor** President Nixon refused to accept the North Vietnamese peace terms. He was committed to a policy of "peace with honor" and believed that there were still military options. He continued a gradual pullout of American troops, and expressed faith in the ability of the Army of the Republic of Vietnam to assume the burden of war. He called his approach **Vietnamization**—U.S. forces would withdraw as ARVN troops assumed more combat duties. The hope was that with continued American aid behind the front lines, the ARVN would fight its own battles to secure South Vietnam.

To reduce the flow of communist supplies to the Vietcong, Nixon ordered the secret bombing of the Ho Chi Minh Trail in Cambodia. This was a controversial move because it widened the scope of the war and helped to undermine the neutral government in Cambodia. In the end, neither Vietnamization nor secret bombings dramatically improved South Vietnam's chances of winning a war against the communists.

 **Checkpoint** How did Vietnamization differ from the war policies of Nixon's predecessors?

# Troubles on the Home Front Intensify

Nixon inherited two things from Lyndon Johnson: an unpopular war and a vocal American opposition to it. The new President wanted "peace with honor," security for America's ally South Vietnam, and international respect for U.S. foreign policy. Antiwar activists wanted the war ended and American troops out of Vietnam—on any terms. Nixon found it increasingly difficult to achieve his goals and satisfy the snowballing antiwar movement.

**American Troops in Cambodia** More than a year into office, Nixon had grown impatient with the snail's pace of the peace negotiations. In 1970, he attempted to break the stalemate by ordering a ground attack on North Vietnamese Army and Vietcong bases in Cambodia. Nixon also hoped to aid the pro-American Cambodian government in its fight against the Khmer Rouge, a communist movement supported by North Vietnam.

On the evening of April 30, Nixon addressed the American people, informing them of his decision to carry the war into Cambodia. He stressed that the war had become a measure of how committed the United States was to preserving freedom around the world:

> **Primary Source** "If, when the chips are down, the world's most powerful nation, the United States of America, acts like a pitiful, helpless giant, the forces of totalitarianism and anarchy will threaten free nations . . . throughout the world."
> —President Richard Nixon, 1970

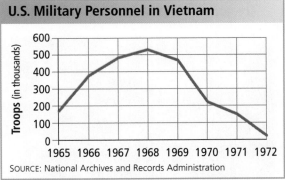

**U.S. Military Personnel in Vietnam**

SOURCE: National Archives and Records Administration

**Vietnamizing the War**
The United States scaled back its commitment of ground troops to Vietnam after 1968. However, while more American troops left for home, U.S. air forces dropped more bombs on communist targets in North Vietnam and along the Ho Chi Minh Trail. *How did the shift in American tactics ensure Nixon's "peace with honor"?*

The next morning, U.S. and ARVN forces crossed the border into Cambodia. These soldiers captured large stockpiles of weapons and supplies, but they did not break the stalemate. North Vietnam remained determined to have peace on its terms or no peace at all.

**Violence Erupts at Kent State** The Cambodian incursion had a profound impact on the peace movement at home. It stirred antiwar activists, who argued that Nixon had widened the war and made the world a more dangerous place. Throughout the country, college campuses erupted with protests. Several demonstrations prompted the police and National Guard to step in to preserve order.

On two campuses, confrontations between students and armed authorities led to deaths. Four days after Nixon's speech, demonstrators at Kent State University in Ohio threw rocks and bottles at members of the National Guard. When one guardsman thought he heard a sniper's shot, he fired his rifle. The shot prompted other National Guardsmen to discharge a volley of gunfire into a group of protesters, killing four youths. The Kent State killings led to demonstrations on other campuses. At Jackson State University, a traditionally African American college in Mississippi, a confrontation between students and police ended with two students dead.

College demonstrations against the war sometimes prompted counterprotests by Americans who supported the President. In response to a May 8, 1970, antiwar rally in downtown New York City, construction workers decided to demonstrate, carrying American flags and chanting "All the Way USA." Believing that some anti-

**Protest and Death in Ohio**
A student photographer at Kent State snapped this photograph moments after the Ohio National Guard opened fire on student protesters on May 4, 1970. *How do you think people reacted to seeing this photograph in the newspaper?*

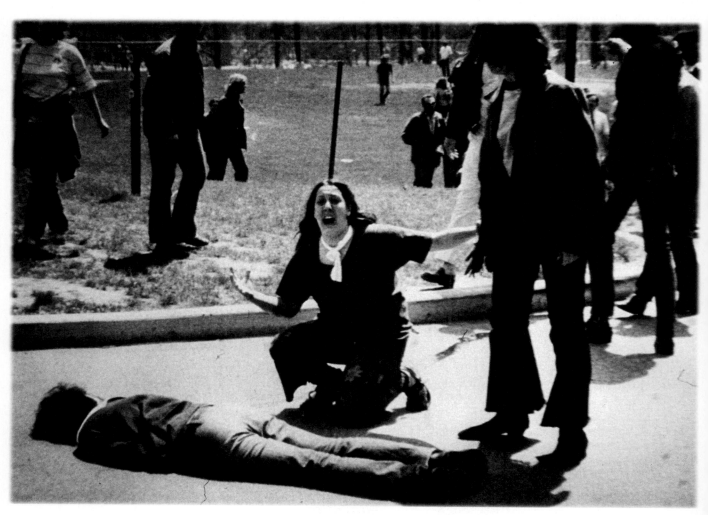

war demonstrators had spit on the American flag, they pushed into the crowd and started hitting protesters. The clash drew national attention. Days later, thousands of construction workers, businessmen, secretaries, and housewives marched peacefully through Manhattan's streets in support of Nixon and the war effort. One man expressed his feelings about the march:

> **Primary Source** "I'm very proud to be an American, and I know my boy that was killed in Vietnam would be here today if he was alive, marching with us. . . . I know he died for the right cause, because in his letters he wrote to me he knew what he was fighting for: to keep America free. . . ."
> —Robert Geary, May 20, 1970

As the fighting continued in Vietnam, the American home front became its own physical and emotional battlefield.

**American Soldiers Kill Civilians at My Lai** In 1971, two events increased the pressure on Nixon to pull U.S. troops out of Vietnam. The first event had roots in a U.S. action in South Vietnam three years earlier. On March 16, 1968, American forces searching for enemy troops in an area with a strong Vietcong presence came upon the village of **My Lai.** By this point in the war, many American troops had been injured and killed by Vietcong fighters posing as civilians. It was a recipe for disaster at My Lai, where Lieutenant William Calley's unit began shooting and killing unarmed civilians. During the assault, U.S. soldiers killed between four and five hundred Vietnamese.

Lt. Calley later maintained that he was following orders, but many of the soldiers present did not participate in the massacre. At least one risked his own life to stop it. The tragedy was made even worse by an inadequate military investigation of the incident. *Life* magazine eventually published photos taken during the event, and in March 1971, a military court convicted Lt. Calley of his participation in the attack. News of the My Lai massacre, the coverup, and Calley's trial shocked many Americans and added fuel to the burning antiwar fire.

**Pentagon Papers Undermine Public Trust** On the heels of My Lai came the 1971 publication of the **Pentagon Papers** in *The New York Times.* The term referred to a classified government history of America's involvement in Vietnam. The study was leaked to *The Times* by one of its coauthors, Daniel Ellsberg. Nixon tried to block the full publication, but in *New York Times* v. *United States,* the Supreme Court ruled against the administration. The study revealed that American leaders involved the U.S. in Vietnam without fully informing the American people and occasionally even lied to Congress.

✓ **Checkpoint** What happened at Kent State and Jackson State universities in 1970?

**Slaughter and Coverup in South Vietnam**
A photographer captured the terror in the village of My Lai as American troops were killing hundreds of civilians. The massacre was followed by a military investigation, but only Lt. William Calley was convicted. *Why were many Americans dissatisfied with the result of the military investigation?*

# The War Finally Ends

The failings of Vietnamization and growing dissent at home forced President Nixon to search for some final way out of the conflict. A 1971 public-opinion poll revealed that two thirds of Americans favored withdrawing American troops, even if it meant a communist takeover of South Vietnam. Sensitive to the public mood, Congress pressed Nixon to bring the troops home. Many believed that to win reelection in 1972, he had to end the war.

**American Troops Leave Vietnam** In October 1972, the United States and North Vietnam came to terms on a peace settlement. One month later, with lasting peace almost at hand, Nixon easily defeated the antiwar Democrat George McGovern for reelection. But Nixon's triumph was short-lived. The Vietnamese peace fell apart when North Vietnam refused to sign the agreement. Talks broke off, but renewed American bombing in North Vietnam finally induced the North Vietnamese to resume negotiations.

At last, in January 1973, the United States, South Vietnam, North Vietnam, and the Vietcong signed the **Paris Peace Accords.** The parties agreed to a cease-fire and a U.S. troop withdrawal from South Vietnam. POWs would be exchanged, but North Vietnamese troops would remain in South Vietnam. The National Liberation Front would become a legitimate political party in South Vietnam, and South Vietnam's noncommunist government would remain in power pending a political settlement. With the war ended, the last American troops came home. Among the returning soldiers were more than 550 POWs, most of whom were pilots shot down during the war.

**Saigon Falls** For the United States, the war in Vietnam was over. For the Vietnamese, however, it continued. Neither North nor South Vietnam honored the cease-fire or worked toward a diplomatic settlement of their differences. In the spring of 1975, minor fighting escalated when North Vietnam launched an offensive against the South. Without American aid and ground support, the ARVN was no match for the Soviet-supplied North Vietnamese Army. By the end of April, the communists had taken Saigon. After decades of fighting and millions of deaths, Vietnam was unified under one flag.

✓ **Checkpoint** What did the signing parties agree to in the Paris Peace Accords?

**Vocabulary Builder**
induce–(ihn DOOS) *v.* to bring about; cause

◄ A Purple Heart is awarded to members of the U.S. armed forces who are wounded or killed by an enemy in combat.

● **INFOGRAPHIC**

# America's Veterans Return From Vietnam

In April 1973, a plane carrying the last American prisoners of war from Vietnam touched down in Hawaii. The flight marked the end of an era that had seen hundreds of thousands of American troops deployed to fight in the Vietnam War. The homecoming for many of these soldiers had been bittersweet. While some came home to exuberant family reunions and community parades, many Vietnam veterans received little or no public acknowledgment of their sacrifices. It was not until nearly a decade later that the nation dedicated the Vietnam Veterans Memorial (see photo at far right) to honor these brave Americans.

◄ A Vietnam veteran takes part in a 1973 parade in New York City to honor those who served in the war.

Some veterans, like this ► man in San Francisco in 1994, faced hard times after they reentered American society.

# The Vietnam War Has a Lasting Impact

More than 58,000 American soldiers gave their lives serving their country in Vietnam; another 300,000 were wounded. Although figures are not exact, the Vietnamese death toll most likely exceeded 2 million. Peace, however, did not mean the end of pain and hardship. The end of the war created other problems in Southeast Asia. The war also affected American attitudes toward world affairs.

**Southeast Asia Suffers Further Turmoil** Many foreign-policy experts in the United States had predicted that if North Vietnam won the Vietnamese civil war, communism would spread to other nations in Southeast Asia. In a limited sense, they were right. Communist regimes eventually came to power in both Laos and Cambodia. In Cambodia, the ruling Khmer Rouge unleashed a genocide on the populace, killing everyone who had ties to the West or previous Cambodian governments. Between 1975 and 1979, upwards of 2 million Cambodians were executed or died in labor camps.

In an expanded sense, however, many American foreign-policy strategists misjudged the spread of communism. They concluded it was a monolithic global movement controlled by Moscow and Beijing. However, as the war's aftermath would attest, communist movements in Southeast Asia were nationalistic and intolerant of outside influences. After the Vietnam War ended, Vietnamese communists went to war against the Khmer Rouge, who in turn received help from Chinese communists to battle the Vietnamese. In this conflict, the United States supported the Chinese.

**Veterans Return Home to Mixed Reactions** The war and the peace divided Americans. Some argued that the United States should never have entered the war and that their leaders had lied to them. Others countered that the war was part of an ongoing struggle against communism and that in the

The families of Americans still missing after the Vietnam War hope that those prisoners and missing will one day be returned to them. ▼

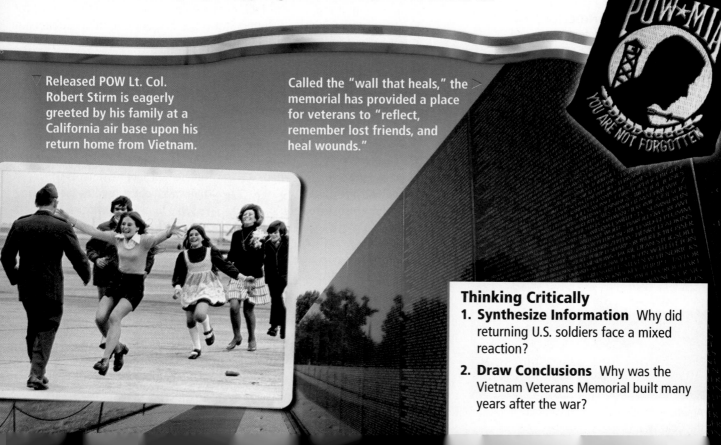

▽ Released POW Lt. Col. Robert Stirm is eagerly greeted by his family at a California air base upon his return home from Vietnam.

Called the "wall that heals," the ▷ memorial has provided a place for veterans to "reflect, remember lost friends, and heal wounds."

## Thinking Critically

1. **Synthesize Information** Why did returning U.S. soldiers face a mixed reaction?

2. **Draw Conclusions** Why was the Vietnam Veterans Memorial built many years after the war?

## TRACK THE ISSUE

**THE ESSENTIAL ? What is America's role in the world?**

At times throughout its history, the United States has tried to avoid getting involved in other countries' affairs. At other times, it has played an active part in world affairs. Today, America is deeply involved around the world. But what should its role be? Use the timeline below to explore this enduring issue.

**1796 Washington's Farewell Address**
President Washington warns against foreign alliances.

**1823 Monroe Doctrine**
President Monroe tells Europe to stay out of the Americas.

**1898 Spanish-American War**
The United States defeats Spain and expands overseas.

**1940s–1980s Cold War**
The United States tries to stop the spread of communism around the world.

**2000s War on Terrorism**
The United States works with other countries to fight global terrorism.

American soldiers fought in Vietnam during the Cold War.

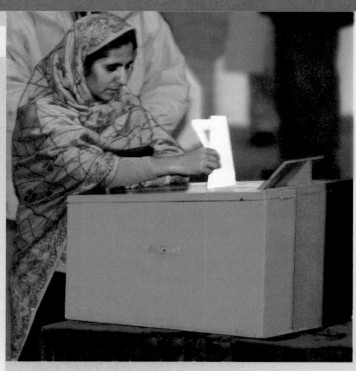

MI 7.2.1c

Since 2001, Afghanistan has labored to remake its government into a stable democracy.

## DEBATE THE ISSUE

**Intervention and Democracy** In 2001, the United States invaded Afghanistan. It toppled the Taliban government and ended its support for terrorism. Since then, the United States has helped to rebuild Afghanistan. Can intervention bring progress to a country?

"The United States and Afghanistan have made great progress. . . . Together we have . . . worked to ensure that Afghanistan will never again be a safe haven for terrorists. The United States has supported the Afghan people as they have established a moderate, representative government."
—Joint Declaration of the United States-Afghanistan Strategic Partnership

"The [George W.] Bush administration has consistently labeled the invasion of [Afghanistan] a success. But reports from humanitarian organizations, United Nations officials and Afghanis themselves paint a very different picture—warlords dominate much of the country, the Taliban is still a force in many parts, and the illegal drug trade is flourishing."
—Seymour Hersh, journalist for *The New Yorker*

**? TRANSFER Activities**

1. **Compare** What does the first quotation say about the results of intervention? What does the second quotation say?

2. **Analyze** What kinds of challenges might leaders from both countries face as they work to create a functioning democratic government?

3. **Transfer** Use the following Web site to see a video, try a WebQuest, and write in your journal. **Web Code:** neh-8902

end, the United States betrayed South Vietnam. An unfortunate result of the controversy was that the nation never fully expressed its appreciation to the returning veterans.

Overwhelmingly, the 2.5 million enlisted men who served in Vietnam did so with honor and distinction. Yet, unlike the soldiers that returned to the United States after World Wars I and II—the famed Doughboys and G.I. Joes—few Vietnam vets enjoyed the warmth and adulation of victory parades. In addition to the indifference that some veterans encountered, some also suffered from physical and psychological ailments for years when they returned home.

Not until almost a decade after the end of the war did Americans begin to fully honor the courage and sacrifice of these veterans. The Vietnam Veterans Memorial, dedicated in Washington, D.C., in 1982, stands as an eloquent testament to the men and women who served and died in Vietnam.

**Vietnam Changes American Policies** The war was costly both monetarily and in the human toll of shattered lives. The war also altered American domestic and foreign policies. Lyndon Johnson's Great Society campaign against poverty and racism fell victim to the conflict. Increasingly, between 1964 and 1968, Johnson could not pay for both the Vietnam War and the Great Society. Paying for more guns left less money to pay for textbooks, school lunches, and prenatal care.

Additionally, the war undermined Americans' trust in their leaders and fragmented the Cold War consensus on foreign affairs. In 1973, Congress passed the **War Powers Act.** The act restricted the President's war-making powers by requiring him to consult with Congress within 48 hours of committing American forces to a foreign conflict. The act was a congressional attempt to check the unilateral formation of American foreign policy and stop the growth of the "imperial presidency."

Finally, the Vietnam War made Americans more suspicious of foreign commitments and less likely to intervene in the affairs of other countries. For the next 30 years, many Americans would view conflicts in Central America, Africa, the Balkans, and the Middle East through a lens tinted by the Vietnamese quagmire. The fear of "another Vietnam" had profound effects on American foreign policy in the postwar world.

✓ **Checkpoint** What did the War Powers Act do?

**NoteTaking**

**Reading Skill: Recognize Effects** As you read, use a concept web to identify the effects of the Vietnam War.

SECTION

# 4 Assessment

**Progress Monitoring *Online***
For: Self-test with vocabulary practice
Web Code: nea-1610

## Comprehension

1. **Terms and People** For each term below, write a sentence explaining its significance.
   - Vietnamization
   - Paris Peace Accords
   - War Powers Act

2.  **NoteTaking Reading Skill: Compare and Contrast** Use your Venn diagram to answer the Section Focus Question: How did the Vietnam War end, and what were its lasting effects?

## Writing About History

3. **Quick Write: Choose Strongest Argument** Consider this thesis statement: Richard Nixon won the Vietnam War. List possible arguments for a persuasive essay that supports this thesis. Review each argument and choose the strongest one. Make sure that factual points from the text support your argument.

## Critical Thinking

4. **Synthesize Information** How did Nixon redirect the peace process when he became President? Did his plan have the desired result?

5. **Explain Effects** What impact did the events of 1970 and 1971 have on Nixon's actions in Vietnam?

6. **Draw Conclusions** Which two effects of the Vietnam War do you think had the biggest long-term impact? Explain.

Chinese and American flags ▶

▲ Nixon and Zhou shake hands in China in 1972.

WITNESS HISTORY 🔊 AUDIO

**A New Era Begins**

When Richard Nixon visited the People's Republic of China in February of 1972, Premier Zhou Enlai greeted the President as he landed in Beijing. Once on the wind-swept tarmac, Nixon walked toward his host with his arm outstretched. Recalling John Foster Dulles's refusal to shake Zhou's hand at the Geneva Conference in 1954, Nixon made certain not to repeat the insult to the Chinese leader. Nixon remembered the occasion in his memoir:

❝When I reached the bottom step, therefore, I made a point of extending my hand as I walked toward him. When our hands met, one era ended and another began.❞

—Richard Nixon

# Nixon and the Cold War

 **Content Expectations**

- **8.1.2a** Evaluate development of U.S. national security establishment.
- **8.1.2d** Evaluate U.S. involvement in Vietnam, foreign/domestic consequences of the war.
- **8.1.2f** Evaluate the arms race.

## Terms and People

Henry Kissinger
realpolitik
Zhou Enlai

Strategic Arms
 Limitation Treaty
détente

## NoteTaking

**Reading Skill: Categorize** As you read, describe Nixon's Cold War foreign policies in dealing with China and the Soviet Union.

| Nixon's Cold War Policies | |
| --- | --- |
| China | Soviet Union |
| • Normalization of relations will drive wedge between China and Soviet Union. | • Diplomacy with China will create Soviet fear of isolation. |
| • | • |
| • | • |

**Why It Matters** As a presidential candidate, Richard Nixon had promised to end U.S. military involvement in the Vietnam War. Recognizing the potency of Soviet power and the increasing unwillingness of many Americans to pay the costs of containing communism everywhere, Nixon developed a new approach to the Cold War. His bold program redefined America's relations with the two titans of global communism, China and the Soviet Union. **Section Focus Question: How did Richard Nixon change Cold War diplomacy during his presidency?**

## Nixon Redefines American Foreign Policy

During his years in office, Richard Nixon fundamentally reshaped the way the United States approached the world. Before Nixon took office, most American leaders shared a common Cold War ideology. They stressed that there existed a basic conflict between democratic, capitalist countries and totalitarian, communist ones. They divided the world into "us" and "them," and they established policies based on an assumption commonly held that "the enemy of my enemy is my friend." Therefore, a country opposed to communism was, by this definition, a friend of the United States. Nixon and **Henry Kissinger,** his leading adviser on national security and international affairs, altered this Cold War policy approach.

At first glance, Richard Nixon's partnership with Henry Kissinger seemed improbable. Nixon was a conservative California Republican, suspicious of the more liberal East Coast Republicans and exhausted with the political and strategic theories of Ivy League intellectuals. Kissinger was a Harvard-educated Jewish émigré from Germany and a prominent figure in East Coast intellectual circles. In several prior presidential campaigns, Kissinger had actually worked against Nixon. However, both men were outsiders, equipped with an outsider's readiness to question accepted orthodoxy.

In foreign affairs, Nixon and Kissinger embraced the idea of **realpolitik,** a German word meaning "real politics." According to realpolitik, political goals should be defined by concrete national interests instead of abstract ideologies. The two statesmen argued that if Americans would put aside their Cold War biases and look at the world with fresh eyes, U.S. global interests could be surveyed not in black and white but in shades of gray. For example, China and the Soviet Union—America's ideological enemies—could actually become excellent trading partners. At the same time, West Germany and Japan—America's ideological friends—were fast developing into economic rivals.

Nixon and Kissinger also questioned some lingering Cold War assumptions. For instance, they concluded that there was no united worldwide communist movement, as Lyndon Johnson and other Presidents had believed. There were important differences between the unique ideologies of the Soviet Union and China and other communist countries, such as Yugoslavia, North Korea, and North Vietnam, which often behaved quite independently. As President, Nixon insisted on a flexible, <u>pragmatic</u> foreign policy that avoided ideological absolutes.

✔ **Checkpoint** How did Nixon and Kissinger reshape America's approach to foreign affairs?

**Vocabulary Builder**
<u>pragmatic</u>—(prag MAT ihk) *adj.* practical; having to do with real actions and results rather than ideas and theories

## Playing the China Card

From his first days in office, Nixon seemed determined to leave his mark on the nation's international affairs. Lyndon Johnson focused primarily on domestic affairs—the nuts and bolts of legislation and political deal-making. Nixon was more a man of the world, fascinated by global politics and shifting alliances. Johnson believed his Great Society would solidify his reputation as a great President. In stark contrast, Nixon thought his reorientation of American foreign policy would cement his legacy in the annals of United States history.

**Reasons for Reaching Out to China** "You're not going to believe this," a Nixon aide told a journalist in 1969, "but Nixon wants to recognize China." It was an odd, almost unbelievable, statement. At the time, the communist People's Republic of China was the most populous country in the world, but it was not officially recognized by the United States. Nor had it been admitted to the United Nations. The China that the United States recognized as the official representative body of the Chinese people was the Nationalist Chinese government exiled on the island of Taiwan. Nixon built his impressive career as a hard-line "Cold Warrior," a vigilant opponent of communism. He was the last politician Americans could imagine to extend the olive branch of recognition—and thus peace—to the communists.

Ever the political realist, Nixon knew that the People's Republic of China could not be ignored forever. He recognized that establishing diplomatic relations with the Chinese communists would benefit the United States. From an economic standpoint, improved relations would

### HISTORY MAKERS

**Henry Kissinger** (b. 1923)

Born in Germany, Henry Kissinger came to the United States in 1938 when his family decided to flee the Nazis' growing persecution of Jews. After serving in the United States Army during World War II, he went to college. A brilliant student, Kissinger earned his bachelor's degree with highest honors and gained a Ph.D. at Harvard in just four years. Kissinger became a noted expert on national security and defense issues and soon impressed Richard Nixon with his foreign-policy analysis. When Nixon became President, he named Kissinger as his top national security adviser. The two worked closely together to end the Vietnam War, open relations with communist China, and shape the new diplomacy of détente with the Soviet Union. Nixon eventually named Kissinger his Secretary of State in 1973.

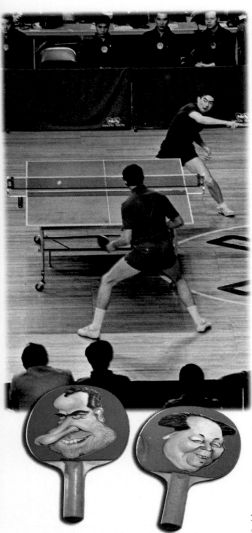

**Ping-Pong Diplomacy**
Nine American table-tennis players journeyed to China in 1971 to play matches against Chinese competitors. Americans commemorated the event with special ping-pong paddles fashioned after Nixon and Chinese leader Mao Zedong.

bring significant trade agreements, especially benefiting California and the Pacific Coast. Politically, U.S. normalization would drive a wedge between China and the Soviet Union, who had strayed from their traditional alliance and become rivals for territory and diplomatic influence. Finally, if the United States forged stronger relations with the Chinese, they might pressure North Vietnam to accept a negotiated peace to end the conflict still raging at the time.

**Nixon Normalizes Relations With China** With so much to gain and so little to lose, Nixon quietly pushed ahead with his plans. In public, the Chinese made symbolic overtures toward a meeting. In April 1971, China invited an American table-tennis team to play against its athletes. This small action demonstrated China's willingness to talk. Henry Kissinger worked behind the scenes, talking with Chinese leaders and ironing out sensitive issues with Premier **Zhou Enlai.** Then, in July 1971, Nixon announced that he would make an official state visit to China.

In February 1972, the President made the trip and toured the Great Wall, the Imperial Palace, and other historic sites. Nixon sat down for lengthy talks with Zhou Enlai and Communist Party Chairman Mao Zedong. He even learned enough Chinese to make a toast in the language of his host country. The visit was a great success and an important step toward normalizing diplomatic relations with China. The following year, American tourists started visiting and American companies set up a thriving trade with China. Nixon's China trip was the high point of his presidency. It bridged, as Zhou Enlai said, "the vastest ocean in the world, twenty-five years of no communication." In 1979, the United States and China established full diplomatic relations.

✓ **Checkpoint** Why did Nixon reach out to China?

## Détente With the Soviet Union

Nixon's trip to the People's Republic of China prompted an immediate reaction from the Soviet Union, which had strained relations with both countries. Soviet leader Leonid Brezhnev feared that improved U.S.-Chinese relations would isolate Russia. Therefore, he invited Nixon to visit Moscow. Nixon made the trip in May 1972. Afterward, the President reported to Congress that he and Brezhnev had reached agreements in a wide variety of areas:

> **Primary Source** "Recognizing the responsibility of the advanced industrial nations to set an example in combating mankind's common enemies, the United States and the Soviet Union have agreed to cooperate in efforts to reduce pollution and enhance environmental quality. We have agreed to work together in the . . . conquest of cancer and heart disease."
>
> —Richard Nixon, speech to Congress, June 1, 1972

Nixon also announced plans to conduct a joint U.S.-Soviet space mission.

However, by far the high point of the summit was the signing of the first **Strategic Arms Limitation Treaty.** Otherwise known as SALT I, the treaty froze the deployment of intercontinental ballistic missiles (ICBMs) and placed limits on antiballistic missiles (ABMs), but it did not alter the stockpiling of the more dangerous multiple independent reentry vehicles (MIRVs). SALT I did not end the arms race between the United States and the Soviet Union. But it was a giant step toward that goal.

The importance of SALT I stemmed first and foremost from U.S. and Soviet efforts to reduce tensions between them. A policy aimed at easing Cold War tensions, **détente** had replaced previous diplomatic efforts based on suspicion and

**Nuclear Arms Treaty**
As Leonid Brezhnev (seated, right) looks on, President Nixon signs the SALT I treaty during his historic visit to Moscow.

distrust. With his visits to China and the Soviet Union, coming within six months of each other, Richard Nixon dramatically altered America's global strategy. He relaxed the nation's inflexible stance toward communism and applied a more pragmatic approach to foreign policy. In the short term, the new relationships he forged helped the United States to end the Vietnam War. In the long term, Nixon's foreign-policy breakthroughs moved the world a step closer to the end of the Cold War.

✔ **Checkpoint** How did SALT I support Nixon's new policy for dealing with the Soviet Union?

---

**Progress Monitoring *Online***
**For:** Self-test with vocabulary practice
**Web Code:** nea-1611

### Comprehension

1. **Terms and People** For each item below, write a sentence explaining its significance.
   • Henry Kissinger
   • realpolitik
   • Zhou Enlai
   • détente

2. **NoteTaking Reading Skill: Categorize** Use your table to answer the Section Focus Question: How did Richard Nixon change Cold War diplomacy during his presidency?

### Writing About History

3. **Quick Write: Write the Essay Body** Choose a topic from the section on which you might write a persuasive essay. For example, you might discuss whether Nixon was a better Cold War President than his predecessors. Write the body of your essay, using a list of points you have made to guide you. Remember to open and close the body of the essay with strong arguments.

### Critical Thinking

4. **Apply Information** How did Nixon's policy toward China reflect the philosophy of realpolitik?

5. **Draw Conclusions** Why did Nixon and Kissinger believe détente was a beneficial foreign policy?

6. **Predict Consequences** Did Richard Nixon position the United States to win the Cold War? Why or why not?

# Quick Study Guide

 8.1.2d

Progress Monitoring *Online*
For: Self-test with vocabulary practice
Web Code: nea-1612

## ■ Roots of the U.S. Action in Vietnam

| French Surrender at Dien Bien Phu | |
|---|---|
| **Before** | **After** |
| • **French-Indochinese War:** French forces battle Vietnamese communists under Ho Chi Minh. | • **Geneva Accords:** France grants independence to former colonies; Vietnam divided. |
| • **Cold War:** Truman helps France in order to maintain Cold War alliance against the Soviets. | • **SEATO:** U.S. assembles coalition to oppose spread of communism in Southeast Asia. |
| • **Domino Theory:** Eisenhower continues aid to French to prevent communist victory. | • **U.S. Intervention:** U.S. supports anticommunist Diem regime and sends troops to Vietnam. |

## ■ Arms Control Agreements

| Year | Agreement | Effect |
|---|---|---|
| 1963 | Nuclear Test Ban Treaty | Banned testing of nuclear weapons in the atmosphere |
| 1972 | SALT I Interim Agreement | Froze existing number of weapons held by each side |
| 1972 | SALT I Anti-Ballistic Missile Treaty | Set strict limits on missiles that could shoot down missiles from the other side |
| 1979 | SALT II Treaty | Set absolute limit on number of weapons each side could hold |

## ■ The Vietnam War, 1969–1972

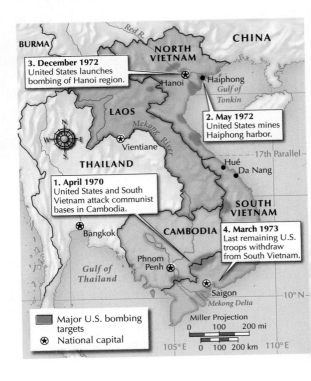

**3. December 1972** United States launches bombing of Hanoi region.

**2. May 1972** United States mines Haiphong harbor.

**1. April 1970** United States and South Vietnam attack communist bases in Cambodia.

**4. March 1973** Last remaining U.S. troops withdraw from South Vietnam.

Major U.S. bombing targets
⊛ National capital

Miller Projection
0    100    200 mi
0  100 200 km

## ☑ Quick Study Timeline

| In America | 1950–1954 **United States aids French war effort in Indochina** | 1954 **United States supports South Vietnam; SEATO forms** | 1963 **American involvement in South Vietnam increases; Kennedy assassinated** |
|---|---|---|---|
| **Presidential Terms** | Harry S. Truman 1945–1953    Dwight D. Eisenhower 1953–1961 | | John F. Kennedy 1961–1963 |
| | **1950** | **1955** | **1960** |
| Around the World | 1950–1953 **Korean War** | 1954 **Dien Bien Phu falls; Geneva Accords** | 1963 **South Vietnamese citizens protest Diem regime** |

# American Issues
●—●—●—● **Connector**

 8.2.4

By connecting prior knowledge with what you have learned in this chapter, you can gradually build your understanding of enduring questions that still affect America today. Answer the questions below. Then, use your American Issues Connector study guide (or go online: www.PHSchool.com **Web Code:** neh-8903).

## Issues You Learned About

● **America and the World** During the Cold War, the United States tried to spread democracy, increase American power around the world, and limit the expansion of communism.

1. Think about the reasons for U.S. involvement in the Vietnam War and the reasons for opposition to America's role in the war. Then, write your own evaluation of whether the United States made the best decision in taking an active role in the Vietnam War. Consider the following:
   • domino theory and its validity
   • Gulf of Tonkin incident
   • implementation of the draft
   • conflict between hawks and doves
   • total of American casualties

● **America Goes to War** Again and again, Americans have faced the tough decision of whether or not to go to war.

2. What steps are usually followed before committing U.S. forces to war? Was this process followed in the Vietnam War? Explain.

3. Why did Johnson follow a policy of "Americanizing" the war effort? How did the war escalate under Johnson?

4. Why did President Nixon order bombing attacks on neighboring Cambodia? Why was this move controversial?

● **Global Interdependence** U.S. leaders often use diplomacy to improve relations with our friends and to reduce tensions with our rivals.

5. How did Nixon's China policy affect relations between the United States and the Soviet Union?

6. Explain the importance of SALT I.

| **Connect to Your World** | **Michigan** |
|---|---|

**Education and American Society** President Johnson's decision to bomb North Vietnam in February 1965 sparked protests on many college campuses, including several protests at the University of Michigan. In response to the bombing, more than 200 faculty members at the University led a teach-in on the night of March 24. From 8 P.M. until 8 A.M., more than 3,000 students listened to lectures, participated in a midnight rally, and joined discussion groups about topics related to the war. As the anti-war movement grew, University of Michigan students organized a sit-in at the Selective Service (draft) office, took over the Administration Building to protest University support for war research, and disrupted recruitment interviews by companies involved in war-related industries. Learn more about student protests on college campuses and write an editorial describing what free speech means to you.

---

**1964**
Gulf of Tonkin Resolution

**1968**
Violence erupts at Democratic National Convention

**1972**
Nixon visits China

Lyndon B. Johnson 1963–1969

Richard M. Nixon 1969–1974

**1965**

**1970**

**1975**

**1965**
Operation Rolling Thunder

**1968**
Tet Offensive

**1973**
Paris Peace Accords

**History Interactive**
**For:** Interactive timeline
**Web Code:** nep-1614

# Chapter Assessment

## Terms and People

1. Who was **Ho Chi Minh**? What role did he play in Vietnam's history?

2. Define **hawks** and **doves.** What generalizations can you make about each group?

3. What was the **Tet Offensive**? Why was it a tactical victory for the Americans but a strategic victory for the communists?

4. Define the **Gulf of Tonkin Resolution** and the **War Powers Act.** What was the relationship between them?

5. Define **realpolitik.** Give an example of realpolitik in the 1970s.

## Focus Questions

The focus question for this chapter is **How did the United States confront communism in East Asia after the Korean War?** Build an answer to this big question by answering the focus questions for Sections 1 through 5 and the Critical Thinking questions that follow.

**Section 1**
6. Why did the United States become involved in Vietnam?

**Section 2**
7. What were the causes and effects of America's growing involvement in the Vietnam War?

**Section 3**
8. How did the American war effort in Vietnam lead to rising protests and social divisions back home?

**Section 4**
9. How did the Vietnam War end and what were its lasting effects?

**Section 5**
10. How did Richard Nixon change Cold War diplomacy during his presidency?

## Critical Thinking

11. **Compare** Compare the involvement of Presidents Truman, Eisenhower, Kennedy, Johnson, and Nixon in Vietnam.

12. **Explain Effects** What impact did the Vietnam War have on the United States domestic economy?

13. **Evaluate Credibility of Sources** In February 1968, a television journalist reported to his viewers that there was a "credibility gap" between Johnson's statements about the war and the reality of the fighting. Why did Americans come to doubt the word of their President?

14. **Analyze Charts** Study the chart below. Why were casualties the highest between 1967 and 1969? Why were casualties much lower in 1972?

### American Casualties in Vietnam

| Year | Killed in Action | Wounded in Action | Missing in Action |
|------|------------------|-------------------|-------------------|
| 1961–1965 | 1,864 | 7,337 | 18 |
| 1966 | 5,008 | 29,992 | 61 |
| 1967 | 9,378 | 56,013 | 113 |
| 1968 | 14,594 | 87,388 | 176 |
| 1969 | 9,414 | 55,390 | 112 |
| 1970 | 4,221 | 24,835 | 101 |
| 1971 | 1,380 | 18,109 | 16 |
| 1972 | 300 | 3,936 | 11 |

SOURCE: National Archives and Records Administration

15. **Categorize** In his efforts to end the Vietnam War, Nixon followed some policies that seemed to lessen U.S. involvement and some that seemed to increase U.S. involvement. Give examples of each type of policy.

16. **Identify Assumptions** Before Nixon took office, what did Cold War foreign-policy strategists believe about the spread of communism? What assumptions did Nixon and Kissinger make when it came to foreign affairs?

## Writing About History

**Writing a Persuasive Essay** From 1954 to 1975, the United States supported South Vietnam in an ultimately losing battle against communist forces from North Vietnam. Write a persuasive essay in which you argue for or against the following thesis: The Vietnam War could have been won by the United States and South Vietnam. Consult page SH16 of the Writing Handbook for additional help.

### Prewriting
- Choose a side of the argument.
- Collect evidence, using a graphic organizer to list points on both sides of the issue.
- Research Internet or print sources to find materials that analyze your position from both sides. Take notes on relevant details, events, and people.

### Drafting
- Clearly state the position that you will argue in a thesis statement. Use the rest of your introduction to provide necessary context about the issue.
- Make an outline to organize your argument and its supporting details. Then, choose information from your research that supports each part of your outline.

### Revising
- Use the guidelines on page SH16 of the Writing Handbook to revise your essay.

# Prepare for the MME

## The 1968 Presidential Race

After the Tet Offensive showed the United States sinking deeper into a stalemate in Vietnam, the antiwar movement took center stage during the race for the White House. Use your knowledge of the election and the following documents to answer questions 1 through 4.

### Document A

"The feud that helped define the public lives of LBJ and RFK also helped shape the two greatest national undertakings of their times—the war on poverty and the war in Vietnam. Consumed by contempt for Kennedy, Johnson transformed a potential ally into an archenemy. . . . As Johnson and Kennedy became ever more bitter enemies, they divided constituencies they once shared, weakening their party by forcing its members to choose between them. They exposed and exacerbated the growing divide within the Democratic Party and American politics in general."

—*Jeff Shesol,* Mutual Contempt

### Document B

"[I]t is true that a house divided against itself by the spirit of faction, of party, of region, of religion, of race, is a house that cannot stand. There is division in the American house now. . . . I should not permit the Presidency to become involved in the partisan divisions that are developing in this political year. With America's sons in the fields far away, with America's future under challenge right here at home, with our hopes and the world's hopes for peace in the balance every day, I do not believe that I should devote an hour or a day of my time to any personal partisan causes or to any duties other than the awesome duties of this office—the Presidency of your country. Accordingly, I shall not seek, and I will not accept, the nomination of my party for another term as your President."

—*President Lyndon B. Johnson, March 31, 1968*

### Document C

Chicago police remove an antiwar protester from a demonstration during the 1968 Democratic National Convention.

### Document D

"For four years America's fighting men have set a record for courage and sacrifice unsurpassed in our history. . . . Never has so much military and economic and diplomatic power been used so ineffectively. . . . I say the time has come for the American people to turn to new leadership not tied to the mistakes and policies of the past. That is what we offer to America. And I pledge to you tonight that the first priority foreign policy objective of our next Administration will be to bring an honorable end to the war in Vietnam. We shall not stop there. We need a policy to prevent more Vietnams."

—*Republican Presidential Nominee Richard M. Nixon, August 8, 1968*

---

1. According to Document B, Johnson has chosen not to run for reelection because he
   A does not believe he can win.
   B is tired of trying to lead a divided nation.
   C has more vital duties to perform.
   D thinks the nation needs new leadership.

2. Which of the documents focus primarily on the causes of divisions within the Democratic Party?
   A Documents B and D
   B Documents A and D
   C Documents C and D
   D Documents A and C

3. The speakers in Documents B and D would most likely agree that
   A ending the Vietnam War is a top priority for the President.
   B the Vietnam War has been badly managed.
   C the United States is on the verge of winning in Vietnam.
   D the United States should pull its troops out of Vietnam immediately.

4. **Writing Task** What were the most important factors that led to the defeat of the Democrats in 1968? Write a paragraph answering this question, using your knowledge of the chapter content and specific evidence from the primary sources above.

# 17

# An Era of Protest and Change

## 1960–1980

## The Hippie Experience

Many young Americans in the 1960s identified with a cultural movement that rejected the social conventions of their parents' generation. Their long hair and flowing clothes set them apart from mainstream America. So did their name—hippies. One journalist and social commentator explains what it meant to be a hippie:

66 The word 'hip' translates roughly as 'wise' or 'tuned-in.' A hippy is somebody who 'knows' what's really happening, and who adjusts or grooves with it. Hippies despise phoniness; they want to be open, honest, loving and free. 99

—Hunter S. Thompson, "The 'Hashbury' Is the Capital of the Hippies"

*Listen to the* Witness History *audio to hear more about the hippie experience.*

◄ A hippie woman dances at the Woodstock music festival in New York, 1969.

**Early logo of the National Organization for Women**

**A Beatles album released in 1969**

 **Content Expectations**

**Chapter Focus Question:** How did the counterculture and the expanding rights revolution of the 1960s and 1970s influence American society?

## Section 1

**The Counterculture**   8.2.1, 8.2.4, 8.3.1b

## Section 2

**The Women's Rights Movement**   8.2.4, 8.3.3, 8.3.4

## Section 3

**The Rights Revolution Expands**   8.2.1, 8.3.3, 8.3.4

## Section 4

**The Environmental Movement**   7.1.3, 8.2.2a, 8.2.4

**Protesters holding up a peace sign**

Use the ☑ **Quick Study Timeline** at the end of this chapter to preview chapter events.

> **Note Taking Study Guide *Online***
> For: Note Taking and American Issues Connector
> Web Code: nee-9001

◄ Some audience members make their own music.

 WITNESS HISTORY 🔊 AUDIO

## Remembering Woodstock

In the summer of 1969, hundreds of thousands of people gathered for a rock concert in Bethel, New York. Most of the media criticized the three-day event because of the concertgoers' widespread use of drugs and open displays of "free love." The people who went to Woodstock felt differently. For them, Woodstock showed that close to half a million people could come together peacefully. Twenty-five years later, many who attended Woodstock still remember their experiences vividly.

❝Woodstock was a time of social changes in human freedom and expression. . . . We learned not to be ashamed of our bodies. . . . We spent time with our kids. . . . That festival set the standards for peace, music, people and expression and showed to the world that all was not just violence and hatred . . . it was LIFE!❞

—Juan C. Morales

◄ A 1969 poster promises "3 days of peace & music" at the Woodstock concert.

# The Counterculture

 **Content Expectations**

- **8.2.1** Use population data to analyze maps that show changes in population distribution, spatial patterns, density.
- **8.2.4** Analyze competing perspectives/ controversies among Americans generated by U.S. Supreme Court decisions.
- **8.3.1b** Analyze Supreme Court decisions/ governmental actions during Civil Rights Movement.

**Terms and People**

| | |
|---|---|
| counterculture | commune |
| generation gap | Timothy Leary |
| Beatles | |

**NoteTaking**

**Reading Skill: Identify Main Ideas** As you read, use a concept web like the one below to record main ideas about the counterculture.

**Why It Matters** Woodstock was a dynamic expression of a **counterculture** that arose in the 1960s. Members of the counterculture adopted values that ran counter to mainstream culture. They rebelled against long-standing customs in dress, music, and personal behavior. The counterculture both challenged the values of mainstream American society and unleashed a movement to reassert traditional values. **Section Focus Question: What was the counterculture, and what impact did it have on American society?**

## The Counterculture Rises

The counterculture was rooted in the social and political events of the 1950s. The Beat movement had emphasized freedom from materialism and the importance of personal experience. The civil rights movement introduced the idea of social and political protest, which stimulated the Vietnam antiwar movement. Both movements prompted many people to question traditional boundaries, whether restrictions on rights or cultural norms in dress or hairstyles. It also heightened distrust of authority, leading some in the counterculture to declare, "Don't trust anyone over 30."

Members of the counterculture valued youth, spontaneity, and freedom of expression. Also called hippies, these young people promoted peace, love, and freedom. They experimented with new styles of dress and music, freer attitudes toward sexual relationships, and the recreational use of drugs. Their values were so different from traditional ones that many social analysts described the resulting situation as a **generation gap,** in which there was a lack of understanding and communication between the older and younger generations. Jerry Rubin, a political activist, described how long hair divided parents from their children:

**Primary Source** "Young kids identify short hair with authority, discipline. . . . Wherever we go, our hair tells people where we stand on Vietnam, Wallace, campus disruption, dope. . . . Yesterday I was walking down the street. A car passed by, parents in the front seat and a young kid, about eight, in the back seat. The kid flashed me the clenched fist sign. [Meaning: He identified with Rubin's long hair.]"
—Jerry Rubin, *America in the Sixties*

The baby boom that followed World War II resulted in a huge student population in the 1960s. By sheer numbers, the baby boomers became a force for social change. The music industry rushed to produce the music they liked; clothing designers copied the styles they introduced; universities were forced to change college courses and rules to accommodate them.

✓ **Checkpoint** What factors influenced the rise of the counterculture?

# Defining the Counterculture

Many people have used the so-called trinity of the counterculture—sex, drugs, and rock-and-roll—to define the youth generation. But the counterculture was also marked by an interest in spirituality.

**Music and Art Shape Youth Culture** By the 1960s, rock-and-roll had become a defining characteristic of the baby-boom generation. When the **Beatles** made a triumphant visit to the United States in 1964, more than 70 million Americans watched the English rock band perform on Ed Sullivan's television show. The Beatles also had an impact on folk musicians like Bob Dylan, whose protest songs highlighted the civil rights and peace movements. As radical musician John Sinclair put it, rock became "a weapon of cultural revolution," urging listeners to reject conventions and, in many cases, the political policies of the government. Even after the counterculture had declined in significance, rock music remained popular among baby-boomers as well as their children.

The art and literature of the 1960s and 1970s also displayed a rebellious side. Andy Warhol's realistic paintings of common items of American culture, such as Campbell soup cans, questioned satirically what was "real." In literature, the novels of Tom Wolfe and Hunter S. Thompson blurred the lines between reporting and political activism.

**The Sexual Revolution** Members of the counterculture rejected many traditional restrictions on sexual behavior in what became known as the "sexual revolution." They called for the separation of sex from traditional family life and often advocated new living patterns. For example, many hippies lived together in **communes,** or small communities in which the people have common interests and share resources. The sexual revolution was one of the strongest indicators of the generation gap. One poll showed that nearly two thirds of all Americans over the age of 30 opposed premarital sex, whereas a majority of those under age 29 did not. Eventually, however, the sexual revolution led to a more open discussion of sex in the mainstream media.

**Rock Art**
The pop art that decorated concert posters, such as this one from the late 1960s, often challenged tradition.

● **INFOGRAPHIC**

# The Generation Gap

In the 1960s and 1970s, many parents and their children had little in common apart from their genes. Parents of boomer children were heavily influenced by the two major events of their own childhoods, the depression and World War II. Part of what was called the "silent generation," they sought stability by conforming, and they started adulthood early, marrying young. In contrast, their baby-boomer children rejected tradition and authority in favor of individuality. Boomers did not want to fit in; they wanted to stand out.

**THE BOOMER GENERATION**
Teens during the 60s and 70s grew up in a time of prosperity. Many embraced activism and symbols of peace, such as flowers and pins. Rock-and-roll music shaped their worldviews and set them apart from their parents. The boomer generation also expressed a new distrust toward tradition and authority, reflected in popular magazines like *MAD*.

**THE SILENT GENERATION**
Parents of boomers grew up in a different world from their children. They had learned to live frugally through years of rationing during the depression and war. As teens, they had listened and danced to the big-band music that their parents had enjoyed. They valued loyalty, authority, and had respect for the military and veterans.

**Age Breakdown, 1964**

**1964**

Under age 17 36%

Over age 17 64%

SOURCE: Federal Interagency Forum on Child and Family Statistics

◀ The boomers' sheer numbers emphasized the growing generation gap. While today youths make up about a quarter of the population, in the mid-1960s they made up more than a third.

**Thinking Critically**
**Draw Inferences** Why do you think the generation of people born between 1925 and 1942 has been called the "silent generation"?

**History** *Interactive* ✱
**For:** More about the generation gap
**Web Code:** nep-1711

**Life in Haight-Ashbury** In 1967, as many as 2,000 people flocked to the Haight-Ashbury district of San Francisco, a center of the counter-culture. Hippies there experimented with drugs, wore unconventional clothing, and listened to rock music and speeches by political radicals like Timothy Leary, a one-time Harvard researcher. He preached that drugs could free the mind, and he encouraged American youths to "tune in," "turn on" to drugs, and "drop out" of mainstream society. The hippies of San Francisco attracted a great deal of media attention, much of it critical of the lifestyles they advocated. Life in Haight-Ashbury did prove to have unwanted effects. As in other enclaves of hippie culture, it experienced high rates of drug abuse which led to increased crime.

**Exploring Different Routes to Spirituality** Some members of the counterculture sought spiritual enlightenment outside of the Judeo-Christian traditions in which they had been raised. Many explored Buddhism and other Eastern religions, while others sought spirituality by living in harmony with nature. Particularly in the late 1960s and early 1970s, some hippies established rural communes, seeking to live off the land as Native Americans had in the past. These beliefs had a lasting impact on the budding environmental movement.

✓ **Checkpoint** What characteristics define the counterculture?

# The Counterculture Ends

By the end of the 1960s, many people, even those within the counterculture, had become disillusioned with some of its excesses. The utopian urge to discover a more authentic way of living had an unfortunate underside. Drug addictions and deaths from overdoses rose. A number of rock musicians, most famously Jimi Hendrix and Janis Joplin, died of drug overdoses while only in their twenties. The downward spiral continued in 1969 with a tragedy at a music festival sponsored in Altamont, California. While the Rolling Stones played, members of the Hells Angels, a motorcycle gang that had been hired to provide security, stabbed to death a black man who had approached the stage. The ugly violence <u>contradicted</u> the values of "peace and love" that many hippies embraced.

At the same time, the movement's values were becoming increasingly shallow and self-centered. When the counterculture fell apart, most hippies abandoned their social experiments and melted right back into the mainstream. Still, the seeds of protest they had sown would influence the growing "rights revolution."

**Vocabulary Builder**
<u>contradict</u>—(kahn truh DIHKT) *v.* to go against expressed views

✓ **Checkpoint** Why did the counterculture fall apart?

**Progress Monitoring _Online_**
For: Self-test with vocabulary practice
Web Code: nea-1711

**SECTION 1 Assessment**

## Comprehension

1. **Terms and People** For each item below, write a sentence explaining how it influenced the counterculture.
   - generation gap
   - Beatles
   - commune
   - Timothy Leary

2. **NoteTaking Reading Skill: Identify Main Ideas** Use your concept web to answer the Section Focus Question: What was the counterculture, and what impact did it have on American society?

## Writing About History

3. **Quick Write: Identify Issues** You are a teenager in the 1960s, and you've been invited to your father's club to give a speech about the values of the youth generation. Identify the issues that you will address, keeping your audience in mind.

## Critical Thinking

4. **Identify Assumptions** What assumptions about mainstream culture were made by the counterculture?

5. **Analyze Information** Explain whether you agree with the following statement: "The counterculture was a form of protest."

6. **Recognize Cause and Effect** How did trends within the counterculture movement contribute to its downfall?

▲ National Organization for Women button

▲ Civil rights leader Coretta Scott King speaks to a group of feminists at a National Women's Conference.

WITNESS HISTORY  AUDIO

### Challenging a Stereotype

"The unspoken assumption is that women are different. They do not have executive ability, orderly minds, stability, leadership skills, and they are too emotional. It has been observed before, that society for a long time discriminated against another minority, the blacks, on the same basis—that they were different and inferior. The happy little homemaker and the contented "old darkey" on the plantation were both produced by prejudice. As a black person, I am no stranger to race prejudice. But the truth is that in the political world I have been far oftener discriminated against because I am a woman than because I am black."

—Shirley Chisholm, Address to the United States House of Representatives, May 21, 1969

# The Women's Rights Movement

 **Content Expectations**

- **8.2.4** Analyze competing perspectives/controversies among Americans generated by U.S. Supreme Court decisions.
- **8.3.3** Analyze causes/course of the women's rights movement in 1960s/1970s.
- **8.3.4** Evaluate major accomplishments/setbacks in civil rights/liberties for U.S. minorities.

## Terms and People

feminism      ERA
Betty Friedan      Gloria Steinem
NOW      Phyllis Schlafly

## NoteTaking

**Reading Skill: Identify Causes and Effects**
Record the causes, effects, and main figures of the women's movement in a chart like this one.

| The Women's Movement | | |
|---|---|---|
| **Causes** | **Proponents/ Opponents** | **Effects** |
| • | • | • |
| | | • |

**Why It Matters** Following World War II, most women gave up their jobs to returning servicemen and went back to their homes to take care of their families. Social analysts and popular culture portrayed women, especially suburban housewives, as the personification of America's achievement of the good life. By the end of the 1960s, however, a broad-based movement to attain sexual equality had arisen. The women's movement fundamentally changed American life—from family and education to careers and political issues. **Section Focus Question: What led to the rise of the women's movement, and what impact did it have on American society?**

## A Women's Movement Arises

Historians often refer to the women's movement of the 1960s and 1970s as the second wave of **feminism,** or the theory of political, social, and economic equality of men and women. They want to emphasize that the struggle for women's rights has had a long history, going back at least to the 1840s, when women drafted the Declaration of Sentiments at Seneca Falls, New York. The phrase *second wave of feminism* also reminds us that the first wave, which culminated with women's winning the right to vote in 1920, ended well before the nation addressed the call for full equality. In the decades that followed, women made little legal or social headway. Several factors influenced the rebirth of the women's movement in the 1960s and 1970s.

**Seeking to Redefine Traditional Roles** The civil rights struggle prompted women to look at the ways in which society judged and discriminated against them as a group. As Casey Hayden and Mary King, two veterans of that movement, put it: "Sex and caste. There seem to be many parallels that can be drawn between the treatment of Negroes and the treatment of women in society as a whole." The civil rights movement both inspired women to demand <u>gender</u> equality and taught them ways to get it. It also brought black and white women together, strengthening their shared cause.

Women also wanted to redefine how they were viewed. Many women objected to the inaccuracy of the housewife stereotype. Some needed to work to support themselves or their families. Others wanted more opportunities than their lives as housewives could offer. **Betty Friedan** powerfully articulated this message in her groundbreaking book *The Feminine Mystique*.

**Vocabulary Builder**
<u>gender</u>–(JEHN der) *n.* a person's sex

> **Primary Source** "The problem lay buried, unspoken, for many years in the minds of American women. It was a strange stirring, a sense of dissatisfaction. . . . Each suburban wife struggled with it alone. As she made the beds, shopped for groceries, matched slipcover material, ate peanut butter sandwiches with her children, chauffeured Cub Scouts and Brownies, lay beside her husband at night—she was afraid to ask even of herself the silent question—'Is this all?'"
> —Betty Friedan, *The Feminine Mystique*, 1963

**Looking for Better Work** Despite the stereotypes, the number of women in the workforce grew throughout the 1950s and 1960s. Yet working women often found themselves in deadend jobs. Even those with training and education had their access to careers or advancement blocked, in many cases, by blatantly discriminatory employers. Sandra Day O'Connor, who ultimately became the first female Supreme Court Justice, graduated near the top of her class at Stanford Law School in the early 1950s. Yet while she found few employment opportunities upon graduation, her male counterparts won job offers at prestigious law firms. Facing such restrictions, women increasingly demanded equal treatment in the workplace.

✓ **Checkpoint** How did the women's movement of the 1960s begin?

# Women Find Their Voices

Several years after she wrote *The Feminine Mystique*, Betty Friedan helped establish the **National Organization for Women (NOW)**. The organization—which dedicated itself to winning "true equality for all women" and to attaining a "full and equal partnership of the sexes"—galvanized the women's movement.

**NOW's Goals and Tactics** NOW set out to break down barriers of discrimination in the workplace and in education. It attacked stereotypes of women in the media and called for more balance in roles in marriages. It had two major priorities. The first was to bring about passage of the **Equal Rights Amendment (ERA)**, an amendment to the Constitution that would guarantee gender equality under the law. The ERA initially had been proposed in the early 1920s but had never passed. The second was to protect reproductive rights,

## HISTORY MAKERS

### Betty Friedan (1921–2006)

Educated at Smith College, where she edited the school newspaper, Betty Friedan did graduate work in psychology before becoming a journalist. She married in 1947 and was fired from her job when she became pregnant with her second child. Friedan raised three children and occasionally wrote articles for magazines. As she was working on one article, she realized that many educated women who had become housewives shared the uneasiness she felt about her life. This led her to write *The Feminine Mystique* in 1963, which helped launch the women's movement by inspiring women to join in the struggle for equal rights. In a later book, *The Second Stage* (1981), she criticized the direction of the women's movement, arguing that it had become too hostile to families.

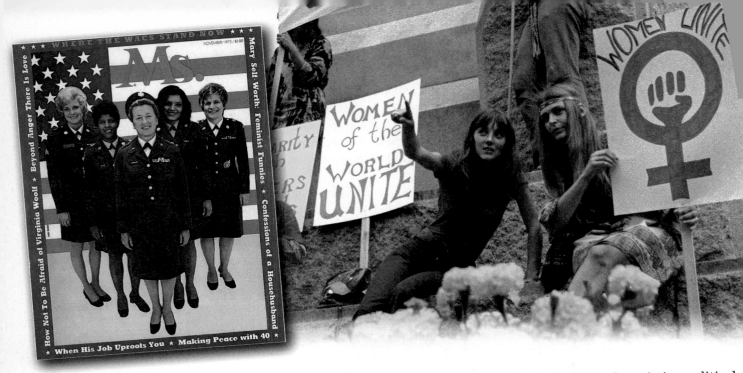

## A Diverse Movement

Women take part in a NOW rally in Washington, D.C., in 1970. A *Ms.* magazine cover from 1972 shows that women from all different backgrounds participated in the women's movement. *What women's issues might have been especially important to women in the military?*

especially the right to an abortion. NOW worked within the existing political system, lobbying for political reforms and readying court cases to compel the government to enforce existing legislation that banned discrimination. For some women, NOW seemed too extreme; for others, it was not extreme enough. Still, NOW served as a rallying point to promote equality for all women.

**Raising Society's Awareness** Finding NOW too tame, radical feminists sought a more fundamental restructuring of society. Rather than seeking legislative change, these protesters sought to show the way society trapped women into adopting restrictive roles. In addition to public protests of the Miss America Pageant, radical feminists engaged in small-scale consciousness-raising efforts. Other feminists sought to raise public awareness by making personal issues political. Charlotte Bunch, for example, wrote that "there is no private domain of a person's life that is not political and there is no political issue that is not ultimately personal."

Some feminists, like **Gloria Steinem,** tried to change awareness through the mass media. After graduating from college, Steinem worked as a freelance writer, including a stint of undercover work at a club run by *Playboy* magazine. While society tended to view Playboy bunnies in glamorous terms, Steinem revealed how much humiliation they had to endure to make a living. In 1972, she helped co-found *Ms.*, a feminist magazine. Its title meant to protest the social custom of identifying women by their marital status rather than as individuals.

**Opposing the Women's Movement** Some Americans—both men and women—openly challenged the women's movement. **Phyllis Schlafly,** for example, is a conservative political activist who denounced women's liberation as "a total assault on the family, on marriage, and on children." She worked hard to defeat the ERA, arguing that the act would compel women to fight in the military, end sex-segregated bathrooms, and hurt the family. Her argument resonated with many conservatives. With their support, the ERA fell three states short of becoming a constitutional amendment.

✓ **Checkpoint** What were the various goals of the women's movement?

# Lasting Effects of the Women's Movement

The women's movement affected all aspects of American society. Women's roles and opportunities expanded. Women gained legal rights that had been denied them. And feminists sparked an important debate about equality that continues today. Yet the issues they raised continue to divide Americans. Some say that women haven't made enough gains. Others fear that the movement has actually harmed society.

**Making Legal Headway** Before the 1960s, there were no federal laws prohibiting gender discrimination. The Civil Rights Act of 1964, however, gave feminists a legal tool. It included a clause, called Title VII, that outlawed discrimination on the basis of sex. The clause was actually inserted by civil rights opponents, who thought it was so outlandish that it would make the entire bill look ridiculous. When the bill actually passed, however, women used Title VII to challenge discrimination. The bill also set up the Equal Employment Opportunity Commission (EEOC) to enforce the federal prohibition on job discrimination.

Enforcing Title VII, even with the EEOC, was often difficult. Still, NOW and other feminist organizations tirelessly filed suits against employers who refused to hire women or to pay them fairly, compelling the federal government to act. President Kennedy established the Commission on the Status of Women in 1961 to examine workplace discrimination. Title IX of the Higher Education Act of 1972 banned discrimination in education. The Equal Credit Opportunity Act, passed in 1974, made it illegal to deny credit to a woman just because of her gender.

## Comparing Viewpoints

## Do Women Need to Fight for Equal Rights?

[Ins]pired by the successes of the civil rights movement, many American women in the late 1960s [ren]ewed their own demand for equal rights. Other women, however, argued that their demand was [des]tructive.

### PHYLLIS SCHLAFLY

[S]chlafly (born 1924) is a lawyer and [p]olitical organizer who first became [f]amous for her anticommunist [v]iews. She became an opponent of [f]eminism.

**Primary Source**

"Feminism is doomed . . . because it [attempts] to repeal and restructure human nature."

"Women have babies and men provide support. If you don't like the way we're made you've got to take it up with God."

### GLORIA STEINEM

Steinem (born 1934) is a journalist who founded political organizations to help women lobby for equal rights. She became the most famous feminist leader of the 1970s.

**Primary Source**

"Sex and race, because they are easily visible differences, have been the primary ways of organizing human beings into superior and inferior groups, and into the cheap labor on which this system still depends."

### Compare

1. What do you think each woman would say about the role that biology plays in women's lives?

2. What is unusual about Schlafly's insistence that women should devote themselves to staying home and raising a family?

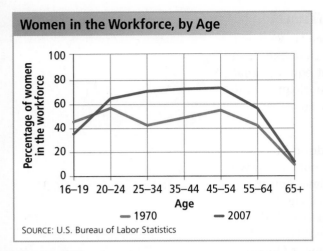

## Women in the Workforce, by Age

SOURCE: U.S. Bureau of Labor Statistics

**Graph Skills** Compare the lines for 1970 and 2007 on the graph. Notice that the 1970 line makes the shape of a letter *m. What factors explain this? Why is the 2007 line different?*

Some feminists considered their most important legal victory to be the 1973 Supreme Court decision in *Roe* v. *Wade,* which assured women the right to legal abortions. Prior to *Roe,* most states outlawed or severely restricted abortion. Some women turned to illegal and often dangerous ways to end their pregnancies. The case and its decision was highly controversial at the time and still is today.

**The Workplace Slowly Changes** The women's movement fostered a shift in attitudes among both men and women, and the American workplace today reflects this change. The percentage of women in the workforce has grown, from about 30 percent in 1950 to more than 60 percent in 2000. So, too, has the number of married female workers. Fields long closed or severely limited to women—such as medicine, law, and accounting—have opened up as well. The general shift in attitudes symbolized by these changes has created a world of possibilities for many young women who never knew a time when women were not allowed to do these things.

Despite these gains, the average woman still earns less than the average man, partly because many women continue to work in fields that pay less. Some people have referred to this situation as a "pink collar ghetto." Whether this is because of discrimination, or because women who shoulder family responsibilities often have limited job choices, remains a matter of debate. Many studies suggest that a "glass ceiling" exists, limiting the advancement of even the most highly educated and skilled women workers.

Most troubling, the United States has witnessed a feminization of poverty over the past 30 years. This means that the majority of the nation's poor people are single women. These are the women in the lowest-paying jobs, with the fewest benefits. Many of these poor women are single mothers, who must bear the costs and responsibilities of raising children alone while also working.

✓ **Checkpoint** What legal and social gains has the women's movement made?

---

**Progress Monitoring *Online***
For: Self-test with vocabulary practice
Web Code: nea-1721

### Comprehension

**1. Terms and People** What is the relationship between each of the following items and the women's movement?
- feminism
- Betty Friedan
- NOW
- ERA
- Gloria Steinem
- Phyllis Schlafly

**2. NoteTaking**  **Reading Skill: Identify Causes and Effects** Use your cause-and-effect chart to answer the Section Focus Question: What led to the rise of the women's movement, and what impact did it have on American society?

### Writing About History

**3. Quick Write: Identify Arguments** Suppose that you are either Betty Friedan or Phyllis Schlafly and you are giving a speech about women's roles in society. Identify and list the main arguments that would support your position.

### Critical Thinking

**4. Draw Inferences** Why did so much time elapse between the first and second waves of feminism?

**5. Identify Assumptions** What beliefs led women to support the women's movement? What beliefs led women to oppose it?

**6. Formulating Questions** Make up two or three questions that will help you decide whether American women have made significant strides toward equality.

# Esmeralda Santiago: *Almost a Woman*

As more Latinos arrived in America, their similar experiences as immigrants drew them together despite having come from many different countries. As Latinos, they faced common challenges: discrimination, lack of opportunity, and a mainstream society in which their differences were ignored and their voices often unheard. In this excerpt from her memoir *Almost a Woman,* Esmeralda Santiago tells what happened to her the first day after her family moved from Puerto Rico to New York.

Esmeralda Santiago

There was no horizon in Brooklyn. Everywhere I looked, my eyes met a vertical maze of gray and brown straight-edged buildings with sharp corners and deep shadows. Every few blocks there was a cement playground surrounded by [a] chain-link fence. And in between, weedy lots mounded with garbage and rusting cars.

A girl came out of the building next door, a jump rope in her hand. She appraised me shyly. I pretended to ignore her. She stepped on the rope, stretched the ends overhead as if to measure their length, and then began to skip, slowly, grunting each time she came down on the sidewalk. Swish splat grunt swish, she turned her back to me; swish splat grunt swish, she faced me again and smiled. I smiled back, and she hopped over.

"*¿Tú eres hispana?*" she asked, as she whirled the rope in lazy arcs.

"No, I'm Puerto Rican."

"Same thing. Puerto Rican, Hispanic. That's what we are here." She skipped a tight circle, stopped abruptly, and shoved the rope in my direction. "Want a turn?"

"Sure." I hopped on one leg, then the other. "So, if you're Puerto Rican, they call you Hispanic?"

"Yeah. Anybody who speaks Spanish."

I jumped a circle, as she had done, but faster. "You mean, if you speak Spanish, you're Hispanic?"

"Well, yeah. No . . . I mean your parents have to be Puerto Rican or Cuban or something."

I whirled the rope to the right, then the left, like a boxer. "Okay, your parents are Cuban, let's say, and you're born here, but you don't speak Spanish. Are you Hispanic?"

She bit her lower lip. "I guess so," she finally said. "It has to do with being from a Spanish country. I mean, you or your parents, like, even if you don't speak Spanish, you're Hispanic, you know?" She looked at me uncertainly. I nodded and returned her rope.

But I didn't know. I'd always been Puerto Rican, and it hadn't occurred to me that in Brooklyn I'd be someone else.

Girls skip rope in a city playground.

## Thinking Critically

1. **Make Inferences** Reread the first paragraph. How does Esmeralda feel about her new surroundings?

2. **Interpret the Literature** What would it mean to come to a new country and be "someone else"?

### From Graffiti to Art

Judith Baca, the daughter of Mexican immigrants, taught art in public schools in a rough Los Angeles neighborhood in the early 1970s. Between her classes, she watched young Latinos hanging out in parks and writing graffiti on the walls. Intrigued by the kids' graffiti, she developed the idea of channeling their creative energy into painting murals. Her idea spread to other U.S. cities, where kids used murals to document and celebrate Latino culture and history. Their work was just one part of a growing movement that sought to educate, respect, and politically organize American Latinos.

◄ A mural from the Philadelphia Mural Arts Program, begun in 1984, honors the great Mexican muralist, Diego Rivera (seated at center).

# The Rights Revolution Expands

### Content Expectations

- **8.2.1** Use population data to analyze maps that show changes in population distribution, spatial patterns, density.
- **8.3.3** Analyze causes/course of the women's rights movement in 1960s/1970s.
- **8.3.4** Evaluate major accomplishments/ setbacks in civil rights/liberties for U.S. minorities.

### Terms and People

Cesar Chavez
migrant farmworker
UFW
Chicano movement

AIM
Japanese American
   Citizens League
Ralph Nader

### NoteTaking

**Reading Skill: Compare and Contrast**
Create a Venn diagram to compare and contrast the Latino and Native American rights movements.

**Why It Matters** Successes in the civil rights and women's movements signaled a growing rights revolution in the United States. Latinos, Native Americans, and Asian Americans engaged in their own struggles for equality during the 1960s and 1970s, fighting to influence laws and government. Meanwhile, activists worked to expand rights for two broad groups: consumers and people with disabilities. **Section Focus Question: How did the rights movements of the 1960s and 1970s expand rights for diverse groups of Americans?**

## The Latino Population Grows

After World War I, the United States passed legislation limiting European immigration. Yet during and after World War II, the country faced a growing demand for cheap labor. At the same time, the populations of Mexico and other Latin American nations grew steadily while job opportunities there declined. The combination of these factors created a steady stream of new immigrants to the United States.

**A Spanish-Speaking Population** People whose family origins are in Spanish-speaking Latin America are called Latinos or Hispanics. They come from many different places, but they share the same language and some elements of culture. Spanish-speaking people lived in many parts of the western United States before settlers from the United States arrived, and their numbers have grown steadily. Mexican Americans, known as Chicanos, have always made up the largest group of U.S. Latinos.

**Mexican Americans Farm the Land** Beginning in 1942, Mexican immigrants came to the United States under the *bracero*, or farmhand, program. This program granted Mexican migrants temporary guest worker status, and over a period of 25 years, more than 4 million of them entered the U.S. The *braceros* played a crucial role in sustaining American agriculture during and after World War II.

Along with Mexicans who had migrated to the U.S. illegally in search of work, *braceros* who had outstayed their permits were targeted for deportation in the 1950s. In 1965, however, the government passed the Immigration and Nationality Act Amendments, eliminating national-origin quotas for immigrants. In the decades that followed, the number of legal Mexican and Asian immigrants surged. More than 400,000 Mexicans arrived during the 1960s, another 630,000 in the 1970s, and more than 1.5 million in the 1980s.

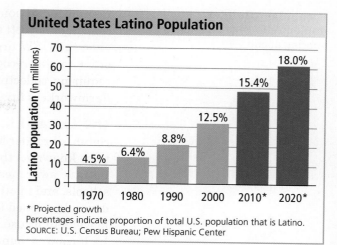

**United States Latino Population**

*Graph shows Latino population (in millions):*
- 1970: 4.5%
- 1980: 6.4%
- 1990: 8.8%
- 2000: 12.5%
- 2010*: 15.4%
- 2020*: 18.0%

\* Projected growth
Percentages indicate proportion of total U.S. population that is Latino.
SOURCE: U.S. Census Bureau; Pew Hispanic Center

**Graph Skills** Describe the growth of the Latino population from 1970 to 2020.

**Emerging Latino Communities on the East Coast** After World War II, large numbers of Puerto Ricans, Dominicans, and Cubans migrated to the United States. As citizens of a United States territory, Puerto Ricans came legally, leaving their homeland in search of better-paying jobs. In contrast, most Cuban and Dominican immigrants came to America as political refugees, fleeing their countries to escape the harsh rule of dictators. Most Puerto Rican, Cuban, and Dominican immigrants settled in urban areas, especially in New York City and Miami, Florida.

✔ **Checkpoint** Why did Mexicans and immigrants from other Latin American countries migrate to the United States?

# Pressing for Equal Rights

Like other minorities, Latinos had long faced discrimination. After World War II, Latino veterans began agitating for equal treatment. Veteran Hector Garcia, for example, formed the American G.I. Forum to battle discrimination. In the 1960s and 1970s, influenced by the growing civil rights movement, Latinos increasingly fought for equal rights. They demanded better working conditions, salaries, and educational opportunities. Like African Americans, they sought federal protection of their right to vote and campaigned to elect politicians who represented their interests.

**Cesar Chavez Organizes Farmworkers** The most influential Latino activist was **Cesar Chavez.** Chavez fought for rights for farm laborers, who were among the most exploited workers in the nation. Because they migrated from farm to farm—and often from state to state—to pick fruits and vegetables, they were known as **migrant farmworkers.** They labored for long hours in deplorable conditions, with no benefits.

In 1962, Chavez organized a farmworkers' union in Delano, California. In the late 1960s, he merged his union with a separate union of Filipino farm laborers to form what became the **United Farm Workers (UFW).**

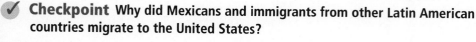

**HISTORY MAKERS**

DON'T BUY CALIFORNIA GRAPES!

**Cesar Chavez** (1927–1993)
Cesar Chavez spent his childhood and youth toiling, like his parents, as a migrant farmworker. In the 1950s, he trained to be a community organizer. His skills led him to be named chief of the group doing the training. In 1962, he formed the National Farm Workers Association. Migrant workers had tried to form unions before and failed; Chavez made the effort succeed. In an impassioned letter to the grape industry, he expressed the workers' suffering and determination. "We are men and women who have suffered and endured much," he wrote. "Generation after generation have sought to demoralize us, to break our human spirit. But God knows that we are not beasts of burden, agricultural implements or rented slaves; we are men."

Committed to nonviolent tactics, the UFW implemented a workers' strike and consumer boycott of table grapes. With the help of Dolores Huerta, Chavez's top aide, the UFW urged people across the nation to boycott California grapes in order to win recognition from the growers. In 1975, California passed a law requiring collective bargaining between growers and union representatives. Farmworkers finally had a legal basis to ask for better working conditions.

**The Chicano Movement Grows** While Chavez focused on farmworkers' rights, a broader Mexican American social and political effort grew, which came to be known as the **Chicano movement.** Part of it was dedicated to increasing Latinos' awareness of their history and culture. At California colleges and high schools, and in other states with a Mexican American population, Chicano students demanded that educators teach more about their heritage. Others in the movement focused on quality of life issues. For example, the National Council of La Raza was founded in 1968 with the goal of reducing poverty and discrimination and providing better opportunities for Latinos.

Much of the movement's energy was concentrated on attaining political strength for Latinos, or what some called "brown power." José Angel Gutiérrez organized the political party La Raza Unida in Texas. The party worked for better housing and jobs, and it successfully supported Latino political candidates. By 1980, six Hispanics sat in Congress, representing districts from New York to California. Moreover, Hispanics gained greater representation in state, county, and city governments.

✓ **Checkpoint** What were some of the demands of Latino groups in the 1960s and 1970s?

A worker picks strawberries at a California farm in 1963. ▼

**INFOGRAPHIC** 🔊 AUDIO

# Migrant Workers
## Seek A Living

In the 1960s, many Americans took for granted the availability of fresh fruits and vegetables in their supermarkets, even during the winter. This luxury was made possible by a group of hardworking and largely silent migrant farmworkers. Moving from farm to farm with the seasons, migrant farmworkers performed back-breaking labor for extremely low wages. They often worked in harsh conditions, without medical care, education for their children, or vacation. Even today, the majority of farmwork is done by migrant workers, often under similar conditions (see table above right).

Labels on produce crates showed stereotypical images of the Mexican farmworkers who harvested the crops. ▶

# Native Americans and Asian Americans Battle Discrimination

Native Americans had a long history of discrimination and suffered high rates of poverty, unemployment, and suicide. Inspired by the struggle for civil rights, they forged their own protest movements in the 1960s and 1970s. At the same time, Asian Americans fought long-standing discrimination.

**Activist Groups Form** As with the civil rights movement, the young took the lead in demanding change for American Indians. In 1961, the National Indian Youth Council (NIYC) formed, with the goal of preserving native fishing rights in the Northwest. Over time, the group expanded its aims to include broad civil rights for Native Americans. In 1968, the Chippewa activists Dennis Banks and George Mitchell founded the **American Indian Movement (AIM).** At first, AIM focused on helping Indians living in urban ghettos. Before long, however, AIM was addressing all civil rights issues, particularly the securing of land, legal rights, and self-government for Native Americans.

**Confronting the Government** As Indians' dissatisfaction with the government grew, their activism became more militant. In late 1969, a group of American Indians occupied the island of Alcatraz, the site of a federal prison in San Francisco Bay that had closed in 1963. Members of the Sioux tribe asserted that the island belonged to them under a treaty provision granting them unused federal land. About 100 American Indians representing 50 tribes joined the occupation. In spite of efforts by the Coast Guard and other federal authorities to evict them, the Indians maintained control of the island until mid-1971.

The 1970s saw another series of confrontations. Led by Dennis Banks and Russell Means, AIM orchestrated a "long march" from San Francisco to Washington, D.C., in 1972. Upon arriving in the capital, they took control

## Migrant Farmworkers Today

- 81 percent are foreign-born; of these, 77 percent are Mexican.
- 52 percent are illegal immigrants.
- The average migrant farmworker is a 31-year-old Spanish-speaking male.
- Half of all migrant farmworkers live far below the poverty level.
- The life expectancy for a migrant farmworker is 49 years.

SOURCE: U.S. Department of Labor; ERIC Digest

◀ Commercial farmers sprayed their crops with chemicals like DDT, exposing workers to serious health threats.

Many migrants call ▶ strawberries the "fruit of the devil" because picking them is difficult and low-paid work.

Mexican *bracero* workers toil in a California field in 1964. ▼

## Thinking Critically

1. **Synthesize Information** Study the table and the images. Why might the average lifespan of migrant farmworkers be only 49 years today?

2. **Contrast** How does the produce crate label contrast with the actual conditions of migrant farmworkers?

### Daniel Inouye (born 1924)

When Hawaii became a state in 1959, Daniel Inouye was elected its first representative to Congress. Three years later, he became the Senate's first Asian American. The son of Japanese immigrants, Inouye entered the army after the bombing of Pearl Harbor. He lost an arm in combat and received the Medal of Honor. Inouye graduated from law school before entering public office. In more than forty years in the Senate, Inouye, a Democrat, has championed the interests of Hawaiians as well as healthcare and education for all children.

### Ben Nighthorse Campbell (born 1933)

The son of a Portuguese immigrant mother and a Cheyenne Indian father, Ben Nighthorse Campbell joined the Air Force and served in the Korean War before entering college. In 1982, he was elected to the Colorado State Legislature. He went on to careers as a U.S. representative and then a senator. He did not run for reelection in 2005. Throughout his years in Congress, he worked for Native American rights and on policy relating to natural resources. Originally a Democrat, Campbell became a Republican in 1995.

of the Bureau of Indian Affairs building. They temporarily renamed it the Native American Embassy, suggesting Native Americans are treated as foreigners.

**Siege at Wounded Knee** In 1970, Dee Brown published *Bury My Heart at Wounded Knee,* about the 1890 massacre of Sioux at Wounded Knee, South Dakota. Brown noted that in all the history of the American West,

> **Primary Source** "Only occasionally was the voice of an Indian heard, and then more often than not it was recorded by the pen of a white man. The Indian was the dark menace of the myths, and even if he had known how to write in English, where would he have found a printer or a publisher?"

The best-selling book raised public consciousness about the historic mistreatment of Native Americans. Building on this momentum, AIM planned a dramatic confrontation at Wounded Knee. In late February of 1973, AIM took over the village and refused to leave until the government agreed to investigate the condition of reservation Indians. Federal authorities put Wounded Knee under siege, and two AIM members died in the resulting gunfire. The standoff ended in May when the government pledged to reexamine native treaty rights.

**Making Legal Headway** Native American activism spurred the passage of several laws in the 1970s. The Indian Self-Determination Act of 1975, for instance, fulfilled one of the main demands of the American Indian movement by granting tribes greater control over resources and education on reservations. Native Americans also continued to win legal battles to regain land, mineral, and water rights. Yet the protests staged by AIM and other militant groups also provoked a political backlash with some contending that the federal government gave special treatment to American Indians. While politicians debated how the government should treat Native Americans, the Indians themselves continued to suffer disproportionately from high rates of unemployment and other social ills.

**Asian Americans Fight Discrimination** Prejudice against people of Japanese and Chinese ancestry, who had come to the United States as laborers, had long been part of the American social and economic climate. The **Japanese American Citizens League,** founded in 1929 to protect Japanese Americans' civil rights, worked for decades to receive government compensation for property lost by Japanese Americans interned in camps during World War II. In the 1960s and 1970s, in the wake of the expanding rights revolution, many other groups formed to combat discrimination and protect the rights of all Asian Americans. The Immigration and Nationality Act Amendments (1965) also aided Asian immigrants.

## NoteTaking

**Reading Skill: Identify Causes**
Identify causes of expanding rights for Asian Americans, consumers and those with disabilities.

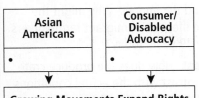

| Asian Americans | Consumer/ Disabled Advocacy |
|---|---|
| • | • |

**Growing Movements Expand Rights**

✔ **Checkpoint** Why did Native Americans work to expand their rights?

# New Rights for Consumers and the Disabled

In the same way that many activists worked to extend rights to women and minorities and to protect the environment, others worked to protect the rights of consumers and Americans with disabilities.

During the Progressive Era, reformers had pushed for measures to protect consumers, ranging from the Pure Food and Drug Act to the Meat Inspection Act. The consumer rights movement reemerged during the 1960s and 1970s. It was led by **Ralph Nader,** a lawyer who began to investigate whether flawed car designs led to increased traffic accidents and deaths. His book, *Unsafe at Any Speed* (1965), attacked automakers whose thirst for profits produced unsafe vehicles that endangered the public. Nader's best-selling book stirred the nation and prompted Congress to pass the National Traffic and Motor Vehicle Safety Act in 1966. Among other things, the act made safety belts standard equipment in all cars. Nader went on to form several consumer advocacy groups. Under his influence, consumer advocacy adopted many of the practices that shape it today, including research and government lobbying. Advocacy for workers began to gain more prominence as well. The Nixon administration proposed the idea for the Occupational Safety and Health Administration (OSHA), which mandated workplace safety regulations.

Historically, the nation had treated people with disabilities as defective. FDR hid the fact that he could not walk because he did not want society to assume he was incapable of serving as President. Yet by the 1970s, Americans with disabilities were making great strides toward expanding their rights. Disabled veterans from the Korean and Vietnam wars took part in this activism. The Kennedy administration called for change by establishing the Panel on Mental Retardation in 1961 to explore ways for the government to help people with intellectual disabilities. The next year, Eunice Shriver, Kennedy's sister, began an athletic camp for young people with disabilities that eventually became the Special Olympics. Over the next few years, the government passed several laws guaranteeing equal access to education for people with disabilities.

**A Winner**
A girl shows her sister the gold medal she won at a 2003 Special Olympics event in South Carolina.

✓ **Checkpoint** How did rights for consumers and people with disabilities expand during the 1960s and 1970s?

---

SECTION **3** **Assessment**

**Progress Monitoring *Online***
**For:** Self-test with vocabulary practice
**Web Code:** nea-1731

## Comprehension

1. **Terms and People** What is the relationship of each of the items below to Latino, Native American and Asian American movements for equality?
   - Cesar Chavez
   - migrant farmworker
   - UFW
   - Chicano movement
   - AIM
   - Japanese American Citizens League

2. **NoteTaking Reading Skill: Compare and Contrast** Use your completed Venn diagram to answer the Section Focus Question: How did the rights movements of the 1960s and 1970s expand rights for diverse groups of Americans?

## Writing About History

3. **Quick Write: Anticipate Opposing Arguments** Suppose that you are going to give a speech in support of making migrant farmworkers legal citizens with full benefits. Anticipate any opposing arguments, and note ways to address them in your speech.

## Critical Thinking

4. **Draw Inferences** How did the government make immigration for Latinos and Asians easier in the 1960s?

5. **Identify Central Issues** Why was it particularly important to Latino activists to gain political rights?

6. **Draw Comparisons** How and why was the Native American struggle for equality different from that of Latinos?

7. **Predict Consequences** Do you think rights for people with disabilities would have been achieved earlier if FDR had openly shown his disability? Explain.

▲ Rachel Carson

A 1962 cartoon shows a man choking on fumes from a pesticide he uses to kill a fly. ▶

WITNESS HISTORY 🔊 AUDIO

### An Environmental Wake-up Call

❝There once was a town in the heart of America where all life seemed to live in harmony with its surroundings. . . . Then a strange blight crept over the area and everything began to change. Mysterious maladies swept across the flocks of chickens; the cattle and sheep sickened and died. . . . There was a strange stillness. The birds, for example—where had they gone? . . . On the mornings that had once throbbed with the dawn chorus of robins, catbirds, doves, jays, wrens, and scores of other bird voices there was now no sound; only silence lay over the fields and woods and marsh. . . . No witchcraft, no enemy action had silenced the rebirth of new life in this stricken world. The people had done it to themselves. ❞

—Rachel Carson, *Silent Spring*, 1962

# The Environmental Movement

 **Content Expectations**

- **7.1.3** Explain/evaluate Roosevelt's New Deal policies.
- **8.2.2a** Describe issues challenging Americans.
- **8.2.4** Analyze competing perspectives/controversies among Americans generated by U.S. Supreme Court decisions.

## Terms and People

Rachel Carson        Clean Air Act
toxic waste          Clean Water Act
Earth Day            Endangered Species
EPA                      Act

## NoteTaking

**Reading Skill: Recognize Sequence** As you read, record major events in the environmental movement in a flowchart like the one below.

| Rachel Carson publishes *Silent Spring* in 1962. |
| :---: |

↓     ↓     ↓

| Americans celebrate the first Earth Day in 1970. |
| :---: |

↓     ↓     ↓

|  |
| :---: |

**Why It Matters** The "rights revolution" of the 1960s and 1970s eventually influenced all aspects of American life—including people's right to a clean and safe environment. The story told by **Rachel Carson** pointed out that human actions were harming not only the environment but people themselves. Public awareness of environmental issues prompted an important debate about the government's role in environmental regulations. **Section Focus Question: What forces gave rise to the environmental movement, and what impact did it have?**

# Environmental Activists Speak Out

In the 1920s, Progressives had worked to conserve public lands and parks. But no one thought to worry much about the ill effects of industrialization. In 1952, however, a blanket of deadly smog, caused by coal fires, engulfed the city of London, killing some 12,000 people. Ten years after the London smog, a book sparked the modern environmental movement.

***Silent Spring* Sparks a Movement** Coal smog is just one kind of **toxic waste,** or poisonous byproduct of human activity. Another is acid rain, or moisture in the air caused by the mixing of water with chemicals produced by the burning of fossil fuels. Toxic wastes are also produced when nuclear power is generated. Throughout the 1960s and 1970s, scientists learned more about toxic wastes and other environmental threats.

In 1962, biologist Rachel Carson's book *Silent Spring* described the deadly impact that pesticides were having on birds and other animals. Her book caused a sensation. Though the chemical industry fought back, the public was convinced by her argument. Carson did more than point to the dangers of chemicals and toxic waste. She also insisted that human activity drastically altered the environment and that humans had a responsibility to protect it. Her work eventually <u>compelled</u> Congress to restrict the use of the pesticide DDT. It also spurred widespread environmental activism among Americans.

When a fire erupted on the Cuyahoga River in Cleveland, Ohio, in 1969, activists instantly spoke out. The fire occurred when a spark ignited floating oil and debris—byproducts of industrialization—on the river's surface. *Time* magazine reported that the river "oozes, rather than flows." Even more luridly, the magazine remarked that in the Cuyahoga, a person "does not drown but decays."

**Inaugurating Earth Day** Events like the Cuyahoga fire seemed to confirm the dire predictions of *Silent Spring*. One response to growing environmental concerns was a nationwide protest called **Earth Day.** Wisconsin senator Gaylord Nelson, who played the leading role in organizing the protest, wanted "to shake up the political establishment and force this issue [environment] onto the national agenda." On April 22, 1970, close to 20 million Americans took part in Earth Day events across the nation. The yearly event attracted the support of many of the same people who had advocated civil and women's rights. It was also backed by a number of grassroots groups, including the Sierra Club, founded by John Muir in 1892, and the Wilderness Society, established in 1935. Historically, these groups had focused on conservation. With the rise of the environmental movement, however, they called for broader environmental protections.

**Vocabulary Builder**
<u>compel</u>–(kuhm PEHL) *v.* to force someone to do something

**Earth Day, Then and Now**
Students march through the streets of St. Louis on the first Earth Day to protest pollution caused by cars (left); students on Earth Day in 2005 rush to break a world record for the most trees planted in an hour.

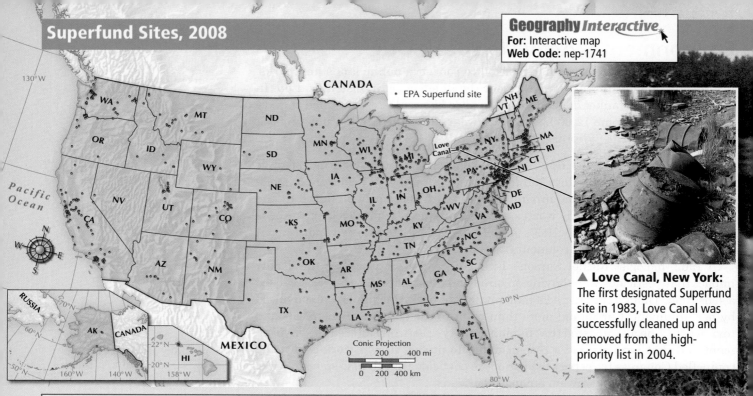

## Superfund Sites, 2008

**Geography** *Interactive*
For: Interactive map
Web Code: nep-1741

• EPA Superfund site

▲ **Love Canal, New York:** The first designated Superfund site in 1983, Love Canal was successfully cleaned up and removed from the high-priority list in 2004.

Conic Projection
0    200    400 mi
0  200  400 km

**Map Skills** In 1980, Congress established Superfund, a program financed by taxes on oil and certain chemicals, to clean up sites that had extreme environmental pollution. Today, more than 1,500 sites remain on the high-priority list.

1. **Identify** In general, where are most Superfund sites located? Why do you think this is so?

2. **Draw Inferences** Do sites in urban areas pose greater risks than sites in rural areas? Explain.

3. **Synthesize Information** Study the bar graph. What varied benefits does repurposing Superfund sites bring that would not be accomplished by just cleaning up the sites?

**A President Turns Environmentalist** In 1969, President Nixon declared that the 1970s "must be the years when America pays its debts to the past by reclaiming the purity of its air, its water and our living environment." Nixon had not come into office as an environmental activist. But the public's increasing concern with protecting the environment convinced him to support environmental reforms.

Under Nixon's leadership, Congress created the **Environmental Protection Agency (EPA)** in 1970. This federal agency's mission was to protect the "entire ecological chain." In addition to cleaning up and protecting the environment, the EPA sought to limit or to eliminate pollutants that posed a risk to the public's health, such as toxic substances that cause cancer. Nixon also signed a number of environmental laws. The **Clean Air Act** (1970) combated air pollution by, among other things, limiting the emissions from factories and automobiles. The **Clean Water Act** (1973) sought to limit the pollution of water by industry and agriculture. The **Endangered Species Act** (1973) promoted the protection of endangered plants and animals.

President Gerald Ford continued in Nixon's footsteps. In 1974, he created the Nuclear Regulatory Commission to make sure nuclear materials would be handled safely without harmful impacts on people or the environment.

✔ **Checkpoint** How did the modern environmental movement grow?

◀ **Bowers Landfill, Before Cleanup:** Bowers Landfill in Ohio was a municipal dump for garbage and hazardous chemical and industrial waste for several decades starting in the 1960s.

**Bowers Landfill, 1991:** After removing all of the contaminated soil, this site was completely restored for use as a wetland.

**Bowers Landfill, Today:** Wetlands provide a safe habitat for a variety of plants and wildlife, and they also protect the surrounding ecosystem by preventing flooding.

**Superfund Cleanup, 2004**

Superfund sites

- 1,750
- 1,500
- 1,250
- 1,000 (900)
- 750
- 500
- 250 (248)
- 0

Site cleanups completed | Sites restored for new uses

One of Superfund's goals is to restore sites in ways that provide economic or environmental benefits to communities.

# Environmental Setbacks

As the 1970s drew to a close, a series of environmental crises made the headlines. They reinforced the public's concern about the environment and produced calls for even more far-reaching actions. Yet, at the same time, a number of people began to wonder if the government had enacted too many regulations. Rather than calling for more federal action, they tried to limit the government's role in environmental protection.

**The EPA Investigates Love Canal** In 1978, a resident of Love Canal, a community near Niagara Falls in upstate New York, hung a sign from his home that read: "Give me Liberty. I've Already Got Death." This sign referred to the fact that residents of the community had exceptionally high rates of birth defects and cancer. Newspaper reporters and EPA investigators determined that these illnesses were caused by thousands of tons of toxic chemicals, which industries had been dumping in the ground for decades. One EPA administrator recalled the scene he witnessed following a heavy rain that sent toxic chemicals percolating up through the ground.

**Primary Source** "I visited the canal area at that time. Corroding waste-disposal drums could be seen breaking up through the grounds of backyards. Trees and gardens were turning black and dying. . . . Puddles of noxious substances were pointed out to me by the residents. Some of these puddles were in their yards, some were in their basements, others yet were on the school grounds. Everywhere the air had a faint, choking smell. Children returned from play with burns on their hands and faces."
—Eckhardt Beck, *EPA Journal*, 1979

The Love Canal contamination, along with other events involving hazardous waste, prompted Congress to establish Superfund (see feature at top) in 1980.

## TRACK THE ISSUE

**THE ESSENTIAL ?**

## How can we balance economic development and environmental protection?

The goals of economic growth and environmental protection are often in conflict. For example, power plants provide energy, but they pollute the air. Dams supply water, but they destroy natural habitats. Finding a balance between growth and conservation may involve trade-offs. Use the timeline below to explore this enduring issue.

 9.1.1

**1872 Yellowstone**
First national park is established.

**1916 National Park Service**
Congress creates the National Park System.

**1962 *Silent Spring***
Rachel Carson's book exposes dangers of pesticides.

**1970 Clean Air Act**
Congress establishes air quality standards.

**1973 Endangered Species Act**
Law offers protection for threatened species.

**1997 Kyoto Protocol**
United States signs international agreement on $CO_2$ emissions, but Congress fails to ratify it.

A herd of caribou grazes on a plain near an oil-drilling facility in Alaska.

## DEBATE THE ISSUE

**The Search for Oil** Alaska's Arctic National Wildlife Refuge (ANWR) is a large nature preserve with an abundance of wildlife. It may also contain large deposits of crude oil. Some people want to drill for this oil, while others believe oil drilling would ruin the pristine wilderness.

" . . . There are good reasons . . . to permit ANWR drilling. . . . It could be done without wrecking the environment. . . . Only 2,000 acres of the 19 million-acre ANWR refuge would be subject to drilling. . . . Drilling could create 250,000 to 735,000 jobs nationwide. . . . [Drilling] in an environmentally sensitive fashion is important insurance against future energy shocks."

—Editorial, *USA Today*, 2005

"Drilling in the Arctic Refuge is not a path to energy independence or lower prices at the pump. The United States Geological Survey estimates that the Refuge has less than a single year's supply of oil that would not reach the market for at least 10 years. Meanwhile, the harm to wildlife and to our greatest wildlife refuge would be irreparable."

—Defenders of Wildlife

## *TRANSFER* Activities

1. **Compare** Why does the first source support drilling in the arctic refuge? Why does Defenders of Wildlife oppose it?

2. **Analyze** How might the first source have responded to the creation of the National Park Service in 1916? Explain.

3. **Transfer** Use the following Web site to see a video, try a WebQuest, and write in your journal. **Web Code:** neh-9002

A view of Yellowstone's Grand Canyon painted in 1872

**Meltdown at Three Mile Island** Shortly after the investigation at Love Canal, an accident occurred in the nuclear energy industry. On March 28, 1979, the core of the nuclear reactor at Three Mile Island outside Harrisburg, Pennsylvania, began to melt after the reactor malfunctioned. When the plant threatened to release radioactive gas, the governor declared a state of emergency and shut it down. To reassure the public that plant managers had contained the accident, President Jimmy Carter and his wife traveled to Three Mile Island and toured the reactor.

Even though the incident was contained and there proved to be no health risks, it had profound effects on America's energy policy. In the wake of the accident, Americans opposed nuclear energy, fearful of possible disasters. The government temporarily stopped building new nuclear power plants. Even though it later lifted the ban, no new American nuclear plants were ordered for more than a quarter of a century. In the 2000s, with energy shortages, many Americans began to call for building new nuclear plants.

**Questioning Environmental Regulation** As more environmental regulations were passed, opposition to them grew. Conservatives complained that they stripped individuals of their property rights by restricting what they could or could not do with their land. Some argued that private property owners would do a better job of protecting the environment than the government because the owners had an interest in preserving the profitability of their land. Many people—and especially industry leaders—also worried that too much environmental regulation would hamper business and jobs by diverting funds to cleaning up the air and water. Therefore, as the 1970s came to a close, Americans remained divided about what role the government should play in regulating industry and protecting the environment.

 **Checkpoint** Why did some people oppose the environmental movement?

---

**Progress Monitoring *Online***
For: Self-test with vocabulary practice
Web Code: nea-1741

## Comprehension

1. **Terms and People** For each item below, write a sentence explaining how it helped expand a right or provide a protection.
   • Rachel Carson
   • Earth Day
   • EPA
   • Clean Air Act
   • Clean Water Act
   • Endangered Species Act

2. **NoteTaking Reading Skill: Recognize Sequence** Use your completed flowchart to answer the Section Focus Question: What forces gave rise to the environmental movement, and what impact did it have?

## Writing About History

3. **Quick Write: Organize the Material** You need to give a speech describing environmental problems in your region and how they could affect the local economy. Outline topics and arguments, remembering to begin with a strong argument or a personal story and to end with your most compelling argument.

## Critical Thinking

4. **Recognize Cause and Effect** How did Rachel Carson's concern about DDT spark the environmental movement?

5. **Make Comparisons** How did the goals and tactics of the environmental movement compare with those of the women's movement?

6. **Identify Assumptions** What basic assumptions about the environment did opponents to environmental regulation have?

# Quick Study Guide

 8.3.4

**Progress Monitoring *Online***
For: Self-test with vocabulary practice
Web Code: nea-1751

## Rights-Expanding Legislation

| | |
|---|---|
| Equal Rights Amendment (ERA) (First proposed 1921; never passed) | Proposed constitutional amendment to guarantee gender equality |
| Panel on Mental Retardation (1961) | Explored ways the government could help people with disabilities |
| Title VII of the Civil Rights Act (1964) | Outlawed sex-based discrimination |
| Immigration and Nationality Act (1965) | Eased restrictions, making immigration easier for Latinos and Asians |
| National Traffic and Motor Vehicle Safety Act (1966) | Mandated safety equipment in cars |
| Environmental Protection Agency (1970) | Established to clean up degraded environments and to prevent further contamination |
| Clean Air Act (1970) | Limited emissions from factories and cars |
| Clean Water Act (1973) | Limited pollution of water by industry and agriculture |
| Endangered Species Act (1973) | Protected endangered plants and animals |
| Indian Self-Determination Act (1975) | Gave Native Americans control over resources on reservations |

## Major Activists and Groups

| Activist/Group | Goal |
|---|---|
| Betty Friedan/National Organization of Women (NOW) | Win true equality for all women; pass ERA; make abortion legal |
| Phyllis Schlafly | Defeat the ERA |
| Cesar Chavez/United Farm Workers | Obtain better working conditions for migrant farmworkers |
| National Council of La Raza | Reduce Latino discrimination |
| La Raza Unida | Support Latino political candidates; obtain better jobs and housing for Latinos |
| Dennis Banks/American Indian Movement (AIM) | Secure legal rights and self-government for Native Americans |
| Rachel Carson | Publicize dangers of chemicals to environment |
| Ralph Nader | Enact legislation and regulations to protect consumers |
| Japanese American Citizens League | Secure civil rights for Japanese Americans |

## Influence of the Civil Rights Movement

**The Civil Rights Movement**

- African Americans push for legal and social equality.
- Groups use different tactics, including protesting, raising social consciousness, and working for political and legal change.
- Important legislation is passed, including the Civil Rights Act of 1964.

→

**The Civil Rights Movement Influences Other Protest Movements**

**Goals**
- Women, Latinos, Native Americans, Asian Americans, and people with disabilities push for legal and social equality.
- Environmental and consumer groups demand legal changes.

**Tactics**
- Women, Latinos, Native Americans, and environmentalists use civil rights protest tactics to support their own causes.

## ☑ Quick Study Timeline

**In America**

| 1962 | 1963 | 1966 | 1969 |
|---|---|---|---|
| Rachel Carson's *Silent Spring* launches environmental movement | Betty Friedan publishes *The Feminine Mystique* | United Farm Workers union is formed | Woodstock festival celebrates the counter-culture |

**Presidential Terms**  John F. Kennedy 1961–1963  Lyndon B. Johnson 1963–1969

**1960**  **1964**  **1968**

**Around the World**

| 1960 | 1963 | 1966 |
|---|---|---|
| Ceylon (now Sri Lanka) elects world's first female prime minister | Soviet cosmonaut Valentina Tereshkova becomes first woman in space | Indira Gandhi becomes India's first female prime minister |

# American Issues
●—●—●—● **Connector**

By connecting prior knowledge with what you have learned in this chapter, you can gradually build your understanding of enduring questions that still affect America today. Answer the questions below. Then, use your American Issues Connector study guide (or go online: www.PHSchool.com Web Code: neh-9003).

## Issues You Learned About

● **Interaction With the Environment** The federal government seeks to balance environmental conservation with development.

1. How did John Muir and Theodore Roosevelt contribute to the early conservation movement in the United States?

2. Give three examples of human activities that have harmed the environment.

3. Give three examples of the way individuals or the government have tried to protect the environment.

● **Women in American Society** Women's movements have organized to demand greater equality in American society.

4. Describe the first wave of feminism, including its leaders and its goals.

5. Explain the goals of the second wave of feminism.

6. What are some reasons that the average woman continues to earn less than the average man?

● **U.S. Immigration Policy** The country's immigration laws change over time, often in response to outside influences.

7. In the past, Congress has passed laws preventing people from certain countries from immigrating to the United States. Identify one of these laws, its provisions, and the people against whom it was directed.

8. Why was the *bracero* program initiated in 1942?

9. What happened as a result of the Immigration and Nationality Acts Amendments?

### Connect to Your World | Michigan

**Interaction with the Environment** On July 27, 1970, Michigan governor William Milliken signed the Michigan Environmental Protection Act (MEPA) into law. The new law allowed individuals and organizations to take an active role in protecting the state's natural resources by filing lawsuits against polluters. Many citizens did just that. In the late 1970s, a citizen lawsuit under MEPA successfully prevented Shell Oil from drilling in the Pigeon River Country State Forest. MEPA's success made it a model for environmental legislation, and nine other states passed similar laws. Do research and create a brief radio, television, or Internet news report about the history of MEPA from 1970 until today.

**1970**
EPA is established

**1973**
Supreme Court legalizes abortion in *Roe* v. *Wade*; AIM confronts government at Wounded Knee

**1979**
Nuclear disaster occurs at Three Mile Island

| Richard M. Nixon 1969–1974 | Gerald R. Ford 1974–1977 | Jimmy Carter 1977–1981 |
|---|---|---|
| **1972** | **1976** | **1980** |

**1971**
Environmental group Greenpeace founded in Vancouver, Canada

**1973**
American involvement in Vietnam War ends

**History Interactive**
**For:** Interactive timeline
**Web Code:** nep-1751

# Chapter Assessment

## Terms and People

Match the following definitions with the items below.

| | |
|---|---|
| counterculture | migrant farmworker |
| generation gap | Chicano movement |
| feminism | toxic waste |

1. The _____ sought to raise cultural awareness among Latinos.

2. Members of the _____ promoted the sexual revolution.

3. Acid rain and the byproducts of nuclear power are examples of _____.

4. The baby boomers' rejection of traditional values set them apart from the older generation, creating a _____.

5. Phyllis Schlafly opposed _____ because she believed it hurt families.

6. Cesar Chavez led a movement to improve working conditions for the _____.

## Focus Questions

The focus question for this chapter is **How did the counterculture and the expanding rights revolution of the 1960s and 1970s influence American society?** Build an answer to this big question by answering the focus questions for Sections 1 through 4 and the Critical Thinking questions that follow.

### Section 1
7. What was the counterculture, and what impact did it have on American society?

### Section 2
8. What led to the rise of the women's movement, and what impact did it have on American society?

### Section 3
9. How did the rights movements of the 1960s and 1970s expand rights for diverse groups of Americans?

### Section 4
10. What forces gave rise to the environmental movement, and what impact did it have?

## Critical Thinking

11. **Recognize Ideologies** How did rock and folk music become, in the words of the musician John Sinclair, "a weapon of cultural revolution"?

12. **Synthesize Information** What underlying problem in American society did the rights movements of the 1960s and 1970s address?

13. **Make Comparisons** How were the lasting effects of the counterculture similar to and different from those of the other rights movements discussed in this chapter?

14. **Analyzing Visuals** Use information from the chapter to explain the data on the graph below.

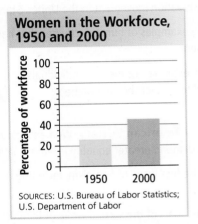

**Women in the Workforce, 1950 and 2000**

SOURCES: U.S. Bureau of Labor Statistics; U.S. Department of Labor

15. **Predict Consequences** Would the rights movements of the 1960s and 1970s have been as successful without the examples of civil rights activists? Explain.

16. **Geography and History** Why was geography a central issue of the Native American movement but not of the other rights movements?

## Writing About History

**Writing a Persuasive Speech** During the 1960s, many people used speeches to draw attention to their causes. Write a persuasive speech from the point of view of one of these people discussed in the chapter: Betty Friedan, Phyllis Schlafly, Cesar Chavez, Dennis Banks, Ralph Nader, or Rachel Carson. Deliver your completed speech to a classmate or to the entire class.

### Prewriting
- Choose the person who most interests you. Take notes about the person's motivations and methods.
- Identify the venue where the speech will be delivered, as well as its audience.

### Drafting
- Develop a thesis, and choose information to support it.
- List arguments that support your thesis, and answer opposing arguments.
- Write the speech, remembering to open with an attention-grabbing statement and to end with your strongest argument.

### Revising
- Use the guidelines on page SH16 of the Writing Handbook to revise your speech.

# Prepare for the MME

## The Voting Rights Act

In 1965, Congress passed the Voting Rights Act, removing the barriers that had kept African Americans disenfranchised. In 1975, Congress amended the act to address voting barriers related to Latino and Native American voters. Section 203 of the law required that voting materials be published in languages other than English in certain areas. Section 5 required that certain counties with a history of discrimination pre-clear any voting changes with the U.S. Department of Justice. Use your knowledge of the civil rights movement and Documents A, B, C, and D to answer questions 1 through 4.

### Document A

Citizens of language minorities have been effectively excluded from participation in the electoral process. Among other factors, the denial of the right to vote of such minority group citizens is ordinarily directly related to the unequal educational opportunities afforded them resulting in high illiteracy and low voting participation. . . . The requirements of the law are straightforward: all election information that is available in English must also be available in the minority language so that all citizens will have an effective opportunity to register, learn the details of the elections, and cast a free and effective ballot.

—*From Section 203 of the Voting Rights Act, 1975*

### Document B

I'm a naturalized citizen now, born in the Philippines and it just put a smile to my face as well as the rest of the people in our household when we get those ballots in Tagalog. We DON'T even have those in the country I came from so the more I appreciate all the efforts of you guys put into making sure every eligible citizen [is] able to understand and get informed with regards to all the candidates and all the measures by sending them tools in their native languages. America is truly the best country in the world to live in. . . . Proud to be a U.S. Citizen. . . . Thanks to all of you and keep up the good work.

—*A voter from San Diego County, California*

### Document C

This nation is still subject to the problem that Section 5 was developed to address. Even today, many jurisdictions still respond to growth in minority political power by restricting minority political opportunity. In Texas and Arizona, for example, the Justice Department continues to interpose a significant number of objections; the deterrent effect of Section 5 stops many discriminatory election changes before they are enacted by covered jurisdictions. Despite what you may hear from opponents of the Voting Rights Act, the emergency that led to the adoption of Section 5 has not passed. Latino voters have not yet closed the gap in voter registration and turnout in the Southwest. . . . I urge you today to reauthorize Section 5 with language clarifying congressional intent to prohibit intentional discrimination and to restore ability to elect. . . .

—*Nina Perales, counsel to the Mexican American Legal Defense and Education Fund, 2005*

### Document D

1. Document B supports the purpose and outcome of which other document?
   A Document A
   B Document C
   C Document D
   D none of the documents

2. In Document C, a lawyer testifies before Congress, urging it to
   A change key provisions of the Voting Rights Act.
   B disallow the Voting Rights Act.
   C reauthorize the Voting Rights Act.
   D amend the Voting Rights Act so that it applies to only Native Americans.

3. In Document D, what is the cartoonist's opinion about American political parties and Latino voting rights?
   A The Democrats alone are concerned about Latino voting rights.
   B The Republicans alone are concerned about Latino voting rights.
   C Both parties are concerned about Latino voting rights.
   D Neither party is concerned about Latino voting rights.

4. **Writing Task** Explain why Latinos have focused on expanding voter participation, the obstacles they have faced, and the successes they have had. Use the documents on this page, along with material from the chapter, to support your assessment.

## A Long National Nightmare

In the late summer of 1974, President Richard Nixon's resignation ended the drawn-out Watergate scandal. However, the nation still reeled from the shadow that Watergate had cast on its President. New President Gerald Ford attempted to set a new tone for the troubled nation:

"My fellow Americans, our long national nightmare is over. Our Constitution works; our great Republic is a government of laws and not of men. . . . As we bind up the internal wounds of Watergate, more painful and more poisonous than those of foreign wars, let us restore the golden rule to our political process, and let brotherly love purge our hearts of suspicion and of hate."

—President Gerald Ford, August 9, 1974

*Listen to the* Witness History *audio to learn more about Nixon's resignation.*

◄ Two tourists in front of the White House read headlines announcing Nixon's intention to resign on August 8, 1974.

Yellow ribbon symbolizing the hope that hostages held in Iran would return home safely

Tape recorder used by President Nixon in the Oval Office

 **Content Expectations**

**Chapter Focus Question:** What caused Americans to suffer a crisis of confidence during the 1970s?

### Section 1
**Nixon and the Watergate Scandal**   8.3.4, 8.3.1b, 8.3.1c

### Section 2
**The Ford and Carter Years**   8.2.2a, 9.1.1, 9.1.2b

### Section 3
**Foreign Policy Troubles**   8.1.2e, 8.1.3, 8.2.3

Sign on a Volkswagen Beetle announces a gas shortage

Use the ☑ **Quick Study Timeline** at the end of this chapter to preview chapter events.

**Note Taking Study Guide** *Online*
**For:** Note Taking and American Issues Connector
**Web Code:** nee-9101

WITNESS HISTORY 🔊 AUDIO

## The Watergate Tapes

Not long after President Nixon's 1972 reelection, the huge Watergate scandal began to unfold. The root of the scandal was a break-in at the Democratic Party's headquarters in Washington, D.C. Tapes of White House conversations later revealed that Richard Nixon and his top aides had tried to cover up the break-in:

❝**H. R. Haldeman [assistant to the President]:**
Now, on the investigation, you know, the Democratic break-in thing, we're back to the—in the problem area because the FBI is not under control, because [FBI Director L. Patrick] Gray doesn't exactly know how to control them [his agents]. . . . [The] way to handle this now is for us to have [Deputy CIA Director] Walters call Pat Gray and just say, 'Stay . . . out of this.' . . .
**President Nixon:** You call them in. . . . Play it tough. That's the way they play it and that's the way we are going to play it.❞
—Taped conversation, Oval Office, White House, June 23, 1972

▲ Nixon and aide H. R. Haldeman

# Nixon and the Watergate Scandal

**MI Content Expectations**

- **8.3.4** Evaluate major accomplishments/setbacks in civil rights/liberties for U.S. minorities.
- **8.3.1b** Analyze Supreme Court decisions/governmental actions during Civil Rights Movement.
- **8.3.1c** Analyze protest movements, organizations, civil actions.

## Terms and People

silent majority
stagflation
OPEC
southern strategy

affirmative action
Watergate
Twenty-fifth Amendment
executive privilege

## NoteTaking

**Reading Skill: Identify Main Ideas** Record Nixon's major domestic policies and goals in a chart like the one below.

| Nixon's Domestic Policies and Strategies ||
| --- | --- |
| New Federalism | Southern Strategy |
|  |  |

**Why It Matters** President Richard Nixon stood at the summit of his long government career when he was reelected President in a landslide in November 1972. Yet, less than two years later, Nixon left office in disgrace, the first time a President of the United States had resigned. The Watergate scandal gripped the nation and shaped the values and attitudes toward government that many Americans hold today. **Section Focus Question: What events led to Richard Nixon's resignation as President in 1974?**

## Nixon's Policies Target Middle America

Richard Nixon's political career had more ups and downs than a roller coaster ride. Brought up in hard times, he worked his way through college and law school. After service in the navy during World War II, Nixon was elected to the House of Representatives in 1946 and then to the Senate in 1950. As Dwight Eisenhower's running mate in 1952, he became Vice President with Eisenhower's victory. Nixon was not yet 40 years old.

Then came the defeats. In 1960, Nixon narrowly lost to John F. Kennedy in the race for the White House. Two years later, Nixon's career hit bottom when he lost an election to become governor of California. In 1968, however, Nixon made a dramatic comeback, narrowly defeating Democrat Hubert Humphrey to win the presidency.

**Nixon Calls for a "New Federalism"** During the campaign for President, Nixon cast himself as the spokesperson for those he called Middle Americans, or the **silent majority.** As Nixon put it at the 1968 Republican convention, he sought to speak for the "non-shouters, the non-demonstrators," the men and women who "work in America's factories . . . run America's businesses . . . serve in the Government . . . provide most of the soldiers . . . [and] give life to the American dream."

Winning the support of Middle America proved a tricky task. Nixon believed that Americans had tired of the "big" government of Lyndon Johnson's Great Society. However, he also believed that the American people still wanted the government to address various social ills, ranging from crime to <u>pollution</u>.

Nixon's solution was to call for the establishment of a "new federalism." As he explained in his 1971 State of the Union address, the nation needed "to reverse the flow of power and resources from the States and communities to Washington and start power and resources flowing back from Washington to the States and communities." Nixon proposed revenue sharing with the states. Under revenue sharing, the federal government gave the states the money to fund social programs. The states then controlled the operations of these programs.

**Nixon Expands the Government's Role** However, while returning power and money to the states, Nixon also sponsored many programs that increased the size and role of the federal government. During his presidency, a number of powerful new federal agencies and laws came into existence. The Occupational Safety and Health Administration (OSHA) regulates workplaces to make them safer for workers. The DEA, or Drug Enforcement Administration, administers the federal war against illegal drugs. The Environmental Protection Agency (EPA) enforces federal environmental standards. The Clean Air Act, signed into law in 1970, gives the EPA the power to set air quality standards.

Nixon's welfare policies also reflected his complicated domestic strategy. To decrease the power of the federal government, Nixon began to dismantle the Office of Economic Opportunity, the cornerstone of Lyndon Johnson's "war on poverty." Yet, Nixon also proposed creating a Family Assistance Plan (FAP), which called for providing a guaranteed or minimum income to every American family. Although the FAP did not become law, federal spending on other social welfare programs, such as Medicare and public housing, grew steadily, especially during Nixon's early years.

**The Economy Struggles** As his presidency progressed, Nixon grappled with an increasingly troublesome economy. After decades of strong growth and low inflation, the U.S. economy experienced both recession and inflation at the same time. These symptoms began during the Johnson administration, but they grew stronger during the Nixon years. The combination of recession and inflation baffled economists and led them to coin a new term, **stagflation,** to describe the dual conditions of a stagnating economy and inflationary pressures.

Stagflation had several causes. Expanding federal budget deficits caused by the Vietnam War produced inflation. Another cause was rising foreign competition, which cost thousands of Americans their jobs. Heavy industries such as steel and auto production, which had enjoyed a dominant position since World War II, proved especially vulnerable to foreign competition. Yet

### An Overwhelming Wave

While inflation drove prices up, most workers' wages stayed the same, causing the money they earned to buy fewer necessary goods. *How would high unemployment make the situation shown in the cartoon even worse?*

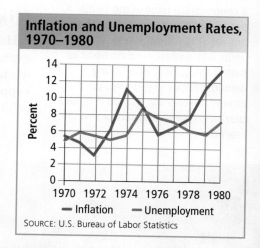

**Inflation and Unemployment Rates, 1970–1980**

SOURCE: U.S. Bureau of Labor Statistics

THE NIXON WAVE

the factor that caused most Americans pain was the rapid increase in the price of oil.

During the 1973 Arab war against Israel, the **Organization of Petroleum Exporting Countries (OPEC),** a group of mostly Arab countries that sells oil to other nations and cooperates to regulate the price and supply of oil, placed an embargo on Israel's allies, including the United States. Dependent on imports for nearly one-thirds of their energy, Americans soon felt the sting of this embargo as oil prices skyrocketed 400 percent in a single year. The embargo lasted until the spring of 1974 and resulted in gas lines at the pumps that stretched for blocks. With the end of the embargo, gas prices remained high.

Nixon fought stagflation in a variety of ways. Most dramatically, in August 1971, he placed a 90-day freeze on all wages and prices. The controls worked for a short time, causing a spurt of economic growth. However, price controls do not work well in a free economy, and the economy went into a tailspin in the mid-1970s.

 **Checkpoint** What was the goal of President Nixon's "new federalism"?

## Nixon Follows a Southern Strategy

Having narrowly won the presidency in 1968, Richard Nixon set out to expand his base of support. He targeted blue-collar workers and southern whites, both of whom had traditionally voted for Democrats. By winning the support of southern whites, Nixon hoped to make the Republican Party a powerful force in the South. Commentators called this Nixon's **southern strategy.**

### Turmoil Over Busing

Court-ordered busing continued to be a controversial issue in the 1970s. A police escort (left) protects a school bus carrying African American students into a white neighborhood as part of the busing. Anti-busing demonstrations (right) went on around the country. *Why do you think that busing provoked such a strong reaction?*

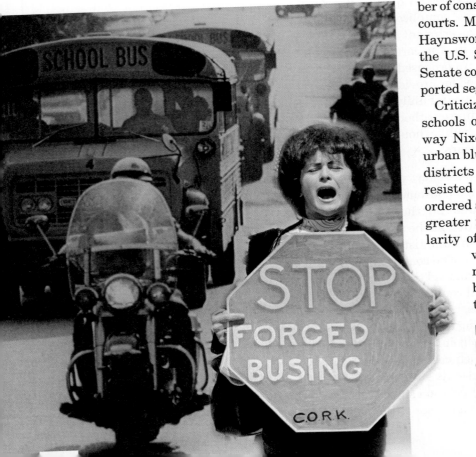

**Controversy Rages Over Busing** As part of his southern strategy, Nixon tried to place a number of conservative southerners as judges in federal courts. Most prominently, he nominated Clement Haynsworth and G. Harrold Carswell to serve on the U.S. Supreme Court. Both men failed to win Senate confirmation, in part because both had supported segregation in the past.

Criticizing court-ordered busing of children to schools outside their neighborhood was another way Nixon reached out to southern whites and urban blue-collar workers. For years, many school districts in both the South and the North had resisted desegregation. In 1971, federal courts ordered school districts to bus students to achieve greater racial balance. Recognizing the unpopularity of busing, Nixon made a nationally televised address in which he called for a moratorium, or freeze, on court-ordered busing. By speaking forcefully, Nixon won the support of many busing opponents.

**Nixon Proposes New Civil Rights Initiatives** Yet, as with much else that he did, Nixon's stance on civil rights was mixed. In 1969, the Nixon administration initiated the Philadelphia Plan, a program that required labor unions and federal contractors to submit goals and timetables for the hiring of minorities. It was a type of **affirmative action,** a policy that gives special consideration to women and minorities in the fields of education and employment, in order to make up for past discrimination. Nixon's Assistant Secretary of Labor, Arthur Fletcher, who designed the Philadelphia Plan, argued:

### Primary Source

"The Federal Government has an obligation to see that every citizen has an equal chance at the most basic freedom of all—the right to succeed. . . . Segregation didn't occur naturally—it was imposed. . . . The gap . . . between black and white . . . was growing wider and wider. . . . Visible, measurable goals to correct [these] imbalances are essential."
—Arthur Fletcher, Assistant Secretary of Labor, speech on affirmative action, 1969

**Nixon's Strategy Succeeds** By the 1972 election, Nixon enjoyed high approval ratings. Some of this popularity was based on his trips to the Soviet Union and China. Some was based on his domestic policies.

Nixon ran a masterful political campaign in 1972, positioning himself as a moderate. He portrayed his opponents—George McGovern, an antiwar senator from South Dakota, and Alabama governor George Wallace—as extremists. (Wallace's campaign was cut short when he was shot and left paralyzed by a would-be assassin.) Nixon and his Vice President, Spiro Agnew, successfully cast themselves as spokespersons for the silent majority. On election day, Nixon won almost 61 percent of the popular vote and nearly all of the electoral votes. He became the first Republican presidential candidate to sweep the entire South.

✔ **Checkpoint** In what ways did Nixon appear to send mixed messages about civil rights?

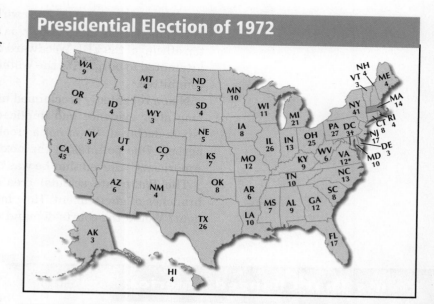

## Presidential Election of 1972

| Candidate (Party) | Electoral Vote | Popular Vote | % Electoral Vote | % Popular Vote |
|---|---|---|---|---|
| Richard M. Nixon (Republican) | 520 | 46,740,323 | 96.7 | 60.7 |
| George S. McGovern (Democratic) | 17 | 28,901,598 | 3.1 | 37.5 |
| Other | 1 | 1,341,502 | 0.2 | 1.7 |

*One elector from Virginia voted for John Hospers (Libertarian)
†McGovern received 3 electoral votes from Washington, D.C.

# The Watergate Scandal Brings Nixon Down

As a triumphant Richard Nixon stood before the cameras on election night 1972, he had no idea that the seeds of his downfall had already begun to sprout. The botched burglary of Democratic Party headquarters at the Watergate complex in June 1972 received little attention at first. But as investigators began to unravel the connections between the burglars and the White House, **Watergate,** as the scandal become known, came to dominate the national news.

The Watergate burglars were tried in 1973. After the trial, one of them, James McCord, charged that administration officials had been involved in the break-in. This led to a Senate investigation and to televised hearings, where numerous witnesses charged that the President and his top aides had taken part in a coverup. From the first news of the break-in, President Nixon denied any wrongdoing. Yet, as time went on, investigators discovered important links between the burglars and top Nixon administration officials.

**Watergate Goes Public** Two young *Washington Post* journalists, Bob Woodward and Carl Bernstein, played a <u>crucial</u> role in lifting the veil of secrecy from

## NoteTaking

**Reading Skill: Identify Causes and Effects** Use a chart like the one below to record the causes and effects of the Watergate crisis.

| Watergate Crisis | |
|---|---|
| **Causes** | **Effects** |
| • Break-in at Democratic Party headquarters<br>• | • Connections revealed between burglars and White House<br>• |

**Vocabulary Builder**
<u>crucial</u>–(KROO shuhl) *adj.* of vital importance

the Watergate scandal. The two reporters followed tips provided by a secret government informant known as "Deep Throat," who was later revealed to be a top official of the FBI. Woodward and Bernstein reported that the men, who had attempted to burglarize the Watergate hotel, had close ties to Nixon's reelection committee.

Nixon repeatedly proclaimed his innocence. For example, in November 1973, long after evidence had implicated his top aides and forced them to resign, Nixon declared, "I am not a crook." Yet the polls indicated that the public disagreed. One poll, taken the next month, showed that fewer than one in five Americans believed that he was being honest about the Watergate affair.

The Watergate scandal created a historic showdown between the three branches of government. How far would Congress go to investigate the President? Would the courts demand that the President turn over information that

**Events That Changed America**

# WATERGATE FORCES NIXON FROM OFFICE

One of the biggest political scandals in American history, Watergate has become synonymous with corruption and abuse of power. It began when President Nixon's reelection committee tried to record the conversations of political opponents, led to a string of coverups at the highest levels of the U.S. government, and ultimately forced Nixon from office. Nixon's role in the coverup shocked the nation.

The public might never have learned of the President's actions without the investigative reporting of journalists Bob Woodward and Carl Bernstein of the *Washington Post,* who broke the story in a series of articles. Their revelations, and those of other reporters, may have left the American people's faith in government shaken, but the aftermath reinforced the public's trust in the constitutional system.

**June 1972**
Five men linked to President Nixon's reelection campaign are arrested for trying to bug the offices of the Democratic National Committee in the Watergate complex (shown here) in Washington, D.C.

**April 1973** Nixon denies knowledge of the Watergate break-in or any coverup.

**May 1973** Archibald Cox is named as the Justice Department's special prosecutor for Watergate. The Senate Watergate Committee begins nationally televised hearings.

**June 1973**
Former White House counsel John Dean (right) tells investigators that Nixon authorized a coverup.

◄ Members of Congress hold a news conference about the scandal in May 1974.

might implicate him? And if the courts sided with Congress, would the President comply with its decisions?

**Revealing the White House Tapes** The Watergate scandal came to a climax with a dizzying array of developments. In the fall of 1973, Vice President Spiro Agnew resigned in the face of an unrelated corruption scandal. According to the procedures established by the **Twenty-fifth Amendment,** which deals with presidential succession, Nixon nominated Gerald Ford to become his new Vice President. Nixon's troubles multiplied when, in the summer of 1973, it was revealed that he had been secretly taping Oval Office conversations for many years. Many commentators speculated that these tapes would show that the President had played a leading role in trying to cover up the break-in.

▼ James McCord demonstrates a phone wiretap.

**July 1973** Nixon, claiming executive privilege, refuses to release the tapes of secretly recorded Oval Office conversations.

**October 1973** Nixon offers investigators summaries of tapes, which Special Prosecutor Cox refuses. Nixon fires Cox. This triggers other firings and resignations in what becomes known as the Saturday Night Massacre.

**March 1974** Former Nixon administration officials are indicted on charges of conspiracy in the Watergate break-in. Richard Nixon is named as an "unindicted co-conspirator."

**July 1974** The Supreme Court rules unanimously that Nixon must surrender all of the White House recordings requested by the new special prosecutor. The House Judiciary Committee recommends impeachment.

**August 1974** Transcripts of tapes show that Nixon ordered a coverup of the Watergate break-in. On August 9, Nixon becomes first U.S. President to resign.

## Why It Matters
While Watergate damaged the public's trust of government officials, the U.S. government's system of checks and balances withstood the crisis. Lawmakers passed laws to prevent similar abuses from happening. The role of the press in bringing the scandal to light reminded the public of the importance of a free press in a democratic society.

Journalists Bernstein ▶ (left) and Woodward (right) with *Washington Post* publisher Katharine Graham

## Public Trust in the Federal Government, 1964–1992

Percentage of Americans who trust the federal government*

| | |
|---|---|
| 80 | |
| 60 | |
| 40 | |
| 20 | |
| 0 | |
| 1964 1968 1972 1976 1980 1984 1988 1992 | |

SOURCE: The American National Election Studies
*Most of the time

## Thinking Critically
How did Congress and the Supreme Court balance the role of the executive branch during the Watergate crisis?

**History *Interactive* ***
**For:** More information about Watergate
**Web Code:** nep-1802

Nixon refused to turn over these tapes to the special prosecutor investigating the scandal. The President justified withholding the tapes by claiming **executive privilege.** Executive privilege is the principle that the President has the right to keep certain information confidential. It took almost a year for the courts to sort out the matter. On July 24, 1974, in the case of *United States* v. *Nixon,* the Supreme Court disagreed that the tapes fell under the principle of executive privilege and ordered Nixon to turn them over. Chief Justice Warren Burger made it clear that the Court rejected Nixon's claim of executive privilege in this instance:

**Primary Source**  "The expectation of a President to the confidentiality of his conversations and correspondence . . . has all the values to which we accord deference for the privacy of all citizens. . . . But this presumptive privilege must be considered in light of our historic commitment to the rule of law [the principle that all citizens are bound by the same laws]. . . . The very integrity of the judicial system and public confidence in the system depend on full disclosure of all the facts, within the framework of the rules of evidence."
—U.S. Supreme Court, *United States* v. *Nixon,* 1974

**Nixon Resigns** When investigators listened to the tapes, they found that crucial parts of the conversations were missing. Nixon claimed his secretary had mistakenly erased them. Still, the tapes provided enough evidence of Nixon's involvement in the coverup to lead the Judiciary Committee of the House of Representatives to vote to impeach the President. The committee charged Nixon with obstructing justice in the coverup of the Watergate break-in, misuse of power, and refusing to comply with House subpoenas. A number of Republican committee members joined the Democrats in voting for impeachment.

Recognizing that the full House of Representatives would vote in favor of impeachment and that many Republicans would vote to convict him in a trial in the Senate, Nixon decided to resign. In a speech to the American public on August 8, 1974, Nixon informed the nation that he would step down the following day in the hope that he "will have hastened the start of that process of healing which is so desperately needed in America." The long ordeal of Watergate had finally come to an end. With it, Nixon became the first and only President to resign the presidency.

Historians disagree about whether Nixon knew beforehand of the decision to burglarize Democratic Party headquarters. However, few doubt that he took part in the coverup. Testimony by his top aides, the Watergate tapes, and evidence gathered in the prosecution of the burglars all show that the President sought to quash the investigation.

Moreover, investigations revealed that Nixon had committed other abuses of presidential power. His reelection team had engaged in dirty tricks to secure his election. He had developed an "enemies list" and used federal agencies to go after his enemies. The President had ordered the FBI to place wiretaps on the telephones of those government employees and reporters he suspected of leaking information unfavorable to the administration.

**Watergate Has a Lasting Impact** In pursuit of personal power, Richard Nixon damaged the reputation of the

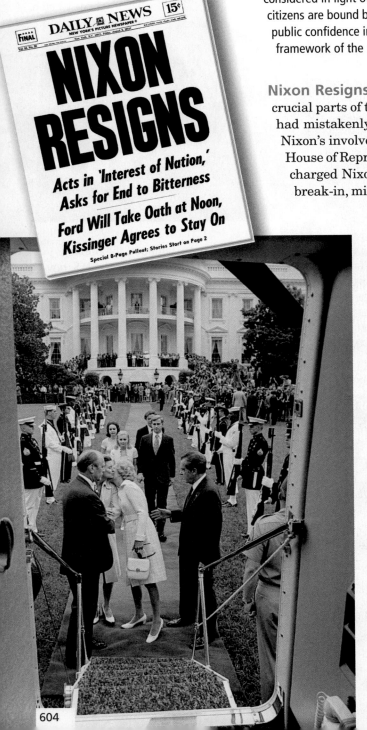

**Nixon Quits**
Nixon and his family bid goodbye to Gerald and Betty Ford as they board a helicopter after Nixon's historic resignation.

FINAL  DAILY NEWS  15¢
NEW YORK'S PICTURE NEWSPAPER

**NIXON RESIGNS**

Acts in 'Interest of Nation,'
Asks for End to Bitterness
Ford Will Take Oath at Noon,
Kissinger Agrees to Stay On

Special 8-Page Pullout; Stories Start on Page 2

presidency and shook the public's confidence in government. One conservative commentator, formerly a supporter of Nixon, echoed the disillusionment of many Americans:

**Primary Source** "The lies, the lies, the lies! . . . What a pity, what a pity! Here was a President who got us out of Vietnam, ended the draft . . . and by his bold overtures to Red China opened new avenues toward world peace. Now the good vanishes in the wreckage of the bad. The swearing-in of Gerald Ford cant come one hour too soon."

—James J. Kilpatrick, *National Review*, August 30, 1974

Polls revealed that from the late 1950s to the mid-1970s, the percentage of Americans who believed in the truth of government statements plummeted from 80 percent to 33 percent.

In the wake of Watergate, Congress enacted numerous reforms to try to restore the public's confidence in government and to prevent abuses of power in the future. It established a procedure for naming an independent counsel to investigate charges against the White House. The Federal Election Campaign Act of 1974 sought to limit the amount of money that individuals could give candidates, in order to prevent the corruption of the political process.

Yet, the Watergate affair also demonstrated that the nation could weather such a crisis. It showed the strength of the system of checks and balances. Both Congress and the Supreme Court had successfully checked the power of the President. According to *Time* magazine, Nixon's resignation represented an "extraordinary triumph of the American system." Watergate demonstrated that no person, not even a President, is above the law. As Gerald Ford said when he became President: "Our great republic is a government of laws and not of men."

✓ **Checkpoint** What role did Richard Nixon and his top aides play in the Watergate scandal?

## Post-Watergate Government Reforms

| | |
|---|---|
| Federal Election Campaign Act Amendments (1974) | Set limit on campaign contributions, provided partial federal funding for presidential campaigns, created the Federal Election Commission to enforce these laws |
| Freedom of Information Act Amendments (1974) | Penalized government officials who withheld documents illegally |
| Government in the Sunshine Act (1976) | Opened meetings of many government agencies to the public. By 1977, all states had passed sunshine laws. |
| Ethics in Government Act of 1978 | Required financial disclosure forms from public officials, restricted government officials' ability to lobby, created the office of special prosecutor |

**A Breach of Faith**
The laws and measures listed above were passed after Watergate to make government more transparent. *Do you think these laws helped to restore the public's faith in government? Explain.*

---

**Progress Monitoring** *Online*
For: Self-test with vocabulary practice
Web Code: nea-1803

### Comprehension

1. **Terms and People** For each term below, write a sentence explaining its relationship to the domestic policy record of the Nixon administration.
   • silent majority
   • stagflation
   • affirmative action
   • Watergate
   • executive privilege

2. **NoteTaking Reading Skill: Identify Main Ideas** Use your chart to answer the Section Focus Question: What events led to Richard Nixon's resignation as President in 1974?

### Writing About History

3. **Quick Write: Write a Resumé** Conduct research on Richard Nixon's life and career, and then create a resumé for the former President that lists his educational background, work experience, and any awards he received.

### Critical Thinking

4. **Summarize** How did Nixon respond to the economic problems he faced as President?

5. **Synthesize Information** In the long run, how successful was Richard Nixon's southern strategy?

6. **Draw Inferences** Opinion polls taken before and after Watergate showed a sharp drop in people's confidence in government. List two other results of the scandal.

# What Are the Limits of Executive Privilege?

8.3.1b

The President's power to keep certain communications with his advisers confidential is called executive privilege. This power is based on the idea that members of the executive branch should be able to advise the President without worrying that their opinions will be revealed to other branches of government or to the public.

## *United States* v. *Nixon (1974)*

| The Facts | The Issue | The Decision |
|---|---|---|
| • Congressional investigation revealed that President Richard Nixon and his aides may have committed illegal acts.<br><br>• Taped Oval Office conversations between President Nixon and his aides were sought as evidence.<br><br>• President Nixon refused to surrender the tapes to the Department of Justice. | President Nixon argued that executive privilege gave him the absolute right to withhold the tapes from the Department of Justice. | The Supreme Court ruled that executive privilege has limits. They said that executive privilege could not protect the President from the judicial process. Nixon must surrender the tapes to prosecutors. |

▲ In this cartoon, the executive and legislative branches fight for power. In *United States* v. *Nixon,* the judicial branch backed the legislative branch.

## Why It Matters

Although not specifically granted by the Constitution, Presidents have long assumed that executive privilege is implied by the constitutional separation of powers. *United States* v. *Nixon* was the test case that allowed the Supreme Court to define executive privilege and to set limits on its use.

In his written opinion, Chief Justice Burger recognized that there is a need for confidentiality in the executive branch, particularly when "military, diplomatic or sensitive national security secrets" must be protected. Under those conditions, the President has the absolute right to keep communications confidential. However, communications between the President and his advisers often concern policy that has nothing to do with national security. In those cases, Burger said, executive privilege is limited. A judge can decide that there is overwhelming government interest in obtaining the President's privileged communications. The due process of law in a criminal case is one example of overwhelming government interest.

A few days after the decision in *United States* v. *Nixon*, President Nixon resigned from office. The Court's ruling had proved that the President is not above the law.

### Connect to Your World

Consider the limits of executive privilege outlined in *United States* v. *Nixon*. During their respective terms in office, recent Presidents Bill Clinton and George W. Bush have applied executive privilege in controversial situations. Research one example and then write a paragraph either defending or arguing against this use of executive privilege.

**For:** Supreme Court cases
**Web Code:** nee-1804

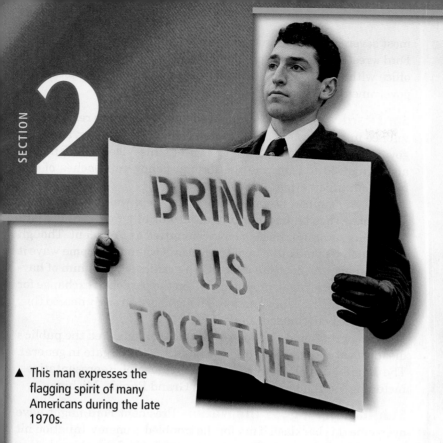

▲ This man expresses the flagging spirit of many Americans during the late 1970s.

### A Crisis of Confidence

On July 4, 1976, the United States celebrated its bicentennial, or two hundredth anniversary. By the end of the decade, however, the celebratory mood had evaporated in the face of a series of crises that tested the nation's spirit. President Jimmy Carter took note of what he called the nation's crisis of confidence.

❝The symptoms of this crisis of the American spirit are all around us. For the first time in the history of our country a majority of our people believe that the next five years will be worse than the past five years. Two thirds of the people do not even vote. The productivity of workers is actually dropping. . . . There is a growing disrespect for government and for churches and for schools. . . . This is not a message of happiness or reassurance, but it is the truth and it is a warning.❞

—President Jimmy Carter, "Crisis of Confidence" speech, 1979

# The Ford and Carter Years

 **Content Expectations**

- **8.2.2a** Describe issues challenging Americans.
- **9.1.1** Evaluate changes in U.S. economy.
- **9.1.2b** Analyze role of evangelical religion in national politics.

## Terms and People

Gerald Ford
pardon
Jimmy Carter

Christian fundamentalist
amnesty
televangelist

## NoteTaking

**Reading Skill: Identify Main Ideas** Create an outline like the one below to record the political, economic, and social problems of the era and their impact on American society.

> I. Gerald Ford's Presidency
>   A. Major Domestic Issues
>     1.
>     2.
>   B.

**Why It Matters** In 1982, historian Peter Carroll published a history of the 1970s entitled *It Seemed Like Nothing Happened.* Compared to the turbulent 1960s, indeed, the 1970s appeared mostly uneventful. Yet, the decade witnessed significant social, economic, and cultural changes. These changes contributed to a growing sense among Americans that something had gone wrong, that the nation had gotten off the right track. This sense of disquiet is even now a part of the nation's political dialogue. **Section Focus Question: What accounted for the changes in American attitudes during the 1970s?**

## Ford Faces Political and Economic Woes

**Gerald Ford** brought a long record of public service to the presidency. A star football player at the University of Michigan, Ford enlisted in the United States Navy and fought in World War II. Following the war, Ford successfully ran for a seat in the U.S. Congress, where he served for 25 years, rising to the position of House Minority Leader in 1965. Democrats as well as Republicans supported Ford's nomination for Vice President because he had a stellar reputation for hard work, integrity, and dependability.

Ford stepped into a delicate situation when he became President after Richard Nixon's resignation. Watergate had scarred the public's faith in government. Furthermore, the nation struggled with the most severe economic problems it had faced since the depression. Ford wrestled with these problems but not very successfully. He left office with the economy still suffering and the public's distrust of government still high.

**Ford Pardons Nixon** Ford moved quickly to try to restore confidence in government. He selected Nelson Rockefeller, a former governor of New York State, to serve as his Vice President. He also promised to continue the foreign policy approaches of the Nixon administration.

Whatever support he gained from these steps was lost when Ford announced that he had **pardoned,** or officially forgiven, Richard Nixon for any crimes he may have committed as President. Though the pardon was meant to heal the nation's wounds, in some ways it achieved just the opposite effect. Ford's critics accused him of having made a secret deal, promising Nixon the pardon in exchange for the vice presidential nomination. Though Ford strongly denied this, his popularity declined dramatically.

The congressional election results of 1974 indicated the public's disapproval of the pardon and the impact of Watergate in general. The Republicans lost 48 seats in the House of Representatives, including Ford's longtime district in Grand Rapids, Michigan.

**Stagflation Plagues the Nation** President Ford might have overcome this backlash if not for the troubled economy. Inflation hit double digits in 1974 and early 1975. To fight skyrocketing prices, Ford promoted a mostly voluntary plan known as WIN, or Whip Inflation Now. Unfortunately, WIN was a clear failure. Instead of improving, the economy took a turn for the worse. Factories closed down, consumer demand for goods dropped sharply, and the rate of unemployment rose steadily. Ford's popularity plummeted.

**WIN Fails**
Despite enthusiastic campaigning by Ford, his WIN plan failed to tame inflation.

✓ **Checkpoint** How did President Ford's WIN program try to address inflation, and how successful was it?

**WITNESS HISTORY DVD**

Watch *The Presidency in Crisis* on the **United States Witness History DVD** to explore what some saw as a crisis in the presidency during the 1970s.

## A Washington "Outsider" Becomes President

Prior to the mid-1970s, few Americans outside Georgia had ever heard of **Jimmy Carter,** a one-time governor of that state. But on election day 1976, Americans elected Carter President of the United States. He won a slim popular majority, receiving slightly more than 50 percent of the vote to Ford's 48 percent. In the electoral college, Carter won 297 votes compared to 240 for Ford.

Carter's rise was the result of several factors. Most important was the turmoil of the 1960s and Watergate, which created a backlash against professional politicians. Carter seized this opportunity by casting himself as a fresh face, with no ties to Washington, D.C. A born-again Christian who taught Sunday school, Carter won the support of many **Christian fundamentalists,** people who believe in a strict, literal interpretation of the Bible as the foundation of the Christian faith. This group became increasingly involved in politics in the 1970s.

**Carter Pays a Price for Inexperience** From the beginning of his presidency, Jimmy Carter sought to portray himself as a "citizens' President." He became the first President since William Henry Harrison to walk all the way from the Capitol to the White House during the inaugural parade. He held town meetings, wore casual clothes, and carried his own suitcase.

However, Carter's inexperience, which helped him get elected, hurt him during the early days of his presidency. As an outsider, he did not have close ties with the Democratic leadership in Congress. He submitted numerous bills to Congress, but few of them passed without major changes by his own party.

Just one day after his inauguration, Carter fulfilled one of his campaign pledges by granting **amnesty,** or political pardons, to Americans who had evaded the draft during the Vietnam War. Carter hoped this act would help the nation move beyond the divisions caused by that war. Yet the war remained an emotional issue, and many Americans criticized the President for forgiving those who had refused to fight. Republican senator Barry Goldwater called the amnesty "the most disgraceful thing that a President has ever done."

**Problems Sap the Nation's Confidence** Like Ford, Carter <u>contended</u> with the energy crisis and severe inflation. Inflation ate away at people's savings, raised the prices of necessities, and made American goods more costly abroad. The U.S. automobile industry, long a symbol of the nation's economic power, became a symbol of its ills. Japanese car companies vastly expanded their sales in the United States by selling better-built and more fuel-efficient cars at reasonable prices. The situation grew so bad that Chrysler, one of the three major American automobile companies, needed a federal loan to survive.

At the center of the nation's economic ills lay the ongoing energy crisis. In 1973, a gallon of gas cost about 40 cents. By the end of the decade, it cost close to $1.20. To make matters worse, the winter of 1976 to 1977 was an especially bitter one in parts of the United States, increasing the need for heating oil. Fuel shortages caused factory closings and business losses.

**Vocabulary Builder**
<u>contend</u>–(kuhn TEHND) *v.* to fight

In 1974, gas stations all over the country ran out of gas to sell motorists.

# RUNNING OUT OF GAS

The energy crisis of the 1970s rocked the American economy and stumped the best efforts of three Presidents to stop it. It made Americans feel powerless and angry, and added to the general crisis of confidence. **Why did the scarcity of oil in the 1970s have such a strong impact on the United States?**

WAIT HERE

ODD NUMBER LICENSE PLATE   10 GALS ONLY

HALF TANK OR LESS

**Price of Imported Crude Oil, 1970–1980**

Dollars per barrel (in 2005 constant dollars)

SOURCE: U.S. Energy Information Administration

The price of gas continued to increase in leaps and bounds throughout the 1970s.

At gas stations that had gas, people waited for hours in long lines that snaked for blocks.

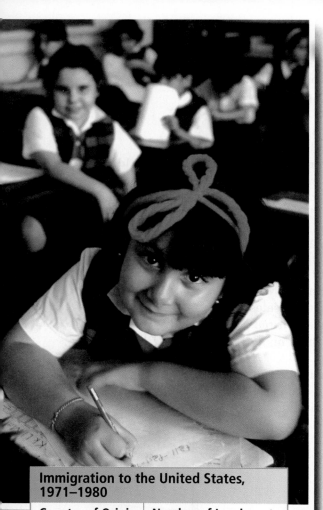

Carter responded to the oil crisis by calling on Americans to conserve and by asking Congress to raise taxes on crude oil, which he hoped would encourage conservation. However, the bill that finally passed in the Senate had few of the President's ideas in it. Critics saw this as one more example of Carter's poor leadership skills.

Carter did implement several domestic policies that his successors would build on during the 1980s. To fight inflation, Carter nominated Paul Volcker to head the Federal Reserve Board. Under Volcker's lead, the Federal Reserve began raising interest rates. In the long term, this policy helped to bring an end to the inflation that had plagued the nation for so long.

✓ **Checkpoint** What challenges did President Carter face?

# Changing Values Stir Unease

Social and cultural changes that had begun in the 1950s and 1960s continued unabated in the 1970s. As a result, by the end of the decade, the United States was a very different society from the one it had been a generation earlier. These differences gave rise to an ongoing debate about the nation's values.

**Demography Affects Politics** The migration of Americans to the Sunbelt and the continued growth of the suburbs, both of which had begun in the post–World War II years, continued during the 1970s. As northern industries suffered, many blue-collar workers and their families moved from the Rust Belt states of the Northeast and Midwest to the Sunbelt of the South and West. They sought work in the oil fields of Texas and Oklahoma and in the defense plants of southern California, the Southwest, and the Northwest. These trends changed the face of the United States.

The elections of Richard Nixon and Jimmy Carter demonstrated the growing political power of the Sunbelt. Earlier in the century, Presidents tended to come from the large northern industrial states, such as New York and Ohio. In the latter decades of the twentieth century, Presidents tended to come from the Sunbelt.

The influx of immigrants from Latin America and Asia represented a different kind of demographic change. Even before the 1970s, hundreds of thousands of Cubans, Puerto Ricans, and Mexicans had migrated to the United States. This migration, especially from Mexico and other Latin American countries, continued to be strong in the 1970s. The growing power of the Latino vote did not escape the notice of politicians. Richard Nixon was the first presidential candidate to seriously court the Spanish-speaking vote.

**The "Me Generation" Comes of Age** During the 1960s, radicals had challenged many of society's traditional values. They questioned restrictions on premarital sex and drug use. They sported casual clothing and long hairstyles that many of their parents' generation found improper. Yet the counterculture remained a relatively isolated phenomenon during the 1960s. By the end of the 1970s, in contrast, these behaviors had become more common. Nationwide, the

### Immigration to the United States, 1971–1980

| Country of Origin | Number of Immigrants |
| --- | --- |
| Mexico | 640,294 |
| Philippines | 354,987 |
| Korea | 267,638 |
| Cuba | 264,863 |
| Vietnam | 172,820 |
| India | 164,134 |
| Dominican Republic | 148,135 |
| Jamaica | 137,577 |
| United Kingdom | 137,374 |
| Italy | 129,368 |
| China | 124,326 |
| Hong Kong | 113,467 |

SOURCE: U.S. Office of Immigration Statistics

## Immigration Changes America

In the 1970s, immigration continued from Southeast Asia and Latin America. Girls from families of Cuban refugees (above) attend a Catholic school in Miami, Florida. *From which region did more people emigrate in the 1970s—Southeast Asia or Latin America?*

## Focus On Geography

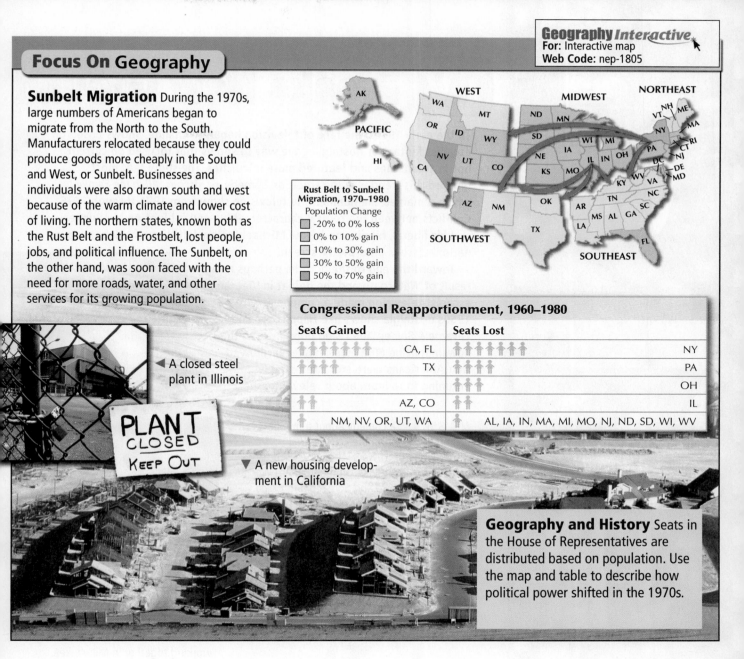

**Sunbelt Migration** During the 1970s, large numbers of Americans began to migrate from the North to the South. Manufacturers relocated because they could produce goods more cheaply in the South and West, or Sunbelt. Businesses and individuals were also drawn south and west because of the warm climate and lower cost of living. The northern states, known both as the Rust Belt and the Frostbelt, lost people, jobs, and political influence. The Sunbelt, on the other hand, was soon faced with the need for more roads, water, and other services for its growing population.

**Rust Belt to Sunbelt Migration, 1970–1980**
Population Change
- -20% to 0% loss
- 0% to 10% gain
- 10% to 30% gain
- 30% to 50% gain
- 50% to 70% gain

◄ A closed steel plant in Illinois

PLANT CLOSED KEEP OUT

▼ A new housing development in California

### Congressional Reapportionment, 1960–1980

| Seats Gained | | Seats Lost | |
|---|---|---|---|
| 👤👤👤👤👤👤 | CA, FL | 👤👤👤👤👤👤 | NY |
| 👤👤👤 | TX | 👤👤👤👤 | PA |
| | | 👤👤👤 | OH |
| 👤👤 | AZ, CO | 👤👤 | IL |
| 👤 | NM, NV, OR, UT, WA | 👤 | AL, IA, IN, MA, MI, MO, NJ, ND, SD, WI, WV |

**Geography and History** Seats in the House of Representatives are distributed based on population. Use the map and table to describe how political power shifted in the 1970s.

divorce rate had more than doubled between 1965 and 1979, and twice as many children were born out of wedlock. To some Americans, the new ways were a sign of troubled times.

Some critics called the 1970s the "me decade" because many Americans appeared to be absorbed with improving themselves. This trend was reflected in the rise of movements like Transcendental Meditation (TM), a practice based in Eastern religious ideas. Those who practiced TM sought to find inner relaxation and vitality by chanting their personal mantras for about half an hour twice a day.

The seventies also witnessed an increasing interest in personal fitness and health. Millions began to jog for exercise and to eat natural, or less processed, foods. In 1970, just over 100 men and women ran in the New York City Marathon. Ten years later, more than 14,000 ran in the race. Body building took off, too, largely due to the influence of Arnold Schwarzenegger. A charismatic personality, Schwarzenegger went on to become one of Hollywood's most popular actors and, later, governor of California.

# TV Breaks New Ground

In the early 1970s, the face of television began to change. Shows based on escapist fantasy or nostalgia gave way to shows that focused on current, hot-button issues and featured more minorities. The show that most typified this trend was the situation comedy, or sitcom, *All in the Family*, which remained the number one television show from 1971 through 1976. Conflicts between the central character—blue-collar bigot Archie Bunker—and his liberal, hippie son-in-law Michael (below left) brought debates over national issues onto the TV screen.

Toward the end of the decade, perhaps as a result of Watergate and the defeat in Vietnam, escapist television made a comeback with 1950s nostalgia shows like *Happy Days* and *Laverne & Shirley*. The rising popularity of the newsmagazine *60 Minutes*, however, showed that Americans were still interested in tuning in to learn about relevant issues.

*M\*A\*S\*H\** ❶, a comedy about a mobile hospital unit during the Korean War, resonated with viewers who were used to watching news reports on the Vietnam War. Shows like *Sanford and Son* ❷ and *Chico and the Man* ❸ proved that viewers would tune in to shows featuring minority characters. *60 Minutes* ❹ was the first television newsmagazine. *Roots* ❺, a graphic historical miniseries that followed the life of a slave and his descendants, fascinated more than 100 million viewers.

*Happy Days* (top) was about a teenager growing up in the 1950s, while its spin-off, *Laverne & Shirley* (bottom), followed two lifelong friends living and working together in Milwaukee.

## Thinking Critically

1. **Identify Central Issues** How did television change in the 1970s?

2. **Determine Relevance** How did these changes reflect broader changes taking place in American culture?

**Conservatives Reassert Traditional Values** The 1970s witnessed a resurgence of fundamental Christianity, partly as a response to the shift in values. To some commentators, it seemed as if the nation was experiencing another Great Awakening, like the great religious movements of the eighteenth and nineteenth centuries. Although the total number of Americans who attended church on a regular basis did not change much, the number of men and women who belonged to evangelical churches rose rapidly. One in five Americans considered himself or herself a religious fundamentalist by 1980.

Evangelical ministers used the media to gain a broader audience. Those who preached on television—known as **televangelists**—such as Jerry Falwell, Oral Roberts, and Marion "Pat" Robertson, reached millions of viewers. Falwell's daily radio broadcasts were carried by 280 radio stations, and his weekly television show was broadcast to 1.5 million viewers.

Religious conservatives firmly opposed many of the social changes begun in the 1960s that had gone mainstream in the 1970s. They opposed the Supreme Court's rulings that legalized abortion and restricted prayer in school. Falwell formed a prominent Christian conservative organization known as the Moral Majority in 1979. He voiced the concerns of many fundamentalists:

> **Primary Source** "We must reverse the trend America finds herself in today. Young people . . . have been born and reared in a different world than Americans of past worlds. . . . They have learned to disrespect the family as God has established it. . . . They have been taught that the Bible is just another book of literature. . . . They have been introduced to the drug culture."
>
> —Reverend Jerry Falwell, *Listen America,* 1980

During the 1970s, religious conservatives began forming alliances with other conservatives. They worked with economic conservatives, who sought to cut taxes and government spending, as well as with supporters of a stronger foreign policy, who favored increasing defense spending. Together, they began forging a new political majority. By 1980, Ronald Reagan, another political outsider, would use this alliance to win election to the White House.

 **Checkpoint** In what ways did the United States change socially and culturally during the 1970s?

---

SECTION

# 2 Assessment

**Progress Monitoring** *Online*
**For:** Self-test with vocabulary practice
**Web Code:** nea-1806

## Comprehension

1. **Terms and People** For each item below, write a sentence explaining its effect on social and economic conditions in the 1970s.
   - Gerald Ford
   - pardon
   - Jimmy Carter
   - Christian fundamentalist
   - amnesty
   - televangelist

2. **NoteTaking Reading Skill: Identify Main Ideas** Use your outline to answer the Section Focus Question: What accounted for the changes in American attitudes during the 1970s?

## Writing About History

3. **Quick Write: List Qualifications** Suppose that you are Gerald Ford applying for the position of Vice President in the mid-1970s. Research Ford's background and skills. Then, list the qualifications that you would highlight to try to get the position.

## Critical Thinking

4. **Demonstrate Reasoned Judgment** Should Gerald Ford have pardoned Richard Nixon?

5. **Identify Point of View** What arguments would you expect people to give for and against President Carter's decision to grant amnesty to Americans who had evaded the draft?

6. **Draw Inferences** How do you think Watergate affected social trends in the 1970s?

# Are Affirmative Action Programs Fair?

 8.3.4

In the 1970s, the government urged employers and schools to adopt affirmative action programs. These programs aimed to increase the number of women and minority group members in college, postgraduate schools, and higher-paying jobs. The goal was to make up for past discrimination against these groups. Did those programs now discriminate against white males?

## *Regents of the University of California* v. *Bakke* (1978)

| The Facts | The Issue | The Decision |
|---|---|---|
| • Allan Bakke, a white man, was twice denied admission to a University of California medical school.<br><br>• Bakke had a stronger academic record than 16 minority group applicants that the school had accepted under a special program. | Bakke claimed that his rights under the equal protection clause of the Fourteenth Amendment had been violated. | • Five Justices agreed that racial quotas violated Bakke's rights.<br><br>• One of those Justices and four others agreed that race could be a factor in admissions decisions. |

### Why It Matters

Some people predicted that *Bakke* would end affirmative action. That did not happen, however. Justice Lewis Powell was the key figure in the Court's complex statements on the issue. He agreed with four Justices that quotas were not acceptable, but he also agreed with the other four that using race as a factor in admissions was acceptable. Powell favored using race as a "plus factor," just like artistic or musical ability, athletic talent, or other factors.

After the Court's decision, universities dropped quota systems. Many also followed Powell's opinion by setting up programs that consider a person's race as one factor among many.

▲ Protesters in Michigan support the University of California.

### Connect to Your World

In 2003, the Court visited the issue again. In *Grutter* v. *Bollinger,* a 5-to-4 majority ruled that a law school's admissions policy met the standards of *Bakke* by using race as part of the process but not as a deciding factor. Read more about the case, then take the role of a newspaper editor and write an editorial agreeing or disagreeing with the Court's decision.

**For:** Supreme Court cases
**Web Code:** nee-1807

◄ Today's college classrooms reflect a greater gender and ethnic diversity in part because of affirmative action policies.

**Human Rights and American Foreign Policy**

As President, Jimmy Carter sought to center America's foreign policy on human rights rather than on anticommunism. Carter outlined his views in 1977:

"For too many years, we've been willing to adopt the flawed and erroneous principles and tactics of our adversaries, sometimes abandoning our own values for theirs. We've fought fire with fire, never thinking that fire is better quenched with water. . . . [I] believe that it is a mistake to under-value the power of words and of the ideas that words embody."

—President Jimmy Carter, Commencement Address at Notre Dame University, 1977

▲ President Carter and Panama's leader General Omar Torrijos in 1978

# Foreign Policy Troubles

## Content Expectations

- **8.1.2e** Evaluate indirect confrontations within specific world regions.
- **8.1.3** Evaluate factors leading to the end of Cold War.
- **8.2.3** Compare/contrast Roosevelt's New Deal initiatives, Johnson's Great Society programs, Reagan's market-based domestic policies.

## Terms and People

| | |
|---|---|
| Helsinki Accords | sanctions |
| human rights | developing world |
| SALT II | Camp David Accords |
| boat people | Ayatollah Khomeini |

## NoteTaking

**Reading Skill: Identify Supporting Details** Use a concept web like the one below to record the main ideas and details about the foreign policies of presidents Ford and Carter.

Gerald Ford — Jimmy Carter — U.S. Foreign Policy

**Why It Matters** The ordeal of the Vietnam War led many to question the direction of American foreign policy. They asked: Why was the United States so concerned with fighting communism that it ended up supporting oppressive anticommunist governments? Should the United States continue to pursue détente with the Soviets? Or should it instead demand that the Soviet government grant its people more freedoms? The echoes of these debates continue to be heard today. **Section Focus Question: What were the goals of American foreign policy during the Ford and Carter years, and how successful were Ford's and Carter's policies?**

## Ford Continues Nixon's Foreign Policies

Relations with the Soviet Union remained central to U.S. foreign policy during the Ford and Carter administrations. Upon assuming the presidency, Gerald Ford made clear that his foreign policy would differ little from that of Richard Nixon's. Ford retained Henry Kissinger as his Secretary of State and continued to pursue détente with the Soviet Union and China.

**Pursuing Détente** Ford and Soviet leader Leonid Brezhnev met in late 1974 and again the next year, when the two leaders endorsed the **Helsinki Accords.** This document put the nations of Europe on record in favor of **human rights,** or the basic rights that every human being is entitled to have. Some thought that President Ford

**Vietnamese Boat People**

These Vietnamese refugees wait in their rickety boat in Hong Kong's harbor in September 1979, having survived the voyage from Vietnam.

would try to compel the Soviet Union to allow more political freedoms, but Ford decided to put arms control ahead of human rights. At his direction, the United States continued disarmament talks with the Soviets. These talks led to an agreement known as **SALT II**, in which the two nations pledged to limit nuclear arms production.

**Trouble in Southeast Asia** Under Ford, the United States sought to put the turmoil of the Vietnam War behind it. When the communist Khmer Rouge government of Cambodia began a genocidal slaughter of civilians, killing about 1.5 million people between 1975 and 1979, the United States did not intervene. The main exception to this policy of noninvolvement came in May 1975, when the Khmer Rouge seized an American merchant ship, the *Mayaguez*, which had been steaming just outside Cambodian waters. Ford responded by sending in some United States Marines, who freed the ship.

During Ford's presidency, South Vietnam fell to North Vietnam. As the communists took over, hundreds of thousands of Vietnamese, many of whom had worked with the United States, tried to escape. Many refugees took to the seas in rickety, unseaworthy boats. These **boat people** represented the largest mass migration of humanity by sea in modern history. Over a 20-year period, more than one million men, women, and children braved storms, pirates, and starvation in search of refuge abroad. Their immediate destinations were in other nations of Southeast Asia, but many eventually found that refuge in the United States and Canada.

 **Checkpoint** How did Ford approach foreign policy challenges during his presidency?

## Carter Changes Course

Early in his presidency, Jimmy Carter proclaimed that as much as possible, American foreign policy would be guided by a concern for human rights. Carter hoped to make his foreign policy into a tool to end acts of political <u>repression</u> such as torture, murder, and imprisonment without trial. This policy direction helped reaffirm the position of the United States as a nation of freedom and justice. However, it undercut the goal of better relations with the Soviet Union.

**Vocabulary Builder**
<u>repression</u>–(rih PREHSH uhn) *n.* the act of suppressing or keeping down

**Relations With the Soviet Union Cool** At first, Carter continued Nixon's and Ford's policies toward the Soviet Union. He worked to achieve détente. He continued efforts at arms control, meeting with Leonid Brezhnev in June 1979 and signing the SALT II treaty.

However, relations between the two superpowers soon took a decidedly frosty turn. The SALT II treaty was bitterly debated in the United States Senate, where its opponents argued that it put the national security of the United States in jeopardy. Then, in December 1979, the Soviet Union invaded the neighboring country of Afghanistan to prop up a tottering communist government. Carter responded by withdrawing the SALT II treaty from Senate consideration and by imposing **sanctions**, or penalties, on the Soviets. The sanctions included a U.S. boycott of the 1980 Summer Olympic Games held in Moscow as well as a suspension of grain sales to the Soviet Union.

**Carter Supports Human Rights in the Developing World** Since the end of World War II, American Presidents had tended to see the **developing world**—the poor nations of Asia, Africa, and Latin America—as another stage for the Cold War. Carter broke with that approach and insisted that foreign policy toward the developing world should revolve around the expansion of human rights. Carter believed that U.S. relations with foreign countries should be determined by how a country treated its citizens.

Carter's <u>emphasis</u> on human rights led him to alter the U.S. relationship with a number of dictators. In Nicaragua, the Somoza family had ruled the country with an iron grip since the mid-1930s, most of the time with the support of the United States. In 1978, a leftist group known as the Sandinistas began a rebellion against the country's ruler, General Anastasio Somoza. His brutal response to the rebellion helped convince Carter to withdraw U.S. support. Without U.S. aid, General Somoza had to flee Nicaragua, and the Sandinistas came to power.

**Vocabulary Builder**
<u>emphasis</u>–(EHM fuh sihs) *n.*
special attention

**Carter's Policies Get Mixed Results in Latin America** The Carter administration briefly sought to improve relations with Cuba, ruled by communist Fidel Castro since 1959. However, U.S.-Cuban relations soured in 1980 when Castro announced that any Cuban could leave the island from the port of Mariel for the United States. However, Castro insisted that any boats headed to the United States would also have to take criminals from the island's prisons. Because of this condition, the Mariel boatlift developed a bad reputation in the eyes of many Americans. Fewer than 20 percent of the people transported had spent time in prison, and many of those were political prisoners. Still, Americans were repelled by Castro's lack of concern for the welfare of the emigrants and by the idea that he would send criminals to the United States.

Carter's most controversial foreign policy move involved his decision to return the Panama Canal Zone to Panama. You will recall that Panama had given the United States control of a wide strip of land across the middle of the country in 1903 that later became the site of the Panama Canal. In 1977, Carter negotiated a set of treaties to return the Canal Zone to Panama by 1999. Many Americans worried that the loss of control over the canal would threaten American shipping and security. Nonetheless, the United States Senate narrowly ratified the treaties in 1978, and all control of the canal was ultimately turned over to Panama.

✓ **Checkpoint** In what ways did President Carter's policies differ from those of Ford?

# Success and Setback in the Middle East

Carter's greatest achievement in foreign policy came in the region that also saw his greatest setback. He helped negotiate a historic peace agreement between Israel and Egypt, but he failed to win the release of Americans held hostage by Iranian radicals.

**Israel and Egypt Agree to Peace** Egypt had opposed Israel's existence since Israel's founding in 1948. As recently as 1973, the two nations had fought a bitter war. By 1977, eager to improve relations, Egyptian President Anwar el-Sadat and Israeli prime minister Menachem Begin met in Jerusalem to negotiate a peace agreement. To help continue the negotiations, Carter invited the two leaders to Camp David, the presidential retreat. For

## HISTORY MAKERS

**Jimmy Carter** (born 1924)
A former navy officer and peanut farmer, Jimmy Carter's presidency began with high hopes and calls for a new emphasis on human rights. Carter lost his bid for reelection but continued to work to promote human rights and democracy around the world. He set up an organization called the Carter Center that promotes peace and human rights, and he has helped several countries' efforts to hold free and fair elections. He even joined Habitat for Humanity to help poor people build and afford new homes.

# IRAN HOSTAGE CRISIS

The Iranian Revolution, which toppled the Shah and brought the Ayatollah Khomeini to power in 1979, had a strong anti-American component. The United States had supported Mohammad Reza Shah Pahlavi, Iran's Shah, to secure a firm ally against communism in the region. However, the Shah's rule grew more oppressive after 1953, when the CIA had helped him control a challenge to his power. Resentment over political interference and foreign involvement in Iran's oil industry boiled over when the deposed Shah entered the United States for medical treatment. Outraged Iranians seized 66 American hostages and held 52 of them for 444 days.

▲ The Ayatollah Khomeini

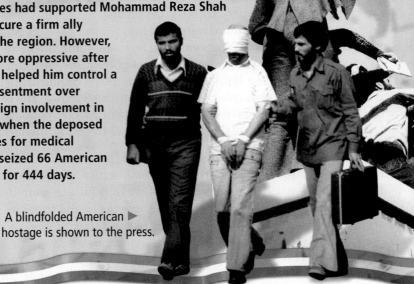

A blindfolded American ▶ hostage is shown to the press.

### The Crisis Unfolds

- **January 1979** The Iranian Revolution forces the Shah into exile.
- **February 1979** Ayatollah Khomeini returns to Iran after 15 years in exile.
- **April 1979** Khomeini takes power.
- **October 1979** The Shah enters the United States.
- **November 1979** Militant students take 66 Americans hostage. Carter halts oil imports and freezes Iranian assets in the United States.
- **April 1980** Carter severs diplomatic relations with Iran and imposes an economic embargo. A military mission to free the hostages ends in disaster.
- **January 1981** On the day of Reagan's inauguration, the hostages are released in exchange for $8 billion in frozen assets and a promise to lift trade sanctions against Iran.

nearly two weeks, the three leaders carried on the difficult negotiations that produced what is known as the **Camp David Accords.** These agreements provided the framework for a peace treaty in which Egypt formally recognized the nation of Israel, becoming the first Arab nation to do so. In return, Israel withdrew its troops from the Sinai Peninsula, which it had occupied since the 1967 war. The preamble to the Accords states:

> **Primary Source** "After four wars during 30 years, despite intensive human efforts, the Middle East, which is the cradle of civilization and the birthplace of three great religions, does not enjoy the blessings of peace. . . . [Israel and Egypt] recognize that for peace to endure, it must involve all those who have been most deeply affected by the conflict. They therefore agree that this framework, as appropriate, is intended by them to constitute a basis for peace not only between Egypt and Israel, but also between Israel and each of its other neighbors. . . ."
> —Camp David Accords, September 19, 1978

**Iran Seizes American Hostages** Carter hoped that the Camp David Accords would usher in a new era of cooperation in the Middle East. Yet, events in Iran showed that troubles in the region were far from over. Since the 1950s, the United States had supported the rule of the Shah, or emperor, of Iran. In the 1970s, however, opposition to the Shah began to grow within Iran.

Dying of cancer, the Shah fled from Iran in January 1979. Fundamentalist Islamic clerics, led by the **Ayatollah Khomeini** (ī yuh TOH luh koh MAYN ee), took power. Carter allowed the Shah to enter the United States to seek medical treatment. Enraged Iranian radical students invaded the U.S. Embassy and took 66 Americans as hostages. The Khomeini government then took control of both the embassy and the hostages to defy the United States.

The hostage crisis consumed the attention of Carter during the last year of his presidency. To many Americans, Carter's failure to win all of the hostages' release was evidence of American weakness. As Peter Bourne put it in his biography of

◄ Iranian students burn an American flag at the U.S. embassy in Tehran; protesters call for the CIA to stop interfering in Iran (right).

▲ The freed hostages arrive in the United States after their ordeal finally ends in January 1981.

**Thinking Critically**

1. **Recognize Causes** What event triggered the seizure of the American hostages in Iran?

2. **Synthesize Information** What actions did Carter take to try to get the hostages released?

Jimmy Carter, "Because people felt that Carter had not been tough enough in foreign policy ... some bunch of students could seize American diplomatic officials and hold them prisoner and thumb their nose at the United States."

The hostage crisis began to change the way Americans viewed the world outside their borders. Nuclear war between the two superpowers was no longer the only threat to the United States. Although the Cold War still concerned Americans, the threats posed by conflicts in the Middle East threatened to become the greatest foreign policy challenge of the United States.

✓ **Checkpoint** How did the seizure of the U.S. Embassy by Iranian students affect Americans' view of the world?

---

SECTION **3** Assessment

**Progress Monitoring *Online***
**For:** Self-test with vocabulary practice
**Web Code:** nea-1808

**Comprehension**

1. **Terms and People** For each item below, write a sentence explaining the way it affected U.S. foreign policy.
   • human rights
   • SALT II
   • boat people
   • sanctions
   • developing world
   • Camp David Accords
   • Ayatollah Khomeini

2. **NoteTaking Reading Skill: Identify Supporting Details** Use your concept web to answer the Section Focus Question: What were the goals of American foreign policy during the Ford and Carter years, and how successful were Ford's and Carter's policies?

**Writing About History**

3. **Quick Write: Present Skills** Put yourself in the place of someone applying to be the U.S. Ambassador to Panama in the mid-1970s. Write a paragraph describing the key qualities needed for the job.

**Critical Thinking**

4. **Draw Conclusions** What do you think were the most important foreign policy accomplishments of Gerald Ford and Jimmy Carter?

5. **Draw Inferences** What did Carter's inability to secure the release of the hostages in Iran symbolize to many Americans?

# Quick Study Guide

 8.1.2d

**Progress Monitoring *Online***
For: Self-test with vocabulary practice
**Web Code:** nea-1809

## ■ Watergate in Review

| Issues | Consequences |
| --- | --- |
| • Presidential abuse of power (FBI wiretaps of "enemies")<br>• Limits of executive privilege<br>• Supreme Court's power to rule on presidential actions<br>• Willingness of Congress to confront presidential power | • Shook public confidence in government<br>• Damaged the reputation of the presidency<br>• Confirmed the independent power of legislative and judicial branches<br>• Demonstrated strength of checks and balances system<br>• Prompted laws to govern independent counsel investigations and reform election finance practices |

## ■ Economic Problems of the 1970s

| |
| --- |
| Slow economic growth |
| Inflation |
| Energy crisis |
| Foreign competition |

## ■ International Relations in the 1970s

| International Relations in the 1970s | | |
| --- | --- | --- |
| **Hot Spots** | **Disputes** | **Improvements** |
| • Vietnam<br>• Cambodia<br>• Afghanistan | • Soviet Union<br>• Cuba<br>• OPEC countries<br>• Iran | • China<br>• Panama<br>• Israel<br>• Egypt<br>• Nicaragua |

## ■ Domestic Controversies in the 1970s

Court-ordered busing — Changing values — **Domestic Controversies of the 1970s** — Antiwar demonstrations — Affirmative action — Vietnam War — *Bakke* case — Nixon's Philadelphia Plan — Amnesty for draft resisters

## ☑ Quick Study Timeline

**In America**

**1970** Clean Air Act becomes law

**1973** OPEC oil embargo causes U.S. energy prices to soar

**1974** Nixon resigns in wake of Watergate scandal; Ford becomes President

**Presidential Terms**  Richard M. Nixon 1969–1974    Gerald R. Ford 1974–1977

**1970**          **1972**          **1974**

**Around the World**

**1970** United States invades Cambodia

**1971** Idi Amin takes power in Uganda

**1972** Terrorists kill Israeli athletes at Munich Olympics

**1975** South Vietnam surrenders to North Vietnam

# American Issues
● — ● — ● Connector

By connecting prior knowledge with what you have learned in this chapter, you can gradually build your understanding of enduring questions that still affect America today. Answer the questions below. Then, use your American Issues Connector study guide (or go online: www.PHSchool.com **Web Code:** neh-9102).

## Issues You Learned About

● **Checks and Balances** Political leaders disagree on how much authority each branch can exert over the others.

**1.** Why is the principle of checks and balances important to the U.S. government? Give an example of checks and balances at work.

**2.** Describe the role of the judicial branch and the legislative branch in the move to impeach President Nixon. What did *Time* magazine mean when it called Nixon's resignation an "extraordinary triumph of the American system"?

● **Church and State** The First Amendment of the United States Constitution, known as the Establishment Clause, calls for the separation of church and state.

**3.** Read the 1787 Virginia Statute for Religious Freedom, which appears in the documents section at the end of this book. What was the importance of this document?

**4.** Since the 1960s, the Supreme Court has made a number of rulings limiting prayers and religious readings in public schools. Why do you think that the Supreme Court banned prayer in public schools?

● **Sectionalism and National Politics** Different regions of the country often can be defined by their political beliefs.

**5.** Why did southern states traditionally vote for Democrats? What was remarkable about Nixon's presidential victory in 1972?

**6.** How did Nixon expand his base of support from the 1968 election? What was this strategy called?

**7.** Why did the Sunbelt gain political power in the 1970s?

### Connect to Your World — Michigan

**Migration and Urbanization** In 1947, Detroit's 3,272 manufacturing companies had more than 338,000 employees. Thirty years later, only 153,300 workers remained at fewer than 2,000 manufacturing companies. In the 1970s and early 1980s, many Michigan businesses failed and unemployment rose. At the same time, the state government's limited budget forced it to cut services. The situation looked more promising in other states, however. Many African American residents moved to the South, an area their families had left a generation earlier. Young Michiganians left their "Rust Belt" state in search of new economic opportunities, while many older Michiganians retired to the Sunbelt region. Work with a group to brainstorm ways to keep the population of Michigan steady. How might you convince current residents to stay? How might people who leave the state be replaced?

---

**1976**
America celebrates Bicentennial

**1977**
President Carter pardons Vietnam War draft evaders

**1979**
Protesters seize U.S. embassy and hostages in Tehran

**History Interactive**
**For:** Interactive timeline
**Web Code:** nep-1811

**Jimmy Carter 1977–1981**

**Ronald Reagan 1981–1989**

1976          1978          1980

**1978**
Egypt and Israel sign Camp David Accords

**1979**
Soviet Union invades Afghanistan

**1980**
Iraq invades Iran

**1981**
Egyptian President Anwar Sadat is assassinated

# Chapter Assessment

## Terms and People

1. Define **stagflation**. What were the causes of stagflation in the early 1970s?

2. Define **executive privilege**. How did the Supreme Court rule on executive privilege in *United States* v. *Nixon*?

3. What is **amnesty**? Why did Carter's granting of amnesty to draft evaders anger some Americans?

4. What is the **developing world**? How did Carter change U.S. foreign policy toward the developing world?

5. Who was the **Ayatollah Khomeini**? How did his actions affect the Carter presidency?

## Focus Questions

The focus question for this chapter is **What caused Americans to suffer a crisis of confidence during the 1970s?** Build an answer to this big question by answering the focus questions for Sections 1 through 3 and the Critical Thinking questions that follow.

### Section 1
6. What events led to Richard Nixon's resignation as President in 1974?

### Section 2
7. What accounted for the changes in American attitudes during the 1970s?

### Section 3
8. What were the goals of American foreign policy during the Ford and Carter years, and how successful were Ford's and Carter's policies?

## Critical Thinking

9. **Synthesize Information** Think about Nixon's approach to new programs and policies designed to ease racial inequality. Would you call him a supporter or an opponent of civil rights? Explain.

10. **Analyze Political Cartoons** Study the political cartoon in the Landmark Decisions of the Supreme Court feature about executive privilege that appears earlier in this chapter. Explain the political issue depicted in the cartoon and the cartoonist's view of it.

11. **Recognize Cause and Effect** Why did Ford pardon Nixon for any crimes he may have committed as President? What effect did this pardon have on American politics over the next few years?

12. **Analyze Information** How did Carter's role as a political outsider both help and hinder him in Washington, D.C.?

13. **Summarize** Summarize the responses of Nixon, Ford, and Carter to the downturn of the American economy, and explain what impact these measures had.

14. **Compare Points of View** Compare Ford's and Carter's foreign policy toward the Soviet Union.

15. **Identify Central Issues** Identify and describe two regions in the world in which Carter's policies had a major impact.

## Writing About History

**Applying for a Job** Throughout American history, many talented individuals have worked in the federal government to try to address the energy and economic problems that have troubled the nation. Write an essay from the point of view of a college graduate in 1977 trying to get a job in the newly established Department of Energy. Explain what your qualifications are and how they are a good fit with the job's needs.

### Prewriting
• Research the skills needed to fill a job in the Department of Energy in 1977.
• Develop the character of a 1977 college graduate based on those skills.

### Drafting
• Write a thesis statement that expresses the key qualifications, skills, and qualities that you (as the college graduate) possess that suit the Department of Energy job.
• Expand upon these positive factors in the body of your essay.
• Close with an effective and well-worded conclusion.

### Revising
• Use the guidelines on page SH16 of the Writing Handbook to revise your essay.

# Prepare for the MME

 8.2.4

## Anatomy of a Scandal

President Richard Nixon's administration was marred by a political scandal, called Watergate, that led to his resignation. What were the roles of the Congress, the press, and the courts in investigating President Nixon's unchecked presidential power? Use your knowledge of the Watergate scandal and Documents A, B, and C to answer questions 1 through 4.

### Document A

### Document B

"If the president, for example, approves something because of the national security, or in this case because of a threat to internal peace and order of significant magnitude, then the president's decision in that instance is one that enables those who carry it out, to carry it out without violating a law. Otherwise they're in an impossible position. . . . [It] has been however argued that as far as a president is concerned, that in war time, a president does have certain extraordinary powers which would make acts that would otherwise be unlawful, lawful if undertaken for the purpose of preserving the nation and the Constitution, which is essential for the rights we're all talking about."

—*President Nixon, from an interview with British TV host, David Frost, May 19, 1977*

### Document C

"The Constitution charges the president with the task of taking care that the laws be faithfully executed, and yet the president has counseled his aides to commit perjury, willfully disregard the secrecy of grand jury proceedings, conceal surreptitious entry, attempt to compromise a federal judge, while publicly displaying his cooperation with the processes of criminal justice. . . . Has the president committed offenses, and planned, and directed, and acquiesced in a course of conduct which the Constitution will not tolerate? That's the question. It is reason, and not passion, which must guide our deliberations, guide our debate, and guide our decision."

—*Barbara Jordan, statement at the U.S. House Judiciary Committee Impeachment Hearings, Washington, D.C., July 25, 1974*

1. What point of view does Document A present?
   A The judicial viewpoint
   B The executive viewpoint
   C The viewpoint of Congress
   D The viewpoint of the press

2. Document B shows the role of the press in the Watergate scandal because it shows
   A that Nixon was accountable to the press.
   B how reporters began to investigate the story.
   C how Nixon was forced to confess his role in the scandal.
   D Nixon's willingness to accuse others of committing minor crimes.

3. In Document C, what was the purpose of Barbara Jordan's statement?
   A It defended the actions of the President.
   B It tried to determine the grounds for impeachment.
   C It clarified Congress's role in the Watergate scandal.
   D It explained that the Constitution tolerated the President's conduct.

4. **Writing Task** Did Congress, the press, and the courts successfully do their jobs in investigating the Watergate scandal that led to President Richard Nixon's resignation? Use your knowledge of the chapter content and specific evidence from the primary sources above to support your opinion.

## MI Connect to Michigan

### Globalization and the Michigan Automobile Industry

In the 1990s and early 2000s, increasing global trade transformed the American automobile industry. Michigan automakers faced new competition, particularly from Japanese manufacturers. American companies had to find new ways to reduce costs and stay competitive in this new global market. Many American automakers moved some of their manufacturing activities to Latin America, China, and Southeast Asia, where labor was cheaper. These relocations meant fewer jobs for Michigan autoworkers.

Other automobile companies tried to stay competitive by merging to form larger companies. In 1998, for example, the German automaker Daimler-Benz bought Chrysler for $35 billion. The companies' leaders hoped that the merger would help Chrysler sell more cars in Europe and increase U.S. sales for Daimler-Benz. High costs and a loss of $1.5 billion in 2006, however, led Daimler-Benz to sell Chrysler for just $5 billion in 2007.

Despite the failed merger, globalization has had some benefits for Michigan. Global competition forced American automakers to improve their products, including focusing on new technologies such as hybrid gasoline-electric engines. Some Japanese and other foreign automakers also started producing vehicles in Michigan. In a 2007 survey, many Michigan business owners and managers favored increasing opportunities for foreign companies like Toyota to invest and create jobs in Michigan.

On July 28, 2005, Michigan Governor Jennifer M. Granholm gave a speech in Tokyo, Japan, about the future of Michigan industries, including the automobile industry. The governor said:

> "We're reshaping Michigan's economy to be the 21st century center of growth in automotive manufacturing, the life sciences, and alternative energy development. . . . Globalization offers Michigan, more than any other state, the possibility and the probability of becoming North America's next great center of growth and opportunity. Our history traces the rise of the global automotive industry. Our highly trained workforce and renowned research institutions give us, uniquely, the know-how to succeed. Our vision is one that embraces globalization and change."
>
> —Governor Jennifer M. Granholm, 2005

In the following chapters, you will read more about the effects of globalization in the 20th and 21st centuries.

# CHANGING AND ENDURING ISSUES

## CONTENTS

In classrooms across
the country, today's
students prepare to be
tomorrow's leaders. ▶

625

## A New Agenda

Americans were tired of the prolonged economic and foreign policy problems of the 1970s. Many looked to Ronald Reagan, the Republican candidate for President in 1980:

❝I cannot and will not stand by and see this great country destroy itself. . . . I don't agree that our nation must resign itself to inevitable decline, yielding its proud position to other hands. . . . The crisis we face is not the result of any failure of the American spirit; it is the failure of our leaders to establish rational goals and give our people something to order their lives by. If I am elected, I shall regard my election as proof that the people of the United States have decided to set a new agenda. . . .❞

—Ronald Reagan, November 13, 1979

*Listen to the* Witness History *audio to learn more about Ronald Reagan.*

◀ Reagan on the campaign trail in 1980

1980 campaign pin

Piece of the Berlin Wall after its fall

 **Content Expectations**

**Chapter Focus Question:** What was the conservative resurgence, and how did it affect the domestic and foreign policy of the United States?

## Section 1
**The Conservative Movement Grows**  9.1.2b, 9.1.2e, 9.2.1

## Section 2
**The Reagan Revolution**  8.3.3, 9.1.1, 9.1.2a, 9.1.2c

## Section 3
**The End of the Cold War**  8.1.3, 8.2.3, 9.2.1

## Section 4
**Foreign Policy After the Cold War**  9.1.2a, 9.2.1, 9.3.1a

Linda Evans and John Forsythe, stars of television's *Dynasty*

Use the ☑ **Quick Study Timeline** at the end of this chapter to preview chapter events.

**Note Taking Study Guide** *Online*
**For:** Note Taking and American Issues Connector
**Web Code:** nee-9201

Frustration over ▶ controversial issues in the 1970s, such as the busing battle featured on this cover of *Time* from 1975, lingered into the 1980s.

WITNESS HISTORY 🔊 AUDIO

### Backlash Against Liberal Programs

By 1980, public discontent with liberal programs, from welfare to school busing, had grown considerably. Many middle- and working-class Americans, in particular, felt that the reforms enacted during the 1960s and carried out in the 1970s threatened the American dream.

“If, during the 1960s and 1970s, there was an elite wisdom that shaped the directions of social policy, there was also a popular wisdom that explained why things were falling apart. . . . The popular wisdom is characterized by hostility toward welfare (it makes people lazy), toward lenient judges (they encourage crime), and toward socially conscious schools (too busy busing kids to teach them to read).”

—Charles Murray, *Losing Ground,* 1984

# The Conservative Movement Grows

### Content Expectations

- **9.1.2b** Analyze role of evangelical religion in national politics.
- **9.1.2e** Analyze role of regional differences in national politics.
- **9.2.1** Explain role of U.S. as a super-power in post-Cold War world.

### Terms and People

| | |
|---|---|
| liberal | unfunded mandate |
| conservative | Moral Majority |
| New Right | Ronald Reagan |

### NoteTaking

**Reading Skill: Summarize** As you read, summarize the rise of the conservative movement in an outline. Use the one below as a starting point.

> I. Two Views: Liberal and Conservative
>   A. Liberal ideas and goals
>     1.
>     2.

**Why It Matters** The 1964 election marked a low point for conservatives in the post–World War II era. Barry Goldwater, favorite of the conservative movement, lost the election in a landslide. Nonetheless, conservatives were not defeated by this loss at the polls. On the contrary, they set out to build an organization and to put forth a clear vision of their goals and values that would enable them to win in the future. By 1980, their plan had worked: Ronald Reagan, the new hero of the conservatives, was elected President. The modern conservative movement spearheaded by Ronald Reagan deeply affected the nation's policies for decades. **Section Focus Question: What spurred the rise of conservatism in the late 1970s and early 1980s?**

## Two Views: Liberal and Conservative

The two major political parties in the United States in the late twentieth century were the Democrats, many of whom were "liberals," and the Republicans, who were often labeled "conservatives." **Liberals** generally favored government intervention to help the needy, whereas **conservatives** generally favored allowing the free market, private organizations, and individuals to do that. Although the two parties did agree on many basic issues, including core American values such as freedom and equality, they diverged on many others. In addition, individual members within both parties did not always conform to their party's majority.

**The Ideas and Goals of Liberalism** In the late 1970s, liberals tended to believe that the federal government should play a significant role in improving the lives of all Americans. They valued social programs that helped the poor, unemployed, elderly, and others. They also sponsored laws that protected the rights of minorities and women, especially in the post–World War II period. They supported greater government regulation of industry. In the foreign policy realm, liberals tended to favor cooperating with international organizations like the United Nations.

**The Ideas and Goals of Conservatism** In contrast, some conservatives felt that a large central government endangered economic growth and individual choice. They felt the liberal policies of the 1960s amd 1970s left a legacy of rising inflation and enormous waste. Futhermore, some conservatives criticized the liberal solution of "throwing money" at social problems. They sought to reduce taxes and limit government regulation of industry in order to promote economic growth. As conservative economist Milton Friedman and his wife Rose Friedman wrote in their book *Free to Choose*, "The story of the United States is the story of an economic miracle. . . . What produced this miracle? Clearly not central direction by government."

Other conservatives, neoconservatives or traditionalists, warned about the dangers posed to society by abandoning traditional values in favor of the new freedoms exemplified by the counterculture and advertised by the mass media. This concern with the perceived <u>degeneration</u> of modern youth dovetailed with many conservatives' religious beliefs.

**Vocabulary Builder**
<u>degeneration</u>—(dee jehn er AY shuhn) *n.* declining in quality

Anticommunism formed the third leg of modern conservatism. Most anticommunists focused on the dangers posed to the United States by the Soviet Union. They questioned the wisdom of the détente policy followed by Presidents Nixon, Ford, and Carter. They also fought against the SALT II treaty in the Senate.

✓ **Checkpoint** How was conservatism different from liberalism in the early 1980s?

# The Conservative Movement Gains Strength

During the 1940s and 1950s, the lines separating Republicans and Democrats had blurred. The two parties had developed a bipartisan foreign policy aimed at containing communism. Both favored a relatively significant role for the government in domestic affairs. However, during the 1960s and 1970s, many Republicans became increasingly critical of the liberal policies of the Democrats. They advanced a new conservative agenda. The differences between the two major parties grew more pronounced. The **New Right,** as the resurgent conservative movement was called, grew rapidly and was a coalition of several different groups with varying ideas and goals.

| Two Viewpoints: Liberal and Conservative | | ✓ Quick Study |
|---|---|---|
| **Issue** | **Liberal Viewpoint** | **Conservative Viewpoint** |
| Role of government in the economy | Favored more government involvement to lessen extreme economic inequalities through<br>• social programs (often leading to higher taxes)<br>• government regulation of industry | Favored limited government involvement in order to stimulate economic growth by<br>• reducing taxes<br>• decreasing regulation of industry |
| Foreign policy | Favored international diplomacy to combat communism in other countries | Favored relying on our own national defense and actively fighting against communism in other countries |

**Liberalism Loses Its Appeal** One reason for the revival of the Republican Party was the unraveling of the Democratic Party. The Vietnam War and urban riots of the 1960s divided the same people who had rallied around President Johnson's vision of the Great Society. The rise of the counterculture had alienated many midwestern Americans and white conservative Christians in the South. Watergate, the oil crises of the 1970s, and the Iran hostage crisis further weakened the public's faith in the federal government.

Just as importantly, the shifts in the economy of the 1970s, including the decline in northern industries, dampened America's optimism about the future. America had supported the Great Society, in part, because Johnson had suggested that the war on poverty and other new programs would not demand higher taxes. When the economy stagnated, liberal ideas lost their pull and conservative beliefs became more attractive.

**The New Right Criticizes Liberal Programs** Many conservatives believed that liberal policies were responsible for stagflation and other economic problems of the late 1970s. They believed that the government taxed citizens and businesses too heavily and spent too much on the wrong programs. They complained about **unfunded mandates,** programs required but not paid for by the federal government.

Some conservatives also criticized federal welfare programs, arguing they rewarded lack of effort. Furthermore, they thought that the Great Society had made the problem of poverty worse not better. They believed that welfare contributed to the rise in the number of children born out of wedlock and therefore encouraged the decline of the traditional family, consisting of a married father and mother and their children. They also felt that affirmative action programs went too far and contributed to reverse discrimination.

Another group that supported the conservative platform was the "sagebrush rebels." Sagebrush rebels were activists who believed that the federal government controlled too much land in the western states. They thought the federal government should give control of this land to the states, to be used to their best economic advantage. Most environmentalists opposed the movement, not wanting to expose preserved lands to possible development.

**Religious Participation Rises** At the same time, concern with cultural change caused more religious groups to become actively involved in politics. The **Moral Majority,** founded by Reverend Jerry Falwell in 1979, was a political organization working to fulfill religious goals. It also worried about the decline of the traditional family. The Moral Majority opposed the 1962 Supreme Court decision *Engel* v. *Vitale,* which forbade religious teaching in schools, as well as the historic 1973 *Roe* v. *Wade* decision, which legalized abortion. It condemned the Equal Rights Amendment and homosexuality.

The Moral Majority boosted the Republican Party's chances of winning the presidency by reaching out to Americans who had traditionally not participated in the political process. With other groups like it, the Moral Majority registered at least 2 million new voters before the 1980 presidential election. One of their tactics was to distribute Moral Majority "report cards" on candidates, which almost always favored Republicans.

**Politics and Religion Meet**
Reverend Jerry Falwell, founder of the Moral Majority, stands in front of his home church in Lynchburg, Virginia, in August 1980. A banner on top of the church's sign encourages members to register to vote. *How was the Moral Majority different from traditional religious groups?*

**Population Trends Boost Conservatism** Demographic, or population, trends also strengthened the conservative movement. Historically, northern cities stood as the stronghold of liberal Democrats. When an increasing number of Americans moved to the suburbs, their attachment to liberalism waned as they struggled financially during the tough economic days of the late 1970s. At the same time, Republicans emphasized issues that they believed would convince moderate liberals to switch their party allegiance. For instance, Republicans attacked school busing as a form of social engineering that threatened the long-cherished ideal of neighborhood schools.

Republicans also benefited from the migration from the Rust Belt to the Sunbelt, which took place in the 1970s, and a historical realignment of white voters in the Deep South. Since the Civil War, most white southerners had voted for the Democratic Party. Following the enactment of civil rights legislation in the mid-1960s, however, many white southerners began to shift their party allegiance. By the 1980s, the Republicans had become the dominant political party in the region.

 **Checkpoint** What were some of the forces that helped the Republican Party grow during the 1970s?

# Reagan Wins the Presidency

The growing conservative movement swept the Republican presidential candidate, a man named **Ronald Reagan,** to victory in the 1980 election. Much more charismatic and polished than Goldwater, Reagan made clear his opposition to big government, his support for a strong military, and his faith in traditional values. Just as importantly, he radiated optimism, convincing Americans that he would usher in a new era of prosperity and patriotism.

**Reagan's Path to the White House** Born in Tampico, Illinois, in 1911, Reagan suffered the hardships of the Great Depression as a young adult before landing a job in Hollywood as a movie actor. Never a big star, Reagan appeared in many "B" or low-budget films. His most famous starring role was in *Knute Rockne,* a film based on the life of Notre Dame's legendary football coach.

When his acting career began to wane, Reagan became a spokesperson for General Electric and toured the nation giving speeches. Although once a staunch New Dealer, Reagan had become a Goldwater conservative. In these speeches he began to criticize big government and high taxes and warned of the dangers of communism. In 1964, near the end of Goldwater's presidential campaign, Reagan delivered a nationally televised address in which he spelled out these views:

> **Primary Source** "This is the issue of this election, whether we believe in our capacity for self-government or whether we abandon the American Revolution and confess that a little intellectual elite in a far-distant capital can plan our lives for us better than we can plan them ourselves."
>
> —Ronald Reagan, "A Time for Choosing," 1964

## HISTORY MAKERS

**Ronald Reagan** (1911–2004) Ronald Reagan's easy communication style, which appealed so much to his supporters, was rooted in his background as an entertainer. After graduating from college, he worked as a radio sports announcer until, in 1937, he signed a contract with a movie studio. In 1954, he began hosting a television show sponsored by General Electric. Soon, he was touring the country for the company, giving speeches that promoted traditional values and American business. As Reagan's views became more conservative, he switched from the Democratic to the Republican Party. He gained political fame in 1964 with a speech supporting conservative senator Barry Goldwater's run for the presidency.

While the speech failed to bolster Goldwater's campaign, it won the admiration of many conservatives. Two years later, Reagan won the governorship of California. He served for two terms as governor and nearly won the Republican presidential nomination in 1976. In 1980, he won the nomination by a landslide. His opponent was Jimmy Carter, the Democratic incumbent.

**Reagan Wins a Close Election** As the election approached, Carter looked like a lame duck. Persistent inflation, the Iran hostage crisis, and the Soviet invasion of Afghanistan made it easy for Reagan to cast the Carter presidency in a negative light. "Are you better off than you were four years ago?" Reagan asked audiences on the campaign trail, knowing that most Americans would say, "No."

The race remained relatively close until about one week before the election, when Reagan and Carter held their only presidential debate. In this debate, Reagan's gifts as a communicator shone. He appeared friendly and even-tempered and calmed fears that he did not have enough experience to serve as President. On Election Day, Reagan won 50.6 percent of the popular vote. Because most states award electoral votes on a "winner-takes-all" basis, Reagan won an overwhelming majority of electoral college votes despite the narrow margin by which he won the popular vote. Even though the Democrats maintained control of the House of Representatives, Republicans captured the U.S. Senate for the first time since 1955. The conservatives were back.

## The Presidential Election of 1980

| Candidate (Party) | Electoral Vote | Popular Vote | % Electoral Vote | % Popular Vote |
|---|---|---|---|---|
| Ronald Reagan (Republican) | 489 | 43,642,639 | 90.9 | 50.6 |
| James Carter (Democratic) | 49 | 35,480,948 | 9.1 | 41.2 |
| John Anderson (Independent) | — | 5,719,437 | — | 6.6 |

✔ **Checkpoint** What did Ronald Reagan promise to do if elected to the presidency?

---

## SECTION 1 Assessment

**Progress Monitoring *Online***
For: Self-test with vocabulary practice
Web Code: nea-1902

### Comprehension

1. **Terms and People** For each item below, write a sentence explaining how it related to the rise of conservatism in the late 1970s.
   - liberal
   - conservative
   - New Right
   - unfunded mandate
   - Moral Majority
   - Ronald Reagan

2. **NoteTaking Reading Skill: Summarize** Use your outline to answer the Section Focus Question: What spurred the rise of conservatism in the late 1970s and early 1980s?

### Writing About History

3. **Quick Write: Choose a Topic** Choose a topic from this section, such as Ronald Reagan's path to the White House, that would suit the creation of a multimedia presentation. Keep in mind that a multimedia presentation is an oral report that is enhanced with artwork, charts, music, videos, and so on.

### Critical Thinking

4. **Compare Points of View** Describe one major difference between liberals and conservatives in the early 1980s.

5. **Identify Central Issues** What policies did members of the New Right criticize?

6. **Summarize** How did the Moral Majority help strengthen the Republican Party?

7. **Draw Conclusions** Why did Americans elect Ronald Reagan to the presidency in 1980?

LET'S MAKE AMERICA GREAT AGAIN
REAGAN '80

WITNESS HISTORY ◆)) AUDIO

**WITNESS HISTORY** ◆)) AUDIO

## Reagan's Vision

During his eight years as President, Ronald Reagan earned a reputation as the "Great Communicator" because of his speaking abilities. In his farewell speech, he expressed his satisfaction with what he had accomplished:

❝After 200 years, two centuries, . . . [America is] still a beacon, still a magnet for all who must have freedom. . . . We've done our part. And as I walk off into the city streets, a final word to the men and women of the Reagan revolution, the men and women across America who for eight years did the work that brought America back. My friends: We did it.❞

—Ronald Reagan, Farewell Address, January 11, 1989

▲ Ronald Reagan and his wife Nancy after his victory in the 1980 election. Above, a campaign button for Reagan.

# The Reagan Revolution

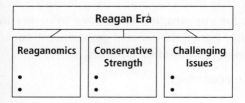

## Content Expectations

- **8.3.3** Analyze causes/course of the women's rights movement in 1960s/1970s.
- **9.1.1** Evaluate changes in U.S. economy.
- **9.1.2a** Growth of conservative movement in national politics/role of Reagan.
- **9.1.2c** Analyze intensification of partisanship.

## Terms and People

| | |
|---|---|
| supply-side economics | Savings and Loan crisis |
| deregulation | voucher |
| budget deficit | AIDS |
| national debt | |

## NoteTaking

**Reading Skill: Identify Main Ideas** Identify the main ideas behind Reagan's policies.

```
              Reagan Era
   ┌──────────────┬──────────────┬──────────────┐
   │ Reaganomics  │ Conservative │ Challenging  │
   │              │  Strength    │   Issues     │
   │  •           │  •           │  •           │
   │              │  •           │  •           │
   └──────────────┴──────────────┴──────────────┘
```

**Why It Matters** Conservatives celebrated Ronald Reagan's election as the fulfillment of their dreams. Some even referred to his coming to power as the "Reagan Revolution." The Reagan Revolution would bring a significant shift in the political direction of the nation. **Section Focus Question: What were the major characteristics of the conservative Reagan Revolution?**

## Reaganomics Guides the Economy

Reagan and his advisers based their economic policies on the theory of "supply-side economics," sometimes called "Reaganomics." The theory of **supply-side economics** rests on the assumption that if taxes are reduced, people will work more and have more money to spend, causing the economy to grow. The government will then collect more in taxes. To cut taxes while still balancing the federal budget, however, Reagan also needed to reduce federal spending on programs favored by both Democrats and Republicans.

**New Policies to Boost the Economy** Congress approved most of Reagan's plan to institute supply-side economics by passing the Economic Recovery Act of 1981, which reduced taxes by 25 percent over three years. The richest Americans received the largest tax cuts. Reagan justified this move by saying that the wealthy would use the money they saved to invest in new businesses, which would

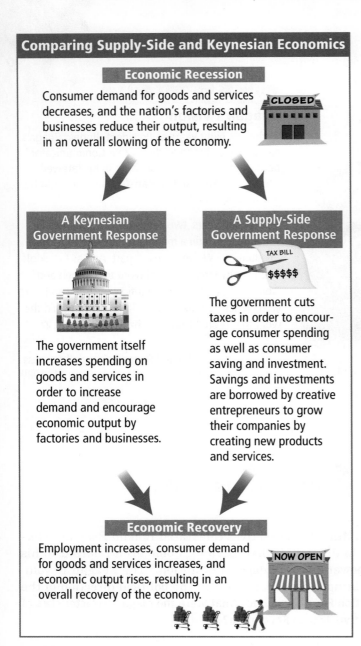

## Comparing Supply-Side and Keynesian Economics

### Economic Recession

Consumer demand for goods and services decreases, and the nation's factories and businesses reduce their output, resulting in an overall slowing of the economy.

CLOSED

### A Keynesian Government Response

The government itself increases spending on goods and services in order to increase demand and encourage economic output by factories and businesses.

### A Supply-Side Government Response

TAX BILL
$$$$$

The government cuts taxes in order to encourage consumer spending as well as consumer saving and investment. Savings and investments are borrowed by creative entrepreneurs to grow their companies by creating new products and services.

### Economic Recovery

Employment increases, consumer demand for goods and services increases, and economic output rises, resulting in an overall recovery of the economy.

NOW OPEN

**Diagram Skills** Can you predict what might be the upsides and downsides of both of the responses shown above?

---

help everyone. Reagan also convinced Congress to cut about $40 billion from the federal budget, mostly by cutting spending for social programs.

In addition to cutting taxes, Reagan also reduced the government's role in the economy by calling for **deregulation,** or the removal of government control over industry. By the mid-1980s, Congress had deregulated the airline, telecommunications, and banking industries. The Reagan administration also cut funding for federal agencies that oversaw many other industries.

**Recession and Recovery** Despite Reagan's economic policies, the economy experienced a severe recession from 1980 to 1982. Unemployment rose to more than 10 percent in 1982. The recession hit blue-collar workers particularly hard. Many farmers, facing overseas competition, lost their farms. The policies that Paul Volcker, as head of the Federal Reserve Board, had introduced to tame the great inflation of the 1970s contributed to the recession in the early 1980s. Beginning in early 1983, however, the economy began to turn around. Inflation fell dramatically. The Gross National Product, or the annual income earned by Americans and American businesses, expanded at a healthy pace. America's economy seemed revitalized.

Despite this, the number of poor people, including the working poor, actually increased. In addition, immigrants from Latin America and Asia continued to pour into the United States. More than 7.3 million legal immigrants and hundreds of thousands of undocumented immigrants entered the country in the 1980s. Many of these newcomers worked in low-paying jobs and struggled to make ends meet. Meanwhile, the richest percentage of Americans grew richer.

**Problems With Budget Deficits** Reagan increased defense spending but failed to win huge cuts in government spending in other areas. This caused the federal **budget deficit,** or the shortfall between the amount of money spent and the amount taken in by the government, to skyrocket from about $79 billion in 1981 to more than $221 billion in 1986. The **national debt,** the amount of money the federal government owes to owners of government bonds, rose to $2.5 trillion.

In response to persistent budget deficits, Congress passed the Gramm-Rudman-Hollings Act in 1985. The act sought to balance the budget by 1990 by requiring automatic cuts in federal spending if the deficit exceeded a certain amount. However, the federal budget deficit set new records into the early 1990s.

The **Savings and Loan, or S&L, crisis** in 1989 exacerbated deficit problems. In the late 1980s, about 1,000 Savings and Loan banks failed, some because of fraudulent behavior and others because they made too many risky loans. Critics blamed Reagan's deregulation policies for encouraging the banks to invest in riskier propositions. To prevent a broader panic, the federal government spent upwards of $200 billion to bail out depositors at the failed banks.

 **Checkpoint** What was supply-side economics?

# Conservative Strength Grows

Despite budget and debt problems, the economic recovery improved the national mood and helped Ronald Reagan's popularity. Reagan used his time in office to strengthen the conservative cause.

**Reagan Wins Reelection in 1984** During the 1984 presidential campaign, Reagan used the phrase "It is morning in America" as a campaign slogan:

> **Primary Source** "It's morning again in America. In a town not too far from where you live, a young family has just moved into a new home. . . . Right down the street one of the neighbors has just bought himself a new car, with all the options. The factory down the river is working again. . . . Life is better, America is back. And people have a sense of pride they never felt they'd feel again."
> —Campaign commercial for the reelection of Ronald Reagan, 1984 🔊 AUDIO

This theme dovetailed nicely with Reagan's upbeat spirit, which he displayed even in his darkest moments. For example, on March 30, 1981, a disturbed man named John Hinckley, Jr., tried to assassinate the President. One bullet from Hinckley's gun lodged in Reagan's chest. According to one account, Reagan joked to his doctors, "I hope you are all Republicans."

Americans voted overwhelmingly to reelect Reagan in 1984. He easily defeated Walter Mondale, the Democratic presidential nominee, and his running mate, Geraldine Ferraro, the first woman to be nominated for Vice President by a major political party. However, Reagan's <u>momentum</u> did not lead to a total triumph for conservatives, as Democrats retained control of the House of Representatives.

**Vocabulary Builder**
<u>momentum</u>–(moh MEHN tuhm)
*n.* forward motion; push

**Conservative Supreme Court Justices and the Equal Access Act**
During his two terms, Reagan appointed judges who he hoped would reverse the liberal drift of the federal courts. He appointed three new Justices—Sandra Day O'Connor, Antonin Scalia, and Anthony Kennedy—to the Supreme Court and elevated William Rehnquist, a well-known conservative, to the position of Chief Justice in 1986. Sandra Day O'Connor, nominated in 1981, was the first female Justice and a moderate conservative. Although she voted with other conservatives on many issues, she consistently voted to uphold *Roe* v. *Wade,* which Reagan opposed.

Near the end of Reagan's first term, Congress passed the Equal Access Act. This act required public secondary schools to allow any group equal access to school facilities. Conservative Christian groups supported the act's passage because many public schools did not allow religious groups to meet on school property. The Supreme Court confirmed the constitutionality of the Equal Access Act in 1990 in *Board of Education of Westside Community Schools* v. *Mergens.*

**George H.W. Bush Becomes President** Reagan used his personal popularity to promote George H.W. Bush, his Vice President for eight years, as Bush campaigned for the presidency against Massachusetts governor Michael Dukakis in 1988. Bush called for a "kinder, gentler nation," yet both candidates attacked the other using negative campaign ads. Bush cemented his support among conservatives by promising not to raise taxes and by casting himself as a defender of

## HISTORY MAKERS

### Sandra Day O'Connor (born 1930)

After getting her law degree in 1952, Sandra Day O'Connor served as a lawyer for many years before becoming involved in Arizona state politics in the late 1960s. She was serving as a judge on the Arizona Court of Appeals when she was nominated to the Supreme Court in 1981.

O'Connor sat on the Supreme Court for nearly 25 years. Her vote was the tiebreaker on several influential court cases, causing her to be called one of the most powerful women in the United States.

Personal Computers: Hot item. ■ See p. A12

# TIMES of the Eighties
## A SNAPSHOT OF THE REAGAN YEARS

**TV Review**
## *Dynasty*: Living large and behaving badly
Fans love the Wednesday night favorite, *Dynasty*, featuring Linda Evans as Krystle Carrington and John Forsythe as Blake Carrington. ■ See p. B6

### Are you a Yuppie?
If you're under 30, live in a city, and work in an office, then *yes*—you're a Young Urban Professional, or Yuppie.
■ See p. A7

# ADA Passed!

- The Americans With Disabilities Act (ADA) was passed by Congress and signed into law by President George H.W. Bush in July 1990.
- The act will ensure that Americans with disabilities will receive the same opportunities in employment and access to public transportation and public places as other Americans.
- The act benefits more than 43 million people and is another stride forward in the quest to protect the rights of all Americans.

## In the Economy

### Trade Imbalance With Japan Deepens
Japan's import restrictions are keeping American goods off of Japanese store shelves.

**U.S. Trade Deficit With Japan, 1980–1990**

U.S. Exports to Japan
Japanese Imports to U.S.

Dollars (in billions)
100
80
60
40
20
0
1980 1982 1984 1986 1988 1990
SOURCE: *Statistical Abstract of the United States*

## Trend Spotting

### VCRs Bring Fitness Craze Home

Videotapes of popular exercise programs, such as Judi Missett's Jazzercise fitness plan, are flying off the shelves.

# Space Shuttle *Challenger* Explodes
## Reagan Comforts the Nation

**CAPE CANAVERAL, FLORIDA** On January 28, 1986, the long-awaited launch of the space shuttle *Challenger* ended in tragedy when the shuttle exploded 73 seconds after take-off. The shuttle carried seven astronauts, including New Hampshire schoolteacher Christa McAuliffe. Her flight would have been the first time a private citizen entered space.

President Reagan spoke to the nation following the tragedy:

**Primary Source** "For the families of the seven [astronauts], we cannot bear, as you do, the full impact of this tragedy. But we feel the loss, and we're thinking about you so very much. Your loved ones were daring and brave, and they had that special grace, that special spirit that says, 'Give me a challenge and I'll meet it with joy.' They had a hunger to explore the universe and discover its truths. They wished to serve, and they did. They served all of us."

The space shuttle *Challenger* exploded shortly after lifting off from Kennedy Space Center. Inset: Schoolteacher Christa McAuliffe (far left) and six career astronauts died aboard the shuttle.

---

## Thinking Critically

1. **Draw Conclusions** How do you think the trade imbalance with Japan affected the American economy?

2. **Summarize** How did new technologies help advance the personal fitness craze?

---

traditional values. However, Democrats won a majority of seats in both houses of Congress.

President Bush sought to control federal spending by encouraging Americans to volunteer. Government, he asserted, could take a smaller role in daily life if, "like a thousand points of light," community organizations and volunteers provided more help to the disabled, illiterate, and poor.

✓ **Checkpoint** How did Reagan try to build upon conservative gains during his presidency?

# Confronting Challenging Issues

Despite Reagan and Bush's successes, the nation continued to face a number of pressing problems. In 1981 when thousands of air-traffic controllers went on strike, Reagan refused to negotiate with the Professional Air Traffic Controllers Organization (PATCO) and fired the striking workers because they were violating a law forbidding federal employees from striking. Many Americans admired Reagan's strong, decisive stance. Some union supporters, however, claimed that Reagan's action represented an assault on the labor movement.

In the 1980s, the rising cost of Social Security caused concern. As the number of elderly people in America grew, the Social Security system began to collect less money than it paid out. In 1983, Reagan signed the Social Security Reform Act, which raised the minimum retirement age and increased payroll taxes for Social Security. It provided a temporary fix but did not solve the long-term problems of the Social Security program.

Many Americans also worried about the state of America's public education system. In 1983, the Department of Education issued *A Nation at Risk*. This study showed that students were consistently scoring lower on standardized tests as time passed. The report argued that America's schools failed to prepare students adequately to compete with students around the globe.

Even before the report appeared, conservatives called for providing **vouchers**, or government checks, that could be used by parents to pay tuition at private schools. Conservatives argued that vouchers would force public schools to improve in order to attract and retain students. Liberals in Congress argued that vouchers would take much-needed money away from public schools.

In addition, the nation faced the threat of a new disease, **Acquired Immunodeficiency Syndrome (AIDS),** which first appeared in 1981. AIDS is the last stage of the Human Immunodeficiency Virus (HIV), which attacks the immune system of its victims. There is no known cure. At first, AIDS spread mainly among homosexual men and intravenous drug users. Later, the virus infected different groups of people. By 1994, AIDS had killed more than 250,000 Americans. President Reagan responded slowly to the AIDS epidemic. During George H.W. Bush's presidency, funding for research on the disease rose substantially.

 **Checkpoint** What were some of the challenges that the nation faced during the 1980s and early 1990s?

## The AIDS Quilt

When the AIDS Quilt was displayed in Washington, D.C., in October 1988, it consisted of 8,288 panels, each created in the memory of a person who had died of AIDS. Today, the quilt has more than 44,000 memorial panels.

---

SECTION **2** Assessment

**Progress Monitoring *Online***
For: Self-test with vocabulary practice
Web Code: nea-1903

### Comprehension

1. **Terms and People** For each term below, write a sentence explaining its significance to the Reagan era.
   - supply-side economics
   - deregulation
   - budget deficit
   - national debt
   - Savings and Loan crisis
   - AIDS

2. **NoteTaking Reading Skill: Identify Main Ideas** Use your chart to answer the Section Focus Question: What were the major characteristics of the conservative Reagan Revolution?

### Writing About History

3. **Quick Write: Create a Storyboard** Create a storyboard that illustrates one of the challenges facing Americans during this period. Use a combination of words and images to express your points.

### Critical Thinking

4. **Summarize** In what ways did Reagan try to fulfill the goal of less government involvement in the economy?

5. **Draw Conclusions** How did Reagan strengthen the conservative cause?

6. **Identify Central Issues** How did Reagan address problems with Social Security?

# Ronald Reagan: *Tear Down This Wall*

On June 12, 1987, President Reagan spoke at the Brandenburg Gate, near the Berlin Wall, in West Berlin, Germany. His speech acknowledged the new Soviet leader Mikhail Gorbachev's efforts at reform in the Soviet Union. However, Reagan was not satisfied with Gorbachev's limited measures. He challenged the Soviet leader to show a real commitment to reform by tearing down the Berlin Wall that had stood between East and West Berlin since 1961. This wall symbolized the division between communism and democracy.

Reagan speaking at the Brandenburg Gate (above); the western side of the Berlin Wall before its fall (below)

In the 1950s, Khrushchev predicted: "We will bury you." But in the West today, we see a free world that has achieved a level of prosperity and well-being unprecedented in all human history. In the Communist world, we see failure, technological backwardness, declining standards of health, even want of the most basic kind—too little food. Even today, the Soviet Union still cannot feed itself. After these four decades, then, there stands before the entire world one great and inescapable conclusion: Freedom leads to prosperity. Freedom replaces the ancient hatreds among the nations with comity [courtesy] and peace. Freedom is the victor.

And now the Soviets themselves may, in a limited way, be coming to understand the importance of freedom. We hear much from Moscow about a new policy of reform and openness. Some political prisoners have been released. Certain foreign news broadcasts are no longer being jammed. Some economic enterprises have been permitted to operate with greater freedom from state control.

Are these the beginnings of profound changes in the Soviet state? Or are they token gestures, intended to raise false hopes in the West, or to strengthen the Soviet system without changing it? We welcome change and openness; for we believe that freedom and security go together, that the advance of human liberty can only strengthen the cause of world peace. There is one sign the Soviets can make that would be unmistakable, that would advance dramatically the cause of freedom and peace.

General Secretary Gorbachev, if you seek peace, if you seek prosperity for the Soviet Union and Eastern Europe, if you seek liberalization: Come here to this gate! Mr. Gorbachev, open this gate! Mr. Gorbachev, tear down this wall!

## Thinking Critically

1. **Demonstrate Reasoned Judgment** How does Reagan support his statement "Freedom is the victor"?

2. **Identify Central Issues** How does Reagan challenge Gorbachev to prove that his reforms are not "token gestures"?

▲ A soldier trains at Fort Dix in New Jersey in the 1980s.

WITNESS HISTORY  AUDIO

**A Strong Approach to Communism**

During the first term of his presidency, Ronald Reagan challenged the Soviet Union by building up America's military and casting the Cold War as a struggle between good and evil:

❝But if history teaches anything, it teaches that simpleminded appeasement or wishful thinking about our adversaries is folly. . . . I urge you to speak against those who would place the United States in a position of military and moral inferiority . . . beware the temptation . . . to ignore the facts of history and the aggressive impulses of an evil empire, to simply call the arms race a giant misunderstanding and thereby remove yourself from the struggle between right and wrong and good and evil.❞

—President Ronald Reagan, March 8, 1983

# The End of the Cold War

 **Content Expectations**

- **8.1.3** Evaluate factors leading to the end of Cold War.
- **8.2.3** Compare/contrast Roosevelt's New Deal initiatives, Johnson's Great Society programs, Reagan's market-based domestic policies.
- **9.2.1** Explain role of U.S. as a super-power in post-Cold War world.

**Terms and People**

Strategic Defense
 Initiative
Contras
Mikhail Gorbachev

*glasnost*
*perestroika*
Iran-Contra affair

**NoteTaking**

**Reading Skill: Sequence** As you read this section, use a flowchart like the one below to sequence major events related to the fall of communism in Europe and the Soviet Union.

| Reagan supports buildup of United States military. |
| --- |
| ↓      ↓      ↓ |
| |

**Why It Matters** President Ronald Reagan believed that the United States had lost its way in the wake of the Vietnam War. Rather than détente, he felt the United States should seek to roll back Soviet rule in Eastern Europe and elsewhere. Reagan believed that peace would come through strength. Although they initially increased tensions between the two superpowers, Reagan's foreign policies contributed to the end of the Cold War. **Section Focus Question: What were Reagan's foreign policies, and how did they contribute to the fall of communism in Europe?**

## Reagan Challenges Communism

President Reagan believed that the United States needed to weaken communism by challenging it as much as possible without provoking war. To this end, he devised policies aimed at toppling communist nations, ranging from building new nuclear missile systems to funding covert operations against Soviet troops and allies around the globe.

**Reagan Builds Up the U.S. Military** Under Reagan, the United States committed itself to the largest peacetime military buildup in its history. Reagan dedicated billions of dollars to the development and production of B-1 and B-2 bombers, MX missile systems, and other projects. In spite of massive protests by the nuclear freeze movement in the United States and abroad, the Reagan administration placed a new generation of nuclear missiles in Europe.

Reagan supported this massive military buildup, in part, because he did not believe that the Soviet Union could afford to spend as much on defense as the United States could. Reagan felt this

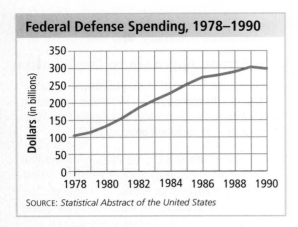

## Federal Defense Spending, 1978–1990

Dollars (in billions)

350
300
250
200
150
100
50
0

1978 1980 1982 1984 1986 1988 1990

SOURCE: *Statistical Abstract of the United States*

**Graph Skills** Reagan's foreign policy stance caused defense spending to increase dramatically. *How much did defense spending increase between 1978 and 1988?*

## The Contras in Nicaragua

After coming to power in 1939, Nicaragua's socialist Sandinista government accepted aid from Cuba and the Soviet Union, alarming the United States. Below, a group of Contras review a map at a base camp along the San Juan River. Contras opposed the Sandinista government. *How did a socialist government in Nicaragua alarm foreign policy officials in the United States?*

applied particularly to the **Strategic Defense Initiative (SDI),** a proposed program in which land- and space-based lasers would destroy any missiles aimed at the United States before they could reach their targets. Some dubbed the missile program "Star Wars," after the popular science-fiction movie trilogy, and claimed that it was unrealistic.

**Reagan Aids Anticommunists** Reagan also sought to weaken the Soviet Union by supporting anticommunist rebellions around the globe. To this end, the United States funded and trained the mujahadeen (moo jah huh DEEN), anti-Soviet rebels in Afghanistan. Reagan's advisers believed that with U.S. help, these guerrillas could drive the Soviets out of Afghanistan. In 1988, Soviet forces finally began to withdraw after years of fierce Afghan resistance.

Closer to home, Secretary of State Alexander Haig feared that the newly formed Sandinista government in Nicaragua provided the Soviets with a "safe house" in America's backyard. To counter this threat, the administration backed a group of anticommunist counterrevolutionaries, known as the **Contras.** At the same time, the United States supported a right-wing government in El Salvador as it battled leftist rebels. Many human rights activists strongly objected to this policy; even U.S. Ambassador Robert White described the legal system in El Salvador as "rotten" and called for the United States to suspend aid to the nation. Instead, Congress made funding for El Salvador's government dependent on the nation making progress on human rights.

In 1983, Reagan acted to counter another perceived threat in the Western Hemisphere. Members of a radical leftist movement, with some help from Cuba, had violently ousted the Grenadian prime minister. On October 25, 1983, U.S. troops invaded Grenada to prevent the island nation from becoming a communist outpost and to protect the lives of American medical students. Even though the legal grounds for this invasion proved questionable, most Americans approved of Reagan's decision.

**Gorbachev Pursues Reform** In 1985, **Mikhail Gorbachev** (mee kah EEL GOR buh chawf) became the President of the Soviet Union. Gorbachev ushered in a new Soviet era by pursuing the twin policies of *glasnost* and *perestroika*. **Glasnost** meant "a new openness," and **perestroika** stood for reforming the Soviet system—for instance, by moving away from a socialist or state-controlled economy. Gorbachev's reforms created an opening for a shift in relations between the two superpowers.

Gorbachev started these reforms mostly because the Soviet Union's economy lay in shambles. The nation faced regular shortages of food. Its factories and workers could not compete with their Western counterparts. A huge chunk of the Soviet economy's money went toward paying for the military. The war in Afghanistan had drained Soviet resources. Gorbachev realized that his nation could not match the military buildup initiated by the Reagan administration.

**The Two Leaders Meet** Gorbachev's policies and personality helped soften the Soviet Union's international image. Reagan responded to this change by moderating his own stance toward the Soviet Union. While the two nations had held no summits during Reagan's first four years in office, their leaders met four times between 1985 and 1989. During their final meeting in Moscow, Reagan and Gorbachev toasted each other at a state dinner, toured the sights like old friends, and held a joint press conference. At the press conference, a reporter asked Reagan about his description of the Soviet Union as an "evil empire." Reagan responded, "I was talking about another era." Then, Gorbachev allowed President Reagan to address students at Moscow State University on the benefits of the free-enterprise system and democracy:

### Analyzing Political Cartoons

**A Bumpy Ride?** In this cartoon, the communist bloc, or the group of Soviet-dominated communist nations in Eastern Europe, is represented by a rickety car headed down the bumpy road of reform.

1. What does the cartoonist seem to think perestroika will do to the communist bloc?
2. Why might economic reforms like perestroika lead to bumpy, or troubled, times?

**Primary Source** "Your generation is living in one of the most exciting times in Soviet history. It is a time when the first breath of freedom stirs the air and the heart beats to the accelerated rhythm of hope, when the accumulated spiritual energies of a long silence yearn to break free. . . . We do not know what the conclusion of this journey will be, but we're hopeful that the promise of reform will be fulfilled . . . leading to a new world of reconciliation, friendship, and peace."
—Ronald Reagan, May 31, 1988

Even before this summit, the two nations had signed a historic nuclear arms pact and had begun negotiations on the START I Treaty, which would reduce the number of nuclear weapons in the world.

 **Checkpoint** What policies toward communism did President Reagan pursue?

# The Cold War Ends

In a little over three years' time after Reagan's speech in Moscow, the Cold War had come to an end. The Berlin Wall came down; Poland, Czechoslovakia, and Hungary held democratic elections; and the Soviet Union disintegrated into numerous separate republics. *Time* magazine observed: "It was one of those rare times when the tectonic plates of history shift beneath men's feet, and nothing after is quite the same."

**Communism Ends in Eastern Europe** More so than any other event, the fall of the Berlin Wall symbolized the end of communism in Europe. For decades, the wall had blocked travel from communist East Berlin to democratic West Berlin. Guards shot those who attempted to escape over the wall to West Berlin. Then, in November 1989, following the fall of East Germany's communist government, East German authorities opened the wall's gates. Thousands climbed atop the wall; some even took sledgehammers and chipped away at the barricade. Within a year, East and West Germany would reunite as one single nation. Communists also lost power in Poland, Hungary, Czechoslovakia, Bulgaria, and Romania in 1989; in Albania in 1990; and in Yugoslavia in 1991.

**WITNESS HISTORY DVD**

Watch *Reagan and the End of the Cold War* on the **United States Witness History DVD** to explore Reagan's role in the end of the Cold War.

America's buildup of weapons, such as long-range nuclear missiles, threatens the Soviet Union.

**The Soviet Union Breaks Apart** In August 1991, hard-liners in the Soviet Union attempted to stage a coup in a last-gasp attempt to maintain communist rule. But when millions of Russians, led by Boris Yeltsin, rallied in the streets of Moscow in support of Gorbachev, the coup fell apart. Not long afterward, the Communist Party lost power, and the Soviet Union separated into 15 independent republics. Boris Yeltsin became the new leader of the largest new republic, the Russian Federation.

Historians do not totally agree on what caused the Soviet Union to collapse. Most acknowledge that Gorbachev's policy of *glasnost* opened the floodgates to rebellions against Soviet domination of Eastern Europe. Likewise, they note that his policy of *perestroika* fostered a challenge to communist rule within the Soviet Union. Yet, a number of scholars give Reagan credit for bringing an end

## Events That Changed America

# THE FALL OF COMMUNISM IN EUROPE

In the early 1980s, Ronald Reagan began to build up the American military. Knowing that the struggling Soviet economy could not match this buildup, Mikhail Gorbachev began reforms in the Soviet Union and sought a better relationship with the United States.

Then came 1989, the "year of the miracle." In that year, the nations of Eastern Europe experienced a series of bloodless revolutions. In June 1989, Solidarity, Poland's anticommunist reform party, swept into power. Its leader, Lech Walesa, was elected President in 1990. In November 1989, the Berlin Wall fell. People were allowed to travel freely from East to West Berlin for the first time in nearly 40 years. Next, massive demonstrations by university students in Czechoslovakia ended communist rule there. Finally, in August 1991, following a failed coup against Gorbachev, millions of Russians led by Boris Yeltsin protested against the central Soviet government, breaking its power. Not long afterward, the Soviet Union ceased to exist. President George H.W. Bush and Boris Yeltsin, the President of the new Russian Federation, established a friendly relationship between their nations.

▲ An American game about the Soviet policy of *glasnost*

▼ Reagan shares a friendly moment with Soviet leader Mikhail Gorbachev.

Lech Walesa, head of Poland's Solidarity movement, kisses the Polish flag as he takes his oath as President. ▼

to the Cold War. By dedicating America to a massive arms buildup, they argue, he hastened the collapse of the Soviet economy. In turn, this compelled Gorbachev to promote reform at home and relinquish control of Eastern Europe.

The key rival, competitor, and enemy of the United States for so many years had suddenly disappeared. President George H.W. Bush met and signed agreements with first Gorbachev and then Yeltsin to scale down and even eliminate certain types of nuclear weapons. Bush and Yeltsin issued a joint statement in 1992 pledging friendship and cooperation. The long Cold War, which had absorbed so much of the energy and resources of the Soviet Union and the United States since 1945, was finally over.

✔ **Checkpoint** What key actions and events brought about the end of the Cold War?

## Why It Matters

Although communism survived in China, Cuba, and a few other nations, the fall of communism in Eastern Europe and the Soviet Union ended the Cold War. American leaders now faced new challenges and daunting questions: Should military spending be decreased? What new direction should American foreign policy take in the post–Cold War world?

◀ West Germans celebrate the fall of the Berlin Wall and the reunification of Berlin.

▲ Bush and Yeltsin meet at Camp David to discuss joint foreign-policy proposals.

◀ Thousands of Czechs hold peaceful protests and candlelight vigils to protest Czechoslovakia's communist regime.

A child plays on a statue of Stalin that has been knocked down in Gorky Park in Moscow. ▼

## Thinking Critically

How did Reagan end up influencing Soviet policy in the mid-1980s?

**History Interactive**

**For:** More images from the fall of communism in Eastern Europe and the Soviet Union
**Web Code:** nep-1904

**Identify Main Ideas** Record the main ideas related to events in the Middle East during Reagan's presidency in a concept web like the one below.

**Vocabulary Builder**
contradict–(kahn truh DIHKT) *v.*
to go against

# Trouble Persists in the Middle East

Even as the Soviet Union collapsed, the United States continued to confront problems in the Middle East. In 1982, Reagan sent a group of 800 United States Marines to Lebanon as part of an international force trying to bring peace to a nation torn by civil war. On October 23, 1983, a truck loaded with thousands of pounds of explosives smashed through barriers at the headquarters of the United States Marines in Beirut (bay ROOT), Lebanon's capital, and into a four-story building that housed hundreds of military personnel. The explosion killed 241 marines. Reagan withdrew the remaining marines in February 1984. The incident illustrated, once again, the complicated nature of Middle Eastern politics.

During the 1980s, the United States often clashed with Libya. Led by Muammar al-Qaddafi (MOO uh mahr al kuh DAH fee), whom Reagan described as "the mad dog of the Middle East," Libya supported terrorist groups. In 1986, following a terrorist attack on a Berlin nightclub, which Reagan blamed on Qaddafi, U.S. warplanes bombed Libya. The air raid killed one of Qaddafi's daughters. Even though Qaddafi was unharmed, his criticism of the United States dwindled.

Reagan's presidency had started with a breakthrough in the Middle East. Twenty minutes after he took the oath of office on January 20, 1981, Iran released all 52 Americans it had held hostage since 1979. But during his second term, the Iran-Contra affair badly tarnished Reagan's reputation.

The **Iran-Contra affair** began when the United States sold weapons to Iran in 1985 in exchange for Iran's promise to pressure terrorist groups in Lebanon to release some American hostages. The plan didn't work, and it <u>contradicted</u> the administration's policy of refusing to negotiate with terrorists. Then, the administration used the money from the sale to fund the Contras in Nicaragua, despite the fact that in 1983 Congress had banned sending funds to the Contras. News of these deals came out in 1986. Although President Reagan accepted responsibility for the actions of his administration, he never admitted to ordering his aides to support the Contras. Ultimately, several leading administration officials and a top aide, Oliver North, were convicted on charges stemming from the scandal, although many of the convictions were later overturned on technical grounds. In spite of this, Reagan left office with extremely high approval ratings.

 **Checkpoint** What was the Iran-Contra scandal?

---

**Progress Monitoring *Online***
**For:** Self-test with vocabulary practice
**Web Code:** nea-1905

## Comprehension

1. **Terms and People** For each item below, write a sentence explaining how the term or person related to the fall of communism in Europe and the Soviet Union in the late 1980s and early 1990s.
   - Strategic Defense Initiative
   - Mikhail Gorbachev
   - *glasnost*
   - *perestroika*

2. NoteTaking **Reading Skill: Sequence** Use your flowchart to answer the Section Focus Question: What were Reagan's foreign policies, and how did they contribute to the fall of communism in Europe?

## Writing About History

3. **Quick Write: Choose Images** Using library books or approved Internet sources, select images and write captions to create a multimedia presentation about the fall of the Berlin Wall.

## Critical Thinking

4. **Draw Inferences** How did Reagan's foreign policy differ from that of Carter?

5. **Identify Point of View** During his first term, Reagan called the Soviet Union an "evil empire," but in his second term, he developed a working relationship with Gorbachev. What accounts for this change in strategy?

6. **Synthesize Information** Why did Reagan order an air raid on Libya?

**A New World Order**

Less than two years after the Berlin Wall fell, the United States found itself involved in another war after Iraq invaded its neighbor Kuwait. President George H.W. Bush spoke about his vision for this war:

**❝**We stand today at a unique and extraordinary moment. The crisis in the Persian Gulf, as grave as it is, also offers a rare opportunity to move toward a historic period of cooperation. Out of these troubled times . . . a new world order can emerge; a new era—freer from the threat of terror, stronger in the pursuit of justice; and more secure in the quest of peace, an era in which the nations of the world, East and West, North and South, can prosper and live in harmony.**❞**

—George Herbert Walker Bush, Address to Congress, September 11, 1990

▲ President Bush and his wife, Barbara, visiting troops in Saudi Arabia during the Persian Gulf War

# Foreign Policy After the Cold War

## (MI) Content Expectations

- **9.1.2a** Growth of conservative movement in national politics/role of Reagan.
- **9.2.1** Explain role of U.S. as a super-power in post-Cold War world.
- **9.3.1a** Compose a persuasive essay on role of U.S. in the world.

## Terms and People

Manuel Noriega
Tiananmen Square
apartheid
Nelson Mandela

divest
Saddam Hussein
Operation Desert Storm

## NoteTaking

**Reading Skill: Summarize** Use a chart like the one below to summarize Bush's major foreign-policy decisions.

| Post-Cold War Foreign Policy | |
| --- | --- |
| America's new role in the world | Persian Gulf War |
| • | • |
| • | • |

**Why It Matters** When the Cold War came to an end, many Americans hoped that a new era of peace would dawn. Yet, America's foreign policy during the Bush years demonstrated that the end of the Cold War would not lead to a new era of peace, but instead to a dangerous era of regional conflicts. **Section Focus Question: What actions did the United States take abroad during George H.W. Bush's presidency?**

## A New Role in the World

When the Soviet Union collapsed, the United States became the only unopposed superpower poised to take a leading role in world affairs under the leadership of President George H.W. Bush. Few leaders entered the White House with as much foreign policy experience as Bush. A graduate of Yale and a veteran of World War II, Bush had served as the U.S. Ambassador to the United Nations, as director of the CIA, and as Ronald Reagan's Vice President. His experience would be put to the test as America faced a series of difficult international crises during the late 1980s and early 1990s.

**Latin America and the War on Drugs** In the late 1980s and early 1990s, Latin America experienced a wave of democracy. In Central America, a peace plan devised by Costa Rican leader Oscar Arias (AH ree uhs) brought free elections in Nicaragua and the end of a long civil war in El Salvador. In Chile, the notorious military dictator Augusto Pinochet (ah GOO stoh pee noh SHAY) gave up power.

# Foreign Policy Under Bush

President Bush faced several foreign-policy challenges. He adjusted his policy depending on each situation. **How did Bush's approach in Somalia differ from his approach in Panama?**

▲ **Promoting Democracy in South Africa**
Bush greets South African leader Nelson Mandela soon after Mandela's release from prison in 1990.

Not all developments in Latin America, however, pleased the Bush administration. Since the Nixon administration, the government had been waging a "war on drugs," or an attempt to stop illegal drug use by going after both sellers and users. Groups of racketeers in Latin America supplied a significant amount of the illegal drugs in the United States. The Bush administration arrested and tried several international drug figures, including Eduardo Martinez Romero, the reputed financier of a Colombian drug cartel. Even more spectacularly, in December 1989, Bush sent more than 12,000 U.S. troops to invade Panama and arrest Panama's dictator **Manuel Noriega.** Brought to the United States for trial, Noriega was convicted of several charges of drug trafficking and sentenced to 40 years in prison.

**China Cracks Down on Critics** Meanwhile, in the spring of 1989, Chinese students captured the world's attention by staging prodemocracy protests in **Tiananmen Square** in the heart of Beijing. Many Americans hoped that these protests might result in the fall of communism in China. Instead, on June 4, Chinese tanks rolled into Beijing, killed hundreds of protesters, crushed the demonstrations, and imprisoned many prodemocracy activists.

The Bush administration condemned this action and suspended arms sales to China. However, Bush did not believe that stiffer penalties would influence Chinese leaders. He made the pragmatic choice to remain engaged with China economically and diplomatically, rather than cut off ties with the country.

**Change Comes to South Africa** While China resisted changes, long overdue ones were taking place in South Africa. For years, the South African government, controlled by whites, had maintained an oppressive system of rigid segregation known as **apartheid.** The leader of the antiapartheid movement, **Nelson Mandela** (man DEHL uh), had been imprisoned since 1962. In the late 1980s, protests against apartheid within South Africa and around the globe grew. In the United States, many private firms **divested,** or withdrew investments, from South Africa. Congress imposed economic sanctions instead of fully divesting, not wanting to destabilize the struggling nation. President Bush met with Mandela after his release from jail in 1990 and endorsed the drive to bring democracy to South Africa. Soon after, apartheid began to be dismantled, and South Africans elected Mandela as their leader in 1994 in their first free elections.

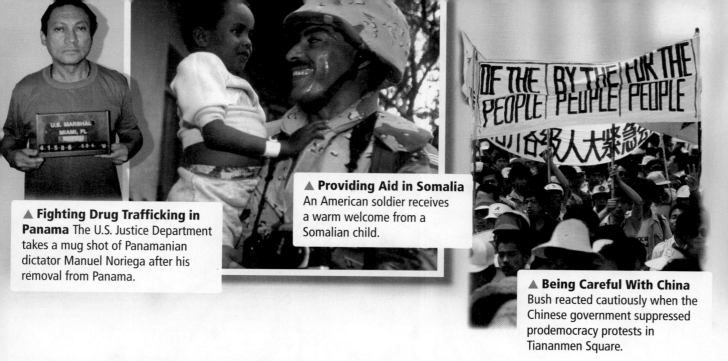

▲ **Fighting Drug Trafficking in Panama** The U.S. Justice Department takes a mug shot of Panamanian dictator Manuel Noriega after his removal from Panama.

▲ **Providing Aid in Somalia** An American soldier receives a warm welcome from a Somalian child.

▲ **Being Careful With China** Bush reacted cautiously when the Chinese government suppressed prodemocracy protests in Tiananmen Square.

**Peacekeeping and Police Actions** With the fall of communism in 1991, the nation of Yugoslavia disintegrated into a bloody civil war. Bush chose not to send troops because he feared that the tangled conflict could embroil the United States in another Vietnam. Not until 1992, however, did he back a modest UN plan to restore peace in Bosnia, one of the new republics carved out of Yugoslavia. By then, more than 150,000 civilians had died.

The Bush administration acted more swiftly to protect human rights in Somalia. As part of "Operation Restore Hope," United States Marines landed in this East African nation in December 1992 to help establish a cease-fire between rival warlords and to deliver food to hundreds of thousands of starving people. The American humanitarian mission reinforced UN efforts at peacekeeping and relief. Even some of Bush's most persistent critics applauded his decision to intervene in Somalia.

✓ **Checkpoint** What domestic problems caused President Bush to order the invasion of Panama?

## The Persian Gulf War

The most important foreign-policy challenge faced by the Bush administration took place in the Persian Gulf. On August 2, 1990, Iraq invaded its tiny neighbor Kuwait. Nearly 150,000 Iraqi troops quickly overran Kuwaiti forces.

**Causes of the War Saddam Hussein,** Iraq's ruthless dictator, had run the Middle Eastern nation with an iron fist since 1979. By invading Kuwait, Hussein sought to take over Kuwait's rich oil deposits. With Kuwait in his power, Hussein would control nearly 20 percent of the oil produced around the world. The United States feared how Hussein would use the influence that controlling such a large amount of oil would give him. In addition, nearby Saudi Arabia possessed even more massive oil reserves. The United States did not want Hussein to seek to gain control of those reserves next. President Bush made it clear that he would not <u>tolerate</u> Iraq's aggression against its neighbor. He worked to build an international coalition and backed a UN resolution demanding that Iraqi troops withdraw.

**Vocabulary Builder**
<u>tolerate</u>–(TAHL er ayt) *v.* to put up with

# The Persian Gulf War, 1991

**Geography** *Interactive*
For: Interactive map
Web Code: nep-1906

**Map Legend**
- Allied air base
- Iraqi air base
- U.S. naval forces
- Allied air attacks
- Allied ground attacks
- Iraqi invasion of Kuwait
- Iraqi Scud attacks
- Iraqi retreat

Map labels: TURKEY, Incirlik, Mosul, SYRIA, Euphrates River, Tigris River, CYPRUS, *Mediterranean Sea*, LEBANON, Beirut, Damascus, IRAQ, Baghdad, IRAN, Haifa, ISRAEL, Tel Aviv, Amman, Jerusalem, JORDAN, Basra, Kuwait City, KUWAIT, 50°E, SAUDI ARABIA, Hafar al Batin, 35°E, EGYPT, *Red Sea*, Dhahran, *Persian Gulf*, Riyadh, 35°N, Miller Projection, 0 100 200 mi, 0 100 200 km

## Major Gulf War Coalition Members, 1991

| Country* | Flag | Country* | Flag |
|----------|------|----------|------|
| Bahrain | | Pakistan | |
| Canada | | Qatar | |
| Egypt | | Saudi Arabia | |
| France | | Syria | |
| Germany | | Turkey | |
| Japan | | United Arab Emirates | |
| Kuwait | | United Kingdom | |
| Netherlands | | United States | |
| Oman | | | |

*Other coalition members who made smaller contributions:
Argentina, Australia, Bangladesh, Belgium, Czechoslovakia, Denmark, Greece, Italy, Morocco, New Zealand, Niger, Norway, Poland, Portugal, Senegal, South Korea, Spain

**Map Skills** The Persian Gulf War consisted mainly of aerial bombardment, with only a brief ground war.
1. **Locate:** (a) Kuwait, (b) Saudi Arabia, (c) Baghdad
2. **Location** Why was Saudi Arabia a strategic ally?
3. **Synthesize Information** From what points did the Allied forces launch air attacks?

As they retreated, Iraqi troops set fire to Kuwait's oil wells, causing great environmental harm (below). General Norman Schwarzkopf, the commander of the coalition's forces in the Persian Gulf, consults with a soldier (right).

**Operation Desert Storm** By late fall, about 700,000 troops had assembled in Saudi Arabia, including nearly 500,000 American forces. Britain, France, Egypt, and Saudi Arabia, among others, also sent troops. Other nations, for example Japan, agreed to help pay for the costs of the operation. Initially, Bush hoped that the presence of these troops, along with the economic sanctions against Iraq, would convince Hussein to withdraw his soldiers. At the same time, the President asked for and received from Congress the authority to use force, if necessary, to back up the UN's resolution that Iraq leave Kuwait.

**Operation Desert Storm,** the name given to the American-led attack on Iraqi forces, began on January 16, 1991. General Colin Powell, the Chairman of the Joint Chiefs of Staff, and General Norman Schwarzkopf devised and executed a strategy that began with five weeks of devastating aerial bombardment on Iraqi forces. Iraq countered by launching Scud missiles on both coalition forces and Israel. Although, these missiles did little serious damage, they struck terror in the hearts of many who feared they were armed with chemical warheads.

On February 23, coalition troops stormed into Kuwait. Easily overmatched, Iraqi troops surrendered or fled, setting fire to Kuwaiti oil rigs along the way. Less than five days after the ground war began, Iraq agreed to a UN cease-fire. It had lost an estimated 25,000 soldiers. American deaths totaled 148. "We've kicked the Vietnam syndrome once and for all," proclaimed Bush. He then chose to limit American actions to enforcing the UN resolution. The coalition's forces would compel Iraq to leave Kuwait but would not continue on to Baghdad, Iraq's capital, to topple Saddam Hussein. As a result, Hussein and his regime survived the war. Bush's public approval rating skyrocketed.

### HISTORY MAKERS

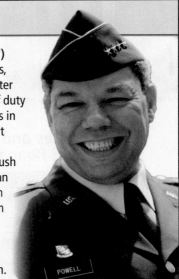

**Colin Powell** (born 1937)
The son of Jamaican immigrants, Colin Powell joined the army after college and served two tours of duty in Vietnam. He held several jobs in the army and in the government during the 1970s and 1980s. In 1989, President George H.W. Bush named General Powell Chairman of the Joint Chiefs of Staff. From that post, he guided the American victories in Panama and the Persian Gulf War. Powell later served as Secretary of State under President George W. Bush.

✔ **Checkpoint** What strategic political and economic interests caused the United States to become involved in the Persian Gulf War?

---

**SECTION 4 Assessment**

**Progress Monitoring *Online***
**For:** Self-test with vocabulary practice
**Web Code:** nea-1907

### Comprehension

1. **Terms and People** For each item below, write a sentence explaining how the term or person demonstrated the new role of the United States after the end of the Cold War.
   - Manuel Noriega
   - Tiananmen Square
   - apartheid
   - Nelson Mandela
   - divest
   - Saddam Hussein
   - Operation Desert Storm

2. **NoteTaking Reading Skill: Summarize** Use your chart to answer the Section Focus Question: What actions did the United States take abroad during George H.W. Bush's presidency?

### Writing About History

3. **Quick Write: Create a Timeline** Plan, draft, and create a multimedia timeline featuring American foreign policy after the Cold War. Consider using a slideshow computer application to present your timeline.

### Critical Thinking

4. **Draw Inferences** Why did President Bush respond differently to the crisis in Somalia than he did to the crisis in China?

5. **Compare** How was the Persian Gulf War fought differently from the Vietnam War?

6. **Draw Conclusions** Why did the U.S.-led coalition decide not to invade Baghdad or try to oust Hussein after driving Iraq out of Kuwait?

# Quick Study Guide

 9.2.1

**Progress Monitoring *Online***
**For:** Self-test with vocabulary practice
**Web Code:** nea-1908

## ■ Key Policies and Actions of Ronald Reagan

| Domestic |
| --- |
| Supported tax cuts and deregulation to stimulate demand under the theory of supply-side economics |
| Took a strong stance on air-traffic controllers' strike |
| Appointed conservative Justices to the Supreme Court |
| Reformed Social Security |
| Increased defense spending |

| Foreign |
| --- |
| Pressured the Soviet Union by building up the American military, including the Strategic Defense Initiative program |
| Aided anticommunist forces in several countries, including Afghanistan and Grenada |
| Signed arms control agreements with Soviet leader Mikhail Gorbachev |
| Sent peacekeeping force to Lebanon |
| Ordered an air raid on Libya because of Libyan leader Muammar al-Qaddafi's involvement in terrorist attacks |

## ■ Key Events in George H.W. Bush's Presidency

- Signed Americans With Disabilities Act into law
- Forged friendly relationship between the United States and the new Russian Federation
- Continued the war on drugs by invading Panama and arresting Panamanian dictator Manuel Noriega on drug-trafficking charges
- Sent humanitarian mission to Somalia
- Headed an international coalition of forces in the Persian Gulf War

## ■ The Fall of Communism in Eastern Europe and the Soviet Union

## ✓ Quick Study Timeline

**In America**

**1981**
**Hostages in Iran released on first day of Reagan's presidency**

**1983**
**Economy starts to recover from recession**

| Presidential Terms | Ronald Reagan 1981–1989 |
| --- | --- |

**1980**        **1982**        **1984**

**Around the World**

**1982**
**Argentina and Great Britain battle for control of Falkland Islands**

**1984**
**Indira Gandhi, prime minister of India, is assassinated**

# American Issues
●—●—●—● **Connector**

By connecting prior knowledge with what you have learned in this chapter, you can gradually build your understanding of enduring questions that still affect America today. Answer the questions below. Then, use your American Issues Connector study guide (or go online: www.PHSchool.com **Web Code:** neh-9202).

## Issues You Learned About

● **America and the World** The Cold War dominated American foreign policy for half a century, starting in the 1940s.

1. When and why was the Berlin Wall constructed? How did the United States respond at the time?

2. Why did Reagan's attitude toward Soviet leader Gorbachev change? What events and policies demonstrated this change?

3. What role do some historians believe the United States played in the fall of the Soviet Union?

● **Sectionalism and National Politics** Most politicians in the United States are members of a political party.

4. What were the first two major political parties in the United States, and what policies did they generally favor? In the late twentieth century, what were the country's two major political parties, and what policies did they generally favor?

5. What complaints did Republicans lodge against Democratic economic policies in the late 1970s?

6. Why had many white southerners changed their historical allegiance from the Democratic Party to the Republican Party by the 1980s?

● **Government's Role in the Economy** Different administrations back their own economic policies, such as raising or lowering taxes and increasing or decreasing funds for government programs.

7. What is supply-side economics? What changes did Reagan's application of supply-side economics bring to taxpayers?

8. What steps did Reagan take to lessen the federal government's role in the economy?

### Connect to Your World | Michigan

**Government's Role in the Economy** When President Reagan took office in 1981, Michigan's automobile industry was going through a difficult time. A combination of high oil prices, a nationwide recession, and an influx of lower-priced Japanese cars led to decreased sales for American automobile companies. On April 6, the Reagan administration released a statement outlining its plan to help the struggling automobile industry. The administration sought to improve the overall economy, reduce environmental and safety regulations, have the government buy additional vehicles, allow automobile companies to collaborate, and limit international competition. Write a newspaper article about the role of government and private companies in overcoming the challenges the automobile industry faced in the early 1980s.

**1987**
**Reagan and Gorbachev sign treaty agreeing to eliminate some nuclear missiles**

**1991**
**United States leads coalition of forces in Persian Gulf War**

George H. W. Bush 1989–1993

| 1986 | 1988 | 1990 | 1992 |

**1988**
**Soviet forces begin to pull out of Afghanistan**

**1989**
**Berlin Wall falls**

**1991**
**Soviet Union breaks up; Cold War ends**

**History** *Interactive*
**For:** Interactive timeline
**Web Code:** nep-1909

651

# Chapter Assessment

## Terms and People

1. What was the **New Right**? Give two reasons for the rise of the New Right.

2. What was the **Savings and Loan crisis**? How did the federal government respond to this crisis?

3. What is **AIDS**? How did Reagan and Bush react to the increase of AIDS in the United States?

4. What were *glasnost* and *perestroika*? What effect did they have on the Soviet Union?

5. Define **apartheid**. What actions did the United States take to end apartheid?

## Focus Questions

The focus question for this chapter is **What was the conservative resurgence, and how did it affect the domestic and foreign policies of the United States?** Build an answer to this big question by answering the focus questions for Sections 1 through 4 and the Critical Thinking questions that follow.

### Section 1

6. What spurred the rise of conservatism in the late 1970s and early 1980s?

### Section 2

7. What were the major characteristics of the conservative Reagan Revolution?

### Section 3

8. What were Reagan's foreign policies, and how did they contribute to the fall of communism in Europe?

### Section 4

9. What actions did the United States take abroad during George H.W. Bush's presidency?

## Critical Thinking

10. **Categorize** Identify the goals of the conservative movement in the early 1980s.

11. **Analyze Charts** Study the chart below. Use it, along with your reading of this chapter, to explain how the conservative movement affected Congress.

### Composition of Congress, 1979–1983

| Year | House of Representatives | | | Senate | | |
|------|------|------|------|------|------|------|
| | Dem. | Rep. | Ind. | Dem. | Rep. | Ind. |
| 1979 | 276 | 157 | 0 | 58 | 41 | 1 |
| 1981 | 243 | 192 | 0 | 46 | 53 | 1 |
| 1983 | 269 | 165 | 0 | 46 | 54 | 0 |

12. **Recognize Effects** Think about the economic policies that Reagan followed. Then, identify and describe one positive and one negative effect that his policies had on the economy.

13. **Identify Central Issues** In the Iran-Contra affair, what actions of several members of Reagan's administration went against the policies of the federal government?

14. **Make Generalizations** Describe the political policies that led to U.S. involvement in Afghanistan, Nicaragua, El Salvador, and Grenada.

15. **Synthesize Information** Reagan's foreign policy was directed at stopping communism. What was the basis of Bush's foreign policy? Give one specific example of this foreign policy.

16. **Draw Inferences** How did George H.W. Bush approach the war against Iraq in 1991?

## Writing About History

**Create a Multimedia Presentation** In the late 1980s and early 1990s, sweeping changes happened in Europe and other places around the world. These changes affected the United States in subtler but still significant ways. Choose one of these changes, and create a multimedia presentation showing what happened and how it affected the United States.

### Prewriting

- Go online to PHSchool.com and enter **Web Code:** nep-1911 to review several presentations that use different types of media to make their points.

- Brainstorm topics and choose the one that you think lends itself best to a multimedia format.

- Outline the main points you would like to make and choose the type of media you will use to make each point.

### Drafting

- Write a draft of your presentation.

- Search for or create images and artwork to enhance your presentation.

- Create storyboards showing how you will blend the text and images in your presentation.

- Consider using a computer application to put together the final presentation.

### Revising

- Use the guidelines on page SH31 of the Writing Handbook to revise your work.

# Prepare for the MME

## Is the National Debt a Problem?

During the 1980s, the Reagan administration lowered tax rates, hoping to pull the economy out of a recession. At the same time, defense spending increased. These factors, in part, led to annual budget deficits that added substantially to the national debt. There remains considerable debate about the costs and benefits of national debt. Use your knowledge of Ronald Reagan's economic policies and Documents A, B, and C to answer questions 1 through 4.

### Document A
**Budget Surpluses and Deficits, 1950–2006**

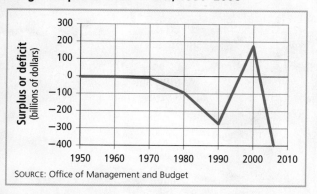

SOURCE: Office of Management and Budget

### Document B
**National Debt as a Percentage of GDP, 1940–2010**

SOURCE: Office of Management and Budget

### Document C

"Large deficits and rising federal debt constrain future economic growth and living standards by reducing the amount of saving in the United States available for private investment. Federal borrowing to finance deficits may also put upward pressure on interest rates, which increases household borrowing costs for such things as homes, cars, and college loans.

In addition to these economic consequences, the budgetary effects of deficits and growing debt reduce the federal government's flexibility in funding various programs and activities. . . . In fiscal year 2003, net interest spending was the sixth largest item in the federal budget—about 7 percent of total federal spending was primarily used to pay interest on debt held by the public rather than to finance other public priorities. . . .

Federal borrowing has both advantages and disadvantages. . . . Borrowing, in lieu of higher taxes or lower government spending, may be viewed as appropriate during times of economic recession, war, and other temporary challenges. . . . Borrowing for such short-term circumstances can permit the government to hold tax rates relatively stable and avoid economic disruptions. Federal borrowing might also be viewed as appropriate for federal investment, such as building roads, training workers, and conducting scientific research, contributing to the nation's capital stock and productivity. . . . In concept, federal spending that is well chosen . . . could ultimately contribute to producing a larger economy from which to pay the interest and principal on the borrowed funds. However, in practice, [the Congressional Budget Office] concluded that many federal investments might not significantly increase economic growth because some are selected for political or other noneconomic reasons and others displace more productive investments by the private sector or state and local governments."

—*from* Federal Debt: Answers to Frequently Asked Questions, *U.S. Government Accountability Office, 2004*

---

1. According to Document A, annual budget deficits
   A remained relatively low during the 1980s.
   B increased dramatically during the 1980s.
   C decreased dramatically during the 1980s.
   D disappeared during the 1980s.

2. According to Document B, national debt
   A was at its lowest point ever during the 1980s.
   B was at its highest point ever during the 1980s.
   C increased during the 1980s.
   D decreased during the 1980s.

3. According to Document C, federal debt
   A makes it easier for individual citizens and companies to borrow money.
   B makes it more difficult for the government to fund other public priorities.
   C is never desirable.
   D always increases economic growth.

4. **Writing Task** Do you think benefits of the increased national debt during the 1980s and 1990s outweighed the costs? Why or why not? Use evidence from the documents and the chapter to support your answer.

# 20

# Into a New Century
## 1992–Today

# WITNESS HISTORY ◄)) AUDIO

## Becoming American Citizens

Every year, hundreds of thousands of immigrants change their lives by taking part in naturalization ceremonies to become U.S. citizens. After declaring their commitment to this nation and renouncing allegiance to their home countries, they join other Americans in lending their talents, skills, and dreams to their new country. President George W. Bush has described citizenship in this way:

"America has never been united by blood or birth or soil, we are bound by ideals that move us beyond our backgrounds. . . . Every immigrant by embracing these ideals makes our country more, not less, American."

*Listen to the* Witness History *audio to hear more about American citizenship.*

◄ Immigrants wait to be sworn in as U.S. citizens during a ceremony in Los Angeles, California, in February 2005.

Saddam Hussein's statue being toppled in Iraq

 **Content Expectations**

A simple "W '04" declares Bush's reelection campaign

**Chapter Focus Question:** What political, social, technological, and economic trends have shaped American life since 1990?

### Section 1
The Computer and Technology Revolutions   9.1.1, 9.3.1a, 9.3.1b

### Section 2
The Clinton Presidency   9.1.2c, 9.2.1, 9.3.1e

### Section 3
Global Politics and Economics   9.2.1, 9.2.2, 9.3.1a

NASA rover exploring Mars

### Section 4
The George W. Bush Presidency   9.1.2a, 9.1.2c, 9.2.2

### Section 5
Americans Look to the Future   9.1.1, 9.3.1c, 9.3.1d, 9.3.1g

Use the ☑ **Quick Study Timeline** at the end of this chapter to preview chapter events.

**Note Taking Study Guide *Online***
For: Note Taking and American Issues Connector
Web Code: nee-9301

◀ Michael Dell with one of his computers

WITNESS HISTORY 🔊 AUDIO

### A Young Entrepreneur

In 1980, a Texas teenager named Michael Dell bought his first computer. He immediately took the computer apart to see if he could rebuild it. Though Dell entered college intending to become a doctor, his real interest lay in the computer company he started from his college dorm room. By 2003, that small company had grown into a global corporation called Dell Inc.—the most profitable company in the computer industry.

❝There were obviously no classes on learning how to start and run a business in my high school, so I clearly had a lot to learn. And learn I did, mostly by experimenting and making a bunch of mistakes.❞

—Michael Dell, 1999

# The Computer and Technology Revolutions

### Content Expectations

- **9.1.1** Evaluate changes in U.S. economy.
- **9.3.1a** Compose a persuasive essay on role of U.S. in the world.
- **9.3.1b** Compose a persuasive essay on national economic policy.

### Terms and People

personal computer
biotechnology
satellite
Internet
globalization
multinational corporation
service economy

### NoteTaking

**Reading Skill: Categorize** As you read, fill in a flowchart like this one to help you categorize technological changes and their impact.

| Technology Revolution | | |
|---|---|---|
| Computers | Communications | Globalization |
| • <br> • | • <br> • | • <br> • |

**Why It Matters** During the twentieth century, the rate of technological change sped up dramatically. New technology touched every aspect of life, including how Americans worked, played, and communicated. At the same time, globalization transformed the American economy, bringing both new challenges and new opportunities. **Section Focus Question: How have technological changes and globalization transformed the American economy?**

## Technology Changes American Life

The 1900s was a century of unparalleled change. In 1903, Orville Wright flew the first airplane. Less than 70 years later, astronaut Neil Armstrong walked on the moon. During that same span of time, television went from a novelty at a World's Fair to a standard household possession, and sophisticated microscopes and telescopes unveiled previously hidden worlds. One of the most important innovations was the development of the computer.

**Developing the Modern Computer** Intense rivalry between enemies during World War II brought about a life-and-death race to develop new technologies, such as the computer. The U.S. government funded research that led to the creation of the first modern computer in 1946. This huge machine occupied the entire basement of the research lab. It calculated artillery ranges and performed computations for the atomic bomb.

Soon after World War II, universities and corporations joined government agencies to develop smaller, faster, more powerful computers that could perform a range of functions. The IBM company developed one of the first commercially successful computers in 1954. In the 1960s, a few companies located south of San Francisco, California, focused on developing improved technology for running the computer. Their efforts led to the microchip, a tiny fragment of silicon containing complex circuits, and the microprocessor, a silicon chip that held a central processing unit. These chips made possible the development of small computers, called **personal computers.**

**Transforming Business and Industry** At first, personal computers were a novelty item, used mainly by hobbyists. But by the 1980s, computers were transforming industries, research labs, and businesses. Personal computers could perform many different tasks but were small and simple enough for the average person to use. The technology that created them eventually spread to many other industries. Video games, cellular telephones, and other electronics all depended on microchips and microprocessors. Entrepreneurs played a large role in accelerating the use of personal computers. Steve Jobs's Apple Computers and Bill Gates's Microsoft made computers and software affordable for millions of Americans. Jeff Bezos's Amazon.com ushered in buying and selling products by computer. Like Andrew Carnegie and John D. Rockefeller a century before, these men amassed great fortunes by pioneering new technologies.

**Revolutions in Science and Agriculture** Medical science also moved ahead by gigantic leaps in the twentieth century, often aided by computer technology. Scientists developed drugs that extended patients' lives, reduced pain, and battled a huge number of diseases. They made artificial hearts and learned how to successfully transplant body organs. Such advancements, along with **biotechnology,** or the use of living organisms in the development of new products, have produced a level of healthcare unknown to any previous generation.

Advances in agricultural technology, including improved machinery, irrigation techniques, and growing methods, have brought profound changes to American society. While farms have grown larger and more productive, fewer people are needed to work them. In 1900, 50 percent of the labor force worked on farms. At the end of the century, only 2 percent did.

☑ **Checkpoint** What was the impact of the personal computer?

# A Communications Revolution

Late in the twentieth century, commentators began to describe their times as the "information age." Access to information, they claimed, was access to power. Computers, cellphones, e-mails, and instant messaging became the tools of the information age. Entrepreneurs who could control these tools became wealthy—and powerful. For example, media executives who decide what gets on television can exert influence on political elections and controversial topics. But computer and communication technologies also have a democratic leveling effect. Anyone with access to a computer can acquire information that was once available only to a few, well-connected leaders.

**A New Form of I.D.**
A vet implants a tiny microchip (inset) into a puppy. If the dog is lost, a simple scan of the chip will reveal its name and its owner's address.

**Satellite Technology** Satellite technology increased the speed of global communications. **Satellites** are mechanical devices that orbit Earth in space, receiving and sending information-filled signals that are then relayed to televisions, telephones, and computers. Originally developed for military purposes during the Cold War, satellite technology was used in the 1970s by businessman Ted Turner to run the first "superstation," broadcasting into cable-equipped households across the country. In 1980, Turner began the 24-hour-per-day, all-news Cable News Network (CNN). Cellular telephones used similar satellite technology, allowing people to communicate away from their homes.

**The Internet Is Born** In the 1970s, various branches of the U.S. government along with groups in several American universities led efforts to link computer systems together via cables and satellites. By the 1980s, the **Internet,** or World Wide Web, had been born, reaching the general public in the 1990s. The Web made communication and <u>access</u> to information almost instantaneous. This breakthrough completely and profoundly transformed commerce, education, research, and entertainment. E-mail provided great advantages over the delays of postal mail and the expense of telephones. The impact has been especially great on people living in rural areas. The Internet's immense storage capacity also changed the world of research. In the 1980s, scientists and scholars primarily used the Internet to share information. By the early 1990s, they were using it as a research tool and an online database.

✔️ **Checkpoint** How did new technology revolutionize communications?

**Vocabulary Builder**
<u>access</u> – (AK sehs) *n.* means of getting or using

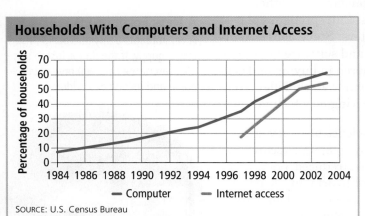

**Households With Computers and Internet Access**

SOURCE: U.S. Census Bureau

**Graph Skills** The graph shows how Americans' access to computers and the Internet has changed over the past two decades. Describe the change. Note that the data for Internet access do not begin until 1997. Why might this be so?

## A Changing American Economy

All of these technological changes had a dramatic effect on the American economy. New technology influenced how and where people did their jobs. In this changing economy, one sector—the service industry—grew rapidly. A lower percentage of Americans than ever before worked on assembly lines or on farms. Instead, they provided services.

**The Impact of Globalization** New communications infrastructures—especially satellites and computers—have made it easier for companies to do global business. This has increased **globalization,** or the process by which national economies, politics, cultures, and societies become integrated with those of other nations around the world. **Multinational corporations** are one example. Such a corporation might have its financial headquarters in one country and manufacturing plants in several others, and may obtain its raw materials from many different places. The company then sells the products it makes to a worldwide market.

Globalization has made more products and services available to greater numbers of people, often at lower prices. It has hastened the development of some nations. But it has also had some drawbacks. Industrial nations have seen their manufacturing jobs flow out to less developed nations. Steel that was once manufactured in Pittsburgh, for example, might now be made in South Korea. In less developed nations, workers often do not enjoy the protections that workers have in industrial nations. Finally, the interconnection of world economies almost guarantees that economic problems in one region will be felt in others.

**Computers Transform Workplaces** Computer technology has also changed the nature of the American economy. Many workers have found that they need computer skills to get jobs. Banking, stockbroking, programming, and the many other occupations dependent on information and computers have added millions of jobs to the service economy. Many white-collar workers in the information economy have seen their jobs radically change. Professional workers are

# The Global Reach of E-commerce

Global communications, especially the Internet, have reshaped ways of doing business. Just 15 years ago, shoppers bought almost everything they needed at local stores, and most things they bought were made in the country where they lived. The Internet and e-commerce—electronic commerce, or business conducted over the Internet—have helped to change that. This illustration shows an example of e-commerce in progress.

**5** Another message to a factory in Shanghai, China, tells workers there to produce more snowshoes and ship them to Los Angeles, CA.

**1** A woman in Minneapolis, MN, shops for a pair of snowshoes online. She has questions about a model she likes and requests to speak with customer service on the Web site.

**4** A message to the Swedish company's U.S. warehouse in Los Angeles, CA, tells workers there to ship the shopper a pair of snowshoes.

**2** A customer-service representative in Bangalore, India, types answers to her questions in real-time.

**3** The customer's order is received and processed by a computer at the sporting-goods company in Stockholm, Sweden. The computer sends messages to two locations.

## Thinking Critically
**Synthesize Information** Use the illustration above to describe the impact of globalization.

**History** *Interactive* ★

**For:** More about e-commerce
**Web Code:** nep-2011

**Chart Skills** Americans' occupations in the next few years will be dramatically different from what they were 100 years ago. *Which two fields are projected to grow the fastest in the next few years?*

linked by a network of computers, fax machines, television screens, and cell phones. They often telecommunicate, holding meetings that involve participants sitting in offices around the world.

**The Service Sector Expands** With the production of services increasing faster than the production of goods, some economists say that America now has a **service economy.** Jobs in the service sector vary widely. Lawyers, teachers, doctors, research analysts, police officers, professional athletes, and movie stars are all service workers, as are salespeople and the people behind fast-food counters. Service workers are among the lowest paid and the highest paid people in the United States.

The transition from an industry-based economy to a service-based one has created opportunities for entrepreneurs. For example, Californians Richard and Maurice McDonald opened their new restaurant in 1948. The brothers emphasized efficiency, low prices, high volume, and quick service. They did away with anything that slowed down the process, including plates, glasses, dishwashing, and tipping. In 1955, Ray Kroc began to franchise the McDonald's system and name. By the end of the century, McDonald's had become the most successful food service organization in history, and the name McDonald's came to stand for low-priced, standardized-quality food.

Other entrepreneurs' names also came to symbolize their businesses. For example, Wal-Mart, a discount merchandising business founded by Sam Walton, became one of the most successful businesses in the late twentieth century.

**Organized Labor Declines** The rise of the service economy and the decline in American coal mining, steelmaking, and automobile manufacturing has had a strong impact on organized labor. At its peak in 1945, about 35 percent of all American workers belonged to unions. In 2000, less than 15 percent of workers did. Blue-collar jobs, once the mainstay of American labor, declined dramatically in the second half of the twentieth century. As a result, the political power of labor unions, as well as farm organizations, has fallen. At the same time, workers' average wages—especially those of nonprofessional workers—have fallen.

✔ **Checkpoint** How has globalization affected the American economy?

---

SECTION **1** Assessment

**Progress Monitoring *Online***
For: Self-test with vocabulary practice
Web Code: nea-2011

**Comprehension**

1. **Terms and People** For each term below, write a sentence explaining its effect on American society or the economy.
   - personal computer
   - biotechnology
   - satellite
   - Internet
   - globalization
   - multinational corporation
   - service economy

2. **NoteTaking Reading Skill: Categorize** Use your flowchart to answer the Section Focus Question: How have technological changes and globalization transformed the American economy?

**Writing About History**

3. **Quick Write: Choose a Topic** Recall all the American issues you have studied in this course. Identify an issue that comes into play in this section, and explain how.

**Critical Thinking**

4. **Draw Inferences** Why are new technologies often developed as a result of waging war?

5. **Recognize Cause and Effect** How has the computer sped up the pace of globalization?

6. **Test Conclusions** Cite evidence to support or refute this statement: A service economy provides more opportunities to entrepreneurs than does an industrial economy.

## Becoming President

In 1963, a high school student named Bill Clinton from Hope, Arkansas, went to the White House as part of a youth leadership conference. He was first in line to shake President Kennedy's hand. Thirty years later, Clinton was sworn in as President of the United States.

66 Thomas Jefferson believed that to preserve the very foundation of our nation, we would need dramatic change from time to time. Well, my fellow citizens, this is our time. . . . And so today, we pledge an end to the era of deadlock and drift—a new season of American renewal has begun. 99
—Bill Clinton, First Inaugural Address, 1993

▲ Sixteen-year-old Bill Clinton meets President Kennedy on July 26, 1963. A campaign button proclaims his own presidential bid nearly 30 years later.

# The Clinton Presidency

## Content Expectations

- **9.1.2c** Analyze intensification of partisanship.
- **9.2.1** Explain role of U.S. as a super-power in post-Cold War world.
- **9.3.1e** Compose a persuasive essay on health care.

## Terms and People

William Jefferson Clinton
H. Ross Perot
Family Medical Leave Act
Brady Bill
Newt Gingrich
Contract With America
Kenneth Starr
impeachment

## NoteTaking

**Reading Skill: Summarize** Create an outline like the one below as you read to summarize information about the Clinton presidency.

> I. The 1992 Election
>  A. Bush's popularity plummets
>  B. Clinton runs as "New Democrat"
>  C. Clinton carries the election
> II. Clinton's Domestic Policies
>  A.

**Why It Matters** The conservative revolution of the 1980s had kept Republicans in the White House for 12 straight years and influenced every branch of government. The election of Bill Clinton to the presidency in 1992 signaled that Americans were ready for a change. Clinton's position as a moderate, practical Democrat had broad appeal for a wide range of voters. **Section Focus Question: What were the successes and failures of the Clinton presidency?**

## The 1992 Election

After the 1991 Persian Gulf War ended, President George H.W. Bush's approval rating reached 91 percent. In less than one year, however, public opinion had changed. Saddam Hussein had stayed in power, continuing to threaten peace in the Middle East. The American economy had gone into recession and the federal deficit had risen. People were angered by Bush's betrayal of his 1988 campaign pledge not to raise taxes. Bush's sinking popularity opened up the way for the Democratic challenge.

**Clinton Raises the Challenge** The Democrats nominated **William Jefferson Clinton,** governor of Arkansas, as their presidential candidate. Clinton was born in 1946 into a humble home and had worked his way through college and law school before being elected governor of Arkansas in 1978. To widen his appeal and distance himself from traditional "tax and spend" liberals, Clinton promoted himself as a "New Democrat." New Democrats were centrists who sought to

**Celebrating Victory**
Newly elected President Bill Clinton, Vice President Al Gore, and their families greet supporters in Arkansas on November 3, 1992.

reconcile liberal and conservative ideals. They believed in strong national defense, tough stands on crime, free trade, welfare reform, and closer ties with corporations. They believed that government was necessary and important but that it had grown large and inefficient. Clinton's centrist position attracted conservative and liberal Democrats as well as moderate Republicans.

**Winning the White House** By 1992, Clinton was poised to capitalize on Bush's political problems. He entered the presidential race along with Texas billionaire **H. Ross Perot,** who led a self-funded independent party and promised to govern by sound business principles. Clinton's campaign focused on economic and social opportunity. Clinton charged that Bush's economic policies had made the rich richer. He also pointed out that, unlike Bush, he came from a family that had struggled through hard times and knew what it was like to worry about paying bills. Bush responded by attacking Clinton's character. Republicans accused the governor of draft-dodging, marital infidelity, and other moral laxities. Bush also suggested that Clinton and his vice presidential candidate Al Gore were too inexperienced to lead the nation.

In the end, Clinton's message carried the election. In the largest voter turnout since 1960, more than one hundred million Americans turned out at the polls. Clinton received 43 percent of the popular vote to Bush's 37 percent and Perot's 19 percent. Democrats also retained control of the House of Representatives and the Senate.

 **Checkpoint** How did Clinton use his stance as a moderate to attract voters?

## Clinton's Domestic Policies

When Bill Clinton took the presidential oath of office on January 20, 1993, he faced a great challenge. Since 1968, Americans had chosen Republican Presidents in five out of six elections. The Republican argument that government was the problem, not the solution, resonated with many Americans. Clinton therefore needed to chart a middle course between the limited role for government advocated by Republicans and the traditional Democratic reliance on government programs to address social problems.

**Signing New Laws** Early in his presidency, Clinton signed the **Family Medical Leave Act,** which had been vetoed by President Bush despite having bipartisan support. The act guaranteed most full-time employees 12 workweeks of unpaid leave each year for the birth and care of a newborn child, to recover from a serious illness, or to care for an immediate family member with one. The Clinton administration also raised the minimum wage, increased access to college loans, and expanded tax credits for higher education.

**Healthcare Reform Fails** Healthcare reform headed Clinton's list of priorities. The United States was the only developed country without national healthcare. Though Clinton did not advocate socialized medicine, he wanted a program that would guarantee care for all Americans. His wife, Hillary Clinton, was appointed to head a healthcare task force to investigate the issue. The task force conducted highly publicized hearings and produced a long, detailed proposal that attracted immediate criticism from diverse interest groups. The bill never won congressional support and was <u>ultimately</u> dropped after about a year of debate.

Clinton had miscalculated Americans' faith in the federal government to solve the country's social problems. Millions of Americans simply did not feel that enlarging the federal bureaucracy and allowing the government to run healthcare was a good idea.

**Dealing With Violence** Clinton also tried to address the issue of violence in American society. In 1993, he signed the **Brady Bill,** a gun-control act named for presidential aide James Brady, who had been wounded in the 1981 assassination attempt on Ronald Reagan. Under Clinton, Congress also passed a $30 billion anticrime bill that increased funding for police and banned several kinds of assault weapons.

Still, violence continued to haunt the nation. In 1995, Americans were horrified by the bombing of a government building in Oklahoma City that killed 168 people and injured more than 800 others. The mass murder was committed, not by foreign terrorists, but by home-grown anti-government extremists. To deal with the threat of terrorism, federal buildings in major cities were surrounded with barriers to ward off similar attacks. New laws were passed to deter terrorism and impose stiffer penalties.

In 1999, yet another act of senseless violence stirred nationwide debate. At Colorado's Columbine High School, two heavily armed students killed 12 fellow students and a teacher, as well as wounding 24 others. In the aftermath of this tragedy, schools across the nation installed metal detectors and other security measures. Many schools instituted new anti-bully policies and "zero tolerance" approaches to school violence.

✔ **Checkpoint** What were Clinton's legislative successes and failures?

# The Republicans Galvanize

After two years in office, Clinton had achieved a few lasting legislative victories. Yet the failure of his healthcare initiative signaled that his popularity, and his control of Congress, was waning. With the 1994 midterm elections approaching, congressional Republicans seized the opportunity to advance their own ideas.

**Vocabulary Builder**
ultimately – (UHL tuh miht lee) *adv.* in the end; finally

## Oklahoma City Bombing
The Oklahoma City bombing of April 1995 was the worst act of domestic terrorism in American history. The victims included a number of children in a day care center.

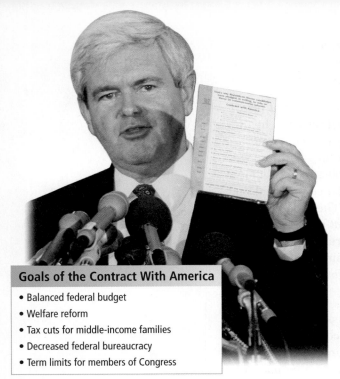

**Goals of the Contract With America**

- Balanced federal budget
- Welfare reform
- Tax cuts for middle-income families
- Decreased federal bureaucracy
- Term limits for members of Congress

**The "Gingrich Revolution"**
Gingrich explains his Contract with America at a press conference in January 1994. *How did his goals attract voters who were opposed to "big government"?*

**Gingrich's Contract With America** Georgia congressman **Newt Gingrich** led the opposition to Clinton. Gingrich was bold and aggressive and not interested in compromising with the Democrats: "We will cooperate, but we won't compromise." Many people thought that Gingrich's goal of the Republicans gaining control of the House of Representatives in 1994 was a nearly impossible task. After all, the Democrats had controlled the House for 58 of the previous 62 years.

Gingrich, however, galvanized Republicans around his **Contract With America,** a plan that attacked big government and emphasized patriotism and traditional values. The Contract With America called for congressional term limits, reduction of the federal bureaucracy, a balanced budget amendment to the Constitution, and large tax cuts, as well as increased defense spending, significant welfare reform, and tough anticrime legislation. The idea was to capture the votes of Americans who felt the federal government was too big, too wasteful, and too liberal.

**Capturing the 1994 Elections** Although most eligible voters did not vote in 1994, there was a strong turnout among Republicans. For the first time in 40 years, the Republicans won control of the House. They also captured the Senate and most of the governorships. *Newsweek* magazine observed:

> **Primary Source** "Last week in one of the most profound electoral routs in American history, Republicans won the right to occupy the Capitol and mount what their . . . commanders think of as a counter-revolution: a full-scale attack on the notion that a central government should play a central role in the life of the nation."

Once in office, Republicans passed most of Gingrich's program, but their attempts to slash Medicare and other government programs proved unpopular. Many Americans were also upset when the government shut down in 1995 because Congress would not pass Clinton's budget. Meanwhile, Clinton incorporated some of the conservative agenda into his own 1996 reelection bid. He signed a bill to reform welfare, passed legislation that appropriated more money for law enforcement, and called for stiffer sentencing for criminals. Finally, he made balancing the budget and reducing the federal deficit a priority.

**Clinton Wins Reelection** Beginning in the mid-1990s, the American economy broke out of recession and began to soar, starting the longest period of sustained growth in the country's history. Americans benefited from low unemployment, low inflation levels, and the government's efforts to balance the budget and reduce the deficit. In 1994, Clinton's disapproval rating had exceeded 60 percent, and few expected him to win a second term. As the 1996 election approached, however, the booming economy meant that few Americans had a compelling reason to change leadership.

The Republicans nominated Senate Majority Leader Robert Dole, a World War II hero and a moderate Republican. H. Ross Perot entered the race as the Reform Party candidate. Clinton skillfully captured the middle ground, labeling Dole as an out-of-touch conservative and Perot as a political quack. On election day, Americans chose Clinton by a wide margin. The House of Representatives and Senate, however, retained their Republican majorities.

✔ **Checkpoint** How did the Republicans take control of Congress?

# Scandals, Impeachment, and Trial

President Clinton had dodged scandals from his first days in office. One, a sexual harassment suit, had stemmed from his years as governor of Arkansas. Another concerned investments that Bill and Hillary Clinton had made in the Whitewater Development Corporation, an Arkansas real estate company, in the 1970s and 1980s.

**Prosecuting Clinton** A special prosecutor appointed by Attorney General Janet Reno investigated the Whitewater investment case and recommended that no criminal charges be filed. However, in July Congress passed a new law requiring that special prosecutors be selected by a three-judge panel from the U.S. Court of Appeals. As a result, in August of 1994 special prosecutor **Kenneth Starr** was appointed to investigate the case again. In seven years of investigation Starr failed to uncover any conclusive evidence of the Clintons' guilt, though some of their associates were convicted.

In the process of prosecuting Whitewater, Starr began investigating Clinton's relationship with a White House intern. Clinton had denied under oath that the two had an affair. Eventually, Clinton admitted that he had lied. The Whitewater case was quickly overshadowed by the new scandal. In 1998, Starr recommended **impeachment** proceedings on a number of counts, all related to the intern scandal rather than to Whitewater.

**Impeaching the President** Most Americans condemned Clinton's actions but opposed impeachment. Congressional Democrats, similarly, did not believe his behavior met the standard of "Treason, Bribery, or other high Crimes and Misdemeanors" required by the Constitution for the impeachment and removal of a President. Nevertheless, the House of Representatives, led by the Republican majority, impeached Clinton on the charges of perjury and obstruction of justice.

In January 1999, the Senate tried the President. The removal of a President requires a two-thirds majority of senators, and from the beginning it was clear that Clinton's opposition did not have the necessary votes. After a short trial, the President was acquitted on both counts on February 12.

 **Checkpoint** What was the outcome of the Clinton impeachment?

---

**SECTION 2 Assessment**

**Progress Monitoring *Online***
For: Self-test with vocabulary practice
Web Code: nea-2021

## Comprehension

1. **Terms and People** For each item below, write a sentence explaining how it relates to Clinton's presidency.
   - H. Ross Perot
   - Family Medical Leave Act
   - Brady Bill
   - Newt Gingrich
   - Contract With America
   - Kenneth Starr
   - impeachment

2. **NoteTaking Reading Skill: Summarize** Use your completed outline to answer the Section Focus Question: What were the successes and failures of the Clinton presidency?

## Writing About History

3. **Quick Write: Form a Main Idea** This section touches on the American issue of social problems and reforms. Compare the scandals surrounding Clinton to historical scandals you have read about. Write down a main idea that you will present in your response.

## Critical Thinking

4. **Identify Central Issues** How did Clinton position himself ideologically in order to win over both Democrats and Republicans in the 1992 election?

5. **Recognize Ideologies** On what domestic issues did Democrats and Republicans differ during Clinton's presidency?

6. **Synthesize Information** Why did Clinton win reelection?

7. **Summarize** Summarize the events surrounding Clinton's impeachment.

SECTION **3**

## Calling for a "Shared Future"

In 2000, the United Nations launched the Millennium Summit. The three-day event, held in New York City, was the largest gathering of world leaders in history. In the Millennium Declaration, they stated:

66We believe that the central challenge we face today is to ensure that globalization becomes a positive force for all the world's people. For while globalization offers great opportunities, at present its benefits are very unevenly shared, while its costs are unevenly distributed. . . . [O]nly through broad and sustained efforts to create a shared future, based upon our common humanity in all its diversity, can globalization be made fully inclusive and equitable.99
—Millennium Declaration, September 8, 2000

▲ Former White House official John Sununu meets with Saudi Arabian government leaders at a dinner during the Millennium Summit in New York City in 2000.

# Global Politics and Economics

### Content Expectations

- **9.2.1** Explain role of U.S. as a super-power in post-Cold War world.
- **9.2.2** Analyze how 9/11 attacks/response have altered American domestic/international policies.
- **9.3.1a** Compose a persuasive essay on role of U.S. in the world.

### Terms and People

EU
NAFTA
GATT

WTO
ethnic cleansing
al Qaeda

## NoteTaking

**Reading Skill: Identify Main Ideas**
Complete a flowchart like this one to help you identify main ideas about global politics and economics.

```
           U.S. Global Policy
    ┌───────────┬───────────┬───────────┐
  Free Trade    Foreign     Middle East
              Intervention
  • NAFTA        •             •
  •              •             •
```

**Why It Matters** With the end of the Cold War, the United States was the sole superpower in a dramatically changing world. No longer defined by its opposition to communism, the United States had to carve out new roles for itself in a world of globalization and increasing regional conflict. President Clinton, the nation's first baby-boomer President, ushered in this new period of American soul-searching. **Section Focus Question: What role did the United States take on in global politics and economics following the Cold War?**

## Competing in the Global Economy

In the 1990s, the United States was both an important promoter of global trade and an example for newly industrializing nations. As more nations participated in economic globalization, the United States tinkered with its own policies to ensure it remained an economic powerhouse.

**The Role of Free Trade** As an economic leader, America has had a major role in globalization. Free trade—the guiding principle of globalization—has been hotly debated in American politics. Americans want the lower costs that free trade creates but worry about the loss of American jobs to other countries. Generally, Republicans have supported the interests of big business and free trade agreements. Democrats have been more sympathetic to labor interests and have often opposed legislation that would cost American workers' jobs. Depending on which party has been in power, free trade has either been encouraged or hindered.

Bill Clinton challenged the traditional Democratic thinking by supporting free trade blocs, which in theory would increase the economic prosperity of particular regions. Europe was an example of such a bloc. In 1993, a number of European nations established the **European Union (EU)** to coordinate monetary and economic policies. By the end of the century, the EU had adopted a single currency, the euro, to promote economic efficiency. The EU's combined resources both encouraged trade among its members and challenged the economic leadership of the United States. North American free trade proponents believed a similar bloc would stimulate their own region.

**America Joins NAFTA** The **North American Free Trade Agreement (NAFTA),** a direct response to the EU was originally proposed during the Bush administration. President Bush and leaders of the other nations signed the agreement in 1992, but Congress blocked it. It called for a gradual removal of trade restrictions among the United States, Canada, and Mexico. NAFTA's supporters maintained that creating a free trade zone in North America would promote economic growth, reduce prices, increase exports, and encourage economic investment. Most labor leaders, environmentalists, and liberal Democrats argued that NAFTA would force American manufacturers to relocate to Mexico, where wages were lower and environmental controls were less rigid. They feared that hundreds of thousands of American jobs would be lost. President Clinton embraced NAFTA and pushed it through Congress. It went into effect in 1994, and since then the three countries have also signed agreements covering environmental protection, safety standards, and workers' rights.

Fourteen years later, with the removal of remaining trade restrictions between the United States and Mexico, the final provisions of NAFTA went into effect in January 2008.

**Expanding Global Trade** Clinton signed a total of 270 free trade agreements, including the revision of the **General Agreement on Tariffs and Trade (GATT)** in 1994 and the accords of the **World Trade Organization (WTO)** in 1995. GATT's goal was to reduce tariffs to promote free trade. The WTO replaced GATT, expanding the organization's authority to negotiate trade agreements, settle disputes, and enforce compliance with them. Clinton also continued the strong U.S. support of the World Bank.

Critics complain that the WTO and World Bank favor business interests over environmental concerns and workers' rights. At the 1999 WTO meeting in Seattle, protesters filled the streets, disrupting the proceedings. Yet most people agree that economic globalization has often had positive effects by exposing people to new ideas, technology, and communications. Nations involved in free trade have often become more democratic. Normalizing trade—engaging in free trade with countries rather than imposing sanctions based on disagreements—can strengthen economic ties. For example, normalizing trade with China has encouraged that country to adopt free market reforms.

**Analyzing Political Cartoons**

This political cartoon appeared as part of an intense national debate about the United States joining NAFTA.
1. What is the cartoonist's opinion about joining NAFTA?
2. Based on the cartoon, how would joining NAFTA affect the United States?

 **Checkpoint** Which trade blocs has the United States become involved with?

# Americans on the Global Stage

When Bill Clinton became President, the more than 40-year-old American foreign policy of fighting communism had just ended. The United States needed to develop a role for itself in the post–Cold War world. Americans were willing to provide economic aid, as they did to nations of the former Soviet Union. But many of them questioned military <u>intervention</u> abroad, fearing a costly commitment like the Vietnam War. With violence surging in regional conflicts throughout the world, however, Clinton found it necessary to intervene. He did so with mixed success.

**Vocabulary Builder**
<u>intervention</u>–(ihn tuhr VEHN shuhn) *n.* becoming involved in the affairs of another nation, often by force

# The World Bank

**T**he World Bank was founded in 1944 to help rebuild war-torn Europe. It still handles reconstruction efforts, as it did in India following a 2001 earthquake. **1** Yet it has increasingly focused on issues facing developing countries, such as healthcare, human rights, debt relief, economic growth, and poverty. In Latin America, the Bank gives loans to people like this Peruvian man so they can own their own homes and businesses. **2** Throughout the developing world, the Bank works to promote education for people like this Bulgarian girl. **3**

The U.S. has taken a primary role in the financing and management of the Bank. The Bank has its headquarters in Washington, D.C. As one of the Bank's most important partners, the U.S. has long seen the Bank and its work as integral to the American economy. Forty-five percent of U.S. exports go to developing countries in which the Bank is active, supporting American jobs. The U.S. also believes that strong and stable developing countries are vital to its own security.

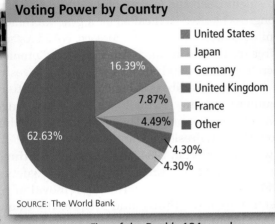

**Voting Power by Country**

- United States
- Japan
- Germany
- United Kingdom
- France
- Other

16.39%
7.87%
4.49%
62.63%
4.30%
4.30%

SOURCE: The World Bank

▲ Five of the Bank's 184 member countries take the lead in setting its direction. The chart shows the voting power for the Bank's Reconstruction and Development department. As with the World Bank's four other departments, the United States has the most voting power.

▼ A Senegalese family picks tomatoes on land that used to be plagued by drought. The Bank worked with governments and local communities to make the land usable and promote agriculture.

## Thinking Critically
1. **Analyze Information** What kinds of work does the World Bank do?

2. **Draw Inferences** Why is it in America's interest to support the World Bank?

**Intervening in Somalia and Haiti** In the late 1980s, civil war broke out in Somalia. By 1991, the government had disintegrated and the fighting had caused widespread famine. In 1992, the United States led a multinational force, later joined by the UN, to bring about peace and distribute food. The coalition fell apart in 1994 when several countries, including the United States, suffered steep casualty rates and withdrew their troops. Eventually, the UN also withdrew, and civil war dragged on for several more years in the devastated country.

Meanwhile, conflict was simmering in Haiti. In 1990, Haitians brought Jean-Bertrand Aristide to the presidency, in the nation's first free elections. Less than a year later, a military coup overthrew Aristide, plunging the country into turmoil. Thousands of Haitians left the country by boat to immigrate to the United States as political refugees. Many were sent back by American immigration officials, causing a public outcry. In 1994, Clinton sent American troops to Haiti to restore Aristide to power. Although American action improved the situation, within a decade Haiti faced a sinking economy and rising rates of disease and crime.

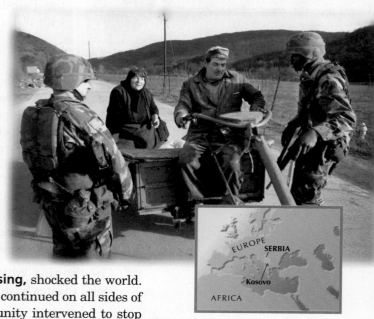

### NATO in the Balkans
American soldiers monitor a border crossing between Serbia and Kosovo in 2001.

## Fighting Ethnic Cleansing in Eastern Europe
In the Balkans, the collapse of communism broke up the country of Yugoslavia. For decades, the communist leader Tito had contained ethnic and religious strife. But his death in 1980, and the collapse of communism in 1989, left the country with no unifying forces. Soon, four of Yugoslavia's six major republics formed their own states, and long-suppressed ethnic and religious hostilities came boiling to the surface.

In newly independent Bosnia, ethnic and religious rivalries among Eastern Orthodox Serbs, Catholic Croats, and Bosnian Muslims eventually led to civil war. Serbs, with the help of Serbia-dominated Yugoslavia, attacked Bosnians and Croats. In many cases, they forcibly removed Bosnians and Croats from their homes and later murdered them. This state-sanctioned mass murder, violence, and rape, known as **ethnic cleansing,** shocked the world. The UN intervened with humanitarian aid. Yet atrocities continued on all sides of the struggle, and years went by before the world community intervened to stop the slaughter.

**Galvanizing NATO Forces** Finally, in the late summer of 1995, Clinton encouraged NATO to bomb Serbian strongholds. This was the first time the organization had gone into combat, and its use of force quickly brought about a cease-fire. In December 1995, the Dayton Accords established a federated, multinational Bosnia. Although the ethnic cleansing had ended, the enforced peace had not solved the problems of the region. In 1998, violence flared up anew—this time in Kosovo, a Serbian province on the Adriatic Sea. The fighting once again involved ethnic cleansing and also spread to the neighboring countries of Macedonia and Albania. NATO forced Serbs to withdraw from Kosovo.

 **Checkpoint** How did Clinton involve the United States in foreign conflicts?

## America and the Middle East
In the 1990s, disputes and fighting between Israelis and Palestinians grew increasingly fierce. Meanwhile, instability had increased in the region as a whole. As Clinton worked to address it, violence originating in the region spread outward, with the United States increasingly a target.

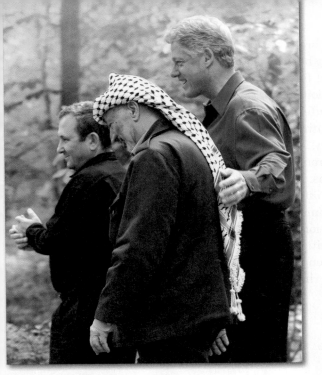

**Camp David Talks**
President Clinton walks with Ehud Barak and Yasir Arafat in the woods of Camp David in July 2000.

**Trying for Peace in Israel** In 1993, Palestinians and Israelis conducted secret negotiations in Oslo, Norway. The resulting Declaration of Principles promised Palestinian self-rule in Jericho and the Gaza Strip, as well as security for the Israelis. The declaration did not adequately address the issues of Israeli settlements in the West Bank, nor did it placate extremists on both sides, who had no interest in compromise. Chronic violence continued even though Israel withdrew from much of the West Bank, and later from Gaza. Israeli prime minister Yitzhak Rabin, who had signed the declaration, fell victim to the fury in 1995 when an Israeli religious fundamentalist assassinated him.

In 2000, Clinton invited Palestinian leader Yasir Arafat and Israeli prime minister Ehud Barak to Camp David to work on a peace agreement. They came close to signing one, but Arafat was not satisfied with any of the proposals. Back in Israel, Barak was ousted by Ariel Sharon, a "hawk" who opposed any concessions to the Palestinians. Palestinian suicide bombings increased, and with them so did crackdowns by the Israeli military.

**Dealing With Terrorism** In 1993, a terrorist group called **al Qaeda** exploded a bomb in the World Trade Center in New York City, killing six people and injuring more than one thousand others. Al Qaeda was led by a wealthy Saudi businessman named Osama bin Laden. Bin Laden had fought in Afghanistan in the 1980s on the side of Islamic fundamentalists who sought to expel the Soviet Union. By the late 1990s, he had formed al Qaeda with the purpose of ending American involvement in Muslim countries. Five years after the U.S. bombing, al Qaeda set off car bombs at American embassies in Nairobi, Kenya, and in Dar es Salaam, Tanzania. The blasts killed 225 people and injured more than 5,500 others. In 2000, al Qaeda bombed the USS *Cole,* an American warship anchored off the coast of Yemen, killing 17 American sailors. These attacks angered Americans and frustrated politicians, who were learning that fighting terrorism would be extremely difficult.

✔ **Checkpoint** What strategic, political, and economic interests did the United States have in the Middle East?

**SECTION** **3** **Assessment**

**Progress Monitoring *Online***
**For:** Self-test with vocabulary practice
**Web Code:** nea-2031

**Comprehension**

1. **Terms and People** For each term below, write a sentence describing what effect it has on the global economy or global society.
   • EU
   • NAFTA
   • GATT
   • WTO
   • ethnic cleansing
   • al Qaeda

2.  NoteTaking **Reading Skill: Identify Main Ideas** Use your completed flowchart to answer the Section Focus Question: What role did the United States take on in global politics and economics following the Cold War?

**Writing About History**

3. **Quick Write: Plan a Structure** Compare the issue of America and the world in the context of this section with how it related to an earlier period in American history. Choose the best way to structure your comparison, such as point by point or topic by topic.

**Critical Thinking**

4. **Identify Central Issues** Why have efforts to reduce tariffs and trade barriers often been controversial in the United States?

5. **Identify Assumptions** What basic assumption about the U.S. role as sole superpower underlies American peacekeeping efforts of the 1990s?

6. **Analyze Information** For what various reasons has the United States become involved in Middle Eastern affairs?

WITNESS HISTORY 🔊 AUDIO

**A Two-Term President**

In 2005, George W. Bush was sworn in as President for a second term. In his inaugural address, he alluded to a remarkable shift in traditional American foreign policy, saying that the cause of advancing freedom and democracy abroad was sufficient reason for the United States to involve itself in conflict overseas.

❝All who live in tyranny and hopelessness can know: the United States will not ignore your oppression, or excuse your oppressors. When you stand for your liberty, we will stand with you.❞

—George W. Bush, Second Inaugural Address, 2005

▲ Bush's casual style attracted voters in both of his presidential races. By his reelection in 2004, he was often referred to simply as "W."

# The George W. Bush Presidency

## Content Expectations

- **9.1.2a** Growth of conservative movement in national politics/role of Reagan.
- **9.1.2c** Analyze intensification of partisanship.
- **9.2.2** Analyze how 9/11 attacks/response have altered American domestic/international policies.

## Terms and People

George W. Bush
*Bush* v. *Gore*
No Child Left Behind Act
Afghanistan

Taliban
Patriot Act
Department of Homeland Security
WMD

## NoteTaking

**Reading Skill: Recognize Sequence** Record the sequence of events in Bush's presidency in a flowchart like the one below.

> The 2000 election is disputed but leads to victory for George W. Bush.

↓　　　↓　　　↓

> Bush launches an ambitious agenda including tax cuts and education legislation.

**Why It Matters** The election of **George W. Bush** to the presidency assured Republican domination of the White House and Congress. When the United States was attacked on September 11, 2001, Bush would use this unity—along with the support of a galvanized American public—to move the nation in a new direction. **Section Focus Question: What was the impact of Bush's domestic agenda and his response to the terrorist attack against the United States?**

## An Election Controversy

The year 2000 brought an end to Clinton's two terms as President. Clinton's legacy of a strong economy coupled with personal scandal polarized voters. As candidates geared up for the 2000 presidential race, it promised to be a close election.

**Three Candidates Run** Clinton's Vice President, Al Gore, Jr., of Tennessee, ran for the Democrats. Gore selected Connecticut senator Joseph Lieberman as his Vice President, making Lieberman the first Jewish person to be on the ticket of a major party. Gore tried to associate himself with the economic record of the Clinton administration while distancing himself from Clinton's personal scandals.

The Republicans chose George W. Bush as their candidate. A son of George H.W. Bush and a former governor of Texas, Bush was popular with party leaders, conservatives, and Christian fundamentalists. As governor of Texas, he had been adept at working with Democrats as well as Republicans. Although he was not a gifted orator, he struck many Americans as down-to-earth and sincere.

Consumer advocate Ralph Nader ran for the Green Party. Saying that corporate interests controlled the two major parties, he claimed he alone represented all Americans.

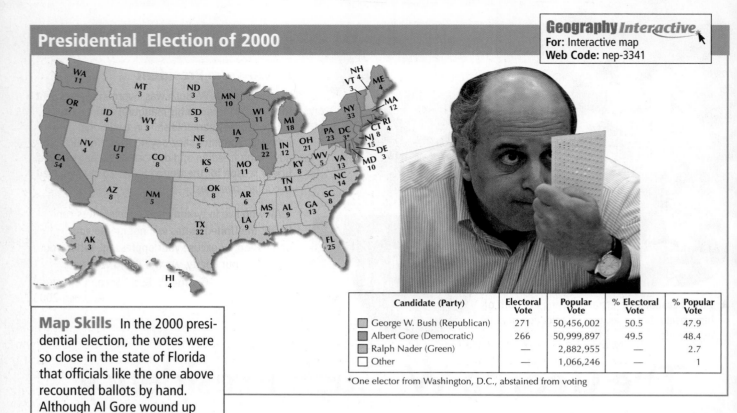

## Presidential Election of 2000

| Candidate (Party) | Electoral Vote | Popular Vote | % Electoral Vote | % Popular Vote |
|---|---|---|---|---|
| George W. Bush (Republican) | 271 | 50,456,002 | 50.5 | 47.9 |
| Albert Gore (Democratic) | 266 | 50,999,897 | 49.5 | 48.4 |
| Ralph Nader (Green) | — | 2,882,955 | — | 2.7 |
| Other | — | 1,066,246 | — | 1 |

*One elector from Washington, D.C., abstained from voting

**Map Skills** In the 2000 presidential election, the votes were so close in the state of Florida that officials like the one above recounted ballots by hand. Although Al Gore wound up winning the popular vote, George Bush captured a greater number of electoral votes, winning him the presidency.

1. **Identify** In general, which regions voted for Bush? Which voted for Gore?

2. **Predict Consequences** How might the dispute over the 2000 election affect future elections?

**A Tight Race** The campaigns focused mainly on how to spend the federal budget surplus. Bush wanted to use it to institute widespread tax cuts, while Gore proposed strengthening Social Security and paying down the national debt. Bush also said that a Republican President would restore morality to the White House. None of the candidates had the appeal of former Presidents Reagan or Clinton. Bush tended to mispronounce words, and Gore appeared dull and cold. On election night, Americans voted mainly by party affiliation.

The vote margin in the Electoral College was razor thin. Although Gore received a half million more votes than Bush, he fell short of winning the 270 electoral votes needed to capture the presidency. So did Bush. The issue was Florida's 25 electoral votes. Gore ran strong in the cities and along the coast, but Bush won the suburbs and the center of the state. The popular vote in Florida was so close that a state law mandated an automatic statewide recount of votes. Bush led by a margin of 327 popular votes. He was awarded a total of 271 electoral votes, one more than was needed to win the election.

**The Supreme Court Intervenes** Given the extreme closeness of the votes, Democrats demanded a hand, rather than machine, recount in several Florida counties. Republicans countered by suing in a Miami district court to prevent the hand recount. For more than a month, confusion reigned as each charge prompted a countercharge. Finally, the Supreme Court ruled on the issue. In the case of *Bush v. Gore*, the court ended the re-recounting by a 5-to-4 decision. On December 12, 2000, Gore conceded defeat, and Bush delivered a conciliatory victory speech. The election showed an interesting geographical pattern. The Democrats captured votes in their traditional strongholds such as the two coasts and large cities. The Republicans had extended their influence, winning voters in a large bloc that included most of the Midwest and the South.

✔ **Checkpoint** Why did the Supreme Court decide the 2000 presidential election?

# Bush Launches an Ambitious Agenda

Once in office, Bush turned to the domestic issues that most concerned him, including using Clinton's budget surplus to finance tax cuts. Like most Republicans, Bush believed that tax cuts would stimulate the economy. He felt they would provide Americans with more disposable income, leading to greater spending, heavier investment, and the creation of new jobs. In 2001, Bush successfully pushed a $1.3 trillion tax cut through Congress. The cut was highly controversial. It did put more money in the hands of consumers. Yet coming on the heels of a declining economy, it also increased federal budget deficits.

Bush's other domestic <u>priority</u> was education. He favored legislation that tied the federal funding of schools to demonstrable academic success. The 2002 **No Child Left Behind Act,** which attracted bipartisan support, held schools accountable by penalizing those that did not reach federal performance standards. It also called for improving teacher quality and for making information about schools more readily available to parents.

Bush also addressed the concern of older Americans who were caught between their relatively fixed incomes and the rising costs of prescription drugs. In 2003, Congress extended Medicare to cover prescription drugs for senior citizens. Like his tax cuts, the measure was controversial. It was expensive, creating further budget deficits, and many seniors found its provisions confusing and its coverage inadequate.

**Vocabulary Builder**
<u>priority</u>–(prī ôr ə tē) *n.* a thing that is considered more important than another

✔ **Checkpoint** What were Bush's domestic priorities?

---

**Comparing Viewpoints**

# Should President Bush's Tax Cuts Be Passed?

President Bush's tax cuts sharply divided Americans into two camps—those who agreed with the cuts and those who opposed them.

Primary Source

Primary Source

**Compare**
1. In the cartoon on the left, the artist mocks Democrats for overreacting to the tax cuts. How does he do this?

2. Who does the artist of the cartoon on the right imply is the main beneficiary of Bush's tax cuts?

**WITNESS HISTORY DVD**

Watch *The War on Terrorism* on the **United States Witness History DVD** to explore how the attacks of September 11, 2001, prompted the United States to wage a wider war on terrorism.

## The United States Is Attacked

Bush had been in office less than a year when the United States was attacked by a foreign enemy for the first time since Pearl Harbor. Following the hijacking and crashing of four commercial airplanes on September 11, 2001, millions of Americans rushed to donate money, supplies, services, and their own blood. As it became clear that the crashes were part of an organized terrorist attack on the United States, Americans responded as they had after Pearl Harbor—as a unified, determined nation. The attack challenged the new President in unforeseen ways and led to a major shift in American foreign policy. On the day of the attacks, President Bush addressed the nation:

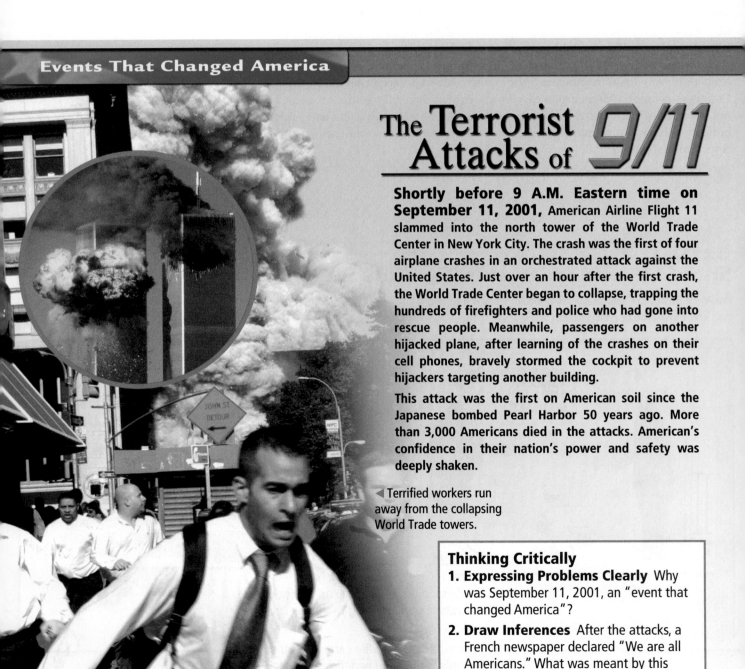

**Events That Changed America**

# The Terrorist Attacks of 9/11

**Shortly before 9 A.M. Eastern time on September 11, 2001,** American Airline Flight 11 slammed into the north tower of the World Trade Center in New York City. The crash was the first of four airplane crashes in an orchestrated attack against the United States. Just over an hour after the first crash, the World Trade Center began to collapse, trapping the hundreds of firefighters and police who had gone into rescue people. Meanwhile, passengers on another hijacked plane, after learning of the crashes on their cell phones, bravely stormed the cockpit to prevent hijackers targeting another building.

This attack was the first on American soil since the Japanese bombed Pearl Harbor 50 years ago. More than 3,000 Americans died in the attacks. American's confidence in their nation's power and safety was deeply shaken.

◀ Terrified workers run away from the collapsing World Trade towers.

### Thinking Critically

1. **Expressing Problems Clearly** Why was September 11, 2001, an "event that changed America"?

2. **Draw Inferences** After the attacks, a French newspaper declared "We are all Americans." What was meant by this statement?

"Today, our fellow citizens, our way of life, and our very freedom came under attack in a series of deliberate and deadly terrorist acts. . . . Thousands of lives were suddenly ended by evil, despicable acts of terror. . . . These acts of mass murder were intended to frighten our nation into chaos and retreat. But they have failed. . . . Terrorist attacks can shake the foundations of our biggest buildings, but they cannot touch the foundation of America. These acts shatter steel, but they cannot dent the steel of American resolve."

—President George W. Bush, September 11, 2001

✓ **Checkpoint** What was the significance of September 11, 2001?

# America's War on Terrorism

In the wake of September 11, Bush and his advisers agreed that the most important priority should be finding and prosecuting the people behind 9/11. This would be just the first step in what Bush called the "war on terrorism."

**Invading Afghanistan** American government officials quickly determined that Osama bin Laden's al Qaeda network had been behind the September 11 attacks. Bin Laden opposed the presence of American troops in Saudi Arabia, the U.S. economic boycott against Iraq, and U.S. support for Israel. He also opposed any governments in the Middle East that he felt were pro-Western. Bin Laden and other al Qaeda leaders were believed to be hiding in Afghanistan, where the Islamic fundamentalist **Taliban** government allowed them to operate training camps for terrorists.

Bush believed that any government that sponsored terrorism, even if it did not itself commit terrorist acts, should be held accountable. He immediately demanded that the Taliban turn over bin Laden to U.S. custody. When the Taliban refused, he quickly sent American forces, joined by Great Britain and other allies, into Afghanistan. Joined by Afghan rebels, the allied forces overthrew the Taliban within three months. Although American troops captured several of al Qaeda's leaders, bin Laden himself escaped. While Afghanistan held its first free elections and wrote a new constitution, the United States still faced the threat of terrorism elsewhere.

**Improving National Security** Bush also moved quickly on the home front to prevent future terrorist attacks. Soon after September 11, Congress passed the **Patriot Act** to give law enforcement broader powers to monitor suspected terrorists. Congress also approved Bush's call for the creation of a new Cabinet-level **Department of Homeland Security** to coordinate domestic security matters among a number of federal, state, and local agencies. Some critics charged that the Patriot Act violated civil liberties, but most Americans were willing to give up some freedoms in return for improved protection against attack.

**Launching Operation Iraqi Freedom** Bush next turned his attention to Iraq. In the decade after the first Gulf War, Iraqi dictator Saddam Hussein had defied UN weapons inspectors. Many people both inside and outside of the Bush administration believed that Saddam was constructing and stockpiling nuclear, biological, and chemical **Weapons of Mass Destruction (WMD)**. Bush contemplated invading Iraq as part of his wider war on terrorism.

Despite many Americans' belief that UN weapons inspectors should be allowed to continue their search for WMD, in October of 2002 Congress authorized Bush to use American military forces against Iraq. On March 19, 2003, American and British military forces invaded Iraq in Operation Iraqi Freedom.

**War in Iraq, 2003**

April 14, 2003 Tikrit falls. Pentagon announces that major combat operations are over.

April 9, 2003 Fall of Baghdad

March 20, 2003 Explosions in Baghdad mark the beginning of U.S.-led operations.

March 23, 2003 First significant casualties during battle in An Nasiriyah.

Predominately Kurdish
Predominately Sunni Arab
Predominately Shia Arab
Advance by the U.S. and allies
Major bombing target

**War in Afghanistan, 2001–2002**

November 9, 2001 Battle for Mazar-e Sharif.

December 7, 2001 Kandahar, the last Taliban controlled city, falls.

October 7, 2001 U.S. and British forces begin aerial bombing campaign of Taliban sites.

Advance by the U.S.
Advance by the Northern Alliance
Major bombing target

U.S. ally
Unstable relations with United States

**Map Skills** In the early 2000s, the United States waged two wars in the Middle East.

1. **Locate:** (a) Baghdad, (b) Kabul, (c) Pakistan, (d) Syria

2. **Location** Describe the location of Baghdad. What difficulty might a Baghdad-based government have keeping peace?

3. **Draw Inferences** Notice the location of Pakistan. Why is it important to the United States that Pakistan remain a reliable ally?

**Geography** *Interactive*
**For:** Interactive map
**Web Code:** nep-2043

Saddam's forces collapsed almost immediately. As the Iraqi capital of Baghdad fell, Saddam and the other Iraqi leaders went into hiding. Bush gave a victory speech on May 1, 2003, in front of a banner reading "mission accomplished." In the months that followed, Saddam and many of his supporters were captured.

✔ **Checkpoint** How did Bush combat terrorism?

## Bush's Second Term

The Iraq war, terrorism, and the budget weighed heavily on Americans' minds as they cast their votes in the 2004 election.

Bush relied heavily on his image as a "war president," saying that the lack of an attack on American soil since 9/11 proved his competency as commander in chief. The Democratic candidate, Massachusetts senator John F. Kerry, was a decorated Vietnam veteran with many more years of political experience than Bush. His message never fully resonated with Americans, however, and Bush defeated Kerry by a comfortable margin. Once again, the U.S. electoral map indicated what many began to call a "red state, blue state" divide, with people along the coasts and in the big cities voting Democratic, and people in the South, Midwest, and rural areas voting Republican.

Iraq remained the major focus of Bush's second term. Saddam's brutal rule kept fighting among Iraq's three major groups: Sunnis, Shi'a, and Kurds in check. With Saddam's overthrow, these groups fought bitterly for power. By the end of 2005, Iraq had written a new constitution and established the beginnings of a democracy. But the chaos continued. Saddam went into hiding, but was soon captured. After a lengthy trial, Iraq's High Tribunal sentenced him to death for crimes against humanity. Saddam was executed in 2006.

By early 2004, the United Nations had determined that Saddam had never possessed nuclear weapons or the materials to make them. Critics of Bush charged that he had exaggerated evidence of WMD and misled Congress and the American people in his effort to win support for the war. Even those who agreed that the war was necessary worried that the United States had gotten itself into a quagmire.

Meanwhile, Bush faced serious domestic challenges. With so much money being spent on Iraq, the federal deficit grew larger. In August of 2005, Hurricane Katrina hit the Gulf Coast, destroying much of the city of New Orleans. The government response to Katrina, which largely affected poor people, was slow. National discontent was reflected in the 2006 Congressional elections in which Democrats, for the first time in 12 years, won control of both the House and the Senate.

During the final two years of his second term, Bush's approval ratings fell dramatically. By 2008 Americans faced serious problems. Wars in Afghanistan and Iraq, possible spread of nuclear weapons, and the continuing threat of terrorists stretched American resources. At home, healthcare concerns, the cost of oil, immigration problems, and the economy added to American worries.

 **Checkpoint** What challenges did Bush face in his second term?

# The 2008 Election

The 2008 election broke new ground in America's political landscape. In the primary campaign, Senator Hillary Rodham Clinton became the first woman to win a major party's presidential primary. She came close to winning the Democratic nomination for president. Meanwhile, Democrat Barack Obama became the first African American to be nominated for president by a major party. Governor Sarah Palin of Alaska was the second woman to be selected as a Vice Presidential running mate. Geraldine Ferraro, the first, ran with Walter Mondale in 1984.

**The Candidates** In the 2008 presidential race, Republican John McCain and Democrat Barack Obama advanced different solutions to key issues such as the wars in Iraq and Afghanistan, the economy, healthcare, and energy policy. But they shared a firm belief in service to their country. McCain, the son and grandson of navy admirals, served as a pilot in the Vietnam War. He also endured six years as a prisoner of war in North Vietnam after his plane was shot down. After his release, he entered politics to continue to serve his country.

After graduating from Columbia University and Harvard Law School, Obama worked as a community organizer on the south side of Chicago. He set up programs to aid minorities and the poor. Like McCain,

## HISTORY MAKERS

### Condoleezza Rice (born 1954)
Condoleezza Rice grew up in segregated Birmingham, Alabama. At age 15, she entered college intending to become a concert pianist but graduated at age 19 with a degree in political science instead. By age 30, she had earned a Ph.D., served as an intern in the Carter administration, and held a professorship at Stanford University. In 2000, Rice was tapped by George W. Bush to become National Security Advisor. In 2004, she became the first African American woman to be named Secretary of State. Dr. Rice has taken an active role in the U.S. rebuilding of Iraq.

In a decisive victory, Barack Obama became the nation's first African American President.

he entered politics to fulfill a commitment to solving America's foreign and domestic problems.

**An Historic Moment** On January 20, 2009, Barack Obama became the 44th President and the first African American to hold the office. Speaking at a huge rally in Chicago after winning the race, his words defined the historic moment. "If there is anyone out there who still doubts that America is a place where all things are possible, who still wonders if the dream of our founders is alive in our time, who still questions the power of our democracy, tonight is your answer."

Obama's victory not only marked a shift in American politics but reflected the changed national mood. The election drew a huge voter turnout, with an unexpectedly large participation of young voters. Along with the economic crisis—nearly 62 percent of voters cited the economy as a major concern—and with the low approval ratings of President Bush, a Republican victory seemed almost impossible.

In Congress, the Democratic Party, which won a majority of seats in 2006, expanded its majority in the 2008 election.

## Banking Crisis

During the last month of the 2008 campaign both candidates faced a disturbing, and potentially disastrous, economic crisis centered on Wall Street and in the banking industry. The causes of the crisis that flared up stemmed from a series of risky bank loans and a general decline in the value of many American homes. As a result, millions of Americans could not pay their home mortgages. Several important banking and investment firms who had engaged in the risky lending policies were either forced out of business or bought by other firms. Congress passed legislation that attempted to solve the problem but the crisis defied any quick-fix solutions. By the time of the election the crisis had spread around the world. The situation was so serious that many people considered it to be the worst economic crisis since the Great Depression.

 **Checkpoint** Why was the 2008 election significant?

---

**Progress Monitoring *Online***
**For:** Self-test with vocabulary practice
**Web Code:** nea-2041

### Comprehension

**1. Terms and People** Using complete sentences, relate each of the following items to the presidency of George W. Bush.
  • No Child Left Behind Act
  • Taliban
  • Patriot Act
  • Department of Homeland Security
  • WMD

**2. NoteTaking Reading Skill: Recognize Sequence** Use your completed flowchart to answer the Section Focus Question: What was the impact of Bush's domestic agenda and his response to the terrorist attack against the United States?

### Writing About History

**3. Quick Write: Provide Details** Choose an American issue that has relevance both to the Bush presidency and to an earlier period of American history. Analyze the issue in both time periods, including details that define the issue and support your points.

### Critical Thinking

**4. Compare Points of View** Compare how Democrats and Republicans viewed the initial results of the 2000 election.

**5. Analyzing Effects** Why do you think the economic crisis in the United States in 2008 had a global effect? Explain.

**6. Identify Assumptions** What assumptions about the United States were conveyed in Bush's speech to the nation on September 11?

**7. Recognize Cause and Effect** How did the September 11 attacks influence American policy in the Middle East?

WITNESS HISTORY 🔊 AUDIO

**Finding the American Dream**

In 1990, Eddie (Duc) and Linda (Lieu) Tran left Vietnam with their young son to start over in Columbus, Ohio. Sponsored by Linda's brother, who had fled Vietnam by boat during the fall of Saigon in 1975, the Trans were aware of the obstacles that faced them in their new country.

❝Learning the English language and finding jobs were our biggest challenges. We listened to the radio and tried to converse as much as possible with our co-workers to learn English. Everyone was helpful. And we were determined never to receive welfare. Linda got a job as a tailor ten days after we arrived. I owned a manufacturing business in Vietnam, but it took me six months to get employed here. Times were hard, and we still work 12-hour days in our restaurant now. But the best thing about this country is freedom. If you work hard, you can achieve the American dream.❞

—Eddie and Linda Tran, 2005

▲ The Trans today (above) with their sons and at their wedding in Vietnam (left).

# Americans Look to the Future

 **Content Expectations**

- **9.1.1** Evaluate changes in U.S. economy.
- **9.3.1c** Compose a persuasive essay on welfare policy.
- **9.3.1d** Compose a persuasive essay on energy policy.
- **9.3.1g** Compose a persuasive essay on civil rights.

## Terms and People

Immigration Act of 1990
bilingual education
Immigration and Control Act of 1986

affirmative action
Violence Against Women Act
privatize

## NoteTaking

**Reading Skill: Identify Supporting Details**
Record supporting details about the changing American society in a table like this one.

| A Changing Society | |
|---|---|
| **Immigration** | **Demographics** |
| • Immigration policies relax | • Family structures change |
| • | • |

**Why It Matters** As the twenty-first century dawned, American society looked very different from the way it had during the previous century. It also faced different challenges. As the nation entered the new millennium, it sought ways to preserve its heritage while at the same time adapting to rapid social, political, and technological change. **Section Focus Question: How was American society changing at the beginning of the twenty-first century?**

## Immigrants Shape a Nation

For two centuries, American protection of religious and personal freedom, along with opportunities for social and economic mobility, has attracted huge numbers of immigrants. Over time, however, the nature of immigration has changed.

**Immigration Policies Change** For years, the government limited immigration to mainly northern and western Europeans. In the 1960s, however, laws began to relax immigration limitations. The **Immigration Act of 1990** increased quotas by 40 percent and eased most remaining restrictions. As a result, the period from the 1990s to the 2000s saw the largest numbers of immigrants in the country's history. During that time, almost one million immigrants arrived in America each year from all over the globe, representing a wide variety of cultures and religions. Today, immigrants account for more than 10 percent of the total American population.

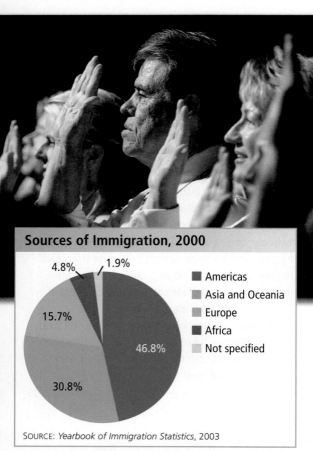

## Sources of Immigration, 2000

- 4.8%
- 1.9%
- 15.7%
- 46.8%
- 30.8%

■ Americas
■ Asia and Oceania
■ Europe
■ Africa
■ Not specified

SOURCE: *Yearbook of Immigration Statistics*, 2003

## U.S. Population by Race, 2000

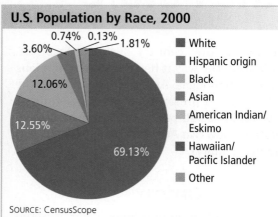

- 0.74%
- 0.13%
- 3.60%
- 1.81%
- 12.06%
- 12.55%
- 69.13%

■ White
■ Hispanic origin
■ Black
■ Asian
■ American Indian/ Eskimo
■ Hawaiian/ Pacific Islander
■ Other

SOURCE: CensusScope

**Graph Skills** Every year, people from all backgrounds are sworn in as U.S. citizens. Study the two pie charts. What was the largest minority group in 2000? How does the Sources of Immigration graph support the data in the U.S. Population by Race graph?

**Latinos Exert Their Influence** Most of the new immigrants were Latinos. In 2000, 27 percent of the total immigrant population were Mexicans, with people from the Caribbean and Central America making up almost 17 percent. Mexicans and Central Americans settled largely in the South and Southwest. Caribbean immigrants, many of them Cubans, settled in Florida. The census of 2000 showed that a third or more of the residents of Texas, New Mexico, Arizona, and California were Latinos.

Like all immigrants, Latinos have varying educational and employment backgrounds. Often they are forced to take lower-paying jobs with no healthcare benefits. However, Latino immigrants have had a profound social, cultural, and political impact. By 2001, Latinos held about 5,000 political offices and 4 percent of the seats in Congress, primarily as Democrats. Cuban Americans in Florida, generally Republican, have had an enormous influence on American political policy concerning Cuba.

**A Surging Asian Population** Asians make up the second-largest source of the new immigration. In 2000, they were nearly 23 percent of the total immigrant population, with the largest numbers coming from China, the Philippines, and India. The majority of Asian immigrants have settled in California, adding to the large Asian population in that state. As a group, Asian immigrants have had widely varying backgrounds, but overall they have the highest level of education. Some came to America with college degrees and marketable skills and found professional jobs. Others came from war-torn countries, with very little education.

**Debating Immigration** Immigration has long been debated in this country. People who would restrict it worry that immigrants take jobs and social services away from native-born Americans. They generally oppose **bilingual education,** in which students are taught in their native languages as well as in English, saying that immigrants must learn English in order to assimilate into American society. Proponents point out that immigrants contribute to the economy, often by taking jobs no one else wants. They also argue that with the U.S. birthrate falling immigrants help the country by maintaining its population.

Much of the debate concerns illegal immigrants. A large number of immigrants to the United States, especially Latinos, have come illegally. They labor in low-paying jobs, such as migrant farmwork, and receive no benefits. The **Immigration Reform and Control Act of 1986** hoped to stop the flow of illegal immigrants by penalizing employers who hired them and by granting resident status to those residing in the United States since 1982. But illegal immigrants still regularly cross U.S. borders. How to treat these illegal—but often necessary—workers is an ongoing debate. In 2008, the Bush administration proposed changes that would make it easier for farm employers to legally hire immigrant workers. He also proposed a process by which illegal immigrants could eventually gain citizenship.

✔ **Checkpoint** How has immigration to America changed over time?

# Changing American Demographics

At the beginning of 2000, Americans were on the move more than ever. Coastal cities as well as the Sunbelt, or the region of warm southern and southwestern states, saw rapid population and economic growth as people left the cold Northeast and the Rust Belt. Meanwhile, the family itself was changing.

**The Changing Family** In 1960, more than 70 percent of American households were headed by a working father and a nonworking mother, neither of whom had ever been divorced. By 2000, fewer than 15 percent of households fit this model. In 2000, one out of every two marriages ended in divorce, and in a high percentage of households both parents worked outside the home. Single-parent households were far more common, with a quarter of all children growing up in a single-parent household. The number of children born to unmarried mothers also rose. In 1960, only 5 percent of children were born out of wedlock. In 2000, one out of every four white babies, one out of every three Latino babies, and two out of every three African American babies were born to unmarried mothers.

**Debating Affirmative Action** In the 1960s, President Johnson introduced the idea of **affirmative action,** or improving opportunities for women and minorities by giving preference to them in school admissions and job applications. Since that time, affirmative action has been hotly debated. Proponents argue that without such initiatives, minorities cannot overcome generations of <u>discrimination</u>. Opponents say that the policy is unfair and discriminates against nonminorities. In 1996, Californians voted to end affirmative action in state hiring and education. That same year, a federal court struck down an affirmative action admissions program at the University of Texas. In 2003, however, the Supreme Court decided in two cases involving the University of Michigan that while race could not be the deciding factor in admissions, it could be one of several factors.

**Expanding Rights for All** At the turn of the new century, African Americans and women continued to make social and political gains. By 2002, 33 percent of African American families enjoyed incomes of at least $50,000, placing them in the middle class. Also in 2002, 17 percent of African Americans over the age of 25 held bachelor's degrees. At the same time, legislation to enforce equal pay for equal work, address child care needs for working women, and end sexual harassment in the workplace has improved the lives of working women. Outside of the world of work, women have also achieved victories. Issues such as spouse abuse and date rape are now widely discussed. Incidents of violence against women are more often reported and more often punished than ever before.

**Vocabulary Builder**
<u>discrimination</u>—(dih skrihm ih NAY shuhn) *n.* unfair bias in the treatment of a particular group

**Graph Skills** While the income gap is slowly narrowing, wages among ethnic groups still vary widely. Study the graph. Which group enjoyed the highest income in the period shown? What might explain this?

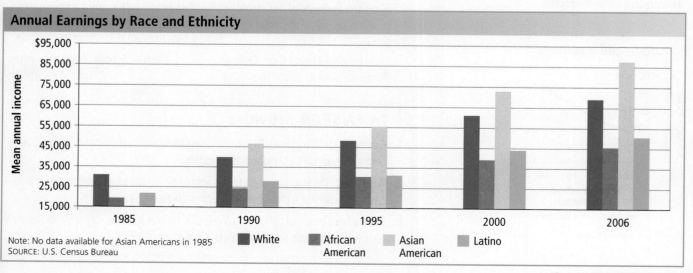

**Annual Earnings by Race and Ethnicity**

Mean annual income

Note: No data available for Asian Americans in 1985
SOURCE: U.S. Census Bureau

White · African American · Asian American · Latino

## TRACK THE ISSUE

### What should be the goals of American education?

Over time, the purpose of American education has changed. From an early focus on religion, schools turned to the promotion of democratic values. Today, they are placing a strong emphasis on performance standards. Use the timeline below to explore this enduring issue.

### 1600s–1700s Colonial Education
Schools emphasize religious study.

### 1852 Public Schools
Massachusetts passes first compulsory school attendance law in the United States.

### 1903 Du Bois-Washington Debate
Scholars debate the role of education in improving African Americans' lives.

### 1926 Scholastic Aptitude Test
The Scholastic Aptitude Test (SAT) is first administered.

### 2001 No Child Left Behind Act
Federal law tries to raise student performance through standardized testing and other measures.

MI 9.3.1f

Students taking a standardized test

### Education and Income

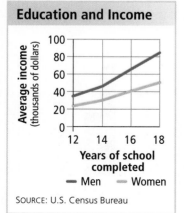

SOURCE: U.S. Census Bureau

## DEBATE THE ISSUE

**Standardized Testing** Standardized tests are used both to assess students and to hold teachers accountable for meeting standards. But critics argue that an emphasis on testing is hurting American schools.

❝We have learned a great deal about the nature of teaching and learning, and we know that students need to have opportunities to construct knowledge and connect that knowledge to what they already know. However, many . . . [standardized tests] still continue to focus on the memory of isolated facts which are destined to be forgotten.❞

—Marilyn Bizar, North Central Regional Educational Laboratory

❝You can't figure out whether schools are doing a good job unless you have some way of measuring how much their students are learning. . . . A guarantee by the national government of a decent education for every child is a noble cause, and so is the idea that all Americans will acquire a common body of skills and knowledge as they come of age.❞

—Nicholas Lemann, writer, *The New Yorker*

### ❓ *TRANSFER* Activities

1. **Compare** Why does Bizar oppose standardized testing? Why does Lemann support standardized testing?

2. **Analyze** Do you think that the increase in standardized testing will cause students' achievement scores to rise? Explain.

3. **Transfer** Use the following Web site to see a video, try a WebQuest, and write in your journal. **Web Code:** neh-9302

The 1994 **Violence Against Women Act** increased federal resources to apprehend and prosecute men guilty of violent acts against women.

**America Grows Older** While the life expectancy of an American born in 1900 was less than 50 years, an American born in 2000 can expect to live to age 77. By 2000, older Americans tended to retire earlier, live longer, and exert more political influence. These factors have strained the country's social welfare system, especially Social Security and Medicare. In 1960, the federal government spent less than $100 billion on social welfare. By 2003, the amount had increased to $1.4 trillion.

With the large baby-boom generation reaching retirement age, the issue of elder care has become critical. Falling birthrates over the past two decades have meant that when the huge population of baby boomers retires, there will not be enough workers to cover their Social Security benefits. Politicians have been debating how to deal with this impending reality. In his second term, President Bush called for **privatizing** Social Security by allowing younger workers to invest some of their earnings in individual retirement accounts. Critics defeated the measure, saying that it would put younger workers at the mercy of fluctuating stock market returns without addressing the shortfall of funds. As Americans get older, the debate continues.

**Facing the Future** As the new millennium began, Americans looked back at a century of great change and technological progress. Looking forward, immense challenges remain. Americans still struggle with basic problems with which societies throughout history have struggled, as well as some new problems unique to the time. Yet with its greatest resource—the American people—the United States faces this new century with strength and optimism.

 **Checkpoint** What challenges have changing American demographics brought?

## HISTORY MAKERS

**George H. W. Bush** (born 1924) **and William Jefferson Clinton** (born 1946)
Both presidents Bush and Clinton (below with the president of Indonesia) have spent much of their lives as public servants. Former political opponents, the two men formed an organization to bring relief to Southeastern Asians in the wake of the 2004 Asian tsunami. Touring the United States, the men raised millions of dollars by appealing to Americans to contribute to tsunami relief. A year later, Bush and Clinton went into action again in the wake of Hurricane Katrina. The former Presidents raised $100 million dollars and immediately set to work rebuilding and providing economic and educational opportunities to Americans devastated by the disaster. At the end of 2005, the former Presidents remarked that "the generosity of people never ceases to amaze us."

---

**SECTION 5 Assessment**

**Progress Monitoring Online**
For: Self-test with vocabulary practice
Web Code: nea-2051

## Comprehension

**1. Terms and People** For each term below, write a sentence explaining its significance to American society in the twenty-first century.
- Immigration Act of 1990
- bilingual education
- Immigration and Control Act of 1986
- affirmative action
- Violence Against Women Act
- privatize

**2. NoteTaking Reading Skill: Identify Supporting Details** Use your completed table to answer the Section Focus Question: How was American society changing at the beginning of the twenty-first century?

## Writing About History

**3. Quick Write: List Details** You are writing an essay that analyzes the American issue of education and American society. List details from this section that support your analysis.

## Critical Thinking

**4. Draw Inferences** How can a nation's immigration policies affect its economy?

**5. Identify Central Issues** Why is an aging population a problem for a society?

# 20

# Quick Study Guide

 9.2.2

**Progress Monitoring *Online***
**For:** Self-test with vocabulary practice
**Web Code:** nea-2061

## ■ World Trade Organization Members and Observers

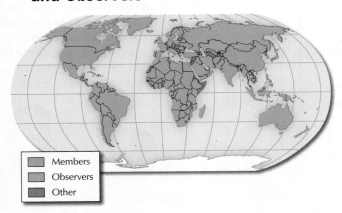

- Members
- Observers
- Other

## ■ Major Events in the Clinton and Bush Presidencies

| President | Event |
|---|---|
| Clinton | **1992** Signed NAFTA; sent forces into Somalia |
| | **1993** Signed Brady Bill; helped negotiate Declaration of Principles |
| | **1994** Sent troops to Haiti |
| | **1995** Sent forces into Bosnia as part of NATO |
| | **1996** Signed bill to reform welfare |
| | **1999** Impeached; cleared of charges |
| Bush | **2001** Pushed for major tax cuts; sent troops to war in Afghanistan; signed Patriot Act |
| | **2002** Signed No Child Left Behind Act |
| | **2003** Sent troops to war in Iraq |
| | **2004** Bush reelected |

## ■ Major Issues of American Society in the New Millennium

**Technology**—Computers, satellites, and advances in agriculture raise productivity and efficiency, but challenge many workers and industries.

**Globalization**—Globalization brings consumers more choices and opportunities, but can result in the loss of American jobs.

**Terrorism**—After September 11, government must work to make America more secure.

**Immigration**—Immigrants continue to enrich American society and fuel its economy, but their increasing numbers spark debate.

**Demographics**—Federal and local governments must find ways to support older Americans, Americans on the move, and nontraditional families.

## ✓ Quick Study Timeline

**In America**

| 1992 Bill Clinton is elected President | 1994 Republicans win control of Congress | 1996 Congress passes Welfare Reform Act | 1998 President Clinton is impeached |

**Presidential Terms** George H. W. Bush 1989–1993    William J. Clinton 1993–2001

1992    1994    1996    1998

**Around the World**

| 1993 European Union forms | 1994 Mandela is elected President of South Africa | 1995 NATO forces restore order in Bosnia; WTO is established | 1998 Indonesian dictator Suharto steps down |

# American Issues
## •—•—• Connector

9.3.1

By connecting prior knowledge with what you have learned in this chapter, you can gradually build your understanding of enduring questions that still affect America today. Answer the questions below. Then, use your American Issues Connector study guide (or go online: www.PHSchool.com **Web Code:** neh-9303).

## Issues You Learned About

● **Education and American Society** American leaders continually try to find new ways to improve the quality of the American education system.

1. Name and describe an educational reform in the United States that you have already learned about.

2. Why do you think the No Child Left Behind Act attracted the support of both Republicans and Democrats?

3. As part of the No Child Left Behind Act, schools must demonstrate success in order to receive federal funding. What are some ways that schools can demonstrate success?

● **Technology and Society** The development of the modern computer has changed the way people live, work, and play.

4. Prior to the computer, what do you think was the most important technological development, and why?

5. What spurred the development of the modern computer?

6. What are some ways that you use personal computers?

● **Global Interdependence** The United States economy depends on trade with countries around the world.

7. What are some of the issues that have caused a debate in the United States over free trade?

8. Why was Clinton's support of NAFTA controversial?

9. What are some of the benefits and drawbacks of globalization?

### Connect to Your World | Michigan

**Government's Role in the Economy** In 1912, the Michigan state legislature passed a bill guaranteeing worker compensation for all workplace injuries. To help provide this new insurance, the state created and operated the Accident Fund of Michigan. By the 1990s, the Accident Fund covered more than 15 percent of Michigan workers' compensation insurance, but some Michiganians felt that privatizing the fund would improve insurance quality and alleviate burdens on the state. In 1995 Blue Cross Blue Shield of Michigan bought the fund for $262 million. The renamed Accident Fund Insurance Agency of America is now one of over 200 private insurance providers available to Michigan employers. Compose a persuasive essay arguing for or against privatizing the Accident Fund.

**2001**
**Terrorists attack United States. The United States invades Afghanistan**

**2003**
**War in Iraq begins**

George W. Bush 2001–2009

Barack Obama 2009–

**2000**

**2002**

**2004**

**2006**

**2008**

**2000**
**Putin is elected President of Russia**

**2002**
**Al Qaeda car bombs kill more than 200 people in Indonesia**

**History *Interactive*****
**For:** Interactive timeline
**Web Code:** nep-2061

# Chapter Assessment

## Terms and People

1. Define **satellite**. What role does satellite technology play in everyday life?

2. Who is **Newt Gingrich**? What were some of his specific proposals during the Clinton presidency?

3. Define **ethnic cleansing**. Where was it used, and by whom?

4. What was the **Patriot Act**? What caused Congress to pass this legislation?

5. What is **bilingual education**? Why are some people opposed to it?

## Focus Questions

The focus question for this chapter is **What political, social, technological, and economic trends have shaped American life since 1990?** Build an answer to this question by answering the focus questions for Sections 1 through 5 and the Critical Thinking questions that follow.

### Section 1

6. How have technological changes and globalization transformed the American economy?

### Section 2

7. What were the successes and failures of the Clinton presidency?

### Section 3

8. What role did the United States take on in global politics and economics following the Cold War?

### Section 4

9. What was the impact of Bush's domestic agenda and his response to the terrorist attack against the United States?

### Section 5

10. How was American society changing at the beginning of the twenty-first century?

## Critical Thinking

11. **Identify Central Issues** How did the rise of the service sector benefit some Americans and harm others?

12. **Draw Inferences** In the 1988 presidential election, 57.4 percent of Americans voted; in 1992, 61.3 percent voted, and in 1996, 54.2 percent voted. What may have contributed to the 1992 spike in voter participation?

13. **Analyze Evidence** In 1996, during his reelection campaign, Clinton announced, "The era of big government is over." Cite evidence supporting or refuting this statement.

14. **Synthesize Information** What foreign policy did the United States adopt in the post Cold War world?

15. **Determine Relevance** How helpful was the Declaration of Principles at resolving problems in the Middle East?

16. **Analyze Visuals** Study the visual below. What event are these newspaper headlines describing?

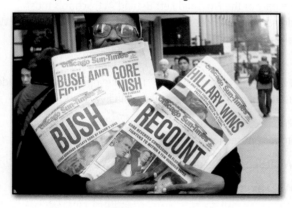

17. **Analyze Information** Did Operation Iraqi Freedom succeed at improving the lives of the Iraqi people?

18. **Explain Causes** Why was affirmative action first introduced in the United States?

## Writing About History

**Writing for Assessment** As Americans head into the new millennium, many of the major issues that have been part of American history for over two centuries remain relevant. Write an essay that traces an important American issue over time. Explain why it became an American issue and how its relevance has changed or remained the same over time.

### Prewriting

• Go online to www.PHSchool.com and enter **Web Code:** neh-2061 to find a list of American issues.

• Eliminate issues about which you are unsure. Choose the one for which you have the most background information or ideas.

• Identify the focus of your essay by forming a main idea.

### Drafting

• Sketch out an organizational plan for your essay. Consider using an outline or other graphic organizer to help you.

• Provide details that define, explain, support, or illustrate your points.

• Strengthen your introduction by including an interest-grabbing sentence.

### Revising

• Use the guidelines on page SH11 of the Writing Handbook to revise your report.

# Prepare for the MME

 9.1.1, 9.2.2

## Media Influence on Political Issues

News coverage of the war in Iraq became news in itself. While editorial writers strongly supported or opposed American policy, other journalists questioned the way the war was being reported. Was the media too critical—or not critical enough? Use your knowledge of media coverage of the war in Iraq and Documents A, B, C, and D to answer questions 1 through 4.

### Document A

"Mr. Bush's 'Plan for Victory' speech was, of course, the usual unadulterated nonsense. Its overarching theme—'We will never accept anything less than complete victory'—was being contradicted even as he spoke by rampant reports of Pentagon plans for stepped-up troop withdrawals between next week's Iraqi Elections and the more important (for endangered Republicans) American Election Day of 2006. The specifics were phony, too. Once again inflating the readiness of Iraqi troops, Mr. Bush claimed that the recent assault on Tal Afar 'was primarily led by Iraqi security forces'—a fairy tale immediately unmasked by Michael Ware, a Time reporter embedded in the battle's front lines, as 'completely wrong.'"

—*Frank Rich,* The New York Times, *December 11, 2005*

### Document B

Over the past few years, the Iraq war has morphed from a war of liberation against Saddam into a civil conflict between Sunnis and Shiites. . . . But the best news out of Iraq last week was that the Sunnis voted joyfully and in large numbers. In what they said and the way they acted, both the Sunnis and Shiites made it clear that while they are engaged in a fierce rivalry, they fervently believe in a democratic and unified Iraq. This is not yet a to-the-death struggle. . . . That's why it's necessary to have a third party—in Iraq, the United States—to cajole the two sides toward the settlement, to enforce the agreement afterward, to nurture a functioning social contract after that, and to prevent

hostile outside powers from spoiling the deal. That's why, again, it is essential that the U.S. remain in Iraq long enough to deescalate the conflict.

—*David Brooks,* The New York Times, *December 18, 2005*

### Document C

### Document D

Fairness and Accuracy in Reporting did a study. In the week leading up to General Colin Powell going to the Security Council to make his case for the invasions and the week afterwards—this was the period where more than half of the people in this country were opposed to an invasion—they did a study of CBS *Evening News,* NBC *Nightly News, ABC World News Tonight,* and the *NewsHour with Jim Lehrer* on PBS. The four major newscasts. Two weeks. Three hundred and ninety-three interviews on war. Three were anti-war voices. Three of almost four hundred, and that included PBS. . . . [T]hey have to provide the diversity of opinion that fully expresses the debate and the anguish and the discussions that are going on all over this country. That is media serving a democratic society.

—*Amy Goodman, "Independent Media in a Time of War," April 21, 2003*

---

1. Which of the documents is critical of the government's positive assessment of the war in Iraq?
   A Document A     C Document C
   B Document B     D Document D

2. According to Amy Goodman, which of the following statements is the most accurate assessment of media coverage of the invasion of Iraq?
   A All the major newscasts tried to present both points of view about the invasion.
   B The media coverage resulted in a national debate about the invasion.
   C Media coverage favored opponents of the war.
   D Media coverage did not reflect the diversity of opinion about the war.

3. What is the main point of the cartoon in Document C?
   A People generally do not trust the mainstream media.
   B Although people claim to distrust the media, they still rely on it for information.
   C The mainstream media is biased.
   D The mainstream media is unbiased.

4. **Writing Task** Think about the political perspectives on the war in Iraq expressed in the media. Do you think the media has played an influential role in shaping American foreign policy in Iraq? Use your knowledge of media coverage of the war, key events in the war, and specific evidence from the primary sources above to support your opinion.

# MI Connect to Michigan

## Michigan's Living History

Americans often depend on the past to guide them through current and future challenges. In Michigan, learning from the past can be as easy as spotting one of the approximately 1,500 historic markers sites around the state.

Michigan started its Historical Marker Program in 1955. The State Historic Preservation Office (SHPO), part of the Michigan Department of History, Arts, and Libraries, continues to run the program today. The markers commemorate people, places, and events that are important in Michigan history. For example, the SHPO has marked places such as the reputed site of Jacques Marquette's death, in Frankfort, as well as the state capitol in Lansing. Each marker offers a glimpse into the events that have unfolded in the towns and cities of the state.

> "HOME OF THE MODEL T Here at his Highland Park Plant, Henry Ford in 1913 began the mass production of automobiles on a moving assembly line. By 1915, Ford built a million Model Ts. In 1925 over nine thousand were assembled in a single day. Mass production soon moved from here to all phases of American industry and set the pattern of abundance for twentieth century living."
>
> —marker commemorating the Ford plant in Highland Park, Wayne County, Michigan.

In recent years, the SHPO has encouraged the people of Michigan to nominate more locations in their state that have either statewide or national significance.

There are other ways that residents and visitors to Michigan can become more familiar with important places, people, and events in the state's past. For example, they can investigate the 35 National Historic Landmarks found throughout the state. The National Park Service designates and maintains these landmarks. Notable national landmarks in Michigan include the French Fort Michilimackinac and Ernest Hemingway's cottage. The Historical Society of Michigan, founded in 1828, also runs programs to highlight the state's history.

As you have read, the United States has a rich, diverse history. You can continue to explore the ways that history shapes the world around us through the state Historical Marker Program and other preservation programs operating throughout Michigan.

# Reference Section

# Five Themes of Geography

The five themes of geography are tools you can use to analyze geographic information given in photographs, charts, maps, and text. Use these themes to determine the role of geography in U.S. history.

**Location** answers the question, Where is it? The answer might be an absolute location, such as 167 River Lane, or a relative location, such as six miles west of Mill City.

**Place** identifies natural and human features that make one place different from another. Landforms and buildings are features that can be used to identify a specific place.

**Movement** answers the question, How do people, goods, and ideas move from place to place?

**Regions** are areas that share at least one common feature. Climate, culture, and government are features that can be used to define regions.

**Human-Environment Interaction** explores the relationship between people and the natural world. Humans often modify their environment, and the environment affects how they live.

## Profile of the Fifty States

| State | Capital | Entered Union | Population (2005) | Population Rank | Land Area (Sq. Mi.) | Electoral Votes |
|-------|---------|---------------|-------------------|-----------------|---------------------|-----------------|
| Alabama | Montgomery | 1819 | 4,557,808 | 23 | 50,744 | 9 |
| Alaska | Juneau | 1959 | 663,661 | 47 | 571,951 | 3 |
| Arizona | Phoenix | 1912 | 5,939,292 | 17 | 113,635 | 10 |
| Arkansas | Little Rock | 1836 | 2,779,154 | 32 | 52,068 | 6 |
| California | Sacramento | 1850 | 36,132,147 | 1 | 155,959 | 55 |
| Colorado | Denver | 1876 | 4,665,177 | 22 | 103,718 | 9 |
| Connecticut | Hartford | 1788 | 3,510,297 | 29 | 4,845 | 7 |
| Delaware | Dover | 1787 | 843,524 | 45 | 1,954 | 3 |
| District of Columbia | —— | —— | 550,521 | —— | —— | 3 |
| Florida | Tallahassee | 1845 | 17,789,864 | 4 | 53,927 | 27 |
| Georgia | Atlanta | 1788 | 9,072,576 | 9 | 57,906 | 15 |
| Hawaii | Honolulu | 1959 | 1,275,194 | 42 | 6,423 | 4 |
| Idaho | Boise | 1890 | 1,429,096 | 39 | 82,747 | 4 |
| Illinois | Springfield | 1818 | 12,763,371 | 5 | 55,584 | 21 |
| Indiana | Indianapolis | 1816 | 6,271,973 | 15 | 35,867 | 11 |
| Iowa | Des Moines | 1846 | 2,966,334 | 30 | 55,869 | 7 |
| Kansas | Topeka | 1861 | 2,744,687 | 33 | 81,815 | 6 |
| Kentucky | Frankfort | 1792 | 4,173,405 | 26 | 39,728 | 8 |
| Louisiana | Baton Rouge | 1812 | 4,523,628 | 24 | 43,562 | 9 |
| Maine | Augusta | 1820 | 1,321,505 | 40 | 30,862 | 4 |
| Maryland | Annapolis | 1788 | 5,600,388 | 19 | 9,774 | 10 |
| Massachusetts | Boston | 1788 | 6,398,743 | 13 | 7,840 | 12 |
| Michigan | Lansing | 1837 | 10,120,860 | 8 | 56,804 | 17 |
| Minnesota | St. Paul | 1858 | 5,132,799 | 21 | 79,610 | 10 |
| Mississippi | Jackson | 1817 | 2,921,088 | 31 | 46,907 | 6 |
| Missouri | Jefferson City | 1821 | 5,800,310 | 18 | 68,886 | 11 |
| Montana | Helena | 1889 | 935,670 | 44 | 145,552 | 3 |
| Nebraska | Lincoln | 1867 | 1,758,787 | 38 | 76,872 | 5 |
| Nevada | Carson City | 1864 | 2,414,807 | 35 | 109,826 | 5 |
| New Hampshire | Concord | 1788 | 1,309,940 | 41 | 8,968 | 4 |
| New Jersey | Trenton | 1787 | 8,717,925 | 10 | 7,417 | 15 |
| New Mexico | Santa Fe | 1912 | 1,928,384 | 36 | 121,356 | 5 |
| New York | Albany | 1788 | 19,254,630 | 3 | 47,214 | 31 |
| North Carolina | Raleigh | 1789 | 8,683,242 | 11 | 48,711 | 15 |
| North Dakota | Bismarck | 1889 | 636,677 | 48 | 68,976 | 3 |
| Ohio | Columbus | 1803 | 11,464,042 | 7 | 40,948 | 20 |
| Oklahoma | Oklahoma City | 1907 | 3,547,884 | 28 | 68,667 | 7 |
| Oregon | Salem | 1859 | 3,641,056 | 27 | 95,997 | 7 |
| Pennsylvania | Harrisburg | 1787 | 12,429,616 | 6 | 44,817 | 21 |
| Rhode Island | Providence | 1790 | 1,076,189 | 43 | 1,045 | 4 |
| South Carolina | Columbia | 1788 | 4,255,083 | 25 | 30,110 | 8 |
| South Dakota | Pierre | 1889 | 775,933 | 46 | 75,885 | 3 |
| Tennessee | Nashville | 1796 | 5,962,959 | 16 | 41,217 | 11 |
| Texas | Austin | 1845 | 22,859,968 | 2 | 261,797 | 34 |
| Utah | Salt Lake City | 1896 | 2,469,585 | 34 | 82,144 | 5 |
| Vermont | Montpelier | 1791 | 623,050 | 49 | 9,250 | 3 |
| Virginia | Richmond | 1788 | 7,567,465 | 12 | 39,594 | 13 |
| Washington | Olympia | 1889 | 6,287,759 | 14 | 66,544 | 11 |
| West Virginia | Charleston | 1863 | 1,816,856 | 37 | 24,078 | 5 |
| Wisconsin | Madison | 1848 | 5,536,201 | 20 | 54,310 | 10 |
| Wyoming | Cheyenne | 1890 | 509,294 | 50 | 97,100 | 3 |

SOURCES: U.S. Census Bureau, U.S. National Archives, *World Almanac*

Atlas

## The World: Political

40°W  20°W  0°  20°E  40°E  60°E  80°E  100°E  120°E  140°E  160°E

**Greenland (Denmark)**

*Arctic Ocean*

Arctic Circle

**ICELAND**

*see inset below*

**EUROPE**

**RUSSIA**

**ASIA**

**KAZAKHSTAN**

**MONGOLIA**

**GEORGIA**
**AZER.**
**ARMENIA**
**UZBEK.**
**TURKMEN.**
**KYRGYZSTAN**
**TAJIKISTAN**

⊗ Tehran

**NORTH KOREA**

Beijing ⊗

Seoul ⊗

**SOUTH KOREA**

**JAPAN**
⊗ Tokyo

**CHINA**

**ISRAEL**
**IRAQ**
**IRAN**
**AFGHAN.**

**JORDAN**
**KUWAIT**
**BAHRAIN**
**QATAR**
**PAKISTAN**
**NEPAL**
**BHUTAN**

*Pacific Ocean*

Cairo
**EGYPT**

Karachi
**U.A.E.**

New Delhi ⊗

Shanghai

**MOROCCO**
**ALGERIA**
**LIBYA**

**SAUDI ARABIA**
**OMAN**

**INDIA**
**BANGLADESH**

**MYANMAR (BURMA)**

**LAOS**

**TAIWAN (Claimed by China)**

Hong Kong

**CAPE VERDE**

**AFRICA**
**CHAD**
**SUDAN**
**ERITREA**
**YEMEN**

Mumbai

**THAILAND**
Bangkok ⊗
**VIETNAM**
**CAMBODIA**

**SRI LANKA**

Addis Ababa ⊗
**DJIBOUTI**
**ETHIOPIA**
**SOMALIA**

**MALDIVES**

**PHILIPPINES**

**BRUNEI**
**MALAYSIA**

**MARSHALL ISLANDS**

**KIRIBATI**

**CEN. AFR. REP.**
**CAMEROON**

*see inset below*

**SÃO TOMÉ AND PRÍNCIPE**
**GABON**
**CONGO**
**DEM. REP. OF THE CONGO**
**UGANDA**
**KENYA**
**RWANDA**
**BURUNDI**

**SINGAPORE**

**INDONESIA**

**FEDERATED STATES OF MICRONESIA**

**NAURU**
**SOLOMON ISLANDS**
**TUVALU**

Jakarta
**TIMOR LESTE**

**PAPUA NEW GUINEA**

*Atlantic Ocean*

**TANZANIA**
**MALAWI**
**ANGOLA**
**ZAMBIA**
**MOZAMBIQUE**

**SEYCHELLES**
**COMOROS**

*Indian Ocean*

**OCEANIA**
**VANUATU**
**FIJI ISLANDS**

**ZIMBABWE**
**BOTSWANA**
**NAMIBIA**
**MADAGASCAR**

**MAURITIUS**

**AUSTRALIA**

Sydney

**New Caledonia (France)**

**SWAZILAND**
**SOUTH AFRICA**
**LESOTHO**

Cape Town ⊗

**NEW ZEALAND**

*Robinson Projection*
0   1,000   2,000 mi
0   1,000   2,000 km

40°E  60°E  80°E  100°E  120°E  140°E  160°E

*Southern Ocean*

*Barents Sea*

20°W  0°  20°E

**ANTARCTICA**

**Western Sahara (Morocco)**

**ALGERIA**

**MAURITANIA**

**MALI**

**NIGER**

**SENEGAL**
**GAMBIA**
**GUINEA-BISSAU**
**GUINEA**

**BURKINA FASO**

**BENIN**
**TOGO**

**SIERRA LEONE**
**CÔTE D'IVOIRE**
**GHANA**

**NIGERIA**

*Atlantic Ocean*

**LIBERIA**

Lagos

*Azimuthal Equidistant Projection*
0   200   400 mi
0   200   400 km

*Gulf of Guinea*

**EQUATORIAL GUINEA**

**SWEDEN**
**FINLAND**

**NORWAY**

*Conic Projection*
0   200   400 mi
0   200   400 km

**ESTONIA**
**LATVIA**

⊗ Moscow

**IRELAND**
**UNITED KINGDOM**
**DENMARK**

*North Sea*

**LITHUANIA**
**RUSSIA**

**RUSSIA**

London ⊗

**NETHERLANDS**

**BELARUS**

⊗ Berlin

**GERMANY**
**POLAND**

⊗ Kiev

*Atlantic Ocean*

**BELGIUM**
**LUX.**

**UKRAINE**

Paris ⊗

**CZECH REP.**
**SLOVAKIA**

*Bay of Biscay*

**FRANCE**
**LIECH.**
**SWITZ.**
**AUSTRIA**
**HUNGARY**

**MOLDOVA**

**SLOVENIA**
**ROMANIA**

*Black Sea*

**PORTUGAL**

**ANDORRA**
**MONACO**
**ITALY**

**CROATIA**
**BOS. AND HERZ.**
**SERBIA**
**MONT.**
**BULGARIA**

Istanbul

Madrid ⊗

**SPAIN**

**SAN MARINO**
**VATICAN CITY**

Rome ⊗

**ALBANIA**
**MAC.**

**Corsica (France)**

**Sardinia (Italy)**

**GREECE**

**TURKEY**

**Gibraltar (U.K.)**
**Ceuta (Spain)**
**Melilla (Spain)**

**Balearic Islands (Spain)**

**Sicily (Italy)**

**MALTA**

*Mediterranean Sea*

**CYPRUS**
**SYRIA**

**MOROCCO**
**ALGERIA**
**TUNISIA**

**Crete (Greece)**
**LEBANON**

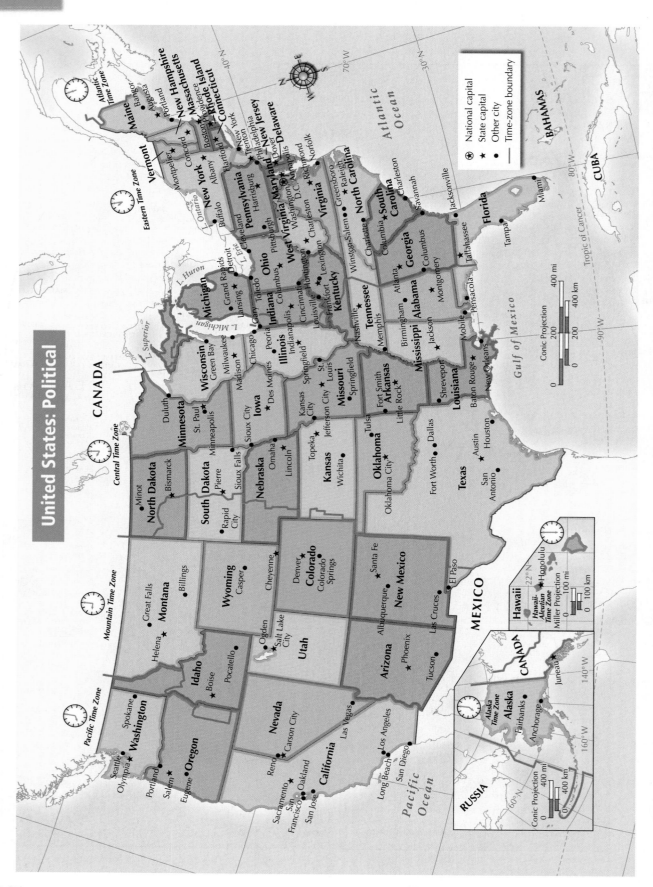

# United States: Political

**CANADA**

**MEXICO**

Atlantic Ocean

Pacific Ocean

Gulf of Mexico

**CUBA**

**BAHAMAS**

**RUSSIA**

Atlantic Time Zone

Eastern Time Zone

Central Time Zone

Mountain Time Zone

Pacific Time Zone

| Legend | |
| --- | --- |
| ⊛ | National capital |
| ★ | State capital |
| • | Other city |
| — | Time-zone boundary |

Conic Projection

400 mi

400 km

0   200   400

**Maine** — Bangor, Augusta, Portland
**New Hampshire**
**Vermont** — Montpelier, Concord
**Massachusetts** — Boston
**Rhode Island** — Providence
**Connecticut** — Hartford
**New York** — Buffalo, Albany, New York
**New Jersey** — Trenton
**Pennsylvania** — Harrisburg, Philadelphia, Pittsburgh
**Delaware** — Dover
**Maryland** — Annapolis, Washington, D.C.
**West Virginia** — Charleston
**Virginia** — Richmond, Norfolk
**North Carolina** — Greensboro, Raleigh, Charlotte, Winston-Salem
**South Carolina** — Columbia, Charleston
**Georgia** — Atlanta, Savannah, Columbus
**Florida** — Jacksonville, Tampa, Miami, Tallahassee, Pensacola
**Ohio** — Cleveland, Columbus, Cincinnati, Toledo
**Michigan** — Detroit, Grand Rapids, Lansing
**Indiana** — Gary, Indianapolis
**Illinois** — Chicago, Peoria, Springfield
**Kentucky** — Frankfort, Louisville, Lexington, Huntington
**Tennessee** — Nashville, Memphis
**Alabama** — Birmingham, Montgomery, Mobile
**Mississippi** — Jackson
**Louisiana** — Baton Rouge, New Orleans, Shreveport
**Arkansas** — Little Rock, Fort Smith
**Missouri** — Jefferson City, St. Louis, Springfield, Kansas City
**Iowa** — Des Moines, Sioux City
**Wisconsin** — Green Bay, Milwaukee, Madison
**Minnesota** — Duluth, St. Paul, Minneapolis
**North Dakota** — Minot, Bismarck
**South Dakota** — Pierre, Rapid City, Sioux Falls
**Nebraska** — Omaha, Lincoln
**Kansas** — Topeka, Wichita
**Oklahoma** — Oklahoma City, Tulsa
**Texas** — Dallas, Fort Worth, Austin, Houston, San Antonio, El Paso
**New Mexico** — Santa Fe, Albuquerque, Las Cruces
**Colorado** — Denver, Colorado Springs
**Wyoming** — Cheyenne, Casper
**Montana** — Great Falls, Billings, Helena
**Idaho** — Boise, Pocatello
**Utah** — Salt Lake City, Ogden
**Arizona** — Phoenix, Tucson
**Nevada** — Carson City, Reno, Las Vegas
**California** — Sacramento, San Francisco, San Jose, Oakland, Los Angeles, Long Beach, San Diego, Eugene
**Oregon** — Salem, Portland
**Washington** — Olympia, Seattle, Spokane

L. Ontario, L. Erie, L. Huron, L. Superior, L. Michigan

40°N, 70°W, 30°W, 80°W, 90°W, Tropic of Cancer

**Hawaii**
Hawaii-Aleutian Time Zone
Miller Projection
Honolulu
22°N
100 mi
100 km
0   100

**Alaska**
Alaska Time Zone
Conic Projection
Juneau, Fairbanks, Anchorage
**CANADA**
140°W, 160°W, 60°N
400 mi
400 km
0   400

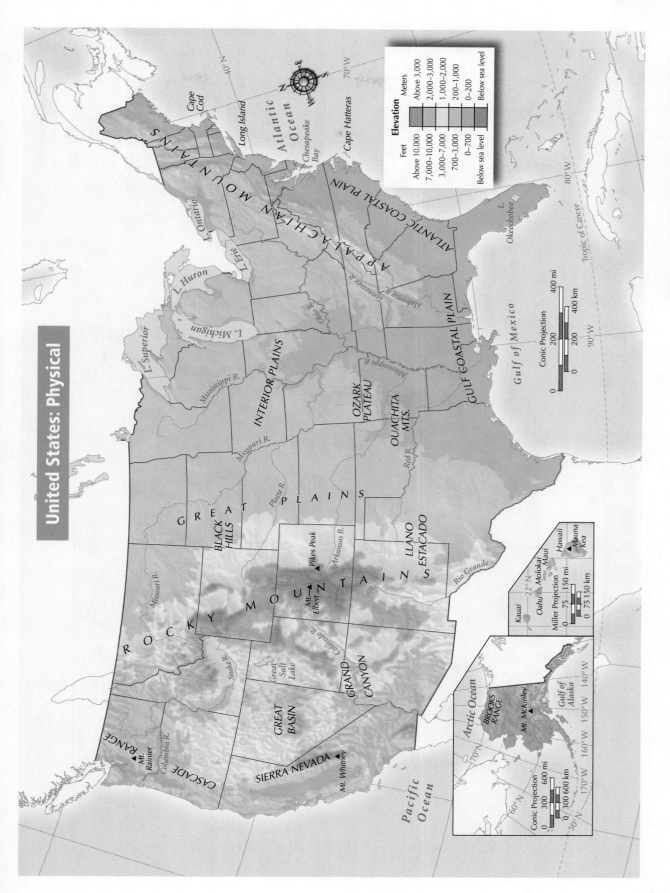

# United States: Physical

**Elevation**

| Feet | Meters |
|---|---|
| Above 10,000 | Above 3,000 |
| 7,000–10,000 | 2,000–3,000 |
| 3,000–7,000 | 1,000–2,000 |
| 700–3,000 | 200–1,000 |
| 0–700 | 0–200 |
| Below sea level | Below sea level |

Cape Cod
Long Island
Atlantic Ocean
Chesapeake Bay
Cape Hatteras
APPALACHIAN MOUNTAINS
ATLANTIC COASTAL PLAIN
L. Ontario
L. Erie
L. Huron
L. Michigan
L. Superior
Tennessee R.
Ohio R.
Alabama R.
GULF COASTAL PLAIN
L. Okeechobee
Tropic of Cancer
Gulf of Mexico
Conic Projection
400 mi
400 km
200
200
0
0
Mississippi R.
INTERIOR PLAINS
OZARK PLATEAU
Mississippi R.
OUACHITA MTS.
Missouri R.
Red R.
GREAT PLAINS
BLACK HILLS
Platte R.
Pikes Peak
Arkansas R.
LLANO ESTACADO
Rio Grande
ROCKY MOUNTAINS
Mt. Elbert
Missouri R.
Colorado R.
GRAND CANYON
Snake R.
Great Salt Lake
GREAT BASIN
CASCADE RANGE
Mt. Rainier
Columbia R.
SIERRA NEVADA
Mt. Whitney
Pacific Ocean

Hawaii
Mauna Kea
Kauai
22° N
Oahu Molokai Maui
Miller Projection
150 mi
75
0 75 150 km

Arctic Ocean
BROOKS RANGE
Mt. McKinley
Gulf of Alaska
70° N
60° N
50° N
170° W 160° W 150° W 140° W
Conic Projection
600 mi
300
0 300 600 km

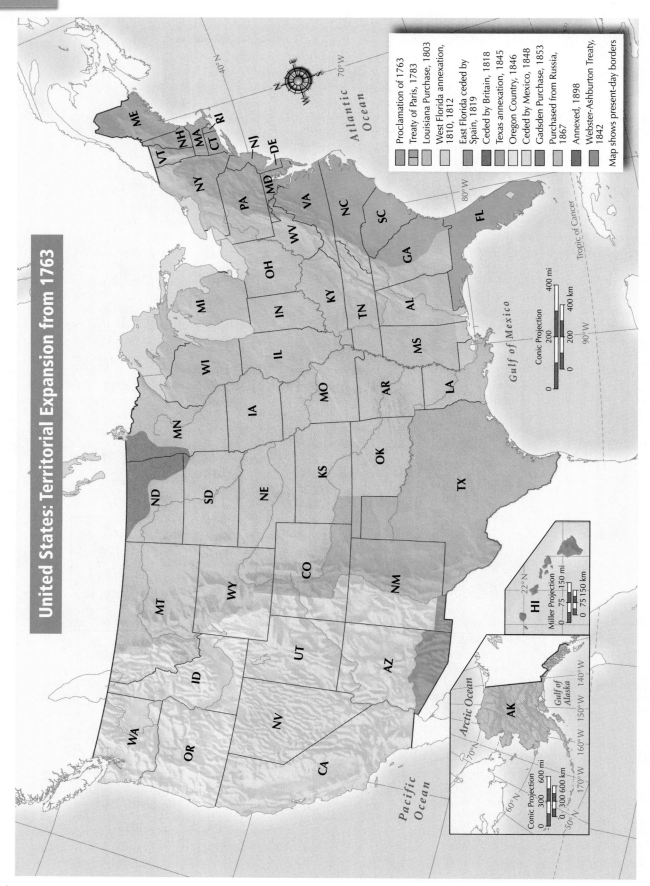

United States: Territorial Expansion from 1763

Proclamation of 1763
Treaty of Paris, 1783
Louisiana Purchase, 1803
West Florida annexation, 1810, 1812
East Florida ceded by Spain, 1819
Ceded by Britain, 1818
Texas annexation, 1845
Oregon Country, 1846
Ceded by Mexico, 1848
Gadsden Purchase, 1853
Purchased from Russia, 1867
Annexed, 1898
Webster-Ashburton Treaty, 1842
Map shows present-day borders

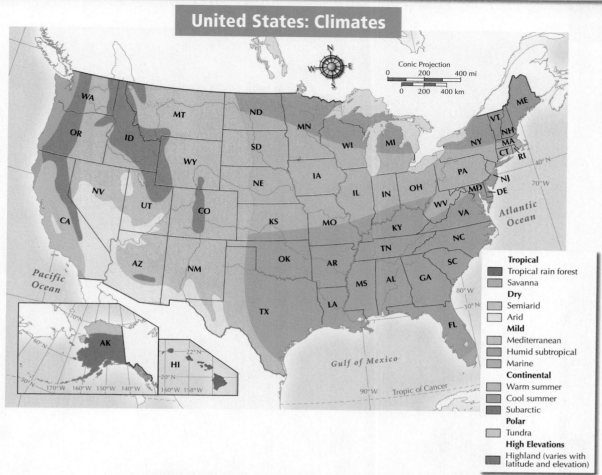

# United States: Climates

**Tropical**
- Tropical rain forest
- Savanna

**Dry**
- Semiarid
- Arid

**Mild**
- Mediterranean
- Humid subtropical
- Marine

**Continental**
- Warm summer
- Cool summer
- Subarctic

**Polar**
- Tundra

**High Elevations**
- Highland (varies with latitude and elevation)

Conic Projection
0   200   400 mi
0   200   400 km

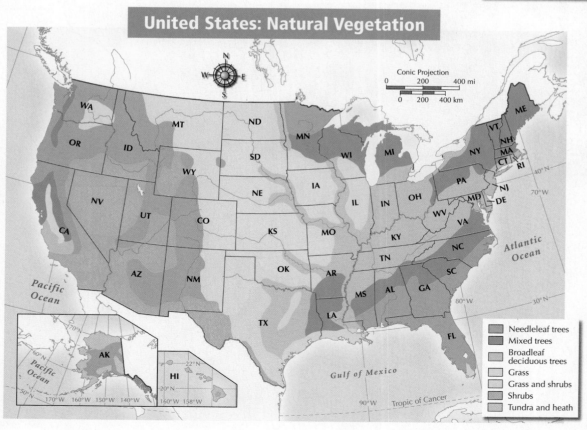

# United States: Natural Vegetation

- Needleleaf trees
- Mixed trees
- Broadleaf deciduous trees
- Grass
- Grass and shrubs
- Shrubs
- Tundra and heath

Conic Projection
0   200   400 mi
0   200   400 km

## United States: Land Use and Land Cover

Farming
Grazing
Forestry
Park, military use
Urban
Desert
Wetland

Atlantic Ocean

Gulf of Mexico

Pacific Ocean

ME
VT
NH
MA
CT
RI
NY
NJ
DE
PA
MD
VA
NC
SC
WV
OH
IN
KY
TN
GA
AL
MS
FL
MI
IL
WI
MN
IA
MO
AR
LA
OK
TX
KS
NE
SD
ND
CO
NM
WY
MT
UT
AZ
NV
ID
CA
OR
WA

Boston
New York
Philadelphia
Washington, D.C.
Pittsburgh
Cincinnati
Detroit
Chicago
Atlanta
New Orleans
Miami
Houston
Dallas
Denver
Minneapolis
Phoenix
Los Angeles
San Francisco
Seattle

L. Ontario
L. Erie
L. Huron
L. Michigan
L. Superior

Tropic of Cancer

Conic Projection
400 mi
400 km
200
200
0
0

HI
Miller Projection
150 mi
150 km
75
75
0
0
22° N

AK
Conic Projection
600 mi
600 km
300
300
0
0
70° N
60° N
50° N
170° W
160° W
150° W
140° W

40° N
30° N
70° W
80° W
90° W

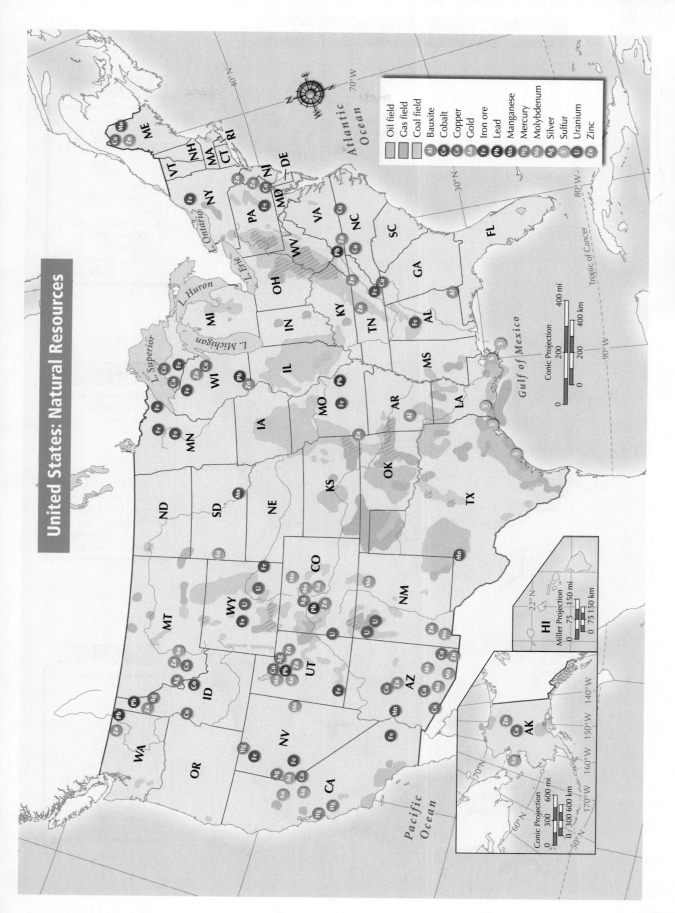

# United States: Natural Resources

## Legend

| | |
|---|---|
| Oil field | |
| Gas field | |
| Coal field | |

| | |
|---|---|
| Al | Bauxite |
| Co | Cobalt |
| Cu | Copper |
| Au | Gold |
| Fe | Iron ore |
| Pb | Lead |
| Mn | Manganese |
| Hg | Mercury |
| Mo | Molybdenum |
| Ag | Silver |
| S | Sulfur |
| U | Uranium |
| Zn | Zinc |

Atlantic Ocean

Gulf of Mexico

Pacific Ocean

Conic Projection

Miller Projection

# United States: Population Density

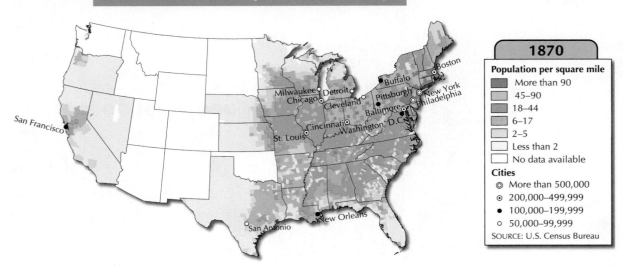

## 1870

**Population per square mile**
- More than 90
- 45–90
- 18–44
- 6–17
- 2–5
- Less than 2
- No data available

**Cities**
- ◎ More than 500,000
- ⊙ 200,000–499,999
- ● 100,000–199,999
- ○ 50,000–99,999

SOURCE: U.S. Census Bureau

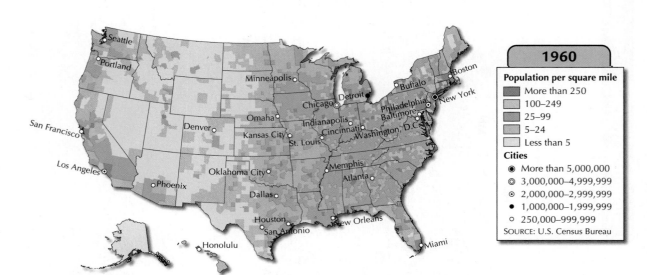

## 1960

**Population per square mile**
- More than 250
- 100–249
- 25–99
- 5–24
- Less than 5

**Cities**
- ◉ More than 5,000,000
- ◎ 3,000,000–4,999,999
- ⊙ 2,000,000–2,999,999
- ● 1,000,000–1,999,999
- ○ 250,000–999,999

SOURCE: U.S. Census Bureau

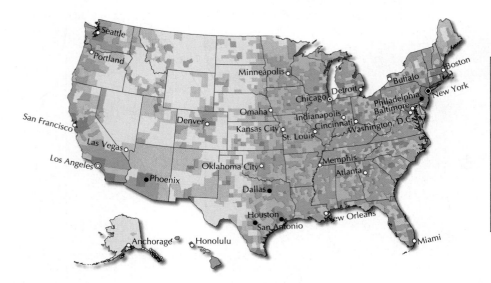

## 2000

**Population per square mile**
- More than 250
- 100–249
- 25–99
- 5–24
- Less than 5

**Cities**
- ◉ More than 5,000,000
- ◎ 3,000,000–4,999,999
- ⊙ 2,000,000–2,999,999
- ● 1,000,000–1,999,999
- ○ 250,000–999,999

SOURCE: U.S. Census Bureau

# Presidents of the United States

**1**

**George Washington**
(1732–1799)

*Years in Office:* 1789–1797
**No political party**

*Elected from:* Virginia
*Vice President:* John Adams

**2**

**John Adams**
(1735–1826)

*Years in Office:* 1797–1801
**Federalist**

*Elected from:* Massachusetts
*Vice President:* Thomas Jefferson

**3**

**Thomas Jefferson**
(1743–1826)

*Years in Office:* 1801–1809
**Democratic Republican**

*Elected from:* Virginia
*Vice Presidents:* Aaron Burr, George Clinton

**4**
**James Madison**
(1751–1836)

*Years in Office:* 1809–1817
**Democratic Republican**

*Elected from:* Virginia
*Vice Presidents:* George Clinton, Elbridge Gerry

**5**

**James Monroe**
(1758–1831)

*Years in Office:* 1817–1825
**National Republican**

*Elected from:* Virginia
*Vice President:* Daniel Tompkins

**6**

**John Quincy Adams**
(1767–1848)

*Years in Office:* 1825–1829
**National Republican**

*Elected from:* Massachusetts
*Vice President:* John Calhoun

**7**

**Andrew Jackson**
(1767–1845)

*Years in Office:* 1829–1837
**Democrat**

*Elected from:* Tennessee
*Vice Presidents:* John Calhoun, Martin Van Buren

**8**

**Martin Van Buren**
(1782–1862)

*Years in Office:* 1837–1841
**Democrat**

*Elected from:* New York
*Vice President:* Richard Johnson

**9**

**William Henry Harrison***
(1773–1841)

*Year in Office:* 1841
**Whig**

*Elected from:* Ohio
*Vice President:* John Tyler

**10**
**John Tyler**
(1790–1862)

*Years in Office:* 1841–1845
**Whig**

*Elected from:* Virginia
*Vice President:* none

**11**

**James K. Polk**
(1795–1849)

*Years in Office:* 1845–1849
**Democrat**

*Elected from:* Tennessee
*Vice President:* George Dallas

**12**

**Zachary Taylor***
(1784–1850)

*Years in Office:* 1849–1850
**Whig**

*Elected from:* Louisiana
*Vice President:* Millard Fillmore

**13**

**Millard Fillmore**
(1800–1874)

*Years in Office:* 1850–1853
**Whig**

*Elected from:* New York
*Vice President:* none

**14**

**Franklin Pierce**
(1804–1869)

*Years in Office:* 1853–1857
**Democrat**

*Elected from:* New Hampshire
*Vice President:* William King

**15**

**James Buchanan**
(1791–1868)

*Years in Office:* 1857–1861
**Democrat**

*Elected from:* Pennsylvania
*Vice President:* John Breckinridge

**16**

**Abraham Lincoln****
(1809–1865)

*Years in Office:* 1861–1865
**Republican**

*Elected from:* Illinois
*Vice Presidents:* Hannibal Hamlin, Andrew Johnson

**17**

**Andrew Johnson**
(1808–1875)

*Years in Office:* 1865–1869
**Democrat†**

*Elected from:* Tennessee
*Vice President:* none

**18**

**Ulysses S. Grant**
(1822–1885)

*Years in Office:* 1869–1877
**Republican**

*Elected from:* Illinois
*Vice Presidents:* Schuyler
Colfax, Henry Wilson

**19**

**Rutherford B. Hayes**
(1822–1893)

*Years in Office:* 1877–1881
**Republican**

*Elected from:* Ohio
*Vice President:* William Wheeler

**20**

**James A. Garfield\*\***
(1831–1881)

*Year in Office:* 1881
**Republican**

*Elected from:* Ohio
*Vice President:* Chester A.
Arthur

**21**

**Chester A. Arthur**
(1830–1886)

*Years in Office:* 1881–1885
**Republican**

*Elected from:* New York
*Vice President:* none

**22**

**Grover Cleveland**
(1837–1908)

*Years in Office:* 1885–1889
**Democrat**

*Elected from:* New York
*Vice President:* Thomas
Hendricks

**23**

**Benjamin Harrison**
(1833–1901)

*Years in Office:* 1889–1893
**Republican**

*Elected from:* Indiana
*Vice President:* Levi Morton

**24**

**Grover Cleveland**
(1837–1908)

*Years in Office:* 1893–1897
**Democrat**

*Elected from:* New York
*Vice President:* Adlai Stevenson

**25**

**William McKinley\*\***
(1843–1901)

*Years in Office:* 1897–1901
**Republican**

*Elected from:* Ohio
*Vice Presidents:* Garret Hobart,
Theodore Roosevelt

**26**

**Theodore Roosevelt**
(1858–1919)

*Years in Office:* 1901–1909
**Republican**

*Elected from:* New York
*Vice President:* Charles
Fairbanks

**27**

**William Howard Taft**
(1857–1930)

*Years in Office:* 1909–1913
**Republican**

*Elected from:* Ohio
*Vice President:* James Sherman

**28**

**Woodrow Wilson**
(1856–1924)

*Years in Office:* 1913–1921
**Democrat**

*Elected from:* New Jersey
*Vice President:* Thomas
Marshall

**29**

**Warren G. Harding\***
(1865–1923)

*Years in Office:* 1921–1923
**Republican**

*Elected from:* Ohio
*Vice President:* Calvin Coolidge

**30**

**Calvin Coolidge**
(1872–1933)

*Years in Office:* 1923–1929
**Republican**

*Elected from:* Massachusetts
*Vice President:* Charles Dawes

**31**

**Herbert C. Hoover**
(1874–1964)

*Years in Office:* 1929–1933
**Republican**

*Elected from:* New York
*Vice President:* Charles Curtis

**32**

**Franklin D. Roosevelt\***
(1882–1945)

*Years in Office:* 1933–1945
**Democrat**

*Elected from:* New York
*Vice Presidents:* John Garner,
Henry Wallace, Harry S. Truman

**33**

### Harry S. Truman
(1884–1972)

*Years in Office:* 1945–1953
**Democrat**

*Elected from:* Missouri
*Vice President:* Alben Barkley

**34**

### Dwight D. Eisenhower
(1890–1969)

*Years in Office:* 1953–1961
**Republican**

*Elected from:* New York
*Vice President:* Richard M. Nixon

**35**

### John F. Kennedy**
(1917–1963)

*Years in Office:* 1961–1963
**Democrat**

*Elected from:* Massachusetts
*Vice President:* Lyndon B. Johnson

**36**

### Lyndon B. Johnson
(1908–1973)

*Years in Office:* 1963–1969
**Democrat**

*Elected from:* Texas
*Vice President:* Hubert Humphrey

**37**

### Richard M. Nixon***
(1913–1994)

*Years in Office:* 1969–1974
**Republican**

*Elected from:* New York
*Vice Presidents:* Spiro Agnew, Gerald R. Ford

**38**

### Gerald R. Ford
(1913–2006)

*Years in Office:* 1974–1977
**Republican**

*Elected from:* Michigan
*Vice President:* Nelson Rockefeller

**39**

### James E. Carter
(1924–)

*Years in Office:* 1977–1981
**Democrat**

*Elected from:* Georgia
*Vice President:* Walter F. Mondale

**40**

### Ronald W. Reagan
(1911–2004)

*Years in Office:* 1981–1989
**Republican**

*Elected from:* California
*Vice President:* George H. W. Bush

**41**

### George H. W. Bush
(1924–)

*Years in Office:* 1989–1993
**Republican**

*Elected from:* Texas
*Vice President:* J. Danforth Quayle

**42**

### William J. Clinton
(1946–)

*Years in Office:* 1993–2001
**Democrat**

*Elected from:* Arkansas
*Vice President:* Albert Gore, Jr.

**43**

### George W. Bush
(1946–)

*Years in Office:* 2001–2009
**Republican**

*Elected from:* Texas
*Vice President:* Richard Cheney

**44**

### Barack H. Obama
(1961–)

*Years in Office:* 2009–
**Democrat**

*Elected from:* Illinois
*Vice President:* Joseph R. Biden

\* Died in office
\*\* Assassinated
\*\*\* Resigned
† Elected Vice President on the coalition Union Party ticket

# Key Economic Questions

In every society, people have access to resources such as water, soil, and human labor. Yet all resources are limited. Economics is the study of how people choose to use their limited resources to meet their wants and needs. Every society must answer three basic economic questions. How a society answers these questions depends on how much it values different economic goals.

## Economic Goals

| | |
|---|---|
| **Economic efficiency** | Making the most of resources |
| **Economic freedom** | Freedom from government intervention in the production and distribution of goods and services |
| **Economic security and predictability** | Assurance that goods and services will be available, payments will be made on time, and a safety net will protect individuals in times of economic disaster |
| **Economic equity** | Fair distribution of wealth |
| **Economic growth and innovation** | Innovation leads to economic growth, and economic growth leads to a higher standard of living. |
| **Other goals** | Societies pursue additional goals, such as environmental protection. |

## Three Key Economic Questions

| What goods and services should be produced? | How should goods and services be produced? | Who consumes the goods and services? |
|---|---|---|
| How much of our resources should we devote to national defense, education, public health, or consumer goods? Which consumer goods should we produce? | Should we produce food on large corporate farms or on small family farms? Should we produce electricity with oil, nuclear power, coal, or solar power? | How do goods and services get distributed? The question of who gets to consume which goods and services lies at the very heart of the differences between economic systems. Each society answers the question of distribution based on its combination of social values and goals. |

**Choices About How to Produce Goods**
This wind farm illustrates a society's decision to produce electricity using the power of the wind. What do you think are the benefits and drawbacks of wind power?

# Economic Systems

An economic system is the method used by a society to produce and distribute goods and services. A society's economic system reflects how that society answers the three key economic questions and what its economic goals are. Different systems produce different results in terms of productivity, the welfare of workers, and consumer choice.

## Modern Economic Systems

| | Description | Origin | Location Today |
|---|---|---|---|
| **Market** (Capitalist, Free-Enterprise) | Economic decisions are made in the marketplace through interactions between buyers and sellers according to the laws of supply and demand. Individual capitalists own the means of production. Government regulates some economic activities and provides such "public goods" as education. | Capitalism has existed since the earliest buying and selling of goods in a market. The market economic system developed in response to Adam Smith's ideas and the shift from agriculture to industry in the 1800s. | Canada, Germany, Japan, United States, and many other nations |
| **Centrally Planned** (Command, Socialist, Communist) | Central government planners make most economic decisions for the people. In theory, the workers own the means of production. In practice, the government does. Some private enterprise, but government dominates. | In the 1800s, criticism of capitalism by Karl Marx and others led to calls for distributing wealth according to need. After the 1917 Russian Revolution, the Soviet Union developed the first command economy. | Communist countries, including China, Cuba, and North Korea |
| **Mixed** (Social Democratic, Liberal Socialist) | A mix of socialism and free enterprise in which the government plays a significant role in making economic decisions. | The Great Depression of the 1930s ended laissez-faire capitalism in most countries. People insisted that government take a stronger role in fixing economic problems. The fall of communism in Eastern Europe in the 1990s ended central planning in most countries. People insisted on freer markets. | Most nations, including Brazil, France, India, Italy, Poland, Russia, Sweden, and the United Kingdom |

**Buyers and Sellers in a Free Market**
In a market economy, buyers and sellers make decisions on the basis of their own self-interest. They may freely buy and sell goods. In a voluntary exchange, both parties expect to gain from the transaction.

# The American Economy

For centuries, people have considered the United States to be a land of opportunity where anyone from any background could achieve success through hard work. Why has the United States been such an economic success? Certainly the open land, natural resources, and uninterrupted flow of immigrant labor have all contributed. But a key factor has also been the tradition of free enterprise—the social and political commitment to giving people the freedom to compete in the marketplace.

## Constitutional Protections of Free Enterprise

**Property Rights**
Property rights are protected by the Fifth Amendment: "No person shall be deprived of life, liberty, or property, without due process; nor shall private property be taken for public use, without just compensation." The Fourteenth Amendment places the same limitation on state governments.

**Taxation**
Congress can only tax individuals and businesses in the ways the Constitution allows. Article 1 gives Congress the power to levy taxes, but Sections 2 and 9 require that direct taxes be apportioned according to population. The Sixteenth Amendment gave Congress the right to set taxes based on income.

**Binding Contracts**
Article 1, Section 10, guarantees people and businesses the right to make binding contracts.

▲ Free enterprise in the United States is founded on ideas so basic to our culture that we tend to take them for granted.

## Flow of Goods, Services, and Money in a Market Economy

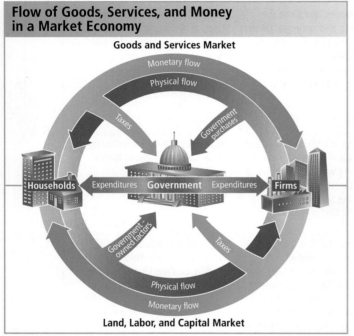

▲ This circular flow model shows how government typically interacts with households and businesses in the marketplace.

## United States Workforce, by Occupation, 2005*

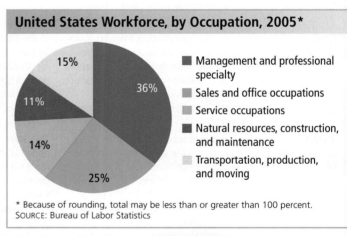

- 36% Management and professional specialty
- 25% Sales and office occupations
- 14% Service occupations
- 11% Natural resources, construction, and maintenance
- 15% Transportation, production, and moving

\* Because of rounding, total may be less than or greater than 100 percent.
SOURCE: Bureau of Labor Statistics

▲ How do you think this snapshot of the United States labor force would have looked in 1800? In 1900?

## Key Events in American Economic History

**1791**
First Bank of the United States chartered

**1834**
Mill girls in Lowell, Massachusetts, protest wage cuts

**1867**
Knights of Labor formed

**1886**
American Federation of Labor formed

**1780**

**1820**

**1860**

**1835**
Strike for 10-hour workday in Philadelphia

**1869**
Financial panic sweeps nation

**1892**
Homestead Strike in Pennsylvania

# Measuring the Economy's Performance

A modern industrial economy repeatedly experiences cycles of economic growth and decline. Business cycles are of major interest to macroeconomists, who study their causes and effects. Economists use many tools to predict changes in business cycles. The leading indicators are a set of key economic variables including stock prices, interest rates, and manufacturers' new orders for goods.

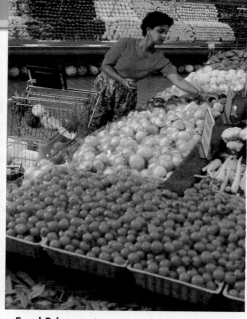

▲ **Food Prices** An increase in the price of food can signal inflation. What impact do rising food prices have on families?

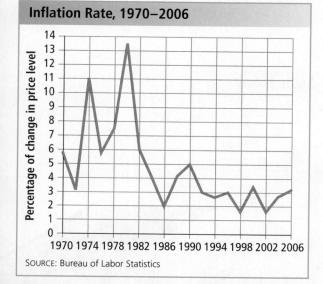

**Inflation Rate, 1970–2006**

SOURCE: Bureau of Labor Statistics

▲ One of the economic indicators economists look at is the economy's level of inflation. Inflation is a general increase in prices. As prices rise, the purchasing power of money declines.

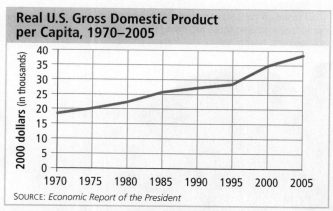

**Real U.S. Gross Domestic Product per Capita, 1970–2005**

SOURCE: *Economic Report of the President*

▲ Gross Domestic Product is the dollar value of all final goods and services produced within a country's borders in a given year. GDP per capita equals the GDP divided by the country's total population. Long-term increases in GDP allow an entire society to improve its standard of living.

**Economics Handbook**

**1913** Federal Reserve System created

**1929** Stock market crash

**1947** Taft-Hartley Act

**1955** AFL and CIO merge

**1980** Savings and Loan crisis begins

**2008** Mortgage crisis leads to increase in home foreclosures

**1900**

**1940**

**1980**

**2020**

**1930** Great Depression begins

**1933** Federal Deposit Insurance Corporation (FDIC) created

**1963** Equal Pay Act

**1997** More than 160,000 ATMs operate in United States

**2001** Office of Faith-Based and Community Initiatives established

# Analyzing Costs and Benefits

Economists point out that all individuals, businesses, and large groups of people make decisions that involve trade-offs. Trade-offs are all the alternatives that we give up whenever we choose one course of action over another. One alternative, though, is usually more desirable than all the others. The most desirable alternative given up as the result of a decision is called the opportunity cost. At times, a decision's opportunity cost may be unclear or complicated. Nonetheless, consumers, businesses, and governments must carefully consider trade-offs and opportunity costs before making a decision.

**Safety Versus Cost and Convenience** Tens of thousands of people are killed every year in auto accidents in the United States. Safety features like antilock brakes, air bags, and seatbelts may save lives, but they also make cars more expensive. Throughout history, government policymakers have had to weigh the costs and benefits of any policy proposal, including those regarding the regulation of business, health, safety, and foreign policy.

| Costs of Auto Safety | |
|---|---|
| **Saftey Feature** | **Cost** |
| Antilock brakes | $600.00 |
| Side-impact air bags | $350.00 |
| Traction control | $1,200.00 |

# The Federal Budget

The federal budget is a written document indicating the amount of money the government expects to receive during a certain year and authorizing the amount the government can spend that year. Government officials who take part in the budgeting process debate how much should be spent on specific programs such as defense, education, and scientific research.

## Federal Revenue, 2007

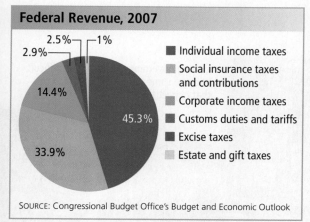

- 2.5%
- 1%
- 2.9%
- 14.4%
- 45.3%
- 33.9%

- ■ Individual income taxes
- ■ Social insurance taxes and contributions
- ■ Corporate income taxes
- ■ Customs duties and tariffs
- ■ Excise taxes
- ■ Estate and gift taxes

SOURCE: Congressional Budget Office's Budget and Economic Outlook

▲ This graph shows the sources of government revenue. What are the largest sources of federal income?

## National Debt as a Percentage of GDP

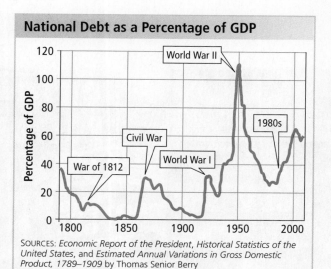

SOURCES: *Economic Report of the President, Historical Statistics of the United States,* and *Estimated Annual Variations in Gross Domestic Product, 1789–1909* by Thomas Senior Berry

▲ If the federal government's spending is greater than its income in any given year, then the budget is said to be in deficit. The government must then borrow money to pay the shortfall. The total of the government's borrowed money over time is added together to form the national debt.

## Government Spending, by Category, 2004

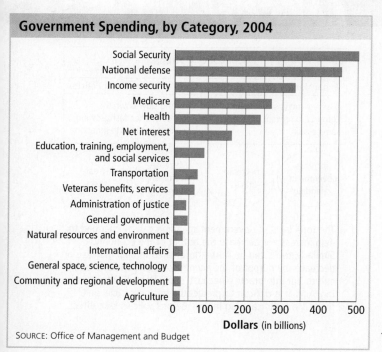

SOURCE: Office of Management and Budget

◄ This graph shows how the government spends its money. What are the largest areas of federal spending?

# Tools for Moderating the Business Cycle: Fiscal Policy

The federal government takes in money to pay for its spending through taxation and borrowing. The decisions the government makes about taxing and spending can have a powerful impact on the overall economy. Fiscal policy is the use of government spending and revenue collection to influence the economy. Fiscal policies are used to achieve economic growth, full employment, and price stability.

▼ Cutting government spending is difficult because some voters will object to cuts that impact their interests.

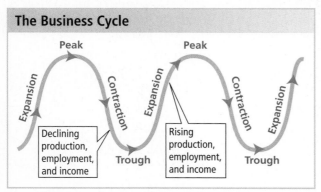

**The Business Cycle**

▲ In a business cycle, a period of rising real GDP reaches a peak, then falls into a contraction. When the contraction reaches the low point, or trough, a new expansion begins. From 1854 to 1991, the United States experienced 31 business cycles. Excluding wartimes, the cycles averaged 48 months.

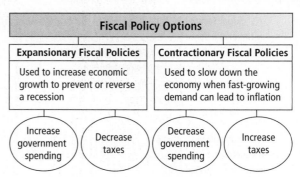

| Fiscal Policy Options | |
|---|---|
| **Expansionary Fiscal Policies** | **Contractionary Fiscal Policies** |
| Used to increase economic growth to prevent or reverse a recession | Used to slow down the economy when fast-growing demand can lead to inflation |
| Increase government spending / Decrease taxes | Decrease government spending / Increase taxes |

▲ The total level of government spending can be changed to help increase or decrease the output of the economy. Similarly, taxes can be raised or lowered to help increase or decrease the output of the economy. Fiscal policies are difficult to put into practice because many laws dictate spending. Also, it is difficult to predict the business cycle, and there is a significant lag in time before policies take effect.

# Tools for Moderating the Business Cycle: Monetary Policy

After the charter of the Second Bank of the United States expired, states chartered some banks while the federal government chartered others. Reserve requirements—the amount of money that banks are required to keep on hand—were difficult to enforce, and bank runs often led to panic. After the Panic of 1907, Congress responded with the Federal Reserve Act of 1913. This act created the Federal Reserve System—a group of twelve independent banks that could lend to other banks in times of need. Monetary policy refers to the actions the Federal Reserve Board takes to influence the level of real GDP and the rate of inflation in the economy.

**Money Creation**

$1,000 + $900 + $810 = $2,710

You deposit $1,000 into your checking account.

Your $1,000 deposit minus $100 in reserves is loaned to Elaine, who gives it to Joshua.

Joshua's $900 deposit minus $90 in reserves is loaned to another customer.

At this point, the money supply has increased by $2,710.

$100 held in reserve
$900 available for loans

$90 held in reserve
$810 available for loans

◀ The Federal Reserve is best known for its role in regulating the nation's money supply. Too much money in the economy leads to inflation. This diagram shows how money is created. By altering the amount of money banks are required to keep in reserve, the Fed can increase or shrink the money supply.

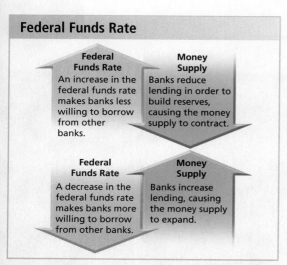

**Federal Funds Rate**

| Federal Funds Rate | Money Supply |
|---|---|
| An increase in the federal funds rate makes banks less willing to borrow from other banks. | Banks reduce lending in order to build reserves, causing the money supply to contract. |

| Federal Funds Rate | Money Supply |
|---|---|
| A decrease in the federal funds rate makes banks more willing to borrow from other banks. | Banks increase lending, causing the money supply to expand. |

▲ The federal funds rate is the interest rate that banks charge each other when they lend each other reserves. An increase in the federal funds rate makes borrowing more costly, and the monetary supply contracts. Banks are more willing to borrow and lend money when the federal funds rate is low.

**Open Market Operations**

| Bonds Circulating | Money Supply |
|---|---|
| Through bond **sales,** the Fed removes reserves from the banking system. | Banks reduce lending, causing the money supply to contract. |

| Bonds Circulating | Money Supply |
|---|---|
| The Fed's **purchase** of bonds increases reserves in the banking system. | Banks increase lending, causing the money supply to expand. |

▲ When the Fed purchases government bonds on the open market, the bond seller deposits the money from the bond sale in the bank. In this way, funds enter the banking system, setting in motion money creation. When the Fed sells government bonds that it holds, bond buyers pay for the bonds using money from their bank accounts. When the Fed receives this money, it is taken out of circulation.

## U.S. Foreign Trade

Foreign trade has played an important role in the U.S. economy. A free-trade zone is a region where a group of countries agrees to reduce or eliminate trade barriers, such as tariffs or taxes on imports. The North American Free Trade Agreement (NAFTA) set the goal of eliminating all tariffs and trade barriers between Canada, Mexico, and the United States by 2009. Supporters of NAFTA point to increased trade among the countries. About 100 regional trading organizations operate in the world today. Many goods are produced globally by multinational corporations, with parts produced in one country and assembled in another.

**U.S. Exports and Imports, by Major Trading Partners, August 2006–August 2007**

SOURCE: U.S. Census Bureau

**Specialization and Trade** International trade occurs when one country provides resources that another country needs. By specializing in the production of certain goods and services, nations can use their resources more efficiently. Do research at the library or online to learn more about absolute and comparative advantage to understand why specialization and trade can benefit all nations—even those with few resources.

## Balance of Trade

The **balance of trade** is the relationship between a nation's imports and exports.

**Historical Context**: According to the theory of mercantilism, a nation could increase its wealth by protecting its own industries from foreign competition through tariffs, or taxes on imports, and by striving to export more than it imports. The American colonies provided a market for British-made goods. American colonists were not permitted to trade with countries other than Britain or to manufacture their own goods.

**Today**: In recent decades, the United States has had an unfavorable balance of trade. It has imported more than it has exported and experienced annual trade deficits. A trade imbalance can be corrected by limiting imports or increasing exports.

### Major Exports and Imports, 2007

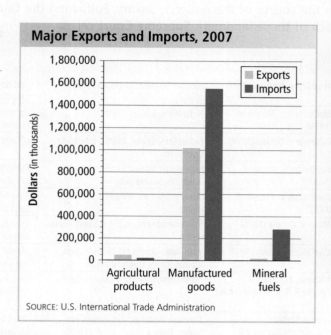

SOURCE: U.S. International Trade Administration

## Major Trade Organization Members

Asia-Pacific Economic Cooperation (APEC)

Caribbean Community and Common Market (CARICOM)

European Union (EU)

North American Free Trade Agreement (NAFTA) and APEC

Southern Common Market (MERCOSUR)

# Landmark Decisions of the Supreme Court

The table below lists key Supreme Court cases, issues, and decisions that have had a lasting impact on the course of the nation's history. Following the table, you will find a more detailed summary of each of these landmark Supreme Court cases.

| The Case | The Issues | The Supreme Courts Decision |
|---|---|---|
| *Marbury* v. *Madison* (1803) | Judicial Review, Checks and Balances | First decision to assert judicial review: the power of the Court to interpret the constitutionality of a law |
| *McCulloch* v. *Maryland* (1819) | Federalism, States' Rights | Upheld the power of the national government and denied the right of a state to tax a federal agency. |
| *Gibbons* v. *Ogden* (1824) | Federalism, States' Rights, Interstate Commerce | Upheld broad congressional power to legislate and regulate commerce between states. |
| *Worcester* v. *Georgia* (1832) | Federalism, States' Rights; Native American Sovereignty | Ruled that Georgia had no power to pass laws affecting the Cherokees because federal jurisdiction over the Cherokees was exclusive. |
| *Dred Scott* v. *Sandford* (1857) | Slavery, 5th Amendment, Citizens' Rights | Ruled that slaves were property, not citizens and, therefore, Dred Scott was not entitled to use the courts. |
| *Munn* v. *Illinois* (1876) | 5th Amendment, Public Interest; States' Rights | Upheld an Illinois law regulating railroad rates because the movement of grain was closely related to public interest. |
| Civil Rights Cases (1883) | 14th Amendment Equal Protection Clause, Racial Discrimination | Stated that the 14th Amendment only applied to discriminatory action taken by states, not to discriminatory actions taken by individuals. |
| *Wabash, St. Louis & Pacific R.R.* v. *Illinois* (1886) | Federalism, Interstate Commerce | Struck down an Illinois law regulating interstate railroad rates, ruling that it infringed on the federal government's exclusive control over interstate commerce. |
| *United States* v. *E.C. Knight Co.* (1895) | Sherman Antitrust Act, Federalism, States' Rights | The Sherman Antitrust Act does not apply to manufacturers located within a single state, because under the 10th Amendment, states have the right to regulate "local activities." |
| *In Re Debs* (1895) | Labor Strikes, Interstate Commerce | Ruled that the federal government had the authority to halt a railroad strike because it interfered with interstate commerce and delivery of the mail. |
| *Plessy* v. *Ferguson* (1896) | Segregation, 14th Amendment Equal Protection Clause | Permitted segregated public facilities, arguing that separate but equal accommodations did not violate the equal protection clause of the 14th Amendment. |
| *United States* v. *Wong Kim Ark* (1898) | Immigration, citizenship, 14th Amendment | Affirmed that under the 14th Amendment, all persons born in the United States are citizens of the United States. |
| *Northern Securities Co.* v. *United States* (1904) | Sherman Antitrust Act, Interstate Commerce | Sherman Antitrust Act could apply to any company that sought to eliminate competition in interstate commerce, including companies chartered within a single state. |
| *Lochner v. New York* (1905) | Labor conditions, property rights, 14th Amendment | Struck down a state law setting a 10-hour day for employees because the law interfered with an employee's right to contract with an employer and violated the protection of liberty guaranteed by the 14th Amendment. |
| *Muller* v. *Oregon* (1908) | Women's rights, Labor Conditions, 14th Amendment | In a departure from the *Lochner* case, the Court upheld a state law limiting women's work hours, viewing women as a special class needing special protections. |
| *Standard Oil of New Jersey* v. *United States* (1911) | Antitrust | Ruled that Standard Oil was an illegal monopoly and ordered that it be dissolved into smaller, competing companies. |
| *American Tobacco* v. *United States* (1911) | Antitrust | Ruled that American Tobacco was an illegal monopoly and ordered that it be dissolved into smaller, competing companies. |
| *Schenck* v. *United States* (1919) | 1st Amendment freedom of speech, national security | The Court limited free speech in time of war, reasoning that freedom of speech can be limited if the words present a "clear and present danger" to the country. |
| *Abrams* v. *United States* (1919) | 1st Amendment freedom of speech, national security | Upheld the convictions of persons who distributed antigovernment literature in violation of the Espionage Act. But Justices Holmes and Brandeis dissented, urging more stringent protection of the 1st Amendment. |
| *Gitlow* v. *New York* (1925) | 1st Amendment freedoms of speech and press, 14th Amendment | Ruled that the freedoms of speech and press were "incorporated" and protected from impairment by the states by the due process clause of the 14th Amendment. |
| *Stromberg* v. *California* (1931) | 1st Amendment freedom of speech, 14th Amendment | Overturned an anticommunist law that banned the public display of a red flag. This was the first time the Supreme Court struck down a state law under the 1st Amendment as applied to the states by the 14th Amendment. |
| *Near* v. *Minnesota* (1931) | 1st Amendment freedom of speech, 14th Amendment | The Supreme Court struck down a Minnesota state law, ruling that it infringed upon freedom of the press, guaranteed by the due process clause of the 14th Amendment. |

| The Case | The Issues | The Supreme Court's Decision |
|---|---|---|
| Schechter Poultry Corporation v. United States (1935) | New Deal, separation of powers, interstate commerce | The Court held that Congress, not the President, has the power to regulate interstate commerce. The National Industrial Recovery Act was declared unconstitutional for exceeding the commerce power that the Constitution had given to Congress. |
| West Coast Hotel v. Parrish (1937) | Minimum wage laws, 5th Amendment | Ruled that the Constitution allowed the restriction of liberty of contract by state law where such restriction protected the community, health, safety, or vulnerable groups. |
| West Virginia State Board of Education v. Barnette (1943) | Pledge of Allegiance, 1st Amendment | The Court found that a state law requiring students to pledge allegiance to the flag violated freedom of speech and freedom of religion. |
| Hirabayashi v. United States (1943) | 5th Amendment, civil liberties, national security | The Supreme Court upheld the legitimacy of travel restrictions imposed on Japanese Americans during World War II. |
| Korematsu v. United States (1944) | 5th Amendment, civil liberties, national security | Ruled that the internment of Japanese Americans during World War II did not violate the Constitution. |
| Everson v. Board of Education (1947) | 1st Amendment, establishment clause | The New Jersey law allowing reimbursement of money to parents whose children attended Catholic schools did not violate the 1st amendment. Some services "are separate from the religious function." |
| Dennis v. United States (1951) | 1st Amendment, civil liberties, national security | The Court ruled that the Smith Act, which prohibited advocation of the overthrow of the U.S. government by force and violence, did not violate the 1st Amendment. |
| Brown v. Board of Education of Topeka (1954) | School segregation, 14th Amendment | The Court found that segregation itself was a violation of the Equal Protection Clause, commenting that "in the field of public education the doctrine of 'separate but equal' has no place." |
| Watkins v. United States (1957) | Rights of the accused, 5th Amendment | The Bill of Rights is applicable to congressional investigations, as it is to all forms of governmental action. |
| Yates v. United States (1957) | 1st Amendment freedom of speech, national security | Ruled that the Smith Act did not forbid persons from advocating forcible overthrow of the government; it only forbade actions to achieve that goal. |
| Cooper v. Aaron (1958) | School segregation, 14th Amendment | The Court ruled unanimously against the Little Rock School Board's efforts to not comply with the Brown decision. |
| Mapp v. Ohio (1961) | Search and seizure 4th and 14th amendments | Ruled that evidence obtained by searches and seizures in violation of the Constitution is inadmissible. |
| Baker v. Carr (1962) | Legislative reapportionment, 14th Amendment | Ruled that federal Courts could direct that election-district boundaries be redrawn to ensure citizens' political rights. |
| Engel v. Vitale (1962) | 1st Amendment, establishment clause | Ruled that the recitation of a prayer in a public classroom was a violation of the establishment clause of the 1st Amendment. |
| Gideon v. Wainwright (1963) | Rights of the accused, 6th and 14th amendments | The Court said that all states must provide an attorney in all felony and capital cases for people who cannot afford one themselves. |
| Reynolds v. Sims (1964) | Legislative reapportionment, 14th Amendment | Extended the one-person, one-vote principle of *Wesberry* v. *Sanders* (1964) to states, ruling that state legislative districts should be roughly equal in population so that every voter has an equally weighted vote. |
| Heart of Atlanta Motel v. United States (1964) | Racial segregation, interstate commerce | Racial segregation of private facilities engaged in interstate commerce was found unconstitutional. |
| Miranda v. Arizona (1966) | Rights of the accused, 5th, 6th, and 14th amendments | Before questioning suspects held in custody, police must inform suspects that they have the right to remain silent, that anything they say may be used against them, and that they have the right to counsel. |
| Swann v. Charlotte-Mecklenburg Board of Education (1971) | School desegregation, busing | Ruled that busing students to various schools is an acceptable way to integrate segregated school systems. The Court said school districts had broad powers to find solutions to the problem of segregation. |
| Tinker v. Des Moines (1969) | Students' rights, 1st Amendment freedom of speech | Students in school may exercise freedom of speech as long as they do not disrupt classwork, create substantial disorder, or interfere with the rights of others. |
| New York Times v. United States (1971) | 1st Amendment freedom of the press | The Court limited censorship through "prior restraint" of the press, noting that it is the obligation of the government to prove that actual harm to the nation's security would be caused by the publication. |
| Roe v. Wade (1973) | Abortion, 9th Amendment, "right to privacy" | Decided that states could regulate abortions only in certain circumstances but otherwise a woman's right to an abortion was protected by her right to privacy. |
| United States v. Nixon (1974) | Executive privilege, separation of powers | Executive privilege was subordinate to "the fundamental demands of due process of law in the fair administration of criminal justice." President Nixon had to surrender audiotapes to a special prosecutor. |
| Regents of the University of CA v. Bakke (1978) | Affirmative action, 14th Amendment, | The Court held that a university could consider an applicant's race in making admissions decisions, but the use of strict racial quotas in affirmative action programs was not permissible. |
| New Jersey v. T.L.O. (1985) | Students' rights, 4th and 14th amendments | School officials, unlike the police, need only "reasonable suspicion" to search students when they believe illegal activity is occurring. |
| Texas v. Johnson (1989) | 1st Amendment freedom of speech | Ruled that desecrating the flag as an act of protest is an act of expression protected by the 1st Amendment. |
| Cruzan v. Director, Missouri Department of Health (1990) | "Right to die," 9th Amendment, 14th Amendment | Individuals have the right to refuse medical treatment, but the State can preserve life unless there is "clear and convincing" evidence that the patient desires the withdrawal of medical treatment. |

# Supreme Court Cases

| The Case | The Issues | The Supreme Court's Decision |
|---|---|---|
| **Board of Education of Westside Community Schools v. Mergens** (1990) | 1st Amendment, Establishment Clause | Allowing students to meet in noncurricular clubs on campus and discuss religion is constitutional because it does not amount to state sponsorship of a religion. |
| **Planned Parenthood of Southeastern Pennsylvania, et al. v. Casey** (1992) | Abortion, 14th Amendment, "right to privacy" | The Court upheld a woman's "liberty" to have an abortion but also allowed for restrictive state regulations as long as they did not create an "undue burden" or "substantial obstacle" for a woman. |
| **Vernonia School District v. Acton** (1995) | Students' rights, 4th Amendment search and seizure | The Court decided that drug testing of student athletes was constitutional; students' rights can be lessened at school if it is necessary to maintain student safety. |
| **Reno v. American Civil Liberties Union** (1997) | Internet, 1st Amendment, freedom of Speech | Ruled that the 1996 Federal Communications Decency Act violated the 1st Amendment's right to freedom of speech by not clearly defining which Internet materials were "indecent." |
| **Bush v. Gore** (2000) | Election rules, 14th Amendment | Following the controversial 2000 presidential election, the Supreme Court held that the Florida Supreme Court's plan for recounting ballots was unconstitutional. |
| **Mitchell v. Helms** (2000) | 1st Amendment, Establishment Clause | Ruled that a federal law providing funds for educational materials to public and private schools, including Catholic parochial schools, does not violate the 1st Amendment's Establishment Clause. |
| **District of Columbia v. Heller** (2008) | 2nd Amendment | The Court rules that a ban on handguns in the District of Columbia violated the 2nd Amendment right to bear arms. |

## Abrams v. United States (1919)

**(1st Amendment freedom of speech, national security)** Jacob Abrams and others distributed leaflets attacking the U.S. decision to send troops to Russia, which was experiencing revolution and civil war. They were found guilty of violating the Espionage Act. The Supreme Court upheld the convictions citing Holmes's "clear and present danger" test. But Justices Holmes and Brandeis published a powerful dissenting opinion. Holmes argued that the "silly leaflet" of "poor and puny anonymities" posed no real danger to U.S. efforts, and thus failed to present a "clear and present danger." He urged his colleagues to enforce the 1st Amendment more stringently.

## American Tobacco v. U.S. (1911)

**(antitrust)** Federal regulators filed an antitrust suit against American Tobacco, controlled by James Buchanan "Buck" Duke. The company controlled more than 90 percent of the world tobacco market. In 1911, the Supreme Court declared the company was a monopoly in violation of the Sherman Antitrust Act and ordered it to be split into five smaller competing companies.

## Baker v. Carr (1962)

**(legislative reapportionment, 14th Amendment)** Rapid population growth had occurred in Tennessee's cities, but the rural-dominated Tennessee legislature did not redraw state legislature districts. Cities with larger populations were underrepresented, while rural communities with smaller populations held the majority of representation. Mayor Baker of Nashville asked for federal court help. The Supreme Court ruled that the apportionment of state legislative districts is within the jurisdiction of federal courts. The Court directed a trial to be held in a Tennessee federal court. The case led to the 1964 *Wesberry* decision, which affirmed voters' right to the equal protection guaranteed by the 14th Amendment and established the principle of "one man, one vote" for the apportionment of congressional districts.

## Board of Education of Westside Community Schools v. Mergens (1990)

**(1st Amendment, establishment clause)** A request by Bridget Mergens to form a student Christian religious group at school was denied by an Omaha high school principal. Mergens took legal action, claiming that a 1984 federal law required "equal access" for student religious groups. The Court ordered the school to permit the club, stating that "a high school does not have to permit any extracurricular activities, but when it does, the school is bound by the . . . [Equal Access] Act of 1984. Allowing students to meet on campus and discuss religion is constitutional because it does not amount to 'State sponsorship of a religion.'"

## Brown v. Board of Education of Topeka (1954)

**(school segregation, 14th Amendment)** Probably no twentieth-century Supreme Court decision so deeply stirred and changed life in the United States as *Brown*. An eight-year-old girl from Topeka, Kansas, was not permitted to attend her neighborhood school because she was an African American. The Court found that segregation was a violation of the Equal Protection Clause, commenting that "in the field of public education the doctrine of 'separate but equal' has no place. . . . Segregation is a denial of the equal protection of the laws." The decision overturned *Plessy*, 1896.

## Bush v. Gore (2000)

**(election rules, 14th Amendment)** Following the controversial 2000 presidential election, the Florida Supreme Court ordered that every county in Florida had to manually recount some ballots. George Bush filed a request for review in the U.S. Supreme Court. The Supreme Court held that the Florida court's plan for recounting ballots was unconstitutional, noting that the Equal Protection Clause guarantees individuals that their ballots cannot be devalued by "later arbitrary and disparate treatment." The Court reasoned that there were too many procedural differences among the various counties for a fair recount to be conducted by the deadline date set by law.

### Civil Rights Cases (1883)

**(14th Amendment Equal Protection Clause, racial discrimination)** The Civil Rights Act of 1875 included punishments for businesses that practiced discrimination. The Court ruled on a number of cases involving the acts in 1883, finding that the Constitution, "while prohibiting discrimination by governments, made no provisions . . . for acts of racial discrimination by private individuals." The decision limited the impact of the Equal Protection Clause, giving tacit approval for segregation in the private sector.

### Cooper v. Aaron (1958)

**(school segregation, 14th Amendment)** President Eisenhower sent troops to Little Rock, Arkansas, to protect black students and enforce court-ordered school integration. But the local school board and state government continued to use delaying tactics. Arkansas officials even claimed that a state governor had the same power as the Supreme Court to interpret the Constitution. African American students appealed to the Supreme Court. The Court reaffirmed the *Brown* ruling that segregation was unconstitutional and boldly affirmed the Supreme Court's authority as the ultimate interpreter of the Constitution.

### Cruzan v. Director, Missouri Department of Health (1990)

**("right to die," 9th Amendment, 14th Amendment)** After Nancy Beth Cruzan was left in a "persistent vegetative state" by a car accident, Missouri officials refused to comply with her parents' request that the hospital terminate life-support. The Court upheld the State policy under which officials refused to withdraw treatment, rejecting the argument that the Due Process Clause of the 14th Amendment gave the parents the right to refuse treatment on their daughter's behalf. Although individuals have the right to refuse medical treatment, "incompetent" persons are not able to exercise this right; without "clear and convincing" evidence that Cruzan desired the withdrawal of treatment, the State could legally act to preserve her life.

### Dennis v. United States (1951)

**(1st Amendment, civil liberties, national security)** Eugene Dennis, a leader of the Communist Party in the United States, was arrested for violation of the Smith Act, which prohibited advocation of the overthrow of the U.S. government by force and violence. Dennis claimed that the law violated his 1st Amendment right to free speech. Reasoning that the Communist Party is a conspiratorial organization with "evil" intent, the Supreme Court upheld the Smith Act and Dennis's conviction. The Court ruled that free speech may be limited if it presents a clear and present danger to overthrow the government of the United States by force or violence.

### District of Columbia v. Heller (2008)

**(2nd Amendment, right to bear arms)** The Supreme Court upheld a Court of Appeals decision overturning a District of Columbia law that made it illegal for private citizens to own handguns. The law also required that other firearms be kept either unassembled or with trigger locks in place, thus rendering them unusable. The Court ruled, 5–4, that this law violated a person's Second Amendment right to lawfully own a firearm. Justice Antonin Scalia stated in the Court's opinion "Few laws in the history of our Nation have come close to the severe restriction of the District's handgun ban. . . . Undoubtedly some think that the Second Amendment is outmoded in a society . . . where gun violence is a serious problem. That is perhaps debatable, but what is not debatable is that it is not the role of this Court to pronounce the Second Amendment extinct."

### Dred Scott v. Sandford (1857)

**(slavery, 5th Amendment, citizens' rights)** This decision upheld property rights over human rights by saying that Dred Scott, a slave, could not become a free man just because he had traveled in "free soil" states with his master. A badly divided nation was further fragmented by the decision. "Free soil" federal laws and the Missouri Compromise line of 1820 were held unconstitutional because they deprived a slave owner of the right to his "property" without just compensation. This narrow reading of the Constitution, a landmark case of the Court, was most clearly stated by Chief Justice Roger B. Taney, a states' rights advocate.

### Engel v. Vitale (1962)

**(1st Amendment establishment clause)** The State Board of Regents of New York required the recitation of a nonsectarian prayer at the beginning of each school day. A group of parents filed suit against the required prayer. The Supreme Court ruled that the recitation of a prayer in a public classroom was a violation of the establishment clause of the 1st Amendment. The Court ruled New York's action unconstitutional, observing, "There can be no doubt that . . . religious beliefs [are] embodied in the Regents' prayer."

# Supreme Court Cases

## Everson v. Board of Education (1947)

**(1st Amendment, establishment clause)** New Jersey allowed for the reimbursement of transportation costs to parents whose children attended private schools, including parochial Catholic schools. Arch Everson, a taxpaying resident of Ewing Township, sued the local school district, insisting that this reimbursement violated both the New Jersey State Constitution and the First Amendment. In a 5–4 ruling, the Supreme Court upheld the law, stating that the "First Amendment has erected a wall between church and state. . . . New Jersey has not breached it here."

## Gibbons v. Ogden (1824)

**(federalism, states' rights, interstate commerce)** Aaron Ogden's exclusive New York ferry license gave him the right to operate steamboats to and from New York. Thomas Gibbons was operating steamboats between New York and New Jersey under a U.S. federal license. Ogden obtained an injunction from a New York court ordering Gibbons to stop operating his boats in New York waters. The Supreme Court invalidated the New York licensing regulations, holding that federal regulations should take precedence under the Constitution's Supremacy Clause (Article VI, Section 2). The decision strengthened the power of the United States to regulate interstate business. Federal regulation of the broadcasting industry, oil pipelines, and banking are all based on *Gibbons*.

## Gideon v. Wainwright (1963)

**(rights of the accused, 6th and 14th amendments)** Gideon was charged with breaking into a poolroom. He could not afford a lawyer, and Florida refused to provide counsel for trials not involving the death penalty. Gideon defended himself poorly and was sentenced to five years in prison. The Court called for a new trial, arguing that the Due Process Clause of the 14th Amendment applied to the 6th Amendment's guarantee of counsel for all poor persons facing a felony charge. Gideon later was found not guilty with the help of a court-appointed attorney.

## Gitlow v. New York (1925)

**(1st Amendment freedoms of speech and press, 14th Amendment)** Gitlow was convicted for distributing a manifesto that called for the establishment of socialism through strikes and other actions. The Supreme Court considered whether the 1st and 14th amendments had influence on state laws. According to what came to be known as the "incorporation" doctrine, the Court argued that the provisions of the 1st Amendment were "incorporated" by the 14th Amendment. The New York law was not overruled, but the decision clearly indicated that the Court could make such a ruling. Later cases extended the incorporation doctrine. Today, the Supreme Court holds that almost every provision of the Bill of Rights applies to both the federal government and the states.

## Heart of Atlanta Motel v. United States (1964)

**(racial segregation, interstate commerce)** The Civil Rights Act of 1964 outlawed racial discrimination in "public accommodations," including motels that refused rooms to blacks. Although local desegregation appeared to fall outside federal authority, the government argued that it was regulating interstate commerce. The Court agreed, declaring, "The power of Congress to promote interstate commerce also includes the power to regulate the local incidents thereof, including local activities . . . which have a substantial and harmful effect upon that commerce." Racial segregation of private facilities engaged in interstate commerce was found unconstitutional.

## Hirabayashi v. United States (1943)

**(5th Amendment, civil liberties, national security)** After the Japanese attack on Pearl Harbor, President Roosevelt issued executive orders to protect the West Coast from espionage and sabotage. As a result of these orders, curfews were established, and Japanese Americans were evacuated to relocation centers. Gordon Kiyoshi Hirabayashi, a student at the University of Washington, was convicted of violating a curfew and relocation order. Did the government policies violate the 5th Amendment rights of Americans of Japanese descent? The Supreme Court upheld the curfew, but evaded ruling on the relocation. The Court considered the vulnerability of military installations on the West Coast and the "solidarity" that persons of Japanese descent felt with their motherland, and reasoned that restrictions served an important national interest. Racial discrimination was justified since "in time of war residents having ethnic affiliations with an invading enemy may be a greater source of danger than those of a different ancestry."

## In Re Debs (1895)

**(labor strikes, interstate commerce)** Eugene V. Debs, a leader of the 1894 Pullman Railroad Car workers' strike, refused to halt the strike as ordered by a federal court. Debs appealed his "contempt of court" conviction. Citing Article 1, Section 8 of the Constitution, the Supreme Court ruled that the government had a right to regulate interstate commerce and ensure the operations of the Postal Service. The federal court had a right to stop the strike because the strikers interfered with the railroad's ability to provide interstate commerce and deliver the mail, which benefited the needs and "general welfare" of all Americans.

## Korematsu v. United States (1944)

**(5th Amendment, civil liberties, national security)** After the Japanese attack on Pearl Harbor, President Roosevelt issued executive orders to protect the West Coast from acts of espionage and sabotage. As a result of these

718    Supreme Court Cases

orders, more than 110,000 Japanese Americans living on the West Coast were forced to abandon their property and live in primitive camps far from the coast. Korematsu refused to report to an assembly center and was arrested. The Court rejected his appeal, noting that "pressing public necessity [World War II] may sometimes justify restrictions which curtail the civil rights of a single racial group" but added that "racial antagonism" never can justify such restrictions. The *Korematsu* decision has been widely criticized, particularly since few Americans of German or Italian descent were interned. In 1988, the U.S. government officially apologized for the internment and paid reparations to survivors.

## Lochner v. New York (1905)

**(labor conditions, property rights, 14th Amendment)** A New York law limited bakery employees' working hours to no more than 10 hours a day or 60 hours a week. Lochner claimed that the law infringed on his right to make employer/employee contracts and violated the Due Process Clause of the 14th Amendment. The Supreme Court struck down the New York law, arguing that states have the power to regulate health, safety, and public welfare, but that the New York law was not within the limits of these "police powers." The New York law interfered with citizens' property rights, guaranteed by the 14th Amendment.

## Mapp v. Ohio (1961)

**(search and seizure, 4th and 14th amendments)** Admitting evidence gained by illegal searches was permitted by some states before *Mapp*. Cleveland police raided Dollree Mapp's home without a warrant and found obscene materials. She appealed her conviction, saying that the 4th and 14th amendments protected her against improper police behavior. The Court agreed, extending "exclusionary rule" protections to citizens in state courts, saying that the prohibition against unreasonable searches would be "meaningless" unless evidence gained in such searches was "excluded." *Mapp* developed the concept of "incorporation" begun in *Gitlow* v. *New York*, 1925.

## Marbury v. Madison (1803)

**(judicial review, checks and balances)** After defeat in the 1800 election, President Adams appointed many Federalists to the federal courts, but James Madison, the new Secretary of State, refused to deliver the commissions. William Marbury, one of the appointees, asked the Supreme Court to enforce the delivery of his commission based on a provision of the Judiciary Act of 1789 that allowed the Court to hear such cases on original jurisdiction. The Court refused Marbury's request, finding that the relevant portion of the Judiciary Act was in conflict with the Constitution. This decision, written by Chief Justice Marshall,

established the evaluation of federal laws' constitutionality, or "judicial review," as a power of the Supreme Court.

## McCulloch v. Maryland (1819)

**(federalism, states' rights)** Called the "Bank of the United States" case. A Maryland law required federally chartered banks to use only a special paper to print paper money, which amounted to a tax. James McCulloch, the cashier of the Baltimore branch of the bank, refused to use the paper, claiming that states could not tax the federal government. The Court declared the Maryland law unconstitutional, commenting ". . . the power to tax implies the power to destroy."

## Miranda v. Arizona (1966)

**(rights of the accused; 5th, 6th, and 14th amendments)** Arrested for kidnapping and sexual assault, Ernesto Miranda signed a confession including a statement that he had "full knowledge of [his] legal rights. . . ." After conviction, he appealed, claiming that without counsel and without warnings, the confession was illegally gained. The Court agreed with Miranda that "he must be warned prior to any questioning that he has the right to remain silent, that anything he says can be used against him in a court of law, that he has the right to . . . an attorney and that if he cannot afford an attorney one will be appointed for him. . . ." Although later modified by *Nix* v. *Williams*, 1984, and other cases, *Miranda* firmly upheld citizen rights to fair trials in state courts.

## Mitchell v. Helms (2000)

**(1st Amendment Establishment Clause)** Chapter 2 of the Education Consolidation and Improvement Act of 1981 provides for the allocation of funds for educational materials and equipment to public and private schools to implement "secular, neutral, and nonideological" programs. In Jefferson Parish, Louisiana, about 30 percent of Chapter 2 funds are allocated for private schools, most of which are Catholic. Mary Helms and other public school parents filed suit alleging that the policy violated the 1st Amendment's Establishment Clause. The Supreme Court disagreed, ruling that Chapter 2, as applied in Jefferson Parish, is not a law respecting an establishment of religion, noting that "the religious, irreligious, and areligious are all alike eligible for governmental aid."

## Muller v. Oregon (1908)

**(women's rights, labor conditions, 14th Amendment)** In 1903, Oregon enacted a law prohibiting women from working in factories or laundries more than 10 hours in any day. After a conviction, Curt Muller claimed that the law violated his freedom of contract, protected by the 14th Amendment. The Court upheld the law, viewing women as a special class that needed special protections. The Court noted that "woman's physical structure and the functions she performs . . . justify special legislation restricting the conditions under which she should be permitted to toil."

### Munn v. Illinois (1876)

**(5th Amendment, public interest, states' rights)** Responding to farmers' complaints about the exorbitant rates they were paying, Illinois passed laws that set maximum rates that railroads and grain storage companies could charge. Munn, a partner in a Chicago warehouse firm, appealed his conviction, contending that the Illinois regulation constituted a taking of property without due process of law. The Supreme Court upheld the Illinois laws, arguing that states may regulate the use of private property "when such regulation becomes necessary for the public good." The case established as constitutional the principle of public regulation of private businesses involved in serving the public interest.

### Near v. Minnesota (1931)

**(1st Amendment freedom of speech, 14th Amendment)** Jay Near published a Minneapolis newspaper whose articles charged that local government and police officials were implicated with gangsters. A local official filed a complaint against Near under a Minnesota law that provided permanent injunctions against those who created a "public nuisance," by publishing, selling, or distributing a "malicious, scandalous and defamatory newspaper." The Supreme Court held that the Minnesota law was an infringement of freedom of the press guaranteed by the Due Process Clause of the 14th Amendment.

### New Jersey v. T.L.O. (1985)

**(students' rights, 4th and 14th amendments)** After T.L.O., a New Jersey high school student, denied an accusation that she had been smoking in the school lavatory, a vice principal searched her purse and found cigarettes, marijuana, and evidence that T.L.O. had been involved in marijuana dealing at the school. T.L.O. was then sentenced to probation by a juvenile court but appealed on the grounds that the evidence against her had been obtained by an "unreasonable" search. The Court rejected T.L.O.'s arguments, stating that the school had a "legitimate need to maintain an environment in which learning can take place," and that to do this "requires some easing of the restrictions to which searches by public authorities are ordinarily subject." The Court thus created a "reasonable suspicion" rule for school searches, a change from the "probable cause" requirement in the wider society.

### New York Times v. United States (1971)

**(1st Amendment, freedom of the press)** In 1971, *The New York Times* obtained copies of classified Defense Department documents, later known as the "Pentagon Papers," which revealed instances in which the Johnson administration had deceived Congress and the American people regarding U.S. policies during the Vietnam War. A U.S. district court issued an injunction against the publication of the documents, claiming that it might endanger national security. On appeal, the Supreme Court cited the 1st Amendment guarantee of a free press and refused to uphold the injunction against publication. The Court noted that it is the obligation of the government to prove that actual harm to the nation's security would be caused by the publication. The decision limited "prior restraint" of the press.

### Northern Securities Co. v. United States (1904)

**(Sherman Antitrust Act, interstate commerce)** In 1901, financiers formed the Northern Securities Company as a holding company that controlled the stock of the Great Northern Railway, Northern Pacific Railway, the Chicago, Burlington & Quincy Railroad, and other railroads. Fearing a monopoly, President Theodore Roosevelt's trust-busting government applied the Sherman Antitrust Act. In response to the question of whether the Sherman Act applied to a company chartered by one of the states, the Supreme Court ruled "It cannot be said that any state may give a corporation, created under its laws, authority to restrain interstate or international commerce. . . . Every corporation created by a state is necessarily subject to the supreme law of the land."

### Planned Parenthood of Southeastern Pennsylvania, et al. v. Casey (1992)

**(abortion, 14th Amendment, "right to privacy")** The Pennsylvania legislature enacted new regulations limiting abortion. Physicians had to provide patients with antiabortion information and wait at least 24 hours before performing an abortion. In most cases, minors needed the consent of a parent, and married women had to notify their husbands of their intention to abort the fetus. The Supreme Court reaffirmed a woman's "liberty" to have an abortion as it had in the *Roe* decision. However, it upheld most of Pennsylvania's provisions, reasoning that they did not create an "undue burden" or "substantial obstacle" for women seeking an abortion. Under this new "undue burden" test, the only provision to fail was the husband notification requirement.

### Plessy v. Ferguson (1896)

**(segregation, 14th Amendment equal protection)** A Louisiana law required separate seating for white and African American citizens on public railroads, a form of segregation. Herman Plessy argued that his right to "equal protection of the laws" was violated. The Court held that segregation was permitted if facilities were equal. The Court interpreted the 14th Amendment as "not intended to give Negroes social equality but only political and civil equality. . . ." The Louisiana law was seen as a "reasonable exercise of (state) police power. . . ." Segregated public facilities were permitted until *Plessy* was overturned by the *Brown* v. *Board of Education* case of 1954.

### Regents of the University of California v. Bakke (1978)

**(affirmative action, 14th Amendment)** Under an affirmative action program, the medical school of the University of California at Davis reserved 16 of 100 slots in each class for "disadvantaged citizens." When Bakke, a white applicant, was not accepted by the school, he claimed racial discrimination in violation of the 14th Amendment. The Court ruled narrowly, requiring Bakke's admission but not overturning affirmative action, preferring to review such questions on a case-by-case basis.

### Reno v. American Civil Liberties Union (1997)

**(Internet 1st Amendment, freedom of speech)** Seeking to protect minors, the 1996 Federal Communications Decency Act made it a crime to transmit obscene or indecent messages over the Internet. The Supreme Court ruled that the "indecent transmission" provision and the "patently offensive display" provision of the Communications Decency Act violated the 1st Amendment's freedom of speech. The Court reasoned the act did not clearly define "indecent." The Internet does not have the special features (such as historical governmental oversight, limited frequencies, and "invasiveness") that have justified allowing greater regulation of content in radio and television.

### Reynolds v. Sims (1964)

**(legislative reapportionment, 14th Amendment)** Voters of Jefferson County, Alabama, filed a suit challenging the apportionment of the Alabama legislature, which was still based on the 1900 federal census. The Supreme Court extended the "one person, one vote" principle that emerged from *Baker* v. *Carr* (1962) and *Wesberry* v. *Sanders* (1964) and applied it to this case, calling for reapportionment based on current census data. Applying the Equal Protection Clause of the 14th Amendment, the Court ruled that state legislative districts should be roughly equal in population so that every voter has an equally weighted vote.

### Roe v. Wade (1973)

**(abortion, 9th Amendment, "right to privacy")** A Texas woman challenged a state law forbidding the artificial termination of a pregnancy, saying that she "had a fundamental right to privacy." The Court upheld a woman's right to choose in this case, noting that the state's "important and legitimate interest in protecting the potentiality of human life" became "compelling" at the end of the first trimester, and that before then,

". . . the attending physician, in consultation with his patient, is free to determine, without regulation by the state, that . . . the patient's pregnancy should be terminated." The decision struck down the state regulation of abortion in the first three months of pregnancy and was modified by *Planned Parenthood of Southeastern Pennsylvania* v. *Casey*, 1992.

### Schechter Poultry Corporation v. United States (1935)

**(New Deal, separation of powers, interstate commerce)** As part of the New Deal, the National Industrial Recovery Act (NIRA) gave the President authority to regulate aspects of interstate commerce. The government convicted Schechter for not observing minimum wage and hour provisions, selling uninspected chickens, and other violations. The Supreme Court ruled that Congress, not the President, has the power to regulate interstate commerce, and that Congress cannot delegate that power to the President. The Court reversed the conviction of Schechter because his business, which operated almost exclusively in New York State, only indirectly affected interstate commerce. The Court also declared the NIRA to be unconstitutional because it exceeded the commerce power that the Constitution had given to Congress.

### Schenck v. United States (1919)

**(1st Amendment freedom of speech, national security)** Schenck, a member of an antiwar group, urged men drafted into military service in World War I to resist and to avoid induction. He was charged with violating the Espionage Act of 1917, which outlawed active opposition to the war. The Court limited free speech in time of war, stating that Schenck's words presented a "clear and present danger. . . ." Although later decisions modified this one, the *Schenck* case created a precedent that 1st Amendment rights are not absolute.

### Standard Oil of New Jersey v. United States (1911)

**(antitrust)** The Standard Oil Company of New Jersey, controlled by John D. Rockefeller, owned virtually all the oil-refining companies in the United States and was extending its stranglehold over oil exploration and retail distribution of refined products. The government therefore prosecuted Standard Oil under the Sherman Antitrust Act. The Supreme Court found Standard Oil to be an illegal monopoly that restrained free competition. It fined Rockefeller and others, and ordered that the company be dissolved into smaller, competing companies.

### Stromberg v. California (1931)

**(1st Amendment freedom of speech, 14th Amendment)** A California state law, enacted in 1919, prohibited the public display of a red flag. Yetta Stromberg, a member of the Young Communist League and a counselor at a camp for working-class children, was arrested for violating the law. Stromberg had led the youth in raising and pledging allegiance to "the workers' red flag." The Court struck down the law, concluding that a law that permitted the punishment of peaceful opposition exercised in accordance with legal means and constitutional limitations was "repugnant to the guarantee of liberty contained in the 14th Amendment."

### Swann v. Charlotte-Mecklenburg Board of Education (1971)

(school desegregation, busing) After the *Brown* decision, school desegregation advanced very slowly. The NAACP took the *Swann* case to the Supreme Court on behalf of six-year-old James Swann and other students in the Charlotte-Mecklenburg, North Carolina, school system where the vast majority of black students attended all-black schools. The Court held that all schools in a district need not reflect the district's racial composition, but that the existence of all-white or all-black schools must be shown not to result from segregation policies. It stated that busing students to various schools is an acceptable way to integrate segregated school systems. The Court said school districts had broad powers to find solutions to the problem of segregation.

### Texas v. Johnson (1989)

(1st Amendment freedom of speech) To protest national policies, Johnson doused a U.S. flag with kerosene and burned it outside the 1984 Republican National Convention in Dallas. He was arrested and convicted under a Texas law prohibiting the desecration of the Texas and U.S. flags. The Court ruled that the Texas law placed an unconstitutional limit on "freedom of expression," noting that ". . . nothing in our precedents suggests that a state may foster its own view of the flag by prohibiting expressive conduct relating to it."

### Tinker v. Des Moines (1969)

(students' rights, 1st Amendment freedom of speech) Marybeth and John Tinker violated a school rule and wore black armbands to school in protest against the Vietnam War. They were suspended. The Tinkers claimed that their freedom of speech had been violated. The Supreme Court agreed, saying that students do not "shed their constitutional rights to freedom of speech or expression at the schoolhouse gate." Students may express personal opinions as long as they do not disrupt classwork, create substantial disorder, or interfere with the rights of others. Since the wearing of black armbands was a "silent, passive expression of opinion" without these side effects, the Tinkers' action was protected by the 1st Amendment.

### United States v. E. C. Knight Co. (1895)

(Sherman Antitrust Act, federalism, states' rights) After gaining control of the E. C. Knight Company, the American Sugar Refining Company controlled more than 90 percent of the American sugar-refining industry. The federal government sued the Knight Company under the provisions of the Sherman Antitrust Act. The Court ruled that the Sherman Antitrust Act does not apply to manufacturers located within a single state, because under the 10th Amendment, states have the right to regulate "local activities," such as manufacturing. In later cases, the Court modified its position and permitted Congress greater power to limit monopolies.

### United States v. Nixon (1974)

(executive privilege, separation of powers) During the investigation of the Watergate scandal, journalists discovered that President Nixon had recorded all of his conversations in the White House, including some with administration officials accused of illegal activities. A special prosecutor subpoenaed the tapes. Nixon refused to release them, citing separation of powers, his need for confidentiality, and executive privilege to immunity from court demands for information. The Supreme Court rejected his arguments and ordered him to surrender the tapes. Executive privilege was subordinate to "the fundamental demands of due process of law in the fair administration of criminal justice."

### United States v. Wong Kim Ark (1898)

(immigration, citizenship, 14th Amendment) The Chinese Exclusion Act of 1882 denied citizenship to Chinese immigrants. Wong Kim Ark was born in 1873 in California to Chinese parents who were resident aliens. In 1894, Ark visited China. When he returned to the United States, he was denied entrance on grounds that he was not a U.S. citizen. The Supreme Court ruled in favor of Ark. Under the 14th Amendment, all persons born in the United States are citizens of the United States. Since he was born in the United States, Ark was a citizen. The Chinese Exclusion Act could not apply to him because he was a citizen by birth.

### Vernonia School District v. Acton (1995)

(students' rights, 4th Amendment, search and seizure) The Vernonia school district of Oregon established a student-athlete drug policy that authorized urinalysis drug testing of student athletes. James Acton refused the urinalysis test and was therefore not allowed to participate in the school's junior high football program. Did the school policy violate the 4th Amendment protection against unreasonable search and seizure? The Supreme Court ruled that the school policy was constitutional. The reasonableness of a search is judged by "balancing the intrusion on the individual's 4th Amendment interests against the promotion of legitimate governmental interests." The school's concern over the safety of students under their supervision overrides the minimal intrusion in student-athletes' privacy.

### Wabash, St. Louis & Pacific R.R. v. Illinois (1886)

**(federalism, interstate commerce)** An Illinois law regulated railroad rates on the intrastate (within one state) portion of an interstate (two or more states) journey. The Supreme Court declared the state law to be invalid, ruling that continuous transportation across the country is essential and that states should not impose restraints on the freedom of commerce. The Court stated that the regulation of interstate railroad rates is a federal power and that states cannot enact statutes interfering or seriously affecting interstate commerce. Soon afterward, Congress created the Interstate Commerce Commission (ICC).

### Watkins v. United States (1957)

**(rights of the accused, 5th Amendment)** In 1954, John Watkins testified in hearings conducted by the House Committee on Un-American Activities. Watkins answered questions about himself but refused to give information on individuals who had left the Communist Party, arguing that such questions were beyond the authority of the committee. After being convicted for refusing to answer the committee's questions, Watkins appealed, arguing that his conviction was a violation of the Due Process Clause of the 5th Amendment. The Supreme Court overturned Watkins's conviction. The Court said that congressional committees had to clearly define the specific purposes of their investigations. Congressional committees must abide by the Bill of Rights. No witness can be made to testify on matters outside the defined scope of a committee's investigation.

### West Coast Hotel v. Parrish (1937)

**(minimum wage laws, 5th Amendment)** The case involved Elsie Parrish, an employee of the West Coast Hotel Company, who received wages below the minimum wage fixed by Washington State law. The issue was whether minimum wage laws violated the liberty of contract as construed under the 5th Amendment and applied by the 14th Amendment. The Supreme Court upheld the constitutionality of the minimum wage legislation, ruling that the Constitution allowed the restriction of liberty of contract by state law where such restriction protected the community, health, safety, or vulnerable groups, as in the case of *Muller* v. *Oregon*, 1908.

### West Virginia State Board of Education v. Barnette (1943)

**("Pledge of Allegiance," 1st Amendment)** The West Virginia Board of Education required that all teachers and pupils salute the flag. Some children did not comply, saying the requirement went against their religious beliefs. The Court held that compelling public schoolchildren to salute the flag was unconstitutional. "Compulsory unification of opinion," the Court held, was antithetical to 1st Amendment values. The decision noted that Americans could not be forced to demonstrate their allegiance to "what shall be orthodox in politics, nationalism, religion, or other matters of opinion."

### Worcester v. Georgia (1832)

**(federalism, states' rights, Native American sovereignty)** Two missionaries were convicted for violating a Georgia law requiring all whites living in Cherokee Indian Territory to obtain a state license. The Supreme Court overturned their convictions, ruling that the state had no power to pass laws affecting the Cherokees because federal jurisdiction over the Cherokees was exclusive. Chief Justice John Marshall argued, "The Cherokee nation, then, is a distinct community occupying its own territory in which the laws of Georgia can have no force. The whole intercourse between the United States and this nation, is, by our constitution and laws, vested in the government of the United States."

### Yates v. United States (1957)

**(1st Amendment, freedom of speech, national security)** In 1951, fourteen members of the Communist Party in California were convicted of violating the Smith Act, which said it was illegal to advocate or organize the forceful overthrow or destruction of the U.S. government. Yates claimed that the law violated his 1st Amendment right to freedom of speech. The Supreme Court reversed the convictions, saying that to violate the Smith Act, a person must urge others to do something, not just believe in something. The Court distinguished between speech promoting an idea and speech advocating direct action.

# Documents of Our Nation

# The Mayflower Compact

▲ Signing of the Mayflower Compact

*T*he Pilgrims arrived at Massachusetts in 1620. Before disembarking, they signed a covenant that established a basis for self-government derived from the consent of the governed. Forty-one men signed the compact, agreeing to abide by the laws of the government. Women, who did not enjoy equal rights, were not asked to sign.

In the name of God, Amen. We, whose names are underwritten, the loyal subjects of our dread Sovereign Lord King James, by the grace of God, of Great Britain, France and Ireland king, defender of the faith, etc. Having undertaken, for the glory of God, and advancement of the Christian faith, and honor of our king and country, a voyage to plant the first colony in the Northern parts of Virginia, do by these presents solemnly and mutually in the presence of God and one of another, covenant and combine ourselves together into a civil body politick, for our better ordering and preservation, and furtherance of the ends aforesaid; and by virtue hereof to enacte, constitute, and frame such just and equal laws, ordinances, acts, constitutions and offices, from time to time, as shall be thought most meet and convenient for the general good of the Colony unto which we promise all due submission and obedience.

In witness whereof we have hereunder subscribed our names at Cape Cod the eleventh of November, in the year of the reign of our Sovereign Lord, King James, of England, France and Ireland, the eighteenth, and of Scotland the fifty-fourth. Anno Dom. 1620.

## *Patrick Henry*
## "Liberty or Death"

*O*n March 23, 1775, Patrick Henry urged a Virginia convention to prepare for war against British forces. Decades later, from the recollections of men like Thomas Jefferson, William Wirt wrote a biography of Henry, including the speech below. Henry's passionate speech caused quite a stir, even if we cannot be certain of his exact words.

. . . It is now too late to retire from the contest. There is no retreat but in submission and slavery! Our chains are forged is Their clanking may be heard on the plains of Boston! T' inevitable—and let it come! I repeat it, sir, let it come may cry,

It is in vain, sir, to extenuate the matter. Gradually begun! The Peace, Peace—but there is no peace. The was to our ears the clash of next gale that sweeps from the north with in the field! Why stand we resounding arms! Our brethren are on? What would they have? Is life so here idle? What is it that gentle nased at the price of chains and slavery? dear, or peace so sweet, as to not what course others may take; but as for Forbid it, Almighty God! e death! me, give me liberty

▲ Patrick Henry addresses fellow Virginians.

Documents of Our Nation

## Thomas Paine
## Common Sense

In 1776, after the battles at Lexington and Concord, Thomas Paine published a fiery fifty-page pamphlet that challenged the authority of the British government and the royal monarchy. Paine appealed to the people of America to seek independence from Great Britain.

. . . As to government matters, it is not in the power of Britain to do this continent justice: The business of it will soon be too weighty, and intricate, to be managed with any tolerable degree of convenience, by a power, so distant from us, and so very ignorant of us. . . .

For as in absolute governments the King is law, so in free countries the law ought to be King; and there ought to be no other. But lest any ill use should afterwards arise, let the crown at the conclusion of the ceremony be demolished, and scattered among the people whose right it is.

A government of our own is our natural right: And when a man seriously reflects on the precariousness of human affairs, he will become convinced, that it is infinitely wiser and safer, to form a constitution of our own in a cool deliberate manner, while we have it in our power, than to trust such an interesting event to time and chance. . . .

▲ Abigail Adams

## Abigail Adams
## "Remember the Ladies"

John and Abigail Adams spent long periods of time apart during the Revolution and the formation of the United States. During this time, they frequently wrote letters to each other, many discussing the politics of the day. In the following letter, written March 31, 1776, Abigail urges her husband to consider the role of women in the new nation.

. . . I . . . long to hear that you have declared an independence. . . . and by the way in the new Code of Laws which I suppose it will be necessary for you to make I desire you would Remember the Ladies, and be more generous and favorable to them than your ancestors. Do not put such unlimited power into the hands of the Husbands. Remember all Men would be tyrants if they could. If particular care and attention is not paid to the Ladies we are determined to foment a Rebellion, and will not hold ourselves bound by any Laws in which we have no voice, or Representation. . . .

## John Adams
## "Free and Independent States"

On July 2, 1776, the Second Continental Congress approved a resolution asserting the right of the colonies to be independent of Great Britain. Two days later, Congress would ratify the official Declaration of Independence. In between these two events, John Adams, a member of the Declaration of Independence draft committee, wrote to his wife expressing his excitement.

Yesterday the greatest question was decided, which ever was debated in America, and a greater, perhaps, never was or will be decided among men. A Resolution was passed without one dissenting Colony "that these United Colonies are, and of right ought to be, free and independent States, and as such they have, and of right ought to have, full power to make war, conclude peace, establish commerce, and to do all the other acts and things which other States may rightfully do." You will see, in a few days, a Declaration setting forth the causes which have impelled us to this mighty revolution, and the reasons which will justify it in the sight of God and man. A plan of confederation will be taken up in a few days.

▲ John Adams

## Thomas Jefferson
## Virginia Statute for Religious Freedom

Thomas Jefferson took great pride in drafting this law in 1777, but it was James Madison who skillfully secured its adoption by the Virginia legislature in 1786. The statute was the basis for the Religion Clauses in the Constitution's Bill of Rights.

. . . Be it enacted by the General Assembly, That no man shall be compelled to frequent or support any religious worship, place, or ministry whatsoever, nor shall be enforced, restrained, molested, or burthened in his body or goods, nor shall otherwise suffer on account of his religious opinions or belief; but that all men shall be free to profess, and by argument to maintain, their opinion in matters of religion, and that the same shall in no wise diminish, enlarge, or affect their civil capacities. . . .

◀ Bruton Parish Church in Virginia

# The Northwest Ordinance

Adopted in 1787 by the Second Continental Congress, the Northwest Ordinance created a method for admitting new states to the Union. While the Articles of Confederation lacked a bill of rights, the Ordinance provided one that included many of the basic liberties that would later be included in the Constitution's Bill of Rights.

. . . **ART. 1.** No person, demeaning himself in a peaceable and orderly manner, shall ever be molested on account of his mode of worship or religious sentiments, in the said territory.

**ART. 2.** The inhabitants of the said territory shall always be entitled to the benefits of the writ of habeas corpus, and of the trial by jury. . . .

**ART. 3.** Religion, morality, and knowledge, being necessary to good government and the happiness of mankind, schools and the means of education shall forever be encouraged. . . .

**ART. 6.** There shall be neither slavery nor involuntary servitude in the said territory, otherwise than in the punishment of crimes whereof the party shall have been duly convicted: Provided, always, That any person escaping into the same, from whom labor or service is lawfully claimed in any one of the original States, such fugitive may be lawfully reclaimed and conveyed to the person claiming his or her labor or service as aforesaid.

▲ Settlers moving to the Ohio Territory

# The Federalist, No. 51

This Federalist paper was probably written either by James Madison or Alexander Hamilton. It argues that the federal system and the separation of powers proposed in the Constitution provides a system of checks and balances that will protect the rights of the people.

. . . In order to lay a due foundation for that separate and distinct exercise of the different powers of government, which to a certain extent is admitted on all hands to be essential to the preservation of liberty, it is evident that each department should have a will of its own. . . .

But the great security against a gradual concentration of the several powers in the same department, consists in giving to those who administer each department the necessary constitutional means and personal motives to resist encroachments of the others. . . . Ambition must be made to counteract ambition. . . .

The constant aim is to divide and arrange the several offices in such a manner as that each may be a check on the other. . . .

In the compound republic of America, the power surrendered by the people is first divided between two distinct governments, and then the portion allotted to each subdivided among distinct and separate departments. Hence a double security arises to the rights of the people. . . .

## Thomas Jefferson
## First Inaugural Address

After the hotly contested presidential election of 1800, some expected that Jefferson's inaugural address would attack the defeated Federalists and their policies. Instead, he extended an olive branch of reconciliation. Jefferson praised a society in which people have full freedom to differ. He urged abidance with the will of the majority and respect for the rights of the minority.

Friends and Fellow Citizens:

. . . All . . . will bear in mind this sacred principle, that though the will of the majority is in all cases to prevail, that will, to be rightful, must be reasonable; that the minority possess their equal rights, which equal laws must protect, and to violate which would be oppression. Let us, then, fellow citizens, unite with one heart and one mind. . . . We have called by different names brethren of the same principle. We are all Republicans—we are all Federalists. If there be any among us who would wish to dissolve this Union or to change its republican form, let them stand undisturbed as monuments of the safety with which error of opinion may be tolerated where reason is left free to combat it. . . .

Still one thing more, fellow citizens—a wise and frugal government, which shall restrain men from injuring one another, which shall leave them otherwise free to regulate their own pursuits of industry and improvement, and shall not take from the mouth of labor the bread it has earned. This is the sum of good government. . . .

You should understand what I deem the essential principles of our government, and consequently those which ought to shape its administration. . . . Equal and exact justice to all men, of whatever state or persuasion, religious or political; peace, commerce, and honest friendship, with all nations—entangling alliances with none; the support of the state governments in all their rights . . . absolute acquiescence in the decisions of the majority. . . .

◀ Campaign banner promoting the election of Thomas Jefferson for President

## Francis Scott Key
## "The Star-Spangled Banner"

**D**uring the War of 1812, a Maryland attorney named Francis Scott Key witnessed the British attack on Fort McHenry, near Baltimore. In the morning, Key was so delighted to see the American flag still flying over the fort that he composed a poem to commemorate the event. Set to the music of a popular folk tune, "The Star-Spangled Banner" was officially made the national anthem by Congress in 1931.

▲ Flag that flew over Fort McHenry during the British attack

O say, can you see, by the dawn's early light,
What so proudly we hail'd at the twilight's last gleaming?
Whose broad stripes and bright stars, thro' the perilous fight,
O'er the ramparts we watch'd, were so gallantly streaming?
And the rockets' red glare, the bombs bursting in air,
Gave proof thro' the night that our flag was still there.
O say, does that star-spangled banner yet wave
O'er the land of the free and the home of the brave?

▲ Frederick Douglass

## Frederick Douglass
## Independence Day Speech

**I**n 1852, Douglass accepted an invitation from the leading citizens of Rochester, New York, to speak at their Fourth of July celebration. Douglass delivered a scathing speech in which he attacked the hypocrisy of celebrating independence and freedom in a nation where millions of people were enslaved.

Fellow citizens, pardon me, allow me to ask, why am I called upon to speak here today? What have I, or those I represent, to do with your national independence? Are the great principles of political freedom and of natural justice, embodied in that Declaration of Independence, extended to us? . . .

What, to the American slave, is your Fourth of July? I answer: a day that reveals to him, more than all other days in the year, the gross injustice and cruelty to which he is the constant victim. To him, your celebration is a sham; your boasted liberty, an unholy license; your national greatness, swelling vanity; your sounds of rejoicing are empty and heartless; your denunciation of tyrants, brass-fronted impudence; your shouts of liberty and equality, hollow mockery; your prayers and hymns, your sermons and thanksgivings, with all your religious parade and solemnity, are, to Him, mere bombast, fraud, deception, impiety, and hypocrisy—a thin veil to cover up crimes which would disgrace a nation of savages. There is not a nation of savages. There is not a nation on the earth guilty of practices more shocking and bloody than are the people of the United States at this very hour. . . .

## Sojourner Truth
## "Ain't I a Woman?"

Sojourner Truth, an African American woman prominent in both the abolitionist and early feminist movements, delivered her famous speech at a women's rights convention in Akron, Ohio, in 1851. The version below was first published twelve years later in the Anti-Slavery Standard by Frances Gage, a celebrated antislavery fighter and president of the Convention. Although recent scholarship questions the exact wording of the speech, it made a great impact at the time and has endured as a classic statement of women's rights.

▲ Sojourner Truth

. . . I think that 'twixt the Negroes of the South and the women at the North, all talking about rights, the white men will be in a fix pretty soon. But what's all this here talking about?

That man over there says that women need to be helped into carriages, and lifted over ditches, and to have the best place everywhere. Nobody ever helps me into carriages, or over mud-puddles, or gives me any best place! And ain't I a woman? Look at me! Look at my arm! I have ploughed and planted, and gathered into barns, and no man could head me! And ain't I a woman? I could work as much and eat as much as a man—when I could get it—and bear the lash as well! And ain't I a woman? I have borne thirteen children, and seen most all sold off to slavery, and when I cried out with my mother's grief, none but Jesus heard me! And ain't I a woman? . . .

## Elizabeth Cady Stanton
## Address to the Legislature of New York

In 1854, Elizabeth Cady Stanton presented this speech to the New York State Legislature. She addressed the inequalities faced by all women under the state laws and discussed the specific challenges met by mothers, wives, and widows.

. . . Gentlemen, in republican America, in the nineteenth century, we, the daughters of the revolutionary heroes of '76, demand at your hands the redress of our grievances—a revision of your State Constitution—a new code of laws. Permit us then, as briefly as possible, to call your attention to the legal disabilities under which we labor.

1st. Look at the position of woman as woman. . . . We are persons; native, free-born citizens; property-holders, tax-payers; yet are we denied the exercise of our right to the elective franchise. We support ourselves, and, in part, your schools, colleges, churches, your poor-houses, jails, prisons, the army, the navy, the whole machinery of government, and yet we have no voice in your councils. We have every qualification required by the Constitution, necessary to the legal voter, but the one of sex. . . .

2nd. Look at the position of woman as wife. . . . The wife who inherits no property holds about the same legal position that does the slave on the Southern plantation. She can own nothing, sell nothing. She has no right even to the wages she earns; her person, her time, her services are the property of another. . . .

## Abraham Lincoln
# The Gettysburg Address

At the Battle of Gettysburg, more than 51,000 Confederate and Union soldiers were listed as wounded, missing, or dead. President Lincoln gave this brief speech at the dedication of The Gettysburg National Cemetery on November 19, 1863. The five known manuscript copies of the speech differ slightly and historians debate which version Lincoln actually delivered. But the address is considered one of the most eloquent and moving speeches in American history. As Lincoln described the significance of the war, he invoked the Declaration of Independence and its principles of liberty and equality, and he spoke of "a new birth of freedom."

Four score and seven years ago our fathers brought forth on this continent, a new nation, conceived in Liberty, and dedicated to the proposition that all men are created equal.

Now we are engaged in a great civil war, testing whether that nation, or any nation so conceived and so dedicated, can long endure. We are met on a great battle-field of that war. We have come to dedicate a portion of that field, as a final resting place for those who here gave their lives that the nation might live. It is altogether fitting and proper that we should do this.

But, in a larger sense, we can not dedicate—we can not consecrate—we can not hallow—this ground. The brave men, living and dead, who struggled here, have consecrated it, far above our poor power to add or detract. The world will little note, nor long remember what we say here, but it can never forget what they did here. It is for us the living, rather, to be dedicated here to the unfinished work which they who fought here have thus far so nobly advanced. It is rather for us to be here dedicated to the great task remaining before us—that from these honored dead we take increased devotion to that cause for which they gave the last full measure of devotion—that we here highly resolve that these dead shall not have died in vain—that this nation, under God, shall have a new birth of freedom—and that government of the people, by the people, for the people, shall not perish from the earth.

▶ Lincoln Memorial statue in Washington, D.C.

## Abraham Lincoln
## Second Inaugural Address

*L*incoln delivered his second inaugural address just over a month before his death. He spoke about the war, slavery, and the need "to bind up the nation's wounds." The speech's closing words of reconciliation and healing are today carved in the walls of the Lincoln Memorial.

. . . On the occasion corresponding to this four years ago all thoughts were anxiously directed to an impending civil war. All dreaded it, all sought to avert it. While the inaugural address was being delivered from this place, devoted altogether to saving the Union without war, insurgent agents were in the city seeking to destroy it without war—seeking to dissolve the Union and divide effects by negotiation. Both parties deprecated war, but one of them would make war rather than let the nation survive, and the other would accept war rather than let it perish, and the war came.

One-eighth of the whole population were colored slaves, not distributed generally over the Union, but localized in the southern part of it. These slaves constituted a peculiar and powerful interest. All knew that this interest was somehow the cause of the war. To strengthen, perpetuate, and extend this interest was the object for which the insurgents would rend the Union even by war, while the Government claimed no right to do more than to restrict the territorial enlargement of it. Neither party expected for the war the magnitude or the duration which it has already attained. Neither anticipated that the cause of the conflict might cease with or even before the conflict itself should cease. Each looked for an easier triumph, and a result less fundamental and astounding. Both read the same Bible and pray to the same God, and each invokes His aid against the other. . . . Fondly do we hope, fervently do we pray, that this mighty scourge of war may speedily pass away. Yet, if God wills that it continue until all the wealth piled by the bondsman's two hundred and fifty years of unrequited toil shall be sunk, and until every drop of blood drawn with the lash shall be paid by another drawn with the sword, as was said three thousand years ago, so still it must be said "the judgments of the Lord are true and righteous altogether."

With malice toward none, with charity for all, with firmness in the right as God gives us to see the right, let us strive on to finish the work we are in, to bind up the nation's wounds, to care for him who shall have borne the battle and for his widow and his orphan, to do all which may achieve and cherish a just and lasting peace among ourselves and with all nations.

## Chief Joseph
## "I Will Fight No More Forever"

In 1877, after being ordered to a reservation, Chief Joseph led some 800 of his Nez Percé people in an attempted escape to Canada. They fled more than 1,000 miles across Idaho and Montana, battling the U.S. Army all along the way. Finally, with fewer than 500 of his people remaining and only 40 miles from Canada, Chief Joseph surrendered. General O.O. Howard reported Chief Joseph's poignant words.

I am tired of fighting. Our chiefs are killed. . . . The old men are all dead. . . . It is cold and we have no blankets. The little children are freezing to death. My people, some of them, have run away to the hills, and have no blankets, no food; no one knows where they are—perhaps freezing to death. I want to have time to look for my children and see how many of them I can find. Maybe I shall find them among the dead. Hear me, my chiefs. I am tired; my heart is sick and sad. From where the sun now stands I will fight no more forever.

▲ Chief Joseph

## Preamble to the Constitution of the Knights of Labor

The Knights of Labor, which adopted its constitution in 1878, was a national labor union that sought the eight-hour day, abolition of child labor, and equal pay for equal work. The organization grew to more than 700,000 workers, but rapidly declined due to unsuccessful strikes and the formation of the American Federation of Labor in 1886.

The recent alarming development and aggression of aggregated wealth, which, unless checked, will inevitably lead to the pauperization and hopeless degradation of the toiling masses, renders it imperative, if we desire to enjoy the blessings of life, that a check should be placed upon its power and upon unjust accumulation, and a system adopted which will secure to the laborer the fruits of his toil; and as this much-desired object can only be accomplished by the thorough unification of labor, and the united efforts of those who obey the divine injunction that "In the sweat of thy brow shalt thou eat bread," we have formed the Noble Order of the Knights of Labor with a view of securing the organization and direction, by co-operative effort, of the power of the industrial classes; and we submit to the world the objects sought to be accomplished by our organization, calling upon all who believe in securing "the greatest good to the greatest number" to aid and assist us. . . .

# Preamble to the Platform of the Populist Party

*T*he People's, or Populist, Party adopted its party platform in 1892 at its national convention in Omaha, Nebraska. The movement, which emerged from the Farmer's Alliance in the 1880s, sought political reforms and a redistribution of political and economic power.

The conditions which surround us best justify our co-operation; we meet in the midst of a nation brought to the verge of moral, political, and material ruin. Corruption dominates the ballot-box, the Legislatures, the Congress, and touches even the ermine of the bench. . . . The fruits of the toil of millions are boldly stolen to build up colossal fortunes for a few, unprecedented in the history of mankind; and the possessors of these, in turn, despise the Republic and endanger liberty. From the same prolific womb of governmental injustice we breed the two great classes—tramps and millionaires. . . .

We have witnessed for more than a quarter of a century the struggles of the two great political parties for power and plunder, while grievous wrongs have been inflicted upon the suffering people. We charge that the controlling influences dominating both these parties have permitted the existing dreadful conditions to develop without serious effort to prevent or restrain them. . . .

We believe that the power of government—in other words, of the people—should be expanded . . . to the end that oppression, injustice, and poverty shall eventually cease in the land. . . .

## *Emma Lazarus*
## "The New Colossus"

*A*t the dedication of the Statue of Liberty in 1886, President Grover Cleveland spoke of the Statue of Liberty as a symbol of Franco-American friendship and American ideals. But Jewish American poet Emma Lazarus saw the statue as a shining beacon to the millions who were migrating to the United States. The poem that she wrote to help raise money for the statue's pedestal is today carved on that pedestal for all to read.

Not like the brazen giant of Greek fame,
With conquering limbs astride from land to land;
Here at our sea-washed, sunset gates shall stand
A mighty woman with a torch, whose flame
Is the imprisoned lightning, and her name
Mother of Exiles.  From her beacon-hand
Glows world-wide welcome; her mild eyes command
The air-bridged harbor that twin cities frame,
"Keep, ancient lands, your storied pomp!" cries she
With silent lips.  "Give me your tired, your poor,
Your huddled masses yearning to breathe free,
The wretched refuse of your teeming shore,
Send these, the homeless, tempest-tossed to me,
I lift my lamp beside the golden door!"

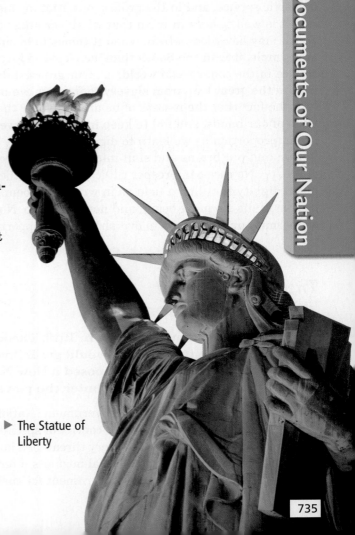

▶ The Statue of Liberty

## Booker T. Washington
## The Atlantic Exposition Address

*I*n 1895, African American leader Booker T. Washington addressed a predominantly white audience in Atlanta. He urged fellow blacks to build friendly relations with whites and to start "at the bottom" by working at "the common occupations of life." Other black leaders rejected Washington's plan and called it the "Atlanta Compromise."

. . . Ignorant and inexperienced, it is not strange that in the first years of our new life we began at the top instead of at the bottom; that a seat in Congress or the state legislature was more sought than real estate or industrial skill; that the political convention or stump speaking had more attractions than starting a dairy farm or truck garden. . . .

To those of my race who depend on bettering their condition in a foreign land or who underestimate the importance of cultivating friendly relations with the Southern white man, who is their next-door neighbor, I would say: "Cast down your bucket where you are"— cast it down in making friends in every manly way of the people of all races by whom we are surrounded.

Cast it down in agriculture, mechanics, in commerce, in domestic service, and in the professions. And in this connection it is well to bear in mind that whatever other sins the South may be called to bear, when it comes to business, pure and simple, it is in the South that the Negro is given a man's chance in the commercial world. . . . Our greatest danger is that in the great leap from slavery to freedom we may overlook the fact that the masses of us are to live by the productions of our hands, and fail to keep in mind that we shall prosper in proportion as we learn to dignify and glorify common labour, and put brains and skill into the common occupations of life. . . . No race can prosper till it learns that there is as much dignity in tilling a field as in writing a poem. It is at the bottom of life we must begin, and not at the top. Nor should we permit our grievances to overshadow our opportunities. . . .

▲ Booker T. Washington

## Theodore Roosevelt
## "The New Nationalism"

*A*t Ossowatomie, Kansas, in 1910, Theodore Roosevelt formulated the themes that would guide his 1912 campaign for the presidency. He proposed a New Nationalism that would promote human welfare and counter the power of big business.

. . . Now, this means that our government, National and State, must be freed from the sinister influence or control of special interests. Exactly as the special interests of cotton and slavery threatened our political integrity before the Civil War, so now the great special business interests too often control and corrupt the men and methods of government for their own profit. . . .

It has become entirely clear that we must have government supervision of the capitalization, not only of public-service corporations, including, particularly, railways, but of all corporations doing an interstate business. . . .

Combinations in industry are the result of an imperative economic law which cannot be repealed by political legislation. The effort at prohibiting all combination has substantially failed. The way out lies, not in attempting to prevent such combinations, but in completely controlling them in the interest of the public welfare. . . .

This New Nationalism regards the executive power as the steward of the public welfare. It demands of the judiciary that it shall be interested primarily in human welfare rather than in property, just as it demands that the representative body shall represent all the people rather than any one class or section of the people. . . .

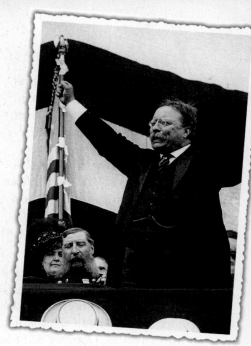

▲ Theodore Roosevelt delivering a campaign speech

## Woodrow Wilson
## "Peace Without Victory"

On January 22, 1917, before the United States entered World War I, President Wilson spoke to the U.S. Senate about his vision for the future. He called for a "peace without victory." His ideas would later influence international cooperation in the League of Nations.

. . . It must be a peace without victory. . . . Victory would mean peace forced upon the loser, a victor's terms imposed upon the vanquished. It would be accepted in humiliation, under duress, at an intolerable sacrifice, and would leave a sting, a resentment, a bitter memory upon which terms of peace would rest, not permanently but only as upon quicksand. Only a peace between equals can last. . . .

No peace can last, or ought to last, which does not recognize and accept the principle that governments derive all their just powers from the consent of the governed, and that no right anywhere exists to hand peoples about from sovereignty to sovereignty as if they were property. . . .

There can be no sense of safety and equality among the nations if great preponderating armaments are henceforth to continue here and there to be built up and maintained. The statesmen of the world must plan for peace, and nations must adjust and accommodate their policy. . . .

I am proposing that all nations henceforth avoid entangling alliances which would draw them into competitions of power, catch them in a net of intrigue and selfish rivalry, and disturb their own. . . . There is no entangling alliance in a concert of power. When all unite to act in the same sense and with the same purpose, all act in the common interest and are free to live their own lives under a common protection. . . .

## Franklin D. Roosevelt
## First Inaugural Address

▲ Franklin D. Roosevelt greets supporters.

*B*y 1933, the depression had reached its depth. Roosevelt's first inaugural address outlined in broad terms how he hoped to govern. He advised Americans "that the only thing we have to fear is fear itself." He reminded Americans that the nation's "common difficulties" concerned "only material things."

. . . This great Nation will endure as it has endured, will revive and will prosper. So, first of all, let me assert my firm belief that the only thing we have to fear is fear itself—nameless, unreasoning, unjustified terror which paralyzes needed efforts to convert retreat into advance. In every dark hour of our national life a leadership of frankness and vigor has met with that understanding and support of the people themselves which is essential to victory. I am convinced that you will again give that support to leadership in these critical days. . . .

I am prepared under my constitutional duty to recommend the measures that a stricken nation in the midst of a stricken world may require. These measures, or such other measures as the Congress may build out of its experience and wisdom, I shall seek, within my constitutional authority, to bring to speedy adoption.

But in the event that the Congress shall fail to take one of these two courses, and in the event that the national emergency is still critical, I shall not evade the clear course of duty that will then confront me. I shall ask the Congress for the one remaining instrument to meet the crisis—broad Executive power to wage a war against the emergency, as great as the power that would be given to me if we were in fact invaded by a foreign foe. . . .

## George Kennan
## "The Sources of Soviet Conduct"

*G*eorge Kennan published this article anonymously in the July 1947 issue of *Foreign Affairs*. He opposed appeasement and promoted firm opposition to the expansion of communism. His ideas on "containment" became the basis for U.S. policy toward the Soviet Union during the Cold War.

. . . In these circumstances it is clear that the main element of any United States policy toward the Soviet Union must be that of long-term, patient but firm and vigilant containment of Russian expansive tendencies. . . .

The Soviet pressure against the free institutions of the western world is something that can be contained by the adroit and vigilant application of counter-force at a series of constantly shifting geographical and political points, corresponding to the shifts and maneuvers of Soviet policy, but which cannot be charmed or talked out of existence. The Russians look forward to a duel of infinite duration, and they see that already they have scored great successes. . . .

The issue of Soviet-American relations is in essence a test of the overall worth of the United States as a nation among nations. To avoid destruction the United States need only measure up to its own best traditions and prove itself worthy of preservation as a great nation. . . .

## The Pledge of Allegiance

The Pledge of Allegiance was first written in 1892. It was revised twice before 1954, when the words "under God" were added, and it became the version that is still recited today.

I pledge allegiance to the Flag of the United States of America, and to the Republic for which it stands, one Nation under God, indivisible, with liberty and justice for all.

▲ A new citizen salutes the flag.

## *Dwight D. Eisenhower* Farewell Address

On January 17, 1961, President Eisenhower delivered his farewell to the American people on national television. To the surprise of the American people, the general who had led America to victory in World War II issued a strong warning about the dangers of the "military-industrial complex."

. . . Until the latest of our world conflicts, the United States had no armaments industry. American makers of plowshares could, with time and as required, make swords as well. But now we can no longer risk emergency improvisation of national defense; we have been compelled to create a permanent armaments industry of vast proportions. . . .

This conjunction of an immense military establishment and a large arms industry is new in the American experience. The total influence—economic, political, even spiritual—is felt in every city, every state house, every office of the Federal government. We recognize the imperative need for this development. Yet we must not fail to comprehend its grave implications. . . .

We must never let the weight of this combination endanger our liberties or democratic processes. We should take nothing for granted. Only an alert and knowledgeable citizenry can compel the proper meshing of huge industrial and military machinery of defense with our peaceful methods and goals, so that security and liberty may prosper together. . . .

## John F. Kennedy
## Inaugural Address

On January 20, 1961, President John F. Kennedy delivered his inaugural address in which he announced to the world that "we shall pay any price, bear any burden, meet any hardship, support any friend, oppose any foe, in order to assure the survival and success of liberty."

... Let the word go forth from this time and place, to friend and foe alike, that the torch has been passed to a new generation of Americans—born in this century, tempered by war, disciplined by a hard and bitter peace, proud of our ancient heritage—and unwilling to witness or permit the slow undoing of those human rights to which this Nation has always been committed, and to which we are committed today at home and around the world.

Let every nation know, whether it wishes us well or ill, that we shall pay any price, bear any burden, meet any hardship, support any friend, oppose any foe, in order to assure the survival and the success of liberty. ...

Now the trumpet summons us again—not as a call to bear arms, though arms we need; not as a call to battle, though embattled we are—but a call to bear the burden of a long twilight struggle, year in and year out, "rejoicing in hope, patient in tribulation"—a struggle against the common enemies of man: tyranny, poverty, disease, and war itself. ...

In the long history of the world, only a few generations have been granted the role of defending freedom in its hour of maximum danger. I do not shrink from this responsibility—I welcome it. ...

And so, my fellow Americans: ask not what your country can do for you—ask what you can do for your country.

My fellow citizens of the world: ask not what America will do for you, but what together we can do for the freedom of man. ...

▲ President Kennedy giving his Inaugural Address

## Martin Luther King, Jr.
## Letter from Birmingham Jail

In 1963, King led a campaign of nonviolent protest against segregation and discrimination in Birmingham, Alabama. Rather than obey a court order to desist, King went to jail. From there, he wrote a response to white Alabama clergymen who were urging King to be more moderate in his struggle. King responded that the wait for civil rights had been too long and that civil disobedience against unjust laws was needed to achieve social justice.

My Dear Fellow Clergymen,

While confined here in the Birmingham City Jail, I came across your recent statement calling our present activities "unwise and untimely." ...

We have waited for more than 340 years for our constitutional and God-given rights. The nations of Asia and Africa are moving with jetlike speed toward the goal of political independence, and we still creep at horse and buggy pace toward the gaining of a cup of coffee at a lunch counter.

I guess it is easy for those who have never felt the stinging darts of segregation to say wait. But when you have seen vicious mobs lynch your mothers and fathers at will and drown your sisters and brothers at whim; when you have seen hate-filled policemen curse, kick, brutalize, and even kill your black brothers and sisters with impunity; when you see the vast majority of your 20 million Negro brothers smothering in an airtight cage of poverty in the midst of an affluent society; when you suddenly find your tongue twisted and your speech stammering as you seek to explain to your six-year-old daughter why she can't go to the public amusement park that has just been advertised on television, and see the tears welling up in her little eyes when she is told that Funtown is closed to colored children, . . . then you will understand why we find it difficult to wait. . . .

You express a great deal of anxiety over our willingness to break laws. . . . The answer is found in the fact that there are two types of laws: There are just and there are unjust laws. I would agree with Saint Augustine that "An unjust law is no law at all." . . .

All segregation statutes are unjust because segregation distorts the soul and damages the personality. It gives the segregator a false sense of superiority, and the segregated a false sense of inferiority. . . .

Let us all hope that the dark clouds of racial prejudice will soon pass away and the deep fog of misunderstanding will be lifted from our fear-drenched communities and in some not too distant tomorrow the radiant stars of love and brotherhood will shine over our great nation with all their scintillating beauty.

Yours for the cause of Peace and Brotherhood,
Martin Luther King, Jr.

▲ A reflective King in his Birmingham jail cell

## *Betty Friedan*
## The Feminine Mystique

**B**etty Friedan's book exploded onto the American scene in 1963. Her work sparked a national debate about women's roles and was a pivotal event in the modern women's movement.

◀ Betty Friedan

. . . It . . . is time to stop giving lip service to the idea that there are no battles left to be fought for women in America, that women's rights have already been won. It is ridiculous to tell girls to keep quiet when they enter a new field, or an old one, so the men will not notice they are there. In almost every professional field, in business and in the arts and sciences, women are still treated as second-class citizens. . . . A girl should not expect special privileges because of her sex, but neither should she "adjust" to prejudice and discrimination.

She must learn to compete then, not as a woman, but as a human being. Not until a great many women move out of the fringes into the mainstream will society itself provide the arrangements for their new plan. . . .

## Lyndon Johnson
## Voting Rights

*P*resident Johnson made this speech to Congress on March 15, 1965, a week after deadly racial violence erupted in Selma, Alabama. He used the phrase "we shall overcome," borrowed from African American leaders struggling for equal rights.

. . . There is no Negro problem. There is no Southern problem. There is no Northern problem. There is only an American problem. And we are met here tonight as Americans—not as Democrats or Republicans—we are met here as Americans to solve that problem. . . .

Many of the issues of civil rights are very complex and most difficult. But about this there can and should be no argument. Every American citizen must have an equal right to vote.

Yet the harsh fact is that in many places in this country men and women are kept from voting simply because they are Negroes. . . .

Wednesday I will send to Congress a law designed to eliminate illegal barriers to the right to vote. . . .

But even if we pass this bill, the battle will not be over. What happened in Selma is part of a far larger movement which reaches into every section and State of America. It is the effort of American Negroes to secure for themselves the full blessings of American life.

Their cause must be our cause too. Because it is not just Negroes, but really it is all of us, who must overcome the crippling legacy of bigotry and injustice.

And we shall overcome. . . .

## Richard Nixon
## Resignation Speech

*I*n the shadow of the Watergate scandal, President Nixon delivered his resignation speech on August 8, 1974. The next morning, he signed the resignation documents, made a final speech to his staff, and stepped onto the Marine One helicopter for the last time, to begin a trip to California as an ex-President.

. . . I have concluded that because of the Watergate matter I might not have the support of the Congress that I would consider necessary to back the very difficult decisions and carry out the duties of this office in the way the interests of the Nation would require. . . .

To continue to fight through the months ahead for my personal vindication would almost totally absorb the time and attention of both the President and the Congress in a period when our entire focus should be on the great issues of peace abroad and prosperity without inflation at home.

Therefore, I shall resign the Presidency effective at noon tomorrow. Vice President Ford will be sworn in as President at that hour in this office. . . .

▲ Richard Nixon leaves the White House after resigning from the presidency.

## Jimmy Carter
## "Crisis of Confidence"

*I*n the 1970s, Americans struggled with the aftermath of the Vietnam War and the Watergate scandal. Economic problems and an energy crisis added to the malaise. On July 15, 1979, in a nationally televised address, President Carter identified what he believed to be a "crisis of confidence" among the American people.

. . . I want to talk to you right now about a fundamental threat to American democracy. . . . It is a crisis of confidence . . . that strikes at the very heart and soul and spirit of our national will. We can see this crisis in the growing doubt about the meaning of our own lives and in the loss of a unity of purpose for our nation. . . .

In a nation that was proud of hard work, strong families, close-knit communities, and our faith in God, too many of us now tend to worship self-indulgence and consumption. Human identity is no longer defined by what one does, but by what one owns. But we've discovered that owning things and consuming things does not satisfy our longing for meaning. . . .

As you know, there is a growing disrespect for government and for churches and for schools, the news media, and other institutions. This is not a message of happiness or reassurance, but it is the truth and it is a warning. . . .

## Cesar Chavez
## Commonwealth Club Address

*T*he Commonwealth Club of California, the nation's oldest public affairs forum, has hosted diverse speakers, including Theodore Roosevelt, Martin Luther King, Jr., Ronald Reagan, and Bill Gates. In 1984, Cesar Chavez spoke about the United Farm Workers and progress for Latinos.

▲ Cesar Chavez

. . . The United Farm Workers is first and foremost a union. . . . But the UFW has always been something more than a union. . . .

The UFW's survival . . . was not in doubt . . . after the union became visible, when Chicanos started entering college in greater numbers, when Hispanics began running for public office in greater numbers, when our people started asserting their rights on a broad range of issues and in many communities across this land. The union survival, its very existence, sent out a signal to all Hispanics that we were fighting for our dignity, that we were challenging and overcoming injustice, that we were empowering the least educated among us, the poorest among us.

The message was clear. If it could happen in the fields, it could happen anywhere: in the cities, in the courts, in the city councils, in the state legislatures. I didn't really appreciate it at the time, but the coming of our union signaled the start of great changes among Hispanics that are only now beginning to be seen. . . .

Like the other immigrant groups, the day will come when we win the economic and political rewards, which are in keeping with our numbers in society. . . .

## William Clinton
## Second Inaugural Address

◀ President William Clinton

**P**resident Clinton took the oath of office for a second term on January 20, 1997. This was the last inaugural address of the twentieth century, and Clinton looked optimistically to the challenges that lay ahead in the next century.

. . . The world is no longer divided into two hostile camps. Instead, now we are building bonds with nations that once were our adversaries. Growing connections of commerce and culture give us a chance to lift the fortunes and spirits of people the world over. And for the very first time in all of history, more people on this planet live under democracy than dictatorship. . . .

Our land of new promise will be a nation that meets its obligations, a nation that balances its budget, but never loses the balance of its values. A nation where our grandparents have secure retirement and health care, and their grandchildren know we have made the reforms necessary to sustain those benefits for their time. A nation that fortifies the world's most productive economy even as it protects the great natural bounty of our water, air, and majestic land. . . .

## George W. Bush
## War on Terror Speech

▼ President Bush addresses rescue at the World Trade Center site.

**O**n September 11, 2001, terrorists hijacked and crashed passenger jets into the World Trade Center in New York City and the Pentagon Building in Washington, D.C. On September 20, President Bush addressed a joint session of Congress and announced to the nation a war on terrorism.

. . . Americans have known surprise attacks, but never before on thousands of civilians. All of this was brought upon us in a single day, and night fell on a different world, a world where freedom itself is under attack. . . .

The evidence we have gathered all points to a collection of loosely affiliated terrorist organizations known as al Qaeda.

The terrorists practice a fringe form of Islamic extremism that has been rejected by Muslim scholars and the vast majority of Muslim clerics; a fringe movement that perverts the peaceful teachings of Islam. . . .

Our war on terror begins with al Qaeda, but it does not end there. It will not end until every terrorist group of global reach has been found, stopped and defeated.

Americans are asking "Why do they hate us?" They hate what they see right here in this chamber: a democratically elected government. Their leaders are self-appointed. They hate our freedoms: our freedom of religion, our freedom of speech, our freedom to vote and assemble and disagree. . . .

Our response involves far more than instant retaliation and isolated strikes. Americans should not expect one battle, but a lengthy campaign unlike any other we have ever seen. . . .

We will rally the world to this cause by our efforts, by our courage. We will not tire, we will not falter and we will not fail. . . .

# A

**abolitionist** reformer who sought to end slavery (p. 36)
   **abolicionista** reformador que abogaba por dar fin a la esclavitud

**Acquired Immunodeficiency Syndrome (AIDS)** a disease with no known cure that attacks the immune system of its victims. It began spreading in the early 1980s and remains a serious global health crisis today (p. 637)
   **Síndrome de Inmunodeficiencia Adquirida (SIDA)** una enfermedad para la que no se conoce cura que ataca el sistema inmunitario de sus víctimas; empezó a extenderse a principios de la década de 1980 y aún hoy sigue representando una seria crisis de salud mundial

**affirmative action** policy that gives special consideration to women and minorities to make up for past discrimination (pp. 600, 681)
   **acción afirmativa** política que da trato especial a las mujeres y minorías para resarcirlas de la discriminación del pasado

**AFL-CIO** in 1955, the American Federation of Labor (AFL) and the Congress of Industrial Organization (CIO) labor unions united (p. 446)
   **AFL-CIO** en 1955 los sindicatos de trabajadores, la Federación Estadounidense del Trabajo y el Congreso de Organización Industrial, se unieron

**Alien Act** 1798 law that allowed the government to imprison or deport aliens (p. 23)
   **Ley de Extranjeros** ley de 1798 que permitió al gobierno encarcelar o deportar extranjeros

**Alliance for Progress** President Kennedy's program which provided economic assistance to Latin America (p. 507)
   **Alianza para el Progreso** programa del presidente Kennedy que daba asistencia económica a América Latina

**Allies** group of countries led by Britain, France, the United States, and the Soviet Union that fought the Axis Powers in World War II (p. 333)
   **Aliados** grupo de países encabezado por Gran Bretaña, Francia, Estados Unidos y la Unión Soviética que peleó contra los Poderes del Eje en la Segunda Guerra Mundial

**al Qaeda** terrorist group established by Osama bin Laden to rid Muslim countries of Western influence (p. 670)
   **al Qaida** grupo terrorista establecido por Osama bin Laden para eliminar la influencia occidental en los países musulmanes

**Alsace-Lorraine** territory lost to Germany by France in 1871 (p. 618)
   **Alsacia y Lorena** territorio que Francia perdió ante Alemania en 1871

**American Federation of Labor (AFL)** labor union that organized skilled workers in a specific trade and focused on specific workers' issues rather than broad issues (p. 71)
   **Federación Estadounidense del Trabajo** sindicato de trabajadores que organizó a los trabajadores calificados en oficios específicos y se enfocó más en los problemas de trabajadores específicos que en aspectos más amplios

**American Indian Movement (AIM)** group that focused on helping Indians, including the securing of legal rights, land, and self-government for Native Americans (p. 583)
   **Movimiento de Indígenas Estadounidenses** grupo que se concentró en ayudar a los indígenas, incluyendo velar por sus derechos legales, tierra y de autodeterminación

**Americanization** belief that assimilating immigrants into American society would make them more loyal citizens (p. 116)
   **americanización** creencia que sostenía que la asimilación de los inmigrantes por la sociedad estadounidense los haría ciudadanos más leales

**amnesty** general pardon for certain crimes (p. 609)
   **amnistía** perdón general de ciertos delitos

**Anaconda Plan** Northern Civil War strategy to starve the South by blockading seaports and controlling the Mississippi River (p. 49)
   **Plan Anaconda** estrategia del Norte en la Guerra Civil de llevar al Sur a la rendición por inanición al bloquear los puertos marinos y controlar el río Mississippi

**anarchist** one who opposes all forms of government (p. 71)
   **anarquista** aquél que se opone a todas las formas de gobierno

**Angel Island** island in San Francisco Bay that served as an immigration station for Asian immigrants (p. 74)
   **Isla Ángel** isla de la bahía de San Francisco que se usó como puesto de migración para los inmigrantes asiáticos

**Anschluss** union of Germany and Austria in 1933 (p. 330)
   **Anschluss** unión de Alemania y Austria en 1933

**Anti-Defamation League** organization formed in 1913 to defend Jews against physical and verbal attacks and false statements (p. 119)
   **Liga Antidifamación** organización formada en 1913 para defender a los judíos contra los ataques físicos y verbales y las falsas declaraciones

**anti-Semitism** prejudice and discrimination against Jewish people (pp. 327, 380)
   **antisemitismo** prejuicios contra las personas judías

**apartheid** political system of strict segregation by race in South Africa (p. 646)
   **apartheid** sistema político de segregación intransigente basada en la raza, en Sudáfrica

**appeasement** policy of granting concessions in order to keep the peace (p. 329)
   **apaciguamiento** política de otorgar concesiones a fin de mantener la paz

**arms race** contest in which nations compete to build more powerful weapons (p. 413)

**carrera armamentista** competencia en la que las naciones se enfrentan para construir armas más poderosas

**assembly line** arrangement of equipment and workers in which work passes from operation to operation in direct line until the product is assembled (p. 213)

**línea de ensamblaje** organización de equipos y trabajadores en la que el trabajo pasa de una operación a otra en una línea directa hasta que el producto queda ensamblado

**assimilate** to be absorbed into the main culture of a society (p. 84)

**asimilarse** ser absorbido por la cultura dominante de una sociedad

**Atlantic Charter** a joint declaration made in August 1941 by Great Britain and the United States, during World War II, that endorsed national self-determination and an international system of general security (p. 338)

**Carta del Atlántico** declaración conjunta de agosto de 1941 entre Gran Bretaña y Estados Unidos, durante la Segunda Guerra Mundial, que aprobaba la autodeterminación nacional y un sistema internacional de seguridad general

**Axis Powers** group of countries led by Germany, Italy, and Japan that fought the Allies in World War II (p. 333)

**Poderes del Eje** grupo de países encabezado por Alemania, Italia y Japón que peleó contra los Aliados en la Segunda Guerra Mundial

# B

**baby boom** increase in births between 1945 and 1964 (p. 435)

*baby boom* aumento de nacimientos entre 1945 y 1964

**Bataan Death March** during World War II, the forced march of American and Filipino prisoners of war under brutal conditions by the Japanese military (p. 345)

**Marcha de la Muerte de Batán** durante la Segunda Guerra Mundial, la marcha forzada de prisioneros de guerra estadounidenses y filipinos en condiciones brutales impuestas por los militares japoneses

**Battle of the Bulge** in December 1944, Hitler ordered a counterattack on Allied troops in Belgium, but it crippled Germany by using up reserves and demoralizing its troops (p. 375)

**batalla de las Ardenas** en diciembre de 1944, Hitler ordenó un contraataque contra las tropas aliadas en Bélgica, pero esto debilitó a Alemania al usar todas sus reservas y desmoralizar a sus tropas

**Battle of Coral Sea** World War II battle that took place in May 1942 in the Pacific theater between Japanese and American aircraft carriers (p. 347)

**batalla del Mar del Coral** batalla entre aviones japoneses y estadounidenses, durante la Segunda Guerra Mundial, ocurrida en mayo de 1942 en el escenario del Pacífico

**Battle of Gettysburg** one of the bloodiest battles of the Civil War, it marked the last major Confederate attempt to invade the North (p. 52)

**batalla de Gettysburg** una de las batallas más sangrientas de la Guerra Civil, marcó el último intento importante de los Confederados por invadir el Norte

**Battle of Midway** turning point of World War II in the Pacific, in which the Japanese advance was stopped (p. 360)

**batalla de Midway** momento decisivo de la Segunda Guerra Mundial en el Pacífico, en que se detuvo el avance de los japoneses

**Bay of Pigs invasion** 1961 failed invasion of Cuba by a CIA-led force of Cuban exiles (p. 508)

**invasión de bahía de Cochinos** invasión de 1961 por exilados cubanos encabezados por la CIA que fracasaron al tratar de invadir Cuba

**beatniks** small group of writers and artists, in the 1950s and early 1960s, who were critical of American society (p. 456)

*beatniks* pequeño grupo de escritores y artistas, en la década de 1950 y principios de los 1960, que criticaban a la sociedad estadounidense

**Berlin airlift** program in which U.S. and British pilots flew supplies to West Berlin during a Soviet blockade (p. 404)

**puente aéreo de Berlín** programa en el que pilotos estadounidenses y británicos volaban llevando suministros a Berlín Occidental durante un bloqueo soviético

**Berlin Wall** dividing wall built by East Germany in 1961 to isolate West Berlin from Communist-controlled East Berlin (p. 510)

**Muro de Berlín** pared divisoria construida por Alemania Oriental en 1961 para aislar a Berlín Occidental del Berlín Oriental controlado por los comunistas

**"big stick" diplomacy** Roosevelt's policy of creating and using, when necessary, a strong military to achieve America's goals (p. 157)

**diplomacia de "mano dura"** política seguida por Roosevelt según la cual se organizaría y usaría, cuando fuera necesario, una fuerza militar poderosa para lograr los objetivos de Estados Unidos

**bilingual education** system in which students are taught in their native languages as well as in English (p. 680)

**educación bilingüe** sistema en el que se enseña a los estudiantes en su idioma nativo así como en inglés

**bill of rights** written list of freedoms guaranteed to citizens by the government (p. 15)

**declaración de derechos** listado escrito de las libertades que el gobierno garantiza a sus ciudadanos

**biotechnology** the application of technology to solving problems affecting living organisms (p. 657)

**biotecnología** aplicación de la tecnología para resolver problemas que afectan a los organismos vivos

**Black Cabinet** group of African American leaders who served as unofficial advisers to Franklin D. Roosevelt (p. 302)

**Gabinete Negro** grupo de líderes afroestadounidenses que fungieron como consejeros extraoficiales de Franklin D. Roosevelt

**blacklist** list of persons who were not hired because of suspected communist ties (p. 422)

**lista negra** lista de personas que no fueron contratadas por sospechas de vínculos comunistas

**Black Panthers** organization of militant African Americans founded in 1966 (p. 493)

**Panteras Negras** organización de militantes afroestadounidenses fundada en 1966

**black power** movement in the 1960s that urged African Americans to use their collective political and economic power to gain equality (p. 493)

**poder negro** movimiento de la década de 1960 que exhortó a los afroestadounidenses a usar su poder político y económico colectivo para lograr la igualdad

**Black Tuesday** October 29, 1929, when stock prices fell sharply in the Great Crash (p. 258)

**Martes Negro** 29 de octubre de 1929, el día en que los precios de las acciones cayeron precipitadamente en la Gran Caída de la Bolsa

**blitzkrieg** "lightning war" that emphasized the use of speed and firepower to penetrate deep into the enemy's territory (p. 333)

*blitzkrieg* "guerra relámpago" que enfatiza el uso de velocidad y capacidad bélica para penetrar muy adentro en el territorio enemigo, usada por Alemania en la Segunda Guerra Mundial

**boat people** refugees who leave their country by boat (p. 616)

**balseros** refugiados que dejan su país en bote

**Bonus Army** a group of World War I veterans who marched on Washington, D.C., in 1932 to demand early payment of a bonus promised them by Congress for their military service (p. 275)

**Ejército del Bono** grupo de veteranos de la Primera Guerra Mundial que marcharon sobre Washington, D.C., en 1932, para exigir el pago anticipado de un bono que les prometiera el Congreso por sus servicios militares

**bootlegger** one who sells illegal alcohol (p. 230)

**contrabandista** quien vende alcohol ilegalmente

**Boxer Rebellion** violence started by members of a secret society in China, which prompted the governments of Europe and America to send troops to squash the rebellion (p. 154)

**Rebelión de los Bóxer** actos de violencia iniciados por miembros de una sociedad secreta en China, que provocó los gobiernos de Europa y América enviaran tropas para sofocar la rebelión

**bracero program** plan that brought laborers from Mexico to work on American farms (p. 363)

**programa de braceros** plan que trajo trabajadores de México a trabajar en granjas estadounidenses

**Brady Bill** law passed in 1993 requiring a waiting period on sales of handguns, along with a criminal background check on the buyer (p. 663)

**Ley Brady** ley aprobada en 1993 que exige un período de espera de cinco días para la venta de revólveres, junto con una verificación de los antecedentes delictivos del comprador

**bread line** line of people waiting for food handouts from charities or public agencies (p. 262)

**cola de alimentación** fila de personas que esperan alimentos gratuitos de obras caritativas o agencias públicas

**brinkmanship** belief that only by going to the brink of war could the United States protect against communist aggression (p. 414)

**teoría del equilibrio del terror** creencia según la que sólo estando al borde de la guerra Estados Unidos podía protegerse contra la agresión comunista

**budget deficit** shortfall between the amount of money spent and the amount taken in by the federal government (p. 634)

**déficit presupuestario** faltante entre la cantidad de dinero gastado y la cantidad de dinero captado por el gobierno federal

**bull market** period of rising stock prices (p. 216)

**mercado alcista** período durante el cual suben los precios de las acciones

**business cycle** periodic growth and contraction of the economy (p. 258)

**ciclo commercial** crecimiento y contracción periódicos de la economía

**buying on margin** margin system of buying stocks in which a buyer pays a small percentage of the purchase price while the broker advances the rest (p. 216)

**compra al margen** sistema de compra de acciones en el que el comprador paga un pequeño porcentaje del precio de compra mientras que el corredor anticipa el resto

# C

**California Master Plan** called for three tiers of higher education: research universities, state colleges, and community colleges, all of which were to be accessible to all of the state's citizens (p. 447)

**Plan Maestro de California** hizo un llamado para la creación de tres niveles de educación superior: universidades de investigación, universidades estatales y centros educacionales comunitarios, los cuales deberían ser accesibles para todos los ciudadanos del estado

**Camp David Accords** 1978 agreement brokered by President Jimmy Carter between Egyptian and Israeli leaders that made a peace treaty between the two nations possible (p. 618)
**Acuerdos de Camp David** acuerdo de 1978 agenciado por el presidente Jimmy Carter, entre los líderes de Egipto e Israel que hizo posible un tratado de paz entre ambas naciones

**casualties** soldiers killed, wounded, and missing (p. 174)
**bajas** soldados muertos, heridos y desaparecidos

**Central Intelligence Agency (CIA)** U.S. intelligence-gathering organization (p. 417)
**Agencia Central de Inteligencia** organización estadounidense para la recolección de inteligencia

**checks and balances** system in which each branch of the government has the power to monitor and limit the actions of the other branches (p. 20)
**controles y equilibrios** sistema en que cada rama del gobierno tiene el poder para vigilar y limitar las acciones de las otras ramas

**Chicano movement** movement that focused on raising Mexican American consciousness (p. 582)
**movimiento chicano** movimiento enfocado en despertar la conciencia de los estadounidenses de origen mexicano

**Christian fundamentalist** individual who believes in a strict, literal interpretation of the Bible as the foundation of the Christian faith (p. 608)
**fundamentalista cristiano** persona que cree en la interpretación estricta y literal de la Biblia como el fundamento de la fe cristiana

**civil disobedience** nonviolent refusal to follow laws that one considers to be immoral (p. 36)
**desobediencia civil** práctica de renuencia pacífica a obedecer las leyes que una persona considera inmorales

**Civilian Conservation Corps (CCC)** New Deal program that provided young men with relief jobs on environmental conservation projects, including reforestation and flood control (p. 288)
**Cuerpos de Conservación Civil** programa del Nuevo Trato que proporcionaba ayuda a los jóvenes con trabajo en proyectos de conservación del medio ambiente, incluyendo reforestación y control de inundaciones

**Civil Rights Act of 1957** law that established a federal Civil Rights Commission (p. 473)
**Ley de Derechos Civiles de 1957** ley que estableció una Comisión Federal de Derechos Civiles

**Civil Rights Act of 1964** outlawed discrimination in public places and employment based on race, religion, or national origin (pp. 484, 518)
**Ley de Derechos Civiles de 1964** conjunto de leyes que prohibió la discriminación en lugares y empleos públicos con base en la raza, religión o nacionalidad

**clan** groups of families related through a common ancestor (p. 5)

**clan** grupo de familias relacionadas a través de un ancestro común

**Clayton Antitrust Act** 1914 law that strengthened the Sherman Antitrust Act (p. 130)
**Ley Clayton Antimonopolio** ley de 1914 que fortalecía la Ley Sherman Antimonopolio

**Clean Air Act** act passed in 1970 that lessened air pollution by limiting the emissions from factories and automobiles (p. 588)
**Ley para el Aire Puro** ley aprobada en 1970 que buscaba disminuir la contaminación del aire al limitar las emisiones de fábricas y automóviles

**Clean Water Act** 1973 law that restricted the pollution of water by industry and agriculture (p. 588)
**Ley para el Agua Limpia** ley aprobada en 1973 que buscaba restringir la contaminación industrial y agrícola del agua

**Cold War** worldwide rivalry between the United States and the Soviet Union (p. 400)
**Guerra Fría** rivalidad mundial entre Estados Unidos y la Unión Soviética

**collective bargaining** process in which employers negotiate with labor unions about hours, wages, and other working conditions (p. 296)
**negociación colectiva** proceso en el que los patronos negocian con los sindicatos sobre los horarios, salarios y otras condiciones de trabajo

**Columbian Exchange** the global exchange of goods and ideas between Europe, Africa, and the Americas after Columbus made his first transatlantic voyage in 1492 (p. 8)
**intercambio colombino** intercambio global de bienes e ideas entre Europa, Africa y las Americas posterior al primer viaje transatlántico de Colón en 1492

**Committee on Public Information (CPI)** government agency created during World War I to encourage Americans to support the war (p. 182)
**Comité de Información Pública** organización creada por el gobierno durante la Primera Guerra Mundial para animar al público estadounidense a apoyar la guerra

**commune** small communities where people share resources (p. 571)
**comunas** pequeñas comunidades en las que las personas comparten los recursos

**Compromise of 1850** agreement designed to ease the controversy over California being admitted as a free state by allowing the residents of other territories to decide the issue of slavery by popular sovereignty (p. 43)
**Acuerdo de 1850** acuerdo diseñado para aminorar la controversia sobre la admisión de California como estado libre, que permitía a los residentes de otros territorios decidieran el tema de la esclavitud por soberanía popular

**concentration camp** camps used by the Nazis to imprison "undesirable" members of society (p. 383)
**campo de concentración** campos usados por los nazis para encarcelar a miembros "indeseables" de la sociedad

**Congress of Industrial Organization (CIO)** a labor organization founded in the 1930s that represents industrial workers (p. 296)
**Congreso de Organización Industrial** organización de trabajadores fundada en la década de 1930 que representa a los trabajadores industriales

**conquistador** one of the sixteenth-century Spanish soldiers who defeated the Indian civilizations of Mexico, Central America, or Peru (p. 8)
**conquistador** en particular, uno de los soldados españoles del siglo XVI que derrotaron a las civilizaciones de México, América Central o Perú

**conscientious objector** person who refuses to fight in a war due to moral or religious beliefs (p. 182)
**objetor de conciencia** persona que rehúsa pelear en una guerra por convicciones morales o religiosas

**conservative** person who tends to support limited government involvement in the economy, favor community help for the needy, and upholds traditional values (p. 628)
**conservador** persona que tiende a apoyar una participación gubernamental limitada en la economía, favorece la ayuda comunitaria para los necesitados y mantiene los valores tradicionales

**consumerism** large-scale buying, much of it on credit (p. 448)
**consumismo** compras a gran escala, la mayoría de éstas a crédito

**consumer revolution** flood of new, affordable goods in the decades after World War I (p. 215)
**revolución de consumo** flujo de bienes nuevos y asequibles durante las decadas posteriores a la Primera Guerra Mundial

**containment** policy of keeping communism contained within its existing borders (p. 402)
**contención** política de mantener el comunismo contenido dentro de sus fronteras existentes

**Contract With America** Republican plan headed by Newt Gingrich that focused on scaling back the government, balancing the budget, and cutting taxes (p. 663)
**Contrato con Estados Unidos** plan republicano encabezado por Newt Gingrich enfocado en la reducción del gobierno, el equilibrio del presupuesto y la reducción de los impuestos

**contraband** during wartime, goods such as weapons and other articles used to fight a war that may be legally confiscated by any belligerent (p. 176)
**contrabando** en tiempos de guerra, bienes, como armas y otros artículos, usados para combatir en la guerra que pueden ser confiscados de manera legal por cualesquiera de los beligerantes

**Contras** anticommunist counterrevolutionaries who opposed the Sandinista government in Nicaragua in the 1980s (p. 640)
**Contras** contrarrevolucionarios anticomunistas opuestos al gobierno Sandinista de Nicaragua en la década de 1980

**convoy** group of merchant ships sailing together, protected by war ships (p. 189)
**convoy** grupo de buques mercantes que navegan juntos bajo la protección de buques de guerra

**cotton gin** machine invented in 1793 to separate the cotton fiber from its hard shell (p. 27)
**desmotadora** máquina inventada en 1793 para separar la fibra del algodón de la cáscara

**counterculture** movement that upheld values different from those of mainstream culture (p. 570)
**contracultura** movimiento que mantuvo valores diferentes a los de la cultura tradicional

**court packing** FDR plan to add up to six new justices to the nine-member Supreme Court after the Court had ruled that some New Deal legislation was unconstitutional (p. 298)
**plan para llenar las cortes** plan de FDR para agregar seis nuevos magistrados a los nueve miembros de la Corte Suprema luego de que la Corte dictaminó que algunas leyes del Nuevo Trato eran inconstitucionales

**"credibility gap"** the American public's growing distrust of statements made by the government during the Vietnam War (p. 546)
**"brecha de credibilidad"** creciente desconfianza del público estadounidense ante declaraciones del gobierno durante la Guerra de Vietnam

**creditor nation** country which is owed more money by other countries than it owes other countries (p. 203)
**nación acreedora** país al que otros países le deben más dinero del que éste les debe

**Cuban missile crisis** 1962 conflict between the U.S. and the Soviet Union resulting from the Soviet installation of nuclear missiles in Cuba (p. 508)
**crisis de los misiles de Cuba** conflicto entre Estados Unidos y la Unión Soviética en 1962, como resultado de la instalación de misiles nucleares en Cuba por parte de los soviéticos

# D

**Dawes Act** law enacted in 1887 that divided reservation land into private family plots (p. 84)
**Ley Dawes** ley promulgada en 1887 que dividió las tierras de reservación en parcelas privadas para familias

**Dawes Plan** agreement in which the United States loaned money to Germany, allowing Germany to make reparation payments to Britain and France (p. 222)
**Plan Dawes** acuerdo en el que Estados Unidos prestó dinero a Alemania, permitiéndole a ésta hacer

pagos de reparación a Gran Bretaña y Francia

**D-Day** June 6, 1944, the day Allies landed on the beaches of Normandy, France (p. 371)

**Día D** 6 de junio de 1944, el día en que los Aliados desembarcaron en las playas de Normandía, Francia

**death camp** Nazi camp designed for the extermination of prisoners (p. 383)

**campo de la muerte** campo diseñados por los nazis para el exterminio de prisioneros

**de facto segregation** segregation by unwritten custom or tradition (p. 468)

**segregación de facto** segregación basada en la costumbre o la tradición no escrita

**deficit spending** the practice of a nation paying out more money than it is receiving in revenues (p. 513)

**déficit de gastos** práctica de las naciones que gastan más de lo que reciben por ingresos

**de jure segregation** segregation imposed by law (p. 468)

**segregación de iure** segregación impuesta por ley

**demobilization** sending home members of the army (p. 435)

**desmovilización** enviar a los miembros del ejército de vuelta a casa

**Department of Homeland Security** Cabinet-level department created by President Bush to coordinate domestic security efforts (p. 677)

**Departamento de Seguridad Nacional** departamento a nivel de gabinete creado por el presidente Bush para coordinar los esfuerzos de seguridad interior

**deregulation** reduction or removal of government controls over an industry (p. 634)

**desregulación** reducción o eliminación de los controles gubernamentales en una industria

**détente** flexible diplomacy adopted by Richard Nixon that sought to ease tensions between the United States, the Soviet Union, and the People's Republic of China (p. 562)

**distensión** diplomacia flexible adoptada por Richard Nixon que buscó aliviar las tensiones entre Estados Unidos, la Unión Soviética y la República Popular China

**developing world** countries that are less economically and technologically advanced than developed countries such as the United States (p. 617)

**mundo en desarrollo** países que son menos avanzados económica y tecnológicamente que los países desarrollados como Estados Unidos

**direct primary** election in which citizens themselves vote to select nominees for upcoming elections (p. 106)

**primarias directas** elecciones en las que los ciudadanos votan directamente para elegir los candidatos para las siguientes elecciones.

**divest** to take away or rid oneself of (p. 646)

**desposeer** quitarse o librarse de algo

**"dollar diplomacy"** President Taft's policy of expanding American investments abroad (p. 161)

**"diplomacia del dólar"** política exterior del presidente Taft que buscaba expandir las inversiones estadounidenses en el exterior

**domino theory** idea that if a nation falls to communism, its closest neighbors will also fall under communist control (p. 534)

**teoría dominó** idea que estipulaba que si una nación cae ante el comunismo, sus vecinos más cercanos también caerán bajo el control comunista

**dove** person who opposed U.S. involvement in the Vietnam War (p. 543)

**"paloma"** persona opuesta a la participación estadounidense en la Guerra de Vietnam

**draftee** young American man drafted into military service during the Vietnam War (p. 544)

**conscripto** varón estadounidense joven reclutado para el servicio militar durante la Guerra de Vietnam

**Dust Bowl** term used for the central and southern Great Plains during the 1930s when the region suffered from drought and dust storms (p. 267)

**Cuenco de Polvo** término usado para describir las Grandes Planicies durante la década de 1930, cuando la región quedó desolada por la sequía y las tormentas de polvo

**Earth Day** annual event of environmental activism and protest, begun in 1970 (p. 587)

**Día de la Tierra** evento anual de activismo y protesta ambiental, empezó en 1970

**Economic Opportunity Act** law passed in 1964 creating the Office of Economic Opportunity to run antipoverty programs (p. 518)

**Ley de Igualdad de Oportunidades** ley aprobada en 1964 que creo la Oficina de Oportunidades Económicas para dirigir programas contra la pobreza

**Eighteenth Amendment** constitutional amendment banning the manufacture, distribution, and sale of alcohol in the United States (p. 229)

**Decimoctava Enmienda** enmienda constitucional que prohibió la fabricación, distribución y venta de alcohol en Estados Unidos

**Eisenhower Doctrine** policy of President Eisenhower that stated that the United States would use force to help any nation threatened by communism (p. 416)

**doctrina Eisenhower** política del presidente Eisenhower que indicaba que Estados Unidos usaría la fuerza para ayudar a cualquier nación amenazada por el comunismo

**Ellis Island** island in New York Harbor that served as an immigration station for millions of immigrants arriving to the United States (p. 74)

**Isla Ellis** isla en el puerto de Nueva York que se usó como puesto de migración para millones de inmigrantes que llegaron a Estados Unidos

**Emancipation Proclamation** decree by President Lincoln that freed slaves in all Confederate territory still in rebellion (p. 50)

**Proclamación de Emancipación** decreto del presidente Lincoln que liberó a los esclavos en todos los territorios confederados aún en rebelión

**embargo** government ban or restriction on trade (p. 24)

**embargo** prohibición o restricción gubernamental del comercio

**Endangered Species Act** law passed in 1973 with the purpose of protecting endangered plants and animals (p. 588)

**Ley de Especies en Peligro de Extinción** ley aprobada en 1973 con el propósito de proteger las plantas y animales en peligro de extinción

**English Bill of Rights** 1689 document that guaranteed the rights of English citizens (p. 11)

**Declaración de Derechos Inglesa** documento de 1689 que garantizó los derechos de los ciudadanos ingleses

**Enlightenment** eighteenth-century intellectual movement during which European philosophers came to believe that all problems could be solved by reason and science (p. 11)

**Ilustración** movimiento intelectual del siglo XVIII por el cual los filósofos europeos llegaron a creer que todos los problemas se pueden resolver a través del razón y la ciencia

**Environmental Protection Agency (EPA)** government agency committed to cleaning up and protecting the environment (p. 588)

**Agencia de Protección Ambiental** agencia gubernamental comprometida con la limpieza y protección del ambiente

**Equal Pay Act** law passed in 1963 that required both men and women to receive equal pay for equal work (p. 513)

**Ley de Pago Equitativo** ley aprobada en 1963 que exigió que hombres y mujeres reciban paga igual por un trabajo igual

**Equal Rights Amendment (ERA)** proposed amendment to the Constitution that guarantees gender equality (p. 575)

**Enmienda de Igualdad de Derechos** enmienda propuesta que garantiza la igualdad entre los sexos

**Espionage Act** act passed by Congress in June 1917 enacting severe penalties for anyone engaged in disloyal or treasonable activities (p. 184)

**Ley de Espionaje** ley aprobada por el Congreso en junio de 1917 que estableció penas severas para cualquiera que participara en actividades desleales o de traición

**ethnic cleansing** systematic effort to purge an area or society of an ethnic group through murder or deportation (p. 669)

**limpieza étnica** esfuerzo sistemático para purgar una zona o sociedad de un grupo étnico mediante el asesinato o la deportación

**European Union (EU)** economic and political union of European nations established in 1993 (p. 667)

**Unión Europea (UE)** unión económica y política de las naciones europeas establecida en 1993

**Executive Order 8802** World War II measure that assured fair hiring practices in any job funded by the government (p. 362)

**Orden Ejecutiva 8802** medida durante la Segunda Guerra Mundial que garantizaba prácticas justas de empleo en cualquier puesto financiado por el gobierno

**executive privilege** principle that the President has the right to keep certain communications between himself and other members of the executive branch private (p. 604)

**privilegio ejecutivo** principio que indica que el presidente tiene derecho a mantener en privado ciertas comunicaciones con otros miembros del poder ejecutivo

**extractive economy** economy in a colony where the colonizing country removed raw materials and shipped them back home to benefit its economy (p. 138)

**economía de extracción** economía de una colonia donde el país colonizador extraía materias primas y las enviaba a la madre patria para beneficiar su propia economía

# F

**Fair Deal** President Truman's legislative program that would strengthen existing New Deal reforms and establish new programs, such as national health insurance (p. 438)

**Trato Justo** programa legislativo del presidente Truman que fortalecería las reformas del Nuevo Trato y establecería nuevos programas, tales como el seguro nacional de salud

**Fair Labor Standards Act** 1938 law that set a minimum wage, a maximum workweek of 44 hours, and outlawed child labor (p. 296)

**Ley de Normas Laborales Justas** ley aprobada en 1938 que estableció el salario mínimo, y una semana laboral de un máximo de 44 horas, y prohibió el trabajo infantil

**Family Medical Leave Act** law guaranteeing most full-time employees 12 workweeks of unpaid leave each year for personal or family health reasons (p. 662)

**Ley de Permiso Médico Familiar** ley que garantiza a la mayoría de los empleados de tiempo completo 12 semanas laborales de permiso sin goce de sueldo cada año por razones personales o de salud familiar

**Federal Art Project** division of the Works Progress Administration that hired unemployed artists to create artworks for nonfederal public buildings and sponsored art-education programs and exhibitions (p. 313)
**Proyecto Federal de Arte** división de la Administración de Progreso de Obras que contrató artistas desempleados para crear obras de arte en edificios públicos no federales y patrocinó programas educativos y exhibiciones artísticos

**Federal Deposit Insurance Corporation (FDIC)** government agency that insures bank deposits, guaranteeing that depositors' money will be safe (p. 287)
**Corporación Federal de Aseguramiento de Depósitos** agencia gubernamental que asegura los depósitos bancarios, garantizando que el dinero de los depositantes estará seguro

**federalism** political system in which power is shared between the national government and state governments (p. 20)
**federalismo** sistema político en el que el poder es compartido entre el gobierno nacional y el gobierno estatal

**Federal Reserve Act** 1913 law that placed national banks under the control of a Federal Reserve Board, which runs regional banks that hold the reserve funds from commercial banks, sets interest rates, and supervises commercial banks (p. 129)
**Ley de Reserva Federal** ley de 1913 que sometió a todos los bancos del país bajo el control de una Junta de Reserva Federal; esta última opera los bancos regionales que mantienen un fondo de reserva de los bancos comerciales, fija tasa de intereses y supervisa a los bancos comerciales

**Federal Trade Commission (FTC)** government agency established in 1914 to identify monopolistic business practices, false advertising, and dishonest labeling (p. 130)
**Comisión Federal de Comercio** agencia gubernamental establecida en 1914 para identificar las prácticas comerciales monopolistas, falsa propaganda y rótulos deshonestos

**feminism** theory that women and men should have political, social, and economic equality (p. 574)
**feminismo** teoría que plantea que las mujeres y los hombres deben tener igualdad politíca, social y económica

**Fifteenth Amendment** 1870 constitutional amendment which guaranteed voting rights regardless of race (p. 56)
**Decimoquinta Enmienda** enmienda constitucional de 1870 que garantizó el derecho al sufragio independientemente de la raza

**filibuster** tactic by which senators give long speeches to hold up legislative business (p. 484)

**obstruccionismo** táctica empleada por los senadores que consistió en hacer prolongados discursos para detener los asuntos legislativos

**fireside chat** informal radio broadcast in which FDR explained issues and New Deal programs to average Americans (p. 287)
**"charla junto a la hoguera"** transmisión informal de radio en que FDR explicaba asuntos y programas del Nuevo Trato a los estadounidenses promedio

**flapper** young woman from the 1920s who defied traditional rules of conduct and dress (p. 236)
**chica "flapper"** mujer joven de la década de 1920 que desafiaba las reglas tradicionales de conducta y atuendo

**flexible response** defense policy allowing for the appropriate action in any size or type of conflict (p. 507)
**respuesta flexible** política de defensa que permite acciones apropiadas en conflictos de cualquier tamaño o tipo

**Foraker Act** law establishing a civil government in Puerto Rico (p. 156)
**Ley Foraker** ley que estableció un gobierno civil en Puerto Rico

**442nd Regimental Combat Team** World War II unit made up of Japanese American volunteers (p. 365)
**Equipo de Combate del Regimiento 442** unidad de la Segunda Guerra Mundial compuesta por voluntarios estadounidenses de origen japonés

**Fourteen Points** list of terms for resolving World War I and future wars outlined by American President Woodrow Wilson (p. 193)
**Catorce Puntos** lista de condiciones planteada por el presidente estadounidense Woodrow Wilson para resolver la Primera Guerra Mundial y guerras futuras

**Fourteenth Amendment** 1868 constitutional amendment which defined citizenship and guaranteed citizens equal protection under the law (p. 56)
**Decimocuarta Enmienda** enmienda constitucional de 1868 que definió la ciudadanía y garantizó por ley a los ciudadanos protección ígual

**franchise business** allows a company to distribute its products or services through retail outlets owned by independent operators (p. 446)
**franquicia comercial** permiso para que una compañía distribuya sus productos o servicios por medio de establecimientos minoristas e independientes

**Freedmen's Bureau** federal agency designed to aid freed slaves and poor white farmers and relieve the South's immediate needs after the Civil War (p. 55)
**Oficina de Libertos** agencia federal diseñada para ayudar a los esclavos liberados y granjeros blancos, y llenar las necesidades inmediatas del Sur luego de la Guerra Civil

**freedom rides** 1961 protests by black and white activists who rode buses through southern states to test their compliance with the ban on segregation on interstate buses (p. 479)

**viaje por la libertad** protesta de activistas afro-estadounidense y blancos que en 1961 viajaron en autobús a través de los estados sureños para probar si acataban la prohibición contra la segregación en autobuses interestatales

**Freedom Summer** 1964 effort to register African American voters in Mississippi (p. 488)

**Verano de Libertad** esfuerzo de 1964 por empadronar a votantes afroestadounidenses en Mississippi

**Free-Soil Party** antislavery political party of the mid-1800s (p. 42)

**Partido Tierra Libre** partido político antiesclavista de mitad del siglo XIX

**fundamentalism** a movement or attitude stressing strict and literal adherence to a set of basic principles (p. 224)

**fundamentalismo** movimiento o actitud que enfatiza un cumplimiento estricto y literal a un conjunto de principios básicos

# G

**General Agreement on Tariffs and Trade (GATT)** international agreement first signed in 1947 aimed at lowering trade barriers (pp. 389, 667)

**Acuerdo General sobre Aranceles y Comercio** tratado internacional firmado originalmente en 1947, diseñado para disminuir las barreras comerciales entre las naciones

**generation gap** lack of understanding and communication between older and younger members of society (p. 571)

**brecha generacional** falta de entendimiento y comunicación entre los miembros más viejos y los más jóvenes de la sociedad

**Geneva Convention** international agreement governing the humane treatment of wounded soldiers and prisoners of war (p. 390)

**Convención de Ginebra** acuerdo internacional que regula el tratamiento humanitario de soldados heridos y prisioneros de guerra

**genocide** willful annihilation of a racial, political, or cultural group (p. 383)

**genocidio** aniquilación intencional de un grupo racial, político o cultural

**"Gentlemen's Agreement"** pact between the United States and Japan to end segregation of Asian children in San Francisco public schools; in return, Japan agreed to limit the immigration of its citizens to the United States (p. 155)

**"Pacto entre Caballeros"** acuerdo entre Estados Unidos y Japón para terminar la segregación de niños asiáticos en las escuelas públicas de San Francisco; a cambio, Japón aceptó limitar la migración de sus ciudadanos hacia Estados Unidos

**Gettysburg Address** speech by President Lincoln in which he dedicated a national cemetery at Gettysburg and reaffirmed the ideas for which the Union was fighting (p. 52)

**Discurso de Gettysburg** discurso del presidente Lincoln durante la inauguración del cementerio nacional en Gettysburg y que reafirmó las ideas por las que la Unión estaba en lucha

**GI Bill of Rights** eased the return of World War II veterans by providing education and employment aid (p. 435)

**Declaración de Derechos de los Soldados** ley que facilitó el retorno de los veteranos de la Segunda Guerra Mundial al brindarles educación y empleo

**Gilded Age** term used to describe the post-Reconstruction era, which was characterized by a facade of prosperity for the country (p. 87)

**Edad Dorada** término usado para describir la era después de la Reconstrucción que se caracterizó por una fachada de prosperidad para el país

*glasnost* Russian term for "new openness," a policy in the Soviet Union in the 1980s calling for open discussion of national problems (p. 640)

*glasnost* palabra rusa que significa "apertura", política de la Unión Soviética de finales de la década de 1980 con un llamado a la apertura y discusión de los problemas nacionales

**globalization** process by which national economies, politics, cultures, and societies mix with those of other nations around the world (p. 658)

**globalización** proceso mediante el cual la economía, política, cultura y sociedad de una nación se mezclan con las de las otras naciones de todo el mundo

**gold standard** policy of designating monetary units in terms of their value in gold (p. 89)

**estándar oro** política de designar las unidades monetarias en términos de su valor en oro

**Gospel of Wealth** Carnegie's doctrine calling for the wealthy to share their riches for the betterment of society (p. 68)

**evangelio de la riqueza** doctrina de Carnegie con el llamado a que los ricos compartieran su riqueza para mejorar la sociedad

**graft** acquisition of money through unethical means, such as bribery and corruption (p. 89)

**concusión** adquisición de dinero por medios no éticos, como sobornos y corrupción

**Great Awakening** religious movement in the English colonies during the 1730s and 1740s, which was heavily inspired by evangelical preachers (p. 12)

**Gran Despertar** movimiento religioso en las colonias inglesas durante las décadas de 1730 y 1740, fuertemente inspirado por los predicadores evangélicos

**Great Depression** period lasting from 1929 to 1941, in which the U.S. economy faltered and unemployment soared (p. 258)

**Gran Depresión** período entre 1929 y 1941 durante el cual la economía de Estados Unidos falló y el desempleo creció

English/Spanish Glossary

# English/Spanish Glossary

Great Migration                human rights

**Great Migration** movement of African Americans in the twentieth century from the rural South to the industrial North (p. 186)
 **Gran Migración** desplazamiento de afroestadounidenses durante el siglo XX desde las zonas rurales del Sur hacia las zonas industrializadas del Norte

**Great Society** President Johnson's goals for the U.S. in the areas of healthcare, education, the environment, discrimination, and poverty (p. 521)
 **Gran Sociedad** objetivos del presidente Johnson para Estados Unidos en las áreas de salud, educación, ambiente, discriminación y pobreza

**Great White Fleet** armada of battleships sent by Roosevelt in 1907 on a "good will cruise" around the world (p. 155)
 **Gran Flota Blanca** armada de barcos de guerra enviada por Roosevelt en 1907 en una "misión de buena voluntad" alrededor del mundo

**guerrilla warfare** form of non-traditional warfare generally involving hit-and-run attacks by small bands of fighters (p. 151)
 **guerra de guerrillas** método de combate no tradicional constituido por ataques de retirada rápida realizados por grupos pequeños de guerreros

**Gulf of Tonkin Resolution** 1964 Congressional resolution that authorized President Johnson to commit U.S. troops to South Vietnam and fight a war against North Vietnam (p. 536)
 **Resolución del Golfo de Tonkin** resolución del Congreso de 1964 que autorizó al presidente Johnson a enviar tropas estadounidenses a Vietnam del Sur y entrar en guerra contra Vietnam del Norte

# H

**habeas corpus** constitutional guarantee that no one can be held in prison without charges being filed (p. 51)
 **hábeas corpus** garantía constitucional para que nadie permanezca en prisión sin que se hayan presentado cargos en su contra

**Harlem Renaissance** period during the 1920s in which African American novelists, poets, and artists celebrated their culture (p. 245)
 **Renacimiento de Harlem** período durante la década de 1920 en el que los novelistas, poetas y artistas afroestadounidenses celebraron su cultura

**hawk** a person who supported U.S. involvement in the Vietnam War (p. 543)
 **"halcón"** persona que apoyó la participación estadounidense en la Guerra de Vietnam

**Hawley-Smoot Tariff** protective import tax, authorized by Congress in 1930 (p. 259)
 **Arancel Hawley-Smoot** impuesto de importaciones aprobado por el Congreso en 1930

**Helsinki Accords** agreement made in 1975 among the United States, Canada, and European nations, including the Soviet Union, in which all nations agreed to support human rights (p. 615)
 **Acuerdos de Helsinki** acuerdo realizado en 1975 entre Estados Unidos, Canadá y las naciones de Europa, incluyendo la Unión Soviética, en que todos países acordaron apoyar los derechos humanos

**Hepburn Act** 1906 law that gave the government the authority to set and limit railroad rates and set maximum prices for ferries, bridge tolls, and oil pipelines (p. 123)
 **Ley Hepburn** ley de 1906 que otorgó al gobierno la autoridad de fijar y limitar las tarifas ferroviarias y fijar los precios máximos para trasbordadores, peaje de puentes y oleoductos

**Hollywood Ten** group of movie writers, directors, and producers who refused to answer HUAC questions about alleged communist ties (p. 421)
 **diez de Hollywood** grupo de guionistas, directores y productores que se rehusaron a contestar preguntas del HUAC sobre supuestos vínculos comunistas

**Holocaust** name now used to describe the systematic murder of Jews by the Nazis (p. 380)
 **Holocausto** nombre usado para describir el asesinato sistemático de judíos por los nazis

**Hoover Dam** dam on the Colorado River, originally named Boulder Dam, that was built during the Great Depression (p. 274)
 **Represa Hoover** represa en el río Colorado, llamada originalmente Represa Boulder, construida durante la Gran Depresión

**Hooverville** term used to describe makeshift shantytowns set up by homeless people during the Great Depression (p. 264)
 **Hooverville** término usado para describir las barriadas de casuchas establecidas por los desposeídos durante la Gran Depresión

**hot line** direct telephone line between the White House and the Kremlin set up after the Cuban missile crisis (p. 508)
 **línea caliente** línea de comunicación telefónica directa entre la Casa Blanca y el Kremlin, establecida luego de la crisis de los misiles de Cuba

**House of Burgesses** representative assembly of colonial Virginia formed in 1619 (p. 11)
 **Cámara Baja de Virginia** asamblea de representantes en la Virginia colonial formada en 1619

**House Un-American Activities Committee (HUAC)** congressional committee that investigated possible subversive activities within the United States (p. 421)
 **Comité de la Cámara de Representantes contra Actividades AntiEstadounidenses** comité del Congreso que investigó posibles actividades subversivas dentro de Estados Unidos

**human rights** basic rights automatically held by every human being, including religious freedom, education, and equality (p. 615)
 **derechos humanos** derechos básicos que tiene todo ser humano automáticamente y que incluyen la libertad religiosa, la educación y la igualdad

## I

**Immigration Act of 1990** law that increased the number of immigrants allowed in the U.S. per year (p. 679)
   **Ley de Migración de 1990** ley que aumenta el número de inmigrantes permitidos en Estados Unidos cada año

**Immigration and Control Act of 1986** legislation that granted resident status to illegal immigrants residing in the United States since 1982 and penalized employers who hired illegal immigrants (p. 680)
   **Ley de Migración y Control de 1986** conjunto de leyes que otorgó la condición de residente a los inmigrantes ilegales que vivían en Estados Unidos desde 1982 y penaliza a los patronos que contratan inmigrantes ilegales

**Immigration and Nationality Act of 1965** law that changed the national quota system to limits of 170,000 immigrants per year from the Eastern Hemisphere and 120,000 per year from the Western Hemisphere (p. 523)
   **Ley de Migración y Nacionalidad de 1965** ley que cambió el sistema de cuotas nacionales para limitar a 170,000 por año los inmigrantes del hemisferio oriental y 120,000 por año los del hemisferio occidental

**impeachment** act of bringing charges against an official to determine whether he or she should be removed from office (pp. 56, 665)
   **impugnación** acción de encausar a un funcionario público para determinar si debe ser dejado en su puesto

**imperialism** political, military, and economic domination of strong nations over weaker territories (p. 138)
   **imperialismo** dominio político, militar y económico de naciones poderosas sobre territorios más débiles

**impressment** policy of seizing people or property for military or public service (p. 24)
   **requisa** política de confiscar personas o propiedades para servicio militar o público

**Indian New Deal** 1930s legislation that gave American Indians greater control over their own affairs and provided funding for construction of schools and hospitals (p. 303)
   **Nuevo Trato Indígena** legislación de 1930 que otorgó mayor control a los indígenas estadounidenses sobre sus propios asuntos y financió la construcción de escuelas y hospitales

**inflation** rising prices (pp. 52, 200)
   **inflación** aumento de los precios

**influenza** flu virus (p. 199)
   **influenza** virus de la gripe

**information industry** businesses that provide informational services (p. 445)
   **industrias de la información** empresas que brindan servicios de información

**initiative** process in which citizens put a proposed new law directly on the ballot (p. 107)
   **iniciativa** proceso en el que los ciudadanos proponen directamente una nueva ley en la papeleta de una elección

**inner city** referred to the older, central part of a city with crowded neighborhoods in which low-income, usually minority, groups live (p. 457)
   **centro de la ciudad** la parte más vieja y central de una ciudad, con vecindarios muy poblados en los que viven grupos de bajos recursos, usualmente minorías

**installment buying** method of purchase in which buyer makes a small down-payment, and then pays off the rest of the debt in regular monthly payments (p. 216)
   **plan de pago a plazos** método de compra mediante el cual el comprador paga un pequeño enganche y luego paga el resto de la deuda con abonos mensuales regulares

**insurrection** rebellion (p. 151)
   **insurrección** rebelión

**Internet** a computer network that links people around the world, also called World Wide Web (p. 658)
   **Internet** red de computadoras que enlaza a personas de todo el mundo, también llamada Red Mundial

**internment** temporary imprisonment of members of a specific group (p. 365)
   **reclusión** encarcelamiento temporal para miembros de un grupo específico

**Interstate Highway Act** 1956 law that authorized the spending of $32 billion to build 41,000 miles of highway (p. 442)
   **Ley de Carreteras Interestatales** ley de 1956 que autorizó el gasto de $32 mil millones para construir 41,000 millas de carreteras

**Iran-Contra affair** political scandal under President Reagan involving the use of money from secret arms sales to Iran to illegally support the Contras in Nicaragua (p. 644)
   **incidente Irán-Contras** escándalo político en la administración del presidente Reagan que involucró el uso de dinero procedente de la venta secreta de armas a Irán para apoyar ilegalmente a los Contras en Nicaragua

**iron curtain** term coined by Winston Churchill to describe the border between the Soviet satellite states and Western Europe (p. 400)
   **cortina de hierro** término acuñado por Winston Churchill para describir la frontera entre los estados satélites soviéticos y Europa Occidental

**"irreconcilables"** isolationist senators who opposed any treaty ending World War I that had a League of Nations folded into it (p. 196)
   **"irreconciliables"** senadores aislacionistas opuestos a cualquier tratado para finalizar la Primera Guerra Mundial que involucrara una Sociedad de las Naciones

**island hopping** World War II strategy that involved seizing selected Japanese-held islands in the Pacific while bypassing others (p. 375)
   **salto de islas** estrategia durante la Segunda Guerra Mundial que involucraba capturar islas selectas que mantenía Japón en el Pacífico a la vez que se evitaban otras

## J

**jazz** American musical form developed by African Americans, based on improvisation and blending blues, ragtime, and European-based popular music (p. 243)
**jazz** forma musical estadounidense creada por los afroestadounidenses y europeos, basada en la improvisación y la mezcla de el blues, ragtime y música popular de origen europeo

*Jazz Singer, The* the first movie with sound synchronized to the action (p. 232)
*El Cantante de Jazz* primera película con sonido y acción sincronizados

**Jim Crow laws** laws passed in southern states that separated blacks and whites (p. 87)
**Leyes Jim Crow** leyes aprobadas en los estados sureños que segregaban a los negros de los blancos

**jingoism** aggressive nationalism; support for warlike foreign policy (p. 145)
**patrioterismo** nacionalismo agresivo; apoyo a una política exterior belicosa

**judicial review** power of the Supreme Court to decide whether the acts of a President or laws passed by Congress are constitutional (p. 23)
**revisión judicial** poder que le permite a la Corte Suprema decidir si los actos del presidente o las leyes aprobadas por el Congreso son constitucionales

## K

**kamikazes** Japanese pilots who deliberately crashed planes into American ships during World War II (p. 377)
**kamikazes** pilotos japoneses que deliberadamente chocaban aviones contra buques estadounidenses durante la Segunda Guerra Mundial

**Kansas-Nebraska Act** 1854 law that divided the Nebraska Territory into Kansas and Nebraska and gave each territory the right to decide whether or not to allow slavery (p. 43)
**Ley Kansas-Nebraska** ley de 1854 que dividió el territorio de Nebraska en Kansas y Nebraska, dándole a cada territorio el derecho de decidir si permitiría la esclavitud o no

**Kellogg-Briand Pact** 1928 agreement in which many nations agreed to outlaw war (p. 221)
**Pacto Kellogg-Briand** acuerdo de 1928 en el que los delegados de muchas naciones estuvieron anuentes a prohibir la guerra

**Kerner Commission** group set up to investigate the causes of race riots in American cities in the 1960s (p. 492)
**Comisión Kerner** grupo que se formó para investigar las causas de los disturbios raciales en las ciudades estadounidenses en la década de 1960

**Knights of Labor** labor union that sought to organize all workers and focused on broad social reforms (p. 71)
**Caballeros del Trabajo** sindicato de trabajadores que procuró organizar a todos los trabajadores y se enfocó en reformas sociales amplias

**Kristallnacht** "Night of the Broken Glass," organized attacks on Jewish communities in Germany on November 9, 1938 (p. 381)
**Kristallnacht** "noche de los cristales rotos", ataques organizados contra comunidades judías en Alemania, el 9 de noviembre de 1938

**Ku Klux Klan** organization that promotes hatred and discrimination against specific ethnic and religious groups (pp. 58, 227)
**Ku Klux Klan** organización que promueve el odio y discriminación contra grupos étnicos y religiosos específicos

## L

**League of Nations** world organization established after World War I to promote peaceful cooperation between countries (p. 194)
**Sociedad de las Naciones** organización mundial establecida después de a la Primera Guerra Mundial para promover la cooperación pacífica entre los países

**Lend-Lease Act** act passed in 1941 that allowed President Roosevelt to sell or lend war supplies to any country whose defense he considered vital to the safety of the United States (p. 337)
**Ley de Préstamo y Arrendamiento** ley aprobada por el Congreso en 1941 que permitió al presidente Franklin Roosevelt vender o prestar suministros bélicos a cualquier país cuya defensa se considerara vital para la seguridad de Estados Unidos

**liberal** a person who tends to support government intervention to help the needy and favor laws protecting the rights of women and minorities (p. 628)
**liberal** persona que tiende a apoyar la intervención gubernamental en la ayuda a los necesitados y favorece las leyes que protegen los derechos de las mujeres y las minorías

**limited war** war fought to achieve only specific goals (p. 410)
**guerra limitada** guerra peleada para alcanzar objetivos específicos

**localism** policy relied on by President Hoover in the early years of the Great Depression whereby local and state governments act as primary agents of economic relief (p. 273)
**localismo** política de la que dependió el presidente Hoover a principios de la Gran Depresión para que los gobiernos locales y estatales actuaran como los principales agentes de asistencia económica

**"Lost Generation"** term for American writers of the 1920s marked by disillusion with World War I and search for new sense of meaning (p. 238)
**"Generación Perdida"** término usado para referirse a escritores estadounidenses de la década de 1920 marcados por su desilusión con la Primera Guerra Mundial y la búsqueda de un nuevo sentido de la vida

**Louisiana Purchase** territory between the Mississippi River and the Rocky Mountains, purchased from France in 1803 (p. 24)
**Compra de Luisiana** territorio entre el río Mississippi y las montañas Rocosas comprado a Francia en 1803

*Lusitania* British passenger liner sunk by a German U-boat during World War I (p. 176)
*Lusitania* trasatlántico británico hundido por un submarino alemán en la Primera Guerra Mundial

## M

**Magna Carta** English document from 1215 that limited the power of the king and provided basic rights for citizens (p. 11)
**Carta Magna** documento inglés de 1215 que limitó el poder del rey y dio derechos básicos a los ciudadanos

**Manhattan Project** code name of the project that developed the atomic bomb (p. 378)
**Proyecto Manhattan** nombre en clave del proyecto que desarrolló la bomba atómica

**Manifest Destiny** doctrine which stated that westward expansion of the United States was inevitable and a God-given right (p. 41)
**Destino Manifiesto** doctrina que establecía que la expansión de Estados Unidos hacia el Oeste no sólo era inevitable sino un derecho divino

**March on Washington** 1963 demonstration in which more than 200,000 people rallied for economic equality and civil rights (p. 482)
**Marcha en Washington** manifestación de más de 200,000 personas que en 1963 marcharon a favor de la igualdad económica y los derechos civiles

**Marshall Plan** economic and foreign policy that offered aid to Western European countries after World War II (p. 402)
**Plan Marshall** política económica y exterior que ofreció ayuda a los países de Europa Occidental después de la Segunda Guerra Mundial

**mass production** rapid manufacture of large numbers of identical products (p. 212)
**producción en masa** fabricación rápida de grandes cantidades de productos idénticos

**massive retaliation** policy of threatening to use massive force in response to aggression (p. 414)
**represalia masiva** política de amenazar con el uso de fuerza masiva en respuesta a una agresión

**Mayflower Compact** agreement for ruling the Plymouth Colony made in 1620 on the ship the *Mayflower* (p. 11)
**Pacto del Mayflower** acuerdo para gobernar la colonia de Plymouth alcanzado en 1620 en el barco *Mayflower*

**McCarthyism** negative catchword for extreme, reckless charges of disloyalty (p. 426)
**McCarthyismo** lema negativo que expresa acusaciones extremas e irresponsables de deslealtad

**Meat Inspection Act** 1906 law that allowed the federal government to inspect meat sold across state lines and required federal inspection of meat processing plants (p. 124)
**Ley de Inspección de Carnes** ley de 1906 que permitió al gobierno federal inspeccionar la carne vendida entre los estados y que exigió la inspección federal de las plantas de procesamiento de carne

**median family income** measure of average family income (p. 448)
**mediana del ingreso familiar** medida del ingreso familiar promedio

**Medicaid** federal program created in 1965 to provide low-cost health insurance to poor Americans of any age (p. 522)
**Medicaid** programa federal creado en 1965 para brindar seguro de salud de bajo costo a los estadounidenses de escasos recursos de cualquier edad

**Medicare** federal program created in 1965 to provide basic hospital insurance to most Americans age 65 and over (p. 522)
**Medicare** programa federal creado en 1965 para brindar seguro hospitalario básico a la mayoría de los estadounidenses mayores de sesenta y cinco años de edad

**Middle Passage** the forced transport of enslaved persons from Africa to the Americas between the 1500s and the 1800s (p. 6)
**Pasaje Medio** transporte forzado de esclavos desde África a las Américas entre los siglos XVI y XIX

**migrant farmworker** person who travels from farm to farm, and sometimes from state to state, to pick fruit and vegetables (p. 581)
**trabajador agrícola migratorio** persona que viaja de una granja a otra, algunas veces de un estado a otro, para la recolección de frutas y vegetales

**militarism** glorification of the military (p. 171)
**militarismo** glorificación de lo militar

**Missouri Compromise** 1820 agreement calling for the admission of Missouri as a slave state and Maine as a free state, and banning slavery in the Louisiana Purchase territory north of the 36° 30 N latitude (p. 38)
**Acuerdo de Missouri** acuerdo de 1820 que establecía a Missouri como estado esclavista y a Maine como estado libre, y prohibía la esclavitud en el territorio de la Compra de Luisiana al norte de la latitud 36° 30 N

**Model T** automobile manufactured by Henry Ford to be affordable on the mass market (p. 213)
**Modelo T** automóvil fabricado por Henry Ford para que fuera asequible en el mercado masivo

**modernism** trend that emphasized science and secular values over traditional ideas about religion (p. 223)
**modernismo** moda que daba énfasis a la ciencia y los valores seculares por sobre las ideas religiosas tradicionales

English/Spanish Glossary

**monopoly** complete control over an industry by one person or company (p. 68)

**monopolio** control total de una industria por una persona o compañía

**Monroe Doctrine** declaration by President Monroe in 1823 that the United States would oppose efforts by any outside power to control a nation in the Western Hemisphere (p. 27)

**Doctrina Monroe** declaración del presidente Monroe en 1823 en cuanto a que Estados Unidos se opondría a los esfuerzos de cualquier poder extranjero por controlar una nación del hemisferio occidental

**Montgomery bus boycott** 1955–1956 protest by African Americans in Montgomery, Alabama, against racial segregation in the bus system (p. 474)

**boicot de los autobuses de Montgomery** protesta de 1955 a 1956 de los afroestadounidenses en Montgomery, Alabama, contra la segregación en el sistema de autobuses

**"moral diplomacy"** Woodrow Wilson's statement that the U.S. would not use force to assert influence in the world, but would instead work to promote human rights (p. 161)

**"diplomacia moral"** aseveración de Woodrow Wilson en cuanto a que Estados Unidos no usaría la fuerza para ejercer su influencia en el mundo, sino que trabajaría en la promoción de los derechos humanos

**Moral Majority** political organization established by Reverend Jerry Falwell in 1979 to advance religious goals (p. 630)

**Mayoría Moral** organización política establecida por el reverendo Jerry Falwell en 1979 para promover objetivos religiosos

**muckraker** writer who uncovers and exposes misconduct in politics or business (p. 102)

**muckraker** escritor que descubre y expone la mala conducta real o aparente de políticos o empresas

**multinational corporation** companies that produce and sell their goods and services all over the world (pp. 446, 658)

**corporaciones multinacionales** compañías que producen y venden sus bienes y servicios alrededor del mundo

**Munich Pact** agreement made between Germany, Italy, Great Britain, and France in 1938 that sacrificed the Sudetenland to preserve peace (p. 330)

**Pacto de Munich** acuerdo de 1938 entre Alemania, Italia, Gran Bretaña y Francia que sacrificó los Sudetes para preservar la paz

**mural** a large picture painted directly on a wall or ceiling (p. 313)

**mural** pintura de grandes dimensiones realizada directamente sobre una pared o cielo raso

**mutualistas** organized groups of Mexican Americans that make loans and provide legal assistance to other members of their community (p. 119)

**mutualistas** grupos organizados de estadounidenses de origen mexicano para ofrecer préstamos y asistencia legal a miembros de su comunidad

**mutually assured destruction** policy in which the United States and the Soviet Union hoped to deter nuclear war by building up enough weapons to destroy one another (p. 413)

**destrucción mutua asegurada** política con la que Estados Unidos y la Unión Soviética esperaban evitar la guerra nuclear al acumular suficientes armas para destruirse mutuamente

**My Lai** village in South Vietnam where in 1968 American forces opened fire on unarmed civilians; during the massacre, U.S. soldiers killed between 400 and 500 Vietnamese (p. 555)

**My Lai** villa en Vietnam del Sur donde en 1968 fuerzas estadounidenses dispararon contra civiles desarmados; durante la masacre, los soldados estadounidenses mataron entre 400 y 500 vietnamitas

# N

**napalm** jellied gasoline dropped in large canisters that explode on impact and cover large areas in flames; dropped by U.S. planes during the Vietnam War (p. 538)

**napalm** gasolina gelatinizada lanzada en grandes latas que explotaban al impactar y dejaban en llamas grandes áreas; lanzadas por aviones estadounidenses durante la Guerra de Vietnam

**national debt** total amount of money that the federal government owes to the owners of government bonds (p. 634)

**deuda interna** cantidad total de dinero que el gobierno federal debe a los dueños de bonos de gobierno

**National Aeronautics and Space Administration (NASA)** government agency that coordinates U.S. efforts in space (p. 417)

**Administración Nacional de Aeronáutica y del Espacio** agencia gubernamental formada para coordinar los esfuerzos estadounidenses en el espacio

**National American Woman Suffrage Association (NAWSA)** group founded in 1890 that worked on both the state and national levels to earn women the right to vote (p. 111)

**Asociación Nacional para el Sufragio de las Mujeres Estadounidenses** grupo fundado en 1890 que funcionó a nivel tanto estatal como nacional para que se otorgara a las mujeres el derecho al voto

**National Association for the Advancement of Colored People (NAACP)** interracial organization founded in 1909 to abolish segregation and discrimination and to achieve political and civil rights for African Americans (p. 119)

**Asociación Nacional para el Avance de las Personas de Color** organización interracial fundada en 1909 para abolir la segregación y la discriminación y avanzar los derechos políticos y civiles de los afroestadounidenses

**National Consumers League (NCL)** group organized in 1899 to investigate the conditions under which goods were made and sold and to promote safe working conditions and a minimum wage (p. 110)

**Liga Nacional de Consumidores** grupo organizado en 1899 para investigar las condiciones en que se fabricaban y vendían los bienes, así como promover condiciones seguras de trabajo y un salario mínimo

**nationalize** to place a resource under government control (p. 416)

**nacionalización** poner un recurso bajo control gubernamental

**National Organization for Women (NOW)** organization established by Betty Friedan to combat discrimination against women in the workplace and education (p. 575)

**Organización Nacional de Mujeres** organización establecida por Betty Friedan para derribar las barreras de la discriminación en el lugar de trabajo y la educación

**National Reclamation Act** 1902 law that gave the federal government the power to decide where and how water would be distributed through the building and management of dams and irrigation projects (p. 126)

**Ley Nacional de Reclamaciones** ley de 1902 que otorgó al gobierno federal el poder para decidir adónde y cómo se distribuiría el agua, mediante la construcción y administración de represas y proyectos de irrigación

**National Recovery Administration (NRA)** New Deal agency that promoted economic recovery by regulating production, prices, and wages (p. 289)

**Administración para la Recuperación Nacional** agencia del Nuevo Trato que promovió la recuperación económica al controlar la producción, precios y salarios

**Nation of Islam** African American religious organization founded in 1930 that advocated separation of the races (p. 492)

**Nación Islámica** organización religiosa afroestadounidense fundada en 1930 que abogó por la separación de las razas

**Neutrality Act of 1939** act that allowed nations at war to buy goods and arms in the United States if they paid cash and carried the merchandise on their own ships (p. 336)

**Ley de Neutralidad de 1939** ley que permitió que las naciones en guerra compraran bienes y armas en Estados Unidos siempre que pagaran en efectivo y transportaran la mercancía en sus propios barcos

**New Deal** programs and legislation enacted by Franklin D. Roosevelt during the Great Depression to promote economic recovery and social reform (p. 285)

**Nuevo Trato** programas y leyes establecidos por Franklin D. Roosevelt durante la Gran Depresión para promover la recuperación económica y reforma social

**New Deal coalition** political force formed by diverse groups who united to support Franklin D. Roosevelt and his New Deal (p. 303)

**coalición del Nuevo Trato** fuerza política formada por grupos diversos unidos para apoyar a Franklin D. Roosevelt y su Nuevo Trato

**New Freedom** Woodrow Wilson's program to place government controls on corporations in order to benefit small businesses (p. 128)

**Nueva Libertad** programa de Woodrow Wilson para establecer controles gubernamentales sobre las corporaciones a fin de brindar más oportunidades a las pequeñas empresas

**New Frontier** President Kennedy's plan aimed at improving the economy, fighting racial discrimination, and exploring space (p. 512)

**Nueva Frontera** plan doméstico del presidente Kennedy dirigido a mejorar la economía, combatir la discriminación racial y avanzar el programa espacial

**New Nationalism** President Theodore Roosevelt's plan to restore the government's trustbusting power (p. 127)

**Nuevo Nacionalismo** plan del presidente Teodoro Roosevelt para restaurar el poder del gobierno de disolver monopolios

**New Right** political movement supported by reinvigorated conservative groups in the latter half of the twentieth century (p. 629)

**Nueva Derecha** movimiento político apoyado por grupos conservadores revigorizados durante la última mitad del siglo XX

**Niagara Movement** group of African American thinkers founded in 1905 that pushed for immediate racial reforms, particularly in education and voting practices (p. 118)

**Movimiento Niágara** grupo de pensadores afroestadounidenses fundado en 1905 que presionó para obtener reformas raciales inmediatas, particularmente en cuanto a la educación y el voto

**Nineteenth Amendment** constitutional amendment that gave women the right to vote (p. 113)

**Décimonovena Enmienda** enmienda constitucional que otorgó a las mujeres el derecho al voto

**No Child Left Behind Act** 2002 law aimed at improving the performance of primary and secondary schools particularly through mandated sanctions against schools not reaching federal performance standards (p. 673)

**Ley Que Ningún Niño Se Quede Atrás** ley del año 2002 destinada a mejorar el desempeño de escuelas primarias y secundarias particularmente mediante sanciones por mandato contra las escuelas que no cumplan las normas federales de desempeño

English/Spanish Glossary

**North American Free Trade Agreement (NAFTA)** agreement signed in 1992 calling for the removal of trade restrictions among Canada, Mexico, and the United States (p. 667)

**Tratado de Libre Comercio de América del Norte (TLCAN)** acuerdo firmado en 1992 para la remoción de las restricciones comerciales entre Canadá, México y Estados Unidos

**North Atlantic Treaty Organization (NATO)** military alliance formed to counter Soviet expansion (p. 404)

**Organización del Tratado del Atlántico Norte (OTAN)** alianza militar creada para parar la expansión soviética

**nuclear family** ideal or typical household with a father, mother, and children (p. 449)

**núcleo familiar** hogar ideal o típico formado por un padre, una madre y niños

**Nuclear Test Ban Treaty** 1963 nuclear-weapons agreement, which prohibited aboveground nuclear tests (p. 510)

**Tratado de Prohibición de Pruebas Nucleares** acuerdo de 1963 sobre armas nucleares que prohibió las pruebas nucleares en la superficie de la Tierra

**Nuremberg Laws** laws enacted by Hitler that denied German citizenship to Jews (p. 381)

**Leyes de Nuremberg** leyes impuestas por Hitler que negaban la ciudadanía alemana a los judíos

**Nuremberg Trials** trials in which Nazi leaders were charged with war crimes (p. 390)

**Juicios de Nuremberg** juicios en los que se acusó a los líderes nazis de crímenes de guerra

### O

**Office of War Information (OWI)** government agency that encouraged support of the war effort during World War II (p. 366)

**Oficina de Información de Guerra** agencia gubernamental que animaba el apoyo al esfuerzo bélico durante la Segunda Guerra Mundial

**Okies** general term used to describe Dust Bowl refugees during the Great Depression (p. 267)

**okies** término general usado para describir a los refugiados del Cuenco de Polvo durante la Gran Depresión

**Open Door Policy** American statement that the government did not want colonies in China, but favored free trade there (p. 154)

**política de puertas abiertas** declaración estadounidense que proclamaba que el gobierno no deseaba colonias en China, pero favorecía el libre comercio

**open range** vast area of grassland owned by the federal government (p. 86)

**praderas abiertas** grandes pastizales propiedad del gobierno federal

**Operation Desert Storm** 1991 American-led attack on Iraqi forces after Iraq refused to withdraw its troops from Kuwait (p. 649)

**Operación Tormenta del Desierto** ataque que comandaron los estadounidenses en 1991 contra las fuerzas iraquíes luego que Irak rehusó retirar sus tropas de Kuwait

**Organization of Petroleum Exporting Countries (OPEC)** group of countries which sell oil to other nations and cooperate to regulate the price and supply of oil (p. 600)

**Organización de Países Exportadores de Petróleo (OPEP)** grupo de países que venden petróleo a otras naciones y que coopera en la regulación del precio y suministro del crudo

### P

**Palmer Raids** the series of raids in the early 1920s initiated by Attorney General A. Mitchell Palmer, against suspected radicals and communists (p. 201)

**Redadas Palmer** redadas de principios de la década de 1920 iniciadas por el fiscal general del estado A. Mitchell Palmer contra personas sospechosas de ser radicales o comunistas

**Panama Canal** human-made waterway linking the Atlantic to the Pacific across the Isthmus of Panama (p. 159)

**Canal de Panamá** vía acuática hecha por los humanos que une el Atlántico y el Pacífico a través del istmo de Panamá

**pardon** official forgiveness of a crime and its punishment (p. 608)

**indulto** perdón oficial de un delito y su castigo

**Paris Peace Accords** 1973 peace agreement between the United States, South Vietnam, North Vietnam, and the Vietcong that effectively ended the Vietnam War (p. 556)

**Acuerdos de Paz de París** acuerdo de paz de 1973 entre Estados Unidos, Vietnam del Sur, Vietnam del Norte y el Vietcong que de hecho finalizó la Guerra de Vietnam

**Patriot Act** law passed following September 11, 2001, giving law enforcement broader powers in monitoring possible terrorist activities (p. 677)

**Ley Patriótica** ley aprobada después del 11 de septiembre del 2001 que otorgó mayores poderes a los agentes de la ley para vigilar posibles actividades terroristas

**Peace Corps** American government organization that sends volunteers to provide technical, educational, and medical services in developing countries (p. 507)

**Cuerpo de Paz** organización del gobierno de Estados Unidos que envía voluntarios para que brinden servicios técnicos, educativos y médicos en países en vías de desarrollo

**Pearl Harbor** American military base attacked by the Japanese on December 7, 1941 (p. 341)

**Peral Harbor** base militar estadounidense atacada por los japoneses el 7 de diciembre de 1941

**Pendleton Act** law that created a civil service system for the federal government in an attempt to hire employees on a merit system rather than on a spoils system (p. 89)

**Ley Pendleton** ley que creó un sistema de servicio civil para el gobierno federal en un intento por contratar empleados con un sistema de méritos en lugar de un sistema de clientelismo

**Pentagon Papers** classified U.S. government study that revealed American leaders intentionally involved the United States in Vietnam without fully informing the American people; leaked to *The New York Times* in 1971 (p. 555)

**Documentos del Pentágono** estudio clasificado del gobierno estadounidense que reveló que los líderes estadounidenses intencionalmente involucraron a Estados Unidos en Vietnam sin haber informado completamente a la ciudadanía estadounidense; lo filtró el *The New York Times* en 1971

*perestroika* policy in the Soviet Union in the late 1980s calling for restructuring of the stagnant Soviet economy (p. 640)

*perestroika* política de la Unión Soviética de finales de la década de 1980 que abogó por la reestructuración de la estancada economía soviética

**personal computer** small computer intended for individual use (p. 657)

**computadora personal** computadora pequeña destinada al uso personal

**Platt Amendment** set of conditions under which Cuba was granted independence in 1902, including restrictions on rights of Cubans and granting to the U.S. the "right to intervene" to preserve order in Cuba (p. 157)

**Enmienda Platt** grupo de condiciones con las que se le otorgó la independencia a Cuba en 1902, que incluían restricciones de los derechos de los cubanos y que otorgaban a EE.UU. el "derecho de intervenir" a fin de conservar el orden en Cuba

**popular sovereignty** concept of permitting the residents of a territory to decide on whether or not to allow slavery (p. 43)

**soberanía popular** concepto de permitir a los residentes de un territorio decidir si permiten la esclavitud o no

**Populist Party** People's Party; political party formed in 1891 to advocate a larger money supply and other economic reforms (p. 89)

**Partido Populista** Partido del Pueblo; partido político formado en 1891 para abogar por mayores ofertas monetarias y otras reformas económicas

**privatize** to transfer from governmental ownership or control to private interests (p. 683)

**privatizar** transferir la propiedad o control gubernamental a intereses privados

**productivity** the rate at which goods are produced or services performed (p. 436)

**productividad** velocidad a la que se producen bienes o se brindan servicios

**Progressive Party** political party that emerged from the Taft-Roosevelt battle that split the Republican Party in 1912 (p. 127)

**Partido Progresivo** partido político surgido de la batalla entre Taft y Roosevelt que dividió al Partido Republicano en 1912

**Progressivism** movement that emerged in response to the pressures of industrialization and urbanization that promoted reforms to bring about social justice (p. 100)

**progresismo** movimiento surgido como respuesta a las presiones de la industrialización y urbanización, que promovía nuevas ideas y reformas políticas para alcanzar la justicia social

**Prohibition** the forbidding by law of the manufacture, transport, and sale of alcohol (p. 229)

**Prohibición** ley para prohibir la fabricación, transporte y venta de alcohol

**Public Works Administration (PWA)** New Deal agency that provided millions of jobs constructing public buildings (p. 289)

**Administración de Obras Públicas** agencia del Nuevo Trato que brindó millones de empleos en la construcción de obras públicas

**pump priming** economic theory that favored public works projects because they put money into the hands of consumers who would buy more goods, stimulating the economy (p. 293)

**cebado de bomba** teoría económica que favorece los proyectos de obras públicas porque ponen dinero en manos de los consumidores que comprarán más bienes, estimulando así la economía

**Pure Food and Drug Act** 1906 law that allowed federal inspection of food and medicine and banned the interstate shipment and sale of impure food and the mislabeling of food and drugs (p. 124)

**Ley de Alimentos y Fármacos Puros** ley de 1906 que permitió la inspección federal de los alimentos y medicinas, y prohibió el transporte y venta interestatal de alimentos impuros así como el rotulado erróneo de alimentos y fármacos

## Q

**quota system** arrangement that limited the number of immigrants who could enter the United States from specific countries (p. 225)

**sistema de cuotas** acuerdo que limitó el número de inmigrantes provenientes de países específicos que podían ingresar a Estados Unidos

## R

**Radical Republican** congressman who advocated full citizens' rights for African Americans and a harsh Reconstruction policy on the South (p. 56)

**Republicano Radical** congresista que abogaba por derechos ciudadanos íntegros para los afroestadounidenses y una política dura de Reconstrucción en el Sur

**English/Spanish Glossary**

**ratify** to approve (p. 17)
   **ratificar** aprobar

**rationing** government-controlled limits on the amount of certain goods that civilians could buy during wartime (p. 366)
   **racionamiento** límites controlados por el gobierno sobre la cantidad de ciertos bienes que podían comprar los civiles en tiempos de guerra

**realpolitik** a foreign policy promoted by Henry Kissinger during the Nixon administration based on concrete national interests instead of abstract ideologies (p. 561)
   **realpolitik** política exterior promovida por Henry Kissinger durante la administración Nixon con base en intereses nacionales concretos en lugar de ideologías abstractas

**recall** process by which voters can remove elected officials from office before their terms end (p. 107)
   **destitución** proceso por el cual los electores pueden remover a funcionarios electos antes de terminar su período

**Reconstruction** federal program between 1865 and 1877 to repair damage to the South caused by the Civil War and restore the southern states to the Union (p. 55)
   **Reconstrucción** programa instaurado por el gobierno federal entre 1865 y 1877 para reparar los daños que causó la Guerra Civil al Sur y reincorporar los estados sureños a la Unión

**Reconstruction Finance Corporation (RFC)** federal agency set up by Congress in 1932 to provide emergency government credit to banks, railroads, and other large businesses (p. 274)
   **Corporación de Financiamiento para la Reconstrucción** agencia federal establecida por el Congreso en 1932 para brindar créditos gubernamentales de emergencia a los bancos, ferrocarriles y otras grandes empresas

**Red Scare** fear that communists were working to destroy the American way of life (pp. 201, 420)
   **miedo rojo** miedo a que los comunistas están empeñados en destruir la forma de vida estadounidense

**referendum** process that allows citizens to approve or reject a law passed by a legislature (p. 107)
   **referendo** proceso que permite que los ciudadanos aprueben o rechacen una ley que ha aprobado una legislatura

**reparations** payment for war damages (p. 194)
   **reparaciones** pago por los daños causados por la guerra

**repatriation** process by which Mexican Americans were encouraged, or forced, by local, state, and federal officials to return to Mexico during the 1930s (p. 269)
   **repatriación** proceso por el cual los estadounidenses de origen mexicano fueron animados, o forzados, por los oficiales locales, estatales y federales a que regresaran a México durante la década de 1930

**reservationists** a group of Senators, led by Henry Cabot Lodge, who opposed the Treaty of Versailles, to end World War I, unless specific changes were included (p. 196)
   **reservasionistas** grupo de senadores encabezados por Henry Cabot que se oponía a terminar la Primera Guerra Mundial con el Tratado de Versalles a menos que éste inlcuyera ciertos cambios

**rock-and-roll** music originated in the gospel and blues traditions of African Americans (p. 453)
   **rock-and-roll** música originada en las tradiciones del gospel y blues de los afroestadounidenses

**Roosevelt Corollary** President Theodore Roosevelt's reassertion of the Monroe Doctrine to keep the Western Hemisphere free from intervention by European powers (p. 159)
   **Corolario Roosevelt** replanteamiento del presidente Teodoro Roosevelt de la Doctrina Monroe, según la cual la política de Estados Unidos era mantener al hemisferio occidental libre de la intervención de las potencias europeas

**Rough Riders** group of men, consisting of rugged westerners and upper-class easterners who fought during the Spanish-American War and are often remembered for the charge up San Juan Hill (p. 148)
   **jinetes rudos** grupo de hombres fuertes provenientes del Oeste y de la clase alta del Este que pelearon durante la Guerra entre España y Estados Unidos, a quienes se les recuerda principalmente por el ataque a la colina de San Juan

**Russo-Japanese War** a war between Japan and Russia in 1904 over the presence of Russian troops in Manchuria (p. 155)
   **Guerra Ruso-Japonesa** guerra entre Japón y Rusia durante 1904 por la presencia de tropas rusas en Manchuria

**sanctions** penalties (p. 616)
   **sanciones** castigos

**satellite** a mechanical device that orbits Earth, receiving and sending communication signals or transmitting scientific data (p. 658)
   **satélite** dispositivo mecánico que orbita la Tierra, y que recibe y envía señales de comunicación o transmite datos científicos

**satellite state** independent nation under the control of a more powerful nation (p. 399)
   **estado satélite** nación independiente bajo el control de una nación más poderosa

**saturation bombing** tactic of dropping massive amounts of bombs in order to inflict maximum damage (p. 358)
   **saturación de bombardeos** táctica de dejar caer cantidades masivas de bombas a fin de infligir el máximo daño

**Savings and Loan crisis** the failure of about 1,000 savings and loan banks as a result of risky business practices (p. 634)

**crisis financiera** fracaso de cerca de 1,000 bancos de ahorro y préstamo como resultado de prácticas comerciales riesgosas

**scientific management** approach to improving efficiency, in which experts looked at every step of a manufacturing process, trying to find ways to reduce time, effort, and expense (p. 213)

**administración científica** enfoque para mejorar la eficiencia, en el que los expertos observaban cada paso de un proceso de manufactura y buscaban formas de reducir el tiempo, esfuerzo y costo

**Scopes Trial** 1925 trial of a Tennessee schoolteacher for teaching Darwin's theory of evolution (p. 224)

**Juicio Scopes** juicio al que fue sometido, en 1925, un maestro de Tennessee por enseñar la teoría de Darwin sobre la evolución

**secede** to withdraw formally from a membership in a group or organization (p. 47)

**secesión** retiro formal de la membresía en un grupo u organización

**Second Great Awakening** religious movement in the first half of the 1800s (p. 35)

**Segundo Gran Despertar** movimiento religioso durante la primera mitad del siglo XIX

**Second New Deal** legislative activity begun by Franklin D. Roosevelt in 1935 to solve problems created by the Great Depression (p. 292)

**Segundo Nuevo Trato** actividad legislativa iniciada por Franklin D. Roosevelt en 1935 para lidiar con los problemas económicos y sociales creados por la Gran Depresión

**Sedition Act** 1798 law that allowed the prosecution of critics of the government (p. 23)

**Ley de Sedición** ley de 1798 que permitió enjuiciar a quienes criticaran al gobierno

**segregation** forced separation of one group from another, oftentimes on the basis of race (p. 59)

**segregación** separación forzada de dos grupos, a menudo con base en la raza

**Selective Service Act** act passed by Congress in May 1917 authorizing a draft of young men for military service (p. 180)

**Ley de Servicio Selectivo** ley aprobada por el Congreso en mayo de 1917 que autorizó el reclutamiento de hombres jóvenes para el servicio militar

**self-determination** the right of people to choose their own form of government (p. 194)

**autodeterminación** derecho de las personas de elegir su propia forma de gobierno

**separation of powers** principle by which the powers of government are divided between the executive, legislative, and judicial branches (p. 20)

**separación de poderes** principio por el cual los poderes de gobierno se dividen entre los poderes ejecutivo, legislativo y judicia

**service economy** an economic system focused on the buying and selling of services (p. 660)

**economía de servicio** sistema económico enfocado en la compra y venta de servicios

**service sector** businesses that provide services rather than manufactured goods (p. 445)

**sector de servicios** empresas que brindan servicios en lugar de fabricar bienes

**settlement house** community center organized to provide social services to the urban poor at the turn of the twentieth century (p. 104)

**casa de asentamiento** centro comunal organizado para ofrecer servicios sociales a los pobres de la ciudad a inicios del siglo XX

**sharecropping** system in which a farmer tends some portion of a planter's land and receives a share of the crop as payment (pp. 56, 81)

**aparcería** sistema en el cual un granjero atiende una porción de la tierra del dueño de una plantación y recibe parte de la cosecha como pago

**Shays' Rebellion** farmers' revolt against high taxes in Massachusetts in 1786 (p. 16)

**Rebelión de Shay** revuelta de los granjeros contra los altos impuestos de Massachussets en 1786

**silent majority** phrase introduced by President Richard Nixon to refer to a significant number of Americans who supported his policies but chose not to express their views (p. 599)

**mayoría silenciosa** frase introducida por el presidente Richard Nixon para referirse a un número significativo de estadounidenses que apoyaban sus políticas pero eligieron no expresar su opinión

**sit-down strike** labor protest in which workers stop working and occupy the workplace until their demands are met (p. 297)

**huelga de brazos caídos** protesta laboral en que los trabajadores dejan de trabajar y ocupan el lugar de trabajo hasta que se satisfacen sus demandas

**sit-in** form of protest where participants sit and refuse to move (p. 477)

**sentada** forma de protesta en que los participantes se sientan y rehúsan moverse

**Sixteenth Amendment** 1913 constitutional amendment that gave Congress the authority to levy an income tax (p. 129)

**Décimosexta Enmienda** enmienda constitucional de 1913 que otorgó al Congreso la autoridad para establecer un impuesto a las rentas

**Smith Act** law that made it unlawful to teach or advocate the violent overthrow of the United States government (p. 421)

**Ley Smith** ley que prohibió la enseñanza o defensa de un derrocamiento violento del gobierno estadounidense

English/Spanish Glossary

**Social Darwinism** the belief held by some in the late nineteenth century that certain nations and races were superior to others and therefore destined to rule over them (pp. 68, 140)

**darwinismo social** creencia de algunos a finales del siglo XIX según la que algunas naciones o razas eran superiores a otras y por lo tanto estaban destinadas a gobernar

**Social Gospel** reform movement that emerged in the late nineteenth century that sought to improve society by applying Christian principles (p. 104)

**Evangelio Social** movimiento reformista surgido a finales del siglo XIX cuyo fin era mejorar la sociedad al aplicarse principios cristianos

**Social Security Act** a 1935 law that set up a pension system for retirees, established unemployment insurance, and created insurance for victims of work-related accidents. It also provided aid for poverty-stricken mothers and children, the blind, and the disabled (p. 293)

**Ley del Seguro Social** ley de 1935 que creó un sistema de pensión para jubilados, estableció un seguro de desempleo y creó seguros para las víctimas de accidentes laborales; también suministra ayuda a las madres y niños pobres, ciegos y discapacitados

**Southeast Asia Treaty Organization (SEATO)** defensive alliance aimed at preventing communist aggression in Asia (pp. 411, 535)

**Organización del Tratado del Sudeste Asiático** alianza defensiva orientada a prevenir la agresión comunista en Asia

**southern strategy** tactic of the Republican Party for winning presidential elections by securing the electoral votes of southern states (p. 600)

**estrategia sureña** táctica del Partido Republicano para ganar las elecciones presidenciales al asegurarse los votos electorales de los estados del Sur

**"space race"** the competition between the United States and the Soviet Union to develop the technology to successfully land on the moon (p. 513)

**"carrera espacial"** competencia entre Estados Unidos y la Unión Soviética en el desarrollo de la tecnología para aterrizar exitosamente en la Luna

**Spanish Civil War** Nationalist forces led by General Francisco Franco rebelled against the democratic Republican government of Spain (p. 329)

**Guerra Civil Española** conflicto en España en el que las fuerzas Nacionalistas dirigidas por el General Francisco Franco se rebelaron contra el gobierno democrático Republicano

**speculation** practice of making high-risk investments in hopes of obtaining large profits (p. 258)

**especulación** práctica de hacer inversiones de alto riesgo con la esperanza de obtener grandes ganancias

**sphere of influence** a region dominated and controlled by an outside power (p. 153)

**esfera de influencia** región dominada y controlada por un poder externo

**Square Deal** President Theodore Roosevelt's program of reforms to keep the wealthy and powerful from taking advantage of small business owners and the poor (p. 122)

**Trato Justo** programa de reformas del presidente Teodoro Roosevelt para evitar que los ricos y poderosos se aprovecharan de los propietarios de pequeñas empresas y de los pobres

**stagflation** term for the economic condition created in the late 1960s and 1970s by high inflation combined with stagnating economic growth and high unemployment (p. 599)

**estanflación** término para la condición económica creada a finales de las décadas de 1960 y 1970 por una alta inflación combinada con el estancamiento del crecimiento económico y el alto desempleo

**Strategic Arms Limitation Treaty (SALT I)** 1972 treaty between the United States and the Soviet Union that froze the deployment of intercontinental ballistic missiles and placed limits on antiballistic missiles (p. 562)

**Tratado de Limitación de Armas Estratégicas** tratado de 1972 entre Estados Unidos y la Unión Soviética que congeló el despliegue de misiles balísticos intercontinentales y puso límites a los misiles antibalísticos

**Strategic Arms Limitation Treaty II (SALT II)** proposed agreement between the United States and the Soviet Union to limit certain types of nuclear arms production; it was never ratified by the United States Senate (p. 616)

**Tratado de Limitación de Armas Estratégicas II** acuerdo propuesto entre Estados Unidos y la Unión Soviética para limitar la producción de ciertos tipos de armas nucleares; nunca fue ratificado por el Senado de Estados Unidos

**strategic bombing** tactic of dropping bombs on key political and industrial targets (p. 359)

**bombardeo estratégico** táctica de dejar caer bombas en blancos políticos e industriales clave

**Strategic Defense Initiative (SDI)** nicknamed "Star Wars," President Reagan's plan to develop innovative defenses to guard the United States against nuclear missile attacks (p. 640)

**Iniciativa de Defensa Estratégica** apodada "Guerra de las Galaxias," plan de 1983 del presidente Reagan para financiar el desarrollo de defensas innovadoras para salvaguardar a Estados Unidos contra ataques con misiles nucleares

**Student Nonviolent Coordinating Committee (SNCC)** grass-roots movement of young civil rights activists founded in 1960 (p. 478)

**Comité Estudiantil Coordinador de la No Violencia** movimiento de base compuesto por jóvenes activistas a favor de los derechos civiles fundado en 1960

**Students for a Democratic Society (SDS)** organization founded in 1960 at the University of Michigan to fight racism and poverty (p. 546)

**Estudiantes a Favor de una Sociedad Democrática** organización fundada en 1960 en la Universidad de Michigan para combatir el racismo y la pobreza

**suburb** residential area surrounding a city (p. 76)

**suburbio** área residencial que rodea a una ciudad

**Suez crisis** attempt by France and Great Britain to seize control of the Suez Canal in 1956 (p. 416)

**crisis de Suez** intento de Francia y Gran Bretaña por apoderarse del control del Canal de Suez en 1956

**suffrage** right to vote (p. 111)

**sufragio** derecho al voto

**Sunbelt** name given to the region of states in the South and the Southwest (p. 443)

**Cinturón del Sol** nombre dado a la región de los estados del sur y suroeste

**superpower** powerful country that plays a dominant economic, political, and military role in the world (p. 388)

**superpotencia** país poderoso que juega un papel económico, político y militar dominante en el mundo

**supply-side economics** economic theory that held that the government should increase the supply of labor and goods to achieve long-term growth, rather than increasing demand through government spending (p. 633)

**economía de la oferta** teoría económica que mantiene que el gobierno debe aumentar la oferta de trabajo y bienes para alcanzar el crecimiento a largo plazo, en lugar de aumentar la demanda por medio del gasto gubernamental

# T

**Taft-Hartley Act** a law that restricted the power of labor unions (p. 437)

**Ley Taft Hartley** ley que restringió el poder de los sindicatos de trabajadores

**Taliban** Islamic fundamentalist faction that controlled most of Afghanistan from 1996–2001 (p. 676)

**Talibán** fracción fundamentalista islámica que controló la mayor parte de Afganistán entre 1996 y 2001

**tariff** tax on imported goods (p. 35)

**arancel** impuesto sobre bienes importados

**Teapot Dome scandal** scandal during the Harding administration in which the Secretary of the Interior leased government oil reserves to private oilmen in return for bribes (p. 220)

**escándalo Teapot Dome** escándalo durante la administración Harding en que el secretario del interior arrendó las reservas de petróleo del gobierno a petroleros privados a cambio de un soborno

**televangelist** minister who uses the television format to preach to millions of people (p. 613)

**teleevangelista** pastor que usa el formato televisivo para predicar a millones de personas

**temperance movement** national organization formed after the Civil War that worked to outlaw the sale and distribution of alcohol (p. 110)

**movimiento por la temperancia** organización a nivel nacional formada después de la Guerra Civil para prohibir la venta y distribución del alcohol

**tenant farmer** one who works land owned by another and pays rent either in cash or in shares of produce (p. 265)

**agricultor arrendatario** aquél que cultiva la tierra propiedad de otro y paga un alquiler en efectivo o en especie con el producto

**tenement** multistory building divided into apartments to house several families, often in unsanitary conditions (p. 78)

**vecindad** edificio de varios pisos dividido en departamentos para albergar a varias familias, a menudo en condiciones poco sanitarias

**Tennessee Valley Authority (TVA)** government agency that built dams in the Tennessee River Valley to control flooding and generate electric power (p. 288)

**Autoridad del Valle del Tennessee** agencia gubernamental que construye represas en el valle del Río Tennessee para controlar las inundaciones y generar energía eléctrica

**termination policy** ended all programs monitored by the Bureau of Indian Affairs; also ended federal responsibility for the health and welfare of Native Americans (p. 459)

**política de terminación** política que cerró todos los programas a cargo de la Oficina de Asuntos Indígenas; también dio por terminada la responsabilidad federal en cuanto a la salud y bienestar de los indígenas estadounidenses

**Tet Offensive** coordinated communist assault on a large number of South Vietnamese cities in early 1968 (p. 547)

**Ofensiva Tet** asalto comunista coordinado contra un gran número de ciudades de Vietnam del Sur a principios de 1968

**Thirteenth Amendment** 1865 constitutional amendment which abolished slavery (p. 56)

**Decimotercera Enmienda** enmienda constitucional de 1865 que abolió la esclavitud

**38th parallel** dividing line between North and South Korea (p. 407)

**paralelo 38** línea divisoria entre Corea del Norte y Corea del Sur

**English/Spanish Glossary**

**Tiananmen Square** site in Beijing where Chinese students' prodemocracy protests were put down by the Chinese government in 1989 (p. 646)

**Plaza Tiananmen** lugar en Pekín donde las protestas de los estudiantes chinos a favor de la democracia fueron aplacadas por el gobierno chino en 1989

**totalitarianism** a theory of government in which a single party or leader controls the economic, social, and cultural lives of its people (p. 324)

**totalitarismo** teoría de gobierno según la que un solo partido o líder controla la vida económica, social y cultural de la población

**total war** war in which a nation uses all of its resources to destroy enemy troops and their resources (p. 54)

**guerra total** guerra en la cual una nación usa todos sus recursos para destruir a las tropas enemigas y sus recursos

**toxic waste** poisonous byproducts of human activity (p. 587)

**desechos tóxicos** productos de desecho venenosos resultantes de la actividad humana

**Treaty of Paris** an agreement signed by the United States and Spain in 1898, which officially ended the Spanish-American War (p. 149)

**Tratado de París** acuerdo firmado por Estados Unidos y España en 1898 que marcó el final oficial de la Guerra entre España y Estados Unidos

**trickle-down economics** economic theory that holds that money lent to banks and businesses will trickle down to consumers (p. 274)

**economía por goteo** teoría económica que mantiene que el dinero prestado a los bancos y empresas llegará a los consumidores

**Tripartite Pact** agreement that created an alliance between Germany, Italy, and Japan during World War II (p. 336)

**Pacto Tripartito** acuerdo que creó una alianza entre Alemania, Italia y Japón durante la Segunda Guerra Mundial

**Truman Doctrine** President Truman's promise to help nations struggling against communist movements (p. 400)

**doctrina Truman** promesa del presidente Truman de ayudar a las naciones en lucha contra los movimientos comunistas

**trust** a combination of corporations or firms bound by a legal agreement, especially to reduce competition (p. 68)

**trust** combinación de empresas o firmas vinculadas por un contrato legal, especialmente para reducir la competencia

**Tuskegee Airmen** African American squadron that escorted bombers in the air war over Europe during World War II (p. 358)

**Aviadores de Tuskegee** escuadrón de afroestadounidenses que escoltaba a los bombarderos en la guerra aérea en cielos de Europa durante la Segunda Guerra Mundial

**Twenty-fifth Amendment** constitutional amendment ratified in 1967 that deals with presidential succession, vice presidential vacancy, and presidential inability (p. 603)

**Vigésima Quinta Enmienda** enmienda constitucional ratificada en 1967 que trata de la sucesión presidencial, vacantes de vicepresidentes e incapacidad presidencial

**Twenty-fourth Amendment** constitutional amendment that banned the poll tax as a voting requirement (p. 490)

**Vigésima Cuarta Enmienda** enmienda constitucional que prohibió el impuesto electoral como requisito para votar

# U

**U-boat** German submarine (p. 176)

**U boot** submarino alemán

**unconditional surrender** giving up completely without any concessions (p. 357)

**rendición incondicional** darse por vencido completamente sin concesiones

**Underground Railroad** support system run by abolitionists to help enslaved people escape to freedom in the North or in Canada (p. 39)

**Ferrocarril Subterráneo** sistema de apoyo dirigido por los abolicionistas para ayudar a los esclavos en su fuga hacia la libertad en el Norte o en Canadá

**unfunded mandate** program or action required but not paid for by the federal government (p. 630)

**mandatos sin fondos** programas o acciones requeridos pero que no paga el gobierno federal

**United Farm Workers (UFW)** labor union of farm workers that used nonviolent tactics including a workers' strike and a consumer boycott of table grapes (p. 581)

**Trabajadores Agrícolas Unidos** sindicato de trabajadores agrícolas que usó tácticas pacíficas, incluyendo una huelga de trabajadores y un boicot por los consumidores de uvas

**United Nations (UN)** organization founded in 1945 to promote peace (p. 389)

**Naciones Unidas (ONU)** organización fundada en 1945 para promover la paz

**Universal Declaration of Human Rights** document issued by the UN to promote basic human rights and freedoms (p. 389)

**Declaración Universal de los Derechos Humanos** documento emitido por la ONU para promover los derechos y libertades humanos básicos

**Urban League** network of churches and clubs that set up employment agencies and relief efforts to help African Americans get settled and find work in the cities (p. 119)

**Liga Urbana** red de iglesias y clubes que estableció agencias de empleo y ofreció asistencia para que los afroestadounidenses se asentaran y encontraran empleo en las ciudades

**urban renewal** government programs for redevelopment of urban areas (p. 457)

**renovación urbana** programas gubernamentales para el desarrollo de las áreas urbanas

# V

**Vietcong** South Vietnamese communist rebels that waged a guerrilla war against the government of South Vietnam throughout the Vietnam War (p. 535)

**Vietcong** rebeldes comunistas sudvietnamitas que hicieron guerra de guerrillas contra el gobierno de Vietnam del Sur durante la Guerra de Vietnam

**Vietnamization** President Nixon's plan for gradual withdrawal of U.S. forces as South Vietnamese troops assumed more combat duties (p. 553)

**vietnamización** plan del presidente Nixon que planteó un retiro gradual de las fuerzas estadounidenses a medida que las tropas sudvietnamitas asumían más deberes de combate

**Violence Against Women Act** law passed in 1994 that increased federal resources to apprehend and prosecute men guilty of violent acts against women (p. 683)

**Ley contra la Violencia hacia las Mujeres** ley aprobada en 1994 que aumentó los recursos federales para arrestar y enjuiciar a los hombres culpables de actos violentos contra las mujeres

**Volstead Act** law enacted by Congress to enforce the Eighteenth Amendment (p. 229)

**Ley Volstead** ley impuesta por el Congreso para hacer cumplir la Decimoctava Enmienda

**Voting Rights Act** law that banned literacy tests and empowered the federal government to oversee voter registration (p. 490)

**Ley de Derechos Electorales** ley que prohibió las pruebas de alfabetismo y dio poder al gobierno federal de vigilar el empadronamiento de los votantes

**voucher** certificates or other documents that can be used as money (p. 637)

**vales** certificados u otros documentos que pueden ser usados como dinero

# W

**Wagner Act** New Deal law that abolished unfair labor practices, recognized the right of employees to organize labor unions, and gave workers the right to collective bargaining (p. 296)

**Ley Wagner** ley que abolió las prácticas laborales injustas, reconoció el derecho de los trabajadores de organizar sindicatos y dio a los trabajadores el derecho a las negociaciones colectivas

**War on Poverty** President Johnson's programs aimed at aiding the country's poor through education, job training, proper healthcare and nutrition, and overall community development (p. 518)

**Guerra Contra la Pobreza** programas del presidente Johnson enfocados en ayudar a los pobres de la nación mediante la educación, entrenamiento laboral, servicios de salud y nutrición adecuados, y el desarrollo comunitario en general

**War Powers Act** 1973 law passed by Congress restricting the president's war-making powers; the law requires the President to consult with Congress within 48 hours of committing American forces to a foreign conflict (p. 559)

**Ley de Poderes Bélicos** ley aprobada por el Congreso en 1973 que restringió los poderes bélicos del presidente; la ley exige que el presidente consulte con el Congreso dentro de un período de 48 horas antes de comprometer fuerzas estadounidenses en un conflicto extranjero

**War Refugee Board** U.S. government agency founded in 1944 to save Eastern European Jews (p. 384)

**Junta de Refugiados de Guerra** agencia del gobierno de Estados Unidos fundada en 1944 para salvar a los judíos de Europa Oriental

**Warren Commission** committee that investigated the assassination of President Kennedy (p. 515)

**Comisión Warren** comité que investigó el asesinato del presidente Kennedy

**"Warren Court"** Supreme Court of the 1960s under Chief Justice Earl Warren, whose decisions supported civil rights, civil liberties, voting rights, and personal privacy (p. 523)

**"Corte Warren"** Corte Suprema de la década de 1960 bajo el mandato del presidente de los magistrados Earl Warren, cuyas decisiones apoyaron los derechos civiles, libertades civiles, derecho al sufragio y privacidad personal

**Warsaw Pact** military alliance of the Soviet Union and its satellite states (p. 404)

**Pacto de Varsovia** alianza militar de la Unión Soviética y sus estados satélites

**Washington Naval Disarmament Conference** meeting held in 1921 and 1922 where world leaders agreed to limit construction of warships (p. 221)

**Conferencia de Desarme Naval de Washington** reunión realizada en 1921 y 1922 durante la cual los líderes mundiales acordaron limitar la construcción de buques de guerra

**Watergate** political scandal involving illegal activities that ultimately led to the resignation of President Nixon in 1974 (p. 601)

**Watergate** escándalo político que involucró actividades ilegales que al final condujeron a la renuncia del presidente Nixon en 1974

**Weapons of Mass Destruction (WMD)** nuclear, biological, and chemical weapons intended to kill or harm on a large scale (p. 677)

**armas de destrucción masiva** armas nucleares, biológicas y químicas destinadas a matar o lesionar a gran escala

English/Spanish Glossary

**welfare state** government that assumes responsibility for providing for the welfare of the poor, elderly, sick, and unemployed (p. 307)
**estado de bienestar** gobierno que asume la responsabilidad de velar por el bienestar de los pobres, ancianos, enfermos y desempleados

**Western Front** battle front between the Allies and Central Powers in western Europe during World War I (p. 173)
**Frente Occidental** frente de batalla entre los Aliados y los Poderes Centrales en Europa Occidental durante la Primera Guerra Mundial

**Wilmot Proviso** proposed but never approved law that banned slavery in the territory won from Mexico (p. 42)
**Condición Wilmot** ley propuesta pero no aprobada que prohibía la esclavitud en el territorio ganado a México

**Women's Army Corps (WAC)** U.S. Army group established during World War II so that women could serve in non combat roles (p. 344)
**Cuerpo Femenino del Ejército** grupo del Ejército de Estados Unidos establecido durante la Segunda Guerra Mundial para que las mujeres pudieran dar servicio en papeles no combativos

**Works Progress Administration (WPA)** key New Deal agency that provided work relief through various public-works projects (p. 292)
**Administración del Progreso de Obras** agencia clave del Nuevo Trato que brindó ayuda laboral a través de varios proyectos de obras públicas

**World Trade Organization (WTO)** international organization formed in 1995 to encourage the expansion of world trade (p. 667)
**Organización Mundial del Comercio (OMC)** organización internacional formada en 1995 para estimular la expansión del comercio mundial

**Yalta Conference** 1945 strategy meeting between Roosevelt, Churchill, and Stalin (p. 386)
**Conferencia de Yalta** reunión sobre estrategia realizada en 1945 entre Roosevelt, Churchill y Stalin

**Yellow Press** newspapers that used sensational headlines and exaggerated stories in order to promote readership (p. 145)
**prensa amarillista** periódicos que utilizaban titulares sensacionales e historias exageradas para promover su circulación

**Z**

**Zimmermann note** telegram written by German Foreign Minister Arthur Zimmermann proposing an alliance between Germany and Mexico against the United States during World War I (p. 179)
**telegrama de Zimmermann** telegrama escrito por el ministro del exterior alemán, Arthur Zimmermann, en el que proponía una alianza entre Alemania y México contra Estados Unidos en la Primera Guerra Mundial

Index

Index

Index

**Index**

**Index**

Index

Index

Index

Index

# Acknowledgments

## Staff Credits
The people who make up the **United States History** team—representing design services, editorial, editorial services, education technology, manufacturing and inventory planning, market research, marketing services, planning and budgeting, product planning, production services, project office, publishing processes, and rights and permissions—are listed below. Bold type denotes core team members.

Ernie Albanese, Mary Aldridge, Diane Alimena, Leann Davis Alspaugh, Michele Angelucci, Jasjit Arneja, **Margaret Antonini,** Rosalyn Arcilla, Alan Asarch, Helene Avraham, Penny Baker, Renée Beach, Peter Brooks, Lois Brown, Kerry Buckley, Pradeep Byram, Rui Camarinha, Lisa Carrillo, Sarah Carroll, Kerry Cashman, Justin Contursi, Jason Cuoco, Harold DelMonte, **James Doris,** Laura Edgerton-Riser, Leanne Esterly, Anne Falzone, Libby Forsyth, Phillip Gagler, Doreen Galbraith, Joe Galka, Kathy Gavilanes, Julie Gecha, Allen Gold, Holly Gordon, Mary Ann Gundersen, Mary Hanisco, Rick Hickox, Karen Holtzman, **Kristan Hoskins,** Beth Hyslip, Katharine Ingram, Linda Johnson, **John Kingston,** Stephanie Krol, Courtney Lane, Mary Sue Langan, Julian Libysen, **Salena LiBritz,** Marian Manners, Grace Massey, Patrick McCarthy, John McClure, Mike McLaughlin, Rich McMahon, Kathleen Mercandetti, Art Mkrtchyan, Karyl Murray, Ken Myett, Deborah Nicholls, Xavier W. Niz, Kim Ortell, Jennifer Paley, Ray Parenteau, **Judi Pinkham,** Linda Punskovsky, Matthew J. Raycroft, Maureen Raymond , **Ryan Richards,** Bruce Rolff, **Laura Ross,** Robyn Salbo, Donna Schindler, Gerry Schrenk, Mildred Schulte, **Melissa Shustyk,** Siri Schwartzman, Ann Shea, Robert Siek, **Laurel Smith,** Lisa Smith-Ruvalcaba, Kara Stokes, Frank Tangredi, Elizabeth Torjussen, Humberto Ugarte, Ellen Welch Granter, Rachel Winter

## Additional Credits
Steve Apple, Karen Beck, Meg Ceccolini, Donna DiCuffa, Lynette Haggard, Stuart Kirschenbaum, Beth Kun, Carol Maglitta, Karen Mancinelli-Paige, Caroline McDonnell, Lesley Pierson, Rachel Ross, Ted Smykal, Alfred Voto, Marc Wezdecki

## Art Credits
Kerry Cashman **SH12,** 7, 19, 26, 28–29, 37, 38, 44, 46, 51, 60–61, 68–69, 75, 83, 92–93, 102–103, 112–113, 115, 122–123, 132–133, 142, 146–147, 152–153, 158–159, 162, 164–165, 171, 176–177, 178, 183, 186, 192–193, 204–205, 214, 226, 228–229, 235, 240–241, 248–249, 256–257, 263, 266, 270–271, 275, 278–279, 285, 294–295, 305, 316–317, 326–327, 342–343, 348–349, 356, 358–359, 368–369, 372–373, 382, 392–393, 403, 414, 418–419, 422–423, 424, 428–429, 436–437, 442–443, 451, 460–461, 474, 479, 482–483, 486–487, 491, 494, 498–499, 514, 519, 520–521, 526–527, 540–541, 549, 556–557, 558, 564–565, 572, 582–583, 590, 592–593, 602–603, 612, 618–619, 620–621, 634, 636, 642–643, 650–651, 668, 674–675, 682, 684–685, 706–707; Ellen Welch Granter 398, 402, 406, 411, 412, 413, 420, 428, 430; Hefflin Agency/Ilene Winn-Lederer 10; Kevin Jones Associates 358–359; Steve McEntee 659; Rich McMahon **C3, C6, C9, C12, C14, C17,** 92, 443, 598, 601, 607, 615, 620, 640, 707, 708, 709, 710, 711, 712, 713; Jen Paley, **SH11, SH12, SH13, SH14, SH15, SH16, SH17, SH18, SH19, SH20, SH21, SH26, SH27, SH28, SH31,** 4, 9, 13, 15, 18, 20, 21, 28, 29, 31, 34, 35, 42, 48, 50, 54, 55, 59, 60, 62, 66, 73, 80, 87, 92, 100, 105, 106, 109, 116, 121, 126, 128, 130, 132, 135, 138, 140, 144, 147, 149, 151, 156, 159, 161, 164, 165, 166, 170, 174, 180, 181, 183, 189, 193, 194, 198, 199, 204, 212, 213, 216, 217, 218, 221, 223, 224, 231, 234, 235, 238, 240, 241, 242, 248, 254, 256, 257, 259, 260, 261, 262, 263, 266, 272, 274, 278, 280, 284, 286, 292, 293, 295, 296, 297, 299, 300, 303, 305, 308, 309, 310, 316, 318, 324, 325, 329, 331, 337, 340, 344, 345, 348, 350, 351, 354, 358, 361, 365, 370, 377, 380, 384, 386, 390, 392, 395, 400, 423, 428, 434, 435, 437, 440, 441, 448, 455, 458, 460, 463, 468, 476, 477, 488, 490, 496, 498, 504, 505, 508, 511, 512, 517, 518, 526, 528, 529, 532, 537, 539, 544, 545, 549, 552, 553, 559, 560, 564, 566, 570, 572, 574, 578, 580, 581, 583, 584, 586, 589, 592, 594, 599, 603, 605, 609, 610, 611, 628, 629, 633, 639, 644, 645, 648, 650, 652, 653, 656, 658, 660, 661, 663, 664, 666, 668, 671, 678, 679, 680, 681, 682, 684, 691, 704, 705, 706, 710, 714–715; XNR Productions, Inc. **SH22,** 5, 11, 13, 24, 26, 28, 40, 46, 53, 85, 114, 125, 129, 141, 149, 158, 160, 162, 164, 172, 176, 186, 191, 195, 200, 214, 266, 281, 287, 306–307, 328, 333, 343, 346, 356, 364, 372, 374, 376, 383, 388, 401, 403, 408, 409, 416, 428, 438, 444, 460, 470, 479, 500, 509, 533, 539, 547, 550, 564, 565, 588, 601, 611, 632, 646, 648, 650, 669, 672, 676, 684, 692, 693, 694, 695, 696, 697, 698, 699, 700, 713

## Photo Credits
**FrontEndsheet:** L, Library of Congress; **FrontEndsheet:** Head, R, Stockdisc/Getty Images; **FrontEndsheet:** Body, R, Dirk Anschutz/Getty Images; **vii:** T, © Bettmann/CORBIS; Inset, © Judith Miller/© Dorling Kindersley/Larry & Dianna Elman; **viii:** BL, Tim Ridley © Dorling Kindersley/Louisiana State Museum; TL, Getty Images; M, Getty Images; R, Bettmann/CORBIS; **ix:** © A724/GAMMA; **x:** L, New York Daily News; R, ©Nathan Benn/CORBIS; **xi:** L, © Peter Turnley/CORBIS; R, © Reuters/CORBIS; **xii:** John Dominis/Time Life Pictures/Getty Images; **xxv:** Bettmann/CORBIS; **xxvii:** © Bettmann/CORBIS; **xxviii:** Library of Congress; Head, R, Stockdisc/Getty Images; Body, R, Dirk Anschutz/Getty Images; **xxx:** Brown Brothers; **SH1:** © Darius Ramazani/zefa/CORBIS; **SH2:** Jose Luis Pelaez, Inc./CORBIS; **SH6:** Tom Stewart/CORBIS; **SH12:** Fox Photos/Getty Images; **SH19:** © Charles Gupton/CORBIS; **SH23:** Bettmann/CORBIS; **SH24:** The Granger Collection, New York; **SH26:** Library of Congress; **SH30:** © Dynamic Graphics Group/IT Stock Free/Alamy; **SH32:** Background, The Art Archive/National Archives Washington, D.C.; BR, © Bettmann/CORBIS; TL, © Reuters/CORBIS; BL, © Bettmann/CORBIS; MR, © Bettmann/CORBIS; TR, The Granger Collection, New York; TM, The Granger Collection, New York; ML, The Granger Collection, New York; **1:** SuperStock, Inc.; **2–3:** Jean Leon Jerome Ferris, ©Private Collection/The Bridgeman Art Library; **3:** M, Colonial Williamsburg Foundation, Williamsburg, VA; T, The Granger Collection, New York; B, National Park Service photo; **4:** The Granger Collection, New York; **6:** T, The Granger Collection, New York; B, The Granger Collection, New York; **7:** T, Sherwin Crasto/Reuters/CORBIS; B, The Granger Collection, New York; **9:** L, The Granger Collection, New York; R, The Granger Collection, New York; **14:** Getty Images; **15:** L, Bettmann/CORBIS; R, National Archives and Records Administration; **16:** © North Wind Picture Archives; **17:** The Granger Collection, New York; **18:** Bettmann/CORBIS; **19:** B, Hulton Archive/Getty Images Inc.; T, Getty Images; **21:** L, The Granger Collection, New York; R, Composite photograph of the almost 200-year-old Star-Spangled Banner, the flag that inspired the national anthem. Smithsonian's National Museum of American History, © 2004; **22:** The Granger Collection, New York; **23:** The Granger Collection, New York; **25:** L, Library of Congress; R, Hulton Archive/Getty Images Inc.; **26:** The Granger Collection, New York; **28:** The Granger Collection, New York; **29:** L, Getty Images; R, National Park Service photo; **30:** The Granger Collection, New York; **D0–C27:** Border © Photodisc/Getty Images; **D0:** B, Courtesy of The Bostonian Society/Old State House; Frame, © Bruce Burkhardt/CORBIS; R, © NTPL/Christopher Hurst/The Image Works; **D4:** The Art Archive; **C1:** L, The Signing of the Constitution of the United States in 1787, 1940, Christy, Howard Chandler (1873–1952)/Hall of Representatives, Washington, DC, USA/Bridgeman Art Library; R, The Art Archive/National Archives Washington, D.C.; **C2:** R, © Royalty-Free/CORBIS; L, © Swim Ink 2, LLC/CORBIS; **C4:** courtesy New York State Historical Association; **C7:** T, The Granger Collection, New York; B, © Bettmann/CORBIS; Inset, The Granger Collection, New York; **C18:** T, ©Michael Kelley/Getty Images; B, © Royalty-Free/CORBIS; **C22:** © Bettmann/CORBIS; **32–33:** Illinois State Historical Library; **33:** T, Getty Images; M, Courtesy of The Oakland Museum of California. Collection of Norm Wilson; BR, © Dave King/Dorling Kindersley Inc./High Impact, BL, Dave King/Dorling Kindersley © Confederate Memorial Hall, New Orleans; M, Courtesy of The Oakland Museum of California; **34:** T, The Picture Desk/Art Archive; B, © Bettmann/CORBIS; **35:** The Granger Collection, New York; **37:** T, Steve Liss/Time Life Pictures/Getty Images; B, The Granger Collection, New York; **38:** TM, The Granger Collection, New York; BR, The Granger Collection, New York; TL, The Art Archive/Culver Pictures; BL, Hampton University Museum, Hampton, Virginia; TR, Bettmann/CORBIS; BM, Getty Images; **39:** The Granger Collection, New York; **41:** Courtesy of California History Room, California State Library, Sacramento, California; **42:** T, The Granger Collection, New York; B, The Art Archive/Culver Pictures; **43:** © Bettmann/CORBIS; **44:** T, Wrangler/Shutterstock, Inc.; B, The Granger Collection, New York; **45:** © Bettmann/CORBIS; **46:** TR, The Lilly Library, Indiana University; BR, The Granger Collection, New York; **47:** United States Dept. of the Interior; **48:** L, © Dorling Kindersley/U.S Army Military History Institute; R, © Bettmann/CORBIS; **49:** Paintings by Don Troiani; historicalartprints.com; **51:** TL, The Granger Collection, New York; BR, The Granger Collection, New York; MR, The Granger Collection, New York; TR, CORBIS; **52:** R, © CORBIS; **54:** © CORBIS; **55:** © 2005 Roger-Viollet/Topham/The Image Works; **57:** T, Corel Professional Photos CD-ROM™; M, istockphoto.com; B, Corel Professional Photos CD-ROM™; BL, The Granger Collection, New York; **58:** © Dallas Historical Society, Texas, USA/Bridgeman Art Library; **60:** © Bettmann/CORBIS; **61:** © Bettmann/CORBIS; **62:** Courtesy of California History Room, California State Library, Sacramento, California; **63:** The Granger Collection, New York; **64–65:** Brown Brothers; **65:** T, Scala/

# Acknowledgments

Art Resource, NY; M, © David J. & Janice L. Frent Collection/CORBIS; The Granger Collection, New York; **66:** Brown Brothers; **67:** R, Bettmann/CORBIS; L, CORBIS; **68:** L, CORBIS; **68–69:** M, William J. Gaughan, Archives Service Center, University of Pittsburgh; **69:** TR, Prentice Hall; BR, Mark Gibson/Index Stock Imagery, Inc.; **70:** T, © Royalty-Free/CORBIS; B, © Kellie Strøm-www.balsko.com; **72:** M, © Mary Evans Picture Library/The Image Works; **73:** Library of Congress; **74:** The Granger Collection, New York; **75:** L, Topham/HIP/The Image Works; TMR, © CORBIS; BMR, © Prentice Hall; BR, © Mary Evans Picture Library/Alamy; TR, © Bettmann/CORBIS; **76:** T, CORBIS; B, Bettmann/CORBIS; **77:** T, Bettmann/CORBIS; B, Library of Congress; **78:** © Bettmann/CORBIS; **79:** R, © Bettmann/CORBIS; L, The Granger Collection, New York; **80:** T, Getty Images; B, The Granger Collection, New York; **81:** The University of Georgia Libraries; **82:** © Christie's Images/CORBIS; **83:** T, AP/Wide World Photos; B, The Granger Collection, New York; **86:** T, Superstock; B, The Granger Collection, New York; **87:** L, Nebraska State Historical Society Photograph Collections; R, © David J. & Janice L. Frent Collection/CORBIS; **88:** The Granger Collection, New York; **89:** Clay County Historical Society, Moorhead MN; **90:** © Bettmann/CORBIS; **91:** T, © Royalty-Free/CORBIS; B, © Bettmann/CORBIS; **92:** The Granger Collection, New York; **93:** L, © Mary Evans Picture Library/The Image Works; R, The Granger Collection, New York; **94:** Getty Images; **95:** Provided courtesy *HarpWeek*, LLC; **96:** TM, The Granger Collection, New York; TL, © Reuters/CORBIS; TR, The Granger Collection, New York; MR, © Bettmann/CORBIS; ML, The Granger Collection, New York; BL, © Bettmann/CORBIS; BR, © Bettmann/CORBIS; Background, The Art Archive/National Archives Washington, D.C.; **97:** © CORBIS; **98–99:** Brown Brothers; **99:** B, The Granger Collection, New York; T, Dartmouth College Library; M, Getty Images; **100:** Bettmann/CORBIS; **101:** Bettmann/CORBIS; **102:** B, The Granger Collection, New York; TL, Library of Congress; BR, The Granger Collection, New York; **103:** B, Hulton-Deutsch Collection/CORBIS; TR. The Granger Collection, New York; **104:** L, Underwood & Underwood/CORBIS; M, The Granger Collection, New York; R, Brown Brothers; **106:** Courtesy of The Rosenberg Library, Galveston, TX; **108:** TR, Dartmouth College Library; B, Brown Brothers; **109:** TR, Lewis W. Hine/George Eastman House/Getty Images, Inc.; TL, Prentice Hall School Division; **110:** Minnesota Historical Society/CORBIS; **111:** The Granger Collection, New York; **112:** TR,

Underwood & Underwood/CORBIS; BL, © David J. & Janice L. Frent Collection/CORBIS; **112–113:** Foreground, Bettmann/CORBIS; Background, Library of Congress; **113:** TL, Courtesy of the Historic National Woman's Party, Sewall-Belmont House and Museum, Washington, D.C.; TR, Bettmann/CORBIS; **114:** Brown Brothers; **115:** B, National Archives and Records Administration; T, Ariel Skelley/CORBIS; **116:** © San Diego Historical Society, EH Davis Collection; **117:** R, Culver Pictures, Inc.; L, Bettmann/CORBIS; **118:** T, The Granger Collection, New York; B, Courtesy of the Abraham Lincoln Presidential Library; **119:** Library of Congress; **120:** Brown Brothers; **121:** L, Brown Brothers; R, Paul & Rosemary Volpp © Dorling Kindersley; **122:** T, Bettmann/CORBIS; TR, The Granger Collection, New York; TL, Bettmann/CORBIS; **123:** R, CORBIS; BR, Courtesy Kansas State Historical Society; L, The Granger Collection, New York; BR, Science Museum/SSPL/The Image Works; **125:** Library of Congress; **126:** Brown Brothers; **127:** The Granger Collection, New York; **128:** R, Brown Brothers; L, Judith Miller/© Dorling Kindersley/Larry & Dianna Elman; **129:** Getty Images; **130:** The Granger Collection, New York; **132:** Library of Congress; **133:** R, The Granger Collection, New York; L, Bettmann/CORBIS; **134:** © David J. & Janice L. Frent Collection/CORBIS; **136–137:** Bettmann/CORBIS; **137:** M, The Granger Collection/New York; T, Getty Images; B, SCHOMBURG CENTER/Art Resource, NY; **138:** R, Brown Brothers; L, Brown Brothers; **139:** BR, CORBIS; L, Bettmann/CORBIS; **140:** Library of Congress; **141:** Getty Images; **142:** T, Victor Jose Cobo/AP/Wide World Photos; B, CORBIS; L, Bettmann/CORBIS; R, Smithsonian Institution; **145:** Pearson Education/PH School; **146:** B, Chicago Historical Society; T, The Granger Collection, New York; **147:** BL, The New York Historical Society; BM, The New York Historical Society; BR, Bettmann/CORBIS; **148:** R, CORBIS; M, SCHOMBURG CENTER/Art Resource, NY; L, © 2002 The Museum of Fine Arts, Houston; **151:** Library of Congress; **152:** R, Bettmann/CORBIS; L, Getty Images; **152–153:** TL, Prentice Hall; **153:** R, Duke University; TM, U.S. Library of Congress; BM, U.S. Library of Congress; **154:** Bettmann/CORBIS; **155:** The Granger Collection, New York; **156:** L, Bettmann/CORBIS; **157:** Bettmann/CORBIS; **159:** L, CORBIS; TR, The Granger Collection, New York; BR, Bettmann/CORBIS; **160:** Bettmann/CORBIS; **162:** M, Getty Images; B, The Art Archive/Culver Pictures; T, Peter R. Westacott; **164:** R, Bettmann/CORBIS; L, CORBIS; **165:** L, The Granger Collection, New York; R, Getty Images; **166:** Bettmann/CORBIS; **167:** T, The

Granger Collection, New York; B, The Granger Collection, New York; **168–169:** National Archives and Records Administration; **169:** B, Brown Brothers; M, Library of Congress; T, © Prentice Hall; **170:** Mary Evans Picture Library; **171:** The Granger Collection, New York; **173:** Bettmann/CORBIS; **174:** Hulton-Deutsch Collection/CORBIS; **175:** The Granger Collection, New York; **176:** T, The Art Archive/Imperial War Museum/Eileen Tweedy; **176–177:** B, Courtesy Motorbuch Verlag and Eberhard Moeller. Photo from *The Encyclopedia of U-Boats; From 1904 to the Present.*; **177:** TR, Three Lions/Getty Images; B, Library of Congress; M, Gary Ombler/Imperial War Museum © Dorling Kindersley; **178:** T, Ceerwan Aziz/Reuters/CORBIS; B, Bettmann/CORBIS; **179:** Hulton Archive/Getty Images Inc.; **180:** R, Stock Montage, Inc.; L, Library of Congress; **181:** Brown Brothers; **182:** Rykoff Collection/CORBIS; **183:** R, Bettmann/CORBIS; BL, CORBIS; TL, Library of Congress; BR, The Granger Collection, New York; **184:** Bettmann/CORBIS; **185:** T, The Granger Collection, New York; B, Culver Pictures, Inc.; **186:** Stock Montage, Inc./Historical Pictures Collection; **188:** T, Library of Congress; B, Bettmann/CORBIS; **189:** L, Library of Congress; R, The Granger Collection, New York; **190:** The Granger Collection, New York; **192:** B, Bettmann/CORBIS; T, Prentice Hall; **192–193:** BL, The Art Archive; **193:** BR, Ann Ronan Picture Library/HIP/The Image Works; M, Liberty Memorial Museum, Kansas City, Missouri; T, Prentice Hall; **194:** CORBIS; **196:** Library of Congress; **198:** Brown Brothers; **199:** R, National Archives and Records Administration; L, Library of Congress; **200:** R, Underwood & Underwood/CORBIS; L, Getty Images; **201:** Bettmann/CORBIS; **202:** Brown Brothers; **203:** T, Bettmann/CORBIS; B, Bettmann/CORBIS; **204:** Liberty Memorial Museum, Kansas City, Missouri; **205:** R, Library of Congress; **206:** T, Library of Congress; B, The Granger Collection, New York; **207:** The Granger Collection, New York; **208:** TM, The Granger Collection, New York; TL, © Reuters/CORBIS; TR, The Granger Collection, New York; MR, © Bettmann/CORBIS; ML, The Granger Collection, New York; BL, © Bettmann/CORBIS; BR, © Bettmann/CORBIS; Background, The Art Archive/National Archives Washington, D.C.; **209:** The Art Archive/Laurie Platt Winfrey; **210–211:** Getty Images; **211:** T, Bettmann/CORBIS; B, The Granger Collection, New York; M, Getty Images; **212:** R, Image courtesy of The Advertising Archives; L, Brown Brothers; **213:** B, Bettmann/CORBIS; **214:** BL, Lake County Museum/CORBIS; BR, Image courtesy of The

Advertising Archives; T, CORBIS; Inset, TL, Blue Lantern Studio/CORBIS; Inset, M, Visions of America, LLC/Alamy; M, © Bettmann/CORBIS; **216:** Museum of the City of New York/CORBIS; **217:** USDA; **218:** L, Bettmann/CORBIS; R, Getty Images; **219:** The Granger Collection, New York; **220:** L, Brown Brothers; R, Bettmann/CORBIS; **223:** L, Library of Congress; R, Getty Images; **224:** Brown Brothers; **225:** The Granger Collection, New York; **226:** T, Ramin Talaie/CORBIS; B, Bettmann/CORBIS; **227:** Library of Congress; **228:** BL, Bettmann/CORBIS; BR, Library of Congress; T, Drug Enforcement Administration; **229:** BM, ProQuest Informaton and Learning Co.; TR, Library of Congress; TL, The Art Archive/National Archives Washington; BL, Dave King © Dorling Kindersley, Courtesy of the New York City Police Museum; **230:** K.J. Historical/CORBIS; **231:** R, The Granger Collection, New York; L, Schenectady Museum;Hall of Electrical History Foundation/CORBIS; **232:** L, Image courtesy of The Advertising Archives; R, Bettmann/CORBIS; ML, Image courtesy of The Advertising Archives; MR, Bettmann/CORBIS; **233:** R, Underwood & Underwood/CORBIS; L, Smithsonian Institution Collections, National Museum of American History, Behring Center; **234:** B, © Bettmann/CORBIS; T, The Art Archive/Culver Pictures; **235:** TR, The Jewish Museum, NY/Art Resource, NY; TL, Bettmann/CORBIS; M, The Granger Collection, New York; B, The Art Archive/Culver Pictures; **237:** L, © Francis G. Mayer/CORBIS; R, The Newark Museum/Art Resource, NY; **238:** T, Getty Images; B, AP/Wide World Photos; **239:** Getty Images; **240:** B, John Springer Collection/CORBIS; M, © Bettmann/CORBIS; **240–241:** T, Bettmann/CORBIS; BL, Sarah Fabian-Baddiel/HIP/The Image Works; BM, The Granger Collection, New York; MR, Bettmann/CORBIS; **242:** SCHOMBURG CENTER, The New York Public Library/Art Resource, NY; **243:** Bettmann/CORBIS; **244:** L, Getty Images; R, Getty Images; M, Tim Ridley © Dorling Kindersley/collection of the Louisiana State Museum, Gift of the New Orleans Jazz Club; **245:** Getty Images; **246:** The Granger Collection, New York; **247:** T, Winold Reiss, Portrait of Langston Hughes (1902-1967) ©1925. National Portrait Gallery, Washington, D.C., USA. Art Resource, NY; B, Brown Brothers; **248:** R, Getty Images; L, Bettmann/CORBIS; **249:** L, Bettmann/CORBIS; R, The Granger Collection/New York; **250:** The Jewish Museum, NY/Art Resource, NY; **251:** Hulton Archive/Getty Images Inc.; **252–253:** CORBIS; **253:** T, Getty Images; M, Conde Nast Publications, Inc.; B, © Prentice Hall; **254:** R, Brown Brothers; L, Getty Images; **255:** The Granger Collection, New York; **256:**

Bettmann/CORBIS; **257:** R, Condé Nast Archive/CORBIS; L, Minnesota Historical Society/CORBIS; **258:** B, The Granger Collection, New York; T, Getty Images; **259:** Bettmann/CORBIS; **261:** Brown Brothers; **263:** B, Bettmann/CORBIS; T, Bettmann/CORBIS; M, The Granger Collection, New York; BR, Horace Bristol/CORBIS; **264:** TL, Library of Congress; B, CORBIS; **264–265:** T, Museum of History and Industry/CORBIS; **266:** AP/Wide World Photos; **267:** The Granger Collection, New York; **268:** Copyright the Dorothea Lange Collection, Oakland Museum of California, City of Oakland. Gift of Paul S. Taylor; **269:** Library of Congress; **270:** B, © Mary Evans Picture Library/The Image Works; **270–271:** AP/Wide World Photos; **271:** TL, The Granger Collection, New York; TR, AP/Wide World Photos; BR, Prentice Hall; BL, CORBIS; **272:** T, Hulton Archive/Getty Images Inc.; B, Prentice Hall; **273:** CORBIS; **274:** CORBIS; **275:** M, Prentice Hall; T, Hulton/Getty Images; B, AP/Wide World Photos; BR, Bettmann/CORBIS; **277:** B, Getty Images; T, Peter Anderson/© Dorling Kindersley; **278:** CORBIS; **279:** The Granger Collection, New York; **280:** Minnesota Historical Society/CORBIS; **282–283:** CORBIS; **283:** M, Blank Archives/Getty Images; B, David J. & Janice L. Frent Collection/CORBIS; T, The Granger Collection, New York; **284:** R, Hulton Archive/Getty Images; L, The Granger Collection, New York; **285:** *New York Daily News*; **286:** R, CORBIS; M, The Granger Collection, New York; TL, Topham/The Image Works; BL, CORBIS; **287:** Bettmann/CORBIS; **288:** R, CORBIS; L, CORBIS; **289:** The Granger Collection, New York; **290:** L, Bettmann/CORBIS; R, Bettmann/CORBIS; **291:** T, AP/Wide World Photos; Inset, no credit necessary; **292:** Minnesota Historical Society/CORBIS; **293:** CORBIS; **294:** TL, Bettmann/CORBIS; BL, Associated Press, AP; BR, Bettmann/CORBIS; TR, Library of Congress; **295:** TR, Monika Graff/The Image Works; L, Michael Newman/PhotoEdit; M, Mark Antman/The Image Works; BR, Dennis MacDonald/PhotoEdit; **296:** B, Bettmann/CORBIS; Inset, CORBIS; **297:** *Celebrate the Century, 1930s FDR's New Deal* © 1998 Used with permission. All rights reserved. Written authorization from the Postal Service is required to use, reproduce, post, transmit, distribute, or publicly display these images; **298:** Library of Congress; **299:** AP/Wide World Photos; **300:** Bettmann/CORBIS; **301:** L, CORBIS; R, Library of Congress; **302:** AP/Wide World Photos; **303:** AP/Wide World Photos; **305:** Tim Boyle/Getty Images; **309:** White House Photo Office; **310:** MGM/THE KOBAL COLLECTION; **311:** BL, Getty Images; BR, Bettmann/CORBIS; M, The Advertising Archive;

**312:** BL, CORBIS; **312–313:** B, Smithsonian American Art Museum, Washington, D.C./Art Resource, NY; **313:** BR, Kelly-Mooney Photography/CORBIS; **314:** The Granger Collection, New York; **315:** ML, SELZNICK/MGM/THE KOBAL COLLECTION; MR, Everett Collection; TR, The Granger Collection, New York; BL, United Artists/Photofest; **316:** L, Hulton Archive/Getty Images; R, Bettmann/CORBIS; **317:** L, CORBIS; R, SELZNICK/MGM/THE KOBAL COLLECTION; **318:** CORBIS; **319:** *International Herald Tribune*; **320:** TM, The Granger Collection, New York; TL, © Reuters/CORBIS; TR, The Granger Collection, New York; MR, © Bettmann/CORBIS; ML, The Granger Collection, New York; BL, © Bettmann/CORBIS; BR, © Bettmann/CORBIS; Background, The Art Archive/National Archives, Washington, D.C.; **321:** Alfred Eisenstaedt/Pix Inc./Time & Life Pictures/Getty Images; **322–323:** Hulton-Deutsch Collection/CORBIS; **323:** T, The Art Archive/Imperial War Museum; B, Deutsches Historisches Museum, Berlin; M, Philip Makanna/GHOSTS; L, The New York Public Library/Art Resource, NY; **325:** Getty Images; **326:** R, akg-images; L, akg-images; M, Bettmann/CORBIS; **327:** L, Bettmann/CORBIS; R, Bettmann/CORBIS; M, Mary Evans Picture Library 2005; **329:** Bettman/CORBIS; **330:** CORBIS; **331:** Bettmann/CORBIS; **332:** L, Bettman/CORBIS; R, Bettmann/CORBIS; **333:** Bettmann/CORBIS; **334:** CORBIS; **335:** L, Bettman/CORBIS; R, Hulton-Deutsch Collection/CORBIS; M, Bettman/CORBIS; **336:** The Granger Collection, New York; **337:** B, Bettmann/CORBIS; T, Time Life Pictures/Getty Images; **338:** AP/Wide World Photos; **339:** Printed by permission for the Norman Rockwell Family Agency Copyright © 1943 the Norman Rockwell Family Entities/CORBIS; **340:** Bettman/CORBIS; **341:** B, Bettmann/CORBIS; T, The Art Archive/Imperial War Museum; **342:** BL, AP/Wide World Photos; TL, Philip Makanna/GHOSTS; **342–343:** BR, Scott Swanson/Archive Inc.; **343:** L, Photo by Three Lions/Getty Images; R, Photo by Three Lions/Getty Images; M, SuperStock, Inc./SuperStock; **344:** Courtesy National Archives and Records Administration, College Park, Maryland, photo no. (NWDNS-208-AA-352QQ(5)); **345:** Brown Brothers; **346:** Getty Images; **348:** Bettman/CORBIS; **349:** R, Photo by Three Lions/Getty Images; L, Bettman/CORBIS; **350:** Bettman/CORBIS; **351:** CORBIS; **352–353:** CORBIS; **353:** T, AP/Wide World Photos; M, Getty Images; B, Peter Wilson/© Dorling Kindersley, Courtesy of the Museum of the Regiments, Calgary; **354:** L, Getty Images; R, Getty Images; **355:** CORBIS; **356:** Background, AP/Wide World Photos; R, National Archives; T,

DRAGESCO-JOFFE, ALAIN/Animals Animals - Earth Scenes; **357:** BR, Bettmann/CORBIS; **358:** L, AP/Wide World Photos; R, Prentice Hall; **358–359:** Background, National Archives and Records Administration; **359:** R, © A724/GAMMA; **360:** Brown Brothers; **361:** T, Library of Congress; B, Time Life Pictures/National Archives/Getty Images, Inc.; **362:** Hulton Archive/Getty Images Inc.; **363:** CORBIS; **364:** R, AP/Wide World Photos; L, Bettmann/CORBIS; **365:** BR, Peter Wilson/© Dorling Kindersley, Courtesy of the Museum of the Regiments, Calgary; **366:** B, Everett Collection; T, Everett Collection; **367:** T, Brown Brothers; B, AP/Wide World Photos; **368:** TL, National Archives; Background, B, AP/Wide World Photos; BR, AP/Wide World Photos; Inset, BL, SuperStock, Inc.; MR, The Granger Collection, New York; **368–369:** TR, Library of Congress; **369:** R, SuperStock, Inc./SuperStock; Background, AP/Wide World Photos; **370:** L, Brown Brothers; R, Time Life Pictures/Getty Images; **371:** Bettmann/CORBIS; **372:** BR, KEYSTONE-FRANCE/ImageState; BL, Prentice Hall; TL, Courtesy Julie Fulmer © Prentice Hall; **372–373:** Background, by ROBERT CAPA © 2001 By Cornell Capa/Magnum Photos; **373:** T, MYCHELE DANIAU/AFP/Getty Images; **375:** T, Bettmann/CORBIS; B, AP/Wide World Photos; **377:** Brown Brothers; **378:** U.S. Air Force; **379:** T, Bettmann/CORBIS; B, Andy Crawford/Dorling Kindersley © By kind permission of The Trustees of the Imperial War Museum, London; **380:** CORBIS; **381:** L, Bettmann/CORBIS; R, Andy Crawford/Dorling Kindersley © Imperial War Museum, London; **382:** M, U.S. Holocaust Memorial Museum. The views or opinions expressed in this book and the context in which the image is used, do not necessarily reflect the views or policy of, not imply approval or endorsement by, The United States Holocaust Memorial Museum.; TL, akg-images; Background, B, USHMM, courtesy of Robert A. Schmuhl; ML, CORBIS; TR, Topham/The Image Works; M, U.S. National Archives/Roger-Viollet/The Image Works; Inset, B, USHMM, courtesy of KZ Gedenkstaette Dachau; Background, T, Keystone/GettyImages; **385:** Vincent Kessler/CORBIS; **386:** LEONE - ullstein bild/The Granger Collection, New York; **387:** Bettmann/CORBIS; **389:** Bettmann/CORBIS; **391:** Brown Brothers; **392:** R, Peter Wilson/© Dorling Kindersley, Courtesy of the Museum of the Regiments, Calgary; L, SuperStock, Inc.; **393:** R, CORBIS; L, Bettmann/CORBIS; **394:** T, Used with permission from the *Stars and Stripes*, a DoD publication. @ 2005 *Stars and Stripes*; B, KEYSTONE-FRANCE/ImageState; **396–397:** Bettmann/

CORBIS; **397:** T, William A. Bake/CORBIS; M, Getty Images; B, CONELRAD Collection; **398:** R, Getty Images; L, Getty Images; **399:** Bettmann/CORBIS; **401:** Solo Syndication/Associated Newspapers; **402:** Bettmann/CORBIS; **403:** Background, Bettmann/CORBIS; T, Keystone/Getty Images; **405:** T, www.ourdocuments.gov/NARA; B, Bettmann/CORBIS; **406:** L, CORBIS; R, William A. Bake/CORBIS; **407:** AP/Wide World Photos; **408:** Bettmann/CORBIS; **410:** Bettmann/CORBIS; **411:** John Nordell/The Image Works; **412:** R, Getty Images; L, CONELRAD Collection; **414:** BL, Jerry Cooke/CORBIS; MR, Bettmann/CORBIS; TL, Bettmann/CORBIS; TR, Jerry Cooke/CORBIS; **415:** Time Inc./Time Life Pictures/Getty Images; **417:** B, Getty Images; T, Sovfoto/Eastfoto; **418:** T, CONELRAD Collection; M, CORBIS; BL, Bettmann/CORBIS; BR, Bettmann/CORBIS; **418–419:** AP/Wide World Photos; **419:** L, BL, Conelrad Collection; TR, Civil Defense Museum; **420:** Conelrad Collection; **421:** The Granger Collection, New York; **422:** Inset, Image courtesy of The Advertising Archives/© 2006 Marvel Characters, Inc. Used with permission; Background, T Conelrad Collection; **422–423:** Conelrad Collection; **423:** R, Allied Artists/The Kobal Collection; L, Courtesy Everett Collection/Everett Collection; Background, T Conelrad Collection; **424:** T, AFP/Getty Images; B, Time Life Pictures/Getty Images; **425:** The Granger Collection, New York; **426:** Marvin Koner/CORBIS; **427:** © Time Life Pictures/Getty Images; **428:** L, Bettmann/CORBIS; R, Bettmann/CORBIS; **429:** B, The Image Works; T, Time Life Pictures/Getty Images; **430:** CORBIS; **431:** The Granger Collection, New York; **432–433:** Getty Images; **433:** M, Dwight D. Eisenhower Library; Bob Paull, Staff Photographer; T, The Granger Collection, New York; B, Bettmann/CORBIS; **434:** Indiana U. Archives & Photographic Services(#47-1082); **435:** Hulton Archive/Getty Images Inc.; **436:** Underwood & Underwood/CORBIS; **437:** L, Associated Press, AP; R, Ewing Galloway/Index Stock Imagery, Inc.; **438:** TL, W. Eugene Smith/Time & Life Pictures/Getty Images; Inset, no credit; **439:** Bettmann/CORBIS; **440:** TL, Photo by J. R. Eyerman/Time Life Pictures/Getty Images; Inset, Richard Wurts/National Building Museum; **441:** Bettmann/CORBIS; **442:** R, H. Armstrong Roberts/CORBIS; L, H. Armstrong Roberts/Robertstock; **443:** R, Philip Gendreau/CORBIS; L, H. Armstrong Roberts/Robertstock; **444:** R. KRUBNER/H. Armstrong Roberts; **445:** CORBIS; **446:** Bettmann/CORBIS; **447:** Brown Brothers; **448:** TL, John Dominis/Time Life Pictures/Getty Images; Inset, Smithsonian Institution

Collections, National Museum of American History, Behring Center.; **449:** BR, Tom Kelley/Hulton Archive/Getty Images; Inset, The Granger Collection, New York; **450:** Bettmann/CORBIS; **451:** BL, Time & Life Pictures/Getty Images; M, Penguin USA; TR, H. Armstrong Roberts/Robertstock; TL, CBS Photo Archive/Getty Images; BR, Getty Images; **452:** TM, Getty Images; M, Image courtesy of The Advertising Archives; TR, CBS Photo Archive/Getty Images; TL, Wrather Corp/Apex Film Corp/The Kobal Collection; **453:** Dunigan/H.Armstrong Roberts; **454:** T, MICHAEL OCHS ARCHIVES.COM; MR, Aardman Animations Ltd.; B, Don Wright/Time & Life Pictures/Getty Images; ML, The Everett Collection, Inc.; **455:** TR, Bettmann/CORBIS; Inset, Touchstone/Simon & Schuster; **456:** Photofest; **457:** L, Bruce Davidson/Magnum Photos; R, AP/Wide World Photos; **458:** Bettmann/CORBIS; **459:** Library of Congress; **460:** L, Library of Congress; R, Richard Wurts/National Building Museum; **461:** B, Touchstone, ©1981; **462:** B, MICHAEL OCHS ARCHIVES.COM; **462:** T, no credit; **463:** R, Collection of the State Museum of Pennsylvania; L, AP/Wide World Photos; **464:** TM, The Granger Collection, New York; TL, © Reuters/CORBIS; TR, The Granger Collection, New York; MR, © Bettmann/CORBIS; ML, The Granger Collection, New York; BL, © Bettmann/CORBIS; ML, The Granger Collection, New York; BR, © Bettmann/CORBIS; Background, The Art Archive/National Archives Washington, D.C.; **465:** © 1976/George Ballis/Take Stock; **466–467:** Bettmann/CORBIS; **467:** T, David J. & Janice L. Frent Collections/CORBIS; B, National Museum of American History, Smithsonian Institution; M, Bettman/CORBIS; **468:** B, CORBIS; T, AP/Wide World Photos; **469:** R, Bettman/CORBIS; L, Magnum Photos; **470:** Time Life Pictures/Getty Images; **471:** Time Life Pictures/Getty Images; **472:** Inset, AP/Wide World Photos; Background, AP/Wide World Photos; **473:** Bettmann/CORBIS; **474:** B, Time Life Pictures/Getty Images; T, Prentice Hall; M, The Granger Collection, New York; **476:** M, Time Life Pictures/Getty Images; B, Bob Daemmrich/The Image Works; T, CORBIS; **477:** L, AP/Wide World Photos; R, AP/Wide World Photos/Montgomery Advertiser; **478:** R, Bettman/CORBIS; L Bettman/CORBIS; **479:** BR, Bettmann/CORBIS; Background, B, Bettmann/CORBIS; T, Bruce Davidson/Magnum Photos; **480:** T, AP/Wide World Photos; B, AP/Wide World Photos; **481:** AP/Wide World Photos; **482:** Time & Life Pictures/Getty Images; **482–483:** Background, Flip Schulke/Black Star; **483:** BR, Flip Schulke/CORBIS; BL, John F. Kennedy Library, National Archives, document MS 2003-036; TR, National Museum of American History, Smithsonian

Institution; **485:** Inset, Time Life Pictures/Getty Images; Background, Flip Schulke/CORBIS; **486:** L, AP/Wide World Photos; **486–487:** B, AP/Wide World Photos; T, Bettmann/CORBIS; **487:** TR, Bettmann/CORBIS; **488:** R, Time Life Pictures/Getty Images; L, David J. & Janice L. Frent Collections/CORBIS; **489:** AP/Wide World Photos; **490:** Flip Schulke/CORBIS; **491:** T, AP/Wide World Photos; B, Flip Schulke/CORBIS; **492:** B, David J. & Janice L. Frent Collections/CORBIS; **492–493:** TL, Bettmann/CORBIS; **493:** TR, AP/Wide World Photos; **494:** Background, T, AP/Wide World Photos; TR, Bob Adelman/Magnum Photos; B, POPPER-FOTO/Alamy; **497:** B, Photofest **498:** R, AP/Wide World Photos; L, Time Life Pictures/Getty Images; **499:** R, Time & Life Pictures/Getty Images; L, Bettman/CORBIS; **500:** AP/Wide World Photos; **501:** AP Photo/Bill Hudson; **502:** L, © Hulton-Deutsch Collection/CORBIS; **502–503:** Bettmann/Sygma/CORBIS; **503:** M, The Peace Corps; T, David J. and Janice L. Frent Collection/CORBIS; B, Time & Life Pictures/Getty Images; **504:** David J. and Janice L. Frent Collection/CORBIS; **505:** Inset, Bettmann/CORBIS; Getty Images; **506:** CORBIS; **507:** R, Paul Conklin Photography/PhotoEdit; L, JP Laffont/Sygma/CORBIS; **509:** CORBIS; **511:** Bettmann/CORBIS; **512:** T, Bettmann/CORBIS; B, CORBIS; **513:** "Eclipse" from *Straight Herblock* (Simon & Schuster, 1964); **514:** MR, NASA; TL, NIX/NASA Image Exchange; TR, GRIN Great Images in NASA; B, GRIN Great Images in NASA; ML, GRIN Great Images in NASA; **515:** Bettmann/CORBIS; **516:** T, stockphoto.com; B, Larry Kolvoord/The Image Works; **517:** Bettmann/CORBIS; **518:** Bettmann/CORBIS; **519:** T, James Leynse/CORBIS; B, Bettmann/CORBIS; **520:** BL, Marty Heitner/The Image Works; T, AP/Wide World Photos; B, Banana Stock/AGE Fotostock; **521:** TL, Sesame Street and associated characters, trademarks and design elements are owned and licensed by Sesame Workshop.© 2006 Sesame Workshop. All rights reserved.; TR, ArenaPal/Topham/The Image Works; B, Hulton Archive/Getty Images; **522:** L, Getty Images; R, Yoav Levy/Phototake; **523:** Bettmann/CORBIS; **525:** Paul S. Conklin/PhotoEdit; AP/Wide World Photos; **526:** National Portrait Gallery, Smithsonian Institution/Art Resource, NY; **528:** Bettmann/CORBIS; **530–531:** The Granger Collection, New York; **531:** M, Library of Congress; B, West Point Museum Collection; T, National Museum of American History, Smithsonian Institution; **532:** Topham/The Image Works; **533:** WolfgangKaehler/CORBIS; **534:** TL, AFP/AFP/Getty Images; TR, Topham/The Image Works; **535:** AP/Wide World Photos; **536:** Pierre-Aux wcoutes, Paris/Rothco Cartoons; **537:**

TR, National Archives and Records Administration, Records of the U.S. Marine Corps; L, West Point Museum Collection; **539:** B, AP/Wide World Photos; **540:** R, Time Life Pictures/Getty Images; TL, National Archives; BL, AP/Wide World Photos; **541:** R, Ullstein Bild/The Granger Collection, New York; M, Associated Press, AP; **542:** Associated Press/Wide World Photos; **543:** T, "Onward And Upward And Onward And" from *The Herblock Gallery* (Simon & Schuster, 1968); **544:** R, Leif Skoogfors/CORBIS; L, CBS Photo Archive/Getty Images; border, Getty Images; **545:** Topham/The Image Works; **546:** Bernard Gotfryd/Getty Images; **548:** Basset/National Archives and Records Administration; **549:** TR, Associated Press, AP; TL, Time Life Pictures/Getty Images; BL, Getty Images; BR, Bettmann/CORBIS; M, Bettmann/CORBIS; **550:** Photo by Bob Peterson/Time Life Pictures/Getty Images; **551:** B, © David J. & Janice L. Frent Collections; T, © David J. & Janice L. Frent Collections; **552:** L, Leif Skoogfors/CORBIS; R, © David J. & Janice L. Frent Collection/CORBIS; **553:** AP/Wide World Photos/USAF; **554:** Getty Images; **555:** T, Photo by Ronald S. Haeberle/Time Life Pictures/Getty; B, Time Inc./Time Life Pictures/Getty Images; **556:** BL, Getty Images; TL, AbsoluteStockPhoto.com/Alamy; R, Charles E. Pefley/Mira.com; **557:** L, Associated Press, AP; BR, Brand X Pictures/Alamy; TR, Prentice Hall; **558:** T, AHMAD MASOOD/Reuters/Corbis; B, stockphoto.com; **560:** L, Bettmann/CORBIS; R, Corel Professional Photos CD-ROM™; M, Corel Professional Photos CD-ROM™; **561:** Bettmann/CORBIS; **562:** B, National Museum of American History, Smithsonian Institution; T, AP/Wide World Photos; **563:** Dirck Halstead/Liaison/Getty Images; **564:** AP Photo/Malcolm Browne; **565:** L, Photo by Terry Ashe/Time Life Pictures/Getty Images; B, Corel Professional Photos CD-ROM™;R, Corel Professional Photos CD-ROM™; **566:** stockphoto.com; **567:** AP/Wide World Photos; **568–569:** Time Life Pictures/Getty Images; **569:** B, Wally McNamee/CORBIS; T, Charles Gatewood/The Image Works; M, Blank Archives/Getty Images; **570:** Background, Time Life Pictures/Getty Images; L, Getty Images; R, John Dominis/The Image Works; **571:** B, © Wes Wilson; **572:** L, The Granger Collection, New York; TMR, Getty Images, Inc.; BL, Henry Diltz/CORBIS; TML, Blank Archives/Getty Images; TR, H. Armstrong Roberts/Robertstock; BR, Jason Reed/Reuters/CORBIS; BML, *Mad* cover #140 image courtesy of Doug Gilford's *Mad* Cover Site - collectmad.com/madcoversite; TL, Prentice Hall; Background R, Prentice Hall; Background L, Prentice Hall; **574:** L, Charles Gatewood/The Image

Works; R, Bettmann/CORBIS; **575:** Bettmann/CORBIS; **576:** R, AP/Wide World Photos; L, © *Ms. Magazine;* **577:** L, Bettmann/CORBIS; R, AP/Wide World Photos; **579:** T, © Frank Cantor; B, Mary Kate Denny/PhotoEdit; **580:** Tribute to Diego Rivera/© 1998 & 2006 Philadelphia Mural Arts Program/Jane Golden/Delia King/Photo by Jack Ramsdale/Reprinted by permission; **581:** B, Time Life Pictures/Getty Images; T, AP Photo/Barry Sweet; **582:** R, Prentice Hall; L, AP Photo; **583:** L, Galen Rowell/CORBIS; Background, AP Photo; R, Ed Kashi/CORBIS; **584:** L, Bettmann/CORBIS; R, AP/Worldwide Photos; **585:** AP Photo/*The Post and Courier*, Mic Smith; TR, Photofest; **586:** TL, Library of Congress; **586–587:** BL, Bettmann/CORBIS; **587:** BR, AP Photo/Nature Consortium,Ron Wurzer; **588:** Inset, CORBIS; **588–589:** Background, Ohio EPA; **589:** L, Ohio EPA; R, Ohio EPA; **590:** T, Copyright © John Warden/Alaska Stock LLC; B, Thomas Moran, The Grand Canyon of the Yellowstone, 1872, The U.S. Department of the Interior Museum, Washington, D.C.; **592:** Time Life Pictures/Getty Images; **593:** Henry Diltz/CORBIS; **594:** Photofest; **595:** © 1998 by Lalo Alcaraz, All Rights Reserved; **596–597:** Bettmann/CORBIS; **597:** Dennis Brack/Black Star/stockphoto.com; T, Connie Ricca/CORBIS; M, AP/Wide World Photos; **598:** **599:** Pelican Publications Company, Inc.; **600:** L, Bettmann/CORBIS; R, Bettmann/CORBIS; **602:** MR, Bettmann/CORBIS; BL, AP/Wide World Photos; BR, Mark Godfrey/The Image Works; TM, Prentice Hall; TR, Prentice Hall; TL, Prentice Hall; **603:** TL, AP Photo/National Archives; TR, Bettmann/CORBIS; BR, Mark Godfrey/The Image Works; BL, Charles Gatewood/The Image Works; **604:** B, Nixon Presidential Materials Project, National Archives and Records Administration. Photo by Oliver F. Atkins; T, *New York Daily News*; **606:** Courtesy *Worcester (Mass) Telegram;* **607:** Mark Godfrey/The Image Works; **608:** T, Bettmann/CORBIS; B, Bettmann/CORBIS; **609:** B, Larry Lee Photography/CORBIS; T, Black Star; **610:** Nathan Benn/CORBIS; **611:** Background, Mark Richards/PhotoEdit; Inset, L, Jeffrey D. Smith/Woodfin Camp; Inset, R, Cleo Photography/PhotoEdit; **612:** #3, Courtesy Everett Collection/Everett Collection; B, Bettmann/CORBIS; #1, CBS/Landov; #2, Courtesy Everett Collection/Everett Collection; #5, © ABC-TV/THE KOBAL COLLECTION; #4, CBS/Landov; TR, Courtesy Everett Collection/Everett Collection; BR, © PARAMOUNT TELE-VISION/THE KOBAL COLLECTION; B, Bettmann/CORBIS; Inset, #4, CBS/Landov; **614:** T, Bettmann/CORBIS; B, Michael Pole/CORBIS; **615:** AP/Wide World Photos; **616:**

Bettmann/CORBIS; **617:** Mark Peterson/CORBIS; **618:** R, Kaveh Kazemi/CORBIS; L, Roger-Viollet/The Image Works; **618–619:** Inset, Bettmann/CORBIS; **619:** L, Wally McNamee/CORBIS; R. AP/Wide World Photos; **620:** L, Black Star; R, Wally McNamee/CORBIS; **621:** Time & Life Pictures/Getty Images; **622:** Dennis Brack/Black Star/stockphoto.com; **623:** from *Herblock: A Cartoonist's Life* (Time Books, 1998); **624:** TM, The Granger Collection, New York; TL, © Reuters/CORBIS; TR, The Granger Collection, New York; MR, © Bettmann/CORBIS; ML, The Granger Collection, New York; BL, © Bettmann/CORBIS; ML, The Granger Collection, New York; BR, © Bettmann/CORBIS; Background, The Art Archive/National Archives Washington, D.C.; **625:** Jose L. Pelaez/CORBIS; **626–627:** CORBIS; **627:** M, Bettmann/CORBIS; T, Pearson Education/Prentice Hall School; B, SPELLING/ABC/THE KOBAL COLLECTION; **628:** Photo by Time Life Pictures/Time Magazine, Copyright Time Inc./Time Life Pictures/Getty Images; **630:** Wally McNamee/CORBIS; **631:** Bettmann/CORBIS; **633:** L, NARA/Ronald Reagan Presidential Library; R, Pearson Education/Prentice Hall School; **635:** AP/Wide World Photos/Ron Edmonds; **636:** MR, AP Photo/Bruce Weaver; BM, Photos12.com/Polaris; TL, SPELLING/ABC/THE KOBAL COLLECTION; TR, STOCKFOLIO/Alamy; M, AP Photo/Barry Thumma; BL, Prentice Hall; **637:** AP/Wide World Photos/Charles Tasnadi; **638:** T, AP/Wide World Photos; B, Time Life Pictures/Getty Images; **639:** Leif Skoogfors/CORBIS; **640:** Bill Gentile/CORBIS; **641:** © Wright, *Providence Journal Bulletin*; **642:** T, CORBIS; M, Prentice Hall; BL, AFP/Getty Images; BR, UK-PRESS/GAMMA; **643:** BR, AP Photo/Lionel Cironneau; TL, Peter Turnley/CORBIS; BL, Charles Steiner/The Image Works; TR, AP Photo/Doug Mills; **645:** J.L. Atlan/Sygma/CORBIS; **646:** Time Life Pictures/Getty Images; **647:** R, Jacques Langevin/CORBIS SYGMA; L, Bettmann/CORBIS; M, Betty Press/Woodfin Camp; **648:** Ben Gibson-Katz/Woodfin Camp; **649:** J A Giordano/CORBIS SABA; **650:** NARA/Ronald Reagan Presidential Library; **651:** T, AFP/Getty Images; B, Bettmann/CORBIS; **652:** AP Photo/Lionel Cironneau; **654–655:** AP/Wide World Photos/Ann Johansson; **655:** M, Mark Avery/Orange County Register/CORBIS; B, NASA/Photo Researchers, Inc.; T, Patrick Robert/CORBIS; **656:** T, Courtesy of Dell Inc.; **657:** B, AP Photo/*The Fort Wayne Journal Gazette*, Samuel Hoffman; T, AP Photo/Steven Senne; **661:** L, Arnie Sachs/CORBIS; R, Pearson Education/PH School Division; **662:** AP/Wide World Photos/Susan Ragan; **663:** Reuters/CORBIS; **664:** T, AP/Wide World Photos/Joe Marquette; B, Najlah Feanny/CORBIS; **666:** AP/

Wide World Photos/Robert Mecea; **667:** Whittemore-Rothco Cartoons; **668:** BL, © Scott Wallace/World Bank; T, ARKO DATTA/AFP/Getty Images; BR, © Scott Wallace/World Bank; M, © Scott Wallace/World Bank; T, Ariadne Van Zandbergen/Lonely Planet/Getty Images; **669:** Tore Bergsaker/Sygma/CORBIS; **670:** Reuters/CORBIS; **671:** R, Mark Avery/Orange Country Register/CORBIS; L, KEVIN LAMARQUE/Reuters/CORBIS; **672:** RHONA WISE/AFP/Getty Images; **673:** R, © 2001. All rights reserved. Reprint permission provided by Mike Peters in conjunction with the Cartoonist Group.; L, STEVE KELLEY Courtesy *San Diego Union-Tribune*; R, © 2001. All rights reserved. Reprint permission provided by Mike Peters in conjunction with the Cartoonist Group.; **674:** Inset, REUTERS/Sean Adair/Files SV; Background, AP/Wide World Photos; T, Reuters/CORBIS; **675:** BL, Mario Tama/Getty Images; TL, Patrick Andrade/Polaris; Background, Steve McCurry/Magnum Photos; TR, REUTERS/Kai Pfaffenbach; **677:** Martin H. Simon/CORBIS; **678:** Morry Gash/Associated Press; **679:** R, Courtesy Linda and Eddie Tran; L, Courtesy Linda and Eddie Tran; **680:** AP Photo/Matt York; **682:** Bob Daemmrich/The Image Works; **683:** SUPRI/Reuters/CORBIS; **684:** AP/Wide World Photos/Susan Ragan; **685:** R, Christophe Calais/In Visu /CORBIS; L, Mario Tama/Getty Images; **686:** T, AP/Wide World Photos; B, AP Photo/Matt York; **687:** © Dan Wasserman, 2005; Courtesy of Tribune Media Services; **688:** Background, The Art Archive/National Archives Washington, D.C.; BR: © Bettmann/CORBIS; ML, The Granger Collection, New York; TM, The Granger Collection, New York; BL, © Bettmann/CORBIS; MR, © Bettmann/CORBIS; TR, The Granger Collection, New York; TL, © Reuters/CORBIS; **689:** Richard Rowan/Photo Researchers, Inc.; **690:** TL, Joseph Sohm, ChromoSohm Media Inc./Photo Researchers, Inc.; TR, © Jim Corwin/The Stock Connection; M, Copyright © DEAN RIGGOTT/Grant Heilman Photography – All rights reserved; TM, © Royalty-Free/CORBIS; B, Jeff Greenberg/Omni-Photo Communications, Inc.; **701:** #1, © National Portrait Gallery, Smithsonian Institution/Art Resource, NY; #2, © National Portrait Gallery, Smithsonian Institution/Art Resource, NY; #3, White House Collection, copyright White House Historical Association; #4, © National Portrait Gallery, Smithsonian Institution/Art Resource, NY; #5, © National Portrait Gallery, Smithsonian Institution/Art Resource, NY; #6, © National Portrait Gallery, Smithsonian Institution/Art Resource, NY; #7, White House Collection, copyright White House Historical Association; #8, White House Collection, copyright White House Historical Association; #9, ©

National Portrait Gallery, Smithsonian Institution/Art Resource, NY; #10, © National Portrait Gallery, Smithsonian Institution/Art Resource, NY; #11, White House Collection, copyright White House Historical Association; #12, © National Portrait Gallery, Smithsonian Institution/Art Resource, NY; #13, White House Collection, copyright White House Historical Association; #14, © National Portrait Gallery, Smithsonian Institution/Art Resource, NY; #15,© National Portrait Gallery, Smithsonian Institution/Art Resource, NY; #16, National Portrait Gallery, Smithsonian Institution/Art Resource, NY **701–703:** Background, Corel Professional Photos CD-ROM™; **702:** #17, White House Collection, copyright White House Historical Association; #18, © National Portrait Gallery, Smithsonian Institution/Art Resource, NY; #19, White House Collection, copyright White House Historical Association; #20, © National Portrait Gallery, Smithsonian Institution/Art Resource, NY; #21, © National Portrait Gallery, Smithsonian Institution/Art Resource, NY; #22, White House Collection, copyright White House Historical Association; #23, White House Collection, copyright White House Historical Association; #24, White House Collection, copyright White House Historical Association; #25, © National Portrait Gallery, Smithsonian Institution/Art Resource, NY; #26, © National Portrait Gallery, Smithsonian Institution/Art Resource, NY; #27, © National Portrait Gallery, Smithsonian Institution/Art Resource, NY; #28, White House Collection, copyright White House Historical Association; #29, White House Collection, copyright White House Historical Association; #30, White House Collection, copyright White House Historical Association; #31, White House Collection, copyright White House Historical Association; #32, White House Collection, copyright White House Historical Association; **703:** #33, White House Collection, copyright White House Historical Association; #34, White House Collection, copyright White House Historical Association; #35, © National Portrait Gallery, Smithsonian Institution/Art Resource, NY; #36, White House Collection, copyright White House Historical Association; #37: White House Collection, copyright White House Historical Association; #38, White House Collection, copyright White House Historical Association; #39, White House Collection, copyright White House Historical Association; #40, White House Collection, copyright White House Historical Association; #41: White House Collection, copyright White House Historical Association; #42, White House Collection, copyright White House Historical Association (Detail); B, The Granger Collection,

New York; Corel Professional Photos CD-ROM™; #43, White House Photo Office, (Detail); #44, Charles Rex Arbogast/Associated Press; **704:** Lester Lefkowitz/CORBIS; **705:** Stockbyte; **706:** © North Wind Picture Archives; **707:** T, Blair Seitz/Stock Connection; B, Getty Images; **708:** Michael Newman/PhotoEdit; **710:** AP/Wide World Photos; **712:** AP/Wide World Photos; **725:** B, Bettmann/CORBIS; T, The Granger Collection, New York; **726:** Bettmann/CORBIS; **727:** T, Réunion des Musées Nationaux/Art Resource, NY; B, The Colonial Williamsburg Foundation; **728:** Copyright © North Wind/North Wind Picture Archives – All rights reserved; **729:** The Granger Collection, New York; **730:** T, Composite photograph of the almost 200-year-old Star-Spangled Banner, the flag that inspired the national anthem. Smithsonian's National Museum of American History, ©2004; B, The Granger Collection, New York; **731:** © Bettmann/CORBIS; **732–733:** AP/Wide World Photos; **734:** © Christie's Images/CORBIS; **735:** Alan Schein/ZEFA/CORBIS; **736:** CORBIS; **737:** Brown Brothers; **738:** Bettmann/CORBIS; **739:** Paul A. Souders/CORBIS; **740:** Bettmann/CORBIS; **741:** T, Bettmann/CORBIS; B, P Laffont/Sygma/CORBIS; **742:** Reuters/CORBIS; **743:** Time Life Pictures/Getty Images; **744:** T, Reuters/CORBIS; B, Reuters/CORBIS

**Text**
**Grateful acknowledgment is made to the following for copyrighted material: About.com** Excerpt from "Why I Support Amnesty for Undocumented Immigrants" from *http://civilliberty.about.com/od/immigrantsrights/a/amnesty.htm* by Tom Head. Copyright © 2008 About.com, a part of The New York Times Company. **The Estate of Stokely Carmichael** From "Black Power" as delivered by Stokely Carmichael, 1966, Berkeley, CA. Copyright © 1966 The Estate of Stokely Carmichael. From "Stokely Speaks," Copyright © 1971 Random House, Inc. Used by permission of the Estate of Stokely Carmichael. www.readyfortherevolution.org. **EMI FEIST CATALOG, INC. (Publishing) and ALFRED PUBLISHING CO., INC. (Print)** OVER THE RAINBOW. Music by HAROLD ARLEN. Lyric by E.Y. HARBURG. Copyright © 1938 (Renewed) METRO-GOLDWYN-MAYER, INC. Copyright © 1939 (Renewed) EMI FEIST CATALOG, INC. All Rights Controlled by EMI FEIST CATALOG, INC. (Publishing) and ALFRED PUBLISHING CO., INC. (Print). All Rights Reserved. Used by Permission. **Employment Policies Institute** Excerpt from "How Do Minimum Wage Hikes Hurt Vulnerable Employees?" from *www.epionline.org*. Copyright © 2008 Employment Policies

Institute. **Amy Goodman** From "Independent Media in a Time of War." Copyright © 2003 by Amy Goodman. Used by permission of the author. **Guardian Newspapers Limited** From "Angry Young Cubans Take Over" by J. Halcro Ferguson. From THE OBSERVER, January 4, 1959. Copyright © 1959 Guardian Newspapers Limited. Used by permission. **Harcourt, Inc.** Excerpt from Chicago from Chicago Poems by Carl Sandburg. Copyright © 1916 by Holt, Rinehart and Winston and renewed 1944 by Carl Sandburg, Reproduced by permission of Harcourt, Inc. All rights reserved. **Alfred A. Knopf, a division of Random House, Inc.** Excerpt from "Beaumont to Detroit" from THE COLLECTED POEMS OF LANGSTON HUGHES by Langston Hughes. Copyright © 1994 by the Estate of Langston Hughes. Used by permission of Alfred A. Knopf, a division of Random House, Inc.; "My People," Copyright © 1926 by Alfred A. Knopf, Inc. and renewed 1954 by Langston Hughes., from SELECTED POEMS OF LANGSTON HUGHES by Langston Hughes. Used by permission of Alfred A. Knopf, a division of Random House, Inc.; "The Negro Speaks of Rivers" From THE COLLECTED POEMS OF LANGSTON HUGHES by Langston Hughes. Copyright © 1994 by the Estate of Langston Hughes. Used by permission of Alfred A. Knopf, a division of Random House, Inc. **Ludlow Music, Inc.** ROLL ON, COLUMBIA. Words by Woody Guthrie. Music based on GOODNIGHT, IRENE by Huddie Ledbetter and John A. Lomax. TRO-Copyright © 1936 (Renewed) 1957 (Renewed) and 1963 (Renewed). Ludlow Music, Inc., New York, NY. Used by permission. **Pat Mounce** Pat Mounce, a Pontococ, Mississippi parent regarding Pro-School Prayer. From www.itvs.org, Independent Television Service: School Prayer: A Community at War. Copyright © ITVS, San Francisco, California. **Music Sales Corporation (ASCAP) and Fred Ahlert Music Corporation** Rosie the Riveter. Words and Music by Redd Evans and John Jacob Loeb. Copyright © 1942 (Renewed Copyright © 1969) John J. Loeb Copmany and Music Sales Corporation (ASCAP). Exclusive licensee for John J. Loeb Company: Fred Ahlert Music Corporation. International Copyright Secured. All Rights Reserved. Reprinted by permission. **The Estate of Jewell Handy Gresham Nemiroff** from "A Raisin in the Sun" by Lorraine Hansberry. Copyright © 1958 by Robert Nemiroff, as an unpublished work. Copyright © 1959, 1966, 1984 by Robert Nemiroff. Random House, Inc. Spanish Language and Electronic Rights used by permission of the Estate of Jewell Handy Gresham Nemiroff. **Next Decade**

**Entertainment, Glocca Morra Music (ASCAP) & Gorney Music (ASCAP)** "Brother Can You Spare a Dime?" by E.Y. "Yip" Harburg & Jay Gorney. Published by Glocca Morra Music (ASCAP) & Gorney Music (ASCAP). Administered by Next Decade Entertainment, Inc. All rights reserved. Used by permission. **The New York Times Company** from "Taking a Long View of the Iraq Conflict" by David Brooks. From The New York Times, December 18, 2005. Copyright © 2005 The New York Times Company. Used by Permission. **Oxford University Press** "Morning In America" from Ronald Reagan's 1980 Presidential Campaign. From PACKAGING THE PRESIDENCY: A History and Criticism of Presidential Campaign Advertising: Third Edition. Copyright © 1984, 1992, 1996 by Kathleen Hall Jamieson. Used by permission of Oxford University Press. **Professor Richard Overy, professor of History, University of Exeter, United Kingdom** Excerpt from World War II: How the Allies Won. Reprinted by permission of Professor Richard Overy, professor of History, University of Exeter, United Kingdom. **Perseus Books, LLC** from "Almost A Woman." Copyright © 1997 by Canto-Media, Inc. Reprinted by permission of DA CAPO PRESS, a member of Perseus Books, LLC. **Progressive Labor Party** from The Great Flint Sit-Down Strike Against GM 1936-1937, Reprint Edition April 1999. Copyright © 1999 Progressive Labor Party. Used by permission. **Random House, Inc.** from "A Raisin in the Sun" by Lorraine Hansberry. Copyright © 1958 by Robert Nemiroff, as an unpublished work. Copyright © 1959, 1966, 1984 by Robert Nemiroff. Used by permission of Random House, Inc. **Saturday Evening Post Society** A Poem capturing the Bull Market Fever Reprinted from The Saturday Evening Post Magazine, Copyright © 1929 Saturday Evening Post Society. Used by permission. **Scribner, an imprint of Simon & Schuster Adult Publishing Group.** Excerpt from the Foreword from Manchild in the Promised Land. Reprinted with the permission of Scribner, an imprint of Simon & Schuster Adult Publishing Group. From MANCHILD IN THE PROMISED LAND by Claude Brown. Copyright © 1965 by Claude Brown.; Excerpt from The Other America. Reprinted with permission of Scribner, an imprint of Simon & Schuster Adult Publishing Group. From THE OTHER AMERICA: POVERTY IN THE UNITED STATES by Michael Harrington. Copyright © 1962, 1969, 1981 by Michael Harrington; Copyright renewed © 1990 by Stephanie Harrington. **Southwest Regional Counsel of Mexican American Legal Defense and Educational Fund** From "Statement Regarding the

Reauthorization of Section 5 of the Voting Rights Act" as delivered by Nina Perales of the Southwest Regional Counsel of Mexican American Legal Defense and Educational Fund to the United States House of Representatives Judiciary Subcommittee on the Constitution, October 25, 2005. **Southwest Voter Registration Education Project** Mission Statement of the Southwest Voter Registration Education Project. Copyright © 2004 Southwest Voter Registration Education Project. **Hunter S. Thompson** Excerpt from The Hashbury is the Capital of the Hippies. First published in the New York Times. Copyright © 1979 by Hunter S. Thompson. **Townnews.com** "1951: American Dream Houses, All in A Row" by John Blackwell from The Trentonian, June 20, 1999. Copyright © 1999 Townnews.com. All Rights Reserved. **University of Exeter Press** Louise Solmitz's Description of an Early Nazi Rally from NAZISM 1941–1945: A Documentary Reader, Volume 1: The Rise to Power 1919–1934, Edited by J. Noakes and G. Pridham, ISBN: 0 85989 598 X. Copyright © 1983, 2000 Department of History and Archaeology, University of Exeter. Used by permission of the University of Exeter Press. **USA Today** Excerpt from "Time to Drill in Alaska" from USA Today, December 20, 2005. Copyright © 2008 USA Today. **Viking Penguin, a division of Penguin Group (USA), Inc.** Excerpt From "Chapter 29" from THE GRAPES OF WRATH by John Steinbeck. Copyright © 1939, renewed © 1967 by John Steinbeck. Used by permission of Viking Penguin, a division of Penguin Group (USA), Inc. **The Washington Post Company** Excerpt from "Debate Could Turn on a 7-letter Word" from The Washington Post, May 30, 2007 by Pamela Constable. Copyright © 1996–2008 The Washington Post Company. **Alice Wine** from Sing for Freedom: The Story of the Civil Rights Movement Through its Songs. Copyright © 1963 Edited and compiled by Guy and Candie Carawan. Song Copyright © 1965 by Alice Wine. **Writers House, LLC as agent for the Estate of Martin Luther King, Jr.** from A Time to Break Silence. Reprinted by arrangement with the Estate of Martin Luther King Jr., c/o Writers House as agent for the proprietor New York, NY. Copyright © 1967 Martin Luther King Jr., Copyright renewed © 1995 Coretta Scott King.; from "I Have a A Dream". Reprinted by arrangement with the Estate of Martin Luther King, Jr., c/o Writers House as agent for the proprietor, New York, NY. Copyright © 1963 Martin Luther King Jr., Copyright renewed © 1991 Coretta Scott King.; From I've Been to the Mountain Top. Reprinted by arrangement with the Estate of

Martin Luther King Jr., c/o Writers House as agent for the proprietor, New York. NY. Copyright © 1968 Martin Luther King Jr., Copyright renewed © 1996 Coretta Scott King.; from Letter from a Birmingham Jail. Reprinted by arrangement with the Estate of Martin Luther King, Jr., c/o Writers House as agent for the proprietor, New York, NY. Copyright © 1963 Martin Luther King Jr., Copyright renewed © 1991 Coretta Scott King.; from Pilgrimage to Nonviolence. Reprinted by arrangement with the Estate of Martin Luther King, Jr., c/o Writers House as agent for the proprietor, New York, NY. Copyright © 1963 Martin Luther King Jr. Copyright renewed © 1991 Coretta Scott King.

**Electronic Selections**
from A Raisin in the Sun by Lorraine Hansberry. Copyright © 1958 by Robert Nemiroff, as an unpublished work. Copyright © 1959, 1966, 1984 by Robert Nemiroff, Random House, Inc. Electronic rights used by permission of the Estate of Jewell Handy Gresham Nemiroff.

Excerpt from "Beaumont to Detroit" from The Collected Poems of Langston Hughes by Langston Hughes. Copyright © 1994 by the Estate of Langston Hughes. Reprinted by permission of Harold Ober Associates, Inc.

"My People," Copyright © 1926 by Alfred A. Knopf, Inc. and renewed 1954 by Langston Hughes., from Selected Poems of Langston Hughes by Langston Hughes. Reprinted by permission of Harold Ober Associates, Inc.

"The Negro Speaks of Rivers" From The Collected Poems of Langston Hughes by Langston Hughes. Copyright © 1994 by the Estate of Langston Hughes. Reprinted by permission of Harold Ober Associates, Inc.

Excerpt From The Other America: Poverty in the United States by Michael Harrington. Copyright © 1962, 1969, 1981 by Michael Harrington; Copyright renewed © 1990 by Stephanie Harrington. Spanish Language and Electronic Rights used by permission of Stephanie Harrington.

Excerpt from "The Hashbury is the Capital of the Hippies." First published in The New York Times. Copyright © 1979 by Hunter S. Thompson. Used by permission of the Wylie Agency.

**Note: Every effort has been made to locate the copyright owner of material reprinted in this book. Omissions brought to our attention will be corrected in subsequent editions.**